Irish Immigrants

IN THE LAND OF CANAAN

WRITTEN &
EDITED BY

Kerby A. Miller

Arnold Schrier

Bruce D. Boling

David N. Doyle

Irish Immigrants

IN THE LAND OF CANAAN

*Letters and Memoirs
from Colonial and
Revolutionary America,
1675–1815*

OXFORD
UNIVERSITY PRESS

2003

OXFORD
UNIVERSITY PRESS

Oxford   New York

Auckland   Bangkok   Buenos Aires   Cape Town   Chennai
Dar es Salaam   Delhi   Hong Kong   Istanbul   Karachi   Kolkata
Kuala Lumpur   Madrid   Melbourne   Mexico City   Mumbai   Nairobi
São Paulo   Shanghai   Taipei   Tokyo   Toronto

Copyright © 2003 by Oxford University Press, Inc.

Published by Oxford University Press, Inc.
198 Madison Avenue, New York, New York 10016

www.oup.com

Oxford is a registered trademark of Oxford University Press, Inc.

Library of Congress Cataloging-in-Publication Data
Irish immigrants in the land of Canaan : letters and memoirs from colonial and
revolutionary America, 1675–1815 / written and edited by Kerby A. Miller . . . [et al.].
p. cm.
Includes index.
ISBN 0-19-504513-0; 0-19-515489-4 (pbk.)
1. Irish Americans—History—Sources.   2. Irish Americans—Biography.
3. Immigrants—United States—History—Sources.   4. Immigrants—United States—Biography.
5. United States—History—Colonial period, ca. 1600–1775—Biography.   6. United
States—History—Revolution, 1775–1783—Biography.   7. United
States—History—1783–1865—Biography.   I. Miller, Kerby A.

E184. I6 I683 2002
973'.049162—dc21   2002030363

1 3 5 7 9 8 6 4 2

Printed in the United States of America
on acid-free paper

IN MEMORY OF

Dennis Clark

E. R. R. "Rodney" Green

and

Franklin Scott

—*Beannacht Dé le hanmmnacha na marbh*

PREFACE ✳

Research for this book began in a sense some thirty years ago, when Kerby Miller first searched for Irish immigrants' letters and memoirs in Irish and North American archives and libraries. In the process, he encountered three other scholars also interested in Irish immigration: Arnold Schrier, a pioneer in the discovery and interpretation of such manuscripts; Bruce Boling, a specialist in Celtic and Hiberno-English philology; and David Doyle, an eminent historian of Irish-America. Over the years we each became increasingly intrigued by *early* Irish migration to the New World—by its complexity and diversity, by the inherent fascination of the first emigrants' few surviving letters and memoirs, and by our growing conviction that some of those documents shed new light on the crucial, formative stages of modern Protestant and Catholic Irish and Irish-American societies and identities. As a result, in the late 1980s we began the formal collaboration that has resulted in this book.

The letters, memoirs, and other documents included here record the experiences and perspectives of men and women who left Ireland for North America between the 1660s—when the authors of the earliest extant letters emigrated—and 1815, when the end of the Napoleonic Wars inaugurated a substantially different migration. We located and selected for publication manuscripts that, we believed, were both historically representative and inherently interesting. Then we conducted extensive background research, in primary and secondary sources, so we could interpret the documents and situate their authors and recipients in historical contexts.

Each of the book's chapters focuses on one or more specific immigrants and on the documents they wrote or dictated. Thus, the chapters constitute a series of historical essays; each can stand alone, but together they represent at once the disparate character, the common themes, and the mosaiclike texture of early Irish migration.

We begin with chapters that focus on letters, written from Ireland, that illustrate the background and causes of emigration, followed by a second set of chapters that present documents that exemplify the processes of Irish migration to the New World. Four other parts follow in which the documents and their immigrant authors are arranged according to the latter's New World occupations: farming; skilled and unskilled labor; commerce;

and the professions. The book's last part is composed of documents that illustrate Irish immigrants' diverse relationships to American political institutions and ideals, particularly in the late 1700s, when revolutionary events on both sides of the Atlantic were critical in shaping American, Irish, and Irish-American political cultures. In each part the chapters are arranged chronologically, according to the periodization of the documents contained therein, with one notable exception: those in part II are organized topically, according to the normal sequence of the migration process, from the emigrants' decisions to leave Ireland through their ocean voyages and initial settlements in the New World.

With the exception of lengthy memoirs that we have abridged, we present the letters and other documents as full texts that replicate, as closely as possible, the original manuscripts. This practice reflects our conviction that the documents are linguistically as well as historically important: that understanding how and why the immigrants expressed themselves in certain ways is crucial to appreciating what they wrote and the cultures that shaped their perceptions and interpretations of experience. However, our reproduction of the documents' original language has required an unusually large number of footnotes to clarify and explain their linguistic features. Those notes, in addition to others that provide historical information, obliged us to sacrifice the usual citations to nearly all the research sources on which the essays are based. Instead, those sources are listed, by chapter, at the end of the book.

We strove of course to uncover and publish documents illustrating the full range of the early Irish immigrant experience. Unfortunately, the low literacy rates that prevailed among poor immigrants and among Irish Catholics and women, generally, determined that members of those groups remain underrepresented, despite our success in locating a number of manuscripts that were dictated by immigrants who were both impoverished and illiterate. We present only one letter that represents Irish migration to what later became the Dominion of Canada. However, prior to 1815 very few Irishmen and -women migrated to mainland Canada, and only a handful of unrepresentative letters survive.[1]

Since the choice of names for Ireland's inhabitants is often freighted with political significance, we must explain that we employ the term *Irish*, without quotation marks, simply to designate any or all of Ireland's inhabitants and emigrants. Likewise, we use the term *Scots-Irish*, also without quotation marks, as purely descriptive of Presbyterians, in Ulster and in North America, whose ancestors had migrated from Scotland to Ireland. We

1. Irishmen and -women emigrated to Canada prior to the American Revolution, but we could locate no letters or memoirs written by either the Catholic fishermen and servants who migrated to Newfoundland or the Scots-Irish farmers who settled in Nova Scotia. At least three caches of letters survive that were written by Irishmen who sojourned in or migrated directly to Canada between 1776 and 1815. One is a collection of letters written by Catholic priests in Newfoundland; see C. J. Byrne, ed., *Gentlemen-Bishops and Faction Fighters: The Letters of Bishops O Donel, Lambers, Scallon, and Other Irish Missionaries* (St. John's, Newfoundland, 1984). The others include letters written by members of the governing élite in early Upper Canada (now Ontario); see the Hugh Hovell Farmar Papers (Public Archives of Canada, Ottawa); and the Joseph Willcocks Letters (Metropolitan Toronto Central Library). These documents are unrepresentative of the few ordinary migrants to British North America, but they also indicate that prior to 1815 Irish migrations to Canada and the United States were quite separate and distinct, as were the social and political contexts in which they settled.

eschew the group descriptive *Ulster Scots* because its modern usage (primarily in Northern Ireland) implies a degree of ethnic continuity and exclusivity, from the 1600s to the present, that cannot be supported by historical evidence.[2] By contrast, the hyphen in *Scots-Irish* reflects the ethnic fluidity and ambiguity that more accurately describes the Ulster Presbyterian experience on both sides of the Atlantic. However, when we employ "Irish" or "Scotch-Irish," in quotation marks, we refer to conscious "ethnic" or "national" group designations (or to their alleged characteristics) that have overt or covert political connotations and that may or may not correspond with their members' actual ancestral origins or religious affiliations.

2. However, we do use the term *Ulster Scots* in a purely linguistic sense to designate the *language* (or dialect—scholars differ on that issue), closely akin to Lowland Scots, that in the eighteenth and early nineteenth centuries prevailed in much of rural Ulster—primarily but by no means exclusively among Scots-Irish Presbyterians (see appendix 1).

ACKNOWLEDGMENTS ✳

In this book's long gestation, we have accumulated many debts. For financial support we are grateful to the Weldon Spring Foundation and the Research Council of the University of Missouri-Columbia, the Irish American Cultural Institute (now in Morristown, New Jersey), the Cushwa Center for the Study of American Catholicism at the University of Notre Dame, the Faculty Scholars Program of the University of New Mexico, the National Endowment for the Humanities, the faculty research support programs at Brown University, the Taft Memorial Fund at the University of Cincinnati, the Modern History Department at the Queen's University of Belfast, and, especially, the late Joseph Gannon of the American Irish Foundation.

For personal research aid, we thank Keith Brown and Mark Graham in Belfast; Robert Doan, Kathleen Ryan, and John Smolenski in Philadelphia; Coreen Hallenbeck of Albany, New York; and Bob Hunt, Mike Gamel, and, especially, Beth Ruffin McIntyre at the University of Missouri. For typing and computer assistance, we thank Cynthia Chermly, Laura Dauer, and Tillian Spitz at the University of Cincinnati and Mike Sullivan at the University of Missouri. Thanks as well to Nora Gibson of Charlottesville, Virginia, for her map-making skills. Special gratitude is due to Linda Brown-Kubisch, Laurel Boeckman, Marie Concannon, and other members of the research staff of the State Historical Society of Missouri. For their herculean efforts to locate the most obscure publications, we warmly acknowledge Josephine Johnson, Dolores Fisher, Sue Halaweh, Pat Holmes, and the other staff of the interlibrary borrowing service at the University of Missouri's Ellis Library. And thanks always to the History Department staff at the University of Missouri: to Patty Eggleston, Melinda Lockwood, Karen Pecora, Marie Sloan, and Nancy Taube.

In the lists of sources at the end of this book, we have tried to acknowledge the aid of all the individuals and institutions that helped us with research for each chapter. However, the assistance given by the following people merits our special thanks: the late J. R. R. Adams; Orlando Albillar; Tom Alexander; Ann Barry; Stefan Bielinski, Tyler Blethen; Maurice Bríc; Katherine Brown; John Bullion; Sharon Carson; Edward Carter; Marion Casey; Bill Crawford; Alun Davies; Jay Dolan; David Fitzpatrick; the late Col. J. R. H. Greeves; Tony Greeves; Beatriz Hardy; Kevin Herlihy; Ron Hoffman; Patricia

Horsey; Joy H. Jones; Tricia Kelleher; Líam Kennedy; John Devereux Kernan; C. I. Mac-Afee; Meg McAleer; C. W. P. MacArthur; John W. McConaghy; Brian McGinn; Ann McVeigh; Tony Malcolmson; Tim Meagher; Polly Midgley; Michael Montgomery; Jim Myers; Alice Naughton; Bruce Norman; Libby Nybakken; Trevor Parkhill; Rev. Donald Patton; Elizabeth Perkins; David Rixse; Barbara Rumsey; Philip Robinson; Mary Shackleton; Neddy Seagraves; Tony Stewart; Charles Stoner; Rev. Paul Thomas; Brian Trainor; Tom Truxes; Paul and Ellen Wagner; Anna Warren; Kevin Whelan, David Wilson; Curtis Wood; and Myrtle Yohe. Likewise, we are particularly grateful to all the staff at the Public Record Office of Northern Ireland; the Historical Library of the Religious Society of Friends in Ireland; the Ulster Folk and Transport Museum; and the National Library of Ireland.

For their patience, faith, and support over more years than they wish to remember, we are very grateful to Susan Ferber, Jessica Ryan, and the other editors and staff at Oxford University Press in New York and in North Carolina. For generous and insightful comments on various drafts and portions of our manuscript, we thank Kevin Kenny, Ted Koditschek, Linda Reeder, Bob Scally, LeeAnn Whites, and John Wigger. A second round of thanks is due to Líam Kennedy for graciously sharing the Irish demographic data that he and Kerby Miller compiled in the mid-1980s; thus, Kennedy shares whatever honors accrue from appendix 2, which presents much of this data for the first time.

None of the individuals just listed is accountable for the accuracy or the analyses of the material in this book. Many will surely disagree with our interpretations, and, indeed, we four collaborators have very different perspectives on many of the historical issues treated herein. Therefore, it should be said that Kerby Miller assumes final responsibility for much of the historical interpretation (especially concerning religion, politics, and identity), while Bruce Boling answers alone for the linguistic data and analyses.

Finally, we wish to express our love and gratitude to the spouses and children who so long endured our preoccupation with Ireland's early immigrants. This book could deservedly have been dedicated to them, but instead we take the opportunity to honor three Irish and immigration historians, former mentors and good friends, who died before they could witness one of the many results of their guidance and inspiration.

CONTENTS ✳

IV ❊
Craftsmen, Laborers, and Servants

V ❊
Merchants, Shopkeepers, and Peddlers

VI ❋

Clergymen and Schoolmasters

VII ❋

Irish Immigrants in Politics and War

Epilogue

Appendices

Sources   *687*

Index   *765*

MAPS ✻

Map Key

1. Drumark and Drumgoon, Killymard parish, Co. Donegal (chapter 2, Alexander Crawford).
2. Desertmartin town and parish, Co. Londonderry (chapter 3, David Lindsey).
3. Loughbrickland town, Aghaderg parish, Co. Down (chapter 4, Henry Johnston).
4. Aughintober, Donaghmore parish, Co. Tyrone (chapter 6, Margaret Wright).
5. Lisreagh, Derryvullan parish, Co. Fermanagh (chapter 7, Anon. Poet).
6. Dungiven town and parish, Co. Londonderry (chapter 8, Rev. James MacSparran; chapter 39, Francis Campble).
7. Ballynahinch town, Magheradrool parish, Co. Down (chapter 10, John Rea).
8. Strabane town, Camus-Morne parish, Co. Tyrone (chapter 11, James Orr; chapter 17, Samuel McCobb).
9. Greyabbey town and parish, Co. Down (chapter 12, John Smilie; chapter 18, Robert Witherspoon).
10. Ballymena town, Kirkinriola and Ballyclug parishes, Co. Antrim (chapter 13, John O'Raw; chapter 60, John Phillips).
11. Drumnashear, Killea parish, Donegal (chapter 15, George Crockett, Jr.; chapter 27, James and Hannah Crockett).
12. Maguires Bridge town, Aghalurcher parish, Co. Fermanagh (chapter 19, James Magraw).
13. Co. Londonderry (chapter 20, Mary Elizabeth McDowell Greenlee; chapter 21, James McCullough; chapter 37, Charles O'Hagan and Mary Dunn).
14. Londonderry city (chapter 22, Elizabeth Guthrie Brownlee Guthrie).
15. Mullaghglass, Ballymore parish, Co. Armagh (chapter 24, John and Jane Chambers).
16. Knockavaddy, Desertcreat parish, Co. Tyrone (chapter 26, Edward and Mary Toner).
17. Comber town and parish, Co. Down (chapter 30, Thomas Ralph).
18. Tamlaght Finlagan parish, Co. Londonderry (chapter 33 and 43, James Patton).

19. Belfast city, Shankill parish, Co. Antrim (chapter 38, Samuel Brown).
20. Newry town and parish, Co. Down (chapter 40, Robert Pillson).
21. Coleraine town, Co. Londonderry (chapter 42, Thomas Shipboy, Jr.).
22. Lisburn town, Blaris parish, Co. Antrim (chapter 45, Mary Cumming).
23. Donegore parish, Co. Antrim (chapter 46, Rev. John Craig).
24. Aughnacloy town, Carnteel parish, Co. Tyrone (chapter 48, Bernard M'Kenna).
25. Aghadowey parish, Co. Londonderry (chapter 49, Rev. James McGregor and John McMurphy).
26. Carrickmacross town, Magheross parish, Co. Monaghan (chapter 53, Rev. Thomas Barton).
27. Leck parish, Co. Donegal (chapter 55, Rev. Francis Alison).
28. Moyallon, Tullylish parish, Co. Down (chapter 56, John Morton).
29. Mullahead, Kilmore parish, Co. Armagh (chapter 57, John McDonnell).
30. Ballymoney town and parish, Co. Antrim (chapter 58, James Caldwell; chapter 68, John Caldwell, Jr.).
31. Slaghtybogy, Maghera parish, Co. Londonderry (chapter 61, Job Johnson).
32. Co. Down (chapter 62, David Redick).
33. Carrowreagh, Burt parish, Co. Donegal (chapter 64, Robert McArthur).
34. Kilmoyle, Ballyrashane parish, Co. Antrim (chapter 65, John Nevin).
35. Culnagrew, Killyman parish, Co. Tyrone (chapter 67, William Heazelton, Jr.).

Map Key by Name

Alison, Rev. Francis (chapter 55): (27) Leck parish, Co. Donegal.

Anon. poet (chapter 7): (5) Lisreagh, Derryvullan parish, Co. Fermanagh.

Barton, Rev. Thomas (chapter 53): (26) Carrickmacross town, Magheross parish, Co. Monaghan.

Brown, Samuel (chapter 38): (19) Belfast city, Shankill parish, Co. Antrim.

Caldwell, James (chapter 58): (30) Ballymoney town and parish, Co. Antrim.

Caldwell, John, Jr. (chapter 68): (30) Ballymoney town and parish, Co. Antrim.

Campble, Francis (chapter 39): (6) Dungiven town and parish, Co. Londonderry.

Chambers, John and Jane (chapter 24): (15) Mullaghglass, Ballymore parish, Co. Armagh.

Craig, Rev. John (chapter 46): (46) Donegore parish, Co. Antrim.

Crawford, Alexander (chapter 2): (1) Drumark and Drumgoon, Killymard parish, Co. Donegal.

Crockett, George, Jr. (chapter 15): (11) Drumnashear, Killea parish, Co. Donegal.

Crockett, James and Hannah (chapter 27): (11) Drumnashear, Killea parish, Co. Donegal.

Cumming, Mary (chapter 45): (22) Lisburn town, Blaris parish, Co. Antrim.

Dunn, Mary (chapter 37): (13) Co. Londonderry.

Greenlee, Mary Elizabeth McDowell (chapter 20): (13) Co. Londonderry.

Guthrie, Elizabeth Guthrie Brownlee (chapter 22): (14) Londonderry city.

Heazelton, William, Jr. (chapter 67): (35) Culnagrew, Killyman parish, Co. Tyrone.

Johnson, Job (chapter 61): (31) Slaghtybogy, Maghera parish, Co. Londonderry.

Johnston, Henry (chapter 4): (3) Loughbrickland town, Aghaderg parish, Co. Down.

Lindsey, David (chapter 3): (2) Desertmartin town and parish, Co. Londonderry.

MacSparran, Rev. James (chapter 8): (6) Dungiven town and parish, Co. Londonderry.

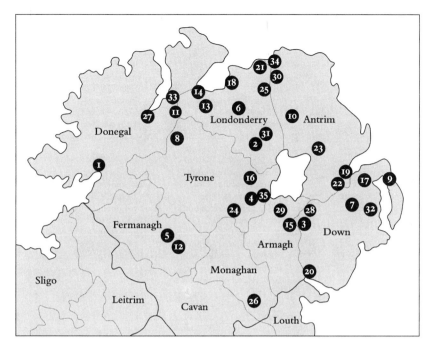

Ireland (north)

Magraw, James (chapter 19): **(12)** Maguires Bridge town, Aghalurcher parish, Co. Fermanagh.

McArthur, Robert (chapter 64): **(33)** Carrowreagh, Burt parish, Co. Donegal.

McCobb, Samuel (chapter 17): **(8)** Strabane town, Camus-Morne parish, Co. Tyrone.

McCullough, James (chapter 21): **(13)** Co. Londonderry.

McDonnell, John (chapter 57): **(29)** Mullahead, Kilmore parish, Co. Armagh.

McGregor, Rev. James (chapter 49): **(25)** Aghadowey parish, Co. Londonderry.

McMurphy, John (chapter 49): **(25)** Aghadowey parish, Co. Londonderry.

M'Kenna, Bernard (chapter 48): **(24)** Aughnacloy town, Carnteel parish, Co. Tyrone.

Morton, John (chapter 56): **(28)** Moyallon, Tullylish parish, Co. Down.

Nevin, John (chapter 34): **(34)** Kilmoyle, Ballyrashane parish, Co. Antrim.

O'Hagan, Charles (chapter 37): **(13)** Co. Londonderry.

O'Raw, John (chapter 13): **(10)** Ballymena town, Kirkinriola and Ballyclug parishes, Co. Antrim.

Orr, James (chapter 11): **(8)** Strabane town, Camus-Morne parish, Co. Tyrone.

Patton, James (chapters 33 and 43): **(18)** Tamlaght Finlagan parish, Co. Londonderry.

Phillips, John (chapter 60): **(10)** Ballymena town, Kirkinriola and Ballyclug parishes, Co. Antrim.

Pillson, Robert (chapter 40): **(20)** Newry town and parish, Co. Down.

Ralph, Thomas (chapter 30): **(17)** Comber town and parish, Co. Down.

Rea, John (chapter 10): **(7)** Ballynahinch town, Magheradrool parish, Co. Down.

Redick, David (chapter 62): **(32)** Co. Down.

Shipboy, Thomas, Jr. (chapter 42): **(21)** Coleraine town, Co. Londonderry.

Smilie, John (chapter 12): **(9)** Greyabbey town and parish, Co. Down.

Toner, Edward and Mary (chapter 26): **(16)** Knockavaddy, Desertcreat parish, Co. Tyrone.

Witherspoon, Robert (chapter 18): **(9)** Greyabbey town and parish, Co. Down.

Wright, Margaret (chapter 6): **(4)** Aughintober, Donaghmore parish, Co. Tyrone.

Map Key

1. Ballychahane, Killoscully parish, Co. Tipperary (chapter 1, James Wansbrough).
2. Ballinlug, Rathconrath parish, Co. Westmeath (chapter 1, James Wansbrough).
3. The Leap, Rossdroit parish, Co. Wexford (chapter 5, Walter Corish Devereux).
4. Ballintrane, Fennagh parish, Co. Carlow (chapter 9, Robert Parke).
5. Dublin city (chapter 14, Thomas Hinds; chapter 30, Michael Wade; chapter 31, John Fagan and John Johnson; chapter 34, Thomas McMahon; chapter 35, James Doyle; chapter 36, Stephen Fotterall; chapter 44, Margaret Carey Murphy Burke; chapter 52, Samuel [and George] Bryan; chapter 66, Thomas Addis Emmet).
6. Galway city (chapter 16, John Blake).
7. Limerick city (chapter 23, Daniel Kent).
8. Ballinclay, Liskinfere parish, Co. Wexford (chapter 25, Joseph and Hannah Wright).
9. Kilmore, Carbury parish, Co. Kildare (chapter 28, Benjamin Chandlee).
10. Cork city (chapter 34, John Justice; chapter 57, John McDonnell).
11. Drogheda city, Co. Lough (chapter 40, Robert Pillson).
12. Clonlisk and Ballybritt baronies, King's Co. (chapter 50, Dr. Charles Carroll).
13. Smithstown, Killeen parish, Co. Meath (chapter 51, Silvester Ferrall et al. [William Johnson]).
14. Tyaquin barony, Co. Galway (chapter 54, Thomas Burke).
15. Co. Galway (chapter 62, Ædanus Burke).
16. Carrignavar, Dunbolloge parish, Co. Cork (chapter 63, Daniel McCurtin).

Map Key by Name

Blake, John (chapter 16): (6) Galway city.

Bryan, George (chapter 52): (5) Dublin city.

Bryan, Samuel (chapter 52): (5) Dublin city.

Burke, Ædanus (chapter 62): (15) Co. Galway.

Burke, Margaret Carey Murphy (chapter 44): (5) Dublin city.

Burke, Thomas (chapter 54): (14) Tyaquin barony, Co. Galway.

Carroll, Dr. Charles (chapter 50): (12) Clonlisk and Ballybritt baronies, King's Co.

Chandlee, Benjamin (chapter 28): (9) Kilmore, Carbury parish, Co. Kildare.

Devereux, Walter Corish (chapter 5): (3) The Leap, Rossdroit parish, Co. Wexford.

Doyle, James (chapter 36): (5) Dublin city.

Emmet, Thomas Addis (chapter 66): (5) Dublin city.

Fagan, John (chapter 31): (5) Dublin city.

Farrell, Silvester (chapter 51): (13) Smithstown, Killeen parish, Co. Meath.

Fotterall, Stephen (chapter 36): (5) Dublin city.

Hinds, Thomas (chapter 14): (5) Dublin city.

Johnson, John (chapter 31): (5) Dublin city.

Johnson, Peter Warren (chapter 13): (13) Smithstown, Killeen parish, Co. Meath.

Johnson, William (chapter 13): (13) Smithstown, Killeen parish, Co. Meath.

Justice, John (chapter 34): (10) Cork city.

Kent, Daniel (chapter 23): (7) Limerick city.

McCurtin, Daniel (chapter 63): (16) Carrignavar, Dunbolloge parish, Co. Cork.

McDonnell, John (chapter 57): (10) Cork city.

McMahon, Thomas (chapter 34): (5) Dublin city.

Parke, Robert (chapter 9): (4) Ballintrane, Fennagh parish, Co. Carlow.

Pillson, Robert (chapter 40): (11) Drogheda city, Co. Louth.

Reily, Charles Lewis (chapter 51): (13) Smithstown, Killeen parish, Co. Meath.

Wade, Michael (chapter 30): (5) Dublin city.

Wansbrough, James (chapter 1): (1) Ballycahane, Killoscully parish, Co. Tipperary; and (2) Ballinlug, Rathconrath parish, Co. Westmeath.

Wright, Joseph and Hannah (chapter 25): (8) Ballinclay, Liskinfere parish, Co. Wexford.

Ireland (south)

Map Key

1. New York City (chapter 5, Walter [John] Corish Devereux [stage 1 of 2]; chapter 32, Francis Burdett Personel [stage 2 of 2]; chapter 40, Robert Pillson; chapter 48, Bernard M'Kenna [stage 2 of 2]; chapter 66, Thomas Addis Emmett; and chapter 68, John Caldwell, Jr. [stage 1 of 2]).
2. Utica, New York (chapter 5, Walter [John] Corish Devereux [stage 2 of 2]).
3. Salem, New York (chapter 6, Margaret Wright [Alexander McNish]).
4. Narragansett, Rhode Island (chapter 8, Rev. James MacSparran).
5. Monroe Co., New York (chapter 4, Henry [Moses] Johnston [stage 2 of 2]).
6. Boothbay, Maine (chapter 17, Samuel McCobb).
7. Fishkill, New York (chapter 29, John Kennedy).
8. Warren, Rhode Island (chapter 41, John O'Kelly).
9. Albany, New York (chapter 42, Thomas Shipboy, Jr.).
10. Nassau Co., New York (chapter 48, Bernard M'Kenna [stage 1 of 2]).
11. Londonderry and Bedford, New Hampshire (chapter 49, Rev. James McGregor and John McMurphy; chapter 59, Matthew Patten).
12. Johnstown, New York (chapter 15, Silvester Ferrall et al. [William Johnson]).
13. Goshen, New York (chapter 15, Silvester Ferrall et al. [Charles Lewis Reily]).
14. Newburgh, New York (chapter 68, John Caldwell, Jr. [stage 2 of 2]).

Map Key by Name

Caldwell, John, Jr. (chapter 68): (1) New York City and (13) Newburgh, New York.

Devereux, Walter [John] Corish (chapter 5): (1) New York City and (2) Utica, New York.

Emmet, Thomas Addis (chapter 66): (1) New York City.

Johnson, Moses (chapter 4, Henry Johnson): Lancaster Co., Pennsylvania, and (5) Monroe Co., New York.

Johnson, William (chapter 51, Silvester Farrell et al.): (11) Johnstown, New York.

Kennedy, John (chapter 29): (6) Fishkill, New York.

McCobb, Samuel (chapter 17): (5) Boothbay, Maine.

McGregor, Rev. James (chapter 49): (10) Londonderry, New Hampshire.

M'Kenna, Bernard (chapter 48): (9) Nassau Co. and (1) New York City, New York.

McMurphy, John (chapter 49): (10) Londonderry, New Hampshire.

McNish, Alexander (chapter 6, Margaret Wright): (3) Salem, New York.

MacSparran, Rev. James (chapter 8): (4) Narragansett, Rhode Island.

O'Kelly, John (chapter 41): (7) Warren, Rhode Island.

Patten, Matthew (chapter 59): (10) Bedford, New Hampshire.

Personel, Francis Burdett (chapter 32): Baltimore Co., Maryland, and (1) New York City.

Pillson, Robert (chapter 40): (1) New York City.

Reily, Charles Lewis (chapter 15, Silverster Ferrall et al.): (12) Goshen, New York.

Shipboy, Thomas, Jr. (chapter 42): (8) Albany, New York.

Wright, Margaret (chapter 6): (3) Salem, New York.

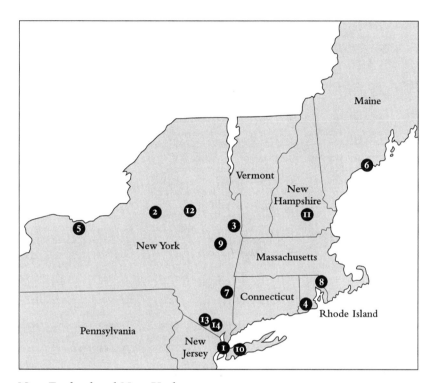

New England and New York

Map Key

1. Cohansey, New Jersey (chapter 1, James Wansbrough [Ann and Thomas Shepherd]).
2. Westmoreland Co., Pennsylvania (chapter 3, David Lindsey; chapter 22, Elizabeth Guthrie Brownlee Guthrie [stage 1 of 2]; chapter 26, Edward and Mary Toner; chapter 30, Thomas Ralph [stage 2 of 2]).
3. Lancaster Co., Pennsylvania (chapter 4, Henry [Moses] Johnston [stage 1 of 2]; chapter 12, John Smilie [stage 1 of 2]; chapter 53, Rev. Thomas Barton [stage 2 of 2]; chapter 62, David Redick [stage 1 of 2]).
4. Chester Co., Pennsylvania (chapter 9, Robert Parke; chapter 23, Daniel Kent; chapter 30, Philip McRory et al.; chapter 47, Rev. Samuel Blair; chapter 55, Rev. Francis Alison [stage 1 of 2]; chapter 61, Job Johnson [stage 1 of 2]).
5. Philadelphia, Pennsylvania (chapter 11, James Orr [John Dunlap]; chapter 14, Thomas Hinds [and son: stage 1 of 2]; chapter 28, Benjamin Chandlee [stage 1 of 2]; chapter 34, Thomas McMahon, William Sotherin, and John Justice; chapter 35, James Doyle; chapter 36, Stephen Fotterall; chapter 37, Charles O'Hagan and Mary Dunn; chapter 38, Samuel Brown; chapter 44, Margaret Carey Murphy Burke [stage 1 of 3]; chapter 52, Samuel [George] Bryan; chapter 55, Rev. Francis Alison [stage 2 of 2]; chapter 56, John Morton; chapter 58, James Caldwell; chapter 61, Job Johnson [stage 2 of 2]).
6. Fayette Co., Pennsylvania (chapter 12, John Smilie [stage 2 of 2]).
7. Paris, Bourbon Co., Kentucky (chapter 14, Thomas Hinds [son: stage 2 of 2]).
8. Shippensburg, Pennsylvania (chapter 19, James Magraw; chapter 39, Francis Campble).
9. Rockbridge Co., Virginia (chapter 20, Mary Elizabeth McDowell Greenlee).
10. Conococheague settlement, Pennsylvania (chapter 21, James McCullough; chapter 33, James Patton [1]).

11. Clarion Co., Pennsylvania (chapter 22, Elizabeth Guthrie Brownlee Guthrie [stage 2 of 2]).
12. Monmouth Co., New Jersey (chapter 24, John and Jane Chambers).
13. Belmont Co., Ohio (chapter 25, Joseph and Hannah Wright [stage 2 of 2]).
14. Luzerne Co., Pennsylvania (chapter 27, James and Hannah Crockett).
15. Cecil Co., Maryland (chapter 28, Benjamin Chandlee [stage 2 of 2]).
16. Burlington, New Jersey (chapter 31, John Grimes, John Fagan, and John Johnson).
17. Baltimore (city and county), Maryland (chapter 25, Joseph and Hannah Wright [stage 1 of 2]; chapter 32, Francis Burdett Personel [stage 1 of 2]; chapter 44, Margaret Carey Murphy Burke [stage 3 of 3]).
18. Emmitsburg, Maryland (chapter 44, Margaret Carey Murphy Burke [stage 2 of 3]).
19. Petersburg, Virginia (chapter 45, Mary Cumming).
20. Staunton, Virginia (chapter 46, Rev. John Craig).
21. Annapolis, Maryland (chapter 50, Dr. Charles Carroll).
22. Carlisle, Pennsylvania (chapter 53, Rev. Thomas Barton [stage 1 of 2]).
23. Northampton Co., Virginia (chapter 54, Thomas Burke [stage 1 of 3]).
24. Norfolk, Virginia (chapter 54, Thomas Burke [stage 2 of 3]).
25. Washington Co., Pennsylvania (chapter 62, David Redick [stage 2 of 2]).
26. Hagerstown, Maryland (chapter 63, Daniel McCurtin [stage 1 of 2]).
27. Chestertown, Maryland (chapter 63, Daniel McCurtin [stage 2 of 2]).
28. Crawford Co., Pennsylvania (chapter 64, Robert McArthur).
29. Pittsburgh, Pennsylvania (chapter 67, William Heazelton, Jr.).

Map Key by Name

Alison, Rev. Francis (chapter 55): (4) Chester Co. and (5) Philadelphia, Pennsylvania.

Barton, Rev. Thomas (chapter 53): (22) Carlisle and (3) Lancaster, Pennsylvania.

Blair, Rev. Samuel (chapter 47): (4) Chester Co., Pennsylvania.

Brown, Samuel (chapter 38): (5) Philadelphia.

Bryan, George (chapter 52, Samuel Bryan): (5) Philadelphia.

Burke, Margaret Carey Murphy (chapter 44): (5) Philadelphia, (18) Emmitsburg, and (17) Baltimore, Maryland.

Burke, Thomas (chapter 54): (23) Northampton Co. and (24) Norfolk, Virginia and Hillsborough, North Carolina.

Caldwell, James (chapter 58): (5) Philadelphia.

Campble, Francis (chapter 39): (8) Shippensburg, Pennsylvania.

Carroll, Dr. Charles (chapter 50): (21) Annapolis, Maryland.

Chambers, John and Jane (chapter 24): (12) Monmouth Co., New Jersey.

Chandlee, Benjamin (chapter 28): (5) Philadelphia and (15) Cecil Co., Maryland.

Craig, Rev. John (chapter 46): (20) Staunton, Virginia.

Crockett, James and Hannah (chapter 27): (14) Luzerne Co., Pennsylvania.

Cumming, Mary (chapter 45): (19) Petersburg, Virginia.

Curry, Edward (chapter 30): (4) Chester Co., Pennsylvania.

Dougherty, Ann (chapter 30): (4) Chester Co., Pennsylvania.

Doyle, James (chapter 35): (5) Philadelphia.

Dunlap, John (chapter 11, James Orr): (5) Philadelphia.

Dunn, Mary (chapter 37): (5) Philadelphia.

Fagan, John (chapter 31): (16) Burlington, New Jersey.

Fotterall, Stephen (chapter 36): (5) Philadelphia.

Greenlee, Mary Elizabeth McDowell (chapter 20): (9) Rockbridge Co., Virginia.

Grimes, John (chapter 31): (16) Burlington, New Jersey.

Guthrie, Elizabeth Brownlee Guthrie (chapter 22): (2) Westmoreland Co. and (11) Clarion Co., Pennsylvania.

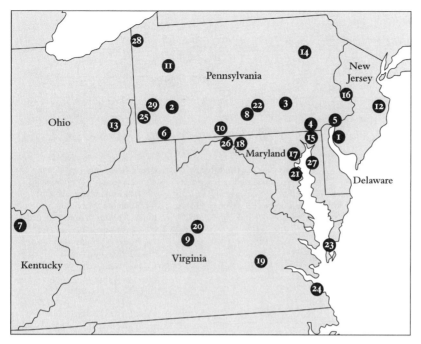

Pennsylvania, New Jersey, and the Upper South

Heazelton, William, Jr. (chapter 67): (29) Pittsburgh, Pennsylvania.

Hinds, Thomas (chapter 14): (5) Philadelphia and (7) Paris, Bourbon Co., Kentucky.

Johnson, Job (chapter 61): (4) Chester Co. and (5) Philadelphia.

Johnson, John (chapter 31): (16) Burlington, New Jersey.

Johnston, Moses (chapter 4, Henry Johnston): (3) Lancaster Co., Pennsylvania, and Monroe Co., New York.

Justice, John (chapter 34): (5) Philadelphia.

Kent, Daniel (chapter 23): (4) Chester Co., Pennsylvania.

Lindsey, David (chapter 3): (2) Westmoreland Co., Pennsylvania.

McArthur, Robert (chapter 64): (28) Crawford Co., Pennsylvania.

McCullough, James (chapter 21): (10) Conococheague settlement, Pennsylvania.

McCurtin, Daniel (chapter 63): (26) Hagerstown and (27) Chestertown, Maryland.

McGee, Ruth (chapter 30): (4) Chester Co., Pennsylvania.

McMahon, Thomas (chapter 34): (5) Philadelphia, Pennsylvania.

McRory, Philip (chapter 30): (4) Chester Co., Pennsylvania.

M'Cullen, Patrick (chapter 30): (4) Chester Co., Pennsylvania.

Magraw, James (chapter 19): (8) Shippensburg, Pennsylvania.

Morton, John (chapter 56): (5) Philadelphia.

O'Hagan, Charles (chapter 37): (6) Philadelphia.

Orr, James [John Dunlap] (chapter 11): (5) Philadelphia.

Parke, Robert (chapter 9): (4) Chester Co., Pennsylvania.

Patton, James (chapter 33): (10) Conococheague settlement, Pennsylvania, and (chapter 43) Asheville, North Carolina.

Personel, Francis Burdett (chapter 32): (17) Baltimore Co., Maryland, and New York City.

Ralph, Thomas (chapter 30): (4) Chester Co. and (2) Westmoreland Co., Pennsylvania.

Redick, David (chapter 62): (3) Lancaster Co. and (25) Washington Co., Pennsylvania.

Shepherd, Ann and Thomas (chapter 1): (1) Cohansey, New Jersey.

Smilie, John (chapter 12): (3) Lancaster Co. and (6) Fayette Co., Pennsylvania.

Sotherin, William (chapter 34): (5) Philadelphia.

Stuart, Rosanna (chapter 30): (4) Chester Co., Pennsylvania.

Toner, Edward and Mary (chapter 26): (2) Westmoreland Co., Pennsylvania.

Wade, Michael (chapter 30): (4) Chester Co., Pennsylvania.

Wansbrough, James (chapter 1): (1) Cohansey, New Jersey [Ann and Thomas Shepherd].

Wright, Joseph and Hannah (chapter 25): (17) Baltimore, Maryland, and (13) Belmont Co., Ohio.

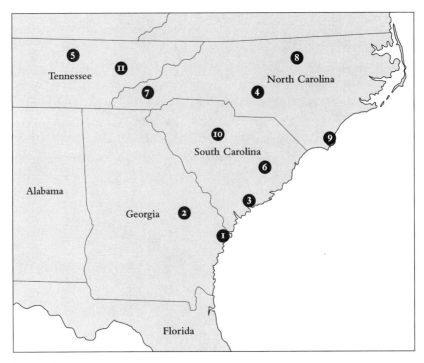

Lower South

West Indies

Map Key

1. Barbados (chapter 16, John Blake).
2. Montserrat (chapter 16, John Blake).

Map Key by Name

Blake, John (chapter 16): **(1)** Barbados and **(2)** Montserrat.

Irish Immigrants

IN THE LAND OF CANAAN

The raisons those unhappey people give for their goeing [to America], as are various, as their Circomstances, ye Richer Sort Say, that if they Stay in Irland, their Children will be Slaves, & that it is better for them to make money of their Leases while they are worth Somthing to inable them to transport them Selves and familys to America, a pleace where they are Sure of better tratement, and although they shold meet with Some hardships, they are very well asured their posterety will be for ever happey. The poorer Sort are deluded by ye acct^s they have, of ye great weages is given there, to Labouring men, . . .

[For the emigrants write home that in America] the rents are Soe Small they can hardly be caled Such, noe Tythes nor Tythmongers, noe County cess   no parish taxes, noe Serviters money, E[a]ster groats, nor Bailifs corn,   these & ye like expressions, I have red in Several of their letters, at ye Same time Setting forth that all men are there upon a levell & that it is a good poor mans Country, where there are no opressions of any kind whatsoeiver. . . .

[Accordingly, here in Ulster t]he Presbiteirian Ministers have taken their Shear of pains to Seduce their poor Ignorant heerers, by, Bellowing from their pulpets against ye Landlords and ye Clargey, calling them Rackers of Rents, and Servers of Tythes, with other reflections of this nature, which they know is pleasing to their people, at ye Same time telling them, that God had appoynted a Country for them to Dwell in . . . and desires them to depart thence, where they will be freed from the Bondage of Egipt and goe to ye land of Cannan.

Rev. Ezekiel Stewart, Portstewart, County Londonderry,
to Michael Ward and the Lords Justices of Ireland
25 March 1729

INTRODUCTION ❋

In 1734 Robert Witherspoon, a child whose Presbyterian grandparents had removed from Scotland to Ulster, Ireland's northern province, scarcely thirty years earlier, migrated with his large extended family to South Carolina, where his parents and uncles prospered as indigo planters and slaveowners. In the same year, John Craig, a Presbyterian clergyman whose ancestors had been settled in Ulster for over one hundred years, crossed the ocean alone and settled initially in Pennsylvania but lived most of his life in Virginia's Shenandoah Valley, ministering to frontier settlers such as Mary Greenlee, whose clan had arrived from northern Ireland a few years before. During her own sojourn in Pennsylvania, Greenlee may have encountered in Chester County the unfortunate Edward Curry, an Irish Catholic indentured servant, or Robert Parke, the brother of Curry's abusive master and a Quaker from southern Ireland. Had Craig been disposed to engage in religious controversies, he could have traveled to Rhode Island and debated his fellow Ulsterman, James MacSparran, a portly and pompous Anglican minister. And MacSparran, always eager for his church's advancement, surely was pleased in 1738 to learn that in Maryland the wealthy Dr. Charles Carroll, scion of one of southern Ireland's most "ancient" Gaelic families, had forsworn his Catholicism and conformed to the Protestant faith.

Robert Witherspoon lived through the American Revolution, and Mary Greenlee survived even longer, through the turbulent 1790s and almost to the War of 1812, and died during James Madison's first administration. Both witnessed the later and larger waves of immigrants from Ireland that followed on the heels of their own generations. In the 1760s and 1770s Ulster Presbyterians such as Job Johnson and Elizabeth Guthrie continued to disembark on the banks of the Delaware, while to the south others such as John Phillips landed their families in Charleston or Savannah. Johnson became a country schoolmaster near Philadelphia; Guthrie a farmer's wife on the Pennsylvania frontier; Phillips a small planter in the Carolina backcountry. During the Revolution, Johnson was an officer in the Continental Army and fought at the siege of Yorktown; Guthrie saw her husband and infant son slaughtered in frontier warfare; while Phillips commanded a Tory militia company and fled to Ireland at the war's end.

After the Revolution, immigration from Ireland surged once more, until interrupted from 1793 by maritime wars between Britain, France, and, in 1812, the United States. In the 1780s Job Johnson died of his wartime wounds in Philadelphia, but he lived to witness the landings at the city docks of more Ulster Presbyterians, such as the laborer James Patton, as well as Catholics like the stocking-weaver Thomas McMahon from Dublin, and other Protestants such as the Methodist Daniel Kent, an indentured servant from Limerick. In the 1790s and early 1800s Patton, now a backcountry trader, was joined on the western frontier by newcomers such as the Ulsterman George Crockett, a Presbyterian merchant in Tennessee; Edward Toner, a Catholic tenant farmer near Pittsburgh; and Hannah Wright, a Quaker townbuilder's wife in frontier Ohio. Meanwhile, Thomas McMahon marketed his stockings to recent arrivals who settled in his own Philadelphia and other eastern seaports: to Samuel Brown, an Anglican glazier from Belfast, and Margaret Carey Murphy, a Catholic innkeeper's widow from Dublin. And from the 1780s ordinary immigrants like Patton and Brown were accompanied at first by a trickle, later a small flood, of political exiles who had agitated or even fought for Irish freedom—by Catholics such as the printer Mathew Carey, Margaret Murphy's brother, and by Protestants like John Nevin, a rebel commander now a fugitive from the shambles of 1798. Ironically, the ships in which they fled often carried other immigrants—such as the Methodist William Heazelton from mid-Ulster—who, loyal to the Crown, had been the exiles' bitterest opponents in Ireland and would remain so in the New World.

Witherspoon, Craig, Greenlee, and the other immigrants whose stories are included in this book were unique in that a few of the letters, memoirs, petitions, or other testaments they penned or dictated have survived the centuries since they were written. In other respects, however, these men and women were broadly representative of the approximately four hundred thousand emigrants from Ireland who settled in North America between the late 1600s and the end of the Napoleonic War in 1815. Perhaps two-thirds of these were Presbyterians, with the rest more or less evenly divided between Catholics and other Protestants; most of the latter were members of the Church of Ireland, with smaller numbers of Quakers, Methodists, and Baptists. The overwhelming majority of Presbyterians, along with perhaps half the Catholics and many of the Anglicans and other Protestants, emigrated from Ulster; most of the remainder probably came from the counties bordering Ulster, in north Leinster and north Connacht, or from the hinterlands of the major southern Irish ports, such as Dublin and Cork. Finally, perhaps two-thirds of these early immigrants were males, and before the American Revolution a large number emigrated as indentured servants.

Taken together these migrations are admittedly small in comparison with the millions who left Ireland in the nineteenth century, but they were enormous in proportion to the contemporary populations of Ulster, Ireland, and North America. In the 1750s Ulster's Presbyterian community probably numbered less than half a million; all of Ireland had merely about 2.4 million inhabitants; and no more than 1.5 million whites and blacks lived in Britain's colonies on the North American mainland. As late as 1790 Ireland's population was only about four million,[1] and the new United States had merely 3.23 million white

---

1. Contemporary estimates of Ireland's population ca. 1790 ranged between three and four million; see K. H. Connell, *The Population of Ireland, 1750–1845* (Oxford, 1950), 4–5.

inhabitants. Consequently, early Irish migrations had dramatic social and even political consequences in Ireland and North America alike. In Ireland, for instance, mass departures by Ulster Presbyterians and southern Irish Anglicans both reduced the size and, in northern Ireland, altered the ethnoreligious configuration of the seventeenth-century Protestant plantations, while early Catholic emigration created the first transatlantic linkages that, in the early and mid-1800s, would draw millions of Catholics to the New World. On the other side of the ocean, the early Irish migrants and their offspring dominated frontier settlement, became a significant presence in many seaports and inland towns, and played major—in some areas predominant—roles in the political tumults, economic developments, social conflicts, and religious revivals that created and shaped the new American nation.

Despite their secular ambitions and material accomplishments, many of the early emigrants—or their descendants—claimed they had left Ireland primarily for religious and political reasons. Such explanations for migration were especially common among Ulster Presbyterians, whose clergymen—as the Church of Ireland minister and magistrate Ezekiel Stewart critically observed—"Bellow[ed] from their pulpits" that "God had appoynted a Country for them to Dwell in," where they would be free from "the Bondage of Egipt and goe to ye land of Cannan."[2] Stewart's Biblical reference seemed an appropriate title for this book, because it illustrates how religious and political concerns were indeed inseparable from economic motives among many, perhaps most, early Irish emigrants. Moreover, this popular scriptural analogy had more than pious implications. After all, the Old Testament Jews had not settled Canaan peacefully; rather, they had conquered its inhabitants and seized their territory—a fate that in the seventeenth and eighteenth centuries befell Ireland's Catholics and North America's natives alike. It was no wonder, therefore, that in the aftermath of Irish Catholics' 1641 Rebellion against British expropriation, Daniel Harcourt, a bishop of the Church of Ireland, had lamented "how dearly the Israelites"—that is, Britain's Protestant colonists in Ireland—had "paid for their cruel mercy in not extirpating the idolatrous Canaanites."[3]

Together, Stewart's scriptural reference and Harcourt's sanguinary analogy suggest that Ireland and North America shared histories that were similar and linked not only by transatlantic migration. Admittedly, however, it was the differences between the two countries that most impressed contemporary observers. For example, the bloodshed and epidemics that accompanied England's conquests of Ireland and the New World did not "extirpate" the island's "natives" as they did nearly all the Indians along America's eastern seaboard. Rather, Catholics remained a large majority of the inhabitants in most of Ireland and a substantial minority even in those parts of Ulster where the English and Scottish plantations were most successful. As a result, and for reasons of security as well as greed, in Ireland Protestant legislators excluded the great mass of the island's inhabitants from politics and government, proscribed their church and clergy, and restricted Catholics' rights to purchase or inherit land and to engage in certain occupations. In British North America,

2. Rev. Ezekiel Stewart, Poststewart, County Londonderry, to Michael Ward and the Lords Justices of Ireland, 25 March 1729 (D.2092/1/3/141, Public Record Office of Northern Ireland, Belfast). 3. Cited in T. Claydon and I. McBride, "The Trials of the Chosen Peoples: Recent Interpretations of Protestantism and National Identity in Britain and Ireland," in Claydon and McBride, eds., *Protestantism and National Identity: Britain and Ireland, c.1650–c.1850* (Cambridge, England, 1998), 23.

by contrast, Catholics (outside formerly French Quebec) composed only a tiny minority of the population, and although they suffered religious and political disabilities, there were few restrictions on their economic activities.

Most important, although in the 1600s British migrations to Ireland had rivaled in size those to the New World, in the early 1700s the former declined sharply, and during the eighteenth century Ireland itself became a fountain of emigrants to North America. The New World's economic abundance and relative social equality—its cheap, purchasable acres, good wages, and plentiful food—contrasted dramatically with conditions in Ireland, where farmers and rural craftsmen struggled under the burdens of rents and tithes, while the opulence of the wealthiest Protestant landlords, a few hundred of whom owned most of the island, contrasted harshly with the dire poverty endured by the masses of rural peasants and urban slum-dwellers alike. In an era when the overwhelming majority of both countries' inhabitants engaged in agriculture, perhaps the most fundamental difference was in the ratios between population and available land. As late as 1790 the former thirteen colonies had fewer than four million whites and blacks living on 240,000 square miles of territory, with another 580,000 square miles, between the Appalachians and the Mississippi, yet to settle. By contrast, contemporary Ireland had roughly the same number of people jostling for space on an island of merely 32,000 square miles—about the same size as New Jersey.

Yet there *were* clear similarities between the two "Canaans." Both were colonies the conquests and settlements of which had involved the military and political subjugation of the natives and the expropriation of their lands. In addition, whatever the legal formalities—their varying degrees of self-government, or the fact that after 1707 the empire was technically "British"—Ireland and North America were essentially *English* colonies. Mercantile regulations devised in London structured Irish and North American economic developments alike, and although the Navigation Acts were perhaps less important or injurious than contemporaries believed, their fundamental purpose was to promote English commercial and manufacturing interests. Furthermore, in both Ireland and America political power and the most lucrative economic opportunities were generally reserved to a political and social élite whose members were of English birth or descent; in Ireland these were invariably—and in North America, outside New England and Pennsylvania, they were usually—communicants of the Anglican church "by law established." In addition, although Ulster Presbyterians' legal disabilities were immeasurably less in North America than they had been in Ireland, often they still felt like second-class citizens overseas—even in colonies, such as Massachusetts and Pennsylvania, that were governed by other non-Anglicans. Finally, all the American colonial assemblies, in emulation of the Irish and British parliaments, passed legislation that denied Catholics political rights, and only Pennsylvania allowed them to worship without penalties or restrictions.

Ironically, during the course of the eighteenth century Ireland and North America in many respects grew closer together.[4] From the late 1600s, and especially after the 1730s,

---

4. Except, of course, for the increasing prevalence of African slavery in the southern American colonies. Although Irish (like American) agitators frequently compared their peoples' political status vis-à-vis England to "slavery" or "bondage," nothing comparable to the plight of American slaves ever afflicted Ireland's (or North America's) white inhabitants, with the notable exception of the Irish political prisoners and "vagabonds" who

the British empire's rapid economic growth created a dynamic, transatlantic market for goods and labor in which both the Irish and the American colonists participated and prospered in varying degrees. Indeed, some historians argue that the expansion of imperial trade and communications during the 1700s resulted in an "Anglicization" of both Irish and North American societies and cultures. To be sure, during the eighteenth century Britain's economic and cultural influence on Ireland, as on North America, increased enormously—as did Irish trade with both the British metropolis and its overseas colonies. However, there were parallel developments, in Ireland and America alike, that might be termed "Hibernicization."

Irish society in the eighteenth century was rigidly stratified, numerically dominated by a mass of impoverished and legally proscribed Catholic peasants, and perhaps therefore unusually vulnerable to economic crises. As a result, Irish economic growth was fragile and uneven, and both the concomitants of growth—such as rising rents and food prices—and its frequent interruptions, as during credit shortages or depressions in Ulster's linen industry, stimulated unprecedented Irish emigration to the New World.

Indeed, between the late 1600s and 1815 the North American mainland witnessed the arrival of many more people from Ireland than from Great Britain itself—at least 150,000 from Ulster and another 50,000 from southern Ireland prior to the American Revolution, and perhaps as many again between the end of that conflict and 1815. In the 1600s the white inhabitants of the North American colonies had been overwhelmingly English, but the eighteenth-century influx from Ireland (as also from Germany and Scotland) altered significantly the ethnoreligious composition of the white population of what became the United States. By 1790 the Irish-born and their descendants constituted between an eighth (New York) and a fourth (Pennsylvania) of the white inhabitants of the Middle Atlantic states, from a sixth (Maryland and Virginia) to more than a fourth (South Carolina and Georgia) of those in the South, between a fourth to a third in Kentucky and Tennessee, and a substantial minority even in northern New England.[5]

Increasingly there were also political parallels and linkages between Ireland and North America. During the 1700s many of Ireland's Protestants increasingly resented what they regarded as the English (after 1707 the British) government's baleful restrictions on Irish economic development and their own pretensions to self-rule. The result was the growth of what some scholars have dubbed "colonial nationalism": an emotional and political association with "Ireland" and at least a tentative willingness to embrace an "Irish" identity that transcended, in varying degrees, the traditional divisions among Anglicans, Dissenters, and even Catholics. Among Protestant liberals these impulses resulted in the constitutional agitation of the late 1770s and early 1780s. Among Protestant and Catholic radicals, inspired by the American and the French revolutions, they culminated in the United Irishmen's Rebellion of 1798. It may not be coincidental that the areas of Ireland most prone to political upheaval were also those that had experienced, and continued to

---

were forcibly transported in the 1600s to the West Indies and the Chesapeake by the Stuart and Cromwellian régimes. Otherwise, the presence of slavery in America surely elevated the legal and probably the social status of even the poorest Irish immigrants.   **5.** On scholars' conflicting assessments of the numbers of early Irish emigrants to North America, see appendix 2.

witness, the greatest outflows of Protestant emigrants to the New World. Not only were the people in those regions most exposed to American influences, but they may also have felt—as did Irish Catholics a century later—that only major political changes could alleviate the economic conditions that obliged or encouraged mass migration.

Meanwhile in North America, similar English influences and colonial resentments produced the agitations that led eventually to revolution and independence. It would be an exaggeration to allege—as did some British and tory observers—that the American Revolution, even in the Middle Colonies, was really an "Irish" or "Scotch-Irish" uprising. Nevertheless there was a distinctively and, in many areas, a prominently "Irish" component in the American rebellion—as there was as well in the succeeding political struggles between Federalists and anti-Federalists over ratification of the U.S. Constitution and later between the Federalist and Republican parties over the very meanings of the Revolution and the Constitution. The revolutionary mixture of late seventeenth-century "commonwealth" and eighteenth-century "liberal" and "radical" ideals informed both Irish and American political agitators and provided opportunities whereby Presbyterians and even Catholics could claim full membership in the Irish and American polities. Indeed, given their histories, it is arguable that eighteenth-century Irishmen were especially attracted (or frightened) by liberating ideas: perhaps more likely than other inhabitants of—or emigrants from—the British Isles to perceive with brutal clarity that, as one wrote, without substantial reform or revolution their societies were merely "combination[s] of those who *have* against those who *have not*."[6]

Thus we contend that from the mid-1700s through the early 1800s there were close affinities between Irish and American economic and political developments, that contemporary Irish migration to the New World both reflected and accelerated those developments, and that out of them emerged modern "Irish" (and "Scotch-Irish") ethnic and political identities on both sides of the Atlantic Ocean. In the late 1700s, as Irish and American political movements interacted and converged, "Irish" became—both in Ireland and in the United States—a more inclusive and more favorable appellation than ever before or since. Temporarily it was associated, whether accurately or not, with those forces of democracy and of personal as well as national liberation that appeared imminently or actually triumphant over the dead weights of aristocracy, deference, and colonialism. However, that moment soon passed. At least by the 1820s and 1830s religious and political conflicts were rife, in Ireland and America alike, between Protestants and Catholics. Once again "Irish" became virtually synonomous with Irish Catholics alone, and among most Protestants, Irish and otherwise, once more the term designated a group laden with negative stereotypes. By contrast, in America the old but formerly ambiguous term "Scotch-Irish" was revived and reformulated, with exclusively favorable connotations, to describe all Protestants of Irish birth or descent. In the process, memories of the earlier liberating and unifying possibilities of "Irishness" were lost or repressed.

We also suggest, therefore, that the following letters and other testaments written by Irish immigrants (or by their correspondents in Ireland) can be read on several levels.

---

6. Cited in D. N. Doyle, *Ireland, Irishmen and Revolutionary America, 1760–1820* (Dublin, 1981), 168.

Certainly, they provide intimate and, we believe, fascinating accounts of the personal experiences of men and women who left Ireland, settled or sojourned in America, and adapted to a wide variety of regional and socioeconomic circumstances. Both the individuality and the ethnic, religious, and social diversity of these early Irish immigrants are remarkable, especially when compared with the apparent homogeneity of the migrants from mid- and late nineteenth-century Ireland. Indeed, for some early immigrants, their Irish origins were of little relevance to their new lives in America—or had only negative implications that might be avoided through strategic conformity to locally dominant cultures. Yet most migrants formed or joined discrete networks and local societies whose members were largely or almost entirely of Irish birth or descent as well as of shared religious beliefs. Moreover, by the last third of the eighteenth century Ireland's immigrants in America—like many of their countrymen at home—were forging more inclusive "ideal" communities and "Irish" identities that were neither entirely confined within the homeland's traditional ethnoreligious boundaries nor completely subsumed in an homogeneous "American" nationalism. Indeed, it is arguable that Irish immigrants' correspondence, memoirs, and other personal testaments not only reflected but even helped create the categories of "Irish" identity that emerged in contemporary political discourse on both sides of the Atlantic.

Of course, when writing letters to Ireland, and especially when authoring their memoirs, Irish immigrants were penning descriptions of their environments and experiences that were inevitably colored by their own expectations, emotions, and prejudices. In the process they were also creating images and constructing "selves" for the edification of their correspondents or their posterity. Many of their "performances" were ritualistic and yet intensely personal: designed to reassure kinsmen at home of the immigrants' continued affection or religious devotion, or to persuade their relatives to join them in America, or to admonish their descendants to emulate the memoirists' alleged virtues and successes. However, these testaments were public as well as private exercises: in the eighteenth century public and private spheres were much less distinct than they would later become, and the "news" in immigrants' letters inevitably circulated beyond their parents' hearths. As early as 1729, Rev. Ezekiel Stewart remarked on the major role the immigrants' letters played in shaping positive, even paradisaical, visions of America—and correspondingly negative opinions of Irish conditions—among their recipients in Ireland, thereby constructing both the cultural and the tangible networks that encouraged and facilitated further emigration. Finally, this era of democratic revolutions (and of counterrevolutions) was an intensely political age. As Stewart's criticism of the immigrants' letters implied, invitations to emigrate, seemingly mundane comparisons between Irish and American circumstances, and even apparently neutral descriptive terms such as "Irish"—could have distinct and even revolutionary political connotations.

Thus, many of these letters and other documents not only reveal the patterns and processes of early migration and immigrant adaptation but also enable an exploration of the dynamics of ethnic identity: of how and why the inclusive and democratic implications of late eighteenth-century "Irishness" emerged, flourished briefly, and then were submerged in America and Ireland alike. In that sense, among many others, these faded manuscripts may be of contemporary as well as historical relevance in a nation and world beset by new forms of imperialism, by mass migrations, and by religious, ethnic, and racial strife. To be sure, in the United States anti-"Irish" (Catholic) prejudice and intra-"Irish" (Protestant vs. Catholic) conflicts have virtually disappeared. In American society generally, however, as in the world at large and in Northern Ireland particularly, the broad question posed by the United Irishmen still awaits resolution: "Are we forever" condemned, they asked, "to walk like beasts of prey over [the] fields which [our] ancestors stained with blood?"[7]

---

7. Cited in N. J. Curtin, *The United Irishmen: Popular Politics in Ulster and Dublin, 1791–1798* (Oxford, 1994), 21.

I ❋
The Causes of Irish Emigration

I ❋

James Wansbrough, 1700–1728

Asingular feature of the history of Irish emigration to North America is that many of
the first emigrants' immediate ancestors had only recently moved to Ireland. In 1649–
1650 Oliver Cromwell's English armies reconquered Ireland from the Catholics who had
controlled most of the island since their rebellion in 1641. During the 1650s the triumph
of Cromwellian religious and political radicalism, plus the availability of confiscated Catholic lands, encouraged many English Protestant Dissenters to settle in Ireland rather than in
America. This was especially true of Baptists and Quakers, who were unwelcome in Puritan New England and the Anglican-dominated Chesapeake colonies. By the 1680s, however, the Cromwellians' Irish-born children and grandchildren were migrating across the
Atlantic. In Irish terms, they were the forerunners of the great movement of Irish Protestants, chiefly Dissenters of Scottish or English descent, who dominated Irish emigration to
the New World from the late seventeenth century through the first third of the nineteenth
century. In American terms, they could be viewed as a delayed and temporarily diverted
stream of the original migration of British Dissenters who had founded New England by
1630 and were settling Pennsylvania and New Jersey in the 1680s.

In the 1650s perhaps as many as 30,000 English and Welsh Protestants migrated
across the Irish Sea. Many remained only a generation or two; some returned to England,
but others emigrated to the American colonies. Among the latter were Ann and Thomas
Shepherd, and several of the earliest surviving emigrants' letters are those addressed to
them in New Jersey by Ann's brother in Ireland, James Wansbrough. The Shepherds and
Wansbroughs had come to Ireland as officers in Cromwell's army and, in return for their
service, had gained estates taken from the defeated Catholics. Several thousand new settlers,
including the Wansbroughs and Shepherds, were Baptists, and after 1654 a larger number,
especially among the lesser grantees and tradesmen, became members of the Society of
Friends, derisively known as Quakers. As in England, the two Irish sects raided each other
for converts (largely ignoring the native Irish) and quarreled bitterly over doctrinal issues.
However, as dissenters surrounded by hostile Catholics and suspicious Anglicans, Irish
Baptist and Quaker families were often closely aligned in marriage, trade, and later remigration to America.

During the early 1650s Baptists were prominent in Ireland's military government,
but they lost power in the latter years of Cromwell's rule and, after the Stuart and Anglican
Restoration of 1660, most went back to England. Like the Quakers, the few Baptists who
remained in southern Ireland congregated principally in major seaports such as Dublin,
Waterford, and Cork, where they engaged in commerce and crafts, but a substantial minority were modest landowners and head tenants in the Irish midlands. Despite their general
prosperity, after the ascension of Charles II (1660–1685) Irish Baptists, Quakers, and other
Dissenters saw their status deteriorate, symbolized by their legal exclusion from politics and

the reimposition of tithes by the reestablished Church of Ireland. Moreover, in the 1680s and early 1690s Irish Catholic resurgence compounded their insecurities and threatened their estates.

However, as the settlers' problems mounted, new opportunities beckoned overseas. In 1667 William Penn (1644–1718), born in Waterford and heir to large Irish estates, converted to Quakerism, and in 1676 he acquired part title to much of West Jersey, as well as to Pennsylvania, and invited British and Irish Friends and other dissenters to settle there. In 1681 a company of Dublin Quakers took lands on the east side of the Delaware River, opposite the site of Philadelphia. This "Irish Tenth" became the nucleus of Gloucester County, and for several generations Irish Quakers would settle on both sides of the Delaware. Also, in 1675 an adventurer named John Fenwick (1618–1683) established a freelance Quaker colony in southern West Jersey, at Salem and at Greenwich on the Cohansey River. Initially this colony stagnated, but after 1683, when Penn purchased Fenwick's disputed claims, the Salem and Cohansey settlements began to fill with Irish Quakers and Baptists, attracted by economic prospects as well as by guarantees of religious freedom and civil equality.

Among these emigrants were James Wansbrough's brothers-in-law, Thomas, David, and John Shepherd. Between the 1680s and 1720s the Wansbroughs, Shepherds, and their Toler cousins extended through the North Riding of County Tipperary, primarily in the baronies of Lower and Upper Ormond and of Owney and Arra, and many of them worshiped at a Baptist church at Cleagh Keating, near the town of Borrisokane.[1] In the 1650s Cromwell's government had confiscated a higher proportion of Catholic lands in Tipperary—77 percent—than in any other county. Owney and Arra and the Ormond baronies, especially, witnessed the plantation of a substantial English minority; for example, by 1659–1660 the population of Killoscully parish, in Owney and Arra, was one-third Protestant. However, these baronies were relatively poor, containing mountains mingled with soils of at best mixed quality. Perhaps this was one reason why by 1700 James Wansbrough had leased his inherited farm at Ballycahane, in Killoscully parish, for £35 per annum and moved 30 miles north to a richer farm at Ballinlug, in the parish and barony of Rathconrath, County Westmeath, where another Baptist community was centered on a church in nearby Rahugh.[2]

In 1683 Wansbrough's brothers-in-law emigrated to West Jersey. After a brief stay in the Irish Tenth, they moved to Salem (later Cumberland) County and settled among other Tipperary Baptists on both sides of the lower Cohansey River, in Greenwich and Fairfield townships. The Irish circumstances that encouraged their emigration probably

---

1. Cleagh Keating (or Cloghkeating, Cloughkeating): a townland in Modreeny parish, Lower Ormond barony. The Wansbroughs, Shepherds, and Tolers were concentrated primarily in the parishes of Killoscully, Loughkeen, Ballingarry, Modreeny, and Kilruane.   2. Rahugh (or Rahue): a townland and parish in Moycashel barony, Co. Westmeath. For demographic data on Killoscully and Rathconrath parishes, see appendix 2.2c, on chapter 1.

included the relative poorness of their lands, political disabilities and resentment of tithes, and fear of the impending ascension of the Catholic king, James II (1685–1688). Indeed, it is likely that the Shepherds were among those Tipperary Baptists who in 1683 fled to New Jersey and Pennsylvania following their implication in the unsuccessful Rye House Plot against James's succession to the throne. Only two years later the Ormond baronies were swept by rumors that the coronation of James II would be attended by a Catholic massacre of Irish Protestants, as had occurred in Ulster in 1641; consequently, declared one local dissenter, "All Sober people here are inclined & pr[e]p[ar]ing to go to West Gursey."

However, James Wansbrough remained in Ireland, although in his Westmeath parish Catholics outnumbered Protestants twenty to one. In 1700 he sent his first letter to his sister Ann and her husband since their emigration. In typically providential terms, he recounted the tumultuous events that had taken place in Ireland in the intervening years—the temporary restoration of Catholic power under James II, the Glorious Revolution of 1688, and the Protestant reconquest by William of Orange in 1689–1691. He also catalogued their dire personal consequences for the Shepherd and Wansbrough families and their relations, many of whom had perished in a conflict that claimed at least 50,000 lives by war and disease and that was especially ferocious in the disputed marchlands of north Tipperary and Westmeath. Yet Wansbrough also related how he had survived these trials and eventually flourished, as the restoration of peace and Protestant power brought renewed English settlement and at least temporary prosperity.

Letter 1.
James Wansbrough, Ballinlug, Rathconrath Parish, County Westmeath,
to Ann and Thomas Shepherd, Cohansey, New Jersey, 4 May 1700

Balenloge[3]   County west meath   may y[e] 4th 1700
Well beloved brother and Cister   theese are to let you under stand that I received
aleter from you with my nevies[4] leter allsoe to our greate satisfaction y[t][5] it hath pleased
allmighty God in his marcy and goodness to preserve you in your far Jorny and to setle
you in agood and peaceable land and allsoe ithath[6] pleased god of Infinite mercy to
deliver us and to bring us through many perels and dangers sence your departure oute
of[7] this kingdom   for after Kingcharles[8] dyed his brother[9] asumed y[e] Crowne and
then popery over swayd this kingdoms and our goods was madee[10] apray[11]   our

---

3. **Balenloge**: Ballinlug townland (Rathconrath parish and barony, Co. Westmeath).   4. **Nevies**: i.e., nephew's. For a discussion of Wansbrough's origins and speech, see appendix 1.   5. **y[t]**: that (as elsewhere in this letter).   6. **ithath**: i.e., it hath; for analytic and (in this instance) synthetic spellings, see appendix 1. 7. **oute of**: from (especially when indicating origin).   8. **Kingcharles**: Charles II (1660–1685).   9. **his brother**: James II (1685–1688).   10. **madee**: made; silent e in a final syllable is occasionally written ee; see **brokee** "broke," **Balmacooghee** "Ballymacue," **pleaseed** "pleased," **whomee** "whom," **scarcee** "scarce" hereafter.   11. **apray**: a prey.

cytes¹² Charters brokee   our peniall laws¹³ teaken away   yᵉ ould propriaters of
Ireland¹⁴ entering in upon all our posesions   our armes¹⁵ Ceased¹⁶ and popish armeys
raised throughout these kingdomes till it pleased god of his bounty ful marcy and good
ness to raies¹⁷ us up a deliverer oute of yᵉ same famyly¹⁸ for our deliverance who was at
yᵗ time prince of Orange and was maried to princes mary King James eldest daughte[r]
who through zeale for yᵉ gospell of our lord Jesus Christ and Honour of god forth with
then when all was at steake Came with asmall army of 14 thousand and in vaded or
landed in England and god Allmighty prospering him hath through greate wars and
danger with yᵉ lose¹⁹ of many thousands of men and great Churge²⁰ obtained peace and
tranquility for himselfe and his sobjects as allsoe he hath been yᵉ Instrument of makeing
peace throughoute all Cristendome and now yᵉ lands is derer²¹ by yᵉ third part then
they ware when you ware heere for the lands yᵗ would agiven yᵘ four shilings pʳ acor²²
will give you six or six and sixpence and wehave more English heere now then we had
before yᵉ ware   and now I will give you some short acount of our owne famyly   my
father dyed at birr²³ after yᵉ first sige of limbrick²⁴ in yᵉ hith²⁵ of yᵉ trobles   brother
Gyles dyed of [y]ᵉ small pox and John whirborn maried Cister bety and he dyed about
yᵉ same time my fa[ther] dyed and now cister bety is maried to simon Ronsall and is
but in anendefarant [wa]y²⁶ and Cosen tho<mas> shephard is larning yᵉ Joyne[rs tra]de
of²⁷ his fatherinlaw and nicolas Conat C[iste]r praxey es²⁸ husband dyed aboute 7 or 8

12. cytes: i.e., cities'; **our cytes Charters brokee**: in 1686–1687, James II's Irish Lord Deputy, Richard Talbot, Earl of Tyrconnel, revoked and redrew the charters of most Irish towns and boroughs; the old charters had ensured a Protestant monopoly of urban government, but two-thirds of the newly appointed aldermen and burgesses were Catholics, as was Talbot.   **13. peniall laws**: penal laws, restricting Irish Catholic civil, economic, and religious activities; repealed by the Catholic-dominated Irish Parliament under James II but reinstated and expanded under his successors.   **14. yᵉ ould propriaters of Ireland**: Catholics whose lands had formerly been confiscated and granted to Protestants; in fact, the "oldest" proprietors, of Gaelic descent, recovered scarcely any of their former estates, and the major beneficiaries of the Protestant conquest's temporary reversal under James II were Catholics of Norman origin, i.e., the "Old English."   **15. armes**: i.e., armies.   **16. Ceased**: abolished, disbanded; see OED s.v. cease, 5. "put a stop to" (obsolete).   **17. raies**: i.e., raise.   **18. a deliverer oute of yᵉ same famyly**: William of Orange, i.e., William III (1688–1702), who ruled jointly with his wife, Mary, James II's eldest daughter, until her death in 1694.   **19. lose**: i.e., loss; see **loses** "losses" hereafter.   **20. Churge**: i.e., courage.   **21. derer**: i.e., dearer "more expensive."   **22. would agiven . . .**: i.e., would have given ("yielded") . . . ; shows the reduction of **have** to **a** between a modal auxiliary (could, should, would, may, etc.) and a past participle and also in the past infinitive (e.g. **to have gone → to a gone**). The form **a** may be further reduced to zero: **would a given → would given**; see Shakespeare, *Coriolanus*, 4.6.36–37: "we should by this . . . found it so" (i.e., **a** found it). See also Robert Burns, *Tam o' Shanter*. The wind blew as 'twad blawn its last (i.e., 'twad **a** blawn). Other instances of this development; n. 84 below; chapter 2, n. 10; chapter 15, n. 42; chapter 26, n. 50; chapter 38, n. 10; chapter 46, n. 40; chapter 51, n. 69.   **23. birr**: Birr town (and parish, Ballybrit barony, King's Co. [now Co. Offaly]); later Parsonstown, now again Birr.   **24. limbrick**: Limerick city, Co. Limerick; William III's first, unsuccessful seige of Limerick occurred in August 1690; the second seige began in August 1691 and ended with the Catholic surrender of the city on 3 October.   **25. hith**: i.e., height; see n. 4.   **26. in anendefarant [wa]y**: in an indifferent way, i.e., only moderately prosperous. For the use of square brackets and other editorial conventions, see appendix 1.   **27. larning . . . of**: learning . . . from.   **28. C[iste]r praxey es**: i.e., sister Praxey's.

weeks after my father and left 3 children t<w>o bo[y]s and one daughter and shee is
maried againe to Daniell dason yᵉ sadler yᵗ lived at Enagh²⁹   Cister lucy maried her
masters stuard and Clark³⁰ aft[er] Cornel buckworth³¹ and they was [v]ery rich   our
brotherinlaws name is richard lockwod   shee dyed in Childbed t<w>o years
sense³²   brother robart wansbrough was a seaman and was prest at bristo<l>³³ to sarve
as seaman and was kild in abatle at sea as we under stand   brother william
wansbrough was Insigne for brudnells regiment and was aboord yᵉ fleete   he dyed
neere aligant³⁴ in spaine   my Cister mary is maried to Pall webster and lives at balen
gary³⁵   Cister rachell lives with cosen thomas towler at balen toty³⁶ and is not
maried   Cister Jain³⁷ liveth at balmacooghee³⁸ with capten baly yᵗ maried mʳ prilyes
eldesᵗ daughter   my mother is maried to mʳ tho<mas> balme yᵗ liveth at
killloughnane³⁹ be twixt raplagh⁴⁰ and grange⁴¹ neere Enagh   I was maried before yᵉ
wars broke oute ayeere⁴² to one Tho<mas> Rol<s> Younge[s]t daughter   Johnathan
wala[n] knowes her cister yᵗ is maried to Joh[n]athan Short of gortin⁴³   and after yᵉ
wars by sick[ness and] loses and yᵉ dept⁴⁴ yᵗ my father owed I was forst to sell my
father<s> lands⁴⁵ for three hundred pound to Cosen nicolas towler   soe after he
posesed it four yeer<r>s It pleaseed⁴⁶ god yᵗ Igot yᵗ favour with my fatherinlaw yᵗ he
advanced 3 hondred pound towards yᵉ purchas and about ahondred pound Ihad myselfe
soe yᵗ it was sould but bought againe   Ihave one daughter and ason   his name is
thomas   my daughter is 12 yeere ould & son is five   my wife is with Child   Ihad
another son Called John but he dyed   this allsoe may carty fie⁴⁷ you yᵗ I received

29. Enagh: now Nenagh town (and parish, Upper and Lower Ormond baronies, Co. Tipperary, North Riding [N.R.]).   **30. stuard and Clark**: i.e., steward and clerk.   **31. aft[er] Cornel buckworth**: after Col. Buckworth's death.   **32. t<w>o years sense** (i.e., since): two years ago. For the use of angled brackets and other editorial conventions, see appendix 1.   **33. prest at bristo<l>**: impressed, i.e., forcibly conscripted, into the English navy at the port of Bristol, England.   **34. aligant**: Alicante, Spain; Wansbrough's form is closer to the Catalan original (Alacant).   **35. balen gary**: Ballingarry townland (and parish, Lower Ormond barony, Co. Tipperary, N.R.).   **36. balen toty**: Ballintotty townland (Lisbunny parish, Upper Ormond barony, Co. Tipperary, N.R.).   **37. Jain**: i.e., Jane; **Jaim** ms.   **38. balmacooghee**: Ballymacue (Kilruane parish, Upper Ormond barony, Co. Tipperary, N.R.); the form has "silent ee" (see n. 10) and silent gh as in **Raplagh** "Rapla" (see n. 40); Wansbrough has dotted the first minim of **m**, making the name appear to be **balinacooghee**.   **39. killloughnane**: Killylaughnane townland (Kilruane parish, Upper Ormond barony, Co. Tipperary, N.R.).   **40. raplagh**: Rapla townland (Kilruane parish, Upper Ormond barony, Co. Tipperary, N.R.).   **41. Grange**: probably Grange Upper townland (Knigh parish, Lower Ormond barony, Co. Tipperary, N.R.).   **42. before yᵉ wars broke oute ayeere**: "a year before the wars broke out."   **43. Gortin**: Gorteen townland (Finnoe parish, Lower Ormond barony, Co. Tipperary, N.R.).   **44. dept**: an interesting case of a "learned" spelling pronunciation. The standard spelling **debt** is itself a purely learned creation based on the antiquarian knowledge that **dette**, the original shape of the French borrowing into English, ultimately reflects Latin de*b*itum. The same phenomenon occurs in chapter 26, n. 33, where we find **Doupt** "doubt" (originally dou*b*t(e), from Latin du*b*itum).   **45. my father<s> lands**: at Ballycahane (Killoscully parish, Owney and Arra barony, Co. Tipperary, N.R.). The form **father** in this phrase may be an archaism: the word belongs to an inflectional class in Old and Middle English which does not formally distinguish the nominative (**father**) and the genitive (**father's**), and this peculiarity may have been preserved here (the same phenomenon is seen in **Lady Day** (i.e., Lady's Day).   **46. pleaseed**: see n. 10.   **47. carty fie**: i.e., certify "inform officially."

apeare[48] of butens of silver from Cosen James shephards wife y[t] was[49] and my mother
and Cisters received twelve pence apeece and Cister rachel aquaife[50] or pin<n>er[51] a
toaken[52] from my Cister   my Cister Rachell and Jane hath either of them aboute
twenty pound apeece of their owne and they say y[t] if they Could get opertunity or
good Company either one or both would goe and scee you in that Contry
allthough we have sceene abondance of troble and received greate Loses yet Ithank god
we have peace and quiatness now and through god allmightys providence and mercy
we have both y[e] law and gospell Reestablished amongst us and Every one EnJoying y[e]
freute of theire labours   this being all at present with my kind love to you and my
dear Cister and Cosen Tho<mas> sheper<d> and y[e] rest of youur Liteleones[53] not for
geting[54] Cosen John and his Children and cosen david and his Cosen Jonathan walen
and his good wife and Children and all y[e] rest of our relations and frinds there y[t] went
alonge with you   my father gyles shepard John whiteho<r>ne[55] is buried[56] by your
Uncle Thomas sheperd in birr   thomas shepard your uncle thomas es[57] son dyed last
yeere at birr   he lived where mr wetherlock lived   his brother james was kild at
teaking of artlone[58]   Joseph is in England   daniell is at home   your ant liveth at
teni kelie[59] & is maried to Joseph Ingrom   liveth & very rich   your father dyed after
y[e] wars   your uncle simon dyed in his exile or banishment   your brother Jonathan
and Jonadab is both ded   they dyed in y[e] wars   Jonathens wife is maried to Gerd[60]
nokes y[t] was prentice to brother gyles sheperd and lives in ormond[61]   they live prety
well[62]   Robart shepard and James shepard your uncle simons sons are both maried and
[is] in an endefrint way of living[63]   mistris Elisbeth wade[64] is maried to alderman heds
sone of water ford[65]   m[s] mary michell is maried and live[s] aboute lim[er]ick
Capten brigges is [de]d   Cornell finch is ded   y[e] bishop of kilalow[66] is ded
Maior[67] Canbe is [d]ed   Capten alen is ded   Roger ho[ld]en bee is ded   samuill
wade ded   henery prithy ded   Leftanant[68] waler ded   parson godfrey ded

48. apeare: i.e., a pair.   49. wife y[t] was: former/deceased wife.   50. quaife: variant of coif "headdress."
51. pin<n>er: a coif provided with flaps.   52. toaken: i.e., token "keepsake" (OED s.v., 9).   53. Liteleones:
i.e., little ones.   54. not for geting: i.e., not forgetting, "including."   55. my father . . . whiteho<r>ne: read
"my father, Gyles Shepherd, and John Whitehorne."   56. burier ms.   57. thomas es: i.e., Thomas's.
58. Artlone: Athlone town (Co. Westmeath); the Williamite army took Athlone, on the river Shannon, from
its Irish and French defenders on 30 June 1691.   59. teni kelie: Tinnakilly townland (Loughkeen parish,
Lower Ormond barony, Co. Tipperary, N.R.).   60. Gerd: Gerard (spelled as pronounced).   61. ormond: the
official name of the Baptist church and settlement at Cleagh Keating; see n. 1.   62. they live pretty well: they
are pretty well-off, fairly affluent or comfortable.   63. in an endefrint way of living: see n. 26.   64. mistris
Elisbeth wade: Elizabeth Wade is probably the daughter of Capt. Samuel Wade, a Cromwellian officer who
helped found Waterford city's Baptist church in the early 1650s; the Cleagh Keating church in north Tipperary
was apparently an offshoot of Waterford's congregation; hed is the English surname Head, mostly associated
with Co. Tipperary (see Edward Mac Lysaght, More Irish Families (Galway, 1960), 119–20.   65. water ford:
Waterford city (Co. Waterford).   66. kilalow: Killaloe diocese (Church of Ireland), the area of which
included the North Riding of Co. Tipperary.   67. Maior: i.e., Major.   68. Leftanant: Lieutenant (as
pronounced).

Leftanant sheldon ded   Capten parker ded   Capten roulstown ye ould man

ded   frank Roulstown y^t maried debrow wade ded   Thomas Casill ded   Capten

powell and his famyly living in ye ould pleace   Capten owataway ded   ould wiliam

freeman ded[69]   ould sargant hardy is living and his ould wife and is weel to live[70]

they live under young Capten harasson[71]   Leftanant foxall ded   Robart alen y^t went

along with you[72] liveth at garan more[73] and is maried   if i should give youe an

acount of all ye tra[ns] actions[74] y^t hath hapened amongst[75] us sence your leving this

Contr[ey a q]uire[76] of peapor would scercely Containe it but if I could by asa[f]e[88]

hand send you abook of ye trans actions and cations[78] of this late Revolution[79]   sence

I Canot teake ye the will for ye deed[80]   Irest your Ever loving brother till deth   I

thank god Iam in a good way of living for Ihave my owne Estate againe   it is set[81] to

three English men   we have 35 pound ayere rent Cleere oute of it besides quitrent

and all other taxes[82] of ye which my mother hath 9 pound ayeere Joynter[83]   I was to

apaid[84] 12 if my father and mother had both lived   Ihave avery good wife Ithank god

and shee is and will be a veery good fortune to me for what I have allredy had and

shall have if shee and I doe oute live her father and mother will be as good Ithink as six

or seven hundred pound[85]   Soe comending you all to ye Providence of all Mighty

god our hevenly father by whomee[86] we live move and have our being desiering y^t he

may in his Infinit marcy in crese Everyone of us in greace[87] wisdom and understanding

y^t we may be truly thankfull for all ye benefits y^t we doe receive at his hands y^t after

this sinfull painfull and mortall life ended we may Every one be parteakers of Etarnell

69. Maior Canbe . . . Capten alen . . . Roger ho[ld]en bee . . . samuill wade . . . henery prithy . . . Capten owataway . . . wiliam freeman: Solomon Cambry (or Cambri), Capt. Stephen Allen, Samuel Wade (see n. 64), Roger Holdenby (or Haldenby), Henry Prittie, Capt. John Otway, and William Freeman: all prominent Cromwellian settlers in north Tipperary's Ormond baronies.   **70. weell to live**: well-to-do, affluent, or comfortable.   **71. they live under young Capten harrasson**: they are tenants (probably head tenants) of the young proprietor, Captain Harrison.   **72. Robart alen y^t went along with you liveth at garan more**: ref. to an emigrant, brother of Capt. Stephen Alen (see n. 69), who accompanied the Shepherds to New Jersey but returned to Ireland.   **73. garan more**: Garrannmore (Youghalarra parish, Owney and Arra barony, Co. Tipperary, N.R.).   **74. tra[ns] actions**: i.e., transactions.   **75. armongst** ms.   **76. [q]uire**: (1) four sheets of paper folded to make eight leaves, or (2) 24 to 25 sheets of paper.   **77. asa[f]e**: i.e., a safe.   **78. cations**: aphetic form of **occasions**; cf. Shakespeare's 'casion, cagion.   **79. this late Revolution**: the Glorious Revolution (1688–1691) of William III.   **80. sence . . . deed**: "since I cannot, [you are to] take the will for the deed."   **81. set**: leased.   **82. besides quitrent and all other taxes**: "after quitrent and all other taxes have been paid"; **quitrent**: annual rent paid by proprietors to the crown.   **83. Joynter**: i.e., jointure, a legal settlement or contractual obligation conferring an annuity. The form **joynter** shows the loss of [y] before an unstressed vowel, a sound change which had taken place by the 16th century and is seen in such forms, for example, as **nater** "nature," **futer** "future," **critter** "creature," **ed(d)ication** "education" and in reverse spellings like **ardure** "ardor." These "y-less" forms penetrated the literary language and are found, for example, in Shakespeare, but they were later censured. By the nineteenth century the older pronunciation had been restored in the standard language, but in non-standard speech and in the dialects the y-less forms have persisted.   **84. to apaid**: i.e., to have paid; see n. 22.   **85. for what I have allredy had . . . six or seven hundred pound**: "because what I have had already and will have . . . will be as good . . . as £600 or £700."   **86. whomee**: whom; see n. 10.   **87. greace**: i.e., grace. For spellings with **ea**, see appendix 1.

rest and felicity is ye harty prayers[88] of your Ever loving brother   fere well till ye next
opertunity

James Wansbrough

if you can get opertunity pray faile not to send and let us heere from you   wee have
had t<w>o leters from you sence your departure   for I think Ishall not Come to you
and sence you are setled Idoe not ad vise you to Come here againe for lands is very
scarcee[89] and deere   I think rat<e>s of goods will fall and rents will behard to bemade
so y^t tenants will <be> slaves to their landlords though sence ye setlement[90] we have
had agood time and mony plenty[91]   a Ould guiny[92] here goes f[or] 26 shilings   4^s
an<d> 9^d for 5^s and 4^d   an English Crown[93] for six shilings   which is all at [present]
f[rom]

J: W

In 1700 James Wansbrough seemed content to remain in Ireland. However, between
1716 and 1728, the date of his last surviving letter, many of his Irish neighbors and
relatives, including one cousin, had emigrated, and in the latter year Wansbrough himself
deliberated whether to take the drastic step for a man of late middle age to join his Shepherd relations in the New World. Economic considerations were probably paramount.
The 1720s were years of severe distress for Irish landlords and tenants alike. Stagnation in
trade, currency shortages, and repeated harvest failures resulted in economic depression
and famine, while the pressure for lands and the expiration of old leases sent rents rocket-
ing. Modest landholders were caught between falling incomes and mounting expenses, and
Wansbrough himself could not renew the lease on his Westmeath farm at a profitable rent.
He also had personal reasons for disenchantment with Ireland: by 1728 Wansbrough's first
wife and all their sons had died, and his second wife, whom he married in 1725, had
relations in America. Moreover, although new English settlers had increased the proportion
of Protestants in Westmeath to an all-time peak of nearly 14 percent, Ireland's Baptist
congregations were shrinking through intermarriage and conversions to the established
church, producing among the remainder a crisis of confidence in the future of their increasingly fragile community.[94] And although official persecution of Irish Dissenters was no
longer as intense as in Queen Anne's reign (1702–1714), the political climate yet remained

---

88. harty prayers and flicity ms. (dittography).   89. scarcee: scarce; see n. 10.   90. sence ye setlement: since
the end of the Williamite wars (1688–1691).   91. we have had agood time and mony plenty: "we have had
prosperous times and money has been plentiful."   92. guiny: i.e., guinea (21 shillings).   93. an English
Crown: coin normally worth five shillings.   94. In the 1650s there were at least 13 Baptist churches in
Ireland, but by 1725 there were only five with settled ministers—Dublin, Waterford, Cork, Cleagh Keating,
and Legacory in County Armagh—plus the "remains" of four others, including Rahugh, that depended on
visiting pastors. In 1725 only the Dublin meeting contained as many as two hundred families, the remainder
having between 60 and 30, and Irish Baptists altogether numbered merely 1,500–2,000. Among the conformists
to the Church of Ireland were Wansbrough's Toler relations, who by the late eighteenth century were among
Co. Tipperary's most powerful families. By 1800 only five hundred Irish Baptists remained, but a surge of

uncertain. However, such troubles did not exist in West Jersey, where Wansbrough, perhaps encouraged by his young wife, thought he might begin the world anew.

Letter 2.
James Wansbrough, Ballinlug, Rathconrath Parish, County Westmeath, to Ann Shepherd, Cohansey, New Jersey, 18 April 1728

Balenlug   Aprill yᵉ 18 1728

Loving Cister   I have Been long Disopointed of sending unto you[95]   I thank god I and my famely is well in helth   soe is two of my Daughters   the youngest I had by my former wife   I have been marid next agust will be[96] three yeers   I have adaughter by my wife   I got onely ahondred pounds with her   she is a very good husef[97] and of a very good famely for thomas Packenham was her mothers brother and his son was night of the Cheere[98] for our County of west meath   she hath aCosen In new york maried unto one Capten Congrave   all my Cisters heere is well onely[99] Jane who is maried to Thomas Barton   she hath been sickly   at last[100] her sickness went to an ague[101]   Cister Praxey lives at balengary[102]   Cister mary and Pall webster is in yᵉ county of Dublen   Cister Rachell and her hosband David Shephard lives at balycahane[103]   she hath four sons   Cister Elisabeth dyed   Lucys son Richard Lockwood is arich man and Justice of yᵉ peace   he is worth five or six hondred pound ayeere   I desier you Dere Cister to write by the first opertunity and let me heere how you and your two sons moses and David <is> and your Daughter and all their famelyes   this hath been avery hard yeere amongst the poore people for Corn failed very much and now wheat is at twenty shillings abarell and other Corne proporsianable[104]   lands is got to an Extrame Rate heere so yᵗ they yᵗ teakes land is likely to be teaken by their lands[105]   I lighted of[106] ahistory of america which gave me avery <h>onest acount of all your Contrey   it sayes yᵗ he yᵗ is worth five hondred Pounds heere laid out and retorned there yᵗ if he have any Induster[107] may live as well

pan-Protestant revivalism soon sparked a remarkable resurgence: in 1800–1841 30 new Baptist churches were founded, and between 1818 and the 1890s membership rose from two thousand to five thousand. However, nearly all this new growth occurred in Ulster; southern Irish Baptist churches continued to atrophy; and by the early twentieth century both the Cleagh Keating and the Rahugh congregations had disappeared.   **95. sending unto you**: sending you a letter by a bearer.   **96. next agust will be**: this coming August.   **97. husef**: housewife (variants in OED: hussive, hussif, huzzif).   **98. night of the Cheere**: i.e., knight of the shire.   **99. onely**: except.   **100. at last**: in the end.   **101. went to an ague**: turned into an acute fever.   **102. balengary**: see n. 35.   **103. balycahane**: see n. 45.   **104. proporsianable**: in proportion, proportionately (see OED s.v. proportionably).   **105. they yᵗ teakes land is likely to be teaken by their lands**: "any person who rents land [at these high rates] will likely be ruined financially."   **106. lighted of**: came across.   **107. Induster**: industry, diligence; the *English Dialect Dictionary* lists **induster** as a verb attested only in Ireland, "to work hard, be industrious," but has no instances of the form as a noun.

as he y[t] is worth six or seven[108] hundred pound ayeere in England   if you or your sons Doe write unto me and give me good Encoragment I will trans port my sellf and famely and soninlaw   I Can teake threehondred pound heere but pray tell me what is y[e] best Comodyty to teake into y[t] Contrey   what meakes me think of goeing is my wife is ayoung woman and would be willing to goe into y[t] Contrey besides agood farm Ihad y[e] lease <of> is Ronoute[109] and <I> Canot get it worth teaking[110]   I have in baly Cahane[111] and this Contrey[112] twenty pounds a yeere   I send this by Cosen frances Parvin whose aunt was maried to my first wives brother   they are honest People and Lives well   your sons may Doe him aCind ness in folloing[113]   Pray <ask> if thomas Green y[t] lived with Isarall Comborton in Philadelpha beliving[114] for his father and mother is very Desierous to know wher[115] he be alive or ded   there was a man left this naibor hood about forty yeer agoe one Owen Daly out of y[e] County of west meath   I was Entreated to Enquier for him if he lives nee[r] you if by chance you or y[e] young men might nnow him   I doe Expect to heere from you by next Crismas   the Creator of us [. . . an]d give my love and servis[116] to my Cosens in generall but Espesially to your own two sons and your Daughter and her hosband not for geting your sellf   my wife gives her servis to you and your Children   I am and Remain your afectinate broth<er> whilst I am

James Wansbrough

if cervants[117] be a good profit Idesier <you> to let me know it or what goods will turn to best acount out of this Contry   I canteake three hondred pounds with me if I doe trans port my sellf into y[t] Contrey[118] and leave five pound ayeer heere to send me every yeere aservant or nesesaryes Duering three lives or thirty yeers to Com[119]   severall of my Cisters sons will Certen be along with me if I doe Com into y[t] Contry   nomore but as a far<e> wel   Dan Towler is worth six hondred ayeere lives at grange[120] where maiar[121] fox lived formerly and Elisabeth weade Daughter to Esquier wad<e> lives at waterford and her hosbond <is> alderman hed of waterford[122]

J. W.

---

108. six or seven: conjectural, written above canc. **five.**   **109. Ronoute**: i.e., run out "expired."   **110. <I> Canot get it worth teaking**: "I cannot get the farm at a rent that would make it economical to take up (renew) the lease." **<I>**: an expected subject pronoun is often dropped in Ulster English in a non-initial clause, especially, as here, when it is identical with the subject pronoun of the preceding clause. This usage occurs frequently in Shakespeare: *King Lear*, 1.4.201: "as you are old and reverend, should be wise."   **111. baly Cahane**: see n. 45.   **112. this Contrey**: the area around Ballinlug (Co. Westmeath); see n. 3.   **113. Doe him aCind ness in folloing**: do him a kindness in the following way.   **114. beliving**: i.e., be living.
115. wher: whether; see n. 4.   **116. give my love**: conjectural; **servis**: respect, duty (OED s.v. service, 9: "[i]n epistolary use, **give my service to** = remember me respectfully to [a third person])."   **117. cervants**: i.e., servants; here = indentured servants.   **118. Contrey** in ms.   **119. Duering three lives or thirty years to Com**: Wansbrough proposes to lease out the remainder of his Irish property at £5 per year for a period of thirty years or the duration of three lives (named in the lease), whichever expires first.   **120. grange**: see n. 41.   **121. maiar**: i.e., Major.   **122. Elisabeth weade . . . alderman hed of waterford**: i.e., Elizabeth Wade . . . alderman Head of Waterford [city]; see ns. 64–65.

Cosen Thomas Toler is ded   Cosen Nicolas toler is awidower   all his Children which is Eleven lives[123]

James Wansbrough was still in Ireland in mid-1732, when his nephew wrote that "uncle James [was] alive and well" in Ballinlug.[124] After that date, he does not appear in New Jersey records, although he may have gone to Pennsylvania, like most Irish Dissenters who emigrated in this period, or joined his wife's cousin in New York. Yet if Wansbrough had joined his Shepherd relations in West Jersey, as planned, he would have found a flourishing settlement. In 1726 Salem County (including the future Cumberland County) contained nearly four thousand white inhabitants, plus 150 slaves. Most whites were "yeomen" farmers who marketed cattle, hogs, wheat, rice, cedar wood, and other produce in Philadelphia. According to one observer, they were "laborious, honest, and industrious" if also "unaccountable obstinate and tenacious."[125] By 1745 Quakers comprised less than a fifth of the area's population, but they were still dominant economically and politically. Although Baptists, the Shepherds (Sheppards in colonial usage) appear to have been equally successful, partly because they were among the first settlers at Shrewsbury Neck, on the banks of the lower Cohansey, which contained some of West Jersey's richest soils. In 1690 the Shepherd brothers founded the first Baptist church in the district, and by his death in 1695 David Shepherd owned a large quantity of land along the river, plus personal property worth £172, while his brother John's family possessed at least three thousand acres. The American-born Shepherds also fared well. One of the sons of Wansbrough's sister Ann, also named David Shepherd, farmed a minimum of 150 acres and in 1702 was nominated by Lord Nottingham for membership in the Governor's Council; likewise, his brother Moses died in 1752 worth over £400 in personal property. Later generations were locally prominent in the American Revolution, perhaps in part because the Anglo-American conflict reignited radical religious and political sentiments inherited from their Cromwellian forefathers. Thus, for over two hundred years the Shepherds multiplied and prospered along the Cohansey.[126] In the late nineteenth century most remained Baptists, although some had become Presbyterians and others had joined the Quakers with whom their ancestors had been contentiously allied during their brief sojourns in Ireland.

123. Cosen Thomas . . . which is Eleven lives and initials J.W. inserted between ms. lines beginning severall of my Cisters and well   Dan Towler.   124. Robert Dawson, Bristol, England, to Moses Shepherd, Cohansey, N.J., 23 July 1732. Dawson was the son of James Wansbrough's sister, Praxey, and her second husband, Daniel Dawson, "yͤ sadler yͭ lived at Enagh" (letter 1); a physician, Dawson emigrated to Philadelphia between 1732 and 1741.   125. Wacker, *Land and People*, 184; see Sources.   126. By 1876 there were at least 25 Shepherd/Sheppard property-owners in Fairfield and Greenwich townships, north and south of the Cohansey River.

2 ✳

Alexander Crawford, 1736

From the late 1600s through the early 1800s, most emigrants from Ireland to America came from the northern province of Ulster. Although Ulster emigration included sizable minorities of Catholics and Anglicans, plus small numbers of Quakers and other Dissenters, by far the largest group was composed of those most commonly known in the United States today as the Scots-Irish: Presbyterians whose ancestors had migrated from Lowland Scotland to Ulster—in numbers ranging perhaps from 80,000 to 130,000—from the beginning of the Ulster Plantation in 1607 through the Scottish famines of the 1690s and in smaller numbers thereafter. Initially, the Scots settled where James I's Scottish "undertakers" or grantees encouraged their plantation on estates confiscated (or, in counties Antrim and Down, purchased) from the province's defeated (or financially distressed) Gaelic lords: primarily in the fertile regions of north Down and south Antrim, in the Lower Bann Valley of north Antrim and east Londonderry,[1] and in the Foyle Valley between east Donegal and west Tyrone, all areas easily accessible from Scottish ports. By the end of the seventeenth century, Scottish and other Protestant settlers had expanded throughout most of Ulster, transforming the province into a religious patchwork of discrete districts dominated by Presbyterians, Anglicans (chiefly of north English origin), or native Catholics. Between 1670 and 1720 the number of Presbyterian congregations in northern Ireland increased from 70 to 148, and by 1732–1733, according to the hearthmoney returns, three-fifths of Ulster's inhabitants were Protestants, of whom a large majority were Presbyterians.

In the 1680s and 1690s, however, even as the last great Scottish migrations to Ulster occurred, some of the Scots-Irish began to move to North America. Between 1680 and 1716 perhaps as many as three thousand passengers left Ulster for the New World, and in 1717–1719 between 4,500 and 7,000 may have emigrated. During the 1720s about 15,000 people, again mostly Presbyterians, sailed from Ulster to America, and perhaps another 50,000 or more emigrated between 1730 and the outbreak in America of the French and Indian War in 1754–1755. Prior to the 1710s the Scots-Irish went primarily to the Chesapeake, next to New England, and from the late 1720s overwhelmingly to Philadelphia and the Delaware Valley, with lesser numbers landing at New York, Charleston, Savannah, and Baltimore.

---

1. In accordance with popular usage, in this book we employ alternatively "Londonderry" and "Derry" to designate both county and city, without reference to the terms' contemporary political implications; prior to the Ulster Plantation, most of Co. Londonderry was known as Coleraine, renamed when James I granted the area to a consortium of London Companies of merchants and manufacturers (Clothworkers, Drapers, Haberdashers, etc.). We will employ "Coleraine" only in reference to the town of that name in northeast Co. Londonderry.

In 1736 one Ulster Presbyterian considering emigration was Alexander Crawford, a tenant in Drumark and Drumgun townlands in Killymard parish, in the barony of Banagh, County Donegal, where he and his brother Hugh rented 240 acres for just under £24 per year (increased from £20 in 1732), as well as additional dues of farm produce and labor, from their absentee landlord, Alexander Murray of Broughton in Kircudbrightshire, Scotland. Most of the Murray estate, some sixty-five thousand acres in all, was inhospitable mountain and bog, suitable only for rough grazing, but the Crawfords' farm was part of a thin belt of Scottish settlers spread for 30 miles along the fertile seacoast of southwest Donegal. According to Murray's agent, Thomas Addi, the Crawfords' and their neighbors' farms were "good for grain and pasture and commodious for fishing herrings, by which in some years they make their whole rent."

The Crawfords' holding should have placed them in at least the middling ranks of west Ulster society, but Alexander's letter to his landlord evinces no sense of well-being but instead catalogues many of the travails that impelled the early eighteenth-century emigration of Scots-Irish and others from Ulster. Crawford's letter complains of the burden of tithes and of the other legal and religious disabilities that Presbyterians and other Irish Dissenters experienced. However, economic adversity was Crawford's paramount concern and the primary factor stimulating Ulster emigration. When old leases expired, competition for new or renewed leases, coupled with landlords' desires for increased revenues, drove rent levels steadily upward; thus, in the early 1730s Addi had boasted of raising the rents of Murray's tenants "by fair or forceable means," despite their attempts to combine against him. Moreover, even in good years the remoteness of southwest Donegal from major markets depressed prices for farm produce and hindered economic development, but throughout Ulster in the 1720s crop failures, cattle diseases, and falling prices reduced tenants' incomes, forced many into linen manufacturing, and caused periodic famines. In 1729 many of Murray's tenants were so poor they abandoned their leases, signed contracts of indenture, and emigrated as servants to New England; and now again in the mid-1730s bad harvests obliged Crawford and many of his neighbors to threaten emigration if their landlord refused to reduce rents and provide assistance.

Alexander Crawford, Drumgun, Killymard Parish, County Donegal, to Alexander Murray, Broughton, Cally, near Gatehouse of Fleet, Kircudbrightshire, Scotland, 21 July 1736

Honred Landlord   Drumgun   July 21th: 1736
                                 I finding this oPortunaty have med this my
Mesenger to Acquent you of ye misrabl Condision that I have Brout myselvef and my famely to In Steying In your oners[2] Land thes yers Past Depending one[3] your Honers

---

2. your oners: i.e., your honor's.   **3. one**: i.e., on.

Promises that you med to me when you were in this Contrey Last and After that
Impost[4] Rents And Burdings[5] that Iame[6] oblig<d> to grone yunder[7] ye Burding therof
when I Can not Provid for my Children But ame[8] obligt to Transport my Self and my
famly to ye Deserts of America and Had it not Ben for depending Upon your Honers
Promise I and my famley might be Living in that Land wher we might be freed from
thos Burdings that we ar Labring yunder   Iame taking thes as Stroks from ye Hand of
god upon ye acount of[9] my not Going with my frends when th<e>y would Ahad me
to Agon[10] wher we might A:livd[11] Hapley But know[12] Ame obligt to venter[13] my grey
hears to ye mersey of god which we must do and ye Dengers of ye seas If not Prevent[14]
by you   And ther has Ben Shuch[15] faymins[16] for Brad[17] in thes Contrys[18] And grat
Daths of Catel and A Cind[19] of deses or morin[20] that ye Contrey Is I<m>povrist by it
which is ye ocesion with rents and tyths to Ca<u>s ye most Part of ye Cuntry to go to
America   we Are As Bound Slevs to Bishop <and> minestor[21] By thire hurying[22] yus
into Bis<h>ops Corts   if we doe not met ther time and Leseur[23] th<e>y may do
What th<e>y Pleas for the<re> is not wan ither[24] to tak Part with yus or to stand ower
Caues[25] or to Plead our Intrest   we Are obligt to your Honers spering yus But at y^e

4. **Impost**: i.e., imposed.   5. **Burdings**: i.e., burdens (reverse spelling; see appendix 1).   6. **Iame**: i.e., I am.
7. **yunder**: i.e., under; for the spelling see **yus** "us" hereafter. The writing of an initial "silent y" is still
characteristic of letters written in the mid–nineteenth century by Ulster authors of Scottish origin, such as the
Sproules of west Co. Tyrone; e.g., **yous** "us," **yout** "out," **yeakers** "acres."   8. **I Can not Provid for my
Children But ame obligt to Transport my Self**: Crawford would normally have said "but is obliged to
transport myself" (Northern Concord Rule; see appendix 1). The form **ame** (i.e., am) may represent an
unconscious slide into the standard language, or it may have been imported from the standard language to lend
the formal tone desirable in a petitionary letter addressed to a social superior (see chapter 6, n. 25). Crawford's
natural usage can be seen hereafter: **ye Havey Burding Contunes** ("continues") **ye seme and Is not Eabel to
Stand it** (i.e., and am not able).   9. **upon ye acount of**: because of.   10. **They would Ahad me to Agon**:
i.e., would have had me to have gone (i.e., would have had me go). When functioning as a complement to a
finite verb in a past tense, the present infinitive can be replaced by its past counterpart (as here: **go** is replaced
by **to have gone**); such usage is particularly popular in the written language of the Early Modern period but is
later largely abandoned. For **would Ahad . . .** see chapter 1, n. 22.   11. **might A:livd**: i.e., might have lived.
12. **know**: i.e., now.   13. **venter**: i.e., venture; see chapter 1, n. 83.   14. **Prevent**: i.e., prevented; **If not
Prevent by you**: if you don't intervene. When the root of a verb ends in **d** or **t**, the ending of the past tense
and the past participle may optionally be dropped in Scots; although the process is obsolescent by Crawford's
time, surviving only in a few forms, among which is the frequently occurring **acquaint** (dialect variant:
acquent) "acquainted, informed."   15. **Shuch**: i.e., such (pronounced [sich]). Because Scots **s** frequently
corresponds to English **sh** (e.g. Scots **sud**, **sall**, **Inglis** = English **should, shall, English**), the graphic symbols **s**
and **sh** can be interchanged in spelling; e.g. hereafter: **Bisops** "bishop's."   16. **faymins**: famines (Scots
pronunciation; see **faimily** "family," **faimish** "famish").   17. **Brad**: i.e., bread. Crawford's Scots pronunciation
was probably [brayd]; see the spelling **grat** "great" hereafter. An alternate pronunciation, depending on dialect,
is [breed].   18. **in thes Contrys**: in these regions, in this area.   19. **Cind**: i.e., kind.   20. **morin**: murrain
(disease of cattle).   21. **Bishop <and> minestor**: i.e., Church of Ireland clergy.   22. **hurying**: harrying,
harassing (probably for failure to pay tithes).   23. **Leseur**: i.e., leisure (here = convenience); transposed spelling
(-eur for -ure).   24. **not wan ither**: not one other; i.e., no one else (Scots forms).   25. **to tak Part with yus
or to stand ower Caues**: "to take our side or defend our cause" (for **yus** see n. 7; **Caues**: transposed spelling,
with -ues for use).

sem time y[e] Havey[26] Burding Contunes[27] y[e] seme and Is not Eabel[28] to Stand it nor would not be Ebel to hold my Land so Long as I did Had it not been for Ason that Ihave[29] whenhee[30] Saw that I was not Ebel to Provid for him hee med to b<u>y yeren[31] and Cep[32] his Credit very well   If It Ley In your Honers Pouer to Put him In Som Beter way of his Busness I would Be yunder singler obligesions to your Honer: I hop you will Pardon thes Prusimtous[33] fevers[34] and my un<con>cidret[35] Lines whish Justly merits Rebuk from your genres good netuer and the kiness of your Honer   Let Humbel Rquests and motivs tak Im Presion upon[36] you And As gods grat Progtive Is to be mersiful so Have mersy at y[e] sencer[37] Request and Answer to this   I ame your Honrs well wis<h>ing frend

And most Hum[l] Sr[t]   Allx[dr] Crawford

Despite his apparent desperation in 1736, as of 1744 Crawford still had not emigrated, as demonstrated by his signature on a petition in that year. Perhaps he had been successful in a ploy, common among tenants, of exaggerating his hardships and threatening to emigrate to wring concessions from his landlord. However, his growing dependence on his son's earnings from weaving or jobbing linen yarn probably indicated real distress, as throughout Ulster tenants and cottagers were turning to linen manufacturing to supplement or supplant agricultural incomes. Although Crawford postponed or even abandoned his plan to emigrate, many others in similar or worse situations went to America at this time, especially from County Donegal and adjacent districts of west Ulster. Indeed, it is likely that Crawford regretted his decision to stay, for in the early and mid-1740s arctic weather and wretched harvests brought severe distress, and in April 1745 Murray's agent reported that many formerly "good tenants" were forced to beg or to emigrate. In the latter half of the century, economic conditions improved significantly, but the earlier crises had "greatly weakened the Dissenting Interest" in southwest Ulster—as a resident of Donegal town, only three miles from Crawford's farm, had warned in 1744—and by 1766 only a handful of the Protestants in Killymard parish were Presbyterians. Even subsequent economic expansion did not stem local Protestants' emigration, as between 1766 and 1831 their proportion of Killymard's population fell from 55 to 36 percent.[38]

26. Havey: i.e., heavy; the spelling suggests the variant pronunciation [hayvee], now confined to Scotland. The more common Scots pronunciation is [hevvee] or [hivvee].   27. Contunes: i.e., continues; may represent a transposed spelling for "contenus," which is a fairly close approximation of the normal Scots pronunciation [kunteenuz].   28. and Is not Eabel: i.e., and I am not able; see n. 8.   29. Ason that Ihave: i.e., a son that I have "one of my sons."   30. whenhee: i.e., when he.   31. yeren: i.e., yern "yarn" (Scots pronunciation; see Scots pairt = English part; Scots lairge = English large, etc.).   32. Cep: i.e., kept; also see [slep] "slept," [uttemp] "attempt," [kunek] "connect," [faak] "fact," etc.   33. Prusimtous: i.e., presumptuous; probably a transposed spelling for prisumtous.   34. fevers: i.e., favors (here = requests for favors/consideration); see appendix 1.   35. un<con>cidret: i.e., inconsiderate.   36. tak Im Presion upon: make an impression upon, not leave indifferent.   37. sencer: i.e., sincere.   38. For demographic data on Killymard parish and its environs, see appendix 2.1a, on chapter 2. Alexander Crawford, 1736.

3 ✷

David Lindsey, 1758

By the mid-1750s emigration from Ulster may have exceeded one thousand per year. Although commerce and industry in northern Ireland expanded after midcentury, so also did population pressures, costs, and expectations. Scots-Irish farmers were increasingly subject to "improving" landlords who granted shorter leases, geared rent levels to anticipated price increases, and demanded that tenants modernize their holdings to increase production. More tenants became dependent on linen manufacturing, and its attendant market fluctuations and social dislocations further stimulated emigration.

Such pressures are obvious in this letter by David Lindsey, a small farmer in the mountainy borderlands between counties Tyrone and Londonderry, near the village and parish of Desertmartin.[1] In the mid–eighteenth century, this was an area in rapid transition. The region's Catholic inhabitants, who in 1766 comprised a slight majority in Desertmartin parish, were still largely Irish-speaking, subsistence farmers. However, among Presbyterians, who dominated the region's Protestant population, the linen trade had grown rapidly, with markets in a network of small towns such as Maghera, Cookstown, and Dungannon, where flax, yarn, and coarse linen cloth were sold and resold for spinning, weaving, bleaching, and eventual export to England and overseas. Economically, the region was oriented to the port of Newry, County Down, whose shippers employed emigration agents around Desertmartin and who sent paying passengers and indentured servants to Philadelphia as well as to New York and elsewhere in the North American colonies. By 1758 the Delaware River had been Ulster emigrants' primary destination for three decades: thus, emigration to "Pennsillvena" was a natural strategy for David Lindsey, and previous settlement there by his Fleming cousins[2] meant he could rely on American kin for encouragement, directions, and perhaps also financial assistance, as his hope that an American relative would purchase or "redeem" his nephew's bonded indenture suggests that at least some branches of Lindsey's family lacked the capital to finance their own emigrations.

> David Lindsey, near Desertmartin, County Londonderry,
> to Thomas or Andrew Fleming, "Pennsillvena," 19 March 1758

---

1. Family tradition locates David Lindsey in Co. Tyrone, probably in the barony of Dungannon Upper. His letter refers only to Desertmartin, a town and parish in Loughinsholin barony in Co. Londonderry, adjacent to Dungannon Upper. For demographic data on Desertmartin parish and its environs, see appendix 2.2b, on chapter 3. **2.** Pennsylvania land-warrant and tax records indicate that the Flemings may have been in Chester Co., in eastern Pennsylvania, as early as 1734 and as late as 1771. However, in 1762 Thomas Fleming appears further west in Cumberland (present-day Huntingdon) Co., where he held 50 acres. By 1775 Thomas had been joined by William Fleming, probably the "Cusen Wᵐ" mentioned in David Lindsey's letter, and by 1781 the former had increased his holdings to 330 acres. After the Revolution it appears that the Flemings again moved westward, to the newly created Westmoreland Co., near Pittsburgh, where in 1791 William Fleming warranted four hundred acres.

Dr Cusen:

　　I had upertunity of reading your letter that was sent to your fatherinlaw, which gave me[3] great satisfaction to here you were all in good health and fortuned so well as to be posessed in so good a bargain of lands.[4] We are all in good health at present I bless God for all his mercies and y^r uncle David is helthy and harty and do all join[5] in our love and Compliments to you and your families and enquiring friends. I expected an account oftener from you, only times being troublesome in that country with wars that we were assured[6] that you were all ded or killed　The good Bargains of your lands in that Country Doe greatly encourage me to pluck up my spirits and make Redie for the Journey, for we are now oppressed with our lands set[7] at 8s per acre and other improvements, Cutting our land in two acre parts and Quicking[8] and only two years time for doing it all—ye<a> we Cannot stand more. I expected a letter from you more oftener, or that Cusen Wm Fleming would come over before this time, but these things does not Discourage me to goe only[9] we Depend on y^e for Derections in the goods fitting to take to that place. I had disappointment[10] of 20s worth of Lining[11] Cloth y^t I sold, and had James Hoskins bond for the money. The merchant ran away, and I had great truble in getting my money, so that <it> was deleavered.[12] Brother John Fleming is dead and brother James Lindsey is married again to one Hoskins and his son Robert has service to[13] his uncle James Martin and desires to know if he will redeem him if he goes over there. He is a good favour[14] and is willing to work for his passage till its paid.

　　Your Cusen<s> in Desert martin is all in health. Cusen Mary <desires> to let you know all my father's family is in helth and joins in y^r[15] love to y^e. My father is very far spent[16] and I expect to see him buried before I leave the place. Your father and my uncle Andrew is but tender in helth. Sarah Rickets desires to be remembered in her

---

3. which gave me: i.e., and it gave me; the use of **which** as a loose sentence connective with roughly the meaning "and" is frequent before the nineteenth century and persists in dialect speech. Cf. Shakespeare, *Timon of Athens*, 5.2.28–33 "They confess towards thee forgetfulness . . . which (i.e., and) now the public body . . . hath sense withal of it (i.e., its) own fail (i.e., failures).　**4. bargain of lands**: lands acquired at an advantageous price; see hereafter: **The good Bargains of your lands.**　**5. and do all join**: and we do all join; see chapter 1, n. 110.　**6. only times being troublesome in that country with wars that we were assured**: read **only** (times being troublesome in that country with wars) that we were assured; **only** (. . .) **that**: except that; **assured**: certain. **wars**: in spring 1754 there commenced in western Pennsylvania the hostilities that soon escalated (especially after General Edward Braddock's defeat near Fort Pitt on 9 July 1755) into what the colonists called the French and Indian War (1754–1763). The war's devastating effects on the Scots-Irish and other settlers on the Pennsylvania frontier are recorded in James McCullough's journal (see chapter 21).　**7. set**: leased (from Lindsey's landlord).　**8. Quicking**: planting a quickset (esp. whitethorn) hedge.　**9. only**: but.　**10. had disappointment of**: lost money on.　**11. Lining**: i.e., linen (reverse spelling; see appendix 1).　**12. deleavered**: delivered, i.e., submitted to the judgment of a court (Scots usage).　**13. has service to**: has a situation as servant to.　**14. favour**: here used in the archaic sense of "object of favor"; therefore **good favour** "a good object of favor, worthy of favor/support."　**15. y^r**: their.　**16. far spent**: far gone, i.e., in health or age.

love to her sister Nelly and other friends. Our living is dear in this place. I conclude with my love to you and all friends there. I am yours till death.

—David Lindsey

As Lindsey noted, in the late 1750s the Pennsylvania frontier was aflame with war between the British and the French and Indians, thereby jeopardizing his connections with his American cousins. However, sometime after 1758 Lindsey did emigrate, and family records indicate that he settled, lived, and died on a "large farm" near Pittsburgh.[17] Two of his four sons[18] fought in the American Revolution: William was killed in North Carolina at the battle of Guilford Courthouse (15 March 1781); and David Jr. served with his Fleming and Martin cousins as a frontier ranger in western Pennsylvania. Sometime prior to 1786 David, Jr., moved to Kentucky, where he later settled in Harrison County, among his Fleming kinsmen, and in 1792 was appointed the county's first coroner. He died in 1814, leaving 12 children, most of whom married the offspring of other Ulster immigrants and subsequently moved to Ohio, Indiana, or Illinois. Not untypically, by the century's end David Lindsey Sr.'s descendants were claiming both noble lineage and that their emigrant ancestor had come directly from Scotland to Pennsylvania, thus ignoring the 50 to 100 years that the Lindseys and their kin had lived in Ireland.

4 ✳

Henry Johnston, 1773–1800

Scots-Irish and other Ulster emigration prior to the American Revolution peaked in 1770–1775, when perhaps 30,000 departed for the colonies, primarily from the east and mid-Ulster counties of Antrim, Down, and Armagh. Among the emigrants was the brother of Henry Johnston, a small farmer, linen weaver, and perhaps once a schoolmaster, in the market town of Loughbrickland, in the parish of Aghaderg and the barony of Upper Iveagh, in west County Down.[1] To the south and west of his parish, in south Down and in Armagh, Catholics comprised half or more of the population, but in Aghaderg Presbyte-

---

17. David Lindsey first appears in the Pennsylvania land and tax records in 1771, as the owner or renter of two hundred acres in Chester Co. Like his Fleming cousins, however, by the time of the Revolution Lindsey had moved westward into Cumberland Co.—where by 1779–1781 he and his son, David Jr., farmed one hundred acres—and after the Revolution he resettled once more in Westmoreland Co., "near Pittsburgh," where in 1783 he again held one hundred acres, plus three horses, four cattle, and nine sheep. Lindsey may have died between 1783 and 1785, for in the latter year "David Lindsey's heirs" were taxed for 250 acres. **18.** Lindsey's other two sons were Hezekiah (b. 1747 in Ulster) and Edward, who settled in North Carolina. **1.** In the 1820s, the Tithe Composition Books recorded only one Johnston or Johnson in Aghaderg parish: John Johnson, holding seven acres in Drumnahaire townland.

rians constituted nearly 60 percent of the households in 1766, with Anglicans another 10 percent.[2] Aghaderg's soil was extremely fertile, lying along the Bann River, but linen dominated the local economy; as late as 1821 nearly 70 percent of the parish's inhabitants were engaged in manufacturing, trade, or other nonfarming pursuits.

In 1772 Henry Johnston's brother, Moses, emigrated with his wife and children to Philadelphia and settled in Leacock township, Lancaster County, Pennsylvania. In 1773 Henry wrote to Moses, congratulated him on his escape to a "Land of Liberty," and recounted the reasons why thousands more were following his example. By the early 1770s extreme specialization in the linen industry, minute subdivision of holdings, and Ireland's highest population densities had reduced most of east Ulster's inhabitants to the ranks of subtenants, tiny farmers and cottier-weavers,[3] often working on the putting-out system, who were totally dependent on the linen trade and highly vulnerable to fluctuating prices and wages and to inflating rents, food costs, and taxes. For several decades, local rents had been rising and evictions becoming more common, and in the early 1770s Lord Donegall, one of the area's largest absentee landlords, imposed substantial fines for lease renewals, allegedly totaling £100,000, on his head tenants, who in turn passed the costs onto a succession of undertenants. This outraged and united farmers and cottier-weavers alike and inaugurated an outburst of violent protests against rents, tithes, and taxes by bands of armed Presbyterians, commonly known as the Hearts of Steel or the Steelboys. In the same years a severe depression in the linen industry put a third of east Ulster's weavers out of employment and caused a succession of failures among major banking houses and traders. Given the general distress, coupled with government repression of the Steelboys (many of whom fled to America), it was little wonder Henry Johnston characterized Ireland as a "Land of Slavery."

2. For demographic data on Aghaderg parish and its environs, see appendix 2.1c, on chapter 4. **3.** Cottiers (or cottagers) were laborers who rented small amounts of land, two acres or less, usually from tenant farmers, in return for their agricultural labor on the latter's farms or, in much of Ulster, for weaving linen yarn which was usually supplied by petty "manufacturers," often the tenant farmers themselves; Ulster cottiers' wives and children also helped pay the rent by spinning prepared flax into linen yarn. In parts of southern Ireland many cottiers were dairymen, but their wives and children also engaged in cottage manufacturing, especially spinning woolen yarn. Cottiers are distinguished from "landless" agricultural laborers (who received monetary wages from farmer-employers and either purchased food in the market or paid cash to rent scraps of land for their families' subsistence) and from farm servants, who lived and boarded with their employers. The socioeconomic and cultural demarcations between cottiers and the smallest tenant or subtenant farmers were indistinct and fluid, and in the late eighteenth century demographic growth and the fragmentation of holdings, especially in Ulster, "pushed" many smallholders' families into the cottier and laboring ranks. Indeed, the desire to escape such a decline, from "independent" to "dependent" status, was a principal motive for emigration among small farmers and their offspring. Likewise, distinctions between cottiers and laborers were often vague, especially in late eighteenth-century Ulster where all the land set for subsistence cultivation in oats and potatoes could not feed its inhabitants and so foodstuffs for sale to the "laboring poor" had to be imported from other parts of the island.

Letter 1.

Henry Johnston, Loughbrickland, County Down, to Moses Johnston, Leacock Township, Lancaster County, Pennsylvania, 28 April 1773

LBland   28th April 1773 three——

Dear Brother}

I see[4] your Letter to my Brother John wrote Immediately after your landing; as also I received yours to my self dated in Novemb[r] and myself my Family and in A word all your Acquaintance in this place are very happy to hear of your safe Arrival with your Family out of A Land of Slavery into A Land of Liberty and freedom; and the more so as this Kingdom is much worse than it was even when you left it; Trading of all sorts and in all Branches[5] Growing worse; and every day opens a new prospect of woe & misery;   I need not tell <you> that Lands is out of measure in high Rents & Tyths; Wool and Woollen Goods Excessive high on Account of the Wooll being transported from hence to France; in Butter Casks[6] and other such ways as can be projected; which practice laves[7] numbers of our Industrious poor without work in the West part of Ireland—and in that part where Thousands ware[8] formarly employed Manafacturing our Wool; they are now without work—And as for our North they are still worse; one unlucky accident after another, has set very sore on Us;[9] in the first place, the Flourishing State of our Linnen Manafacture for many years past Raised the price of Lands in the North of this Island to A monstrous pitch;[10] which while Trade flourish[d] the poor would Easily pay; these Rents are yet Expected by our Landlords tho' Trade is now Sunk to A Very low Ebb;   the first heavy stroak we got was; by Lord Donegall; who its thought Carried away one Hundred Thousand pounds of our ready Specie,   then the Failure of Fordice & Company Bankers of London; Just before our June Market last, Spoiled it Entirely   the September Market no better, & the December one still worse. I was in the Hall[11] for 15 Days & Could scarcely see any man to look on A Piece of Linnen; in Concequence of which Very Few Men was able to buy A Brown Webb; which makes many of our Bleach Yards Idle   not one sing<l>e peice in them; what it will Turn to God only knows; but at present looks very Ill; Failures alway[12] hapning.   the other day S[r] George Colebrook & Company

---

4. see: saw; the past tense form **see** is characteristic of the Ulster Scots and mid-Ulster dialects, while mainland Scots has mostly **saw, seed,** or **sauch. 5. Branch:** subdivision, "department." **6. transported . . . to France; in Butter Casks:** ref. to the smuggling of Irish woolen goods, disguised as butter, to France. Henry Johnston employs semicolons instead of commas. **7. laves:** i.e., leaves [layvz] (Ulster Scots pronunciation); the predominant mainland Scots variant is [leevz]. **8. ware:** i.e., were (rhymes with "car"; for the spelling see **whare** "where" hereafter, which also rhymes with "car" and is frequently spelled **whaur**). **9. has set very sore on Us:** "has hit us very hard." **10. pitch:** level (OED, s.v., 22.a). **11. Hall:** the local linen hall, where weavers sold their webs of woven **brown** (unbleached, see hereafter) linen to bleachers. **12. alway:** always "still, continually" (Scots usage); **alway** is either the archaic variant of **always** or is imported from the Bible. The form **alway** occurs again hereafter for **always** in the standard meaning "at all times": **to him** [= God] **alway be thankfull.**

Bankers of London stopt payment   Davis & Gennings Marcht[s] of Dublin   Will[m]
Wallace of Belfast and numbers more—12 Hundred[13] webbs now [. . .][14] 15[d] to 18[d] &
so on [. . .][15]   One thing indeed is very happy for us   Victualing is Low   Petatoes
from 6½ to 10:[d] ⅌ Bushel & very plenty;[16]   Oat meal from 9 to 10 Shillings ⅌
Hundred   Butter at 5½[d] ⅌ Lb—Flesh is naturaly high this season of the
Year   Beef & Mutton 4[d] to 4½[d] ⅌ LB   Flour is highest; our County of Louth Flour
sells at 17 to 18[s]/6[d] ⅌ Hundred in Newry Market; Best Slain[17] or Haylands at 19[s] ⅌
H[d][18] and 13 Casks of America Flour which was all that I hear of coming into Newry
this season; sold to the Baker I deal with at 19[s]:6 ⅌ C[t].[19] Flax seed selling at 7[s]:6[d] to 8[s]
the Bushel——The Hearts of Oak Steel Gold[20] or what ever you please to Call them
are all Quiet; some few was tried in Carickfergus[21] and Down<patrick>;[22] and all
acquit[23] Except four or five whose Crimes was Felony & suffered; but all that was
taken for the Roiet[24] at Gilford was transmitted to Dublin, and took their tryal[25] there
which was well for them; the citizens was very kind to them when in Goal;[26] and on
tryal Every Soul was acquit[27]——It's now time to turn to Family affairs; thank God
Weare[28] in Tolarable Good health   Dav:[d] married about the time you sail[d] to Ja[s]
Robisons Daughter   Bob & Jn[o] Young are well; as is Hugh Cupples & Family; His
Son James is the Person by whom I send these, in the Ship Needham Capt[n]
Chevers,   I shall send you another Letter by the Ship Minerva Capt[n] M[c]Cullough lest
one should miscarry,   there is Eleven Ships Intended to sail from Newry & Belfast for
Philadelphia & newcastle[29] this Spring; I hear Brother John wrote to you by Capt[n]
M[c]Cullough from Belfast who sail[d] 15 days since   I hope you will not forget to write
when opportunity serves; if to Belfast Direct to me to the Care of M[r] Thomas
Sinclaire; if to Newry to the care of M[r] Geo: Anderson   I hope Dear Moses (tho' you

13. Hundred: measure of the fineness of the weave.   14. Ms. torn (six to eight words missing).   15. Ms. torn
(six to eight words missing).   16. plenty: plentiful, abundant.   17. Slain: Slane town (and parish, Upper Slane
barony, Co. Meath); site of the largest flour mills in Ireland (built 1763–1767).   18. H[d]: hundred (see the
foregoing: County of Louth Flour sells at 17 to 18[s]/6[d] ⅌ Hundred). A shortening of "hundredweight" (112
lbs., or in the case of the long hundred, 120 lbs.); also abbrev. as Hun[d], e.g. 1st Flour 40[s] ⅌ Hun[d] (letter 3
hereafter). Not to be confused with hogshead (abbrev. hhd.), which is a measure of volume, only rarely used
of flour but common with liquids, granular substances, and meat.   19. C[t]: hundredweight (see n. 18).
20. Hearts of Oak Steel Gold: in parts of counties Down and Armagh, the Hearts of Steel were sometimes
known as the Hearts of Oak (the name of another secret agrarian society that had operated in east and mid-
Ulster in the 1760s) or as the Hearts of Gold.   21. Carickfergus: Carrickfergus town, parish, and (then)
county (now part of Co. Antrim), on Belfast Lough.   22. Down<patrick>: Downpatrick town (Down parish,
Lecale Upper barony, Co. Down).   23. acquit: i.e., acquitted; see chapter 2, n. 14.   24. Roiet: i.e., riot;
reverse spelling (most instances of Standard [oy] correspond to [ey] in Scots; e.g. Standard boil [boyl] = Scots
[beyl], Standard join [joyn] = Scots [jeyn], etc.).   25. took their tryal: stood trial.   26. Goal: i.e., gaol "jail."
27. the Roiet at Gilford . . . Every Soul was acquit: the "riot" was an attack by Steelboys on the house of
Richard Johnston, a zealous magistrate in Gilford town, Co. Down, in early March 1772. Although Johnston
escaped, one of his supporters, a Presbyterian minister, and several Steelboys were killed. The authorities
transferred the accused to Dublin for trial, assuming convictions would be more easily forthcoming there than
in east Ulster, but were disappointed when the Dublin jurors refused to convict.   28. Weare: i.e., we are.
29. newcastle: New Castle, Delaware.

have Changed your nativity for a strange Land) You will be very carefull to remember that Kind & mercifull God who has Created & preserved you; whose Goodness you have seen displayed in a Clear manner; in your preservation in your late Voyage; be carefull to repent of your Sins & with all your Heart and Soul turn unto the Lord; set a Good and Religious Example to your wife & Children knowing that there is no [re]pentance in the Grave; I am Dear Br[other] yours till Death

H Johnston

When normal commerce recommenced after the American Revolution, Moses and Henry Johnston quickly reestablished communications. However, although Ulster emigration rapidly resumed at the war's end, with over 10,000 departures in 1784 alone, Henry Johnston was reluctant to consider leaving Ireland: "my son Jack is sometimes Talking of going to america," he wrote, "but I would be glad to know how things go on [there] before he w^d do it."[30] Johnston's hesitation stemmed from several causes. First, he was disappointed in the paucity and vagueness of information received from Moses, in regard both to general American economic conditions and to the latter's own situation. Apparently, in fact, Moses had not done very well. In the early mid–eighteenth century, large numbers of Scots-Irish farmers had emigrated to the Lancaster County frontier, mostly settling the upland districts where forests were easier to clear than in the more fertile bottomlands. However, by the time Moses arrived in 1772 Lancaster County was thickly inhabited, increasingly by German immigrants whose superior capital and farming skills had pushed the Scots-Irish south and west in search of cheaper lands. In 1782 only 13 percent of the county's population was of Irish birth or descent, and in that year local assessors recorded Moses Johnston as among the county's lowest category of taxpayers, owning no land, two horses, and two cattle. At best, he was a small tenant farmer, perhaps also a schoolmaster, in a highly commercialized, wheat-producing district where rising land prices precluded his chances of becoming a substantial land-owner. Nor had Moses established himself politically: his only other appearance in local records was as a member of the county militia in 1782, but his name does not appear on the earlier muster rolls of companies that actually fought in the Revolution. Henry Johnston's suspicion of his brother's lack of success was obvious: "if you have made money as fast as numbers Say they do in America you might now be able to Send over some F[lax] Seed and Get any of this Countrys Goods you might Stand in need of in Return."[31]

Another reason for Henry's reluctance to emigrate was his belief that recent political changes in Ireland augured well for economic improvement at home. In 1778–1783 a Volunteer movement, led by "Patriots" among disgruntled members of the Protestant gentry and merchant classes, successfully pressured the British government to repeal restric-

---

30. Henry Johnston, Loughbrickland, Co. Down, to Moses Johnston, Leacock township, Lancaster Co., Pa., 5 March 1784. 31. Henry Johnston, Loughbrickland, Co. Down, to Moses Johnston, Leacock township, Lancaster Co., Pa., 3 June 1784.

tions on Irish trade and grant legislative autonomy to the Irish Parliament. Thus, in his 5 March 1784 letter Johnston enthused over "the wonders our Volunteer army has wrought in this Country, to obtain our Freedom & to get the making our own Laws." However, the so-called Revolution of 1782 proved disillusioning: the Irish Parliament itself remained unreformed, corrupt, and unrepresentative of Dissenters and of middle- and lower-class Protestants, generally (as well as Catholics), and still subordinate to the British government. Moreover, rising rents, food costs, and taxes, despite overall economic expansion, continued to press hard on Ulster tenants, stimulating more emigration. By 1790 several of Henry and Moses Johnston's relatives were eager to join Moses in America. For example, the brothers-in-law James and Thomas Young, weavers who rented merely seven acres of "verey in[different] Land" for 18s. per acre, begged Moses to inform them "if ther would Be aney incoridgment for Wavers in a Merrica for we he[a]re in this Contrey that one Man Cane Make as Much as fore Men Can Make here At Waving."[32] Also, in his own letters of that year, Henry Johnston referred to the increasing sectarian polarization in Ulster, particularly in neighboring County Armagh, which gave additional stimulus to emigration. In the mid- and late 1780s, political tensions and intense competition for land and employment caused the volatile mixture of Protestants and Catholics in mid-Armagh to explode into violence, as armed bands of poor Protestants—primarily Anglicans—called Peep o' Day (or Break o' Day) Boys fought pitched battles with Catholics, who in turn formed an organization known as the Catholic Defenders. The consequent "Armagh Outrages," when thousands of Catholics were driven from their homes, were a nasty prelude to the "very troublsome times" that Johnston predicted lay ahead.[33]

Letter 2.

Henry Johnston, Loughbrickland, County Down, to Moses Johnston, Leacock Township, Lancaster County, Pennsylvania, 16 April 1790

Dear Brother   LBLand 16th April 1790
            Your Very pleasing Letter dated in Novr 1789 and also one to Bror John
I recd by Mr Thos Hawthorn   he returns by the same Ship & by him I send this   he
is taking aSon of Davd Tullys an Aprentice with him   my self and Family (thank God)
enjoy a Tolarabl good state of health as does Brother John and Family. We have had a
good deal of Disturbance here in this Neighbourhood of Late; for two Years past a set

---

32. James and Thomas Young, "Lesnow" [or "Lesmore," "Lesnord"?], probably Clonduff parish, Co. Down, to Moses Johnston, Leacock township, Lancaster Co., Pa., 4 April 1790.   **33.** Demographic data spanning the 1766–1831 period suggests that a combination of loyalist violence, selective leasing by Anglican landlords, and economic circumstances may have combined to drive very large numbers of disaffected Presbyterians, as well as Catholics, out of the mid-Ulster region of west Down, Armagh, and east Tyrone in the 1780s, 1790s, and early 1800s. If so, such intra-Protestant conflicts remain unknown or unexplored by historians, despite their obviously important implications for the development of Ulster unionism. See appendix 2.1c.

of Idle Ill disposed young Fellows assembled in the Night and went under the Name of B<r>akaday Boys[34]   they said their design was to take the Arms from the Roman Catholicks[35] some of which they did take and <did> some mistchief both to the People and their property   the Catholick<s> endeavour^d to defend them selves and goes under the Name of Defenders   these two parties have been snarling at Each other some months but on the 1st of July last aparty of the Protistants or Brakaday Boys assembled to Celebrate the Memory[36] of the Battle of the Boyne[37] and with arms in their hands and Coulours Flying march^d tho'[38] this Town and took the road to Gilford but about a mile from hence at aplace call^d Lisnagade where is a forth[39] there was a Great Number of the Defenders assembled and as the others pass^d by they fir^d on them   the Protestants return^d the fire and a brisk Ingagement began which lasted about 5 hours   there was many wounded & some few Catholicks Kill^d, and ever since they are snarling at Each other and I doubt if things does not take aspeedy turn that there will be very troublsome times in Ireland before long —— We have had Very uncommon weather these twelve months,   the Summer was Exceeding wet, from Novr till Jany some Wet moderate no Frost, Jany moderate, Feb^y, March, and what is pas^d of April Very dry,   no rain these 2 Months   smart[40] frosts now in the morn^{g}[41] and what Spring we had is fail^d, and Very sore Labour to get the Potatoes Cover^d as to the Books you mention Ihave two English Dicksonarys[42] and am making search for them and <the> Confesion of Faith[43] will be bought in Belfast & Mr Thos promis^d to for ward it toyou   I am Your Loving Brother

Hen Johnston

From 1789 the example of the French Revolution—and the high costs of the subsequent Anglo-French wars—galvanized middle- and lower-class Irish discontent against the governing establishment, especially among many Presbyterian merchants, farmers, weavers, and other artisans in County Down and elsewhere in east Ulster. In October

---

34. B<r>akaday Boys: Break o' Day Boys, i.e., Peep o' Day Boys.   **35. to take the Arms from the Roman Catholicks**: during the Volunteer movement of 1778–1783, and particularly in its later stages, the liberal Presbyterians who controlled many of east and mid-Ulster's Volunteer companies had allowed local Catholics to join their ranks and parade with arms, in violation of the Penal Laws, which (until 1793) restricted firearms to Protestants; in 1784–1785 disarming such Catholics was one of the Peep o' Day Boys' immediate objects—or at least a plausible excuse for raiding Catholics' homes and driving them out of mid-Ulster. **36. Memory**: commemoration.   **37. Battle of the Boyne**: William of Orange's celebrated victory, on the banks of the Boyne River, Co. Meath, over the Irish and French armies of James II on 12 July 1690 (1 July old style).   **38. tho'**: i.e., through; initial cluster thr shows a tendency in Ulster Scots to lose the r, creating doublets **through** : **thoo**, **throat** : **thoat**, etc.   **39. forth**: (ancient) earthworks, rath (Ulster Scots form). The fort or rath of Lisnagade is near Tanderagee town (Lisnadill parish, Fews Lower barony, Co. Armagh); the confrontation described by Johnston occurred in July 1789.   **40. smart**: intense, sharp.   **41. morn^g**: morning. **42. Dicksonarys**: the spelling represents a common Ulster (Ulster Scots and mid-Ulster) pronunciation ("dixonaries").   **43. Confesion of Faith**: the Westminster Confession of Faith (1647), to which most Presbyterian clergy and laity in Ulster, Scotland, and America still subscribed in the eighteenth century.

1791 Belfast and Dublin radicals formed the Society of United Irishmen to agitate for parliamentary reform. Driven underground by official repression, the United Irishmen prepared for revolution with French assistance and strove to unite disaffected Ulster Dissenters with Catholic Defenders in a rebellion to create a democratic, nonsectarian Irish republic. For several years their chances appeared promising, as high wartime taxes and food prices increased popular distress and disaffection, while the war itself closed the safety valve of overseas emigration. By 1797 County Down contained some twenty-eight thousand United Irishmen, over a fourth of Ulster's total. However, among poor Anglicans and other Protestants in mid-Ulster, where Catholics comprised large minorities or majorities of local populations, fears of armed "papists" and of the United Irishmen's democratic vision outweighed resentments against a landlord ascendancy and a government that, however exploitive, guaranteed their physical safety and "ancient privileges." Thus, in 1795 the Peep o' Day Boys and other Protestant bands coalesced into the Loyal Orange Order and launched a pogrom against local Catholics and their radical allies. And in 1797, after the failure of a French invasion at Bantry Bay in west Cork (December 1796), the government unleashed the army and mobilized the Orangemen and other loyalists into Yeomanry Corps to purge Ulster of suspected United Irishmen. Their "dragooning of Ulster" was so effective that when the remnants of the United Irishmen finally rose in May–June 1798, in Antrim and Down as well as further south, the result was disastrous, as Henry Johnston related in his last surviving letter to brother Moses.

Letter 3.
Henry Johnston, Loughbrickland, County Down, to Moses Johnston,
Northumberland, Northumberland County, Pennsylvania, 11 May 1800

Dear Brother   [11]th May 1800——
            As I have not heard from you for Some Years, I concluded you ware Either dead or left the Country whar you was formarly Settled But having by chance seen Mr Alexander Greer, who call^d here on his Way to Newry to take passage for himself and the Family he Left her\<e> when he Left this 16 years agoe   He tells me he was some time in you\<r> House, when he went first to America\<,> that he understood you had purchas^d 400 acres \<of> Land many Miles from whare you liv^d and that you took a Journy to See your New purchase, & took Sick, & return^d, that your wife, & a Daughter died about \<the> Same time, that he does not know whither[44] You are gone to your New purchase or Not——My dear Wife departed this Life in Decr 1795   Since that time there is nothing here but disturbance, confusion, & in many Places Rebelion;   in the Counties of Wexford Wicklow &c many Thousand have been Kill^d some in Battle and many by the Sword of the Law, and yet there are many

---

44. whither: whether (Scots).

atrying[45] which are mostly Transported,[46]   The Low part of County of Antrim was greatly involv^d in the Troubles, Some Kill^d in Skrimiges with the Millitary, Some tryed & Shot, Some hang^d and not ended yet   this day about 30 was march^d Thoug<h>[47] this Town to Dublin from that Quarter,[48] And in this Coun[ty at] Ballinghinch[49] they had a Battle in which many lost thier Lives, and many [innoce]nt People lost thier all, by plundering House burning & desolations such as are the Natural concequences of Civil War

Thank God the Troubles did not come Just to our door, but much too near,   one Man out of this Town was hang^d to <a> Sign-post in Belfast[50]   The dreadfull concequence arising from So much disturbance was a great Check to Agriculture, togather with a Very Wet & cold Spring, in 1799, the summer Wet and unaturill & a Very Wet & scanty Harvest;   Provisions of all sorts a monstrous price   1st Flour 40^s ℔ Hun^d   Oat meal 36 to 37 Shilling & not good   Potatoes from 2^s.2^d to 2^s.8^d ℔ Bushel & I hear that some time ago the<y> sold in Dublin at Eliven Shilling a Hund^rd   I enjoy a tolorable good health considering my age   Jack is well, but Es^t has been Some time past Very Ill but now some what better   I wish to know whether you have gone to your New place, wher it is Situate, how much of it, what it is fit to produce, and what the Rent is, & what Tenure——I have reason to hope from What I heare from America, & what I see here that you Left this in Good time   may God enable you & Family to work tho'[51] the Fatigues which no doubt is great, and to him alway be thankfull   May The Great Director of all Event<s> bless & prosper you in Your Journey Though[52] Life is Sincere prayer of Your Loving Brother—

Hen^y Johnston

℔ favour of Alex^r Greer who says he will forward it safe to you

---

45. atrying: i.e., a trying "being tried;" an instance of the use of the present participle with the prefix **a** to convey a passive sense. Such usage is attested in Shakespeare (e.g., *Macbeth*, 3.4.33: "while 'tis a making" (= while it is being made), and continues in Ulster well into the nineteenth century, although it is clearly obsolete. Another instance of the pattern will be found in chapter 55, n. 18. The present participle with this sense also occurs without the prefix **a**; see chapter 24, n. 13; chapter 40, n. 26; chapter 55, n. 37; and chapter 67, n. 14.   **46. which are mostly Transported**: i.e., most of those convicted of treason were sentenced to transportation and penal servitude overseas, primarily in the new British penal colony at Botany Bay, New South Wales; others were transported to the West Indies, to serve in the British army's "condemned regiments."   **47. thoug<h>**: through; see also **tho'** and **Though** hereafter and n. 38.   **48. Quarter**: area (here the aforementioned **The low part of County of Antrim**).   **49. Ballinghinch**: Ballynahinch town (Magheradrool parish, Kinelarty barony, Co. Down); the battle of Ballynahinch occurred on 11 June 1798. The reverse spelling here (**ng** for **n**) probably represents a pronunciation "Ballinhinch" (see appendix 1).   **50. one Man out of this Town was hang^d to <a> Sign-post in Belfast**: William Magill of Loughbrickland, court-martialed in Belfast on 2 June 1798, on the charge of swearing British soldiers into the United Irishmen, was found guilty and hanged on a lamppost opposite the market house.   **51. tho'**: see n. 38.   **52. Though**: see n. 38.

Moses Johnston indeed had "Left [Ulster] in Good time." Not only had he escaped the political strife and rampant food price inflation of late eighteenth-century Ireland, but sometime in the 1790s he improved his economic position dramatically. After a brief sojourn in Northumberland County, Pennsylvania, by 1800 Moses had moved north to the Genessee country of western New York, a rich and thinly settled frontier region on the verge of rapid development. Perhaps, as Henry had heard, the death of Moses's first wife and an advantageous second marriage had brought him the capital and confidence necessary to recommence pioneering in late middle age. Whether he indeed owned four hundred acres is uncertain, but the 1800 New York state tax lists recorded his ownership of $800 in real and personal property, which placed him among the top twenty property holders (apart from speculators worth $3,000 or more) in Northampton township. In 1810 he was living in Riga township in the future Monroe County, scarcely 15 miles from the growing town of Rochester. Either Moses or his children formed marriage alliances with prosperous west New York families such as the Parishes and Trumbulls, and the coming of the Erie Canal and the region's booming prosperity lay just ahead. After disappointments both in Ireland and in Pennsylvania, Moses Johnston had finally found his "best poor man's country."

5 ※

Walter Corish Devereux, 1798

In the seventeenth century, southern Irish Catholics probably constituted a large majority of the relatively few emigrants from Ireland, perhaps 30,000–50,000 in all, who crossed the Atlantic and settled primarily in the West Indies and the Chesapeake region. In the eighteenth century Catholics still comprised between one-fifth and one-fourth of the permanent Irish migrants to the New World; increasingly they came from Ulster, embarking with their Protestant neighbors from towns such as Newry and Derry, as well as from the hinterlands of southern Irish ports like Dublin and Cork. Also in the 1700s, thousands of Catholics from Ireland's southeastern counties left Waterford to work as seasonal migrants in the Newfoundland fisheries, and at least a few remained on the Grand Banks or remigrated to New England. Before the American Revolution, the great majority of Catholic emigrants were poor indentured servants, and a significant flow of more affluent or skilled Catholics did not commence until the 1780s and 1790s. In the latter decade and in the early 1800s, such emigration was often stimulated or at least politicized by the United Irishmen's Rebellion of 1798, the failure of which forced at least three thousand Irish to take immediate flight to America and encouraged thousands more to follow in succeeding years. Prominent among these were Henry Johnston's radicalized Presbyterian and Catholic neighbors in east Ulster, but they also included large numbers of Catholics from south Leinster counties such as Wexford, Wicklow, and Carlow.[1]

Walter Corish Devereux of County Wexford, in southeastern Ireland, was one Catholic whose emigration overseas was clearly related to the tumultous events of the late 1790s. Devereux was born in 1772 or 1773 at the Leap, a modest estate straddling three townlands[2] in Rossdroit parish, in Bantry barony, which his father, Thomas Devereux, leased from Abraham Fitzpatrick of Waterford.[3] Formerly among Wexford's most prominent Old English families, the Devereuxs were descended from Anglo-Norman settlers who had followed Strongbow's invasion in 1169–1170 and gained estates at the expense of the displaced Gaelic Irish. In the seventeenth century, however, Protestant conquests and confiscations fractured the family's fortunes: some branches converted and retained their estates, but Walter Devereux's ancestors remained Catholic and lost their property. By the late eighteenth century, they had reemerged as "gentlemen farmers," leasing portions of their former estates from Protestant landlords and forming part of Wexford's large subgentry class of fairly prosperous but often embittered and politically active Catholic middlemen and merchants.

Perhaps the emigration of Thomas Devereux's sons should not be viewed exclusively in political terms. After all, Walter's younger brother and his correspondent in 1798, John Corish Devereux (b. 1774), emigrated in 1796, two years before the rebellion. However, Walter's departure from Ireland was certainly precipitated by political developments, although the precise depth of his involvement in the United Irish conspiracy is uncertain. The epicenter of the 1798 rebellion lay along the north Wexford–south Wicklow border, and in mid-Wexford Old English Catholics such as the Devereuxs of the Leap, who had partly recouped their fortunes, tended to be conservative. However, the younger generations of such families were more politically aggressive than their parents, more receptive to revolutionary ideals, and more likely to join the Society of United Irishmen. The Devereuxs' own blacksmith reportedly made arms for the insurgents, and the high probability that Walter wrote his letter from Dublin suggests he may have visited the capital to coordinate local strategy with the Society's leaders.

The Wexford rebellion—and the Devereuxs' involvement—can be attributed to several causes: radical idealism (as Walter's letter suggests), inspired by the French Revolution and spread locally by the United Irishmen; brutal repression of suspected radicals by the government and its local Protestant allies, organized into the Orange Order and the Yeomanry; competition for lease-renewals between Protestant and Catholic farmers; the general economic context of rising rents, high wartime taxes, and economic depression; and, in the case of the Devereuxs and similar families, devotion to Catholicism, resentment

---

1. See chapter 4, Henry Johnston, 1773–1800. Other clear examples of Ulster Protestant and Catholic fugitives from the "troubles" surrounding 1798 are documented in chapters 48, 65, and 68; on the Leinster exile Thomas Addis Emmet, see chapter 66. 2. Davidstown, Coolamurry, and Moneyhore. 3. For demographic data on Rossdroit parish and its environs, see appendix 2.2a, on chapter 5.

FIGURE I
Portrait of John Corish
Devereux (1774–1848) of
Utica, New York, brother of
Walter Corish Devereux.
Photograph courtesy of
Matthew Garrett and John
Devereux Kernan, Hamden,
Connecticut.

against the Protestant Ascendancy, and dreams of regaining their former estates. However, when Walter wrote his brother on 1 April 1798, the prospects for a successful revolution were already slim. Most of the Society's Dublin leaders had recently been arrested, and the government had declared the island in a state of rebellion. Three weeks later, on 27 April, martial law was proclaimed in Wexford, and on 26 May the insurrection commenced at Boolavogue, only fifteen miles from the Devereux farm. Without the promised French assistance and despite remarkable early successes, in less than a month the Wexford rising was thoroughly crushed, with great loss of life, confirming Walter's premonition that emigration—or death—was his likely future.

Walter Corish Devereux, [Dublin?],
to John Corish Devereux, New York City, 1 April 1798

Dear Brother   April 1 1798
    It is with much Pleasure I Embrace this Opirtunity of Sending my love to you   on last Christmas I Was in the Cuntry When your letter Arrivd   it would be impossible to tell the Joy it Created in the Whole familey Particuley my Mother Who Cryed with Joy   Dear John it is the Greatest Happyness to you that you left this

Unfortunate Cuntry now the pray of Orange and Castle[4] Bloodhouns   almost Every County in Poor Old Ireland under Martial Law and the Poor Cuntry Pesants Shot or hanged or Basteeled[5] without Law or form of Tryal   all our Respectable and honest Cuntry men in the Goales[6] of the Kingdom such as A. O. Conner,[7] Oliver Bond[8] & Charles Fitzgerald<,>[9] Sweetman <the> Brewer[10] and Severall Others but thank god that Irish men have Resolution and can Suffer more and Will Be free   I Would send you a more full Ac[t] of <it> Onely that I hope it will not Be long un till it will be none[11] and Praised throw the Whole World   Dear John Send no Remittance to Ireland Untill you heare of her freedom and then When you Do Your Honest Friends[12] Shall Onely Receive the Benefit   Your Old frend D. Murphey is also out of the way of his Enemees   If the times are not Settled Before Next August I Certanley will then leave this Land of tiriney and Seek a land of Liberty but for a man hear to Promise himselfe a Single Day to live would be Presumption<,> for nothing but god and the Majestey of the People can Save us from What Every Irish man Abhors and

---

4. **Castle**: ref. to Dublin Castle, seat of the British-controlled executive branch of the Irish government, headed by the lord lieutenant (**Lord Leftenant** hereafter) or viceroy.   5. **Basteeled**: i.e., bastilled "imprisoned" (after the Bastille, the French royal prison in Paris, the fall of which on 14 July 1789 signaled the beginning of the French Revolution).   6. **Goales**: i.e., gaols "jails."   7. **A. O. Conner**: Arthur O'Connor (1763–1852); born into an affluent Protestant family at Mitchelstown, Co. Cork; graduated from Trinity College, Dublin, 1782; member of the Irish Parliament, 1791–1795; joined the United Irishmen in 1796 and became a leading member of the Society's provincial and national executives; on 28 February 1798 he was arrested while on a mission to English radicals; imprisoned at Fort George, Scotland, 1799–1802; after his release he went to France, where he lived in exile the rest of his life. Significantly, the United Irishmen whom Devereux names in his letter—O'Connor, Bond, Fitzgerald, and Sweetmen—were among the most radical of the Society's Dublin leadership; in 1798 they favored immediate revolution, even before the arrival of French military assistance, unlike more cautious leaders such as Thomas Addis Emmet, with whom O'Connor quarreled bitterly both before and after the rebellion (on Emmet, see chapter 66).   8. **Oliver Bond** (1760?–1798): son of an Ulster dissenting clergyman, Bond settled in Dublin, where he became a wealthy woolen merchant; he joined the United Irishmen at the Society's inception and became a leader of the Leinster and national directorates; arrested in his own house on 12 March 1798, with over a dozen other prominent United Irishmen, Bond was tried for treason, found guilty, and sentenced to death but died in prison of unknown causes before his execution.   9. **Charles Fitzgerald**: Devereux erred in writing *Charles* Fitzgerald (1765–1810), instead of the name of Edward Fitzgerald (1763–1798), Charles's younger brother. Seventh and twelfth sons, respectively, of James Fitzgerald (1756–1810), Earl of Kildare and first Duke of Leinster, Charles and Edward Fitzgerald both served in the British forces during the American Revolution, but afterward their careers were strikingly different: Charles was an outspoken loyalist in the 1790s and later became Baron LeCale, whereas Edward was radicalized by the French Revolution and became a leading United Irishman and the Society's military commander; on 19 May 1798 he was arrested in Dublin and died on 4 June 1798 of wounds suffered during his arrest.   10. **Sweetman <the> Brewer**: John Sweetman (1752–1826): born into a wealthy Dublin Catholic family, Sweetman inherited a prosperous brewery on Francis Street, where many of the United Irishmen's secret meetings were held; with O'Connor, Bond, and Fitzgerald, Sweetman was a member of the Society's Leinster Directory; arrested on 12 March 1798 at Oliver Bond's house, Sweetman spent 1799–1802 in prison at Fort George, after which he was exiled to the continent; in 1820 he was allowed to return to Ireland, where he died at Swords, Co. Dublin.   11. **none**: i.e., known.   12. **Your Honest Friends**: i.e., your relatives who are United Irishmen rather than loyalists.

Will shortley Endevere[13] to Crush to the Earth as they Do us   in your next Let me
<k>now what things would be Best for Me to Bring to America for let what will
happen[14] I Certainley will go to you if life Permits Me to Do and also <let me know>
the Bisness you follow[15] and how you git your helth[16] <and> the trade of that Part of
the Cuntry   Prase the hapey ness of the Goverment and Wish that I Should go to you
and Rite my Mother to let me go   your Poor Old feble Father has not long to
live   he is Realey turned childish god help[17] him   Miss. E. Nowla[n]d[18] is
D<e>ad   all your Friends hear Never forget You and Send you there love   So
Concludes wishing to See all we Expect happiley Compleated and Dear John Also To
See you is the onley t<w>o wishes of your Ever loving Brother[19]

Also we have a great Deale of Short haird People hear which Our Blessed Goverment
Calls Cropps[20] which the<y> are Very much Afeard of and Yesterday our Lord
Leftenant Passed a Bill Proclaiming the hole Kingdom in a State of Rebellion
9 O. Clock is the Ower[21] all must be in Bed and no lights to be Seen throu out the
Cuntrie Parts and in Some Cityes   Aney Person Suspected to be Disafected to be
takend Up and Cramed into Goale and tryed by a Coart Martial and Aney Person that
concealed Arms is found with[22] to Be Shot   So Conclude Ever Wishing a good
Under Standing to the World and a live Eagress [. . .] I Reman your etc.[23]

Walter C. Devoreux

N[. . .]   McNabb is not in town

In February 1800 John Devereux in America heard from his mother, Catherine, for the
first time in a year and eight months. Clearly she did not approve of "the Wicket
Rebellon" in which three of her sons had fought. Walter, her eldest son and the author
of the preceding letter, had fled via Liverpool to Martinique, disguised as a sailor, and was
never heard of again. Another son had been killed in battle, and her husband had died,
perhaps in prison, leaving her a widow with two daughters and three young sons.[24] In her

---

13. **Endeveres** ms.   14. **let what will happen**: "let happen what will" (= whatever happens).   15. **follow**:
pursue (a profession) (*English Dialect Dictionary*, s.v., 2); **the Bisness you follow**: "the line of work you
pursue."   16. **how you git your helth**: how your health is; see chapter 9, n. 12; also chapter 5, n. 16, and
chapter 9, n. 12.   17. **held** ms.   18. **Nowla[n]d**: conjectural (ms. torn).   19. **So Concludes . . .** : mixture of
two constructions: So Concludes (= I conclude), (1) wishing to See all we Expect happiley Compleated, *and* (2)
wishing to See all we Expect happiley Compleated and Dear John Also To See you is the only t<w>o wishes
of your Ever loving Brother.   20. **Cropps**: i.e., Croppies, so called because the United Irishmen and their
sympathizers wore their hair short in emulation of the French revolutionaries.   21. **Ower**: i.e., hour.
22. **Aney Person that concealed arms is found with**: "any person who is found to have secreted arms" (**that
. . . with**: with whom).   23. **live**: conjectural (ms. blurred); [. . .]: perhaps three words illegible; **your etc.**:
conjectural (ms. blurred); the complimentary close appears to be abbreviated, as is often the case.   24. No
essay on the 1798 Rebellion in Wexford would be complete without mentioning the massacres, at Scullabogue
Barn and Wexford Bridge, of several hundred loyalist (primarily Protestant) prisoners by vengeful rebels near
the end of the rising. However, there is no evidence that Walter Devereux or his immediate kinsmen
participated in the killings—although at least one member (also named Walter) of another branch of the

letter she described the continuing postwar repression in County Wexford—including a spate of Catholic chapel-burnings by vengeful loyalists—and declared her intention to emigrate, for "if We Dont get Some Relife the Cathlicks Cant live here."[25] In fact, Walter's mother never emigrated, dying in Ireland in 1813, but her three youngest sons joined their brother John in New York.

After six years' labor as a dancing instructor in New England and New York City, during which he reportedly saved $1,000, in November 1802 John Devereux moved to Utica, New York, then a village of only 90 houses and two hundred inhabitants, and established a dry goods and grocery business. In 1806 he began to bring over his three brothers: Thomas, who returned to Ireland after two years; Luke, who died a wastrel in Natchez, Mississippi; and Nicholas (b. 1791) who, although John's junior by 17 years, became his business partner and proved his equal in enterprise. The withdrawal from trade of their main competitor; the coming of the Erie Canal built from 1817, with largely Irish crews by 1820; and the consequent quickening of commerce and settlement, which increased Utica's population to 3,000 by 1820 and to 8,300 by 1830, all brought prosperity to John and Nicholas Devereux as they expanded from local merchandising into commodity exporting to Europe, banking, manufacturing, land speculation, large-scale farming, and canal and railroad promotion. Both brothers married into wealthy native families and became pillars of Utica society, but they also comprised part of the first leadership of the Irish-American Catholic community that emerged in the early nineteenth century. They contributed heavily to the Catholic Church's expansion in upstate New York, and Nicholas established St. Bonaventure College on his estate near Buffalo. Likewise, the brothers' Utica Savings Bank originated in the safekeeping of Irish canal workers' wages, and unknown numbers of later emigrants found encouragement and employment from Devereux & Company. When John and Nicholas Devereux died, in 1848 and 1855, they were worth at least $450,000 and $300,000, respectively.

Wexford Devereuxs apparently did so. Moreover, the scale of these atrocities, although featured prominently in loyalist propaganda at the time and in most historical accounts ever since, pales in comparison with the thousands of rebels and noncombatants, among Catholics and Ulster Presbyterians alike, who were slaughtered in cold blood by British troops, by the Irish militia and yeomanry corps, and by Orangemen and other loyalist vigilantes shortly before, during, and immediately after the United Irish Rebellion. Contemporaries estimated that as many as one hundred thousand died in the Rebellion, and historians generally agree that between at least 20,000 and 30,000 people died, that a large majority of the dead (perhaps 90 percent) were killed because of their real or alleged involvement with the United Irishmen or their Catholic Defender allies, and that most of them did not perish in actual combat but had surrendered or were defenseless when murdered or executed.
25. Catherine Devereux, The Leap, Co. Wexford, to John C. Devereux, New York City, 14 February 1800.

6 ✳

Margaret Wright, 1808

The 1798 Rebellion convinced Ireland's Anglican gentry to abolish the Irish Parliament and consign their interests and legislative representation to Westminster, depending henceforth on the British government and the United Kingdom's Protestant majority to defend their property and privileges against Irish Catholics' and Dissenters' demands for substantive reform. However, despite official predictions that the consequent Act of Union (1800) would also bring Ireland prosperity, pressures for emigration continued to mount, particularly among Presbyterian small farmers and artisans in densely populated mid-Ulster. In 1806 John Kerr, a smallholder and weaver in southwest County Tyrone, described local conditions to his uncle, Alexander McNish, who had emigrated over thirty years earlier. Food was cheap, Kerr reported, but taxation and rents were soaring: "for as . . . population encreaseth every necessary of life encreaseth in proportion, for land at present is become remarkably high and still seems to encrease in price and in demand, so that very few are capable of entering on farms which occasions numbers of our Inhabitants to transport themselves to America." However, escape to what Kerr called "the land of freedom, of privilege and of right and equity," was now difficult.[1] The Napoleonic and Anglo-American wars of 1803–1815 and 1812–1815, respectively, disrupted the emigrant trade, as did the U.S. Embargo Acts of 1807–1810 and British laws, such as the 1803 Passenger Act, that were designed to curtail departures, especially by skilled workmen. Consequently, in 1800–1814 emigrants from Ulster probably averaged only a few thousand per year, as compared with the 20,000 who crossed the ocean in 1815–1816, as soon as the wars ended.

However, Margaret Wright, John Kerr's cousin, hoped to circumvent the costs and difficulties of wartime emigration through successful dependence on her American uncle, Alexander McNish. Born about 1754, McNish had emigrated in the early 1770s, about the same time and probably for much the same reasons as Moses Johnston of west County Down.[2] Unlike Johnston, McNish quickly found a permanent home—among relatives and former neighbors at New Perth in Washington County, New York, a frontier colony of Seceding Presbyterians from mid-Ulster, established in 1764 by Rev. Thomas Clark of Ballybay, County Monaghan, on land purchased from the De Lancey family along the present New York–Vermont border.[3] Each family received 88 acres, and although the soil

1. John Kerr, Aughintober, Co. Tyrone, to Alexander McNish, Salem, N.Y., 22 March 1806. 2. On Moses Johnston, see chapter 4. 3. Rev. Thomas Clark (1720–1794): born at Paisley, Scotland; studied at the University of Glasgow and in 1748 was licensed to preach by the Glasgow Associate (Seceder and Burgher) Presbytery; minister of the Burgher Presbyterians in Cahans and Ballybay, Co. Monaghan, 1749–1764; imprisoned for two months in 1752 for his refusal to kiss the Bible when swearing oaths, as required by law but which Seceders regarded as idolatrous; emigrated in 1764 to New York with ca. three hundred Presbyterians, primarily members of his congregation; ministered to part of his flock at New Perth, N.Y., from 1764 to 1782, when he removed to Long Cane, S.C., where he died among the rest of his former parishioners

was not rich, which persuaded some colonists to remigrate to South Carolina, those who remained achieved moderate prosperity.

Alexander McNish arrived at New Perth by 1773, accompanied by his aged father. Behind in County Tyrone McNish left his mother and at least five sisters, who later married small farmer-weavers like John Kerr's father or day laborers such as Margaret's father, Jimmy Wright. The related families lived in Donaghmore parish in the barony of Dungannon Middle, about two miles from Dungannon town, the largest linen market in mid-Ulster. The soils in this rolling drumlin country were fairly rich, but the farms had been fragmented by repeated subdivision to accommodate the burgeoning population. For example, John Kerr's holding in Aughintober townland, rented from Lord Ranfurly,[4] contained merely 11 acres of mediocre land, and most of the parish's inhabitants were employed primarily in linen manufacturing and illegal whiskey distillation rather than agriculture. In 1764 the parish's population was about 8,900, only a third of them Protestants, divided roughly between Anglicans and Presbyterians.[5] Most of the latter, including the Kerrs, Wrights, and their kin, were Seceders: rigid Calvinists who were torn between their deep dislike of the Anglican establishment and what John Kerr called the "despotick government"[6] on one side and their traditional animus against the "popery" of the local majority on the other. For such families, the success of the American Revolution and the Irish troubles of the 1790s only heightened the New World's attractions, as emigration to a "promised land" fortuitously linked economic opportunities, escape from an untenable political position, and millenarian hopes of earthly deliverance from Anglican-landlord oppression ("Egyptian bondage") and "papist" foes alike.[7]

from Ulster. Clark strongly supported the American Revolution as well as union between the Seceder and Reformed (Covenanting) Presbyterian churches in America—an alliance that was partly consummated in 1782. **4.** The Earl of Ranfurly's estate totaled about 9,500 acres and in 1771 yielded a rent of £6,660. **5.** For demographic data on Donaghmore parish and its environs, see appendix 2.1c, on chapter 6. **6.** John Kerr, Aughintober, Co. Tyrone, to Alexander McNish, Salem, N.Y., 10 May 1810. **7.** In 1731 the Seceding or, more formally, the Associate Presbyterians broke away from the Church of Scotland. By 1736 the Seceders had planted or recruited several congregations in Ulster (they had nearly forty by 1770), but in 1747 they split into Burghers and Anti-Burghers over whether to take a loyalty oath imposed by the government. In general, Ulster's Seceding Presbyterians were humble folk—smallholders, artisans, laborers, and poorer tradesmen—with a much smaller proportion of educated and middling-income members than the dominant Synod of Ulster could boast. According to some early sources, Seceder families had migrated to northern Ireland quite recently, in the late seventeenth or even the early eighteenth centuries, and were thus more attuned to Scottish popular religion and doctrinal disputes than were members of the Ulster Synod. Although Anti-Burghers were more dogmatic than Burghers, Seceding Presbyterians generally adhered rigidly to the Westminster Confession of Faith, regarded the Ulster Synod's doctrinal flexibility as rank heresy, and favored evanglical exhortations over "paper preaching" by college-trained clergy. Despite their hostility to the Church of Ireland and their formal adherence to the early seventeenth-century Scottish Covenants (which claimed the primacy of God's true church over civil authorities), in the 1780s and 1790s the Seceding clergy's fear of "popery," rivalry with the Synod of Ulster, and desire for a share of the Regium Donum (the official stipend paid to Ulster Synod ministers since the reign of Charles II) led them to conspicuous displays of loyalism to court favor with the government and the landlord class. However, some Seceders (and even a few of their ministers) supported

McNish's success in America provided the ties and encouragement for his relatives' and former neighbors' emigrations. One sister, Isabella Hunter, arrived with her family in 1789, and in the early 1790s Charles Beatty,[8] McNish's uncle and a lay preacher, reported a "Great Emergration from this Country," as "Multitudes" in Donaghmore and adjacent parishes were "Seling their freehold leases to go" to America.[9] Between 1806 and 1810 John Kerr debated emigration, ultimately deciding to remain, although at least one of his sons departed later. However, Margaret Wright had no land and few alternatives. The daughter of a day laborer, her family's downward mobility was so great that she was forced to seek service with another kinsman when poverty caused even her brothers to distance themselves from her. Her situation may also reflect the increasing difficulty which young women, especially those without dowries, had in finding suitable husbands in districts where high rents and the fragmentation of holdings made it almost impossible for most young men to secure viable farms and marry. Given her social status and the fact that as late as 1841 over half the women in County Tyrone were illiterate, it may be that her letter—distinguished by its grace, economy, and scriptural references—was penned by a male relative such as John Kerr or perhaps by a local minister or teacher. Yet the sentiments and tone of desperation were surely Margaret Wright's own, although perhaps to offset popular prejudice against emigration by young, single women, she (or her amanuensis) adopted a submissive posture that reflected traditional gender roles as well as her own dependent position.

Margaret Wright, Aughintober, Donaghmore Parish, County Tyrone, to Alexander McNish, Salem, New York, 27 May 1808

Aughintober   May 27th 1808

Dear Uncle,   Imprest with a deep sense of your love and Kindness to your Relations and of your readiness to impart anything that would seemingly conduce to their welfare & happiness I have embraced this oppertunity of soliciting your hitherto[10] proposed favour hoping that the same goodness the same disinterested freinship will influence you in your behaviour to me as I never more Stood in need of the kindly

---

the United Irishmen, and John Kerr's and Margaret Wright's remarks suggest that ordinary parishioners— perhaps more alienated than their clergy from the political and religious establishment—projected hopes for liberation onto the new American republic.   **8.** In 1771 Beatty rented 22 acres in the townland of Gortlenaghan and Derrykeel, on Lord Ranfurly's estate, for £14 11s. per year. However, the 1826 tithe assessment recorded him as holding merely four acres, suggesting the consequences of partible inheritance in mid-Ulster.   **9.** Charles Beatty, Gortlenaghan, Co. Tyrone, to Alexander McNish, Salem, N.Y., 4 April 1793. **10. hitherto**: here not "until now" but "previously" (not given as a possible meaning by the OED). Apparently, Wright had successfully solicited McNish's aid to emigrate earlier but had delayed accepting his offer of help for reasons explained in her letter.

fostering hand of freinship in what ever charactar it might appear than at present being now deprived of any one that would superintend my conduct or regard[11] my undirected footsteps.   my Brothers I may say being[12] now involved in family concerns I alone[13] am left to act according to my unexperienced discretion on the vast Stage of this troublesome world & believe me my dear Uncle there is nought but trouble and vexation attending our lives in this countrey and more especially at this time as provisions are remarkably high, and they who have nought to Support themselves but their daily labour are hardly enough dealt withal[14]   America with us bears the character of [15] the land of freedom and of liberty and is accounted like the land of promise flowing with milk and honey   thus how desirable would such a place be to those labouring under Egyptian bondage encreasing and seemingly to encrease every day without the smallest gleam of hope   Such is the state of this Countrey and such are our sentiments with respect to america   Now my desire is that you would Substantiate[16] your former proposal & by some means or other procure me an entrance into that land of happiness where I might by industry obtain a competence in life without being dependent on the mercenary and covetous for a miserable and wretched support;[17]   And think not that it is any temporary conviction for the non-acceptance of your kind proposal, arising from the disagreeableness of present circumstances but I assure you it is not,[18] for from the first moment that I heard your sentiments concerning our distressed family & that you wished to assist us in getting to you desire hath still encreased[19] and often hath my heart throbbed with pleasure and Joyfulness in anticipating the happiness of that land of freedom & of visiting your peaceful habitation and of becoming an inmate of your family where I might participate of that freindship in a more abundant measure which extended even across the Atlantic but till now I was under the influence of my brothers who as I mentioned before are all become regardless[20] of me being mindful of their own interest[21] alone   If you could procure a passage for me I would faithfully serve untill I should redeem myself either with yourself or any one you would recommend me to[22]   I live at present with old Daniel McNees of Mullyrodden[23] & never was better than now but there is nothing here but the appearance[24] of trouble and calamity.   William & John Kerr & familys are well

---

11. regard: pay attention to.   **12. bein being** ms.   **13. & I alone** ms.   **14. are hardly enough dealt withal:** "have quite a hard time of it."   **15. bears the character of:** has the reputation of being.   **16. Substantiate:** make good, put into effect.   **17. where I might by industry obtain a competence in life without being dependent:** "where I might by my diligence get a sufficient livelihood to escape being dependent."   **18. And think not . . . I assure you it is not:** "do not think that it is any passing feeling of regret for not accepting your kind proposal, arising from the disagreeableness of present circumstances; I assure you it is not." **19. hath still encreased:** has continually increased.   **20. regardless:** heedless.   **21. interest:** good, profit. **22. I would faithfully serve . . . recommend me to:** "I will faithfully serve you, or anyone else to whom you would recommend me (as a servant), in order to repay you (**redeem myself**) for the cost of my passage." **23. Mullyrodden:** Mullyroddan townland (Killeeshil parish, Dungannon Lower barony, Co. Tyrone), adjacent to Donaghmore.   **24. appearance:** likelihood (OED, s.v., 9; obsolete).

and desires[25] to be remembered   John wrote last year and has got no answer the year[26] at which he greatly wonders   All your relatives are well my Brothers included and all hope this to find you in the Same which that it may is the ardent wish and sincere prayer of Margaret Wright

PS If you write direct to John Kerr   for the rest[27] you know yourself

McNish's response was positive, as John Kerr's subsequent letters to his uncle reveal: "We got your letter in which you gave Peggy Right such encouragement to go & promised so fair"; however, he added,

> the nonintercourse act[28] was so strict and so few going to America that there was no op-portunity of <her> getting there last year & this year we have tried several but there was none willing to take her upon the mere force of your letter   She would be will-ing to go her self I believe and I doubt not but she would fit America very well as she is very quiet & is very industrious.[29]

Unfortunately, it is not certain whether Margaret Wright reached America: the 1820 census shows no fewer than five unnaturalized foreigners in Alexander McNish's household, two of them young women, yet her name does not appear in Washington County's marriage or death notices as recorded in 1799–1880 by the local newspapers.

Between the American Revolution and the time of Margaret Wright's possible ar-rival, Washington County had grown rapidly, from 4,456 inhabitants in 1786 to 42,269 in 1810. By the latter year New Perth (renamed Salem in 1787) had risen from a cluster of log cabins to a small market town with five hundred to six hundred people, a courthouse, academy, and two Presbyterian churches (one for the Scots-Irish, the other for settlers from Connecticut). McNish himself served in the Revolution with distinction,[30] married Sarah McCoy in 1778, and in the early nineteenth century pioneered in the breeding of Merino sheep and became a prominent local Jeffersonian Republican politician, holding most of Salem's town offices and serving in 1816 as a presidential elector for James Monroe. By his death in 1827 McNish and his sons owned farms of at least 130 acres, valued in

---

25. desires: instead of Standard English **desire** (Northern Concord Rule; see appendix 1). The writer has slipped out of the very elevated and literary style of her petition into colloquial Ulster speech in the more personal concluding portion of the letter.   **26. the year**: this past year.   **27. for the rest**: for the remainder of my address.   **28. the nonintercourse act**: the Non-Intercourse Act, passed by Congress on 1 May 1809, banned all trade between the United States and Great Britain.   **29.** John Kerr, Auchintober, Co. Tyrone, to Alexander McNish, Salem, N.Y., 25 August 1810.   **30.** In late 1776 McNish, then aged 22, participated in the ill-fated American expedition, led by the Irish-born General Richard Montgomery (1738–1775), against Montreal and Québec; later he helped build a fort at New Perth to counter British General John Burgoyne's invasion (June–October 1777) and was seriously wounded in the campaign that led to Burgoyne's surrender at Saratoga, N.Y., on 17 October. On Montgomery, see chapter 59, n. 91.

1823 at $5,000. Eschewing the partible inheritance that had dissipated family fortunes in mid-Ulster, McNish willed his holding to one son; two others, one a physician trained in the local academy, migrated to Ohio. Thus, although much less affluent than the Devereux brothers in nearby Utica, Alexander McNish was sufficiently prosperous to aid Margaret Wright and other relations to emigrate for better opportunities in an expanding economic yet familiar religious environment.

II ❋
The Processes of Irish Emigration

7 ✳

Anonymous Poet, Mid- to Late 1700s

Sources that reveal how ordinary Irish Catholic countryfolk regarded the prospect of emigration to America in the eighteenth century are rare. One of these is the following poem, framed in the Irish language—which makes it doubly rare. The poem has become part of the Ulster folksong tradition and cannot be dated precisely, but its style and substance suggest the mid- or late 1700s. The poet himself may not have traveled to America but clearly had one or more informants who had emigrated and returned to Ireland, perhaps after demobilization from the British army or completion of a term of indentured servitude.

The poem suggests why, as contemporaries noted, relatively few Catholics went to the New World before the American Revolution. The traits of the American scene that the author describes—loneliness, absence of community, vast distances, uncultivated land and people—contrast profoundly with the social and physical landscape left behind in Ireland and also with the dense socioeconomic and familial networks that Irish Protestant emigrants, such as the Shepherds, Lindseys, and McNishes, were creating in the colonies to attract and absorb their brethren. Although by the time the poem was composed such descriptions may have become literary commonplaces, the exotic portrait of America could not have appealed to the singer's audience. Few who heard it sung or recited at *céilithe* (evening gatherings) would have responded enthusiastically to the pitch of emigration agents canvassing the Ulster market towns.

An tOileán Úr

Rinne mé smaointiughadh in mo intinn is lean me dó go cinnte
Go n-éalóchainn ó mo mhuintir anonn un Oileáin Úir;
D'iarr mise in mo impidhe ar an Árd Rígh bhí ós mo chionn-sa
Le mo shábháil as gach chontabhairt go gcríochnóchainn mo shiubhal.

Shiubhail mé fiche míle, is ní chasadh orm Críostaidhe,
Capall, bó, no caora a dhéanfadh ingheilt ar an fhéar;
Acht coillte dlútha is gleanntan, is búirtheach bheithidhigh alltan,
Fir is mná gan snáithe ortha a chasfá fá do mhéar.

Tharlaidh isteach i dtoigh mé is casadh orm daoine
D'fhiostraigh siad cár b'as mé nó an tír 'nár tógadh mé;
Labhair mé leobhtha i mBéarla gur tógadh mé i n-Éirinn
Ar láimh le Loch Éirne i gcoillidh Lios na Raoch.

Bhí sean-bhean ins a' chlúdaigh, agus í 'na suidhe go súgach;
D'éirigh sí go lúthmhar agus chraith sí liom-sa lámh;
"Mo sheacht n-anamh fear do thíre, dá bhfaca mé 'riamh de dhaoinibh,
Gur tógadh mise i n-Éirinn i mBaile Lios Béil' Átha.

"Is iomdha lá breagh pleisiúrdha a chaith mé thall i n-Éirinn
Ar láimh le Loch Éirne i gcoillidh Lios na Raoch;
O Bhreatain go Beinn Éadair chan fheicfeá-sa a léithid
Nó ó Chorcaigh i n-a dhiaidh sin go Lios Béil' Átha."

Nuair a chonnaic mé na daoine is annsin a rinne mé smaointe
Gur mhéannair dá mbéinn i n-Éirinn is mé sínte faoi chlár;
Nó sin an áit a bhfuighfuinn aos óg bheadh laghach aoibhinn
Chaithfeadh liom-sa oidhche agus páirt mhór de'n lá.

The New Island [English translation]

I once took a notion that I would leave my people and depart for the
New Island,[1] and so I did. As I left I prayed the High King of Heaven
to preserve me through all dangers to the end of my journey.

Once there I walked twenty miles and never met a Christian[2]—
No, nor even a horse or a cow or a sheep grazing on the meadow.
There was nothing but dense woods and deep glens resounding with
the roar of wild beasts, and the people wore no more clothes than would
amount to a thread twisted between the fingers.

Then I chanced upon a house, and the people there asked me where I came
from and in what country I had been reared. We spoke in English, and
I answered that I had been brought up in Ireland—in the wood of Lisreagh,
beside Lough Erne.

No sooner had I spoken than an old woman rose from her cozy nook beside
the fire and came over to shake my hand. "God bless you of all the people
I've ever met—for I myself was reared in Lisbellaw.[3]

"Many were the pleasant days I spent in Ireland and beside Lough Erne
in the wood of Lisreagh; there's no other place like it from Wales to
the Head of Howth[4] or from Cork to Lisbellaw."

---

1. the New Island: the New World, America; as early as the 1490s the term "the New Isle" was current in
England as a synonym for the New World.   2. a Christian: a "civilized" human being (i.e., a European).
3. Lisbellaw town (Cleenish parish, Tirkennedy barony, Co. Fermanagh).   4. the Head of Howth: a
promontory at the tip of the Howth peninsula, north of Dublin city, facing Wales across the Irish Sea.

> When I saw these people I made up my mind that I would be happier to live
> the rest of my life and die in Ireland, for that is where I would find kind
> and delightful young folk to pass the time with me by day and by night.

Since the author declares himself to be from the shores of Lough Erne, near Lisbellaw town, *Lios na Raoch* is probably Lisreagh, a townland of 233 acres in Derryvullan parish, in the barony of Tirkennedy, County Fermanagh. Although the north and south shores of Lough Erne had been settled by English and Scots, respectively, in the seventeenth-century plantation, Tirkennedy had been left largely to the native Irish and in the late eighteenth century was still Irish speaking, albeit bilingual. Thanks to British settlement, between 1659 and 1732 the Catholic share of Fermanagh's inhabitants fell from 75 to 42 percent, but after that date differential emigration began to deplete the county's Protestants.[5] Thus, between 1744 and 1777 the Catholic proportion of Derryvullan's population rose from 34 to 41 percent—by 1831 it was 46 percent—perhaps an illustration of the native reluctance to emigrate, as portrayed in the poem, contrasting with Protestant willingness to leave.[6]

8 ❈

Rev. James MacSparran, 1752

In 1753, at roughly the same time that "An tOileán Úr" was composed on the shores of Lough Erne, Rev. James MacSparran, an Irish clergyman in Rhode Island, published in Dublin a much more detailed but equally negative description of America in a series of letters that constitute the only known Irish emigrant's guidebook printed in the eighteenth century.

MacSparran was born in 1693 in County Londonderry, in the barony of Keenaght and the mountainous parish of Dungiven, over half of whose inhabitants were Irish-speaking Catholics.[1] He was raised in the Presbyterian faith by a minister of that church, his uncle Archibald MacSparran, "a man of good estate." However, James MacSparran was not a typical Ulster Presbyterian of Lowland Scottish descent. Traditionally, the MacSparrans were Scottish Catholics and closely allied with the MacDonnells of the Isles, Gaelic-speaking Highlanders (often called "Irish" by Protestant Lowlanders) who were royalists or rebels as suited their interests, and who in the 1640s were finally driven by their Scots Presbyterian enemies across the Irish Sea to northeast Ulster. James MacSparran's own

---

5. On Protestant emigration from Co. Fermanagh in the 1730s, see chapter 19. **6.** For additional demographic data on Derryvullan parish and its environs, see appendix 2.1d, on chapter 7. **1.** For demographic data on Dungiven parish and its environs, see appendix 2.1b, on chapter 8.

FIGURE 2
Portrait of Rev. James
MacSparran (1693–1757) of
St. Paul's Church,
Narragansett, Rhode Island,
painted in 1735 by John
Smibert (1688–1751).
Photograph courtesy of the
Bowdoin College Museum
of Art, Brunswick, Maine.

ancestors apparently avoided expulsion by conforming to Presbyterianism, but in the 1670s or 1680s they migrated to Dungiven from the Mull of Kintyre in Argyll, where Scots Gaelic (then interchangable with Ulster Irish) was still the dominant language. Almost certainly MacSparran learned Scots Gaelic at home in Dungiven, thus explaining his later boast that he could read, write, and preach in Irish. From Dungiven MacSparran went to Derry city, where he attended Dr. Blackhall's academy, and thence to the University of Glasgow where he received his M.A. degree in 1709, aged merely 15, being styled in his diploma "ingenuus et probus adolescens" (an honorable and upright youth). Subsequently, he studied for the Presbyterian ministry, was licensed to preach, and apparently spent several years as a clergyman in Derry city.

Why MacSparran emigrated is unknown, but there is a suggestion that doctrinal or personal irregularities ruptured his association with Derry's Presbyterian ministers. In any event, he landed in Boston in June 1718 and, while visiting a relative in Bristol (then in Massachusetts, later in Rhode Island), was asked to preach in the local Congregational church. MacSparran made a favorable impression and was invited to become the church's regular pastor at an annual salary of £100. However, somehow he aroused the enmity of

Boston's most eminent Puritan clergyman, Cotton Mather,[2] and in 1719 MacSparran faced charges of profanity, drunkenness, and sexual immorality. Although both an investigating committee and the Bristol town meeting exonerated him, MacSparran's enemies also spread rumors that his credentials were fraudulent. In October 1719 MacSparran returned to Ireland to secure their confirmation, promising he would return the following June. However, either because his credentials were indeed suspect or because of disillusionment with his treatment first by Derry's and now by New England's dissenting clergy, MacSparran never returned as a Presbyterian minister. Instead, after securing testimonials from the archbishop of Dublin, the bishop of Down and Connor, and other Church of Ireland clergymen, he crossed the Irish Sea to England and requested ordination in the Episcopalian faith, in what he called "the most excellent of all Churches."[3] In 1720 MacSparran was ordained a deacon by the bishop of London and as a priest by the archbishop of Canterbury, and at his request was licensed by the Society for the Propagation of the Gospel in Foreign Parts (S.P.G.) as missionary to the parish of St. Paul in the Narragansett country of Rhode Island. On 28 April 1721, "after a very dangerous tedious and expensive passage,"[4] MacSparran arrived in the parish he would serve as rector for the next 37 years.

MacSparran was one of several Irish-born representatives of a religious crusade that the Anglican church had launched in the colonies at the end of the seventeenth century.[5] Between 1680 and 1720 Anglican reformers built and furnished over one hundred new churches overseas; by the latter date the S.P.G. (est. 1701) had sent more than 60 missionaries to the New World, while its sister organization, the Society for the Propagation of Christian Knowledge (est. 1699), furnished them with thousands of books, tracts, and pamphlets. Ostensibly, the S.P.G.'s primary mission was the conversion of slaves and Indians, but critics charged that the Church of England's real goals were to impose its bishops, ecclesiastical courts, and tithes on all the colonies, to overthrow the Congregational establishments in Massachusetts and Connecticut, and to subvert what American Dissenters regarded as their religious and political liberties.

2. Cotton Mather (1663–1728): minister of Boston's Second Church, prolific writer, and a key figure in the Salem witchcraft trials (1692). Mather had numerous Irish connections: in the late 1650s his father, Increase (1639–1723), preached at Magherafelt and Ballyscullion, Co. Derry, and studied at Trinity College, Dublin (M.A., 1658), and his two paternal uncles, Samuel and Nathaniel, spent their entire careers in Ireland and were successive pastors of the Independent (Congregational) church at New Row, Dublin. In 1717–1720 Cotton Mather also encouraged Ulster Presbyterian ministers to emigrate with their flocks to Boston; however, he was disappointed by the allegedly clannish, contentious, and "profane" nature of many Presbyterian clergy who came to New England, and the cultural distance between him and the Irish-speaking MacSparran, of possibly recent Catholic origins and from the wilds of Dungiven, may have been too great for Mather's comprehension. (On early Ulster emigration to New England, see chapters 17 and 49).   **3.** MacSparran to Col. Henry Cary, 20 August 1752, in *America Dissected*, 44.   **4.** Church Wardens and Vestry, St. Paul's parish, Narraganset, R.I., to the S.P.G., London, 23 May 1721, in S.P.G. Letterbooks, series A, vol. 15 (microfilm reel 5).   **5.** Of the 433 Anglican clergy licensed for the North American colonies between 1710 and 1744, seventeen (8.7 percent) of the 195 whose birthplaces can be determined were born in Ireland.

Rhode Island, unlike New England's other provinces, was neither a Puritan nor a royal colony. Its charter granted religious toleration and full civil rights to all but Catholics and Jews, and most of its inhabitants were Quakers, Baptists, and other Dissenters who felt especially threatened by the "invasion" of a church that proved almost irresistably attractive to the colony's economic and political élites. Thus, whereas in 1700 the Church of England had scarcely existed in Rhode Island, by 1721 Rev. James Honeyman (1675–1750), another S.P.G. missionary, had transformed Newport's Trinity Church into the province's wealthiest and most fashionable congregation. Likewise, although most of MacSparran's own parishioners were ordinary farmers, his "elegant," "commodious," and well-furnished church of St. Paul's was founded (ca. 1702) and dominated by men who were "exceptionally cultured, well-to-do . . . and secure in the conviction that to be a Narragansett Planter, with large estates and troops of slaves, was a sufficient patent of aristocracy."

In outward respects, MacSparran's pastorate on the southwestern shore of Narragansett Bay was very successful. Although his first year in Rhode Island was marred by fresh charges of intemperance and sexual improprieties, MacSparran quickly married Hannah Gardiner, daughter of his wealthiest and most influential parishioner, and won his flock's esteem and affection through his erudition and diligence. Within two years of his arrival, St. Paul's congregation had doubled in size, to three hundred members, and by the end of his pastorate he had been instrumental in founding Anglican churches at Bristol, New London, and elsewhere in the region. MacSparran's biographer describes him as one of the S.P.G.'s ablest missionaries; at least three of his sermons merited publication; and in 1737 Oxford University awarded him a doctorate in sacred theology for his "talents, learning, good deportment, judgment and gravity." Likewise, MacSparran moved comfortably in the colony's highest circles, entertaining the celebrated Anglo-Irish bishop and philosopher George Berkeley (1685–1753) during his 1729 sojourn in America, yet also was solicitous for the spiritual welfare of Narragansett's impoverished Indians and slaves—ten of whom MacSparran owned himself.

However, MacSparran was never reconciled to remaining in America. He hated the extremes of New England weather; the care of his parish, which covered a territory 20 by 25 miles square and included three other churches, was extremely arduous for a "portly" man; and his annual salary of £70 was barely sufficient to maintain a lifestyle commensurate with his social pretensions. While congenial with his flock, he was also pedantic, pompous, egotistical, and intolerant—characteristics that embroiled him in continual controversies with New England's Dissenters, who despised him as both a "hireling priest" and an Irish "Teague."[6] MacSparran's strong advocacy of an American episcopacy infuriated the Congregationalists; at least one of his sermons touched off a bitter pamphlet war; and over

6. **Teague** (as in MacSparran's text): a derogatory term for a Catholic Irishman; present in English since at least the seventeenth century, it is a borrowing of the Irish Christian name Tadhg, which lacks an exact English counterpart but is usually equated with Timothy/Tim or Thaddeus/Thady; the vowel rhymes with the -ea- of "great" (for Hiberno-English speakers) or that of "league" (for speakers of Standard English).

the course of 30 years he spent over £600 of his own money in an ultimately fruitless lawsuit to wrest possession of a three-hundred-acre glebeland from its Puritan claimant. Plagued by nightmares of permanent separation from his Irish friends, by the mid-1740s MacSparran was actively soliciting patronage sufficiently influential to secure him a position as a clergyman in Ireland. In 1751 news of the death of his only brother, who had settled in Pennsylvania, only increased MacSparran's dissatisfaction and homesickness: "O yᵗ I were well settled in my own Country," he confided to his diary.[7] This was MacSparran's frame of mind when, a year later, he penned to his former schoolmates in Derry the three letters that in 1753 were published in Dublin and sold for sixpence as *America Dissected, Being a Full and True Account of All the American Colonies*.[8]

America Dissected is considered to be the first Irish emigrant's guidebook, yet it was written not to encourage or facilitate departures but as "a Caution to Unsteady People who may be tempted to leave their Native Country." Indeed, on his title page MacSparran promised to expose the "Intemperance of the Climates; excessive Heat and Cold, and sudden Changes of Weather; terrible and mischievous Thunder and Lightning; bad and unwholesome Air, destructive to Human Bodies; Badness of Money; Danger from Enemies; but, above all, the Danger to the Souls of the Poor People that remove thither, from the multifarious wicked and pestilent Heresies that prevail in those Parts."[9]

Rev. James MacSparran, Narraganset, Rhode Island,
to the Hon. Col. Henry Cary, Esq., Ireland, 20 August 1752,
in *America Dissected* . . . (Dublin, 1753)

Narraganset, *in the Colony* of Rhode
Island, *in* New England,

7. MacSparran diary, entry of 18 November 1751, in Goodwin, *A Letter Book* . . . (see Sources for this chapter). **8.** MacSparran's published letters were addressed to Col. Henry Cary; his cousin, Rev. Paul Limrick; and William Stevenson. Only the letter to Cary, by far the longest of the three, is published here in abridged form. The Carys (or Careys) owned nearly three thousand acres in Moville parish, in Inishowen barony, Co. Donegal. Limrick (or Limerick, Lymerick) was born in Derry city, the son of an innkeeper, attended Trinity College, Dublin, and from 1723 to 1754 was rector and vicar of Kilmoe and Scull in Co. Cork; he died in Cork city 1755. His son (or nephew) and namesake also graduated from Trinity College and in 1778–1788 was deacon and (from 1781) curate of St. Anne, Shandon parish in Cork city, where he tutored the future United Irishman and American exile and playwright John Daly Burk (see chapter 63). Data on Stevenson cannot be discovered, but doubtless he, like Cary and Limrick, attended Dr. Blackhall's school in Derry. **9.** To facilitate reading MacSparran's text, we have not reproduced in our transcription the rather distracting "long s" or f (used, in continuation of medieval manuscript practice, through the eighteenth century in print and well into the nineteenth in handwriting instead of regular s at the beginning and in the middle of words and as the first character in the cluster -ss-). All instances of "long s" have accordingly been replaced here by regular s.

SIR,   August 20, 1752.

BY the Hands of Mr. *Robert Hamilton*, Son of *Ballyfattan*, near *Strabane*,[10] I did myself the Honour, a few Years ago, of writing you a Letter, giving an Account of myself, with a short Sketch of the Country where I have resided so many Years: But, as I am equally at a loss, whether that Letter reached your Honour, or was acceptable, if it did, I have presumed to put my Pen to Paper, to give you as curt an Account as I can of the *English American* Dominions; which, if it does not minister to your Entertainment, will, nevertheless, from its Intention, entitle me to your Pardon. . . .

Barbadoes is the windermost[11] of all the *English* Intertropical[12] Sugar-Islands; as *Antego*,[13] *Monserat*,[14] *St. Christopher's Nevis*,[15] *Jamaica*,[16] with many other lesser ones, are called the *Leeward Islands*. Your *Irish* Trade furnishes you with so distinct a Knowledge of the Religion, Government, Trade, and Commerce, of those Islands, that it would be but holding a Candle to the Sun to interrupt[17] you with a Detail of them . . .

I will now pass over to the Main-Land, where the first *English* Province that presents is *Georgia*. . . . Its first Inhabitants were, too many of them, the Sweepings of the Streets of *London*, and other populous Places; and though, as yet, it can boast of no very profitable Returns to the Mother-Country, it may, however, plume itself on this, that it eased *England* for that Time of some useless Hands, which doubtless are a dead Weight upon every Country. . . . As it is a Frontier, 'twill be always exposed to *Spanish* Insults[18] in Time of War; and to *Indian* Incursions, whenever their *Spanish* Masters have a Mind to incite them to annoy the *English* . . .

Northerly of *Georgia*, lies the flourishing Province of *South Carolina*. . . . Ever since [1720, when South Carolina became a royal colony], this Province has throve at a prodigious Rate; so that, besides their Home Consumption, it takes above 200 Sail of Ships, and other Top-sail Vessels, to export their annual Overplus. Their principal Produce is *Rice*; besides which, they export *Indian* Corn, (alias Maize) Pitch, Tar, Turpentine, Beef and Pork barrelled, tanned Leather, raw Hides, and other Articles. . . . The Church of *England* is established there by Provincial Law. . . . There are but a few

---

10. *Ballyfattan,* near *Strabane*: Ballyfatten townland (Urney parish, Strabane Lower barony, Co. Tyrone), near Strabane town. In 1876 the Hamiltons of Ballyfatten still held three properties totaling 216 acres.
11. windermost: furthest to windward. McSparran's statement claims that Barbados lies furthest to the windward (which, in the case of the Windward Islands, of which Barbados is a part, means furthest to the south) of the Greater and Lesser Antilles. In fact Grenada is the "windermost" of these islands, whereas Barbados, lying between St. Vincent and Grenada on a north–south axis, is well to the east of any of the chain.
12. Intertropical: lying between the Tropic of Cancer and the Tropic of Capricorn.   **13. Antego**: Antigua (one of the Leeward Islands). Judging by the spelling **Jamaico** (n. 16) the pronunciation was probably [anteegu]. The use of final o(w) with this phonetic value has its origin in forms like **window, follow,** in which the original final [oa] has developed to [u] ([windoa] → [windu], [feloa] → [felu].   **14. Monserat**: i.e., Montserrat (one of the Leeward Islands); on the Irish in Montserrat and elsewhere in the West Indies, see chapter 16.   **15. St Christopher's Nevis**: i.e., St. Christopher's (commonly St. Kitts) and Nevis (two of the Leeward Islands).   **16. Jamaico**: i.e., Jamaica (largest of Britain's West Indian island colonies).   **17. interrupt**: break in upon, bother, impose upon.   **18. Insults**: assaults, incursions.

Dissenters, and those of the *Independent* and *Antipædobaptist*[19] Persuations, who are mostly seated in *Charles-Town*, the Metropolis. . . . The Inhabitants are gay[20] and expensive[21] in their Furniture,[22] Clothing, Equipage, and Way of Living; an Observation that will but too well apply to all the *English* Colonies. The *Irish*, *Dutch*, *Palatines*, and other *Germans*, are as yet the only Exception to this Remark; but I think one may foretel, without a Spirit of prophecy, that, by the Symptoms beginning to shoot out[23] on the Offspring of the Wealthy and Thriving among them, their Posterity will fall into the like destructive Indulgencies.

More North, and North-Easterly, and on the *Atlantic* Shore, lies *North-Carolina*, granted also in 1663, by King *Charles* the Second, to a Company of Proprietors. Their Charter provides, That the Church of *England* shall be the only established Religion, and entitled to the public Encouragements.[24] This Province does not contain more Inhabitants than from 15,000 to 20,000, who live in Plantations scattered at great Distances. They have but few compact Towns, besides the small ones of *Edentown*, the Metropolis, and Cape *Fear*, by which Means[25] Religion has gained but little Ground. Two Clergymen, who are the Society's[26] itinerant Missionaries here, are all the Advantages they are yet under respecting Religion; and, though their Travel and labours are excessive, it can't be supposed but the greater Part of the People are necessarily rude[27] and illiterate, irreligious and prophane. There are a very small Number of Presbyterians, with some Quakers; and wherever these are, at least predominate,[28] you shall never fail to find Immoralities and Disorders prevail. Believe me, Sir, wherever Distinction of Persons is decried, as among that People, Confusions will follow: For Levelism is inconsistent with Order, and a certain Inlet[29] to Anarchy; as, when there was no King in *Israel*, every-one did what was right in his own Eyes. There are, however, sundry well-disposed Gentlemen, who from Time to Time have made laudable Efforts to promote True Religion among their *neighbours*; but what with their Colony Confusions and an *Indian* War some Years since, they have been able to make no great Advances. The Climate subjects the Inhabitants, especially New-Comers, to vernal and autumnal Agues[30] and Fevers of the mortal Kind. They export *Indian* Corn, and Pork, fatted in the Woods, with what, by a general Name, is called *Mast*; that is, Acorns, Walnuts, Chestnuts, other Nuts and wild Fruits; which makes it oily and unpalatable. But their greatest and most profitable Produce is of the Terebinthinate Kind, viz. Pitch, Tar, and Turpentine, which they ship off in great Quantities; as also Whalebone and Oil, some Seasons, from Cape *Fear*. Upon the whole, this Province may still pass for a pretty wild and uncultivated Country; and,

---

19. *Independent*: Congregationalist; *Antipædobaptist* (or hereafter, *Anabaptists*): Baptist(s).   20. gay: showy, flashy.   21. expensive: extravagant.   22. Furniture: furnishings.   23. shoot out: put out shoots, come into bloom.   24. Encouragements: support.   25. by which Means: "and because of this."   26. the Society: the Society for the Preservation of the Gospel (S.P.G.).   27. rude: uncultivated, uncivilized.   28. predominate: written by mistake for "predominant."   29. a certain Inlet: "a sure opening."   30. Agues (in connection with fevers): chills.

excepting a few of the better Sort, its white Inhabitants have degenerated into a State of Ignorance and Barbarism, not much superior to the native *Indians*.

Along the same Shore, and North-Easterly, lies the old famous Colony of *Virginia*; so called from the Virgin-Queen *Elizabeth*, in whose Reign it seems to be first settled. The first Adventurers to those Parts were mostly Gentlemen of Family and Fortune, and firmly attached to the *English* Church. . . . This was the last of all the *American English* Plantations that submitted to *Oliver's*³¹ Yoke; nor was it without a Struggle and force, at last, that they put on that Usurper's Chains. . . . From this Province, and *Maryland*, its next Neighbour, all *Europe* is supplied with Tobacco. . . . There are many Gentlemen of large Demesnes³² and Fortunes in *Virginia*, and are as remarkable for their open and free Hospitality, as for their great Numbers of Negro Slaves; several having Hundreds, and some above a Thousand, of such Servants, so that I believe the Blacks do in number equal, if not out-do, the Whites. As Hanging seems to be the worst Use Men can be put to, it were to be wished, that a Period were put³³ even to the Transportation of Convicts from *England* and *Ireland* to *Virginia* and *Maryland*. Though some of these Felons do reform, yet they are so few, that their Malversation³⁴ has a bad Effect upon the Morals of the lower Class of Inhabitants: Great Pity, therefore, it is, that some Punishments worse than Death or Transportation could not be contrived for those Vermin. . . . There has lately been made, upon and behind the Mountains of *Virginia*, a new *Irish* Settlement, by a Transmigration of sundry of those that, within these thirty Years past, went from the North of *Ireland* to *Pennsylvania*. As the Soil in that new *Irish* Settlement is natural and friendly to Grass, they will, for many Years to come, raise great Quantities of neat Cattle,³⁵ as the Climate is benign, and their Outlets on Commonages large. . . . ³⁶

Along-side of *Virginia*, and more north-easterly, lies *Maryland*, through which runs the great river *Susquehannah*. . . . This tract, or province, was granted to the great *Calvert*, Lord *Baltimore*, an *Irish* nobleman, by Queen *Mary*, wife of *Philip* of *Spain*; and, in honour of her, called *Maryland*. . . . As the late Lord *Baltimore* was the first *Protestant* peer of the *Calvert* family,³⁷ his predecessors (as it was natural they should) first peopled this province with a colony of *Irish Catholicks*. These, having the start, in point of time, of the after-settlers, are also, to this day, a-head of them in wealth and substance; by which means, the first and best families are, for the most part, still of the *Roman* communion. Tho' this province have a succession of secular clergy sent them, chiefly

---

31. Oliver's: refers to Oliver Cromwell, who governed the British Isles in 1653–1658.   **32. Demesnes**: estates.   **33. that a Period were put**: "that a stop/halt were put."   **34. Malversation**: bad behavior. **35. neat Cattle**: neat (i.e., bovine) livestock.   **36. their Outlets on Commonages [are] large**: "the number of cattle let out onto common pastures is large."   **37. the great *Calvert*, Lord *Baltimore***: George Calvert (ca. 1580–1632), first Lord Baltimore; in 1632 he persuaded Charles I—not **Queen Mary** (reigned 1553–1558), as MacSparran erroneously wrote—to grant him what became Maryland; **the late Lord *Baltimore***: Charles Calvert (1699–1751), fourth Lord Baltimore.

from *Ireland*, who subsist on the free-will offerings of those to whom they administer; yet is the Country cantoned[38] into Parishes and Precincts, over which preside, by legal Establishment, a competent Number of Clergymen of our Church, handsomely provided for. . . . There are some *Quakers* here, in Consequence of its bordering on *Pennsylvania*; and some *Irish Presbyterians*, owing to the Swarms that, for many Years past, have winged their Way Westward out of the *Hibernian* Hive. One Mr. *Hugh Conn*, of *Macgilligan*,[39] My Senior, but former Acquaintance, when I was a School-boy at *Foghan-veil*, and Minister to a *Presbyterian* Congregation in *Maryland*; as he was preaching, a few Months ago, upon the Subject of a sudden Death, dropped down dead in his Pulpit,—a melancholy and, indeed, remarkable Verification of the Truth he was inculcating on his Audience. He has Relations in the Place of his Nativity; and this, perhaps, may be the only Intimation they may have of his Demise. . . . As to the Produce, Exportations, and Commerce of this Colony, they are so much the same with *Virginia*, that they need no Repetition. The Inhabitants are all Tenants to Lord *Baltimore*, upon a small Quit-rent;[40] and yet so prodigiously have the Planters extended themselves, that his Lordship's Quit-rents are computed at 8000£. sterling per Annum; and if the *Irish* go on, but a few years more, to people the upper and inland Parts of the Province, as they have begun, it will soon raise his Rents to double that Sum.

Next to *Maryland*, and north-easterly of it, lyes *Pennsylvania*, so called from the famous *William Penn*, a noted Quaker, of a family of that name in *Ireland*. . . . The first *English* settlers here were *Quakers*; for above of two thousand of these people went out of *England* at one embarkation, with *William Penn*, and began the city of *Philadelphia*, and the plantations contiguous to it. Since that time, great numbers, of other nations, and of different notions in religion, have chose this province for their habitation; not to avoid any violence to their persons or principles, (as is more *commonly*, than *truly*, alledged, in *New-England* especially) but to improve their fortunes in those parts. Soon after this colony had a little increased, as an *English* civil government became necessary, and as it could not be safely trusted in, nor its powers agreeably executed by, any but *English* hands, they were reduced to a sad delemma. A statute of *William* and *Mary*,[41] in conformity to their own avowed tenets, had disqualified *Quakers* from the exercise of any civil authority; and, as there were few fit among them for offices, but persons of that persuasion, they petitioned the crown for a dispensation of the statute; and their prayer was heard. Thus let into the administration, they soon shewed, that Nature is

---

38. cantoned: divided (of land). **39.** *Hugh Conn,* **of** *Macgilligan*: born ca. 1685 in Magilligan parish, Co. Londonderry; studied at **Foghan-veil** (Faughanvale townland and parish, Co. Londonderry), and graduated from the University of Glasgow; Presbyterian minister at Patapsco, Md., near Baltimore, 1715–1719, and at the East Branch of the Potomac (now Bladensburg, Md.) from 1719 until his death on 28 June 1752 while preaching a funeral sermon. **40. Quit-rent**: a small payment made annually, in lieu of service, to the landlord or the sovereign. **41.** *William* **and** *Mary*: ruled jointly 1689–1694.

often too powerful for principle: And, tho' they declaim against dominion, yet, when they are once entrusted with power, they won't easily let go their hold. . . .

I believe I need not tell you, that *Pennsylvania* is an absolute stranger to an uniformity in religion; for the different countries, that contributed to the peopling of this province, carried their respective preachers and opinions along with them. The Church of *England* entered no earlier here than 1700; but God's blessing upon the few labourers employed as missionaries among them, has given the church a large and promising spread. The Society for the Propagation of the Gospel in Foreign Parts maintain at present eight missionaries among them, to have the care of treble that number of churches, besides where they officiate in private houses. In the city of *Philadelphia* there is a large church, where the Society maintain Mr. *Sturgeon*, their catechist; but the incumbent (the worthy and Reverend Dr. *Jenny*, son of Archdeacon *Jenny*, in *Waney-Town*, in the North of *Ireland*) is maintained at the expence of his own Auditors.[42] There is a public and open Mass-house[43] in this City; which I note, there being none allowed to the Northward of it, in all the *English* Plantations. The *Irish* are numerous in this province; who, besides their Interspersions among the *English* and others, have peopled a whole County by themselves, called the County of *Donnegal*,[44] with many other new Out-towns and Districts. In one of these Frontiers, on the Forks of *Delaware*, I assisted my Brother[45] (who left *Ireland* against my Advice) in purchasing a large Tract of Land, which, by his and his Wife's Demise, about a Year ago, descends to his Children. This puts me in mind to intercede with your Honour, in Behalf of his eldest Daughter, married to one *Gamble*, and who, I hear, resolves to return again, to receive them to your Favour, if you find they deserve it, as descended from Ancestors who lived happily under your Father and Grandfather, and Great Grandmother, the Hon. Lady *Cork*.[46] The Exportations from this Province are principally Wheaten Flour, which they send abroad in great Quantities; and, by the Accessions and Industry of the *Irish* and *Germans*, they threaten, in a few Years, to lessen the *American* Demands for *Irish* and other *European* Linens. . . .

Next to *Pennsylvania*, and on the East Side of the River *Delaware*, lies the Province which goes by the Name of the *East* and *West Jerseys*. . . . The first Inhabitants were Quakers and Anabaptists, and Sabbatarian Baptists . . . but, at present, its

---

42. Archdeacon *Jenny*: Robert Jenny (1687–1762); S.P.G. missionary in New York, 1722–1742; rector of Christ's Church, Philadelphia, 1742–1762; however, MacSparran apparently erred in that the only *Waney-Town* (recte Weneytown) that appears in the 1851 Irish townland index is in Co. Wexford (Duncormick parish). **Auditors**: congregants. **43. Mass-house**: Roman Catholic chapel (that is, church). **44. the county of Donnegal**: Donegal: a Presbyterian congregation and township (not a county), then in Cumberland (now Dauphin) Co., Pa. **45. my Brother**: Archibald MacSparran, James's eldest brother; sold the family homestead in Dungiven and emigrated to New Castle, Del.; settled in New Londonderry township, Chester Co., Pa., where he died ca. 1750. **46. the Hon. Lady Cork**: probably Dorothy, elder daughter of the Marquess of Halifax; in 1720 married Richard Boyle (d. 1753), fourth earl of Cork and Orrery; or her mother-in-law, Juliana, daughter of Henry Noel, second son of the third Viscount Campden; in 1687/8 married Charles Boyle (d. 1703), the third earl.

Inhabitants are generally *Dutch* and *Irish* Presbyterians, *New-England* Independents, Quakers, and Baptists of divers Sorts. The Church of *England*, however, began to enter here in 1702, and its Success and Progress yields Matter of great Thanksgiving to God. . . .

The next Province we proceed to is that of *New-York*. . . . A little Time after [the English] Conquest,[47] great Numbers of *English* came into this Country, and, by After-accessions, it is become a well-cultivated and extensive, and, in consequence, a rich and populous Province. . . . Several Gentlemen have taken out Patents for large Tracts up in the Country, which they are settling as fast as they can; and, in an Age[48] or two, (if, before that, we should not be drove into the Sea by the *French*) will be profitable Estates. Sir *Peter Warren*, the Admiral,[49] and our Countryman, is one of those who own much of these Lands. The Exportations from this Province are principally Furs, Flour, Bread, Wheat, *Indian* Corn, pickled Beef and Pork, Rye, Buck-Wheat, and other Articles. . . . The first public Beginning of the Church of *England* in the Province of *New-York*, was *Anno Domini* 1693; but so remarkably has God appeared against Schism and Heresy, and in Behalf of the truly Apostolic Faith and decent Worship of the Church of England, that at this day there are ten Missionaries, who officiate in more Churches. . . .

Next to *New-York*, in proceeding East and by North, we enter on the Country called *New-England*. . . . *Connecticut* is that Part of *New-England* next to *New-York*. The first *English* Settlers of this Colony were Puritans, who transported themselves hither in 1630. They formed themselves into a *Civil Society*, by an Instrument of Government of their own making; and, by so doing, became, by strictness of Law, liable to the Penalties of Treason; and into an Ecclesiastical Society, by a Platform partly borrowed from the *Brownists*[50] of *Plymouth*, who come nine years before them, and partly by Additions or Inventions of their own, and so became Independents, and, if you please, Schismaticks. When *Cromwell* began the exercise of Sovereign Power, without the Character and Style of King, these Sectarian Settlements soon submitted to his Yoke; and their fulsome and fawning Addresses, stuffed with the odious Cant peculiar to the Age and People, are at this Day offensive to a loyal and pious Ear. . . . *Independency*, by a more creditable Nick-name, called *Presbyterianism*, is the Religion of the State; but, of late Years, some *Quakers*, more *Anabaptists*, and a still greater Number of *Churchmen*[51] have crowded into, or rather, conformed in, that Colony; and, by present Appearances, one may fortel, that the Members of our Church will, in a Century more, amount to a major Part of the whole. . . . As to the Character of the Independent Teachers, those

---

47. **Conquest**: the English permanently conquered New York, then New Netherland, from the Dutch in 1674. 48. **Age**: generation. 49. **Sir Peter Warren, the Admiral**: of Warrenstown, Co. Meath, from whom MacSparran unsuccessfully solicited patronage appointments in the mid-1740s; for more data on Warren, see chapter 51. 50. **Brownists**: Separatists (Pilgrims). 51. **Churchmen**: Anglicans; members or clergy of the Church of England or the Church of Ireland.

who have undertaken to draw their Picture, have represented them as noted for Enthusiasm,[52] and those affected Inspirations, which for the most part begin in *Folly*, and often (if not always) end in *Vice*. Some Pens[53] have distinguished them for a grave Hypocrisy, Phlegmatick Stiffness, and Sacerdotal Tyranny; and the Laity, for Formality and Preciseness, and covering over ill Arts and Acts with a Cloak of Religion. But I think this Picture wears too harsh Features; tho' it must be owned not to be absolutely void of Resemblance. . . . *Connecticut* is a Colony remarkable for Industry, and a tolerably good Soil; and no Place this way can boast of larger Exportations, in proportion to its Extent and Inhabitants. . . .

Travelling Eastward, the next Region that rises to View is the little Colony of *Rhode-Island*, &c. where Providence has fixed me, and where I have resided in Quality of Missionary thirty-one Years last *April*. . . . In *Connecticut*, I observed to you, that Independency was the Religion of the State; but in *Rhode-Island* no Religion is established. There a Man may, with Impunity, be of any Society, or of none at all; but the Quakers are, for the most part, the People in Power. . . . [A]s Quakerism prevailed, Learning was decried, Ignorance and Heresy so increased, that neither *Epiphanius*'s, nor Sir *Richard Blakmore*'s[54] Catalogues, contain more heterodox and different Opinions in Religion than were to be found in this little Corner. . . . In 1700, after Quakerism and other Heresies had, in their Turns, ruled over and tinged all the Inhabitants for the Space of forty-six Years, the Church of *England*, that had been lost here through the Neglect of the Crown, entered as it were, unobserved and unseen, and yet not without some Success. A little Church was built in *Newport*, the Metropolis of the Colony, in 1702, and that in which I officiate in *Narraganset*, in 1707. There have been two Incumbents before me; but neither of them had resolution enough to grapple with the Difficulties of the Mission above a year a-piece. I entered on this Mission in 1721; and found the People not a *Tabula rasa*, or clean Sheet of Paper, upon which I might make any Impressions I pleased; but a Field full of Briars and Thorns, and noxious weeds, that were all to be eradicated, before I could implant in them the Simplicity of Truth. However, by God's Blessing, I have brought over to the Church some Hundreds, and, among the Hundreds I have baptized, there are at least 150 who received the Sacrament at my Hands, from twenty Years old, to seventy or eighty. *Ex Pede Herculem*.[55] By this, you may guess, in how uncultivated a Country my Lot fell. . . . [W]ould to God I could boast of more Success! but Toil and Travel has put me beyond my Best; and, if I am not rewarded with a little Rest in *Europe*, where my Desires are, I have strong Hopes of infinitely more desirable Rest from my Labours, in those celestial

---

52. **Enthusiasm**: (extreme) religious emotionalism, as associated from 1734 with the colonial revivals collectively known as the First Great Awakening. **53. Pens**: "writers." **54. Epiphanius . . . Sir Richard Blakmore** (recte Blackmore): Epiphanius of Constantia (or of Salamis; ca. 315–402) was the author of the Panarion, a tract against heretics, in which eighty varieties of heresy are discussed and refuted; he was particularly opposed to Arians and Origenists. Sir Richard Blackmore (d. 1729) brought out two works against Arianism, both in 1721: *Just Prejudices against the Arian Hypothesis* and *Modern Arians Unmasked*. **55. Ex Pede Herculem**: Latin proverb; "you can get an idea of Hercules' size by looking at his feet."

Mansions prepared by my dear Redeemer. . . . The Produce of this Colony is principally Butter and Cheese, fat Cattle, Wool, and fine Horses, that are exported to all Parts of the *English America*. . . . There are above 300 Vessels, such as Sloops, Scooners, Snows, Brigantines, and Ships, from 60 Tons and upwards, that belong to this Colony; but, as they are rather Carriers for other Colonies, than furnished here with their Cargoes, you will go near to conclude[56] that we are lazy and greedy of Gain, since, instead of cultivating the Lands, we improve[57] too many Hands in Trade. This indeed is the Case. There are here, which is no good Symptom, a vast many[58] law-Suits; more in one Year than the County of *Derry* has in twenty. . . . The Novanglians[59] in general, the *Rhode-Islanders* in particular, are perhaps the only People on Earth who have hit on the Art of enriching themselves by running in Debt. This will remain no longer a Mystery, than I have related to your Honour, that we have no Money among us, but a depreciating Paper Currency. . . . Indeed, a new Act of the *British* Parliament, ill-penned,[60] passed last Winter, to restrain us: But . . . we shall go on, I doubt,[61] in our Way of paper Emissions,[62] unless the Lord, in Mercy to us, should dispose the sovereign Power to vacate our Patent, and prevent our Destruction, by taking us out of our own Hands . . .

The next Province to *Rhode-Island* is the Province of *Massachusets-Bay*, whose Metropolis is *Boston*, a Town containing about 20,000 Inhabitants. . . . They are obliged to other Colonies for many of the Necessaries of Life, yet they have a great Trade to *England* with Whalebone, Oil, Pitch, and Tar; and to *Portugal*, *Spain*, and *Italy*, with dried Fish; to the *West-Indies*, with Cod, Mackarel, Boards, Frames for Houses, and other Sorts of Lumber. They have one College at *New Cambridge*, and many petty,[63] ill-taught Grammar-Schools; yet, under these mean Advantages, they are a more polite and regular People than some of their Neighbours. This is a very large and populous Province, and has many *Irish* Settlements in the Out-Towns on the *French* Frontier; so that our Countrymen, tho' less esteemed than they ought to be, are yet their Barrier in Time of War.

New-Hampshire Province lyes Eastward of the *Massachusets*, and is absolutely under the King. 'Tis from hence the Royal Navy is furnished with Masting, Yards, Spars, and Oars; and whoever is Master of this, and the Provinces Eastward of it, must be Master at Sea in Europe. . . . [W]ere all the Colonies immediately under the Crown, as this is, the Church would gain Ground faster than She does. In this Province lies that town called *London Derry*, all *Irish*, and famed for Industry and Riches.

Next you enter on the Province of *Main*, which in its Civil Government is annexed to the *Massachusets*, as *Sagadahock*[64] also is; and both rather by Use than Right.

---

56. you will go near to conclude: "you will almost conclude." **57. improve**: employ, make use of. **58. a vast many**: a very great many; the use of **vast(ly)** as an intensifier was common in the eighteenth century. **59. Novanglians**: New Englanders. **60. ill-penned**: badly worded. **61. doubt**: suspect, apprehend. **62. Emissions**: issues of currency. **63. petty**: insignificant. **64. Sagadahock**: Sagadahoc, an area in southwest Maine.

In these two Eastern Provinces many *Irish* are settled, and many have been ruined by the *French Indians*, and drove from their Homes. It is pretty true to observe of the *Irish*, in general, that those who come here with any Wealth are the worse for their Removal; though, doubtless, the Next Generation will not suffer so much as their Fathers; But those who, when they came, had nothing to lose, have throve greatly by their Labour. He that lies on the Ground can fall no lower; and such are the fittest to encounter the Difficulties attending new Settlers. . . .

As the *Jews* had their *Nazareth*, the *New-Englanders* have their *Ireland*;[65] but, as what is always due to too national a Spirit, they are as much despised in the other *English* Plantations, as any *Teague*[66] is by them. This country might be made greatly serviceable to the Mother-Country by proper Management; but *false*, I had almost said *fatal* Policy, has overlooked both the civil and religious Interests of *English America*. Indeed, the Society for Propagation, &c. has done Wonders; but nothing less than Royal and National Attention is equal to the Thing. If our Accounts from Home may [be] depended upon, Religion runs low, and Ireland is like to regain its ancient Name of *Insula Sanctorum*,[67] compared with the greater Island. The Revolution,[68] which happened before you or I were born, might be thought a wise and necessary Measure; But, we see, it has been followed with some bad Consequences; to get free from Popery, we have run into Infidelity and Scepticism. . . . Except the little Revival Religion had in Queen *Ann*'s Reign,[69] the Church has gained no Ground, but in *America*, since that Period. . . . If I should ever be settled in *Europe*, and have a little Leisure, I would employ my Pen in a small History of the *English* Plantations; but, if that is not my Fate, I may *leave*, perhaps, but can't with safety *give*, the Public what may be helpful to an abler Hand. The Share of Satisfaction which a Man of my Age can promise himself in this World, is small, and hardly worth Attention; and yet I should be glad, were it God's will, to end my Days nearer to where I began them than I now am. . . .

In coasting[70] the country, I've said nothing of the climate. . . . In general, the Air is infinitely more clear and serene than in *England* or *Ireland*; and our Nearness to the Sun occasions more frequent and loud Claps of Thunder, and sharper Lightning, than you have. It is no unusual Thing for Houses, and Stacks of Hay, and Grain, to be Burnt; and Men and Cattle are often killed by the sharp Lightning. In *New England*, the Transitions from Heat to Cold are short and sudden, and the extremes of both very

---

65. As the *Jews* had their *Nazareth*, the *New-Englanders* have their *Ireland*: reference to *John* 1:46, "And Nathaniel said unto him, Can there any good thing come out of Nazareth?" That is, the Hebrews' contempt for Nazareth and its inhabitants, as "backward" and "uncivilized," is analogous to the New Englanders' contempt for Ireland and those who come from there (whatever their religion). **66. *Teague*:** see n. 6. **67. *Insula Sanctorum*:** "Isle of the Saints"; a designation of Ireland since the early medieval era. **68. The Revolution:** the Glorious Revolution (1688); MacSparran's ambivalence about the Glorious Revolution was not uncommon among Anglican clergymen in England, less so in Ireland with its large Catholic majority. **69. Queen *Ann*'s Reign:** 1702–1714. **70. coasting:** making the rounds of, traversing.

sensible:[71] We are sometimes frying, and others freezing; and as Men often die at their Labour in the Field by *Heat*, so some in Winter are froze to Death with the *Cold*. . . . Though I am 900 Miles to the Southward, and you Fifteen Degrees to the Northward of me, yet will it freeze Fifteen Times so much in a Night here as I ever observed it to do in *Ulster*. But I must not indulge my Inclination to gratify you with Accounts of this New World; but break off with begging Leave to assure you, that I am,

With the most perfect Sincerity,

And profound Veneration,

Your Honour's

Most obedient, humble Servant,

J. M. S. . . .

MacSparran's last efforts to escape America ended tragically. In 1754 he persuaded his wife to accompany him on a visit to England and Ireland, either to seek "a provision on that shore for the rest of his days" or, as he may have been led to believe, to be consecrated the first American bishop. However, MacSparran's wife died in London of smallpox and he returned to Rhode Island empty-handed, purportedly declaring that "he would rather dwell in the hearts of his parishioners, than wear all the bishop's gowns in the world." Two years later, on 1 December 1757, MacSparran, aged 64, died at his house in South Kingstown and was buried under the communion table of St. Paul's.

Over one hundred years after his death, New England's Episcopalians still memorialized Rev. James MacSparran as the "Apostle of Narragansett." His legacy in Ireland, however, and, indeed, even his primary motive for publishing his letters there, remain ambiguous. Whether *America Dissected* had dissuaded many potential emigrants is improbable, for the very conditions that MacSparran condemned in the colonies—their social fluidity and especially the weakness of royal and ecclesiastical authority—were more likely to attract than repel the Dissenters who comprised the great majority of eighteenth-century Irish emigrants.

On one hand, *America Dissected*, like the sermons MacSparran sent to Irish churchmen, must be interpreted in the context of MacSparran's continued efforts to "raise me up Friends, and restore me to my native Land."[72] Certainly, MacSparran's attempt to discourage emigration was calculated to please both Anglo-Irish bishops and Ulster gentry such as Col. Henry Cary, the recipient of his longest letter, who feared further losses of Protestant parishioners and tenants. Yet there is no doubt that MacSparran's strictures on America were sincere and reflected his instinctive distaste for the crudity, heterodoxy, and lack of hierarchy and deference that characterized colonial society. Thus, *America Dissected* was designed particularly to discourage emigration by others such as himself: genteel, con-

---

71. sensible: palpable.   **72.** MacSparran to William Stevenson, 21 August 1752, in *America Dissected*, 52–3.

servative, and pious but "Unsteady"[73] young Anglicans who lacked patronage sufficient to sustain or improve in the colonies the privileged position they had enjoyed in Ireland.

More broadly, both the vagaries of MacSparran's career and the tone of *America Dissected* may reflect attempts to resolve issues of identity that were intensely personal as well as inevitably political and inextricably linked to his social aspirations. It is intriguing, for example, that MacSparran's writings, both private and published, display a strong sense of "Irish" identity that transcends ethnoreligious distinctions and includes, in his applications of the term "Irish," Anglicans, Presbyterians, and Catholics alike. In *America Dissected* varieties of "Irishness" are distinguished, if at all, only by religion, and earlier or subsequently common "racial" or national designations—such as (the) "English in Ireland"; "Scotch-Irish"; "British"; and "Irish" as synonymous with Catholics *only*—are strikingly absent. Indeed, because of his immediate ancestry and cultural background, MacSparran must have appeared, in the eyes of most Ulster Presbyterians and American dissenters, more suspiciously "Irish" than conventionally "Scottish." And although in 1716 Ulster's General Synod had designated MacSparran's own Dungiven as a center for clerical training in the Irish language, Presbyterian missionary efforts were paltry, as most ministers had little but contempt for a language they identified with the "popery" and "barbarism" of the Scottish Highlands and Ireland alike. It may be that MacSparran's conversion to Anglicanism was in part a defensive or even a defiant response to such suspicions and prejudices.

To be sure, joining a church commonly associated with High Tory principles may have come naturally to a man whose religious and political origins were so at variance from most Ulster Presbyterians' historical experience and mythology. Whereas the latter gloried in their ancestors' persecutions at Stuart hands and their defence of Derry's walls for William of Orange, MacSparran's kin had fought for Charles I against both Scots Covenanters and Cromwell's Puritans, while he himself was more than skeptical concerning the benefits of the Glorious Revolution. Perhaps even more important, however, was that MacSparran's conversion to Ireland's legally established church enabled him to submerge *and* employ his rich but dangerously confusing cultural legacy in ways that were assertively "Irish" yet also politically and socially advantageous. For the Church of Ireland, although "English" in its origin and subordination to Westminster and Canterbury, nonetheless claimed the mantle of St. Patrick, and as Ireland's "national" church it proclaimed—and sporadically pursued—the quixotic goal of obliterating the island's most profound religious and civil distinctions by converting not only Protestant Dissenters but also the "native" Catholics, and that through the medium of their own language, which MacSparran knew intimately. Ironically, then, by embracing the Church of Ireland, MacSparran could both be "Irish" and achieve a social and political status denied by law to Irish Dissenters and Catholics alike.

---

73. MacSparran, *America Dissected,* title page.

Despite his rather unusual background, MacSparran reflected a general trend: the early eighteenth-century transformation among Ireland's Protestants from a "settler" mentality to what some historians have called "colonial nationalism"—an increasing emotional and political identification with "Ireland" and "Irish" interests, coupled with a growing estrangement from the English (after 1707 the British) government and its legal and economic restrictions on Irish Protestant aspirations. The herald of attitudinal change was the 1698 publication in Dublin of *The Case of Ireland . . . Stated* by William Molyneux (1666–1698), an Anglican lawyer, and after 1714—when the Hanoverian succession entrenched a hostile Whig oligarchy in power at Westminster—Ireland's Protestant gentry and Church of Ireland clergy became more vocal in their "national" or "patriotic" objections to British policies and patronage in Ireland. Thus, MacSparran resembled his friend, Bishop Berkeley, and Jonathan Swift (1667–1745), dean of St. Patrick's Cathedral in Dublin, in both his High Tory principles and his bitter resentment against London's appointments of Englishmen to the most lucrative posts in the Irish church and civil administrations. MacSparran equally resented British Whigs' insistence that the Dublin legislature repeal the Penal Laws against the Irish Protestant Dissenters, whom he—like Swift—now despised.[74] Thus, *America Dissected* must be viewed in the broad context of political conflict between the Irish and the British oligarchies, and it may represent a minor contribution to the Irish "pamphlet war" occasioned by the Money Dispute of 1752–1753. For MacSparran's stated opposition to a proposed legislative union between Ireland and Britain clearly expressed his alienation from the British administration in Dublin Castle and his support for the "patriot" or "country" party that voiced (however cynically) the opinions of most Irish landlords and members of the Irish House of Commons.[75]

To be sure, MacSparran was angling for Irish patronage. In addition, among Irish Protestants, generally, this early growth of Irish national sentiment should not be exagger-

74. In doctrinal and social terms, MacSparran—like many Church of Ireland clergymen—felt greater affinity for Irish Catholics than for Irish Protestant dissenters. Consoling his cousin, Rev. Paul Limrick, on the apparent marriage of Limrick's son to a Catholic, MacSparran wrote that, after all, "Papists are Christians, and to be preferred to many Protestant Heretics I could name to you" (*America Dissected,* 48). In Ireland Protestant-Catholic marriages were then (and until 1792) subject to severe legal penalties. Ironically, however, the Church of Ireland recognized the validity of marriages conducted by Catholic priests but *not* those officiated by Presbyterian and other dissenting clergymen.   75. The Money Bill dispute of 1753 culminated a parliamentary power struggle between Henry Boyle, earl of Shannon and speaker of the Irish House of Commons, and his "patriot" or "country" allies on one side, and the adherents of the lord lieutenant, the duke of Dorset, the Anglican primate George Stone, and the Ponsonby family, representing the "English" or "court" interest on the other. In his letter to Limrick, MacSparran wrote: "Our attention here has been for some Time taken up with the News of Measures on Foot to unite *Ireland* to *England,* as *Scotland* is. I pray God they may never take Effect; for if they do, farewell Liberty. You are greater Slaves already than our Negroes; and an Union of that Kind would make you more Underlings than you are now. . . . [I]f ever you come into a closer Connection with the more eastern Island, Corruption will increase, Pedlars be promoted to Power, but the Clergy and landed Interest will sink into Disesteem. I suppose those that are sent to rule with you, like those who sometimes are sent here, imagine fleecing to be a better Business than feeding the Flock" (*America Dissected,* 50).

ated. Although they sought validation of their status by reference to Hiberno-Norman or even Gaelic precedents, the members of Ireland's Anglican ascendancy defined "Irish" interests in their own terms, and in the 1780s-1790s their interests would make most of them fervent loyalists to Britain in opposition to new, more democratic expressions of Irish nationalism espoused by Presbyterian and Catholic reformers and radicals. Moreover, even in the mid–eighteenth century, ecumenical interpretations of "Irishness" could flourish better in the New World than in Ireland, with its deep ethnoreligious divisions and large Catholic majority. Hence it is possible that MacSparran discovered his "Irishness" overseas—and that residence in America (and particularly in New England), where colonists of English descent often ignorantly or willfully conflated Irish Protestant and Catholic immigrants, encouraged his adoption of the one "Irish" identity that enabled him to claim superiority over local Dissenters, despite their numerical majority and political power. Yet just as MacSparran's religious and political beliefs alienated him from the heterodoxy of American culture, so also his heightened identification with Ireland accentuated his homesickness for his "native Land."[76] Thus, less instinctively but no less sincerely than the anonymous composer of *An tOileán Úr*, MacSparran expressed in *America Dissected* a cultural or even a "national" aversion to emigration that contrasted markedly with Irish Dissenters' millennial vision of the colonies as a new "Canaan."

9 ✳

Robert Parke, 1725

Despite promotions by shippers, agents, and colonial governments, transatlantic correspondence played the major role in encouraging and directing Irish emigration. This was perhaps especially true in the early eighteenth century, before the transatlantic servant trade between Ireland and America became fully commercialized, when alternative information sources were few and unreliable, and when the patterns of chain migration were first being established. For the same reasons, early emigrants' letters tended to be extremely detailed, and those of Irish Quakers particularly so by reason of their superior education and determination to reconstitute their exclusive familial and religious communities in North America. Hence this missive by Robert Parke (1695–1737), an Irish Quaker in Pennsylvania, serves as an excellent example of an eighteenth-century letter that encouraged emigration by kinsmen and coreligionists and that helped create the alluring image

---

76. Other Irish Protestant immigrants reacted quite differently, however, to Anglo-Americans' tendencies to confuse them with Irish "papists," and some scholars have argued that the origins of "Scotch-Irish" identity in the New World stemmed from their desire to emphasize the distinction. For different responses, as determined by changing socioeconomic, cultural, and political circumstances, both in Ireland and America, see hereafter, especially chapters 49, 53, 58, and 64.

of an American "land of promise," a bountiful arcadia, that captured the imaginations of Irish Protestants—especially of Dissenters—and, much later, of Irish Catholics.

On 21 May 1724, Robert Parke, aged 31, emigrated with his parents and siblings from Dublin to Delaware Bay, on a stormy voyage that lasted three months. His father, Thomas Parke (1660–1738), had rented several hundred acres in three separate farms,[1] each in a different parish of County Carlow, but he and his wife Rebecca[2] lived at Ballintrane in Fennagh (or Feenagh) parish, in the barony of Idrone East, where they raised 10 children, all but one of whom survived infancy.[3] Unlike the rapidly dwindling Baptists, the Quakers of early eighteenth-century Ireland remained a significant community, as between the 1650s and 1700 migration from England and exceptionally high birth rates had increased their numbers to perhaps 6,500—over a third of them in Leinster, a tenth in Dublin city—with over one hundred weekly meetings. In Dublin, Cork, Waterford, and other cities, wealthy Quakers were prominent in trade and manufacturing, but most southern Friends were farmers like the Parkes or artisans and small tradesmen. Despite their general prosperity, however, in the early 1680s Irish Quakers began to emigrate to New Jersey and Pennsylvania, later to the Carolinas, and by 1750 between one thousand and two thousand had removed to North America.

It is difficult to separate religious, political, and economic reasons for Quaker emigration. Like other Irish Dissenters, the Quakers conflated spiritual and material concerns, and in southern Ireland, where they were surrounded by Catholics, the Friends' self-image as a "peculiar" and a persecuted people was naturally heightened. To be sure, the Parkes and other mid-Leinster Quakers did not suffer the extreme isolation that threatened the Baptist James Wansbrough in contemporary Westmeath.[4] County Carlow had the maximum Protestant settlement outside Ulster (nearly 15 percent in 1732), and despite emigration as late as 1766 Protestants still comprised at least a sixth of Fennagh's inhabitants.[5] However,

---

1. Parke's farms were in the adjacent townlands of Coolasnaghta (Fennagh or Feenagh parish, Idrone East barony) and Ballaghmore (Myshall parish) and Ballyleen (Ballon parish), both in the barony of Forth. Together these townlands comprised nearly 2,200 statute acres, but it is very doubtful that Parke was their only lessee. **2.** Née Ward or Ware, Warr (ca. 1672–1749), of Ballyredmond (Moyacomb parish, St. Mullins Upper barony), Co. Carlow; she and Thomas Parke married on 21 October 1692. **3.** Thomas and Rebecca Parke's children were: (1) Mary (b.1693), m. Thomas Valentine (d.1747) of Ballybromhill (or Ballybrommell), Fennagh parish, in 1715; emigrated in 1728 with her husband and children, and settled in New Providence township in Philadelphia (now Montgomery) Co. (2) Robert: see text. (3) Susanna (b. 1696), remained in Ireland and never married. (4) Rebecca (b. 1699), m. Hugh Stalker in Chester Co., Pa. (5) Rachel (b. 1700); m. William Robinson, from Co. Wicklow, in Chester Co. (6) Jean or Jane (1703–1705). (7) Thomas, Jr. (1705–1758), m. Jane Edge in 1759 in Chester Co.; farmed 276 acres in Caln township and owned the "Ship" tavern, on the main Philadelphia–Lancaster road. (8) Abel (1707–1757); m. Deborah (?); farmed one hundred acres in Caln township and built and operated the "Ship" tavern, later owned by brother Thomas; for his troubled relationships with Irish-born indentured servants, see chapter 30. (9) Jonathan (1709–1767); m. Deborah Taylor in 1771 and farmed two hundred acres, given by his father-in-law, in East Bradford township, Chester Co. (10) Elizabeth (1711–1746); m. John Jackson of Chester Co. **4.** For James Wansbrough, see chapter 1. **5.** For demographic data on Fennagh parish and its environs, see appendix 2.2a, on chapter 9.

the Parkes and other Friends stood aloof from the Anglicans, who comprised the overwhelming majority of southern Ireland's Protestants, and in the 1720s they were still barred by law from holding office and were harrassed, and occasionally even imprisoned, for refusing to pay tithes to Church of Ireland clergy.[6] Hence the allure of William Penn's colony, which Quakers and their political allies would govern down to 1776. Pennsylvania's flourishing and self-confident Quaker communities contrasted sharply with their decline in Ireland. In the early 1700s heavy Quaker emigration constricted marriage opportunities and so encouraged young Friends to "marry out" of the Society. By so doing, they incurred disownment and expulsion, which in turn further reduced Quaker numbers and generated a spiritual and psychological "inward retreat" that made Friends even more isolated and vulnerable to emigration.

Yet in the commercially depressed and famine-ridden 1720s and 1730s, when Quaker emigration first peaked, economic causes were probably paramount for families such as Thomas Parke's. Although the soil in central Carlow was well-drained lowland, rising rents and his large number of surviving children made it unlikely Parke could guarantee them good livelihoods and suitable marriages in Ireland; his son Robert's failure at shopkeeping in Dublin may have represented the family's last attempt to diversify its economic base and so avoid emigration. During the first half of the eighteenth century, emigration rapidly depleted south Leinster's rural Quaker communities. More Friends left Carlow than any other county except Dublin and Armagh and Antrim in Ulster. Thus, by 1724, when the Parkes arrived in Pennsylvania, Carlow Quakers were already well settled in Chester County, where their New Garden monthly meeting, established in 1712 and named after one at home, was the largest in the colonies.

After a brief stay in the town of Chester, the Parkes first leased two hundred acres nearby from another Irish Quaker. However, in late 1724 Thomas Parke paid £350 to purchase five hundred acres further inland at the new settlement of Caln, in the Great Valley of Chester just west of Downingtown, although the family continued to live on their rented farm until mid-1726. Chester County then had about ten thousand inhabitants, mostly crowded along the Delaware, but in the western districts where the Parkes settled the population density was less than 10 persons per square mile. Nevertheless, their purchase of so much rich, if almost entirely uncleared land only two dozen miles from Philadelphia, in what became the most densely settled and prosperous part of Penn's colony, suggests the Parkes's considerable means as well as their affinity with the county's English Quaker majority.[7] From the first the Parkes enjoyed an organized Friends' meeting in Caln township, established in 1715, and Robert's brother Thomas served as trustee when two

---

6. During the reign of George I (1714–1727), the annual value of Irish Quaker goods distrained for nonpayment of tithes averaged £1,731, as compared with £1,350 under Queen Anne, £1,055 under William and Mary, and merely £109 under Charles II.   **7.** Beginning about 1710, Ulster Presbyterians had heavily settled some of Chester County's western townships, but by the 1720s the Scots-Irish (with other early settlers in Chester) were moving further west to uncleared lands in Lancaster and Cumberland counties.

new meetinghouses were built nearby in the 1740s and 1750s, the second on land owned by a Cork Quaker. Thus, Irish Quakers achieved prominence in the Great Valley just as they had earlier in their New Garden settlement near the Delaware.

When Thomas Parke emigrated, he left two daughters in Carlow, one of them Mary who in 1715 had married Thomas Valentine of Ballybromhill.[8] In the autumn of 1725, after little more than a year in Chester County, Robert Parke wrote the following letter to his sister and brother-in-law. Obviously, the Valentines were hesitant to emigrate (they had failed to come out earlier, as expected), and Parke wrote to repersuade them, conscious that returning ne'er-do-wells had carried back false reports that the Parkes were discontented—and even that Pennsylvania's governor intercepted overseas letters to prevent negative accounts of the colony from reaching the British Isles! Thus, Parke was aware that much future Quaker emigration depended on his letter's credibility, as he recalled that when in Ireland he had hungered for specific, reliable information from the New World. Consequently, he strove to reassure putative emigrants on every aspect of emigration, providing a virtual and personalized guidebook that named a trustworthy Quaker captain for the voyage, advised which goods to bring for use and for sale, and provided reassurance as to the country's healthiness and information as to the affordability of land, cleared and uncleared, as well as particulars as to farming methods, crop yields and prices. In only one respect, perhaps, was Parke's portrait too rosy, for his experience of American farming was still confined to a rented and already developed farm, complete with brick house, and he and his father had not yet tackled the arduous task of clearing the forest from their newly purchased land.

Parke's letter also illumines the early eighteenth-century Irish trade in indentured servants. Although slaves had largely displaced temporary bondsmen and -women as fieldhands in the southern plantation colonies, in eastern Pennsylvania a labor shortage in agriculture, as well as in urban crafts, meant that indentured servants remained both necessary and profitable. Transatlantic fares were then £5 to £7 (£9 in Pennsylvania currency), but indentured servants sold for £12 to £35, depending on their age, sex, skills, and length of service, and so males with five years to serve would repay their passage costs several times over. Thus, Parke advised that Samuel Thornton, a Carlow Friend of limited means, could emigrate as a redemptioner and, if unable to redeem his family's passage after arrival, might indent several children to defray the costs. In addition, Parke urged Thornton to bring four servants, as he could recover the fares of the two he kept for himself by selling the services of the others—also a practice common among early Irish Protestant emigrants.[9]

---

8. Ballybromhill (or Ballybrommell): a townland and also a town in Fennagh parish.   9. Such clever use of the system by emigrants is not noted in the historical literature, which usually distinguishes only redemptioners (who sold their own or their family members' time on arrival to cover passage) and indentured servants proper (whose contracts were at the disposal of the ships' captains or owners' agents). For more data on—and examples of—Irish indentured servants, see part IV, especially chapter 30.

Robert Parke, Chester Township, Chester Co., Pennsylvania,
to Mary and Thomas Valentine, Ballybromhill, Fennagh Parish, County Carlow,
October 1725

Chester Township the < . . . >[10] of the 10th Mo:[11] 1725

Chester &c

Dear Sister

Mary Valentine

This goes with a Salutation of Love to thee, Brother Thomas & the children &
in a word to all friends, Relations & well Wishers in Generall as if named, hoping it
may find you all in Good Health, as I with all our family in Generall are in at this
present writing, & has been Since our Arival, for we have not had a days Sickness in
the family Since we Came in to the Country, Blessed be god for it,   my father in
Particular has not had his health better[12] these ten years than since he Came here his
Ancient age considered. Our Irish Acquaintance in general are well Except Tho[s]
Lightfoot[13] who Departed this Life at Darby in a Good old age about 4 weeks
Since   Thee writes in thy Letter that there was a talk[14] went back to Ireland that we
were not Satisfyed in Coming here, which was Utterly false;   now let this Suffice to
Convince you,   In the first place he that carried back this Story was an Idle fellow, &
one of our Ship-Mates, but not thinking this Country Suitable to his Idleness; went
back with Cowman[15] again   he is a Sort of a Lawyer, or Rather a Lyar as I may term
him   therefore I wod not have you give Credit to Such false reports for the future,[16]
for there is not one of the family but what likes the Country very well and Wod If we
were in Ireland again Come here Directly[17] it being the best Country for working
folk & tradesmen[18] of any in the world, but for[19] Drunkards & Idlers, they Cannot live
well any where   it is like to be an Extrardin<ary> Country;[20]   We were all much
troubled when we found you did not Come in with Cap[t] Cowman as Expected nor
none of our acquaintance Except Isaac Jackson & his family[21]   tho, at first Coming

10. The blanks left for dates, the numerous cancellations and substitutions, and the absence of the formulae
constituting the complimentary close indicate that the manuscript transcribed here is a preliminary draft.
11. 10th Mo: October.   12. has not had his health better: has not enjoyed better health; see chapter 5, n.
16; chapter 23, n. 37; and chapter 61, n. 9.   13. Tho[s] Lightfoot: a prominent Quaker minister; born ca. 1645
in Cambridgeshire, England; moved to Ireland and settled first in Co. Antrim, near Lisburn, and by 1694 at
Moate, Co. Westmeath, whence he emigrated in 1716 to New Garden township, Chester Co.; he removed to
Darby township shortly before his death on 4 September 1725. His son, Michael, also born in Ireland, was
provincial treasurer at his death in 1754.   14. talk: rumour.   15. Cowman: Jeremiah Cowman, captain of the
Sizaragh of Whitehaven, which brought the Parkes, Valentines, and many other Irish Quaker families to
America during the 1720s.   16. for the future: in future.   17. there is not one of the family but what likes
the Country very well and Wod . . . come here Directly: "there is not one of the family who does not like
the country very well and would not . . . come here directly." well and & Wod ms.   18. working folk &
tradesmen: written above canc. people that have amind to work.   19. for: as for (particularly after and and
but).   20. like to be an Extrardin<ary> Country: written above as healthy a Country as any in the world.
21. nor none of our acquaintance Except Isaac Jackson & his family: written above canc. I wod not have
you mind Every flying story that is reported of this Country.

in[22] one thinks it Something[23] odd but that is Soon over,   Land is of all Prices Even from ten Pounds; to one hundred pounds a hundred,[24] according to the goodness or else the Scituation therof, & Grows dearer every year by Reason of Vast Quantities of People that Come here yearly from Several Parts of the world,   therefore thee & thy family or any that I wish well, I wod desire to make what Speed you can to Come here the Sooner the better,   we have traveled over a Pretty deal[25] of this country to Seek for Land, & (tho) we met with many fine[26] Tracts of Land here & there in the Country, yet my father being Curious & somewhat hard to Please Did not buy any Land until the Second day of 10th mo: Last[27] and then he bought a Tract of Land Consisting of five hundred Acres for which he gave 350 pounds,   it is Excellent good land but none Cleared[28] Except about 20 Acres, with a Small log house, & Orchard Planted,   we are going to Clear some of it Directly, for our next Sumers fallow   we might have bought Land much Cheaper but not So much to our Satisfaction,   We stayed in Chester 3 months & then we Rented a Place 2 mile from Chester, with a good brick house & 200 Acres of Land for 1 pound a year where we continue[29] till next may   we have Sowed about 200 Acres of wheat & 7 acres of rye,   this Season we Sowed but a bushel an acre   3 pecks is Enough on new ground   I am grown an Experienced Plowman & my brother abell is Learning,   Jonath<an> & thy Son John drives for us   he is grown a Lusty[30] fellow Since thou Saw him   we have the finest plows that Can be,   We plow up our Sumers fallows in may & June, with a Yoak of Oxen & 2 horses & the<y> goe with as much Ease as Double the number in Ireland,   We[31] plow & like wise Sows our wheat with 2 horses,   a boy of 12 or 14 years old Can hold Plow[32] here,   a man Comonly hold<s> and Drives himself,   they Plow an Acre, nay Some Plows 2 Acres a day,   they Sow wheat & Rye in August or September.   We have had a Crop of oates, barley & very good flax & hemp Indian Corn & buck wheat all of our own Sowing & Planting this Last summer   we also Planted a bushel of white Potatoes Which Cost us 5 shills & we had 10 to 12 bushels In Crease   this Country yields Extrardinary Increase of all Sorts of Grain Likewise for Nicholas hopper[33] had of 3 acres of Land & at most 3 bushels of Seed Above 80 bushels Increase, so that it is as Plentifull a Country as any Can be if people will be Industrious,   wheat is 4 Shills a bushell, Rye 2s: 9d oats 2s: 3 pence, barley 3 Shills, Indian Corn 2 Shills all Strike measure,[34]   Beef is 2 a pound Sometimes more & Sometimes less, mutton 2·½, Pork 2·½ ℔ pound   Turnips 13 pence a bushel heap'd

22. Coming in: immigration; written above canc. **When one Comes in to this Country they.**
23. Something: somewhat. **24.** hundred: elliptical for **hundred acres**. **25.** a Pretty deal: a fair amount.
26. fine: written above canc. **a Noble**. **27.** 10th mo: Last: last October; written above canc. **this Instant December**. **28.** but none Cleared: written above canc. **& Covered with woods**. **29.** continue: stay on.
30. Lusty: strong, in rude health (so elsewhere in text). **31.** Cross canc. after **We**. **32.** Can hold Plow: can guide/control a plow. **33.** hopper: i.e., Hooper. **34.** Strike measure: measurement by use of the **strike**, an instrument which levels off the commodity to be measured; opposed to **heaped measure** (hereafter).

ROBERT PARKE

measure,[35] & so Plenty[36] that an acre Produceth 200 bushels,   all Sorts of provisions
are Extrardinary Plenty in Philadelphia market where Country people bring in their
Comodoties   their Markets are on 4th days and 7th days[37]   this Country Abounds in
fruit   Scarce an house but has an Aple, Peach, & Cherry Orchard,   as for Chesnuts,
Wallnuts & hazel nuts Strawberrys, Billberrys & Mulberrys they grow wild in the
woods & fields in Vast Quantities,   they also make great Preparations against[38]
harvest,   both Roast & boyled, Cakes & Tarts & Rum, Stand at the Lands End,[39] so
that they may Eat & Drink at Pleasure,   a Reaper has 2 shills & 3 pence a day,
a mower has 2 Shills & 6 pence & a Pint of Rum beside meat & Drink of the best, for
no workman works with out their Victuals in the bargain throughout the Country,
a Labouring man has 18 or 20 pence a day in Winter,   the winters are not so Cold as
we Expected nor the Sumers so Extreme hot as formerly, for both Summer & Winter
are moderater than ever they were known,   in Summer time they wear nothing but a
Shirt & Linnen Drawers & Trowsers which are breeches & Stockings all in one made
of Linnen[40]   they are fine Cool wear in Summer,   as to what thee writt about the
Governours Opening Letters[41] it is Utterly false & nothing but a Lye & any one Except
<a> bound Servantt may go out of the Country when they will & Servants when they
Serve their time may Come away If they please but it is Rare that any are such fools as
to leave the Country Except[42] mens business Require it,   they pay 9 Pounds for their
Passage (of this mony[43]) to go to Ireland   there is 2 fairs yearly & 2 markets weekly in
Philadelphia also 2 fairs yearly in Chester & Likewise in Newcastle, but they Sell no
Cattle nor horses nor no Living Creatures but altogether[44] Merchants Goods, as hatts,
Linnen & woolen Cloth, handkerchiefs, knives, Scizars, tapes & treds[45] buckles,
Ribonds & all Sorts of Necessarys fit for our wooden[46] Country & here all young men
and women that wants[47] wives or husbands may be Supplyed.   Lett this suffice for our
fairs   As for meetings they are so plenty one may ride to their choice of 10 or a
Dozen in 6 morning[48]   I desire thee to bring or Send me a bottle of good Oyle fit for
guns,   thee may buy it in Dublin,   Martha weanhouse[49] Lives very well[50] about 4

---

35. heap'd measure: a dry measure used for certain commodities, which are heaped up in a cone above the
brim of the measuring container.   **36. Plenty**: abundant, plentiful, numerous (so elsewhere in the text).
37. 4th days and 7th days: written above canc. **Wednesdays & Saturdays**. (Parke belatedly recalls that as a
Quaker he should not employ the "pagan" names for the days of the week and immediately makes the
necessary correction.)   **38. against**: in anticipation of, in time for, for.   **39. at the Lands end** (= land-end):
on a piece of ground at the end of the "land," one of the strips into which a field has been plowed.
40. Trowsers which are breeches & Stockings all in one made of Linnen: "trousers consisting of legs and
stockings in one piece, made of linen."   **41. about the Governours Opening Letters**: about Pennsylvania's
governor intercepting and opening letters sent back to Ireland or Britain.   **42. Except**: unless.   **43. this
mony**: Pennsylvania currency.   **44. altogether**: exclusively.   **45. treds**: i.e., threads (Southern Hiberno-
English pronunciation; see **Trives, triving** hereafter).   **46. wooden**: wooded, forested (probably in a slightly
pejorative sense, "rustic, backward"; see the citations in OED, s.v., 3.b).   **47. wants**: lacks, needs.
48. meetings: Quaker meetings; **6 morning**: Friday morning.   **49. Martha weanhouse**: Martha Wainhouse
(see n. 71).   **50. Lives very well**: lives in very comfortable circumstances.

mile from James Lindlys;[51]   we Live all together Since we Came into the Country Except hugh Hoaker & his family who Lives 6 or 7 mile from us & follows his trade   Sister Rebecka was Delivered of a Daughter y^e < . . . > day 11 month Last past   its name is mary   Abels wife had a young Son 12 months Since   his name is Thomas;   Dear Sister I wod not have thee Doubt the truth of what [I] write, for I know it to be true tho I have not been Long here   I wod have you [c]loath your selves very well with Woolen[52] & Linnen, Shoes & Stockings, & hats, for Such things are dear hear, & yet a man will Sooner[53] Earn a Suit of Cloths here than in Ireland, by Reason workmens Labour is So dear,   A wool hat costs 7 Shill^s, a pair of mens Shoes 7 Shill^s, wemens Shoes Cost 5 Shill^s & 6 pence, a pair of mens Stockings yarn costs 4 Shill^s   feather beds are very dear here and not to be had for money. Gunpowder is 2 Shill^s & 6 pence a pound   Shott & Lead 5 pence a pound,   I wod have you to bring for your own use 2 or 3 good falling Axes,[54] a pair of beetlerings[55] & 3 Iron wedges, for they are of good Service here,   your Plow Irons will not answer[56] here, therefore you had better bring 1 or 2 hundred[57] of Iron,   you may bring your Plow Chains as they are < . . . >[58]   also a good [awnd][59] Iron   There[60] other Letters going to you that gives you an Accompt what to bring into the Country & also for your Sea Store or else I should not omitt it but besure you come[61] with Capt Cowman & you will be well Used for he is as honest a man & has as Civill Saylors as any that Cross the Seas which I know by Experie[nce]   the Ship[62] has been weather bound Since before Chirstmass by reason of frost & Ice that floats about in the River & the Saylors [being] at a Loo[se E]nd came down to C[hester] to See us [&] we have given them < . . . >[63]   Dear Sister I desire thee may tell my old friend Samuel Thornton[64] that if he could give so much Credit to my words, & find no Iffs nor ands in my Letter, that in Plain terms, he could not do better than Come here, for both his & his wife's trade are Very good here,   the best way for him to do is to pay what mony he Can Conveniently Spare at that Side & Engage himself to Pay the rest at this Side[65] & when he Comes here if he Can get no friend to lay down the mony for him, when it Comes to the worst, he may hire out 2 or 3 of <his> Children, & I wod have him Cloath his

---

51. James Lindlys: see n. 68.   **52.** Woolen: i.e., woollen "cloth or other fabric made of wool or chiefly of wool" (OED, s.v., B; now rare).   **53.** Sooner: not "rather" (the usual meaning after "would") but "more quickly."   **54.** falling Axes: i.e., felling axes; the form is based on nonstandard use of **fall** in the meaning "cut down" (OED, s.v. fall, 54.c).   **55.** beetlerings: metal rings used in fashioning a beetle, a mallet- or pestle-like instrument used in washing or fulling cloth and in beating flax to improve its luster.   **56.** answer: be serviceable, do the job.   **57.** hundred: hundredweight.   **58.** Sentence not completed.   **59.** [awnd]: reading conjectural; **awndiron** is an older form of andiron.   **60.** There: i.e., there are.   **61.** besure you come: i.e., be sure you come; a more truncated version of this phraseology can be seen in chapter 24, n. 8, where it has become virtually a grammatical form, functioning as an emphatic imperative.   **62.** the ship: i.e., the *Sizaragh*, Captain Cowman's vessel.   **63.** Sentence not completed.   **64.** Samuel Thornton apparently followed Parke's advice to emigrate, for in 1753 and 1765 he or his son and namesake paid taxes on forty acres (adjoining Robert Thornton's eighty-five acres) in West Bradford township, Chester Co.   **65.** at that Side . . . at this Side: "at that end . . . at this end."

ROBERT PARKE

family as well as his Small Ability will allow,　thee may tell him what things are
Proper to bring with him both for his Sea Store & for his Use in this Country　I wod
have him Procure 3 or 4 Lusty Servants & agree to pay their passage at this Side,　he
might sell 2 & pay the others passage with the mony,　I fear my good will to him will
be of Little Effect by reason he is So hard of belief,[66] but thou mayest Assure him from
me that if I had not a Particular Respect for him & his family I Should not have writ
so much for his Encouragement,　his brother[s] Joseph & Moses Coats[67] Came to See
us Since we came here　they live about 6 or 7 miles apart & above 20 from where we
live,　Unkle James Lindly[68] & family is well & Trives[69] exceedingly,　he has 11
Children & Reap'd last harvest about 800 bushels of wheat,　he is as triving a man as
any where he lives,　he has a thousand Acres of Land, A fine Estate,[70]　Unkle
Nicholas hooper lives very well　he rents a Plantation & teaches Scool & his man
martin hobson[71] dos his Plantation work　Dear Sister I think I have writ the most
needful to thee, but Considering that when I was in Ireland, I never thought a Letter
to<o> Long that Came from this Country, I wod willingly give thee as full an Account
as Possible, tho I Could have given thee a fuller Accompt of what things were fit to
bring here, but only I knew[72] other Letters might Suffice in that point,　I desire thee
may Send or bring me 2 hundred Choice Quils for my own Use for they are very
Scarce here, & Sister Raichell Desires thee wod bring hir Some bits of Silk for
trashbags[73]　thee may buy them in Johns Lane[74]　also 6 yards of white Mode[75] or

---

66. he is So hard of belief: he has such great difficulty believing/is so hard to convince (the phraseology is
now obsolete except in the expression **hard of hearing**).　**67. Moses Coats**: Moses Coates; emigrated in 1717
from Co. Carlow with his wife, Susanna, and their children; in 1731 he purchased a farm at the site of
Phoenixville, Charlestown township, Chester Co., where in 1766 his son and namesake paid taxes on 282
acres, five horses, five cattle, and 17 sheep, adjacent to one hundred acres held by another son, Benjamin.
68. James Lindlys: James Lindley (d.1726): in 1713 he emigrated from Carlow Friends' meeting with his wife,
Eleanor, a sister of Thomas Parke; in 1713 he purchased two hundred acres in New Garden township and in
1722 an additional four hundred acres in London Grove township, where he was styled a blacksmith in the
deed; he was appointed Chester Co. assessor in 1725. In 1724 it was Lindley's brother Thomas, probably a
blacksmith in Philadelphia, who sold to Thomas Parke the five hundred acres in East Caln township on which
the Parke family settled. Also see n. 70.　**69. Trives**: i.e., thrives (Southern Hiberno-English pronunciation;
see also **triving** "thriving" hereafter).　**70. James Lindly . . . has . . . A fine Estate**: see n. 68. In 1774 a James
Lindley, probably a grandson of Robert Parke's uncle of 1725, held only forty acres (adjacent to 150 acres held
by Jonathan Lindley) in London Grove township, Chester Co., suggesting how quickly the practice of partible
inheritance, common among the first generation of Irish Quakers in Pennsylvania, could fragment an
immigrant ancestor's "fine Estate" of one thousand acres.　**71. martin hobson**: Hobson was probably related
to Francis Hobson (1686–1766) of Grange, Co. Armagh, who in 1712–1713 emigrated and settled in New
Garden township, Chester Co.; in 1716 he married **Martha Wainhouse**, who had emigrated from Dublin in
1714 (see n. 49).　**72. but only I knew**: "except that I knew."　**73. trashbag**: "Apron, wherein are seuerall
pocketts . . . to place the seuerall implyments . . . which the Angler hath occasion to use" (OED, s.v., quoting
R. Holme, *Armoury* [1688]).　**74. Johns Lane**: also St. John's Lane; a Dublin street forming the north
boundary of the close of Christchurch Cathedral and running between Fishamble St. and Winetavern St.,
parallel to Skinner Row (now Christchurch Place).　**75. Mode**: thin, glossy silk used for hoods and scarves
(= **alamode**; OED, quoting *MacSparran Diary* [1751]); obsolete. On Rev. James MacSparran, see chapter 8.

Silk for 2 hoods & She will Pay thee when thee Comes here,   I wod have brother Thomas to bring a good new Saddle with a Crooper[76] & housin[77] to it by reason the horses sweat[s] in hot weather for they are very dear here   a Saddle that will cost 18 or 20 Shill[s] in Ireland, will cost 50 Shill[s] or 3 pounds & not so good Neither   he had better get Charls Howell to make it   Lett the tree[78] be well Plated & Indifferent[79] Narrow for the horses here are not So large as in Ireland but the best drawers[80] & finest Pacers in the World   I have known Several that could Pace 14 or 15 miles in a hour   I write within Compass,[81]   as for womens Saddles, they will not Suit so well here,   I wod not have thee think much at[82] my Irregular way of writing by reason I writt as it offerd to[83] me, for they that write to you should have more witt than I can Pretend to < . . . >[84]

Much is known about the Parkes in Pennsylvania, a clear indication of their moderate success, although as a rural family in both Ireland and Chester County they had little or no connection with Philadelphia's wealthy Irish Quaker merchant families whose trade linked Pennsylvania's capital and the Irish ports.[85] In 1727 Robert Parke revisited Ireland, returning the following year accompanied by six servants and by Mary and Thomas Valentine, who settled near the Parkes in the Great Valley, where their son Robert (1717–1786) would long serve as minister to Chester County's Quakers. As for Robert Parke, he farmed the 124 well-watered acres that his father had portioned to him from the 1725 purchase and also worked as a clerk and conveyancer, serving as county recorder of deeds and as county coroner before 1737, when he died unmarried, aged 43, a year before his father. Two of Robert Parke's brothers became tavernkeepers, thus perhaps displaying habits more stereotypically Irish than Quaker. The paths taken by members of the later generations diverged dramatically. One of Thomas Parke's grandsons, Thomas III (1749–1835), was educated in London and Edinburgh, became a physician to the Philadelphia Hospital, a member of the American Philosophical Society, and president of the College of Physicians. By contrast, Thomas Parke's great-grandson Abiah joined the British in the Revolution, fled to Canada, married a Shawnee, and fathered a tribal chieftain (Joseph Parke, d.1857) who led his defeated people from Ohio to Kansas.[86]

76. **Crooper**: i.e., crupper "a leathern strap buckled to the back of the saddle and passing under the horse's tail, to prevent the saddle from slipping forward" (OED, s.v., 1).   77. **housin**: i.e., housing, a cloth or leather covering for a horse, usually attached to the harness.   78. **tree**: framework of a saddle.   79. **Indifferent**: indifferently "tolerably, fairly" (OED, s.v., 5; now rare).   80. **drawers**: draught animals (cf. OED, s.v. draught, 47.a).   81. **within Compass**: without exaggeration (?).   82. **think much at**: pay much attention to.
83. **offerd to**: i.e., offered to "occurred to, came to."   84. Letter breaks off without complimentary close (see n. 10).   85. For an example of such merchants, see chapter 56.   86. Thomas Parke III was the son of Thomas Jr. and Jane Parke; Abiah Parke was the son of Joseph and grandson of Robert Parke's brother Jonathan and his wife Deborah (see n. 3).

John Rea, 1765

Although family ties and the market for indentured servants were of primary impor-tance in encouraging or facilitating early Irish migration, some movements from Ul-ster to colonial America were organized and promoted as business ventures by colonial land speculators and their Irish agents. The cooperation of the brothers John and Matthew Rea (or Rae) offers an excellent example of this pattern.

The eldest son of David Rea, a farmer at Ballycreen, John Rea was born about 1708 and raised near the linen market town of Ballynahinch, in the religiously mixed parish of Magheradrool, in the barony of Kinelarty, County Down. By 1765 his brother Matthew lived ten miles north in the solidly Presbyterian parish of Drumbo,[1] Upper Castlereigh barony, in the Lagan Valley near Lisburn.[2] In 1734 John Rea and his wife, Catherine,[3] emigrated to Savannah and settled on the Georgia frontier, where he became a prosperous rancher and Indian trader, dealing with the Creeks and Cherokees at his private fort near Augusta and investing his profits in cattle, land speculation, and slaves.[4] As he aged he withdrew from the "Fatigue" of frontier trading, left a half-brother, Robert, in charge of his Augusta concerns, and moved south to the vicinity of Savannah, where in 1760 he purchased an estate, Rea's Hall, managed his rice plantations and other businesses in and around the colonial capital, and earned the title "Esquire" by serving as justice of the peace as well as an occasional term in the Georgia Assembly.

After 1763, when the Peace of Paris ended Spanish threats to Georgia's borders, Rea and another Ulster-born Indian trader, George Galphin (d.1780), developed a scheme to colonize Ulster settlers in the empty lands along the Ogeechee River, forty miles southwest of Augusta and the South Carolina border, following precedents set in 1731 and 1761 when South Carolina's colonial legislature had made land grants to attract Ulster Protestants and other colonists to frontier regions. In 1764–1766 Georgia's Assembly adopted a similar policy, to extend the colony's narrow band of settlement along the Savannah River west-ward, and in 1764–1765 Rea and Galphin secured land grants totaling about eighty thou-sand acres along Lambert's Creek, just across the Ogeechee from the Indian territories. Immediately Rea began his promotional efforts, which included the following letter that

---

1. As late as 1863 members of the Rea family still held small parcels of land totaling over 50 acres in Ballylessan, Drennan, and Mealough townlands in Drumbo parish.   **2.** For demographic data on Magheradrool and Drumbo parishes and their environs, see appendix 2.1, on chapter 10.   **3.** Catherine Rea's maiden name is not known, but she and John Rea had six, perhaps seven, children: Jane (born ca. 1739; married John Sommerville, later one of Rea's business partners); John, Jr. (born ca. 1740); William (killed by Indians in 1760); Mary; Elizabeth; Isabella; and perhaps Peter.   **4.** As early as 1738 Rea, then a river trader between Savannah and Augusta, had joined in petitioning Georgia's Trustees to legalize slavery; in 1759 Rea owned at least 36 slaves, and during the next decade he bought considerably more.

his Irish brother Matthew published in the 3 September 1765 issue of Ulster's leading newspaper, the *Belfast News-Letter*, after appending his own assurances to prospective emigrants.

John Rea, Esq., Rea's Hall, near Savannah, Georgia, to Mathew Rea, Drumbo Parish, County Down, 15 May 1765

Rea's-Hall, May 15, 1765.

In my last Letter to you by Way of London, I informed you that I had procured a Grant from the Governor and Council of Georgia for fifty thousand Acres of Land in this Province, for any of my Friends and Countrymen that have a Mind to come to this Country and bring their Families here to settle. The Land I have pitched upon[5] lies on a fine River called Ogichey, near to which I have my large Cow-pens of Cattle settled, which will be very convenient for new-Comers-in, to be supplied with Milk Cows; I can also furnish them with Horses and Mares, any Number they may want. I am likewise in Hopes of obtaining a Bounty at their Arrival; but as this is a young Colony, and of Course not rich, they cannot expect so much as Carolina gave to the People who come over with my Servants,[6] who are all well and hearty. The land I have chosen is very good for Wheat and any Kind of Grain; Indigo, Flax and Hemp will grow to great Perfection; and I do not know any Place better situate for a flourishing Township than this Place will be. Now, Brother, if you think a Number of good industrious Families will come over here I will do every Thing in my Power to assist them; for nothing will give me more Satisfaction than to be the Means of bringing my Friends to this Country of Freedom; there are no Rents, no Tithes here, only the King's Quit Rent,[7] which is only two Shillings Sterl, per hundred Acres: Who would desire a cheaper Rent? We have settled a firm Peace with the Indians around us, and have agreed on boundary Lines betwixt us and them, so that all is settled with them.

The Method of granting Lands to Settlers in this Country, is one hundred Acres to the Head of the Family, be they Man or Woman, and fifty Acres to every Person in the Family, big and little. The Distance of this Township from the Sea will be about one hundred Miles, that is to say, the Town of Savannah, where the Shipping[8] come

---

5. **pitched upon**: decided on (OED, s.v., 16). **6. my Servants**: In the October and November 1763 issues of the *Belfast News-Letter*, John Rea advertised for "six or eight young men, Tradesmen or Labourers, and two young Women, well recommended for making good Butter and Cheese, both Men and Women well testified: They will find the following Encouragement by applying to Matthew Rea of Drumbo, who is wrote to by said John for to pay their Passage and indent with each Person for Four years Service; they will be paid 5 Pounds Sterling yearly, Bed and Board, they are also to receive their own Bounty, which is four Pounds Sterling, and one hundred Acres of Land for each Person." **7. Quit Rent**: a small rent paid to the landlord, who was sometimes the sovereign in lieu of services. **8. Shipping**: ships (in particular, those calling regularly at a given port).

to, which is the Capital Town of the Province, and it grows very fast, and soon will be a great Place of Trade. I have Lots and Houses in Town, and Rea's Hall is about four Miles out of Town, but a Ship can come up the River Savannah to my Door, and large Boats go from hence to my House at Augusta, which is two hundred and seventy Miles by Water. The Township is about forty Miles from Augusta, nearer this Way.[9]

Now I have told you the Encouragement[10] and Situation of the Township, I will now say something of the Climate:—Which is, that it is very hot for four Months, June, July, August, and September, and in these last, People that live on the low Land near the Sea are subject to Fevers and Agues;[11] but up high in the Country, it is healthy, and fine Springs of good Water.

As I would gladly obtain Credit[12] by this Undertaking both here and in Ireland, I should be sorry to say any Thing but what may be depended on. The Winter is the finest in the World, never too cold, very little Frost, and no Snow.[13] The People that I would advise to come to this Country, are those that have large Families growing up, that they may get Land and assist each other; likewise Tradesmen of all Sorts, for that will draw a Trade amongst them from other Settlements, by which they will get Money. I would have them bring a Clergyman with them, and a School-master that may be Clerk, for they are scarce here, and they will have Land given them, and what the People can afford, with my Mite, may procure him a Living.

Dear Brother, I do not expect to have the Pleasure of seeing you in this Country, nor would I advise any Person to come here that lives well in Ireland; because there is not the Pleasure of Society that there is there, and the Comfort of the Gospel preached; no Fair nor Markets to go to; but we have greater Plenty of good Eating and Drinking: For I bless God for it I keep as plentiful a Table as most Gentlemen in Ireland, with good Punch, Wine and Beer. If any Person that comes here can bring Money to purchase a Slave or two, they may live very easy and well. A good Slave will cost about fifty Pounds Sterling. As soon as I can procure a Bill I will send you one hundred Pounds Sterling, to be laid out by you in the Education of my late Brother's Children: Pray give them the best of Education, and I will pay for all. A Young Man that is a good Scholar may not fear[14] a good Living in this Country. I am, &c.   JOHN REA

I Matthew Rea, on Behalf of my Brother John Rea, do hereby promise and engage, That my said Brother shall give every Person who shall go and settle in the above mentioned Township, the Use of a Cow, Horse, or Mare, for the first five Years gratis, to each individual Man, Woman, and Child, they returning at the End of said Term as good a Beast, or the Value such Beast was of when first received. Given under my Hand, this 26th Day of August, 1765.

MATTHEW REA

---

9. nearer this Way: in this direction (toward Savannah).   10. the Encouragement: the attractions, the "good points."   11. Agues: (in connection with a fever) chills.   12. Credit: credibility, good reputation.   13. Show ms.   14. fear: be anxious/worried about.

John Rea's settlement, Queensborough township in St. George's parish, was not a great success. In 1768 the British government, perhaps fearful of "dispeopling" Protestant Ireland, disallowed the Georgia law which had granted Rea and Galphin additional lands for settler promotion. Moreover, although the Georgia Assembly voted £560 to assist Rea's emigrants, who were arriving unaware of London's decision, the brothers' efforts made slow progress. The only ship they brought out expressly for the scheme, the *Prince George*, arrived in December 1768, carrying 34 families who took up land grants in the township, plus house lots in Queensborough itself. In late 1769 Matthew Rea organized the voyage from Belfast to Savannah of the *Hopewell*, which carried 166 emigrants, only 24 of whom settled in Queensborough. In 1770–1773, Rea promoted four additional voyages to Georgia, but many of the newcomers went to South Carolina and few who stayed in Georgia took up lands in Queensborough township. Unfortunately, some settlers sent back unflattering reports: in 1770 the *Belfast News-Letter* published an accusation by one of the *Hopewell's* passengers that "one half and more" of Rea's promises "were lies," as he and Galphin merely intended Queensborough "to be a hedge" or barrier between their personal cattle ranges and the Indians.[15]

Indeed, in 1772, the year of John Rea's death, violence broke out between the newcomers and the natives, as the Queensborough settlers' aggressive behavior toward the latter destroyed the friendly relations that Rea and Galphin had cultivated. In addition, the Reas were members of the Church of Ireland, and religious conflicts between Georgia's Anglican establishment and the staunchly Presbyterian settlers may have hindered Queensborough's development.[16] For whatever reasons, only about 95 families, totaling about 250 individuals, settled on 20,000 of John Rea's acres, merely a fourth of the land granted by the Georgia legislature, and in 1775 only 70 families lived in Queensborough town and perhaps another two hundred in the vicinity. And although John Rea's son and namesake, as well as the old settler's two half-brothers, Robert (d. 1779) and James (d. 1789), served as officers in the Revolution against Britain, many of the Queensborough settlers were loyalists—and, in revenge, the victors not only confiscated their estates but also eradicated the original name of John Rea's settlement.

Despite Queensborough's failure, upward of one thousand emigrants came to Savannah on the six relevant voyages, and in the early 1770s Matthew Rea acted as agent for other sailings to Charleston and continued his efforts to persuade those emigrants to move further south to Georgia. Between 1760 and 1770 the colony's white population increased from around 9,000 to over 25,000, and by 1790 Georgia had a white population of 82,500—*and*

---

15. *Belfast News-Letter*, 11 January 1770. 16. Curiously, in 1771 John Rea was found guilty of manslaughter in the death of a woman named Ann Simpson, and on 18 December of that year he petitioned the Governor's Council for a pardon, appealing to his hitherto "unblemished character" and claiming that Simpson's death had been "without any Malice" and "rather an Act of Indiscretion, than bad intention." Rea died the following year, and it is unknown whether he received a pardon or, more to the point, whether Rea's conflict with Simpson was related to his troubled relationships with the Queensborough settlers. If Georgia's royal government did not pardon Rea, and if he died in prison, that may help explain why in 1776 his son and half-brothers became revolutionaries, despite the family's long and profitable links to crown officials.

the highest proportion of inhabitants of Irish birth or ancestry in the 13 states, with estimates ranging above 26 percent. A natural overflow from Ulster settlements in South Carolina partly accounts for this, but so too does the Reas' propaganda for the Queensborough project.

II ✳

James Orr, 1811

During the colonial and revolutionary periods, Irish emigrants often carried one or more documents to the New World. Sometimes these included official passports required by Irish and, after 1800, British laws designed to restrict emigration by mechanics and artisans.[1] More commonly, the emigrants took letters of introduction or testimonials as to their religious affiliation, marketable skills, family connections, and personal "character." Although by 1760 most emigrants were already joining established kin or friends, others who lacked such close ties still usually sought communities of former neighbors or coreligionists, as well as enhanced economic opportunities, and so needed references to establish claims to aid and fellowship. Thus, Irish Friends' monthly meetings regularly provided transfer certificates to Quaker emigrants in good standing, and Presbyterian and Anglican clergymen often wrote similar documents for their parishioners.[2] Much more usual, however, were private references, written on behalf of emigrants to relatives who had left Ireland decades earlier and thus had little or no personal knowledge of the new arrivals. Such a letter was written in 1811 by James Orr of Strabane, County Tyrone, to John Dunlap of Philadelphia, on behalf of the latter's nephew John Rutherford.

Eighteenth-century Strabane was a major west Ulster market town, whose merchants shipped the grain, beef, and linen produced in the Finn and Morne valleys up the Foyle River to Londonderry city for export to Britain or America. John Dunlap (1747–1812), the son of a Presbyterian saddler and farmer in Strabane, emigrated as a boy to Philadelphia, where he learned the printing trade from his uncle William, an in-law of Benjamin Frank-

---

1. For instance, before he could remove his family to Pennsylvania in 1762, William Stewart, a linen weaver in the town of Clough, Co. Down, was obliged to secure from George Rogers, justice of the peace, a formal passport that affirmed his and his wife's "verry fair Character and Good Reputation, having behaved themselves very honestly and inoffensively," and that permitted them "to pass and repass from hence to New Castle or any Part of His Majesty's Brittish Dominions . . . without Let Hindrance or Molestation" (George Rogers, [Belfast?], 7 July 1762); see Sources, chapter 11. 2. One example is the testimonial penned in 1762 by Benjamin Holmes, the Church of Ireland clergyman in Donaghmore parish, Co. Donegal, that recommended the bearer, Thomas McNaire (or McNear) of Ballynacor, as "descended of an antient Protestant Family deservedly esteemed in their Country," as industrious and of "an Unexceptionable Moral character," and as "admitted to Church Priviledge with us" (Benjamin Holmes, Donaghmore, 20 August 1762); see Sources, chapter 11. McNair settled in Hanover township, Lancaster Co., Pa., where in 1790 he was still receiving letters from relatives in Ballynacor. Undoubtedly, Catholic clergy also wrote such references, but very few survive for this or later periods.

lin's wife.³ He became wealthy as publisher of the *Pennsylvania Packet* (America's first daily newspaper), as official printer to the Continental Congress, and through federal and state government contracts and job-printing, as well as by land speculation. Like many of Philadelphia's Scots-Irish politicians, during the Revolution Dunlap also profited from bargain purchases of property confiscated from Irish Quakers and other loyalists.⁴ After the Revolution, he speculated heavily in western lands; he and his brother James held at least 98,000 acres in Kentucky by 1794, when, as a moderate revolutionary turned conservative Federalist, he commanded the government's cavalry against his poorer follow countrymen in western Pennsylvania during the Whiskey Rebellion.

John Rutherford (born ca.1784–1785), the subject of Orr's letter, was a younger son of Robert Rutherford⁵ and Molly Dunlap, John Dunlap's sister and recently deceased in 1811. In 1785 Dunlap had invited John Rutherford's older brother, William, to emigrate to Philadelphia, and several years later he had urged that all "the young Men of Ireland who wish to be free and happy should leave it and come here as quick as possible, [as] there is no place where a man merits so rich a reward for good conduct and industry as in america."⁶ However, by 1811 Dunlap was 65 and had been away from Strabane for over half a century; his last close link to the town had died with his sister. Thus, to approach so distant and formidable a patron, John Rutherford was wise to rely on the testimony of James Orr, a wealthy Strabane merchant and one of Dunlap's kinsmen or old acquaintances,⁷ as to his character and industry.

James Orr, Strabane, County Tyrone, to John Dunlap, Philadelphia, 1 June 1811

Strabane   1 June 1811

Mʳ John Dunlap

Sir   Tho I was not favoured with a reply to the last letter I wrote you on the death of your Sister I feel it my duty to address you again for the purpose of

---

3. On William Dunlap, see chapter 35.   4. For an example of an Irish Quaker whose property may have been seized by Pennsylvania's revolutionary government and later purchased by Dunlap or his associates, see chapter 56.   5. Robert Rutherford's occupation is unknown, but he may have been related to Matthew Rutherford, high sheriff for the city and county of Londonderry in the 1770s.   6. John Dunlap, Philadelphia, to William Rutherford, Strabane, 12 May 1785; quotation from Dunlap, Philadelphia, to Robert Rutherford, Strabane, 12 May 1789. John Dunlap's correspondence; see Sources, chapter 11.   7. During the 1770s and 1780s prominent representatives of the Orr family who were roughly the same age as John Dunlap apparently shared his political liberalism, whereas in the 1790s at least some members of the younger generation engaged in the kind of revolutionary radicalism of which Dunlap's Federalist associates in America did not approve; thus, in the early 1780s, two officers in Strabane's Volunteer forces were named James Orr, but so was a "notoriously disaffected . . . [local] United Irishman" who was arrested in 1797 and perhaps was related to Joseph Orr, a wealthy brazier in Derry city and a member of the United Irishmen's national executive committee before he fled to France in late 1797. In 1820 *Pigot's Irish Directory* lists James Orr, Esq., among Strabane's "gentry," and James Orr, Jr., & Co. as a timber and general merchant firm on the town's Main St., succeeded by William Orr & Co. in 1824. Thomas Orr of Philadelphia, perhaps a kinsman, appears in that city's directories, 1793–1811, as a merchant at 52 South Front St.

FIGURE 3
Portrait of John Dunlap
(1747–1812) of Philadelphia,
painted by Rembrandt Peale
(1778–1860). Photograph in
John H. Campbell, *History of
the Friendly Sons of St. Patrick
and of the Hibernian Society for
the Relief of Emigrants from
Ireland* (Philadelphia, 1892).

introducing to you a very worthy young Man your nephew John Rutherford who considers himselfe called upon by duty & affection to be the protector and Supporter of his two Sisters whome his Worthy Good Mother left in his Charge   He is a good Clark and from every information[8] is as good a Currier & Tanner as ever left this Country   that business has of late years been so Cloged[9] by heavy Duty on leather together with heavy Taxes of every kind that he expects to do better for his own & Sisters support in America as he has been Informed by different People from that[10] of his Trade being a good one there   He is Sober Industrious & Steady   therefore I have no fear of[11] his Success   His Sisters and he leave this[12] with the best wishes of all that know them for their prosperity and Happiness   John has left with me One Hundred Pounds as Guineas have got so scarce that they could not be had under 15 ₩ Cent which I advised him not to pay but to draw upon me which I expect you will

---

8. **from every information**: from all reports.   9. **Cloged**: i.e., clogged.   10. **from that**: from there; in reference to place *that* in Hiberno-English means "there" and in reference to time "then." In such cases *that* is usually construed with a preposition; e.g., as here, **from that** "from there"; **since that** "since then." In the meaning "there" *that* can also be the complement of a verb; e.g., **I left that** "I left there."   11. **fear of**: fear/ anxiety for.   12. **this**: here; the use of **this** parallels the use of **that** described above in n. 10: this = here = now.

have no Hesitation to take from him or endorse his bill on me for that Sum[13]

He and his Worthy Sisters hav the good Wishes of Mrs Orr and of y^r Hub Ser^t[14]

James Orr

if it is not convenient to pass a Bill on me Here he may draw paym^t in London

After a voyage of 63 days, on 31 August 1811 John Rutherford, his sisters Mary and Sarah, and 53 other passengers arrived in Philadelphia aboard the ship *Fame,* commanded by William Pollock of Londonderry. Thereafter no information can be discovered, as neither John Rutherford nor his older brother, William, appear in early Philadelphia directories.[15] Perhaps they went west to help develop John Dunlap's land speculations, and, if they survived to maturity, a reasonable assumption is that they achieved at least modest prosperity, partly through Dunlap's patronage and partly because their trades and superior educations were indeed more marketable in early nineteenth-century America than in contemporary Ulster.

In Strabane, meanwhile, although the Orrs remained and prospered, the loss of middle-class Protestants such as the Dunlaps and Rutherfords had a dramatic cumulative impact.[16] In the early nineteenth century the town's population was almost perfectly stagnant, at about four thousand inhabitants, and between 1765 and 1831 the relative strengths of the Presbyterian and Catholic communities in the local parish, Camus-Morne, were radically reversed, as the Presbyterian share declined from 40 to 29 percent, while the Catholic proportion rose from 30 to 48 percent.[17] High taxes during the Napoleonic Wars (as Orr's letter testified) and severe commercial and industrial depression afterward, coupled with the dramatic change in the local religious balance, further drained the Strabane region of Protestant, and especially Presbyterian, farmers, traders, and artisans. And the transatlantic links preserved over generations—between prerevolutionary Scots-Irish emigrants such as Dunlap and their kinsmen and former neighbors in Ulster—continued to encourage and facilitate departures by new emigrants such as John Rutherford.

13. John has left with me One Hundred Pounds . . . for that Sum: "since guineas have become so scarce that they cannot be obtained for less than a 15 percent surcharge, I have advised John to lodge a sum of £100 with me. I expect you will not hesitate to accept from him a bill drawn on me for that sum or to pass it on with your endorsement."   **14.** Hub Ser^t: i.e., humble servant.   **15.** It is intriguing, however, that Francis White's *Philadelphia Directory* of 1785 lists an Alexander Rutherford as a tanner in Philadelphia, at the docks between Spruce and Union streets. This is probably the Alexander Rutherford who from 1758 was a leading member of the city's "Ancient" Masonic Lodge No. 2, with which John Dunlap (alongside many others with Scots-Irish as well as "native" or "Catholic" Irish names) was also affiliated from 1768. If Alexander Rutherford was a relative of the Strabane Rutherfords, as his Masonic links with John Dunlap suggest, one might surmise that his death in 1791 obliged John Rutherford of Strabane to rely for assistance on his uncle Dunlap in 1811.   **16.** Unfortunately, there are no Ordnance Survey memoirs for Strabane or Camus-Morne parish, but *Pigot's Irish Directories* of 1820 and 1824 list no Dunlaps or Rutherfords as resident in Strabane or vicinity.   **17.** For demographic data on Camus-Morne (Strabane) parish and its environs, see appendix 2.1a, on chapter 11.

12 ❋

John Smilie, 1762

Irish emigrants' first letters home frequently contained detailed accounts of their transatlantic passages, but most correspondents merely described a "tedious" routine of dietary monotony and mild discomfort, occasionally punctuated by frightening but usually brief encounters with storms and other hazards and "wonders," such as massive icebergs in the north Atlantic. Nevertheless, voyage conditions often ranged from inconvenient to extremely unpleasant. Delays of weeks, even months, in sailing from Irish ports were common, which obliged prospective passengers to expend their meagre capital on lodging and provisions before their ships embarked. Overcrowding was also prevalent, as in their advertisements to prospective passengers, shipowners and shipping agents often exaggerated, sometimes by 100 percent or more, the tonnage or carrying capacity of their vessels. During the eighteenth and early nineteenth centuries, very few ships were specifically designed to carry emigrants, forcing all but a few affluent cabin passengers to subsist in steerage or between decks, in spaces less than five or even four feet high, and to sleep two to a bed in berths a mere 18 inches wide. Before the American Revolution, portholes and other forms of ventilation were virtually unknown, and in such damp, cramped conditions, diseases such as smallpox, typhus, and dysentery sometimes assumed epidemic proportions. Finally, although during this era shippers commonly supplied foodstuffs, usually salt beef, biscuits, and potatoes, to both paying passengers and indentured servants, considerations of profit encouraged shipowners and captains to skimp on provisions, which led to severe hardships during prolonged voyages. Before the Revolution, British officials consistently disallowed the few attempts by colonial legislatures to protect emigrants against abuse, and it was not until 1803 that Parliament passed the first Passenger Act that regulated steerage conditions, limited the number of passengers to a fixed percentage of a ship's registered tonnage, and required specific amounts of provisions. However, the American states did not pass similar legislation until the 1820s, and although ostensibly a humanitarian measure, the 1803 British law's real purposes were to exclude American ships from the trade and to limit emigration by raising fares beyond the means of artisans and laborers.

In general, however, eighteenth-century Irish emigrants did not experience the horrors that frequently marked contemporary German migration to America. On passages from Ireland, and especially from Ulster, deaths occurred rarely, primarily among infants; shipwrecks were few; and water and provisions—often supplemented from the passengers' own "sea stores"—were usually adequate unless storms or calms caused exceptional delays. Voyage length was the single most important determinant of passenger safety and comfort, and by the early 1770s passages from Belfast and other Ulster ports to Philadelphia averaged only seven weeks, four days, in length, down from the 8 to 10 weeks' duration that had been common in the 1720s. Thus, the voyage in 1762 described here by John Smilie was decidedly atypical, for he and his companions endured a miserable crossing nearly 15 weeks long, under a captain who was apparently a pirate as well as a miser and a brute. Nevertheless, Smilie's account dramatically illustrates why eighteenth-century emigrants feared the potential "Villany of Ship Masters," as well as the normal "Tryles, Hardships, and Dangers of the Seas."

John Smilie was born in north County Down, in or near the town and parish of Greyabbey, in Lower Ards barony, on 16 September 1742, the son of Robert Smilie, a Presbyterian farmer or trader of probably middling circumstances.[1] On 24 May 1762 John Smilie, aged 19, embarked from Belfast for New Castle, Delaware, aboard the ship *Sally*, captained by James Taylor and owned by a consortium of Philadelphia merchants.[2] Perhaps Smilie had been attracted by a notice in the 2 March 1762 issue of the *Belfast News-Letter*, which described the *Sally* as a vessel of 250 tons burthen, promised ample provisions, and assured prospective passengers of the very best treatment from a well-known and experienced shipmaster. In fact, the *Sally*'s officially registered tonnage was merely 80 tons,[3] and the deaths by starvation of 64 emigrants and crew members during Smilie's voyage gave the lie to the rest of the advertisement. Smilie himself luckily survived and on 11 November 1762, from the safety of what was then Lancaster (in 1785 Dauphin) County, Pennsylvania, he wrote this account of his ordeal to his father, Robert, who in turn published it in the 13 May 1763 issue of the *Belfast News-Letter*, in order, he wrote, to warn his emigrating countrymen against such "barbarous and inhumane" treatment as his son had endured.

John Smilie, Fishing-Creek on Susquehanna, Lancaster Co., Pennsylvania, to Robert Smilie, Greyabbey, County Down, 11 November 1762

Fishing-Creek on Susquehanna,
Nov. 11. 1762

Honoured Father,

I Account it my Honour and Duty, to give you an Account of myself and my Proceedings since I left you; which have, I confess, been a little extraordinary. On the next Tuesday after I left you, I came on Board the S—y, on the Monday following, being the 24th of May last, we sailed for America: On the 31st we lost Sight of Ireland, having been detained 'till then by Calms and contrary Winds, which seemed to be the doleful Presages of our after unhappy Voyage. We had our full Allowance of Bread

---

1. Efforts to discover more information about Smilie's Irish background have been unsuccessful, but in the early nineteenth century most families named Smilie (Smyley, Smiley) were concentrated in a handful of townlands in the Co. Down parishes of Bangor and Newtownards, adjacent to Greyabbey, and of Magheradrool. For demographic data on Greyabbey parish and its environs, see appendix 2.1c, on chapters 12 and 10.   2. Built in Pennsylvania, the *Sally* was captained by James Taylor of Belfast but owned by William and John Murray, John and Robert Carey, and Robert Wilcox, all of Philadelphia.   3. On 12 December 1761, the *Sally* was registered in Philadelphia at 80 tons burthen; however, to avoid colonial customs duties shippers and captains were at least as prone to underestimate the tonnage of their vessels in America as they were to exaggerate when advertising for emigrants in Irish ports.

and Water, only for the first Fortnight; then we were reduced to three Pints of Water per Day, and three Pounds and a Half of Bread per Week, to each Person; which it never afterwards exceeded, the whole Passage. We had a South-west Wind, which drove us so far North, that our Weather became extremely Cold, with much Rain and hard Gales of Wind: On the 5th of July we had a hard Squal of Wind which lasted 3 Hours, and caused us to lie to;[4] on the 6th we had a Storm which continued 9 Hours, and obliged us to lie to under bare Poles;[5] on the 12th we espied a Mountain of Ice of a prodigious Size; on the 13th our Weather became more moderate; on the 16th we espied a Sail, which was along Side of us before either saw the other; she, having the Wind right aft, crowded Sail,[6] and bore away; we gave her Chace, and fired six Guns at her, but the Fog soon hid her from us. In this Manner did our Captain behave, giving Chace to all Ships he saw, whether they bore off us[7] East or West, it was all alike, the Motives of which caused various Conjectures. August the first our Weather became extremely warm, and the Crew very weak: The 10th Day our Allowance of Bread came to two Pounds and an Half per Week to each Passenger; next Week we had only one Pound and an Half; and the next twelve Days we lived upon two Biscuits and an half for that Time, and half a Naggin[8] of Barley each, which we eat[9] raw, for want of Water to boil it in: We had Beef, but could make no Use of it, for Thirst; for we were a Week that we had but half a Pint of Water per Day[10] for each Person. Hunger and Thirst had now reduced our Crew to the last Extremity; nothing was now to be heard aboard our Ship but the Cries of distressed Children, and of their distressed Mothers, unable to relieve them. Our Ship now was truly a real Spectacle of Horror! Never a Day passed without one or two of our Crew put over Board; many kill'd themselves by drinking Salt Water; and their own Urine was a common Drink; yet in the midst of all our Miseries, our Captain shewed not the least Remorse or Pity. We were now out of Hopes of ever seeing Land. August 29th we had only one Pint of Water for each Person, which was all that we Passengers would have got, and our Bread was done: But on that Day the Lord was pleased to send the greatest Shower of Rain I ever saw, which was the Means of preserving our Lives. After this we had fair Winds, and, for most Part, Rains every Day; and tho' we had no Bread, yet, we thought, we lived well. On the first of September we sounded,[11] and found ourselves in forty Fathom Water, and the next Morning, about eight O'clock, we saw Land, to the inexpressible Joy of all our Ship's Crew; and on Sunday Morning the 4th of Sept. we came to an Anchor off Newcastle; so that we had a Passage of fourteen Weeks and

---

4. **lie to**: come nearly to a standstill by backing and shortening sail (OED, s.v. lie, 29.a); **backing**: adjusting the yard so that the wind blows directly on the front of the sail, stalling forward motion.   5. **under bare Poles**: "with all sails furled."   6. **crowded Sail**: "hoisted more than the usual number of sails."   7. **bore off us**: "steered away from us."   8. **Naggin**: noggin (a small cup, commonly holding a quarter of a pint).   9. **eat**: past tense, pronounced [ett] (Standard British and Southern Irish).   10. **we were a Week . . . per Day**: "for a week we had only a half pint of water per day."   11. **sounded**: "measured the depth of the water."

six Days. You may judge of Capt T——'s Temper and Character by this, that, notwithstanding all the Straits we were in for Bread and Water, neither he, nor his Mistress, nor five others that were his Favourites, ever came to Allowance.[12] We had now, since the Time of our setting sail, lost sixty-four of our Crew by Death. Monday the fifth I came on Shore, and by the Blessing of God, in three Weeks Time I got perfectly well; but indeed, few of our Ship's Crew were so strong as I; for notwithstanding all I suffered I enjoyed a good State of Health the whole Passage.

I am your dutiful Son,

JOHN SMILIE.

Whether John Smilie's letter deterred future emigrants from trusting their fate to Captain Taylor is unknown, but at least as late as 1765 the *Sally* was still advertising for and carrying emigrants to the colonies. As for Smilie himself, in economic and political terms his American career was highly successful, despite his "fretful and unquiet temper" and poor relationship with his wife and children.[13] In 1771, nine years after arriving in Lancaster County, Smilie owned merely 80 acres, plus two horses and two cattle, in Dromore township, but the social and political fluidity engendered by the American Revolution enabled his rapid rise to wealth and influence. In 1775 Smilie was a member of Lancaster County's revolutionary committee, and in 1776 he became a militia sergeant and a member of the provincial congress that met in Philadelphia. In 1778 and 1779 Lancaster's voters elected him to the Pennsylvania General Assembly, but in 1781 he moved his family over the mountains and settled in Tyrone township in what was then Westmoreland (from 1784 Fayette) County. By 1783 Smilie owned three hundred acres, three horses, four cattle, and 13 sheep; from occupying merely the ninth decile of property-holders in Dromore township, Smilie was now part of a frontier élite, and in subsequent years he purchased at least 660 additional acres in western Pennsylvania. His political career also flourished in the backcountry. Between 1783 and his death on 29 December 1813, Smilie won election to the state's Council of Censors (1783), the General Assembly (1784–1789 and 1795–1798), the state's Supreme Executive Council (1786–1789), the convention that ratified the federal Constitution in 1787, the state constitutional convention of 1789–1790, the state Senate (1790), and the U.S. House of Representatives (1793–1795 and 1798–1813).

Yet despite his new status and affluence, Smilie was a faithful representative of the Scots-Irish radicalism that generally prevailed in Pennsylvania's backcountry during and after the Revolution. Following the lead of the Dublin-born Presbyterian politician,

---

12. ever came to Allowance: "were ever reduced to accepting limited/restricted rations." **13.** The Pennsylvania state senator John Roberts, who knew Smilie personally as well as politically, recorded that the latter's wife, Jane, "did not rise with [her husband]," that his children "were not smart," and therefore Smilie was "impatient and unreasonable" with them, and turned to politics in part to escape the disappointments of domesticity. R. C. Henderson, "John Smilie, Anti-federalism, and the 'Dissent of the Minority,'" WPHM, 77 (1988), 242–44.

George Bryan of Philadelphia, Smilie defended Pennsylvania's ultrademocratic 1776 constitution, supported the state's abolition of slavery in 1780, strongly opposed adoption of the
U.S. Constitution, which he condemned as "a device of despotism," was accused by his
Federalist opponents of helping instigate the Whiskey Rebellion of 1794, and eventually
became a staunch Jeffersonian Republican.[14] Although his political opinions were by no
means unique among the Scots-Irish in western Pennsylvania, one may speculate whether
Smilie's suffering aboard the *Sally* in 1762 might have helped engender the deep animosity
toward Philadelphia's merchant élite that marked his subsequent career.

13 ❋

John O'Raw, 1809

Like John Smilie's 1762 journey, John O'Raw's transatlantic passage in 1806–1807 was
exceptional in its length and misery. O'Raw's voyage from Belfast to Charleston,
South Carolina, consumed nearly 22 weeks, including his time spent stranded in Bermuda,
whereas normal passages from Ireland to Charleston averaged only nine weeks. However,
O'Raw's harrowing account illustrates several prevalent hazards of emigration in the eighteenth and early nineteenth centuries: not only the threats of storms and shipwreck but
also the dangers of impressment into the British navy—a not uncommon fate among Irish
passengers during Britain's frequent wars with France, Spain, and, later, the United States—as
well as the often-fatal "seasoning" process that emigrants, especially to southern American
ports, had to endure after exposure to unfamiliar diseases such as malaria and yellow fever.

John O'Raw was born in 1783, the son of Bryan O'Raw (1751–1831) and Nellie
Mcmanus, and, unlike most Ulster emigrants of the period, he was Catholic. Members of
the O'Raw family were small traders, craftsmen, and farmers in and around Ballymena
town, in the parishes of Kirkinriola and Ballyclug, especially in Ballylesson townland, in
County Antrim.[1] The O'Raws were closely allied to—and probably tenants of—the
O'Haras of Crebilly, former chiefs of this region prior to the Ulster Plantation.[2] In 1659
west Antrim's population was still largely Catholic, but in the late seventeenth and early
eighteenth centuries Scottish settlement was so extensive that by 1732 Presbyterians comprised a large majority of the area's inhabitants.[3] However, if Bryan O'Raw indeed leased
the tolls and customs charged in the Ballymena or Crebilly markets, as his son's letter
indicates, his family must have been fairly prosperous and influential, despite their Catholi-

---

14. E. Everett, "John Smilie . . . ," 84; see Sources, chapter 12. On revolutionary and postrevolutionary politics
in Pennsylvania, generally, see chapters 52, 53, 55, 56, 58, 62, and 63. On George Bryan, see chapter 52.
1. Kirkinriola and Ballyclug parishes were in the baronies of Lower Toome and Lower Antrim, respectively.
2. In the early nineteenth century the O'Haras remained prominent landlords in Crebilly, Ballylesson, and
adjacent townlands; in 1876 their holdings in this region still totaled nearly 1,700 acres.   **3.** For demographic
data on Kirkinriola parish and its environs, see sppendix 2.1f, on chapter 13.

cism, as suggested also by John O'Raw's high literacy and obvious educational advantages. In this part of Antrim, relations between Presbyterians and the Catholic minority, both alienated from the established church, were relatively good, as indicated by their mutual participation in the United Irish rebellion and by John O'Raw's own reliance on Presbyterian friends, former neighbors, and fellow rebels, as well as on the O'Haras and other Catholics, for assistance in America. Although merely 15 years old, in June 1798 O'Raw himself joined the Antrim rising, led by Presbyterian merchant Henry Joy McCracken (1767–1798), and fought in the battle of Antrim town. Captured and taken to be hanged in his mother's doorway, O'Raw escaped and lay hidden on Knockanour hill until his father, who had remained loyal, could intercede on his behalf. Thereafter, he lived in the Ballymena area until 1806 when, aged about 23, he embarked for Charleston.

The Belfast firm of Joy & McCracken had long been involved in trade with South Carolina, and such connections may have facilitated O'Raw's departure. However, Charleston was still a popular destination for Ulster emigrants generally, although less so than in the eighteenth century, when the city had been the primary destination in the lower South for Irish passengers and servants. The trade resumed after the American Revolution and may even have expanded for a time, as the growth of Belfast's cotton industry, coinciding with the great expansion of cotton cultivation in inland South Carolina after the cotton gin's invention (1791), both increased commerce between Ulster and the lower South and heightened emigrants' opportunities there. Most Irish emigrants to Charleston were Presbyterians, but some were Catholics, and relations between them were congenial. The city's first Irish Society was established in 1749, and in 1799 Irish Protestants and Catholics founded the local Hibernian Society. By the late 1770s O'Haras were merchants in Charleston; in 1791 Daniel O'Hara[4] was among the Irish-born trustees who incorporated St. Mary's, South Carolina's first Catholic church; and by 1820 the Catholic presence was large enough to warrant Rome sending John England (1786–1842) from Ireland as the city's first bishop. Thus, despite the fact that in 1810 a majority of Charleston's population (24,711) was composed of slaves and free blacks, South Carolina was not an illogical place for John O'Raw to settle, especially given the kinsmen and friends who had preceded him.

John O'Raw, Charleston, South Carolina, to Bryan and Nellie O'Raw, ca. Ballymena, County Antrim, 1 April 1809

Charleston   April 1st 1809

My Dear Father & Mother

Through the mercy of divine Providence I am still in existence after innumerable Misfortunes & dangers & is[5] in good Health & happy & must ask forgiveness of the

---

4. In 1783 Daniel and David O'Hara, merchants, petitioned for U.S. citizenship, "having resided some time in this country."   5. & is: i.e., and am (Northern Concord Rule; see appendix 1).

Almighty, & of you my dear parents in prolonging[6] writing to you, but I trust you will not attribute it to ingratitude as my Heart still flows with the most affectionat & ardent emotions of Filial Affection,   On the 18th Inst[7] I Rec^d a letter from you & one from my Sister Kathy by the Brig [. . .] 75 days from Belfast which was the best I ever rec^d   you mention you wrote twice before but I never was so happy as to get any of them,   you say that your Health & my Dr Mothers is in a declining state which grieves me to the Heart to hear particularly as you say it is principally on Acc^t of never hearing from me—But I trust that that God which has Hitherto spared you will yet prolong your days to your poor Children—My Cause of not writing before this was owing to been[8] so situated & unsettled since I came here that I never could think of writing with any satisfaction to you or myself till the present——I am now happy to inform you that I am in an eligible[9] Situation in this City, in a large Grocery & Liquor Store in the employment of a Mr Phelan[10] an Irishman   my Salary is 200 Dollars a year found in Boarding & Washing[11]——I arrived in this City from the Country in the middle of January last   I came in prospect of getting into a Situation & got the one I am in now through the recommendation of Mr Henry OHara[12]——I have great reason to thank God that I was so fortunate as since the Embargo[13] was laid on little or no Business has been doing & many young men Tradesmen &c for want of employment is in distress——As you will be desirous to hear an Acc^t of my unfortunate passage & my situation Since my arrival here, I shall endeavour to give you as Short and Correct an Acc^t as I can—On the 24th Nov 1806 we Sailed from the White House roads,[14]   we passed the Island of Raughtry[15] on the third day after we Sailed——We now had most Boisterous Stormy weather & I began to grow Sea Sick——On the morning of the tenth Day after we Sailed, before daylight, a light was descried from the deck & when day began to dawn we found ourselves close in upon the land, when we thought we had been a considerable way at Sea,   Here that providence which still protected us saved us from an almost inevitable death,   we were drifting in—in the night upon a dangerous lee shore & it blowing so heard[16] that it was almost impossible to think that the Ship or our lives could be saved when fortunately about 9 OClock in the morning

---

6. prolonging: delaying, postponing (OED, s.v. prolong, 3; obsolete).   **7. Ins^t**: i.e., instant "current month." Since his letter is dated 1 April, O'Raw should have written **ultimo** "last month," but his mind is still in March.   **8. been**: i.e., bein' "being."   **9. eligible**: desirable.   **10. Mr Phelan**: Col. Edmund M. Phelan, in 1801 a grocer and liquor dealer at 225 Meeting St. and a member of the Hibernian Society; by 1810 a prominent trustee of St. Mary's Catholic church; and in 1815–1819 a leader of the "Charleston schism" (see text hereafter).   **11. found in Boarding & washing**: with board and laundry provided.   **12. Henry OHara**: Henry O'Hara, in 1801 a merchant at 128 Broad St. and a member of Charleston's Hibernian Society. **13. the Embargo**: the American Embargo Act (1807), which interdicted all trade between the United States and Great Britain.   **14. White House**: a suburb of Belfast on the Antrim side of Belfast Lough; **roads**: a place in open water calm enough for ships to ride at anchor.   **15. the Island of Raughtry**: Rathlin Island (off the north Antrim coast); **Raughtry** is a variant anglicization of the Irish original.   **16. heard**: i.e., hard; since the Scots correspondent of the standard past tense form **heard** (rhymes with **herd**) is **hard** (rhymes with **lard**), the adjective **hard** can be spelled both **hard** and **heard**.

the Wind Shifted & we Stood[17] along shore & passed in between the County
Donegal & Tory Island & then stood out[18] to Sea,   I now took the last view of my
Native Country——We encountered the most dangerous Storms & head winds for
three Weeks & was[19] driven into the bay of Biscay of<f> the coast of France   a great
many of our passengers now took the Flux[20] & one child died of it,   the weather
continued most dreadful for 6 Weeks during which we were frequently carrying away
our Yards & rigging[21] in dangerous Storms of Thunder & lightening   the Cap[n] said
he never was at Sea in such before,   I was for 4 Weeks that I was almost reduced to
the point of death by Sickness,   I now for the first time found myself from
Home[22]   we had fair Weather from the 10th January to the 22nd of the same Month,
when on the morning of that day about 4 OClock going Nine Knots an Hour we
struck on the rocks of<f> the Island of Bermudas[23] 12 miles from Shore   the Cries of
Men Women & Children at this Awful period of our lives will never leave my
ears,   it now began to blow very heard & we were in immediate expectation of the
Ship going to pieces but fortunately as if the Almighty wished to Save us in the midst
of our greatest dangers, it calmed,   when day light began to appear we Hoisted a
Signal of distress, which was Answered by One of the Forts on the Island, but we
could see no Assistance come to us till about 10 OClock & by 12 OClock there was
upwards of 200 Boats about the Ship   the Negroes in the Boats when coming on
Board began to tear open Boxes of Linen passengers Chests &c   I went ashore in the
Second Boat & landed about 3 OClock in the afternoon fully impressed with the
goodness of God in thus preserving my life   we had now to go through difficulties
on land almost as distressing as the dangers we had encountered at Sea   6 of the
passengers immediately on landing was pressed[24] & put on Board British Ships of war
among which was Jn[o] Boyds two eldest Sons & Rob[t] Gibson from near Crebilly   I
would of Shared the Same fate of those poor fellows had I been along with them as
the<y> went to S[t] Georges the principal Town on the Island & I went to a Country
part of it——the Cap[n] now told us we would have to all do for ourselves for that he
had done with us,[25] & we never Rec[d] anything more from the Ship from the day we
left her   passengers that had Money was now obliged to live at their own expence &
what[26] had not was obliged to live on[27] Charity   Bermuda is one of the dearest parts
in the World for provisions & the expence I was at was Consequently enormous——
The Rem[d][28] of the passengers that was not pressed was Summoned to appear before

---

17. Stood: rode at anchor.   **18.** stood out: left shore for open water.   **19.** & was: i.e., and were (see n. 5).
20. Flux: dysentery.   **21.** carrying away our yards & rigging: "losing our yards and rigging."   **22.** I now for
the first time found myself from Home: "now for the first time I realized that I had left home (for good)."
23. the Island of Bermudas: Bermuda (a British-owned sugar island in the Atlantic Ocean, ca. 570 miles
southeast of Cape Hatteras, North Carolina).   **24.** pressed: impressed, recruited by force, conscripted.
25. for that he had done with us: "because he was finished with us"; see chapter 65, n. 20.   **26.** what: those
who.   **27.** own ms.   **28.** Rem[d]: remainder.

the Governor to give an Acc^t of themselves & the Cause of leaving their own Country——I was Summoned twice to appear before the Governor but seen him neither times but I was examined by his Secretary who ordered me to appear on another day when his Excelency the Governor would have leisure—but this I declined as I understood it was their intention to put me on Board a man of war, & I now Kept myself Retired in obscure & remote parts of the Island, Seldom Sleeping at night & often in want of the Necessaries of life which I could heardly procure for money, & almost reduced to a Skeleton by the Flux which I took very ill a few days after my landing——It is[29] almost unnecessary to mention the most inhuman & cruel manner in which the Cap^n treated the Passengers after suffering Ship wreck by denying them every Article of life when the\<y\> were cast away in a remote & distant part of the World & leaving them to Starve or depend on the charitable donations of the Humane,   the Cargo of the ship was all saved, & she was got off[30] & condemned as unfit for Sea from the damage she had Sustained   the Captn Sold all the Cargo & made off for New York   the potatoes sold for 16/0 a Bushell some of the linen at 7^s/ 6^d the yard,   what passengers of us Remained now chartered a Sloop for Charleston for 450 Dollars & to lay in all our own provisions   My part with my sea Store came to 40 dollars   we Sailed from Bermuda on the 1st April & after being 3 days out was obliged to put back with the loss of our Bowsprit having carried it away in a Storm   Misfortune now seemed never to forsake us   we got the Vessel Repaired & again sailed on the 6th of April after remaining in Bermuda from the 22^d January,   our passage now was the most disagreeable that imagination can conceive from[31] the accommodations in so Small a Vessel & the greatest danger we ever yet was in at sea happened on the 14th of April, when we were in a Violent Storm hove down[32] almost Keel up—2 inches more would have Consigned us to Watery graves, as the Hatches was open & the water running into them   the Cup of Misfortune Seemed now to have been full & only to Submit to the divine will, but that good & Merciful God which had brought us through all our former dangers now saved us at this dreadful Moment,   after being on her broad side for 4 Hours she began to upright & we got the Ballast which was almost hove out[33] of her Hatches put to rights,[34]   we were now a perfect Wreck having carried away our Boom & the greatest part of the Rigging Boat & every thing swept off the decks   the weather coming[35] good we got her so far Repaired that we were enabled to proceed   I arrived in this port after a passage of 18 Days & 59 Days from Belfast to Bermuda & 76 Days I remained in Bermuda——I was three Weeks in this City before I got into any Situation   after my arrival Ch^s & Henry OHara[36] procured me one but it was not a good one as it took all my Salary to pay for my Boarding which is 6 Dollars a Week here,   the Summer coming

---

29. as ms. **30. got off:** that is, off the rocks. **31. from:** because of. **32. hove down:** riding down in the water. **33. hove out:** floating out. **34. wrights** ms. **35. coming:** becoming. **36. Ch^s & Henry OHara:** Charles O'Hara, in 1802 a merchant at 9 Smith's Lane, Charleston; on Henry O'Hara, see n. 12.

on[37] to be very Sickly & in a poor state of Health after the Fatigue & hardships I had undergone I thought it prudent to leave Charleston as it commonly proves fatal to Europeans to Stay here the first summer after coming in   I left charleston the latter end of July & went by Savannah to Augusta in Georgia with an intention of living with Wm Bones[38]   I was only one night in Savannah & Seen Jno Moorehead there   he was friendly to me   when I got to Augusta (which is 130 Miles from Savanah & Savanah 130 Miles from Charleston) I was unable for[39] any Business   I staid in Augusta only 3 Weeks & went to newberry[40] in this state   I went from Charleston to Savanah by Sea & from Savanah to Augusta in the Stage Coach   it was with the greatest difficulty I could make to[41] Newbury to where Jno Boyd lives from Weakness & it was Eighty Miles I had to travel,   a few days after my arrival at Jno Boyds I took ill of a fever, in which I lay for 9 Weeks   my life was the most of the time despaired of   I was Seldom Sensible during the time   Oh My Dr Parents now was the time that I Knowed the want of you[42]   dear Suzy Boyd acted the part of a Mother to me,   I was 4 Months before I was able to go about,   when I began to recover I was in so weak a Situation that I was unable to leave the Country & was advised to Stay in the Country for some time & teach School which I was now obliged to do through Necessity 12 Miles from Jno Boyds & teached for one year,   I Boarded 7 months with a Sister of Jno Crawfords your neighbour   her first Husband McCollum is dead   she is now married again———Johnny Boyd has bought 130 Acres of land for 300 Dollars   he is very contented & happy   he has made a good change   he will in a Short time be Rich which he never would have been in Ireland,   he came from Bermuda in the Man of War that his 2 Sons was in   the<y> touched at this port & landed him & his Family here except his 2 Sons that was pressed   on his Arrival here which was 3 Weeks before mine there was a Subscription made for him in consequence of the loss of his sons   Jno Boyds oldest son Thomas has got home to his Father & Mother   he deserted & left his Brother in Halifax Novascotia & got his way made good here[43]———on my first arrival in Charleston Alex^r OHara formerly of Belfast was Just come from Africa,   he brought with him 4 Negroes for which he got about 1200 Dl^s & bought a Vessel but not being a Citizen of the United States he could not clear her out in his own name & got a man to clear

---

37. coming on: "come so as to prevail disagreeably" (OED s.v. come, 66.c).   **38. Wm Bones**: members of the Bones family, Reformed (i.e., Covenanting) Presbyterians and United Irishmen from Ballygarvey, near Ballymoney, in north Co. Antrim, fled to the United States in the immediate aftermath of the 1798 Rebellion, settling as merchants and planters in Augusta, Georgia, and in Fairfield Co., South Carolina.   **39. unable for**: incapable of.   **40. newberry** (also **Newbury** hereafter): Newberry, the county seat (pop. 200 in 1810) of Newberry Co.; located in the South Carolina piedmont, Newberry Co. prior to the Revolution was part of the Ninety Six District, heavily settled by Scots-Irish migrants in the 1760s and 1770s.   **41. make to**: proceed toward.   **42. now was the time that I Knowed the want of you**: "it was now that I understood fully how much I missed/needed you."   **43. got his way made good here**: "Succeeded in making his way here"; see I hope he has got his way made to some part of this country hereafter.

her out for him who took her away to another port and sold her & never gave OHara a farthing   the man Returned again but OHara could do nothing with him,   when I came to charleston he borrowed 5 Guineas from me as I then thought there was no Risque in lending it to him having brought four Slaves with him from Africa   I however never Rec^d a Farthing of it nor never will   he was afterwards in a poor Situation in this City Borrowing from every person he could get from & at last put in Jail for his Boarding   he is now back some where in the Country   Alex^r McQuillan brother to Jenkins is in Fairfield district[44] in this State teaching School   I am told he makes out[45] wonderfully   Robt Phillips son to the Co^l is also in Fairfield district[46] & is married   he makes out as bad as in Ireland   I heard he was lately in Jail for debt——Thos Banks is married about Eight days ago   his Matrimonial Speculation has been but a poor one   he has now Joined a man in partnership to Keep a Tavern   Ja^s McCay is well & does not he tells me intend going home at this time   William Jno Swan is well & is one of the finest smartest young men in this City——on the 15th Ultimo[47] the Embargo was taken off & a Non intercourse Act[48] passed in place of it which forbids all intercourse with England & France   it is generally thought here that a war with England is inevitable,   this Country has made great preparations for defence   Recruiting for the Army & Navy is carried on brisk   this country is distracted by two contending parties viz Federalist & Republican   the Federalists is distinguished by their partiality to England their opposition to the Embargo & the measures of the late <a>dministration & Hatred to France   The Republicans was Strenuous Supporters of the Embargo & Mr Jeffersons administration & has the greatest hatred to England   Mr Jefferson has retired from the helm of Affairs with the Blessings of his Country & Mr Maddison another Republican has been elected president of the United States by the Republicans,[49]   I seen George Savage Some time ago in this City,   I saw him pass several times in the Street but did not Speak to him,   he had a Ragged Shabby appearance——when you write let me Know what is become of Frank Kenedy   I hope he has got his way made to some part of this Country, likewise F. Dobbin,   Ch^s Kenedy son to W^es Kenedy of Belfast is a Soldier at Fort Johnston below this City   he has been ten years in the United States Service   he lives very

44. Fairfield district: Fairfield Co., prior to the Revolution a part of Camden District, in the South Carolina backcountry. **45. makes out**: is getting on/managing (well or badly) (OED, s.v. make, 91.c [b]); the text illustrates both poles of the basic meaning: **he makes out wonderfully** vs. **he makes out as bad as in Ireland** (hereafter). **46. Robt Phillips son to the Co^l . . .** : Robert Phillips, son of Col. John Phillips, prominent leader of the South Carolina backcountry's Irish loyalists during the American Revolution; see chapter 60. **47. Ultimo**: the preceding month. **48. a Non intercourse Act**: the Non-Intercourse Act, passed by Congress in May 1809, banned all American trade with Britain and France. **49.** Thomas Jefferson's second term as president ended in March 1809; he was succeeded by his fellow Virginia Republican, James Madison, elected in November 1808.

well[50]   he is Armourer   I will write shortly to my Brother Francis[51] & to my Sister Kitty & you may from this forth[52] expect to get at least 3 or 4 letters in the year from me,   I will give you a full Acc^t of this Country in my next as this letter chiefly is taken up with my passage,   do not neglect one day after you Receive this to immediately write to me & also I hope Francis will write to me immediately a long letter giving me an Acc^t[53] of every thing has happened about Ballymena since I left it   you did not mention if you yet held the customs[54]   Remember me to Mr Fitzsimons   tell him I will write to him   also to Mr Clark & in a particular manner to Mrs Hill & all the Mulhollands & my Cousin Kitty & their children   to my dear Brothers & Sisters my Heart flows with affection for them   I have not Room to say more but my Earnest prayer my Dr Father & Mother shall be ever to God for your Health Happiness & welfare from your late Undutiful but now dutiful & affectionate Son

John O Raw

Despite his initial trials, O'Raw slowly improved his fortunes in Charleston. In 1812 he was still merely a grocer's clerk, but between 1816 and 1825 city directories recorded him as a grocer on his own account, with an establishment in Meeting Street. According to family tradition, based on now-lost letters, O'Raw fought in the American navy during the War of 1812, and in 1815 he became a U.S. citizen. By 1820 he was sufficiently prosperous to own two slaves, an adult male and a female child. However, O'Raw never married, and sometime between 1825 and 1829 (when he disappears from city directories), he returned permanently to County Antrim, where he died in 1841. Perhaps he returned to care for his aged father or to rejoin the richer social life enjoyed by the relatively prosperous and interconnected Catholic and Presbyterian families of O'Raws, O'Loans, McAuleys, and Moores in west and mid-Antrim. For while Ballymena was industrializing and growing (by 103 percent between 1821 and 1841), and the size of its Catholic minority increasing, Charleston was stagnating economically and demographically, far outstripped by New Orleans, Baltimore, and even Mobile as Southern centers of trade and Irish immigration.[55]

---

50. lives very well: is very prosperous.   **51. my Brother Francis**: in *Pigot's Irish Directory* of 1824, a Francis O'Rawe, perhaps John's older brother, was listed as a sadler and harness-maker in Church Street, Ballymena. As late as 1862 Bryan and Barnard Orawe rented houses in Ballymena's Fair-Hill Lane and Fountain Place, respectively.   **52. from this forth**: from now on; see chapter 11, n. 10.   **53. & Acc^t** ms.; the use of the ampersand here shows that **an** and & "and" were pronounced alike, i.e., **un**.   **54. customs**: usually "tolls and customs": i.e., the tariffs levied on market transactions in privately owned towns or villages; John O'Raw asks whether his father still leased (**yet held**) from the local landlord the right to charge and collect the tolls and customs traditionally imposed in either the Ballymena or the Crebilly market, where local weavers, spinners, and farmers, among others, sold their goods, produce, livestock, etc.   **55.** Between 1821 and 1841 Ballymena's population increased from 2,740 to 5,549. Religious data for the town itself do not exist in this period, but between 1766 and 1831 the size of Kirkinriola parish's Catholic minority rose from less than a twentieth to

More broadly, O'Raw's return "home" suggests how even a prosperous immigrant might resolve the tensions inherent in an "Irish-American" identity, particularly one that was complicated by potential conflicts between religious and political allegiances. In Charleston O'Raw was a faithful communicant in St. Mary's Catholic church yet also a member of the city's ecumenical Hibernian Society, which was dominated by Ulster Presbyterian immigrants, many of whom were former United Irishmen. Thus, when Archbishop Leonard Neale (1746–1817) of Baltimore tried to impose on St. Mary's an ultra-royalist French priest, a refugee from the French Revolution, O'Raw and the church's other Irish parishioners (many of them, like O'Raw, formerly associated with the 1798 Rebellion) refused to accept Neale's nominee, thus precipitating the "Charleston schism" of 1815–1819. Significantly, their objection was not to the French priest's nationality but to his outspoken animosity toward the radical principles for which they and their Protestant countrymen had fought in Ireland.

After 1819 the personal tact and republican spirit of Charleston's new bishop, the Cork-born John England, defused the crisis. Within a few decades, however, few Irish-American Catholics (particularly men as "respectable" as O'Raw) would dare to defy their church's leaders so openly and vigorously, for by then Irish Catholics on both sides of the ocean regarded religious loyalty (and sharp distinctions from Protestants) as paramount and integral to their conceptions of Irish identity and nationalism. Indeed, when he returned to County Antrim in the late 1820s, O'Raw surely discovered to his sorrow that sectarian relations, generally, were already much more polarized than when he had emigrated, due to the effects of Daniel O'Connell's crusade for Catholic emancipation and, among Presbyterians and other Protestants, the growth of evangelicalism and of the Loyal Orange Order.[56]

nearly a fifth of the inhabitants. By contrast, although between 1800 and 1810 Charleston's population had grown from 18,711 to 24,711, in 1826 its inhabitants numbered merely 24,817, and no appreciable increase in the city's small Irish Catholic population would occur until the Famine immigration of the late 1840s. **56.** In 1823 Daniel O'Connell (1775–1847) founded the Catholic Association, the first mass-based political organization in the British Isles. His crusade for Catholic emancipation (i.e., repeal of the Penal Laws, which prohibited Catholics from sitting in Parliament and holding other civil and military offices) intensified in 1826–1828 and was successful in 1829 when the Tory government reluctantly passed the Emancipation Act. O'Connell's campaign coincided with and spurred the Orange Order's expansion among frightened Protestants, generally, as well as bitter theological and political divisions within the Presbyterian Synod of Ulster between evangelical conservatives who opposed and New Light liberals who supported Catholic civil rights. Thus, the growth of "triumphalism" among Irish Catholics and of evangelicalism among Protestants helped submerge the rationalism and ecumenical nationalism that in the 1790s had inspired many United Irishmen of both faiths. ¶In the early 1840s O'Connell launched his last great political crusade, for repeal of the Act of Union (of 1800) and the restoration of Irish legislative independence. Although O'Connell still had a handful of prominent Protestant supporters, primarily among members of the so-called Young Ireland group, most Irish Protestants were antagonistic to repeal. Moreover, in 1845–1847 even the Young Irelanders repudiated O'Connell's leadership, in part because they sought to emulate the United Irishmen and thus embraced more radical and revolutionary forms of Irish nationalism than O'Connell could abide but also because they rejected what they regarded as O'Connell's and most of his followers' apparent equations of "Irish" identity with Catholicism and of Irish interests with those of the Catholic Church.

Yet had O'Raw lived a long life in Charleston, he might have been equally dismayed by the growing distance between the South's Ulster Presbyterians and Irish Catholics, especially by the former's increasing tendency to identify themselves as "Scotch-Irish," to distinguish themselves from their "Irish"—that is, Catholic—countrymen. In large part that trend was a long-term result of evangelicalism's steady growth among Southern (as among Northern) Protestants, heightening as it did their religious sensibilities and traditional prejudices. In the 1840s, however, the popularity of "Scotch-Irish" identities among the South's Ulster-stock Protestants was no doubt accelerated—and by not only the embarrassing arrival of poor Catholic refugees from Ireland's Great Famine (1845–1852) at Charleston and other Southern ports but also Daniel O'Connell's espousal of Northern abolitionism and his denunciations of slavery from the other side of the Atlantic. Indeed, O'Connell's attacks may have climaxed long-held Southern suspicions concerning Irish immigrants' loyalty to the South's "peculiar institution," for as early as 1800 frightened Virginians had accused Irish republican emigrés of involvement in Gabriel's slave rebellion (allegations later repeated in Mississippi and elsewhere), and in the Nullification Crisis of 1832–1833, South Carolina's only Irish-American newspaper, the Charleston *Irishman and Southern Democrat,* was strongly opposed to the Nullification movement. In retrospect, then, perhaps John O'Raw had been wise to return to Ireland in the late 1820s—before his ethnic identity became even more complex and conflicted than it had been a decade earlier during the Charleston schism.

14 ✳

Thomas Hinds, 1795

Thomas Hinds's petition demonstrates how easily newcomers' expectations could be blighted by breaks in the transatlantic connections that were so vital for chain migration, especially during the eighteenth and early nineteenth centuries when mail services were uncertain and expensive, and when unanticipated moves by emigrant relatives might not be known in Ireland for years, if ever. Not until the mid–nineteenth century did Irish-American newspapers, such as the *Boston Pilot,* publish "missing friends" columns to assist new arrivals to locate relations. In the 1790s disappointed emigrants such as Thomas Hinds and his wife could only apply for assistance to the few Irish charitable organizations in America's seaport cities. By far the most active of these was Philadelphia's Hibernian Society for the Relief of Emigrants from Ireland, founded in 1790 by members of the city's Friendly Sons of St. Patrick and motivated primarily by the idealism and energy of Mathew Carey (1760–1839), the Society's secretary between 1790 and 1800.[1]

---

1. For additional biographical data on Mathew Carey, see chapters 44 and 63; more petitions to Carey as the Hibernian Society's secretary can be found in chapters 34–37.

Like Thomas Hinds and his lost son, Carey had been a member of Dublin's artisan classes—a journeyman printer, bookseller, and radical newspaper publisher before 1784, when he fled to Philadelphia to avoid official prosecution for his seditious editorials, one of which specifically blamed the plight of "50,000 starving [Irish] manufacturers" on Ireland's "damning connexion with Britain." Thanks to Catholic migration from the Irish countryside, by the late eighteenth century Ireland's capital was no longer a "Protestant city."[2] However, Dublin's guilds of skilled tradesmen remained wholly or largely Protestant, although increasingly apprentices and journeymen were Catholic, as was Carey himself. The Hinds family probably belonged to the Church of Ireland, but in the late 1700s, as most southern Irish industries declined in the face of British competition, both Protestant and Catholic artisans were compelled to seek advancement abroad, often in American seaports. This may have been especially true in a small industry like brass manufacturing, where entry was tightly controlled by the exclusive practices of master craftsmen. After emigrating in 1770, Thomas Hinds's son probably worked in one of pre-Revolutionary Philadelphia's several small brass foundries, whose workers marched on 4 July 1788 to celebrate the

---

2. For demographic data on Dublin city, see appendix 2.2b, on chapter 14. See Rowe, *Mathew Carey*, 15; see Sources.

ratification of a Constitution that created a national government able to pass tariff laws to shelter American manufactures. However, Hinds may have departed the city by then, for the glut of British imports in the mid-1780s may have left him unemployed and spurred his migration to Kentucky—which in turn later obliged his elderly and impoverished parents to apply for assistance to Carey and the Hibernian Society.

Thomas Hinds, Philadelphia, to Mathew Carey, Philadelphia, 30 June 1795

Sir

I make bold a Second time[3] to Bring my Self to your view telling you I am a Native of Ireland where I had a Son bound to a brass founder & from the Cruelty of his master (who probably you may know) he came to this country in the Year 1770   he Settled Some years in this City And Carried on Said Business   he wrote Several inviting Letters to me to come hither   I co.[d] not then come <and> Rested Satisfied & Determined to come hither when I could,   I accordingly with my Wife came with Captain Gaddas of the Ship General Washington and to my utter Ruin & disapointment I found my Son was gone to live in the Western country to a Town called Paris or Bourbon in Kantucky and by his absence am left without friends or Money   I am therefore to Request to know if you think me Entitled to any Relief from the Hibernian Society as it is my fate in this very dear[4] Country to come under the Exact condition of the Emigrants mention'd in the Rules of the institution   I should be p<er>fectly Satisfied to Reimburse any primary relief I might receive as I only mean to be Subsisted till my Sons arrival who was in this town 6 or 8 Months ago & Sold a Waggonload of fir[5] of Wild beasts for 7,000 dollars,   I only mention this to Shew you or give Some room to think 'im[6] Rich & able to take care of me if I co.[d] once See[7] 'im   I wrote to 'im a month ago and I am informed another month may bring me an answer or 'imself in person which is the most likely   if your good father or mother were here they w[d] leave nothing in their power undone to Serve my wife who lived 7 years with the Rev[d] Doctor Dabzack at Rathmines[8] near Dub<lin>: with a Reliance on you good Sir I am Your Most Respectfull & most devoted H<um>ble Serv[t],

Thomas Hinds

30th of June 95

---

3. a Second time: Hinds's first petition to Carey has not survived.   **4. dear:** expensive.   **5. fir:** i.e., fur.
6. 'im: him.   **7. See:** meet up with and talk to (OED, s.v., 12.a,b).   **8. Rev[d] Doctor Dabzack at Rathmines:** Rev. Henry Dabzack, D.D. (Trinity College, Dublin, 1792); probably of French Huguenot, Alsatian, or German Palatine descent; Church of Ireland clergyman in Rathmines, then an independent village south of Dublin; and Regius Professor of Greek, modern history, and laws at Trinity until his death in 1790. Mrs. Hinds's former association with Dabzack indicates she and her family were Anglicans, but she herself may have been a convert from Catholicism, as well as a servant, as suggested by the alleged relationship between her and Carey's parents.

No doubt Carey, who had served his own Dublin apprenticeship under "a hard, austere master of the most repelling manners,"[9] was sympathetic to the Hinds's plight, for without certainty as to their son's whereabouts, it is unlikely an aged and poor couple could have traveled over six hundred miles inland. Thomas Hinds cannot be traced in Philadelphia's directories, so it is likely he went west to search for his son, but neither can be identified with certainty in early Kentucky records. In 1785 the Virginia legislature had created Bourbon County, in the heart of Kentucky's Bluegrass Region, and in 1790 had established the county seat variously known as Bourbonton or Paris—thus justifying Thomas Hinds's confusion as to its name. Despite nearly constant warfare with the Indians, in the late 1780s and early 1790s the Bluegrass Country grew rapidly, thanks to infusions of Philadelphia capital and of settlers—called "Tuckahoes" if they came from eastern Virginia or "Cohees" if they were Scots-Irish from west Virginia, Pennsylvania, or the Carolinas.[10] By 1790 at least a fourth and perhaps a third of Kentucky's seventy-four thousand inhabitants were of Irish birth or descent. Land hunger inspired most migrants, but the territory's numerous corn mills and whiskey distilleries also needed the skills of artisans such as the younger Hinds.

The Hinds family's apparent absence from Kentucky land, tax, and other records is not surprising. Although promoters touted the central Bluegrass plain as "the Canaan of the West," Bourbon County epitomized both the fluidity and the growing inequalities of western life. Well before 1792, when Kentucky became a state, a few wealthy grantees—mostly scions of Virginia's gentry—had already engrossed the best lands for speculation or hemp plantations. In the early 1790s two-thirds of Kentucky's household heads were landless, and by 1810 Bourbon County's planter élite had quadrupled the local slave population, which in turn so curtailed employment for free craftsmen and laborers that in 1800 the village of Paris had merely 377 inhabitants, only nineteen more than in 1790. And in 1794 the Whiskey Rebellion brought political turmoil to the area, while in 1801 the great Cane Ridge revival, only a few miles from Paris, shattered established denominational boundaries. Thus, the former Dublin artisan had not merely left his craft and, temporarily at least, lost his parents, but had entered a world of shifting occupations, political loyalties, and even religious identities—a world in rapid transition from the open and abundant frontier

9. Rowe, *Mathew Carey*, 11.   **10. Cohee** (Coohee, Kohee, Quo'hee): inhabitant of the Shenandoah Valley and elsewhere in Virginia west of the Blue Ridge Mountains; derived from the phrase *Quo he*, a shortened form of *quoth he* "said he"; see F. G. Cassidy, *Dictionary of American Regional English* (Cambridge, Mass., 1985–), s.v. The term was once very frequent in Scots and Ulster Scots narrative speech but is now obsolescent (*Scottish National Dictionary*) and mostly derogatory, indicating that the person so designated is a bumpkin; see C. I. Macafee, *A Concise Ulster Dictionary* (Oxford, 1996), s.v. *quohee*: "they're nothing but oul' gossips—quo-hein and quo-shein all nicht." **Tuckahoe**: inhabitant of eastern Virginia; derived from the name of a root that the Indians in the Virginia Tidewater ground and baked into bread; see OED, s.v., 2, and the citation given there: "[The Blue Ridge] divides the Ancient Dominion into two nations, called Tuckahoes and Quo-hees, the former inhabiting the lowland"; P. H. Nicklin, *Letters Descriptive of the Virginia Springs* (Philadelphia, 1835), pp. 16–17).

of hunters and trappers to the settled society of planters and lawyers who increasingly monopolized the region's resources.

Yet there is tantalizing evidence that the younger Hinds may have tried to achieve a degree of social stability and, perhaps, political patronage by ingratiating himself with Kentucky's propertied "friends of order." For it is possible that Thomas Hinds's lost son was the William Hinds who in July 1794 enlisted (and in October reenlisted) in the Kentucky militia to help suppress the Whiskey Rebellion—a possibility enhanced by the likelihood that a combination of religious background (probably Anglican) and a fur trader's links with Philadelphia's Federalist merchants may have predisposed the younger Hinds to support national authority against backcountry defiance. However, if that record suggests Hinds's commitment to Federalist standards of order and hierarchy, another reflects frontier fluidity and instability, for in 1844 an elderly Mrs. Hinds, an early settler in Paris, Bourbon County, complained that her unnamed husband had long since "went off & left her w[ithou]t any reason whatever." Indeed, if the younger Hinds really was engaged in the fur trade, as his father believed, it is not unlikely that by 1795 or thereafter he had moved even farther westward, following the retreating "Wild beasts," and thus further complicating his parents'—or any abandoned wife's—efforts to find him.

15 ✳

George Crockett, Jr., 1797–1807

If Thomas Hinds's petition illustrates the danger of breakdowns in transatlantic communication, the following letters by George Crockett, Jr., of County Donegal and Gallatin, Tennessee, demonstrate how ambitious emigrants could guide and reconstruct prosperous family settlements in the New World.

By at least the 1720s the fertile parishes of east Donegal, on the west bank of the Foyle River, were a major source of Presbyterian emigration that continued and perhaps accelerated after the American Revolution. From the mid-1700s the region's low rate of population increase, especially among Protestants, suggests that the Foyle valley's tenant farmers early adopted impartible inheritance and emigration to keep their holdings intact and economically viable.[1] Certainly they did not limit the size of their families. George Crockett, Sr. (d. 1829), who farmed 75 acres in the townland of Drumnashear, in Killea parish and Raphoe barony, a few miles upstream from Derry city, had at least 10 children, six of whom emigrated to the United States between 1796 and 1817.[2] In 1830 the Crockett

---

1. For demographic data on Killea parish and its environs, see appendix 2.1a, on chapter 15. 2. George Crockett of Drumnashear and his wife, [Catherine?] Gamble, married about 1766 and had at least the following children: (1) George, Jr. (ca.1767–1848), subject of this chapter; (2) James (1768–ca.1855), on whom see chapter

FIGURE 5
Painting of George and James Crockett's family home at Drumnashear, Killea
Parish, County Donegal. Photograph courtesy of James Crockett, Heversham,
Cumbria, England, and the late Mrs. Elizabeth Reeve, Orient Point, New
South Wales, Australia.

property, rented from Sir Robert Ferguson, was valued at £66.12s. and included a substantial two-story stone farmhouse. Clearly, in the time of George Crockett, Sr., the holding was prosperous enough to provide at least some of his children with superior educations, passage money and startup capital to those who emigrated, and apprenticeships, dowries, and money to purchase tenant-right[3] for those who stayed at home.[4]

Between 1796 and 1811 five of the sons of George Crockett, Sr.—George, Jr., James, William, David, and Robert—came to America, and in 1817 a sister, Eliza, went to Baltimore but died of fever a year later. In 1796 the two oldest brothers, George, Jr., and James,

27; (3) John (ca.1770–1825); (4) Samuel (ca.1772–1806); (5) William (b. ca.1775); (6) David (b. ca.1780); (7) Robert (ca.1785–ca.1855); (8) Eliza (ca.1790–1818); (9) Alexander (b. 1794); and (10) Catherine (b. ca.1796). **3.** "Tenant-right": under the so-called Ulster Custom, a sum of money given by a new tenant (or the landlord) to the former occupier or lessee, ostensibly to compensate the latter for the improvements he had made on the farm during his tenure but in reality to enable the new occupant to secure peaceable possession of the holding, i.e., to secure the former tenant's "good will." Outgoing tenants often used the money to finance their families' emigration to North America. **4.** Of the children of George Crockett, Sr., who remained in Ireland, Alexander married a cousin, Sarah Gamble, in 1819 and took control of the family farm; Samuel became a sadler in Derry city; Catherine's dowry of £80 plus "a good featherbed" enabled her to marry another Gamble cousin, James; and John took over a small farm at Edenmore, Co. Tyrone, on the east side of the Foyle, whence some of his own sons later emigrated, joining their uncles in Tennessee in the early 1830s.

emigrated—yet did so separately, to Baltimore and New York, respectively. Perhaps they were estranged by family disagreements over James's marriage, perhaps by George having received a superior education—as his letters (comparatively free of Ulster Scots dialect) indicate. At any rate, the distance between them increased in America, for all the brothers but James followed George to Tennessee and settled there at least temporarily, drawing in their wake various cousins and nephews from Ireland or Baltimore.[5]

Prior to the American Revolution members of the Drumnashear Crockett family and their Gamble, Fulton, and Donaghy relations had emigrated to the colonies.[6] As we have shown, intergenerational links among families such as those of Moses Johnston, John Dunlap, and Margaret Wright transcended the conflict of 1775–1783 to facilitate subsequent departures.[7] However, the Crockett kin who left Ireland in 1796–1811 formed their own networks that linked more closely with the migrations that followed the Napoleonic Wars than with those that had preceded the Revolution. The Crockett brothers' letters provide exemplary evidence of this renewed outflow, as they detail family and kinship connections in migration and settlement over time. They describe efforts, especially by George, Jr., to rebuild a family "plantation" through interlocked business enterprises in Tennessee, but they also reveal the fragmentation of family fortunes as the Crockett kin responded more or less successfully to the opportunities and perils of an early nineteenth-century American capitalism that sifted them into distinct groups of the advantaged and the ordinary, of the settled and the impermanent.

Ulster obligations to siblings and other relatives ("friends" in Irish usage) provided help and starts but did not confine kinsmen to exclusive or disadvantageous partnerships. For instance, as an ambitious entrepreneur, George, Jr., did not seek out his long-settled but apparently poorer relations in rural western Pennsylvania[8] or in backcountry North Carolina—where, he complained, markets were too remote and the local Scots-Irish communities too crude and egalitarian. Instead he first settled near Baltimore and worked with more recently emigrated and more upwardly mobile cousins, such as David Fulton, Jr., an innkeeper, and his brother, John Fulton, who had already explored even greater opportunities in Kentucky and later moved there.[9] In 1797 George, Jr., likewise believed his future lay in "Caintuckey" or in the Cumberland country of Tennessee, linked as they were by

---

5. On James Crockett's American career, especially as a farmer in Pennsylvania, see chapter 27.   6. No known connection exists between these Crocketts and the famed David Crockett (1786–1836), whose Ulster-born grandfather in 1771 fled with the defeated Regulators from North Carolina to eastern Tennessee, where he was killed by Indians during the American Revolution. On the North Carolina Regulators, see chapters 54 and 57.   7. See chapters 4, 6, and 11.   8. For example, one relative, Samuel Alexander, was listed merely as a "renter" in the 1798 and 1802 tax lists of Westmoreland Co., Pa.   9. According to the Crockett letters, David and John Fulton were sons of "old David Fulton," who married a sister of George Crockett, Sr., emigrated to America in the late 1780s or early 1790s, and settled in Cecil Co., Md., near Baltimore. David Fulton, Jr., migrated to Tennessee before 1817, engaged in trade and banking in Nashville and Gallatin, and died in Florence, Ala., in 1829.

navigable rivers to New Orleans and thence to eastern seaports, with dynamic economies thus better suited to advance men of "good conduct and behaviour."

The letters of George Crockett, Jr., are almost wholly concerned with inseparable material and familial concerns. Largely absent are the religious reflections and political strictures that explained or justified emigration for so many of the Presbyterians who left Ulster in the 1790s. Yet northeast Donegal had long been a source of educated religious leadership for America's Scots-Irish—first by Francis Makemie (ca.1658–1708), later by Francis Alison (1705–1779)[10]—and in the 1810s Crockett's own cousin, also named George, and the latter's business partner, David Park, played prominent roles in building the Cumberland Presbyterian Church in Nashville, Tennessee.[11] After their own moves to Gallatin, Tennessee, George, Jr., and his brothers apparently also became Cumberland Presbyterians, thus abandoning their father's strict Calvinism for a new church that rejected the doctrine of predestination; however, they were not as active in religious affairs as their Nashville cousin, perhaps because they were less affluent.

Nor, with one exception, were the Crockett brothers ideologically engaged by political issues, either Irish or American. During the 1790s east Donegal's Presbyterians were disaffected to the Crown and to the Anglican establishment. However, most were not as actively disloyal as their coreligionists in east Ulster, perhaps because they were more apprehensive of east Donegal's Catholics, whose proportion of the region's inhabitants increased between 1766 and 1831 from about a third to nearly half and who comprised a growing majority of the entire county's population.[12] Thus, although what another east Donegal Presbyterian decried as political "oprestions . . . & imposisions"[13] may have conditioned the decisions of George, Jr., and James Crockett to emigrate in 1796, such discontents did not inspire rebelliousness at home but rather their urge to seek prosperity and religious harmony under what the former called the "happy and unparalleled Constitution" of the United States. Once in America, George adjusted easily to the dominant political

---

10. Francis Makemie: born of Scottish parents near Ramelton, Co. Donegal, ca. 1657–1658; attended the University of Glasgow from 1676; licensed to preach in 1681 or 1682 by Co. Donegal's Laggan Presbytery, which in 1682 sent him to minister to the Scots-Irish emigrants on the eastern shores of Maryland and Virginia, where he formed churches at Rehoboth and Snow Hill, among others; during the next two decades Makemie became the largest landowner in Accomack Co., Va., but also performed exhausting labors as a missionary in North Carolina, Pennsylvania, and Barbados; in 1706 he took the leading role in forming the first American Presbytery. Makemie was involved in several major religious and political controversies, in 1692 with Pennsylvania's governor, George Keith, and in 1707 with New York's governor, Edward Hyde, Lord Cornbury, who arrested him for preaching without a license; Makemie's acquittal in the subsequent trial is celebrated as a milestone in American legal and religious history. On Francis Alison, see chapter 55.
11. George Crockett of Nashville, cousin of George Crockett, Jr., of Gallatin, was born in Co. Donegal during the late 1780s, the son of William Crockett, a brother of George Crockett, Sr., of Drumnashear. The Crocketts' Cumberland Presbyterian Church was established near Gallatin, Tenn., in 1810, by Scots-Irish clergymen who refused to subscribe to the Westminster Confession of Faith.   **12.** See appendix 2.1a, on chapter 15.   **13.** James Steele, Tops, Raphoe Parish, Co. Donegal, to Ephraim Steele, Carlisle, Pa., 19 April 1796.

culture and, unlike more radical Presbyterian emigrants, in 1797 he echoed Federalists' fears that the French would invade the United States as well as Ireland.[14] Only his youngest brother, Robert, who in Irish adolescence had imbibed French revolutionary and United Irish ideals, would later in America avow strong anti-British sentiments and upbraid his father for opposing Catholic emancipation: "Was it because their property was confiscated in times of Old that you are affraid they would try to get back their just dues[?]" he asked.[15] By contrast, George, Jr., apparently shared his father's pragmatism, and so the events in Ireland of 1796–1797 only increased his urgency to plan his kinsmen's emigration and relocation in the New World.

Letter 1.

George Crockett, Jr., Cabarrus County, North Carolina,

to George Crockett, Sr., Drumnashear, Killea Parish, County Donegal, 2 June 1797

Captⁿ Paul Phifers   Cabarrus County   June 2^d 1797

Dear Father   I write you these few lines to let you know that I am in good health hoping that they will find you and all the rest of my friends in the same, When I wrote you last Cousin John Fulton and I intended to go Westwardly but upon later considerations we came Southwardly into the State of North Carolina where I now am, Cousin John being gone to the Northward to bring out more goods and I have the care of the store until he returns,   There was a Man pas<s>ed here about the first of January last who (according to the description he gave) told us that he had seen My two Uncles Samuel Al<e>xander and Al<e>xander Donaughey,[16]   the<y> live westward in the State of pensilvina at a place caled redstone old fort on the

<hr>

14. By contrast, see chapters 62–64.   15. Robert Crockett, Gallatin, Tenn., to George Crockett, Sr., Drumnashear, Co. Donegal, 23 December 1825. Such "truly Republican views" (same, Nashville, Tenn., to same, 3 February 1825) were more safely expressed in America than in Ireland, but Robert Crockett's political sentiments were typical of many Scots-Irish emigrants of the early nineteenth century who became ardent Jeffersonians and Jacksonians. Hence the passage in his letter of 23 December 1825 is worth reading in full: see appendix 3. ¶Significantly, Robert Crockett did not share the evangelicalism that later swept many Scots-Irish into the Tory party in Ulster and the Whig party in the United States; for example, in 1830 he opposed a Presbyterian petition asking Congress to ban Sunday mail delivery, arguing that "People must become holy by persuasion, not by force." However, by this time Crockett was fully aware that his political opinions (he condemned the Orangemen as a "disgrace") were too "severe" for his correspondents in Protestant Ulster, most of whom had "ceased to wright" (Robert Crockett, Nashville, Tenn., to his brother, Alexander Crockett, Drumnashear, Co. Donegal, 18 January 1830). Thus, in his later letters (1837–1850), written when he was old, half-blind, palsied, and financially dependent, Crockett tempered his political reflections as he angled to return to his brother's home in Drumnashear, where he died about 1855.   16. Samuel Alexander: see n. 8; probably the Samuel Alexander who in 1778–1783 was a member of the company of Westmoreland Co. frontier rangers captained by William Guthrie, second husband of the unfortunate Elizabeth Brownlee (see chapter 22); in 1783 Samuel Alexander of Westmoreland Co. owned no land but had two horses, two cattle, and three sheep; in 1786 his tax assessment of 8s. was one of the lowest in Derry township. Alexander Donaughey could not be located in Pennsylvania records.

Monongahelio River,[17]   he was to return he said some time in April, when Cousin John and I both intended to write to my Uncles by him, but we have not seen him since therefore we had no opportunity,   I have been informed since I came to this part[18] of two men of my name that lived about forty miles from here one Robert and the other Al<e>xander Crocket[19] who according to every account must be my Grandfathers two Brothers,   Roberts sons lives here yet   I had an opportunity of sending them a few lines by a neighbour of thers informing them according to the best of my recollection who I am and that I expected they were my friends,[20]   Shortly after[21] I received a letter from one of them informing me that according to the account that I gave of my people he was fully satisfyed I was his friend as every instance I mentioned agreed with what he had heard his father say of his friends in Ireland. He gave me an invitation to go and see him   I sent him word that I could not make it convenient[22] untill C<ousin> John would return and then if it was in my power I would, which I intend to do. Al<e>xander never Maried but the old men <are> both dead. The Crockets here I am told are very respectable people and of tolarable good circumstance as much so as any in this part, but people here are nearly on an equality one with another scarsely any distinction amongst them except what is acquired by good conduct and behaviour which is a thing very much taken notice of in this Country,   This is not a good part fore tradsmen of any kind as almost every Man makes out[23] to do his own buisness so that they are all tradsmen but in fact there is hardly a right[24] workeman amongst us,   neither is it very good for Laborers   the most of that Buisness is done by Negros and those that has none contents themselves by raising as much crops as will support their familyes,   as for Rent it is entirely out of the question here and the Taxes are but trifling but the distance of Market is a great inconv<en>ience to this part,   Land here is low but it is not reckoned so good as upon the westeren waters[25] away by Cumberland and Caintuckey but there it is got to be purty high where it is any way improven[26] or well watered,   this is avery healthy

---

17. **redstone old fort on the Monongahelio River**: Redstone Old Fort (later Brownsville): a fortified Scots-Irish settlement established in 1765–1770 and situated on the east bank of the Monongahela River, at the junction of Redstone Creek, in Fayette (formerly Westmoreland) Co., in southwestern Pennsylvania; population ca. five hundred in 1795. In 1781 the 23 congregations in this region were organized into the Presbytery of Redstone.   18. **Part**: (here and elsewhere in Crockett's letters) place, neighborhood, area. Standard English prefers the plural **parts** in this meaning.   19. **Robert . . . Crockett**: In the 1790 census for Salisbury District, Mecklenburg Co., N.C., Robert Crockett is listed as head of a nonslaveowning family comprised of two males (one under 16 years) and seven females, living near an "Archabeld" Crockett whose family owned two slaves; both families were also present in the 1800 Census. No **Alexander Crockett** could be located.   20. **friends** (here and elsewhere in Crockett's letters) relations.   21. **after**: afterward.
22. **I could not make it convenient**: I could not find a time that was convenient.   23. **makes out**: manages, contrives, succeeds.   24. **right**: proper.   25. **waters**: rivers and the adjacent habitations (northern British usage; OED, s.v., 12.c,d); here refers to the **westeren** (western) settlements along the Ohio, Tennessee, and Cumberland rivers and their tributaries, west of the Appalachians, that flow ultimately into the Mississippi.
26. **improven**: improved (Scots form).

THE PROCESSES OF IRISH EMIGRATION

part and very good water here nearly as good as any I have seen in Ireland,   Our public prints[27] has given us several accounts of the French making a descent upon England and Ireland but that the<y> were in every attempt disapointed   however the<y> have not laid aside their plan of invading you   Now I think from the dread of a foreign Invasion with the internal commotion of the Country that you must live in the utmost disqui<e>tude   these considerations induces me to wish that all my friends were in this Country   here we enjoy the blessing of peace in its fullest purity under our happy and unparalleled Constitution,   We have had some apprehensions of a rupture with France but that seems to be dying away and I hope it will come to nothing,   The French if they invade us may expect a purty stiff opposition as the[28] people here are very unanimous and very much exasperated against them,   There is no prejudice or partiality reins in the breasts of individuals respecting Religion here   every man is regarded according to his merit   if hes a clever fellow his Religion is never called in question nor is it the least obstacle to his holding any office or trust whatsoever,   I have not heard one word from my Brother James since I came to this Country nor is there any chance of getting any untill one of us finds out where the other is,   I wrote twice to cousin Thomas Crocket desireing him if he got any account of him or Cousin James when he wrote to let me know but I rec^d no ans<we>r nor I dont expect to hear from him untill he or I by means of your Letters find each other out,[29]   I live at Captn Phifers[30] Cabarrus County State of North Carolina about 500 Miles South of Philadelphia and 20 of Salisbury on the great Road leading to Charlestown.[31] Cousin David Fulton lives now in Baltimore keeping Tavern   you direct your Letters to his care and you can inform Brother James to do the same and any of my Brothers that comes over can by directing to him soon give me word but this is not the part I would recommend for them to come to,   the North and west is much better,   I add no more at present but with love to my Mother Brothers and Sisters and all my friends I remain your affectionate Son

George Crocket

NB[32]   I can not conclude without repeating what I mentioned in my last that if Brother John is still single I would recommend him to raise what money he could and

---

27. public prints: newspapers.   **28. they** ms.   **29. find each other out**: discover each other's whereabouts. **30. Captn Phifer**: probably Martin Phifer, captain of a company of North Carolina Light Horse Cavalry in 1777–1880; the Phifers were of German descent; large numbers of German immigrants settled in and around Salisbury in Mecklenburg Co., which in 1764 was represented in the colonial Assembly by an older Martin Phifer and in 1776 at the state constitutional convention by John Phifer, who also signed the famous Mecklenburg Declaration of 20 May 1775.   **31. Salisbury**: seat of Rowan Co., just north of Cabarrus Co., in southwestern North Carolina; the town's population in 1797 was ca. 560. **the great Road**: formerly an Indian trail, from the 1730s the Great Road (sometimes called the Great Path or the Irish Road) was a highway of Scots-Irish and other migrants who moved south by stages from Pennsylvania's Cumberland Co. through western Maryland and Virginia's Shenandoah Valley and into the backcountries of North and South Carolina. **Charlestown**: Charleston, S.C.   **32. NB**: *nota bene;* lit. "note well," i.e., "take note of, pay attention to the following"; often employed in correspondence as the equivalent of "P.S." (postscript).

leave that crowded place hes in and as I said before if he and Brother James and William were to stick togeather they might soon fix themselves on a good plantation[33] back on the western waters where the land is good, which might be an introduction[34] to all the Family   Most of <the> people living in a country place here are at a great loss for want of Education   <a> great many of our best farmers can scarsely wright their own name and as to figures they <k>no<w> very little,   Therefore you ought to endeavour to make the young boys as good Scholars[35] as possible as a man of good Learning or a treadsman can not be at a loss in this Country

your affectionate son

George

By 1807 George Crockett, Jr., had moved to Gallatin, in Sumner County, Tennessee, and his ambitious plans were coming to fruition. Hugh Rogan, Sumner County's pioneer trader, had moved there from Donegal during the American Revolution; after the war his letters and his visit home in 1796–1797 may have drawn the Crocketts and other west Ulstermen to the Cumberland Valley.[36] However, George, Jr.'s immediate reason for migrating to Tennessee was his business association with Major James White of Abington, Virginia. First as White's employee, then as his partner, Crockett helped establish a trade in cotton and other goods that linked Gallatin with New Orleans and Baltimore. Meanwhile, around 1805 his brothers William and David came to Baltimore and New York, respectively, where both worked in the leather trades. Late eighteenth-century Irish methods of tanning and currying leather were innovative, and Ulster emigrants like the Crocketts found ready markets abroad for their expertise in this hard and dirty but profitable trade. George himself invested substantial sums in a large tanning yard at Gallatin, and later David and William left the East Coast and migrated there to finish and market George's leather goods, thus enabling him to dissolve his partnership with White. Finally, in 1811 cousin George Crockett emigrated and settled in nearby Nashville.[37] Accompanying him to America were Robert Crockett, the youngest brother of George, Jr., and a cousin, George Culbert; they were also tanners, and in 1812–1815 they too joined George, Jr., in Gallatin, as did yet another cousin, Thomas Culbert.[38] All this was prefigured in George of Gallatin's letter home of early 1807, when already he was predicting "a handsome

---

33. plantation: farm, especially in a newly settled area.   **34. introduction**: the meaning seems to be a place that would attract emigrating family members, where they could stay while getting acclimated to the new country, and that would provide a secure base from which they could launch their American careers. **35. Scholars**: students, pupils.   **36.** Hugh Rogan (1747–1814) was from Glentourne, Co. Donegal; after emigrating in 1775 he worked as a weaver in North Carolina before 1780, when he joined James Donalson's expedition to the Cumberland and became a legendary Indian-fighter; returned to Donegal for his wife and son in 1796–1797; settled on 640 acres in Sumner Co., where he constructed a one-story limestone dwelling, "Rogana" (which still stands), to the precise dimensions of a Donegal farmhouse. Rogan was a devout Catholic, and his farm was the center of Catholic devotions in the area until a church was built in Gallatin during the 1840s.   **37.** See n. 11.   **38.** George and Thomas Culbert were the sons of [John?] Culbert and a sister of George Crockett, Sr., of Drumnashear.

business in this place" and was "making arrangements" for his kinsmen to share and expand his enterprises.

Letter 2.
George Crockett, Jr., Gallatin, Tennessee, to George Crockett, Sr., Drumnashear, Killea Parish, County Donegal, 29 January 1807

Gallatin   Jany 29th 1807

Dear Father

You no doubt by this time begin to conclude that I am no more,[39] or that I have forgotten you, but be assured its by no means the case, although I can give no excuses that would be satisfactory to you why I have not been more mindfull of my duty, as you may with justice Suppose that no engagement whatever aught to divert my mind or take my attention So much as to make me forget my obligations to you,   I must therefore plead guilty and endeavour to make amends in future,   Spring last I left Abingdon[40] and came out to this place (Cumberland) w<h>ere I Started with a Boat loaded with Cotton (37000 lb) and went down with it to New Orleans a distance of a bout 1300 Miles from where I first took water on Cumberland River,   I Sold the Cotton at New Orleans and went by water round from thence to Baltimore and had the pleasure of doing the whole buisiness very much to my employers (Maj^r White) Satisfaction   Maj^r White and me formed a partnership before I left him and I on coming to Baltimore purchased an Assortment of Goods and brought them out to this place in (Cumberland in the State of Tennessee) where I now do business under the firm of White & Crocket   I laid in about 10000 Dollars worth of Goods have made tolerable good Sales So far, and I make no doubt in time to do a handsome business here in this place,   the great dificulty in doing business here is the distance we have to go to market   The produce or staple commodity of this Country is Cotton which has all to be taken to Orleans and we have about 750 Miles to waggon our goods from Baltimore here,   this is I Suppose the richest Country for Land in America   it is Settling very fast and I think will in Some time be the richest Country in the world in every respect,   Brother William & Cousin Thomas Culbert have been in Baltimore now about 16 months working at the Currying Business and are now compleat in that Branch,[41]   I am making arrangements for their establishing a Tanyard in this place which I expect to accomplish in the course of next Season at farthest,   I also expect to have Brother David established in his business here,   David writes me he is in very good employ at new york,   I have this day received a Letter from Cousin John

---

39. **no more**: deceased.   40. **Abingdon**: the seat of Washington Co., in the Allegheny Mountains of southwestern Virginia, about ten miles north of the Tennessee border; population 250 in 1795 and 362 in 1800. 41. **compleat in that Branch**: fully accomplished in that skill.

GEORGE CROCKETT, JR.

Crocket (Uncle Williams Son) informing me of his Arrival at new york and that he was not likely to fall into business there   I have therefore wrote him to come immediately out to me and I would either give him employ my self or get him in with Some other Merchant in this Country,   but if he thinks proper to live with me he may, as I expect from the opportunity he has had he must be purty Smart at Business or at least I can Soon make him acquainted with it,   your last letter to me informed of Mothers indisposition   I Sincerely hope She has got over it or Should it pleased[42] God to have taken her to himself I trust your good Sense enabled you to bear the Shock with becoming fortitude and that you Still find consolation in what of your family Still remains with you,   as you are now become old you aught not to expose yourself but make the Boys attend to all the out business,[43] whilst you at home in the Society of the girls may have all your cares lull[d] to rest and Spend your last days in harmony and ease,   I have heard of Brother Samuels death but never had any certainty of it[44] but Cousin John can now inform me   I was truly Sorry to hear it as I knew you and Mother had both formed pleasing hopes of him but I have Still Some hope that it is not the case,   Should it be so we have only to be resignd to <the> great author and it is very striking how little difference it makes as to the Situation a person may be placed in, as I have Since I left you been exposed to many climates and could you often times have Seen me you would have thought me in great danger but thank God I am now in as good health and I believe a Stronger man than ever you Saw me   remember me to all my Brothers and Sisters and all our friends and let me know the Situation of your own family in every part   in hop<e>s this will find you all well remains your affectionate Son

George Crockett

direct your letter to me Merchant of Gallatin[45] Tennessee

For the energetic George, Jr., family reconstitution and good business were closely linked. His own success in Tennessee was symptomatic, as was that of cousin George Crockett of Nashville, who became a prosperous trader and banker in the state capital. By 1810–1820 almost a third of Nashville's leading businessmen were Irish born, as were many lesser traders. Like the Crocketts of Gallatin, most were merchant middlemen, with full title to the goods they transshipped and traded both wholesale and (in general stores) retail. Specialization secured markets and cut costs but few achieved it; dependence on their own small banks, or those of their networks of friends, was thus vitally important, albeit often precarious, especially after the financial panic of 1819. At first in concert, the two George Crocketts built up merchandising and banking networks, employing both Robert Crockett

---

42. Should it pleased: i.e., should it have pleased; shows the frequently occurring loss of a, the unstressed variant of **have** (should it have pleased → should it a pleased → should it pleased). See chapter 1, ns. 22 and 84, and chapter 2, n. 10.   **43. the out business**: the outdoor work.   **44. any certainty of it**: any sure facts about it (OED, s.v. certainty; expression obsolete).   **45. Lallatin** ms.

and George of Gallatin's cousin and brother-in-law, David Fulton, Jr., from Baltimore. After dissolving his business ties with White, George, Jr., made Fulton his partner, and around 1819 the two began to engage in branch banking. By 1822 Fulton had left Gallatin and become treasurer of their more affluent cousin George's Nashville bank; he continued, however, to assist George of Gallatin, who partnered another bank with General James Winchester.[46]

Politics also helped these Ulster immigrants, as Scots-Irish family factionalism merged with nascent Jacksonianism. In 1815 William Fulton, the brother of David, Jr., first came to Sumner County, then went to Nashville to study law with Andrew Jackson's partisan, Felix Grundy,[47] and in 1818 served as Jackson's private secretary during the Seminole campaign. The liberal state banking law of 1817, which allowed petty banks, originated in such circles. Later in 1835 the Gallatin connections helped persuade President Jackson to appoint William Fulton as territorial governor of Arkansas.[48] Ironically, however, as the Crocketts and similar families rose, the Irish share of Tennessee's population was probably shrinking, as in nearby Kentucky, from about one-third in 1790 to only one-fourth by 1820. Thus, George of Gallatin had established his little plantation at precisely the right time, when Ulster Irish influence in the Cumberland region was still at its height.

Ultimately, however, Gallatin failed to fulfill its early commercial promise. In the era of steamboats, Gallatin lacked the river frontage and the political advantages that made Nashville prosperous yet was too close to the capital city to dominate its own trading hinterland. In 1830 Gallatin had merely 666 inhabitants (234 of whom were slaves), while Nashville had 5,566, and in 1834 the former had only 12 stores compared with the capital's 79. The advent of railroads only increased Nashville's lead: by 1850 that city had 15,000 inhabitants and Gallatin merely 1,050. As a result, before his death in 1848 George of Gallatin's affluence never equaled that of his Nashville cousin and namesake, who boasted "The Mansion" as his address and whose children enjoyed society weddings. Yet by 1830 George of Gallatin had achieved at least modest prosperity. He and his wife, cousin Mary

---

46. James Winchester (1752–1826): born in Carroll Co., Md.; captain in the Revolution, after which he moved to Sumner Co., Tenn., settled on a plantation, "Cragfont," near Gallatin, and engaged in trade, banking, and politics; brigadier general in the War of 1812 but suffered total defeat at Frenchtown, Mich., on 22 January 1813; active in town promotion in early Memphis.   47. Felix Grundy (1777–1840): celebrated criminal lawyer, jurist, and politician, initially in Kentucky, from 1806 in Nashville, Tenn.; elected to Congress, 1811 and 1813, as a "war hawk"; promoted debtor relief after the Panic of 1819, in opposition to Andrew Jackson with whom he had an ambivalent political relationship; U.S. senator, 1829–1838 and 1839–1840; President Van Buren's attorney general, 1839.   48. William Savin Fulton (1795–1844): born in Cecil Co., Maryland, where he received a classical education; served in the War of 1812, after which he migrated to Tennessee, studied law with Felix Grundy, and practiced in Gallatin until he joined Jackson in the Seminole War of 1818; afterward, with his brother David, Jr. (see n. 9), he moved to Florence, Ala., where he edited the *Florence Gazette* and served in the state legislature; appointed by President Jackson as secretary of the Arkansas Territory in 1829 and as its last territorial governor in 1835; when Arkansas was admitted to the Union in 1836, Fulton became one of its first U.S. senators; he died in office.

Ann Fulton,[49] whom he married in 1815 when she was 18 and he perhaps 45, had a large family and ran a still larger household, for he owned and hired out several slaves.

George's brother William, a Gallatin tanner, was also sufficiently affluent to own slaves. However, the two brothers' children had very different careers, illustrating how the boom-and-bust capitalism of the late Jacksonian era, punctuated by the Panic of 1837, could disperse family members and differentiate their achievements. George's oldest son and namesake became the partner and legal adviser of Colonel A. R. Wynne,[50] who flourished in hotel, slave-trading, wholesaling, horse-raising, and merchandising businesses in the Gallatin area; George's daughters Catherine and Eliza also married into these prosperous connections. In contrast, by 1850 William's sons had disappeared from all save family concern: one of them became a migratory farmer, eventually settling in Texas, another a Mississippi steamboat engineer, a third a Gallatin carpenter, and the last a farmer in Missouri.[51] Likewise, George's idealistic brother Robert had little success and worse health in Tennessee, and he eventually returned to die in Ireland. Finally, brother David Crockett remained in Gallatin only about five years before moving his family to Ohio, where by the late 1820s he had vanished from Crockett family correspondence and knowledge.

Perhaps David—like his older brother James, who never visited Tennessee but took up farming in Pennsylvania—preferred to be independent of the patronage of George, Jr. Or perhaps, like some Ulster Presbyterians, he simply disliked slavery for moral or economic reasons. However, the "Southern" orientation of the family's most enterprising and ambitious members was well established. Between 1815 and 1833 a new generation of nephews and cousins, Crocketts and Culberts, came out from west Ulster to Gallatin and Nashville and proved at least moderately successful, demonstrating how the processes of chain migration and mutual aid could survive and flourish far beyond the initial phases of emigration and settlement.[52]

---

49. Mary Ann Fulton was a daughter of "old" David Fulton and a sister of David Fulton, Jr., and of William Savin Fulton, territorial governor of Arkansas in 1835–1836 (see ns. 9 and 48).   50. Alfred Royal Wynne (1800–1893): born in Wilson Co., Tenn.; son-in-law of James Winchester (see n. 46), whose business and political connections helped Wynne prosper in slave-trading and other enterprises, despite Wynne's notoriously careless habits.   51. William Crockett's sons were: George W., who died in Texas in 1880; Thomas of Mississippi; William Nariah, who remained in Gallatin; and John, who went to Missouri.   52. For example, about 1832–1833, after their father's death in Ireland, Richard and George Crockett, sons of John, brother of George, Jr., emigrated to Tennessee, eventually settling in Benton, Miss., near their cousin Thomas, the steamboat engineer who was the son of William of Gallatin, brother of George, Jr.

III ✻
Farmers and Planters

16 ❈

John Blake, 1675–1676

During the seventeenth century, most of the few Irish migrants to the New World were Catholics from southern Ireland: primarily indentured servants, laborers, and craftsmen who ventured to the West Indies, accompanied by a small, affluent minority who established plantations and mercantile concerns in Barbados, the Leeward Islands, and Jamaica. No letters or memoirs of the impoverished and illiterate majority of seventeenth-century Irish settlers and sojourners survive, but the following documents, penned in the late 1670s by John Blake, merchant and planter in Barbados and Montserrat, may represent the earliest extant transatlantic correspondence by Irish emigrants.

John Blake was the third son of John Blake fitz Nicholas (d. 1680–1681), one of the most prominent members of the "Galway Tribes": 14 merchant families, all but two of Norman descent, that had comprised the ruling oligarchy of Galway city and its environs from the late thirteenth century onward. Of the Tribes, the Blakes were probably second in wealth and importance only to the Lynches, with whom they were linked—as also with the Bodkins, Brownes, Darcys, Frenches, Kirwans, Martins, and Skerretts—through a complex web of marriage alliances. Fiercely proud of membership in an "auncient English femilie" that had lived in Galway for hundreds of years "without chandge of language, manners or habit," the Blakes held themselves aloof from Connacht's native Irish and Hibernicized Norman families, such as the O'Flahertys and the Clanricard Burkes, and prospered by trading in hides, wool, wine, and salt with England and the European continent. Despite their Catholicism, the Blakes and their kinsmen grew even wealthier during the Reformation: in the late sixteenth and early seventeenth centuries they expanded into banking and into North American commerce, trading Irish provisions for West Indian and Chesapeake tobacco; they purchased, leased, and took mortgages on vast estates in Galway and adjoining counties; and they sent their sons to London to gain the legal training and court influence that the Tribes used to thwart royal and Protestant challenges to their property titles and privileges.

In 1639 John Blake's father was elected to the Irish Parliament for the borough of Athenry; in 1640 he proved the validity of his ancient title to the Kiltullagh estate in east Galway, thus frustrating the crown's confiscatory designs; and in 1646 he was elected lord mayor of Galway city. However, the Irish rebellion of 1641 and the subsequent conflict among the royalists, the Catholics allied in the Kilkenny Confederation, and the English parliamentary forces proved disastrous. Most of the Blakes and other Tribesmen remained loyal to Charles I and only reluctantly and belatedly joined the Confederation. However, after Oliver Cromwell's army captured Galway in 1652, Catholics were expelled from the city, and in 1655 the Commonwealth's Irish commissioners confiscated John Blake fitz Nicholas's ancestral estate as well as his urban property, compensating him with—and in 1656 transplanting him to—the smaller property of Mullaghmore in the barony of Tyaquin. The return of the Stuart monarchy in 1660 did not restore Blake to his lost estates. However, in the late 1660s the Tribes were permitted to return to Galway city and resume their mercantile careers, and during the next several decades the Blakes, Lynches, and others struggled to restore their position by purchasing or leasing country estates and by rebuying their town holdings from the Protestant grantees of the 1650s. Thus, it was to recoup their family's fortunes, as well as to establish their own economic independence, that in about 1668 John Blake fitz Nicholas's three younger sons, Henry (d. 1704), John, and Nicholas (d. 1693), emigrated to the West Indies.

Little is known of Nicholas's activities during his brief sojourn in the Caribbean, but soon after their arrival John and Henry Blake purchased a sizeable plantation, probably between five hundred and one thousand acres, in St. Anthony's parish on Montserrat, one of the smallest and least developed of the Leeward Islands. Until 1676 Henry resided in Montserrat, managing their property, while John lived in Bridgetown, the capital of Barbados, and engaged in trade. The Blake brothers joined a large and varied Irish Catholic population in the West Indies, led by a handful of affluent planters and merchants—including numerous cousins and brothers-in-law from Galway—but dominated numerically by thousands of bonded laborers and of small farmers and craftsmen who had survived their indentures. Settled from the 1620s, the English colonies in Barbados and the Leewards had always been a receptacle for Irish indentured servants and a magnet for smaller numbers of free Irish migrants; in addition, during the Cromwellian period, at least several thousand Irish Catholic prisoners, "rogues," and "vagabonds"—many of them from Galway—were forcibly transplanted to the islands.[1] In 1678 the Irish comprised 70 percent of Montserrat's 2,682 white inhabitants, more than a third of the whites in Barbados, and between 10 and 26 percent of those in St. Christopher, Antigua, and Nevis. However, conditions in the islands were extremely harsh, especially for poor Irish servants and laborers: mortality rates were astronomically high; males overwhelmingly outnumbered females; and the tremendous expansion of sugar cultivation at the expense of tobacco and indigo (in Barbados after 1640, in the Leewards after 1670) resulted in the consolidation of plantations and massive slave imports, which reduced the availability of land and work for freed servants. In addition, bitter hostility between English and Irish settlers, and between landowners and servants, generally, engendered harsh repression and periodic rebellions. Indeed, the initial Irish settlement of Montserrat in the early 1630s stemmed from the efforts of St. Christopher's governor to cleanse his island of disloyal and turbulent "papists." Likewise, it was an uprising of Irish servants that in 1667 enabled the French to conquer Montserrat. The French occupation was brief but devastating to the island's planters, many of whom lost their slaves and fled to Jamaica, never to return. Probably it was their consequent distress—

---

1. Estimates range as high as 6,400 Irishmen, women, and children shipped by Cromwellian officials to Barbados between 1651 and 1655; in addition, in 1655 Henry Cromwell, his father's lord deputy in Ireland, authorized the shipment of two thousand Irish boys and girls to Jamaica, although it is uncertain how many were actually sent.

plus encouragement by William Stapleton, the Tipperary-born governor of Montserrat (1668–1671) and later of all the Leewards (1672–1685)—that enabled John and Henry Blake to purchase what was probably an abandoned plantation.

Both Blake brothers left wives and children in Ireland, where they intended to return after paying their debts and amassing sufficient capital to purchase Irish estates. In 1673–1675 Henry Blake's letters mainly concern such payments, usually made in the form of shipments of tobacco and indigo handled primarily by his eldest brother, Thomas, a merchant in Galway town. Thus, when harrassed by importunate creditors who threatened "to come hither & discredit me," Henry declared, "I doe not care for them, for I thanke God, I carryed meselfe soe honest & civil theise years I live here that they nor 100 more of them can doe me any hurte; I tould long since to the Generall & best of these partes, that my liveing here was to recruite my greate losses whereby I should be enabled to pay my debts at hoame, which I am ready to doe according to the statutes & customes of this countrey, which is noe discredit in theise p[ar]tes of the world, as long as a man complyeth honestly in his dealings here."[2] Henry also provided assistance to kinsmen who came to the West Indies, and he sent remittances to Galway to finance his children's education and to succor his father, who in 1675 was struggling to hold onto Mullaghmore despite a cousin's "tiranicall usadge and uncharitable proceedings."[3] Yet, despite these drains on his income, Henry managed to squeeze "a good plentifull liveing" out of the Monsterrat plantation,[4] and by spring 1676 he was ready to return to Ireland—as had brother Nicholas a year earlier.

Brother John, however, had apparently been less successful in Barbados. Despite—or perhaps because of—his "very greate creditt for his honesty," John Blake struggled to get "cleere of the dutch"[5] merchants whose illegal trade, in collusion with corrupt English officials, dominated West Indian commerce in the late seventeenth century. Perhaps he struggled as well to keep up a genteel appearance on an island where, by the 1670s, fabulous wealth was concentrated among a few English planters and merchants whose lavish hospitality and "Sumptous Houses" were exceeded only by their rapacity and disdain for Irish Catholics. By 1675 it appears that John Blake was resigned to permanent residence abroad, as he arranged for his wife[6] to join him in Barbados—accompanied by an Irish servant woman whose reputation for promiscuity gave brother Henry great concern: "I am very much troubled for that whore (as I am credibly informed) come out along with my Brother John's wife," wrote Henry to Thomas in Galway; "I am afraide she may be the occasion of his confusion by her seducem[t]. I pray God preserve him."[7] In the following letter, written after his wife's and her servant's arrival in Barbados, John Blake strove to

2. Henry Blake, Montserrat, to Thomas Blake, Galway, 22 July 1673.   3. John Blake, Mullaghmore, Co. Galway, to Henry Blake, Montserrat, 8 January 1675.   4. Henry Blake, 22 July 1673.   5. Henry Blake, 22 July 1673.   6. The name of John Blake's wife is unknown. The only woman with that surname listed in the Montserrat census of 1677–1678 was Honora Blake, but she was then resident on a neighboring plantation. 7. Henry Blake, Montserrat, to Thomas Blake, Galway, 29 May 1675.

explain his household arrangements—the unsavory appearance of which may have helped persuade Blake's relatives to keep his young son in Ireland.

Letter 1.
John Blake, Bridgetown, Barbados,
to Thomas Blake, Galway, County Galway, 1 November 1675

Bridge in Barbados, 1st Nob^r 1675.

Deare Brother

Yours of the 26th of Augst last I have on the 28th ultimo[8] rec^d. I am glad you rec^d the moneys mentioned in your s^d[9] letter;   Seeing that yourselfe and nearest relations are against the sending hither of my sonne I doe willingly submitt to your better judgements   wherefore let him remaine there of whom I most earnestly intreat you to be most carefull and to see him decently provided with all necessaries for which purpose I will not from time to time faile to remitt you moneys by the way of London. Mr Nicho. Lynod the schoole master at Mace[10] hath written me that he would be very kind to him for which cause if you & my father in law will thinke it convenient let him remaine under his tuition; for whom is one of the incloseds[11] to whom pay plentiefully what you will think fit, that he may be the more encouraged to take paines about the childe: the inclosed for my s^d Father in law peruse and reseale I pray you, and deliver it if you can with your owne hands. I am very glad of my brother Nicho. and nephew Martin's safe arrival: To my Father and mother I pray you remember me and my wife, whose blessings I most humbly crave; as likewise I pray you remember my kind love to Father Daniell.[12]   The wench come over along with my wife; I am most sensible what my brother Henry hath written me heretofore of her as likewise what you intimated p.[13] your s^d letter, to which I say that though I find her as yet most vitious[14] lesse here perhaps deterred through the most severe correction I keepe her under yet because of s^d bad reports I would not at all abide her under my roofe but I thereunto am as yet inevitably compelled by reason[15] my wife being as I find her[16] of a very weake constitution cannot discharge[17] all herself; for washing starching making of drinke and keeping the house in good order is no small taske to undergoe here;   if I would dismisse her another I must have which may prove tenne times worse than her; for untill a neger wench I have be brought to knowledge[18] I cannot considering my present charge[19] be without a white maid. I hope all will doe

---

8. **ultimo:** of last month (here = October).   **9. s^d** (here and elsewhere in Blake's letters): said.   **10. Mace:** there are two townlands in Co. Galway named Mace: (1) in Moyrus parish, Ballynahinch barony; and (2) in Annaghdown parish, Clare barony.   **11. incloseds:** enclosures.   **12. Fr. Daniell:** a Catholic priest in Galway. **13. p.** (here and elsewhere in Blake's letters): per; probably written as ꝑ in the original ms.   **14. vitious:** vicious "having bad habits."   **15. by reason:** because.   **16. as I find her:** "as I consider her."   **17. discharge:** acquit oneself of, perform.   **18. be brought to knowledge:** "be trained."   **19. present charge:** "my present responsibilities, all the things I have to do at present."

well for I have as much peace and tranquilitie in my house as any one in the world can desire for which the Lord of heaven be for ever praised. Trading groweth dayly here worse and worse, onely that provitions now and then, as now it is,[20] <are> very scarce and deare; vizt beefe sold at 35^s p. barr: and some new beefe lately come in at 40^s p: barr: which prices I am sure will long continue because provitions doe now beginne to come in from New England and some few from Bermudos. If you could at any time send hither 10 or 20 barr: or more of good beefe and finding freight at a moderate rate you may expect thereby reasonable profit. The last Hurricane we had here which was on the last day of August last hath at least by a third part made this Island worse than it was,   God Allmightie grant us patience. My wife remembered herselfe very kindly to you and to my sister your wife, and so doth,   being all at present

Your most faithfull brother and serv^t
John Blake.

I am exceeding glad to heare of my daughter's improvement which I hope through the innocencie of her mother God Allmightie will dayly increase, to which purpose her father's dayly prayers will not be wanting. I pray you remember my most humble service to[21] your worthy brother Mr James Blake to whom I am most thankfull for his kind letters to myselfe and wife: his nephew Thomas the Lord be praised doth enjoy very well his health whereof I was most fearefull because of the thinnesse of his complection but he doth well as afores^d and doe not doubte under God but he will prove in time a sufficient[22] man. I pray you likewise acquaint our cousin Francis Blake fitz Martin that I will send his letter to me to my brother Henry who I am sure will not willingly wrong him or anybody else, for his honest dealings are, the Lord be praised, well known to the world.

On 11 May 1676 John Blake purchased Henry's half of their plantation for 106,889 pounds of sugar—then valued at more than £445—and prepared to settle in Montserrat, as he relates in his second and last surviving letter to Galway. Blake's decision to leave Barbados may have been prompted entirely, as he wrote, by lack of sufficient "imploym^t" in Bridgetown, but there may have been other reasons as well. As Blake related, in August 1675 one of the worst hurricanes in Barbadian history destroyed most of the capital and many plantations on the leeward side of the island. Moreover, in the same year a slave rebellion, in which planters suspected Irish complicity, worsened Anglo-Irish relations and may have persuaded Blake to seek security in an island dominated by his Catholic countrymen. Blake also may have decided that his wife's fragile health would improve in Montserrat, whose mountainous terrain was far more salubrious than "hot, humid, and

---

20. **as now it is**: "as is now the case."   21. **remember my most humble service to your worthy brother**: "remind your worthy brother of my most humble expression of respect" (that is, "convey my respects to your worthy brother").   22. **sufficient**: competent, able; as in Shakespeare, *Othello*, 3.4.88: "Come, come, you'll never meet a more sufficient man."

airless" Bridgetown. And, if Henry's fears of his brother's "seducem^t" had been realized, John Blake's *ménage à trois* would be safer from censure on a remote frontier island than among the pretentious gentry of "little England."

Letter 2.
John Blake, Bridgetown, Barbados,
Thomas Blake, Galway, County Galway, 28 July 1676

Bridge in Barbados, 28 July 1676.

Deare Brother

My last unto you was on the 14th of x^{br}23 last by the way of London since which I did till now forbeare to trouble you with any unnecessarie lines;   yours of the 17th of Feb. last with its inclosed acc^t I have rec^d. For your great care and paines taken about my children I am to you infinitely beholden for which I render you all possible thankes: I hope God Allmightie will reward your great charitie extended towards me and mine the continuance whereof I most earnestly begge. I have p. this convenience ordered my correspondent at London by name Nathaniell Bridges to remitt you £25 sterl. towards the reliefe^{24} of my children which is little enough; but this our present croppe proving so extreame bad as it doth and my purchasing of my brother Henrys share of the plantation that was in halves betweene us at Montserrat, hindered me from sending a larger reliefe according to my ardent desire, for which I am exceedingly grieved; however by sending any more than the said summe I cannot otherwise help myselfe at present. I hope God Allmightie will for the future enable me to provide more plentifully for them, which to bringe to passe, my utmost industrie will never be wanting: here inclosed is a couple of lines from Mr Carpenter^{25} according your desire;   to my honoured Father and mother I pray you present my must humble dutie^{26} whose blessings I most humbly crave   whom be pleased to acquaint that my wife and myselfe doe injoy very well our healths, for which the Lord of Heaven be ever praised. To my Father I would have written but that I am loathe to trouble him with the perusall of frivolous lines, whose sight I most vehemently long for, which if I had competent meanes to remove from hence I would quickly attempt to injoy; in the meantime I must have patience: the inclosed for my sister Mary I pray you cause to be delivered and the inclosed for my brother Henry who is homeward bound I leave open^{27} that you may understand of^{28} part of my grievances. If further imploym^t will

---

23. x^{br}: October.   24. reliefe: relief "financial assistance, aid."   25. Probably William Carpenter, owner of estates in Ireland, Barbados, Montserrat, and Antigua, who sold his West Indian property and returned to the British Isles in August, 1675.   26. present my humble dutie: "convey my respects"; see remember my most humble service (in the foregoing letter).   27. open: unsealed.   28. understand of: "get a proper idea of, form the correct interpretation of."

not come upon me more than now I have, I am resolved as soon as I can discharge myself from hence,[29] to remove for Montserrat and there to settle myselfe for some years to ye end I may in time gaine something for to bring me at last home. My wife remembered herself most kindly to you & to your wife my sister, to whom & to her Reverend Parents and her brothers James and Patricke I pray you present my most faithfull love & service: your nephew Thomas is well in health, who I hope will doe well in time,   being all at present from

Your most faithfull Brother & humble serv^t
John Blake

In 1678 Henry Blake used his West Indian earnings to buy a six-hundred-acre property at Lehinch, County Mayo, and two years later he purchased from the Earl of Westmeath an estate of at least five thousand acres at Renvyle, near Letterfrack, in west County Galway, thus reestablishing, albeit on much poorer land than the Cromwellians had confiscated, the fortunes of a family that would dominate much of Connemara through the late nineteenth century. As for his brother John, whether from jealousy or resentment over the "grievances" alluded to in his 1676 letter, apparently he rarely or never communicated with Galway after his removal to Montserrat. However, John Blake seems to have prospered there with the rise of sugar cultivation. Between 1675 and 1700 the amount of sugar shipped from Montserrat to Britain increased from 2 million to 29 million pounds, and Blake became a member of the local oligarchy, lording it over both his slaves and the island's Irish-speaking white majority, much as his Norman ancestors had done in County Galway. Blake's plantation, still known today as John Blake's Village, on the slopes of George's Hill in east-central Montserrat, was located in the parish that had the richest soil on the island, and in 1677–1678 his work force comprised 38 male slaves—almost a quarter of those in the area. Despite penal laws that restricted office-holding to Anglicans, during the early 1680s Blake served as a member of Montserrat's legislative assembly (as assembly speaker in 1681) and of the Leeward Islands' general council. In 1684 he astutely (and perhaps sincerely, given his family's traditional loyalties) signed governor Stapleton's address to Charles II, congratulating the king on his "deliverance" from the "Popish Plot" of 1678–1679—a fictitious conspiracy, but one that brought severe persecution to leading Catholics in Ireland.

John Blake died in Montserrat around 1692 (his will was dated 18 September), leaving £1,000 and his plantation to a daughter, Catherine, who had married Nicholas Lynch, probably a cousin, who owned sugar estates on St. Christopher and Antigua. By 1745 the nucleus of Blake family wealth in the West Indies had been transferred to those more fertile islands, while the firm of Blake & Lynch became one of the great London commission houses in the sugar trade. Despite Galway's rapid decline as a transatlantic port, in the

---

29. discharge myself from hence: "get clear of my responsibilities here."

early eighteenth century these links continued to draw Blakes and other young Tribesmen to the West Indies—with a "few letters of recommendation and a genteel transportation," as one planter complained[30]—and the Galway interest remained the largest Irish connection in the Caribbean, extending by the mid-1700s even into the French, Dutch, and Spanish islands. However, between 1678 and 1713 the white population of the Leewards fell from 10,408 to only 7,311, while the number of slaves rose from 8,449 to 23,500; likewise, on Montserrat between 1678 and 1730 the number of white servants declined from 1,600 to merely 90 as the number of slaves increased from 991 to nearly 6,000. Thus, the advance of sugar and slavery made the West Indies increasingly unattractive for ordinary Irish emigrants and indentured servants as well as for the early Irish settlers' Caribbean-born children, who directed their ambitions to the North American mainland—to Maryland, for example, where the Catholic Bodkins established tobacco plantations, and to South Carolina, where as early as the 1670s the Moores (O'Mores) and other Anglicized Irish families had led remigration from Barbados.

17 ✳

Samuel McCobb, 1729–1772

Since the late seventeenth century, small numbers of Ulster Presbyterians had trickled across the Atlantic, settling primarily along the banks of the Cheasapeake. However, the first "great wave" of Ulster emigration sailed to New England, led by Presbyterian clergymen from the Bann and Foyle valleys, who anticipated—wrongly, as it transpired—a friendly welcome from fellow Calvinists in Massachusetts. Between 1718 and 1720 about forty vessels from northern Ireland disembarked at Boston perhaps 2,600 Scots-Irish migrants, most of them farmers with families and some capital. Despite their relative affluence, they met a hostile reception from Puritans who regarded them as "foreigners," confused them with "papists," and feared that the "confounded Irish will eat us all up" as provisions were already "most extravagantly dear & scarce of all sorts." Most of the newcomers left Boston as soon as possible, in search of farmland. A substantial minority of the 1718 arrivals went to Maine and spent a miserable winter at Casco Bay before moving south in spring and establishing what would be New England's most successful Scots-Irish settlement at Nutfield, later Londonderry, New Hampshire.[1] The rest scattered throughout New En-

---

30. From L. M. Cullen, "Galway Merchants in the Outside World, 1650–1800," in D. Ó Cearbhail, ed., *Galway: Town and Gown . . .* , 70; see Sources.   1. On the Scots-Irish in Londonderry and Bedford, New Hampshire, see chapters 49 and 59.

gland, but Puritan hostility prevented most from founding Presbyterian churches or discrete communities that could attract later migrants.

As later in Pennsylvania and South Carolina, however, the Massachusetts government was eager to plant colonies of Scots-Irish and other settlers on the frontier, as a buffer against attacks by the French and Indians. During the seventeenth century, Boston officials and land speculators had encouraged perhaps six thousand farmers, fishermen, and timber workers to locate along the coast of the province's "Eastern parts" of Maine, but most of those settlements had been wiped out or abandoned between 1689 and 1713, during King William's and Queen Anne's wars. After the Treaty of Utrecht (1713), efforts to resettle the area intensified, and although the government's attempt to plant Casco Bay with the Scots-Irish who arrived in 1718 was unsuccessful, by 1720 agents for various proprietary companies had located about one hundred families, most of them Ulster Presbyterians, on the east side of the Kennebec River and around Merrymeeting Bay. But again, between 1722 and 1725 a local conflict with the "eastern Indians" raged along the Kennebec, and by the end of the decade few settlers remained.

In 1729 an Irish-born adventurer, David Dunbar, arrived in Maine as surveyor general of the King's Woods (delegated to protect New England's white pine forests for the royal navy) and with a vaguer commission as governor of the territory between the Kennebec and the St. Croix rivers. It is uncertain whether Dunbar was an agent of those who wanted to expand the recently conquered colony of Nova Scotia southward, preempting Massachusetts's claims to Maine, or whether he aspired to create a new, separate province called "Georgia." In either case, Dunbar began to recruit Scots-Irish migrants—both newcomers from Ulster and earlier, dissatisfied settlers from elsewhere in New England—to settle the Pemaquid region, particularly the peninsula and islands between the Sheepscot and Damariscotta rivers, far to the northeast of any existing settlement. Dunbar was bold and energetic: ignoring the fact that at least eight proprietary companies, based in Massachusetts, already claimed the Pemaquid region, he laid out two-acre townlots in a coastal settlement he named Townsend and granted ample farmlands, on generous terms, to attract colonists; he also built a fort, manned with soldiers from Nova Scotia, to protect the settlers against both the Indians and Massachusetts's outraged officials and land speculators. By 1731 nearly 20 Presbyterian families, all direct or indirect migrants from Ulster, had settled in Townsend.

Unfortunately, the Pemaquid district, as its settlers later testified, was "a howling wilderness, . . . an inhospitable desert, in the midst of Savage beasts, and yet more savage men":[2] the vast pine forests, that grew almost to the water's edge, were dark and forbidding and provided easy cover for Indian attacks; the soils along the narrow coastline were thin and stony; and the winters were long and bitter, permitting a growing season that was a full month shorter than that of southern New England. Far worse, however, was the

2. Petition of the Inhabitants of Boothbay [1774], in J. P. Baxter, ed., *Collections . . .* (1910), 166; see Sources.

fact that Dunbar had greatly exceeded his authority and angered powerful interests in Massachusetts, whose agents in London secured his dismissal in late 1731 and confirmed the Bay Colony's ownership of Maine. In 1732 both Dunbar and the soldiers in Fort Frederick withdrew from the Pemaquid, abandoning the Scots-Irish settlers in Townsend. A few of the families also migrated elsewhere, but most remained to struggle, without assistance, against climate, soil, Indians, and incessant harrassment from rival claimants, backed by Boston officials, to their lands.

This deposition by Samuel McCobb relates the story of the Scots-Irish inhabitants of Townsend, grudgingly incorporated as Boothbay by the Massachusetts general assembly in 1764—with the reservation that "incorporating them as a Town is not to be understood to give countenance to any Persons claiming property in said lands."[3] Born in 1707, probably near Strabane, County Tyrone,[4] in west Ulster, McCobb emigrated from Londonderry port in 1728, aged 21, with his brother James and a number of Scots-Irish families who apparently intended to go to Philadelphia but instead, for some unknown reason, disembarked at the mouth of the Kennebec and settled at Arrowsic, Maine. Despite his youth, in 1729–1730 McCobb and his brother were instrumental in persuading many of the Arrowsic settlers to accept Dunbar's inducements and move northeast to Townsend. There Samuel McCobb settled on one hundred acres at Lobster Cove and built a log house with a thatched roof. About 1738 he married the daughter of a fellow settler, and they had nine children[5] who intermarried with the Beaths, Fullertons, McFarlands, and other families who had come with him from Ulster in 1728 or, in the case of the Beaths, had emigrated in 1718, temporarily settled in Massachusetts, and later remigrated to Townsend at Dunbar's and McCobb's behest. If nothing else, the Pemaquid district's climate and social isolation proved remarkably healthy, for McCobb and most of the other patriarchs among the original inhabitants lived well into the late eighteenth and sometimes even into the early nineteenth century. In 1770–1772 McCobb and several other elderly settlers decided to record their community's experience in the form of legal depositions, no doubt designed to protect them and their descendants against the threat of eviction from "these our Ancient possessions."

3. Although the overwhelming majority of Townsend's settlers appear to have been Ulster Presbyterians, at least a few early families in Pemaquid—such as those of Morgan McCaffrey and Timothy O'Neill—were probably of Catholic origins. From F. B. Greene, *History of Boothbay . . .* , 136; see Sources. 4. According to the 1732 hearthmoney returns, the population of Strabane barony was 49 percent Protestant; on the demographic effects of subsequent emigration from the region, see chapter 11 and appendix 2.1 on chapter 11. 5. Samuel McCobb's wife was Mary, surname unknown. Their children were: William (1740–1815), a successful merchant and shipchandler in Boothbay, who m. [?] Beath; John (1744–1831), an "early merchant in town" who in 1775 m. Mary Beath; James (b. ca. 1746), m. Sarah Allen in 1777; Jean (b. ca. 1748), m. (1) John Fullerton in 1769, and (2) James Carven of Burnham; Frances (b. 1753), m. James Auld; Mary (b. 1753), m. John Auld; Samuel, Jr. (1753–1832), m. Sarah McFarland in 1784; Mary (b. 1753?); David (1757–1805), who in 1776 m. Elizabeth McFarland and inherited most of his father's land at Lobster Cove; and Beatrice, named after her father's mother, who probably immigrated in the 1740s with Samuel McCobb's younger brother, George, and who died in Lincoln Co., Maine, in 1750.

Samuel McCobb, Lobster Cove, Lincoln County, Maine, legal deposition
sworn before Thomas Rice and John Stinson, Justices of the Peace,
Boothbay, Maine, 23 October 1772

Samuel McCobb aged 64 years testifieth and saith,[6] that in the year 1729 Col.
David Dunbar came with a Commission from his most excellent Majesty George the
Second, with Instructions to take possession of and to settle with inhabitants, in Behalf
of the Crown the Lands lying to the Eastward of Kennebeck River in said
Province,   that with a Number of Men and Necessaries[7] he arrived at Pemaquid in
the said year, and forthwith proceeded to Survey and settle Several Towns[8] around,
publickly inviting His Majesty's Liege Subjects to come and settle thereon, promising
them ample Encouragement in the Name of the King his Master.[9]

In Consequence of which Encouragement unto this Deponent,[10] with more than
forty others, <he> applied to the said Dunbar, and by him were brought to and settled
on a certain Neck of Land, bounded on the Sea & lying between the Sheepscutt and
Damariscotty Rivers, the which Lands the said Dunbar had laid out in parallel Lotts of
twelve Rods[11] broad containing two Acres apiece and ordered the Settlers to cast Lotts
for their respective places, which being done the said Dunbar did in the King's Name
and Behalf put them in Possession of Lotts they had respectively drawn, and promised
that on Condition of their building an house Eighteen feet long and clearing two Acres
within the Space of three years, he would give them an Addition of forty Acres in one,
and one hundred in another Division as contiguous to the first two Acres as possible in
fee simple[12] for ever, and likewise to add thereto another division devising to each
Settler any Number of Acres besides, less than one thousand which he should request.
A Number having complied with these Terms, the said Dunbar offered to give them
Deeds of said Lands, but the Execution thereof was delayed and in the year 1733 he
was removed, to New Hampshire.

The lands being naturally broken and poor, & more especially then in their wild
uncultivated State, and the Settlers coming there generally in low Circumstances,[13] and
most of them (as being from Britain and Ireland) utterly unacquainted with the Mode
of managing Lands in that State, little of the necessaries of Life was raised from the
Soil—their whole living depended on cutting firewood and carrying it to Boston and
other Towns more than one hundred and fifty miles from them—hence the Settlers

---

6. testifieth and saith: archaic legal formula typically used in depositions.   **7. Necessaries**: supplies and
equipment necessary to a given task (in this instance, probably including farm implements and seed, as well as
provisions).   **8. Towns**: i.e., townships.   **9.** No paragraph in ms. The original deposition consists of only
three paragraphs, the second of which begins "The lands being naturally broken and poor . . ." and the third
with "These things this deponent testifieth . . . " To improve the readability of McCobb's deposition, the
editors have created additional paragraphs.   **10. Deponent**: person making a deposition (here = McCobb).
11. Rod: 5½ yards.   **12. in fee simple**: in absolute possession, willable to any heir.   **13. in low
Circumstances**: i.e., in an impoverished condition.

lived from the first exposed to the utmost Extremities of Indigence and Distress, and at the same Time in almost continual Alarms[14] from the Savages all around, till in the year 1745 when their Murders and Depredations in their Borders[15] forced them from their Habitations to Seek Shelter in the Westward,[16] where they were Scattered in a strange Country at near 200 miles distance from their homes for four years.[17] In October 1749 as soon as the News of peace reached them this deponent with many of his former Neighbours ventured back to their said Settlements where they had scarce finished the Repairs of their wasted Cottages & Improvements when in a year or thereabouts, the Indians, tho' in a Time of Peace fell on their Neighbourhood, burnt Barns, killed many Cattle, attacked the little Garrisons kept by the People and carried away a Number of Men, Women & Children into Captivity—by this the deponent and his Neighbours were obliged to flee to little Fortresses they had raised for themselves, where they lived and defended themselves, as they might, not daring to look after their Plantations, by which means the little provisions then growing for their Support the next Winter, were chiefly destroyed, whereby when they returned to their places, little better than the Horrors of Famine were in prospect—Many were obliged to live by Clams only which they dug out of the Mud when the Tides were down; thus they subsisted in general till the late War with France[18] broke out, when tho' their Cries were sent up to the Government for some Protection on this Settlement which they still held in the King's Behalf, and from which should they be again driven they knew not where to seek a place of abode, yet no defence or Assistance even to a Morsel of Bread was allowed them, but such as they found for themselves, by Garrisons and Guards of their own where their Families lived in continual Terrors and Alarms from the Savages who ranged the Wilderness all around till the late Peace was concluded when their Settlement increased much by new Comers from the Western Parts—

Thus happily rid of French & Indians they were not long suffered to rest,—for three or four oppisite Setts of Claimers (part claiming by Indian Deeds never approved according to Law and part by pretended ancient Occupation[19] & other Pretexts never justified in Law)[20] at diverse Times came among them, demanding the possession of the said Lands or requiring a purchase for them—these imposing on the credulous Simplicity of some of the Inhabitants by fair Promises and terrifying others with Threats

---

14. Alarms: surprise attacks. 15. their Murders and Depredations in their Borders: their (= the Indians') murders and depredations within their (= the settlers') territory. 16. the Westward: i.e., Massachusetts, New Hampshire, and other Western Parts (hereafter) of New England, all of which lie to the (south) west of Maine, which, from a Bostonian perspective, is "down east." 17. These Indian attacks occurred shortly before, during, and for a time after what the colonists called King George's War (1740–1748), known in Europe as the War of the Austrian Succession. Most of the Townsend settlers fled to Boston, where they subsisted largely on public charity until their return to the Pemaquid. 18. the late war with France: the French and Indian War (1754–1763) in colonial usage, known in Europe as the Seven Years' War.
19. pretended ancient Occupation: i.e., claimed on the pretence of a former/sometime occupation. 20. ms. no parentheses.

of Law Suits for which the poor Settlers were ill provided,[21] so far prevailed that the generality were fain to contract with[22] & buy their Lands from one or another of them, and Some bought of them all successively, and such as have not done So are still harassed by the said Claimers & threatned by each in his Turn with Law Suits, Ejectments if not Imprisonment and Ruin, whilst those of[23] whom they have bought have never done any thing to defend them from competing Claimers, and all have left them to become a prey to whoever comes next.[24]

However by the help of God they continued on their said possessions till the year 1764 when desirous of obtaining the Benefit of Order and the Enjoyment of the Gospel they applied to the General Court of this province and were legally incorporated into a Town by the Name of Boothbay, and tho the Generality of them are yet in very low Circumstances, many in Extreme Indigence, and very few able to raise on their farms Provisions to suffice their Families for nine Months in the year, yet in the year 1765 without any help from the Publick, they at their own Cost and Charge[25] erected a Church, in the year 1766 settled a Gospel Minister and still endeavour to support the Gospel amongst them and likewise to contribute their required part towards the defreying the publick Charges of government, & in all other Respects to demean themselves as peaceable and loyal Subjects of his Majesty King George the Third

These Things this deponent testifieth as facts within his own proper Knowledge having had Occasion to be personally present and intimately interested[26] therein and he declareth that this deposition is not given with any injurious Intent towards any person whatsoever

Samuel McCobb

Given the colonists' unfavorable situation after Dunbar's departure in 1732, it was understandable why only a handful of new immigrants from Ulster—primarily members of the Reed and Murray families from the Glens of Antrim—joined the Townsend settlement prior to the English conquest of Canada in the French and Indian War. After 1760, however, a large number of migrants, including some newcomers from Ulster but primarily Congregationalists of English descent from Massachusetts and New Hampshire,

---

21. ill provided: poorly prepared (i.e., due to straitened circumstances).   **22. the generality were fain to contract with . . .** : "the majority (of the settlers) were willing to make the best of a bad situation and contracted with . . . " (OED, s.v., fain, 2).   **23. of**: i.e., from.   **24.** Indeed, McCobb and his Scots-Irish neighbors often must have wondered if they were still in Ireland. Not only were they harassed over lands, taxes, and church fees by members of an alien, absentee establishment, but also the local agents of their putative landlords, the Kennebeck Proprietors in Boston, were Anglo-Irish middlemen, such as the Norths from King's Co. and the Coopers from west Cork, whose exploitation of the Pemaquid settlers combined the traditional arrogance of the Irish gentry with the parvenu ruthlessness of their Irish Cromwellian ancestors. In 1774–1776, when the Norths and Coopers became wholehearted supporters of the American Revolution, it was little wonder that McCobb and his fellow Scots-Irish in Boothbay were lukewarm at best.   **25. Charge**: responsibility.   **26. interested**: involved.

located on the peninsula—part of a great influx of settlers that increased northern New England's population by some 90,000 by the eve of the Revolution.[27] Between 1764 and 1775 the number of adult male inhabitants of the newly incorporated town of Boothbay rose from seventy-five to nearly two hundred, although as late as 1771 a tax appraiser described nearly 70 percent of the settlement's 98 dwellings as mere "log houses" or "camps." In 1765–1766, as McCobb related, the settlers built a church and persuaded Rev. John Murray (1742–1793), born in County Antrim and educated at the University of Edinburgh, to settle among them. Murray proved an energetic leader, both in the Lincoln County religious revival of 1767 and later in the American Revolution. However, most of Boothbay's Scots-Irish families approached the crisis of 1775–1776 cautiously: after all, their tenuous hold on their properties depended on Dunbar's old grants in the king's name, whereas Boston's patriot leaders included many who claimed competing titles to their farms.[28] In the end, it may have been only the British blockade of the Maine coast, which "cut off all this people from their wonted resources of the necessaries of life, by a total suppression of trade and fishing," as Boothbay's inhabitants lamented,[29] that pushed them into a revolutionary—or at least a defensive—alliance with Boston's radicals against the crown.

Despite the influx of new settlers from southern New England in the late eighteenth century, the old Scots-Irish families remained dominant in Boothbay. For example, the town's revolutionary Committees of Correspondence and Safety consisted largely of McFarlands, Reeds, and McKowns, while Samuel McCobb's eldest son, William (1740–1815), held virtually every town office between 1773 and 1798 and served almost continuously as Lincoln's County's representative in the Massachusetts legislature from 1785 to 1811. Old Samuel McCobb, the last of the original settlers, died on Christmas Day, 1801,[30] having lived long enough to witness the transformation of a starving frontier settlement into a relatively prosperous farming and trading community. However, he did not see the

---

27. Between 1760 and 1820 several hundred Irish Catholics (primarily from south Leinster and east Munster) also settled in Lincoln Co., and by 1790 at least 5 percent of Maine's 96,168 inhabitants were of "native" Irish birth or descent, and at least another 8 percent were Scots-Irish (the highest concentrations of Irish Catholics north of Pennsylvania and of Scots-Irish north of New York); intermarriage between members of the two groups was common, as were conversions to Protestantism among early Irish Catholic settlers. 28. Thus, in 1774 McCobb and his sons and in-laws joined over a hundred Boothbay settlers in a petition to the crown, begging for confirmation of their land titles and reassuring "your Majesty . . . that we are as truly loyal, dutiful, and affectionate Subjects, as any others in your Majesty's Dominions, [and] that we have never taken part in any of the seditious proceedings, for which many in the Provinces have rendered themselves justly obnoxious to your Royal displeasure. . . . [A]s Protestants, decended from Ancestors many of whose lives and fortunes have been sacrificed in the cause of religion and the Royal House of Hanover, and who are still prompt to prove themselves not unworthy to be called their Sons, by standing ever ready to devote our lives to the defence of your Majesty's Royal person, family, and Government; Permit us Great Sire, to cast ourselves, our Wives and helpless little ones, at your Majesty's royal feet . . . and earnestly to beseech your Majesty to take our case into your most gracious Consideration." See n. 2. 29. From F. B. Greene, *History of Boothbay . . .* , 216; see Sources. 30. There is some dispute concerning the year of McCobb's death; local Boothbay historian Barbara Rumsey suggests that he died in 1791.

final resolution of the town's legal problems. Indeed, legal harrassment from agents of competing land claimants escalated after the Revolution, culminating in mob violence (its patterns reminiscent of the Oak- and Steelboys' agitations in late eighteenth-century Ulster) and murder in 1810–1811, when a commission appointed by the Boston government finally disallowed the old land grants and confirmed McCobb's descendants and their neighbors in possession of Boothbay.[31]

18 ✳

Robert Witherspoon, 1734–1780

By 1732–1736 most Ulster emigrants were debarking at Philadelphia or New Castle and settling in the Middle Colonies. However, in those years a significant minority of Scots-Irish, perhaps several thousand, responded to the South Carolina colonial government's inducements and sailed directly to Charleston, where they were the forerunners of a much larger—albeit still secondary—migration from northern Ireland to the Lower South that began in the 1750s and accelerated between the French and Indian War and the outbreak of the Revolution. This memoir by Robert Witherspoon records Ulster Presbyterians' initial settlement on what was then the South Carolina frontier. Although Witherspoon was only six years old when his family emigrated and did not pen his account until 1780, his portrait of the travails of early settlement, of his family's efforts to rebuild a Scots-Irish community in the southern wilderness, and of the religious fervor that informed their labors, appears accurate both in sentiment and in nearly all details.

Robert Witherspoon was a grandson of John and Janet Witherspoon (both b. 1670; m. 1693), Scots Presbyterian weavers and farmers who lived at Biggardie, near Glasgow, until 1695, when, fleeing economic distress and—their descendants alleged—religious persecution,[1] they joined the great Scottish migration to Ulster of 1690–1710 and settled in

31. Ironically, the same conflicts with Massachusetts land speculators that inclined Boothbay's Scots-Irish and other settlers to loyalism in the Revolution's early days would transform them into ardent anti-Federalists in the 1780s and Jeffersonian Republicans in the 1790s and early 1800s. Ironically also, whereas during the 1790s and early 1800s many of western Pennsylvania's Presbyterian clergy employed evangelicalism on the Federalists' behalf and against Scots-Irish Jeffersonian radicalism, on the Maine frontier religious enthusiasm, primarily under Baptist and Methodist leadership, served to inspire or at least morally legitimate Scots-Irish and other farmers' agrarian rebellion against the agents of the Ulster-American land speculator Henry Knox and other members of Boston's Federalist élite. 1. Given the rapid reestablishment of Presbyterianism in Scotland following the Glorious Revolution of 1688, it is difficult to credit religious persecution as a motive for the Witherspoons' migration from Scotland to Ulster in 1695—unless they were radical Covenanters and thus alienated from all secular forms of government. According to W. W. Boddie's version of his memoir, Robert Witherspoon alleged that his grandfather had "a great aversion to Episcopacy" and, "<b>eing one who followed field-meetings, he and some others of his kindred were much harassed by the Papists" during the reign of James II (James VII of Scotland). If Witherspoon's grandfather was a Covenanter, as the reference to "field-meetings" suggests, he would have been "harrassed" by the Scots Protestant bishops imposed on the Church of

Knockbreckan townland, in the parish of Drumbo and the barony of Castlereigh, in what became an overwhelmingly Presbyterian district of County Down. In 1725 their Irish-born third son, James (1700–1768), a weaver and reed-maker, married Elizabeth McQuaid (1705–1777), also from Scotland, and settled at Cunningburn Mills, in the parish of Grey-abbey on County Down's Ards Penninsula,[2] where four of their seven children were born—including Robert, the memoirist, on 20 August 1728. In 1732 Robert's grandparents, albeit aged 62 "again resolved to seek relief from civil and ecclesiastical oppression by removing to" South Carolina.[3] Thus, in 1732, 1734, and 1736, 33 members of the Witherspoon clan, accompanied by kinsmen and neighbors, migrated in three separate voyages from Belfast to Charleston. Young Robert sailed in September 1734, on the ship *Good Intent,* with the largest number of relatives, including his grandparents and parents, and the families of one uncle, David Witherspoon, and a married aunt, Jane Fleming, along with at least 17 other households.[4]

The Witherspoons' emigration was not spontaneous. In the early 1720s John Barnwell (1671–1724), an Irish-born Indian trader and colonial official in South Carolina, had urged London to establish a new line of forts and settlements to secure Charleston against the Indians and their French and Spanish allies. In 1731 the government instructed the colony's new royal governor, Robert Johnson, to implement Barnwell's schemes by establishing 11 scattered townships, each 20 miles square, on various rivers in an inland arc around Charleston, and by inticing Protestant settlers with assisted passages, grants of 50 acres per person, tools, and a year's provisions. Ulster's Presbyterians were offered special encouragement: although officially South Carolina was an Anglican colony, Scots-Irish settlers were granted a subsidized Church of Scotland minister, plus guarantees against intrusions by the established church. The Witherspoons responded to these inducements, advertised widely in Ulster; after all, the entire Witherspoon clan was entitled to a minimum of 1,650 acres, plus town lots, and in fact they received considerably more. However,

Scotland after the Restoration of Charles II (1660–1685), not by Scottish Catholics (a small, powerless minority) or later by James II (1685–1688), who tried in vain to court Scottish (and Ulster) Presbyterian support by extending religious toleration to all but Scotland's most militantly antimonarchical Calvinists. Retrospectively, then, Robert Witherspoon may have tailored his family history to comport with the "official" Scottish and Ulster Presbyterian tradition of eternal conflict with "popery," thus obscuring the religious and political struggles within the Protestant community itself. Also, Witherspoon's rather oblique reference to his grandfather's affiliation with the Covenanters may have reflected a desire to obscure the Covenanters' (and, by extension, his family's) marginal and radical position within Scottish and Ulster Presbyterianism, perhaps especially because Covenanters, generally, rejected slavery on principle and, if they emigrated to America, often refused to participate in the "peculiar institution," whereas the Witherspoons in South Carolina clearly abandoned, if they ever shared, such scruples. **2.** In 1725 Greyabbey parish was in Ards barony, later divided into Lower Ards (including Greyabbey) and Upper Ards baronies. For demographic data on Greyabbey and Drumbo parishes, see appendix 2.1c, on chapters 12 and 10. The citation at the end of the following paragraph is from Greaves, *God's Other Children,* p. 135; see Sources. **3.** Mary Stevens Witherspoon, "Genealogy of the Witherspoon Family" (1894); see Sources. **4.** David Witherspoon (1697–1739); in 1723 m. Ann Pressley (1705–1772); an original elder of the Williamsburg, S.C., Presbyterian church (org. 1736). Janet Witherspoon (1695–1761); in 1715 m. John Fleming (1696–1750), also a founding elder.

despite these provisions, and despite the fact that relatives and friends had preceded them two years earlier, Robert Witherspoon's family found their first months in Williamsburg township—named for William of Orange (William III), Protestant Ireland's putative savior in 1688–1690—a disorienting experience, located as they were in an almost unchartered wilderness along the Black River, over one hundred miles by sea and river from Charleston.[5]

Robert Witherspoon Memoir, Williamsburg Township, Prince Frederick's Parish, South Carolina, 1734–1780

We went on ship-board the 14th Sept and lay wind bound in the Lough at Belfast 14 days.[6] On the second day of our sail my grandmother died and was interred in the raging Ocean which was an afflicting sight to her offspring. We were sorely tossed at sea with storms which caused our ship to spring a leak—our pumps were kept incessantly at work day and night for many days.

Our marriners seemed many times at their wits ends but it pleased God to bring us all safe to land about the first of Dec. Three weeks before christmas we landed in Charleston. . . . There were four of us children David Robt. John and Sarah. Sarah died in Charleston and was the first person burried at the Scotch Meeting House Grave-yard.[7] . . . The inhabitants were very kind and we remained in town until after Christmas.

We were then put on board an open boat with tools and a years provision and one still mill for each family.[8] They allowed each person over sixteen one ax, a broad ax, one narrow hoe. Our provisions consisted of indian corn, rice, wheaten flour, beef<,> pork, rum and salt   we were much distressed in this part of our passage as it was the dead of winter and we were exposed[9] to the inclemency of the weather day and night and what added to the grief of all pious persons on board was the Atheistical blasphemous mouths of our patrons[10]   they brought us up as far as Potatoe Ferry on

---

5. In 1732 Williamsburg was in Craven County, one of South Carolina's four original political divisions. In 1734 the county was divided into parishes; Williamsburg became part of Prince Frederick's Parish, in Georgetown District, until after the Revolution, when its boundaries were redrawn as Williamsburg County. **6.** Our transcript of Robert Witherspoon's memoir is a melding of Mary Stevens Witherspoon's "Genealogy of the Witherspoon Family" (1894), a manuscript in the South Caroliniana Library, University of South Carolina, Columbia, and a published version in the *History of Williamsburg* (Columbia, S.C., 1923) by W. W. Boddie, who purportedly made a "true copy" of the original manuscript, then in the possession of "the descendants of the late Dr. J. R. Witherspoon, of Alabama." Linguistically, the unpublished ms. version of Robert Witherspoon's memoir appears most accurate, but Boddie's text includes important material not found in Mary Stevens Witherspoon's "Genealogy." Significant variations from, or additions to, the ms. version are identified in notes hereafter.   **7.** Rearranged here for continuity, the two sentences beginning **My father brought** appear later in Boddie's published text.   **8. still mill:** probably = still, i.e., distillery. **for each family** from Boddie's text.   **9. ex/exposed** ms.   **10. patrons:** person in charge of a ship or boat; also occurs as **patroon** (OED, s.v. patron, 3; now rare).

Black River, about twenty miles from Georgetown[11] and turned us on shore where we lay in Samuel Commander's barn[12] for some time while[13] the boat wrought[14] her way up as far as the king's tree[15] with the goods and provision—which was the first time a boat ever came up so high. Whilst we lay at Mr. Commanders, our men came up[16] to build dirt houses or rather like potato houses[17] to take their families to. They brought some few horses with them. Through what help they could get from the few inhabitants in order to carry children and other necessaries up, as the woods were full of water and the frosts most severe, it was very severe on women and children. We set out that morning the last of January[18]   some got no further that day than Mr Mc Donald's   some got as far as Mr Plowdens   some to James Armstrongs and some to uncle Wm James'[19]   their little cabins were as full that night as they could hold and the next day every one made their way best they could to their own place. . . . [20]

On the first of Feb 1735, when we came to the Bluff three miles below the King's Tree[21] my mother and us children were still in expectation that we were coming to an agreeable place—but when we arrived and found nothing but a wilderness, and instead of a comfortable home, no other than a very mean dirt house[22] our spirits quite sank and to add to our trouble Our pilot that we had with us from uncle Wm. James left us when he came in sight of the place. Father gave us all the comfort he could, by telling us that we would get all these trees cut down and in a short time there would be plenty of inhabitants so that we could see from house to house   Whilst we were talking our fire that we brought from Ox swamp went out. Father had heard that up the River swamp was the King's tree although there was no path neither did he know the distance, yet he followed up the swamp, until he came to the branch[23] and by that means[24] he found Roger Gordon's place.[25] We all watched him as far as we could see for the trees and then returned to our dolorous hut, never

---

11. on Black River, about twenty miles from Georgetown in Boddie's text.   12. Samuel Commander: Samuel, John, and Joseph Commander were very early Presbyterian or Baptist settlers on the Black River. 13. while from Boddie's text; ms. has and.   14. wrought: worked (common form of the past tense and past participle in Ulster).   15. king's tree (or kingstree): King's Tree: the first village in Williamsburg township; named after an unusually tall white pine, of the sort reserved by law to provide masts for the British navy, on the banks of the Black River.   16. came up: i.e., went up (to the King's Tree).   17. potato houses: small, crude huts for storing potatoes.   18. the last of January from Boddie's text.   19. Mr Mc Donald . . . Mr Plowden . . . James Armstrong . . . and . . . Uncle Wm James: Adam McDonald, Edward Plowden, James Armstrong, and William James emigrated together from Belfast in 1732, in the first of the Witherspoon family voyages. James (1701–1750), of Welsh parentage, in 1725 m. Elizabeth Witherspoon (1703–1750), the memoirist's aunt; in 1736 one of the founding elders of Williamsburg's Presbyterian church and later one of its wealthiest settlers, ranging large cattle herds in the swamps near Kings Tree.   20. Genealogical data omitted here and relocated earlier in the text.   21. On the first of Feb 1735, when we came to the Bluff three miles below the King's Tree from Boddie's text; ms. has When we came to the Bluff.   22. Boddie's text reads found nothing but a wilderness, and instead of a comfortable house, no other than one of dirt. Ms. reads found nothing but a very mean dirt house.   23. branch: stream, brook.   24. means from Boddie's text.   25. Roger Gordon's place from Boddie's text; ms. has Rogers garden. Roger Gordon: emigrated from Belfast in 1732, in the first Witherspoon voyage.

expecting to see him, nor any human being again. After some time he returned and brought fire and we were somewhat comforted. As evening came on the wolves began to howl on all sides   we then feared being devoured by wild beasts, having neither gun nor dog, not even <a> door to our house—how be it we set to work and gathered fuel and made a good fire and so passed the first night.

The next day being a clear warm morning we began to stir about—about mid-day there was a cloud in the South-west attended with high wind thunder and lightening—the rain quickly penetrating through the poles that formed the roof brought down the sand that covered it over in such quantities it seemed to threaten to cover us alive. The lightening flash with the claps of thunder were awful and lasted a good space of time. I do not remember to have ever seen a more severe gust[26] than that was. I believe we all sincerely wished ourselves again at Belfast. This fright was soon over and the evening closed and it cleared up warm and comfortable. The boat that brought up the goods arrived at the Kingstree. The people were much oppressed in bringing their things   as there was no horse there, they were obliged to toil hard, as they had no other way but to car<r>y them on their back. The goods consisted of their bed-clothing chests provision tools pots &c.   At that time there were no roads   every family had to travel the best they could, which was double distance to some for their only guides were swamps and branches. After a time the men got sufficient knowledge of the woods as to blaze paths, so the people learned to follow blazes from place to place.[27]

As the winter season advanced there was but a short time for preparing land for planting—but the people were strong and healthy   All that could do anything wrought diligently and continued clearing and planting as long as the season would admit. So they made provisions for that year.[28]   their beasts were few and as the range was good there was no need of feeding creatures for some time to come.[29]

The first thing my father brought from the boat was the gun<,> one of queen Anne's muskets<,> loaded with swawn shot.[30] One morning while we were at breakfast a travelling oppossum on his way passed the door. My mother screamed out   there is a great bear   we hid behind some barrels at the other end of our hut   Father got his gun and steedied[31] it on the fork that held up the end of the hut and shot him about the hinder parts[32] which caused poor opossum to grin and open his mouth in a frightful manner. Father having mislaid his shot could not give it a second bout, but at last ventured out and killed it with a pail.

Another thing which gave us great alarm was the Indians   when they came to hunt in the Spring they were in great numbers and in all places like the Egyptian locast

---

26. gust: windstorm.   **27. from place to place** from Boddie's text.   **28. All that could . . . for that year** from Boddie's text.   **29. for several years** from Boddie's text.   **30. swawn shot**: swan shot: a large size of shot, originally fashioned to shoot swans.   **31. steedied**: steadied (one of several possible Scots pronunciations). **32. about the hinder parts** from Boddie's text.

ROBERT WITHERSPOON

but they were not hurtful.[33] Besides these things we had a great deal of trouble and hardships in our first settling, but the few inhabitants were favored with health and strength. We were also much oppressed with fear on divers other accounts, especially of being massacred by the Indians, or bit by snakes, or torn by wild beasts, or of being lost and perishing in the woods, of whom there were three persons who were never found.[34]

My uncle Robert,[35] with his second wife and two children, Mary and John, arrived here near the last of August, 1736.[36] He came on the fine ship called the "New-built," which was a ship of great burthen and brought a great many passengers, who chiefly came and settled here and had to travel by land from Georgetown, and instead of being furnished with provisions, etc., as we were, they had money given them by the public.[37] When they arrived, our second crop had been planted and was coming forward, but the season being warm and they much fatigued, many were taken sick with ague and fever, some died and some became dropsical and also died.

About August or September 1736[38] the people began to form into a religious society, built a church[39] and sent to Ireland for a minister, one came whose name was[40] Robert Herron he stayed three years and then returned to Ireland.[41] In the Fall of 1737 my Grandfather John Witherspoon[42] took the rose in his leg[43] which occasioned a fever of which he died. he was the first person buried at the Williamsburg Meeting House which he had assisted to erect.[44] He was a man of middle stature firm healthy constit<ut>ion somewhat bandy-legged had a fair complexion, he was well acquainted with the scriptures—had a voluability of expression in prayer and was a zealous adherent to the reformed protestant principles of the church of Scotland, he had a great aversion to episcopacy—and whoever reads impartially the History of the times of his younger years in Scotland may see that his

33. hurtful: harmful. 34. We had a great deal of trouble . . . three persons who were never found from Boddie's text. After hurtful, the ms. has Besides these things we had great dread of snakes, and of being lost in the woods—of the last there were three persons. 35. The paragraph beginning My uncle Robert is located at this juncture in Boddie's text; it does not appear in the ms. copy in the South Caroliniana Library. 36. uncle Robert: Robert Weatherspoon (1705–1758); in 1736 m. second wife Hester Jane Scott (1716–1756); left a cash estate of £1,000 to his seven surviving children. 37. By 1736 South Carolina's bounty money for Scots-Irish settlers had been exhausted, but Robert Weatherspoon and his fellow immigrants were supported by public subscriptions raised in Charleston. Voyagers arriving in 1737 were forced to beg for funds to move inland. 38. August or September 1736 from Boddie's text; ms. has About this time. 39. religious society: i.e., a Presbyterian congregation. into a religious society, built a church and sent . . . from Boddie's text; ms. has into societies and sent . . . 40. whose name was from Boddie's text. 41. At this point, Boddie adds: The first [i.e. next] call was made out for Reverend John Willson of Scotland, author of the "Mother's Catechism," "A Practical Treatise on the Lord's Supper," and of the "Discourses on the Atonement." However, according to local church records, Rev. Heron (or Herron), who returned to Ireland in 1740 or 1741, was succeeded not by Rev. John Willson (or Wilson) but instead (in late April 1743) by Rev. John Rae from the Presbytery of Dundee, Scotland. Rae died in spring 1761, and between that date and the Revolution he was succeeded by clergymen named [?] Simpson, David McKey (or McKee), Hector Alison, and Thomas Kennedy. 42. my Grandfather from Boddie's text. 43. the rose in his leg: erysipelas. 44. which he had assisted to erect from Boddie's text.

prejudices[45] were not without foundation as it was his lot to live in a time of great distress to the persecuted church in the reign of James 7th of Scotland and second of England. As he was one of those who followed field-meetings some of his kindred and himself were much harrassed by the Papists,[46] yet notwithstanding his younger years were attended with trouble, he enjoyed great peace and tranquility in his after life. Excepting the death of my grandmother, he never knew what it was to part by death in his own family a blessing which few have enjoyed.

About the same time, 1737, my father had a daughter, Elizabeth, that died, aged three years, born at the place called the Bluff, where we lived. . . . <Later it> pleased God—in the last awful epidemic that prevailed in Williamsburg in the year 1749 and 1750, usually called the "Great Mortality," and which had carried off near eighty persons, many of them the principal people or heads of families—to remove by death my elder brother, David, and my sister, Jane, both in the year 1750. My father being then in a very feeble and infirm state of health and unable to attend to his own business, I left my own to take care of his. I remained with my parents until 1758, when, on the 2nd of March, I married Elizabeth Heathly, a young lady then in the eighteenth year of her age, and settled for myself four miles below King's Tree and near the River.[47]

I afterwards removed and settled one mile higher up the River nearer King's Tree, in 1761, and immediately on the public road leading from that place to the Lower Bridge on Black River. Here I had a more comfortable and healthy residence, and here also, I expect to spend the remainder of my days. . . .

My honored mother departed this life on the 22nd day of January, 1777, in the seventy-second year of her age, and was the last surviving branch of the old stock of our family.[48] Of the members of the Old stock of our family I have an opportunity of having a personal knowledge of their lives and deaths. I bear them this testimony. They were servers of God,   they were well acquainted with the scriptures and were much in prayer, strict observers of the Sabbath. In a word they studied outward piety and inward purity. God blessed this settlement at first with a number of godly pious men of which I choose to set down their names. William Wilson, David Allen, Wm. Hamilton, John Porter, Wm. James, Robert Wilson,[49] John James, James McClelland, Robert Paisley,[50] James Bradley, John Turner,[51] Wm. Frierson. My own father, James Witherspoon and my three uncles, David, Robert, and Gavin.[52] These were men of

---

45. predjuices ms.   46. by the Papists from Boddie's text (see n. 1).   47. This paragraph and the following one (including some omitted genealogical data) appear only in Boddie's text.   48. This sentence appears only in Boddie's text.   49. David Wilson ms.   50. Robert Pressly ms.   51. John Lemon ms.   52. William Wilson . . . Wm. James . . . David Wilson . . . and my three uncles, David, Robert, and Gavin: for David and Robert Witherspoon and William James, ns. 3, 18, and 35. Gavin Witherspoon (1712–1773) emigrated in 1732, but the others named came on the 1734 crossing with the memoirist's family. David Wilson (1700–1750) was a 1732 emigrant and husband of Mary Witherspoon (1705–1765), the memoirist's aunt; William and Robert Wilson were his brothers.

great piety and indeed they were men of renown. May the glorious king and head of the ch<urch> for His own glory still ma<i>ntain and keep up men of piety and holiness as a blessing to this place and congregation to the latest posterity is the heart<felt> request of the unworthy scribe.[53]

Witherspoon's memoir indicates how naturally the open-range maintenance of live-stock first emerged in the Carolinas, eventually developing into the "cowpens" system of cattle ranching. In its piety, however, the document fails to suggest the Witherspoon clan's rapid transition from subsistence farming to commercial agriculture. Within a few years Kings Tree was linked to Charleston by road, reducing the traveling distance from 120 to merely sixty miles—the difference between the two distances revealing the contrast between the early hardships that Robert described and the family's quick rise to prosperity, especially after the introduction of indigo cultivation in the early 1750s. As South Carolina's first historian, David Ramsay (of Ulster parentage), noted in 1809, although the Williamsburg settlers "remained for several years in low and distressing circumstances," some dying "debilitated in body and dejected in spirit," merchant credit from Charleston soon enabled many to purchase slaves and transform their clearings into "fruitful estates."[54] Thus, Williamsburg should not be confused with the later up-country Piedmont settlements at Ninety-Six and the Waxhaws, settled by the Scots-Irish from the 1750s. The Witherspoons' older backcountry was on the fertile semitropical coastal plain, rich in pine, oak, and good soil and with ample river frontage. Production of corn, timber and pitch, cattle, and especially indigo soon thrived. By 1756 two-thirds of Williamsburg's taxpayers owned five or more slaves, and here as elsewhere on the coastal plain, slaves were soon a majority, if not so overwhelmingly as in the cotton and rice lands of the tidewater. By the early 1770s, three thousand wagonloads of wheat, indigo, and tobacco flowed annually from South Carolina's prosperous backcountry to Charleston.

Scots-Irish emigration to South Carolina helped fulfill Governor Johnson's expectations: from the 1730s the population expanded rapidly beyond the tidewater, tripling the colony's inhabitants from 10,000 whites (and 20,000 slaves) in 1730 to 31,000 (and 52,000) in 1760. The Witherspoons adjusted all too happily to the slave majority, whose labors quickly rescued them from the hoe and loom and brought them to indigo-based affluence and power. From 1734 to 1749 Robert Witherspoon's parents remained at the Bluff, moving thereafter to a new three-hundred-acre plantation at Thorntree Creek, where his father James built an impressive home on what was known as the "English" or "Virginia" model. When James Witherspoon died in 1768 his library alone was worth £63 ($3,150 in 1977 terms); he left his plantation to a younger son, also named James (1743–1790) but willed £500 (or $25,000 in 1977) to Robert and smaller sums and slaves to his other children. Robert's uncles' and aunts' families prospered on similar estates. Robert himself first

53. keep up men of piety . . . of the unworthy scribe in Boddie's text; ms. has keep us men of piety is the hearts request of the unworthy Scribe. **54.** D. Ramsay, *The History of South Carolina from 1670*, vol. 1, 109–10; see Sources.

worked as a weaver, then as a slave overseer and, as he related in his memoir, as manager of his aged father's plantation. In 1758 he married Elizabeth Heathly[55] and established his own plantation some miles further along the Black River, at Ox Swamp, where his nine children were born.[56] Robert was a ruling elder in the Williamsburg Presbyterian church, at King's Tree, which his grandfather had established, and during the Revolution, one son, Captain James Witherspoon (1759–1791), served alongside cousins and other relations in Marion's Rangers. Robert Witherspoon died at his plantation on 5 April 1788. His slaves' opinions are unrecorded, but his tombstone inscription described him as an "excellent man," in whose character "humility of mind, benevolence of heart and undissembled piety shone conspicuous,"[57] and in the nineteenth century the entire clan's many descendants numbered among South Carolina's prominent politicians, lawyers, physicians, and Presbyterian ministers.

19 ✳

James Magraw, 1733

In the late 1710s the Armagh-born Quaker, James Logan (1674–1751), William Penn's chief colonial agent and himself an avid land speculator, invited Ulster Presbyterians to settle in Pennsylvania, thinking that "it might be prudent," as he later wrote, "to plant a settlement of such men as those who formerly had so bravely defended Londonderry and Inniskillen" on the colony's Indian frontiers[1]—and in the process to increase the value of his and the Penn family's estates. Responding to the lures of cheap land, religious toleration, and civil equality, "shoals" of Scots-Irish and other emigrants from northern Ireland were soon landing on the Delaware and migrating beyond the crowded precincts of Philadelphia, westward into Chester County and northward, along the east bank of the Susquehanna River, into what would later become Lancaster (est. 1729) and Dauphin (est. 1785) counties. There, in the 1720s, they formed townships and Presbyterian congregations with familiar Ulster names such as Donegal and Derry. By 1730 at least a hundred Ulster-born families had moved north of Derry and settled in Paxton township, where John Harris's ferry afforded the best river crossing westward into the Cumberland Valley. Most of Paxton's settlers were squatters, and in the early 1730s conflicts between them and Logan's and the Penns' surveyors encouraged the Scots-Irish to cross the Susquehanna.

James Magraw was a member of one of the first parties of Ulster immigrants to ford the river and settle in the future Cumberland County (est. 1750), and his letter to his

---

55. Elizabeth Heathly (1740–1820), daughter of William Heathly (1715–1743), an emigrant from England, and Mary Hamilton (1718–1769), daughter of one of Williamsburg's earliest Scots-Irish settlers. **56.** Robert and Elizabeth Witherspoon's children were: James (1759–1791); Thomas (1761–1765); Ann (1763–1786); John (1765–1767); Robert, Jr. (1767–1837); Mary (1769–1803); Elizabeth (1771–1816); John Ramsey (1774–1852); and Thomas (1776–1836). **57.** J. B. Witherspoon, *History and Genealogy of the Witherspoon Family . . .* , 93; see Sources. **1.** Cited in Leyburn, *Scotch-Irish*, 191; see Sources.

brother John, who remained behind in Paxton, describes the Valley's early settlement. Not until 1736 did the Penn family's treaty with the Iroquois Nations extinguish Indian claims to the west bank of the Susquehanna, but from 1726 Pennsylvania officials had encouraged the area's exploration and had granted special licenses to prospective settlers: in part to create a buffer of Scots-Irish settlement against the Indians and in part to secure the region against rival claims from Maryland.

In June, 1730, 12 families of Ulster immigrants crossed the River at Harris's Ferry and, after a week's travel on Indian trails through the Valley, pitched camp near Middle Spring, establishing a settlement that later would be named Shippensburg. Among these pioneers were Alexander Steen, John McCall, and Hugh Rippey, his wife, and children— all mentioned in the following letter. Magraw and his wife did not join them until mid– 1733, but the Middle Spring area was then still a wilderness, heavily forested with oak and walnut, interspersed with prairie or "barrens," and inhabited by Delawares and Shawnees. Initially, Magraw and his companions had left the neighborhood of Maguire's Bridge, a market town in Aghalurcher parish and Magherastephana barony, County Fermanagh. In Pennsylvania all were Presbyterians, but in the mid–eighteenth century the great majority of Aghalurcher's Protestant inhabitants were members of the Church of Ireland (and about 46 percent of the parish's entire population were Catholics). Thus, it may be that the Magraws, Rippeys, and other early settlers merely conformed to the Cumberland Valley's dominant faith.[2]

James Magraw, Middle Spring, Cumberland County, Pennsylvania,
to John Magraw, Paxton Township, Lancaster County, Pennsylvania, 21 May 1733

May 21st, 1733

Dear John:

I wish you would see John Harris at the ferry[3] and get him to rite to the governor[4] to

---

2. The mixed ethnic origins of Middle Spring's early Ulster settlers illustrate how the "Scotch-Irish" community was created in America rather than simply transplanted from northern Ireland. Among the most prominent early families, for example, those of Magraw (Mac Graith) and McCall (Mac Cathmhaoil) were of Gaelic or native Irish and Catholic backgrounds, whereas the Steens were probably Presbyterian emigrants from Scotland to Co. Fermanagh (although the name was sometimes Gaelicized as O'Steen or Osteen), and the Rippeys were probably Anglicans of English origin. In addition, the degree of sociocultural mingling and intermarriage that may have prevailed in their part of Co. Fermanagh even prior to emigration is suggested by the low estimate of the proportion of Irish-speakers—less than 10 percent—among those born in Magherastephana barony during the 1770s, although the total population was then ca. 43 percent Catholic. For demographic data on Aghalurcher parish and its environs, see appendix 2.1d, on chapter 19.   **3. John Harris at the ferry**: John Harris (1673–1748), probably born in Yorkshire (although some sources attest a northern Irish birthplace) and a brewer in London before emigrating to Philadelphia, where he gained the patronage of Edward Shippen (1639–1712), a prominent Quaker and Pennsylvania official. About 1727, Harris moved to Paxton, on the east bank of the Susquehanna, where he operated a ferry and engaged in fur-trading, general merchandising, farming, and land speculation on the future site of Harrisburg (laid out in 1784 by Harris's son, John, Jr.).   **4. the governor**: Magraw was referring either to Patrick Gordan, Pennsylvania's lieutenant

see if he cant get some guns for us   theres a good wheen[5] of ingens about here and I
fear they intend to give us a good deal of troubbel and may do us a grate deal of harm.
We was three days on our journey coming from Harrisses ferry here   we could not
make much speed on account of the childer   they could not get on as fast <as> Jane
and me   I think we will like this part of the country when we get our cabbin bilt   I
put it on a level peese of groun near the road or path in the woods at the fut of a
hill   there is a fine stream of watter that comes from a spring a half a mile south of
where our cabbin is bilt   I would have put it nearer the watter but the land is lo &
wet   John McCall Alick Steen & John Rippey bilt theres near the stream   Hugh
Rippeys[6] daughter Mary berried yesterday   this will be news[7] to Andrew Simpson
when it reaches Maquires bridge   he is to come over in the fall when they were to be
married   Mary was a verry purty gerl   she died of a faver[8] & they berried her up on
rising groun north of the road or path where we made choice of a peese of groun for a
grav yard   she was the first berried there   poor Hugh has none left now but his wife
Sam and little Isabel   Theres plenty of timmer[9] south of us   we have 18 cabbins bilt
here now and it looks a town[10] but we have no name for it   Ill send this by John
Simpson when he goes back to paixtan[11]   come up soon   our cabbin will be ready
to go into in a week and you can go in till you get wan[12] bilt   we have planted some
corn & potatoes   Dan McGee John Sloan & Robert Moore[13] was here and left last
week   remember me to Mary and the childer   we are all well   tell Billy Parker[14] to

governor in 1726–1736, or to Thomas Penn, chief proprietor and son of the colony's founder, who in
1732–1741 was resident in Pennsylvania. On Penn, see chapter 53.   **5. a good wheen of ingens**: a fair
number of Indians; the Scots word **wheen** shows the same semantics as Standard English **few**: wheen = few =
not numerous, but **a good wheen = a good few** = fairly numerous (see John Barbour, *The Bruce*, ed. by
A. A. M. Duncan (Edinburgh, 1997 ed.), 2.247: thocht thai war **quheyn**, thai war worthy "though they were
few, they were bold").   **6. John McCall**: in 1751 listed, with James McCall, as a taxpayer in Lurgan
township, Cumberland Co. **Alick Steen**: probably a kinsman of Robert Steen, who warranted 150 acres in
1734. **John Rippey** (d. 1758): in 1751 listed as a taxable inhabitant of Lurgan township; son of **Hugh Rippey**
(d. 1750), who in 1744 warranted one hundred acres. Hugh Rippey's other children included Samuel
(1713–1791, **Sam** hereafter), who farmed 212 acres in what became Southhampton township, Franklin Co.,
and Isabella (**little Isabel** hereafter), who died unmarried in 1778. For additional references to the McCalls,
Rippeys, and other early settlers in the vicinity of Shippensburg, see chapter 39.   **7. news**: several early
published transcriptions read **[sad] news**.   **8. gerl . . . faver**: girl . . . fever, spelled as pronounced ([gerl
(rhymes with *peril*)], [fayvur]).   **9. timmer**: i.e., timber; Scots does not develop a [b] between [m] and [r] or
[l], e.g., **chaulmer** "chamber," **nummer** "number," **grummle** "grumble," **tremmle** "tremble."   **10. it looks a
town**: "it looks like a town"; in Standard English **look** now usually takes a noun complement with **like**.
11. paixtan: i.e., Paxton; the spelling **ai** indicates that Magraw has given a Scots pronunciation [paykstun] to
the word; as in Scots **naig**, **aipple** (note the spelling) = Standard English **nag**, **apple**.   **12. wan**: one.
13. John Sloan: warranted two hundred acres in 1734 (as did George Sloan the same year). **Robert Moore**:
warranted 250 acres in 1741.   **14. Billy Parker**: William Parker, warranted 250 acres in 1744 and 50 more in
1745.

come up soon and bring Nancy with him   I know he will like the country   I
forgotto tell you that Sally Brown was bit by a snaik but she is out of danger   come
up soon

yr aft brother[15]

James Magraw

Life for Middle Spring's first settlers was far more primitive than in contemporary Fermanagh. The nearest flour mill was a week's journey distant, and Magraw and his companions at first lived largely on game and fish. A few months after writing his letter, Magraw's fears of the Indians were realized when one settler was killed. After 1734, however, families from Ulster began to pour into the Cumberland Valley: in 1735 the Middle Spring area was organized as Hopewell township; in 1737 Edward Shippen[16] patented the land that, in 1749, would be platted as Shippensburg village; in 1740 the inhabitants built the Middle Spring Presbyterian church; and in December 1741 alone some 60 families—including Hugh Rippey's brother-in-law—came to the settlement directly from Antrim, Londonderry, and Fermanagh.[17] By midcentury the entire Cumberland Valley had over five thousand inhabitants, all but a handful of Ulster origin. The region suffered severely from Indian attacks during the French and Indian War (1754–1763) and Pontiac's subsequent uprising (1763), but by 1775 Shippensburg was a thriving trade and supply center, boasting some five to six hundred inhabitants, a hotel, and a distillery, and surrounded by farms of one hundred to two hundred acres. Unfortunately, James Magraw cannot be traced after 1733, beyond the knowledge that a Pennsylvania state treasurer was among his descendants.[18] However, the Rippeys, McCalls, and Steens flourished as farmers, tradespeople, and professionals in and around Shippensburg at least through the early nineteenth century, although by then more efficient German farmers had largely displaced the Scots-Irish throughout much of Lancaster, Dauphin, and Cumberland counties, as most of the latter had long since moved west and south in search of fresh lands.

---

15. **yr aft brother**: your affectionate brother.   16. This Edward Shippen (1703–1781), a prominent jurist and land speculator, was a grandson of the Edward Shippen who patronized John Harris (see n. 3); known as Edward Shippen of Lancaster to distinguish him from his related namesakes. Also see chapter 39.   17. See chapter 39.   18. The descendant was Henry S. Magraw, according to William H. Egle, *Notes and Queries: Historical and Genealogical*, series 1, part 4 (Harrisburg, 1881). In other late nineteenth- and early twentieth-century published sources, there is some confusion as to whether the surname of the 1733 letter-writer was Magraw or Magaw. In June 1730 a David Magaw was one of the first settlers at Middle Spring, and subsequently the Magaws were very prominent in nearby Carlisle, Pa. However, none of these Magaws was named James, and Egle, who was intimately familiar with the history and genealogy of the Cumberland Valley's early settlers, handled and published James Magraw's letter and made no reference to a connection between the two families, which surely he would have done had any relationship existed.

Mary Elizabeth McDowell Greenlee, 1737–1754

Only a few years after crossing the Susquehanna, large numbers of Ulster Irish began to leave Pennsylvania and move south through the Great Valley of the Appalachians, across the Potomac River, and into the Shenandoah Valley of Virginia. This initiated an inland, southwesterly migration of Ulster immigrants and their American-born offspring that eventually would scatter Scots-Irish settlements and Presbyterian churches as far south as the Carolina and Georgia backcountries, joining or coexisting with communities founded by Ulstermen and -women who, like the Witherspoons and John Rea's colonists,[1] emigrated directly from Ireland to Charleston and Savannah.

As early as 1719 a few families from Ulster had settled in the northernmost reaches of the lower Shenandoah Valley, lured by its natural beauty, fertile soil, and relative absence of Indians. However, large-scale migration to western Virginia did not commence until the late 1720s and the 1730s, when Lord Fairfax, proprietor of the Northern Neck, and William Gooch, colonial governor in 1727–1749, granted huge parcels of Valley land to speculators on condition that they plant actual settlers on their tracts. In 1735–1736 Gooch and his council granted 118,500 acres to William Beverley, an influential tidewater planter, and another one hundred thousand acres to Benjamin Borden, Sr., an adventurer from New Jersey. Both grants were located in the southern or upper Valley: Beverley's Manor within the boundaries of the future Augusta County (est. 1738 but not formally organized until 1745); and Borden's adjacent tract to the south, in the future Rockbridge County (separated from Augusta in 1778). The grants were free, subject only to quitrents and to the stipulation that the grantees plant at least one family or "cabbin" per one thousand acres within two years.

Both grantees advertised extensively for settlers, but Beverley's superior political and commercial connections facilitated his efforts, and by the end of 1738 he had made several large grants of his own to two rather unsavory Ulstermen—John Lewis (1678–1762), a substantial tenant in County Donegal who had fled to Pennsylvania in the late 1720s, purportedly after killing an oppressive landlord,[2] and James Patton (1692–1755), a sea captain from County Londonderry who had absconded to Virginia after defrauding successive employers in Scotland and England. Both Lewis and Patton imported Scots-Irish settlers, from Pennsylvania as well as directly from Ireland, on Beverley's behalf. By contrast, in

---

1. See chapters 18 and 10. **2.** All published accounts of John Lewis repeat the family tradition that he killed the landlord and steward who had tried to evict him unjustly and who, in the process, had murdered his brother. However, in the 1880s Mary Elizabeth McDowell Greenlee's great-great-granddaughter claimed that tradition was false—that Lewis had indeed killed a man in Ireland but that the true story was too "ugly" to be told. Mary Davidson, "Descendants of Mary E. McDowell" (Davison Papers, ms. 113, Folder 11); see Sources.

mid-1737 Borden was still unsure even of his grant's precise location, and on 3 November he petitioned Virginia's government for a one-year extension, pleading that "unforseen Accidents & Difficulties"[3] had prevented him from planting the requisite number of settlers. However, in the autumn of 1737, while searching for his property in the wilds of the Shenandoah, Borden had the good fortune to encounter the family of Mary Elizabeth McDowell Greenlee (b. 17 November 1711), and it was largely through their efforts that Borden was able to populate his holdings and, in 1739, receive a royal patent for 92,100 acres in the upper Valley.

By contemporary accounts and conventional standards, Mary Greenlee was an exceptional woman—bold, resourceful, and independent. According to family tradition, the McDowells were Covenanting Presbyterians who had fled Scotland during the reign of Charles II and settled in west Ulster, where in 1689 Mary Elizabeth's father, Ephraim McDowell (1673–ca.1774), fought at the seige of Derry against the armies of James II. Either a minor landowner or a head tenant, McDowell was nearly 60 years old when in 1729 he left County Londonderry and emigrated to Pennsylvania with his sons John and James, his daughters Mary Elizabeth and Margaretta, and numerous other relatives. At first the McDowells settled in Chester County, but they soon moved across the Susquehanna to the village of Carlisle, where in 1736 the "remarkably handsome"[4] Mary Elizabeth married her cousin James Greenlee (b. 1707), who had accompanied the McDowells to America. A year later, the McDowells and Greenlees packed their belongings on horseback and migrated south on the Great Path to the upper Shenandoah Valley, enticed by reports from their kinsman, John Lewis, that they could secure larger amounts of land in Beverley Manor than in Pennsylvania and at only a third of the cost. When they embarked on their journey, the McDowells had never heard of Borden's tract, but their chance meeting with its grantee both altered their plans and secured them even more land than Lewis had promised.

Over 50 years after the McDowells first met Benjamin Borden, his heirs began a long, complicated, and acrimonious legal dispute concerning the ownership of his unsold lands. In 1806, in the course of that lawsuit, Mary Elizabeth McDowell Greenlee, by then the oldest white settler in the Shenandoah Valley, made the following deposition. Her testimony, described by an early historian as Rockbridge County's "charter document," provides a unique account of the terms on which the Scots-Irish initially settled the upper Valley and by which her own kinsmen and their allies came to dominate its economy and society.

---

3. Cited in W. Couper, *History of the Shenandoah Valley*, vol. 1, 282; see Sources, chapter 20.   4. Cited in R. S. Greenlee and R. L. Greenlee, *Genealogy of the Greenlee Families*, 222; see Sources.

Mary Elizabeth McDowell Greenlee, Forks of the James River,
Rockbridge County, Virginia, legal deposition in *Peck v. Borden,*
before Joseph Walker and J. Grigsby, 10 November 1806

... Mary Greenlee being sworn deposeth and saith[5]   That she with her husband James Greenlee settled in Bordens large Grant as near as she Can recollect in the fall of the Year 1737—her son John was born the 4th of October in the next year after they Settled in <the> Grant, and by the register of his birth kept in the family Bible, to which <she> has had recourse to refresh her memory, it appears he was born on the 4th of October 1738—shortly before her Settlement in <the> Grant she together with her husband, her father Ephraim McDowell (then a very aged man),[6] and her brother John McDowell were on their way to Beverly manor and were advanced as far as Lewises creek, intending to stop on the South river having at that time never heard of Bordens Tract   (she remembers of her brother James having the Spring before Gone into <Beverly> manor and raised a crop of Corn on the South river above Turks near what was Called Woods Gap)[7]   about the time of their Striking up their Camp in the Evening, Benjamin Borden the Elder came to their Camp and proposed Staying all night   In the course of conversation Borden Informed them he had about 10<0>,000 acres of land on the waters of James River or the forks if he could ever find it and proposed Giving 1000 acres to any one who would conduct him to it.[8] . . . Borden . . . had been at William<s>burg[9] and some one, perhaps the Governors son in law (by name Needler as well as she Can recollect), and his other partners had in a frolick[10] Given him their Interest in said Grant—She understood there were four of them: The Governor (Gooch), his son in Law and two others whose names she does not recollect who were Interested[11] in the order of Council for said land and that Borden got it from them. . . .

<hr/>

5. By its nature, Mary Greenlee's deposition is replete with legal terms and phrases that impede the readability of the text. We have omitted these without indication, to avoid cluttering the text with elipses and footnotes. Thus, "the said Benjamin Borden" usually becomes merely "Benjamin Borden," and phrases such as "further deponent saith," "as aforesaid," and "as she understood" are omitted in nearly all cases, as are also numerous instances of "said" and "that." In addition, because of the deposition's disjointed format and awkward phrasing, and because it does not represent Mary Greenlee's own writing, we have taken the liberty of editing this document far more extensively than the others in this book. For instance, some passages of text have been rearranged to improve continuity and comprehension, while other passages have been omitted entirely; these deviations from the original ms. are indicated by elipses and footnotes. Modern punctuation is silently inserted when deemed helpful to understanding.   6. Parentheses inserted.   7. Parentheses inserted.   8. The following passage, separated by elipses from the rest of the text, appears much later in the original ms. and is inserted here for continuity. The original text resumes with <W>hen a light. Parentheses inserted.   9. William<s>burg: the capital of colonial Virginia.   10. in a frolick: on a whim; and/or during a party or drinking bout.   11. were Interested in: had a legal/pecuniary interest in.

<W>hen a light was made <Borden> produced his papers and satisfied the Company of his rights   The deponents brother John McDowell then Informed Borden he would conduct him to the forks of James River for 1000 acres and shewed Borden his Surveying Instruments &c, and finally it was agreed that McDowell should conduct him to the Grant, and she thinks a memorandum of the agreement was then made in writing   They went on from thence to the house of John Lewis, in Beverly manor near where Staunton[12] now Stands, who was a relation of deponents father—They remained with him a few days and there further writings were entered into, and it was finally agreed they should all settle in Bordens Tract   John McDowell was to have 1000 acres for conducting them there agreeable to the writing entered into, and the Settlers were moreover to have 100 acres for every Cabbin they should build, even if they built forty Cabbins, and they might purchase any quantity adjoining at 50/[13] per hundred acres   Borden was Interested[14] in these Cabbin rights, as they were Called, for every cabbin saved him 1000 acres of land   These Cabbin rights were afterwards counted and an account returned to the Government, then held at W^msburg, and She has heard about that time many Tests[15] of the manner in which one person by Going from Cabbin to Cabbin was Counted and Stood for several Settlements

She recollects particularly of hearing of a Serving Girl of one James Bell named Millhollen who dressed herself in mans cloaths and saved Several Cabbin rights, perhaps five or Six, calling her self Millhollen but varying the Christian name—These Conversations[16] were Current in that day—[17] . . . it was Immaterial where the Cabbins were built—they were to entitle the builder to 100 acres wherever he Chose to lay it off, and he had a right to purchase at 50/ any larger quantity—One John Patterson was employed to Count the Cabbin rights   He was accustomed to mark[18] the Setlers on his hat with Chalk and afterwards deliver the account to her brother John McDowell, and <she> remembers to hear that her Brother had expressed his Surprise at so many people by the name of Millhollen being settled on the land, but which was afterwards explained by the circumstance of the Servant Girl, and was a Subject of General mirth in the Settlement   She does not Know whether this plan of saving several Cabbin rights by one person appearing at different Cabbins was suggested by Borden the Elder or not   every person Saving a Cabbin right Got 100 acres for each right so saved, as Borden was <obliged> to have a Cabbin for every 1000 acres[19]

When the party with which she travelled came (as they Supposed)[20] into the

---

12. **Staunton:** Augusta's county seat from 1745, Staunton grew between 1750 and 1790 from fewer than two dozen houses to nearly two hundred houses and ca. 800 inhabitants; by the 1760s it was an important market center, boasting at least six merchants.   13. **50/:** 50 shillings (50s.).   14. **was Interested in:** see n. 11.
15. **Tests:** statements of evidence.   16. **Conversations:** kind of behavior/way of dealing.   17. **She knows nothing of the fact but from Information—She understood that . . . :** omitted.   18. **to mark the Setlers on his hat with Chalk:** i.e., to count or number each settler's cabin by making a chalk mark on his hat.
19. Paragraphing inserted.   20. Parentheses inserted.

Grant, they Stoped at a Spring near where David Steele now lives and Struck their Camp—Her brother and Borden having Gone down <the> branch[21] until they were satisfied it was one of the waters of James River   The Balance of the party remained at that Spring until her brother John and Borden went down to the forks formed by the waters of the south and north River and having taken a Course thro the Country returned to Camp   They then went on to the place Called the red house[22] where her brother John Built a Cabbin   her brother built and setled where James McDowell now lives—The first Cabbin her husband built was by a Spring near where Andrew Scott now lives, but when <she> went to see it she did not like the Situation, and they then built and settled at the place afterwards Called Browns   They sold this after some short time and purchased the land on which her Brother James had made an Improvement (now Called Templetons)[23] and where she resided untill about the year 1780, being within sight of where her Father (then near 100 years of age) resided. This was the first party of white people that ever Settled in the Grant[24]

Borden the Elder remained in the Grant from that time for perhaps two years and more obtaining Setlers, and she believes there were more than 100 Setlers before he left them—she believes he was in the Grant the whole time from his first coming up until he left it before his death[25] but how long before his death he left it she does not Know   He resided some time with a Mrs Hunter (whose daughter afterwards married one Quin)[26] and to whom he Gave the Tract whereon they lived   when Borden left the Grant he left his papers with her Brother John McDowell, to whose house a Great many people resorted to See about Lands, but what authority her brother had to Sell or whether he made sales or not she does not Know   Her brother John McDowell was Killed about Christmas[27] before her son Samuel (her first son of that name) was born   He was born, as appears by the register of his birth in the Bible, about April 1743.[28] . . .

---

21. branch: stream, tributary.   22. the red house: John McDowell's homestead—known as the Red House for the ochre-based paint that covered its timbers—was just south of the future village of Fairfield and adjacent to the Great Path (later the Great Road) that was the main conduit for migrants through the Valley.
23. Parentheses inserted.   24. Paragraphing inserted.   25. Borden the Elder . . . his death: Benjamin Borden, Sr. (1692–1743).   26. Quin: rendered as Green in several old histories of the Shenandoah Valley—e.g., J. L. Peyton, History of Augusta County, Virginia (Bridgewater, Va., 1953 ed. [1882]), and W. Couper, History of the Shenandoah Valley, vol. 1 (New York, 1952)—perhaps intentionally, to delete from the historical record those early settlers whose non-Scots-Irish names suggested a native or Catholic Irish presence; also see n. 37.
27. John McDowell was Killed about Christmas: John McDowell (b. 1714?), captain of the Augusta Co. militia and, according to his followers, a man of "Hart and Curidg," was killed in a skirmish with the Iroquois on 18 December 1742. In 1743 his widow, Magdalena Woods (1716–1782), married Benjamin Borden, Jr., who died of smallpox in 1753; a year later she married Col. John Bowyer, 20 years her junior. One of McDowell's sons, Judge Samuel McDowell, was president of the Kentucky state constitutional convention in 1792, and a grandson, James McDowell, was governor of Virginia (1843–1846) and a member of Congress.
28. Several sentences re proof of her son's birthdate omitted. Paragraphing inserted following the omitted sentences.

Young Ben Borden[29] Came into the Grant before her brothers death   she recollects this from the Circumstance of his being then in ordinary plight[30] and such that he did not then seem much respected by her brothers wife, and when <her brother's widow> afterwards married him she could not but reflect on the Change of Circumstances—<for> he was altogether illiterate   Benjamin Jr lived with her Brother John Whilst in the Grant but returned to his fathers before the death of John, and after his father's death <he> returned fully empowered by his Fathers will to Complete Titles and sell lands, and then married the widow of her Brother and continued to live at the place where her Brother settled until his death.[31] . . .

<A>s to the Value of the lands remaining unsold by Ben Borden <Jr.>—one Hardin . . . was an Executor . . . <Hardin came to> this Country after the death of young Ben Borden and after John Bowyer had married <Borden's> widow. . . . <Harden> was Setling Bordens Business but she does not Know by what authority[32]   Hardin offered to her Brother James the unsold lands for a bottle of wine if he would clear him of the quit rents—her Brother consulted with her father about the proposition, <but her father> advised him to have nothing to do with it for it would probably run him into Jail   This was Shortly after Bowyers marriage[33]

She does not Know whether Benj[n] Borden J[r] was distressed on account of the quit rents[34] or not, <b>ut <she> recollects that shortly before his death, <when> Col[o] Patten[35] was at her house, a horse of Bordens broke out and came there. . . . Patten wished to have <the horse> caught <so> that he might take him for some claims against Borden. . . . <However,> she had <Borden's> horse sent home, fearing that as there had been some misunderstanding between <her> husband and Borden about their Land, he might think they had aided in <the> Seizure—her husband purchased 1000 acres of land of old Borden at an early day for 50/ per hundred which he had located on the Turkey Hill, <but> after the death of old Borden his son Benjamin disputed Giving a deed for the whole quantity there, alledging it was all Valuable Land, and afterwards for the sake of peace it was agreed that a part should be taken there[36]—a part

---

29. **Young Ben Borden:** Benjamin Borden, Jr., son of Benjamin Borden "the Elder."   30. **in ordinary plight:** rather undistinguished/mediocre.   31. Repetitious data in ms. omitted from the rest of this paragraph. Most of the subsequent paragraph in the original deposition, concerning the later land dealings of Joseph Borden, the second son of Benjamin, Sr., is also omitted, except for a few sentences integrated elsewhere, as indicated, in our text.   32. Ms. reads: **She states that one Harden who was an Executor and who was in this Country after the death of young Ben Borden and after John Bowyer had married the widow and who she understood was Setling Bordens Business . . .**   33. Paragraphing inserted.   34. **quit rents:** a quit rent is a small payment (per acre or per a certain number of acres) due to the Crown in lieu of services. 35. **Col[o] Patten:** Col. James Patton, next to Borden and Beverley the largest landholder in the upper Valley; in 1742 appointed colonel of Augusta County's militia by Governor Gooch; also a justice of the peace and later county lieutenant and member of the House of Burgesses; killed by Indians in 1755.   36. **that a part should be taken there:** i.e., that the Greenlees should only take possession of a portion (actually, two portions) of the disputed land.

Joining Robert Cullens,[37] which was sold to one Buchanan, and a part near John Davidsons—This arrangment was made at the time Hardin was present. <He> seemed willing to give the land and advised <her>, whose husband was then abroad,[38] to agree to take it at those places, which she did   all the land purchased by her husband was purchased from old Borden   Indeed he had purchased this thousand acres before they came to the Tract at Lewises,[39] provided he liked the land when he saw it—which he did.[40] . . .

<T>he people paid no quit rents[41] for two years from the time the grant was first settled   this exemption was Granted by the Governor at the instance of one Anderson a preacher[42]   When they had to pay quit rents they raised money by sending butter to New castle, to W^mburg and other markets below, and Got also in return their salt Iron &c.[43] . . . The people who first Settled and purchased did not always have their lands Surveyed at the time of the purchase   some had their lands surveyed & some had not, but when it was not Surveyed they described it by General boundaries. . . . <For example, her> brother[44] James <McDowell> purchased a considerable Tract, perhaps four or 500 acres, either at or below where Stuarts mill now stands   It run on a large Hill but whether in one or two Tracts she Knows not—This tract he sold to some person but <she> does not Know who   She does not Know whether he<r brother> had it surveyed or not but supposes it was merely designated by General boundaries   She thinks if She was on the land She could point out the tree whereon his name was Cut If it is yet standing   it stood near a deep hole in the Creek   she Knows not how he acquired it but understood he had built a Cabbin on it and saved a Cabbin right   <she> never saw the Cabbin nor does she Know where it stood, but the land was Called his very shortly after they went to the Grant and in the lifetime of old Borden.

From their bargain with "old Borden," the McDowell and Greenlee families gained three thousand acres outright, plus additional acres for every cabin they built and permission to purchase still more land for less than the price charged other settlers. To be

---

37. Cullen: older, published texts of Mary Greenlee's deposition often render this Hiberno-Norman (and usually "Catholic" Irish) surname as the Scots-Irish name, **Coulter** (or as **Cueton**); see n. 26.   **38. abroad:** away from home.   **39. he had purchased this thousand acres before they came to the Tract at Lewises:** i.e., when she and her husband were still at Lewis's house and before they came to the Borden tract, her husband had purchased this thousand acres.   **40.** Passages in ms., concerning details of disputed land purchases by other settlers, omitted.   **41. quit rents:** see n. 34.   **42. one Anderson a preacher:** Rev. James Anderson: in 1738 sent by the Philadelphia Synod to the Shenandoah; preached the first sermon in the upper Valley, in John Lewis's house; on behalf of the Valley's Presbyterians, Anderson successfully petitioned Governor Gooch for religious toleration.   **43.** Passages detailing disputed land sales and cabin rights omitted here. The following sentences, separated by elipses from the rest of the text, appear earlier in the original ms. and are inserted here for continuity. The original ms. resumes with **<For example, her> brother James . . .   44. My brother** ms.

sure, neither Borden nor his son and namesake was particularly scrupulous, and the pragmatic marriage of John McDowell's widow to Benjamin Borden, Jr., was designed to ensure he would not renege on his father's promises. Nevertheless, it was largely through the efforts of the McDowell brothers and James Greenlee, as the Bordens' land agents or middlemen, that the Borden tract was speedily settled: by McClungs, McCues, McCowns, and other McDowell kinsmen and former neighbors from Pennsylvania and Ulster, as well as a sprinkling of native Irish families, such as the O'Doghertys, Maguires, and O'Neals.[45] By the 1740s their settlement was so heavy that the upper Valley was known as the "Irish tract," and despite subsequent in-migration by Germans and eastern Virginians, in 1775 the Scots-Irish (and their Irish neighbors of Catholic or Anglican[46] origins) comprised about three-fifths and three-fourths, respectively, of the inhabitants of Augusta and Rockbridge counties. In 1745 Augusta County, which then included the entire upper Valley and all the land west to the Ohio River, contained nearly five thousand people; 10 years later its population exceeded nine thousand; and by 1800 Augusta and Rockbridge together included nearly 17,000 whites and over three thousand slaves, although by 1800 both counties were much smaller in size than Augusta had been at midcentury.

Despite their distance from major markets in Philadelphia and eastern Virginia, improved roads, stock-raising, and the production of hemp, tobacco, and, after 1770, wheat and flour soon raised the Shenandoah Valley's landowners from subsistence farming to commercial prosperity. Although less stratified than in Ulster or in the northern Shenandoah, society in the upper Valley was far from egalitarian or democratic—despite the criticisms of genteel outsiders such as George Washington, who described the inhabitants as "a parcel of barbarians."[47] Indeed, thanks to their early arrival and to their favorable connections with both the original patentees and the tidewater gentry, the McDowells, Greenlees, Lewises, Pattons, and a handful of other families constituted a frontier aristocracy, employing their control over land distribution and their near monopoly of political offices to enrich themselves and marginalize later arrivals. By 1745 nearly 87 percent of the land patented in Augusta County had been granted, in tracts of a thousand or more acres, to merely thirteen families, who, during the next three decades, either traded it among themselves, to consolidate their holdings, or, less frequently, sold it to newcomers at prices that escalated from £2 18s. per one hundred acres in the early 1740s to more than £34 by the eve of the Revolution. By 1782 less than 2 percent of Rockbridge County's landown-

---

45. Men with native or "mere" Irish names were far more common among the Valley's indentured servants than among its farmers.   46. Even more "hidden" than the Irish of native–Catholic Irish origins among the Ulster Presbyterian majority of frontier settlers were those Irish immigrants of Old English (Hiberno-Norman) or New English (Elizabethan, Cromwellian, and later) descent. For example, a prominent settler in colonial Virginia's Lunenburg Co. was Walter Newman, an Anglican from Dublin, whose American-born sons joined Welsh Baptist congregations. Newman, by name and/or religion alone, would never be designated "Irish" by historians seeking to identify ethnicity in early census, tax, or land records. For other examples of seemingly unlikely "Irish" (but not Scots-Irish) patronyms, see chapters 1, 9, 14, 23, 36, and 53.   47. Cited in T. P. Slaughter, *The Whiskey Rebellion: Frontier Epilogue to the American Revolution* (New York, 1986), 79.

ers owned over a thousand acres; nearly 85 percent held fewer than four hundred acres; and over half the titheable men—and perhaps three-fourths of all the county's adult white males—owned no land at all.

By contrast, between 1737 and his death twenty years later, James Greenlee had parlayed his initial grant, subsequent land speculations, and mercantile interests into an estate that covered thousands of acres in the upper Valley and in North Carolina. In 1763 his personal property alone, including six slaves, was valued at over £845 in Virginia currency, at a time when fewer than 5 percent of all estate inventories in the Valley were assessed at more than £500 or included even a single slave. Perhaps because of his illiteracy, Greenlee never attained the political honors achieved by his brothers-in-law, John and James McDowell, who became magistrates and militia officers. Nevertheless, he served five years as county constable and was a leading member of the Timber Ridge Presbyterian church; in 1754 his subscription to the minister's salary was the fifth largest of the congregation's 47 members. Augusta County court records clearly indicate Greenlee's steady rise in social status: from "yeoman" in 1746 and "Mr." in 1751 to "Gent[leman]" by the time he died in 1757.

Mary Elizabeth McDowell Greenlee outlived her husband by more than 50 years and buried at least two of their eight children.[48] After her father's death around 1774 she moved from the McDowell family homestead at Timber Ridge to the forks of the James River, where she operated a tavern and traded by flatboats with Lynchburg and Richmond until her last years, when she retired to her son David's house near Natural Bridge. Thrifty, resourceful, "[e]ndowed with powers of mind beyond the ordinary measure," and, despite her more than two hundred pounds, possessed of great physical stamina, Mary Elizabeth managed her late husband's estate with great success and bestowed "handsome" fortunes on her children.[49] Even in old age she rode on horseback throughout the Valley, attending to her many business concerns, and her memory remained so accurate that the courts frequently relied on her testimony to settle old land claims. Yet there was also a dark side to her reputation. Although her descendants claimed that she was "remarkably kind" to her slaves, in 1777 the county court freed one of her bondsmen because she had enslaved him illegally and treated him inhumanely. Likewise, "an early disappointment in love" allegedly "gave a peculiar turn to the action of her mind," and a caustic tongue persuaded her "more simple-minded" neighbors to charge her with witchcraft. Her kinship with the McDowells and Lewises protected her from prosecution but not from malicious quips, such as:

---

48. James and Mary Greenlee's children were: John (1738–ca.1785), Rockbridge Co. sheriff before the Revolution; James (1740–1813), member of the 1788 North Carolina constitutional convention; Samuel (b.1743), d. in infancy; Mary (b.1745), moved to Kentucky; Margaret (b.1748); Grace (b.1750), married successively two Revolutionary War generals, d. in North Carolina; David (1752–1820), of Natural Bridge, Va.; and Samuel (1757–1824). **49.** The descriptions of Mary Greenlee in this and the following sentences are cited in W. H. Foote, *Sketches of Virginia, Historical and Biographical*, 93; and R. S. Greenlee and R. L. Greenlee, *Genealogy of the Greenlee Families*, 222–23; see Sources.

Mary Greenlee died of late;
Straight she went to Heaven's gate:
But Abram met her with a club,
And knocked her back to Beelzebub![50]

It is impossible to determine whether Rockbridge County's poor folk truly feared Mrs. Greenlee's personal eccentricities or merely projected their anger at her family's wealth and power onto a woman whose financial acumen and "independence of character" defied conventional gender roles.[51] In the end, she probably outlived all her critics, dying on 15 March 1809 in her ninety-seventh year—the last survivor of the first party of white settlers in what her family had helped make "the most distinctively Scotch-Irish county in America."[52]

21 ❋

James McCullough, 1748–1758

Prior to the American Revolution, over 85,000 Ulster Presbyterians and other Irish emigrants settled in Pennsylvania, primarily as farmers and frontiersmen, and at least half again that number took up farms in the backcountry regions of the southern colonies. Since no letters that these pioneers sent to Ireland appear to have survived, the following diary or journal written by James McCullough, a Scots-Irish farmer and weaver on the

---

50. Cited in O. F. Morton, *History of Rockbridge County, Virginia*, 255; see Sources. Other versions of this doggerel substitute the devil for Abram. **51.** In 1729 Rev. Ezekiel Stewart of Portstewart, Co. Londonderry, complained to Ireland's Lord Justices that aggressive, ambitious women were "a great cause" of early Ulster emigration, for "The Masters of Ships," he wrote, "tell ye women, that y^e are much more desireable there <in America> than ye natives of ye Country, because they are much better Housewifes and . . . y^t ye men there use their wifes like gentelwomen,   this makes ye women that have daughters to marry to prevail wth their Husbands to go thither in hopes of makeing them Gentlewomen, and those women that have noe daughters, are in hopes of getting rid of their Husbands & getting better ones" (Stewart, 25 March 1729, in D.2092/1/3/ 141, PRONI). ¶Stewart's criticisms are perhaps more reflective of early eighteenth-century Ulstermens' patriarchal notions as to women's "proper," submissive roles than of emigration's actual causes, but Mary Greenlee's defiance of such conventions may have generated popular resentment. Likewise, in a colonial society where gentility was supposed to accompany economic and political power, both Greenlee and her illiterate husband may have lacked the refinement—the "moral" or cultural qualities—that normally bolstered élite status and helped to ensure lower-class deference. In early eighteenth-century communities that both were traditionally religious *and* were experiencing rapid socioeconomic change, as in Ulster and on the Ulster-American frontier, accusations of witchcraft were not uncommon. Nor were they unusual among early colonial Virginia's "anxious patriarchs," especially among the lower classes, whereas the infamous episode at Salem, Massachusetts, in 1692 demonstrated that even solid yeomen and Harvard-educated Calvinist ministers could succumb to, and suffer from, a witchcraft hysteria that primarily targeted women and others who challenged communal norms. **52.** W. F. Dunaway, *The Scotch-Irish of Colonial Pennsylvania* (Chapel Hill, 1944), 105.

Pennsylvania frontier, is extraordinarily valuable. Between 1748 and 1758, McCullough kept a random account of his farmwork, weaving activities, and economic transactions, interspersed with personal notes, religious reflections, and a record of local casualties in the early years of the French and Indian War (1754–1763), during which many of his closest neighbors were killed and two of his own sons, John and James, were kidnaped. Unfortunately, McCullough's diary is not complete and is difficult to decipher: pages are missing; some entries are illegible and many are undated; and, for reasons now unclear, McCullough compounded the historian's trials by writing a few entries in code, substituting numbers for letters of the alphabet. Nevertheless, McCullough's jottings, reordered chronologically and slightly abridged here, provide an unusually intimate view of the everyday life and concerns of a Scots-Irish pioneer on what was then the westernmost edge of the British frontier in colonial America.

According to family tradition, James McCullough was a native of County Londonderry. On 27 April 1745, he paid £6 to Arthur Burns of Belfast for his and his wife Martha's passage to the New World, although they may not have departed until December. Probably to avoid the Pennsylvania tax levied on Irish immigrants, McCullough and his wife apparently disembarked at the port of New Castle, Delaware, instead of Philadelphia. The McCulloughs evidently remained in Delaware for the next four or five years, probably renting farmland and engaging in weaving, for their first son, John, was born in New Castle County in May 1748. However, in or about 1750 James McCullough moved his wife, son, and daughter, Jean or Jane, westward into Pennsylvania's Cumberland Valley and purchased, at sheriff's auction, a two-hundred-acre tract near the west branch of Conococheague Creek, in Antrim township of the just-established Cumberland County, a mile or two from the present village of Upton. Apparently, he was accompanied by several relations, for the names of other McCulloughs, including his brother Archibald, appear in the diary.

The Scots-Irish had been settling in the future Franklin County (divided from Cumberland in 1784) since about 1730, their migration encouraged by Pennsylvania authorities—who wanted to secure the colony's southern border against Maryland claims—and led by Benjamin Chambers from County Antrim, who established the region's first farm and mill at Falling Spring, the future site of Chambersburg. In the mid-1730s, other Ulster families, attracted by the area's numerous springs and by the ease of clearing the relatively treeless "barrens" or prairies that dominated the landscape, began purchasing or, more commonly, squatting on farms in what became known as the Conococheague settlement. Within a few years, the settlers established several Presbyterian congregations, which in turn soon divided in response to the fervent revivals of the Great Awakening during the late 1730s and 1740s.[1] An adherent to the antirevival "Old Side" Presbyterians, James McCullough joined the Upper West Conococheague church, which had been established in 1738 but did not enjoy the services of a permanent pastor until 1754.

---

1. On the First Great Awakening among the Presbyterians in the Middle Colonies, see chapters 46 and 47.

From 1748 through mid-1755, McCullough's diary primarily records the mundane events of Scots-Irish frontier life. As in contemporary Ulster, the agricultural cycle coexisted with a thriving local trade in yarns and textiles, and McCullough both employed poorer immigrants, such as Denis McFall, to work in his fields and at the loom and labored himself for earlier settlers like Thomas Montgomery. However, on 9 July 1755, General Edward Braddock's defeat at the Monongahela by the French and their Indian allies exposed the Scots-Irish in the Cumberland Valley to the vengeance of the Delawares and the Shawnees. Both local authorities and private individuals, such as Benjamin Chambers and Reverend John Steele, McCullough's minister, hastily organized militia companies and erected a chain of small forts to protect the settlers. Despite these efforts, during the next two years, while Pennsylvania's Anglican proprietors and Quaker-dominated Assembly bickered over how to finance frontier defense,[2] repeated Indian attacks—starkly recorded in McCullough's diary—devastated the Conococheagues and other backcountry communities. McCullough himself joined thousands of western pioneers who hid their possessions, temporarily abandoned their farms, and fled eastward to older settlements in York and Lancaster counties, but not before his own sons were kidnaped in an Indian raid on 26 July 1756. Not until late 1758, when McCullough's journal entries began to dwindle, did a renewed British military presence on the frontier reduce the danger of Indian attacks and enable the Scots-Irish to return and reestablish their decimated congregations.

James McCullough Journal, 1748–1758

James Mᵃ Cullogh his Book[3] . . .

```
1   2   3   4   5   6   7   8   9
a   e   i   o   u   l   m   n   r
1   2   3   4   5   6   7   8   9
```

3172s 7ᶜ C464gh h3s h18d 18d p28 38 h48 t4 728d   3f 7y p28 w292 1 63t26 b2tt29 3 C456d 72<nd>[4] . . .

---

2. On the political struggles between Pennsylvania's Proprietary and Quaker parties, see chapter 53.   3. To the best of the editors' ability, McCullough's diary entries have been rearranged in chronological order, with ellipses indicating that entries have been reordered. This is an abridged rendition of the original diary: entries that were largely undecipherable, had little or no contextual significance, or predated 1748 or postdated 1758 have been omitted. In the original manuscript, the earliest and latest entries are dated 1745 and 1767. However, the overwhelming majority of diary entries are dated 1749–1758 and are reprinted here.   ¶The rows of numbers and alphabetical letters at the beginning of the text constitute McCullough's own key to the code that he employed sporadically. Discerning readers will note that McCullough used his code most consistently to record the matings or "bulling" of his cows, but whether he did so out of prudishness or because he perhaps utilized the services of his neighbors' bulls surreptitiously, without their owners' consent or reimbursement, can only be conjectured.   4. 3172s 7ᶜ C464gh h3s h18d 18d p28 38 h48 t4 728d   3f 7y p28 w292 1 63t26 b2tt29 3 C456d 72: Iames ᵐᶜ Colagh his hand and pen in hop<e> to mend   if my pen were a litel better I Could me<nd>.

a Cubit a fo<o>t and a half . . . a peas⁵ 5 fo<o>t   a furlong 125 peaces   a mile 1000
peaceses   a Sabath days jurney 600 paces   a firkin 4 gallans and a half . . . a Log⁶ half
a pint   a Span - 9 inches   a talant 62 pounds

2 Cronics - 19 & 6 of Judges⁷
2 Chronicls - 18 - 0 22 of ly<ing> Spirits⁸
Judges—13-of yᵉ birth of Samson
Hebrews 6 - 17 of an oath Confirm<ed>⁹
2 Samuel 21–20 of a gient man¹⁰
2 Kings - 13-21-a deed to live¹¹
Judges - 9—53 - a milston Cast by a Woman at Abimelich¹²
Christ Coming riding on an ass   Zachariah - 9 - 9¹³
against the man that is my fellow   Zachariah 13—7¹⁴

1	March¹⁵	31
2	Apriel	30
3	May	31
4	Jun	30
5	July	31
6	Agust	31
7	September	30
8	October	31
9	November	30
10	Desember	31

5. **peas**: i.e., pace (also **peaces**, **peaceses**, **paces** "paces" below).   6. **Log**: "about three quarters of a pint" (OED).   7. MacCullough's lists, here and later in the diary, of biblical passages, names, and stories suggest that, for him and other eighteenth-century Ulster Presbyterians, the Bible not only was spiritually inspirational and even historically accurate but also provided a series of examples, types, or analogies that paralleled and could guide contemporary, individual behavior.   8. 1 Chronicles 18:22: "Now therefore, behold, the Lord hath put a lying spirit in the mouth of these thy prophets, and the Lord hath spoken evil against thee."
9. Hebrews 6:17: "Wherein God, willing more abundantly to shew unto the heirs of promise the immutability of his counsel, confirmed it by an oath."   10. 2 Samuel 21:20: "And there was yet a battle in Gath, where was a man of great stature, that had on every hand six fingers, and on every foot six toes, four and twenty in number; and he also was born to the giant."   11. 2 Kings 13:21: "And it came to pass, as they were burying a man, that behold, they spied a band of men; and they cast the man into the sepulchre of Elisha: and when the man was let down, and touched the bones of Elisha, he revived, and stood up on his feet."   12. Judges 9:53: "And a certain woman cast a piece of a millstone upon Abimelech's head, and all to brake his skull."
13. Zechariah 9:9: "Rejoice greatly, O daughter of Zion; shout, O daughter of Jerusalem: behold, thy King cometh unto thee: he is just, and having salvation; lowly, and riding upon an ass, and upon a colt the foal of an ass."   14. Zechariah 13:7: "Awake, O sword, against my shepherd, and against the man that is my fellow, saith the Lord of hosts: smite the shepherd, and the sheep shall be scattered: and I will turn mine hand upon the little ones."   15. McCullough lists the months according to the Old Style dating, by which March 25 was the first day of the new year. The British empire's official conversion to the New Style occurred in 1752; at the same time the Julian Calendar was replaced by the more accurate Gregorian, which added eleven days to the Julian reckoning. The shift from Old to New Style explains the dating of some of McCullough's diary entries as, for example, March 1750/51 and 1751/52.

JAMES MCCULLOUGH

11 Jenuary 31

12 feberwary[16] 28

in Leap year 29

in on\<e\>[17] year - 365 days

in one year is - 8775 \<h\>ours . . .

John m^a Cullogh[18] was born may 27 - 1748 - it being friday about one o Clock and on the 12th day of the moons age

the red Sea is 15 mils broad and 35 fadom[19] deep . . . the wall of babl was 87 fot wi\<d\>th[20] . . .

Alexander elder to[21]   two bushel of Ray[22] July 27 - 1749   mor[23] two bushels of Ray Agust 25 . . .

---

16. The spelling of some of the months in this list indicates Scots pronounciation: **Apriel** [upreyl], **Agust** [aaagust], **Jenuary** and **Jeneary/Jenewry** hereafter [jeni(w)eri], feberwary [febuweri].   17. on\<e\>: on is the more frequent spelling of one in the ms., but because its formal identity to the preposition on is distracting to the reader, the editors have normalized to the modern spelling throughout. Conversely, the preposition on is often spelled one in the letters, reflecting the Scots pronunciation (rhymes with **own**).   18. John m^a Cullogh: James McCullough's eldest son.   19. fadom: fathom (six feet; Scots form).   20. wi\<d\>th: for the loss of [d] in the cluster [dth] see John Craig's **breath** "breadth" (chapter 46).   21. Alexander elder to: Most of the entries in McCullough's diary can be classified into two broad categories: (1) narrative and (2) commercial. The first type records events, while the second lists transactions involving goods, services, and money. The second category is by far the more numerous and falls into three subtypes, as follows: ¶1. Notations of money or goods received (eight instances), e.g., **Receved ten Shillings from Joseph Holland for Corn November y^e 27th**. ¶ 2. Notations of accounts payable or disbursements (14 instances), e.g., **I ow\<e\> 7^s and on\<e\> peny to James friers vendo** (i.e., vendue "sale"), **Jeneway the 12 to   one gallon and on\<e\> half of melases——— 3^s-9^p**. ¶ 3. Notations of accounts receivable (91 instances). These are mostly expressed in terms of a formula: NAME OF DEBTOR (+ to) + GOODS/SERVICE (+ *AMOUNT DUE*) (+ *DATE*). The parentheses here indicate an optional component and the italics indicate a moveable component. E.g., **Agust the——16——1749   James Frier——to——63 yeards of Linne\<n\> Woven . . . on\<e\> pound eleven Shillings and Six pence**, and **feberwary y^e 19 1752   patrick borns to   on\<e\> half bushel of Corn**. This formula continues in use today—minus the archaic to (see OED, s.v.) but otherwise unchanged in form and content—as the standard format for accounts receivable in bookkeeping entries, with the specific shape: Date + Name of debtor + Goods/service + Amount due. ¶It is clear from a reading of the accounts receivable entries in McCullough's diary, as well as the notations of money and goods received, that besides being a farmer he was a craftsman and businessman, primarily a bespoke weaver (the very large amounts of cloth involved in the various transactions alone support the conclusion that McCullough was selling woven cloth rather than buying for his own needs) but also a general provisioner, hardware merchant, and (not least) moneylender. The importance of weaving for sale in McCullough's economy is seen in his anxiety to conceal the expensive and hard-to-replace parts of his loom from marauding Indians. McCullough's business activities and the products involved, as mentioned in his diary (there were probably others) are as follows. *Weaving*: linen, bagging, shirting, linsey-wolsey, girthing, woolen cloth, hickory, blankets, tow cloth, bed coverings, winding (or winnowing) cloth. *Produce*: rye, potatoes, onions, corn, buckwheat, oats, butter, pork, straw. *Hardware*: buckles, backbands, mattocks. *Services*: moneylending, "bulling," fulling, farm labor, pasturing. *Outfitting*: wallets, hats, shoes.   22. Ray: i.e., rye; the spelling is archaic (early Scots) and is seen mainly in a small number of monosyllables that rhyme with "eye" (e.g. **pay**, **way**, now usually spelled **pey**, **wey**, like **hey** "hay").   23. mor: i.e., more; in bookkeeping style "in addition, plus." Used optionally in multiple entries of accounts receivable to introduce the second and subsequent items (mostly replaced by **item**, itself now quite obsolete).

Agust the - 16——1749   James Frier - to - 63 yeards of Linnen Woven[24] . . . on<e>
pound Eleven Shillings and Six pence   James frier   8 bushels of ray . . .

1749   Sara mᶜCullogh forty yeards of bagin[25] and 9 yeards of lincy[26]   7 yeards
Stript[27] and 3 yeards of Shirtin[28]   mor - 40 yeards of linin   mor 40 yeards of linin . . .

I ow<e> 7⁵ and on<e> peny to James friers vendo[29]   John mᶜCullogh 15 Shillings and
a 11 - pence[30] to James friers vendou . . .

an Account of Charges Laid out During our travel to yᵉ BackCountry   31725 ⁷ᶜ
C4664ch[31]   loss £1-3-3 . . .

John mc Collogh to   40 yeards of Linen   mor—43 yeards of bagin   mor—15
yeards of lincey   mor—72 yeards girthing[32]   more two bushels of ray and one peck
of pretes[33]   mor on<e> bushel of ray and 3 yeards of Lincy Striped   more—on<e>
peck of inins[34] 8p and - 4 pence to John goforth   more of Smith Work   more 20
yeards of bagin

Jeanwary yᵉ - 7ᵗʰ 1750   Dines mᶜ fall[35] 3 yeards of Linen at 2S and 6 pence per yeard
to be payable the Latter End of march Next . . .

Jeneary yᵉ 13 1750   avery great rain and a great frost and Sno<w> . . .

Peter Crall[36] to - 26 yeards of Wollen   Jeneway yᵉ - 15 - 1750   13 Shill<ing>s . . .

I did Sow flex[37] march 31 and oats Apriel the 3 1750 . . .

E.g. **John mc Collogh**   **to 40 yeards of Linin**   **more**——**43 yeards of bagin**   **mor**——**15 yeards of**
lincey   **more**——**72 yeards girthing**. The use of **more** and **item** (and both together) have a long pedigree;
see Muriel St. Clare Byrne, ed., *The Lisle Letters,* vol. 6 (Chicago, 1981), no. 387 (from 1535): **first   vj pair**
of hosen . . . **item ij caps** . . . **more   a yard and a half frisado** ("fine frieze"). . . .   However,
McCullough's employment of the form **more** betrays some education; one expects the Scots form **mair**, as
found for example in the Glasgow burgh records of 1589 (OED, s.v. more): **item   fyvetene schillingis for**
the price of ane hogheid   item mair   twentie sex schillingis viijd. for ane lang courchay. . . .   **24.** 63
yeards of Linnen Woven: "the weaving of 63 yeards of linen." This formula, which occurs very frequently in
McCullough's diary and is probably a bookkeeping cliché, corresponds closely to the Latin formula exemplified
by **ab urbe condita**, literally "since the city founded," i.e., "since the foundation of the city." The spelling
yeards indicates Scots pronunciation (yerdz); see **yerds** hereafter.   **25. bagin** (below also **baging**): i.e.,
bagging (a coarse woven fabric used to make bags).   **26. lincy** (below also **lincey**): i.e., linsey or linsey-
woolsey "a coarse, sturdy fabric made of wool and linen (or cotton)."   **27. Stript**: i.e., striped.   **28. shirtin**:
i.e., shirting "cloth used to make shirts."   **29. vendo** (below also **vendou, vendu**): i.e., vendue "sale of goods,
especially by auction."   **30. a 11 - pence**: i.e., "a leven" (= eleven) pence.   **31. 31725 ⁷ᶜ C4664ch**: Iames
ᵐᶜ Colloch.   **32. girthing** (hereafter also **girth web**): woven material used to make horse girths.   **33. pretes**:
i.e., praties; this and its many variants are the most common designations for "potato" in Hiberno-English, as
well as in the speech of Scotland and the north of England.   **34. inins**: i.e., inions "onions" (Scots form).
35. Dines mᶜ fall: i.e., Denis McFall.   **36. Peter Crall**: Peter Craul, in 1751 a taxable inhabitant of Antrim
township, Cumberland Co.   **37. flex**: i.e., flax; spelling shows the frequent Scots raising of [a] to [e], e.g.,
[nestay] "nasty", [shedday] "shadow", [jekk] "Jack". [eftur] "after." See chapter 43, n. 13; chapter 29, n. 12.

I had my house Covered may the 25 - 1750 . . .

Chirly to bull[38] may the 26 - 1750

I Did Reap ray Jun 18 and Wheat Jun the 23[39] . . .

I did hall[40] in Wheat July the 3 and <s>owed flex and buck Wheat Jun - 28 and I
Sowed buck Wheat July - the 11th—1750 and thrush[41] flex July the - 12th . . .

I did Sow turneps July the 4th and Rept[42] oats July the 5th . . . I did Sow turnips July
the 23

I Did pay 10 Shillings to thomas Willemson July the 24th 1750 . . .

I did begin to plow fother[43] agust 10   I did begin to Sow Wheat agust the 29 - 1750
and I had don[44] Sowing September yᵉ 13th . . .

mary Patan - to   12 yeards of Wolling[45] Septr 14th . . .

I got in[46] all Corn and fother october the 20 1750 . . .

october yᵉ - 15 - 1750   Mary Harper Dettor to James mᵃ Collogh 4 Shillings and - 8
pence being for one pece of Lincey Woven   Receved ten Shillings from Joseph
Holland for Corn november yᵉ 27th . . .

. . . an ACount of goods gotten from thomas montgomrey[47]
october the < . . . > - 1750——two y<ard>ˢ and 3 quarters of Chaker[48]   9-2[49]
2 handCurchies 5<s.> and 2 dito Cottin 3-0
one Wisted[50] Cap 2-4
1 half yeard of linin and one quarter and ahalf of Camrick[51] 0-3-9
November-26——
to one new tes<t>ament 2-4

---

38. Chirly to bull: Chirly (Shirley), one of McCullough's cows, was sent to and mated with a bull that
probably belonged to one of McCullough's wealthier neighbors, although later McCullough's own farm seems
to have been able to provide this service (see hereftter **Robert Mᶜ C<a>rrs Whit hefer did take bul may yᵉ
28ᵗʰ 1775**). **39. the Jun** ms. **40. hall**: i.e., haul. **41. thrush**: Scots past tense of **thresh**. **42. Rept**: i.e.,
reaped (rhymes with **gaped**). **43. fother**: fodder "cattle feed" (general Hiberno-English form). **44. had don**:
was finished; see chapter 65, n. 20. **45. Wolling**: i.e., wollen (any cloth or fabric made of wool). **46. got
in**: gathered in, secured (the harvest), "saved" (in Irish usage). **47. thomas montgomrey**: Thomas
Montgomery, in 1743 a tax collector in Hopewell township, Cumberland Co. **48. chaker**: i.e., chequer or
checker "a fabric with a checkered pattern"; also = **checkery** "checked cloth." **49. 9-2**: sequences of two
numbers of the pattern **x-y** or **x y** are to be read "x shillings, y pence." Whenever this is not the case, the
exception will be noted. Sequences of three numbers of the pattern **x-y-z** (or **x y-z** or **x y z**) are to be read "x
pounds, y shillings, z pence." **50. wisted**: worsted "a smooth compact yarn made from long wool fibres used
especially for firm napless fabrics and knitting." **Wisted** is an Ulster variant of the more common Scots form
worset. **51. camrick**: i.e., cambric "a fine thin white linen fabric." The spelling shows the Scots preservation
of the cluster [mr]; see **timmer** "timber."

to one quarter yeard of green Cloth[52] 1-3ᵖ

Jenwary the 12 to   one gallon and on<e> half of melases[53]———3ˢ-9ᵖ . . .

I did begin to the great Swamp to Clear[54] December the 3 1750 and I did finis[55] the Swamp at the barens[56] Jenewary the 5ᵗʰ 1751 . . .

December the 11 1750   Willem Carson[57] to   Work don - 24 yeards of Lincey Woven 3 yᵈ Striped with 2 Shitels[58] and 6 yeards and a half with 3 Shitels more— 11S-5d / 7 yeards of baging

december yᵉ 25   mor to—11 yᵈ of hikrey[59]   mor to 14 yˢ of Strip<t>   mor to 12 yeards of blankets . . .

I had on<e> hog from mrs James———20 Shillings and 4 pence   John mᶜ Cullogh to   on<e> hog from mʳ James — 16 Shillingss and - 8 - pence . . .

Willem Willson[60]   3 pence behind[61] of that first Lining[62] Web I wove to him   more 17 yeards of to<w> Clouth[63] betwen his wife and Widow Wormingtown Which the Sᵈ willem wilsons wif<e> toke away Which I Receved no pay for yet - 5 Shilings and 8 pence and 4 pence for two tim<e>s Lining[64] because of work of filling[65]   more 9

---

52. green cloth: i.e., green cloth or greencloth "a kind of linen." **53. melases**: molasses; occurs also below as **meloses** (transposed spelling of "moleses"). **54. I did begin** . . . : the sentence reproduces Irish syntax exactly (Irish pattern: BEGIN + to + [Object + to + Verb] = McCullough's sentence: **I-did-begin** + to + [the-great-Swamp + to + clear]), but it is difficult to understand why McCullough would resort to such syntax, when he otherwise (naturally) employed the English and Scots pattern (e.g., the foregoing **I did begin to plow fother**), and his speech does not betray a strong presence of substrate phenomena. **55. finis**: finish (Scots form; rhymes with **Innes**); see **Inglis** "English" and, with reverse spelling **Cleavish** "clevis" (see n. 127). **56. barens**: i.e., barrens (prairies or clearings, unforested land). **57. Carson**: the Carsons were among the first settlers in the vicinity of what became Greencastle (laid out in 1782), in Antrim township, Cumberland Co. The spelling **Willem** indicates the Scots pronunciation; see n. 72. **58. shitel**: shuttle, an instrument containing thread wound on a bobbin, used in weaving to carry the thread back and forth through the threads that run lengthwise (the warp), thus creating the weft; in the case described here each shuttle used contains a different color of thread, and alternating the shuttles produces striped cloth. **59. hikrey**: compare **hickory shirt** "a coarse and durable shirt worn by laborers, made of heavy twilled cotton with a narrow blue stripe or a check" (OED, s.v. hickory). **60. Willem Willson**: William Wilson, in 1751 a taxable inhabitant of Peters township, Cumberland Co. **61. behind**: in arrears, overdue. **62. Lining**: i.e., linen (and elsewhere hereafter). **63. to** (below also **too**) **clouth**: i.e., tow cloth (cloth made from the shorter, lower-quality flax fibers, called "tow" or "hurds," separated by heckling from the longer, higher-quality fibers, called "line"). The spelling **clouth** here and **cloath** below indicates the pronunciation [kloth], which alternates with the more common Scots form **claith** [kleth]. **64. two tim<e>s Lining**: i.e., double lining (see n. 65). **65. work of filling**: work conjectural (ms. blurred); **filling**: i.e., fulling, here probably referring to the process of cleaning newly woven cloth, which would normally still contain oils and dirt, by beating it with wooden mallets and washing it with fuller's earth; see *Piers Ploughman*, B.15.445 (ModE trans. of quotation in OED, s.v. full): "Cloth that comes [directly] from being woven is not fit to wear / until it is fulled." The expression **two tim<e>s lining** (i.e., double lining; see n. 64) probably refers to strengthening (**lining**) the cloth to undergo this process. The spelling **filling** has its origin in the fact that a preceding [f] often causes [i] to change to [u] in Scots, which allows a reverse spelling of [u] as if it were an original [i].

yeards of bed Covering – 9 Shilings   more on<e> hors<e> paster[66] on<e> night – 6 pence   more two hors<e> paster two days and 2 nights – 2 Shilings   3 yeards of lining 18 pence   <total> 18-3 . . .

I Did Sow flex march yᵉ 20 1751 . . . and finist Sowing flex march 29 . . .

mathew paton[67] to   29 yeards of Shirtin march yᵉ 23 – 1750/51 . . .

I Receved 20 Shillings from Alexander Geddes and did give of Said money 10 Shillings to Widow mc Sorley and 8S and 3 pence to gets[68]   J173s 7ᶜ C464ch h3s h18d[69]

I did get twenty Shillings from patrick Cafrey[70] and I did pay – 11 Shillings & 8 pence of Said money to mʳ James[71] / and 6S and 6 pence to Samul[72] Killpatrick / I did get 6s-11ᵈ from Charity Cortney and 5S and did give Said money to James frier march the 28 – 1751 . . .

Apriel 1 – 15 pence to tomas montgomry for wages . . . and 15 pence to thomas montgomrey Apriel yᵉ 1[73] for meloses and 22 yeards of Lining – Jun 29th . . .

began to plant Corn Apriel yᵉ 23 1751 and finist 29 . . .

June the 1-1751   Jane mᶜ Collogh to   7 yᵈˢ of Shirtin Woven . . .

Jun yᵉ 1 1751   Sara mᶜ Collogh to   7 yeards of Shirtin woven and 9 yeards of Lincey – 5 yeards Striped agust yᵉ 24th . . .

James mᶜ Collogh, Junier[74] Was born Jun yᵉ 11th 1751 . . .

in the year 1751 I Did begin to reap ray Jun the 17 and Wheat Jun 26 – and I got all in July the first   had on<e> hundred and 26 Shoaks[75] of Wheat and 23 Shoaks of ray and did thresh flex July yᵉ 19—did Sow buck Wheat Jun yᵉ 22 and 29th   I did Cut hey[76] July yᵉ 11 and did reap oats & I Did Sow my New medo<w> Agust yᵉ 16 and 17th 1751   We begin to Sow Wheat Agust 26 and finist September the 11th—— . . .

---

66. on<e> hors<e> paster: pasturing for one horse; for the significance of the spelling **paster** see chapter 1, n. 83.   **67. mathew paton**: Mathew Patton, settled or patented Pennsylvania land in 1737; in 1751 a taxable inhabitant of the Great Cove settlement in Peters township, Cumberland (later Bedford) Co., to the west of the Scots-Irish enclaves at Conococheague Creek.   **68. gets**: Geddes (a neighbor).   **69. J173s 7ᶜ C464ch h3s h18d**: James mᶜ Coloch his hand.   **70. Cafrey**: conjectural (ms. blurred).   **71. mʳ James**: mʳ conjectural (ms. blurred).   **72. Samul**: the spelling shows the loss of [y] before an unstressed vowel in Scots pronunciation: [samyul]→[samul]. The same change has taken place in the Scots form **Willem** "William" [weelum]; see chapter 1, n. 83.   **73. I** conjectural (ms. blurred).   **74. James mᶜ Collogh, Junier**: the writer James McCullough's second son.   **75. shoaks**: i.e., shock, a gathering of sheaves stood upright against each other to dry and ripen. The spelling indicates Scots pronunciation with unlowered vowel (rhymes with **oak**); see **loag** "log" hereafter.   **76. hey**: hay (Scots form, rhymes with **high**); see n. 22.

Jean m^c Collogh to 7^S and on<e> penny to tomas montmogomerey[77] Jean m^c Collogh on<e> pound and three Shillings and Seven pence to thomas montgomrey in ye year 1751 November ye 5th . . .

November ye 14 1751 gorg bennet to 1 bushel of Corn and a bushel & half of buck wheat & on<e> pound butter and half a Crown in Cash and 2 bushels of Corn november 26 and 2 bushels of Corn December ye 11th and 2 bushels dito December 28 . . .

December ye 11th 1751 Charety Courtney to - 16 yeards of Lincey woven 3 yeards plane[78] and 8 yeards Striped with 3 Shitels and 2 yeards with 2 Shitels . . .

Joseph Holand to 5 bushels of Corn Joseph Holand to 36 bushels of Corn Jenewary y^e - 7th 1751/2 . . .

feberwary ye 1 - 1752 Denos m^c fall agreed With me for his boarding at 3^s and 6 pence per week first week - 7 meals 2<nd> week - 4 hol<e> days and 3 meals and all ye rest of ye month in full march ye first week 4 hol<e> days 2 week - 5 hol<e> days & one meal 3<rd> week - 2 days & one half bushel of Corn and 1^s & 10 pence half peny in Cash lent 4<th> week onley on<e> day & 2 days in march Last . . .

Feberwary ye 13—1752 James John to 37 yeards of shirtin woven more to - 17 yeards of hikrey feberwary y^e-15—1752 more Apriel ye 27th to 12 yeards £1-10 & on<e> quarter of Lincy woven 5 yeards & on<e> half Striped With 4 Shitels & on<e> half yeard with 2 Shitels & 3 yeards and on<e> quarter plean wite linen 0-6-10 . . .

feberwary ye 19 1752 patrick borns to on<e> half bushel of Corn

march ye 16th - 1752 Willem Carson to 33 yeards of Shirtin woven— 13^S-9 . . .

feberwary ye 20 1752 Samul Enos detter to me 3^S & 8 pence in boot[79] between Shoo buckls and 18 pence for back bands[80] and 3^S & 6 pence for Straw £0 8-10 . . .

Feberwary ye 22 1752 John Wats to 34 yeards of to<w> Cloath woven & 3 yeards Striped with 3 Shitels—0 11-10 . . .

---

77. montmogomerey: a "running" correction from the written form (Montgomery) to the spoken, which has been reshaped to fit the Irish pattern of surnames beginning with M(a)c (as if **McGomr(e)y**); see the form mcgomeres "Montgomery's" (hereafter). **78. plane**: plain white cloth (e.g., below **plean wite linen**). **79. boot**: the difference in value between items exchanged in barter, usually settled with a cash payment (Scots usage). The amount due is said to be "in boot." **80. back band**: i.e., backband (a leather strap or iron chain, used to hold the shafts of a cart or wagon; fits over a pad or "cart saddle" placed on the horse's back).

mathew paton vendu March the 2   Mathew paton - 44 yeards of Cloath . . . more
to - 34 yeards of Shirtin woven   march yᵉ - 5ᵗʰ - 1752 . . .

March yᵉ 23 - 1752   Patrick Born to   one half bushel of Corn one Shilling . . .

March yᵉ 24ᵗʰ Samul Enos to   one bushel of potatous 3 Shill<ings> and one bushel &
on<e> half of oats   2ˢ - 3   I did plow Nine days and a half my Self in Corn . . .

Archibald mᶜ Cologh to   amatick[81] 3ˢ 2 pence and to a bel<l> - and to a wolat[82]—1ˢ-
6ᵖ and - 6 pence Lent to his wife in tomas mcgomeres and a hat 6-2ᵖ and [. . .]
bushels of ray[83] & a half of oats   march yᵉ 25-1752 . . .

Apriel yᵉ 11ᵗʰ 1752   Willem Carson to   32 yeards of Linen woven——0 16ˢ-0
Charety Cortney 20 yeards of Linen winding[84] and weaving   Jun yᵉ 1 1751 Sara mᶜ
Collogh to 7 yeards of Shirtin woven and 9 yeards of Lincey - 5 yeards Striped and 15
pence to thomas montgomrey Apriel yᵉ 1 for meloses and 22 yeards of Lining - Jun
29th . .

Apriel yᵉ 17ᵗʰ Denes mᶜ fall to   on<e> half bushel of Corn & one half bushel of
oats & one peck of Corn . . .

Apriel yᵉ 22ᵈ 1752   Willem mᶜ mehen to - 8 yeards of Shirtin   0 3 4 . . .

Apriel yᵉ 27ᵗʰ   John Wats to   6 yeards <of . . . > and 3 yeards of Lincy Woven - 3
yeards & 3 quarters Striped with 2 Shitels   0-3-3½   John Wats to 27 yeards of hikrey
woven July yᵉ - 15ᵗʰ   0-9-0   more to - 30 yeards of Wolling September yᵉ 27 . . .

may yᵉ 4—1752   Denes mᶜ fall to 3 Shilings & 9 pence in Cash Lent   you r not to
go to go[85]

I did Sow 9 bushels and on<e> half of oats 1752 & planted 2 bushels of Corn   I did
finis[86] planting Corn may yᵉ 7ᵗʰ & planted Potatous Said day   13 <days> plowing &
hoing before planting & 3 Spels plowing in yᵉ uper field   2 <days> plowing & 4 Spels
in yᵉ far field & 3 Spels in yᵉ field over yᵉ medow   2 Spels in buck wheat ground & 1
harrowing Corn over yᵉ medow . . .

We had don moulding[87] Corn Jun yᵉ 11ᵗʰ 1752 . . .

I did begin to Cut hay Jun yᵉ 15—1752 . . .

---

81. amatick: i.e., a mattock "an agricultural tool used for loosening hard ground, grubbing up trees, etc."
82. wolat: i.e., wallet (not a billfold but a bag similar to a knapsack).   **83.** [. . .] **bushels of ray:** ms. blurred;
numeral illegible; **ray** conjectural.   **84. winding:** winding cloth, used either for wrapping a corpse or for
winnowing.   **85. r:** i.e., are; one or more words illegible after **go**.   **86. finist** ms.   **87. moulding:** cultivating
by covering with earth ("mould").

My daughter Jean Did Enter to Skool[88] Jun ye 15th & did only 6 days at that
time   July ye Last week 2 days   agust ye 1<st> week 2 days   agust ye 2<nd> week –
4 days   agust ye 3<rd> week 2 days—4th week – 4 days   5<th> week—5 days . . .

We Did Sow turnips July – 22 . . .

Agust y^e-15th-1752   Alexander Robison[89] to   21 yeards of Shirtin woven – 8^S & 9
pence . . .

September ye 23   Dines mc fall indeted to me – 13 Shillings in ballance of aCounts &
one Shilling for hay & 1 bushel of Corn 2^s 6 pence & 4 pound and on<e> half of
backon[90] & 6 pence in Cash   0-18-10

october y^e – 5th – 1752   Willem man[91] to   one Cow hide – 42 pounds   mor to   a
hide – 45 pounds . . .

october ye 5th 1752   Nethanel evens to   one pot of butter waying 22 pounds & a
half . . .

october ye 17th 1752   James m^c Ellot to   27 yeards of Shirtin woven   <£>0- . . .

November ye 27   Willem m^c Maghen to   one pound of Candels   <£>0 9<s.> . . .

December ye 6 – 1752   Sara m^c Collogh to   12 yeards of Lincey – 5 yeards Striped
with 3 Shitels   £0-6-3 . . .

James John Creadit – 36 and 14 yeards of tikin[92] and 13 yeards of lincey [. . .][93] wol
and 41 yeards of tick   I had a hog of James John at – 1 pound – 4 Shillings . . .

I had on<e> hog from Jams John at 1 pound – 4Sh   and one Dosen and 10 Cuts of
yern[94] to Sara and 2 Cuts in the web[95] in Spring and one hank[96] to James frier 14
pence   to John ^mc Collough opon James acount and 3 yeards of Shirtin – 15
pence   and 69 pounds of Be<e>f at two pence half pen<ny> per pound . . .

---

88. **Skool**: i.e., school; also **Scol, Scoll, Scull** hereafter.   89. **Robison**: the usual Ulster form of **Robinson**
(pronounced as if spelled "Roabyson" or "Robbyson"). An **n** between an unstressed vowel and **s** is regularly
lost in Scots; see hereafter **Shipistown** and **Shipestown** "Shippensburg"; see also **Chrissenmas** "Christmas"
(pronounced "krissymas").   90. **backon**: i.e., bacon.   91. **man** (i.e., **Mahon**) conjectural (ms. blurred); see m^c
mehon, m^c **meghan** hereafter. For the loss of **M(a)c** see such doublets as **Cafrey** (hereafter): **McCaffrey**;
El(1)iot(t): m^c **Ellot** (hereafter); **Carr**: m^c **C<a>rr** (hereafter); **Crery**: ^mc **Crerie**, ^mc **Crere**, m^c **Crery** (all
hereafter); **Enos** (foregoing): **McGuinness**; **gouley** (i.e., Gawley; hereafter): **McGawley**.   92. **tikin** (also
tickon, ticken, tick hereafter): tick or ticking (a strong, hard linen or cotton material used to make pillows and
mattresses).   93. One word illegible.   94. **Cut**: quantity of yarn, usually containing 12 hanks (see n. 96); **yern**:
i.e., yarn (Scots form).   95. **web**: the fabric produced on the loom.   96. **hank**: a definite length of yarn,
varying according to material (e.g., for cotton, 800 yards; for worsted, 560 yards).

JAMES McCULLOUGH

167

Willem Carson to   9 yeards of Lincey   Mor to - 28 yeards of Shirtin and 31 yeards of Lining and - 16 year<ds> of Wolling and 4 ye<ards> of Covring[97] . . .

Jenwary y^e - 10th 1753   John Robison to   37 yeards of Lincey Woven   £0-15-5

O greatley blest
o greatley blest ye peopel are
ye Joyfull Sound that know   in
Brightness of thy face o Lord
that Ever on Shall go[98] . . .

Jun ye 10th—<17>53   mary Kelley to   5 yeards of tikon 2-1-6 & in Cash lent —
0-3-6 at Crist[n]en[99] for Rum & on ye 18 of Agust —0-2-0 in Cash lent to hugh . . .

Jun ye 21 1753   Willem tomson[100] to   20 Shillings in Cash lent   Agust ye 17 to ten yeards of Shirten Woven . . .

Jun ye 21st Ch392y was b56d ye y219 1753[101] . . .

748dy J58-26   a g921t g5st[102] . . .

Benjemen ye Son of ye Right hand   Barak Lightening   Biltiak old or feading   booz in power or Strenth   Calob as on<e> hart   Canan a marchent[103]   Seph a saltar[104] . . . Cush black or Ethipone[105]   Damanies a littel   Daniel ye Judgment of God   David beloved   Enos m<e>an or misarbel   Ephraim frut full   Esaw working   Ezekel Strenth of ye lord   Ezra a helper   goliath a Captive   habakuk a wresler

Jun ye 28   David Anderson to   44 yeards of Shirten and 20 yeards of Shirten July the 8th—<17>53 . . .

I Did S45 b5ck[106] Wheat July the 3 . . .

Jean m^c Coloch did Enter to[107] John Robisons Scol upon tusday ye 17th of July & Was 4 days ye first Week at Scull—— 2<nd> Week in full   3<rd> Week-5 days   4<th> Week 5 days   5<th> Week 4 days   6<th> Week 5 days   7<th> Week 1 days   ye 1753

---

97. covring: i.e., covering "cover-cloth, cloth used as a cover"; see the foregoing **bed covering**.   98. Psalm 89:15, *Scottish Psalter*, 1650 ed., repr. in *The Psalter in Metre*, rev. version (London, 1929).   99. Crist[n]en: i.e., christening.   100. Willem tomson: William Thompson, in 1745 a tax collector and in 1751 a taxable inhabitant of Hopewell township, Cumberland Co.   101. Ch392y was b56d ye y219 1753: Chirley [i.e., Shirley] was bul<le>d ye year 1753; see n. 38.   102. 748dy J58 - 26   a g921t g5st: Mondy Jun<e> - 26 a great gust ("wind storm, cloudburst").   103. feading   booz . . . Strenth . . . marchent: i.e., fading . . . Boaz . . . strength . . . merchant.   104. Several words illegible after **saltar**; saltar: i.e., psaltar.   105. Ethipone: i.e., Ethiopean.   106. S45 b5ck: Sou (i.e., sow) buck.   107. Enter to: start, begin.

o that men to ye Lord Would give prais for his goodness then and for his Works of Wonder unto ye Sons of men[108] . . .

Agust ye 14 — 1753   Robert Warnok to   one Small pot of butter waying Eleven pound . . .

ye Belfast Ship did Land   Agust 25—1753

Neley tomson Departed this Life September ye 8th ——— 1753 . . .

September ye 11 1753   James Linsey[109] got one month in November & December & [. . .] last[110] Week & ye 2<nd> Week in Jenewa<r>y in full & 4 days ye 3<rd> Week & ye 4<th> Week in full   ye first week in febery 1 day & 30 days at Scoll and 17 days at his own hand[111] & one day to Charety Cortney . . .

John Woods to   22 yeards of Lincey Woven Jenewary ye 21st - 1754   more to   41 yeards of girth web feberwary ye 29th   £0 18 0

Ephram Smith to   4 bushels of Wheat and one bag £1-3-6   to 16 yeards of Linen———1-12-0 . . . to one Pek of Salt - 0-2-0   to one Shilen and 6 pence of old debt - 0-1-0 . . .

Feberwry ye 29   John Armstong to 5 yeards and a half of Linen at 2 Shillings per yeard . . .

May 1754   Adam Armstrong[112] to   Weaving of Shirtin 15 Shillings   to 8 yeards bagin July ye 8th of   to 2 days Reaping ray   to one days Reaping ray   to one days reaping July ye 17   to one days reaping wheat   to 35 yeards of Lincey woven in feberwary 1755[113] . . . to 20 yeards of Shirten in may to 26 yeards of too Cl<o>th . . . <total> £2 - 0 - 7 . . .

Received 2 bushels of Wheat & one bushel dito from A^mStrong July ye 5 . . .

June 1754   John Woods[114] to   15 yeards baging Woven   mor to - 16 yeards of to<w> Cloath & one day & ahalf Reaping & one dozen of to<w> yearn Spining . . .

Jun 1754   Archibald m^c Coloch to   19 yeards of Linen Woven . . .

---

108. o that men . . . : occurs as verses 8, 15, 21, and 31 of metrical Psalm 107, corresponding to the same verses in the original psalm; see any edition of the Presbyterian *Psalter and Church Hymnary*. In the King James Bible, the psalm reads: "Oh that men would praise the Lord for his goodness and for his wonderful works to the children of men." 109. James Linsey: James Lindsay, in 1751 a taxable inhabitant of Guilford township, Cumberland Co. 110. [. . .] last: first word or numeral illegible; last conjectural (ms. blurred). 111. at his own hand: free, at his own disposal. 112. Adam Armstrong: in 1751 a taxable inhabitant of Peters township, Cumberland Co. 113. 1755: last numeral in date conjectural (ms. blurred). 114. John Woods: in 1751 a taxable inhabitant of Peters township, Cumberland Co.; killed, along with his wife and mother-in-law, by Indians on 9 November 1756 (see hereafter).

Peter Crall to   39 yeards of to<w> Clouth Woven Jun yᵉ-15—1754

Cormick dorman to   3 days reaping wheat . . .

I did Reap ray at Samul torintines[115] & Cut my leg Said day July yᵉ 6 - 1754   to one
day & a half[116] reaping July yᵉ 15 & 16ᵗʰ days . . .

7y Ch392y t4k b566 J467 yᵉ 14—1754[117] . . .

I did reap ray Agust yᵉ 8ᵗʰ 1754 . . .

Ephraim Smith to 1754   25 yeards of Shirton Woven & on<e> days howing   to 7
yeards of baging woven   to 2 days reaping & howing   to 1 days reaping ray by
Dark   to 2 days reaping wheat   to 32 yeard of Lincey   £0 10-5   Receved 5
bushels of ray from Ephraim Smith agust yᵉ 15th . . .

I did Begin to Clear yᵉ Dear[118] patch Agust yᵉ 15ᵗʰ 1754 . . .

Agust yᵉ - 16 — 1754   a verey great rain atended With thunder and Lightening . . .

had don Seeding Wheat October yᵉ 22 - 1754 . . .

Samul torintine to   21 yeards of blankets Woven   December yᵉ 25ᵗʰ 1754

A memerandum of Smith Work between Arter Lockert[119] and me in year 1754   and
first a huk[120] to a littel pot of my own ir<o>n   one Coulter[121] 12 pounds weight and
on<e> Likup[122] to a two hors<e> tree[123] of my ir<o>n and one Stepel[124] to a tree
and[125] my ir<o>n & two plow pleats[126] of my ir<o>n & on<e> Cleavish[127] welded
le<a>d   a Shir[128] onst Lead and mend on the Shoulder[129] . . . 3 Shillings   and a Shir
onst Sharped and a Coulter twice Sharped . . . 9 Shillings more   a Shir Sharped

---

115. torintine: i.e., Torrington.   116. & a half: conjectural (ms. blurred).   117. 7y Ch392y t4k b566 J467
yᵉ 14—1754: my Chirley to<o>k bull Joly yᵉ 14—1754; see n. 38.   118. Dear: i.e., deer.   119. Arter
Lockert: Arthur Lockhart; Arter represents the Scots pronunciation of the name.   120. huk: i.e., hook.
121. Coulter: the knife-like part of a plow that cuts the topsoil.   122. Likup: i.e., lick-up, part of the tackle
that attaches the horse to the plow; specifically, a clasp fitted to the swingletree to hold the traces.   123. a two
hors<e> tree: a swingletree for a two-horse plow.   124. Stepel: i.e., staple or steeple (part of the horse
tackle).   125. and: conjectural (ms. blurred).   126. plow pleats: i.e., plow plates, the metal plates that
comprise the plowshare and/or the mould board (see hereafter).   127. Cleavish (cleaves hereafter): clevis (a
U-shaped piece of iron with a pin or bolt, used to connect a plow with the horse tackle). See n. 55.
128. Shir (also Shear hereafter): [plow]share, the part of the plow that cuts the earth below the top soil; the
share is positioned between the coulter and the mould board. (The mould board throws up the soil and casts it
to one side.) The spelling shir reflects the Scots pronunciation; see cheer "chair"; the more common Scots
term is sock.   129. a Shir onst Lead and mend on the Shoulder: "a share once laid and mended on the
shoulder." When the plow plates, comprised of the plowshare and mould board, become worn with use, the
addition of new metal is known as laying; when the new metal is added, the share of mould board is said to be
laid. The shoulder is the top edge of the share. The significance of onst (once) is simply that during 1754
laying had to be performed only once. The pattern mend (infinitive) : mend (past passive participle) is
modeled on send : send.

£0-4-0 and mended -1-3   two plou pleats 0-1-8 a Shir and Coulter twice Sharped 0-1-0   <subtotal> 8-0 . . .

Colen Spence[130]   60 ye^{ds} of Linen Woven in march <17>55 & 14 ye^{ds} of baging in Apriel & 10 yeards of Covering & 1 bushel of flexSeed & 2 yeards of girthing and 25 yerds of Linen - Jun<e>   19 yeards of hickrey in may £3-19-10   [. . .][131] yeards of hikrey   18 yerds of Lincey 9 0 . . .

Ephram Smith to   3 yeards of Linen woven march ye 30th—1755 . . .

Thomas Deveson[132] to 58 yeards of Linen Woven may ye 14 - - - - 1755 . . .

94b29t 7^c C99s[133] Whit<e> hefer did take bul<l> may ye 28th 1755 . . .

I did begin to plow Corn Jun ye 12   had 803 Dozen in ye new Land   did get all in July ye 19 . . .

I Did begin to reap ray July ye 2^{td}   put all in July 19 1755

July ye first 1755   Widou Rortey to   12 yeards of to<w> Cloath woven . . .

July ye 12 1755   Was put to flight by a fals Alarm from ye Ingens[134] July ye^e 12

ye fort at ye meting hous Was begun July ye 30[135] . . .

Was put to flight by a false report of ye Indins agust ye Sixth . . .

Cornel Denbar and his Armey did Camp at henrey poulens agust y^e - 13 - 1755[136] . . .

We did begin to <build> ye fort at John Alls house agust ye 14 . . .

Cormick Derman to   41 yeards of Linen Woven Agust ye 27th - 1755 and 2 yeards of lincey & 11 yeards of Wollen Jeneway ye 12 <17>56 . . .

I did begin to Sow ray September y^e-3 1755 and Wheat y^e—6th . . .

<Ephram Smith> to   10 yeards of Wolen october ye 21   to one bushel of flexSeed   to one peck of potatous   4s 9p . . .

---

130. **Colen Spence**: Collin Spence, in 1751 a taxable inhabitant of Peters township, Cumberland Co.
131. **Numbers illegible. 132. Deveson**: i.e., Davidson (Ulster Scots form). 133. **94b29t 7^c C99s**: Robert M^c C<a>rrs. 134. **Ingens**: variant pronunciation of **Indians. 135. ye fort at ye meting hous**: Fort Steele, commanded by Rev. John Steele (1716–1779), Ulster-born pastor of McCullough's Upper West Conococheague Presbyterian church ("meeting house"). 136. **Cornel Denbar and his Armey** . . . : after the French and Indians defeated General Braddock's army near Fort Duquesne (Pittsburgh) on 9 July 9 1755, Colonel Thomas Dunbar led the surviving soldiers eastward through the Conococheague settlement to Philadelphia. Dunbar's retreat exposed the Pennsylvania frontier to the merciless attacks that followed. **henrey poulens**: Henry Pauling (or Pawling), in 1751 a taxable inhabitant of Antrim township, Cumberland Co.

y^e great Cove Was burnt Nove\<m\>ber y^e first & our flight to ma\<r\>sh Creek was Novr y^e 2^137 . . .

Cam\<e\> all hom\<e\> from marsh Creek December y^e 17 . . .

\<Archibald m^c Coloch\> 4 yeards lincey Woven December y^e 27 1755 . . .

Colen Spence indeted to me 5 Shillings 10\<d.\> in ballance of acounts in y^e year 1755 . . .

John Creag^138 \<and\> Richert and John Cocks Was taken by the Indins feberwary 11 . . .

We did move all to Anttetem   Apriel y^e 19 - 1756^139 . . .

I did hide Welingers^140 and Som\<e\> Shafts^141 in a holow tree upon y^e top of y^e hill above y^e garden and a Wolen Reed^142 in a holow tree above y^e barn amongst y^e Wheat and a pitch fork and ge\<a\>rs and puley Stocks^143 in a tree over agginst y^e Sheep hous East Ward and a [gune] and Salt unde\<r\> y^e uper berreck next y^e Corn Recks^144 and a great deal of other youtencels in a gume \<tree\> in the head of a prato furr\<ow\>^145 below y^e Stubel^146 and a Plow Shear and Cleaves in a tree or loag before y^e Calf house do\<o\>r Within y^e field . . .

John Was^147 killed may y^e 26 in y^er \<17\>56 . . .

John and James m^c Coloch Was taken Captive by y^e indins from Canagogige^148 July y^e 26th - 1756 . . . Weep y^e not for the dead neither bemoan him but weep sore for him that goeth away for he shall return no more nor see his native country^149 . . .

---

137. great Cove . . . ma\<r\>sh Creek: the Indians' massacre of the Scots-Irish settlers at Great Cove (see n. 67), just west of Conococheague, panicked McCullough and most of his neighbors. The Scots-Irish settlement at Marsh Creek was about 35 miles east of Conococheague, across the South Mountain in present-day Adams (then York) County. James McCullough may have sought shelter with a relation, as a Samuel McCullough had farmed at Marsh Creek since 1741.   138. John Creag: John Craig, in 1753 settled on land in Peters township. 139. Anttetem: on this occasion McCullough's family fled southward to the Scots-Irish settlement on Antietam Creek, near the Maryland-Pennsylvania line.   140. Welingers: i.e., willying gears (gears of a willying machine, a device for cleaning wool, flax, or cotton).   141. Shafts: part of a loom; the shafts each lift or depress one half of the warp threads so that the shuttle carrying the weft threads can be thrown across the warp.   142. Wolen Reed: i.e., wooling reed; in a loom, the reed is an iron bar across which the warp is threaded; the reed regulates the space between threads, thus allowing fine or coarse weaving. A wooling reed is one specifically used for weaving woolens.   143. puley Stocks: i.e., pulley stocks (the cases and wheels through and over which the ropes are threaded).   144. Reck: i.e., rick (large stack of hay, wheat, corn, etc.). The spelling reflects the Ulster lowering of i to e or a.   145. prato: potato; the spelling may reflect either **prata** or **pratay** or **prato** (see the varying Scots pronunciations of **window**: windo, wanday, winda. **furr**: furrow (Scots form).   146. Stubel: i.e., stubble.   147. McCullough's failure to provide **John** with a surname suggests that the murdered man was a close relative; however, the author of one, old published transcript of this part of the diary substituted **Watson** for **Was**, perhaps basing his change on other local records or memories.   148. Canagogige: Conococheague.   149. Weep ye not for the dead . . . nor see his native country: according to viewers of the diary in the early twentieth century, this passage from Jeremiah 12:10 was

John Coks Escaped from ye indins agust the 14 1756 . . .

Agust y^e ^{27} a verey great Slaughter at putmock^{150} by ye indins Wherin was 39 persons killed and taken Captives   16 killed at a burring^{151} and 7 killed loading a Wagon in ye field . . . and Indins did Carey away one prisoner from ye South mounten   agust y^e- 27th <17>56 . . .

god bless King gorge wher ever he <be> . . .

Robert Clogston his son bettey Ramsey hir Son and Croper^{152} Was killed Agust ye 28 <and> hir daughter taken away . . .

patrick m^c intire^{153} to   24 yeards of Linen woven September ye 23-1756   Receved from patrick mctire five Shillings said day . . .

tomas Deveson to   22 yeards of Stuf   to 3 days reaping   october ye 18 1756 . . .

November ye 9   John Woods his wife and mother in Law and John Archers Wife Was killed and 4 Children Carried off and 8 or 9 men killed near m^c Dowels fort^{154} <17>56 . . .

Jenewary ye 21 1757 - Willem Heron to - 14 Shillings and 9 pence of Cash Lent . . .

Cullen Spence to - 18 yeards of Lincey Woven feberwarey y^e - 10th . . .

march ye 29th^{155} 1757   ye indines made a breach at Rockey Springs Wherein was on<e> Woman killed and all Carried away Captives

Apriel ye 2   Willem m^c kiney and his S48 Was killed near Car8ell Chambers fort^{156} year <17>57

Apriel ye 17 or 18th Jeremiah Jeck Near putomock Was taken Captive his two Sons killed and one man and a Woman drounded in putomock making ther Escape   year <17>57

written by McCullough immediately following the entry noting his children's capture by the Indians. Today, the page on which the passage was written is missing, as are many others, from the diary. The passage was also underscored in the McCullough family Bible.   **150.** putmock (also **putomock** hereafter): i.e. Potomac.   **151.** burring: i.e., burying "burial."   **152. Croper:** i.e., cropper (tenant farmer or farmer on commission).   **153.** patrick m^c intire (also mctire, **McIntire, McTier** hereafter): Patrick McIntire, in 1751 a taxable inhabitant of Antrim township, Cumberland Co.   **154.** m^c **Dowels fort:** built by John McDowell at the site of his mill in Peters township, Cumberland Co.; in 1754 its fortifications were improved by Lt. Col. John Armstrong of the Pennsylvania Militia. Many of the "forts" mentioned in McCullough's journal were not constructed by the British or by the Pennsylvania government, as was Fort McDowell, but instead were small, ephemeral, and privately built blockhouses.   **155.** 39th ms.   **156.** S48 . . . **Car8ell Chambers fort:** Son . . . Carnell (i.e. Colonel) Chambers fort: a private fort built by the Antrim-born Benjamin Chambers, one of the first settlers west of the Susquehanna, and the site of the future Chambersburg.

Apriel y[e] 23   John marlen[157] and Willem blear was killed and patrick m[c] Cleland Wounded Near max Wells fort   year <17>57

May y[e] 11[158]   mager[159] Cambel and tussey Was killed or Carried away Captives With 14 other persons near putomock <17>57

y[e] Isrelits Was onst Within 11 days treavel[160] of Canan but ther murmiring against god Caused them to Wander 40 years in the Wilderness . . .

may y[e] 12th   John marten[161] and Andrew paul taken Captive by y[e] indins from Canagogige   <17>57

May y[e] 13   two men killed near m[c] Cormicks fort on Canadeqnet[162] <17>57 . . .

may y[e] 15 or 16th   11 persons killed at paxton[163] by y[e] indins - 1757 . . .

may y[e] 17th 1757   David Stoner[164] Credit to 6s 6p for three yeards of Linen . . .

moved to y[e] Caben at Willem [mc]Creries   may y[e] 19—1757[165] . . .

may y[e] 28th—1757   the Reagelors did begin ther march from Langkester towards herrices ferrey[166]

Jun y[e] 6th   2 men killed and 5 men taken Captives near Shipistown[167] 1757 . . .

Jun y[e] 8th   Willem baxter to   one pair of Shoes   0–7–6

Jun y[e] 9th   James Haledy[168] and 14 men killed and taken Captives   james Longs Son and one other man killed in a Quarey at fort fredreck and 19 killed in a mill on Quitapahcaley[169]   one man and a Woman made ther EScape throu y[e] mill

---

157. **John marlen**: John Morlan, in 1751 a taxable inhabitant of Peters township, Cumberland Co.
158. **11**: conjectural (ms. blurred).   159. **mager**: i.e., Major.   160. **treavel**: i.e., travel; spelling indicates Scots pronunciation (**travyl** or **trevl**).   161. **John marten**: John Martin, in 1751 a taxable in Peters township; in 1771 a taxable at Little Cove, Cumberland (later Bedford) Co.   162. **Canadeqnet**: Conodoguinet (or Candoquinette) Creek.   163. **paxton**: Paxton township, Lancaster (later Dauphin) Co.; see chapter 19.
164. **David Stoner**: a German settler in the Conococheagues; ancestor of the present owner of McCullough's diary.   165. This entry and that of 1 July 1757 indicate that McCullough and his family fled eastward a second time to the Marsh Creek settlement, where William McCreary had lived since 1740. However, this was their third move in all, as they had fled to Antietam on 19 April 1756 (see earlier).   166. **the Reagelors . . . herrices ferrey**: Regulars (British soldiers). This was the vanguard of General John Forbes' British army, marching to the frontier from Lancaster (**Langkester**), across the Susquehanna at Harris's Ferry (**herrices ferrey**; the future Harrisburg), and on to Carlisle (**Carlile** hereafter; see entry of 22 June 1757) and beyond. Eventually, the presence of these troops would sharply reduce French and Indian attacks in the Cumberland Valley, but the main British campaign did not get underway until July 1758. The spelling **Reagelors** reflects the loss of [y] before an unstressed vowel, as in **jointure [joyntyoor]** → **joynter [joyntur]** (chapter 1, n. 83).
167. **Shipistown**: Shippensburg, Pa. For the significance of the spelling, see n. 89.   168. **James Haledy**: James Holiday, in 1751 a taxable inhabitant of Peters township, Cumberland Co.   169. **Quitapahcaley**: Quitapahilla (or Quetapahely) Creek, in Lancaster Co.

Wh<e>ells   and 4 men killed at Shear man velley / and 8 batto men[170] killed going to Shimoko[171] all in one Week / together With 2 men killed and 5 taken prisoners near m^c Cormicks fort   1757

St21t62y t4k b566 Ju8 ye 16th 1757[172] . . .

Jun ye 17th one man killed at Culbertsons fort turning gees out of a medow   4 men Shot at him the ingen ye time[173] he Was Scalping him

Jun ye 22 Joseph Willem to   10 yeards and a half of Linen   £0 6-6   <17>57

ye men did begin ther march from Carlile   Jun ye 22[174]

Jun ye 24th   Alexander miller[175] Was killed and 2 of his Children taken away Captives from Canagogige and John kenedy badley Wounded and killed[176] or taken and geret pendergras Daughter killed at fort Litteltown[177]   1757

July ye 1st - I did plow ye Corn at W36627 7^c C9292s[178] 1757 . . .

July ye 2   a Woman and 4 Children taken from trents[179] gape & ye house burnt . . .

July ye 2   one SpringStons killed Near Loagens mill Canagogig

July ye 9^t - trouper Willsons Son killed Near Antitem—1757 . . .

July 10   Solgers killed at Clapems fort[180] by pretended frend<ly> indins in y^e - 1757 . . .

B93862 t4k b566[181] July ye 14 - 1757 . . .

July ye 18 - 6 men killed or taken away from a field reaping

July ye 19 - 19 men killed and taken away reaping in a field Near Shipistown

July y^e <?>   4 men killed near Bakers <fort> dr<i>ven[182] Wagons to fort fredrick   <17>57 . . .

July ye 27th   one mc Kissen Wounded and his Son taken Captive from ye South mounten—1757

---

170. batto men: i.e., batteau men "boatmen."   **171. Shimoko**: the Indian "capital," on the Susquehanna, below the mouth of the North Branch; near the present site of Sunbury.   **172. St21t62y t4k b566 Ju8 ye 16th 1757**: Steatley (i.e., Stately) to<o>k bull Jun<e> ye 16th 1757; see n. 38.   **173. ye time**: while. **174.** See n. 166.   **175. Alexander miller**: in 1751 a taxable inhabitant of Antrim township, Cumberland Co. **176.** Words scratched out between and and killed.   **177. fort Litteltown**: Fort Littleton (or Lytleton), at Sugar Cabins, Cumberland Co.   **178. W36627 7^c C9292s**: Will<i>am Mc Creres (McCreary's). **179. trents**: conjectural (ms. blurred).   **180. Clapems fort**: Clapham's Fort; probably named after Col. William Clapham of the Pennsylvania Militia.   **181. B93862 t4k b566**: Brin<d>le (cow) to<o>k bull; see n. 38. McCullough's coded spelling (Brinle) reflects the Scots preservation of the cluster [nl]; see **kennle** "candle." **182. dr<i>ven**: i.e., driving.

Agust ye 15   Willem manson and his Son killed Near Croses fort[183]   <17>57

agust ye 17th   Willem Waghs Barn was burnt in ye trak[184] york County by indines . . .

Agust ye 18 or 19   14 peopel Killed and taken away from m^r Sinkeys Congregation[185]
. . .

Agust ye 19 - one man killed Near Herrices ferrey   <17>57 . . .

Septemb ye 2   one man Killed Near bigers gape[186] and one inden killed

September ye 9th   one boy and a girel taken away from diney gall[187] - 1757 . . .

Willem boyl to   3 days reaping and one day Staking grean[188]   more to 29 yeards and
on<e> half of ten hundred Woven /[189] . . . more to 43 yeards of 8+ hundred
Woven   September ye Eleventh £0 10 9 / 1757 . . .

September ye 26th—1757   Robert rusk and Johnne Craken With five others killed
and taken Captive Near Chamberses fort . . .

Willem bool to   15 Shillings in Cash Lent September ye 30th - 1757   receved de<b>t
by his daughter mary . . .

october ye 2nd 1757 a very great Slaughter near opickin[190] in virginey 60^ty od<d> killed
and taken captiv . . .

I did get my money from fort fredrick   october ye 5th <17>57 . . .

Willem Baxter to - 17 yeards of too Cloth Woven December y^e - 20th 1757 . . .
December - ye 20 Receved one bushel of Corn from Willem Baxter . . .

December ye 30th 1757   Samul gettey[191] to   15 Shillinngs in Cash Lent by me James
m^c Colock . . .

Willem m^c Crerey to - 11 yeards of Wolling woven in December - <17>57   more to
<m^c> Crery   Nine yeards of Stuf   jenew<ary 17>58 . . .

---

183. Croses fort: Cross's Fort, in the Conococheague settlement.   **184. ye trak**: the Tract. The spelling
shows the Scots loss of final t following a consonant; see **effeck** "effect," **attemp** "attempt."   **185. m^r Sinkeys
Congregation**: the Irish-born Rev. Richard Sankey (1736–1790); in 1737–1760 his Presbyterian congregations
were located at the Hanover church, on Manada Creek, and at the Old Stone church at Carlisle, Cumberland
Co. Sinkey is a reverse spelling based on the Ulster lowering of **i** to **e** or **a**; cf. **sank/senk** "sink."
186. bigers gape: Bigger's Gap.   **187. diney gall**: Donegal township, Lancaster Co. The spelling represents
the Scots pronunciation of Donegal, which of course is also the westernmost county in Ulster.   **188. Staking
grean**: i.e., stacking grain.   **189.** Several words illegible after **Woven**.   **190. opickin**: Opequon, a Scots-Irish
and German settlement in the northern (lower) end of Virginia's Shenandoah Valley.   **191. Samul gettey**:
Samuel Getty, settled at Marsh Creek in 1739.

Jenewary ye 8th - 1758   then Receved two bushels of Ray from Willem Boyl 2 days at rasing ye barn[192] . . .

Feberwary ye 13-1758   Maren Love to   7S and 6d in Cash Lent by me James m^c Colock . . .

Feberwary ye 24 1758   a Sor<e>[193] bloing Snow . . .

march ye 16th—1758   Willem moore[194] to   2 Shillings and Six pence in Cash lent by me James m^c Colock

march ye 22^d James gouley[195] to   3 Shilling in Cash lent by me   James m^c Colock 1758 . . .

Apriel ye 2nd - 1758   two men killed and one taken Near Shipes town

Apriel ye 5th one man killed and 10 taken near bla<c>ks gape

Apriel ye 13   one man killed and 9 taken near Archibald beards at South mounten   1758 . . .

did begin to plant Corn may ye 4^t——1758   did Soo flex Apriel ye 28   had d48 7456ding C498 Ju8 y^e - 15[196]   James m^c Collogh . . .

May ye 21st one Woman and 5 Children taken Captive from yealou bretches[197]   1758

may ye 23^d Joseph gelledy[198] killed   his Wife and one Child taken from Canagogige   1758 . . .

We did so<w> oats may ye 24 - 1758 . . .

Archibald m^c Coloch to   19 yeards of Linen Woven may y^e - 29th 1758   mor to 2 yeards of too Cloath Woven Jun ye 20th . . .

may ye 29th one dinwodey and Crawford Shot by 2 indins in Carels trail   1758 . . .

we ded re<a>p <and> Cut Corn may ye 31 - 1758 . . .

192. Perhaps to be read as **then <I> Received two bushels of Ray from Willem Boyl <in return for> 2 days <work/help> at rasing ye barn**. 193. Sor<e>: severe. 194. Willem moore: William Moore, in 1751 a taxable inhabitant of Peters township, Cumberland Co. 195. gouley: (Mc)Gawley; conjectural (ms. blurred); for the spelling see **poulen** (Pauling/Pawling) earlier. 196. had d48 7456ding C498 Ju8 y^e - 15: had don<e> moulding Corn Jun<e> y^e - 15. 197. yealou bretches: Yellow Breeches Creek; the spelling **bretches** reflects the Ulster lowering of i to e or a. 198. gelledy: i.e., Gildea.

1758 J58[199] yͤ 15 Robert Erven and John Jeck[200] Was purshued[201] by indins near Antetim . . .

July yͤ 20 - one boy plo<w>ing at Swatara[202] was Shot at by indins killed one of his horses and wounded yͤ other   <17>58 . . .

did Sow turneps Agust yͤ 2ᵈ 1758. . . .

In late November, 1758, General John Forbes's army forced the French to abandon Fort Duquesne (later Pittsburgh), a British victory that led to sharply diminished Indian assaults on Pennsylvania's borderlands. Shortly afterward, James McCullough exchanged his farm in Antrim township for another further west, in Peters township, a few miles from Mercersburg, where he lived the rest of his life. In 1763 Pontiac's Rebellion once more decimated the Conococheagues and other western settlements, and on 26 July 1764 a band of Indians massacred the local schoolmaster, Enoch Brown, and 10 of his pupils; only McCullough's nephew, Archie, survived, although he was bludgeoned and scalped. However, in December 1764 McCullough's grief turned to joy when one of his two kidnaped sons, John, was returned from captivity. The fate of James, Jr., was never determined.

In 1767, when the Upper West Conococheague church was permanently reestablished, the congregation comprised 130 families, and a year later Cumberland County's tax assessor listed James McCullough, his wife, and five surviving children as possessing two hundred acres, 32 of them cleared, plus three horses, four cows, and 10 sheep. McCullough lived to see two of his sons, John and Hance, fight in the Continental Army during the American Revolution, and, according to family tradition, he died on 19 December 1781—although his will was not proved until early 1786. McCullough's wife inherited his "large Bible, Whatsens body of devinity and Browns Explanation of the Romans,"[203] while John and Hance were to share their father's "plantation." Hance apparently died in 1786, but John, the redeemed captive who had to relearn English and the white man's ways after more than eight years among the Indians, lived until 1823 on the family farm, became a

---

199. J58: Jun<e>.   **200. Robert Erven**: Robert Erwin (or Irvine), in 1751 a taxable inhabitant of Antrim township, Cumberland Co. **John Jeck**: John Jack, in 1751 a taxable inhabitant of Hopewell township, Cumberland Co.   **201. purshued**: pursued; Scots form.   **202. Swatara**: Creek and township, also Fort Swatara near Swatara Gap, in Lancaster Co.   **203.** Will of James McCullough, signed 2 May 1778 (Will Book A, p. 66, in Kittochtinny Historical Society, Chambersburg, Pa.; courtesy of Lillian Colletta). **Whatsens body of devinity**: *A Body of Practical Divinity: Consisting of Above One Hundred Seventy Six Sermons on the Lesser Catechism Composed by the Reverend Assembly of Divines at Westminster: with a Supplement of Some Sermons on Several Texts of Scripture* (London, 1692), by Thomas Watson (d. 1686), an English Presbyterian divine, who at the Restoration (1660) was ejected from his church, St. Stephen's, Walbrook, for Nonconformity, although in 1672 he regained a preaching license. Revised editions of Watson's most famous work were published as late as 1855 under the title *A Body of Divinity*. ¶**Browns Explanation of the Romans**: *An Explanation of the Epistle to the Romans* (1679), by Thomas Brown (1610?–1679); born in Kirkudbright, Scotland, from 1655 Brown was minister of Wamphray in Annandale, in Dumfriesshire, but in 1662 he was arrested and banished for opposing Charles II's interference in Presbyterian church affairs; exiled in Holland, Brown became minister of the Scots church in Rotterdam.

ruling elder in his father's church, and had six children whose descendants still lived and farmed in Franklin County in the early twentieth century.

22 ✳

Elizabeth Guthrie Brownlee Guthrie, 1755–1829

Mary Elizabeth McDowell Greenlee[1] was unique in her aggressive personality and public image. In early America the condition of Scots-Irish and other women usually was determined by the men on whom, by law and custom, they were dependent—on their fathers prior to marriage, and on their husbands thereafter. The life and the following petition of Elizabeth Guthrie Brownlee Guthrie (1755–1842) dramatically illustrates the potentially dire consequences of female subordination, for although Guthrie's father was a relatively prominent figure in the Pennsylvania backcountry, successive "unlucky" marriages brought violence and tragedy to her youth and, for the remainder of her long life, the hardscrabble poverty of a squatter's wife on the Pennsylvania frontier.

Guthrie's parents represented the last great wave of Ulster Presbyterian immigrants who pushed beyond the Cumberland Valley and settled in Pennsylvania's southwestern corner immediately prior to the American Revolution. The petitioner's father, John Guthrie (ca. 1720–1797), was the second youngest of seven brothers, Covenanting Presbyterians from Londonderry city, who emigrated to the American colonies. Accompanied by his wife, Mary Jane Reed, and their six children, John Guthrie arrived in Pennsylvania in 1771 and soon moved to the colony's far western frontier, to what in 1773 became Westmoreland County. There he took up land along Loyalhanna Creek, near the ill-fated village of Hannastown, the first county seat, where he also served as a justice of the peace.

The Guthrie family history also reveals how the last prerevolutionary settlers from Ulster overlapped and intermingled with earlier Scots-Irish emigrants and their American-born children on the trans-Appalachian frontier. Robert Guthrie (b. 1711), John Guthrie's oldest brother and a carpenter, had come to Pennsylvania in the early 1740s, and subsequently both he and his descendants moved west in stages. After his arrival, Robert Guthrie lived successively in Philadelphia, Chester County, Lancaster, and Carlisle. By the eve of the Revolution, Robert's son, James, owned a 264-acre farm on Back Creek, in Cumberland County. Not until 1780 did James Guthrie join his uncle John in Westmoreland County, where he grew wealthy through land speculations. Prior to the Revolution, however, at least two of James's children preceded him across the Alleghenies and settled in Westmoreland. There in 1784 one of James Guthrie's sons, William, would become the second husband of John Guthrie's daughter, Elizabeth the petitioner. This marriage of

1. See chapter 20.

second cousins thus reunited the two branches of the Guthrie family, sundered by emigration from Ireland, on the banks of the Loyalhanna.

The French and Indian War and Pontiac's rebellion had delayed white settlement in southwestern Pennsylvania. It was not until 1769, after the first treaty of Fort Stanwix (1768) formally extinguished tribal claims to the area, that large numbers of Scots-Irish, the American-born from the Cumberland Valley as well as new immigrants from Ulster, applied for land warrants, crossed the mountains on Forbes's military road, and took up farms in the vicinity of Fort Pitt (formerly the French Fort Duquesne), along the Allegheny River and its tributaries. There they encountered another stream of migrants from Virginia, including some of Ulster origin, whose settlement was encouraged by Lord Dunmore[2] and the Ohio Company to assert Virginia's title to the region. Dunmore's claims led to local conflicts between magistrates, militia, and settlers loyal to Virginia or Pennsylvania, and in 1774 his aggression toward the tribes in the Ohio country precipitated "Dunmore's War," which exposed the Westmoreland settlements to Indian attacks.

Despite this internal strife, Westmoreland's inhabitants united to support the American Revolution, and in July 1776 Elizabeth Guthrie's first husband, Joseph Brownlee, and her future second husband, William Guthrie, joined their kinsmen and neighbors and enlisted in the Eighth Pennsylvania Regiment of the Continental Army. However, their enthusiasm soon soured when Congress ordered the Regiment to march east, in the dead of winter, to join Washington's forces in New Jersey, thus leaving their families almost defenseless against British, Tory, and Indian assaults on the western frontiers. In 1778 the Eighth Pennsylvania was transferred back to Fort Pitt, but its efforts to secure the Ohio country were largely unsuccessful. In desperation, local men such as Brownlee and Guthrie built small stockades and formed official and irregular ranger companies to patrol the frontiers, but their hatred of Indians was so great that their butchery rivaled that of their foes and antagonized even friendly tribes. Their efforts could not prevent the last major assault by Canadian riflemen and Seneca warriors, who destroyed Hannastown and captured Brownlee and his family on 13 July 1782. The Indians' recognition of Brownlee as one of their most ruthless foes, quickly sealed his and his young son's fate, leaving his grieving wife to endure the hardships that she described, nearly 47 years later, in the following petition to the Pennsylvania legislature, begging for a pension as a Revolutionary soldier's widow.

Elizabeth Guthrie Brownlee Guthrie, Redbank Township, Clarion County, Pennsylvania, petition to the Pennsylvania Assembly, Harrisburg, 5 February 1829

That your petitioner was born in the city of Londonderry, A.D. 1755; that she emigrated to this country with her father, John Guthrie, in the year 1771;[3] that in less

---

2. John Murray (1732–1809), Earl of Dunmore and Virginia's colonial governor immediately prior to the Revolution. **3.** For demographic data on Londonderry city and its environs, see appendix 2.1a, on chapter 22.

than one year thereafter, the said John Guthrie, with his family moved to Westmoreland county, settled near Poke Run;[4] (then beyond the frontiers;) had no other neighbors than the savage nations, and during the time of what is called "Dunmore's war" was frequently obliged to fly to Hannastown fort: In 1775 she married Joseph Brownlee, then a lieutenant in Captain Irwin's company of riflemen.[5] Shortly after the company was called to the state of New Jersey, Lieutenant Brownlee, her husband, was taken prisoner at the battle of Long Island:[6] he was afterwards exchanged and annexed to Colonel Broadhead's regiment, marched to the Big Island in the Susquehanna, and to Wyoming, where they routed the Indians from their hiding places and then returned to Carlisle; from thence they were ordered to Fort Pitt, thence down the Ohio to the place where Fort Lawrence stood, which fort they erected.[7] At this place a party under the command of Lieutenant Brownlee were sent as a scout after the Indians, when he got a stab in his foot, which disabled him from performing any other active service. He then returned home and resided with his wife (your present petitioner) near Greensburgh, until the burning of Hannastown by the Indians. He was then at Miller's fort, about two miles distant, and with most of the settlers in the neighborhood endeavored to make their escape; he, with his son[8] in his arms, your petitioner with a child at her breast, and a number of others, who were overtaken by the savages, at the sight of whom Mrs. Hanna exclaimed, "O, Captain Brownlee!"   The savages on hearing his name, instantly fell upon him and murdered him and his son, together with nine other persons; petitioner, her infant and the aforesaid Mrs. Hanna, only escaping[9] their murderous tomahawks. Your petitioner with her little child in her arms was dragged along as prisoners.[10]

4. **Poke Run**: a stream in present Washington township, Westmoreland Co.   5. **Captain Irwin's company of riflemen**: Joseph Irwin was captain of a company of riflemen, raised in Westmoreland Co. in March 1776; the company was part of the Eighth Pennsylvania Regiment, commanded by Col. Daniel Brodhead (**Broadhead** hereafter), which fought in the Battle of Long Island (17 August 1776) and also in the American defeats at Brandywine, Paoli, and Germantown. The Regiment passed the terrible winter of 1777–1778 at Valley Forge, but in summer 1778 was sent back to Fort Pitt to guard the western frontiers, pausing en route in Carlisle to seek for the British and Iroquois who had massacred the settlers in the Wyoming Valley on 3 July. Three hundred soldiers who had gone east with the Eighth Regiment never returned to Westmoreland Co.   6. **the battle of Long Island**: a major defeat for Washington's army, which thereby failed to prevent the British occupation of New York City on 15 September 1776; see n. 5.   7. In October 1778, General Lachlan McIntosh, American commander at Fort Pitt, took an army of 1,300 soldiers, Westmoreland militia, and then-friendly Delaware Indians on a vain expedition to capture the British base at Detroit. They got no further than the Tuscarawas River, in the Ohio country, where McIntosh constructed an outpost named Fort Laurens (**Fort Lawrence**). In summer 1779, Col. Broadhead, who had succeeded McIntosh as commander, abandoned Fort Laurens and relied primarily on rangers such as Brownlee and Guthrie to secure the frontier but with no greater success.   8. **his son**: Guthrie family records indicate that John was the name of Joseph and Elizabeth Brownlee's four-year-old son. Their daughter, aged four months when captured with her mother, was named Jane.   9. **only escaping**: "being the only ones to escape."   10. Hannastown was about three miles northeast of Greensburg and of Brownlee's farm. When the attack occurred, on 13 July 1782, many of the settlers, including the Brownlees, were attending a wedding feast at Miller's Station, about two miles south of Hannastown. The British officer who ordered the attack later reported that his forces killed "15 of the Enimy

Her suffering during thirteen days march through the wilderness of that country, (part of which is in the same state to this day,) can be better conceived than described, at which time they arrived at Cateragus,[11] with several prisoners from various places, when she was kept two weeks on[12] the pith of young cornstalks, of which she had but a small quantity allowed her daily. She was marched from Cateragus to Buffalo,[13] during which period she was taken with the fever and ague,[14] when a council was called to determine on the mode of putting her to death! At this council was a white man who had the command of a party of Indians, who was called Capt. Lottridge.[15] He told them that she was so far reduced that she could affort them no amusement in dying by any mode of torture they could inflict; but advised them to take her to Niagara and exhange her for rum, and that would afford them more amusement than her death could possibly do—his counsel was adopted and her life spared.

They remained at Buffalo nearly four months in a very low state of health, uncomfortable lodgings and scant provisions. Before she could be removed to Niagara, where she was about to be removed, they found she was unable to carry her child; but they tied it on her back, gave her a stick and in that manner drove her along before them past Fort Slusher[16] on to Niagara, where they sold her for 20 dollars and 2 gallons of rum and her child for 10 dollars.—Being purchased by a British officer, she was taken in his family and attended to in such a manner that in two weeks her health was so far restored that she was put on board a vessel and taken to Carlton Island,[17] in Lake Ontario—was then put on board of an open boat and after traveling two cold days in the month of November she arrived in a perishing condition at Montreal. There she was kept a prisoner seven months, and compelled to live on musted[18] meal and stinking meat until peace was declared and a general exchange of prisoners took place. She was then, with many others, sent to St. John's on the Sorrel river, thence by Crown Point to Ticonderoga, where an American officer received the prisoners. She then returned

and took 10 Prisoners," in addition to destroying "between three and four Hundred head of horn'd Cattle, 70 Horses, [plus] Sheep and Hogs innumerable." (cited in Anna L. Warren, *A Captive's Tale* . . . , 15; see Sources). However, although Hannastown itself was burned to the ground, most of the inhabitants fled in time to the safety of the village stockade. Besides those killed or captured at Miller's Station, one of the few additional casualties was Elizabeth Guthrie Brownlee's youngest brother. ¶**Mrs. Hanna**: Elizabeth Kelly Hanna, wife of Robert Hanna, whose tavern was the nucleus of the settlement; she and her daughter were taken prisoner but later exchanged and returned to Westmoreland Co.   **11. Cateragus**: Cattaraugus, a Seneca village near the eastern shore of Lake Erie.   **12. was kept**: was maintained; see chapter 24, n. 13.   **13. Buffalo**: Buffalo Creek, an Indian village just below the headwaters of the Niagara River.   **14. ague** (in connection with fever): chills.   **15. Captain Robert Lottridge**: an officer in Col. John Butler's notorious Rangers, who accompanied the Indian raiding party that attacked Hannastown. His own wife and children were prisoners of the Americans, which may account for his sympathetic treatment of Elizabeth Guthrie Brownlee.   **16. Fort Slusher**: Fort Schlosser, built in 1759 to guard the Upper Niagara; located on the east bank of the Niagara River north of Grand Island.   **17. Carleton Island**: an island in Lake Ontario at the headwaters of the St. Lawrence River, which was fortified by the British and used as a military supply base during the Revolution. **18. musted**: mouldy.

by Skeensborough, Saratoga, Fort Anne, Fort Edward, the Half Moon Battery, Albany, New York, Philadelphia, &., to the ruins of Hannastown, in the county of Westmoreland, emaciated, sickly, without the consolation of her husband, without money, without friends, who could afford her relief, her house and furniture burned by the savages, together with all her husband's papers and accounts.[19] She supported herself and child by her own industry for two years, at the expiration of which time she married Capt. William Guthrie, who then commanded a company of rangers, for the protection of the frontiers, until peace was fully and finally established.[20] His habits of life were not well calculated to make a comfortable living by farming, and he was unable to commence any other business   consequently he remained in great want of the indispensable necessaries of life, until he obtained a pension a few years since from this commonwealth. But through an accidental fall of a wagon a few months ago from a high bridge, he was killed.[21]

Thus your petitioner is now left in her old days destitute of everything that could make her comfortable in this world. She therefore prays your honorable body to grant her the same pension which was received by her late husband. And she will ever pray, &c.[22]

Her petition's closing lines suggest that Elizabeth Guthrie found the 44 years after the Hannastown raid almost as miserable as her one year's captivity in Canada. Hannastown's dispirited inhabitants never rebuilt their village, and although Joseph Brownlee had owned six hundred acres in Westmoreland County, apparently his widow could recover none of his property, which was sold for debt. By all accounts, Elizabeth's life with her second husband, the impecunious and perhaps alcoholic William Guthrie, was fraught with insecurity. Pennsylvania land records indicate that between 1784 and 1799 William took out warrants on various parcels of Westmoreland County land totaling over one thousand acres, but evidently he was less successful in his speculations than his father had been, and by the early 1790s Westmoreland's was an increasingly stratified society, in which a majority of the inhabitants owned little or no land. Thus, in 1806 (or 1810—accounts differ)

19. Elizabeth Guthrie Brownlee and her daughter, Jane, returned to Westmoreland Co. in the late summer of 1783, after an ordeal of about thirteen months.   **20. William Guthrie** enlisted in May 1776, served in the battles of Trenton and Princeton, and was discharged in January 1777. In 1780 he reenlisted and served one year as lieutenant in Capt. Mathew Jack's company of frontier rangers and a second year as captain of his own company. According to Guthrie family records, William married Elizabeth Brownlee in 1784, although her petition says that she delayed remarriage for two years after her return from captivity. Since their first child was born in April 1785, perhaps her descendants' circumspection necessitated a 1784 marriage.   **21.** William Guthrie died, as his widow described, on 10 March 1828. In about 1825 he had applied for and received a pension for his own military services from the state of Pennsylvania.   **22. and she will ever pray, &c.**: the petitioner conventionally prays at the end of the petition for the health and long life of the person or body petitioned.

William Guthrie dragged his wife and their nine surviving children,[23] plus Elizabeth's daughter by Joseph Brownlee, north to what was then Armstrong County (est. 1800), later Clarion County (est. 1839), where they squatted in an unsettled wilderness at the mouth of Leatherwood Creek, near the future village of Smithfield in Redbank, later Porter, township. Apparently, however, William's ventures on this new frontier were equally unprofitable, and only his Revolutionary soldier's pension from the Pennsylvania government (secured ca. 1825) kept his family above dire poverty prior to his death in 1828.

In 1829 Elizabeth's own petition to Harrisburg was successful, as on 23 March the Pennsylvania Assembly passed an act that authorized the state treasurer to pay "to her order sixty dollars immediately, and an annuity of sixty dollars, payable half yearly during life." After her husband's death, she lived on a farm in Redbank township, with her youngest son, Joseph Brownlee Guthrie, until she died, aged 87, on 11 February 1842. By this time, Elizabeth's daughter, Jane, who had shared her Canadian captivity, had long since married and moved to Ohio.[24] However, in 1847 Joseph and her other surviving children by William Guthrie applied for and, two years later, received a federal pension as orphans of Elizabeth's first Revolutionary soldier-husband, Joseph Brownlee.

23 ✳

Daniel Kent, 1786–1794

Many early eighteenth-century Irish emigrants—like the Parkes, Witherspoons, and McDowells[1]—could sell their leases or otherwise amass sufficient capital to transport entire families across the Atlantic and immediately commence homesteading in the colonies. However, increasing numbers of those who emigrated later, just prior to and after the American Revolution, were less affluent and traveled singly, often as indentured servants. Except perhaps as squatters in the backcountry, relatively few Irish servants were able to establish themselves as farmers after their indentures expired.[2] This was especially true of craftsmen or laborers who were born and raised in Irish cities and hence unaccus-

---

23. Elizabeth and William Guthrie's children were: (1) William (b. 21 April 1785), died at Smithland, Armstrong Co., Pa.; (2) James (1786–1851), settled on a large farm near Summerville, Jefferson Co., Pa.; (3) Elizabeth (b. 1788), married a Mr. Boles, had 10 children, and moved to Ohio; (4) Mary (1789–1809), died unmarried; (5) Jane, twin to Mary, died in infancy; (6) Jennie (b. 1791), married a Mr. Matthews and "moved east"; (7) name unknown (b. 1793); (8) Nancy (1794–1826), married a Mr. Coon, died of consumption—her daughter was raised by Elizabeth Brownlee Guthrie; (9) Joanna (b. 1796), married Alexander Brown; and (10) Joseph Brownlee Guthrie (1798–1883), who in 1837 married Mary Ann Fleming and lived at Licking, Porter township, Clarion Co., Pa.   **24.** According to family records, Jane Brownlee married James Hugle, Hughes, or Jesse Hukel (as her husband's name was variously recorded) and with him moved to Muskingum Co., Ohio.   **1.** On the Parkes, Witherspoons, and McDowells, see chapters 9, 18, and 20, respectively.   **2.** On Irish indentured servants in rural America, see chapter 30.

tomed to the demands of agriculture. Yet one exception was Daniel Kent, a journeymen cutler and a Methodist from Limerick city, who in 1785 shipped as a servant to Philadelphia. Through his remarkable adaptability, work ethic, religious conversion, and fortunate marriage, Kent eventually became the owner of a snug farm in Chester County, Pennsylvania. For his self-transformation, however—for the abandonment of his Irish associations and inherited faith—Kent may have paid a psychological price greater than he could ever acknowledge.

Daniel Kent was born 11 July 1765, the eldest of the 11 children of Ann and William Kent, a master cutler whose home and shop were near St. John's Gate, in St. Mary's parish, in the old Irish Town section of Limerick.[3] Kents from England had settled in Munster since the late 1500s, but Daniel Kent's ancestors probably came to Limerick after the Cromwellian wars, with the great influx of New English Protestants who in 1659 comprised over half the city's population. By the last quarter of the eighteenth century, however, Protestants probably numbered only a fourth or fewer of Limerick's approximately 35,000 inhabitants, and although the city's merchant community flourished in its elegant new Georgian development, Newtown Pery (built from 1769), Protestant craftsmen in "noisome" or increasingly marginal trades, such as cutlery, were left behind, economically and socially, in the narrow, congested streets of medieval Limerick's Irish and English towns.[4] By the 1780s these were squalid, impoverished neighborhoods, where the Kents and other Protestant artisans were increasingly outnumbered by Catholic migrants from the surrounding countryside. Such circumstances were ideal for the growth of Irish Methodism. Ever since John Wesley's first visit to the city in 1749,[5] Methodism's emphasis on diligence, frugality, and respectability, as well as its fervent loyalism and anti-Catholicism, had considerable appeal for middling- and lower-rank Protestants in southern Irish towns such as Limerick, beleaguered as they were by economic distress and by the rise of Catholic competitors in trade and petty manufacturing.[6] By 1789, when Wesley last visited Ireland,

---

3. The Kents' other children were: John, who enlisted in the English artillery during the French wars and died in December 1797 at St. Domingue (Haiti); George (1771–1794), a lieutenant in the English navy who died shortly after returning from a voyage to China; Anne (Nelly), who ca. 1788–1789 married Thomas Quin, nailor, of Limerick; Mary, who ca. 1799 married William Byrne, nailor, of Limerick; William (b. 1774), who became a cutler in Limerick; Richard (b. 1778), a journeyman cabinetmaker ca. 1800; Thomas, his father's halfwit shop assistant ca. 1800; Joseph (b. 1784), so disabled by smallpox he was incapable of working; and Charles (b. 1789), in 1806 an assistant to his uncle Richard Kent, a naval ship's surgeon stationed at Sheerness, at the mouth of the Thames.   **4.** For demographic data on Limerick city, see appendix 2.2b, on chapter 23.
5. John Wesley (1703–1791): English clergyman, evangelist, and, with his brother Charles (1707–1788), founder and organizer of Arminian Methodism in Britain and in Ireland, where he visited and preached 42 times from 1747, as recorded in his detailed journals. Wesley also evangelized in America, most notably in Georgia in the late 1730s.   **6.** In 1771 John Wesley visited Limerick city and reported that he "found no Society in Ireland, member for member, so rooted and ground in love," although the same year a local informant confessed that "the bulk of the Society" was too poor to help cover the debt that incumbered the "new preaching house" built in 1764–1765. In 1775 Wesley discovered only 101 Methodists in the city, "being 7 less than two years

Irish Methodists numbered over 14,000, a 500 percent increase since 1770, and almost half of them lived in cities and market towns in Leinster and Munster.[7]

Methodist fervor could not stem emigration from southern Irish Protestant communities, however; indeed, Wesley's emphasis on education and uplift may have fostered ambitions that could not be satisfied at home.[8] Certainly, Daniel Kent received a "tender Education"[9] and was exceptionally literate, and, years after his emigration, his aunt remembered how, as a child, he "used to be asking about America."[10] However, there were other, more immediate causes for Kent's precipitous departure from Ireland, an act of "foolish infatuation"[11] that startled and dismayed his parents: mounting frustration with "the badness of Trade"[12] as he tramped from Limerick to Cork and on toward Dublin, vainly seeking employment; conflict with his brother William, an apprentice or journeyman cutler in his father's shop; perhaps a desire to escape parental restraints on "the Liberties that the folly of Youth is subject to," as Limerick's Methodist elders suspected;[13] or, more likely, given Kent's exemplary behavior in Pennsylvania and his own later admonitions, a pious urge to seek "a sober Virtuous way of Living in America" and to break from the "gross vices" that he and his "old Companions" had indulged in Ireland.[14]

In any case, in May 1785, unable to find work in Waterford city and "hearing that there was A Vessel Ready to Sail" for the New World, Kent was seized—as he later claimed—by such "a Strange notion Coming In My head of Going on Board that I could not Get Over it," despite his friends' dissuasion.[15] Accordingly, on 21 May he signed an indenture with the ship's captain, John Johnston, agreeing to serve the latter or his assigns for three years in return for passage to America, plus "Meat, Drink, Apparel and Lodging, with other Necessaries during the said Term," and "the usual Allowance,[16] according to the Laws and Customs of that part of America they may arrive at." On 23 May Kent and

previously," but in 1778 he found the local "congregations good and well sustained, and . . . more alive to God and more loving than he had known them to be for many years." E. R. Ware, ed., *The Works of John Wesley*, vol. 22 (1993), 274, 450; and C. H. Crookshank, *History of Methodism in Ireland*, vol. 1, 295–96, 318; see Sources. **7.** In the late eighteenth century a majority of Irish Methodists lived in Ulster, particularly in the "linen triangle" bounded by Lisburn, Dungannon, and Newry; e.g., see chapter 67. **8.** In the 1750s many of the Protestant German refugees from the Palatine, who had been settled in rural Co. Limerick during Queen Anne's reign (1702–1714), converted to Methodism and, beginning in 1760, began to remigrate to British America, primarily under the leadership of lay preacher Philip Embury (d. 1773), who founded in New York City one of the first Methodist churches in the New World. After the British evacuated New York at the end of the Revolution, much of Embury's predominantly loyalist congregation, including his widow and children, moved once again and resettled in Canada. **9.** William and Ann Kent, Limerick, to Daniel Kent, West Bradford, Pa., 25 January 1786. **10.** William Kent, Limerick, to Daniel and Esther Kent, East Fallowfield, Pa., 12 May 1804. **11.** Ja[c]ques Ingram et al., Limerick, reference for Daniel Kent, 24 January 1786, in Daniel Kent's letters; see Sources, chapter 23. **12.** William and Ann Kent, 25 January 1786. **13.** Ja[c]ques Ingram, 24 January 1786. **14.** Daniel Kent, East Caln, Pa., to William and Ann Kent, Limerick, 1 October 1789. **15.** Daniel Kent, West Bradford, Pa., to William and Ann Kent, Limerick, 7 January 1787. **16.** Allowance: "freedom dues": money, clothes, tools, etc., which masters were contractually and legally obligated to give their servants at the termination of their contracts, provided the latter had served "faithfully." The passages quoted in this sentence are from Kent's indenture, in Daniel Kent's letters; see Sources, chapter 23.

about 50 other indentured servants sailed for Philadelphia aboard Johnston's brigantine, *Asia*, arriving on 26 July after a voyage of nine weeks and two days. In the following letter, the second and the most detailed of his earliest communications with his parents, Kent described his passage and his initial experiences in Pennsylvania.

Letter 1.

Daniel Kent, West Bradford Township, Chester County, Pennsylvania,
to William and Ann Kent, St. John's Gate, Limerick, 20 May 1786

W Bradford In Pennsylvania   1786

Dr Parents   America   5th Mo 20th

Imake bold to trouble you with these lines In hopes they Will find you and the family In A State of Health Eaqual To my Desires,   I wrote to you Before this the 11th of the 11<th> Month 1785 In which Igave you an Account of my Passage & Settlement here But Got no Answer,   However Iwait Impatiently for it,   But least[17] you have not Rec^d my letter I shall Send you Some Account In this,   Iwrote to you Before I left Cork of my Intention of Going to Dublin And Set of<f> In A Couple of Days After. When I Got As far as Clonmell[18] Iwas much fatagued with the Walk And was Resolved to go to Waterford by Water Which I did & found Thomas Quin Cutler At Work there But the trade Being Bad there Icould Get no Work. Iheard that there was A Vessel there Ready to Sail for this Continent freighted With Passengers[19] On Which Iwent On Board Being Seventh <day> Afternoon And We weighed Anchor first day Being the 23^d of the 5th Month   Ihave nothing Remarkable to Relate Concerning Our Passage but that we had some Bad Weather In which Our Bowsprit was Sprung & Our foremast Nearly taken Away,   We Cast Anchor Near Philadelp<h>ia The 26th of the 7th Month & lay there four weeks During which time Most of Our Company was taken Away.[20]   we then Went Up the Country (being About 20 In Number) towards this place (the Mate of the Vessel Being withus) Where I found Such Aman as I wished for, Whom Iam to Serve three years from the time the Vessel Cast Anchor Here,   His Name is Joseph Hawley By Profession A Quaker & Occupation Afarmer & has a large Plantation   There is not Many In these parts of my

---

17. least: i.e., lest (here = in case).   **18. Clonmell**: Clonmel, a major market town on the River Suir, in south Co. Tipperary.   **19. freighted With Passengers**: with passengers as cargo.   **20. Most of Our Company was taken Away**: i.e., about thirty of the fifty indentured servants aboard the *Asia* were sold in Philadelphia, while the ship lay in the Delaware River. Technically, Kent was a would-be "redemptioner": according to his contract, had Kent been able to pay Johnston £10 sterling within 20 days of arriving in America, he would have been able to void his indenture. Unable to find his own master and redeem himself, however, Kent and about 20 other unsold servants were transported by Johnston's first mate into Chester Co., where their contracts were sold to farmers such as Joseph Hawley.

D A N I E L   K E N T

Profession.[21] However I attend Quaker Meetings Mostly once A week And Seem to Like the Way of Silent Worship Very Well,

You need not Be uneasy At my Situation for I Am not   I am Quite Contented

My Business Is of little Use here,   Blacksmiths, Carpenters Shoemakers, Bricklayers, & taylors Are the Chief trades here. But there is Enough of Each trade here Already,[22]

Kent was indeed fortunate to be settled in Chester County and indentured to Joseph Hawley (1735–1817), who on 27 August 1785 had purchased Daniel's indenture from Johnston for £14 10s. At least a fourth of Chester's inhabitants were of Irish birth or descent, and the wealthiest farmers among them were generally Quakers.[23] In addition, the farms along the branches of the Brandywine River were fertile and prosperous, and traditionally servants in eastern Pennsylvania were treated much better than further south, in Maryland or Virginia. Also, Hawley himself had several reasons to be sympathetic to his young Irish servant. Both shared an artisanal background, for although in 1785 Hawley owned 150 acres in West Bradford township (plus another 50 acres in East Bradford), until 1782, when he inherited his father's lands, he had been merely a "taylor" with a smallholding. Moreover, in her youth Hawley's own wife had been an orphaned, indentured servant from England.[24] Finally, it appears that at least one of Hawley's daughters, Esther, found her father's new employee romantically attractive.

At least equally important for Daniel Kent's future prospects was his quick embrace of the Hawleys' religious culture. Apparently Kent found the serenity of his master's Quaker worship spiritually satisfying, but the high status that local Friends enjoyed surely impressed him as well. Since the late 1600s Quakers had been socially and culturally dominant in Chester County. By contrast, when Kent arrived in Philadelphia the few hundred Methodists there and in rural east Pennsylvania's scattered ironworks were generally poor laborers, as their bishop admitted, while most of their ministers were poorly educated itinerants. Moreover, whereas in Ireland by the 1780s the Methodists' political conserva-

---

21. **My Profession**: i.e., Methodists.   22. The cover page of the letter is inscribed, in Daniel Kent's handwriting, "2nd Copy," hence its abrupt ending, lack of complimentary close, etc.   23. At the time of the Revolution, perhaps a fifth of Chester Co.'s inhabitants were of Ulster Presbyterian birth or background; including Irish Quakers, Anglicans, and Catholics (the latter primarily indentured servants), at least a fourth, perhaps even a third, of the county's population was variously "Irish"—although rural Chester's Irish Quakers (usually of English origins) identified and associated more closely with their coreligionists of English and Welsh descent than with the Scots-Irish or with Irish Anglicans or, certainly, with Irish Catholics. In Philadelphia, however, pan-Irish associations, at least on formal levels, were more common; see chapters 56 and 58.   24. Elizabeth Spackman Hawley (1735–1796): daughter of a Wiltshire, England, wool-comber, who died ca. 1746 and whose widow and orphans were brought to America about 1750 through the charity of her maternal uncle, William Beale (1709–1800), of West Whiteland township, Chester Co. She married Hawley in 1762 and had eight children. ¶Hawley's own father, Benjamin (1703–1782), emigrated from England in 1722 and may also have been an indentured servant in Chester Co. before becoming a schoolteacher and, by 1767, a farmer of 140 acres in East Bradford township.

tism had generally won them acceptance among other Protestants, in America their social and racial egalitarianism were still often viewed as threats to social order. Thus, as his preceding letter indicates, Kent adopted Quaker ways—such as their manner of dating days and months—shortly after entering Hawley's household, and in 1789 he became a full member of the Bradford monthly meeting. For an ambitious youth, isolated without kinsmen or friends in Chester County, rapid acculturation and conversion were natural, perhaps inevitable, strategies—as they had long been for most Irish servants of Catholic and Anglican origins in the backcountry regions where Scots-Irish Presbyterians predominated.

Back in Limerick, however, old William Kent was distressed to learn of his son's situation, especially when he heard that "some of those People who sailed with you have met since their arrival in America with the severest Cruelty and hardship."[25] While admitting that "trade is very bad here" in Ireland, Daniel's father could not imagine how a genteelly educated urban craftsman could find the labor of a bound farm worker congenial or even bearable: "Nature must allow," he wrote, "that y^r low situation in life must give no unknown trouble to think that one of y^r tender rearing should voluntarily plunge yourself in the state of a slave." Kent prayed "to the Almighty in his good time to extricate"[26] Daniel from his plight but also begged all the "Persons of Consquence" whom he knew in Limerick for a testimonial to his son's character, which he quickly sent to Chester County in hopes of elevating Daniel's status in the eyes of his master and new neighbors.[27] However, Daniel Kent himself sent nothing but glowing reports to his parents, such as the following letter written toward the close of his indenture.

Letter 2.
**Daniel Kent, West Bradford Township, Chester County, Pennsylvania,
to William and Ann Kent, St. John's Gate, Limerick, 6 April 1788**

West Bradford In Chester County

Dr Parents   Pennsylvania   4th Month the 6th 1788

I received your Letter of the 21st of March of 1787 After Six or Seven Months Passage which Gave me the Greatest Pleasure and Satisfaction to hear you are all In health. I enjoy Good Health at Present thanks be To god for it. Iam sorry to hear trade is so bad, but I am in hopes it will Revive again.   I am Likewise Sorry To hear of my Brother John's Ill Luck with his Master And the Death of his Mistress, But Iwould

25. William and Ann Kent, Limerick, to Daniel Kent, West Bradford, Pa., 21 March 1787.   26. William Kent, Limerick, to Daniel Kent, West Bradford, Pa., 31 July 1786.   27. William and Ann Kent, 25 January 1786.

advise you To keep him to his Trade.[28]   As for my part Istill Rem^n Contented And Satisfied In my Present Situation   Ishall be free the 26th of the 7th Month Being then Three years from the time the Ship which I came In Cast Anchor In America.   Ishall Like to follow My trade If Ican fall Into Business   Other wise Ishall follow Plantation Work Except Some Easier[29] Way of Life should Present itself   However your Good advice would be very Acceptable to me In your Next Letter Which Ihope you will forward upon Receipt of this,   This Country at Present Is quiet And Peaceable. Provisions are very Low And Money Very Scarce. Ilike the Country Better than Idid at my first Settlement here So Ithink Icould spend my Lifetime here And Though I have to work Harder here than at home my Wages being proportionable[30] I Choose this Country Before my Native Country   I think itis Preferable to Ireland for an honest Industrious Man yet Iwould not advise you to send any more Servants here As they Cannot Behave themselves better   There are but four or five out of twenty And Upwards that Came to this part of the Country With me that have Stayed with their Masters,   the Rest Ran away   Some have Been taken up and Condemned to serve a Longer time,   Ihave no more to write at Present But Conclude with my Love and Duty to my Grandmother And Desires for her Good Health and Long Life   my Love to my Brothers & Sisters To My Cousin Zachariah And Margret My Aunt Deacon Cousin Polly and Nancy   My Best Respects to Uncle Richard And to you In particular So

     Remain your Dutiful Son

                  Daniel Kent

     My love to All Enquiring Friend<s>

NB   I should have wrote to you Before now but there is no Ships Sails from here In the winter——

On 26 August 1788, Joseph Hawley freed Daniel Kent, gave him his freedom dues in clothing and cash, and certified that Kent had "Served the S^d Indented time Honestly" and without blemish in his "Conduct and Conversation."[31] However, as the closing of Kent's preceding letter suggests, few ships traveled regularly between Limerick and Philadelphia, especially as the provision trade between southern Irish and North American

---

28. Brother John's Ill Luck . . . to his Trade: John (or "Jack") Kent had been apprenticed to a tradesman in Dublin, but on 21 March 1787, his father had written that John's master and mistress had moved to Limerick "where they remain about 3 Months which time we had Jack mostly, when out of A Drunken frolic his Master went of[f] again leaving your Brother behind without A Fee or very little of his Trade." Eventually, John Kent joined the British army.   **29. Some thing Easier** ms.   **30.** A second, incomplete copy of this letter reads as follows: "Ilike the Country better than Idid at my first Settlement here so Ithink Icould Spend my lifetime here and If Ihave to work harder here my wages are higher in Proportion than In Ireland   Icould Save more In a year here If Icould Get Constant work than Icould in Two years In Ireland So Ithink Its a good Country for an Industrious honest man. . . . "   **31.** Joseph Hawley's endorsement of Kent's indenture, 26 August 1788.

ports rapidly declined after the American Revolution. Hence Daniel had not received an answer to his appeal for advice of 6 April 1788 before he wrote the following letter in late 1789, describing his new career as a hired farm laborer, struggling to acquire sufficient capital to rent, and eventually purchase, his own homestead.

Letter 3.
Daniel Kent, East Caln Township, Chester County, Pennsylvania, to William and Ann Kent, St. John's Gate, Limerick, 1 October 1789

East Caln In Chester County Pennsylvania

Dr Parents   10th M^o the 1st 17<89>

Ihave not heard from you these Two years which makes me very uneasy.   I expect you wrote but your Letters has miscarried   However Iam In daily Expectation of receiving one from you.   Iwrote to you Last Eleventh Month by a country man of mine that was going to Ireland which I expect you have got, and Ishould have wrote sooner, but waiting for your Answer delayed me.   Iam free Above Ayear and has left my Old Master. Iam hired for a year with a Man Named Isaac Coats[32] about 7 Miles from my Old Master to work Plantation work, which time is nearly Expired   Ibelieve with Care I may Keep myself as Decent here as ever Iwas   Ihave more Cloaths now than Ever Ihad at Once[33] Though there is not so many foolish fashions on them   I Keep my self out of bad Company   I work pretty constant but do not spend my Earnings foolishly yet Ido not deny myself of the Necessary's of Life. Ihave not drank a pint of Spirits this 10 Months and hope IShall Keep myself so as Ibelieve they are very hurtful to the Constitution   Iheard from my Uncle Richard About 3 Months Ago Which was as follows,   He wrote to afriend of his In Philadelphia Named William Brown to Enquire After me which said Brown did and IReceived aletter from him With the letter my Uncle sent to him enclosed in it and Isent a letter to William Brown to Be forwarded to my Uncle[34]   He was then About Jamaica on Board the Cygnet & was In health

---

32. Isaac Coats: Isaac Coates, in 1774 farmed 120 acres in East Caln township, just north of West Bradford; member of an affluent Quaker family (Thomas and Moses Coates had larger farms in East Caln), almost certainly related to Isaac Coates, "brick-maker" of Philadelphia Co., whose tax assessment was ca. £120 in 1769–1774 and who was double-taxed £161 for his pacifism in the American Revolution.   **33. at Once:** at the same time; see George Gascoigne, *The Steele Glas, a Satyre* (London, 1576), p. 70: more clothes **attones** than might become a king (quoted OED, s.v. at once, 3).   **34. my Uncle:** Richard Kent, ship's surgeon, then on the *Cygnet* with the British naval squadron stationed at Port Royal, Jamaica, and a major benefactor to the family in Limerick. On 24 August 1789, Richard Kent wrote his nephew, Daniel, in Chester Co., admonishing him, "you need never have been a Servant if you had Consulted your Parents, or me, . . . but Perhaps you have done best both in <u>temporal & Spiritual Affairs</u>, [although it] is rather a strange Transition from a Tolerable Cutler to a Farmer, <u>Alias Labourer</u>, or from a Protestant to a Quaker."

this Country is very Peaceable at present   Provisions Is Very Plenty and
Cheap   Mens wages has got much lower than they were when I come in the
Country first   Cloathing Keeps[35] midling high   Linnen of about 15 Cuts[36] to the
pound is 3 Shillings a Yard   1^s-6^d for Making A Shirt   4 or 5 shillings for Knitting a
pair of Coarse yarn Stockings   10 Shillings for a pair of Shoes   about 18^s for making
a suit of Cloaths   from 30 to 45 Shillings for a good Hat   a Common Wool hat
about 7^s-6^d And Every thing Else InProportion So that a Man had need to be saving
here,   I enjoy my health very Well[37] since I came to here   Ihad not above two
weeks sickness Since my Arrival In this Country,   Ishall now Conclude with my love
and Duty to my Grand Mother and Wishes for her Good health   My love to my
Aunt Deacon Cousin Mary & Cousin Nancy to Cousin Worrell and Wife & all that
family, to my Brothers And Sisters,   My love to my old Companions   my desire for
them is that they may Break off From the way of life the<y> Lived in Whilst Iwas
With them & turn to a sober Virtuous way of Living, to turn to that Inward principle
of Light in their hearts which giveth them Secret trouble and grief for their Evil ways
and Which will give them Peace of mind and Comfort If they turn from those Evil
ways and live a Virtuous Life, & this Ican say from my own Experience   And My
love to my Dr Parents In Particular And Rem^n Your Dutiful and Affectionate Son,
My love to All Enquiring Friends   Daniel Kent
                                    Direct to me as Usual[38]

Although Kent's father was pleased that Daniel's indentured service was over, he still
hoped his son would return to Ireland or, at the least, abandon the drudgery of farm
work and resume his trade: "My Dr Son," he wrote, "we are grieved to think you are so
laboriously employed and we earnestly wish you could change it. . . . [W]ould it not be
possible for you to get employment at your own Business[?]" William Kent was equally
distressed by his son's conversion to Quakerism and begged, "if your lot should ever be
cast where there are Methodists[,] get acquainted with some of them who are experienced
in the Grace of God[,] read their Books and perhaps . . . if you pray earnestly you will find

---

35. Keeps: remains, continues to be.   **36. Cut:** see chapter 21, n. 94.   **37. enjoy:** "Sometimes used
[inappropriately] with an object denoting something *not* pleasurable or advantageous. Chiefly in expressions like
"to enjoy poor health," "to enjoy an indifferent reputation," where the noun has properly a favourable sense,
qualified adversely by the adjective. (See the similar use of *jouir de*, censured by French grammarians.)" (OED,
s.v., 4.a). The pattern is analyzed (incorrectly) as **enjoy——health/reputation**, in which the slot is occupied
indifferently by an affirmative or a negative adjective, reducing **enjoy** to a neutral sense of "experience." A
very commonly used variant of this pattern is **have/get one's health**; for examples see chapter 5, n. 16 and
chapter 9, n. 12.   **38.** On a separate sheet, apparently accompanying this letter to his parents, Kent wrote the
following verse: *The Prayer of Agur the Son of Jaketh* | Two things I ask of thee (O God most High) | Deny me
not of them Before I die | Remove far from me Lus[t] and Vanity | Give me not Riches, Neither poverty |
Be pleased to feed me with Convenient food | (Luxurious Diet for Man is not Good) | Lest I be full and say
who is the Lord | (And thus abuse the Blessings thou Afford) | or Lest I Steal And take thy Name In Vain |
And thus thy Holy Just Command Profane

their principles far more agreeable to Scripture and Antiquity than that of the Quaker."[39] In reply, Daniel apologized profusely for causing his parents grief, patiently explained the tenets of the Society of Friends, and declared, "I am so far from thinking that farming is as Laborious as you Imagine it to be that I think it is the Sweetest Employment in the World, and I know not of Any Trade or Calling Whatsoever that I would Change it for so long as It shall Please God to give me health & strength to Work at it[.] I take Delight in it," he concluded, and "therefore it is easy to me, and I believe it is my Place to follow it."[40]

Perhaps out of exasperation, Kent did not write his parents again for several years, and by late 1794, at the time of his last surviving letter, he had married Esther Hawley (1763–1816), eldest daughter of his former master, and begun a family and was renting a farm in East Bradford township.[41] Word of his progress had already reached Limerick, and in this letter Kent not only described his transition from farm laborer to tenant, and consoled his aged parents in their increasing infirmities, but also, in a postscript, appended a few lines to his brother-in-law, Thomas Quin, who had inquired "how the nailing business Goes in America."[42]

Letter 4.
Daniel Kent, East Bradford Township, Chester County, Pennsylvania, to William and Ann Kent, and to Thomas Quin, St. John's Gate, Limerick, 21 December 1794

East Bradf^d 21st of 12 M^o 1794

Dr Parents

I once more address you with that Duty & Respect which is ever due from Children to Parents Ardently desiring these may find you in a state of good Health of which we have no great cause to Complain _ the Last letter we Rec^d from you was dated the Last day of the year 1792 which gave us much Satisfaction to hear that you Enjoyed a midling state of Health as you are now pretty well advanced in years   according to the Course of Nature you cannot expect that the Strenght[43] and Vigour of youth Will

39. William Kent, Limerick, to Daniel Kent, East Caln, Pa., 14 November 1789. **40.** Daniel Kent, West Town, Pa., to William and Ann Kent, Limerick, 17 October 1790. **41.** Daniel Kent and Esther Hawley married on 28 April 1791 at the West Bradford meetinghouse. They had seven children, whose birthplaces chronicle the locations of their father's farms: (1) William (b. 1792 in East Bradford township; d. 1860); (2) Joseph (b. 1794 in same; d. 1863); (3) Elizabeth (b. 1796 in Kennet township; d. 1848); (4) Anne (b. 1798 in East Fallowfield township, where all the remaining children were born; d. 1872); (5) Mary (1800–1870); (6) Daniel (1803–1881); and (7) Benjamin (1805–1881). Except for Anne, who married into a farm in Little Britain township in adjacent Lancaster Co., all the Kent children married, farmed, and died in Chester Co. **42.** Thomas Quin's postscript to William Kent, Limerick, to Daniel and Esther Kent, West Bradford, Pa., 30 December 1792. **43. Strenght** ms.

follow you, it flies from you as fast as you Advance in years & we all should look upon every Indisposition as a Prelude to that which will take us from works to Rewards & as Amerciful call from our maker to prepare for our latter end,——It is with sorrow Iheard of the Death of my Grandmother & Cousin Worrell the Latter Especially as her loss will be more felt in her young family but we must Learn to be Content with the will of Providence who IBelieve orders all things for the better If we will best take them so——Since our last Letter to you we have been Blest with another Son whom we have Call<ed> Joseph after his grandfather Hawley he is now near six months old and is Alusty Boy William is growing a fine Boy he is near 2 years & five months Old

Now as to my own circumstances After Imarried Iworked my Fatherinlaw's farm for 2 years but finding Icould not make out much[44] I Rented a farm about 4 miles distant from his I Bought Stock And farming utensils & went in debt for most of them I pay 30£ Pr year Rent we make Butter & Cheese which we take to market to Philadelphia With Veal, Pork, Mutton & Whatever else we can Spare all which has Sold well these 2 yrs past the manner of our going to market here is thus We Carry our Load on horseback and set off about Sunset We Ride nearly all night (the weather being to<o> hot to go in the Daytime) and so gets to the City against Morning sells our Marketing Early & Comes home the next Day We are about 25 Miles distant from market, We have now got Apretty Good Stock Eight Cattle four Horses a score Sheep Pigs &c. All which we got by our own Industry So that I think your Prayrs for the Blessing of God on our Undertakings is heard far more than we Deserve or Can expect.——I am Glad to hear my Brothers & Sisters is Like to do well IConfess Iam some times desirous to have some of the family Here and Almost tempted to give Some of my Brothers some encouragement to Come over the family is Large and Ithink you might Spare One for Company for me Shoemaking is Good business here Iwould be glad to hear Particularly from my Uncle Richd & Brother George & desires to Send my Kind Love to them——
And Conclude with great Affection your Dutifull Children

Danl & Esther Kent

To Brother Quin

In Compliance to thy request Imay Inform thee that Nailing is Good Business here there being a great Demand for Large Nails such as is used in Covering houses we call them Shingle Nails theyare some thing Larger than a twelvepenny Nail If you Can Come so as to Set up for yourselves it may answer very well My Kind love to you Both & am your Affectionate

Brother

Daniel Kent

44. **make out much**: make much of a living.

Daniel Kent and his father continued to exchange letters at least through April 1806, although the doting William was the more faithful correspondent. In early 1801 Daniel informed his father that three years earlier he had purchased for £800 a 122-acre farm in East Fallowfield township.[45] This news finally reconciled old William to his son's emigration and career choice, if not to his new religion. After all, William Kent's last letters from Ireland contained a chronicle of woe: from the "horrid acts of cruelty . . . against the Protestants"[46] in the 1798 Rebellion to the wartime depression in trade, which, coupled with potato-crop failures, had brought severe distress to Limerick's poor artisans. "[D]aily may be seen almost starving Tradesmen in our streets," William reported, with "meagre ghastly countenances [that] bespeak the want of the necessaries of life."[47] Indeed, the members of his own family were in such "a struggling state" that he was forced to beg for financial assistance and to urge his younger sons to follow Daniel to America.[48] "Indeed it was a blessed day that ever you left this wretched Country," William at last admitted, for "had you stayed here since you could not call a single foot of land your own."[49]

Apparently, Daniel Kent could not send aid to his father, citing the "embarassed Circumstances"[50] occasioned by mortgage payments, and neither his brothers' nor his sisters' families ever joined him in Pennsylvania. However, Daniel Kent and his own family flourished on his farm in the East Fallowfield hills. In 1803 Kent became an American citizen, and in 1810 he was appointed justice of the peace, a post he held for 20 years. When Kent's wife Esther died in 1816, he married a second time,[51] and he remained on his farm until old age obliged him to sell and move to the home of his unmarried daughter, Elizabeth, a produce dealer in Upper Oxford township. There he died on 26 January 1844, leaving a personal estate worth nearly $4,400 in "bonds and obligations," furniture, bedclothes, and a silver watch he had brought from Ireland nearly 60 years before.

Kent's descendants later remembered their "Irish Grandsire" as "a stout, heavy set, medium height man, who set his feet down as though he had an undisputed right to put all his weight on the earth," who composed spontaneous rhymes for the children's amusement, and who was never ill until the day he died—after chopping wood at age 78! However, they also recalled Kent's mercurial temper, vividly reflected in a face either "open and inviting and wreathed in smiles or stern and forbidding almost to the point of repulsion." Yet they learned, too, that they could dispel their grandfather's dark moods by pointing out Limerick on the old man's Irish map and persuading him to reminisce about

---

45. Kent purchased his farm from Jesse Gilbert, "yeoman," and Sarah, his wife. In 1810 Kent and a partner purchased an additional 20 acres from Jesse Kersey.   **46.** William Kent, Limerick, to Daniel and Esther Kent, West Bradford, Pa., 4 June 1799.   **47.** William Kent, Limerick, to Daniel and Esther Kent, East Fallowfield, Pa., 28 March 1801 (this letter was actually penned by Daniel's brother, Richard).   **48.** William Kent, Limerick, to Daniel and Esther Kent, East Fallowfield, Pa., 7 March 1803.   **49.** William Kent, Limerick, to Daniel and Esther Kent, East Fallowfield, Pa., 12 May 1804.   **50.** William Kent, Limerick, to Daniel and Esther Kent, East Fallowfield, Pa., 6 April 1806.   **51.** In 1818 Kent married Pamela Ives (d. 1842) in the East Fallowfield meetinghouse.

his Irish past.[52] Through emigration and conversion Daniel Kent had rejected old authorities and submitted to new ones, and although the results were materially and even spiritually rewarding, apparently his recreated "self" could not entirely jettison fond memories of—and perhaps bitter regrets for—what he had left behind in Ireland.

24 ✳

John and Jane Chambers, 1796

Most of the preceding documents in this part illustrate the travails of frontier farming. The letter of John and Jane Chambers, however, like those by Daniel Kent, demonstrates another pattern common among Irish immigrants: settlement, hired agricultural labor, and farm tenancy in an eastern area, close to markets and long-settled, before purchasing their own holding. Sufficiently affluent to avoid indentured servitude but too poor to buy farmland on arrival, John and Jane Chambers located temporarily in central New Jersey—in a district inhabited by earlier emigrants, coreligionists, and perhaps kinsmen or former neighbors—in order to amass capital, gain familiarity with American agricultural techniques, and, as their letter clearly indicates, to create a first home, near a major seaport with direct mail and passenger connections to Ireland, that could welcome the relatives they invited to join them in the New World. Unlike Daniel Kent, however, John and Jane Chambers did not intend to settle permanently in or near their initial staging-ground but instead pursued a plan of secondary migration to purchase new and cheaper lands on one of America's northwestern frontiers.

John and Jane Chambers probably came from the townland of Mullaghglass, in the predominantly Protestant and largely Presbyterian parish of Ballymore, in east County Armagh's Orior Lower barony.[1] Certainly, in 1796 John's apparently widowed mother, Mrs. Thomas Chambers, and his brother lived near Tanderagee, a market town also in Ballymore parish, on the border of counties Armagh and Down, and a mile from the Newry Canal, whose construction from 1730 had quickened commercialization among local farmers and weavers. Probably Mrs. Chambers was a small tenant or subtenant of the

---

52. Cited in D. Kent, *Letters and Other Papers of Daniel Kent . . .* , 73–75; see Sources.   **1.** Confusingly, John and Jane Chambers's letter is addressed to "Mrs. Thomas Chambers, c/o James Stewart, Moneyglass, near Tanderagee." However, in 1851 the only townland named Moneyglass is in Co. Antrim, in Duneane parish, which is quite far from Tanderagee, Co. Armagh. Moneyglass may have been the name of a small area, a former townland or a subdivision of same, known locally in the 1790s but officially disappeared by 1851. Alternatively and (we believe) more likely, the Chambers' "Moneyglass" is the same unit as Mullaghglass, a townland situated in the same Co. Armagh parish, Ballymore, as Tanderagee. On the religious composition of Ballymore parish, see n. 3.

Duke of Manchester, whose properties covered most of the parish.[2] Economic difficulties may have occasioned John and Jane Chambers's emigration, for in 1790–1791 tenants' rent arrears doubled on the Ballymore estate. In addition, Armagh was Ireland's most densely populated county, and sharp competition—increasingly sectarian and violent—for land and employment may also have spurred the Chambers's departure.[3]

No surviving official records indicate when John Chambers and his wife arrived in the United States, but their 1796 letter suggests they had left Ulster only two or three years before.[4] John Chambers first worked as a farm laborer and then rented a farm nine miles from the seacoast at Middletown Point, in Freehold township, Monmouth County, in eastern New Jersey. Since the mid-1600s Monmouth County had been farmed by the Dutch and later by transplanted New Englanders, followed by large numbers of Presbyterian settlers from Scotland and Ulster since the early 1700s. By the early eighteenth century, Monmouth's New England settlers had shifted from a Congregational to a Presbyterian church organization, which facilitated the acculturation and absorption of the Scots-Irish, especially after both groups embraced the revivals of the Great Awakening. In 1790 Monmouth and contiguous Middlesex counties had New Jersey's highest proportions of inhabitants of Scots-Irish or Scottish (36 percent) and Irish (20 percent) descent, the former centering on Freehold township and village. Among local Scots-Irish farmers were several Chambers households, one of whose heads, William—a Revolutionary War veteran—had emigrated from the Newry-Tanderagee area.

Perhaps these were the connections that lured John and Jane Chambers to Freehold and made the township a redistribution point for them and other postwar immigrants. Certainly, by the 1790s Freehold was no frontier, either for newcomers or for many of its native-born, as after the Revolution land prices had soared, farms had become larger, and—as early as 1780—at least half the township's adult males were landless. However, the region did offer certain economic opportunities to poor but industrious immigrants. Adjacent to sandy uplands and pine barrens, Monmouth County's rich, well-drained bottomlands and its proximity to the New York City market, promoted a prosperous, unspecialized farming pattern that combined rough pasturage for livestock with a shifting cultivation of wheat, rye, and barley for sale—and of maize for local consumption—that required little manuring or proper crop rotation. And whereas New York could absorb virtually all of

2. The Duke of Manchester's rent rolls for 1790–1792 list numerous tenants, on the Ballymore and contiguous Kernan estates, named Chambers, Johnston, and Purday. Most held fewer than 15 acres. In 1792 the total rental of the Ballymore estate was £2,519.   3. For demographic data on Ballymore parish and its environs, see appendix 2.1c, on chapter 24. On sectarian and political violence in west Co. Down and in Co. Armagh during the 1780–1800, see chapter 4.   4. The historian Michael Durey, in his *Transatlantic Radicals and the Early American Republic* (Lawrence, Ks., 1997), misidentifies this "John Chambers of County Armagh" as a United Irishman "who was swept up onto a Belfast prison tender only days before the Ulster rebellion [of 1798] broke out" (p. 200). However, since the subject of this chapter emigrated prior to 1796, it is highly unlikely that he was implicated in the United Irish Rebellion, unless he returned to Ulster after writing this letter.

Freehold's agricultural surplus, John Chambers's transplanted expertise in weaving could at least cut his family's living costs, if not provide additional income. In short, both his Ulster background as a small farmer-weaver and his new American environment demanded and, in New Jersey, rewarded the versatility that John Chambers demonstrated in this letter.

> ## John and Jane Chambers, Freehold Township, Monmouth County, New Jersey, to Mrs. Thomas Chambers, Mullaghglass, Ballymore Parish, County Armagh, 20 March 1796
>
> Honoured Mother   sunday March the 20th 1796
>   freehold to<w>nship   Monmoth County   East New Jersey   North A Merica
> I take this opertunity of Letting you know that I and My family are in good health at
> Pres<en>t thanks be to God for all his Continued Mercies to us and I trust you all
> share the Same Blessing   since I Came to this Country I had two children Both
> Doughters   the oldest[5] Name is Betty for My Brothers Wife   the other is Now two
> weeks old and My wife is up and well   her Name is Jane   the<y> were Both Born
> on friday   I Now Live within thirty seven Miles of Newyork Near the shore and has
> rented A house and Place for one year and after that is expired I intend for to go a little
> farther Back[6] to albony[7] where the Land is Better and cheaper   I would of gone Long
> before this but I still expected Letters from you as I wrote often to you and as I Like
> this Country very well and every thing seems to Doe very well with Me<,> Dear
> Mother I want you to Come here very Much and live with Me and you Can Live
> better than in <the> Best Mans house in ireLand and My Brother and Dear Mother
> you Must Come To Me without fail and if your <money> is Low agree with the
> Captain for your Passage and he to allow you twenty Days to send Me word after you
> Land in Newyork and I will Come there and Bring you home   the Steerage is the
> Best Part in the ship for you   be sure Lay[8] in plenty of seastore Bread Butter cheese
> eggs Cofie and three gallons of Porter some spirits Potatoes   Dont treat the sailors to[9]
> you be some time out at sea and be saving[10] for fear of A Long Passage   be sure Bring
> Me some Black potatoes for seed if it is ever so fue[11]   when you Land in New york
> enquire for Barnard Burns store keeper front Street New york and enqire for Boats
> Comeing to Midletown point and I live within 9 Miles of it   if you write Direct To
> John chambers to the Care of Colonel Conover freehold Near Middletown point and I
> will soon get it then   send me word how My Cousin John tate and all his Brothers is

5. **oldest**: i.e., oldest's.   6. **Back**: inland, away from heavily settled areas (on the seaboard).   7. **albony**: Albany, New York.   8. **be sure Lay**: the construction **be sure + imperative** here functions essentially as a grammatical form (emphatic imperative: **lay** "lay!" vs. **be sure lay** "be certain/don't forget to lay!")   9. **to**: until.   10. **saving**: sparing, economical.   11. **fue**: i.e., few: "bring me some black potatoes for seed—just a few will do."

and all My relations   let[12] My uncle Richard know that <I had a letter? heard?> from
my Cousin Billy two weeks ago and he and his family is well and my wife wishes to
know how her sister Nelly and two sons is <also> John Johnston and family and
Prudy   I have 2 Cows two hogs a fine horse of three years old worth thirty five
Pounds and Can <run> very well   he has run two Races and won both and is Now
keeping[13] for another and when he is five years old he will Bring one hundred
pound   Last <month? year?> I and another Man Jointly Bought a young hor<s>e for
fifty pounds   Dear Brother Come here without fail as you Can work at your trad and
take Care of these horses as I work out[14] sometimes from home   the<re> are good
prices her<e> for weaveing   you Can get a shilling a yard for weaving any thing from
afour hundred to Nine   Bring reeds[15] from four to ten hundred al <a> y^d wide Coarse
shuttles sheers and temples[16]   this <is> a good Country to trad in Cattle   I Bought A
Cow for six pounds and sold her the Next year for thirteen pounds   I reased two
hogs since I came here and sold them Both for twelve pounds each   the People
wondered To see them and I have one at Present that I e<x>pect will do the
same   we hear of war being at home   be sure send Me word how Times is
there   here we have Peace and plenty   Prices of grain are such   Wheat sixteen
shilling Per Bushel   Rie[17] ten   indian Corn eight   Barley Nine   oats four and
wages are ackording[18]   I had all winter six shillings per Day for threshing and eight
shillings for Mowing   wages high and work plenty[19]   Dear Mother and Brother
Come   wait for Nobody   besure Come to Newyork and if you Cant Come this
year besure write to Me and My Wife and Me Joins in Love[20] To all friends and
relations and Remains your Dutiful son and Daughter Whilst <living>[21]

John, and Jane chambers

Dear Brother   if you have any spare Money Bring Me a Good Rideing saddle as
there[22] Deer here and Bridle   A light saddle suits Best   Likwise Croper   tea kettles
is very Dear hear   buy two or three and use them once and you wont Pay any Duty
for them   feather Beads is very Dear here   Bring Me one if in your Power   Dont

---

12. Tell ms. (either a transposed spelling or a crossed construction: "tell my uncle Richard that . . . " crossed
with "let my uncle Richard know that . . . ").   **13. keeping**: being maintained/cared for (see chapter 22, n.
12); an example of the archaic use of the present participle with a passive meaning, as seen for example in "the
barn is building" (= being built); see chapter 4, n. 45.   **14. out**: construed with **from home**.   **15. reed**: part
of a loom, consisting of two parallel bars of wood between which are fixed reed strips (later, metal wires);
through the interstices of these strips or wires are run the threads of the warp, and as the number of interstices
varies from reed to reed, so the fineness or coarseness of the cloth is regulated. Before reaching the reed the
warp threads are run through the heddles, which serve, by raising one half of the warp and lowering the other
half, to fashion a "shed," through which the shuttle containing the weft threads is thrown. Each newly shuttled
weft thread is "beaten up" against the existing weft by a vigorous pull on the reed, which is attached for this
purpose to two vertical bars.   **16. temples**: toothed flat rods used to keep cloth stretched at a uniform width
on the loom.   **17. Rie**: i.e., rye.   **18. ackording**: in proportion.   **19. plenty**: plentiful.   **20. and My Wife
and Me Joins Me in Love** ms.   **21. Whilst <living>**: a common phrase in the complimentary close.
22. there: i.e., they're.

sell any Sacks or Coarse Cloth for the<y> will be very usefull here   Good check[23]
sells well here   the Last I heard from My sister she was well   I hope to see you[24]
Next fall and I hope My Brother will be her<e> to goe with us[25]

John Chambers's absence from later New Jersey records suggests he and his family migrated beyond Albany as planned, perhaps following the lead of older Chambers relatives who, as Revolutionary War veterans, had received land grants in upstate New York. On the frontier Chambers could purchase cheap if uncleared lands, and his weaving skills would be in greater demand. However, it is doubtful whether initially his income in upstate New York would be as high as it was in Freehold. Prior to the War of 1812 and the building of the Erie Canal, central New Jersey's easy accessibility by water to the New York City market ensured Monmouth County's farmers wheat prices that were four times higher than those in the Genessee country—where Irish "tea kettles" and "feather Beads" would be even more difficult to procure.

25 ❈

Joseph and Hannah Wright, 1801–1817

In 1801 Joseph Wright was one of many emigrants, often of urban and mercantile backgrounds, who dreamed of founding a prosperous rural "colony" of kinsmen and coreligionists on the American frontier. Wright's goals were not impossible, despite his advanced age. Possessing far more capital and affluent connections than most contemporary emigrants, Wright would not need to spend years in tenant farming, as did Daniel Kent and John Chambers, before purchasing his own acres.[1] And although Joseph's personal speculations eventually failed—in 1836 the ambitious "town" he platted in the Ohio wilderness had merely 150 inhabitants—he succeeded in transplanting much of his family to the New World, and when he died in 1844 most of his sons and nephews were achieving at least modest success as farmers, traders, and politicians in Ohio, Illinois, and Missouri.

Like the Devereux brothers, Joseph Wright (ca. 1757–1844) was born in County Wexford and left Ireland in the wake of the 1798 Rebellion.[2] Unlike the Catholic Devereuxs, however, Wright was a member of the Society of Friends, and he went to America not because of political persecution but to flee economic disgrace and to recoup his fortunes. Wright was the second of the 11 children of John Wright (1735?–1811) and Abigail

23. check: checked cloth. 24. you conjectural; if Chambers' reference is to My sister, then the pronoun in question is probably her. 25. us conjectural. 1. See chapters 23 and 24. 2. On the Devereuxs and the 1798 Rebellion in Co. Wexford, see chapter 2.

Smithson (d. 1807),[3] who farmed over 136 acres at Ballinclay townland, in Liskinfere parish and Gorey barony, in north Wexford.[4] As his older brother, John, Jr., inherited the family holding,[5] around 1780 Joseph moved to Dublin and set up shop on Skinner's Row (later Christ Church Place), perhaps sponsored by his wealthy uncle, the merchant Nehemiah Wright. There in 1783 Joseph married Mary Jenkinson, with whom he had four children— Joseph, Jr. (1785–ca. 1807), John (b. 1786), James (b. 1788), and Nehemiah (b. 1790)—before she died in her last childbirth. In 1798 he married again, to Hannah Green,[6] and their first two children were also born in Dublin: Benjamin in 1799 and Abigail in 1800.

Unfortunately, sometime in the late 1790s Joseph Wright failed in business and was disowned for his debts by the Quakers' Dublin meeting. Clearly, it was these economic reverses that determined his hasty decision to emigrate where he could escape his creditors. Yet there may have been subtler considerations as well. Irish Quakers were notoriously strict in discipline, and after the French Revolution many of them became increasingly conservative in doctrine and politics. However, in 1797–1801 a minority of "Irish New Lights," led by Abraham Shackleton, a schoolmaster in Ballitore, County Kildare, and inspired by Hannah Barnard, a missionary from America, denounced the legalism dominant among Irish Friends and preached a rational, individualistic Quakerism that their critics denounced as deistic and republican.[7] Given his personal difficulties, Wright may have endorsed liberal Quakerism while still in Ireland; certainly, similar views later flowered

3. John and Abigail Wright's children were: (1) John (1756–1828), inherited Ballinclay; (2) Joseph (1757–1844), subject of this chapter; (3) Abigail (1761–1846), married William Knott; (4) Nehemiah (1763–1855), a Dublin trader, wed Susannah Gatchell; (5) Thomas (1765–1807), married Mary Johnson; their son William went to Ohio in 1807, after his father's death; (6) Margaret (1767–1821), married William Watson; (7) Benjamin (1769–1801), wed Julia [?], emigrated with brother Joseph, and died in Baltimore; (8) William (1771–1853), married Anne [?] and emigrated to Ohio in 1825; (9) Mary (1775–1813), wed William Beale of Mountmellick, Queen's Co.; (10) Samuel (1776–1817), married [?] Wilson; (11) Martha (1780–1865), lived in Dublin with brother Nehemiah and died unmarried.   4. For demographic data on Liskinfere parish and its environs, see appendix 2.2a, on chapter 25.   5. After John's death in 1828, the Ballinclay farm passed into the hands of Joseph Waring (or Warring). In 1853 the townland comprised only the Waring farm and the Friends' burial ground; in that year the Wright/Waring holding, farmhouse, and farm buildings were assessed at the high annual valuation of £96 (£75 for the land alone).   6. Hannah Wright was the daughter of Benjamin and Sarah Green of Forest, Taghmon parish, Co. Wexford.   7. In this context, the term "New Lights" does not have evangelical connotations; rather, in its emphasis on rational, individual judgment—and in its liberal or even radical political implications—New Light Quakerism was akin to the New Light Presbyterianism that flourished in Dublin and in much of Ulster during the 1700s, until swamped by evangelicalism and loyalism in the early 1800s. Perhaps significantly, New Light Quakerism was strongest among Ulster Friends. ¶Abraham Shackleton: in 1779 he succeeded his father, Richard (1728–1792), as master of the famous Ballitore school which his grandfather, Abraham (1697–1771), had founded and in which the young Edmund Burke was educated; he was also sister to Mary Shackleton Leadbeater (1758–1826), poet and author of the *Annals of Ballitore* (1862). ¶Hannah Barnard (1754–1825): born a Baptist in Dutchess Co., N.Y., she converted to Quakerism at age 18 and married Peter Barnard, a Quaker wagoner in Hudson, N.Y. Self-educated and strongly influenced by the French Revolution, in 1798–1802 she visited England, Scotland, and Ireland, where she preached an egalitarian, quasi-unitarian message that "New Light" Irish Friends welcomed but that in May 1800 earned her condemnation by the powerful London yearly meeting. After returning to America in late

among his family and the Friends in his own frontier settlement. Moreover, at least a few members of Wright's family were more overtly estranged from the Irish political establishment, as later in America his eldest son, Joseph, Jr., acknowledged that he "formerly used to support" the "cause . . . [of] free Gover^t for Ireland." And although by 1805 Joseph, Jr., had renounced "such romantic notions of liberty," those ideals flourished among some Wright kinsmen in Ohio and Illinois.[8]

For several reasons, therefore, Joseph Wright, Sr.'s elders may have been glad to send him packing, and so in 1801, at age 44, he and his younger brother, Benjamin (1769–1801), who had also been disowned for "marrying out," left their families in Ireland, crossed the Irish Sea from Dublin to Liverpool, and on 1 July embarked on the American ship *Sally* for Baltimore, arriving on 28 August. Benjamin quickly secured clerical employment in Baltimore but died suddenly in the street, apparently from heatstroke, leaving Joseph in shock and without relations in "this strange land," as he lamented in his first letter home.[9] Ironically, however, it was his successful effort to secure Benjamin's burial in the Quaker graveyard that brought Joseph into contact with the Baltimore Friends who directed his steps to the Ohio frontier. By the time Wright wrote a second letter to his wife, although merely the day after his first, grief had been dissipated by his envisioned prospects in what was then still called the Northwest Territory.

Letter 1.

**Joseph Wright, Baltimore, Maryland,
to Hannah Wright, Dublin, 18 September 1801**

Baltimore   9^{Mo} 18th 1801—4 O'Clock

My Dearly beloved   in the morning

Wife & children

      Yesterday morning I wrote you a long letter for to send you by the same Vessell we came here in, (the Sally); which the Captain is to drop at Dover on his way to Rotterdam (he d'ont sail for a Week)   I expect it will get safe to my dearest Hannah, who will I Know rejoice to receive it;   as this may perhaps[10] get first to hand[11] it may suffice to say it contained an account of my Welfare & also of our Dear

---

1802, Barnard was disowned as a deist and a follower of Tom Paine by her Hudson, N.Y., meeting—an action that the monthly and yearly meetings refused to reverse. Subsequently, Barnard wrote widely on religion and political economy, and during the War of 1812 she founded a peace society. **8.** Joseph Wright, Jr., McMahon's Creek, Ohio, to Martha Wright, Dublin, 11 January 1805. Wright's remarks accompanied his denunciation of Robert Emmet's failed Dublin rebellion of 1803 as the act of "a lawless banditti." However, around 1828 his Irish-born brother, James, would name one of his American-born sons Emmet. **9.** Joseph Wright, Sr., Baltimore, to Hannah Wright, Dublin, 17 September 1801. **10.** ^{per}Perhaps ms. (i.e., the abbreviation for the word **per** is used for the letter **p**). **11. get first to hand**: reach its destination/arrive first; frequent variants of this idiom are **go to hand** (said by the sender) and **come to hand** (said by the receiver).

Brother Benj[ms] Decease, who died quite Suddenly Yesterday week in the evening from not being used to this Warm Climate & drinking Cold Water; I wrote in my letter of Yesterday as full an account of it as I well could; it has been a very great trial to me from its being so sudden & in this Strange & distant part of the world; However I hope he is gone to a better place.— Ah! my love in what a moment did thy two letters come to ease my anxious mind by receiving in this remote place a line from thee informing me of thy welfare as also that of my dear Children & Relatives— But my dear thee did not say how thy dear Mother was or how she bore it; the day before yesterday I called at J & J Roberts's[12] to enquire for a letter & there was none. so I wrote thee the letter mention'd above & I believe forgot dating it; its directed for[13] Brother Knott.[14] I expected getting out of town yesterday but fortunately by the taking of my Clothes to a friends house (Jos[h] Townsend) I was delayed so long as to put off my going until early this morning & on getting back to my lodging I met J Roberts who told me he thought I was out of town & that he had some letters; that he had received his Brother James's trunk by the Phoenix that arrived on first day;[15] that his Brother was to have come in her but did not.— I returned with him & to my heartfelt Joy received thy two welcome letters of the 18th & 20th of 7[mo] the one thou mentioned having wrote before I have not rec[d].— on[16] the 30th of 7[mo] Dear Brother Benj[m] & I wrote by a Lieu[t] of an English Frigate who boarded us at Sea I hope they will get safe[17] as they would be some little gratification to poor afflicted Julia[18]——This letter I am to leave (as I set out on my Journey) at J Roberts's who made me promise to take breakfast with him; he is to Send it with his letters by the Harriot that sails for Liverpool in a week— So my Dear it's more than probable one[19] of these will salute thee.——My Dearest Hannah from Capt[n] Hutchensons representation of us to W Wilson (a most respectable man here & who has from almost nothing acquird a large fortune) the partner in the House of Wilsons & Maris he has behaved uncommonly Kind to us; it was he procured the situation for my Brother & has given me a letter to a friend of his in Genessee[20] but I have declined going there as I am informed the Ohio or[21] the part of it I am going to which is <a> place called Wheeling[22] is still more healthy than Genessee.— However my dear ask twenty people & they will perhaps every one have a different Idea of places; from accounts they have had.— I shall be very particular getting my information & have a list of Friends &c to apply to for it that I expect will not deceive me— But indeed they

12. **J & J Roberts's**: John & James Roberts, Irish Quaker merchants in Baltimore, apparently linked by blood or marriage to the Wrights and engaged in trade between Baltimore and Dublin. 13. **directed for**: addressed to. 14. **Brother Knott**: William Knott: husband of Joseph Wright's sister, Abigail. 15. **first day**: Sunday. 16. **one** ms. (written confusion between **on** and **one** is common in mss. of the Early Modern period). 17. **get safe**: arrive safely. 18. **Julia**: Benjamin Wright's widow. 19. **on** ms. (see n. 16). 20. **Genessee**: the Genessee country, in western New York. 21. **of** ms. 22. **Wheeling**: in western Virginia, across the Ohio River from Belmont Co., Ohio, where Joseph Wright's family eventually settled.

mostly seem to encourage one to settle where their connections are as they like Company backwards[23]— However many disinterested sincere people are to be met with as much so as I have ever seen in the old Country as they call it here—but it's best to See the Country myself & shall more particularly inform thee when I return which may be in about 5 Weeks   I have to walk there & back which is in all ab[t] 540 Miles   my love will think <it> a long Journey but now my dear it seems no more to me than crossing Fishamble St[24] since my mind is relieved by thy letters— I would be greatly gratified by receiving one from my Dear Jos[h] who will I hope with the rest of my poor children be dutiful to thee & remember their Creator in the Days of their Youth[25]   My love was one of the Six to stay behind the<r>e & not come here   I could not tell which to mention & I quite approve that thee should not Stay behind when thou may be favord to get away— for your Encouragement I think any Industrious person[26] may do well here & <at> Baltimore altho: in some respects <it is> not pleasant (on acc[t] of Sickness &c) yet on the whole it's a pleasing place & aplace that with a little Money in Business say £100 Eng[s] and care there would be a far Greater likelyhood of Doing well as business is not Carried on in the Same line Althogather[27]   My Dear from every thing I See & hear I would hope if thee & the Children were here & a little to begin with we could do extremely well   I am Sure thee thy self could nearly Support us by Baking,   I Shall my Dear never look for Great things   the Shops here have more than Double the profits in Dublin & often Thrible[28] and then they pay well for labour or any thing they get Done   the poorest people thee would meet look as Clean <u>as a very decent</u> Servant in Dublin, even the poorest Kind[29] of Black people & Since I have been here I dont think I Saw 3 Begging,   the Times in town are not as Good as Usual with the Merchants & large shops in Town[30]   ab[t] 12 M[os] Back there was a great Many Failures— My love must understand that I am in the power of my Creditors in this Country Same as in Ireland which would make me willing to Settle Back[31] in this Country where the Climate is healthy & if near a place where we could Carry on a little Dealing & Rent a little Clear Ground which would be low & Could near it purchase a Good Ground at 9[s]/ Eng[s] ℔ acre near it which we could be Clearing in a few years[32]   at first the greatest Difficulty Would be as New Settlers as[33] New Settlers will find it Different after leaving

---

23. backwards: in the backcountry, on the frontier.   **24. Fishamble St.:** in Dublin; runs from the eastern end of Skinner(s) Row (now Christchurch Place) to Wood Key; formerly the site of a fish market ("fish shambles"). Handel's *Messiah* had its first performance in a newly opened theater in this street in 1742. **25. remember . . . :** "Remember now thy Creator in the days of thy youth, while the evil days come not, nor the years draw nigh, when thou shalt say, I have no pleasure in them" (Ecclesiastes 12:1). **26.** ℔erson ms. **27. Althogather:** spelling influenced by **altho'**; see **altogather** hereafter. **28. Thrible:** i.e., treble (spelling influenced by **three** and **triple**). **29. King** ms. **30. (in Town)[2] (& large shops)[1]** ms. (the superscript numerals provided by the writer indicate the order in which the parenthesized phrases are to be read). **31. Back:** in a remote area; away from the urban seaboard. **32. which we could be Clearing it is a few years** ms. **33. as:** i.e., since.

their Settled habitations   now my Dear if that[34] we were altogather I mean all the family that proposed Coming here <we> would be Society for one another & could rent a place which is easy got, (near ground we might purchase) of Good ground at a Moderate Rent   or the way it is Common there—is if a Man takes a farm he gives a Certain part Say one Half the produce to the landlord & the landlord finds Seed, or $\frac{1}{3}$ if He finds Seed himself, or it is Customary for to get one or Two hundred acres of Woody land for the Customary price of Purchase in the neighbourhood & to be improving & living on it & at the end of Seven years to Keep it & pay up the purchase Money perhaps for Good land 9^s/ Eng^s ℔ acre or to give it up to the Owner,   in many places it bring<s> without any Manure 40 Bushels of wheat to the acre & 50 to 60 Bushels of Indian Corn which makes Bread good enough for any one and the Rye makes good Bread also— Labour so high is what Distresses farmers But My Dear a very little Cleared ground would produce Sufficiency & Plenty of every Kind for the Belly   the Cows even in this City Kept by any person if I had one now I might turn her out on the Commons in the Morning & she would come home in the Evening of herself & no Expence except to give her in Winter food at home,   I think Bro Jno Cousin's Business would answer well if he can procure the Cotton Twist[35] & Silk at any rate   Several Frd^s thinks it would answer well back where I am Now going some Branches of his Business[36] & from what I now see & every thing Considered I would expect we would do well here & if Settled althogather where we could assist on<e> another and be much happier than we could in poor Ireland altho my attachment to it is great and if not overdone[37] would be preferable to this country from its very temperate climate— I think the Americans the little rising generation seem very delicate in this place but it's in part oweing to the bring<ing> up   it's not so much so in the country parts— Any young Man or Woman to come over to be servants could live happy & respected & have a prospect here not to be met with in Ireland—and a Man able & Willing to work & Carefull might live as happy as he could

---

34. if that = if (archaic); the sentence begun here is lengthy, complex, and rather loosely constructed, and the following modernized version may be helpful in understanding it: <I>f we were altogether (I mean all the family that proposed Coming here), [we] would be Society for one another & [we] could rent a place of Good ground at a Moderate Rent, which is easy got, near ground we might purchase.   [O]r, the way it is Common there [in Ohio]——Is if a Man takes a farm, He gives a Certain part (Say one Half) [of] the produce to the landlord, & the landlord finds [i.e., furnishes] Seed; or [the farmer gives the landlord] $\frac{1}{3}$ [of the produce] if He [the farmer] finds Seed himself. [O]r it is Customary for [a farmer] to get one or Two hundred acres for the Customary price of purchase in the neighborhood & to be improving & living in it, & at the end of Seven years, to Keep it & pay up the purchase Money, [which] Perhaps for Good land [would amount to] 9^s/ Eng^s ℔ acre, or to give it [the land] up to the Owner [i.e. the landlord].   **35. Cotton Twist**: cotton thread made by twisting two or more filaments together, often used, because of its greater strength, for the warp; the collocation of cotton and silk here may refer to the making of a variety of poplin (silk warp with cotton weft). **36. Several Frd^s** . . . : "several Friends (i.e., Quakers) think that in the backcountry where I'm going there would be a good market for some of the things he stocks." **37. if not overdone** . . . : i.e., if my attachment to Ireland does not tempt me to exaggerate, [I believe] it would be preferable to this country.

wish Labourers get one dollar ꝑ Day that's 4^{s}/6^{d} english or 7^{s}/6^{d} this currency in town Carpenters from 7^{s}/6 to 10/ this currencey and find themselves[38]

My dear will be ready to come perhaps[39] in 1st or 2^{d} Month or to wait longer if our dear relations may come & all the children thee asks if Kitty had best come I think well of it & that it would be greatly to her advantage or any young Woman that would take care of themselves, most of the servant girls here are blacks the white girls are almost above being servants but may if they act properly get husbands suitable with their assistance to maintain a family decently washing Stockings 5^{d} ꝑ pair Shirts 5^{d} & handkerchiefs the Same of this Currency which is equal to 3^{d} Eng^{s} Money if Polly & Jinny Reily were here they Might live on Dainties to[40] What they Do I wish the<y> was here & Many other poor strugling creatures a Man having 2 horses & Carts would earn with 2 Men to follow them they would earn for him 18^{s}/ Eng^{s} Currancy ꝑ Day or 30^{s}/ of this Currency Horses Much the Same as in Ireland Some provisions are high bou^{t} In Smalls[41] but by laying in a Stock its pritty low Best American flour 7½ to 8 Dollars at 4/6 Eng^{s} Each Dollar ꝑ Barrell of 1^{C}-3^{qrs}-O[42] the price the labourer pays for his Diet[43] is 2½ Dollars ꝑ Week that is what I pay for My Diet & lodging its very Good Drinking people here are not at all requested[44] nor cant expect doing any good every thing in the Cloathing way comes high & house rent in this place much Dearer than in Dublin the person who goes with Me to Wheeling is a Welsh lad he has been Waiting for Me these two Days, I must my love send a few lines to P Tudor who has been used[45] So Badly I Can in Truth Say with no intention to injure him altho it turned out otherways & also to the Society when I feell ability of the Almighty to do so, the Acc^{t} of My Dear parents being in health is very Consoling to Me as also our Frd^{s} & Relations in General I must give My love to them all without Naming them is not for want of feeling Near Affection for them, Ah My Beloved And Affectionate Wife I hope we will Soon Meet and until that happy time farewell & with My Dear Children Accept the Best wishes of thy loving & Affectionate Husband——

Jos^{h} Wright

Pure coincidence may have directed Joseph Wright to the fertile, hilly, oak- and hickory-forested country, just across the Ohio River from Wheeling, that was organized as Belmont County, Ohio, in September 1801. However, after the Northwest Ordinance

38. this currency . . . find themselves: American currency . . . provide their own board. **39. ꝑhaps** ms. **40. to**: compared to. **41. bou^{t} In Smalls**: bought in small amounts; see OED, s.v. small, B.5.c. (**in smalls** "in small amounts"; marked as archaic and Scottish). **42. Barrell of 1^{C}-3^{qrs}-O**: i.e., each barrel contains one and three-quarters hundredweight (Wright's "C" for the more common **cwt.**) of flour; used alone as a unit of weight **quarter** signifies specifically a quarter of a cwt. (28 lbs.). **43. Diet**: meals, board. **44. Drinking people are not . . . requested**: i.e., they do not receive invitations, their company is not sought after. **45. used**: treated.

(1785), Joel Wright, a Baltimore Quaker of Ulster parentage and perhaps one of Joseph's distant relatives, was a prominent surveyor of Ohio lands; in 1798 he was also the Ohio agent of the Baltimore Friends' meeting, and later—in 1813—he became town planner of Columbus. In addition, after 1800 the federal government redoubled its efforts to market Ohio lands, establishing land offices at Steubenville and Marietta. Certainly, Joseph Wright was so entranced by Ohio that he minimized the difficulties of settlement in this letter[46] he wrote to his wife, shortly after returning to Baltimore from his journey westward, urging her and his children to join him.

Letter 2.
Joseph Wright, Baltimore, to Hannah Wright, Dublin, 12 November 1801

Baltimore   11 M⁰ 12th 1801—

My Dearly beloved Hannah

On my arrival here from the western Territory the 3rd Instant I got at J. Roberts's thy very welcome letter of the 7 M⁰ 6th which tho: written befor the two I Rec^d just as I started on my journey; afforded me great satisfaction; which a line from my truly beloved Hannah must at all times give me.— I may now my dear with thankfulness inform thee that I am in perfect Health & have been so since I wrote thee two letters about 9 M⁰ 17th one went ♃ the Sally for Dover & the other to Liverpool; which I hope have reached my dear 'ere this, to relieve her distressed mind, which I trust will be supported under her tryals.— Ah! my dear I wish these few lines were now in thy possession: the vessell is to sail for Cowes,[47] on first day the 15th Ins^t she is a Prussian vessell called the Krohn Printz,   I wish her a speedy passage & intend writing also by a Vessell that sails for Liverpool in a few days.— On the 10th Ins^t the ship Ardent from Londonderry arrived with Passengers & was out only 42 days.— There is a vessel expected from Dublin every day which I am anxiously waiting for, as I am almost sure of a letter from thee;   my dear Hannah may well know how I must feel myself in this distant land situated as I am & separated from thee & my dear Children but the thoughts of seeing you ere long keeps up my drooping spirits.— My two letters to thee before mentioned contained the sorrowful account of my dear brother Benj^{ms} decease, & the particulars of it;   I hope Sister Julia has been enabled to bear that vary great tryal & that she & her poor children are well   his death & the manner of it, was to me in this strange land very afflicting indeed being left quite alone but I hope he is now in a better place.— My dear I shall now give thee a little sketch of my walk back to the western Territory & my opinion

---

46. Ms. copy, made in Dublin by Joseph Wright's brother, Nehemiah Wright, who forwarded it to their father in Ballinclay, Co. Wexford.   47. **Cowes**: on the Isle of Wight, Hampshire, England; now a venue for yachting.

of this country as I am now better able to inform thee & write something for the Government[48] of our near & dear relatives that were speaking of coming over with thee & my dear children.— after making every enquiry & getting from sundry friends, & others the best information I could about this country: I concluded on directing my course from this place in a west direction to that part of the Western Territory which lies over the Ohio River opposite a town on this side of the river called Wheeling.— I set out from this place in company with a young man from near Wales that came over in the same ship: he returned with me for his clothes & went back yesterday to settle there

    The land about this place (Baltimore) is very poor & bad not at all like the land in the Western Territory; where altho: its in general hilly,—the roads are bad being rough & stoney in many places—

    We travelled through Fredericks town, Williams fort, Cumborland,[49] crossed the Allegany mountains & got to Redstone & Old fort,[50]   about these two last places is very good ground but it can't be purchased (nearly cleared) under from £5 to £10 this currancy ℔ acre,   the land is never manured & brings from 20 to 40 bushels of Wheat ℔ acre & from 40 to 60 Bushels of Indian Corn.— Mens Wages there about half a Dollar ℔ Day   from this we went on through Washington county[51] to Wheeling on the Ohio river & crossed over into the Western Territory;   there are several families of friends settled about seven miles over from Wheeling, that have come there from South Carolina, & other places, three or four of whom are accounted very great Ministers;   they were generally at the Yearly meeting in Baltimore when I was there & had not returned when I left that Quarter— This Territory is of large extent & likely in a short time to form another state,   it's now regulated by the laws of Pensylvania;   Congress is disposing of the land (which is at present generally covered with Timber) in sections of a Square mile which contains 640 English acres the purchase of which is two Dollars ℔ acre   the terms of payment ¼th on taking the section   ¼th in 2 years after   ¼th in 3 years & ¼ in 4 years,   one year after is allowed & in case of the full payment not being made in the 5th year the land is taken possession of by congress & forfeited by the purchaser——This part of the Country is very healthy & comes as near Ireland in regard to the climate as any place we would <be> likely to meet with here;   The Country is hilly but by no means mountainous being mostly rising grounds descending into little Valleys;   on most sections there is good water which is generally the case on hilly ground;   The soil is very rich in the low ground or vallies & produces when cleared[52] grass in abundance & produces from 40 to 50 Bushels of Indian corn ℔ acre; but it is too rank for wheat or other small

48. Government: guidance.   49. Fredericks town, Williams fort, Cumborland: Frederick, Williamsport, and Cumberland in western Maryland.   50. Redstone & Old fort: Redstone Old Fort (later Brownsville), on the Monongahela River in Fayette Co., Pa.; see chapter 15, n. 17.   51. Washington county: in southwestern Pennsylvania; on Irish settlers there, see chapters 3, 12, 26, and 62.   52. cleared: conjectural.

grain;— the high ground is very good for wheat or other kinds of grain & brings good Potatoes (which several parts of America does not)   the produce of wheat is from 25 to 40 Bushels ℔ acre;   they generally plough only about 3 Inches deep for their wheat   the soil is quite soft & black on the rising ground;   such a Section in Ireland when cleared I think would bring 40ˢ or 2 £s ℔ acre yearly & be counted cheap;— here it can be purchased out for ever in it's present State at 9ˢ/9ᵈ Irish money ℔ acre; very little taxes to be paid & no tithe man coming with his demand.——This season has been remarkably dry; since I came to America I have not seen more than 3 days rain.—— Wheeling is about 300 Miles from Baltimore & I went about 20 miles beyond it; where we met with an honest Welshman of the name of Jnᵒ. Edwards who behaved extremely Kind to us & entertained us about 3 days;   he Settled there in 8 Mᵒ 1800 & bought a Section on which he has a good house nearly finished; at least it's looked on in that part of the country as such.—— My dear I have mentioned to thee how cheap & good the land is; but even with these advantages they who live comfortable in poor Ireland will on coming here think it very odd & perhaps at first not be well satisfied;   on coming here into the Woods for 2 or 3 years there will be many things to encounter;—— A very middling habitation must answer them perhaps   but in a very few years people get independant & can provide for their families in a manner not to be done in Ireland (except by chance<)>.— It is my opinion if a few of us were settled on a section which would answer 3 or 4 Families, that we could be as one family to assist each other & for a while be satisfied to take with53 plenty but not of dainties & with accomodations not of the best; but such as through mercy54 I have been used to for some time back & would be as happy as I could wish if my dear Hannah & my dear Children were with me.—— it would add greatly to our comfort if brothers Wᵐ, Jnᵒ Cozins E Pitts, J Green & their families came over; we might form a little colony & in a little time I hope be happy together.— J Green could get plenty of Wild Turkeys & Bears, to shoot with Deer, Patridge,55 Pheasants, &c.——On the road I saw Dear's,56 Turkey's, Patridge's, Pheasant's, Snipe's Squirrell's &c.——I Knocked down with my stick one evening as I was travelling a fine Pheasant as large as a pullet which served me & my fellow traveller next day for dinner.——Baltimore seems to be an excellent place for business & there is good profits on what is sold in general; but I find it an unhealthy place to what Dublin is;   altho its not above ¼ as large as Dublin, I think more People die in it57 in the year;   nothing of the yellow fever has appeared in it this summer yet the inhabitants very much dreaded it the weather being so extremely hot & not having experienced so warm a Summer these several years past;— On my journey to the Ohio I could wring the sweat out of my waistcoat as if it was just taken out of the

---

53. take with: accept, put up with (see OED, s.v. take, 75).   **54. through mercy**: "by God's grace"; an expression in common use among Quakers.   **55. Patridge**: variant of **partridge**.   **56. Daer's** ms. (transposed spelling).   **57. in in** ms.

washtub & it has been never dry for a week together; the morning<s> are very cold.———There was such numbers of people moving to the back country, we would be some times oblidged to lye all night on the boards & often Beds little better;   I think I am now hardy enough to travel anywhere;   returning I generally got one good meal in the day, carried some bread with me & would get a pint of Cider with it or sometimes Milk;   I suffered a good deal by my feet blistering & most of the way I walked in very great pain;   in every other respect was thro: mercy as well as I could possibly be in my health & not at all tired.— J. Roberts told me he had orders to pay me 10 Guineas & the same to my brother Benj,   I have got from him some part of mine as I had not more than carried me back to this place & I thought I should have been oblidged to have sold thy watch in the country & should only I took as cheap a way of travelling as I found would carry me on.— I intend remaining here until thee & the children comes which will I hope be as soon as you possibly can, as I can't be happy untill that wished for time comes, when I think we would set off for the Western Territory.———The Welshman I before mentioned desired me on your arrival not to mind[58] writing to him but immediatly set off & we should have house &[59] room with him & welcome & he would assist in looking out for a suitable Section against[60] spring as I told him if my friends came over that I expected not less would do.— If I knew they would not come over I would on getting the 10 G^s from J Roberts, have parted with the watch & returned back & get some[61] for ourselves & try to be clearing it to have some Indian corn against harvest next but then I would have to come back against Spring to conduct thee & my little Family back.— I hope to get something to do here to Support me as this City is a very dear place altho: provisions at the first hand[62] are low   fine flour 8 Dollars for 1^C 3^{Qr} 01^b; Beef 3^d ℔ lb Irish Money, Fish cheap, Milk 4^d ℔ Q^t Irish Money   Salt butter 10^d ℔ lb.   I hope My Dear thee has been enabled to bear the heavy burden which has been thy lott; they[63] occupy a good deal of thy Dear Joseph's thoughts but he cannot lessen them   let me my dear have a letter by every vessell from Dublin or by Post under cover to J & J Roberts Market S^t.———As soon as my dear Knows what vessell she will come in, she will please write ℔ post to acquaint me & if no vessell is coming here if one offer'd for Philadelphia[64] to come in her & to write ℔ post from dublin to me here acquainting me with her name & when she will be likely to sail;   but a Vessell to Baltimore will answer best & take less to carry us to the W. Territory[65] which will come very high

---

58. mind: think of, contemplate, "bother."   **59. &:** conjectural.   **60. against:** toward, by; see **against harvest next** hereafter.   **61. get some:** i.e., would get some (say, land).   **62. provisions at the first hand:** provisions bought directly rather than through a middle man.   **63. they:** i.e., the burdens.   **64. if one offer'd for Philadelphia:** if there should happen to be one bound for Philadelphia.   **65. but a Vessell to Baltimore . . . :** but a vessel to Baltimore will best serve the purpose, and from there our transportation to the Western Territory will cost us less [than from Philadelphia].

not less I suppose than 100 Dollars.— Everything in the earthen ware & ever<y>thing necessary for housekeeping very dear here,   plates about 3/ ℔ Doz Irish money,   Tin Ware, dear, as is Clothing Stockings, & Hatts & I wish I had my old Boots   a new pair here worth 9 Dollars——If E Pitts was coming he could get several little tools for very little that would be of great use here & cost a good deal to get them——A nest of Drawers[66] on board would be very handy to keep things in & handy to take them out.— Beds very dear & Bed Clothes,   it would be much better to bring such articles over than to buy them here— Pins & Needles would be good articles to sell here   If possible my Dear strive to come in a vessell that won't be crowded with Passengers, as the way that some vessells are crowded & badly provided by the Captain it risques the lives of the passengers very much— I'm sorry Ja^s. Roberts alter'd his Plan of being in Dublin in 12 M^o. as thou mentioned——thou should have a great plenty of Potatoes, good bacon with two pots of Essence of Spruce[67] to make on board, a cask of Water, Oatmeal, Flour, Wine Spirits, some Bottled Porter, bring several heads of cabbage— Ah that you were all safe over in this country— My Dr Love to all my Dear Ralations & to thee my dearest Hannah with all my Dear children whom I often think of & hope yet to be happy together & my Dear will believe me to be in the tenderest ties of affection thy loving Husband

Jos Wright

Through the winter and spring of 1801–1802 Joseph Wright remained in Baltimore, unemployed, drawing on the credit of relations and Friends and entreating his wife, children, and other kinsmen to come help him establish a self-sufficient Quaker colony near the banks of the Ohio. However, back in Ireland it was his wife, Hannah, who bore the burdens of organizing the family exodus, winning removal certificates from the Dublin meeting's hesitant elders and persuading skeptical relatives to finance the journey and her husband's schemes. Finally, on 2 June 1802 Hannah and all Joseph's children, save Joseph, Jr. (who sailed in September), arrived at New York City. After a month enjoying the society of Baltimore Friends—although criticizing their wives and daughters as "so vain as to wear Earrings" to weekly meeting[68]—Hannah and the children embarked with Joseph on the long trek to their forest settlement, the initial stages and costs of which she bravely described in a letter to her brother- and sister-in-law in Ireland.

66. **nest of Drawers**: a set of drawers enclosed in a single container (see OED, s.v. nest, 6.a.).   67. **Essence of Spruce**: probably the concentrated ingredients of spruce beer, to which water would be added to make the beverage, "a powerful diuretic . . . and . . . a wholesome beverage for the summer" (OED, s.v. spruce beer, 1.b, quoting T. J. Graham, *Modern Domestic Medicine*, 6th ed., 1834, p. 180).   68. Hannah Wright, Baltimore, to John and Abigail Wright, Ballinclay, Co. Wexford, 1 July 1802.

Letter 3.

Hannah Wright, "N.W. Territory" [Belmont County, Ohio],
to William and Anne Wright, [Ballinclay, County Wexford?], 24 September 1802

N.W. Territory   9mo 24th 1802

My dear W^{m} and Anne

      I told you in my last that I would if I had an oppertunity inform you from this place what I thought of this new settlement and I should be tempted to wish you were here only so much self[69] might apear in it and another great objection with me is the difficulty of getting along some of the worst roads I beleive in the known world   there are nothing almost from Baltimore hear but Hills and Hollows and so much mountains & ridges as they call them here, yet we were favoured to get on uncomonly well,   My Jos^{h}[70] with the boys walk'd all the way and was not as much fatigued as going to dear Ballinclay on foot would occation, their feet not even blistered, and we had several very wet days with uncomon thunder and lightening and once our waggon over set and we in it but received no material injury except the children's faces a little scratchd,   I was able to help to unload the waggon while my Joseph was calling Ralph Heath & Wm Philpot to assist us who had gone on before us, but that was only a common accident,   we had five of the best Horses to it I ever saw togather so much so that I do not remember to see the driver ever give them the whip up the worst of the mountains,   now could these difficulties be got over and the danger of the seas—I think there would be a fair chance of setling down comfortably for life if one could have about 100£ & 50£ clear of expence here as there is no such thing even in this new settlement as any one wanting the nessessarys of life,   they have abundant crops without manure and with very little cultivation   one horse will plough ground that has been broken before, but it requires two to begin to cultivate   oxen are much used in this place   I am not my dear Anne urging your trying this country or leaving that dear old Ireland but my promise was to give you an impartial account of this,   the people sent us an abundance of french beans, cucumbers, and sometimes potatoes and squashs gratis and ears of indian corn which resemble peas when boil'd a little in flavour— the children are very fond of them and these articles which save us laying out money come from loghouses not larger than you<r> parlour, and we have one neighbour here a dutchman that gives us plenty of milk twice in the day for both our families and has lent them horses many times to go to the section where[71] I hope we shall be able to move to—the latter end of next week—as we wish to have a door and floor laid before we go into it,   its to be lofted one story[72] but some of them has two story in them,   they serve at the first setting

---

69. self: selfishness (OED, s.v., C.I.5).   70. My Jos^{h}: her husband, Joseph Wright, Sr.   71. when ms.
72. its to be lofted one story: an upper story is to be added.

out[73] for parlour and Kitchen but the beds can be over head,   my Joseph has been out all day inviting the people to come on third day[74] next to raise their houses and I expect they will have thirty men,   this is attended with expence as they are to be maintaind,[75]   I wish we had our dear Joseph hear before all the little articles his father has is sold as it would help to introduce him to the sale of them under his fathers inspection and a deal can be done here by taking skins of wild beasts and grain &c &c in exchange while his father and brothers would be preparing grain for use,   my Joseph bought a little mare yesterday with part of the price of my watch which brought 33 dollars what it cost five years back   I sold it to a freind the name of Howord a very religious man   we had a letter to him from Richard R Laurence of Newyork and on the receipt of it he came immediately to offer us any assistance in his power and is to survey the land gratis and devide the section,   I wish thou were one of the partiners in it without the hardship which thy dear Anne would find in coming provided your parents could freely give you up for life,   some land that was bought of congress two years back for 1½ doller per acre brings now ten at second hand rate and I think in a little time there will not be any to be disposed of in this territory which is an healthfull situation,[76]   I am through mercy now quite recovered and equal to the task of washing again and getting our little business done tho for some weeks I hardly expected ever to write to you again   altho I have had no[77] information from any of our dear relatives since I parted you I hope to hear and is anxiously waiting the post that comes regularly here and John Roberts & Joseph Desy was to forward any that might come to their care but I wish any future ones might come to John Roberts who has proved himself my Josephs best friend,   I must beg to have our dear love and warmest gratitude presented to Unkle Jo Smithson with Aunt and dear James Morison and his Eliza and Also to Unkle John Smithson and his family and besure say how thy Anne & your little Ellen is and whether my dear Unkle and Aunt Thomas are well to whom our dear love is also presented with the boys and to John and Jane at Cookfield[78]   I met a freind at Baltimore so like Jane that I could hardly keep from kissing her at our first meeting and we found on further aquaintance with her that she exceeded even my expec<ta>tion   she is clark to the womens-meeting and is I beleive a very religious woman   her name Rebecca Proctor,   I write so much in haste that it carries me from subjects that I wish not to omit   its now near 2 oclock at night and my Joseph will have to go I suppose ten miles to the freind tomorrow that is going to Baltimore to attend the yearly meeting there,   my Joseph is fatter then he was when we landed notwithstanding all his fatigue and was never threw divine favour in better health   Ah! I must close and once more bid you my dear brother & sister farewell when I assure you that time or situation cannot alter the affection that fills our bosoms

---

73. **at the first setting out**: at the outset. 74. **third day**: Tuesday. 75. **they are to be maintaind**: they are to be paid their keep. 76. **an healthfull situation**: a healthful place to live. 77. **not** ms. 78. **Cookfield**: probably Cookesfield, in Offerlane parish, Queen's Co.

for you to which the children desire to have their joint love presented and beleeve me your very affc^te sister in law

Hannah Wright

My dear William

I mention'd in my letter to Susan that our expence of getting here and having to buy our provisions for one year would run us so hard that I much fear we shall not be able to make up the next payment of the section and yet I feel quite ashamed after all our freinds done for us to ask for an hundred and twenty Dollars more though I am well convinced the<y> would not think much about it and my Joseph may have it yet in his power to repay it if he is spared

In 1800 only 8,158 adult white males inhabited what in 1803 became the state of Ohio. During the next two decades, however, over thirty thousand newcomers per year poured into the state, which by 1820 had become the fifth most populous in the Union. Thus, Joseph Wright's timing was ideal, as he was one of the earliest settlers in Ohio's Seven Ranges, the first lands surveyed under the Northwest Ordinance and sold under the Harrison Land Act (1800). In September 1802 Wright and two other Dublin Quakers, William Philpot and Ralph Heath, who had accompanied Joseph and Hannah from Baltimore, took a section of land on McMahon's Creek in Belmont County. Wright's share, one third of the section, comprised 215 acres and was located only three miles from the Friends' weekly meetinghouse at Plainfield although over 15 miles from the monthly meeting at Short Creek. Aided by his four teenage sons and local Friends, Wright built a house, cleared forests, and planted crops: "every thing now begins to grow familiar," Hannah Wright wrote, "& we look as if we ware at home."[79] He also began selling store goods, purchased on credit from John Roberts in Baltimore, to his neighbors, but apparently his income from dealing was not sufficient to cover the costs of pioneer farming and payment for his land. Thus, in September 1803 Joseph Wright wrote to his parents, describing his considerable accomplishments but also begging for more capital.

Letter 4.
Joseph Wright, McMahon's Creek, "N.W. Territory" [Belmont County, Ohio], to John and Abigail Wright, Ballinclay, County Wexford, 25 September 1803

N.W. Territory 9mo 25th 1803

My Dear & Honoured
Parents

When in Baltimore last 2nd month I wrote you, since which we have not wrote till by the present oppertunity nor has received any letter or ans[80] from you or any of our friends in Ireland which I may say is cause of uneasiness & distress to

---

79. Hannah Wright, Belmont Co., Ohio, to her brother, Ireland, undated [1803].   **80. an^s**: answer (reply).

us at times, being now sofar distant from our near & Dear Connections that a corrispondence seems the only way for us to know of Each others welfare & to us it would be highly gratifying, & render us much consolation   I may now tell my Dear Parents we are in our House ab^t 2½ months & been working on the Plantation since 4$^{\underline{mo}}$ last,   we with our Neighbours assistanc[81] raised the shell of a Log House 20^F By 24-, & have now got it fitted up pritty comfortable for the time[82]   there is one good Room Below & 2 Small ones—& overhead when divided will make three little appartments,   its as snugg a Cabbin as most any I see out in the woods———When a man moves out to this back Country he generaly raises a Cabbin to get into & often moves his family into it without fire place, floor or Doors & keeps an open House   if its in Spring he gets ab^t Clearing[83] land for Indian Corn which should be planted in 5$^{\underline{mo}}$ & is ripe in 10$^{\underline{mo}}$ or late this month— if he comes out later gets Ground prepared for Wheat, Rye, Potatoes or meadow— the manner of clearing, Generally is by deadening the large timber which is done by cutting with an ax ab^t 18 Inches from the ground, thro' the sap all round the tree when the leaves if on wither[84] & the tree dies   then the land begins to melerate[85]   next all the Saplins & Small trees to<o> large to grub are cut down chop'd into lenghts & the land grubb'd & the grubbs[86] Saplins &c burn'd— also the large decay'd trees that lye on the Ground are cut, & rolld by the assistance of the Neighbours   Such land as ours would take a good workman ab^t 5 days to an acre to prepare as above mentiond— & the Fence used is rails of 10½ or 11 feet long & is laid in this form ab^t 6 rails High   2 lengths of rails thus put up make one perch (16½ feet) of Fence by which thee will see it takes 196 rails to a 10 Acre field or 40 Perch Square,   a Man if the timber splits well would cut down trees maul[87] the Rails & put 'em up in ab^t 10 days or less—@ 3/ ⅌ Day   in Breaking up new Ground two Horses is generaly used with a Plow somewhat Simaler to thyne calld a Barshiere[88]—& sometimes with a Small Coulter plow so calld from having a Sharp Coulter perpendicular from the Beam to the ground & no sock[89] & is used by one Horse & cutts thro the roots surprisingly but dont turn up any sod & after with a Shovel plough[90] also drawn by one Horse   with the last two ploughs mentiond I prepar'd my Turnip Ground & Brushed them in with the Branch of a tree & the ground was very mellow[91]   all our plowing in future we can do ourselves but had to pay for plowing ab^t 7 acres which is under Corn & potatoes which are both doing

81. asststanc ms.   82. time: season.   83. he gets ab^t Clearing: he sets about clearing.   84. when the leaves if on wither: at which point the leaves, if they are still on the tree, wither.   85. melerate, i.e., meliorate: get better (= ameliorate).   86. grubs: roots left in the ground after clearing (OED, s.v., 7).   87. maul: split rails with a maul and wedge (OED, s.v., 1.b).   88. Barshiere: bar-share (pron. bar-*shear*) plow; "a plough with a wooden mould-board on which thin bars of iron were nailed to save the board from wear," Bennett Wood Green, *Word-Book of Virginia Folk-Speech* (Richmond, 1912), quoted in *Dictionary of American Regional English*, ed. by Frederic G. Cassidy et al. (Cambridge, Mass., 1985–).   89. sock: plowshare (OED, s.v.; northern and Scots).   90. Shovel plough: implement used to clear weeds from cultivated fields (see OED, s.v. shovel, 7.b (b)).   91. mellow: soft, rich, loamy (OED, s.v., 2.a).

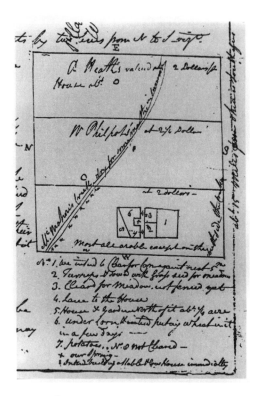

N° 1. We intend to Clear for Corn again<s>t next 5mo

2. Turnips—& sowed with Grass seed for meadow

3. Cleard for Meadow, not fenced yet

4. lane to the House

5. House & Garden North of it ab^t ⅙ acre

6. Under Corn & intend puting wheat in it in a few days

7. potatoes . .   N°. 8 not Cleared—

x our Spring—

: Intend building aStable & Cow House immediatly

FIGURE 6

Map of Joseph and Hannah Wright's farm in Belmont, Ohio Territory, drawn by Joseph Wright in his letter of 25 September 1803. Permission to print courtesy of the Historical Committee, Religious Society of Friends in Ireland (Yearly Meeting), Dublin.

well— its not necessary to plow more than 3 or 4 Inches deep—& in sowing down for Grass seed only clear the Ground & Harrow it & Sow the seed which is frequently done in the Snow when the<y> find it likely to be a thaw & leave it so—which answers very well,   the Horses are under much better command than with thee   no such thing as a driver used & the Horses go between the Standing trees so tractable that it w^d astonish thee   a man ploughs ab^t one acre ℔ Day— the Section is divided in 3 parts by two lines from N to S—vizt[92] as thee may have some imperfect Idea of by the annex'd plot,[93]— on every Side Except the South we are like to have this part very thickly Settld shortly & ab^t 2 miles South the land is Greatly Broken or Hilly to the Ohio so as to be unfit for tillage pritty much or at least so little land on the Section fitt for tilling that people dont find it their advantage to take up the whole Section, & so[94] less is made— if they alter their plan & Sett less, or Sett the levell part of it we may get Some Settlers there——A new Town is Laid off ab^t 2½ Miles north of us   if it

92. vizt: ref. to Joseph Wright's diagram of his and his partners' section of land. **93. plot:** diagram. **94. no** ms.

gets forward[95] <we> expect it will be of use to us—to sell any Surplus we may
have   We have under Corn ab^t 6 acres, Potatoes & Turnips ab^t 2 acres.   our Garden
produced us abundantly Kidney Beans, Cucumbers, Melons & without any manure, or
almost any preperation of the ground & Cabbage— Pumpkins we did not sow any not
having time or seed,   K Beans & Melons Squashes & Pumpkins are planted among
the Corn & grow without farther trouble which causes a great plenty in a family &
makes a little flesh meat go a good ways— I often wonder how we have done as well
as we have as we had nothing untill the vegetables Came in but as we are oblidgd to
buy & our family is pritty large   however if some few years were over I hope we w^d
be enabled to live comfortably as to the necessarys of Life more so than we might
expect in Ireland— I was sorry to find warr had again commenced between France &
G Brittain.[96]   I hope my native Land may remain undisturbed—& that an
accomadation may soon take place to Stop the Havock of the desolating Sword— I
have sometimes wished you safe here in this wooden[97] Country where there is more
satisfaction to be met than any one might expect   when people have a Competence
to buy Land & a little money to help to improve it, the loss of ones near Connections
is the only thing they w^d have to regrett—In most other respects the<y> may be very
happy here.   we have got into a Situation—which is like to be a very pleasing
Settlement   the Settlers are for the most part friends[98]   when we came out here
first, there might be ab^t 12 or 14 at our Meeting on first day in a Friends
house,   Now we have ameeting House ab^t 24 feet Square & expect to make an
addition of the same dementions to it very soon & perhaps from 40 to 70 at meeting
on firstdays   some freinds are Settled ab^t 6 miles west of us & got a meeting
established also—& North of us ab^t 17 miles there is 2 mee<t>ings Settled which place
was the first Settlement of Friends in this country[99] one Short Creek & the other
meeting Concord—& a few miles partly N:East of that a meeting Call'd
Plymouth,   our Meeting is calld Plainfield— all belong to the Same M^o
Meeting[100]—but are ab^t being Divided into two   I may indeed say was it not for
been[101] away from our Relations we might feel at home.   Several friends has been
here to see us & are very kind & has Invited us to see them in a most friendly
manner—& take a good dale of notice of the Boys—— we are all thro' mercy favour'd
with good Health for which I wish we may be enough thankfull to the auther of every
blessing whose supporting arm has been near us or I dont know how we would have
been long since   Jo's[102] Letters will say how he likes the Country   it was very odd
to him at first as it was to us all   My Dear Hannah & the Boys write to several
of their relations which its like<ly> my D^r father & mother may see   we Send

95. gets forward: is successful.   96. In May 1803 the Peace of Amiens (1802) broke down irrevocably and
war recommenced between Britain and Napoleonic France.   97. wooden: wooded, heavily forested; see
chapter 9, n. 46.   98. friends: Quakers.   99. country: area, region.   100. M^o Meeting: monthly meeting.
101. been: i.e., being; spelling reflects pronunciation.   102. Jo's: Joseph Wright, Jr.'s.

these letters by afriend of this meeting who goes to attend the yearly meeting at Baltimore & by whom I am expecting to recive some Letters that may have arrived to Jn⁰ & James Roberts, in whose Care he leave<s> these to forward—& whose attention & care has been extended to us in many respects   (Dear Father   Jo was telling me thou intended Still to leave me some farther assistanc for my family in thy will;   Its with reluctance I think of requesting any thing that way, & of what much greater advantage it might afford us all if it could be convenient at all to thee to order something to be pᵈ to us by Jn⁰ & James Roberts, as it wᵈ help us over difficulty's & further us much in divers respects,   I dont wish to say much to urge the feeling of a Father I know to be almost to<o> willing to assist his Children & that the distance wᵈ not lessen thy inclination to afford any assistance)——I may say My Hannah & the Boys truly unite with me in Dʳ Love to thee & My Dear Mother, Sister Martha & Samˡ to Bro Neᵃ[103] & his family Uncle Josʰ Smith<son> & Aunt with Cousins James Morison & Eliza & all our enquiring relations & remains thy Dutiful & affecᵗ Son

Jos Wright

(Please Dʳ Father write soon & direct under cover to Jn⁰ & James Roberts who will forward it)

Between 1803 and 1817 Joseph Wright apparently prospered. His land lay on the Zanesville Trace, the first road west from Wheeling through central Ohio, and later the National Road and the Baltimore and Ohio Railroad would be constructed near or across his farm. Thus, Wright's situation indeed appeared an ideal "field . . . for speculation," and in 1808 he laid out much of his holding in lots for a town—first called Wrightstown, later Belmont—in hope that the county seat might be transferred there. Despite his 51 years of age, Wright's dream, shared by thousands of other would-be townbuilders in the early nineteenth-century West, was not entirely unrealistic. Between 1800 and 1820 Belmont County's population soared from 600 to 20,300, and although the Scots-Irish were most numerous, there was also heavy settlement by Quakers from the Southern states, in flight from the consequences of their antislavery testimonies. In 1818 Wright's town gained a stagecoach service, and in the same year he won appointment as local postmaster.

However, the human costs had been high. Wright's incessant attempts to sponge money alienated his parents and other Irish relations, especially in 1805 when he drew two drafts of £50 from Baltimore merchants on his father and brother without their permission—which apparently caused a 12-year break in his correspondence with Ireland. Wright's own family suffered as well to create his "plantation." In 1803–1806 his eldest son, Joseph, Jr., wrote several letters to his maiden aunt, Martha, in Dublin. He did not complain of his and his brothers' hard, unceasing labor, and he appreciated the "harmony"

---

103. Neᵃ: Nehemiah.

and "equality" that prevailed among local Friends, but the settlement's relentless rusticity made him long for Irish society: "our only amusement is hunting or going to Raisings, Bladings,[104] Huskings &c," he wrote.[105] His escape came in 1805, when his father apprenticed him as clerk to Baltimore merchants at a salary of $450 per year, but he lamented that the city's Quakers were "too much absorbed in business" and lacked "the Sociability of the Children of Erin."[106] Unfortunately, Joseph, Jr., died two years after moving to Baltimore, perhaps of the ague or malaria he had contracted in Ohio. His stepmother, Hannah, had tried to protect the children against overexertion—"we are not as able to work as them brought up to it nor do I let the poor boys do as much as the[y] want to do,"[107] she wrote; however, on 25 May 1805 she herself died of "an inward weakness,"[108] a year after the birth of her last child, William. Shortly afterward, Joseph Wright married for a third time, to Eleanor Evans, a Welsh Quaker, and had three more sons: Smithson (b. 1807), a second Joseph (b. 1808), and Joel (b. ca. 1810). Thus, in 1817 Joseph, Sr.'s enthusiastic account of his settlement's progress glossed over the travails and sacrifices of the preceding 14 years.

Letter 5.
Joseph Wright, Belmont, Belmont County, Ohio,
to Martha Wright, Dublin, 27 June 1817

Belmont in Belmont County   this 6mo 27th 1817

My Dear Sister
Martha Wright

Thy welcome letter of 4[mo] 1815 I received and ought <to> have answered it sooner but hope to make amends in future by writing more frequent— Thou mentioned that Brother W[m] had wrote me previous to thyne letting me know of my Dear Parents removal,   it never came to hand,   the news of our much honour'd Fathers decease was very unpleasant to me, but the almighty's will must be submited to,   my Dear Mothers death I heard of through my Son James— I am much pleased my Dear Sister that thou has been so particular in Stating how our Relatives were— I am sorry my Sister watson[109] has been so afflicted with the Rheumatism but hope she is now much better, and very Glad to hear that Brother W[m] Knott & Sister with the

---

104. Bladings: form not attested in OED or the *Dictionary of American Regional English*, but the meaning is clear: "blades" are leaves of Indian corn (growing from the ear downward), which are used with the "tops" of the same plant (leaves growing upward from the ear) as fodder for cattle; bladings would be the gatherings organized to collect and store the blade-fodder (in "blade-houses"), analogous to husking and house-raising parties and like them probably accompanied by recreations of various sorts. **105.** Joseph Wright, Jr., McMahon's Creek, Ohio, to Martha Wright, Dublin, [?] September 1803. **106.** Joseph Wright, Jr., Baltimore, to his aunts, Dublin, 2 May 1806. **107.** Hannah Wright, Belmont Co., Ohio, to her brother, Ireland, undated [1803]. **108.** Joseph Wright, Jr., McMahon's Creek, Ohio, to Martha Wright, Dublin, 3 June 1805. **109. Sister watson**: Margaret Watson; Joseph Wright's sister and wife of William Watson.

family are so well. I am sorry to hear of the Death of uncle & aunt Smithson, also uncle Josʰ Cousin Peter Doyle & his Sister Martha— I wrote aletter last < . . . >ᵐᵒ to my Brother Nehemiah¹¹⁰ respecting what thou said was in Sister watsons hands by my Dʳ Fathers will for me— I therein requested he would forward me a Bill on Baltimore for abᵗ 45£ Irish—and the Ballance to send me in Sundry articles of which I sent him a memorandum— in case my letter to Brother Nehemiah has not got to hand and that this does, he will please to send, a Bank post Bill or order in favour of Jnᵒ Hayes Merᵗ Baltimore and enclose one half of it in a letter to Jnᵒ Hayes Merᵗ. Gough Sᵗ. near Bond Street Baltimore—and the other half under cover to Isaac Procter Merᵗchᵗ. Baltimore, for the whole amount Coming and not mind¹¹¹ sending any goods—and write to Jnᵒ Hayes letting him know its for my accᵗ and also to write to me under cover to Jnᵒ Hayes who will forward it me. I have an engagement¹¹² to meet in 11ᵐᵒ for which I shall want some of it very much— my Son Jnᵒ now lives in Pitsburgh abᵗ 80 miles from this   he is married & his wife was here to see us abᵗ 3 weeks ago,   I went home with her when she was returning & Saw Jnᵒ who I did not see for near 3 years,   he is well and keeps Store there & is doing well in that line,   he married out¹¹³ & dont attend meeting,   however there is no friends meeting in Pitsburgh——James I have not seen for more than five years   when I last saw him it was in Baltimore   he has been mostly at Sea & trading to the W India Islands & is now Settled in the Island of Cuba at Sᵗ. Jago¹¹⁴ where he is in partnership with a young Spaniard in the Commission buisiness & does a great dale¹¹⁵ for merchants in Baltimore & New york, in Selling Cargoes & making returns in goods   abᵗ 5 weeks ago a Captain Darrell who sails from Baltimore was out in this western Country & by James's Directions calld to See us   he saw James in 4ᵐᵒ last when he was loaded by him,   he says he had one order from a House in N York to purchase 800 Hogsheads of Sugar & that he is making money fast & that he says he will not Stay there long,   he is not married— on my way to Pittsburgh & from it I calld at Nehemiahas   he and his family well. I expect him & abiggil his wife & their two children a boy & Girl to see us in afew days   he told me he wrote to Thee— my Son Benjamin is apprentice to him,   he has some thought of Selling his property where he lives & coming to live here in this Town— I wish Brother Willᵐ was here & Samuel,¹¹⁶   its a fine place for a Farmer & Store keeper   in afew years aperson would make a Fortune— I have Laid off a Town thro' my land Named Belmont and

---

110. **my Brother Nehemiah**: in Dublin.   111. **mind**: think of, "bother."   112. **engagement**: financial obligation, promise to pay (see OED, s.v., which cites this meaning only in the plural, e.g., "to have engagements").   113. **married out**: i.e., did not marry within the Quaker community, which was meant to be endogamous.   114. **Sᵗ. Jago**: Santiago de Cuba.   115. **dale**: i.e., deal; the phonetic spelling shows that Wright had the Hiberno-English pronunciation [dayl]. See chapter 67, n. 9.   116. **Brother Willᵐ . . . and Samuel**: Joseph's brother William and his family emigrated and settled in Belmont in March 1825. On 18 September 1844 (see n. 121) Joseph's son, James, wrote that his uncle William "is doing very well indeed, he is perfectly steady and orderly [perhaps implying he had not always been so], and has near 100 acres of very good land,

has sold Several Lots   Each Lot Contains ab^t 28 Rods Eng^s Measure   the$<$y$>$ Sell at
from 40 to 100 Dollars ℔ Lot & I expect the Town will thrive— I first Sold them at 12
dollars Back Lots & 20 for front Lotts,   we petition'd Congress for a post office &
expect to have one here in 2 or 3 month as the Establishment is granted— we have
some good brick Houses erected and a Clever[117] Brick meeting House for
Friends   several buildings are going on and I expect we will have a handsome Town
here,   its in a most excellent Settlement mostly Virginians but some from most parts
of the world,   they mostly profess with Friends & Methodists— the alterati$<$o$>$n here
since my Settling in the woods is truly astonishing   in the Township in which I Live
(Goshen) when I came there was only one Cabbin—& there is now as many as 150
families living in it— a Township Contains 6 miles Square— I think if my Dr Sister
was here she w^d be more at home than she imagines,   altho I have never encouraged
any of my Relations to come to this Country I must still confess I often wish to see
many of them here believing it w^d be for their advantage and their childrens and altho
I know I am much preposessed in favour of my Native land I must give this Country
the preference in many respects— there is afield here for speculation in so many ways
that a man with a little money may advance himself much easier than in Ireland with
the same means— and people are more on a level, their money not being so much
looked at, as the manner they conduct themselves in   a man with 100 Dollars looks
on himself as good as a man with Thousands— I read in the news paper afew days ago
of a vessell Coming to Philadelphia from Holland with about 2000 people coming from
thence, all friends, and that a vessel had saild from Antwerp with 300 Friends— The
Emigration to this western Country is immense both from Europe & from the old
Settled States in this Country— in the Course of 2 weeks back we have had in this
Town as many as 60 children innoculated with the Kine pock[118]   four of mine were
in the number   the Small pox has been very little in this neighborhood since I came
here   my wife & abigail & the children unite with me in Dear love tothee all my
Brothers & Sisters as if particularly named and Relations and believe me thy truly
affectionate Brother

Jos^h Wright

Unfortunately, by 1821 Joseph Wright's Irish nemesis, insolvency, caught up with him,
as with thousands of others, when the bottom fell out of his western speculations
following the Panic of 1819. Owing $5,642—a sum indicative of excess trading inventories
and of defaulting customers and town-lot buyers—Wright transferred most of his unsold
lots and much of his other property to two men for resale to pay off his many creditors;

which he is putting in prime order by lime, and is considered by every one, as one of the best farmers in the
country." Joseph's youngest brother, Samuel, never emigrated.   **117. Clever**: neat, handsome, convenient
(OED, s.v., II, III; in these meanings either dialectal or archaic).   **118. Kine pock**: cow pox (OED, s.v. **kine**).

the fact that his farm implements were included suggests that his debacle was total. Wright's dream of a prosperous "plantation" had been reduced to a single family store in a village with fewer than 75 inhabitants. He appears to have deeded his remaining holdings to his son, Nehemiah, a prosperous farmer whose lands in 1836 were valued for taxes at $889. However, when Joseph died in 1844, his possessions were sold to pay his debts.

In the meantime, Wright's harmonious Quaker community had also disintegrated. Most of Ohio's 8,500 Friends were concentrated in the Seven Ranges, but their farmsteads were too dispersed and scattered among settlers of other faiths to sustain the endogamy required by the Quaker prohibition against intermarriage with others, and the pressures toward worldly speculation could not be balanced, as in Philadelphia, by community discipline and tradition. The result was what Wright diagnosed in 1825 as a "kind of division in Sentiment"[119] among local Friends, but it was symptomatic of a nationwide conflict between urbanized, evangelical Orthodox Quakers, with their emphasis on hierarchical and scriptural authority, and the rural followers of Elias Hicks,[120] who represented a more relaxed trust in the old Quaker traditions of "inner light." By the fall of 1828 both sides in the so-called Hicksite schism were literally battling for control of Belmont County's meetinghouses. The Hicksites' nondogmatic attitude to discipline and outmarriage probably appealed to Joseph Wright and his family. At least three of his sons had been discharged for "marrying out"—as was his third wife, indicating that Joseph himself was not in good standing with his monthly meeting—and one of his offspring may have been the unnamed Irishman who reportedly called the Orthodox elders "dogs" at their riotous confrontation with the Hicksites at the Short Creek meeting in 1828. As in Ireland, there may also have been a political dimension to this theological conflict. Most Friends in southwestern Ohio were Federalists until long after the War of 1812. However, Joseph Wright's appointment as federal postmaster in 1818, during James Monroe's first presidency, suggests that his political affiliations differed from those of the local Quaker majority.

The final word on the local schism—and on the Wright family's varied fortunes—belonged to its most remarkable and successful member: James S. Wright, Joseph's third son, who in 1807 had followed Joseph, Jr., into trade in Baltimore, prospered in commerce with Cuba, moved there, converted to Catholicism, sent generous sums to support his father and brothers in Ohio, and in 1844 was appointed U.S. consul in Santiago. In July of that year he visited Belmont,[121] just in time for his father's death, as he wrote to his

119. Joseph Wright, Sr., to his sister, Martha Wright, Ballinclay, Dublin, 19 September 1825.   120. Elias Hicks (1748–1830): by trade a carpenter and farmer in Hampstead, Long Island, Hicks was poorly educated but an avid reader and an eloquent preacher; from 1815 he was recognized as the foremost champion of liberal Quakerism in America; despite his gentle, almost saintly manner, in 1827–1828 opposition from conservative, evangelical "Orthodox" Friends precipitated the Hicksite Schism that bitterly divided Quaker meetings throughout the northern states.   121. En route from Cuba to Ohio, James S. Wright disembarked in Philadelphia shortly before the the city's nativist riots of 6–10 May 1844, in which 16 people died and two Irish Catholic churches and numerous homes were destroyed by native and Irish Protestant mobs. "I arrived in

aged aunt Martha in Dublin. Belmont, he reported, contained "about 300 inhabitants, . . . but the schism among friends, has done much evil, as respects their religious feelings & faith and I must in truth say, that in no part of this country have I seen less of the spirit of devotion than here."[122] Individually, however, most of Joseph Wright's children had done passably well. Nehemiah owned three hundred acres in Belmont County, and one of his sons was studying medicine in Cincinnati. John, a storekeeper in Pittsburgh and later St. Louis, had died, as had William, Abigail, and, presumably, Joel.[123] The second Joseph, Jr., was a local tailor: "a very liberal open hearted man, too much so to get along fast as regards the wages and means of life, but . . . well respected in the community." Smithson was a storekeeper in Columbus, "a very industrious moral man," and was elected mayor on the Whig ticket. Finally, Benjamin was a local farmer of over one hundred acres and "a great politician on the [D]emocratic side," albeit unsuccessful in his candidacy for the state legislature.[124]

Indeed, if any of the United Irishmen's radical idealism *had* inspired Joseph Wright's emigration, it was transmitted to Benjamin, a convert to his wife's Presbyterianism, who somehow combined rabid Jacksonian and fervent antislavery convictions, and to Benjamin's sons, also Presbyterians, who became substantial farmers near Rock Island, Illinois. By the late 1870s Benjamin's offspring venerated and mythologized their Irish grandfather not only as the patriarch of a prosperous settlement in the Ohio wilderness but also as a 1798 exile for Ireland's freedom! Thus, Benjamin's family had appropriated through marriage, and adapted to their Quaker ancestors' more complex political history, traditions of Scots-Irish radicalism that in the 1790s and early 1800s had flourished on the western Pennsylvania and eastern

that city," he wrote on 18 September, "formerly called by way of distinction 'of brotherly love,' as I may say in the midst of one of those detestable riots, which have latterly changed that appellation, to one more consonant to the present temper of its inhabitants, that is to say, of mob rancour,   during thirty years residence in Santiago, I never saw any thing a tenth, no, not a hundredth part as bad, and the apathy and indifference of the respectable part of the community to such a sad state of things, I considered as more foreboding of future evil, than even the discontented and riotous spirit of the lower classes,   even Friends spoke of it a good deal in the following style; 'well! certainly I agree, that all such acts are to be deprecated, but it must be allowed that the Catholic party merited punishment, and the laws won't touch their unworthy doings'; and my firm persuasion is, that while the upper orders feel thus, the lower will continue to act wrong." James S. Wright, Belmont Ohio, to Martha Wright, Dublin, 18 September 1844.   **122.** James S. Wright, 18 September 1844.   **123.** According to Joseph Wright, Sr.'s letter of 19 September 1825, to his sister Martha Wright in Dublin, in that year his son John was married and living in St. Louis, earning "a good salary," having moved there from Pittsburgh just a few months previously. John's death by 1844 is suggested by James S. Wright's reference (in his letter of 18 September 1844) to himself and Nehemiah as the "two remaining brothers" who were sons of their father's first wife. Likewise, in 1825 William Wright was in St. Clairsville, Belmont Co., apprenticed to a Quaker physician and studying medicine; but by 1844 he was dead and his widow and their two children were living with her father. In 1825 Abigail and her husband, James Gregg, resided in Belmont with their three children, but in 1844 her motherless family lived in Warsaw, Illinois, with her widowed husband who, according to James S. Wright, led a "desultory life." In 1825 Joel Wright lived with his parents in Belmont, but later letters give no indication of his fate.   **124.** James S. Wright, 18 September 1844.

Ohio frontiers but that, ironically, by the 1870s had long since dissipated on both sides of the ocean—except when preserved in the relative isolation of rural America.

26 ✳

Edward and Mary Toner, 1818

Edward Toner, like John and Jane Chambers, was an Ulster emigrant who rented farmland in the United States. Unlike most early Ulster-American farmers, however, Toner was not Presbyterian but Catholic: one of the pioneer settlers of that faith west of the Allegheny Mountains in Pennsylvania. Toner and his wife and cousin Mary, née Donnelly, emigrated from Knockavaddy townland in the religiously mixed parish of Desertcreat, near the linen market towns of Cookstown and Dungannon, in the barony of Dungannon Upper, County Tyrone.[1] Their correspondence, with its marginal English dialect and strong Irish language influence, suggests that the Toners and their kin were small farmers and weavers, although their connection with Rev. Henry Conwell, vicar-general of the Catholic diocese of Armagh, also indicates their respectable status in mid-Ulster's truncated Catholic society.[2] Evidence in his letters and in Pennsylvania records suggests that Edward Toner was born about 1770–1775 and emigrated, doubtless to Philadelphia, around 1810. Toner apparently left Ulster under some duress; perhaps he had been evicted or involved with the outlawed Ribbon Lodges.[3] By 1818, however, when he wrote the first of his two surviving letters to Ireland, he had become an American citizen and no

---

1. For demographic data on Desertcreat parish and its environs, see appendix 2.1c, on chapter 26. **2.** Edward may have been an uncle of the Hugh Toner who in 1825 paid tithes on 10 acres of land in Knockavaddy townland. In 1859 Peter Toner, perhaps Edward's elderly brother but more likely a younger kinsman, held 20 acres of land, valued at £12 15s., in Knockavaddy, rented from the Misses Bailie of Cookstown who owned 1,798 acres in Co. Tyrone; also recorded was a John Toner who rented a house worth 10s. The Donnellys were a prominent Catholic family in Pomeroy parish, adjacent to Desertcreat, but both parishes were poor and mountainous, Pomeroy especially so. The smallness of the Toner and Donnelly farms, if situated in Leinster or east Munster, would have placed them well below the ranks of Catholic strong farmers and wealthy graziers. In mid-Ulster, however, even the most respectable Catholics were usually smallholders, artisans, and shopkeepers, and the two families' apparent connection with the Catholic vicar-general suggests an above-average status based on piety, reputation, and perhaps marginally superior levels of material comfort. **3.** The Ribbon Lodges were secret Catholic societies that emerged, primarily in mid- and south Ulster, after the failure of the United Irish Rebellion of 1798. The Ribbonmen, as their members were known, were successors to the Catholic Defenders of the mid-1780s and 1790s, and their organization, with its shadowy national directory, was the Catholic counterpoint to the Loyal Orange Order. Although the Catholic Defenders had been allied with the United Irishmen and had absorbed at least some of the latter's republican idealism, the Ribbonmen's rhetoric and activities—especially their frequent, bloody clashes with the Orangemen—were at least partly responsible for the increasingly virulent sectarianism of early nineteenth-century Ulster.

FIGURE 7
Portrait of Rev. Charles
Bonaventure Maguire,
O.F.M. (1768–1833), of
Westmoreland County and
Pittsburgh, Pennsylvania.

longer regretted his fate: "for them that Appered to Be My greatest Enemy was My Best friend in helping Me to this Contery," he acknowledged.[4]

Both secular concerns and religious convictions probably determined Toner's place of settlement in western Pennsylvania. Former neighbors from County Tyrone, including many of his wife's relations, had settled on farms in Westmoreland County, around Greensburg and Latrobe. And Unity township, where Toner farmed, was the first place in southwestern Pennsylvania to provide permanent Catholic services—at Sportsman's Hall (later known as St. Vincent's)—ever since the arrival in 1787 of German-speaking migrants from Berks County, followed by Irish settlers and a resident priest in 1789. However, although Westmoreland was then "the seat of Catholicity" in western Pennsylvania, the

4. Edward Toner, Unity Township, Westmoreland Co., Pa., to Peter Toner, Knockavaddy, Desertcreat Parish, Co. Tyrone, 21 January 1819. Toner became a U.S. citizen on 21 November 1817.

bulk of the county's 30,572 inhabitants in 1820 were Ulster Presbyterians, who had been clearing the forests and farming since the late 1760s.[5]

Edward and Mary Toner's letters illustrate some intriguing patterns of early Irish community- and identity-formation. The Toners' correspondence, as well as western Pennsylvania marriage and baptismal records, emphasize their exclusively Catholic connections, both in Ulster and in America, which contrast with the interdenominational or at least interethnic networks of neighbors, acquaintances, and sometimes even kinsmen revealed by the letters and testaments of James Magraw, Mary Greenlee, and John O'Raw in the Pennsylvania, Virginia, and South Carolina backcountries, respectively.[6] Certainly, this reflects the Toner-Donnelly migration strategy—in family groups and with sufficient numbers and capital to create a rural settlement that could promote endogenous marriages and attract additional kinsmen and coreligionists. At least equally important was the availability of cheap land and its location near one of the backcountry's few Catholic churches with a resident priest. Thus, the Toners and Donnellys avoided the early frontier conditions that had obscured and eventually erased the presence of earlier Irish Catholic settlers—usually single males, often indentured servants to Protestant masters—who lived in overwhelmingly Scots-Irish regions that lacked Catholic chapels or even occasional missionaries.

However, the ethnic exclusivity revealed in the Toner-Donnelly letters and records may also reflect the high degree of religious segregation that prevailed in late eighteenth-century County Tyrone and elsewhere in a mid-Ulster region where Catholics and Protestants were roughly equal in numbers and often fiercely competitive. To be sure, Toner and his Protestant neighbors exhibited similar economic characteristics on both sides of the Atlantic. In Desertcreat and in Westmoreland County alike, small farmers of both faiths struggled to raise crops on marginal hillside land and distilled whiskey to turn small grain surpluses into a marketable and transportable commodity.[7] Likewise, the weaving, tailoring, and other skills that Catholics as well as Protestants brought from northern Ireland found rewards in the relative isolation of frontier Pennsylvania. However, despite the United Irishmen's fragile alliance between mid-Ulster's Catholics and Presbyterians, sectarian conflict had intensified from the mid-1780s, exploding into violence then and again in the 1790s, and was perpetuated in the early 1800s by frequent, bloody clashes between Orangemen and Ribbonmen. Hence the contemporary McNish-Beatty-Wright letters, written by Seceding Presbyterians in Tyrone's Donaghmore parish, just south of Desertcreat, exhibit an ethnoreligious tribalism similar to that revealed by the Toner correspondence.[8] By contrast, the letters that reflect more inclusive networks and attitudes were usually authored by emigrants from regions, such as the Foyle Valley and north and west Antrim, that boasted large Protestant—especially large Presbyterian—majorities and, not

---

5. On early Scots-Irish settlers in Westmoreland Co., see chapters 3, 12, and 22. **6.** See chapters 19, 20, and 13. **7.** Indeed, in 1794 Westmoreland and neighboring Washington Co. had been the center of the Whiskey Rebellion, mediated by the Scots-Irish politician William Findley, who had helped found Unity township's first Presbyterian church back in 1776. On Findley, see chapters 52 and 62. **8.** See chapter 6.

coincidentally, low levels of sectarian strife and, in the 1790s, high levels of participation in the United Irishmen.[9]

By 1818, as Toner noted in his first surviving letter, mid-Ulster's small farmers and craftsmen suffered severe economic distress, which in turn only heightened local conflicts and—as Toner anticipated—reduced Ulster Catholics' proverbial reluctance to emigrate. However, most of Toner's letter is devoted to religious concerns: Toner urges his brother-in-law, Patrick Donnelly, to study for the priesthood and seek ordination in the United States. In the process Toner provides a unique description of Irish Catholicism on the American frontier—thus complementing Bernard M'Kenna's contemporary account of Catholicism in urban America.[10] More important, Toner's correspondence reveals the transition taking place in rural Catholicism in Ireland itself: the early stages of the "devotional revolution" whereby the clergy institutionalized and "Romanized" popular religion, in the process abolishing or bringing under clerical auspices the traditional and often only quasi-Christian beliefs and practices—for example, the "patterns" or pilgrimages to ancient sites sacred to local (and clerically unsanctioned) "saints" and the archaic customs at wakes and funerals—that for centuries had expressed Irish peasants' relationship with the supernatural. Clearly, however, Toner's "modernized" Catholicism—centered on collective, clerically controlled rituals and on officially sanctioned icons—was strikingly different in substance and tone from the religiosity of traditional Scots-Irish Calvinists, for whom only the Scriptures mediated between helpless man and angry God, from evangelical Protestants' emphasis on individual conversions experienced through revivalism, and from the "rational" and humanistic beliefs held by many Irish Protestants (and by some Catholics such as John O'Raw and Daniel McCurtin)[11] who had been influenced by the Enlightenment.

Scholars have debated whether such religious differences were so profound as to doom the United Irishmen's political project from its inception or whether common interests and antipathies, radical republican ideals, and similar millenarian traditions were effective in creating an ecumenical alliance among rural Ulster's "men of no property." However, once French aid had failed and the 1798 Rebellion was smashed, conservative clergymen, both Catholic and Protestant, strove to reassert their churches' respective authorities and purge their flocks of French radicalism, in the process reinforcing the religious tribalism that the United Irishmen had striven, with some success, to overcome. Inadvertently, therefore, Toner's letter also suggests how, in the early 1800s, American Catholic bishops—like their peers in Ireland, increasingly conservative in response to events in Paris and Rome—could rely on Irish Catholic immigrants' renewed devotion and deference to their clergy, not only as a bulwark against resurgent Protestantism but also against "republicanism," as promoted by lay trustees, within the American church itself.[12] Thus, in the United States as in Ireland, churchmen mobilized popular Irish piety to affirm an exclu-

---

9. E.g., see chapters 13, 27, 58, 64, 65, and 68. **10.** See chapter 48. **11.** See chapters 13, and 63. **12.** On the Catholic clergy and/or lay trusteeship, see chapters 13, 44, 48, and 63.

sively and even militantly Catholic "Irish" identity that would alienate even sympathetic Irish Protestants and so help dispel the United Irishmen's dream on both sides of the Atlantic.

Edward and Mary Toner, Unity Township, Westmoreland County, Pennsylvania, to Patrick Donnelly, ca. Pomeroy,[13] in care of Rev. Henry Conwell,[14] Dungannon, County Tyrone, 7 June 1818

Unity Township   Weastmooreland County   June the 7[thd] 1818
Dear Brother & Couzen   I Recaved your Letter and My Loveing Brother Peters Letter on one day that was the 27[thd] of May Last which surprized Me Much to Read The Contents thereof Concerning the Distress and poverty of Ireland which is[15] a greavious heareing to Me to think of the Distress and want of that Contery and More so when I do think[16] of My friends and Relations to sufer[17] there in Destress and hardship and is not Able to Rach to[18] a free Contery Like this is   I understand that Edward Muldoon[19] was the Barer of them Two letters   he was here a long time Before them After spending the winter in Lancaster for he Entrusted them to Another Man which was[20] Neglected   if he had posted them there I should have them in six Day<s> Time   therefore when you send Any More Letters Desire them to Be posted in Philidelphia or Lancaster and I Shall have them in a short Time for I can take Care of Any Letter that is sent in My Care for I am Better Aquent[21] there Now that I ever was in Pomproy[22]   sir I understand your Uneasyness Concerning ordination But you Need not be in the Least Uneasy   only Dedicate your self to the will of god for if you ware A priest the Night you ware Born no Man Can Deprive you of it only this that you Must Be as pure as the Ceder of Lebannan which Is Encoruptable wood   I

---

13. Pomeroy town (Pomeroy parish, Dungannon Middle barony, Co. Tyrone).   **14.** Rev. Henry Conwell (ca.1745–1842): in 1818 vicar-general of the Archdiocese of Armagh; from 1820 bishop of Philadelphia, where he struggled vainly with rebellious priests and lay trustees. For more information on Conwell, see chapter 48. Albeit much better educated than Edward Toner, Bernard M'Kenna (subject of chapter 48) was also a devout Catholic emigrant from east Co. Tyrone, and his letter complements Toner's in its description of urban American Catholicism.   **15. which is:** "and it is."; see n. 20 and chapter 3, n. 3.   **16. when I do think:** Gaelicism; the use of a form of **do** + infinitive in Hiberno-English dialects corresponds to the use in the Irish verbal system of the consuetudinal aspect, which expresses habitual or repeated action or stasis (in this instance, "whenever I think").   **17. to sufer:** Gaelicism; "suffering." Corresponding to a single nominal form of the verb in Irish (the "verbal noun") are two forms in English, the infinitive (e.g., **to suffer**) and the gerund (e.g., **suffering**). Toner, speaking a dialect of English strongly influenced by the adstrate (or substrate) Irish of the area, has a certain difficulty with the distribution of the two English forms, at times using the infinitive when the gerund is appropriate and vice versa.   **18. Rach to:** i.e., reach to "get to" (OED, s.v. reach, 16). **19. Edward Muldoon:** still resident in Unity township on 10 February 1823, when he and Edward and Peter Toner witnessed the marriage of Margaret Toner and Patrick McKenna in the Catholic church at Sportsman's Hall.   **20. which was:** "and they were"; see chapter 3, n. 3.   **21. Aquent:** i.e., acquainted "personally known [to others]" (OED, s.v., 1; obsolete).   **22. Pomproy (pumproy** hereafter): Pomeroy town (see earlier).

have the Advice of three pr<i>est<s> Concerning you Coming[23] to this Contery
Which is the one half of the Cleargy of this state as the<y> have Told Me   first the
Rev^d M^r O Brine priest of pitsburg[24] Who Allows that you will get free Collage in this
Contery if you Didedicate your self to the service of the state or otherwise tatch[25] A
Lower Class if you are Able and Live independente and study[26]   Likewise that is to
Be A secular priest[27] which I Belive would be your Desire   if you would wish to Be a
Regular priest[28] the Revrend Charles M^cguire[29] from the Coale Iland[30] who Left there
30 years Ago and Came here Last Chrismus to Be our priest after Trevling All catholick
Conterys   he was in Etily france & germiney in the Nine provences of Netherlans and
Last of All in Bohemia   he Can preach in five Defirent Languges   he has Been
professor in several Colageges   he is a friar of the order of st frances—he says that if
he had five Boys he would study[31] them himself But the<y> Must have Letters of
Recomendations Along[32] and you Must have the same Along so do not Neglecte
it   The Reverend M^r flen thinks that the jesuat^s friers is the strongest Body and
likewise in riches But there is no Doupt[33] if you ware here and To Be well
Recommended But you would Be Recaved in Baltimore or georgia or Any other part

23. Concerning you Coming: see n. 17 and see hereafter: **Besides her Children to have a Chance of Arriveing to perfaction** (instead of: **Besides her children having . . .**).   **24. Rev^d M^r O Brine priest of pitsburg**: Rev. F. X. O'Brien, in 1808–1820 priest in Pittsburgh, where he built St. Patrick's Church (finished 1811); d. 1832 in Maryland.   **25. tatch**: i.e., teach.   **26. you will get free Collage in this Contery if you Didedicate your self to the service of the state or otherwise tatch A Lower Class if you are Able and Live independent and study**: Toner advises his nephew to complete his training for the priesthood through formal study, or through teaching (if **Able**) and independent study, at one of the new American seminaries, Georgetown at Washington, D.C., or St. Mary's in Maryland. The grievous shortage of priests in the United States compelled American bishops to offer generous inducements to persuade Irish, French, and other foreign-born seminary students and priests to embrace the American mission—what Toner erroneously (but perhaps revealingly, given traditional church-state relationships in Europe) calls **the service of the state**. **otherwise**: alternatively; **tatch**: i.e., teach; **Lower**: elementary.   **27. Likewise that is to Be A secular priest**: "the conditions are the same if you want to be a secular priest." Toner's language here appears garbled, but may be a calque on Irish **mar an gcéanna é bheith i do shagart paróiste**: "it's the same to be/being a secular priest." **28. a Regular priest**: i.e., a member of a religious order, such as the Franciscans or the Jesuits (below **jesuat^s**), as opposed to **A secular priest**.   **29.** What immediately follows in the next several lines is parenthetical; Toner's original thought resumes with **he says that if he had five boys**.   **30. Revrend Charles M^cguire from the Coale Iland**: Rev. Charles Bonaventure Maguire, O.F.M. (1768–1833), from Coalisland, near Dungannon, Co. Tyrone; student and lector in philosophy and theology at Irish Franciscan colleges in Louvain and Rome before their closure during the French Revolution; tutor to a noble family in Bohemia and Vienna; came to America in 1817, at the invitation of siblings who had emigrated in the 1780s and prospered in Ebensburg, Pa.; in 1817–1820 priest at Sportsman's Hall, Unity township; in 1820–1833 priest and (from 1822) vicar-general in Pittsburgh, where he laid the foundations of St. Paul's cathedral. Maguire's royalist or at least antirepublican sympathies were common among Irish and, especially, French priests and bishops in the early nineteenth-century American church, although some of the former exhibited strong republican attitudes that helped precipitate several of the conflicts and schisms over lay trusteeship that rent many dioceses and churches in Philadelphia, Charleston, and elsewhere. On the "Charleston schism," see chapter 13.   **31. study**: educate, train; see **to be studied** "to be educated" (OED, s.v., 8.b obsolete).   **32. have . . . Along**: have with one, have brought along.   **33. Doupt**: see chapter 1, n. 44; also see n. 68 hereafter.

that there is A Collage in the United States so do not fret But make the Best speed you Can for its very Likely that your Luck or fortune was not laid out for you in that Contery   do not Be Like A greate Many that I had knowed Myself there in Ireland   if the<y> would only build A New End to thire house the<y> Could not find from thire heart to lave it[34] Much Like the snaile when he Lives in his Box all winter and when he is Laveing it in the sumer time he Trailes it Along untill that he gets quite weried[35] for he takes it to Be one of the greatest pallices in the world   this hould<s>[36] in Comparison to[37] A greate Many there   In the year 1811 I was in Philedelphia Agreeing About[38] my son Arthur[s] passage[39]   I got your Name on the List with the Rev[nd] priest kinay To Be Advanced to Bishop Eagin[40] as soon as you should Land and Michiel Flinn Likewise and I had Left the Chuseing of the third To My B<r>other petter Toner[41] that Three of you should be Recaved in haveing your Recomendations Along that you ware to Embrace a free Collag in Case you wood find yourselves in Cloathing[42]   But I was thinking that your Mother was the Mains[43] of keeping you there as she thought that Any one that would Come to AMaraca Was totaly Lost   But I Recommend you Much to Ade and Asist your sister Nancy and her fatherless Children which I Regreat[44] Very Much for thire father[s] Death and so Dus Mary for he was an Upright Man   I think you would Act Very proper if you and that Litle familly Could get Coming[45] Togather for if she was here shee was no More A Trouble[46] to you for if she had Nither friends or Relation<s> Before her she would fetch herself through Deasenly[47] When she Could get a Bushel of good wheat for the spining of four or five Dozens of yearn of thire Own stuff Besides her Children to have a Chance[48] of Arriveing to perfaction[49] which the<y> Never would Arrived[50] to in that Contery Let thire fortune Be Ever so good   therefore put your Whole Dependence in the Allmighty god and Invoke the Coort of heaven to Be your guide   do as the Litle Huny Bee Dus when shee gos out in the time of storme shee Cary[s] A Litle gravel

---

34. the<y> Could not find from thire heart to lave it: Gaelicism (cf. Irish ní bhfaighinn óm chroí é sin a dhéanamh "I couldn't find from my heart to do that" = "I couldn't find it in my heart . . . "). **35. weried**: i.e., wearied. **36. hould<s>**: holds true, is valid. **37. in Comparison to**: i.e., with respect to. **38. Agreeing About**: entering into an agreement about, arranging for. **39. my son Arthur**: Arthur Toner; records place him in Unity township in 1818–1826. **40. Rev[d] priest kinay . . . Bishop Eagin**: Rev. Anthony Kenny, priest and associate of Rev. C. B. Maguire in Pittsburgh; Rev. Michael Egan, Galway-born bishop of Philadelphia (1808–1814) and, like Maguire, a Franciscan. Toner's ignorance of Bishop Egan's death in July 1814 indicates his rural community's physical and social distance from the seaboard centers of American Catholicism. **41. petter Toner**: Peter Toner, Edward's brother, then in Kockavaddy; see n. 79. **42. in Case you wood find yourselves in Cloathing**: "with the provision that you would furnish your own clothing"; **in Case**: Gaelicism (see Irish **i gcás go**, lit. "in case that" = provided that). **43. Mains**: i.e., means "instrument." **44. which I Regreat**: whom I sympathize with. **45. Could get Coming**: were able to come; Gaelicism (the Irish verbal root **faigh-** means not only "get, find" but also "be able"). **46. Trouble**: burden. **47. Deasenly**: i.e., decently "with a competence." **48. Besides her Children to have a Chance**: see n. 17. **49. Arriveing to perfaction**: achieving full proficiency (?). **50. would Arrived**: i.e., would have arrived; see chapter 1, n. 22.

Along to Balance[51] her in the Are[52]   so paus on this and Beg <God> to grant yo<u>
so Much grace as will gard you Against the snares and Temptations of this Life As it is
well Becoming a Man in your state of Life and situation to Be an example of Virtue To
Both old and young—which I Expect it will be the Case with you   you know it
would Be our glory to here and see of your wellfaire and to proceed[53] in what you
Underwent[54]

In this Contery I have seen A part[55] of the Boanes of the 12 Apostlys in Relecks[56]
Most Curiously[57] Cemented in frames of glass and Embroyderd with gould and Even
the garment of our Blessed Redemer A part of them and of the garmets which his
Mother Ever Virgin wore in this world   I had the Hapiness of kissing them   when
the shedow <of> s[t] petter & the Napken of s[t] paul Did Cast out[58] Devils what less
Virtue would thire Boones have   if you would see the profoile of the Bless<ed>
Virgin & of her Enfant jesus Most Curious<ly> Drawed out[59] in waxed work in A
frame Likewis Embroyderd with gould   the Rev[nd] Charles Boneventure M[c]guire
Collected all thes Relicks in his Trevels   We have great satisfaction for we Live on
the Nixt plantation to him   he is one of the greatest pratchers that Ever I hered in My
Life   Catholick Clergy gets fine Liven[60] in this Contery   there are several places Laid
out for A priest and non to Embrace it   there are so Many other Chances for Lerned
Men in this Contery which Makes so few Embrace the Church Unless such as are
Enspired with pyety or Devotion to the Catholick fath   our priest got 500 Acrs of first
Reate land Besides his Congregation subscribes[61] Better than 500 Dollars yearly
solarry   his Brothers had wrote him <in> Bohamia and incouraged him to this
Contery but it would take a seacon<d> Mosses[62] to Drag Any of the Clargy that was
Reased there here Altho the<y> are in herdships and want in it[63]—no More on that
subject   we are in good helth thanks be to god   your sister Mary is younger and
frasher Lookin than shee Was the day she Left Ireland   shee Carrys her Age Better
than I do for Many a hard days work I got sinc I left there which Left My head
gray   I k<n>ew[64] Myself often wett[65]   still I had my Own Dew[66] A good Bed to
Lye on and plenty to Eat and Drink But I had got A complant with the grief and

---

51. Balange ms.   **52. Are**: i.e., air.   **53. to proceed**: i.e., proceeding; see n. 17. **proceed**: advance, get on,
prosper. With the substitution of the gerund the sentence reads: it would be our glory to see and hear of your
welfare and of your prospering in whatever you have undertaken.   **54. Underwent**: undertook (OED, s.v., 8;
now rare). The presence of the simple past here, rather than the expected perfect ("have underwent"),
represents a Gaelicism, Irish having a single past tense covering the semantic area split between two forms in
English.   **55. A part**: some; Gaelicism (Irish **cuid** "part, some").   **56. Relecks**: here "reliquaries"; hereafter
"relics."   **57. Curiously**: skilfully, exquisitely (OED, s.v., 3; archaic).   **58. Did Cast out**: see n. 16.
59. Drawed out: outlined.   **60. gets fine Liven**: "can live very well."   **61. Congregation fo subscribes** ms.
62. Mosses: i.e., Moses.   **63. in it**: there; Gaelicism (Irish **ann** "in it, there").   **64. k<n>ew**: saw,
experienced.   **65.** Ms. torn; several words lost after **wett**.   **66. Dew**: i.e., due.

Trouble I was In when I was in Ireland Viz A pain in My Bowels that works[67] Me in the Maner of a Collick which some times I am Douptfull[68] will shorten My Days Altho I live hapy and well and Expects so[on] to B<u>y A place of My Own which is still My Look out[69]   simon Donely is Making out well in greensburg   he gets as high as ten Dollars for Maken A greate Coate and James is Distilling in this Nibourhood   the<y> Meet with Me here Very often   John Donelly from shesaugh Donoughey is here and Dooing well at his Trade[70]

I send My love to My brother petter and Let him know that I sent him A letter Januar[y] last to All My Brother[s] in Law   I Expect that My sister peagy and paul Mallon will here this Letter Read as I am Told the<y> live in pumproy   I should wish that the<y> were alle to Come to this Contery   therefor I conclude with My best Respects to all My friends and wellwisher<s> in that Contery

Edward Toner and Mary Toner

In the Main Time[71] I am pening these few Lines I have an Extract of A letter from A Man in Dundalk in the County Louth to his friends in this Contery Relateing the Barbarity Tyrony Hardships and hard usage of the poore Enhabitants of them parts   the said Letter Expressly says that the<y> are hanged and gebigeted Burned with Roach'd Lime in the goile yeards<,>[72] that Numbers of heads of familyes <are> Transported for Exiles[73] and Especily Roman Catholkcks when the<y> are so Unfortunate as to fall into thire hands<,> that Caracture is of no Use to them<,> that the<y> are the Most Degradeingest[74] people in the world all By the pride and

---

67. works: affects.   68. Douptfull: apprehensive; see n. 33.   69. Look out: desire (OED, s.v., 4.a; obsolete). 70. simon Donely . . . James . . . John Donelly from shesaugh Donoughey: Simon Donnelly of Greensburg, Westmoreland Co., d. 1827, age 28. James Donnelly, brother of Simon. John Donnelly, from Sessiadonaghy townland, Pomeroy parish, Co. Tyrone: "a gentleman of fine scholarship and culture"; perhaps eldest brother of Simon and James Donnelly: emig. 1798 and lived in Derry township, Westmoreland Co.; m. Margaret Atchison (d. 1853) who, in 1820, age 42, publicly "renounced the Calvinistic heresy" and received Catholic baptism; d. 1826; survived by nine children, one of whom, William (b. 1817) became a Democratic member of the Pennsylvania legislature (1877–1878). Albert, *Westmoreland Co.*, 606; *Catholic Baptisms in Western Pennsylvania . . .* , 83; see Sources, chapter 26.   71. Main time: i.e., meantime; in the meantime "at the same time as, while" (OED, s.v., A.1.a.).   72. gebigeted: i.e., gibbeted. The bodies of the executed were publicly displayed, hanging for weeks or even months on a gibbet or gallows, as a warning to prospective law-breakers. Burned with Roach'd Lime in the goile yeards: Irish authorities commonly buried the bodies of executed criminals in quicklime pits in the jailyards (goile yeards), rather than return them to their kinsmen for interment in consecrated ground—thereby outraging the latter's religious sensibilities.   73. Transported for Exiles: for "as"; i.e., transported to the penal colony at Botany Bay in New South Wales, Australia; after the American Revolution, Irish (later British) authorities could no longer transport Irish convicts to Maryland and to Britain's other former colonies on the North American mainland, but between 1788 and 1853 over 40,000 Irish convicts were transported to eastern Australia.   74. Degradeingest: i.e., degradenest "most degraded," referring to Irish Catholics. The spelling ng to represent the sound [n] is the same as seen, for example, in the spelling taking for taken. The form degraden is the attributive adjective derived from the past passive participle: degraded (past passive participle) → degraden (attributive adjective); for the usage see *I have mowed*

Aristocricy of the Nobility of England and Ireland   it[75] has Rached over the globe and no Doubt But it has Rached heaven—for the Cryes of the Dying Enocent Must Rach that holy Coort as the said Letter allows[76] that the\<y> Declaire thire Inocency to the Last[77]

O n 21 January 1819, seven months after writing to Patrick Donnelly, Edward Toner penned a second letter to his own brother Peter, also in Knockavaddy. Anticipating the American financial panic of 1819, Toner complained that "this Contery is Much poluted with Insolvent Banks and . . . speckalaters," and he also reported the recent, accidental death of his daughter Nancy's husband.[78] Yet despite these setbacks, Toner urged his brother to "place your Dependence in your Maker" and emigrate.[79] "A good Taylor Can make well out here," Toner advised, and opportunities in other trades were also "Excelent." Indeed, he declared, "Any Man of A traid will Not Be Exposed to hard work here."

By contrast, recent reports from home had convinced Toner that "there is a Disolation Aproching to England and Ireland. . . . [T]hire time is nerely At an End." Indeed, in 1814–1815, with the end of the Napoleonic Wars, Irish farm prices collapsed, cottage industries failed, and much of mid-Ulster began to resemble a densely populated rural slum. In Toner's youth, however, the region's economic growth had encouraged, among Catholics as well as Protestants, ambitions that now found outlets in America. And Ulster traits of diligence and adaptability were only reinforced by the challenges and opportunities of frontier farming and early industrialization in areas such as western Pennsylvania. Thus, like the Presbyterian Crocketts,[80] Edward Toner believed that America rewarded emigrants bred to labor and penalized those with genteel pretensions and fallacious expectations. "[T]hire is No people," Toner wrote, "that this Contery Comes Less strange to them[81]

---

the grass vs. *I like the look of newly **mown** grass.* This derivational process, mostly employing the suffix -(e)n, is no longer productive in Standard English but persists in some nonstandard dialects. For details see Otto Jespersen, *A Modern English Grammar on Historical Principles,* pt. 6, *Morphology* (Copenhagen, 1942).   **75. it:** i.e., news of their plight.   **76. allows:** asserts.   **77.** Toner undoubtedly refers to the mass executions in early 1818 at Dundalk, Co. Louth, of 24 Catholics, members of the outlawed Ribbon Society, for the 30 October 1816 massacre of the Lynch family of Wildgoose Lodge at Corcreagh (Reaghstown), Co. Louth—a story immortalized by the Tyrone-born novelist William Carleton (1794–1869), in "Wildgoose Lodge," first published in Caesar Otway's evangelical Protestant newspaper *The Christian Examiner* (Dublin), later in Carleton's *Traits and Stories of the Irish Peasantry* (New York, 1864).   **78.** Nancy (or Anna) Toner: married cousin Matthew Toner, by whom she had two children, Anthony and Mary (b. 1817); in 1822 she apparently remarried, to James Heeny, at Sportsman's Hall church.   **79.** Peter Toner did emigrate, and on 10 October 1822 he was a witness at the wedding of Edward Toner's son, Meredith, at Sportsman's Hall (see n. 85).   **80.** See chapter 15 and, especially, chapter 27. For similar remarks on the characteristics required for American success (and with respect to Irish distress and "despotism"), also see the 1817 and 1825 letters by Ulster Presbyterian immigrants David Robinson and Robert Crockett, respectively, in appendix 3.   **81. that this Contery Comes Less strange to them:** to whom this country seems less strange; **that . . . to them:** to whom (Gaelicism).

than those that had Been in other Meen Employ[82] in the old Contery for when the[y] get here hard work is no Object to them no nor the Clamency or inclamency of the weather." However, he warned, many from Ireland were

> not Acustomed to work there and When the[y] get in here and Aquent[83] with the Custom of the Contery the[y] Begin to speckalate on some Idle Employ sooner than work—some to gamling   some to follow Women   some others to hard Drinking   others to forgery and passing Bad Notes and from thence the[y] are Senten[c]ed to the Cells and workhouse for which the[y] are A Disgrace to thire Contery and An Upcast[84] to those that is well behaved.

Toner's moral strictures were typical of Catholic Irish-America's nascent, property-owning middle class, and in his 1819 letter Toner reiterated his hope to purchase "A place of My own . . . with gods Asistance." Surviving records, however, do not indicate that Toner ever owned a farm, and although at his death in 1849 he possessed a house and lot in the crossroads village of Youngstown, these had to be sold to meet his debts. Yet Toner's work ethic apparently fourished among his descendants, for whereas in 1826 his son Meredith[85] was merely a carter in Pittsburgh, his grandson, Joseph M. Toner (1825–1896), became an eminent physician in Washington, D.C., as well as a historian of American Catholicism and medicine. However, like Meredith and his son, most of the Toners and their Irish Catholic neighbors were unable to carve out permanent niches in Westmoreland County's rural economy and in a Scots-Irish subculture that, like its Irish Catholic counterpart, became increasingly sectarian as United Irish and Jeffersonian radicalism waned under the impact of evangelicalism and the disintegration of the first American party system. Whether for economic or cultural-political reasons, well before the middle of the nineteenth century most Ulster-stock Catholics had left Unity township and moved to Pittsburgh, and by 1843 only 1,350 Catholics comprised merely 3 percent of Westmoreland's population, leaving the Scots-Irish overwhelmingly dominant among the county's farmers.

---

82. **Meen**: i.e., mean (lowly, manual); **Employ**: occupations.   83. **get . . . Aquent**: become acquainted.
84. **Upcast**: source of reproach/embarrasment (Scots).   85. **Meredith** (or "Murty") Toner: born in Co. Tyrone, he emigrated in 1810 and first settled in Unity township, where, in 1818, he declared his intention to become a U.S. citizen; in 1822 he married Ann Layton in the Catholic church at Sportsman's Hall and subsequently moved to Pittsburgh.

James and Hannah Crockett, 1822

Few sibling contrasts among Ulster emigrants can have been greater than those between James Crockett of Pennsylvania and his older brother, George Crockett, Jr., of Tennessee.[1] Both were born in the late 1760s (James ca.1768) on their father's prosperous farm at Drumnashear, in east County Donegal, but, judging from their letters, George was by far the better educated. Both emigrated in 1796, but they came separately, George to Baltimore and James to New York, and apparently never met again and corresponded only rarely. Whereas George was a successful entrepreneur and planner of his extended family's settlement in America, James spurned George's and his other brothers' offers to join them in urban Tennessee and instead made his way alone as a pioneer farmer in an undeveloped region of Pennsylvania. Yet James's success, although more modest, may have been more lasting. In the end, James not only outlived George but at age 82 was hearty enough to take care of his decrepit younger brother, Robert, after relatives in Tennessee could no longer do so.[2]

Although Presbyterian, James Crockett had much in common with his contemporary Ulster Catholic emigrant to Pennsylvania, Edward Toner. Both were shrewd, unvarnished, persistent men, harshly critical of "genteel" emigrants too pretentious to work with their hands. "[T]his is a verry fine Countrey," Crockett wrote to his father in 1800, "but it is abuest by a class of young mens that cums from among you that is too lasey to woork at home and is not scholar anuf to get other busness and is too proud to work."[3] To be successful, he noted three years later, an emigrant needed "a good hart."[4]

James Crockett apparently possessed the qualities he praised, for he endured 13 years of hard labor before he amassed the capital necessary to purchase a farm. In 1796, shortly after disembarking, Crockett hired out as a farm laborer, at £3 per month, five miles from New York City, but by 1800 he was working "on the Bridge" near Newark, New Jersey, probably as a quarryman or stonemason, for £42 per year.[5] Through "frugalety and economy," by 1803 Crockett had accumulated savings and, despite his father's criticism, had invested in a quarrying venture at Newark. James was now able to fulfill his father's old order for several bushels of American flaxseed, but he was weighted down by unsold stones and admitted that "it is verry killing on nature to woork out[doors] in this countrey."[6] By the summer of 1806, according to his brother David, then a saddler in New York City, Crockett "had purchased a sloop and was in the stone trade betweenst this [city] and New

---

1. See chapter 15; and for demographic data on the Crocketts' east Donegal, see appendix 2.1a, on chapter 15.
2. On Robert Crockett, see chapter 15 and appendix 3.   3. James Crockett, Newark, N.J., to George Crockett, Sr., Drumnashear, Killea Parish, Co. Donegal, 30 January 1800.   4. James Crockett, Newark Bridge, N.J., to George Crockett, Sr., Drumnashear, Killea Parish, Co. Donegal, 20 June 1803.   5. James Crockett, 30 January 1800.   6. James Crockett, 20 June 1803.

Ark" and was "doing very well."[7] And three and a half years later, the same brother reported that "James and his wife is gone to Pennsylvania to live . . . on the Susquehanna river   he has bought an hundred acres of land and thinks he can live more Independent on that than he could Expect to live here."[8]

Although already about 40 years old, James Crockett settled on hilly, uncleared land in Huntington (later Union) township, between the north branch of the Susquehanna River and Shickshinny Creek, in central Pennsylvania's Luzerne County. Historical ironies had made Luzerne County less developed and settled than Toner's Westmoreland County farther westward. The Indians had ceded the region late, in 1768, and for the next 30 years settlement was delayed by premature and ill-considered land speculations: first by the Connecticut-based Susquehanna Company and thereafter by Pennsylvania officials such as Robert Morris and James Nicholson.[9] The latters' speculative schemes collapsed, landing both men in debtor's prison, and creditors eventually sold off Luzerne County lands at $2 per acre—the same price that, a decade earlier, had attracted Joseph Wright to much superior, federally owned land in southeastern Ohio.[10]

Unfortunately, disputed titles became the nightmare of many Luzerne County settlers, including James Crockett. Moreover, at first Crockett's shortage of capital and labor led him to rely on brother David for financial assistance—and to urge brother Robert, then still in Ireland, to come "help me with my harvest."[11] But although Robert emigrated in 1811, he went instead to Tennessee, as did David, to join their more ambitious brother George. In 1816 George also invited James to come south, but the latter never budged, finally determined to build his livelihood in one place. "I now live happy and contented," James had written in 1810;

> I had a good crop this year which gives me great encouragement to prepair for another   I lick[12] it well   I mack no dout but it will turn out to our advantage   it is good for grass   I think in a few years we could make medow anuf to kep 50 head of cattle   we are not afraid of the landlord takeing them for the rent . . . hear all we have to pay is our necery[13] taxis which we do with pleashur.[14]

One senses that James Crockett relished personal as well as economic freedom from Irish impositions. His long breaks in correspondence with his father in Ireland stemmed not only from the latter's disapproval of his earlier involvement in quarrying but, more profoundly, from the old man's adamant opposition to James's choice of a Catholic

---

7. David Crockett, New York City, to George Crockett, Sr., Drumnashear, Killea Parish, Co. Donegal, 22 August 1806.   8. David Crockett, Elizabeth, N.J., to George Crockett, Sr., Drumnashear, Killea Parish, Co. Donegal, 28 December 1809.   9. On Robert Morris, see chapters 52 and, especially, chapter 58.   10. See chapter 25.   11. James Crockett, Huntington, Pa., to George Crockett, Sr., Drumnashear, Killea Parish, Co. Donegal, 11 November 1810.   12. lick: like (Scots form).   13. necery: i.e., necessary.   14. James Crockett, 11 November 1810.

wife, Hannah [McCarten?], from near Drumnashear. Attempting to extend patriarchal authority across the Atlantic, George Crockett, Sr., commanded James to "part with" Hannah or cease writing home. Responding in 1810, James refused to leave his "most exlant wife"—"conscience forbad it," he declared—and so he "was obliged to submit to the disagreable task of not writing."[15] The lapse in correspondence lasted over 11 years, until 1822, when James finally penned the following latter—proudly recounting his physical and legal struggles to secure the farm he had purchased 12 years earlier.

James and Hannah Crockett, Union Township, Luzerne County, Pennsylvania, to George Crockett, Sr., Drumnashear, Killea Parish, County Donegal, 14 January 1822

Union   January 14ᵗʰ 1822

Dear Father,

it is a long time since I had the plashure of writing or hearing from you, which you no dout will think the same   I must confes I have been negl<ec>tfull about riting nor can I Make aney excuse for my self,   thairfore I think it better to confess my falts than smuther the truth   I had aletter from Brother George   he let me know that you had agreat desire to hear from me and how I was coming on[16]   I shall endevor to satisfy you as far as I can   about twelve year ago I bought alot[17] of land the place[18] I now live   it was wild land   what I mean by wild land is oncultiveted land   the lot contain 109 acres   I gave 2 Dollars per acre,   it lookt a wild looking place to get aliving as the<re> were nothing but trees and bushes to be seen,   I began to doubt whither I could get aliving of the land or not as I was onaquented with the method of cleering land,   I thot it would not doo to stand and look at them[19]   I went to woork with my ax and grubing hoe,   I soon got down as many logs as laid up[20] my house,   the<y> wer laid up horizantly in pers[21]   the roof made of shingls split out of wood and naild to the lath,   I went on verry well for too or three years till it was rumord a bout that my title would bee disputed   I did not belive it as I did not wish to but I soon found it to bee true,   the sherrif made me <a> viset and served me with an Ejectment by A Mᵣ Bidle   he said the rite was in him[22] and not in me   I said I would stand him a trial for it   I went to Wilksbree[23] the county town where our corts holds and employd two la<w>yers to carry it on for me,   Mᵣ Bidle did not come forward to have it brought on[24]   it lay still[25] for five years although I wisht to have it tryd as thair is no feeling so painfull as suspence when

15. James Crockett, 11 November 1810.   16. **coming on**: progressing (OED, s.v. come, 66.b)   17. **a lot**: not "a great deal" but "a parcel, portion."   18. **the place**: where.   19. **them**: that is, the trees and bushes mentioned earlier.   20. **laid up**: erected, built (OED, s.v. lay, 60.a; archaic).   21. **pers**: i.e., pairs.   22. **the rite was in him**: he had the juster claim.   23. **Wilksbree**: Wilkes-Barre, the county seat; population 1,225 in 1818.   24. **brought on**: brought into action (OED, s.v. bring, 20.c).   25. **still**: dormant, inactive.

the result[26] is to determin a mans all whither it is lost or gaind   I got an ordor out at
coart to have it brought to tryal the nixt coart   it was brought on and desidet in my
fevor and left M͞r Bidle A hansum bill of cost to pay,   my layers beheved with great
faith[27] and libarality to me   M͞r Mallery in purticylar[28] advanced his own money and
waited on me til I could replece it   I now begin to feel better since I gaind the
land   I have about 30 acres cleerd and I am now going to tell what you will s<c>arce
give me credet for, that is I have not hyred but thre<e> mo<n>ths woork on the
place   I done all my own woork   I hav built a lerge Barn 41 feet by 30 that I hyred
all done   if my Barn is large my house is small   I have now got thrue with the
historical part of my letter,   I must now give you som acount of my Famely affairs   I
have got one Son and no Daughters   my son is six years old avery fine boy   his
name is George Alaxandor Cro<ckett>   he and his Mother desires to be
remem<bered> to you,   when you write to me derect your letter to James Crockett
Union care of M͞r Jarius Herrison Huntiongton Luzerne County Pennsylvania   I wish
to be remembert to all my Brothers and Sistors and all the rest of my frends   I remain
your very affectionete son

James Crocket

Honnored Sir
after presenting you my humble dutys I request you to write to us and let me know if
my aunt M͞cCarten is still alive

Hannah Crocket

Apparently, this letter never elicited a response from George Crockett, Sr., before his
death in 1829, and so it marked James's last attempt to reestablish direct contact with
his family in Drumnashear. Fortunately, despite the lack of subsequent letters written by
James or Hannah, the story of their struggles to wrest a living from their Luzerne County
farm can be documented from other sources. As James had written in 1822, he and his
wife had only one child, George Alexander. For a pioneer farmer in early nineteenth-
century Pennsylvania, Crockett's small family was exceptional—and also economically disadvantageous, as the usual five to eight children were necessary to boost farm productivity
much above subsistence level. Thus, as brother Robert reported in 1827, after visiting
Pennsylvania, James had "to work hard": prices were too low to enable him to hire labor,
and his 11-year-old son was only "able to help a little."[29]

During the 1830s and early 1840s, James Crockett probably raised wheat and cattle.
In those years, however, Union township was "a very dull place," remote from markets,
with little or "no demand for the produce of farmers" who, increasingly, competed with

---

26. ruselt ms. (transposed spelling).   **27.** faith: trust, confidence (OED, s.v., 1.a).   **28.** purticylal ms.
29. Robert Crockett, Gallatin, Tenn., to George Crockett, Sr., Drumnashear, Killea Parish, Co. Donegal, 26
January 1827.

Midwestern grain and livestock producers. But by 1848, as James's son, George, reported, "the extensive coal business that is carried on in this county and those adjoining keeps our market good" and "our Canall . . . thronged with boats."[30] Indeed, by midcentury the economy of Pennsylvania's Susquehanna-Schuylkill-Wyoming region had been radically transformed, as a crazy quilt of hard-coal mines and iron furnaces was imposed on its hills and hollows, ridges and valleys, leaving some of them quiet and agrarian, making others a smudge of slag heaps and shanties, with Union township a mixture of both.

In response to growing local demands, James and his son probably shifted their farm's production to a mixed-grain, herding, and dairying emphasis. Yet if industrialization provided profits for local farmers, it also brought an influx of Irish Catholic laborers, many of them poor peasants in flight from Ireland's Great Famine of 1845–1852. Between 1830 and 1850 Luzerne County's population more than doubled from 27,000 to 56,000, and the proportion of its foreign-born inhabitants—most of them Irish Catholics—soared from merely 3 percent to over 22 percent. Thus, before one society had time to mature, another was thrust upon it. The result was political revolution: almost the entire region, consistently Jeffersonian and Jacksonian in its voting patterns from 1799 to 1851, went Whig in the latter year, as nativist politicians deliberately mobilized the Scots-Irish and other, once-insurgent small men of the postfrontier against the Irish Catholic newcomers' interests, religion, and drinking habits.

Religion, culture, and social distance sharply divided rural Pennsylvania's old and new Irish—the established farmers from the Famine-era miners.[31] However, the former's hostility may also have stemmed from economic anxieties, as many second-generation Ulster-American families strove with only moderate success to hold their farms and find livelihoods for their children. Certainly, James Crockett had little leisure in his latter years. As his son, George, admitted, "our land is not as smooth and easy worked as the river bottoms"[32]—although its location was healthier—and in 1850 brother Robert observed that James "works hard for a man of his age" of 82![33]

By midcentury George had developed a farm of his own, in nearby Ross township, where James—and, briefly, James's brother Robert—settled in old age. And, at his father's death, George would almost certainly inherit any balance left over from the old holding in Union township, which James continued to farm into the late 1840s. In addition, George taught school in winters and served as a local magistrate. Unlike his father, however, George and his wife, Ann, had at least six children. Thus, although George was "very

---

30. George A. Crockett, Ross, Muhlenberg Co., Pa., to Robert Crockett, [Nashville, Tenn.?], 14 February 1848. **31.** The social distance of Scots-Irish farmers from Irish Catholic miners, blast furnace workers, and laborers was so great that a William [O']Rourke (b. 1840), an immigrant from Co. Tyrone who escaped the coalfields, married a local farmer's daughter, converted to Protestantism, and became a farmer on Shickshinny Creek, would later claim "Scotch-Irish" heritage by asserting that *his father* had been a Scot who had migrated to Ulster. **32.** George A. Crockett, 14 February 1848. **33.** Robert Crockett, Union, Luzerne Co., Pa., to Alexander Crockett, Drumnashear, Killea Parish, Co. Donegal, 19 February 1850.

active and a fine hand to work on the farm" (and his spouse "a very smart industrious woman"), according to his uncle Robert, "[i]t will be all they can make to support them."[34] Indeed, sometime after 1850 financial exigencies finally obliged James and George to pack Robert off to Ireland, on funds sent from Drumnashear.

Yet despite these travails, the elderly James Crockett may have been saddened to find Ulster's social and sectarian tensions transposed onto his new home. The fact that brother Robert—with his outspoken Irish nationalist and republican sympathies that dismayed his Irish correspondents[35]—found a congenial if temporary home with James's family suggests that the two men may have shared similar opinions, forged in the politically exciting Ulster of the 1790s. And although many of Luzerne County's new settlers were impoverished, illiterate Irish-speakers from the boggy shores of west Donegal and Mayo, perhaps James Crockett's own marriage to an Irish "papist"—in defiance of his father's and his community's traditional strictures—prepared him to resist, however feebly in his old age, the sectarian trends that increasingly segregated and alienated Irish Protestants and Catholics in America and Ireland alike.

---

34. Robert Crockett, 19 February 1850.   **35.** E.g., see chapter 15, and appendix 3.

IV ✳
Craftsmen, Laborers, and Servants

28 ✳

Benjamin Chandlee, 1705

Although the great majority of Irish emigrants to eighteenth-century America became farmers, significant numbers were artisans and unskilled laborers, attracted by the higher wages, steadier work, and greater opportunities for comfortable subsistence or even upward mobility that the New World offered. Although the colonial gentry and wealthy overseas merchants often denominated artisans and laborers, collectively, as the "lower sort" or the "humbler orders," in fact they comprised two distinct although very fluid and heterogeneous groups, as reflected in their Irish origins, migration patterns, and American experiences. For example, although both craftsmen and laborers usually emigrated as indentured servants, the former's superior skills normally commanded better terms and treatment as servants and, after their indentures had expired, enabled many to achieve "independence" as farmers, independent tradesmen, or even merchants.[1] By contrast, unskilled immigrants generally fared much less successfully in the New World, especially if they were of "native" or Catholic Irish origins, or women, or, worst of all, transported criminals or "vagabonds."

Certainly, skilled craftsmanship was much in demand in British North America, especially in the Middle Colonies, where a diverse, export-driven economy generated a variety of ancillary enterprises both to service transatlantic trade and to provide consumer goods that could be produced in the colonies, with its abundance of raw materials, more cheaply than they could be imported from Great Britain. Benjamin Chandlee, an Irish Quaker, was one immigrant who took full advantage of American opportunities. He also penned several of the earliest surviving Irish immigrants' letters; indeed, his is the only extant transatlantic correspondence written by an Irish artisan prior to the American Revolution. Yet Chandlee had emigrated under certain disadvantages. Apparently, he possessed no special skills when he left rural Ireland. Moreover, he was the first and only member of his immediate family to emigrate to the colonies, and probably he traveled as a redemptioner—pledging as many as five to seven years' service to an American employer in return for the cost of his passage. However, Chandlee was more fortunate than many young immigrants without trades or capital, for, as a member in good standing of the Society of Friends, he was able to use the transatlantic Quaker network to secure a good master, training in a profitable and highly specialized trade, a favorable marriage, and upward mobility to the status of manufacturer—eventually founding in America the nucleus of a

---

1. For two examples of Irish craftsmen who eventually became American farmers, the former rising from indentured servitude, see chapters 23 and 27. Several of the skilled and unskilled immigrants chronicled in this section, including the subject of this chapter, achieved "independence" as manufacturers, shopkeepers, or merchants; see chapters 33, 35, 36, and 38.

mixed farming-industrial community similar to those established by Quakers at Ballitore, County Kildare, and elsewhere in Ireland.

Born in 1685, Benjamin Chandlee was the eighth child of Joanna and William Chandlee, Jr. (d. 1723), a miller in Kilmore townland, in the united parishes of Carbury, in Carbury barony, in western County Kildare. Benjamin's grandfather was the English-born William Chandlee, Sr. (1591–1694), who came to Ireland with Oliver Cromwell about 1649, supervised the English army's stores in Trim, County Meath, was "convinced of ye blessed truth" preached by William Edmundson, the first Irish Friend,[2] and lived the remainder of his 103 years near Edenderry town, in King's County, just across the border from Kilmore in County Kildare. By 1700 there were still at least 450 to 500 Quaker families in Ireland, but the devastation wrought by the recent Williamite War (1688–1691), plus migration to Dublin and Philadelphia, had already eroded rural communities of Friends in Kildare, King's, and other Leinster counties.[3] In 1702 the ascension of Queen Anne (d. 1714) brought Irish Quakers a last period of severe persecution—much relaxed by 1724, when Robert Parke's family left nearby County Carlow—but as a younger son, with few prospects for inheritance, Benjamin Chandlee's solitary emigration was probably occasioned primarily by economic concerns and personal ambition.[4]

In any case, on 28 November 1702, Benjamin Chandlee, aged about 17, secured from the Edenderry monthly meeting a removal certificate, recommending "him to friends care where his lot may fall we knowing him to be an innocent youth & of good conversation."[5] Judging from his 1705 letter, written two years after his emigration, Chandlee probably embarked from Dublin aboard a ship bound for Maryland and then traveled by land, sloop, and ferry to Philadelphia. In 1703 Penn's capital was only three years older than Chandlee himself and contained merely five thousand inhabitants; however, by 1720 its population would double and both its trade and the prosperity of its hinterland would surpass those of Boston and New York.

Perhaps 10 percent of Pennsylvania's early Quaker settlers were Irish-born, but upon

---

2. William Edmundson (1627–1712): b. in Westmoreland, England; orphaned very young and apprenticed as a carpenter in York; served in the Cromwellian army ca. 1647–1651, where he first encountered the Quakers, whose faith he embraced formally in 1653; emigrated to Ireland ca. 1652, first settling at Antrim and Lurgan, in Ulster, where he preached and organized the first Friends' meetings in the island; frequently arrested and imprisoned for his faith, in about 1660 Edmundson removed to a farm at Rosenallis, Queen's Co., in southern Ireland, where he experienced more harassment; in 1671–1672 he accompanied George Fox, the English Quaker leader, on a missionary trip to the West Indies and the mainland colonies; despite his unflagging charity to all the combatants, Edumndson's family suffered extreme hardships during the Williamite War (1688–1691), and restoration of the Anglican ascendancy only brought renewed official persecution that made miserable his declining years. Remarkably, Benjamin Chandlee, as well as his grandfather and father, would surely have known Edmundson personally. Quotation from E. E. Chandlee, *Six Quaker Clockmakers*, 5–6; see Sources, chapter 28. **3.** For demographic data on Carbury parish and its environs, see appendix 2.2c, on chapter 28. **4.** On contemporary Quaker emigration from southern Ireland to Pennsylvania, see chapter 9. Perhaps Benjamin Chandlee's status, as his parents' eight child, precluded their ability to establish him as a farmer in the Irish midlands or even as an apprentice to a Dublin Quaker tradesman. **5.** Cited in E. E. Chandlee, *Six Quaker Clockmakers*, 31; see Sources, chapter 28.

or shortly after his arrival Chandlee was apprenticed to a Friend from Devonshire, England: Abel Cottey (1655–1711), a clockmaker who had emigrated in 1682 and settled in Philadelphia when the town was founded. The long pendulum clock was only invented in England in 1676, and Cottey was probably the first to apply that knowledge in Pennsylvania. William Penn himself was one of Cottey's customers, and by 1703 Chandlee's master had achieved considerable prosperity, owning a house and lot on Second Street, as well as other town property, and purchasing in that year the first parcels of what would eventually be a thousand-acre estate in the "Nottingham Lots," on the disputed border between Chester County, Pennsylvania, and Cecil County, Maryland.

In 1704 or early 1705, one of Chandlee's younger brothers, Jonathan, expressed interest in emigrating, and Chandlee sent the following letter to his elder brother, Ephraim (1676–1710) in Dublin, to answer Jonathan's inquiries.[6] Although Chandlee's letter is silent about the conditions of his apprenticeship, the letter provides considerable information about the processes of early Irish emigration—for example, about routes, shipboard provisions, and artisanal tools and supplies for use or for marketing abroad; parenthetically, it also suggests the remarkable prominence of potatoes in the southern Irish diet, as early as the late 1600s and even among comfortable Protestants. Perhaps most important, Chandlee's letter illustrates early colonial America's occupational and social fluidity, as he ranges over economic and legal issues of concern to prospective farmers and land speculators, merchants, and craftsmen alike.

Benjamin Chandlee, Philadelphia, to Ephraim Chandlee, Dublin, 28 August 1705

Philadelphia   Pensilvania y[e] 28th: 8[mo]:7 1705

D[r] Brother

This w[th]: the Salutation of my Dear Love to thee[8] & Sister Martha,[9] & also my Duty remembred[10] to my dear ffather & tender Mother & all dear Brothers & Sisters in generall; thine and Brother Jonathans Irecd[11] from the hands of John Barrows   I also recd one the 5[mo]: last dated y[e] 23[d]: 7[mo]: 1704   one Irecd from Brother

---

6. Whether Jonathan Chandlee sojourned in America is unknown, but if so, he had returned to Ireland by 1712, when he married Sarah Cherry of Cashel, Co. Tipperary.   7. 8[mo]: eighth month ("August"); see the 5[mo] last ("last May") hereafter.   8. This w[th]: the Salutation of my Dear Love to thee . . . : formulaic, but seemingly not attested outside the Quaker community; see the opening of the letter of Robert Parke nearly a generation later (chapter 9).   9. Sister Martha: Martha Hill, daughter of William Hill of Dublin; married Ephraim Chandlee in 1701.   10. my Duty remembred: "my respects having been conveyed." This epistolary formula was archaic by Chandlee's time and appeared only in very conservative or provincial letter-writing practice; it seems to have been a staple of Quaker letter-writing. The formula was very frequently followed by an equally conventional reference to the state of the correspondence; see Cely letter no. 115 (13 May 1481): "[A]fftyr dew recommendaschon I louly recommend me vnto yowre masterschypp, etc. Furdermore pleseth it yowre masterschypp to vnderstond that I have reseyued an letter ffrom yow" (i.e., "having duly recommended myself to your attention, I humbly convey my respects, etc. Further, please be informed that I have received a letter from you"). In Alison Hanham, ed., *The Cely Letters, 1472–1488* (London, 1974).   11. Irecd: i.e., I received.

Thomas,—four in all I Recd writ by thy own hand;   Dear Brother at this p^{r}sent writeing I am hearty and well the which I bless God ffor,[12]   Now as to Brother Jonathans Concerns for his intended voyage,   as to Small nourishing things Such as I brought[13] wth: me may be Convenient[14] but whatever he brings of that Sort let him to bring Some good beere & good potatoes abord wth: him,   alittle good beere Ilonged dearly for & could not have when nothing Else would go downe when Sick,[15] & as to Some perticulars[16] Ihad Iwould give them all for potatoes,   I haveing good butter on board It would have been more Serviceable[17] wth: potatoes to me than any thing Ihad beside[18]   I longed so much for them y^t:I dreamed night after Night y^t: Ileft the Ship & got home & there Iwas Sacking them up in barrell Sacks——now as to Commodityes good Shag,[19] Muzlins, black hoods for women ready made, good ding[ed],[20] spockled[21] hancarchiefs, plain Calimincoes,[22] fine Camlets,[23] good linnen cloth ye Largest bredth will be ye Most proffitt & best to bring hither,   if he doth bring any hats let them be of the best Sort   felts will Scarcely give[24] Any thing here   lamblack[25] when at the cheapest here p^d[26] twelve pence ℔ barrell ye dearest 20^d or 2S ℔ bar^{ll}:   Ihave not Known Any at 12^d Since Icame hither,   tell him to bring afew good hansome wigs wth: him pretty plaine and Naturall   they will be proffitable,   if he intends to Settle here I think it would not be amiss for him to bring pewter and brass for houshould goods wth: him, & bring a good larg Iron pot or two wth him   one for himself & another for me   Such things he'l find very dear here,   but one Commodity is plenty[27] Enough here y^t:[28] is Young women,   young women Come[29] Over to these parts Especially to this Country[30] to Advantage

---

12. at this p^{r}sent writeing . . . the which I bless God for: another archaic epistolatory formula, used when reporting on health or prosperity; see Cely letter no. 35 (6 October 1478): "at the makyng of thys lletter howre ffather and mother wer in good helle ['health'], blyssyd be God." (For the source of the Cely letters, see n. 10.) **13. Such as I brought**: "those that I brought." **14. Convenient**: suitable, appropriate. **15. when Sick**: "when I was sick." **16. perticulars**: i.e., particulars "things, articles." **17. Serviceable**: suitable to be served (OED, s.v., 2; obsolete and rare). **18. any thing Ihad beside**: "anything else I had." **19. Shag**: a worsted cloth, sometimes with a nap of silk or velvet. **20. ding[ed]**: meaning with respect to cloth making uncertain but possibly "embossed"; see the use of the word in metalworking to mean "repoussé." **21. spockled**: meaning unknown, but perhaps a cross between **spottled** "spotted, thickly dotted" and **speckled**.
22. Caliminicoes: i.e., calamancoes, woolen materials with a glossy surface, woven with a satin twill, checkered in the warp; popular in the eighteenth century (OED). **23. Camlets**: fine fabrics of mixed materials such as silk, wool, linen, angora goat's hair, and camel's hair; popular in the making of clothing from the twelfth through the nineteenth century (OED, s.v.: C. M. Calasibetta, *Fairchild's Dictionary of Fashion*, 2nd ed., 1988). **24. give**: yield; see hereafter: y^t I brought wth: me will not yeald 20S here. **25. lamblack**: lampblack. **26. p^d**: either "priced" or, more likely, "paid" (i.e. "sold for"). **27. plenty**: plentiful. **28. y^t**: that. **29. Come**: "who have come"; the sense is that any young women who come to America expecting therby to improve their situation (**Advantage themselves**) or to have a better chance of finding a rich husband are deluding themselves. Chandlee's strictures concerning an excess of female emigrants and their alleged motives were common in seventeenth- and early eighteenth-century Ireland; however, they are of very doubtful veracity, given what scholars know about the proponderance of males among contemporary Irish emigrants, both free and indentured, and they most likely reflect the challenge that emigration by even a few young, unmarried Irishwomen, unaccompanied by parents, posed to conventional gender roles in a patriarchal society. **30. Country**: the particular region in which one lives, "area."

themselves or get Rich husbands will be mistaken   that time was but is not now,[31]   guns are of Small value Except they be very good & hansome   y^t I brought wth: me[32] will not yeald 20S here,   Idesire him to bring a clever[33] hansom good one wth: him for me about 4 foot long in the barr^{ll}: & good Store of powder & shot,   his trade will Answer[34] very well here   <t>here is whale fishing here,   Oyle is plenty here,   <t>here is No Wash lether Dressing here,   Sheeps pelts ar very cheap there being No use made of them here Except Some Sorts of herdsmen maketh Aprons of them   <t>here is not Aman glover in Philadelphia Only All women & poor work they Make,[35]   I had Afew lines from Coz: Joshua Carleton[36] this Spring from Corke, concerning their Land   According to his desire Iwent to the Mans house & did walk over great part of the Land   it is two hundred and ten Acres in Number,   it lyes in the Midst of agood neighbourhood & is good land and well timbred,   he writ to me to Signifie[37] if the timber on it would defray the Charg of takeing more Land up   the Law here is not to Cut atree downe Except the Owner was here p^{r}sent, & with out A new letter of Atturney there Can be no more land taken up,   I wonder Some of them do not Come over About it,   <t>here Can be no more <land> taken up where It Lyeth no nearer than 40 or 50 miles off the Said land[38]——<t>here landed this Spring Mary Cherry Sister to Richard Cherry[39] y^t was Marryed wth:[40] Brother thomas in our meeting at Waterford,   She and Georg Preste Came in here together
[. . .][41]   Georg is deceased ye last weeke [and d]ecently buryed,   what Effects[42] ye Sd. Georg had is put[43] Into the Governors hands by reason of the Shortness[44] of A will being made not haveing but one Evidence[45] w^{ch}: would not Do,   so Idesire thee Send Afew lines to Caleb Jacobs In Corke y^t his poore wife may understand what is become of him & She May send Aletter of Atturney for ye Recovery of these goods Againe,   she lives in Corke,

Dear Brother from this last line Ilet this by[46] neer a weeke not Expecting what happened Since;   ye Mans name was Henry Clifton w^{ch}: ye Charge of ye Effects[47] was Commited to,   he hath Since as ISaid got the Effects in his own hands againe So Idesire thee to Send Afew lines to Corke & signifie to Caleb to direct the Answer to Saml: Carpenter for Henry Clifton;   Mary Wilson that lived wth: James Pedegrea Arrived here this Spring Sister to Anne Wilson y^t belonged Once to Edenderry

---

31. **that time was but is not now**: the time that that was possible is long gone.   **32.** **y^t I brought wth: me**: "the one I brought with me."   **33.** **clever**: handy, convenient to use.   **34.** **Answer**: be suitable, serve the purpose.   **35.** **<t>here is not Aman glover . . . they Make**: "all the glovemakers in Phildelphia are women, and their work is inferior."   **36.** **Joshua Carleton**: youngest brother of Deborah Carleton, who married John Chandlee, Benjamin's brother.   **37.** **Signifie**: indicate.   **38.** **where it Lyeth . . . the Said land**: "if it is situated more than forty or fifty miles from the land in question."   **39.** **Cherry**: the Cherry family was from Cashel, Co. Tipperary; at least two Cherry sisters married brothers of Benjamin Chandlee.   **40.** **Marryed wth**: married to.   **41.** ms. torn.   **42.** **Effects**: property left after death.   **43.** **put**: conjectural.   **44.** **Shortness**: defectiveness.   **45.** **not haveing but one Evidence**: "having only one witness."   **46.** **Ilet this by**: "I laid this aside."   **47.** **ye Effects**: i.e., of the late **Georg Preste** (see n. 42).

meeting,   she is hearty and well & has her Love Remembred to[48] her Old Master &
all her[49] ffriends y^t may Enquire after her——they were but twenty nine days between
land and land at Comeing hither   I believe it would be Much better for Brother
Jonathan to go Over to England & there buy goods & there take his passage & come
Right up our River up straight to Philadelphia for if he takes his passage at Dublin he
has his passage but to Maryland, & from thence to Philadelphia he'l find it more
troublesom than All his Vioge[50] before if it were twice as far againe;[51]   In the first
place After the Vessel has Cast anchor there is Asloope for Removeing his goods then a
carting[52] by land then fferrying here near three Slow miles[53] & adeal more Cost besides
trouble and Exercise & also A damnifying[54] his goods & further let him not Concern
him self in the Least w^th: Any Servants y^t may be Consigned to Isaac Sharp[55] or
Anybody Else whatever,   It will all his Voyage Looke but Ascandalous thing besides
adeal[56] of Exercise[57] and trouble more than Any of you may think of——I desire him
to bring me agood bible and Some good Shag for apair of brekes[58] & bring aset of
Small buttons Such As you Commonly wear for y^t [. . .][59] good writeing paper &
Stock himself well w^th: goose quills   <t>here is adeal here but not good,   & bring
me a doz: or two duz: pound of whited yarn[60] for my trade,   Thomas Watsons family
Are well all John Hugs in generall and Old Willm: Albersons & Thomas
Denises[61]   they all in generall have their kind Loves remembred to[62] you all in
generall and to All Loving ffriends y^t may Inquire After them——So haveing Inlarged[63]
As fully As Ithink needfull, So do Conclude w^th: my Unfeigned Love to thee & all my
dear Parents and Relations in generall & to all Loving ffrds[64] in Generall

Benjamin Chandlee

48. she . . . has her Love Remembred to: "she . . . asks that (the expression of) her love be conveyed to."
This is a somewhat mangled remnant of an archaic formula of commendation that makes use of the verb **have**
in the passive voice with the unusual sense of "perform"; see Stonor letter no. 89: "aftyr all dew
recommendacyon had . . . " "with all due expression of regard performed . . . " = "having duly expressed my
regards . . . " For the use of **remember** in the sense of "inform, convey information to" see Stonor letter no.
189: "lyke it youe to be remembered that . . . " "please be informed that . . . " In Christine Carpenter, ed.,
Kingsford's Stoner Letters (Cambridge, England, 1996).   **49. herws** ms.   **50. Vioge**: i.e., voyage (transposed
spelling for "voige").   **51. if it were twice as far againe**: "even if it (= the voyage) were twice again as long."
52. casting ms.   **53. miles**: conjectural.   **54. A damnifying**: indemnifying ("insuring"). The creation of a
form **adamnify** beside **indemnify** is supported by such genuine doublets as **appeach : impeach** (both having
the same meaning) and by the existence of the unstressed variant **a** of the preposition **in** (in expressions like **a**
God's name "in God's name").   **55. Isaac Sharp**: probably the son of Anthony Sharp (1643–1707), a wealthy
Dublin merchant and Quaker leader; born in 1681, Isaac Sharp settled in New Jersey in 1700 and inherited
from his father property in Ireland, England, and America worth £10,000.   **56. adeal**: a deal (with mass
nouns, as here, "a large amount"; with count nouns, as hereafter [modifying **goose quills**], "a large number").
57. Exercise: exertion "bother."   **58. brekes**: i.e., breeks "breeches, trousers" (Northern British form).
59. Five or six words obscured by crease.   **60. yarn**: probably "catgut" or silk yarn used for hanging the
weights of clocks.   **61. Watsons . . . John Hugs . . . Thomas Denises**: the Watsons were from Carlow; John
Hugg settled in the Quakers' Newtown settlement in Carlow where in 1683 he purchased five hundred acres;
Thomas Dennis procured a removal certificate from Moate, Co. Westmeath.   **62. have their kind Loves
remembred to**: see n. 48.   **63. Inlarged**: dilated, expanded.   **64. ffrds**: friends.

If old Isabell Scot hath A mind to Send Atoken[65] to
Catherine John Hugg let her get it but up to Dublin[66] &
Brother Jonathan may bring it hither Easily with out
Any trouble   she was talking of sending acheese w[th]:
me,   Ithought it troublesome   so did shee, but Iknow
the trouble will be next to Nothing,   it will be as
Acceptable as So much Gold to her——

{give y[e] Inclosed to
Sharpless but first Seal
it}

On 25 March 1710, at the Philadelphia Friends' meetinghouse, Chandlee realized every apprentice's dream and married his master's daughter, Sarah Cottey. Abel Cottey died a year later, and in 1712 Chandlee and his wife and mother-in-law moved from Philadelphia to the Quaker settlement in the Nottingham Lots.[67] When Cottey's widow died in late 1713 or early 1714, she willed nearly all her late husband's estate, valued at £240, to Benjamin Chandlee. Blessed with ample water power, the Nottingham Lots quickly evolved into a protoindustrial community of Irish and English Friends who combined farming with furniture- and coffin-making, grain- and paper-milling, and a variety of other trades.[68] The settlement was also close to supplies of copper, crucial for making brass clockworks, and although at first Chandlee manufactured farm implements, brass cowbells, and other household goods, he founded the clockmaking industry that his sons and grandsons later developed on a larger scale. Clockmaking required such skill and precision that between 1714 and 1730 Chandlee probably made only about 40 tall clocks, which increased in height and ornamentation as his customers became more prosperous. At least six of Chandlee's clocks still survived as late as 1943, most of them still owned locally by the descendents of the original purchasers.

In 1741 Chandlee and his wife sold part of their lands and moved to Wilmington, Delaware, where apparently he died in 1745 and was interred in the Friends' burial ground. Of their six children, three sons—Cottey (1713–1807), William (1721–1791), and especially Benjamin, Jr. (1723–1792)—remained in Nottingham and expanded the family business, which in turn passed to Benjamin, Jr.'s children. Thus, for nearly one hundred years, the firm of Chandlee & Sons manufactured tall clocks, surveyors' compasses, and other brass implements, but their trade did not pass to a fourth generation, for the high costs and standards of their craftsmanship could not compete with the wooden clockworks that Eli Terry and other Connecticut clockmakers began to mass-produce after 1800.

---

65. token: keepsake.   66. let her get it but up to Dublin: "all she has to do is get it up to Dublin."
67. When Charles Mason and Jeremiah Dixon completed their survey of the Pennsylvania-Maryland border in 1767, most of the "Nottingham Lots," including Chandlee's property and the Quaker meetinghouse, became part of Cecil Co., Md.   68. Chandlee's community may have been the prototype for Joseph Wright's much later Quaker settlement in Ohio, urged on Wright by Baltimore Friends who would have been well aware of the former's success. See chapter 25.

John Kennedy, 1753

By the mid-eighteenth century, the North American economy was expanding rapidly and generating increasing demands for immigrant craftsmen, especially for coopers whose kegs, barrels, casks, and hogsheads were indispensable in both domestic and trans-atlantic trade. In the winter of 1753–1754 alone, for example, the New England and, primarily, the Middle Colonies shipped 17,180 hogsheads of flaxseed—an 829 percent increase since 1733–1734—to Irish ports such as Belfast, Newry, and Dublin. On their return voyages, most flaxseed vessels carried Irish immigrants, including coopers who fled low pay and high production costs at home for a land where wages were higher and timber was plentiful. Sometime around 1750 one of these ships brought John Kennedy, an Irish cooper born about 1721, and his wife and children, from east Ulster to New York City.[1] Perhaps to escape competition or guild restrictions among seaport coopers or perhaps hoping to acquire farmland, Kennedy moved his family up the Hudson and settled six miles from the river in the village of Fishkill, in Rombout precinct, Dutchess County, where he engaged in "Cuntrie Cooperi[n]g" for the farmers along Fishkill Creek and in the adjacent hills.

Dutchess County was organized in 1683 but settlement was slow—in 1731 the county contained merely 1,727 people—because most of the land was held by Dutch patentees who, like Irish landlords, preferred to rent their manors rather than sell land to prospective settlers. Beginning in the 1730s, however, the population rapidly increased, and in 1756 Dutchess County had over 14,000 inhabitants (including 859 slaves), and its economy—based largely on farming and milling for the New York and West Indian markets—was "populous and flourishing."[2] Numerically, the Dutch still dominated the riverfront precincts, centered on Fishkill Landing and Poughkeepsie, as well as the upper reaches of the county's economy and political life, but recent migrants from Britain, Ireland, and New England comprised a majority in the eastern districts, where the first Presbyterian (and non-Dutch) church in the county was organized, two miles east of Fishkill, in 1746.

Thus, Kennedy settled in a growing and rapidly commercializing area, and by 1747 Rombout was Dutchess County's second wealthiest precinct. However, local society was also increasingly stratified: at midcentury the top third of the county's taxpayers held three-fourths of the taxable wealth; and most inhabitants were poor tenants, squatters, and laborers. Thus, in 1753 the lure of potential profits, or the pressure of mounting debts, may

1. Kennedy's 1761 militia roll attests to his Irish birth; linguistic evidence (see n. 12) indicates east Ulster origins; most likely Kennedy was Presbyterian.   2. Cited in J. H. Smith, *History of Duchess County . . .* , 59; see Sources, chapter 29.

have persuaded Kennedy to compromise the Irish craftsman's dream of "independence" for a hazardous venture into the expanding regional and transatlantic flaxseed market. In the summer and autumn of 1753 the merchants of New York port required over 11,000 casks or hogsheads to transport locally grown seed to Ireland during the coming winter, and it was the task of upcountry storekeepers and commission merchants, such as John Campbell and Peter Bogardus, Sr., of Dutchess County, not only to purchase seed from local farmers but also to contract with coopers like Kennedy to construct the containers for shipment downriver and overseas.[3] As the following document attests, Kennedy believed that Campbell had cheated him by refusing to pay the price agreed for making 28 casks—representing perhaps a month's labor. Consequently, he sent a semiliterate petition, begging for justice, to William Kempe, a transplanted Englishman and the colony's new attorney general.[4]

John Kennedy, Fishkill, Dutchess County, New York, to William Kempe, Attorney General, New York City, 16 September 1753

Fish Killns   16 Sep[br] 1753

The hum[bl] Compleant & Suplication of Jn[o] Kennedy a[n][5] a piel[6] of (apoor Macink[7] Late from y[e] old Cuntry Who Came in Wi[th] my Wife & Childrin to Leabour honestly @[8] my tread[9] for a Living & being a stranger I am Likely to be Ill used)——

To The Rig[t] hon[bl] his Majesty King George his atturney[10] Gen[l] for y[e] provence of new York this Greeting——

Whereas one John Campble requested me to Leave of<f> Cuntrie Cooperi<n>g Which I had plenty of & make apersel[11] of flexseed[12] Casks   I ask[d] @ What price   he said Campble told me[13] the price that pitter[14] Bogardus Wou[d] pay in York[15] he Was

---

3. The Bogarduses were one of the oldest Dutch families in New York. In the 1640s Dominie Bogardus was the first clergyman in New Amsterdam; the wife of Francis Rombout, the original patentee of the Dutchess Co. precinct bearing his name, was first married to a Bogardus; and in the early and mid-1700s family members were prominent merchants in both Albany and New York City. Peter [Petrus] Bogardus, Sr., of Fishkill Landing, appears in the Dutchess Co. tax lists from 1748 to 1779; he died ca. 1781–1784. Less is known of John Campbell: probably of Scottish or Scots-Irish origin, he appears in the Rombout precinct tax lists in 1739 and in 1754–1761; his will was proved in 1762.   **4.** William Kempe: a "Gentleman from England" and an appointee of the Duke of Newcastle, served at New York's attorney general from 1752 until his death in 1759, when he was succeeded by his son. Margaret Heilbrun, library director, New-York Historical Society, to authors, 7 December 1995.   **5.** ms. torn.   **6.** a piel: i.e., appeal.   **7.** Macink: i.e., mechanic "craftsman."   **8.** @: at.   **9.** tread: i.e., trade.   **10.** King George his atturney: i.e., King George's attorney.   **11.** apersel: a parcel ("a few, several"; in American colloquial speech "a passel"). Scots form [pairsel].   **12.** flexseed: i.e., flaxseed; see chapter 21, n. 37. Since this sound change does not occur in the south of Ireland, its appearance here suggests that Kennedy is of Ulster origin.   **13.** he said Campble told me: "he, the said Campbell, told me."   **14.** pitter: Peter.   **15.** York: New York (City).

bringing to Some of yᵉ Cuntrie merchᵗˢ16 &ᶜ   When bogardus Came to yᵉ Store Wᵗʰ yᵉ York Casks: Said Campble Came to me & told me my price Was to be 4ˢ-york mony & bid me work away   th\<e>y Wouᵈ take all I Couᵈ make: Which bargen I Depended on & no outher———Now he desirs me to go & Sue pepol who had them from him Who never Spock for17 aCask to me & tels me th\<e>y will give me no mor then th\<e>y Sold them for in york Wᵗʰ yᵉ flexseed   Some Will give: 18ᵈ—Some Will give 2ˢ:6ᵈ—in Stead of my bargen Wᵗʰ Campble to Witt his own makeing18 4ˢ- as aforesaid   How If19 th\<e>y Can make a second price as they pleas\<?>   Wourthy Sʳ you yᵗ. Came from the Sate20 of Justice I hubˡʸ aply to for the Same21 for hear I Can have non\<e>   my mony amounts \<to> 5£: 12ˢ-York Curancey for 28 Casks @ 4ˢ ℔ Cask   Grate Sʳ Your answer I Expect how I Shall act on Sigᵗ22 & Your Derictions I Will Punctuley obsarve   This23 I make bold in hopes You Will over look my fealings24 & aid & asist me to my own25 & be payᵈ for Yᵒʳ truble   Wourthy Sʳ I am Your Hubˡᵉ Serᵛᵗ J. K\<ennedy>

To The Rigᵗ honᵇˡᵉ his Majsteys atturney Gen.ˡˡ for the province of New York

If Kempe took any action on this petition, no record of it survives, and thus it is impossible to determine whether Kennedy's "Compleant" was justified. Casks for storage in the holds of transatlantic vessels had to be watertight, and perhaps Kennedy's products were simply inferior in quality. Conversely, the flaxseed trade was highly speculative, and a sudden, sharp fluctuation in the price of seed may have forced Campbell, who perhaps was being squeezed by Bogardus in turn, to renege on his promise to Kennedy and secure cheaper casks, perhaps ones made by slaves in New York City. Whatever the merits of his case, however, Kennedy was probably correct in asserting he could expect no justice locally. In the 1740s and 1750s litigation in Dutchess County increased sharply, but the poor were at a great disadvantage. Legal fees were high and the contests uneven: ordinary farmers and artisans such as Kennedy appeared in court rarely as plaintiffs and much more often as defendants prosecuted for debt by the county's wealthier inhabitants. Moreover, Bogardus was a member of one of the oldest, largest, and most influential families in Duchess County, and the local magistracy was tightly controlled by representatives or allies of the original Dutch grantees. Indeed, Kennedy's petition is but a minor indication of a much broader socioethnic and political conflict between the region's largely Dutch oligarchy and a New England–born and Irish Protestant middling and lower strata. And in 1766 these

---

16. the price . . . Some of yᵉ Cuntrie merchᵗˢ: "he (Campbell) was offering to some of the country merchants the same price that Peter Bogardus would pay in New York."   17. Spock for: i.e., spoke for ("bespoke, ordered").   18. to Witt his own makeing: "namely, the bargain he himself made with me." 19. How If . . . : what will happen/what can we expect if . . . (see *Romeo and Juliet*, 4.3.30: "How . . . if I wake before the time?").   20. Sate: i.e., seat.   21. the Same: i.e., justice.   22. Your answer I Expect how I Shall act on Sigᵗ: "I await your answer upon receipt ('on sight') of this, telling me how I am to act." 23. This: thus (?).   24. fealings: i.e., failings.   25. my own: "what is due to me."

tensions would erupt in the violence of the Anti-Rent War—led in Duchess County by William Prendergast, a poor tenant farmer from Waterford or Kilkenny.[26]

Whether Kennedy participated in the riots and skirmishes of 1766 is unknown, but, despite his troubles with Campbell and Bogardus, he remained in Duchess County. In 1755–1762 he appeared (as "John Cannady the cooper") on the county's tax lists; in 1761 he enlisted in Captain Isaac Terbush's local militia company, when he was recorded on the muster rolls as well above average in both age (40) and stature (six feet). However, whereas Kennedy's militia service indicates permanent settlement, his inability to hire a substitute also suggests poverty, and there is no record of his ever owning or even renting land in the county. After 1762 Kennedy may have given up and migrated elsewhere; no death records can be located for him or for members of his family. Yet perhaps the Fishkill cooper was the same John Kennedy who in the summer of 1775 enlisted in a Duchess County regiment (the New York Fourth) in the Continental Army. If so, he had remained to witness the union of the county's ethnic groups against a common foe, and subsequently he may have had the pleasure of persecuting one of his former nemeses, Peter Bogardus, Sr., who that summer refused to swear allegiance to the Continental Congress.

30 ✳

Philip McRory, Ruth McGee, Edward Curry, Rosanna Stewart, Patrick M'Cullen, Ann Dougherty, Thomas Ralph, and Michael Wade, ca. 1735–1774

Prior to the Revolution, more than half and perhaps as many as two-thirds of Irish immigrants came to America as indentured servants, contractually bound to serve colonial masters for an average of four to five years in return for their passage to the New World. Bonded servants comprised a large proportion of the Scots-Irish and other Irish Protestants and the overwhelming majority of those of Catholic background. After mid-century, an increasing percentage of Irish servants were indentured to urban masters, but by far the greatest number were hired by farmers and engaged in agricultural labor: alongside slaves in tobacco fields and rice plantations in the southern colonies; in lumberwork

---

26. New York's Anti-Rent War of 1766, analogous to the contemporary Oakboy and Whiteboy disturbances in northern and southern Ireland, respectively, was a tenants' revolt against rising rents, evictions, and semifeudal dues and services; the initial focus was Beverly Robinson's Dutchess Co. manor, but the agitation quickly spread from Westchester to Albany, targeting wealthy landlords of British descent, such as the Livingstons, as well as the old Dutch proprietors. William Prendergast (1727–1811), along with Samuel Munroe, William Finch, Stephen Crane, and several others, was the leader of the dissident tenants; of Hiberno-Norman origins, Prendergast was married to Mehitabel Wing, a Quaker of Scottish descent.

and land clearance on the frontier; and in general farm work in the longer-settled, mixed-farming regions in the eastern parts of the Middle Colonies. In the latter region, as indentured servitude evolved between 1680–1720 and 1720–1775 from an informal, personal institution into a strict, legally structured, market relationship, the proportion of Irishmen and -women in the servant population increased sharply. In 1682–1687, for example, only 12 percent of Pennsylvania's indentured servants were Irish-born, whereas by 1741–1746 nearly 94 percent hailed from Ireland. In turn, the increasing ethnic and religious differences between most masters and servants resulted in harsher treatment by the former and greater alienation among the latter, as measured, for instance, in longer terms of servitude, a sharp rise in the numbers of runaway servants, and increasing interventions by colonial courts in master-servant relationships.

In the nearly total absence of surviving correspondence or memoirs by Irish indentured servants, colonial court records provide virtually all the extant documentation of the lives of these largely illiterate and otherwise anonymous members of the first Irish-American working classes. Uniquely, the archives of Chester County, in southeastern Pennsylvania, preserve large numbers of petitions and testaments that Irish servants submitted to the justices of the county's quarter sessions court that met every three months in Chester town. Published hereafter are eight examples of such manuscripts, written between the 1730s and early 1770s by poor Irishmen and -women who therein revealed some fugitive fragments of biographical data that cannot be fully reconstructed.

Judging from their statements or, in most cases, their surnames, all but one of these eight petitioners came from Ulster (the other from Dublin), as did the great majority of eighteenth-century Irish immigrants.[1] To be sure, it is arguable that the experiences recorded in these documents are atypical, since most indentured servants never complained to colonial courts—perhaps especially in Pennsylvania, where their treatment was reputedly superior to that meted out to bondsmen and -women in the South. However, in Pennsylvania as elsewhere the Irish comprised a disproportionately large number of those servants who absconded from their masters, suffered severe abuse, or for other reasons found themselves in court. At least a fifth, perhaps a fourth, of Irish-born servants became runaways—as did at least two of the eight petitioners described here—and between 1728 and 1796 fully 40 percent of *all* the fugitive servants advertised in the *Pennsylvania Gazette* had been born in Ireland. In addition, Chester was a rural county, at least six of the eight petitioners engaged in farm work, and throughout the colonies servants who were agricultural laborers were much more likely to appear before magistrates, either as complainants or defendants, than were servants in urban centers such as Philadelphia. Likewise, the forced intimacy between masters and servants in Chester County, where farmers, albeit

---

1. According to Edward MacLysaght, *The Surnames of Ireland*, 6th ed. (Dublin, 1991), the surname McRory is most common in counties Tyrone and Derry; McGee in Donegal and Antrim; Curry (var. of [Mac]Corry or -Corrie) in Tyrone and Fermanagh; Stewart in east Ulster; M'Cullen in Monaghan; and Dougherty (or O'Doherty) in Donegal. Ralph and Wade give their origins as Co. Down and Dublin city, respectively.

generally prosperous, rarely owned more than one or two bonded laborers, produced at least as many conflicts and complaints to local courts as did the conditions of Southern gang labor. Indeed, such proximity may have heightened the prejudice of masters, usually Quakers of English origins, toward Presbyterian and Catholic servants, who were indiscriminately labeled "Irish" and stigmatized as "St. Patrick's Vermin."

For their part, Irish-born servants in Chester County as elsewhere may have been unusually alienated and prone to disputes with masters that resulted in court cases. Although some Catholic servants spoke only Irish, and although the "broad Scotch" of many Ulster Presbyterian servants was barely intelligible to many English-stock colonists, nevertheless the great majority of Irish servants, unlike German bondsmen, were not insulated from native prejudice by ignorance of English. In addition, whereas laboring-class Irish were accustomed to employers' abuse in Ireland, the drudgery of colonial farmwork—especially clearing heavily forested land—in the severe American climate often proved intolerable, particularly for the children of Irish farmers and tradesmen, who were unused to hard labor and often resented their lowly status in the New World. Finally, although sharp increases in Irish servant emigration, as in the 1720s, early 1740s, and early 1770s, usually coincided with famine or severe economic depression at home, during normal years many prospective servants—such as Thomas Ralph, a petitioner in 1753—signed indentures and emigrated with false notions of what awaited them, lured by the blandishments of emigration agents and merchants eager to fill the holds of flaxseed ships with profitable cargoes of servants for the return voyage to America. Thus, the most widely circulated promotional letter in early and mid-eighteenth-century Ulster, purportedly written—to reassure the ignorant—to a Presbyterian minister in County Tyrone, promised the Irish poor that "God ha[d] open'd a Door for their Deliverance" in America and alleged that many former Irish bondsmen were "now Justices of the Piece."[2] No doubt many were bitterly disillusioned to discover that the good fortunes of Benjamin Chandlee and Daniel Kent were exceptional.[3]

Even Pennsylvania's colonial Assembly, dominated by affluent Quakers who themselves employed large numbers of indentured servants, admitted that many of the latter, "after having faithfully discharged their duty," found it difficult or impossible to collect "freedom dues" from their former masters—and this despite the fact that the Assembly itself had progressively reduced the value of such dues, from the 50 acres initially promised by William Penn to what came to be known, rather flexibly, as "the custom of the coun-

---

2. James Murray, New York, to Rev. Baptist Boyd, Aughnacloy, Co. Tyrone, in the *Pennsylvania Gazette*, 27 October 1737; ed. by E. G. Swem and published as *Letter of James Murray of New York* (Metuchen, N.J., 1925). 3. On Chandlee and Kent, see chapters 28 and 23. To be sure, a celebrated few Irish indentured servants or redemptioners did enjoy spectacularly successful American careers, including the elder Daniel Dulany, Maryland's attorney general; Charles Thomson of Philadelphia, secretary to the Continental Congress; and George Taylor of Pennsylvania and Matthew Thornton of New Hampshire, signers of the Declaration of Independence.

try": at most, two suits of clothing, one new, plus two hoes and an axe—or their cash equivalent.⁴ Thus, by far the greatest number of petitions from Irish servants in Chester County were similar to that of Philip McRory, who in 1749 asked the quarter sessions court to force his former master, James Miller, a member of one of the wealthiest Quaker families in New Garden township, to fulfil his contractual obligation.⁵

Document 1.

Philip McRory, [30 November] 1749

To The Honourable Justices of the County of Chester in the Province of Pensilvania

The Humble Petition of Philip M^{cc}Rory Sheweth,⁶

That in the Year of our Lord God, one Thousand, Seven Hundred and Thirty nine, in the latter end of September, your Petitioner landed at New-Castle upon Delaware under the Power and at the Disposal of one James Harvey Merchant from Londonderry.⁷   That said Harvey did bind out⁸ as an Apprentice for the Space and Term of three Years and three Months to James Miller Farmer, in the Township of New garden and County aforesaid, the said Philip M^{cc}Rory, which Term of time he faithfully and honestly served in such Service as his Master was pleased to exercise him.

That some time after he was set free, he was informed, he was justly entitled to all such Freedoms⁹ as the Custom of the Country did Allow, and having requested the same of James Miller, he refused, saying he would not give them, till the Law would oblige him.

This is therefore to beg of this honourable Bench of Justices to take Your Petitioners Case into Consideration, and to allow him all such Necessaries as he may justly require by the Law made and provided for securing the Rights and Properties of Servants.

philip m^{cc} Rorey

And Your Petitioner as in Duty bound will pray.¹⁰

---

4. These requirements prevailed in Pennylvania during nearly all the colonial period, but in 1771 the Assembly even deleted the legal clause obliging masters to provide farm tools to former servants. Quoted phrases are legal formulae, as cited, for example, in C. A. Herrick, *White Servitude in Pennsylvania . . .* , 286–308; see Sources, chapter 30.   5. The Millers were Irish Quakers and among the earliest settlers in Chester Co. However, the father of James Miller (1708–1758), McRory's master, had emigrated from Co. Kildare and settled in New Garden township only in 1729. By 1765 the entire Miller (or Millar) clan in New Garden owned over 2,600 acres, and James Miller himself was assessed for 250 acres, five horses, four cattle, seven sheep, and one servant.
6. Sheweth: petitionary formula: "alleges, declares."   7. Harvey probably landed McRory and other Irish servants at New Castle, Delaware, instead of Philadelphia, to avoid paying the 20s. tax that the Pennsylvania Assembly levied in 1722 on imported Irish and other "foreign" servants—yet another indication of the Quaker élite's aversion to Irish servants, despite their colony's pressing labor needs.   8. bind out: indenture.
9. Freedoms: freedom dues (articles owed by contract and/or law to the indentured servant on expiry of the term of service).   10. And your Petitioner as in Duty bound will pray: petitionary formula; the petitioner prays not that his petition may be granted but that the person or persons petitioned may enjoy long life, prosperity, etc.

McRory's complaint was successful, for the court ordered Miller to provide his former servant with "a new and Compleat Suite of apparel."[11] However, many petitions similar to McRory's met much less sympathetic responses. Twenty-five years later, for example, Ruth McGee made the following request for "freedom dues" from her former master, Josiah Hibberd, also a Quaker, who farmed 150 acres in East Whiteland township.[12]

Document 2.
Ruth McGee, 21 May 1774

To the worshipful the justices of the court of Quarter Sessions held at chester the last tuesday in may

The Humble Petition of Ruth McGee Humbly sheweth that your petitioner is poor and not Sufficient to Earn her living by reason of achild she hath to maintain   your Petitioners Master Josiah Hibberd refuseing to Let your Petitioner have her freedom Dues Which is mentioned in apair of Indentures (Viz) A new Suit of clothes for freedoms and five Pounds in Money and Eight months schooling of which schooling I received but four months and twenty two Days   Likewise your Petitioners Said Master Josiah Hibbard detains your Petitioners cloths that she had whilst she your Petitioner Lived with Said Master that is to say one quil<t>ed peticoat Short Gown and Apron   Likewise your Petitioner had seven years and six weeks to serve and your Petitioner had but two months to serve her Said Master Josiah Hibbard When your Petitioner was Sent to the Goal[13] of this county   furthermore your petitioner having Suffered the rigour of the Law your Petitioner apprehends she should not be detained from her said freedoms Dues but that your Petitioner should [have them][14] for her Support in this your Petitioner<'s> Poor condition   So your Petitioner Layeth this her Humble Petition before your worships for redress of said Grievances and your Petitioner in Duty bound Shall Ever Pray

May the 21st Anno Domini 1774

The court's response to McGee's petition is unknown, but there are several reasons to assume it was unfavorable. In general, farmers and magistrates in colonial America regarded female servants as less productive and more "troublesome" than males. Conse-

---

11. Court scribe's notation on McRory petition; see Sources, chapter 30.   12. Josiah Hibberd (usually spelled Hibbard, sometimes Hibbert, in colonial records) was the eldest son of Benjamin Hibberd (b. 1707), whose own father had emigrated to Pennsylvania, probably from England, in the early 1680s. In 1767 Josiah Hibberd of East Whiteland owned 150 acres of farm- and woodland valued at £61, plus four horses, four cows, and six sheep, on all of which he paid a county tax of £1 5s.3d. In 1779 he still owned 150 acres, in addition to two horses and seven cattle.   13. Goal: gaol "jail."   14. have them conjectural (line blurred)

quently, women never comprised more than 20 to 30 percent of Pennsylvania's servant population; their labor was devalued while, compared with male servants, their terms of servitude tended to be longer. More specifically, McGee seems to have borne an illegitimate child while bound to Hibberd, and Pennsylvania law not only punished fornication and bastardy by whipping and incarceration—the latter apparently McGee's fate—but also required a lengthening of service, up to two years beyond the original term, to compensate masters for the loss of their servants' time during and immediately after their pregnancies. It appears that Hibberd wanted rid of McGee and demanded no additional service, but considered himself justified in denying her freedom dues and in retaining her clothes. Given her past transgressions and present helplessness, it is probable that Chester County's male magistrates agreed.

Although McGee cannot be found in Chester County's poor-relief rolls or other records, female ex-servants, especially those with illegitimate children, often fell into poverty and required public charity. Somewhat better documented is the unhappy career of Edward Curry (or Corry), whose undated submission to the quarter sessions court, probably written about 1735, illustrates another category of servants' petitions: those begging for release from their indentures on the grounds that their masters had physically abused them or had violated some clause in the provincial statutes governing master-servant relationships. In the following petition, Curry recounts the "Barbrous usage" he allegedly received from Abel Parke, an Irish-born Quaker who farmed one hundred acres in East Caln township.[15] According to Curry, Parke had not only violated William Penn's injunction that servants "be both justly and kindly used" but also had tricked his bondsman into an extended indenture.

Document 3.
Edward Curry, ca. 1735

To the Honnourable Bench
The Humble pet<i>tion of Edward Curry Servant unto Abel parks who Hath Been most unReasonable used by my S^d Master for In the first place he Bought me for ye term of four years where with him I Lived the Space of two years in a misirable Condition By his most Barbarous usage for I was Abused time Affter time and keept out of Doors when the Snow was on the Ground till I have Been almost pershed with Cold and all through and he By his Cuning Intragues gott me Drunk and made me to Singe[16] an Indenture two years and a half more then I had to Serve and when y^r poor

15. Abel Parke (1706–1757) was born in Co. Carlow and emigrated to Pennsylvania with his father Thomas, brother Robert, and other siblings in 1724. In addition to the East Caln farm, inherited from his father in 1738, Abel Parke also co-owned with brother Thomas, Jr., the "Ship" tavern on the main road from Philadelphia to Lancaster. On the Parke family, see chapter 9.   16. Singe: i.e., sign.

pertitinor Came to a Right Under Standing of the matter Spoke to him about itt and Iwas aBused for So doing and then I toulde him I would make my application to amagistrate and then he falsly aCused me with Stealing of his wheat to the quanty of two Bushells which y^r poor petetionner is Clear from[17] any Such Action   therefore y^r humble pertetiner Beggs that ye Honnourable Bench will take into Considoration and y^r poor pertesiner Shall Be Ever Bound

      To pray

Although Abel Parke compiled a record of bad relationships with Irish bondsmen—in 1735 another servant, Ann Byrn, fled his household—their social and ethnic biases, plus Edward Curry's own subsequent history, might suggest that Chester County's magistrates probably ruled in Parke's favor, crediting his claim that Curry was both a liar and a thief. The court's specific decision is not recorded, but Curry must have been returned to Parke, who in turn sold his servant into New Jersey where, on 14 June 1739, Abraham Bryan of Burlington advertised him as a runaway in the *Pennsylvania Gazette*, describing him as "aged about 26 Years, short and well set, thin visag'd, brown complexion'd, and has the Brogue on his Tongue." "He served a Time in Chester County," Bryan added, "and was some time in Chester Goal." It is uncertain whether anyone claimed Bryan's "Twenty Shillings Reward" for "tak[ing] up the said Servant," but three years later Curry was back in Chester County, where in August 1742 he was convicted of counterfeiting "a certain Brief to collect Charity" and sentenced to stand one hour in the pillory. Curry was fortunate—his accomplice, George Duke, received "fifteen lashes well laid on his bare back"[18]—and after this episode he apparently left Chester County for good, as he does not appear in subsequent records.

Of course, it is impossible to determine when a servant's incorrigible behavior invited a master's harsh treatment, or when systematic abuse drove a servant to rebel, abscond, or commit acts of retaliation that unsympathetic magistrates treated as criminal offenses. A particularly pathetic instance of the latter may be the case of Rosanna Stewart (or Stuart).[19] On 25 August 1772 Stewart's master, Dr. Thomas Whitesides of Oxford township, petitioned the justices of the quarter sessions court to exend her term of servitude as punishment for stealing his wife's clothes and running away to Philadelphia, where

17. **Clear from**: innocent of.   18. Chester County Quarter Sessions Court docket, August 1742; see Sources, chapter 30.   19. None of the documentation of Rosanna Stewart's case clearly identifies her as Irish. However, it is extremely likely that she was Irish-born (and probably from Ulster), as were ca. 80 per cent (11 of 14) of the runaway servants named Stewart, Steward, or Stuart who were advertised and whose ethnicity was identified in the *Pennsylvania Gazette* between 1728 and 1796. In addition, the petitioner's own use of "Stewart," as opposed to the Chester court officials' "Stuart," is notable, as the former spelling was usual in Ulster and the latter very uncommon there. Finally, in the early 1770s **James Rea** (hereafter), who took Rosanna Stewart from Philadelphia to Chester Co., regularly transported inland for resale large groups of recently arrived servants, virtually all of them from Ireland.

he had found her confined in the workhouse.[20] Six days later, while incarcerated in Chester County's jail awaiting trial, Stewart submitted a counterpetition in which she pled extenuating circumstances, described months of mistreatment from a succession of cruel or indifferent masters, and begged the magistrates to take her "Melloncholy Condition into Consideration."

Document 4.
Rosanna Stewart, 31 August 1772

To the Worshippful the Magistrates Assembled at Chester this 31st of August 1772

The humble petition of Rosanna Stuart Humbly Sheweth

That your petitioner was brought up to these parts by A Certain James Rea[21] who bought her in Philadelphia & brought her to Campbells tavern in Little Britain, & he kept me there from the Second of November till the first of January Dureing which time Your pet[r] had no bed to lie on & likewise the Victuals I got was very bad so that I could not live on it. Afterward the S[d] James Rea Sold me to one of <the> people Call'd Quakers with whom Istaid from about Christmas untill May, when one of my legs broke out in Several places by reason of the usage Ireceived, for which My Master would not keep me but returned me back to the S[d] James Rea, who went up to Philadelphia to return me back to the Merchants he bought me of,   but they Refusing to take me from him, on this Account as they Suspected of the bad usage I had reieved which was the reason of My leg breaking out, he sold me to Doctor Whitesides, and the Doctor promised to Cure my leg,   after Some Considerable time the S[d] Doctor Whiteside Sold me to m[r] David Dunkin[22] for A Sound Woman, when at the Same time my leg was only Skinned over[23] for the pain was never taken out.

In respect of My running away from Doctor Whitesides for which I am to be judged, the hardships I Suffered was So great, that I was not able to bear up under it, for the Winter before Iran away I had no bed for ten or Eleven weeks but the Cold Earth to

---

20. Dr. Thomas Whitesides, a Reformed (Covenanting) Presbyterian of Ulster or Scottish origin, lived on Conewago Creek on the margins of Oxford township in Chester Co. and Little Britain township in Lancaster Co.; in 1774 he was assessed in Oxford for merely four acres and a cow but in 1780 for one hundred acres, two horses, and four cattle; in 1781 he paid £2 0s.2d. in state taxes.   **21. James Rea:** see n. 19. In the indentured servant trade, Rea was what was known as a "soul-driver," in some respects comparable to the infamous domestic slave traders in the nineteenth-century South. Ironically, in his youth Rea himself had been a servant, probably from Ireland, who in 1746 had been indented for six years to a Philadelphia butcher.
22. David Dunkin: perhaps David Duncan of Lower Chichester township; a "shopkeeper" taxed for 15 acres, a horse, and a cow in 1768. Oxford and Lower Chichester townships are located in the extreme southwest and extreme southeast corners, respectively, of Chester Co., and it is unclear how Stuart ran away "from Doctor Whitesides" after he had sold her to Duncan; presumably, her transfer to Duncan had not yet taken place, and perhaps she absconded in order to prevent it.   **23. Skinned over:** healed over by the growth of new skin.

lie on, & my Victuals & Cloathing was Agreeable to[24] my bed, So that I was Apprehensive I Could not endure it Another Winter,   And I hope that your Worships will take my Melloncholy Condition into Consideration, & grant your pet[r] Such Relief in her Distress'd Circumstances as Your Worships in your Wisdom Shall see fit and you<r> pet[r] as in Duty bound will ever Pray

Rosana
Stewart[25]

A large minority, perhaps a fourth or more, of Pennsylvania's Irish servants were indentured to masters or mistresses who were themselves Irish-born or of Irish parentage. However, there is little evidence that common origins, even if acknowledged, softened master-servant relationships. Even a shared Presbyterian background—as most likely existed between Stewart and Whitesides, the former almost certainly from Ulster, the latter of Scottish or Scots-Irish descent—obviously did not guarantee decent treatment. Moreover, when masters were Irish Protestants and their servants native Irish Catholics—or, less frequently, when the usual Irish roles were in America reversed—a legacy of communal conflict in Ireland could engender private injustices in the colonies. Such may have influenced the relationships between Irish Quakers Miller and Parke and their respective servants McRory and Curry. It may also help explain Patrick M'Cullen's alleged mistreatment by Robert Allison, a wealthy Scots-Irish farmer in Uwchlan township,[26] as described in the former's petition to the court in late 1756.

Document 5.
Patrick M'Cullen, [November] 1756

To The Worshipfull the Justices of the Court of Quarter Sessions for the County of Chester——
        The Petition of Patrick M'Cullen
    Most Humbly Sheweth

                                That your Petitioner on or about the Month of October in the Year of our Lord One thousand Seven hundred and Fifty-Two came over to this Province from the Kingdom of Ireland an indented Servant for the Term of Four Years and was purchased by a certain Robert Allison of this County

---

24. **was Agreeable to:** matched.   25. Stewart's signature is in a shaky, childlike handwriting different from that of the text of the petition, which was probably written by a court official. Unfortunately, as in most of these cases, there is no extant documentation of the court's decision in *Whitesides v. Stewart*; nor does Stewart appear in later county or provincial records.   26. In 1766 Robert Allison of Uwchlan township was taxed on 309 acres, three horses, five cattle, six sheep, and one servant; by 1771 he owned 550 acres. In February 1748, he was commissioned lieutenant in a Chester Co. militia company raised out of Uwchlan and four other townships.

for the Sum of Fifteen Pounds.   That your Petitioner served the said Robert faithfully
and honestly for the Term of one Year, during which time the said Robert used your
poor Petitioner in the most cruel and Barbarous Manner and frequently Beat whipt and
abused your Pet.ʳ most inhumanly without any reasonable Cause, so that he
apprehended his Life to be in great Danger,   that the s.ᵈ Robert often in the s.ᵈ Time
solicited your Pet.ʳ to execute an new Indenture to him for a longer Time and in
Order to compel your Pet.ʳ to comply with his unjust request, falsely charg'd him with
committing a Rape on his Daughter a Child of six Years old and threaten'd to have
him tried for his Life   That your Pet.ʳ at last tired out with the ill Usage of his s.ᵈ
Master did consent to give a new Indenture for a longer Time but without any
Consideration paid to him for that Purpose where upon the s.ᵈ Robert Allison in the
Fall <of> Seventeen hundred and Fifty Three sold your Pet.ʳ to James Benson[27] of this
County for the Term of Five Years for the Sum of Twenty Pounds, and your Pet.ʳ to
get out of the Power of the said Rob.ᵗ executed a new Indenture to the s.ᵈ James
Benson for that Term accordingly.   That your Pet.ʳ having now served out the
compleat Time of his first Indenture apprehends & is advised he is intituled both in
Law and Justice to his Freedom, and humbly prays your Worship's Relief in the
Premisses and your poor Pet.ʳ as in Duty bound will ever pray &c

his
Patrick   X   M Cullen
Mark

Unfortunately for M'Cullen, on 30 November 1756, the magistrates ruled against his
bid for freedom, upholding the sanctity of M'Cullen's second contract, regardless of
the duress under which it had been signed. However, the court did not credit Allison's
allegations of rape against M'Cullen, who took up permanent residence in Uwchlan township after his indenture to Benson finally expired. In 1768 he appeared in the Uwchlan tax
lists, under the name Patrick Cullen, as a hired agricultural laborer, but his last documentation was on 22 February 1777, when he enlisted as a private in Captain Jeremiah Talbot's
company of the Seventh Pennsylvania Regiment of the Continental Army. On this occasion, the ex-servant reassumed his native-Irish patronym, M'Cullen, for although the Seventh Pennsylvania was an overwhelmingly Scots-Irish regiment, it also included a large
minority of Irish soldiers with "Catholic" names.[28] When he enlisted, M'Cullen was still
without taxable property, like most ex-bondsmen even two decades after the termination

27. **James Benson**: also of Uwchlan township; described as a "Yeoman of Chester" in 1746, when he paid
£15 10s. for the four years' indenture of another Irish servant, Patrick Harkill. Between 1765 and 1768,
Benson increased his taxable landholdings from 190 to 280 acres, perhaps by inheritance or other transfers from
kinsmen William or Jno. Benson, also listed with James among the 1753 Uwchlan taxables. **28.** For example,
M'Cullen's comrades in Capt. Talbot's company included Patrick Boyle, Francis O'Hara, Patrick Doyle, and
Felix O'Neal.

of their indentures. However, although he may have joined the Revolutionary War for lack of better economic prospects, it is also likely that, given his experiences in 1752–1756, the word "freedom" had for him more than abstract significance.

Four years after M'Cullen's failed petition, Ann Dougherty's appeal to the quarter sessions court—in this case, for the freedom of her indentured child—may have been more successful. Dougherty's petition not only illustrates another form of abuse by unscrupulous or hard-pressed employers but also provides an early example of Irish emigration motivated by desperation rather than ambition—a pattern more common a century later, during the Great Famine of 1845–1852.

Document 6.
Ann Dougherty, 25 August 1760

> To the Honourable Court of Quarter Sessions held at Chester, &c. The humble Petition of Ann Dougherty Plainly Sheweth——
>
> That Your Petitioner (an Indigent Woman) about Six years ago was thro' Necessity oblidged to transport her Self and three Small Children from Ireland to Pennsylvania; & not able to Defray the Expence of their Passage, was oblidged to bind them Servants to A Captain —— Mullen, who was obligated that they Should be landed, and Serve in the Province of Pennsylvania; who after Landing, Sold one of them to Robert Powell,[29] of the great Valley in Chester County.——Now the Said Robt Powell, without the Poor Womans Knowledge, has sold, and Delivered the Said Child to a Certain Trader, and Inhabitants of the Province of Virginia—
>
> Now—the humble Request of your Poor Petitioner, is, that the Honourable Court would take the matter into their Consideration; and if Robert Powels Proceedings, are Repugnant to the Laws of this Province, that they will give order for Redressing the Poor Womans Grievance; as they in their Wisdom Shall think most Proper
>
> For Which Your Petitioner Shall Pray, &c.——
>
> Whiteland.
> 25th 8th mo: 1760}

Robert Powell had clearly violated the Pennsylvania statute that forbade a servant's sale outside the province without the approval of two magistrates and the consent of the servant—or, if the servant was a minor, as in this case, of his or her parents. Conse-

---

29. **Robert Powell**: of East Whiteland township; a vestryman of St. Peter's Anglican church in Chester County's Great Valley, in 1766 Powell was taxed for 140 acres, four horses, seven cattle, and two servants. However, economic problems may have persuaded him to violate Pennsylvania law by selling Dougherty's child out of the province, as in 1774 Powell owned only 54 acres and by 1780 merely four acres.

quently, on 26 August 1760 Chester County's judges ordered Powell to attend the next court session. Unfortunately, however, the records do not say whether Powell was fined £10 as the law required or, more important, whether Ann Dougherty actually recovered the custody of her child, who was probably laboring far away by the waters of the Shanandoah.

Thomas Ralph, from Comber, County Down, and almost certainly a Presbyterian,[30] may also have been successful in his appeal to Chester's magistrates. Ralph's petition is uniquely valuable in that it provides an unusually large amount of autobiographical data, including a detailed description of how, as a naive and adventurous youth, he was enticed to run away from home and sign an indenture for America: a decision he later rued when he found himself "Constantly at hard Labour" for a Pennsylvania farmer instead of learning "the Taylor's trade" as his seducer had promised.

Document 7.
Thomas Ralph, 1753

> To the honourable Justices of the Court of Gen[l] Quarter Sessions to be held at Chester for the County of Chester the 29th of May 1753.
>
> The Petition of Thomas Ralph of the said County——
> Most humbly Sheweth
>   That Sometime in the Month of April in the Year 1751, Your Petitioner met with one Arthur Kennedy in Cumbortown, in the Kingdom of Ireland, (being the town where your Petitioner's Father then dwelt),   That the said Arthur Kenidy used many Persuasions and fair Promises, to Entice your Petitioner to leave his Parents, and Go to Pennsylvania with him, Promising to Learn him the Taylor's trade and give him two Suits of Cloaths and Money when he was free, By reason of which Promises, your Petitioner was over Persuaded to leave his Parents (who knew nothing of the agreement, nor that he was going to Come away from them) & He being but 15 Years old at that time;   And so after the said Agreement, Your Petitioner was Secreted by the said Kennidy for about a Month, till the Vessell was ready to Set Sail for Pennsylvania, and then he Embarked, on Board the Vessell, with the said Kennidy, and came to this province, and Indented himself to the said Kennidy for the term of Six Years & ahalf;——That the said Kennidy kept your Petitioner a Year and ahalf, at the Taylor's trade, after his arrival here as aforesaid, after which the said Kennidy threatned to Sell your Petitioner to a Farmer, to work at a Plantation, if he would not Indent him for Seven Years, to him, which your Petitioner, after a Greatt many

---

30. Eighteenth-century demographic data for Comber (or Cumber) town and parish, in Lower Castlereigh barony, Co. Down, does not exist, but in 1831 the parish's population was over 98 percent Protestant and 91 percent Presbyterian.

Persuasions Comply'd with, rather than to go to hard labour, and accordingly Signed an Indenture, to the said Kennidy for the Term of Seven Years from the first day of May in the Year 1752;——

That the said Kennidy Sometime in March last Past, Assigned over your Petitioner to a Certain Ezekiel Moore,[31] of said County Yeoman, for the remainder of the said Term of Seven Years then to come, and unexpired; Who keeps your Petitioner Constantly at hard Labour.——

Your Poor Petitioner therefore most humbly Prays that your honours would be pleased to take his Case under Your Wise Consideration, and if it be possible, to Set him, Free from said Moore So that he may work for himself, at his trade, Or if that cant be done, Your Petitioner prays that Your honours would be pleased, to Order that he may be free at the End of the Six Years and ahalf, being the time he was to Serve the said Arthur Kennidy, by the first Indenture.——Or otherwise to do those things which to you, in your Wisdoms Shall Seem most[32] Proper.

And your poor Petitioner (as duty bound) Shall

> Ever pray &c
>
> thomas Ralph

It is unclear under which Pennsylvania statute Ralph appealed for his freedom to the quarter session court, but the magistrates responded favorably, ordering Ezekiel Moore "to Shew Cause, if any he hath, Why the said Thomas Ralph ought not to be discharged from his said Servitude."[33] Indeed, Ralph appears to have been doubly fortunate, as he was one of a small minority of ex-servants who later appeared as a landowner in provincial records. Like thousands of other Scots-Irish settlers, after the French and Indian War Ralph moved to southwestern Pennsylvania, where in 1783 he owned two hundred acres, two horses, two cattle, and three sheep in Westmoreland County's Huntington township.

Unfortunately, the fate of Michael Wade, a servant from Dublin, may have been more typical, although his career had begun auspiciously. Apparently, Wade served his time without incident, learned at least the rudiments of the mason's trade, and subsequently married and left Chester County. Instead of moving west like Ralph, Wade migrated to New York City, no doubt hoping to employ his construction skills in that flourishing seaport. However, Wade's testimony suggests he experienced only unemployment and poverty, as the £6 annual rent he paid for a "Tenement"—probably a shabby garret near the waterfront—was far less than the minimum £50 rent that the city's craftsmen and

---

31. Ezekiel Moore: on the West Fallowfield taxables list in 1753, but the size of his farm cannot be determined, and he does not appear in subsequent Chester Co. lists of taxable property–owners. Ironically, if Ralph's master in 1753 was the same Ezekiel Moore who in 1783 owned merely 25 acres in Westmoreland County's Springhill township, then by the latter date Ralph, with two hundred acres in the same county, may have surpassed his former owner in prosperity. **32. Seemost** ms. **33.** Court scribe's notation on Ralph petition; see Sources, chapter 30.

shopkeepers paid for the smallest houses. By 1766 Wade had gone blind, had become an object of public charity, and had been shipped back to Chester County by New York's poor-relief officials.

According to Pennsylvania's poor laws, either the township in which an ex-servant had been bound for the first 60 days or the one in which he or she had served for 12 months thereafter was deemed to be his or her "legal settlement" and hence responsible for providing poor relief if the former servant later became a public charge. Naturally, each township's overseers of the poor strove to minimize local taxes by shunting paupers onto another locale, and it was to resolve the issue of Wade's place of legal settlement that in 1766, helpless and impoverished, he gave the following account of his life during the previous 16 years.

Document 8.
Michael Wade, 21 April 1766

Chester   Apr. 21, 1766[34]

The Examination of Michael Wade /Aged thirty two years / taken Before us, two of his Majesties Justices of the peace, in & for the County of Chester this 21[s] day of April AnnoDo 1766——

This Examinent, upon his Solumn Oath, Saith, that he was born in Dublin, in the Kingdom of Ireland and About sixteen Years ago he Arived at philedel[a] In the Hornet snow[35] Jn[o] Slade Master, & in a few days was Sould & Assign[d] over before the Mayor of Philadelphia to one James Moor[36] of the Township of Uwychland & County of Chester, & Contin'd with him not Exceeding one week, when the s[d] Moor Sold him to one James M'Clare[37] of the s[d] Township, But was not Assign'd over before a Justice; And Living with S[d] M'Clear the term of Six or seven Months /as he Believes/ when James M'Clear sold him to Jonothan Howall[38] of Whiteland Township; & was Assign'd

---

34. **Apr. 21, 1766**: in a handwriting different from the petition's text.   35. **snow**: a small vessel resembling a brig.   36. **James Moor**: James Moore, listed in 1750 as a "freeman," without taxable property, in Uwchlan township; perhaps the James Moore, Esq., on the 1774 landowners' list (next to James McClure, see n. 34) for West Nantmeal township, adjacent to Uwchlan.   37. **James M'Clare** (below **M'Clear**): James McClure, on the Uwchlan township list of taxable property-holders in 1753. Several McClure kin held land on the border of Uwchlan and West Nantmeal townships, and their property was sometimes assessed in one, sometimes in the other. In 1753 James McClure appeared on the Uwchlan list of taxable property-holders, but in 1771 and 1774 he was assessed for two hundred acres in West Nantmeal.   38. **Jonothan Howall**: Jonathan Howell, member of a Quaker family that emigrated from Cheshire, England, in 1683. In 1753 Howell appears on the Whiteland township taxables list and again in 1781 as owning one hundred acres, two horses, and four cattle in East Nantmeal township. Jonathan was almost certainly kin of Israel Howell and Thomas Howell who appeared on the Thornbury township taxables list in 1753 and 1774, respectively.

over Before Saml Lightfoot Esq^r39 & Resided with his s^d Master in the s^d Township
five weeks, & then was Sent down into the township of Thornbury to work at a
Plantation his Master had Lately bought & served the Remainder of his time there;
Which this Examinent believes was upwards of four years; this Examinent having
Given his s^d Master New Indentures with an Addition of one year in Consideration of
Lerning the Mason Trade & some schooling;   there was no^40 Notice Given to the
overseers of the poor of any of the several TownShips as this Examinent knows or
believs and About Ten years ago he Married & Lived in Thornbury neer Twelve
Months; Then Moved to New york with his wife; who is now Living; and There
Rented of one Mayers a Tenement of Six Pounds for one year; Then Rented at the
Rate of Six pounds a year Sundry Tenements for the Space of Seven or Eight years in
s^d place but paid no taxes or poor Rates; And is now Return'd into the Township of
Thornbury friendless^41 poor, Blind & unable to Support & Maintain himself & stands in
need of Relief——

And further Sayeth not——

Taken & Subscribed before				his	
us the Day & year Afores^d			Michael	X	Wade
William Parker				Mark	
Jno Hann[?]					

Unfortunately, it cannot be determined how long Wade, only 32 years old in 1766,
eked out a miserable subsistence on Chester County's grudging charity. Indeed, he
may have been denied relief—a victim of jurisdictional conflicts compounded by anti-Irish
prejudice. In Wade's case, as in those of the other petitioners, most questions remain
unanswered. Eighteenth-century officials were usually more concerned to punish than to
relieve the poor, and not until after the Revolution would urbanized Irish-Americans of
élite and middling status create benevolent societies to succor their own unfortunates.
Thus, as the following two essays demonstrate, often more is known about the lives of
those few Irish servants who died on the gallows than of the great majority whose careers
terminated in less spectacular fashion.

39. Saml **Lightfoot** Esqr: Chester Co. justice of the peace; owner of four hundred acres in Pikeland township
in 1765; and prominent surveyor who in 1750 helped settle the Pennsylvania-Maryland boundary dispute;
almost certainly a descendant of Thomas Lightfoot, a Quaker from Co. Carlow, mentioned in Robert Parke's
1725 letter (see chapter 9).   **40. now** ms.   **41. friendless** conjectural (ms. blurred).

John Grimes, John Fagan, and John Johnson, 1765

Given the illiteracy that prevailed among the poorest Irish immigrants—and their consequent historical anonymity—the autobiographical confessions of John Grimes, John Fagan, and John Johnson, hanged for burglary at Burlington, New Jersey, in 1765, are uniquely valuable. Despite the problematic nature of such evidence, their testaments provide a rare glimpse of an Irish-immigrant demimonde in colonial America. Although it is arguable that Grimes's, Fagan's, and Johnson's behavior and fate were atypical, the criminal charges levied against several of the Chester County petitioners, chronicled in the previous chapter, suggest that for Irish immigrant laborers—and especially for Catholics—conventional distinctions between "honest" workers and "vicious" criminals were often blurred: by dire necessity among the poorest Irish themselves; and by social, ethnic, and religious prejudices among colonial masters and public officials.

Between eleven o'clock and midnight on 13 July 1765, Grimes, Fagan, and Johnson, "armed with Guns, and having their Faces painted," robbed the isolated house of Joseph Burr, perhaps the richest farmer and manufacturer in Burlington County, stealing money, silver, clothes, and linens. Their meager disguise was of little avail, for the subsequent hue and cry described them by name and appearance. Johnson, "a very lusty Man, . . . wore a Beaver Hat, Leather Breeches, with broad Knee Bands, and Buckles"; Fagan "had a Hat half worn, Check Shirt, and striped Trowsers"; and Grimes, the shortest of the three at five feet, four inches, "wore a Beaver Hat, Check Shirt, and had black curled Hair." Even more revealing was "the Brogue on their Tongues," which singled them out in a county where 85 percent of the inhabitants were English and Welsh farmers, mostly Quakers like Burr, whose ancestors had settled the area in the late seventeenth century. Within a few days, Grimes, Fagan, and Johnson were confined in Burlington gaol, where they confessed and claimed membership of "a numerous and dangerous Gang" that operated in and between New York City and Philadelphia. On Tuesday, 20 August, the three men were tried, found guilty of burglary, and sentenced to be hanged the following Wednesday. During their last weeks of life, someone—probably Rev. Colin Campbell,[1] the Anglican minister of Burlington's St. Mary's church—elicited from the condemned confessional memoirs that were published in broadside form.

In the American colonies, as in eighteenth-century England, the lives, last words, and dying confessions of convicted criminals were commonly issued as pamphlets or broadsides, sold on execution day, and widely circulated. Such testaments played major roles in elaborate

---

1. Rev. Colin Campbell (1707–1766); born at Earnhill, Scotland; educated at Inverness and at the University of Aberdeen (M.A. 1729); a missionary for the Society for the Propagation of the Gospel at Nevis in the West Indies (1738); at Bristol, Bucks Co., Pa. (1741); and at Burlington, N.J. (1742–1766). Quotations in this paragraph from *Pa. Gazette*, 25 July and 1 August 1765; see Sources, chapter 31.

execution rituals, in which the majesty of the law, the triumph of social order, and the personal drama of penitence and redemption were represented by church and state to edify and warn those assembled at the gallows. Consequently, such documents must be examined cautiously, for those who transcribed them were usually public officials or clergymen who ignored the social contexts of criminal behavior and shaped the stories and purported repentence of the condemned into formulaic moral lessons on the wages of individual sin.

Nevertheless, there are reasons to believe that the confessions of the Burlington hanged reveal at least as much about their own experiences as about the hegemonic imperatives of the colonial élites. Such documents could subvert as well as buttress prevailing systems of property, order, and morality, and their final, published forms were the products of an unusual dialogue between representatives of subterranean and polite or official cultures. Of course, given their circumstances, the relationship between Rev. Campbell and Grimes, Fagan, and Johnson was decidedly unequal. However, Campbell himself, as an Episcopalian from the Scottish Highlands, was a relative "outsider"—both in his homeland and in Burlington County; in addition, it is likely he could speak Scots Gaelic, then closely akin to Ulster Irish, which may have facilitated his communication with at least one of the prisoners. Thus, although allegedly "a man of strict and severe honesty," Rev. Campbell was perhaps less condemnatory, more aware of the difficult conditions that had shaped his informants' character, and more respectful of their individuality and cultural backgrounds than most of his peers.[2] It may be suggestive that, of the three criminals, only Fagan's testimony was made to conform to the conventional demands for extensive expressions of abject repentence, while by contrast Grimes's almost boastful account of his prison exploits in New Castle resembles the picaresque tales of "bold rapparees"[3] and daring highwaymen that were a staple of popular literature in contemporary Ireland and the Highlands alike.[4]

2. During and after the Glorious Revolution, Scottish Episcopalians, concentrated in the Gaelic-speaking Highlands around Aberdeen, Banff, Inverness, and Argyle (the origin of Rev. James MacSparran's family, see chapter 8), suffered mob violence and legal persecution from Scotland's Presbyterians during and after the Glorious Revolution, which overthrew the Scottish episcopacy imposed by Charles II. Persecution intensified in the wake of the 1745 Jacobite invasion, which many Scottish Episcopalians welcomed. In addition, the latter were assiduous in preserving traditional Scottish music and poetry, believing that their religion gave them greater continuity with the Scottish past than did Presbyterianism. Thus, although Scotland's Episcopalians were by no means Scoto-Catholics, after 1688 there *were* similarities between their experiences and outlooks and those of Ireland's Catholics. Quotation from *Pa. J.*, 14 August 1766; see Sources, chapter 31.   3. "Rapparees" was a generic term applied to Irish Catholic outlaws—often former soldiers in the armies of James II and Patrick Sarsfield—who turned to highway robbery during and after the Williamite War of 1688–1691. In eighteenth-century Ireland, popular books such as John Cosgrave's *Irish Rogues and Rapparees* and *The Lives and Adventures of the Most Notorious Irish Highwaymen* celebrated their exploits.   4. However, it must be noted that all three confessions conformed to stock formulas by which such testaments were designed, by civil and religious leaders, to restore familial, as well as public, order. Most confessions (such as Fagan's and Johnson's) depicted condemned criminals as youthful rebels against the authority of "good parents," led astray by "bad company" such as "youths of corrupt morals" and "loose women" (e.g., see chapter 32). Grimes's confession illustrated another pattern: self-exculpation by blaming negligent or overly indulgent parents for the criminal's subsequent descent into sin and law-breaking.

Moreover, the autobiographies of the three men closely match the profiles of transported Irish convicts (and of runaway Irish servants) that historians have constructed from colonial legal records and newspaper advertisements. For although only Grimes was actually shipped to America as a convict, Fagan and Johnson were nearly so, having fled to the colonies in an ultimately vain attempt to avoid arrest and punishment. Indeed, the transatlantic world of eighteenth-century Britain's real or potential criminals—a "floating population" of footloose individuals—appears to have been disproportionately Irish. Often made homeless in Ireland by landlord clearances or jobless by the deskilling of crafts, they or their parents drifted from rural hamlets or country towns into the major Irish and English ports. There they settled, at least temporarily, in crowded, impoverished neighborhoods, such as Dublin's Liberties and London's St. Giles in the Fields, where flourished groggeries, brothels, and more opportunities for crime than for gainful employment.

Many died at the hands of Irish or British hangmen: late eighteenth-century Dublin averaged nearly a dozen public executions per year; and between 1703 and 1772 London's Irish-born inhabitants provided at least 14 percent of the nearly 1,200 felons hanged at Tyburn. More fortunate were those who absconded—as indentured servants or stowaways—or were forcibly transported as convicts to the American colonies. During the 1700s some 14,000 felons and vagabonds were shipped directly from Ireland, and a large minority of the 50,000 convicts transported (like Grimes) from London and other English ports were also Irish. Of the latter, most served their 14-year sentences—the normal punishment for eighteenth-century Britain's and Ireland's long list of capital crimes—on plantations and ironworks in Maryland and elsewhere in the Chesapeake, where their treatment was so harsh that many (again, like Grimes) fled their masters.

Like Grimes, Fagan, and Johnson—and like most ordinary, runaway Irish servants—Irish convicts in colonial America usually were males in their teens or twenties; most were unskilled and illiterate laborers (Grimes) or craftsmen (Fagan and Johnson); and, according to their masters' advertisements, many were scarred, physically and psychologically, by abuse, alcohol, and diseases such as syphilis. A majority were from Leinster, often Dublin-born like Fagan and Johnson or, like Grimes, temporary residents in the Irish capital; judging by their names, a large number were Catholics (Grimes and Fagan) or at least of Catholic ancestry, although Dublin's "lower orders" still included a large minority of Protestants, primarily Anglicans such as Johnson.[5] Like Fagan, many were former British soldiers, demobilized and unemployed after 1763, at the end of the Seven Years' War. All suffered the effects of postwar depression in the colonies, when the numbers of transported convicts, fugitive servants, and executions for crimes against property soared. Many convicts who completed their terms settled peacefully, if not prosperously, in the American backcountry, as did most ex-servants. But others—especially the runaways—congregated in the dockyard slums of seaports such as New York where, in the mid-1760s, respectable

5. On eighteenth-century Dublin city's religious demography, see appendix 2.2b, on chapter 14.

citizens attributed a wave of "Pillages and Robberies"[6] to men such as Grimes, Fagan, and Johnson.

> "*The Last* Speech, *Confession, Birth, Parentage and Education, of* John Grimes, John Fagan, *and* John Johnson, *alias* Johnson Cochran, *who were executed at* Gallows-Hill, *in the City of* Burlington, *on* Wednesday *the 28th of* August, 1765, *for Burglary and Felony, committed in the County of* Burlington."

I *JOHN GRIMES,* aged Twenty-two Years, was born in the West of *Ireland,* in a small Village, of low, mean Parents, who had neither Ability nor Opportunity to give me any Education, so that from my Infancy I was brought up to Idleness and Thieving, which, instead of being corrected in me, was rather encouraged; at last I became so notorious, that I was obliged to leave that Part of the Country, and come to *Dublin,* and being bred to no Business, worked on board Ships at the Keys, but following my old Trade, I was dismissed from all Employment for Dishonesty and Thieving; I subsisted some Time in that City by joining a Gang of Street Robbers and Pick Pockets, but Justice overtaking them, and the Heads of the Gang being hanged, and others impeaching me,[7] I was once more obliged to abscond, and from thence went over to *Liverpool,* but being known there, I travelled to *Bristol,* and from thence to *London,* following my Trade of Thieving all along; and there turning Foot Pad,[8] and robbing a Gentleman at *Temple-Bar,*[9] I was taken and committed to *Newgate,* and tried at the *Old-Bailey;*[10] and as it was the first Crime I was known to be guilty of, I was cast for Transportation,[11] and accordingly came over in the *Dolphin,* Capt. *Cramer,* to *Patapsco,*[12] in *Maryland,* and was sold as a Servant to an Iron-Work, but I soon run away from them, and carried off with me as much Goods out of a Store I had broke open, as made me pass for a Pedlar, when I came into *New-Castle;*[13]   from *New-Castle* I went to *New-York,* where I associated with a Gang who for a long Time had infested

---

6. Bridenbaugh, *Cities in Revolt,* 113; see Sources, chapter 31.   **7. impeaching me**: informing on me.
8. Foot Pad: highwayman who robs on foot.   **9.** *Temple-Bar*: when first mentioned in 1293, a chain ("Bar") hung between two posts at the point where the Strand becomes Fleet Street, marking the westernmost limit of extramural land controlled by the City of London. The name, subsequently applied to the immediate neighborhood, derived from the adjacent house of the Knights Templar ("The Temple"). By 1351 the chain had been replaced by a gate, with a prison above. In the early 1670s Christopher Wren rebuilt the gate, but in 1878 it was demolished as an impediment to traffic.   **10.** *Newgate*: London's most notorious prison ("a habitation of misery . . . a bottomless pit of violence") for "ordinary" criminals, a five-story structure dating from the fifteenth century. Adjacent to Newgate was **the Old-Bailey**, a complex of buildings, constructed after London's great fire of 1673, that housed the eight annual courts ("sessions") that tried criminal cases for the City of London and Middlesex Co. Both Newgate and the Old Bailey were located in east London, across the city from the execution grounds at Tyburn.   **11. cast for Transportation**: condemned to transportation.
12. *Patapsco*: then in Baltimore Co., Maryland, and site of one of the colony's largest ironworks. Between 1745 and 1775, former ironworkers comprised nearly a fourth of colonial Maryland's runaway male convicts.
13. *New-Castle*: in northern Delaware; then a major debarkation port for immigrants.

that City; but being obliged to leave that Place, I returned to *New-Castle*, where I pretended to be an Irish Pedlar newly come over; but I could not help following what was almost natural to me, but once more took to Thieving and House-breaking, and after performing several Exploits in that Way, I at last stole a Horse, for which I was apprehended, tried, and burnt[14] in the Hand; while I lay in this Gaol, I could not resist the Temptation of Stealing, the Evil was so ingrafted in my wicked Heart; the Affair was this, a Man being in that Gaol, under Sentence of Death, the Sheriff procured a Person to execute him, and paid the Money before hand; but to secure the Fellow from running away before he had done the Job, he put him in Gaol, where he had not lain long before I robb'd him of all his Money, which I spent idly:[15] I lay a considerable Time in this Gaol, till a Gentleman from *Maryland*, upon my signing an Indenture to serve for some Time for the Fees, took me out, but instead of fulfilling my Engagement, I robbed the Gentleman of his Horse, and all he had about him, and again push'd for *New-York*. In the Gaol at *New-Castle*, I had Information from a Prisoner who was well acquainted in *New-Jersey*, of the House of *Joseph Burr*, for the robbing of which I now suffer. In the City of *New-York* I first became acquainted with my unhappy Fellow-Sufferers;[16] from that City we travelled in Company towards *West-Jersey*, and parted near *Mount-Holly*, when I went across *Delaware*, into *Pennsylvania*, and there stole the Watch of *Edward Hill*, and then returned into the *Jersies*, met my old Comrades, and with them planned and executed the aforesaid Robbery, we then stole Horses to carry us off, but getting drunk, we quarrelled in the Woods about dividing our Booty, when I was beat in so terrible a Manner that I was not able to make my Escape, and the other two going to sleep, during which Time the Country being alarmed, we were apprehended and brought to *Burlington*, and now are deservedly to suffer for this and our former Crimes. I die a Member of the *Roman* Catholic Communion, and in Peace and Charity with all Men, hoping GOD will pardon all my Sins and Offences, and forgive my Enemies.

I *JOHN FAGAN*, was born in the City of *Dublin*, in the Kingdom of *Ireland*, in the Year 1737, of poor but honest Parents, who brought me up in the Roman Catholick Religion, till I arrived at the Age of Fourteen, when I was put an Apprentice to a Joiner and House-Carpenter, with whom I lived between 4 and 5 Years, and falling into bad Company, I fell first from my Duty towards GOD, and then towards Man; for in a small Space of time, Drunkenness, Sabbath-breaking and the Conversation[17] of lewd[18] and disorderly[19] Women, became the fatal Objects of my Thoughts as well as Practice.

---

14. burnt: branded. **15. idly**: frivolously, to no useful purpose. **16. my . . . Fellow-Sufferers**: my accomplices condemned to die with me. **17. Conversation**: company, society. **18. lewd**: low(-class), vulgar, common; also, lascivious, unchaste. **19. disorderly**: prone to offend against public order and morality.

This Course of Life not answering my Purpose, and fearing the fatal Consequences that might attend my Stay, I thought it safest to embark for *America*, which I did in the Year 1756, where I had not been long till I engaged in his Majesty's Service, wherein I continued till the Troops were discharged, after which I engaged to Work at my Trade at the *Highlands* above *New-York*, where I wrought[20] some Time, but my Inclinations still hankering after lewd Company, I frequented bad Houses, in one of which I became acquainted with my unhappy Fellow-Sufferers; and after some short Acquaintance, we left *New-York* together, and travelled into *New-Jersey*, where we committed many Crimes, particularly robbing the House of *Joseph Burr*, near the City of *Burlington*, and the same Night with my Accomplices, stole three Horses, in Order to make our Escapes to *New-York*, but getting Drunk by the Way, we fell out, and was presently after[21] apprehended, and brought to *Burlington* Gaol, where we were confined, and several Times attempted an Escape, but was prevented. *Good People*, Take Warning by my Fate,   I am, you see a young Man, who by my Sins have shortened my Days, and brought myself to this shameful (but deserved) Death. Take heed to yourselves how you lead your Life. Live not as I have done, lest you come to the sad and untimely End I am now come to. Break not the Sabbath Day, and keep not Company with wicked Men, and lewd Women, as I have done. Those are the great Evils which have brought this Sorrow upon me. Avoid all Manner of Sin, even the smallest, for from one little Sin, Men easily fall to the Commission of greater ones. I die in the Faith of the *Roman* Catholick Profession, and I pray heartily to God to keep you from all Evil: And I beseech you to pray for me, that God would have Mercy upon my poor Soul.

I *JOHN JOHNSON*, alias *Johnson Cochran*, was born in the City of *Dublin*, in the Kingdom of *Ireland*, of very good Parents, who brought me up to good Learning, in the Protestant Religion, and never did profess any other: I was put to School till I was 15 Years of Age; after which I was put an Apprentice to a Silver Smith, but having too good a Master and Mistress, I left them and got acquainted with many idle and wicked Men, and lewd Women, who led me into all Manner of Vice, particularly Shop-lifting: In breaking open the House of *Joseph Jennings*, in *Waterford*, I very narrowly escaped being taken as I was getting out at the Window, from whence I stole some Cash, Cloaths, and many other Articles; and then made off towards the North of *Ireland*.

After having collected a considerable Booty by Means of such Villanies, I embarked on board of the Ship *King George*, Capt. *Mackie*, bound for *Philadelphia;* here I continued some Time, and not finding any Encouragement at my Trade, I betook myself to my former Way of Living, *viz:* Whoring, Drinking, and such like Vices; and

---

20. wrought: worked (the normal form of the past tense and past participle in Ulster English).   **21. presently after**: shortly afterward.

getting acquainted with some lewd People, I fell to picking of Pockets, and stole many Pocket Books and Watches, to a considerable Value, but finding *Philadelphia* too hot to hold me, I removed to *New-York*, where I soon became acquainted with People of the same dishonest Profession as myself; and having good Encouragement, joined with a Company of them, and robbed several People in the Street, of Money and Effects, and shared them amongst my Accomplices,   after some Time I became acquainted with my Fellow-Sufferers, who were of the same Profession, and we all three agreed to travel together into *New-Jersey;* and our Inclination still leading us to Mischief, we made several Attempts on different Persons on the Highway, and finding but little Encouragement, we moved farther into *West-Jersey*, where we followed the like Courses, but with little Success.

After which, from the Information of one of my Fellow-Sufferers, the House of *Joseph Burr* was thought worthy of our Attention, which Robbery we effected the 13th of July, at Night; then returned to the City of Burlington, and stole three Horses, with a Design to make an Escape to New-York, but losing our Road, and getting Drunk and quarrelling, we were pursued and apprehended the 18th Day of the same Month, and committed to *Burlington* Gaol, and on the 20th Instant, took our Trials,[22] and received Sentence of Death. To this I shall add, I heartily wish that the Number of Malefactors, may not encrease, but diminish; so I pray God to convert all those that abandon themselves to wicked and illegal Courses: I now die in the Faith of the Protestant Religion; and I pray God to have Mercy upon my Soul.

As Fagan admitted, he and his comrades made several attempts to break out of Burlington gaol. According to the *Pennsylvania Gazette* of 5 September 1765, they nearly "effected it, having got off their Irons, and made a Hole in the Wall, large enough to get out at, but were discovered by the Watch, just as every Thing was ready for their Escape." Perhaps this failure persuaded them to cooperate with Rev. Campbell's homiletic endeavors, but neither Grimes's black humor, Fagan's apparently sincere repentance, nor Johnson's effort to distance himself from his Catholic confederates, by proclaiming his Protestant faith, won reprieves. On 28 August 1765, they were "launched into eternity" on Burlington's Gallows Hill. Ironically, almost precisely a year later, Rev. Colin Campbell followed the miscreants to the grave. Perhaps the sight of their miserable deaths had hastened the decline of a man described in his funeral sermon as "a lover of peace."[23]

22. **took our trials**: stood trial.   23. *Pa. J.*, 14 August 1766; see Sources, chapter 31.

32 ✳

Francis Burdett Personel, 1773

Francis Burdett Personel was one of a minority of Irish indentured servants who had fled to America for highly individualistic, rather than economic, reasons—to escape familial authority or personal embarrassment. Once in New World, however, it is probable that such immigrants, like Personel, frequently absconded, after discovering American servitude to be as constraining as the Irish conditions they had fled, and after finding that the colonies offered greater opportunities to pursue whatever desires for "freedom" had impelled their departures. Thus, like John Grimes,[1] Francis Burdett Personel ran away from his master in Maryland and ended his young life on the gallows, leaving a confessional memoir to edify contemporaries and give historians a tantalizing glimpse of Irish life among the American colonies' "lower orders." Unlike Grimes, however, Personel was not an illiterate, professional criminal but a highly skilled and articulate if wayward youth, whose hapless relationships with women brought him both to America and to an untimely end.

Personel's primary purpose in recounting his story was to repent his sins and admonish readers to avoid his example; thus, over half the text in his 20-page pamphlet was devoted to pious exhortations. Nevertheless, his memoir is particularly valuable for its detailed portrayal of the travails of an runaway Irish servant in a colonial society where the dangers of apprehension were balanced by exceptional opportunities for anonymity and mobility. Despite his eventual execution, in most respects Personel's situation was not unusual. Six out of every seven European emigrants to eighteenth-century Maryland (and probably nine-tenths of the Irish) arrived in bondage, and although historians estimate that fewer than 10 percent of servants absconded from their masters, newspaper advertisements indicate that among the Irish the figure was much higher. Unfortunately, in his account Personel identified neither his trade nor his regional and religious origins in Ireland. However, the ease with which Personel avoided recapture and changed locations, occupations, and even identities in the colonies suggests that—in addition to his skills and literacy—it was a Protestant (probably Church of Ireland) upbringing, plus further Anglicization in England itself, that enabled him to achieve a greater degree of acculturation and assimilation than usually was possible for Irish servants who had "the Brogue on their Tongues."[2]

Personel was born in Ireland about 1747 and "tenderly raised by careful and industrious parents," who provided their only child with eight years' education before apprenticing him to a "good trade."[3] After mastering his craft, Personel went to Bristol, in England, and lived a "considerable while" in Shepton-Mallet, Somersetshire, until his father's death, when he succumbed to his mother's entreaties and returned home. Although at first "very

---

1. See chapter 31. 2. E.g., see chapter 31. 3. *An Authentic and Particular Account of the Life of Francis Burdett Personel* . . . (New York, 1773). Unless otherwise cited, all subsequent quotations are from this source.

careful about worldly affairs, and . . . remarkably sober," the "continual admonitions" of a nagging mother—"a passionate woman" who "loved [him] beyond measure"—drove him to seek independence: first in Ireland among "lewd women" and eventually in America, where he sojourned for 18 months before returning to his mother's house "in a poor and miserable condition." For a year after his return, Personel lived "very comfortably" with his mother, avoiding "the sinful appetites of the flesh," until she insisted he accept an arranged marriage with a woman "of an honest family," without "the least blemish in their characters." Personel refused, despite the promise of a "handsome dowry" and his mother's threat to disinherit him. "Thinking the young woman not handsome enough, nor fancying her in the least, [and] knowing myself to be but young, I resolved not to have her, let what would happen." Instead, he signed a contract of indenture and "through disobedience . . . came off to America a second time, and have never since returned."

An Authentic and Particular Account of the Life of Francis Burdett Personel,
Written by Himself. Who was executed at New-York, September 10th, 1773;
in the Twenty-sixth Year of his Age, for the Murder of Mr. Robert White
(New York, 1773)

. . . I lived in Baltimore county, in Maryland, for eighteen months, as a servant, and served but so much of four years due for my passage.[4] Being now in want of clothes, as those I brought from home were wore out, and those I had of my master but indifferent,[5] though far better than what other servants got for common.[6] At length, I took a thought to run away, and accordingly did in a foolish manner; one morning, after breakfast, my master came home, and shewing me what was to be done; I worked a little after his departure, then took my ax with me, went about a mile through the woods, and seated myself on the top of a hill till night, it being then the spring of the year, though the trees were not yet green. I travelled that night but slowly, my shoes being bad and the roads very deep, as it had rained. I got within a mile of Baltimore by day-light, and then, for fear of being discovered, went and laid me down in the woods; but, having only a shirt, jacket, and a pair of trowsers upon me, and it raining very much, I could not sleep, being cold, wet and hungry. I now repented of my running away, and would have returned home, had I not recollected that I had heard my master say, he would treat a runaway that returned, worse than one that used his endeavour to get off;[7] therefore, I would not go home, nor tell that I was a runaway, but wished to be taken up;[8] and, with an expectation of being taken, came on the high road at mid-day, and went into Baltimore Town. As nobody questioned me, I enquired for a

---

4. and served but so much of four years due for my passage: "I served merely eighteen months of the four years [of indentured servitude] that I owed in return for my passage [to America]." **5. indifferent**: average, mediocre. **6. common**: allowance; here "clothing allowance." **7. used his endeavour to get off**: "bent his efforts to get away/escape." **8. taken up**: apprehended (by legal authority), arrested.

certain tavern, where I had heard my master say he used to put up at; coming there, I mentioned my master's name, and said, that he desired me to get a dinner there; the landlord asked me if my master had given me a note. I said, no: Then said he, I cannot let you have dinner. I wished to be taken up, yet would not inform him I was a runaway.

      I then walked through the town, and came to a road that leads to Annapolis,   I reached the river by sun-set, where I waited till two Gentlemen came who wanted to get over; they asked me to whom I belong? I said to Squire Carroll of Annapolis,[9] which was false; but he living in Annapolis, and I wanting to get there if possible: They examined me no farther, knowing that <he> whom I called my master had several farms, and his servants continually going from one to another: I travelled with this lie in my mouth till I came to Annapolis; it was evening when I came to town, and I had neither money, friends, nor clothes, I walked about hoping somebody noticed me. Going to a Gentleman's house, I laid me down under the stoop,[10] hoping that some one from within would examine me, but there came none. The next morning I walked out of town very feeble and hungry not having eat[11] for a long time. I then wandered I know not where, steering partly by the sun, travelled by day on the high road, caring not much whether I was then taken up or no, but was resolved to keep going whilst I was able. I met several people, and saluted them, and so passed on: At length, I saw a Gentleman on horseback coming towards me, which daunted me, fearing he was in pursuit of me,   I saluted him, passed on, and sometimes after met his brother, who questioned me; I told him I was just free,[12] and my master was such a villain, that he would not give me my freedom dues,[13] and that I came to Annapolis, in search of a friend, to acquaint him how my master served[14] me. But unhappily, I told him, my friend had left town before I came, and having no money I left town, with an intent to get work in the country; he replied his brother wanted a workman but could get none this while past,[15] therefore, desired me to call at his brother's house, told me his name, and gave proper directions, and desired me to tarry there till his brother came home, where I went, and spoke to the Gentlewoman, who ordered me a dinner, which was very welcome to me just then: When the Gentleman came home, I engaged with him for four months under the name of James Alkins,   having been with him a week or two, pleasing him, being handy at any sort

---

9. Squire Carroll of Annapolis: Charles Carroll of Annapolis, son of Charles Carroll "the Settler" (1660–1720) from King's Co., Ireland, and father of Charles Carroll of Carrolton (1737–1832), Maryland revolutionary leader and signer of the Declaration of Independence; see chapter 50. **10. stoop**: "an uncovered platform before the entrance of a house, raised, and approached by means of steps. Sometimes incorrectly used for *porch* or *veranda*" (*Century Dictionary*, quoted in OED). **11. eat**: past tense, pronounced [ett] (Standard British and Southern Irish). **12. I was just free**: "I had just been freed." **13. freedom dues**: the clothes, tools, cash, etc., as stipulated in the contracts of indenture or by Maryland law or custom, that masters were required to give servants at the termination of their service. **14. served**: treated. **15. this while past**: for some time past.

of plantation work,[16] he let me have necessary apparel; with him I lived till after harvest, but he not letting me have my earnings, lest I should leave him before my time was expired, and I fearing my master would hear of me, <I> borrowed a coat, hat, and other necessaries suitable, under a pretence of visiting a friend, and went off, being provided with a pass I had written myself, and signed a Magistrate's name to it, changing my name to Patt Percy; having now some money, I delayed not till I got into Virginia; and, being well dressed, could write a passible hand, and understood some figures, I set up for a Schoolmaster,[17] accordingly I got a school, where I taught for some time, was very well regarded by my neighbours, some gave me credit for one thing and some for another.[18] I lived very happy, as I thought, just then, and could go out on a evening after school and serve the devil with delight. I continued this practice for some time, till I went to hear the Baptists called by some New Lights.[19] I went more out of curiosity than any thing else, having heard much of them: The first sermon I heard pricked my heart. I went to hear them often, wrestled against sin in a measure,[20] and would not commit such as appeared base in the world, and as few others as possible.

I had a desire to leave off all sin; but depended on the broken staff of my own strength, therefore could not do it: I obtained the name[21] of being a religious young man by some, who knew not what it was; and I myself was deceived, thinking I was converted when only convicted,[22] and wanted to join the church, but was not accepted, upon which the young men derided me: yet I continued to hear preaching, and, to appearance, had I staid there, would have been brought to the knowledge of God through Christ: But two men, who suspected me to be a runaway, saying they would take me up, occasioned my leaving this place, being unwilling to return to Maryland to my master. I went to a widow, whom I was bound in oath to be married unto, borrowed a mare, bridle, and saddle of her, under a pretence to go to town for some things; from whence I went, calling myself Francis Personel, *alias* Burdett Personel, and never returned. About an hundred miles therefrom I sold the mare, bridle and saddle, and travelled to Pittsburg, nigh which I tarried for some time.

P ersonel did not describe his sojourn in Pennsylvania, although his anonymous editor noted the rumor that Personel "was tried at Lancaster, after he left Virginia, for horse-stealing, in company with another." Sometime thereafter, he moved to the seaport of New

---

16. plantation work: farm work.   **17. I set up for**: "I went into business as."   **18.** On Irish schoolmasters in early America, see chapter 48.   **19. New Lights**: the contemporary, generic term in America for evangelical Protestants associated with the First (and, later, the Second) Great Awakening.   **20. in a measure**: to a moderate degree.   **21. name**: reputation.   **22. convicted**: i.e., convicted of sin; **convince/convict of sin**: to declare guilty of/bring to acknowledge sin. See John 8:48: "Which of you convinceth me of sin? And if I say the truth, why do ye not believe me?"

York, where in 1773 he married for love a woman who "had followed a loose way of life" and, although beautiful in Personel's eyes, was of course precisely, and perhaps intentionally, the opposite sort of woman whom his mother had wished him to wed. Yet Personel, still influenced by his "genteel" upbringing despite his frequent resorts to crime, "could not bear to think of her following that course [prostitution] any longer" and strove to support his wife through his own earnings. Shortly after their marriage, however, he was taken ill and became unable to work, and his wife returned to the taverns and "prostituted her body as usual." At first Personel acquiesced in "[t]his abominable practice," but soon he was overcome with shame and jealousy. On the night of 16 May, enraged and humiliated, he attacked one of his wife's wealthy customers, Robert White, Esq., and unintentionally killed him.

According to the editor of his confession, and the official proclamation calling for his apprehension,[23] Personel ("otherwise called Francis Parsells") "went off" after White's murder, fleeing to New Haven, Connecticut, where he was arrested about six weeks later. On 31 July a New York court sentenced Personel to death for murder but granted his plea for six weeks to prepare his soul for execution. With the aid of Methodist preachers and other clergymen, Personel finally achieved in gaol the conversion experience and the freedom from carnal desires that had previously eluded him. Now filled with the Holy Spirit, Personel penned his final testament, denouncing his former self and the "fornicators" and "daughters of hell" who allegedly had led him astray. Fully "resigned to the King of Terrors," and after a last exhortation to "young sinners," Personel was hanged in the town green on the evening of 10 September 1773.

Ironically, the large crowd that witnessed Personel's execution assembled near the city's Liberty Pole, a symbol of social and political dissatisfaction. And, indeed, Personel's assault on a "Gentleman" who was, in effect, exploiting the economic vulnerability of New York's humblest inhabitants, could have been seen to have radical implications—as an instance of popular outrage against the colonial élite and the hierarchical order that its laws imposed on the city's poor. Perhaps of necessity, therefore, New York's newspapers portrayed Personel as merely a common "Murderer," his action devoid of any larger significance, and Personel himself died affirming what the historian Daniel Williams calls "the order that condemned him."[24]

23. The proclamation calling for Personel's apprehension was published in the 21 June 1773 *New-York Gazette*. Notices of his arrest, trial, conviction, and execution were published in the *New-York Journal* of 1 July, 5 August, and 9 and 16 September 1773 and of his execution in the *New-York Gazette* of 13 September.
24. D. E. Williams, *Pillars of Salt . . .* , 205; see Sources, chapter 32.

33 ❋

James Patton (1), 1783–1789

In the 1780s Irish emigration to the new United States, stifled since 1775 by the American Revolution, increased markedly, while simultaneously the old transatlantic traffic in indentured servants began a steep decline. This new outflow was largely composed of emigrants less affluent than the Witherspoons, McDowells,[1] and others who, in the early 1700s, had transported entire families overseas and purchased American land, but not so poor as many had been during the decades immediately prior to the Revolution, when indentured servitude had represented their only hope of reaching the colonies. Thus, James Patton, although an Ulster Presbyterian like most of his predecessors, represented a different kind of Irish emigrant: one whose parents had sufficient means to afford passage-money for at least one of their unmarried sons but whose lack of additional capital, highly marketable skills, or close relations in America precluded immediate entry into a farm or business and instead necessitated years of hard labor before the goals of "independence" and family reunion might be achieved.

James Patton was born on 13 February 1756 in the parish of Tamlaght Finlagan, in the barony of Keenaght, near the shores of Lough Foyle in west County Londonderry. In 1766 Tamlaght Finlagan had about 3,900 inhabitants, a large (but declining) majority of them Presbyterians[2] who combined farming with extensive involvement in the linen trade—centered locally in nearby Newtown-Limavady, on the main coach road from Belfast to Londonderry city. Of "poor, but respectable parentage,"[3] Patton's father was a Presbyterian tenant farmer, probably on the Limavady estate, who fathered at least 10 children (James was the third oldest of eight sons) before three years of bad health, culminating in his death when James was 14, plunged the family into poverty. For the next 14 years, Patton lived at home, "learned the Weaver's trade, and worked at it for about five years," to help support his mother and siblings. However, in 1781 the Limavady estate changed hands[4] and the rents were increased, which, Patton wrote, "together with the many difficulties laboured under in Ireland, induced a wish on my part, to try my fortune in some other part of the world." One of Patton's brothers joined the East India Company, but James obtained his mother's consent to emigrate to the United States, "for the purpose

1. See chapters 18 and 20. 2. For demographic data on Tamlaght Finlagan parish and its environs, see appendix 2.1a, on chapter 33. 3. This and subsequent quotations are from Patton's memoir, written in March 1839 and subsequently published, initially in 1845 (Racine, Wisc.) by his son William, as *Letter of James Patton, one of the first residents of Asheville, North Carolina, to his children.* 4. In the mid-1830s, the Limavady estate was owned by Robert Ogilby, Esq., of Dungiven, Co. Londonderry, but much of it was held (on perpetually renewable leases) by middlemen who sublet to tenant farmers who in turn frequently sublet to cottiers. In 1876 James Ogilby of Dungiven owned 2,087 acres, valued at £604, and the representatives of R. L. Ogilby of Newtown-Limavady held 9,735 acres, valued at £3805, all in Co. Londonderry.

of procuring the necessary means of bringing herself and family to this land of liberty, where we would no longer feel the oppression of haughty landlords."

In early summer, 1783, Patton traveled to the seaport of Larne, on Ulster's east coast, and took ship for Philadelphia, hoping that his "virtue and good conduct" would give him "a passport to the highest stations in [American] society." However, by the 1780s the Cumberland Valley of Pennsylvania, where Patton first resided, was long settled by earlier generations of Scots-Irish and German immigrants: land prices were high and wages low, especially in the years immediately following the Revolution, and although Patton found friends and employers among a network of second- and third-generation Ulstermen in Pennsylvania, he had no close relations there who could advance his interests. Nor had his Irish experiences prepared him for American farmwork, which, at age 28, he found physically difficult as well as unremunerative. Consequently, it took Patton six years of unremitting labor, in a variety of skilled and unskilled trades, before he could overcome poverty, sickness, disappointment, and—as he admitted later—his own dissipation; could embark on a new entrepreneurial career that in time would secure his fortune; and could fulfill his promise to send for his mother and siblings. Decades later, aged 84 and prosperous, Patton penned a lengthy "letter" to his children, recounting the story of his early trials and eventual successes. Ultimately inspired by the Calvinist urge to self-examination, and modeled—consciously or unconsciously—on John Bunyan's *Pilgrim's Progress* and Benjamin Franklin's *Autobiography*, Patton's memoir is didactic, moralistic, and self-serving, as well as being written from hindsight. Nevertheless, its first pages (reprinted here) provide an intimate, detailed account of the travails and temptations that Irish immigrant laborers faced, and sometimes failed to surmount, in late eighteenth-century America.

James Patton Memoir, 1783–1789

> . . . I embarked at Lairn,[5] in the County of Antrim, on the 4th day of June, 1783, and landed at Philadelphia on the 3rd day of August following. When I left Ireland, my mother furnished me with two suits of clothing, two dozen shirts, and other things necessary, so that I would be enabled to save all the money that I might make; calculating that I would return in two years and bring them to America, but sickness prevented the execution of this plan. After I landed, I remained in Philadelphia ten days; I then left my chest and clothing at the house where I boarded, and went into the country to the house of a Mr. Green (a Quaker) fifteen miles from the city: the first night, I recollect, that he observed to me—"If thee have as good luck as thy countryman Robert Kerr,[6] thee will do well. He rented a small house at an early day in

---

5. **Lairn**: Larne, Co. Antrim; spelling indicates Scots pronunciation (rhymes with **cairn**).   6. **Robert Kerr**: between 1769 and 1780 Robert Kerr of Middle (later Mulberry) Ward, rose from an untaxed shopkeeper to a property-owner whose holdings were valued at £19,000, on which he was taxed £68 12s. (in inflated Pa. currency). In 1782 his property was valued at £202. However, the lists suggest that Kerr's rise owed at least as

Philadelphia, and worked at hard labour on the streets, and now, by his perseverance of himself and his wife, he owns nearly a whole square[7] in the city." He made many other observations, which occur to my mind, when I am lying on my bed. I told him, that I came to this country for the purpose of amending my condition in life, and that I would try to do so. The remarks of Mr. Green, together with my own observations, soon convinced me that the Americans were not composed of Lords and Dukes and belted Knights, (as Burns says).[8]

The next night I went to the house of Mr. Green's son, and undertook to clear out a small piece of land for him at the end of a field; and not being acquainted with such work, I hurt myself so much the first day, that I was not able to do anything the next. Mr. Green mentioned, that the work could be done in two or three hours, but as I knew nothing about it, I could take no advantage of the grubs,[9] and therefore I spent the whole day at it. From this I went to deliver a letter which I had promised, and then engaged to weave for some time with a Mr. Chafin; during the time I was here, an Englishman (a Tinker)[10] came along; he asked me, what I stopped[11] here for? and told me to quit the place; intimating some unfavorable things respecting the people; accordingly, I left Chafin's and went to a Thomas Wilson's[12] and wove some time for him. During that winter, I worked at different kinds of business, but principally threshing. The Americans at this time were generally poor, having been stripped of almost everything by the British during the Revolutionary War, consequently the price of labor was very low.

Not being afraid of sickness, I went the next spring to the Delaware River, where hands were employed in embanking.[13] There I was attacked by the dumb ague[14] (as it was called in that country) and was sick for nearly twelve months; in consequence of which the small pittance I had earned, and the clothing my mother had given me, had all to go for Doctor's bills and board. When I became able to work again, I had nothing left but the clothes on my back, one shirt, and a dollar in my pocket.

I had boarded some time with a Mr. Shaw, a countryman of mine, and when I left his house, he took two horses and assisted me along the road for some distance. He

---

much to a fortunate marriage as to his own industry, for in 1780 he was also taxed £63 (in 1782 £3 2s.6d.) for "John Gansell's estate," valued in 1780 at £18,000 (in 1782 at £600), which probably was his father-in-law's property.   **7. square**: (in Philadelphia) block.   **8. Lords . . . Knights**: Patton's reference is to the fourth stanza of "For A' That and A' That" (1795), a poem by Robert Burns (1759–1796), the radical Scottish bard whose compositions, both in English and Scots, were extremely popular—for political as well as for aesthetic reasons—among Presbyterians in late eighteenth- and early nineteenth-century Ulster. The stanza cited by Patton reads: "A prince can mak a belted knight, | A marquis, duke, and a' that; | But an honest man's aboon his might, | Guid faith, he mauna fa' that."   **9. I could take no advantage of the grubs**: "I couldn't get the better of the roots" (i.e., "the task of getting the roots out defeated me").   **10. Tinker**: a transient, often a craftsman who mends pots, kettles, and other metal household implements.   **11. stopped**: stayed.
12. Thomas Wilson: a Quaker of Irish birth or descent.   **13. embanking**: confining the flow of a river by building stone or earthen mounds or dykes.   **14. the dumb ague**: malaria.

inquired where I was going? I told him I was going to Canada, that my mother had told me, she had an uncle and brother in that country, who had become rich; and that I would endeavor to find them out.[15] But this was not my real motive. I was really afraid that nothing awaited me but misery and poverty, and that news would reach Ireland that I was in a most destitute situation, and being naturally of a proud spirit, I wished to go where I would not be known by any person. My health was at this time so bad, that I was unable to do anything for myself; but thanks to the great and mighty God! I had a mind that enabled me to surmount all difficulties. When Mr. Shaw left me, I went off the roads into the woods, sat down by an oak tree, and gave vent to a torrent of tears.

Just reflect on my situation at this time: a stranger in a strange land, an ocean rolling between me and every relation I had on earth, without a friend to advise or protect; health precarious and funds exhausted; misfortunes seemed to thicken around me and in whatever direction I would turn my head, I could see nothing but misery staring me in the face. My situation was truly disconsolate,[16] but the Lord was my strength and my shield,[17] and to Him I ought ever to be thankful for strength of mind capable of supporting me under such severe trials. That night I went to the house of Mr. John McCall, on the Susquehanna River (a countryman of my own),   he treated me kindly and would have nothing[18] for my lodging, but wished me to stay some days with him; he had seen me at Mr. Shaw's and knew that I was sick. When I left his house, he advised me to go to a Mr. James Patton's (a namesake of mine) and live with him until I would recover my health; I accordingly went and found him to be a very friendly man, but he had a young wife of whom I did not form so good an opinion.

At this time I had but one dollar, and as I could not travel long on that, I went to a canal that had been commenced on the Ball Friar Ferry on the Susquehanna River;[19] there I engaged to work, and got into a mess[20] of eight men—old soldiers, and the very refuse of the army. It was very disagreeable to me to associate with such people, and therefore applied to the employer for a part of the canal that was clear of rocks, and not so difficult to work; I got an Irishman to join me. We worked at it for three months and boarded ourselves. During the summer I enjoyed tolerable health, with the exception of three weeks, and worked about[21] in different parts of the country.

I was advised to go to some moral and orderly part of the country; but it will appear from what follows, that I had not done with[22] misfortune yet; on my way to the

---

15. to find them out: to discover their whereabouts.   16. disconsolate: gloomy.   17. the Lord was my strength and my shield: Psalms 28:7: "The Lord is my strength and my shield; my heart trusteth in him, and I am helped: therefore my heart greatly rejoiceth; and with my song will I praise him."   18. would have nothing: refused to take anything (in reimbursement).   19. a canal . . . : Maryland's Susquehanna Canal: chartered in 1783, but in 1803 only eight miles were open for navigation.   20. mess: a company of persons of the same employment who are assigned to eat together; the term is most familiar in its use by the armed forces.   21. about: here and there, up and down.   22. had not done with: was not finished with; see chapter 65, n. 20.

section of country I had in view, I stopped at a Dutchman's house in York County, Pennsylvania, and it then being in the winter, I engaged to work for him for three months at a guinea[23] per month. I dug a well for him, 52 feet in depth, in a very short time. When I first went to his house, I handed him all the money I had, except three dollars. Calculating that he would return the same when I wanted it, and also pay me for my labor like an honest man. One night when I returned from work, he and others were throwing dice and drinking: he kept a public house[24] and would always give me spirits when I came in from work. He proposed to me to join their party, and that he would be my partner, and thought it would be a money-making business; I refused, and told him that I knew nothing about gambling. He said that it was not gambling, that his little son could do it as well as a man. He gave me some more liquor (that wily destroyer of the human race), which had the desired effect, and I took my chance among them. He and I were fortunate for some time: at last luck changed (as gamblers say) and I lost all. Too late I discovered that they had two sets of dice, and instead of those we commenced with, they had a set of their own which threw up twelve at every throw. I then found out that my partner had been acting the scoundrel, in connection with the others. It almost deranged me to think that I had lost all my hard-earned wages, by the influence of drink, and by the persuasion of a villain in whom I had placed confidence. I accused the company of cheating me. We all became angry, and consequently an affray took place: fearing nothing in my then distracted situation, I took up the tongs and paid some of them in hard coin;[25] the balance of the night I passed without sleep. When we went out to work the next morning, the Dutchman's son appeared disposed to amuse himself at my expense, and I thought proper to give him a little of the same sort of change, and I told him to go and tell his father what I had done.

I then left the house: having the character of a faithful laborer, a great many persons wished to employ me. From this, I went to Yorktown,[26] Pennsylvania, and set into work with an honest Dutchman (Phillip Kissinger,[27] a brickmaker by trade), and remained with him during the spring and summer;   during the time I was with Mr. Kissinger, two young Irishmen came to the brickyard on their way to a canal on the Potomac River;[28] they urged me to go, and said that I would get two dollars per day. I was flattered with the prospect of speedy gain, and requested Mr. Kissinger to let me off, as I had but about six weeks to stay with him; he refused, as I suited his business,

---

23. guinea: 21 shillings (English).   24. public house: inn, tavern, or hostelry (usually licensed).   25. paid some of them in hard coin: "some of them earned very dearly the (re)payment they received from me." 26. Yorktown: York, seat of the county of the same name, had 2,076 inhabitants in 1790.   27. Phillip Kissinger: brickmaker and German Lutheran, in Spring Garden township, York Co.; in 1799 an organizer of the county's Democratic-Republican party; in 1814 elected an overseer of the county almshouse.   28. a canal on the Potomac River: in 1785 the Potomac Company began constructing a series of five short canals, eight miles long, around the falls above Georgetown.

but at last agreed, on condition that he could get hands in the place of another Irishman and myself; he got hands and let us go. We got fixed for the journey and made a start. We stopped in Yorktown to take a parting glass with our countrymen and some others, and they all drank freely; it was almost daylight before I could get them off. We had gone but a few miles from town, when they all laid down to take some sleep by the side of the road; I sat there like a wild goose watching, while the flock would be feeding. This put me to thinking. I asked myself, if this was the kind of company I ought to keep? No, said I!—I will part from such people, and accordingly the next morning started to the Canogege settlement,[29] a rich section of country about 150 miles from Philadelphia, and settled by a moral and orderly people.

I had now been in America about three years, and through sickness, misfortune, and one imprudent attempt at gambling, I had very little more than when I landed.[30] . . . In the Canogege settlement, I made my home at a Mr. Walker's, an excellent man and a member of the Presbyterian Church. He was very kind, and would always let me have a horse to ride to preaching with himself and his wife. He would often laugh at me, and say, "Jimmy, you will be a rich man yet! Never mind, Jimmy, you will be a rich man yet." Said he, "The grandfather of that young man (alluding to a young lawyer), came to this country a very poor man; he had as much money when he landed as bought a bed and a cow in Philadelphia. He placed his clothes on the cow's back, and milked her at night." He also said, that his own father, Mr. Dickey and many others were in the same situation when they came to America. I first cleared ten acres of land for Mr. Walker, and agreed to wait for the payment until he could make it out of the first crop of wheat which he raised on the land. I made my home at his house for three years and worked about in the country, at various kinds of business, such as blowing rocks,[31] digging wells, &c. . . . [32] [F]or a great portion of the time I worked in this part of the country—I got only about 26 cents per day; a hand in the harvest field could not get more than 31¼ cents per day. This shows that the price of labor was very low at that time. I made it a rule to be always employed, and for three years was scarcely ever seen anywhere except at my work or at Church.

I soon discovered the difficulty of clothing myself decently, and making money merely by hard labor alone; I would therefore try to make a little besides[33] when an opportunity offered. I once bought one hundred bushels of rye from a man who

---

29. the Canogege settlement: i.e., the Conococheague settlement, in Franklin Co., Pa., where James McCullough had settled ca. 1750, just south of James Magraw's Shippensburg. Several of the family names mentioned by James Patton (e.g., McCall, Patton, Stoner) also appear in Magraw's letter and McCullough's journal; see chapters 19 and 21.   **30.** Omitted: Patton's story of how, eight years later, when he was an affluent cattle drover, he revisited Coffield, the former employer who had cheated him at gambling, and found him in poverty, with "no way of supporting his wife and two children, but by her making straw hats and he selling them."   **31. blowing**: blasting.   **32.** Omitted: Patton's account of a later visit to the Walker family; apparently Walker and his wife hoped that Patton would marry one of their daughters; however, he wrote, "I had commenced trading and it did not suit me at that time."   **33. besides**: in addition.

needed some money and had it distilled, the distiller giving me six quarts and a pint for every bushel I delivered at the mill; I made something by this speculation. I also bought a field of wheat of a man who wished to move away; it was covered with snow when I bought it; in the spring it looked very yellow, and Mr. Walker would laugh and tell me, I was cheated, although he knew better at the time.

When the wheat was ready to cut, the neighbors and their daughters came, and assisted me. They brought plenty of everything to eat, and I had plenty of rye whiskey, of which I gave them freely. The wheat was ripe two weeks sooner than any in the neighborhood, on account of its being sowed on slate land.[34] I had understood that there was a premium offered in Baltimore for the first load of good new flour that might be delivered in that market, a premium for the second, and also a premium for the third, and I was determined to compete for one of them. The neighbors were all anxious that I should be successful, and Mr. Dickey had his mill put in the best kind of order by the time my wheat was ready. I had it cleaned and ground as soon as I possibly could. I hired a young man to haul it, and agreed to give him something extra to hurry him, but he was so slow in his movements that I lost the premium by about one hour. The neighbors were much mortified that I did not get it, and ridiculed the young man very much for he could have gotten there in time, if he had pushed his team.

I had worked hard and used great economy, and all I had at the end of the three years that I had lived in the Canogege settlement was two hundred dollars. In the meantime I kept myself decently clothed, which I always would do, if I had nothing left. From the long spell of sickness which I had—the effects of which I can feel to this day—I was unable to work constantly at hard labor (for I could eat no strong diet), and therefore concluded that I would turn my attention to some other business.

Patton's decision to foresake the physical and moral dangers of canal labor for the stability and domesticity of the Conococheagues was probably crucial in determining his fate in the New World. In autumn 1789, inspired by an ambitious, entrepreneurial spirit—perhaps first imbibed in west Ulster's highly commercialized Foyle Valley but certainly encouraged by the thrifty, market-oriented farmers of settled Pennsylvania—James Patton invested his $200 in dry goods and launched a career as an itinerant trader, eventually a wealthy merchant, in the North Carolina backcountry.[35] In his life and his memoir, Patton would not only replicate the rags-to-riches story of Robert Kerr, whose example had been held before him by his first American employer, but in the process would help transform both the reality and the image of the Scots-Irish in the United States—from crude, hard-drinking subsistence farmers, frontiersmen, and laborers to industrious, pious members of

---

34. **slate land**: land in which the topsoil is underlain by slate or stone (usually connotes "poor" land). **35.** See chapter 43.

a rising middle class. As a result, by the middle of the nineteenth century, the intemperance and turmoil that often characterized laborers on American canals and other worksites would be associated almost exclusively with Irish Catholic immigrants, not with Ulster Presbyterians such as James Patton.

34 ❋

Thomas McMahon, William Sotherin, and John Justice, 1789–1793

In the 1780s and 1790s, Irishmen and -women comprised over half the European immigrants to Philadelphia. Despite the decline of indentured servitude, and although Scots-Irish artisans and would-be farmers still predominated, growing numbers of "new Irish" were poor, Catholics, or both. Certainly, most new arrivals quickly left Philadelphia, yet it appears that a larger minority, among both the skilled and unskilled, were settling in the city (and in other seaport towns), continuing an urbanizing trend that had begun after 1763 and became more pronounced after the Revolution. Thus, a surname analysis of city directories for Philadelphia—as well as for New York and Baltimore—suggests that between 1785 and 1805 a quarter to a third of their populations were of Irish birth or extraction, still chiefly Ulster Presbyterians but increasingly diverse. Among unlisted and unestablished new arrivals in boarding houses—and among poor journeymen, apprentices, day laborers, and servants, generally—the Irish share would have been larger and would have included more Catholics from Ireland's southern provinces, as well as from the north. However, although urban opportunities for employment and even upward mobility were considerable, given Philadelphia's rapid growth and, after 1791, the infusion of federal tax expenditures, so also were the dangers of joblessness and poverty, especially for newcomers who lacked kinsmen or patrons in the New World.

In the 1780s and 1790s, an estimated 10 to 15 percent of Philadelphia's white population was both poor and largely Irish—the latter congregating especially in the city's Southwark and Northern Liberties districts. After the Revolution, Philadelphia society had become increasingly stratified, and the polemics that accompanied the Federalists' removal of the nation's capital to that city in 1791, and their dismantling of Pennsylvania's radical unicameralist government there after 1790, placed the newer Irish in the firing line of an antipopular resurgence. To be sure, some pre-Revolutionary Irish immigrants—largely but not exclusively Ulster Presbyterians, such as John Dunlap and the Caldwells[1]—comprised part of the city's new postwar élite. Class, and class-and-ethnicity, lines were not frozen; nor were sectarian divisions among the Irish as rigid and volatile as they would later be-

---

1. See chapter 11 and chapter 58.

come. Yet even the achieving "new Irish"—ambitious tradesmen and master craftsmen—felt excluded. And poor, recent arrivals suffered from prejudice as well as economic insecurity at the hands of the governing mercantile and professional classes—many of whom, as one new immigrant complained, regarded a "Hibernian" as "an Obnoxious being."[2] Between 1796 and 1798 (admittedly, during the height of Federalist hysteria over "wild Irish" fugitives from revolutionary Ireland), nearly two-fifths of all those found guilty of crimes by Philadelphia's mayor's court were Irish-born, although natives of Ireland probably comprised only about a tenth of the city's population. Indentured servitude and its abuses, low wages and casual employment, harsh antidebtor laws (requiring imprisonment and self-maintenance therein), penal provisions against breaches of apprenticeship or journeymen conditions, a legal system presuming guilt among the Irish, and a generally distant and at times hostile social situation: all these conditions had characterized urban life among poor Irish Catholics, and even poor Protestants, in the pre-Revolutionary colonies. The three petitions in this chapter—and those in the following essays—demonstrate that such problems and prejudices persisted long after 1776.

In the absense of effective or humane provisions for public poor relief, in 1790 Mathew Carey[3] and other "respectable and influential"—if not quite élite—Irish Philadelphians created the Hibernian Society for the Relief of Emigrants from Ireland. The Society enabled poor migrants, increasingly arriving without kinfolk or "connections" in America, to seek aid within the bounds of an ethnic community that was broadly defined to include all the Irish-born, regardless of religion. It also allowed poor newcomers to avoid the city's almshouse—a fifth of whose inmates were Irish-born in the early 1800s[4]—as well as official scrutiny and native contempt. However, the Society itself had paternalistic and moral functions, as Carey and its other officers interviewed ship captains concerning the immigrants' "character" and, like the agents of official and Protestant charities, sought to distinguish between the deserving and undeserving poor. After all, Carey ascribed his own success to "inflexible honesty, unceasing industry, and rigid economy"—the virtues he had imbibed from his father, a respectable Dublin manufacturer—and in Philadelphia he boasted of always paying his debts "in good season" and of having never "entered a tavern . . . in a single instance for the [sole] purpose of drinking."[5]

The Hibernian Society required poor Irishmen and -women to make personal appeals for assistance. This system demanded a certain deference, and petitioners quickly learned to emphasize their diligence and sobriety, as well as their national origins and desperate circumstances, in order to win immediate relief or the support of patrons who could further their ambitions. The following petitions, sent to Carey in his capacity as secretary of the Society, are published here together because of their brevity and because they exemplify the range of obstacles that faced Irish newcomers who were alike in their distress but diverse in back-

2. Patrick Morgan, Philadelphia, petition to the Hibernian Society, 17 December 1796. **3.** On Carey (1760–1839), also see chapters 14, 44, and 63. **4.** See Peter O'Connor's 1797–1798 letters to Carey from the Philadelphia almshouse, in appendix 3. **5.** M. Carey, *Autobiography* (Brooklyn, 1942), 1–2, 24–25, 42; also cited in McAleer, "'Civil Strangers,'" 199; see Sources, this chapter.

grounds and skills: Thomas McMahon, an unemployed artisan from Dublin and probably a Catholic; William Sotherin, a bankrupt shopkeeper imprisoned for debt, whose name suggests Leinster origins and Hiberno-Norman or even Huguenot stock but whose children's burial records indicate he too was Catholic;[6] and John Justice from Munster, religion indeterminable, a servant or laborer enticed to Philadelphia and then cut adrift by a "Gentleman from Cork," probably after the latter's own speculative enterprises had failed.

Petition 1.

Thomas McMahon, Philadelphia, to Mathew Carey, Philadelphia, 21 February 1791

Sir

I hope you will excuse the liberty I take in writing to you but the necesety of my case & haveing no friend in this City Obliges Me to it   I am from Dublin which place I left the 25th day of march last by Trade a Hosier   unfortunate for me the<y> wont trade in this City as there is no work but for the summer Season[7] & then the<y> can earn little more than clears there Board <and> of course can lay nothing up for these times,[8]   hearing of your goodness & readiness to Serve your Country men emboldend me to apply to you,   if you would be so good to procure me any decent employ you will relieve the distresͭ

yͬ Hum͟b Servͭ

Feby 21ˢᵗ 1791—   Tho͢s MͨMahon

will call for Answer any time you Appoint

Petition 2.

William Sotherin, Debtors' Prison, Philadelphia, to Mathew Carey, Philadelphia, March 1791

M Carey   Sec'ry to the Hibernian Society
Sir,

As the Institution to which You are Chosen Sec'ry is Established for the Relief of Your Fellow Creatures, and as None Stands in More Need off assistance than

---

6. According to the indexes to the Tithe Applotment Books (1821–1826) and to Griffith's Valuations (1850–1854), in the Public Record Office of Northern Ireland, Belfast, and the National Library of Ireland, Dublin, the rare surname Sotherin (Sotheran, Southern, Sothern, etc.) was most frequently found in Co. Wicklow, less often in Queen's and King's counties. On 4 September 1789 and 12 August 1790, two unnamed children of "William Southern" were interred in the burying ground of St. Mary's Catholic church in Philadelphia; Southern's payments for their burials of 7s 6d and 10s, respectively, indicate that he was not then in dire financial difficulties.   7. the<y> wont trade . . . as there is no work but for the summer Season: "they (i.e., hosiers) won't [be able to] get regular trade (i.e., business, employment) . . . because work is available only in the summer season."   8. clears there Board: pays for their food and lodging; can lay nothing up for these times: can save nothing for the winter months (e.g., February, when McMahon wrote his petition).

Myself—Having the Honor to be a Hibernian—I flatter myself I can lay Claim to Your Assistance which the Institution You have Established Convinces me of Your Goodness & Humanity, and fills me With the Greatest Veneration for all that worthy Society. Unavoidable Events lays me under the Necessity of Applying to Your Goodness and to hope that You as Well as the other Gentlemen of the Society will use Your Influence with the Judges of the Court of Common Pleas to give me a hearing <before> this Court, that I may Be Enabled By my Industry to Endeavour to Support a Wife and three Small Children who Have been labouring—Under the Greatest distress Immaginable this Nineteen Months Past (the Time I have been Confined)—and having a Claim upon Every Member of that Society—One of Whose Pillars is Benevolence & Charity, That I flatter my Self You will use Your Influence to Obtain My Releasement——

It is Objected on the Part of my Creditors I have been Guilty of Fraud—But as I and Many others Conceive this Objection Cannot be Supported, as I can Assure You its without the least Foundation—and having Made Every Overture[9] to my Creditors that Was in My Power—But in Vain—as I am Still in Confinement <with> No Possible Means of Relief—without Your Friendly Assistance which Joind to that of His Excellency the President Gov. Mifflin, Bishop White, Revd Doctors Hellmot & Pilmore &^{c} Cannot fail of Having the Desired Effect.[10]——Nothing Gentlemen Can give You a More Striking Idea of My Distress and Inability to Pay My Creditors than the Necessity my Family Labors Under and Was it Not that the Overseers of the Poor Messrs Robt Wharton, W. Malory &^{c} had undertaken to Support them, Certainly they Must have perished[11]   At the foot[12] is a list of My Creditors, with whom I wish You Also to Use Your Influence.—and beg leave to Subscribe Myself with Respect——

Sir,

Debtors Apartment	Your Most Obd^t Servt
Philad^a March 1791	William Sotherin

Benjamin Fuller—
Mordecai Lewis & Co.   } Creditors[13]
John Nixon—

---

9. **Overture:** proposal, proposition, offer (with a view to negotiating a settlement).   10. **Gov. Mifflin, Bishop White, Revd Doctors Hellmot & Pilmore:** in 1791 Thomas Mifflin (1744–1800), a former member of the Constitutional Convention, was governor of the state; and the Rt. Rev. William White, D.D. (1748–1836), was bishop of the Episcopal Church in Pennsylvania. In 1791–1793 Rev. Henry Helmuth, D.D., was professor of German at the University of Pennsylvania and minister of St. Michael's German Lutheran Church at 60 N. Fourth St.; and Rev. John B. Pilmore was minister of the Third Presbyterian Church on Pine St., between Fourth and Fifth sts.   11. **Robt Wharton, W. Malory:** no information can be found on Malory, but in 1785–1793 Robert Wharton was a flour merchant and grocer at various locations; in 1803 he was an alderman of the city.   12. **foot:** bottom (of the page).   13. **Benjamin Fuller . . . Mordecai Lewis . . . John Nixon:** in 1791 Benjamin Fuller (d. 1799), a native of Cork, was a merchant on 162 South Front St.; Mordecai Lewis was

Petition 3.
John Justice, Philadelphia,
to Mathew Carey, Philadelphia, no date [1789–1793]

The petition of John Justice a Native of Ireland,

Humbly Sheweth

That poor petitioner is under the necessity of imploring relief,   The case is as follows   That petitioner being brought over here by a Gentleman from Cork, and [14] meant to do for me as I understood, <but> when we came here he told me he had no further occasion[15] of me, and desired me to go and provide for myself, which accordingly I was obliged to do, which I thought very hard after his promise to me before we came away,   Now I am left here without either friend or Relation house or home, nor no place of residence,   Your goodness on this occasion to help me to some little employment for a livelihood shall be ever Remembered, And poor petitioner shall for ever Pray   John Justice

Unfortunately, we cannot determine what, if any, actions Carey and the Hibernian Society took in response to these pleas. However, fleeting evidence suggests that Carey did aid John Justice and Thomas McMahon. In 1794 and in 1798 Philadelphia directories list Justice at various addresses as a maker of ceramic pipes and chimney pots, and by 1800 he had promoted himself to house- and sign-painter, resident at 79 Race Street. Moreover, the same year Philip and Joseph Justice were listed separately as house carpenter and plasterer, suggesting that John, once established, had brought his kinsmen to the city and helped direct them to skilled trades during a decade when artisans' wages peaked, in 1798, at nearly $2 per day. As for Thomas McMahon, between 1793 and 1802 city directories list him as a stocking weaver (with Hugh McMahon, also a stocking weaver and perhaps his brother, in 1793). Although that trade was one of the city's least remunerative, in 1800 McMahon was one of only four stocking weavers in Philadelphia, and between 1803 and his last entry in 1808, directories list him in Elmsley's (or Elmslie's) Alley as a "stocking manufacturer," which may indicate a rise to employer status. William Sotherin's fate, however, is unknown. Unfortunately, no city directories were published during the years immediately prior to his imprisonment in 1789, and he does not appear in the lists subsequent to 1791. Given that his creditors were three of Philadelphia's most influential

a merchant at 112 South Front and a director of the Hand-In-Hand Fire Insurance Co.; and John Nixon (1733–1808), of Irish descent, was an alderman and a director of the Bank of North America. In 1793 Lewis was a director of both the Bank and of the Philadelphia Library, and Nixon was the Bank's president. Both Fuller and Nixon were members of the Friendly Sons of St. Patrick, and Nixon was at this time president of the Hibernian Society. On Nixon, also see chapter 58.   **14. and**: Justice means to write "who" ("who, as I was given to understand, intended/proposed to provide for me"—i.e., "employ me **here**" [in Philadelphia]"). **15. occasion**: use, need.

citizens—and that one of them, John Nixon, was a director of the Hibernian Society!—
Carey may have found it impolitic to intervene on Sotherin's behalf. We can only speculate that, unless he died in debtors' prison or during Philadelphia's yellow fever epidemic
of 1793, Sotherin probably fled the scene of his embarrassment and moved west or returned
to Ireland.

35 ✳

James Doyle, 1789

At least after Benjamin Franklin's earlier years, printing in colonial America was an
indigenous and self-sustaining trade. Yet from the 1740s there was a significant trans-
atlantic migration of Irish printers, appraised of the latest London fashions and techniques.
Some emigrated from Ulster, including Hugh Gaine (1726–1807), founder in 1752 of the
New York Mercury (from 1768 the *New-York Gazette, and Weekly Mercury*), and William
Dunlap (d. 1779) of Philadelphia, uncle of the John Dunlap who became printer to the
Continental Congress.[1] The great majority, however, came from Dublin—the British em-
pire's second city and publication center—as did James Doyle and his more famous coun-
tryman, Mathew Carey.

Most Irish immigrant printers were journeymen, seeking higher wages, steadier employment, and greater opportunities to achieve the status of master printer—all of which
were declining in Ireland during the 1780s, when Dublin's journeyman printers' union
complained that the city was flooded with "improperly trained" journeymen and apprentices from country towns. Hard-pressed by fierce competition and high taxes on imported
paper, the capital city's master printers reduced costs by hiring such workmen at wage rates
significantly below those in Dublin, London, or America. Facing frequent unemployment
or, at best, poor wages for working days that averaged more than 12 hours, Irish journeymen organized collectively but also emigrated individually, responding to the dramatic
growth in the late eighteenth century of America's publishing industry.

Political circumstances often hastened or colored Irish printers' migration overseas.
Beginning in the 1760s, the sharp polarization of Irish political journalism meant that for
Dublin's printers there was often little distinction between voluntary emigration and forced
exile. Perhaps the most celebrated fugitive was Charles Lucas (1713–1771), whose "patriotic" essays obliged his flight to France in 1741.[2] Yet another was Mathew Carey himself.

---

1. William Dunlap, born in Ulster, was a printer and bookseller in Lancaster, Pa. (1754–1757), Philadelphia
(1757–1766), and Barbados (1766), before he went to England, became an Anglican clergyman, returned to
America, and served as rector in Stratton Major (1768–1778) and Hanover (1778–1779) parishes, in Virginia,
before his death in 1779. On John Dunlap, see chapter 11. **2.** On Lucas, see chapter 52.

In 1784 the threat of official prosecution for publishing his radical *Volunteer's Journal* prompted Carey's departure for Philadelphia, where the Marquis de Lafayette's financial assistance enabled him to establish the *Pennsylvania Herald,* followed by his *Columbian Magazine* and the *American Museum.*

James Doyle's letter to Mathew Carey, although written a year before its recipient founded the Hibernian Society, indicates that by 1789 Carey had already become a sort of American mentor to nearly all Irish immigrant printers—and to Belfast Protestants as well as to Dublin Catholics such as Doyle. However, although Doyle had actually worked for Carey in Ireland, he apparently owed his start in the United States to the Dunlap network, for his American-born employers—Francis Childs and John Swaine, publishers of the New York *Daily Advertiser* (established in 1785)—had been William Dunlap's apprentices and, in consequence, may have felt some obligation to Irish journeymen. Moreover, during the 1790s Childs's and Swaine's two newspapers (in 1792 they took over Philip Freneau's *National Gazette* of Philadelphia) were harshly critical of "silk and satin" Federalism, and their sympathy for the French Revolution and for the emergent Jeffersonians cut them off from government printing contracts and forged a natural affinity with Irish radicals such as Carey and Doyle.[3]

After the American Revolution, the new nation's printing and publishing trades had expanded at a tremendous rate. Between 1786 and 1796 the number of printers in Doyle's New York City rose from 15 to 68, in Carey's Philadelphia from 37 to 81, and between 1790 and 1800 the number of American newspapers increased from less than 100 to more than 230, although most survived for only short periods. Thus, during the 1780s Philadelphia had merely 19 newspapers, whereas in the 1790s the city boasted no fewer than 42! Nevertheless, Doyle's letter suggests that his own position was rather tenuous. In America as in Ireland, wider markets coupled with precarious finances obliged the owners of printing shops to expand their workforces and cut labor costs by employing poorly trained and underexperienced "half-journeymen," runaway apprentices, and foreigners with questionable qualifications. Apparently, one of Doyle's New York workmates—the "boy of the name of Patten"—accused him of fitting at least one of those descriptions, perhaps (Doyle implied) to divert attention from his own bad record. Clearly, Doyle's situation was already too marginal to allow such accusations to pass unchallenged. For although he claimed to be an all-round printer-compositor, Doyle worked for Childs and Swaine as a mere pressman—the hardest and most monotonous job in an age of hand presses (before steam and cylinder presses came in the mid-1820s)—and in 1789 his weekly salary was at the bottom of the printers' scale of $5 to $10. Thus, wage levels, quality of work, and permanent employment were all at stake in Doyle's plea that Carey verify his "Character" and refute Patten's damaging allegations as to his lack of experience and training in Ireland.

3. On Carey's political opinions and affiliations in the late 1780s and 1790s, see chapter 63.

The exploitation of printers in post-Revolutionary America engendered the earliest examples of strikes and union formation—in Philadelphia in 1786 and 1788, respectively—and in 1794 Doyle's fellow journeymen formed the New York Typographical Society. However, Doyle's style was less confrontational. Without patronage from master printers, journeymen's opportunities to advance were few—and for an Irish Catholic immigrant probably even less. Hence Doyle turned to his established countryman, coreligionist, and former Dublin employer, and sought to ingratiate himself with Carey by referring to the latter's Irish friends and enemies—favorably in the case of John Magee, proprietor of the radical *Dublin Evening Post,* and sarcastically with respect to John FitzGibbon (1748–1802), the attorney general who had prosecuted Carey and who, in 1789, was elevated to the peerage as a reward for his implacable opposition to reform. Even more pointedly, Doyle associated his own persecutors with Carey's chief American adversary, Col. Eleazar Oswald of Philadelphia, the anti-Federalist editor of the *Independent Gazetteer,* with whom Carey, who had championed ratification of the U.S. Constitution, fought a near-fatal duel in 1787. Finally, perhaps Doyle's most effective appeal was the remark that his "Yankee" workmates were "by no means fond of the Irish." And, indeed, it is probable that anti-Irish Catholic prejudice played a major role in Doyle's troubles with Patten (whose name suggests Scots-Irish origins), as they had in the English-born Oswald's attacks on Carey. In short, Doyle's concerns reflected no mere office quarrel but went to the heart of his—and Carey's—economic and political survival in the intimate yet rancorous, even dangerous, late eighteenth-century world of transatlantic printing.

James Doyle, New York City,
to Mathew Carey, Philadelphia, 17 October 1789

New York, Octr 18th 1789,——

Dr Sir,

I am inclined to think you may be surprised to receive the letter I wrote you the other day,[4] but Sir, I shall beg leave to inform you of the reason of my taking the liberty of troubling you, and I am induced to hope your goodness will excuse me,——I am at present employed in the Office of Messrs Childs and Swaine,[5] to work their News Paper at Press,[6] for which I receive a Salary of 5 Dollars ⅌r Week,   In the same office is a man or rather aboy of the name of Patten, who was apprentice to Mr Pritchard,[7] but ran away from him, and as I am informed,

---

4. **the letter I wrote you the other day**: Doyle's previous letter to Mathew Carey has not survived.
5. **Childs and Swaine**: Francis Childs (1763–1830), born in Philadelphia, where he was apprenticed to Dunlap, was a printer and bookseller in New York (1785–1796; in partnership with John Swaine in 1791–1794), where he published the *New York Daily Advertiser* (1785–1796); in Philadelphia (1795–1796); and in Vermont (1803–1830). John Swaine (b. 1762?); died in November 1794, in New York City.   6. **to work their News Paper at Press**: to work as a pressman at their newspaper.   7. **Mr Pritchard**: William Pritchard (or Prichard), bookseller and printer in Philadelphia (1782–1791, 1797), New York (1795–1796), and Richmond, Va. (1796–1809).

stole a Quantity of Paper from him at different times and otherwise behaved in every respect as abad apprentice,   this fellow Sir, is a strenuous supporter of M[r] Oswald[8] with whom I understand you had some difference,   the day of the Date of my first letter, a Conversation arose in the office relative to the Volunteer's Journal, and the Proprietors of it<,> and on my declaring that you was the real owner and Sole Proprietor of it, and giving as a reason for my knowledge of the same, my being employed on said Paper, he made answer and said that you were only aPartner, and also asserted that He was informed that I never worked on said Paper, and also that I never served atime[9] to the Business, and on my saying that you and M[r] Rice[10] could prove I did, and could also give me a Satisfactory character[11] as having always behaved myself and lived genteely,[12] he said he would lay two Dollars that neither of you knew me,   I have accordingly closed the Bet,[13] and in Presence of the Office wrote the letter you have received and also agreed that your answer should be read before them employed in said Office,   I also informed him I would request of you to wait on[14] M[r] Pritchard and M[r] Hall[15] and get a Portrait[16] of his Character during his Continuance[17] in their Service, which D[r] Sir, I would ever be thankful to you if you would be so kind as to do, and also send it with your kind answer to me as directed,——I am exceedingly sorry to be under the necessity of giveing you this trouble, but such language tho' it cannot be in any respect hurtful to me, yet it might be made aSubject of derision not very agreeable,—My Character from M[r] Louden[18] where I worked before I came to M[r] Child's, is unexceptionable and he was sorry I left him,   My Character also from M[r] Child's both as to knowledge of business and behaviour, will be found the same,   But Sir, the Prevailing number of our hands are Yankees who are by no means fond of the Irish,——I saw in the Promotions in Ireland[19] your friend Fitzgibbon is highly advanced, and by alate Dublin Evening Post, I see Magee and the Sham Squire are at great variance,[20]   I hope soon to be in Philadelphia when I shall

---

8. M[r] Oswald: Eleazer Oswald (1755–1795): born in Falmouth, England; emigrated to New York, where he was apprenticed to John Holt, printer, whose daughter he married; served in the American Revolution; published the *Maryland Journal* in Baltimore (1779–1781); the *Independent Gazeteer* in Philadelphia (1782–1795); and the *New-York Journal* in New York City (1785–1787); served as officer in the army of the French Republic (1793–1795).   **9. served atime**: served a term as apprentice.   **10. M[r] Rice**: John Rice: probably born in Dublin; bookseller and/or printer in Philadelphia (1784–1796); in Dublin (1796–1803); in Baltimore, Md. (1803–1805); and again in Philadelphia (1805–1806).   **11. character**: character reference.   **12. genteely**: in a respectable way.   **13. closed the Bet**: concluded, agreed on the terms of, the wager.   **14. wait on**: call on.   **15. M[r] Hall**: Parry Hall (1755?–1793): printer and bookseller in Philadelphia (1785–1793), in partnership with William Pritchard in 1787–1791; see n. 7.   **16. Portrait**: description.   **17. Continuance**: tenure.   **18. M[r] Louden**: Samuel Loudon (1727?–1813): born in Ireland; ship chandler in New York City (1760–1772); bookseller and printer there from 1773 until his death; published the *New-York Packet* (1776 in New York; 1777–1783 in Fishkill, N.Y., during the British occupation of New York City; and in 1783–1792 again in New York); and the *Diary* (1792–1795 in New York).   **19. Promotions in Ireland**: notice or list of Irish government promotions (published in the newspaper).   **20. are at great variance**: are having a great dispute. Doyle here refers to Magee's oftimes hilarious conflicts with John Scott, Irish lord chief justice and later earl of Clonmell, derided by his detractors as the "Sham Squire"; like FitzGibbon, Scott was an enemy of press freedom, political reform, and Catholic emancipation.

JAMES DOYLE

do myself the Pleasure to wait upon you,   I seen Mr Devan afew days since,[21] who informed me Mrs Devan and M^r & Mrs Donovan were gone to Ireland,   I believe poor Mrs Devan was sorry she ever left it,——I request you may remember me to Harry Rice and until I hear from you I remain Dr Sir

> Your's &c &c——
> James Doyle,

P.S. If you have any business to do in this town,
I Shall be happy to do it for you, if directed as Per
first letter,——Mr Gay informed me you were in Town
lately and I was very sorry I did not see <you>,——Adieu,——

It is uncertain whether Mathew Carey responded to Doyle's plea for assistance. In the early American republic journeymen printers were highly mobile, moving from city to city, state to state, in search of work. Likewise, despairing of advancing to master printer by traditional means, or of improving their lot through collective action, they often turned to speculative publishing of books or newspapers—for although riskier than job- or contract printing, speculative publishing offered chances for greater, quicker rewards, especially if they could appeal to a specialized but profitable market. Thus, it is likely that the humble petitioner of 1789 was the same James Doyle who in the spring of 1790 took over the Georgetown, Maryland, *Weekly Ledger* from Alexander Doyle (perhaps his kinsman) and in 1792–1793 published *The Potomack Almanack* and, for his fellow Catholics, *The Pious Guide to Prayer and Devotion*—thus emulating Carey's own success as a publisher of Catholic Bibles and other religious works. Unfortunately, Doyle disappears thereafter—perhaps he died in one of the decade's frequent yellow fever epidemics—leaving only a tantalizing glimpse of an articulate Irish artisan coming to terms with the craft, ethnic, and political rivalries of American printing.

36 ✳

Stephen Fotterall, 1791

Like Francis Burdett Personel,[1] Stephen Egan Fotterall was a runaway indentured servant whose background made him ill-suited for—and resentful of—hard labor and who spent time in an American jail. Unlike Personel, however, Fotterall found influential friends, won release from both prison and his master, and ended his career not on the gallows but as a leading member of the Hibernian Society, which had aided him.

Fotterall, the son of James Fotterall and Mary Blakely, was born in Dublin, on 4 July 1772. His religion is unknown, but his surname (usually Fottrell and very rare in Ireland)

---

21. since: ago, past. **1.** See chapter 32.

was held chiefly by propertied Catholics of medieval English descent in the province of Leinster; thus, although in his petition Fotterall claimed to come from Belfast, this may have been in deference to the preponderant Scots-Irish composition of Philadelphia's Irish and their aid societies.[2] Despite his youth, Fotterall allegedly served in the British army in Dublin, and perhaps it was a wish to escape the army that persuaded him, in 1788 and at age 15, to bind himself to a shipmaster for a five-year term of indentured servitude in the United States, where his immediate expectations of genteel, urban employment were bitterly disappointed.

When Fotterall arrived in Philadelphia, indentured servitude there was in steep decline, in part because the post–Revolutionary War depression severely afflicted the city's master craftsmen, formerly the largest urban employers of indentured servants. Thus, although in 1732 bonded servants had comprised over a third of Philadelphia's workforce, between 1775 and 1800 that proportion declined from 13 to only 1 percent. This shrinking urban market for indentured servants, increasingly replaced by free workers such as John Justice,[3] helps explain why Fotterall's services (like Daniel Kent's)[4] were sold to a master in rural Pennsylvania, where laborers were relatively scarce and, if free, comparatively well paid. It was also Fotterall's misfortune to tangle with one of Pennsylvania's more powerful families: the Hubly clan was one of the most prominent in Lancaster borough; and between 1783 and 1787 Adam Hubly—a wealthy merchant on Philadelphia's Water (later Front) Street, and a relative of Fotterall's master—was a member of the state's executive council. Perhaps this (plus Fotterall's alleged Belfast origin) was why Fotterall addressed his petition not to Carey, the Hibernian Society's secretary, but to its more influential president, Thomas McKean, of Ulster parentage and then Pennylvania's chief justice and its future governor.[5]

> **Stephen Fotterall, Philadelphia, to the President of the Hibernian Society, Philadelphia, 15 June 1791**
>
> To the President of the Hibernian Society
>
> The Humble Petition of Stephen Fotterall A Native of Ireland &[6] was Brought up in Belfast in the Countey of Antrim, Setting forth that your humble petitioner was in the mont\<h\> of April in the year of our Lord 1788 advised to come to America by Captain Blair then commander of the Ship, Rising Sun, then belonging to Gurney & Smith Merchants in Philidelphia who promised if I would Bind Myself for five Years to him

---

2. According to the surname indexes compiled for genealogical researchers, by the Public Record Office of Northern Ireland and by the National Library of Ireland, from the Tithe Applotment Books (1825–1835) and from Griffith's Valuation (1850–1864), the name Fotterall (Foterall, Fottrell, Fotheral, etc.), although very rare generally, was then most commonly found in counties Kildare, Dublin, Meath, and Queen's in Leinster, much less frequently in counties Down and Cavan in Ulster. **3.** See chapter 34. **4.** See chapter 23. **5.** On Thomas McKean (1734–1817), see chapter 55, n. 42. **6.** &: "who."

that he would put me in Gurney & Smiths Office to Act as a Clerk in the Office which I verry readiley Embraced against all my Relations endeavours to hinder Me at which time your humble petitioner was onley Fifteen year Old, but when I came here to my utmost Disapointment I was Sold to a Mr Hubley who Lived at the Middle Ferry on Schuylkill, when I found I was So ill used[7] by Captain Blair that I did Not know what to Do, for I Lived with the utmost discontent for two years & three months Never been[8] used to Such buissnes as I had for to doe there which time Mr Hubley canot say but I behaved[9] both faithful & Honest to him,

About the 14th or 15th of Last September Mr Hubley Sent Me To Philidelphia to pay a sum of Money to the Bank which Sum I paid and Gote a Receipt for the same and returned home to the ferry & then I was sent in with ten dollars Cash & to receive a Sum to add to it, which time I took the oppertunitey of leaving him and sending him a Letter to acquaint[10] him that I was a Goeing[11] to try to get home to Ireland and that I would Remit him what he had Lost by me which was the Rema<in>ing part of my time[12] & ten dollars Cash of his that I took with me he paid fifteen pounds penselvenia Currensy for my time at first after I had made my escape from him I went to Baltimore and their was neve<r>[13] a vessel bound for Ireland and I went from there to Norfolk in Virginia and their was no vessel there for the vessel that I was to goe in was at Norfolk but had Sailed, after I arrived at Norfolk I got into an office as a Clerk and Stayed ther for Eight Months and in that time I Remited Mr Hubley fifteen pounds pens^a Curr^y[14] thinking that it would satisfy him for my time having lived with him for better than two years and promised to remit him more when I could afford it—Mr Hubley after Receiving the fifteen pounds was Not Satisfied but Said he would Not Give up my indentures till I paid Some more to him, but Sent Me a Receipt for the money he had received in the followin Manner—

Received the 13th of December 1790 by the hands of Mr Hales Richardson Fifteen pounds penny^y Curr^y On Acc^t. of Stephen Fotterals time he had to Remain with me £15.0.0

At the expiration of the Eight months I came back to philidelphia supposing that the Receipt was a sufficient discharge and after I came here I went out to see Mr Hubley Expecting that he would give up my indentures but instead of that he employed a

---

7. **ill used**: badly treated.   8. **been**: i.e., being (spelled as pronounced).   9. **but I behaved**: "that I did not behave."   10. **acquaint**: inform (OED, s.v., 6.b; latest citation, 1775).   11. **a Goeing**: a rare example in writing of the prefixed present participle with an active meaning; cf, Shakespeare, *Love's Labour's Lost*, 1.1.96: "the spring is near when green geese are a breeding." The BE + a + ——ing construction enjoyed a great vogue in the nineteenth century, and became a hallmark of rural Southern American English. Because of its regional distribution in the U.S., the pattern has been regarded as originating in Ulster; however, it seems to have rapidly flowered and as rapidly withered in northern Ireland, leaving little trace. See chapter 47, n. 27. 12. **time**: contracted term of servitude.   13. **neve<r>**: not; Ulster English regularly replaces **not** with **never** in the past tense: "You ate my ice cream." "I never."   14. **pens^a Curr^y** (below **penny^y Curr^y**): Pennsylvania currency.

Constable and Sent me to Gaole which place I now Remain being Commited here as a Run away Servent, and having No friends nor relations in America to assist Me in my Distress I was advised to Petition the Hibernian Society which I am acquainted[15] is errected[16] for the Relief of Irish Emigrants, and your petitioner hoping you will take his case into Consideration and be So kind as to assist him in his Distressed Situation and hopeing you will Let me have an answer to know what my Distressed situation will come to[17]

Philidelphia Gaol   }   Stephen Fotterall
June 15ᵗʰ 1791

Apparently, Carey took up Fotterall's moving yet politically awkward case; perhaps the fact that Adam Hubly was Carey's neighbor on Front Street, and that both were associated with the popular politics of the old state constitution, enabled Carey to win Fotterall's release. In any case, Fotterall was a fortunate youth. In 1745–1746 four-fifths of the Irish servants bound in Philadelphia could be located later in the city's poor relief or tax deferment records; for them, Irish servitude had led only to Irish-American poverty. By contrast, Fotterall's subsequent career was positively meteoric. About 1794–1795 he married Catherine Coutance (1775–1845), a widow, perhaps with money, for in 1796 city directories list him as a shopkeeper in partnership with several associates. Although Fotterall was careful to take the naturalization or loyalty oath, to forestall the Alien and Sedition Acts (1798), he rose to influence as the Federalist political tide receded and as most Irish Philadelphians combined to support the Jeffersonian Republicans. In March 1798 Fotterall was elected ensign of the Light Infantry Company, Third Philadelphia Regiment, and from 1801 through at least 1806 he was ranking officer of the Southwark Light Infantry, the militia unit of the city's premier if poor Irish suburb, and an associate of such key city Irish as General John Shee and William Duane[18]—who later became an executor of Fotterall's estate.

During the War of 1812, Fotterall held the colonelcy, in succession, of two regiments of Philadelphia troops, and from 1819 to 1821 he served on the excecutive committee of the Hibernian Society. In his later decades, Fotterall was a shipping merchant at 224 Vine Street, and when he died at his residence, the old Cormac mansion at the corner of South Third and Union streets, on 26 September 1839, aged 67, he left a remarkable estate of

---

15. acquainted: informed; see n. 10.   16. is errected: has been established.   17. what my Distressed situation will come to: "what will be the outcome of my distressed situation."   18. John Shee (d. 1808): born in Co. Westmeath, Shee emigrated with his father and brother ca. 1742–1745, settled in Philadelphia, and engaged in shipping as Walter Shee & Sons; supported the Revolution and commanded the Third Pennsylvania Regiment (1776–1777); was appointed member of Pennsylvania's Board of War (April 1777); was Philadelphia city treasurer (1790–1797); was appointed Philadelphia port collector by President Jefferson; and was an Anglican (albeit of native Catholic origins) and (in 1771) an original member of Philadelphia's élite Friendly Sons of St. Patrick and, after the Revolution, of the Society of the Cincinnati. ¶On William Duane (1760–1835), exiled Irish radical and Democratic-Republican journalist and politician, see chapters 38 (esp. n. 45), 63, and 64.

$38,840 to his wife, two sons, three adopted grandchildren, and numerous other relatives. However, Fotterall had lived high: his household furniture alone was valued at $5,531, his horses and carriage at $600, so that, unsurprisingly, most of his estate (as much as $28,900) went to settle outstanding debts, mortgages, and funeral costs. Thus, through political and trade connections, this once-exploited Irish indentured servant had managed to reproduce in Philadelphia the self-indulgent lifestyle of late eighteenth-century Dublin's more prosperous merchant-gentlemen.

37 ❋

Charles O'Hagan and Mary Dunn, 1796

Mary Dunn, the last of Mathew Carey's supplicants included in this part, was an impoverished Catholic—albeit allegedly of "respectable" and "industrious" parentage—who emigrated from County Londonderry about 1794, according to the following appeal on her behalf by Charles O'Hagan—also from County Derry, judging by his claim to know her family.[1] Unfortunately, almost no information can be discovered to corroborate O'Hagan's account of Mary Dunn's plight, but, if true, it provides fascinating evidence on several topics: the beginnings of domestic service among unmarried Irish Catholic women in America—at a time when the wages in Philadelphia for such work were merely $1 per week; the manner in which female subordination to fathers and brothers and their household needs could actually enable young women to break the traditional injunction against their migrating separately;[2] and the poverty into which unestablished and unmarried spinster immigrants could fall in late eighteenth-century America. For in the late 1700s and early 1800s, two-thirds of those seeking shelter in Philadelphia's almshouse were females, as were a third of its Irish-born inmates, and—as with Mary Dunn—the latter's distress usually stemmed from a combination of illness, poorly paid or no employment, and the absence (through death or desertion) of the husbands or other male relatives on whom they had depended.

> **Charles O'Hagan (on behalf of Mary Dunn), Philadelphia, to Mathew Carey, Philadelphia, 5 February 1796**
>
> Lambart St.[3] Fber 5th 96
>
> Dear Sir
>
> As a man of Philanthropy, I sollicit you in behalf of the Bearer Mary Dunn (a

---

1. According to the indexes to the Tithe Applotment Books and to Griffith's Valuation, in the early and mid-1800s the names Dunn (or Dunne) and O'Hagan were most common in the Co. Londonderry baronies of Tirkeeran and Loughinsholin. However, the two baronies are far distant: the former is in the northwestern part of the county, adjacent to Derry City, whereas the latter is in southeastern Co. Derry, bordering on Lough Neagh. On emigration and population change in both baronies, see appendices 2.1a, on chapter 33, and 2.1b, on chapter 3. **2.** For another example of Irish single-female emigration through dependence on familial networks and needs, see chapter 6. **3. Lambart St.:** Lombard Street.

Catholic)   She is the daughter of respectable parents in the County of Londonderry
N: of Ireland of middling Circumstances a numerous family being of them,[4] and a
brother of the Bearer's a Docter some years ago came to this Country and was doing
very well till about 3 years ago he broke loose[5] and led since a dissipated life,   he
wrote for the bearer to keep house for him, thro' which[6] She unfortunately prepared &
came over ab^t two years ago, but to her double mortification found that he co^d not
receive her agreeable to his encouragem^t, & her expectations,   She always was but
tender in health, but rather than starve She was forced in her languishing state to go to
Service, that She w^d acquire one part of the time by her insupportable Struggles
<what> was required to afford her barely a sustenance of nature whilst confined to her
bed another part of the time, till now at length[7] She is no longer capable to use any
more efforts of Industry &c— Thus forlorn, healthless, Oppressed in Spirits and
destitute of means to Support herself, has no other alternative but to return home, if
She co^d——

But understanding the Hibernian Society (of w^h I hear you are a member) will not
assist any to return, I take the Liberty of recommending her to you, truly represented,[8]
that you may from your wanton[9] clemency divise some means thro' your influence that
might assist her much desired ret^n[10]   if a private Collection co^d be raised to pay her
passage She w^d leave it in your hands till her passage w^d be agreed for in the first Vessel
for the North of Ireland—It is y^r humane Character that emboldens her to apply and
me to write to you on a Subject so momentously feeling—God will reward your
laudable interference in heaven & can only be acknowledged on earth by the
Applicant—

I am on a Slender acquaint^{ce}

Sir Yours most Respectfully

Charles O Hagan

P:S:

If a certificate[11] is necessary She can procure it;
only that I am myself struggling with wind
& tide, endeavouring to pay a great rent &c and
Support a family on a very Slender footing, I
w^d not hesitate to pay her passage, from

---

4. **a numerous family being of them**: the syntax is un-English and may reflect underlying Irish usage (perhaps
something like **agus líon ti mór a bheith ann acu** "there being a big family of them").   5. **broke loose**:
departed from social conventions, deviated from moral restraints, "went to ruin" (perhaps implying bankruptcy,
among other conditions).   6. **thro' which**: as a result of which.   7. **to go to Service, that . . . till now at
length . . .** : This complicated phrase may be best understood as follows: "to enter domestic service, in which
employment she was able, through great effort, to earn a bare subsistence for part of the time, but the rest of
the time she was confined to bed (with sickness), until finally now . . . "   8. **truly represented**: truthfully
portrayed/described.   9. **wanton**: unrestrained, extravagant; however, the writer may mean *wonted*
"accustomed."   10. **ret^n**: return.   11. **certificate**: recommendation, reference, "character."

the long knowledge of her good behav[r] & the

respectable Character of her industrious parents

In 1796 a Charles Hagan was listed in Philadelphia directories as a scrivener or copyist. This may have been Mary Dunn's petitioner, for in the eighteenth century Irish Catholics regularly dropped the "O" in their surnames, except on those rare occasions—as when addressing Carey—when emphasizing native Irish origins might prove beneficial.[12] According to the directories, Hagan's business was "between 102 and 103 Race Street"—probably the address of a street stall, which in turn suggests he may have written Mary Dunn's letter as much for profit as for philanthropy. On 20 February 1798 he became an American citizen, five days before Stephen Fotterall,[13] in the rush of naturalizations at the Pennsylvania Supreme Court (controlled by the Jeffersonian Irish leader Thomas McKean)[14] to avoid the requirements of the new Aliens Act. Perhaps by 1800 O'Hagan had won his struggle against "wind & tide," for that year's directory listed him (with the "O" restored—a sign of greater prosperity and confidence) as a grocer at 169 Lombard Street, but his absence in subsequent directories may indicate that his victory was only temporary.

However, although these few records rescue O'Hagan himself from total obscurity, his account of Mary Dunn and her scapegrace brother cannot be verified and, in some respects at least, may be questioned. As a result of eighteenth-century penal legislation (only recently repealed) in both Ireland and the American colonies, Irish Catholic doctors on either side of the Atlantic were rare, even after the Revolution.[15] Likewise, it seems most unlikely that all Philadelphia city directories of the 1790s would have omitted Mary Dunn's brother if he were a physician—even one in decline and dissipation, as O'Hagan alleged. On the other hand, Dunn's sibling may have been one of those few Catholics who somehow had studied medicine in Dublin or, as was more common, in Europe. In addition, O'Hagan did not state specifically that the doctor resided in Philadelphia; his failure elsewhere may have driven his sister back to her probable port of entry and the nation's largest Irish Catholic urban community. Yet there were established Dunns in Philadelphia—such as Benjamin Dunn, the wartime privateer, and Thomas Dunn, door-keeper and messenger to Congress in 1796–1800—who might have aided her. Indeed, in 1791 (before O'Hagan's client allegedly immigrated) there was even a Mary Dunn living in Southwark, the district of the Irish poor. Perhaps this "spinster" (as she was listed) *was* O'Hagan's client, fallen on hard times for reasons that were best disguised from Carey and that forfeited sympathy from her own relations in the city. Perhaps O'Hagan was stretching the truth, or inventing information, to help the daughter of an old friend.

---

12. Or when functioning in exclusively "Catholic" circumstances, for on 29 December 1794 a child named Sarah O'Hagan, probably the 1796 petitioner's infant daughter, was buried at St. Mary's Catholic church, Philadelphia, at the cost of 10d.   13. On Fotterall, see chapter 36. O'Hagan applied for naturalization on the same day as Samuel Brown, the glazier from Belfast in chapter 38.   14. On McKean, see chapter 36, but especially chapter 55, n. 42.   15. See chapter 50.

Apparently, Mary Dunn never made it home to Ireland, dying instead in Philadelphia in early September 1796, only seven months after O'Hagan petitioned on her behalf.[16] Unfortunately, we will never know her own version of her travails, for in 1796 convention (and perhaps illiteracy) prevented Mary Dunn from telling her story to Carey, and today we can only see her as the helpless (and innocent) victim whom O'Hagan sought to portray. Nevertheless, the very anonymity of Mary Dunn, by contrast with her lowly male benefactor, itself sheds light on the origin and character of early unmarried Irish women's migration to America.

38 ✳

Samuel Brown, 1793–1815

The world of the urban artisan in the early American republic was dynamic but precarious, as the traditional household system of production steadily eroded before the advance of the subcontracting, putting-out, and factory systems. Recent research indicates that only one of every three journeymen eventually achieved independent status as a master craftsman or shopkeeper, while the rest remained mere employees, their ambitions thwarted and livelihoods reduced by poor pay and the steady fragmentation and deskilling of their crafts. Conventional wisdom suggests that recently arrived immigrant artisans would be doubly disadvantaged. In this era of early American industrialization, however, craft skills and business acumen learned in Irish cities were often superior to those of the native-born. Thus, the knowledge and experience gained in Belfast, rather than family connections in Philadelphia, may best explain the success of Samuel Brown—his rise from glazier and house-painter to contractor and tea merchant—although once established, his own modest prosperity drew a steady stream of relations across the Atlantic. Indeed, after the second Anglo-American conflict of 1812–1815, as Philadelphia became the epicenter of a new postwar Ulster immigration, the examples of men like Samuel Brown played a major role, showing that by skillful use of fairly limited education and capital, at least a few immigrant artisans could not merely outflank the proletarianizing tendencies of early American industrialization but even rise above them.

Samuel Brown was born around 1770–1775, perhaps in Ballymena, County Antrim, although obviously he learned his trade in Belfast, in the family business apparently owned (at least from 1793) by his brother David, to whom he wrote nearly all his surviving letters.

---

16. On 13 September 1796 a Mary Dunn was interred in the burying ground of St. Mary's Catholic church, Philadelphia. We surmise that she was the subject of O'Hagan's petition, although another Mary Dunn was also buried at St. Mary's on 7 November 1797. Neither woman was interred in a pauper's grave, as someone paid $4 for each burial.

In 1813 Thomas Humphry's *Irish Builder's Guide* condescended from its Dublin perspective that although Belfast's buildings lacked adornment, thanks to their purchasers' proverbial parsimony, "[n]o town in Ireland produces better bricklayers, stone masons, . . . plasterers, plumbers, glaziers, painters and smiths, or men who will execute a pile of buildings in less time."[1] The Browns' painting and glazing business was in Mill Street, which, although not downtown, ran eastward into High Street, the old city hub that reached the wharfs, and westward into Belfast's industral Lagan Valley hinterland. On either side, Mill Street looked north and south to expanding streets, brickyards, and small businesses. This combination of trade and place prepared Samuel Brown and his almost equally successful brother, Thomas, to make the most of their opportunities in the New World, for when Samuel emigrated in late June 1793, Belfast and Philadelphia—both centers of Irish Presbyterian society and politics—were at similar stages of economic development and were remarkably alike in physical appearance and architectural styles.[2] Thus, in his first letter from America to his brother David in Belfast, written in December 1793, Brown did not decry novelties in Philadelphia's building or window design: the plain Georgian brick fronts and six- to twelve-paned windows were quite familiar—only details, not basic tasks were distinctive— and during the next two decades the city would become even more like Belfast with the adoption of the Anglo-Irish terrace or row house method of house construction.

Nevertheless, Samuel Brown's venture to America was not without great initial hardships. After embarking from Belfast, his ship ran aground, sprang a leak that rendered "our Bread . . . scarsely sufficient for Dogs,"[3] and had to be repaired in Derry city before proceeding to Philadelphia—where he arrived in the midst of the worst yellow fever epidemic in the city's history. It was no wonder, then, that at first Brown strongly considered returning to Belfast by the following autumn, after the summer's construction work in Philadelphia was over—a common pattern of seasonal migration, judging from his letter, among Belfast artisans in American seaports.

Letter 1.
Samuel Brown, Philadelphia,
to David Brown, Mill Street, Belfast, 23 December 1793

Philadelphia   Dec[r] 23rd 1793

Dear Brother
    I take this opertunity of Wrighting you Afew Lines to Lett you know that I am

---

1. Cited in J. C. Beckett and R. E. Glasscock, eds., *Belfast . . .* , 74; see Sources, chapter 38. 2. In 1800 Belfast had about 20,000 inhabitants, Philadelphia 41,220 (and including its industrial suburbs—Kensington, the Northern Liberties, and Southwark—about 66,600). For additional demographic data on Belfast, see appendix 2.1c, chapter 38. 3. Samuel Brown, "Lough Sooly" [i.e., Lough Swilly], Londonderry, Co. Derry, to David Brown, Belfast, 28 June 1793.

in good health at Preasent thanks be to god and hopeing these Lines Will find you and My sister And the Children Injoying the seam[4] as is My Ever sinser Wish—

D[r] David I hope you[5] not think me Neglectfull not Wrighting to you Sooner for the times hav been So very Disagreeable sins I Came hear I Detianed[6] to give you as full account of this Cuntry as possable   I had avery Good passage of Eight Weeks and two days With out the Least sickness on the passage   there Was a feavour aboard but Not mortal   Wee Landed at New Castle[7] on the Eight Day of September on account of a Feavour that Prevealed[8] in Philadelphia   Thomas Stewart and Tho[s] Smyth and I thought it better to Detain there for a few days to[9] Wee Could Hear a better acount[10] of the sickness Which I think was Very fortunate for us only that I took A Feavour Which Continued for Near Four Weeks   I Would Seen[11] more of this Cuntry only on that acount[12] for the feavour Was so shocking in Philadelphia   I stoped[13] there for Eight Weeks Which Cost Me ten Guineas With out[14]—I Came to this Sitty on the 7th of Nov[b] Which Was Nearly the end of the Sickness   When I got the acount of So many of My aquentanses being dead Shocked me Verry Much[15]   amongst these Was M[r] Faulkner and Andrew Sprouls Carpenter and W[m] Campble Stone Cutter & Medole the Beaker[16] and Russal the Plummer and John Morrow Cabnit Meaker and A great Nomber two numerous to Mention   the Number in Whole Died[17] from the first of Agust to the 15th of Nov[b] is Concluded to be 6500 People   this sitty is Verry Much hurted by the Sickness and is thought by many it has a chance to[18] brake out against[19] the Spring   it has Spoiled all Kind of Trade   there has numbers Left the sitty on Acount[20] and not Coming back to after Spring   I should not Came here only on the acount of the Lead I brought[21]   on our arival here <it> put me to a studdy[22] Whether to Leave the sitty or stay to Spring   Wee took a Room and shop But finding the Pay being so Very bad Wee thought better to Work For an Imployer Where Wee ar Paid Every Week   the Room Wee Keep only so that if sickness apears We Intend to Remove to New york[23]

---

4. seam: i.e., same.   5. you[l]: you'll (contractions, though certainly pronounced, occur rather infrequently in written form).   6. Detianed: i.e., detained "waited, delayed"; transposed spelling, with -ia- for-ai-.   7. New Castle: on the Delaware River, south of Philadelphia.   8. Prevealed: i.e., prevailed "was general."   9. to: till, until.   10. acount: i.e., account "report."   11. I Would Seen: i.e., I would have seen; other examples of the reduction of the auxiliary **have** to phonetic zero in this construction occur hereafter: **I should not Came** "I should not have come," **I Should been** "I should have been." See chapter 1, n. 22.   12. only on that acount: "except for that."   13. stoped: i.e., stopped "stayed, remained."   14. With out: without meals, washing, etc. (i.e., lodging only).   15. When I got the acount . . . Verry Much: a cross between two constructions: (1) "when I got the account . . . it shocked me very much" and (2) "the account . . . shocked me very much."   16. Medole the Beaker: i.e., McDowell (Ulster form) the baker.   17. Died: "who died."   18. it has a chance to: "it is very likely to"; Gaelicism (seans go . . . "chances are that . . . ").   19. against: toward.   20. on Acount: elliptical for "on that account."   21. the Lead I brought: i.e., to make paint and/or for window-glazing.   22. <it> put me to a studdy: "it caused me some doubt."   23. the Room Wee Keep . . . to Remove to New york: "we continue to live in the room (rather than getting something more permanent) so that we can (easily) move to New York if the epidemic breaks out again."

SAMUEL BROWN

305

This Sitty I Like Midling Well and has My health as Well[24] as I Ever had t<h>anks be
to god   our Weages is Five Shilling and sixpense ℔ Day Each   Wee both Fell to
Work In one shop[25] the third day after our Coming here   Imployers prices[26] here is
Very good In Peanting and glazing but Long Trust Gleasing[27] is Done here by the
pean[28] or Light acording to the size   the General Sizes is 10^l[29] by 8^l Which is one
shilling and 10^l by 12^l is 2^s and 9^l by 11^l is 1^s 6^d this Corrensy[30]   there is Larger Peans
so Large as 11^l by 20^l them is found[31] by the owner of the Building   I am Gleazing
a Large hous at Preasent for the Imployer and for Priming and Putty and Work
Manship 1^s 6^d ℔ Light or Pean   the Gleasers here is but Verry bad at the Buisness for
the<y> Both Peant and Gleaze   the Man that I work for is Verry Hapy he Mett With
Mee and I Believe Would find Me In Constant Imployment at the Gleazing onley[32]
but the summer time the Weages Is better   I beleive a Doller a Day is the
hig<h>est   Boarding is Very Dear from two dollers to three Pr Week   a doller is
7^s 6^d this Corensy   as for Carpenters Weages Jurneymen has from six shillings to a
Doller p^r Day from sun up to sun Down but by Peise Work the<y> Can Meake 10
Shillings ℔ Day[33]   there is three Months in the year that all Treads[34] is bad from
December to March——there is a Great Demand for Leabourers at a Kinall[35]   their
Weages in Winter is 4^s 6^d & 5^s ℔ Day Where you^l find some of your Verry
Respectfull[36] Irish men that you Would be sorry to see——Vittling is Dear   Beef is

24. has My health as well as . . . : "am in as good health as . . . "   25. Wee both Fell to Work In one
shop: "we both chanced to find work in the same shop."   26. prices: rates of pay.   27. Long Trust (=
Trussed?) Gleasing: meaning uncertain, but possibly one of the various systems of fitting glass into the frame
(as, for example, the modern systems: British Challenge, Mellowes, Perfection, Invincible, etc.).   28. pean:
i.e., pane or (window) light.   29. 10^l: 10 inches.   30. this Corrensy: i.e., this currency "in American
money."   31. them is found: "those are supplied"; them: standard in Ulster dialect for "those" and followed,
because it is not a *personal* pronoun, by the singular of the verb (see appendix 1).   32. Would find Me In
Constant Imployment at the Gleazing onley: "would provide me steady employment doing nothing but
glazing."   33. by Peise Work the<y> Can Meake 10 Shillings ℔ Day: "by piecework they can earn 10s. per
day." Brown's reference to craftsmen earning higher income through piecework than through fixed daily or
weekly wages challenges conventional assumptions that piecework pay was inherently exploitive and imposed
by cost-cutting employers rather than (at least initially) welcomed and bargained for by the most skilled and
productive workmen. In his letter of 10 December 1810 Samuel Brown's recently arrived nephew, James, also
expressed a preference for piecework wages in his first trade, cotton weaving, but in a few decades masters'
reductions in the piece-rate pay would transform Philadelphia's largely Ulster-born cotton weavers into a
symbol of employer exploitation and working-class militance.   34. Treads: i.e., trades.   35. Kinall: canal
(spelling reflects Ulster pronunciation, the last syllable rhyming with standard English all); probably one of
Robert Morris's schemes to link the Schuylkill with the Delaware and Susquehanna rivers, projected in 1789
but a failure by the mid-1790s.   36. Verry Respectfull: very respectable; Brown's reference to the Irish canal
laborers as some of your Verry Respectfull Irish men that you Would be sorry to see is probably sarcastic,
likely a reference to poor Irish immigrant workers (perhaps specifically to Catholics), whose drinking and
boisterous habits embarrassed aspiring immigrants such as Brown and James Patton (chapter 33); conversely,
Brown's remark may be a lament that substantial farmers' sons from home were often reduced to day laborers
in America.

from 5^d to 8^d p^r Pound in Market   Butter is 1^s 10^d p^r Lb   Potatoes 6 Shillings ℔ Bushel   Mutton 5^d to 6^d ℔ pound and Milk by the Quart is 6   Beer by do[37] 8^d Porter by Do Bottled 11^d Spirits by the Quart 1^s 10^d out of the Stores and taverins 16^d p^r half pint   Oat Meal Here out of the stores is 11^d ℔ Quart   Shoes is from 8^s in the Market to 11^s:3 bespoke[38]——Meaking of Cloase is Dear   a Coat from 2 Dollers to 20^s Small Close[39] is 12^s Each——as for My part I heave not the smalles Right to dispise this Cuntry but I Know agreat Many Wishes to be in Irland again So from this you^l be a gudge[40] your self

Dear David

I hope as Soon as this Comes to hand you^l Wright To Me and Give me a full acount of Belfast and Lett me Know if your Treade is as good as before I Left you and if its Better I intend Coming Nixt faul if God spears Me health   I Received your Letter by Mr Irvin Which give Mee the Greatest Pleasure I Met With sins I Came here to hear your[41] all Well   you Wright to Me about Thos Steel and sinse I heave heard by Robert Longs Letter that he saw thomas Smyth and Thomas Steel In Baltimore   I amediatly Wrot to Robt Long to Lett thomas Steel Know that I Wished to See him not Mentioning Any thing that Would Provent him   Remember Mee to all My old aquenteanses and Lett Mr Smyth Know that Thomas Left Mee In new Castle In good health to go to his brother on acount getting no Work   he Was in tended[42] going hom this faul after seeing his brother but I find he has stoped in Baltimore   Remember me to Jack Mequillon and Peggy Bannin   I am sinserly your Afectnate Brother

Samuel Brown

Despite his early hesitations, Samuel Brown settled permanently in Philadelphia. In 1806 and 1808, city directories listed him as a painter on Lodge and New Bank streets, respectively, but by 1810 he had established his home and business at 73 Chestnut, between Second and Third streets, close to the city quays and surrounded by the shops of other craftsmen and small merchants, where he resided for the rest of his life.[43] Sometime in the early 1800s Samuel's brother, Thomas, came from Belfast and established a grocer's shop just around the corner, on South Second Street. By 1810 their recently arrived nephew, James Brown—a cotton weaver who earned $10 a week until uncle Samuel took him into his painting and glazing business—was able to report, to one of his cousins in

---

37. Beer by do: "beer by ditto" (i.e., by the quart).   **38. bespoke**: made to order.   **39. Small Close**: i.e., small clothes "knee-breeches."   **40. gudge**: judge; for the spelling see **gaol** "jail," **Gorge** "George."   **41. your**: i.e., you're.   **42. he Was in tended**: i.e., . . . intended "he was resolved" (OED, s.v. intended, 3; archaic).   **43.** In 1795 Edmund Hogan's Philadelphia directory listed 73 Chesnut Street as the residence of another Samuel Brown, perhaps an older kinsman.

Belfast, that Samuel also "Caeps[44] a large tea Store . . . has four fine children . . . [and] is worth 4 or 6 thousand Dollars," while uncle Thomas Brown "is keepping a large dry good Store What you call a Cloth Shop at home."[45]

Samuel Brown's economic success in Philadelphia may be attributable in part to political connections, just as the prosperity of his family's firm in Belfast was linked to that city's Anglican patronage network, which secured brother David lucrative contracts to paint and glaze Church of Ireland and public buildings. Yet although the Browns' probable Anglicanism may explain brother Thomas's political conservatism—for example, his alleged support for the British during the War of 1812—the letters of Samuel Brown and his nephew James indicate they were ardent Jeffersonian Republicans.

Late eighteenth- and early nineteenth-century Philadelphia was stratified politically along social and ethnoreligious lines. During the 1790s the Federalists represented established wealth, gained primarily in transatlantic commerce, banking, and the professions, whereas the Republicans represented a coalition of rising men—lesser merchants and ambitious manufacturers, excluded from the Federalists' inner circles—with the city's "old working class," composed of smaller shopkeepers, master craftsmen, and journeymen. The Federalists also aligned Quakers, Anglicans, and others of largely English descent against Presbyterians, evangelicals, and secularists of Scots-Irish, German, and other backgrounds, led by Jeffersonians such as the Scots-Irishmen Thomas McKean and Blair McClenachan, the exiled Irish journalist William Duane (a convert from Catholicism), and the German-American physician Michael Leib.[46] Most Irish immigrants, whether Catholics like Mathew Carey[47] or Anglicans like Samuel Brown, also fit into this latter "democratic" group,

---

44. Caeps: i.e., keeps. The spelling indicates a pronunciation rhyming with **capes**, at odds with the expected form rhyming with **heaps**. Mainland Scots shows the expected form; the Ulster form attested here (and in other letters from Ulster) is an analogical innovation: thus, Standard English **leave** is to Ulster **lave** as Standard **beat** is to Ulster **bate** as Standard **keep** is to Ulster **kape** (or **cape**, here **caep**).   **45.** James Brown, Philadelphia, to James [Brown], c/o David Brown, Belfast, 10 December 1810.   **46.** On Thomas McKean, see chapter 55, n. 42. On Blair McClenachan, see chapter 63, n. 11. ¶William Duane (1760–1835): born of Irish Catholic immigrant parents in upstate New York (now Vermont), in 1765 Duane returned with his widowed mother to Clonmel, Co. Tipperary, where he apprenticed to the printing trade before moving to London. In 1787 Duane joined the East India Company and subsequently lived in Calcutta, where he edited two newspapers in which he praised the French Revolution and supported Company soldiers' complaints against their officers. Expelled from India in 1795, Duane returned to London and engaged in revolutionary politics until 1796, when he fled to Philadelphia. There he joined the staff of the *Aurora*, the city's major Jeffersonian newspaper, eventually married its owner's widow, and became the primary spokesman for Philadelphia's radical Republicans and Irish workers. After 1800 Duane, with the sometime congressman Michael Leib (1760–1822), led the ultrademocratic "Old School" or "Philadelphia" faction of the city's Republicans, but the lack of federal and state patronage from conservative Republicans, as well as the structural changes wrought by industrialization that fragmented Duane's "old working class" constituency, eventually eroded his and Leib's influence. In 1822 Duane sold the *Aurora* and embarked on a tour of the South American republics, whose independence he had long championed. After his return to Philadelphia, Duane revived his newspaper to support President Jackson's "war" against the Second Bank of the United States, but he eked out only a modest income until his death. Also on Duane and his political affiliations, see chapters 63 and 64.   **47.** On Carey, see chapters 14, 34, 44, and especially 63.

as confessional rivalries from the old country were largely overcome by a need for solidarity among those whom the city's Federalist élite disdained as "outsiders," "upstarts," and, comprehensively, "wild Irish."

In addition, Samuel Brown had emigrated in 1793, in the heady early years of the French Revolution, and probably he had imbibed the radical enthusiasm that swept much of Belfast's middle classes into the United Irishmen. By contrast, brother Thomas apparently left home after the 1798 Rebellion caused Anglicans to reemphasize their faith's traditional loyalism. Once in Philadelphia, the strongly democratic and masonic elements among the city's Jeffersonians (which probably included and advanced Stephen Fotterall)[48] may have alienated Thomas Brown—perhaps even from his own brothers, for Thomas complained to his nephew in Ireland that Samuel was "very unshosable" and that his siblings in Belfast never wrote to him.[49] Although prosperous on his own account, Thomas's economic gains never quite matched those of his brother. By contrast, Samuel obviously benefited, materially and politically, from his connections to Philadelphia's new Jeffersonian establishment of aspiring and successful "small men," and his own rise from the "hard Industry" of the artisan to the gentility of the tea merchant helps explain his enthusiasm by 1815 for his adopted country—and for its second war with Britain, which the city's Republicans supported so ardently.

Letter 2.

Samuel Brown, Philadelphia, to David Brown, Belfast, 12 March 1815

Philadelphia   March 12th 1815

Dear Brother David

    I take this oppertunity of Writing you a few lines hoping them to find you and All the famely in Good health and all my Brothers and Sisters   I hope you will Excuse my neglect of not Writing Sooner   you will not fail in giving my kind Love to all my Brothers and Sisters and there famelys   I have long Wished to hear from them   My famely all Enjoys Good health Except our oldes Daughter Eliza   She has been in Bad[50] health this two Years and Litle hopes of her living many Days unless a Change[51]   I was exceedingly Sorow[52] to hear of the Death of Sister Betty But god Who has the Rooling of all things and his Will must be Done[53]   We must not reflect[54] for What is Our Loss is theire gain   But While we ar in this trouble Some Worald While the almighty Spairs us and gives us Good health it is our Duty to Provide for our Children and live in fear of god that we when Called on be prepared for the Worald to Come When we Will then find all our Departed Relations in that

---

48. See chapter 36.   **49.** Thomas Brown, Philadelphia, to James Brown, Belfast, 7 December 1813.   **50. Bat** ms.   **51.** Eliza Brown died a month later, according to her father's letter of 25 December 1815.   **52. Sorrow:** i.e., sorry.   **53. God who has . . . must be Done:** cross between two constructions: (1) "God has the ruling . . . " and (2) "God who has the ruling . . . "   **54. reflect:** reproach, blame, "criticize."

Hapiness Which I believe all good Christians Enjoys   We have Lost two of our Children When young and has four Left the youngest a fine Little Boy of four years old Just got well of the Hoping[55] Caugh   I suppose you have heard I have Kept Tea Store[56] for Som time,   I have took James Brow<n> in Partnership two Years ago and he Does Very well and When I get him Perfectly acquaint with the Customers I intend giving him up[57] the Whole of the Painting   the Almighty has been Kind to me and although I have Wrought[58] very hard I Enjoy as good health as I Ever Did and I hope with Care and Attention to the Tea Buisness With What I have meade by hard Industry to live Without Working hard and Bring up our family genteel   I have been fortunate During the Late unfortunate War and although I never Wished for it I Was One Who allways Suported it in Money believing it to be the Be<s>t goviriment in the Worald   I purtched[59] During the Last nine months Which Was the time to try the friends of a Republickan Goverment thirteen thousand Dollars Worth of Stock at from 75 to 87 D[rs] for One Hundred and the Intrest Paid four times a year and is now at Near par   your Brother Thomas Keeps Dry good Store and having a Large stock on hand When the News of Peace Came fell one half in price Will Loose Much But he is Strongly Attached to the goverment of England Still believing the<y> Would Destroy Our Navy and Bring us to Make a peace on their own terms   he has been Disapointed   him and My Self Canot <a>gree on Politics   Had the War Continued Many years I Should been a looser in House Rents and Goverment taxes at Least four hundred Dollars ℔ year   this City has been more favoured than any other During the war   We Scarcely Ever feeled the War to[60] the English Burned the City of Washington if Worth Calling it a City but that Was a fortunate Day for this Country   than[61] the opisite Party[62] as is Called Joined us and With one Voice Every man Turned out in the City to the Amount of twenty Thousand   James Was amongst them and Marched from the City towards Baltimor Where the<y> Lay in Camp for 4 Months and Such as Stayed in the city turned out to Make fortifications not Less than fifteen Hundred to two thousand Daylie for two weeks, Even the Sabath Day, and One Day the Sons of Eran alone amounted to twenty five Hundred So that We bid Defyanc to all the men the<y> Could Send[63]   the Day the news Came that they Were

---

55. **Hoping**: i.e., whooping.   56. **I have Kept Tea Store** (and, hereafter, **your Brother Thomas Keeps Dry good Store**): Though readily understood, these phrases exhibit a rather peculiar construction not elsewhere attested in the letters presented in this compilation. They are clearly based on the ("incorporating") construction seen in **keep store, keep bar, keep house**, which normally does allow any specification of the kind of store, bar, or house, since the construction is meant precisely to convey a generic sense.   57. **giving him up**: "making over to him."   58. **Wrought**: worked (the normal form of the past and past participle in Ulster English).   59. **purtched**: i.e., purchased.   60. **to**: till, until.   61. **than**: then (Scots form).   62. **the opisite Party**: the Federalists.   63. **the Sons of Eran . . .** : on Sunday and Monday, 11–12 September 1814, some 2,550 Irish Americans, formally organized as the Sons of Erin, helped construct fortifications to protect Philadelphia against an anticipated British attack.

Defeated at Baltimore and Genl Ross[64] Shot was great Joy here   We have Lost many Valueable lives here But nothing to Compare With What the English has Loosed[65]   the<y> Must have loosed By Land and Sea not Less than from fifteen to Eighteen thousand men at the Whole Battle at New Orleans[66]   the<y> Acknoladged their Loss was five thousand nine hundred and not an officer Left to lead them <and> By a few untrained men With a few Bales of Cotton for Brestwork Piled up Hastely   an[67] the Whole I hope the English government Will find the<y> never Can Doe any thing With this Country When Every Man has His own property to Defend and fireside——Dear David I Remain Your

    Loving Brother   Saml Brown

Hannah and Children all Joins in Love to you and all the famely

Before their deaths in 1836 and 1851, respectively, Thomas and especially Samuel Brown assisted the emigrations from Belfast of several nephews and nieces in addition to the aforementioned James, who in 1817 became a full partner in Samuel's painting and glazing firm. However, the same spirit that, in business, kept Samuel Brown at one address from 1810 to 1851 also found expression in his cautious approach to would-be emigrants among his Belfast kin: "it is an old creed of mine never to insist on any one of my Relations to come here," Brown wrote to another inquiring nephew in late 1816, "But if they do come they shall not want a friend." In part, Brown's hesitation stemmed from the economic effects of immediate post-war recession—"this country is altred very much," he wrote, "all the young men that has come here lately would be glad they had not come here"[68]—but perhaps also by his knowledge that by this time Belfast's growth was beginning to outpace Philadelphia's.[69] Thus, whereas emigrants such as the Crocketts and Kerrs,[70] from mid- and west Ulster's declining rural economies, had no real alternatives to emigration, Brown's nephews could afford prudence and delay—especially when their ill-considered arrivals could strain his hopes of raising his own children "genteel." Indeed, the Browns' emotional distance—between Samuel and Thomas in Philadelphia and be-

---

64. Genl Ross: General Robert Ross, cocommander of the British forces that captured and burned Washington, D.C. (24–25 August 1814) and attacked Baltimore (12–14 September 1814), where he was mortally wounded.   **65. Loosed:** i.e., lost.   **66. Battle at New Orleans:** the victory on 8 January 1815 of the American forces led by Gen. Andrew Jackson, of Ulster parentage, over an invading British army commanded by the Anglo-Irish general Sir Edward Packenham; British losses were 2,036 men killed (including Packenham) and wounded, against American casualties of 8 killed and 13 wounded.   **67. an:** i.e., on.   **68.** Samuel Brown, Philadelphia, to James Brown, Belfast, 30 December 1816. This James Brown was a cousin of Samuel's nephew, of the same name, who had emigrated to Philadelphia ca. 1809–1810 and in 1817 became his uncle's business partner.   **69.** Between 1800 and 1831 the population of Philadelphia rose from 41,220 to 80,462 (an increase of 95 percent), while that of the city plus its industrial suburbs (Kensington, the Northern Liberties, and Southwark) had increased from ca. 67,000 to 144,074 (a rise of 116 percent). By contrast, Belfast had grown from ca. 20,000 inhabitants in 1800 to 53,287 in 1831—a 166 percent increase—and by 1841 the city would have a population over 75,000. See n. 2.   **70.** On the Crocketts, see chapters 15 and 27; and on the Kerrs, see chapter 6.

tween both and their relations in Belfast—suggests that the greater opportunities and exigencies of urban life, both at home and overseas, may have eroded the kinship solidarity on which rural families, such as the Crocketts, depended so heavily.

More broadly, during the same period the strains of early industrialization were also eroding the political and ethnic solidarities that in the 1790s had united Philadelphia's upwardly mobile and working-class Irish behind the Republican party's opposition to Federalist pretensions and prejudices. Jefferson's triumph in 1800 had precipitated sharp divisions between merchant-Republicans, such as Thomas McKean and Mathew Carey, and the more radical "Old School" Jeffersonians, led by William Duane and Michael Leib, who wanted to restore the ultrademocratic provisions of Pennsylvania's 1776 constitution and who warned that American industrial and finance capitalism, unless publicly regulated, would reproduce in the New World the deep social divisions, exploitation, and poverty that characterized British urban society. As early as 1805–1806 conflict between the city's journeymen cordwainer's union and local shoe and boot manufacturers—ranging employers and workers of Irish birth and parentage against each other—and the journeymen's subsequent trial and conviction for conspiracy to restrain trade signaled what Duane characterized as the first shot in a class war that ultimately would destroy the Jeffersonian coalition.[71] Indeed, the War of 1812 provided only a temporary respite to the local Republicans' internecine political warfare, and in the following years most of Philadelphia's ambitious master craftsmen (including, most likely, Samuel Brown) joined the promanufacturing and probanking "New School" or "Quid" Republicans, thus isolating Philadelphia's emerging proletariat in Duane's and Leib's Old School faction and decisively crushing the latter in the 1818 city and county election.

Irish- and British-born craftsmen were often more experienced in labor organization and protest than their American peers, and one response by Philadelphia's Irish and other workers to their defeat at the polls was to accelerate the formation of trade unions and strike actions and to experiment with radical workingmen's parties. However, in the late 1820s the latter were overwhelmed by most workers' misplaced faith in—and by the general Irish enthusiasm for—Andrew Jackson and the new Democratic Party. Likewise, although in the mid-1830s local trade unionism achieved some spectacular successes, the Panic of 1837—coupled with the steady growth among the city's lower-middle and working classes of Protestant evangelicalism, fed by and reinforcing the militant sectarianism of many new Ulster immigrants—broke the city's unions and produced vicious tribal warfare among its Irish Protestant and Catholic workers, most spectacularly in the great riots of May and July 1844. Henceforth, Irish workers in Philadelphia, as in other American industrial cities, would largely be ranged in opposing political parties and in religiously exclusive "ethnic" communities, whose bourgeois leaders, whether "Scotch-Irish" or Irish Catholic,

---

71. In 1809 a similar strike by—and conspiracy trial of—New York's journeymen cordwainers heralded the growing social divisions among that city's Irish and other inhabitants; see chapter 66.

had little interest in the structural causes of working-class poverty. Formerly the Jeffersonians' and the United Irishmen's ideologies of economic and political liberalism had united the Irish and others, across social and denominational boundaries, against old British and Federalist "aristocracies." Now, however, under the impacts of industrialization and evangelicalism their once-emancipating doctrines of enterprise and individualism became tests of "moral character," which, coupled with traditional religious and cultural prejudices, served to divide the successful "Irish" from the unsuccessful, the "deserving" from the "undeserving," along ethnoreligious as well as class lines.

To be sure, in the 1840s some Ulster Presbyterian immigrants, such as the distiller and tavern-keeper Robert Smith,[72] remained prominent in a local Democratic party that, at least until the 1844 riots, still included many Irish Protestants as well as virtually all of the city's Irish Catholics. Indeed, Samuel Brown's will indicates he was a modest prototype of the Philadelphia Irish construction tycoons-turned-gentlemen merchants who, as Protestant Ulster-American "bosses," dominated much of the city's Jacksonian Democracy until the nativist surge and sectional conflicts of the 1850s and 1860s channeled most of them into the local Republican party "machine." Thus, in 1849, two years before his death, Brown's personal estate was inventoried at nearly $20,000, three-fourths of which consisted of shares in the Bank of North America, the Farmers' & Mechanics' Bank, the Union Canal Company, and various insurance companies. In addition to his own dwelling and shop on Chestnut Street, Samuel also owned at least five other houses—two of them four-story—and lots on South Fourth Street and elsewhere in the city. His semiestranged brother, Thomas, did almost as well. Despite severe losses following the peace of 1815, by his death in November 1836 Thomas Brown's total real and personal property was worth $12,000, and although the estate was equally divided among his wife and 10 children, even such modest legacies were significant in a city where, between 1800 and 1860, the top decile of local taxpayers increased its share of Philadelphia's wealth from 50 to 90 percent and where by the eve of the Civil War, 1 percent of the taxpayers owned half the taxable property.

---

72. On Robert Smith from Moycraig, Co. Antrim (immig. 1837; d. in Philadelphia 1846), see his letters, 1837–1845, in D. 1828 in PRONI.

V ❋
Merchants, Shopkeepers, and Peddlers

39 ❈

Francis Campble, 1737–1742

In the eighteenth century fewer than 10 percent of white Americans—and probably a smaller proportion of Irish immigrants—engaged primarily in business or commercial trading. They were a diverse group: in seaport towns they ranged from fabulously wealthy transatlantic merchants and financiers to modest traders, petty retailers, clerks, and other employees; in the countryside they included a few affluent traders but primarily a host of less prosperous, often part-time, shop- and inn-keepers, factors and other middlemen, hawkers, and peddlers. Yet despite their small numbers and varied functions, eighteenth-century traders played a crucial role in the American economy's remarkable expansion, beginning especially in the 1740s, as soaring British, West Indian, and southern European demands for American produce generated in turn an enormous growth in colonial consumption of British imports. The result was what the historian T. H. Breen has called a transatlantic "empire of goods"—the transport, advertising, and marketing of which increasingly linked the most modest households in rural America to the richest countinghouses in Philadelphia and London. And, as eighteenth-century American society became more commercialized—and more stratified as well, despite the general rise in white colonists' living standards—another consequence was that merchants, traders, and their professional retainers (especially lawyers) became increasingly dominant socially, culturally, and politically—particularly, but not exclusively, in the Northern and Middle colonies.

From the 1740s eighteenth-century Ireland also participated in this economic growth, especially through its export trades in linens and agricultural goods. Indeed, prior to the American Revolution—and despite mercantile restrictions—both direct and indirect trade between Ireland and the mainland colonies steadily increased. However, Ireland's commercial expansion was punctuated by frequent depressions; moreover, Irish society's widespread poverty, especially among Catholics, and its relatively rigid social, religious, and political stratification made it particularly vulnerable to such crises and, in general, inhibited both investment and consumption. Thus, economic advances could not keep pace either with Ireland's demographic growth or with the ambitions that commercialization generated among its nascent middle classes. One result was a small but significant emigration to the American mainland by entrepreneurially minded Irishmen who, formerly, had often pursued careers in Europe or the West Indies.[1] Some were agents of Irish trading concerns: of provisions merchants in southern Irish ports, for example, but more commonly of linen merchants and manufacturers in Ulster and Dublin. Others were the

---

1. Indeed, among eighteenth-century Irish immigrant entrepreneurs, Catholics (such as Stephen Moylan of Philadelphia) often represented earlier Irish merchant enclaves in France, Spain, or (as in the case of the Blakes' descendants and, perhaps, John O'Kelly) the West Indies. On the Blakes, O'Kelly, and Moylan, see chapters 16, 41, and 58, respectively.

sons of commercial farming families that were themselves branching into trade and industry. Irish capital and connections often helped establish and sustain these immigrant traders in the New World, as considerations of profit usually overlapped with those of family, religion, and, increasingly, shared "national" identity. This was especially true for those who engaged in transatlantic commerce, but ethnoreligious linkages—with Irish-American partners, middlemen, consumers—also facilitated the careers of many who dealt largely or exclusively in domestic trade. Such linkages also ensured that immigrant merchants, shopkeepers, and so on, played major roles in shaping and directing early Irish-American networks and communities.

For example, Irish-born entrepreneurs enjoyed great social prestige and political influence, as well as economic leverage, in the heavily Irish-settled districts of the colonial backcountry, where they functioned as crucial intermediaries between the farmers and the seaport merchants—a significant minority of whom were also of Irish birth or descent. To be sure, the colonial frontier's most famous Irish traders, Sir William Johnson and George Croghan,[2] specialized in commerce and diplomacy with the Indian nations. More typical, however, was Francis Campble (or Campbell), a pioneer merchant in Shippensburg, a fledgling town in Pennsylvania's Cumberland Valley—the inhabitants of which were, during most of Campble's career, overwhelmingly of Ulster birth or descent. Like his customers, Campble was also from the north of Ireland. He was born around 1700–1705 near the town of Dungiven in County Derry,[3] the third son of Arthur Campble, who had returned to Ulster and purchased a farm with the "considerable wealth" he had acquired in the West Indies. Francis received a "collegiate education," perhaps in Spain, but his father's death in 1733 obliged him and an older brother to emigrate to Philadelphia in the summer of 1734. For two years Campble assisted his brother in trade in Philadelphia. In the 1730s, however, Irish merchant networks in American seaports were still too small and undercapitalized to absorb and promote most ambitious newcomers, and so it was the patronage of the Boston-born Edward Shippen (1703–1780) that furthered Campble's career and directed him to Pennsylvania's frontier. Shippen was already one of Philadelphia's wealthiest merchants and land speculators when, in early 1737, he purchased from the Penn family over 1,300 acres in the Cumberland Valley and invited Campble to visit his acquisition and serve as his agent. Impressed by the region's beauty and economic potential, Campble located permanently in the Middle Spring settlement, the nucleus of which later became the village of Shippensburg, while his brother in Philadelphia supplied him with goods for retail to the Valley's earlier settlers such as the Magraws and Rippeys.[4]

The surviving fragments of Campble's journal cover his first years in Middle Spring–Shippensburg, which he describes from an entrepreneurial perspective, keenly assessing the

---

2. See chapter 51.   3. For demographic data on Dungiven and adjacent parishes in Co. Derry, see appendix 2.1b, on chapter 8. Quotations in this and the following sentence are cited in W. H. Burkhart, *Cumberland Valley Chronicles . . .* , 2; see Sources, chapter 39.   4. See chapter 19.

settlement's economic potential and growth, yet also—after his initial burst of enthusiasm for the area's landscape and inhabitants—decrying the physical insecurity and social instability that might inhibit future development and the security of capital investments. Thus, Campble's account provides evidence of early commercialization and urban growth on a raw and often turbulent Ulster-American frontier, of the deteriorating relations between newcomers and Indians that would flame into warfare in the 1750s, and, finally, of the western settlers' resentments against colonial officialdom that, in turn, would help inspire the Paxton Boys to violence in late 1763 and the entire Pennsylvania backcountry to revolution in 1775–1776.[5]

Francis Campble Journal, 1737–1742

September 14th, 1737. I came here ten days ago, not as a matter of necessity, but as a matter of choice, and I find the country all that my friend, Mr. Shippen, represented it to be. . . .[6] It is not the grandeur of rocks, cascades and romantic glens, but it is the beautiful panorama of forest and plain spread out in all their beauty which meets you everywhere, and which will, at no very far distant day, become the happy home of intelligent, God-fearing people, when the savage shall have passed forever from its borders. This is the kind of grandeur which surrounds me, and this is what attracted me hither. New settlers are arriving here weekly, most of them have scattered out and settled along the streams and in the woodlands. They are generally a hardy, industrious, intelligent and pious people, who are well fitted to endure the privations and overcome the difficulties that must ever be encountered in the formation of a new settlement. The entire people of this settlement is of Irish origin and Presbyterian in faith. I have been told by some of the first settlers that there is not a single family here who are not natives of the Province of Ulster.

April 10th, 1738. We have a little hamlet here of a few houses, in one of which I live and keep a little stock of goods for sale. Some of my time, however, is occupied in surveying, and in other duties. If my employments are not very lucrative, they are healthful; with this, and the blessings of God, I shall be happy. James McCall,[7] to-day, in sinking the well in front of his house, deeper, he struck a fine stream of good water, which will be of great advantage to us all. Mr. John Reynolds[8] this morning proposed selling me a portion of his plantation, lying south-east of our little hamlet; but whilst

---

5. On the Paxton Boys and the coming of the Revolution in frontier Pennsylvania, see chapter 53.
6. Omitted: additional descriptive material.   7. **James McCall**: with John McCall, in 1751 a taxpayer in Lurgan township, Cumberland Co.; see chapter 19 for earlier references to the McCalls, Rippeys, and other settlers mentioned in Campble's journal.   8. **John Reynolds**: warranted 400 acres in 1735, 950 acres in 1738, and 200 in 1746—thus justifying Campble's reference to Reynolds's holding as a "plantation"; probably a kinsman of **William Reynolds** (hereafter). In 1751 John Reynolds paid taxes in Antrim township, Cumberland Co., but by 1778 a John Reynolds and James Reynolds owned only 74 and 70 acres, respectively, in Lurgan township.

there is still so much land in the hands of the Penns, which can be had without paying a profit to a first purchaser, it would be a mistaken policy to buy his.

June 4th, 1740. Our settlement is increasing rapidly, and our village, which has been named Shippensburg, has several substantial houses in it. The stone house of Samuel Perry, in which the Widow Piper now keeps tavern, together with that of Daniel Duncan, just finished, are both good substantial two-story houses. The stone house at the Branch, built by Samuel Rippey,[9] two years ago, is also a very fine house. In addition this Mr. R<ippey> is now erecting along the Branch, a few rods[10] below his house, a large, square, stone building for a distillery. These, with the two-story, log houses which have recently been erected, lead us to believe that we shall have, ere long, a town of some importance.

Oct. 10th, 1740. The building of our little fort, and the digging of the well within its enclosure, has been a good work. Had it not been for the recent killing of young Alex'r Askew, near to where Robert McInnis was shot seven years ago, the friendship of the Indians might not have been suspected, and this very necessary work might have been postponed until a more serious calamity would have overtaken us. I have no confidence in the friendship of these savages, and have always felt that we have been warming a viper which will some day show us its fangs. Our only safety, in my opinion, depends wholly upon our vigilance and the preparation we make in our defence. A portion of Fishburn's[11] Brewery was damaged by fire to-day.

May 1st, 1741. Mr. Shippen has written to me that he intends soon to lay out his town, which he intends naming Shippensburg or Shippenstown, by both of which names it has already been called. Whether it will be laid out in the direction of the Spring, or whether it will follow the crooked path made by the Indians, now the road, he has not stated, and probably will not know himself until he comes to make the survey. I sold to-day, to Richard Long[12] for £6 16s, the heavy pine logs I bought from Mr. Shippen, and cut along the run[13] east of us with which I had intended building a house. With these logs Mr. Long will build a large, two-story house. This afternoon we had one of the most terrific thunder storms it has ever been my lot to witness. Several trees in the vicinity were stuck with lightening, and the rain fell in torrents, flooding

---

9. Samuel Perry: in 1778 he or his namesake held 21 acres in Hopewell township, Cumberland Co., and William Perry paid taxes on 31 acres in Lurgan township; in addition, "Perry and Duncan" held five hundred acres in Newtown township. **Widow Piper**: in 1778 several individuals named Piper held farms, ranging from 45 to 85 acres in size, in West Pennsborough, Newtown, and Hopewell townships. **Daniel Duncan**: in 1778 he or his namesake paid taxes on 422 acres in Lurgan township, Cumberland Co., and 172 acres in Newtown township. **Samuel Rippey** (1713–1791), son of **Hugh Rippey** (hereafter), one of Middle Spring's first settlers, from Maguire's Bridge, Co. Fermanagh, d. 1750; see chapter 19. In 1778 Samuel Rippey paid taxes on 70 acres in Lurgan township. **10. rod**: 5½ yards. **11. Fishburn**: transcript has **Fairbai[rn]**, but in 1778 a Conrad Fishburn held 147 acres in Lurgan township, adjacent to the holdings of the Rippeys, Duncans, Reynolds, etc. **12. Richard Long**: in 1751 Robert Long and Thomas Long were taxpayers in Lurgan and Antrim townships, respectively; in 1778 various Longs held 35 acres in Antrim, 263 acres in Guilford, 112 acres in Peters (adjacent to Francis Campble's holdings), and 74 acres in Lurgan township. **13. run**: small stream or brook.

the low lands around us. The woods from the foot of the hill east of us, to the hill beyond, is now one sheet of water; and the flat below the Spring on the west is impassable. Mrs. Jean Morrow[14] died this morning, aged 86 years.

December 20th, 1741. I this day completed the survey of the road leading from the Widow Piper's tavern, through the woods, past Cessna's[15] plantation. This is a continuation of the road which I surveyed from a point beyond the church on Middle Spring,[16] past Andrew Culbertson's,[17] into the village, opposite the said tavern. A severe and disgraceful fight took place today, at William Reynolds' tavern, between Neil McLean and John McCall,[18] in which both were badly injured. Both are stout men, and are disposed to be quarrelsome when under the influence of liquor, which is too often the case. David Magaw[19] was badly injured yesterday by a kick from his horse, but I think he is not dangerously or fatally injured. A number of families arrived here yesterday from Ireland, most of whom are from Antrim and Derry; one is from Down. Two of these families are named McCullough, two Thompson, one McConnell, one McNair, one Maxwell, one Jenkins, and one Linn.[20] Last week a man, with his family, named McComb,[21] a brother of Hugh Rippey's wife, arrived from the

---

14. Mrs. Jean Morrow: perhaps a kinswoman of Charles Morrow, who in 1754 joined Campble, Reynolds, and other inhabitants of Cumberland Co. in petitioning the governor's council for protection against Indian attacks; in 1778 Richard Morrow held 54 acres in Lurgan township, and Samuel Morrow owned 48 acres in Newtown township.   **15. Cessna**: probably John Cesna, who in 1751 paid taxes in Lurgan township and in 1754 joined Campble, Charles Morrow, John Reynolds, etc., in their petition to the governor's council; perhaps a kinsman of William Cesny, who in 1778 owned 61 acres in Letterkenny township.   **16. the church on Middle Spring**: Middle Spring Presbyterian church, built in 1740.   **17. Andrew Culbertson**: probably a kinsman of the numerous Culbersons who in 1751 were taxpayers in Peters and, primarily, in Lurgan township; in 1778 Culbersons (none named Andrew) held land in Cumberland County's Armagh, Guilford, Hopewell, Lurgan and, primarily, Letterkenny townships, in parcels ranging from 24 acres (John, in Lurgan) to 283 acres (Joseph, in Letterkenny).   **18. Neil McLean**: Neal McClean: in 1778 he or his namesake held 24 acres in Hopewell township, as did Robert McClean. **John McCall**: listed (with James McCall) in 1751 as a taxpayer in Lurgan township, but no McCalls could be located in Cumberland Co. in 1778.   **19. David Magaw**: warranted three hundred acres in 1737; among Cumberland County's petitioners to the governor's council in 1754.   **20. McCullough**: in 1778 a James McCullough paid taxes on 96 acres in West Pennsborough township, Cumberland Co. **Thompson**: in 1751 John and Joseph Thompson were listed as taxpayers in Lurgan township, and Moses Thompson paid taxes in Antrim township; by 1778 John Thompson owned 61 acres in Lurgan, and other Thompsons held land (ranging from 20 to 135 acres) in Antrim, Guilford, Hopewell, Lack, Letterkenny, Newtown, and West Pennsborough townships. **McConnell**: in 1751 Robert and William McConnell were listed as taxpayers in Lurgan, as was James McConnell in Peters township; in 1778 George McConnell held 248 acres, and John McConnell 87 acres, in Lack township, and James and Robert McConnell owned 48 and 35 acres, respectively, in Letterkenny township. **McNair**: in 1778 John and Alex McNeare held 35 acres apiece in Teboyne township. **Maxwell**: in 1778 Patrick Maxwell owned 120 acres, and James Maxwell, Esq., 132 acres, in Peters township. **Linn**: in 1751 William, William, Jr., and David Linn were taxpayers in Lurgan township, where in 1778 William, Jr., owned 159 acres.   **21. McComb**: probably John, Mahan, or Thomas McComb (McCombs), all of whom were listed in 1751 as taxable inhabitants of Lurgan township; in 1778 John, Thomas, and William McComb[s] owned 38, 128, and 46 acres, respectively, in Lurgan (near Samuel and William Rippey's farms), while Robert McComb held 132 acres in Newtown township.

county of Fermanaugh. These families form a total of about sixty persons. Andrew Gibson, who has taught school during the Summer season, for the past four or five years, in McCall's barn, died last night, aged about 40 years. Governor Thomas,[22] in company with some other Colonial officials, paid our village a visit last week, and remained over night at the Widow Piper's tavern. Were I permitted to express an opinion of those who occupy high official positions, I would say that there is something rather too stately in the Governor's manner and bearing—something which smacks too much of the tyrant—to make him popular with the people. It may not be just to form an opinion of a man, based upon an acquaintance of but a single evening; and yet I have found that first impressions are seldom wrong. Our fort has not been occupied since the Governor ordered the withdrawal of the soldiers from it last Spring. Yesterday we put Thomas Edmonson[23] and his family into it to take care of it. His wife is a careful woman, and he, when sober, is trustworthy and reliable. Throughout the day he has been drinking too much, and is somewhat jolly, and has christened his new home Fort Edmonson. When returning home from surveying, we met two wolves in the woods not half a mile from the village. At first they did not appear to be much alarmed; but when they found we were advancing toward them, they struck eastward, growling.

March 10th, 1742. A quarrel occurred last night out at the Spring amongst a party of drunken Indians, during which, four of their cabins were set on fire, and burned to the ground. One of the Indians, named Bright Star, a desperate man, was seriously injured in the fight, and will likely die of his wounds. I saw him not an hour ago, and considered him then in a dying condition. These savages will give us trouble yet.

Despite Campble's optimism, Shippensburg grew slowly at first—in part because of the Indian wars of the 1750s and early 1760s—and Shippen did not plat his town until 1749 or give formal leases until 1763. However, Francis Campble flourished as a trader, surveyor, and farmer, eventually owning a minimum of five town lots, over six hundred acres of farmland,[24] a spacious two-story stone house, and a popular tavern and

22. **Governor Thomas**: George Thomas, deputy governor of Pennsylvania, 1738–1747; despite Campble's criticisms, Thomas, a former planter in Antigua, was very popular with the Quaker-dominated colonial legislature.   23. **Thomas Edmonson**: Thomas Edmondson: in 1737 warranted one hundred acres of land in Cumberland Co. Also, in 1743 a Robert Edmondson warranted three hundred acres; by 1778 he or his namesake still held 148 acres in West Pennsborough township, and a John Edmonston owned 48 acres in Peters township.   24. In 1778 Francis Campble (listed as Campbell) was taxed £41 7s. for 483 acres in Cumberland County's Hopewell township, second only to Edward Shippen's assessment of £196 for one hundred acres in the same township. In the same year, kinfolk James, Martha, Patrick, Robert, and William Campbell held a total of 635 acres in Peters township.

hotel named "The Indian Queen." Twice married, Campble had at least nine children.[25] In the late 1750s, during the anti-"papist" hysteria occasioned by the French and Indian War, rumors spread that Campble had been born a Catholic and even educated in Spain for the priesthood. Perhaps the allegations were true—Campble's first wife was reportedly "a Spanish woman"—but in Shippensburg he fully conformed to his neighbors' faith, was an elder of the Middle Spring Presbyterian church, and educated one of his sons for the ministry. According to an early biographer, Campble was "tall and slender in person, . . . graceful in his manners, . . . dignified in all his intercourse with his fellow men," and an "elegant and forcible writer" with "wonderfully brilliant conversational powers."[26] On at least one occasion Campble employed these qualities to mediate among his neighbors and prevent mob violence, and in 1764 and again in 1769 he was appointed a county magistrate. Campble served in the militia during the French and Indian War, and with the onset of the Revolution he helped form the militia companies in which two of his sons served. He died on 1 March 1790, leaving a personal estate (including a sizeable library and six slaves) valued at £648, and having witnessed Shippensburg's growth from a cluster of cabins to a thriving village of six hundred inhabitants.

40 ✳

Robert Pillson, 1764

Despite the Navigation Acts' restrictions, trade between Ireland and Britain's North American colonies doubled between 1730 and 1760 and doubled again by the outbreak of the American Revolution, as Irish linens, salted beef and pork, and indentured servants were exchanged for American flaxseed, rum, wheat and flour, staves, and lumber. By the mid–eighteenth century, sizeable communities of Irish merchants had emerged in the major American ports—especially in Philadelphia, New York, and Baltimore—organizing and servicing this transatlantic commerce and providing economic opportunities for ambitious new immigrants such as Robert Pillson.

Pillson was probably a Presbyterian, perhaps from near Downpatrick or Saintfield, County Down (where Pilsons still owned land in the 1870s), who in the mid–eighteenth

---

25. By his first wife (name unknown), Campble had two sons: John (1752–1819), educated at Princeton, an Episcopalian minister at York, later at Carlisle; and Robert, an officer in the Revolution, who died in the militia riot at "fort Wilson," Philadelphia, on 4 October 1779. By his second wife, Elizabeth Parker, Campble had seven children: Francis, Jr. (d.1808), a merchant in Shippensburg;, Ebenezer, a merchant in Shippensburg, later in Washington Co., Pa., and in Ohio; Nancy, who married Robert Tate; James, a lawyer in York, Pa., and Natchez, Miss.; Parker (d. 1824), a lawyer in Washington, Pa.; Elizabeth, died unmarried sometime after 1821; and George, alive in 1790, when mentioned in his father's will. **26.** Cited in W. H. Burkhart, *Cumberland Valley Chronicles*, 2; see Sources, chapter 39.

century had migrated to the flourishing manufacturing and commercial port of Newry, where he may have clerked for Edward and Isaac Corry, wealthy merchants active in the flaxseed and linen trade with America. On 10 May 1764, shortly after the conclusion of the Seven Year's War, Pillson sailed from Newry to New York aboard the same ship that carried Rev. Thomas Clark's Seceding Presbyterian congregation.[1] Pillson may have been associated with Clark's followers, for in 1765 he joined them in petitioning New York's executive council for a land grant near Lake George. However, most of Clark's parishioners settled instead in Washington County, and Pillson did not join them, preferring to invest his capital in transatlantic trade.

Pillson's ambitions were not unrealistic. To be sure, New York lagged behind Philadelphia, Boston, and even Charleston in her total volume of maritime trade. However, with about 17,000 inhabitants in 1767, New York was second only to Philadelphia in its population, in the importance of its Irish-American trade, and in the size of its Irish merchant community.[2] Indeed, from the 1750s through the early 1770s between a fourth and a third of New York's transatlantic export tonnage was shipped to Ireland. Clearly, also, Robert Pillson was both well-educated and well-connected, and in the preceding decade other young Ulstermen such as Waddell Cunningham and George Folliot[3] had migrated to New York and grown rich in Irish-American commerce, as well as through wartime contracting, privateering, and smuggling.

Pillson never attained such wealth and influence. However, in early 1764 Pilson wrote—to Harry Brabazon, a merchant in the port of Drogheda, County Louth—what is

1. On Rev. Clark's immigrant congregations in New York and South Carolina, the former joined by Alexander McNish in the early 1770s, see chapter 6. 2. At its peak, in the late 1760s and early 1770s, New York's Irish community of transatlantic merchants numbered about 30, compared with Philadelphia's 60 or so. 3. Waddell Cunningham (1729–1797): born in Killead parish, Co. Antrim, into a Presbyterian farming family with close ties to the linen trade; in the early 1750s he migrated to New York City, where he became a merchant on Queen St.; from 1756 he was in partnership with a leading Belfast merchant, Thomas Greg (1718–1796), forming Greg & Cunningham, which, by the mid-1760s, was one of the largest shipowners in New York and the most successful Irish-American trading firm in the colonial era; in the Seven Years' War Cunningham prospered through military contracts, smuggling, and privateering; the firm continued until 1775, but in 1764 Cunningham returned to Belfast; within a decade he was Belfast's wealthiest merchant and active in its civic life. In the early 1770s Cunningham and Greg helped Belfast's proprietor, Lord Donegall, raise large sums of money by paying him large fines for the renewal of leases on his Co. Antrim estates; they recouped their costs by raising tenants' rents and evicting those who refused to pay, thus precipitating mass emigration and an agrarian revolt by the so-called Hearts of Steel or Steelboys, who invaded Belfast and destroyed Cunningham's house (see chapter 4). In the late 1770s Cunningham helped found the Volunteer movement, and in 1783 he won election to the Irish Parliament, as the "patriot" candidate for Carrickfergus, but was unseated on petition; however, in 1792 he sided with moderates and conservatives in rejecting both the United Irishmen's radicalism and the demand for full Catholic Emancipation. ¶George Folliot (1730–1810): born in Derry, the grandson of one of the town's leading merchants; in 1753 Folliot emigrated to New York; two years later he formed a partnership with Archibald Cunningham of Derry; the firm, Cunningham & Folliot, prospered in the flaxseed and linen trades, as well as in smuggling; in May 1775 Folliot was elected to New York's provincial congress but refused to serve; as a loyalist, his property was confiscated, and, at the Revolution's end, he returned to England, claiming £66,000 in losses.

perhaps the single best surviving letter by an Irish-American merchant in the colonial period.[4] Pilson's correspondence exemplifies the parameters of eighteenth-century Irish-American trade, especially in colonial flaxseed and in Irish linens and foodstuffs. At midcentury Drogheda had about five thousand inhabitants and, with easy access up the Boyne River to the great mills at Slane, County Meath, was an important trading center for grain and flour, as well as for beef and livestock. Moreover, the town had a prosperous linen market and the largest linen-manufacturing capacity outside Ulster. However, the dearth of quality flaxseed in north Leinster oriented Drogheda's merchant-manufacturers, such as Brabazon, both to North American supplies and to Newry, mid-Ulster's main transatlantic port and Pilson's former residence. Pilson's letter thus illustrates how an Irish immigrant with "small Capitall" sought to draw on and expand these connections in personally profitable ways, by establishing with Brabazon the kinds of transatlantic commercial relationships that had enriched men such as Cunningham and Folliot.

Robert Pillson, New York City, to Harry Brabazon, Drogheda, County Louth, 5 April 1764

M[r] Harry Brabazon   New york 5th April 1764
Dear Sir

As I am at this Season addressing myself to such of my Friends and acquaintances in Ireland, as are in the Mercantile way, <I> take this opportunity of Introducing a correspondence; but notwithstanding that business did not lead me thus to Commence an Epistolary acquaintance, yet I look upon myself, as being bound by the tyes of gratitude, at least to render you & M[rs] Brabazon an acknowledgment for the kindness, and friendship, which I have experienced from you whilst among you,[5] and of which I shall always Entertain a gratefull sense, and wish to have it in my power to make a suitable return. My prospect in comeing to this Country, was from the Encouragement of several of my friends in Ireland, particularly Mess[rs] Corrys of Newry,[6] who have since my comeing here manifested their good Inclinations to serve me, by giving a considerable order for shipping Flaxs[d7] which has

---

4. The Brabazons were Protestant converts of Norman or "Old English" descent, the most prominent of whom were earls of Meath. Harry Brabazon was probably a representative of a lesser branch of the family whose members held estates in Termonfeckin parish, Co. Louth, and served on the city council in nearby Drogheda. For demographic data on Drogheda, see appendix 2.2b, on chapter 40. For additional trade-oriented correspondence by Irish transatlantic merchants, see especially chapter 56. **5. which I have experienced from you whilst among you:** "which I experienced/enjoyed while I was in your company." **6. Mess[rs] Corrys of Newry:** Edward and Isaac Corry were among Newry's leading merchants; Edward's son, also named Isaac (1755–1813), became a prominent politician, first (from 1776) as a "patriot" member of the Irish Parliament, but after 1789 as a government supporter and placeman, capping his career with membership in the Irish and, later, the British privy councils in return for his general loyalty and, in 1800, his support for the Act of Union. **7. Flaxs[d]:** flaxseed.

been Executed with several others from same place,[8] Belfast & Derry and as I mean to continue in doing business in the Commission way shall always endeavour to transact it in such a manner as to give my Friends Satisfaction, by holding their property Committed to my care in the highest Esteem, and pay due attention in all respects to their Interest, which I hope will intitle me to the favour of their Commands[9]——As I make no doubt you are well acquainted with such of your Towns-people as do any business in this City, <I> must entreat you to recommend me to their notice, in putting what business they can into my hands, and I shall alway deem it as a particular favour; and you may at same time assure them that think it their Interest[10] to commit any transaction to my care they may rely on having it compleated as much to their content as they cou'd wish, and in order that they may be satisfy'd as to their safety in corresponding with me,[11] I must beg leave to referr them to my particular friends the Messrs Corrys, to Messrs Melling & Glennys & Mr David Gaussan of Newry,[12] for whom I have done some business since I came to this Country, and for the better enabling me to send my Irish friends such Flaxseed as I know answers[13] that Market, I am now getting a very compleat Machine erected for cleaning,[14] that will Cost upwards of £300 this money,[15] which I purpose[16] shall go thro' every operation under my own Inspection——My liveing in Newry so long where that trade was carried on largely,[17] afforded me Repeated opportunitys of knowg[18] the different good qualitys necessary in Seed in order to Recommend it to the Country people,[19] who I know are often hard to please even with the best——Seed of a small Grain, bright coloured, clean, and free from Spirry[20] is the kind that answers your Market, and such grows here upon a dry, Sandy soil, and is only rais'd on Two particular Islands, viz. Long Island, and Connecticutt: but it generally commands from 2d to 3d ℔ Bushell in price, more than any other Seed brought to this Market on acct of the qualitys abovementioned.——By all accounts from Ireland their last Summer has prov'd very moist, which must consequently have produced you large quantitys of butter, and as the Exportation of that article is prohibited from Ireland to England induces me to think it must be laid in reasonably by[21] you,   therefore I immagine a quantity ship'd from your place for this could not fail of turning out well   the present price 14d ℔ bl by single Casks, and 3d by that quantity   if you, or any of your Friends should deem it prudent to adventure therein, I would recommend their shipping it so as to be here early in the fall,   Beef now sells from 65 to 70/ ℔ Barrell (I mean Irish) being in much greater esteem than

---

8. **same place:** i.e., Newry.   9. **Commands:** orders, directions (as in trade), "business."   10. **Interest:** advantage.   11. **safety in corresponding with me:** "security in doing business with me."   12. **David Gaussan of Newry:** David Gaussan & Company was one of several Irish firms (like Gregg & Cunningham) that combined investments in linen manufacturing, overseas trade, and emigration.   13. **answers:** suits. 14. **for cleaning:** i.e., for cleaning flaxseed, prior to shipping it to Ireland.   15. **this money:** i.e., New York currency.   16. **purpose:** propose.   17. **largely:** extensively.   18. **knowg:** knowing.   19. **Country people:** i.e., Irish farmers (engaged in growing flax).   20. **Spirry:** i.e., "spiry," var. of **spret** "sprouts" (Scots).   21. **laid in reasonably:** i.e., stocked at a reasonable price; **reasonably by:** conjectural.

what is cured here, as it is found by experience that the Irish Beef, (when well cured, and honestly made up) always commands both a preference, and a higher price at the West India Markets.——Irish Mault answers well[22] here, when good, and well Malted it sells now @ 25/ ℔ barrell of 12 Stone, and expected higher soon, on acc^t of a Stop[23] being put to the Exportation of Corn from England; if you or your friends incline sending any to this Market, the safest conveyance w^d be in Sacks, made of the Coarse Ticken[24] manufactured with you, which wou'd bring a handsome proffitt here.——was not my own small Capitall otherwise occupy'd at present, I shou'd have ordered over some Mault, and butter on my own acc^t as I really dont know any thing in which there's a better prospect of makeing money; Coarse linnen & Sheeting[25] much Wanted for about 3,000 provinciall Troops now raiseing[26] to protect our Frontiers.——I shall be extreamly glad to be favoured with a letter from you when opportunity serves, and to have it in my power[27] to render you, or any of your friends what services I can here being with much Esteem Dear Sir Your sincere & obed^t Servt

Robt Pillson

pray my Complem^{ts} to Mrs Brabazon Miss Brabazon & Mr P. B.; the hurry of business prevented my writing you by a Vessel that Sail'd from hence for your place——inclosed you have prices Curr^{t28} of this Market——Jamaica Rum . . . 4/6 Antigua d^o . . . 3/6 New Eng. d^o . . . 2/6 Melasses . . . 2/ Rice . . . 14/ Best Flour . . . 12/ 2^d d^o . . . 11/ Irish Beef . . . 65 to 70/ ℔ barrell d^o Pork . . . 95 to 100/ d^o Butter . . . 14^d ℔ bl in demand d^o Linnens from 13 to 20^d Irish ℔ y^d in great demand for the provincial Troops——Coarse Sheeting in demand

In the summer of 1765, Pillson received his first consignment of "102 Pieces of Linnen" from Drogheda. However, as he reported to Brabazon, spoilage during a long, stormy voyage had made the cargo "quite Rotten."[29] Bankruptcies among colonial merchants were frequent, and, for a trader just beginning on limited means, this disaster may have been economically fatal. Yet Pillson faced even greater obstacles to success. The timing of his migration had been unpropitious, for New York's economy was suffering the effects of a temporary but sharp postwar depression. Moreover, with his small resources, Pillson could hardly compete with the established firms that dominated New York's Irish commerce—much of which (unlike Philadelphia's) was in the hands of non-Irish merchants.

22. answers well: "does well, sells well." **23. Stop**: halt, cessation (in this case, because of a legal obstruction). **24. Ticken**: tick or ticking (a strong, hard linen or cotton material used to make pillows or mattresses). **25. Sheeting**: stout cloth of linen or cotton, as used for bed linen. **26. raiseing**: "being raised"; see chapter 4, n. 45. **27. power**: conjectural. **28. Curr^t**: current. The sequences of periods in the following list of goods and prices (e.g. **Jamaica Rum** . . . 4/6) are not elipses but appear in Pillson's ms.; 4/6 = four shillings, six pence; 11/ = eleven shillings even, etc. **d^o**: ditto; ℔ **bl**: per barrell; ℔ **y^d**: per yard. **29.** Robert Pillson, New York City, to Harry Brabazon, Drogheda, Co. Louth, 8 June 1765.

As a Presbyterian, Pillson may also have faced political and religious obstacles, as nearly all of New York's prominent merchants (both the American- and the Irish-born) who engaged in Irish trade were Anglicans and thus enjoyed special favor with the colony's governing élite.[30] Finally, despite Drogheda's economic importance, its transatlantic trade was already oriented to Philadelphia and too small to support Pillson's ambitious attempt to rechannel it to New York; indeed, Pilson's own correspondent, Brabazon, was merely a dabbler in American commerce. Thus, there were many possible reasons why Pillson's attempt to become even a minor figure in Irish-American trade seems to have failed. For in late October 1765 he sold his New York property (including, no doubt, his "very compleat Machine" for cleaning flaxseed) and afterward disappeared completely from the historical record.

41 ❋

John O'Kelly, 1773

During the eighteenth century, the southern New England colonies had little direct trade with Ireland, and relatively few Irish Protestants—and even fewer Irish Catholics—settled there. Both were discouraged by the lack of available land in that densely settled region and by Puritan hostility to Ulster Presbyterians and especially to Irish Catholics, who from 1729 were denied civil rights even in the tolerant and predominantly Baptist and Quaker colony of Rhode Island.[1]

Indirectly, however, southern New England—especially Connecticut—and Long Island played major roles in Irish-American trade, for the area's farms produced the largest quantity and the best quality of the flaxseed that was shipped to Ireland and sold to the farmers who raised flax to supply Ulster's burgeoning linen industry. Every autumn, through a system of bookkeeping barter, Yankee farmers exchanged flaxseed—for salt, West Indian provisions, and manufactured goods—with country storekeepers such as John O'Kelly of Warren, Rhode Island. They in turn sold the seed to their suppliers—to

---

30. New York's dominant De Lancey family was staunchly Anglican, and the De Lanceys and their allies certainly furthered the career of Sir William Johnson (see chapter 51)—and probably those of Irish-born merchants George Folliot and Hugh Wallace, also Anglicans and future New York loyalists. However, if Robert Pillson was, indeed, a Seceding Presbyterian (as suggested by his early association with Rev. Clark's congregation), it is doubtful that De Lancey connections would have aided him, as in the late 1760s and early 1770s the De Lanceys were embroiled in bitter political and religious disputes with New York's leading dissenters, who, when the Revolution occurred, played prominent roles in the new state government that confiscated the properties of Johnson, Folliot, Wallace, and the De Lanceys alike. 1. On anti-Irish prejudice in New England, see chapters 8, 17, and 49.

wealthy merchants such as Christopher Champlin of Newport[2]—who then dealt the flax-seed to Irish export traders in New York or Philadelphia for winter transport across the Atlantic.

On the eve of the American Revolution, Ezra Stiles,[3] the minister of Newport's Second Congregational Church, noted in his diary that John O'Kelly was the only Irish Catholic in Warren, a small (ca. eight hundred inhabitants) but flourishing seaport, whaling, and ship-building center at the north end of Narragansett Bay. O'Kelly had arrived in Rhode Island sometime prior to 9 April 1769, when he married Elizabeth Cole, daughter of one of Warren's earliest and most prominent Baptist families.[4] Most of the few Irish Catholics in eighteenth-century New England came from southeastern Ireland, via the Newfoundland fisheries; in January 1774 alone, for example, some 60 Irish from Newfoundland settled in Newport. However, nearly all the Newfoundland migrants were illiterate and impoverished servants and laborers, whereas O'Kelly's advantageous marriage and modest prosperity indicate much higher status, and his surname suggests that he had emigrated from County Galway, where the O'Kellys had been dispossessed in the Cromwellian confiscations. In the late 1760s Irish emigration from Galway port to North America had resumed, after a hiatus of nearly four decades, and it is likely that O'Kelly made his way to Rhode Island via the trade in Irish provisions and West Indian molasses that linked Galway, Jamaica (where several Kellys and O'Kellys were lawyers, planters, and merchants), and Newport, then the fifth largest seaport in the mainland colonies. In any case, prior to the Revolution John O'Kelly combined school teaching with shipwrighting and, especially, storekeeping: purchasing flaxseed from local farmers and forwarding it either to Newport or to Providence merchants, depending on price and demand.

O'Kelly's letter does more than illustrate one aspect of the flaxseed trade. Eighteenth-century commerce, both within the colonies and with foreign ports, was based almost entirely on credit and, consequently, on networks of personal contacts and trust that were largely shaped by familial ties and ethnoreligious affinities. The lack of such linkages, plus legal disabilities, helps explain why it was so difficult for Irish Catholic immigrants to secure credit and engage in profitable trade, especially in New England where commerce

---

2. Christopher Champlin, Jr. (1731–1805): wealthy Newport merchant, shipowner, financier, and Anglican vestryman, eldest son of Col. Christopher Champlin and Hannah Hill, whose two-thousand-acre estate on Rhode Island's Narragansett Bay adjoined St. Paul's church, pastored by the Tyrone-born Rev. James MacSparran (see chapter 8), who baptized Champlin, Jr., and had married his parents. Champlin, Jr., proclaimed his loyalty to the crown in December 1776, when the British occupied Newport, as did most of the port's Anglican merchants, but later fled the town and supported the Revolution; in 1784 he was elected an alderman, in 1791 became grand master of Rhode Island's Masonic Lodge, and in 1795 was the first president of the Bank of Rhode Island.   3. Rev. Ezra Stiles (1727–1795), leader of Connecticut's Congregational clergy, noted astonomer, and later president of Yale College; also see chapter 55.   4. O'Kelly may have been present in Warren as early as 1765, when a John Kelley was taxed 15s. 8d. on local property. More certainly, in 1774 the subject of this chapter, listed as John O'Kelley, was taxed 5s. 12d. In 1774 Edward Cole of Newport, a tanner, was twelfth on that city's assessment list of taxpayers, with a tax of £10 3s., and in 1786 Ebenezer Cole, Sr., of Warren, probably O'Kelly's father-in-law, was taxed £2 10d.

and capital were monopolized by Puritan or (in Newport) Anglican oligarchies whose members, as O'Kelly's letter to Champlin suggests, were instinctively hostile to Irish Catholics or, at the least, suspicious of their honesty.[5]

John O'Kelly, Warren, Rhode Island, to Christopher Champlin, Newport, Rhode Island, 20 October 1773

M[r]. Christophor Champlin }   Warren   Octob,[r] y[e]. 20th -1773
Sir

   Since I have Seen you, I bought 20 Casks of flaxseed, Which I am to pay for this week, or Else it will be sold To Providence People, Whom plauges me aboute Getting Away what they Can from me, as I am Confident they will Give 7 Shillings ℔: Bushel for it, before Newport Men will have it, as they are Collecting for Newyork.[6] You told me you would Give me but 1 Dollar a Bushel for Seed deliverd in Newport,[7] and freight, which is athing I cant Get it for, all to[8] about 10 Casks I have in my own

---

5. O'Kelly's only other surviving correspondence are two business letters that he wrote (on 4 May and 6 July 1772) to Aaron Lopez (1731–1782), Newport's wealthiest merchant, for whom he was building a brig at Warren. Perhaps significantly, O'Kelly's letters to Lopez evince none of the defensiveness that marks his correspondence with Champlin, perhaps because Lopez was a Portuguese Jew whose religion, like O'Kelly's, also made him an "outsider" in Rhode Island law and among Newport's Protestant élite. **6.** Since the allusive, not to say cryptic, style of O'Kelly's letter to Champlin may impair a full understanding of its contents, we offer the following version, which translates the sense of the text while attempting to remain faithful to the original. ¶Sir ¶Since I saw you last I have bought 20 casks of flaxseed [from local farmers], which I have to pay for this week or they will sell it to agents acting for merchants in Providence. These Providence people torment me with threats that they will carry away as much of this flaxseed as they can buy, and I have no doubt they will pay up to 7s. a bushel for it in order to keep Newport agents such as myself from getting it, since they are now buying for the New York market. You proposed giving me $1.00 (i.e. 5s.) a bushel plus payment of freight charges to Newport for any flaxseed I send you (except for the ten casks I have in my private store, which are intended for payment of my outstanding account with you and to cover my draft on you in the amount of $40.00 to the order of Mr. Kinnicut), but that price leaves me no profit. If you think I am good for a credit of $100.00 and won't abscond to Ireland, send the goods [see n. 7] to me with Capt. Shearman together with a box of 6 × 8 window panes. I will discount the $100.00 for the amount owing to me for your purchase of the flaxseed and repay the rest as soon as I can get the order together, etc. I don't think I will have to draw on you for even a penny additional credit before paying off the current balance due. ¶Sir, I am [with] due respect your most humble servant ¶John O'Kelly ¶P.S. You may be reluctant to trust an Irishman in this transaction, but don't worry—if you can't see your way to undertaking it, there will be no hard feelings on my part. **7.** Although O'Kelly gives the value of the flaxseed in cash amounts (1 **Dollar a Bushel**), the actual exchanges were made in store goods, as demonstrated by the following lines from Asa Champlin's 17 September 1773 letter to his brother, Christopher: "The seed Cant be purchased Deliverd at the Harbour [Newport] under 5/ or 6 shillings per Bushel, as there never was so much Salt giveing for Seed as they [country merchants, such as O'Kelly] give this Year, two Bushels and half and 3 giveing for one of Seed. Niether could the Seed be Collected in 14 Days as they [the farmers] wont Thrash the Seed in general until they want the Salt to salt their winter's provision." **8. all to:** Gaelicism meaning "except for" and corresponding to the Irish preposition **go dtí**, which means "(all the way up) to," and is common in quantitative expressions; e.g., **do chuid airgid go dtí scilling**, lit. "all your money up to a shilling" (i.e., "all your money *except for* a shilling").

Store, Which Belongs to you, in Regard of the Ballence Due on Book Acc^tt: and my ord^r. of forty Dollars in feav^r. of Kinnicutt,[9]   but however, if you doant think Ile Run Away to Ireland, or Else, I ant[10] Worth 100 Dollars, Send them to me, by Capt. Shearman, with a Box of Glass six by Eight which I shall Discount the Whole with you As Soon As I can Get my flaxseed Together—&c &c   I doant think I shall draw one Copper[11] more on you, Until you have Value Rec.^d of the Above Sums mentioned,—

　　　　Sir   I am <with> Due Respect y^r. most humble Servt

　　　　　　　　　　　　　　　　　　　　　　　　　　　　John O:Kelly

N.B.

Doant Stress y^r. self as I know perhaps, you will be Very Loath To trust an Irish man with the Above; if you think you Cant Conveniently do it, without hard thoughts—

Rhode Islanders supported the American Revolution almost unanimously, and O'Kelly joined his neighbors and served in the Rhode Island militia, mostly guarding the bayshores against invasion but also, in August 1778, fighting in the battle of Rhode Island under General John Sullivan of New Hampshire,[12] son of another Irish immigrant schoolmaster, to expel the British from Newport. O'Kelly survived both that engagement and the British sacking of Warren itself. However, the Revolution ruined O'Kelly's trading concern, and he died insolvent, of unknown causes, on 30 May 1781, two years before Rhode Island granted Catholics the right to vote. O'Kelly left three children[13] and a widow who twice remarried—and was twice rewidowed[14]—before 1838 when, aged 89, she successfully petitioned the Rhode Island legislature for a pension based on O'Kelly's military service to the patriot cause.

42 ❋

Thomas Shipboy, Jr., 1774

In the colonial era, aspiring Irish entrepreneurs generally enjoyed greatest success when they could avail themselves of commercial networks organized on ethnoreligious and familial lines—and/or when they could specialize in branches of trade not already controlled by exclusive, non-Irish merchant oligarchies. Thus, Francis Campble could flourish

---

9. Kinnicutt: perhaps Shubeal Kinnicut of Warren, R.I., who later married O'Kelly's widow.
10. ant: i.e., ain't.   11. one Copper more: "a single penny/halfpenny more" (both denominations struck in copper).   12. General John Sullivan (1740–1795); see chapter 59, n. 83.   13. O'Kelly's children (and their birthdates) were: Mary (1770), Martin (1773), and Elizabeth (1775).   14. Elizabeth O'Kelly's second and third husbands, both of Warren, R.I., were: Marmaduke Mason (m. 12 December 1782; d. 28 June 1798); and Shubeal Kinnicut (m. 4 November 1802; d. 13 August 1810).

on Pennsylvania's Scots-Irish frontier, and even John O'Kelly could find a small but modestly profitable niche in New England's flaxseed trade. By contrast Robert Pillson's failure probably owed as much to the opposition of New York's Anglican élite and its dominance of that city's Irish-American trade as to the damaged goods he received from Drogheda.[1] Similarly, in upstate New York the Shipboys from County Londonderry found their economic prospects threatened by the hostility of Albany's entrenched Dutch oligarchy toward the town's newly formed Ulster Irish and Scottish merchant community. The agitation that produced the American Revolution, with its complex and shifting local alliances, only further complicated the Shipboys' situation. Although one brother survived that crisis and subsequently prospered, another did not, and their young cousin, recently arrived from County Derry, quickly abandoned the struggle and, apparently, returned to Ireland even before the Revolution began.

In the early eighteenth century, the Shipboys (or Shipbuoys) farmed at Dooeybeg, in the seacoast parish of Agherton (or Ballyaghran), near the mouth of the Bann River. Although the family continued to lease land in Dooeybeg from 1744 at least through the 1790s, sometime after midcentury the children of Thomas Shipboy (d. 1773) moved three miles into Coleraine, in 1766 a thriving port of about five hundred households (95 percent of them Protestant), where they engaged in trade and, apparently, left their parents' Presbyterianism and joined the local Church of Ireland.[2] By the early 1770s Robert Shipboy (d. 1787), who himself had ventured briefly to New York in 1766, and his wife, Elizabeth (d. 1795), a dressmaker, were retailing a variety of dry goods and groceries from their store and home on Coleraine's Church Street. In 1774 Robert's brother, Thomas, Jr., emigrated to Albany, hoping to clerk or peddle goods for his "Cuzen Shipboy," also named Thomas, who had left Ireland some 20 years earlier.[3]

"Cuzen" Thomas Shipboy was one of many Ulster Irish and Scottish entrepreneurs who migrated to Albany during the Seven Years' War (1754–1763), initially to provision the British forces that occupied what had been an insular frontier village, dominated by a handful of wealthy Dutch families. After the war, many of the newcomers remained, and some prospered, as between 1757 and 1779 the populations of Albany town and county increased by 60 percent (to ca. 3,000) and by nearly 400 percent (to 42,700), respectively, and as the conquest of Canada opened the fur trade of the Great Lakes region to the merchants of northern New York. For a time, "Cuzen" Thomas shared in this expanding commerce, first in partnership with fellow Ulsterman Robert Henry and after 1763 with his brother John Shipboy, in a prime location on State Street where they sold imported linens, wines, and other goods. In 1767 "Cuzen" Thomas's property was assessed at the high value of £86; in 1768 he was a founding member of Albany's second Masonic lodge;

---

1. On Campble, Pillson, and O'Kelly, see chapters 39–41. 2. For demographic data on Coleraine parish and its environs, see appendix 2.1g. 3. "Cuzen" Thomas Shipboy and his brother, John, were the sons of James Shipboy of Dooeybeg (d. 1771), the brother of Thomas Shipboy, Sr., of Ballywillin, whose sons included Robert, the Coleraine trader, and Thomas, Jr., who ventured to Albany in 1774.

and in 1769 he and his brother joined with others to speculate in one hundred thousand acres on the south side of the Mohawk River. Indeed, the prosperity of "Cuzen" Thomas Shipboy and his brother John seemed assured, as they were social as well as business associates of the Irish-born Sir William Johnson, a fellow Anglican and Mason and the most powerful official and wealthiest Indian trader in the Mohawk Valley.[4]

However, at midcentury the Swedish traveler Peter Kalm had remarked on Albany merchants' notorious "avarice . . . selfishness" and dishonesty, and the town's Dutch burghers bitterly resented the Irish and Scottish interlopers and used their power in the town government and the courts to harrass their competitors. "[T]here is no justice to be expected by any [Briton] in this country, nor never will," Sir William Johnson complained, "whilst the bench of judges and justices is entirely Dutch."[5] Although in 1767 "Cuzen" Thomas Shipboy had married a Dutch widow, her relations were not members of Albany's oligarchy.[6] In addition, the local agitation that led to the Revolution bedeviled the Shipboys' position. Initially, most members of Albany's Dutch élite joined the town's Sons of Liberty in supporting anti-British measures, thus ranging the Anglican Shipboys—allied with the loyalist Johnson—in logical opposition for reasons grounded in ideology as well as ethnic competition. However, in the late 1760s and early 1770s leadership of the local agitation became increasingly radical, targeting Albany's political and economic aristocracy as well as British taxation, and thus alienating many of the town's Dutch burghers from the antiimperial cause. Accordingly, "Cuzen" Thomas and his brother had to be very cautious: in 1766 the former signed the constitution of the Albany Sons of Liberty, but thereafter neither sibling appears on the lists of those who supported, served in, or opposed the Revolution. Apparently, however, the Shipboys' studied neutrality during the impending crisis did not save them from Dutch animosity or from consequent bankruptcy—as the recently arrived Thomas Shipboy, Jr., bitterly recounted in late 1774, in the following letter to his brother and sister-in-law back in Coleraine.

Thomas Shipboy, Jr., Albany, New York,
to Robert and Elizabeth Shipboy, Coleraine, County Londonderry,
9 November 1774

                                                   Albany Novr 9 1774

    Dear Brother and Sister

                      I Wrote you By the way of London Aquainting you of
my passage to this Contry   I Live at present with my Cuzen Shipboy but does Not

---

4. On Johnson, see chapter 51. **5.** P. Kalm, *Travels into North America* (Barre, Mass., 1972), 333; Johnson cited in Greenberg, *Crime & Law*, 67; see Sources, chapter 42. **6.** On 25 April 1765, Thomas Shipboy took out a marriage license to wed Annatie Van Vechten (née Williams; d. 1838, age 65), widow of John Van Vechten, a major in the provincial militia who died ca. 1762–1763. The Van Vechtens were an old Dutch family but merely tenant farmers of below-average wealth.

Intend to Stay Longer then Spring as he his[7] a Clark alredy By the year;[8]   he had to Give up his Books[9] and mony To the value of Nine Thousand pounds upon the Account of[10] his Brother But he is Now in as Good tread[11] as Ever;   I Intended to Joyn the Traveling with Goods;[12] But as this None Importation[13] his taking[14] place it his Raised the goods to Such a Rate[15] that there is nothing to be made by that Busness here now;   there is no goods to be Imported from England or Irland after the first day of December Next nor otherwise Exported from this kingdom to any of these parts untill they open the docks of boston that they have blockt up;   it is not known how these matters will be Settl[d] But I hope it is the Beginning of a ware;[16]   what the Contry has been I know not; But them that Comes here to make a fortune Now must Alow themselves to be Slaves to the Dutch which is two hard for any young man of Spirit to do   But for my part if things dow Not offer to my mind[17] again[18] the Spring I Intend to try Some other part of the worald   as for Clarks you may Shingle the houses with them they are So plenty[19] here   mathew Steel is about Seventy miles up the Mohawk River and is Teaching a hye dutchmans[20] Childer for the winter at ten pounds   Robart Kare is in the Same Imployment twenty Miles from this town; I left the Stockings I had for m[r] Robert dodd with his friend John lalor in philedelpha how[21] would forward them the first oppertunity;   I Seen James Thompso<n> when he Come from Detroyt how told me that John m[c] Nyer Lives there But by What I understd you may Credit him on the Back of the Book for What he owes you[22]   Give my Compliments to Samuel Larance[23] and Let him know that he will have as much pleasure with his Doge and Gun as he would have in Seeing America

---

7. his: i.e., has (Scots).   **8. By the year:** i.e., "Cuzen Shipboy" has already engaged a clerk for the year, at an annual salary.   **9. Books:** accounts (receivable).   **10. upon the Account of:** because of.   **11. tread:** i.e., trade.   **12. the Travelling with Goods:** journeying from place to place with merchandise for sale, peddling. **13. None** (i.e., non-)**Importation:** on 18 October 1774 the First Continental Congress adopted the Continental Association, which pledged the colonists to cease all importations from Great Britain and Ireland on 1 December, in retaliation for Parliament's Coercive Acts (31 March–20 May 1774), one of which, as Shipboy said hereafter, **blockt up** the port of Boston.   **14. taking:** i.e., taken (reverse spelling; see appendix 1).   **15. Rate:** price.   **16. I hope it is the Beginning of a ware:** it is impossible to determine whether Thomas Shipboy, Jr.'s desire for **ware**, expressed solely in terms of his family's animosity to the Dutch, reflected support for or opposition to revolution against British rule. His Anglicanism and recent arrival from Ireland would support a loyalist interpretation of his remarks, and most younger members of Albany's broadly defined "Scottish" merchant community became Tories during the Revolution. However, Shipboy's political sympathies were probably formed primarily or only in opposition to those of his family's specific Dutch competitors, and the latter's precise identities cannot now be discovered.   **17. offer to my mind:** turn out according to my expectations.   **18. again:** with expressions of future time, "by."   **19. plenty:** plentiful. **20. hye dutchman:** High Dutchman = German (as opposed to a Low Dutchman "Netherlander").   **21. how** (and in the following sentence): who.   **22. you may Credit him on the Back of the Book for What he owes you:** meaning not altogether clear, but perhaps: "you can write off what he owes you."   **23. Larance:** the Lawrences were prominent merchants in Coleraine, related by marriage to the Wyllys who traded with and emigrated to Georgia and the West Indies; Alexander Lawrence of Coleraine was part-owner of two ships, the *Rainbow* and the *Providence*, that carried passengers to America prior to the Revolution.

I have Nothing more meterial to aquaint you of; but my Kind Love to you and your agreeable wife and Childer and m^r Dodd and famely   Remember me to All my old Neabers and in particuler the yong Ladys of my aquaintence   you may let m^r Colman know that I Called for him at the halfway hous but he was Not So kind as to treat me to one Can²⁴ of Beer tho I was very Dry at the Same time²⁵ and for that Reason I will Not Drink one half kenn in his house this year   his Brother is Well But Did not see him   hugh hezeltin²⁶ and hugh hameltin was well when I left them in philedelpha and Intends going home   I seen James nalson last Satterday and he taches²⁷ Schule in Schenactdy²⁸   you may Let John Renkin of Ballywelenn know that his Son²⁹ is well and treads with the Indans at Detroyt   I Seen James Boys Which Concluds this Episel——

Dear Brother and Sister I Remain y^r
Ever Loving Brother while I am
Thos Shipboy

When you write; write me suner and to the Care of Cambell & Gott n<ew> york

Thomas Shipboy, Jr., does not appear in subsequent Albany records. Given his antipathy to America, his cousins' inability to employ him, and the general depression caused by the First Continental Congress's ban on British and Irish trade, it is likely he followed his inclination "to try Some other part of the worald." However, his kinsmen remained in Albany. Prior to the American Revolution, "Cuzen" Thomas—with Sir William Johnson's aid—appears to have recouped at least part of his fortune, and during the war he served as a bailsman for several Irish and Scottish merchants jailed as Tories; perhaps his Masonic connections enabled him to weather the conflict by retaining favor with both sides.³⁰ After the war at least one of Thomas's children married locally, into a rising Dutch family that had been prominent in the patriot cause,³¹ and in 1798 he died in Albany. His brother, John, was less fortunate: in 1791 the courts seized for debt £865 worth of his real and personal estate; and by 1802 he was a recipient of public charity. Unlike his brother's

---

24. Can (kenn hereafter): drinking vessel, of various materials and measures.   25. at the Same time: here emphasizes the adversative force of the preceding tho.   26. hugh hezeltin: probably related to Thomas Hazelton, a prominent merchant in mid-eighteenth-century Coleraine.   27. taches: i.e., teaches.
28. Schenactdy: Schenectady, then in Albany Co., N.Y.   29. John Renkin . . . : John Rankin's son was probably David Rankin, a partner of the Ulster-born fur trader George McBeath at Detroit and, in 1781–1783, at Mackinac; by 1785 he was in business at Montreal. Ballywelenn: Ballywillin (or Milltown) parish, Co. Londonderry, adjacent to Coleraine and Agherton parishes.   30. In 1779 Thomas Shipboy was assessed at $700 on the tax rolls; either this was an indication of considerable wealth or his property was under attack by the patriots who controlled the new state government.   31. In 1800 Rosanna Shipboy (d. 1838), daughter of Thomas and Annatie, married Sebastian Visscher, son of Mattheus (or Matthew) Visscher (d. 1792), a self-taught lawyer and secretary of Albany's Committee of Safety during the Revolution; the Visschers were a rising political family, with links to the Clintons. Another daughter, Margaret, died unmarried in 1810.

children, John's offspring apparently fled Albany for western New York, as the 1800–1840 censuses list Shipboys living in Otsego, Herkimer, and Chautauqua counties.

43 ✳

James Patton (2), 1789–1839

Most of the Irish immigrants described in this section began their entrepreneurial strivings shortly after they arrived in the New World. However, the continuing saga of James Patton from County Londonderry,[1] written in his eighty-fourth year for his childrens' edification, demonstrates how minimal capital—combined with dogged determination, reformed habits, and good luck—could propel an immigrant artisan and farm laborer into a profitable commercial career, thus creating a prototypical success story for the "Scotch-Irish" eulogists of the nineteenth and early twentieth centuries.

In November 1789, after six years of hired labor in the Conococheagues and elsewhere in Pennsylvania, Patton decided to invest his ambition and his $200 savings in "some other business" than farmwork and weaving. After purchasing a pony and a variety of dry goods, he headed south on the Great Wagon Road to western Virginia and North Carolina, peddling his wares for cash or, more frequently, for furs, indigo, beeswax, feathers—whatever his backcountry customers offered in exchange—before returning in spring to Philadelphia for more goods. Between 1789–1790 and 1791–1792, Patton made three such trips, steadily increasing his volume and variety of sales and purchases, before establishing his mercantile concern permanently in western North Carolina, first near Wilkes Court House (now Wilkesboro), later in Asheville, in the newly created Buncombe County, on the edge of the settlers' incursions onto Cherokee lands. In this excerpt from his 1839 memoir, Patton details the cautious albeit flexible course of his peddler's progress to wealth and prominence on the North Carolina frontier.

Since the 1730s, a steady stream of Scots-Irish and others from Pennsylvania's Cumberland Valley, joined by a minority of new immigrants from Ulster, had flowed south down the Great Road, settling first in the southern regions of the Shenandoah Valley and the Valley of Virginia and later, by the 1750s, moving into the North and South Carolina uplands. In the 1780s the mountainous region of far western North Carolina was still largely unsettled, but after the Revolution a series of treaties with the Cherokees, culminating in their almost total expulsion in the 1830s, steadily opened the area to penetration by pioneers from the Virginia and North Carolina Piedmont. In 1790 even Wilkes County, settled prior to 1776, had merely 8,157 inhabitants, but by 1840 there were approximately

1. On James Patton's earlier career in the United States, see chapter 33.

34,000 people in Buncombe and its adjacent counties along the North Carolina–Tennessee border. By 1850 Asheville, which had only 38 inhabitants in 1800, boasted a population of 700. A large proportion of these settlers were of Ulster ancestry: in 1800 an estimated 43 percent of the nearly nine hundred families settled along the Swannanoa and French Broad rivers were Scots-Irish. Their share of the population declined as the frontier moved westward, and after about 1810 the rapid growth of the Baptists and Methodists in western North Carolina completely overshadowed the local Presbyterian church.[2] Nevertheless, the region's wealthiest landowners and most prominent traders and political leaders remained disproportionately of Scots-Irish origins.

Ulster-born entrepreneurs, like Francis Campble before and James Patton after the Revolution, played vital roles in both the early settlement and the subsequent commercialization of the trans-Appalachian frontier, helping to establish a chain of major and subsidiary market centers from Shippensburg and Chambersburg in Pennsylvania, through Winchester and Staunton in Virginia, and further south to Camden and Augusta in South Carolina and Georgia. What some of them, like Patton, initially lacked in capital they gained from their versatility and from their reliance on personal credit and connections with their fellow countrymen and coreligionists, among both their rural customers and their suppliers and financial backers in Philadelphia, Baltimore, and other seaports. The less successful remained itinerant traders or died of malaria or yellow fever (Patton's likely fate had he gone to New Orleans, as first planned), but the more enterprising and fortunate—like Patton—grew wealthy as the Southern backcountry became, through their efforts, increasingly market-oriented.

James Patton Memoir, 1789–1839

. . . . The first thing that suggested itself to my mind was to get three or four young men to unite their small capitals with mine, purchase a boat load of flour, and take it to New Orleans; but in this I was disappointed. In the same year that I intended to start, a difference took place between the Spaniards and Kentuckians, which prevented all trade from passing down the river.[3] Having failed in this scheme, I (contrary to the advice and wishes of all my friends) concluded to lay out the little money I had in dry goods, and vend them over the country as well as I could. The principal objection that was urged against this plan was the scarcity of money. I told them that I could get something else that would answer in the place of money. About this time I wrote for

---

2. By the early 1840s there were 37 Baptist and 32 Methodist congregations in southwestern North Carolina, compared with only six Presbyterian churches that together had fewer than three hundred members. **3. a difference took place between the Spaniards and Kentuckians . . .** : after the failure of the Jay-Gardoqui negotiations (1785–1786), Spanish officials temporarily barred American farmers and traders from shipping their goods down the Mississippi through New Orleans.

my mother and family, and mentioned in my letter that I had been unfortunate from[4] sickness, but that I now saw the way clear before me. Accordingly, in the month of November, 1789, I went to Lancaster, Penn., and bought my goods of an old German: he told me, that he and his wife had both been servants, and had served out their time, and that he started in the world on very little. The old woman furnished a piece of Russia Duck,[5] took it to the Saddler's and had it made in the shape of saddle bags. The old German wrapped up the goods in the best manner. I paid for the whole of them, taking nothing on credit; I was so little acquainted with the nature of trade that I did not ask for credit; neither did I expect that it would be extended to me, as I was poor and had no friends to assist me. When I was ready to start, I placed the pack on the back of my pony and drove her before me, with my staff in my hand, whistling and singing in the highest spirits: I thought that I was a very rich man, or was in a fair way to become so; but misfortune seemed to await me at every turn: I had not gone more than three miles when I met with an awful defeat at the millpond of a Mr. Stoner.[6] The road passed over the end of the mill dam, my pony stopped to drink, after drinking, instead of keeping the road, she[7] dashed into the pond, but could not get through; she stuck fast in the mud at the bottom of the pond, got her head upon a stump, and thus saved herself from drowning. Imagine (if you can) my distress, at seeing my whole fortune on the back of my pony in the middle of a mill pond, and he stuck fast in the mud and unable to get out; it looked like a bad beginning to the mercantile business; there was no time to be lost, so Mr. Stoner procured some kind of a craft for the purpose of rescuing my pony and goods. He wished to release the pony and let her go out with the pack on her back, but I said no!   we will save the goods if the pony should be lost; so we took out the pack of goods first, and then the pony. The goods had been so carefully wrapped up that they received no material injury. That night I went to the house of a widow woman, one mile and a half from Mr. Stoner's at the forks of the road, one leading to Anderson's Ferry, the other to Wright's Ferry (now called Columbia)[8] on the Susquehanna River. She furnished me with a good room and lines to hang my wet goods upon. I sat up all night drying my goods and cleaning my buckles and buttons with my brush and chalk, so that they looked as well as they did at first.

Having put all in good order, I proceeded on my way: I met with a young Dutchman[9] who wished to purchase a pair of silver lockets; he asked me the price of them: I fearing that they were probably too high,[10] asked him the price of such in

4. from: because of.   **5. Russia Duck:** a type of canvas.   **6. Mr. Stoner:** a descendant of David Stoner, an immigrant from Germany and, in the 1740s, a neighbor of James McCullough in the Conococheagues settlement, later Franklin Co., Pa.; see chapter 21.   **7. she:** referred to as "he" below ("and *he* stuck fast").   **8. Columbia:** in Lancaster Co., Pa., on the east bank of the Susquehanna River; population five hundred in 1810.   **9. Dutchman:** likely "German."   **10. high:** first attested in the sense of "expensive" in 1737 (OED); this acceptation has persisted in American English, but in British English and Hiberno-English has been replaced in most contexts by "dear."

town. However, I sold them to him at 13 or 14 cents advance:[11] this was the first profit that I realized from the sale of my goods.

The next night I went to the honest Dutchman's Philip Kissinger,[12] at whose brickyard I had worked, got all my goods hung upon lines in the stove-room, where he and his wife slept: I went to bed and took a sound sleep. The next morning, Mrs. Kissinger took a dozen of my cotton handkerchiefs and sold eleven of them for me at about 13 cents advance on each, and for her trouble and kindness, I gave her the twelfth and last one. I had now made about $1.43 on my handkerchiefs, which money I laid out for the same sort, and got as good a bargain as I did for the first.

I then steered my course for North-Carolina. Fifteen miles from the place I had lived, I met a young man who had been out with $500 worth of goods to the same section of country I intended to go to. I said, hie, hie Elick,[13] sold all and returning, and I doing nothing? Yes, said he, it is well I met you here. I would advise you to sell your goods and go to work; there is no money in the back country, and I sold my goods to a merchant in Virginia for the same they cost me in Philadelphia. I said to him, Elick, did you call at every house and all the cabins on the road? He said, he did not: that he only called at the best looking houses, where he expected to find something. I told him that he was wrong, that money was sometimes to be found in cabins, where there was none to be had at fine houses. Sir, said I, you are too finely dressed, you should have gone out in your common clothes; a man should always be dressed to suit his business, and don't suppose show will make money. The people took you for some collegian going to College with a load of books. No sir, said I, they would laugh at me if I were to go back, if I cannot get money I will try to get something else, and was determined that I would not be turned[14] by him.

I proceeded on my way and got in company with Mr. James McIntyre, of Morgantown,[15] Burke County, North Carolina, near Chambersburg,[16] Pennsylvania. We travelled together and camped out at night, as he had a wagon loaded with goods. My forming an acquaintance with him, was the cause of my coming to this part of the country. I formed a good opinion of him; he was kind and advised me what to do. We parted in Botetourt County, Virginia, and I took the road to the head of the Holston.[17] After beating about for some time in that part of the country, I crossed the mountain into the county of Surry; thence, into Wilkes, Burke, and Buncombe. To show how

---

11. advance: rise in value or price (i.e., profit).   **12. Philip Kissinger:** see chapter 33, n. 27; **I went to the honest Dutchman's Philip Kissinger** "I went to the house of the honest Dutchman (i.e. German), Philip Kissinger."   **13. hie, hie Elick:** "hey there, Alec!"; see chapter 21, n. 37.   **14. turned:** deflected.   **15. James McIntyre:** James McEntire, an early Irish immigrant and settler in western North Carolina, who in 1790 owned five slaves; father of Dr. John McEntire (1791–1852), prominent local physician and North Carolina state legislator. **Morgantown** (usually Morgonton): seat of Burke Co., N.C.; population 150 in 1790–1795. **16. Chambersburg:** seat of Franklin Co., Pa.; population one thousand in 1795–1797.   **17. the head of the Holston:** the headwaters of the Holston River, which flows west into east Tennessee, are in the mountains of southwestern Virginia, south of **Botetourt County** at the southern end of the Shenandoah Valley.

slowly I got along in my business, I will inform you that I travelled in the section of country now called Ashe County,[18] for ten days, and got but three dollars in money. I could have purchased fur skins, but was not willing to risk it, as I did not know their value. During this trip I met with poor success in the sale of my goods.

I will here mention an incident which occurred to me at Morgantown; it will show you the kind of stuff I was made of. An Act of Congress had been passed to pay the Revolutionary soldiers for their services; I found that the certificates were selling very low, and I thought that something could be made by buying them; accordingly I purchased some of them, and paid part in goods and part in money.[19] When I was going from Wilkes to Burke County, the Entry Taker of Wilkes,[20] a Mr. Fletcher, requested me to take an £80 note of his, (as he called it) and dispose of it along with my own. When I got to Morgantown, I showed it and some other notes to several persons in the public square, and they all refused to receive them, as the note I had gotten of Fletcher proved to be a raised note[21] from £8 to £80. I then stepped into Mr. <Mc>Intyre's and had scarcely seated myself, before a man came in and told me to make my escape, that I had bad money and would be taken up in an hour; said I, thank you sir, for your information, but I never went to a place yet, where I would go out of the back door if the front door was open, for any crime which I have ever committed. I told him that I would go immediately to the gentlemen; they were not dispersed, but were talking together and probably laying some plan to secure me. I said, gentlemen, I am told that I have bad money, if I have, I don't know it. I am informed that this £80 note is raised from £8 to £80, if so shew it to me; and that you intend to put me in jail; I told them that I hoped they would not do that, that the jail was never made for me; you can take my horse, my money and all I have, until I satisfy you better. I had become acquainted with Mr. Wallace Alexander,[22] a lawyer of

18. Surry . . . Wilkes, Burke, . . . Buncombe . . . Ashe: counties in western North Carolina, along the Virginia and Tennessee borders; Surry, Wilkes, and Burke were created prior to the 1790 census, Buncombe and Ashe between 1790 and 1800. 19. In late 1789, Congress passed the Invalid Pensioners Act, by which the new federal government assumed from the states the responsibility (for at least one year) of paying pensions to wounded Revolutionary War veterans. However, Patton probably refers to the Congressional passage, on 26 July and 4 August 1790, of the proposals by Alexander Hamilton, secretary of the treasury, that the federal government should fund the national debt and assume the state debts incurred during the Revolution; these proposals did not compensate soldiers per se but rather the current owners of U.S. and state bonds; since many of the latter were speculators, who (like Patton) were busy purchasing the bonds at a discount from their original owners (unaware of Congress's decision to redeem the bonds immediately and at full value), Hamilton's proposals were very controversial, especially in the Southern states, which may help account for Patton's erroneously vague description of their purpose. 20. the Entry Taker of Wilkes: i.e., the recorder of deeds for Wilkes Co., N.C. 21. raised note: a banknote the value of which has been increased by counterfeiting. 22. Wallace Alexander: a kinsman of Dr. Nathaniel Alexander (1756–1808), of Mecklenburg Co., who was a North Carolina state legislator (1797–1802), congressman (1803–1805), and governor (1805–1808).

Mecklenburg County, North-Carolina, at Wilkes Court<-house>,[23] previous to this time; he was in Morgantown; I told him that I had gotten that note from Fletcher in Wilkes County, and that I had no suspicion at the time, that it was not good. He said, gentlemen, I believe what Mr. Patton says; he then told me that he would take the note, and put it out of their power to do me any harm. I told him he could have it, if he would stand between me and danger, and let Fletcher have the note if he wanted it. Now you see, that I possessed a proud, independent spirit and was not to be alarmed at trifles, when I was conscious of my integrity; and remember, a clear conscience will carry a person through difficulties when every thing else fails. When I returned to Wilkes, I told Fletcher that he had done very wrong in giving me that note; that I was not only near getting into trouble, but was in a fair way of having my character injured, as I was a stranger in the country. I told him that he could get his note if he would apply for it; he said, let it go.

I now made preparations to return to the North, which was in the spring of 1790. On my way, I bought 200 pounds of indigo at Fincastle[24] in Virginia, and made almost as much profit on it, as I had done on my goods. I also bought a few fur skins of different sorts, to see what each kind would bring; I shewed them to eight or ten different hatters, told them not to be offended before I opened them. This way of proceeding learned[25] me the value of the different kinds of fur, and was of great service to me the next year, and many years afterwards, when I had a store in Wilkes. This shows with what caution I acted in my trading: I was unwilling to risk anything, even in the smallest matters, without some certainty of profit. During this trip, I called upon my old friend Mr. Walker, with whom I had lived for three years.[26] I had at that time two good horses; I took the best care of them, and they were in fine order. I purchased another from Mr. Walker, and went down to the Federal City,[27] and the adjacent country, with an old Mr. McCall, who had a small drove of horses also. I sold one horse and swapped the other two for an old horse, and got the difference in their value; the one that I got was poor[28] but strong.

I now discovered that there was something to be made by buying feathers and taking them up the country. Accordingly, I purchased some, made a large cloth sack and filled it, and loaded my horse and started. You see, children, nothing was too humble for me that was honest; I was not ashamed of anything that soap and water would wash out.

On my return I bought an old Jersey wagon for about $30, which was not worth

---

23. Wilkes Court<-house>: Wilkesboro, seat of Wilkes Co., N.C., on the Yadkin River; population only 150 in 1840.　24. Fincastle: seat of Botetourt Co., Va.; population 250 in 1795–1797.　25. learned: taught; in Hiberno-English learn means both "learn" and "teach."　26. with whom I had lived for three years: i.e., in the Conococheagues settlement, Franklin Co., Pa.; see chapter 33.　27. the Federal City: Patton probably refers, with hindsight, to Washington, D.C., although Philadelphia was the nation's capital from 1790 to mid-1800.　28. poor: shabby.

thirty shillings, except for iron. This shews that a person should not touch on matters of which he is not a judge. It was a bad time for me to pay high for my schooling,[29] as I had but little to go on: however, I got my wagon so repaired that I got it to Lancaster,[30] Pennsylvania. There I had to get it made almost entirely new, no part of it being worth anything except the body and some of the irons. As I was going to the North this trip (of which I have been speaking), I met two young men on the way; one of them said to the other, does not that man (alluding to me) favor[31] old Mrs. Patton and family who came in the vessel with us? I then made some inquiry about them, and asked the men if they could name them? They soon satisfied me that it was my good mother and family; this was the first information I had received of their arrival. The next night I arrived at the place they were, and we had a joyful meeting. I then went to Philadelphia and bought as many goods as I was able to pay for, and $90 worth on a credit besides, which I did not ask. When I looked over the bills, I discovered that they would take too much of my money, and prevent me from buying other goods on which I could make more profit, and requested the merchants to take some of them back, and told them my reasons. These merchants were Quakers. One of them said to the other, don't thee think James will come back and pay us? O, yes, said the other. I thought he was amusing himself with me at the time. I took the goods, and this was the commencement of a credit that would afterwards have commanded twenty thousand dollars or more, if I had asked it, at that house and others. I happened to see a young man in Philadelphia at this time, who was going to Ireland and to the very neighborhood in which I had lived in that country; I sent a small amount of money by him to defray the expenses of my brother Thomas and family to this country, which he received and came in the next summer. When he arrived, the whole of the family were in this country, except one brother who had gone to the East-Indies.[32]

I now left Philadelphia with all my goods, for the State of North-Carolina; sold all I could on the road, and would stop a day or two at a place for that purpose. When I came to North River,[33] Rockingham County, Virginia, I stopped at an honest German's house by the name of Jacob Singer, and staid there three weeks. With what I had gotten before and during this time, I had upwards of three hundred dollars in cash, and also some fur skins and beeswax. The fur skins and beeswax I left at that place until

---

29. schooling: (gaining of) experience.   **30. Lancaster:** seat of Lancaster Co., Pa.; population 4,500 in 1795; on Lancaster prior to the Revolution, see chapter 53.   **31. favor:** resemble, have similar features to. **32.** James Patton's siblings included: Thomas, who married Jane Shaw in Ireland and died in Coffey Co., Tenn.; William, died a bachelor; John, settled and died in the "Calhoun Settlement," Abbeville District, S.C.; Daniel, died in Bedford Co., Tenn.; Neely, who enlisted in the British East India Company's service, returned from India, and died near London; Joseph, died in Asheville, N.C.; George (1769–1843), married Mary Jane McDonald and died near Franklin, Macon Co., N.C.; Rosanna, married a Mr. Campbell of Pennsylvania; and Jane (b. 1770), who married Col. Andrew Erwin (see n. 46).   **33. North River:** the North Fork of the Shenandoah River, in Rockingham Co., at the northern (or lower) end of the Shenandoah Valley.

I would return. I laid out what money I had on hand in Staunton,[34] Augusta County, Virginia: this was in the fall of the year: I bought such goods as I thought would sell readily in the country; I got them on very good terms, and had at this time a pretty good assortment. The last purchase I thought would help to sell the first. I travelled on by the way of Lexington,[35] Pattonburg, Fincastle, Pepper's Ferry on New River, to the head of the Holston. On my way I frequently stopped from six to twelve days at a place; would send out word beforehand, that I would be at such places at the time appointed. By this means the people would get their trade ready, such as fur skins, beeswax, &c., and some money. I sometimes left money with men on whom I could depend, to purchase fur skins, beeswax, &c., for me at such prices as I directed them to give. This year I took in fifteen hundred skins of different sorts, and made a handsome profit on them, having the year before made myself acquainted with the prices of all kinds, from a rabbit skin to an otter skin. I left my wagon on the south fork of the Holston and packed my goods on horseback; came to Roan's creek, thence into Ashe, Wilkes, Burke and Buncombe counties.

I returned to the North the first of the next summer. I left my small wagon and got a light four horse wagon. I purchased as many goods as I was able, and returned the same road that I had travelled the first two years, stopped at the same places, and sold double the amount of goods that I did the first two years. I drove my own wagon, until I came to the North River, Rockingham County, Virginia; then I hired a little simple Dutchman and kept him until I got to the head of the Holston; he was so much of a fool, and withal[36] so lazy, that I would not have him any longer. I now met with Andrew Erwin, let him have about $150 worth of goods to trade on, sent him into the country and directed him where to go, and to meet me at Wilkes Court-house, which he did. He transacted the business as well as I expected; I did not calculate on his doing much, as he was only nineteen years of age, and had little experience; but I found he was honest: this has caused me to overlook many errors of young men, all my life. I have had a great many in my employment from this time until I quit business; for I touched at everything that I thought would be profitable—gathering ginseng, snake root, purchasing deer skins, bear skins and driving large numbers of cattle.

During this and the preceding trips, I had frequently stopped at the house of a man by the name of Jonathan Tompkins, in the county of Wilkes, a member of the Baptist Church, and apparently[37] a very pious man. He told me, that his land was under execution, and that £40 would save it; that his brother had gone to South Carolina for money, and would be certain to get it, but for fear that he might be detained by high water or some accident, wished me to let him have it, which I did. I knew so little of

---

34. Staunton: seat of Augusta Co., Va., in the heart of the Shenandoah Valley; population eight hundred in 1790–1797; on this region prior to the Revolution, see chapters 20 and 46.   **35. Lexington**: seat of Rockbridge Co., Va., in the upper Shenandoah Valley, between Augusta and Botetourt counties; population five hundred in 1795–1797.   **36. withal**: in addition.   **37. apparently**: seemingly.

mankind at that time, that I took no obligation on him for the money, but merely made a memorandum of it in my pocket-book. This single circumstance is sufficient to show my great want of qualification for business at that time. I then attended Burke Court, and on my return, this same man came to where I was stopped by high water, and told me that I would lose my money, and he would lose his land if I did not pay £40 more. He therefore proposed to let me have a part of his land, and he would have a good crop raised on it for me, if I would pay the other £40, to which I agreed, as I intended to move my mother and family to that part of the country.

This summer I intended to go to Philadelphia to dispose of my furs, and purchase goods to enable me to buy a handsome drove of cattle, but finding it would be too late before I could go and return, I stopped at Staunton, Augusta County, Virginia, and employed three hatters to work up a part of my fur into hats, and paid them in fur for their labor. I returned to North Carolina with my hats in boxes, packed upon horses. I purchased all the cattle I was able to pay for, in the counties of Wilkes, Burke and Buncombe, and started for Philadelphia; stopped at Staunton, Virginia, and took on the balance of the furs which I had left there. I purchased in Philadelphia as many goods as I was able to pay for, and returned to North Carolina with two wagons, one loaded with goods, and the other with my mother and family. We moved to the piece of land which I got of Tompkins, in Wilkes County, North Carolina, fifteen miles from the Court-house on Lewis' Fork, near the foot of the Blue Ridge. This was in the winter of 1792; at that time there was no building of any kind on the place; but I got the assistance of the neighbors who were very kind, and in two weeks had a comfortable house a story and a half high to move into. It was built of pine logs and covered with clapboards. I put my goods on the second story of the house. My principal reason for commencing business at my mother's was to procure such things as were necessary for the family. We never lived better in our lives, and had plenty of everything that was comfortable. By this time I had fully seen the value of a good parent who strove so hard for the comfort and happiness of her children.

The ensuing fall[38] I moved my goods to Wilkes Court-house. The next year in the fall, I moved my brother Thomas and family to Wilkes County, and settled him on the top of the Blue Ridge, ten miles from my mother's. I let him have cattle and horses to make a beginning on, and he lived well though at a distance from neighbors; he had but three children and they were small; his wife was an excellent woman, I always esteemed her highly: she was a high-minded honorable woman, and endeavored to instil pure principles into the minds of her children. Brother Thomas was a weakly[39] man, but he did all he could for his family. I gave them all the assistance in my power, but it could not be expected that I could do much for them in so short a time from my

---

38. The ensuing fall: autumn 1792; **fall**: from the mid–nineteenth century on, mostly replaced by "autumn," except in Ulster and the United States.   **39. weakly**: delicate, not robust.

little beginning of two hundred dollars; however, I put them all in a way to support themselves and raise their families decently. They are now respectable, which is well known by those who are acquainted with them.

The first year after I moved my mother to Wilkes County, I bought a small drove of horses and took them to the Federal City, and from that[40] to Baltimore. I also bought a house and lot in Staunton, Virginia, from a man who lived in Wilkes County, North-Carolina, and agreed to give him two young negroes for it. Indeed, before I bought it, I had sold it on condition that I would make a right to it.[41] If a man will help himself he will always find friends. The merchants of Staunton saw that I was making a better use of my small beginning, and some of them became my security for a title, before I had bought it myself. I made something by the speculation. I also bought some other negroes, besides the two that I paid for the house and lot. The money was all paid down for the house and lot, and I intended to lay it out for cattle. You will observe how careful I was; I knew how much I would have to pay for negroes, and also knew what I could get for the house and lot before I made the trade.

About two years from the time that I moved my mother to Wilkes County, I was married to your good and great mother.[42] She was the daughter of Francis Reynolds, a man of little property, but as honest and respectable as any man in the County of Wilkes. He was one of the first settlers on the Yadkin River in that county; he had twelve children, of course he was not able to give her much;[43] all she ever got did not amount to more than three hundred dollars. When we were married, she was in the bloom of youth and very handsome; amiable and sensible. There was great disparity in our ages; she was twenty years and five months younger than myself. She was ambitious to excel in all the duties of a wife, and assisted me greatly in my business. She saw that I was using all the exertions in my power, and having confidence in my judgement, it gave an increased impulse to her industry.

Her Mother (Mrs. Reynolds) was a superior house-keeper; it was from the management of her domestic concerns, the neatness of her house, and the nice arrangement of everything about it, that I took a fancy to my wife, and I was not disappointed. She was everything I expected and looked for—prudent, industrious and economical, ready at all times to receive advice—cheerful, but not ostentatious. I gave it as my opinion, that it would be imprudent for myself and her to appear at Church and other public places in superfluous dress,[44] or to appear at any time above our neighbors; not only because I dislike vain show, but my principal reason was, that as we were just starting in the world, and were dependent on the public for our success, it might have an improper influence on their minds, and excite prejudices very much

---

40. that: see chapter 11, n. 10. **41. make a right to it**: secure a title to it (i.e., the house and lot in Staunton). Patton was allowed to buy the property and resell it without waiting for the title but on the promise that he would secure it. **42.** James Patton married Ann Reynolds in 1795. **43. give her much**: i.e., as a dowry or wedding present. **44. in superfluous dress**: overdressed.

against our interest. My motto was, plainness and neatness; and this is as far as any one should go, however prosperous their circumstances may be; a beautiful exterior may dazzle the fancy for a short time, but solid worth depends entirely on a well trained and virtuous mind.

I made it a rule to consult my wife on all weighty and important matters that I thought she could comprehend, and when I deviated from her opinion, I generally found that I was in error. I would advise all married men to consult their wives in every important undertaking. If they cannot fully understand the whole of any matter that may be presented to their consideration, they will be certain to catch at parts, and make some observations that will set their husbands to thinking. My opinion is, that women have never been allowed their just weight in society; were they permitted to use that influence in society to which I consider them entitled, they would contribute much more to the success of business through life, than is generally imagined, and particularly to domestic prosperity and happiness.[45]

During the third year after I had commenced trading, I took Col. Andrew Erwin in, to assist me in my business. The second year that he was in my employment, he married my sister.[46] About twelve months after his marriage, I took him into full connection with me in trade, although he had nothing at the time; I had two reasons for it, one was, on account of the high regard I had for my sister—she was a high-minded honorable young woman; the other was, that I wished to encourage him, as he had married my connexion. At this time my capital was greater than his by twenty-eight hundred dollars, after all I had done for my good mother and family.

It gives me consolation at this time, to think that I did not grasp all, and prevent others from coming forward, which (it is well known) I had no disposition to do. I find fault very much with wealthy men, for not taking poor young men by the hand, and putting them in a way to do well, when they find them honest, trusty and capable. I had now lived in Wilkes County, North-Carolina, twelve years, and my health had become so greatly impaired, that I took a dislike to Wilkesborough, and resolved to leave the place; accordingly, I rented my possessions to Waugh & Finley (merchants) for seven years. We then moved into the county of Buncombe in 1807, and settled on the farm where my son Thomas now lives, three miles from Asheville, where we lived for seven years. We then moved from the farm to Asheville, where we lived together thirteen years and six months, before your mother died. She had been afflicted with a liver complaint for several years, which finally took her off. I think I can date her indisposition back to the birth of your sister Jane Hardy, who died the past winter in Charleston, South Carolina; she then took cold, and was more or less indisposed from that time until her death. From the time we were married, until the death of your

---

45. No paragraph break between **happiness** and **During the third year** in Patton's published *Letter*.
46. Andrew Erwin was born in Wythe Co., Va., in 1723 and died in Bedford Co., Tenn., in 1834; in 1793 he married Jane Patton (b. 1770).

mother, was thirty-two years and ten months. We had eleven children, of whom we raised ten. At the time we moved to Asheville my son James was 11 years of age, my second son John 9, Franklin 7, and Thomas 5 years old. You can judge from this that I had to contend with many disadvantages when I commenced public house-keeping.[47]

Col. Erwin and myself were in partnership for twenty years, and made a complete dissolution in one day, to the astonishment of every person of understanding; it was effected in the following manner. As he was the active partner, I told him to make a division of the whole, accompanied with a statement on paper, and give me my choice, which he did; and in this way we came to an amicable settlement at once.

Col. Andrew Erwin was a man of clear head and a good heart, but too credulous and too easily imposed upon by bad men. I was like the little boat spoken of by Dr. Franklin,[48] I would always keep near the shore; I would not venture far out to sea for fear of accidents, therefore, I always endeavored to find out whether a man was deserving of confidence, before I trusted much in his hands.

I have thought it unnecessary to extend this narrative any further, as my principal object has been to give you some knowledge of my low beginning in the world, more than any thing else: and my dear children, having thus endeavored to give you a short sketch of the struggles and difficulties which I have passed through in life, I can assure you that I have not done it by way of boasting, but quite the contrary. It would be vain and foolish in me to suppose that it would be of any advantage to me as an individual, for at my time of life I have no disposition to indulge any such feelings; but I have thought that if it should never be of any benefit, it would perhaps afford satisfaction to some of my posterity to know from whence they sprang. You could not reasonably expect, that I would be able at my advanced age (being now in my 84th year) to give you an exact and accurate account of the various vicissitudes of my life, merely from memory. I know that I have omitted many things worthy of notice, but I could not from recollection alone, embody them in a way calculated either to please or instruct; but imperfect as it is, I hope it may be profitably read by some of you when I am no more. You will see that I had many hard trials to endure, and difficulties to encounter. You will also observe how much can be accomplished by industry and frugality. To the exercise of these virtues is mainly to be attributed the little success I have had in life, for I was possessed of very moderate qualifications for the business in which I was generally engaged; but I had a firm mind, which by the assistance of a kind providence enabled me to surmount the many obstacles which were in my way. . . . [49] [W]ith all the trials and misfortunes that have come my way, I never desponded; I always looked onwards and suffered nothing to arrest my progress; if I met with troubles, I consoled myself with the reflection, that it was the common lot of

47. **public house-keeping**: managing a tavern or an inn—in this instance Patton's hotel at Warm Springs (see hereafter). 48. **Dr. Franklin**: i.e., Benjamin Franklin, after whom Patton named his third son. 49. Omitted: Patton's account of an accident, which fractured both his legs, when he was 80 years old.

man, and endeavored to profit by it in the future. The little success I have had in life, was owing (as I before mentioned) to industry and frugality, for I settled in the upper part of North-Carolina, at that time the poorest part of the country I ever saw to make property; but I do not entertain the same opinion now. Changes and improvements have taken place, which have convinced me that there are few sections of country superior to the western part of North-Carolina. I am thankful that the Almighty blessed my weak means and enabled me to do as much as I have, and I have the consolation at this day to think, that I never made anything at the expense of the widow and the fatherless. I have never sold the widow's cow or the poor man's land. . . . [50]

During their 20-year partnership, Patton and his brother-in-law, Andrew Erwin, prospered, establishing branches in western North Carolina's small villages in addition to their primary store and inn at Wilkesboro. In 1800–1801 Erwin represented Wilkes County in the state legislature; in 1803 he moved to Asheville and took over the business of Jeremiah Cleveland as merchant and innkeeper. In 1807 Patton joined Erwin in Buncombe County, where he combined farming and land speculations with commerce and manufacturing. In Asheville, Patton built a store, a tanyard, and the Eagle Hotel. Patton's judgement of Erwin's credulity may have been accurate, for after they dissolved their partnership in 1814, his brother-in-law moved to Augusta, Georgia, and failed in several ambitious enterprises. However, after moving into Asheville the same year, Patton's wealth continued to increase. In 1824 he and two partners gained a contract from the North Carolina legislature to lay out what became, in 1828, the Buncombe Turnpike, which ran from Greeneville, Tennessee, to Greenville, South Carolina, along the banks of the French Broad River. The Turnpike inaugurated the great livestock drives of cattle and hogs from the mountains of eastern Tennessee and western North Carolina to new markets in Charleston, Columbia, and Savannah. However, those who grew wealthiest from the drives were not the farmers and drovers but the men who owned inns, taverns, hotels, and livestock "stands" or feedlots along the route. Patton already owned one such facility in Asheville, and in 1831 he purchased the land and medicinal waters at Warm Springs, near the Tennessee–North Carolina border, and built a luxurious hotel, with accommodations for 250 guests, which catered to wealthy summer visitors, seeking cool air and health in the Blue Ridge Mountains, as well as to the autumn crowd of livestock drovers. In 1835, when he made his will (with the assistance of his friend, David Swain, then governor of North Carolina),[51] Patton estimated his personal property alone at $45,000, although he had already turned control of his businesses over to his eldest son, James W., and bestowed large legacies on his other children.

---

50. Omitted: Patton's lengthy, detailed, and somewhat repetitious advice to his children and grandchildren; for a summary and excerpts, see hereafter. **51.** David Swain (1801–1868); born in Asheville; lawyer and politician; elected governor of North Carolina (the youngest ever) in 1832; president of the University of North Carolina from 1835 until his death.

James Patton died in his ninetieth year on 9 September 1845 and was buried in the graveyard of the Asheville Presbyterian Church, under a marble obelisk that described him as "the founder of his family in America; an honest and persevering man, accumulating much property without grinding the poor—prudently assisting his poor relations, as well as bringing forward in the world many deserving young men." He left behind in his memoir not only his life's story but pages of Franklinesque injunctions to his descendants, advising them to be industrious and public-spirited; to shun litigation, ostentation, speculation, and his own former failing, intemperance; and to treat poor relations, debtors, tradesmen, and "servants" (Patton's euphemism for his slaves) with kindness and charity.[52]

44 ✳

Margaret Carey Murphy Burke, 1798

Margaret Carey Murphy Burke's career and her correspondence with her famous brother Mathew Carey of Philadelphia are unusual in several respects: she was exceptionally literate among early Irish immigrant women; and, despite being twice widowed, she strove with some success to achieve a rare degree of economic independence. Yet Margaret's life and letters also exemplify several broad themes in early Irish-American history. As a city-dweller in America (as in Ireland before her emigration), Margaret symbolized Irish-America's nascent urbanization and social-class formation. Likewise, as a Roman Catholic her career revealed the vital and symbiotic, albeit often ambivalent, relationships between the Church and the Irish-American Catholic middle classes—a relationship

---

52. Patton's last pages of parental advice included the following injunctions: "Let all your intercourse with the world be marked by honesty and integrity. . . . Don't strive to be the richest people in the country, by grasping at too much you may lose all. Therefore, never engage in uncertain speculation. Wealth is generally the result of patience, industry, and frugality. . . . Make use of all honest and honorable means of gain, and God will give the blessing. Treat every person with kindness and respect, be plain and decent both at home and abroad, and you will have the good opinion of your poor relations and neighbors. . . . Be charitable to your poor relations and neighbors, and as God has enjoined, that we must earn our bread by the sweat of the brow, we must be industrious. In my opinion, a man cannot be a good Christian, unless he be industrious; and I know without industry he cannot be a good citizen. . . . Give your children a good education, impress upon their minds principles of industry and morality, but above all set before them pious examples and encourage them to follow the same. . . . As I have passed through life I have often reflected on my hard lot, and wondered that my father had not exerted himself more for the good of his children when he had it in his power, but he was like many others, he did not think properly until it was too late. He died when his children were all small, I have often felt the consequences of his neglect, which has stimulated me to do all that I could for you. . . . Be charitable to the poor. . . . [E]xercise a good degree of judgment in determining who are proper objects of charity, and who are not . . . ; but . . . the unfortunate drunkard . . . should be taken by the hand and encouraged to do well. . . . I was often fond of spirits when a young man, and even after I was married, and frequently drank too much, and never can be too thankful that I did not become the victim of intemperance."

that eventually facilitated their mutual ascent to respectability and their mutually reinforcing hegemony over the impoverished immigrant masses.

Margaret Carey's story also has important implications for the history of women in the late 1700s and early 1800s. For instance, although Margaret was obliged by misfortune to pursue economic self-sufficiency, as a widowed immigrant her engagements in business were by no means unique. In addition, Margaret Carey's struggles for a sense of personal worth, as well as for financial independence, revealed the constraints—internalized as well as externally imposed—endured by most women in a patriarchal society. According to the prevalent "doctrine of separate spheres," women were consigned to the ideally sheltered realm of domesticity—to housewifery and motherhood. In reality, the domestic sphere rarely provided its promised securities—especially to the widowed or to poor women, generally—yet the ideology denied women's ability to engage successfully in commercial enterprise or the propriety of their attempting to do so. Moreover, it is possible that middle-class Irish-American Catholic women experienced greater burdens and constraints than their Protestant contemporaries. In part this was because many such women, like Margaret Carey Murphy, were involved in business concerns such as tavern-keeping, which many native Americans considered disreputable. More important, although in the early 1800s the wives and daughters of middle-class Protestants increasingly "feminized" their churches and extended their "domestic" duties into "society" by creating and participating in philanthropic and reform organizations, among Catholics in the United States—as in Ireland—similar activities became the responsibility of societies of women religious. In the early nineteenth century communities of nuns or sisters proliferated in both Ireland and America, with the result that the kinds of "public" activities in which middle-class Protestant women independently engaged were, among Catholics, institutionalized in the Church itself and under the immediate authority of priests and bishops. Although not without protests by strong-willed mother superiors, by midcentury male clergymen had sharply limited whatever freedom of action and innovation the nuns initially had enjoyed. Ironically, therefore, although Margaret Carey Murphy Burke eventually achieved a measure of freedom from both financial insecurity and the supervision of her own male relatives, she did so only through an increasing association with a hierarchical and male-dominated Catholic church on which she became more emotionally as well as economically dependent.

Margaret Carey was born in Dublin in 1772, 12 years later than her brother Mathew. Apparently she was the only daughter and also the youngest of the six surviving children of her parents, Christopher, a prosperous baker, and Mary Sheridan Carey, who lived at 2 Redmond's Hill, on the south side of the River Liffey that divided Ireland's capital city. Although Mathew later claimed to have received in his youth only an indifferent education, Margaret's ability to read and converse fluently in French indicates that her schooling was far superior to that attained by the great majority of her peers. In the late 1700s Dublin boasted several schools for "young ladies," but only a few convent schools had survived the Penal Laws to cater for the children of the city's growing Catholic business and professional classes. Perhaps that was why Margaret's parents sent her to an exclusive convent school in Cork city, where for eight years she boarded with the Ursulines, members of a French order of nuns whom Nano Nagle (1718–1784), a wealthy Catholic philanthropist, had persuaded to come to Ireland in 1771. However, Margaret Carey's later letters reveal a forcible if not contentious personality, and she may have rebelled against the seclusion of convent life—or, more generally, against what brother Mathew recalled as their parents' "austere system" of childrearing. For whatever reason, in 1789 or 1790, when she was merely 16 or 17, Margaret married a fellow Catholic named John Murphy, perhaps in a "runaway" match. Margaret and her husband had at least two children, including a daughter named Maria born about 1791, before she and her family emigrated to the United States in 1794.

Almost 10 years earlier, Mathew Carey had left Dublin in flight from prosecution for sedition, and when Margaret's family joined him in Philadelphia he had already achieved eminence as a bookseller, publisher, political pamphleteer, and secretary to the city's Hibernian Society—although his financial affairs long remained precarious.[1] The Murphys lodged temporarily with Mathew—an imposition that was later the source of much recrimination—while Margaret's husband explored opportunities in weaving and then in retailing dry goods and groceries. By 1795, however, the Murphys had settled in premises at 6 Læticia (later Leticia) Court, a lane 30 feet wide and two hundred feet deep, off High or Market Street, where between 1795 and 1798 city directories listed John Murphy as the keeper of the "Leopard"—an "inn," a "tavern," and finally a "tavern & oyster house." To achieve this status so quickly, the Murphys must have brought some capital from Ireland—whether Margaret's or John's is unknown—but in Philadelphia they also relied on familial and ethnoreligious patronage: on loans from Mathew and also from James Gallagher, a wealthy Irish-American merchant, trustee of St. Mary's Catholic church, and Mathew's own creditor.[2] Yet at this time neither the Murphys' residence nor their occupation was distinctively "Irish": according to Philadelphia directories, in the 1790s only three or four of Læticia Court's eleven householders—occupied by a medley of small proprietors, craftsmen, sailors, laborers, and one "gentlewoman"—had recognizably Irish surnames, as did only about a tenth of the city's approximately 250 inn- and tavernkeepers, most of whom were native or German Americans.

Catering to Philadelphians' then almost insatiable appetite for drink was a lucrative trade, and Margaret and her family initially flourished. "Murphy keeps a tavern & thrives," Mathew Carey reported in 1795; "He has grown industrious"—perhaps implying he had not been so in Ireland—"& he & his wife are both very saving; so there is little doubt of

---

1. On Carey's career in Ireland and Philadelphia, see chapters 14, 34, and 35 and especially chapter 63.   2. On James Gallagher, also see chapter 63.

their doing well."[3] Margaret's family continued to grow: among her children who survived infancy, Charles was baptised at St. Joseph's Catholic church in early 1797, followed by Teresa in mid-1798. However, Mathew Carey—perennially concerned for his family's reputation—did not in fact approve of his sister's and brother-in-law's occupation or the state of their premises: "I rarely go to taverns . . . ," he sniffed, "and when I do, I wish to go to those which have at least the recommendation of Cleanliness."[4] Indeed, by 1797 Margaret's and Mathew's quarrels over old debts and disputed family responsibilities had deteriorated their relationship to such an extent that, although they resided only a few blocks apart, they communicated only through formal and abusive letters.

Both siblings were hot-tempered and extremely sensitive to perceived slights and insults. Perhaps Margaret's status in the Carey family—as youngest child and only daughter—exacerbated a sense of injustice or insecurity that may have stemmed ultimately from the discrepancy between a precarious sense of self-worth and a woman's social and legal subordination to male authority. As for Mathew, a cripple from a childhood accident, he retained bitter memories of his schoolmates' taunts and henceforth personalized conflicts over economic and political issues. In addition, both Mathew and Margaret may have shared the generalized resentment felt by many ambitious Irish and Irish-American Catholics who had been born under the Penal Laws and still suffered social scorn if not legal disabilities.

In any event, by early 1798 Margaret and Mathew had repaired their relationship. Indeed, although their estrangements were nasty and brutish, usually they were relatively short. In Margaret's case, periods of alienation alternated with fulsome declarations of affection and of gratitude for financial assistance—the necessity and memories of which must have galled her later, if not at the time. More destructive to her family's well-being, however, were Philadelphia's frequent epidemics of yellow fever. Læticia Court may have been an exceptionally unhealthy environment—18 residents had perished of that disease in 1793—and in the mid-1790s Margaret buried one, and probably at least two, of her own children. In late summer 1798 one of the worst yellow fever epidemics struck the city, and by late September there were as many as nine burials per day in the graveyard of St. Mary's Catholic church alone. One of the earliest victims was Margaret's husband, John Murphy, who was interred in St. Mary's burying ground on 29 August, only five weeks after the birth of their youngest daughter.

In the late 1700s and early 1800s about 10 percent of all the adult women in Philadelphia were widows. In general, their prospects were not promising: more than 80 percent never remarried, and the poorest—a disproportionate number of whom were Irish—tried to find refuge in the city's almshouse. However, Margaret Murphy was fortunate in several respects. Her intelligence, her tavern, and her connections to the Carey and Gallagher

3. Mathew Carey, Philadelphia, to James Carey, [Savannah, Ga.?], 31 August 1795. **4.** Mathew Carey, Philadelphia, to Margaret Carey Murphy, Philadelphia, 12 August 1797.

families ensured her financial survival. And those assets, plus her youth—she was only about 26 when Murphy died—made her eminently eligible for remarriage. Moreover, it was not uncommon for widows to manage their late husbands' businesses, often quite successfully, and in 1800 at least 15 percent of Philadelphia's inn- and tavern-keepers were widows. On the other hand, none of her children was old enough to be of much help—the eldest was merely eight or nine. In addition, John Murphy had died intestate, and in such circumstances Pennsylvania law determined that the widow could inherit merely one third of her husband's estate—even if "his estate" was comprised largely or entirely of property that she, herself, had brought to the marriage—and then only after all her husbands' creditors had been satisfied. The remaining property and cash would be divided among the deceased's children, but when all were minors, as were Margaret's offspring, the estate would be administered by the local Orphan's Court, which in turn would appoint one or more male trustees—in this case, her brother Mathew—to invest and otherwise oversee the children's legacies until they came of age.

These arrangements had important implications for Margaret Murphy's future. Certainly they wounded her pride and exacerbated her sense of grievance, for she now found herself largely dependent on the good will and business acumen of a sibling with whom she already had an ambivalent relationship. In the future this would lead to further periods of bitter estrangement, and Margaret would later accuse her brother, apparently without clear cause, of mismanaging her children's money and, with perhaps more justification, of "act[ing] the despot" by withholding funds or credit she wanted to pursue various business opportunities.[5] More immediately, however, her husband's death meant that Margaret now had to manage her greatest remaining asset—the "Leopard" tavern and oyster house— with hired help, without the capital tied up in the Orphan's Court, and while striving simultaenously to raise her children and to maintain her own health and reputation. In the following letter to brother Mathew, written less than three months after John Murphy's demise, Margaret addressed in detail some of the problems that a young widow faced in operating an establishment that catered to the drinking habits of an almost-exclusively male clientele of artisans, laborers, and sailors.

Margaret Carey Murphy, Philadelphia,
to Mathew Carey, Philadelphia, no date [received 17 December 1798]

    Dear Brother
        You will I hope excuse me for not profiting of your pressing invitation but the state of mind I at present feel disheartens me from leaving home or intruding my trouble on those who are themselves happy,   When you were with <me> I was

---

5. Margaret [Murphy] Burke, [Horsham, Pennsylvania?], to Mathew Carey, Philadelphia, no date [1802?].

to<o> full[6] to be able to communicate to you a plan which I had yesterday
formed —— if possible to be executed,[7]   1st I have this night to abolish card-playing
which will rid the house of a vast deal of trouble prevent late sitting up & be attended
with satisfaction, if not so profitable will make it more comfortable[8] for hou[ses] where
cards are not permitted are more peaceable than where they are — 2nd if possible to
find a person who can give security for the property in the house to allow him half
profit for a few months which I would pass in the Country if possible to restore my
health — Connor[9] I could entrust for honesty but he is too rough & uncouth in his
manner to please the company — the abolishing of cards will keep quietness as
gamblers are the only <patrons> who misbeheave & make a noise about their
money   Sunday nights always are comfortable, no loud talking   every man comes in
takes what he pleases makes no stay & goes off early,   week nights one comes in so
does another then a third a fourth make up a card table play sometimes
for money sometimes for Supper or liquor perhaps for all three stay late, perhaps
agree[10] or perhaps not —— generally speaking card-players are the poorest
customers,   Sunday Nights, do not generally speaking, turn out as much money as
other nights but I have not half the fire or candles used as other nights,   go to bed by
Eleven O Clock instead of two;   from all these circumstances I infer that it is possible
(if in good health with a good assistant) I could live tolerably happy where I am, for
here I am sure of being able to advance in the world ——

One circumstance more I will state which to me seems favourable — the river in all
apearance will in a day or two, close   there are two boat loads of good Oysters, in at
present   my neighbour[11] who like me sells Oysters is not able to lay in a Stock,   I
am   consequently if I loose[12] my card customers my Oyster ones will encrease   I
have not as yet laid in a stock & seems doubtful whether I will or not —— I attempted
yesterday to advise with M[r] Gallagher[13] but found the subject too weighty on my mind
to be able to proceed —— You may if you please consult with him   he is a better
judge of my business than you are — Whatever plan you can both fix on I will agree to
follow if compatible with my health which call<s> immediately for my absence from
here —— As for buying the bake-house I am nearly resolved not   I think it would

---

6. full: two possible meanings here: "occupied, engrossed" or "full of emotion."   **7. if possible to be
executed . . . :** the writer's inconsistent punctuation (when it exists) may put a barrier in the way of
understanding, which the following paraphrase may remove: " . . . if possible to be put into effect as follows:
(1) this very night I will have to abolish cards, which will rid the house of a great deal of trouble . . . ; although
perhaps lowering my profits, it will make things quieter . . . ; (2) I need to find a person who will manage the
operation and be able to give security for the business during the few months that I will be in the country."
8. comfortable: tranquil, peaceful.   **9. Connoll:** Margaret Murphy's hired man; probably the same person as
Connor hereafter.   **10. agree:** do not get into disputes.   **11. my neighbour:** probably John Cross, listed in
the Philadelphia city directories as a tavernkeeper at 9 Leticia Court in 1795–1801, joined by Mary Foot,
tavernkeeper at 10 Leticia Court in 1801.   **12. loose:** i.e., lose.   **13. advise with:** seek advice from; **M[r]
Gallagher:** probably James Gallagher (earlier).

be madness to sink my money & fasten myself to a place which might, or might not, turn out well. I am well aware that it would be difficult to find a person whom I could entrust with my[14] property but I do not despair such a one might be found   in the meantime Connoll might remain & I go immediately to the Country for nothing else will save my life —— When you have fixed your opinion you will please commit it to writing & send it to me for I have not resolution enough to converse calmly on the subject,   if possible let me hear from you this night for by Wednesday morning I expect the Oysters will be all either sold or bespoke[15]   Adieu   excuse the Scrawl I am Y[rs] M Murphy

Margaret Murphy's letter clearly evinces her pragmatism and sound business sense. Despite the concern for propriety that she shared with brother Mathew, apparently she was untroubled by the alleged "wickedness" of either drinking or gambling, although both were increasingly criticized by apostles of Christian morality, health reform, and capitalist efficiency. Rather, her primary concerns were that cardplayers commonly purchased little drink or food, "misbeheave[d]" and thus drove away better customers, and raised her fuel costs by staying up all night. Indeed, Murphy seemed quite content to profit by many Philadelphians' preference for liquor over bread, as she dismissed the notion of trading her tavern for a bakery as financial "madness." Yet Margaret's letter also exposes a psychological dilemma that was probably common among many contemporary women who were torn between a sense of their own potential and the submissive roles that society expected them to fulfill. Thus, Margaret the capable and ambitious businesswoman forcefully stated her desire "to advance in the world" through her own efforts, whereas one paragraph later the economically dependent sister, bereaved widow, and overwrought mother collapsed rhetorically in "feminine" dependence on male "wisdom" as to her economic affairs—proclaiming her lack of "resolution enough to converse calmly on the subject[s]" about which she had just written so ably. "I will be entirely ruled by your opinion," wrote Murphy to her brother a short time later, as "I have not strength of mind enough to form any determined plan[,] for when I find myself laying projects for futurity my fortitude escapes me."[16]

Of course, it is possible that in such letters Margaret was consciously manipulating male expectations of "feminine weakness" for her own advantage. In other communications she was forceful and insistent, as when demanding that Mathew turn over the money he held on her children's behalf. Or perhaps rapid alternation between passive and aggressive postures had simply become fundamental to Margaret's personality—an unconscious survival mechanism of a strong-willed woman frustrated by male insistence on her "natural" as well as legal incapacity. In either case, it may not be surprising that on 7 April 1799,

---

14. my: conjectural; ms. blurred.   **15. bespoke**: spoken for, contracted for.   **16.** Margaret Murphy, Philadelphia, to Mathew Carey, Philadelphia, no date [early 1799?].

less than eight months after her first husband's death, Margaret resolved these tensions—and escaped in part from dependence on her sibling—through a second marriage with the Irish-born James Burke (or Burk), "a sea captain with whom I have had a very long acquaintance," as she informed her astonished brother.[17] Their first child, John, was born scarcely nine months later, in early January 1800, and at least two more children followed: James in 1802, and a daughter, Cecilia, in 1806. Shortly after remarriage, Margaret Burke relinquished the burdens of tavern-keeping,[18] and although the 1799 city directory still listed her as proprietor of the Læticia Court establishment, by 1800 the newly rechristened "beef stake and oyster house" was owned by Daniel Dunn.

Unfortunately, marriage to a sea captain did not provide Margaret or her children much permanency or security. Judging from her letters, Captain Burke had poor health and was frequently at sea for long periods—trading with Londonderry and Belfast, among other ventures—leaving Margaret to agonize over reports of storms, shipwrecks, and the depredations of privateers. During his absences, Margaret Burke's finances were often precarious, obliging her to borrow money from Mathew and to move frequently among Philadelphia, its outlying villages, and Burlington, New Jersey, to secure cheap lodgings and to evade demanding landlords. Finally, she decided to set up a boarding school or "Academy for young Ladies," and in 1802 she was back in Philadelphia as a "schoolmistress" at 61 South Third Street. These efforts apparently failed, however, and she was deeply discouraged: "I have made no progress in School-keeping & fear I am to remain so," she admitted to her brother;

> I am greatly dejected at it as I know it will cast a gloom on Capt Burke when he returns to find so heavy a family dependant altogether on his endeavours. I drew more satisfaction from the thought of pleasing him by my exertion than even from my personal emolument, but all my plans have proved abortive—What step I shall take next I know not or whether I shall ever make another effort for I have set it down as a certainty, that were I [to] turn hatter no one would buy hats.[19]

Margaret Burke's despondency was only temporary, and by mid-1803 her relationship with Mathew had again become venemous, as by now she had determined to "put [her] children's money into trade"—she proposed to purchase a house and operate a dry goods store—and she upbraided her brother for allegedly mismanaging the funds and thus

---

17. Margaret Murphy, Philadelphia, to Mathew Carey, Philadelphia, no date [March 1799?].   18. On 21 April 1799, shortly after Margaret Murphy's marriage to Captain Burke, the Philadelphia *True American* reported that the "noted Tavern and oyster house the Sign of the Leopard in Letitia court, lately occupied by Mrs. John Murphy," was "to let," along with "a stock of liquors and wines to be disposed of, likewise household and kitchen furniture which the tenant is required to pay for."   19. Margaret Burke, [Philadelphia?], to Mathew Carey, Philadelphia, no date [1802?].

"prevent[ing her] design."[20] By 1805, however, Margaret's correspondence with Mathew had again become affectionate—perhaps out of gratitude for occasional infusions of cash or perhaps because she and captain Burke had achieved at least enough prosperity to warrant a permanent Philadelphia residence at 151 Mulberry Street. Indeed, she even sent her eldest daughter, Maria Murphy, on one of Burke's Irish voyages, to visit her Carey and Sheridan kin. Yet Margaret's travails were by no means over, for sometime in the summer or early fall of 1806 her second husband died.[21] Burke left her a small pension from the "Captain's Club," an insurance society to which he had belonged, but now Margaret was not only bereaved again—and with six young children to care for—but once more heavily dependent on her brother's generosity.

Remarkably, the twice-widowed Margaret Burke was still relatively young—merely thirty-five or so when the captain died. However, she would never remarry, and the initial years of her second widowhood were much more arduous than her short period of mourning for John Murphy. Historians generally agree that, as American society became increasingly commercialized and industrialised, economic opportunities for single or widowed women declined proportionately: unable to command capital or credit, their representation among urban shopkeepers and craftsmen steadily declined. Likewise, as sectarian and ethnic tensions increased in American cities, in part a result of the steady influx of Irish Catholic laborers, even Catholic schoolmistresses faced new difficulties, as Protestant parents feared their children's proselytization, while most new migrants from Ireland lacked funds sufficient to pay for their children's education. Perhaps it was to escape such problems that, after a failed effort in 1807 to establish a millinery shop at 119 South Second Street, Margaret swallowed her pride and persuaded Mathew to purchase for her a strawberry farm outside Philadelphia. Yet this venture, too, proved disastrous: "for one fall & the ensuing spring," she later recalled, "with cold & num[b] fingers I sat with my little Children on the cold damp ground from morning 'till night weeding with the pleasing thought of reaping in Summer the fruit of our Labour[,] but Alass when summer came there were no Strawberries to pick. . . . [T]he disappointment . . . was keen & poignant," she concluded, "& . . . I saw nothing but Ruin awaiting me & my little Dear Children."[22]

Soon after this episode, however, Margaret and her family were saved from poverty by what she subsequently described as an almost miraculous set of circumstances. Sometime in 1808 both she and her eldest daughter, Maria Murphy, met Fr. Pierre Babad (or Babade, 1763–1846), a member of the French Order of St. Sulpice. After 1789 many Sulpician priests had fled the French Revolution to Baltimore, Maryland, where they became educa-

---

20. Margaret Burke, [Philadelphia?], to Mathew Carey, Philadelphia, several undated letters of 1802–1803, especially one marked "received 10 June 1803." **21.** Neither the date nor the cause of James Burke's death can be determined (Philadelphia has no death record). However, on 8 October 1806 Philadelphia's Registry of Wills processed the administration of Burke's estate, with a sworn affidavit from his widow that he died possessed of property worth no more than $500. Like John Murphy, Burke also died intestate. **22.** Margaret Burke, St. Mary's Mountain, Emmitsburg, Md., to Mathew Carey, Philadelphia, 22 May 1810.

tors and missionaries in the farflung Baltimore archdiocese of John Carroll (1735–1815), the United States' first bishop. In several respects Babad, an extraordinarily sensitive soul given to weeping while conducting mass, symbolized the "romantic" or baroque style of European Catholicism—lavish and emotional yet clericalist and hierarchical—that in this period often clashed with the "enlightened" ideals and republican principles of many middle-class Irish-American laymen, such as Mathew Carey, who as church trustees often rebelled against authoritarian-minded priests and bishops.[23] However, Margaret and Maria encountered Fr. Babad and his fellow Sulpicians not through the Carey connection but instead through the family of Matthias O'Conway (1766–1842), an impecunious translator and lexicographer from Galway. Like Mathew Carey, O'Conway was a self-proclaimed "democrat" and "republican," with at least a tinge of anti-clericalism. Yet his cultural and religious sensibilities were at bottom profoundly traditional—in his reverence for the Gaelic past, for example, and in his family's associations with the mystical devotionalism of Spanish and Spanish-American Catholicism—in which the O'Conways had been immersed in New Orleans and Havana, prior to their settlement in Philadelphia. Even before they met Fr. Babad, Cecilia O'Conway (1787–1865), Matthias's eldest daughter, and her equally devout soulmate, Maria Murphy, had resolved to abandon the world and seek cloistered lives as nuns in Spain. Babad encouraged their pious devotion but directed them instead—and through them Maria's mother—to Elizabeth Ann Seton's fledgling order of women religious in Maryland.

"Mother" Seton (1774–1821), as she liked to be called by her followers, was remarkable for her piety (she was canonized in 1975) but also for her forceful personality. Christened Elizabeth Ann Bayley, the daughter of an affluent Episcopalian physician in New York City, in 1794 she married William Magee Seton—a prosperous merchant until the late 1790s, when his fortune and health went into steep decline. In 1803 Elizabeth accompanied William to Italy where he died and where she began the spiritual pilgrimage that culminated, after her return to New York, in a public conversion to Catholicism. Seton's conversion outraged most of her relatives but delighted Baltimore's Bishop Carroll and other Catholic clergymen, who prayed that similar accessions to the Church might help fortify America's miniscule Catholic middle class against the dangers of proselytization, "mixed" marriages, and inundation by Irish Catholic immigrants who were either lowly in status or "contaminated" by republican beliefs.

Carroll and the Sulpicians soon proposed that Seton abandon New York, where sectarian tensions were mounting, and move to Maryland with its strong Catholic traditions. There she should establish a new order of women religious whose primary responsibility would be the education of Catholic "young ladies," who in turn would preserve the faith among their husbands and children. Seton's own yearnings perfectly accorded with these proposals, and in June 1808 she and her daughters moved to Baltimore, where Fr.

---

23. For examples and further discussions of such conflicts, see chapters 13, 48, and 63.

Babad became her spiritual adviser. A few months later, Babad journeyed to Philadelphia and recruited Cecilia O'Conway and Maria Murphy to be Seton's first novitiates in a new order called the Sisters of Charity. In 1809 Mother Seton, Cecilia O'Conway, Maria Murphy, and several other recruits took their vows in Baltimore and then abandoned its comforts for the rigorous seclusion of Emmitsburg, high in the Maryland mountains, where another French Sulpician, Fr. John Dubois (1764–1842), had already begun to build what became Mount St. Mary's Seminary and a similarly named boys' academy (now Mount St. Mary's College). A short distance away, Seton and her followers—with Dubois's heroic assistance—established their first convent and a girls' school in a complex of log cabins they called St. Joseph's House.

Ironically, at first Margaret Burke was not at all pleased by Maria Murphy's vocation. Indeed, Maria had left her Philadelphia home without her mother's consent, and Margaret hastened to Maryland to retrieve her daughter. Angry and tearful, Mrs. Burke confronted Mother Seton, but eventually she not only acquiesced in her daughter's decision but became involved in Seton's and Dubois's spiritual and educational projects. Seton—roughly Margaret's age and also a widow—successfully appealed to the latter as a fellow "child of Affliction."[24] Perhaps more important, Seton and the Sulpicians gained Margaret's acquiescence by promising her economic security and superior educations for her other children. According to their agreement, Teresa Murphy—Maria's young sister—would be schooled by the nuns at St. Joseph's, while Fr. Dubois would take Margaret's sons, Charles Murphy and John and James Burke, as students in Mount St. Mary's boy's academy, where they could remain until they reached age 18. In return, Margaret would pay the Society of St. Sulpice only $1500 for her sons' maintenance and education—less than a third of the amount normally charged, with the Sulpicians absorbing the difference. Finally, Dubois hired Mrs. Burke herself at Mount St. Mary's Academy as "Superintendent of the boys' Necessaries," as she described her position, at a salary that she gauged sufficient to maintain her and Cecilia, her youngest daughter, "on a very respectable footing."[25]

At first, Margaret Burke seemed very pleased by these arrangements—finalized once Mathew Carey, after much badgering, succeeded in getting from the Philadelphia Orphan's Court the $1500 to pay the Sulpician Fathers in Baltimore. She now enjoyed a greater measure of financial security than she had known for many years; her children were receiving exceptionally good educations; and Fr. Dubois, she claimed, "promises to be every thing to me my warmest heart could wish"—"as loving friendship he says should exist between us as Brother & Sister." Thanks to Dubois's generosity, she assured Mathew, she would "never again be a tax" on her brother's purse, for "the idea of obligations conferred always sat a heavy burden on my mind & the impossibility as things seemed to turn out

24. Elizabeth Ann Seton, St. Joseph's House, Emmitsburg, Md., to Margaret Burke, [Baltimore?], 21 March 1810. **25.** Margaret Burke, St. Mary's Mountain, Emmitsburg, Md., to Mathew Carey, Philadelphia, 7 February 1810.

of being ever able to requite them was a much heavier burden which my temper could never brook."[26]

Given her history and temperament, however, perhaps it was predictable that Margaret would become discontented and would remain at Mount St. Mary's only a short time, although most of her children would stay there much longer.[27] By 1813 she was teaching her own school in nearby Emmitsburg village, and in 1815 she moved to Baltimore where she was a schoolmistress and lived for the rest of her long life. Gaps in her correspondence with brother Mathew make it impossible to do more than surmise why she abandoned what seemed an ideal situation at Fr. Dubois's academy. However, early on Margaret herself had recognized one of the dangers: "I have every reason to hope that my stay will be permanent," she had written, "yet I have not been long enough tried in the school of adversity to make the quality of dependant or Secondary set very well with me. . . . [Fr. Dubois] tries to persuade me I am not considered in that light by any one," but "my Irish pride feels it."[28] Given the bargain she had struck for her children's education, it is not unlikely that Margaret resented the slightest implication that she and her offspring were objects of charity. Moreover, even the saintly but aristocratic Mother Seton and Fr. Dubois had ethnic and social prejudices they may not have been able to conceal.[29] In addition, life on "the Mountain" was rustic and primitive, particularly for a woman who had spent nearly all her life in Dublin or Philadelphia. It was also remarkably unhealthy: within a few years of St. Joseph's foundation both of Seton's sisters-in-law, two daughters, and several other nuns had died, mostly from tuberculosis. Finally, on 12 March 1812 the "angelic" Sr. Maria Murphy, Mrs. Burke's eldest daughter, died of consumption, and perhaps this was the blow that severed Margaret's relationship with Mother Seton and Fr. Dubois.

However, although Margaret Burke left the Mountain, she did not loosen the close emotional and institutional ties she had formed there with the Catholic Church. Indeed,

---

26. Margaret Burke, St. Mary's Mountain, Emmitsburg, Md., to Mathew Carey, Philadelphia, 22 May 1810.
27. In 1813 Charles Murphy, whom one of his teachers described as "void either of any talents or of any application," left Mount St. Mary's Academy, during the War of 1812, to join the crew of a privateer. By contrast, John and James Burke were good students and remained on the Mountain until August 1817. In 1814–1815 Teresa Murphy had applied for admission to the Sisters of Charity but was "not admitted on account of health tho' her piety & amiable conduct are such as would at any time be recommendation." In September 1815 she was living in Baltimore with her mother and her half-sister, Cecelia, who later returned to the Sisters of Charity, at St. Joseph's House in Emmitsburg, for her own education.   28. Margaret Burke, St. Mary's Mountain, Emmitsburg, Md., to Mathew Carey, Philadelphia, 18 February 1810.   29. Seton had converted to Catholicism despite her personal revulsion to the "poor, red-faced Irish" she encountered at New York's St. Peter's church (however, between 1790 and 1850 nearly a fourth of the Sisters of Charity at Emmitsburg were Irish-born). Dubois's condescending attitude alienated at least one of his Irish students at Mount St. Mary's, John Hughes from County Tyrone, and after 1826, when Dubois became bishop of New York, helped spark bitter conflicts with the Irish priests and trustees in his diocese. Hughes got his revenge when, as Dubois's coadjutor in 1837–1842, he treated his elderly bishop with the same ruthlessness that he meted out to New York's rebellious clergy and laymen. On Hughes, also see chapter 48, n. 83.

it is arguable that she depended on them for personal and financial sustenance for the rest of her life. In contrast to her earlier letters, which were entirely secular in tone, from 1809—when she first moved to Maryland—her correspondence with Mathew Carey was suffused with pious reflections, and these only increased after she left Mount St. Mary's. Moreover, it is clear from her last surviving letter to him, written from Baltimore in September 1815, that her plans for "battle thro' this busy world" were now more dependent on assistance from influential Catholic clergymen than from brother Mathew. In her efforts to secure both better lodgings and more students for her fledgling school, she turned to Fr. Babad and to Archbishop Carroll, each of whom had "promised . . . to exert himself for me."[30] Apparently their efforts—and those of their successors among Baltimore's clergy—were successful.[31] According to Baltimore's city directories, in 1816 Margaret Burke was teaching school at 46 North Liberty Street, only a half-block from the archbishop's own residence at Old St. Peter's Cathedral. From 1819 until her apparent retirement from teaching around 1830, Margaret resided on Paca and Mulberry streets, in the heart of the twelfth ward—the most "Catholic" in the city—and so close to St. Mary's College that it is likely she was affiliated with either the St. Mary's Free School for Girls or the Cathedral Parish School, operated by Mother Seton's Sisters of Charity. After 1831, if not before, Margaret lived in her own two-story, red-brick house at 123 Mulberry Street, between Paca and Greene, only four blocks from the new Cathedral of the Assumption.[32] And it was in the Cathedral cemetery that she was buried, beside her daughter Teresa, on 28 May 1852, when she died at the age of 80.

The church had supported Margaret Burke's struggles to become "independent" as well as to negotiate her personal "vale of tears": the demise of two husbands and the early deaths of all her children by 1828, the memories of which were refracted through her enduringly bitter conviction that—in contrast to her new friends among the Catholic clergy and sisters—her "near kindred [had] never showed any affection or kindness to [her] family." It was no wonder, then, that in old age she rejoiced in the triumphs of what she called the "Church militant"—"notwithstanding the vituperation of the Sectarian papers, magazines & pulpits"—and supported in return its efforts to sustain and "uplift" the thousands of poor Irish Catholics who poured into Baltimore during her life there.[33] At her death Margaret Burke left an estate valued at nearly $7,000, the bulk of which consisted

---

30. Margaret Burke, Baltimore, to Mathew Carey, Philadelphia, 4 September 1815. **31.** Margaret Burke was also fortunate in that her life in Baltimore coincided with a tremendous growth in that city's Catholic population: from less than 10,000 out of 35,600 inhabitants in 1810 to between 50,000 and 60,000 out of 169,000 by midcentury. **32.** Margaret Burke's achievement was remarkable, particularly for an independent woman, as between 1798 and 1850 the proportion of Baltimore's white inhabitants who owned real estate declined from about 10 to less than 2 percent. In 1841 Burke also owned a female slave, her house servant. **33.** Margaret Burke, Baltimore, to Cecelia O'Conway [Sr. Marie de l'Incarnation], Ursuline Convent, Quebec, 15 March 1829 and 22 August 1841; see Sources, chapter 44. ¶In 1815 Charles Murphy had returned from the War of 1812 and was living with his mother in Baltimore. He returned to the sea, however, and in 1818 he died at Samarang, on the island of Java, in the Dutch East Indies. John Burke also resided with his mother in

of her house and lot worth $1,250 on Mulberry Street and of almost $5,000 worth of stock in the Baltimore and Ohio Railroad and in Baltimore's City Corporation. Her will provided about $1,000 to relatives in Ireland and America and about the same amount to various friends and associates, nearly all female, in Baltimore—including $30 "and Some of my old cloathes" to Agnes Whelan, "my Coloured Wash Woman." However, she left the great bulk of her estate to the Catholic Church and to Catholic charities: $150 to the priests of St. Mary's College; $400 to Fr. Edward McColgan for his "poor school" and "for the relief of poor Roman Catholic Irish Emigrants"; $500 to Fr. James Dolan's orphan school for boys in St. Patrick's parish at Fell's Point, the heart of Baltimore's Irish slum district; $100 to St. Mary's Roman Catholic Orphan Asylum; $150 to the Roman Catholic Charitable Relief Society; $100 to the Young Catholics' Friend Society; $100 to the St. Alphonsus Sisters' poor school; and, perhaps most appropriately, her house and lot to the "Rev^d. directors of the Roman Catholic Cathedral," to provide "an Asylum [for] Roman Catholic Widows."

45 ※

Mary Cumming, 1814–1815

The last Irish emigrant in this section, Mary Cumming (née Craig), was the young wife of William Cumming, also from Ulster and a tobacco merchant in southeastern Virginia. Surprisingly, Mary Cumming's letters to Ireland have survived whereas her husband William's correspondence has not. This represents a reversal of the usual pattern which reflected not only lower literacy among Irishwomen than among their male peers,[1] but also the patriarchal custom whereby even literate married women often deferred to their husbands in communicating with Irish kinfolk.[2] For instance, although wives of wealthy Irish immigrants were more likely to be letter-writers than were the spouses of ordinary farmers and artisans, when Hannah Wright in frontier Ohio addressed her Irish relations, she wrote primarily on her husband's behalf—begging for money to fund his speculations.[3]

Baltimore until 1822, when he perished of yellow fever while visiting a cousin, an American naval officer, at Norfolk, Virginia. Cecelia Burke apparently lived in Emmitsburg in 1825, when she died of typhus fever less than four months after her marriage. Teresa Murphy was a lifelong invalid, unable to marry or work outside her mother's home, but she survived until February 1828, when she died of consumption. Twelve weeks later, James Burke, Margaret's last living child, died in Washington, D.C., also of a pulmonary disease and, like his sister Cecelia, after only a few weeks of matrimony; in April 1830 James's widow followed him to the grave. None of Margaret Burke's children had any offspring. **1.** See chapter 6. **2.** E.g., see chapters 24, 26, and 27. Similarly, see Charles O'Hagan's petition on behalf of Mary Dunn (chapter 37). **3.** On Hannah Wright, see chapter 25.

FIGURE 8
Portrait of Mary Cumming
(1790–1815) of Petersburg,
Virginia, painted in 1812
by an unknown artist.
Photograph courtesy of Tom
McDonald, Impact Printing,
Ltd., Coleraine, County
Londonderry, Northern
Ireland.

Thus, Mary Cumming's letters are relatively unique. In general, they provide an affluent, married woman's perspective on emigration, on upper-class life in urban Virginia, and, most poignantly, on the problems of sickness and premature death that beset many Irish immigrants, particularly in the South. Mary's surviving correspondence was written to family members in Ireland, mostly to her older sister Margaret, in an intimate, conversational style—as if "I am talking to you," she explained. As one might expect, its focus is primarily on domestic and family concerns—on husband and home in Petersburg, Virginia, but also on her father and siblings back in Ulster. Indeed, and despite her warm relationship with William, Mary Cumming's letters were riven with an almost inconsolable homesickness, so much so she could scarcely bear to end each letter—for, as she exclaimed to her sister, "it is like a second parting with you for me to quit writing."[4]

Yet in spite of the intensely personal nature of her correspondence, Mary Cumming's letters indicate that her life was by no means confined to an exclusively private domain. In this era what would later be called "middle-class" families were in transition: family and work were no longer combined in patriarchal households, but they were not

4. Mary Cumming, Liverpool, England, to Margaret Craig, Strawberry Hill, Lisburn, Co. Antrim, 30 August 1811. Strawberry Hill, the Craig family home, actually lay about a mile outside Lisburn, on the Co. Down side of the Lagan River, which separates Antrim from Down.

yet entirely separated into distinct "private/feminine" and "public/masculine" spheres. Thus, during their first year in Petersburg, Mary and her husband resided under the same roof with his clerks, and although they later moved their home to an élite suburb, Mary's letters continued to demonstrate her remarkably detailed knowledge of William's business affairs. To be sure, unlike her older contemporary, the twice-widowed Margaret Carey Murphy Burke,[5] Mary Cumming was never an *independent* economic agent (for that matter, neither was William), and the tobacco she marketed was a gift from her husband; however, it is clear that she was thoroughly engaged in her husband's commercial concerns and employed her own capital and family networks in Ireland to promote his trading ventures. Likewise, Mary's domestic production—of clothes and lacework, for example— contributed significantly to the Cummings family economy, as did also her reluctant management of William's domestic slaves. And, finally, even Mary's participation in affluent Petersburg's social whirl—its seemingly endless balls and dinner parties—served to reinforce her family's status and advance William's career, while her participation in élite women's charitable activities, such as the local Female Orphan Asylum, complemented her husband's more overt involvement in the "male" worlds of business and formal politics. Thus, it is the paucity of letters, such as those of Mary Cumming, that often gives the erroneous impression that the wives of affluent Southerners were not engaged in commercial and public affairs—although, admittedly, Mary's economic roles may have been enhanced by her and her husband's desire to amass sufficient capital, as quickly as possible, to enable them to return permanently to Ireland at the earliest opportunity.

The future Mary Cumming was born on 6 December 1790, the second child of Rev. Andrew Craig (1754–1833), a Presbyterian minister in the thriving linen-market town of Lisburn, County Antrim, and Mary McCully (1760–1807), daughter of "an ingenious experimental farmer" who lived near Newtownards, County Down.[6] Although her mother died when Mary was only 17, she and her siblings, Margaret (1789–1850), James (1793–1845), and Rachel (1798–1860), apparently enjoyed an idyllic life at Strawberry Hill, their father's country manse just outside Lisburn. It was at Strawberry Hill, on 8 August 1811, that Mary Craig, aged 20, married William Cumming. For several years Cumming had resided at Petersburg, Virginia, and the wedding took place during one of his trips to visit relations in Armagh town, where his elder brother was a clergyman. Cumming was employed in Petersburg as a commission merchant, purchasing tobacco, cotton, and flour for the export-import firm of Alexander Brown & Sons. The elder Brown (1764–1834) had been a wealthy linen merchant in Belfast before 1798, when he was implicated in the United Irish rebellion and emigrated to Baltimore—at that time the fastest growing seaport

---

5. See chapter 44. 6. Lisburn town is located on the Co. Antrim side of the parish of Blaris (or Lisburn), which is divided between Co. Antrim's Upper Massereene barony and the baronies of Lower Iveagh (Upper Half) and Upper Castlereagh in Co. Down. For demographic data on Blaris parish and its environs, see appendix 2.1c, chapter 45. Quotation cited in J. Irvine, ed., *Mary Cumming's Letters Home . . .*, 28; see Sources, chapter 45.

FIGURE 9
Painting of "Strawberry Hill," Mary Cumming's family home near Lisburn, County Antrim, made in 1934 by W. J. Carey. Photograph courtesy of Tom McDonald, Impact Printing, Ltd., Coleraine, County Londonderry, Northern Ireland.

in America.[7] There he became a millionaire as his business expanded from commerce into ship-building and banking, with branches in Liverpool, New York, and Philadelphia. His Cumming cousins also prospered, as both William and his younger brother, James, served as company agents in Petersburg, while other members of the Cumming family represented the firm in Liverpool and Savannah.

Shortly after their wedding, Mary and "Mr. Cumming"—as she referred to her husband in her first six letters—sailed from Warrenpoint, County Down, to Liverpool, "encountering the danger of a tempestuous sea and the most dreadful sickness I ever endured."[8] After crossing the Irish Sea, the Cummings resided temporarily in Liverpool with William Brown, one of Alexander Brown's four sons and business partners, and made a brief visit to London. Despite her stern Calvinist heritage, Mary enjoyed the London theatre and was entranced by the city's high fashions and "magnificent buildings." However, she disliked Liverpool's dirt and bustle and, although she found the English countryside "charming"—and its cottages "so neat and clean" compared with their Irish equivalents—she missed the mountains of her "darling Ireland."[9] After three weeks' delay, on 28

7. Between 1790 and 1820 Baltimore's population rose from 13,503 to 62,738, and before the War of 1812 the city surpassed Philadelphia and rivaled New York in prosperity and trade with Europe and the West Indies.
8. Mary Cumming, 30 August 1811. 9. Mary Cumming, Camden Town, London, to Margaret Craig, Strawberry Hill, Lisburn, Co. Antrim, 7 September 1811.

September the Cummings embarked from Liverpool on the *Lydia*, sharing first-class state-rooms with William Brown and his own young bride. Only six weeks later, on 7 November, they arrived in New York City, but despite their comfortable accommodations, Mary Cumming, already pregnant, had spent most of her short but miserable voyage confined to her berth. "Our passage . . . was very rough," she related; "indeed it blew a constant gale . . . for most of the time." "It would be impossible almost to conceive the delight I felt when again I set my foot on land."[10]

After recuperating in the New York mansion of Robert Dickey—another Cumming-Brown cousin and United Irish exile who had become "immensely rich" in American trade[11]—Mary and William traveled by steamboat to New Brunswick, New Jersey, then by stagecoach to the Delaware, down the river by sail to Philadelphia and Newcastle, overland by stage to the head of Chesapeake Bay, and once again by sailboat to Baltimore. There they tarried for several days at Alexander Brown's mansion, where they met Robert Oliver, a Lisburn Quaker who had emigrated in 1783 and amassed a fortune in trade, and Rev. William Sinclair, who in 1787 had officiated at the wedding of Mary's parents and, like Dickey, had been exiled overseas in 1798.[12] Finally, on 17 November the Cummings embarked by stagecoach south to Alexandria, Richmond, and Petersburg. Mary found American cities "much handsomer than . . . expected," and she enjoyed "travelling through the American woods very much," but her long journeys left her "very much fatigued" and weighing only 105 pounds, 21 fewer than when she left Lisburn.[13]

Nevertheless, Mary Cumming's first impressions of her new home were very favorable. "[A]fter encountering the troubles and dangers of a sea and land voyage," she reported, "here I am at last comfortably fixed in a very pleasant house which I may call my own":

> Oh, my darling friends, how I wish you saw how happily I am settled in this nice little
> place,   there is everything in it I could possibly wish for. The house is extremely neat
> and convenient. . . . The first floor is entirely taken up with the office and store and

---

10. Mary Cumming, New York City, to Margaret Craig, Strawberry Hill, Lisburn, Co. Antrim, [8 November 1811]. 11. Robert Dickey was a native of Ballymena, Co. Antrim; his brother, James Dickey, had been less fortunate, forfeiting his life on the gallows for his involvement with the United Irishmen and the 1798 Rebellion. Quotation from J. Irvine, ed., *Mary Cumming's Letters Home* . . . , 41; see Sources, chapter 45. 12. Rev. William Sinclair: a graduate of the University of Glasgow (1775), in 1785 he was ordained as Presbyterian minister of Newtownards, Co. Down; Sinclair was associated with other New Light and nonsubscribing clergymen in the Presbytery of Antrim, and in the 1790s he became a major figure among Co. Down's United Irishmen; in 1798 Sinclair was found guilty of treason and transported to America, sailing on the same ship that carried John Caldwell of Ballymoney (see chapter 68); because of Sinclair's doctrinal liberalism and political radicalism, he was "embargoed" by the General Assembly of the Presbyterian Church in the United States; however, the Presbytery of Baltimore accepted him, and he spent the rest of his life ministering to a congregation in that city, as did another United Irish exile, the Rev. John Glendy from Maghera, Co. Derry. 13. Mary Cumming, Petersburg, Va., to Margaret Craig, Strawberry Hill, Lisburn, Co. Antrim, 25 November and 6 December 1811.

room for the young men[14] to sleep in. Above stairs there is a very neat parlour about the size of the sitting one of my own sweet Strawberry Hill, [plus] a very handsome drawing room in front with three windows . . . very neatly furnished indeed. You go out of the parlour into a little passage which leads to my sleeping room, which is a very pleasant apartment. On the same floor there is a very nice high dressing-room which I intend making a china closet of. Next to that there is a back stairs which leads you through a little shrubbery to the kitchen, which is at a little distance from the house. There is another little room with shelves all round it where the cold meat and bread are kept. In the third story there are three excellent sleeping-rooms all as neat as I could wish for. There are fireplaces in all the chambers except one. . . . Mr. Cumming has got plate,[15] china and glass, etc., in great plenty,   indeed it does not look much like a bachelor's establishment.[16]

Mary Cumming shared the house not only with William and his clerks but also with at least six black "servants"—"I cannot bear the word slaves," she admitted[17]—whom she managed, apparently, with both kindness and success: "the servants appear to be all regular and well behaved," she wrote, and one of them, Nancy, "is so good a cook that I have only to tell her in the morning what I wish for dinner."[18]

Superficially, early nineteenth-century Petersburg seemed an ideal place to be young, wealthy, and Irish. With 5,668 inhabitants (half of them slaves and free blacks), Petersburg in 1810 was Virginia's third largest town (behind Richmond and Norfolk), the leading tobacco port for the southern part of the state and for much of North Carolina, and a major flour-milling and manufacturing center. It was also a rigidly stratified society: in 1820 the top 10 percent of Petersburg's taxpayers held nearly 60 percent of all taxable property. To be sure, Petersburg's main streets were not paved until 1812, and religion was reportedly "at a low ebb"; the first permanent Presbyterian congregation was not established until mid-1812, which obliged Mary to endure "dry, uninteresting" sermons in the local Episcopal church.[19] However, the town boasted a flourishing social and cultural life, centered around what was reputedly the oldest theatre in North America, the race track, and balls and card-parties in the gentry's "elegant and well-built houses," as one traveler described them.[20] Moreover, the Irish presence in Petersburg was especially strong: economically, as after the Revolution Ulster-born merchants largely supplanted the Scottish factors who formerly dominated the tobacco trade; and culturally, as resident Irish literati such as the 1798 exile, John Daly Burk,[21] published volumes of history and Irish music, and wrote plays for the town's theatre. Intelligent, charming, and well-connected,

---

14. the young men: William Cumming's two clerks.   15. plate: dinner utensils or vessels made of silver.
16. Mary Cumming, 25 November 1811.   17. Mary Cumming, Petersburg, Va., to Margaret Craig, Strawberry Hill, Lisburn, Co. Antrim, 24 February 1812.   18. Mary Cumming, 25 November 1811.
19. J. G. Scott and E. A. Wyatt III, *Petersburg's Story* . . . , 100; see Sources, chapter 45. Mary Cumming, 6 December 1811.   20. Scott and Wyatt, 42.   21. On Burk, see chapters 63 and 64.

Mary Cumming enjoyed a prominent place in this society: "I like the country," she enthused, "and I admire the people whom I have met with extremely. The American ladies are in general gentle and elegant in their manners, and most of those I have the pleasure of knowing appear to be accomplished and well-informed."[22]

Most rewarding was her seemingly idyllic relationship with a devoted husband: "My dear William . . . is everything to me my heart could wish for," she wrote; "the longer I know him I love and esteem him more."[23] The Cummings apparently enjoyed what historians have called a "companionate marriage"—increasingly common among the genteel classes in Britain and America—that was based on free choice and mutual affection and respect rather than on patriarchal authority, parental compulsion, or purely economic calculations. Clearly, Mary and William delighted in each other's company: they attended parties together; read to each other on chilly evenings; and shared interests in gardening, politics, and William's commercial ventures, in which Mary herself invested. Thus, what she called her domestic "rapture" seemed complete when, on 1 May 1812, she gave birth to a "darling little daughter."[24]

Yet, despite every comfort, Mary Cumming was desperately homesick. After she and her husband moved to an even grander house in Petersburg's upper-class suburb of Blandford, "William tells me sometimes that . . . I will get so fond of the place that I will not like to leave it"; however, she vowed, "there is not the least danger in that respect": "a cottage in Ireland for me, before a palace in any other country."[25] In part, Mary's longing for "dear Strawberry Hill" stemmed from her initial belief that, after merely a few years in Petersburg, her husband would make his fortune and return to Ireland—thus relieving her of the need to adjust psychologically to the possibility of permanent emigration.[26] Unfortunately, and despite William's assurances, on 18 June 1812 her worst fears were realized when war commenced between the United States and Great Britain. The War of 1812 not only imperiled transatlantic communications but also made going home impossible: "I now feel as if I was a prisoner in this country," Mary lamented; "I much fear that the time for our return to my dear native land is now more uncertain than ever. . . . I cannot bear to think of it."[27] The outbreak of hostilities also endangered the status of Petersburg's alien residents, and despite their families' many associations with United Irish refugees, both Mary and her husband were loyal "Britons."[28] Thus, although she

22. Mary Cumming, 6 December 1811.   23. Mary Cumming, Petersburg, Va., to Margaret Craig, Strawberry Hill, Lisburn, Co. Antrim, 9 January 1812.   24. William and Mary Cumming, Petersburg, Va., to Margaret Craig, Strawberry Hill, Lisburn, Co. Antrim, 2 May 1812.   25. Mary Cumming, Petersburg, Va., to Margaret Craig, Strawberry Hill, Lisburn, Co. Antrim, 26 May 1812.   26. Mary Cumming, 30 August 1811.   27. Mary Cumming, Petersburg, Va., to Margaret Craig, Strawberry Hill, Lisburn, Co. Antrim, 24 June 1812.   28. It is intriguing that, despite her own Ulster childhood during the 1790s, and despite her family's close ties to former United Irishmen, in none of her letters did Mary Cumming ever allude to the 1798 rebellion, even when she encountered its exiles in America. Since she wrote freely and informatively on other political issues, her reticence cannot be ascribed to conventional gender roles but rather to the loyalism of her own immediate family (one of her brothers-in-law was a Church of Ireland minister) or, more broadly, to the self-imposed

readily admitted that "[t]he people of this country certainly enjoy many blessings,"[29] she assured her father, "I do not feel pleasant when I hear old England spoken of disrespect-fully."[30]

However, most alienating and ultimately disastrous were the effects of what one early visitor called Petersburg's "extreme unhealthiness." As another traveler wrote in 1786, the town "stands upon the River Appomattox, the water thereof is almost stagnant . . . [and] the Vapors arising from it contaminate the air with the most pestilential disorders. Agues and fevers of Every kind prevail."[31] Conditions were no better during Mary Cum-ming's residence, and the local Female Orphan Asylum—of which she was elected a direc-tor in 1814—was necessitated by the high mortality from malaria, yellow fever, and other diseases. Thus, more than conventional piety obliged Mary to preface her hopes for the future with the phrase, "if we live." She was weak from the beginning and unaccustomed to America's climatic extremes, and Mary Cumming's health deteriorated rapidly during her first hot, "sickly season," when she contracted "a bilious fever" and, more devastating, when her "sweet infant" died of a "bowel complaint."[32] Mary never really recovered from this first major illness, and the following autumn another bout with "bilious colic" caused the stillbirth of her second and last child.[33] To make matters worse, if possible, "the severe remedies" prescribed by Petersburg's physicians were, she lamented, "almost as bad as the diseases themselves": "bleeding, blistering, salivating, are three of the most favourite cures for bilious complaints," she reported, and the doctors induced salivating by forcing her to drink calomel, a compound of mercury.[34] By January 1814, when she composed the fol-lowing letter home, Mary Cumming had regained strength sufficient to observe, if not participate in, the events of the social season. However, her preoccupation with local funeral customs reflected her own precarious health as well as the shadow of premature death that fell over all Petersburg society.

Letter 1.
Mary Cumming, Blandford, Virginia,
to Margaret Craig, Strawberry Hill, Lisburn, County Antrim, 2–9 January 1814

Blandford, January 2, 1814
Many happy returns of the year to my dear Margaret, and all the beloved inmates

silence on the subject that characterized much of Ulster Presbyterian society after 1798.   **29.** Mary Cumming, Blandford, Va., to Rev. Andrew Craig and Margaret Craig, Strawberry Hill, Lisburn, Co. Antrim, 29 January 1813.   **30.** Mary Cumming, Blandford, Va., to Rev. Andrew Craig, Strawberry Hill, Lisburn, Co. Antrim, 20 December 1813.   **31.** Cited in J. G. Scott and E. A. Wyatt III, *Petersburg's Stoy . . .* , 24, 41; see Sources, chapter 45.   **32.** Mary Cumming, Blandford, Va., to Margaret Craig, Strawberry Hill, Lisburn, Co. Antrim, 17 November 1812.   **33.** Mary Cumming, Blandford, Va., to Margaret Craig, Strawberry Hill, Lisburn, Co. Antrim, 7–14 November 1813.   **34.** Mary Cumming, 7–14 November 1813. Mercury, of course, is lethally poisonous.

of Strawberry Hill. When or how this letter will be sent I know not, but as I intend it shall be a very long one I will write a little now and then till I hear of an opportunity of sending it. Occasionally I think of something which I wish to tell you, of which I forget when I am in haste to send off my letter. I wrote a very long letter to you in the beginning of November which has not left this country yet, and another to my Father last month which I expect he will receive before you get yours, as I sent it by another conveyance.

I have been very anxious to hear from home for a long time, and indeed if I did not know that vessels at this season of the year have sometimes very tedious passages I should be very uneasy. The last letter I had from home was from Rachel, dated June. The one she said you had written to me at the same time has not come to hand yet. Before I finish this letter I hope I shall have the happiness of telling you I have received a packet[35] from Ireland. I am now so well that I was able to be at no less than two balls last week,   one of them was at Major Taylor's,[36] a very near neighbour of mine,   the other was a public one held at the hall which is within a hundred yards of us. I danced a little but I have not the pleasure now I once enjoyed in that amusement. I get so soon tired owing to my want of strangth that it is rather a toil for me to go through a reel, and I feel more pleasure to sit and look at others than to join them in the dance. "How you are changed" you will say, but believe me I have no idea my dancing days are over. When I go home you will see me I hope as active on the floor as ever. I do not like the reels they dance here,   it is the same or nearly the same figure[37] over and over again. They seem to me to pay no attention to the music and begin at the last of the line as soon as at the beginning. Country dances are not much liked here. In Richmond and the Northward cotillions[38] are the most favoured dances,   balls are always well attended and young and old join in the dance. It would amuse you to see Mrs. Moore[39] going through a reel,   she is an uncommonly large woman, dresses very gay, and seems to enjoy herself more than anyone I know. The American ladies in general dress very well, a good deal in the French style, which I do not admire. There are a number of very pretty girls in Petersburg,   most of the American ladies I have seen are remarkably fair, with scarcely any colour, owing to the warmth of the climate, I suppose. My sweet little Agnes Freeland is an exception,   she is as blooming as any Irish girl,   she has beautiful hair and dark eyes,   I have not

---

35. packet: package or parcel (of letters).   **36. Major Taylor**: George Keith Taylor, Petersburg's leading attorney and a Virginia state legislator. His wife (**Mrs. Taylor** hereafter), a sister of the U.S. chief justice John Marshall (1755–1835), was primarily responsible for establishing the local Female Orphan Asylum.   **37. figure**: dance movement.   **38. cotillion**: a dance of French origin, now a variety of quadrille.   **39. Mrs. Moore**: in her letter of 6 December 1811, Mary Cumming had described Mrs. Moore as an Irishwoman who, although she had lived 20 years in America, was still "completely Irish in her manners, which I like very much. She is a great, large, fat, bouncing-looking woman, appears to be prefectly good-natured, and extremely obliging to me indeed, but I come from Ireland, and that is my recommendation with Mrs. Moore. . . . She is a complete national character."

seen her here so often of late, owing to her mother's health, which I am sorry to say is very bad. She is now confined to bed, and I am very much afraid her disease will end in a consumption. She has been long threatened with it, and she has met with so many misfortunes lately that I fear it has increased the complaint. Within the last year she lost her husband and an only sister. Mr. Freeland died very suddenly,   her sister (who was a charming woman) died a few hours after the birth of her boy. Mrs. Freeland has an uncommonly strong mind, but I fear her health will suffer,   I do not know what I would do if I was to lose her,   she says she looks on me as if I was her daughter and she has always treated me as if I was really so, but I hope from my heart she will soon get better,   I cannot bear to think of losing her. I have attended four funerals since I came to this country, I believe. The persons all died during the last year,   they were all acquaintances of ours, and what is singular, all Scotchmen. I like the manner that funerals are conducted here very much,   I think they are extremely solemn and impressive. It is a mournful subject, but as this is Sunday I will therefore tell you as well as I can how they are arranged. The day after the decease of the person their friends send notes to as many of their acquaintance as they wish to attend, mentioning at what hour the funeral will take place. The ladies all go in carriages, the men on horseback   when you get to the house every place looks mournful, the coffin put on a large table in the middle of the room, covered with white, the ends tied with black,   all the pictures and mirrors are covered in like manner. When all the company have assembled the clergyman reads the funeral service, which is altogether the most affecting scene I have witnessed these many years. After he has finished six of the deceased's most particular friends bear the coffin to the hearse, the company attend to the place of interment, all alight and proceed to the graveyard where the clergyman again delivers a short prayer over the spot. No person could possibly help being affected during this solemn scene.

There is always a quantity of what is called funeral cake, made on the occasion. It is like our Naples biscuits, each piece is rolled up in mourning paper and sealed with black. I think this is a curious custom,   even the baskets which it is handed round in are all covered with white. I shall now bid my dear Margaret adieu for the present.

Thursday, January 6th

I again take up my pen to have a little conversation with my dear Margaret, and to tell her we have all been on the tip-toe of hope and expectation for these last few days past. A cartel[40] has arrived at Annapolis and brought a messenger from the British Government, who is now at Washington. The general opinion is that the message is of a pacific nature and that peace is not far distant. From my soul I hope it is not. William is in fine spirits at the good news. If it does take place I think I shall see my beloved friends sooner than I once expected. Do you know I am going to commence tobacco

---

40. cartel: a ship commissioned in time of war to exchange prisoners.

merchant? William gave me for my Christmas gift a quantity which I intend shipping off when peace takes place. If I succeed in my first attempt I shall go on in the same manner till I return to Ireland. William and myself were talking of a plan if we should have peace which he would advise my Father to think of. It is for him to get James Cumming[41] or some other person to purchase some fine and coarse linens, send them to W. Brown of Liverpool to be shipped to America. William will sell them for him and if he pleases lay the proceeds out in tobacco so that if all would turn out well my Father would make by[42] both purchases. William says if we had peace many merchants will be ruined,   some have speculated very largely[43] in tea and sugar when both articles had got[44] an exorbitant price in expectation that the war would last a long time. I am glad to say William never thought it would last very long. I have the happiness of telling you Mrs. Freeland is much better since I wrote last and I trust will soon be quite well. My acquaintance is now very numerous indeed,   my health has been so bad lately that I have not been able to visit any except my most particular friends. There are about eight families with whom I am very intimate, and those are quite enough for me. I do not care for a large circle of acquaintances, a great many of whom I do not care for. Several of my most intimate friends are as elegant accomplished women as I ever met with, so much so that I can find no fault with them, but I must give you some description of Mrs. Taylor, a lady who visited me about a twelve month ago, and who is my nearest neighbour, as I have nothing better at present to tell you. Perhaps it may amuse you. You must not say I am satirical,   I shall not exaggerate nor "set down aught in malice." Often before I had the pleasure of knowing this lady I had heard of her. I was told she was extremely lively, witty, and sensible,[45] keen in her remarks, and will have her laugh no matter at whose expense. From these accounts I thought I should feel rather afraid of her, but my opinion changed the first time she came to see me,   I found her lively, cheerful, and agreeable, seemed very desirous.[46]

I really think this long epistle will try your patience, but I wish you to send me one just as long. Peace is still spoken of as not being far off,   I feel quite anxious now for William's return to hear all the news. If we have peace he will make a very handsome sum of money by a purchase of flour which he bought the other day,   it was quite a sudden thought;   he had heard some report of the good news, and therefore bought eight hundred barrels of flour at four dollars and a half a barrel. This was lower than it has been here for a long time, and yesterday he would have got six for it. If we have peace it will be up eight or nine dollars, so that at any rate he will make.

---

41. **James Cumming**: William's brother, who had left Petersburg and returned to Ireland shortly after Mary and her husband arrived in Virginia.   **42. make**: profit by.   **43. largely**: widely, heavily.   **44. got**: commanded, sold for.   **45. sensible**: endowed with good sense, intelligent, judicious; also, possessed of sensibility ("romantic").   **46. desirous**: (socially) desirable "eligible."

I have a delightful plan in view to expend the profits of this little speculation, and if all goes on well I hope to see it accomplished. I wish William to take me on in the gig[47] next summer to Philadelphia, spend some time there, and get the man who made the gig to exchange it for a handsome carriage, as the former is of very little use to us now, since William is so much engaged. I should like to spend some time in Baltimore also. Carriages are very necessary in this country in the Summer to protect you from the immense heat and in Winter from the cold. We have had some piercing weather lately, but I do not mind, as I am always better in cold weather. It is the sudden changes we have which are so injurious. You have not said anything of the Cairds in your letters lately, I hope they are well. I do not know what all the Lisburn girls are about,[48] not a girl of my acquaintance married since I left Ireland. Tell Margaret Byers I have not had a letter from her this long time. J.C.[49] deserves his ears boxed. Oh, my beloved Margaret, how happy we shall all be when I return to Ireland. I suppose Dublin will be our place of residence, and then I will have you and Rachel always with me, or I will be with you. My dear Father must come very often and stay with me. I fancy Rachel will be his housekeeper before that time comes. I should like M. Cumming to be mistress of the house at the bridge, as for Miss Rachel I want her to be planted beside me. What do you think of these plans?

This is a great day in Petersburg, the inhabitants are to give a dinner to the volunteers.[50] I was awakened this morning by the firing of cannon, some of the democrats[51] have styled them "the Spartan band." I suppose it will be "Much ado about Nothing." William subscribed, but he would not dine with them. The suppers we have at the public balls are very superb. The ladies never pay, each gentleman's ticket is four dollars, and he may take as many ladies with him as he chooses. I like this plan, it is considered enough for them to honour the balls with their company without paying anything. The girls in general strip[52] very much at these places, the frocks are made very low, without very often a shoulder strap; their hair, ever since I came to this country has been worn in what is called an Indian knot. It is twisted in this form as close to the neck as possible, I did not like this fashion much at first, but I am reconciled to it now. The Americans dress much more in the morning than is customary in Ireland, I have seen ladies fine enough to go into a ball-room paying morning visits. Perhaps this is owing in some measure to their using carriages so much. There is a beautiful kind of silk to be got in this country, called the French Levantine, it is much richer than the English sarsnet,[53] as soon as I have an

---

47. gig: a light two-wheeled one-horse carriage.   **48. about**: engaged in, "up to."   **49. J.C.**: James Craig, Mary's younger brother, who was studying law at Trinity College, Dublin.   **50. the volunteers**: i.e., the officers and members of Petersburg's militia company.   **51. the democrats**: i.e., local leaders of the Republican party.   **52. strip**: expose/bare a fair amount of flesh (see **very low** hereafter).   **53. sarsnet**: var. of sarcenet: a soft thin silk of oriental origin.

MARY CUMMING

opportunity I will send you and Rachel frocks of it, for it is not to be had with you.[54] I got a very handsome figured[55] pink one for the last birth-night ball, which I paid fifteen shillings a yard for. Mercy upon us! how the cannons are firing! If they were going to give a dinner to Lord Wellington[56] there could not be a greater fuss. I think they had better not waste any more powder, as they are very often at a short for[57] some when they are fighting. I believe in my soul many Americans wish old England was sunk in the sea, but she will flourish great and free, the dread and envy of them all.

You cannot conceive how very much my white tippet[58] is admired, it is the only one in Petersburg of the kind. I have told many people how it was done, but they are afraid to begin so troublesome a job. Pelisses[59] of fine cloth trimmed with gold and gold buttons are very much worn here. This I think is too showy a dress for the street. I have never seen any velvet as handsome as mine. I send you a little bit of the trimming Agnes Freeland taught me to do. Perhaps Rachel or you will find out the way to do it, it is very easy, but I fear unless you saw it done you will not succeed. However you can try, and I will endeavour to give you the best description of how it is done that I can. You take a piece of cotton (the kind we used to knit with will do) about a yard long, put the one end of it between the first finger and thumb of the left hand, put the thread once around the left hand, and with the right take the other end and work the cotton which is over the left hand something like the way you make a button-hole. When you have about sixteen stitches on try if it will draw,[60] which forms the little loop, which you may make large or small by putting more or less stitches on. The only trouble is to learn to make it draw, which you may be able to find out from what I have said, though I wish I could make it clearer to you. Do not be discouraged if you do not succeed at first, for I am sure I tried forty times before I could get it to draw with me. There are a great variety of ways of making it, but this is the most simple kind I have sent you. I will with pleasure teach you all the others when you can do this, but you must learn to make it draw before you can do any kind, It is called tatting[61] and makes a very neat trimming. I have done a great quantity of it. When your cotton gives out you must knot it close to the little loop.

January 9th, Sunday.

This is a very wet day. William is gone to town and I have been engaged writing to Mr. Gilmour. We had a snow storm last week, but if this rain continues it will soon

---

54. it is not to be had with you: it is not available where you are (i.e. in Ireland).   **55. figured**: patterned.
56. Lord Wellington: Arthur Wellesley (1769–1852), of Dangan Castle, Co. Meath: victorious general in the Napoleonic Wars, first duke of Wellington, and Tory prime minister (1827–1830) during the crisis over Catholic emancipation, which he opposed; his more liberal elder brother, Richard Colley, Lord Wellesley (1760–1842), was governor-general of India in 1797–1805 and Ireland's lord lieutenant in 1820–1828 and 1832–1834.   **57. are at a short for**: lack an adequate supply of.   **58. tippet**: a shoulder cape of fur or cloth.
59. pelisse: a long cloak or coat made, lined, or trimmed with fur.   **60. draw**: in tatting (see n. 61) to pull on the thread to cause the stitching to form into a ring.   **61. tatting**: a kind of knotted lace, used for edging or trimming.

disappear. I did a little bit of the tatting last night, which I send you,   you will find if you draw the long end of the cotton which I have left it will form the little loop. The trimming makes a handsome finish to any kind of work,   it always looks well round the sleeve or neck of a morning gown. If you cannot find out the manner in which it is done, as soon as I have an opportunity I will send you and Rachel some. Perhaps she could describe something she learned at school to me, so that I could find it out. What pleasure I shall take in teaching my beloved sisters all the little things I have learned during my stay in this country. I never saw such elegant baby-clothes as the ladies make here. I took much pains making mine the last time, but alas! I had no occasion for them. Tatting done with fine cotton looks very well round the ruffle of little shirts. You see I am telling these things as perhaps you may have use for them some time or other. I have got some beautiful patterns for working, which I would like to send you. Does Rachel make her frocks?

And now my beloved Margaret, I shall bid you adieu! having told you everything I could think of, and I hope I may soon receive a letter from you, as long as this is. I shall write to Rachel very soon. God bless you my darling sister, and grant you every happiness, is the sincere prayer of your

Mary Cumming

William sends a thousand loves to you all.

Mary Cumming's hopes for Anglo-American peace and a speedy return to Ireland were continually frustrated. Thus, in summer 1814 William tried to console her with what she hoped would be "a charming excursion, from which I hope to enjoy health and a great deal of pleasure,"[62] to the fashionable medicinal springs at Balltown (now Ballston Spa), near Saratoga, New York. Unfortunately, she reported after her visit, "whether it was owing to the fatigue of travelling or some other cause I did not derive the benefit . . . which I expected; on the contrary I think I got weaker during my stay."[63] Indeed, by the time Mary and William reached Baltimore on their return journey, she was too ill to travel further and was forced to remain at Alexander Brown's house while her husband continued to Petersburg. She rejoiced that William "has now determined on returning to Ireland," as "I suffer so much from the climate that he will not run the risk of keeping me longer in it."[64] Yet despite the ministrations of the city's "most skillful physician," Mary Cumming never left Baltimore, and by mid-March 1815, when she penned her last letter to her sisters in Lisburn, her joy at the "most wonderful news"[65] of

---

62. Mary Cumming, Blandford, Va., to Margaret Craig Ward, Lisburn, Co. Antrim, 4 June 1814 (in March 1814 Mary's sister, Margaret, had married James Ward of Lisburn).   **63.** Mary Cumming, Springfield, Md., to Rev. Andrew Craig, Strawberry Hill, Lisburn, Co. Antrim, 14 October 1814 (Springfield was the rural suburb of Baltimore where Alexander Brown's country home was located).   **64.** Mary Cumming, 14 October 1814. **65.** Mary Cumming, Baltimore, Md., to Margaret Craig Ward, Lisburn, Co. Antrim, 9 February 1815.

peace between the United States and Britain was canceled by the certainty of her impending death.

Letter 2.
Mary Cumming, Baltimore, Maryland,
to Margaret Craig Ward and Rachel Craig, Strawberry Hill, Lisburn,
County Antrim, 15 March 1815

Baltimore, 15 March 1815

My ever beloved and darling Sisters,

As I have been getting weaker every day since I wrote to my dear Margaret, I again take up my pen to try to write a few lines.[66] Thank God that I feel a little stronger today than I have done for some time past. Oh my beloved Sisters, I too well know what you will all feel when this letter reaches you, but I hope and trust that Providence will enable you to bear the mournful news with composure. I hope I shall be quite so before Providence thinks fit to remove me out of this world of care and sorrow. I do all I can to be so. I find it a hard trial to think of leaving this world with all the prospects of felicity which I thought I had to find in it. These are now all over and I must try and prepare myself for another and better state where I believe I am now soon going.

My dear dear friends I have a great deal to say to you. I wish I had strength sufficient to write to you all but that I have not at present.

It is possible that this letter will be given you by my beloved darling William. Oh my friends, if ever you loved your poor Mary, show it in your attention to one that was dearer to her than life. Try to cheer and comfort his dear heart which I know will oppress him for the loss of one whom he always treated with the most unremitting affection, kindness and regard, but I know you will do this with the greatest pleasure. His own worth will secure him the regard of all who have the happiness of knowing him. Talk to him of me for this will please him. He has been my comfort and support during all the sickness and sorrow which I have had and he is now the soother of every moment of my life. I hope and trust we may be united in a better world, never more to part. I cannot speak of the happiness I promised myself on my return this Spring to my native country and to the beloved friends I left,   that is over now.

William will take you a few seeds and roots. My dear Rachel will show him what I once called my garden where I want them to be planted. Let him have it to cultivate when he is with you. He is fond of flowers and this will help to amuse him. Try and keep him with you in Ireland,   I think he would be much happier than here. I know my ever dear and beloved Father will do all in his power to comfort and amuse one so every way deserving of his kindness and affection.

66. This letter is a contemporary transcript of Mary Cumming's letter, made by her brother James.

My illness has not been a severe one. I hardly suffer any pain as yet. It seems to be a kind of gradual decline. For this I am, I hope, very thankful and it will be a consolation to all my friends to know that I have had the very best advice that America could give. I have met with every attention from this family that I could have had even at home and if an All Wise Providence now thinks fit to take me, I trust to a better world, I must endeavour to be resigned to his Will. My attachment to this world was very great, it is so still, but my dear friends, I look forward to a blessed reunion. Any and every circumstance you may wish to hear, my dear William will take pleasure in telling you, if you ask him.

There are a few little trifles which it is my wish should go to you to be divided between you in any way you think right. It is not for their value but that there is a good deal of your poor Mary's work on them.

I send back my dear James's brooch which I have always kept with great regard. Give him now a sister's blessing who always adored him. Tell him I hope he will prove an ornament to his family and name. Give him some of my hair which you will receive by my love.

But what shall I send to my adored Father, that father who took such pains with me? Oh that I could think of something. He will require nothing, nothing to remind him of me. I hope all his good instructions have not been bestowed on me in vain. I can leave him nothing but my blessing, and may every blessing this world can bestow light on his beloved head. God bless him.

You would wonder if you saw how thin I am, that I could write with such a steady hand, but so it is. You will give my most affectionate love to my dear and very kind friends in Armagh, to my ever kind and most attentive relation Miss McCully, and to my once lively and dear early companion and friend Margaret Byers. I think with great affection and regard on the many many friends I have left in Lisburn,   please remember me to them all.

Do not you remember, my beloved Sisters, some kind of Spring Evenings I used to be particularly fond of? They were in the latter end or beginning of April. On some such evening as I shall attempt to describe take a walk to Charles Grove with my dear William and talk of me. Soft, mild and calm, the twilight stealing on, the Bat flittering about and the Beetle humming through the air. You will think then of me.

I gratify myself writing these lines and this moment I feel quite composed and perhaps I am more fanciful than usual.

May God bless, protect, help and support you all through this transient world and grant us all a happy meeting in a better beyond the grave, is and will be, the last prayer of

M. Cumming

Mary Cumming died in Baltimore in early April 1815, so beloved that relatives as far away as Londonderry and Genoa named ships after her and composed elegies in her honor. After her death, William Cumming visited the Craigs at Strawberry Hill[67] but returned to Petersburg in December. According to one source, William died of fever or a broken heart in April 1816, but the fact that his will was not recorded in Petersburg until 17 March 1825 suggests that his death occurred shortly before the latter date. Cumming's real and personal property was valued at $23,000, including 134 cotton bales ($7,814), eight slaves ($2,210), his and Mary's pew in the new Presbyterian church ($75), and all their household goods. William generously bequeathed £500 each to Mary's father and two sisters in Ireland, and the same to his Cumming relations in Dublin and Armagh. The final tragedy, however, was that to yield those sums the entire estate had to be sold—including the slaves for whom Mary Cumming had had such sympathy and affection.

67. "Go to our beloved country," Mary Cumming had written to her husband, in her last letter of 24 March 1815; "there you will find peace. Talk to my beloved friends of me. Tell them we will all meet in a better world. If I can I will hover round and bless you wherever you go."

VI ✳
Clergymen and Schoolmasters

46 ✳

Rev. John Craig, 1734–1769/70

In 1734 when the future Presbyterian minister John Craig emigrated from Ulster to New Castle, Delaware, he was following a well-worn path, first blazed in 1683 by Rev. Francis Makemie (1658–1746) of County Donegal, the "father of American Presbyterianism." From its origins the Presbyterian church in colonial America was heavily dependent on foreign-born and -trained ministers, a majority of whom were born in Ulster and educated in Scottish universities. Between 1680 and 1750 more than half the Presbyterian clergy in America were foreign-born and over one-third were from Ireland. In the years 1711–1740, when the colonial church grew from about 35 to over 160 congregations, the proportions were even higher: during those decades two-thirds of the American clergy had been born abroad and nearly half in Ireland (plus another fifth in Scotland). After midcentury clerical emigration abated: Ulster's economic expansion enabled Presbyterian congregations to pay their ministers better and more punctually than in the early 1700s, thus encouraging the latter to seek livings at home; while in America after 1758 the clerical faction that controlled the Synod of New York and Philadelphia refused to accept many Ulster-born and Scottish-trained licentiates and clergymen, suspecting them of harboring "lukewarm" or heretical—that is, non-Calvinist—convictions. In general, however, the impressive growth in the eighteenth century of America's Presbyterian churches, to nearly six hundred congregations by 1776,[1] was due not only to the influx of Scots-Irish laity but also, in large measure, to the devoted efforts of Ulster-born clergymen.

John Craig was born on 17 August 1709 in mid–County Antrim, in the barony of Upper Antrim and the parish of Donegore, nearly all of whose inhabitants were Presbyterians[2] and, Craig later recalled, "Remarkable for the[ir] Modest Sober Religious Conduct."[3] His parents, probably David Craig and Agnes Park, were "Rich" farmers, tenants of Lord Donegall and members of the Donegore Presbyterian church, which their ancestors had helped establish during the first Ulster Plantation and maintain through the native rebellions and Anglican persecutions of the seventeenth century. In later years, Craig would rejoice that God had allowed him to be born in a "time & place when & where Ignorance & Barbarities are No More, and popish Cruelties Ra[c]k Stake & flames for Sake of Consience and Cause of Christ was at an End." However, a sense of guilt that he had

---

1. In 1776 the great majority of the approximately six hundred Presbyterian congregations in the new United States were affiliated with the Synod of New York and Philadelphia; about one hundred others represented the transplanted Scots-Irish and Scottish faiths of Associate (Seceder) or Reformed (Covenanting) Presbyterians.
2. In 1666 the hearth money returns showed a John Craige, perhaps the future emigrant's grandfather, living at Doagh Grange, a vicarage attached to the united parishes of Donegore, Kilbride, and Nalteen (or Nilteen) Grange. For demographic data on Donegore parish and its environs, see appendix 2.1f, on chapter 46.   3. This and the following quotations are from Rev. John Craig's memoir, written in 1769–1770.

been spared "all these temptations & fiery trials" helped persuade him to prove his own spiritual mettle on the American frontier.

Indeed, Craig appears to have been an exceptionally pious youth, even by the most exacting Calvinist standards. Although his parents doted on him, as the last child of their old age, he later recalled that "early instructions in the principles of religion . . . had strong effects on my young and tender mind . . . and engaged me to fly to God with prayers and tears in secret, for pardon, peace, guidance and direction." Convinced of his sinfulness when merely five years old, at age 14 Craig was baptized and admitted to "yᵉ Lords Table which prov'd a mighty Support against temptations and gave much Delight Comfort & Consolation[. M]any a Sweet Communion Sabbath I Enjoy'd in my Native Country," he recounted, "Some times brought to the Banqueting house . . . Ravished with love" for God. Craig's youthful piety "raised" his parents' "pleasing hopes" that God had destined him for the ministry, and so they determined, "contrary to their former designs, to bestow upon [him] a liberal education." Although shocked by the "vice folly and wickedness" of his schoolmates, Craig proved a model student, studying "Reading Algebra, Mathematicks, Logicks, MetaphySicks, pneumaticks, Ethics . . . Geography & history both Ecclesiastick and prophane" under "yᵉ care of able masters" who never had cause, he claimed, to give him "one Stroak or So much as a Sharp Rebuke."

After eight or nine years of schooling in Ulster, Craig went to Scotland, where he attended the University of Edinburgh. By his own account, Craig was very "Carefull in Choosing my Companions, frugal as to my Expense, and Diligent in my Studies." However, Craig's pious resolve was soon shaken by his classmates' scorn for the ministry, by "the low opinion I had Conceived of my own abilities for Such an important office," and by the prospect of an ample inheritance from his parents and an offer from a Scottish uncle of "a Little Laird-ship worth about Sixty pounds a year." Thus, after receiving his M.A. degree in 1732, Craig returned to his parents' house secretly determined to study medicine, "attend yᵉ Phisicians hall," and become a doctor instead of a clergyman. Yet within a few months, his "Consience Roar'd like a Devouring Lyon, . . . in a most Sharp and terrible manner accusing me of my Deceitfull & unsteady Dealing with God." While clumsily practicing his "new Skill" at medicine on himself, he contracted a "Mortification" which "Swel'd" his arm "to a wonderfull Size." Anticipating "that in a few hours I must be in Eternity" and "fully Convinc'd of yᵉ Evil of my New Design," Craig tearfully repented of his "Pride [and] Self Conceit," promising his angry God that, if his life was spared, he would embrace the ministry—although it was a "Laborious Difficult and a Despised office amongst yᵉ fashionable part of the world." Within six months, Craig was both physically cured and spiritually renewed: "Patrimony & Estate" no longer mattered, and Craig was "Now willing to Serve God in any office Station or Relation he pleased to fit me for & Call me too; or in any place where he pleased to Send me." And so, he wrote, "I Cast my Self upon his Care and Earnestly pray'd for his Direction."

Over a third of a century later, in the winter of 1769–1770, Craig penned the following memoir, in part to edify his children but also to explain his life as the unfolding of

God's will, as the triumph of faith over trials and temptations, and to rededicate himself—despite "Distress want . . . poverty" and the increasing afflictions of old age—to the steps remaining on his path of duty. "[O]h Give Strength & Courage Now when Nature fails," he prayed, "to fight ye Good fight of faith and to finish my Course with Joy; Not fearing Even the King of terrors thro Christ his Conquerer ye Captain of my Salvation ye foundation of all my hopes." Unfortunately, the first and last pages of Craig's memoir have been lost since the mid–nineteenth century, but enough remains to illuminate much of the inner as well as the outer life of a Scots-Irish clergyman on the Virginia frontier.

The excerpt here begins in 1734, after Craig's recovery from illness, with the implementation of his decision to emigrate and seek ordination in America. In 1738, after four years of theological studies and school-teaching in the colonies, Craig was licensed to preach by the Presbytery of Donegal, which then covered most of Pennsylvania west of Philadelphia as well as the entire southwestern frontier. For two years Craig temporarily supplied vacant pulpits in western Pennsylvania, Maryland, and Virginia's lower Shenandoah Valley, until 1740 when he accepted a call to minister among the Scots-Irish settlers at the Triple Forks of the Shenandoah, in the recently established Augusta County, thus becoming the first permanently settled Presbyterian clergyman west of the Blue Ridge Mountains. There he remained for the rest of his life, serving a congregation scattered over 1,800 square miles and preaching alternate Sundays in two churches over 10 miles apart—the Augusta Stone Church (still standing near Staunton) and the Tinkling Spring Church (near Fisherville)—until he relinquished the latter charge in 1764.[4]

The life of a Presbyterian clergyman in the colonial backcountry was not easy, and, in addition to the normal hardships of frontier settlement, Craig faced and recounts in his memoir at least four trials or crises peculiar to his profession and its presumptions of authority. First, unlike Ireland, where since 1672 Presbyterian ministers had received a stipend or *regium donum* directly from the crown, in nearly all the colonies dissenting clergymen were entirely dependent on their congregations' good will and voluntary contributions.[5] Throughout his tenure in the Shenandoah, Craig struggled unsuccessfully to secure his promised salary from his parishioners, some of whom had been barely churched in Ulster, were even less attentive to religion on the American frontier, and often still harbored folk beliefs in magical cures and witchcraft; even those who attended church regularly, Craig lamented, suffered "repeated lapses from the path of virtue."[6] Moreover, from the begin-

---

4. Craig's pastorate covered most of Beverley Manor and the northern reaches of the Borden Grant. In the early days of his pastorate, before his churches were constructed, Craig preached in the house of Benjamin Borden, Sr., to congregations that undoubtedly included the Greenlee and McDowell families. On the early Scots-Irish settlement of this region and the upper Shenandoah Valley, generally, see chapter 20. **5.** Except in Connecticut and Massachusetts, where Congregationalism was by law established, non-Anglican clergy received no support from colonial authorities and encountered varying degrees of hostility in colonies, such as Craig's Virginia, where the Church of England was legally preeminent. **6.** Rev. John Craig's baptismal and church record; copy in the archives of the Presbyterian Church (U.S.A.), Presbyterian Historical Society, Montreat, N.C.

FIGURE 10
Rev. John Craig's Augusta Stone Church (or Old Stone Church), Fort Defiance, near Staunton, Virginia, in the late nineteenth century. Photograph courtesy of Augusta Stone Presbyterian Church, Fort Defiance, Virginia.

ning of his pastorate Craig found himself caught in a power struggle between John Lewis and James Patton, the two most affluent, influential, and ruthlessly ambitious members of his Tinkling Spring congregation. Their animosity undermined Craig's authority, reduced his income, and subjected him to vicious legal and personal attacks that lasted at least until 1755, when Patton was killed in a skirmish with the Indians.[7]

Second was the crisis precipitated by the so-called First Great Awakening, colonial America's first great wave of religious enthusiasm. Between 1741 and 1758 the Awakening's tumultuous revivals formally split the colonial Presbyterian church between their New Side supporters and their Old Side critics, engendering a bitterness—among both clergy and laity—that lasted for decades. Historians have debated whether the colonial revivals of the late 1730s and 1740s represented a transplanted expression or an "American" repudiation of traditional Scottish and Ulster Presbyterian religious practices and beliefs. It is arguable, however, that both the emotional piety of the New Side evangelicals and the reasoned morality of their Old Side opponents were rooted in Scottish and Scots-Irish Presbyterianism. As early as 1625–1633, during the first stage of the Ulster Plantation, Craig's own Donegore parish had witnessed northern Ireland's first great religious revival, at Six-Mile Water. Moreover, Ulster Presbyterian communion services, held only once or

7. On John Lewis and James Patton, also see chapter 20.

twice yearly, were often scenes of fervent piety; frequently, these "holy fairs" were conducted jointly by several clergymen who preached and administered the sacraments in stages to hundreds, even thousands, of people, seated at long tables in the fields. However, there had always been tensions between Scottish and Scots-Irish Calvinism's pietist and legalist tendencies, between its dual emphases on man's "affections" and "reason" as the paths to understanding God and experiencing conversion. And in general, during the late seventeenth and early eighteenth centuries, Ulster's university-trained clergy and its more affluent laymen had become increasingly averse to emotional outpourings of the Holy Spirit, although evangelicalism or "lively preaching" remained popular among ordinary Presbyterians in the Synod of Ulster (and among members of splinter sects, such as the Seceders and Covenanters) who were less affected by Enlightenment rationalism.

Thus, by the 1730s and 1740s both the supporters and the critics of the First Great Awakening could claim to speak not only as Calvinists but for Scots-Irish traditions. Consequently, Ulster-born clergymen were found on each side of the schism that the First Great Awakening precipitated among Presbyterians in the colonies. On the one hand, evangelicals such as Gilbert Tennant, Samuel Blair, and Samuel Finley spearheaded the New Side revivalists' "invasions" of Old Side congregations, denouncing their clerical opponents as unconverted "enemies of Christ" and of "true religion." Conversely, Francis Alison, John Craig, and John Thomson—Craig's mentor and surrogate father in America—condemned the revivals as devilish and disorderly, and in 1741 they signed the protestation that expelled Tennent and the other New Side clergy from the Philadelphia Synod.[8]

Despite internal dissension, Craig's own congregation—unlike many in Pennsylvania and New Jersey—was not split asunder by the First Great Awakening.[9] Indeed, it appears that revivalism was most popular in eastern congregations, where Scots-Irish Presbyterians were longer-settled and inhabited ethnically and religiously mixed areas—relatively far from threats by Indians but in close proximity to the official representatives of alien Quaker and Anglican establishments—and where commercialization, coupled with the rise to adulthood of an American-born generation, rendered socioeconomic status more fluid and parental authority less secure than in the old country. Thus, in the Middle Colonies' eastern districts the Great Awakening may have reflected not only a nascent individualism but perhaps also a reaffirmation as well as a reconfiguration of threatened ethnoreligious

8. The activities of Tennent, Finley, and especially Blair are discussed more fully in chapter 47. On Alison, see chapter 55. ¶Rev. John Thomson (or Thompson): born in Ireland, in 1715 Thomson emigrated to New York; successively, he was Presbyterian pastor at Lewes, Delaware (1717–1729), New Castle, Delaware (1729), Middle Octorara, Pennsylvania (1729–1731), and Chestnut Level, Pennsylvania (1732–1744). In 1744 Thomson joined Craig, whom he had tutored in theology at Chestnut Level in 1734–1738, as a missionary to the Shenandoah Valley. He died in North Carolina in 1753. Next to Alison, Thomson was perhaps the most able of the Old Side clergy. 9. In many congregations, the revivals enabled assertive or ambitious laymen to challenge the traditional authority of their Old Side ministers. However, it is significant that apparently neither James Patton nor John Lewis used revivalism as a weapon in their struggles against Craig or each other, preferring more traditional, secular levers of power such as the magistracy.

identities. By contrast, newcomers from Ulster felt their traditional, tribal identity less endangered in the overwhelmingly Scots-Irish and perhaps more hierarchical and patriarchal settlements in the upper Shenandoah Valley, where Anglican churches and officials were still virtually nonexistent; perhaps there also, as on the seventeenth-century Ulster frontier, they had less inclination to divide among themselves, given the omnipresent threat of Indian assaults. For example, although in 1755 Braddock's defeat by the French and Indians precipitated yet another crisis in Craig's ministry, the consequent threat of imminent Indian attacks also enabled him to reassert the authority that Ulster's Presbyterian clergy had first assumed in the seventeenth century, when their congregations had faced native Irish rebellions and Anglican proscriptions. At great personal expense, Craig fortified his churches (the Augusta Stone Church became "Fort Defiance") and, drawing on communal memories of 1641 and 1688–1689, he rallied his frightened parishioners and kept them safe from danger throughout the French and Indian War.

However, if the First Great Awakening did not exile Craig from his pulpit, while Thomson and many other Old Side clergy were expelled from theirs, it may have encouraged some disaffected parishioners to poison his livestock and charge him with witchcraft. More important, that religious controversy only increased Craig's sense of isolation and loneliness, exacerbating his chronic self-doubt and fear of social inferiority—the latter evidenced by his defensive and almost obsessive references to his personal "interest" and material "Estate," as well as by his conflicting concern for his spiritual relationship with a demanding deity. Most likely it was these insecurities and unresolved internal conflicts that in 1745 precipitated Craig's greatest personal crisis: the bout of acute depression—occasioned by the impending birth of his first child, but rooted in his harsh Calvinist condemnation of his own "Deceitfull treacherous and Backsliding" heart—that momentarily tempted him to abandon ministry, family, and faith itself. Yet only the same uncompromising faith enabled him to overcome this mental illness, as in 1733–1734 it had helped him surmount his physical afflictions and persuaded him to abandon the familiar comforts of County Antrim for a life of trial and sacrifice in the colonial wilderness.

Rev. John Craig Memoir, 1734–1769/70

America was then Much in my mind accompany'd with this Argument, that Service would be most pleasing and acceptable, where most Needful & wanting, which rais'd in me a Strong Desire to See that part of the world

But I had Resolved Never to be Rash in determining affair<s> of weight<y> importance any more, and began to think of that affair deliberatly. to Leave my Dear and most affectionate Parents Now very old, my Relations acquaintances & sweet Companions Some of them very Dear to me with all my prospects of a way of Living and thousands of Dangers & Difficulties appearing in yᵉ way which appear'd hard to Get over, but for these things, my mind was Determined believing it to be my Duty to venture thro all opposition   I Consulted my parents & friends who Did not much

hinder my Design but grieved at my thoughts of Leaving them   but above all I
Earnestly Cry'd to God for his Direction that he would Restrain or Encourage me as
he saw would tend to his Glory & my happiness   Still my mind was steady

at that time I had a Dream or vision Representing to me, as it were in Minature
the whole that has happened to me of any importance these thirty five years yea the
very place I have been Settled in these thirty years,   I knew it at first Sight & have
Done here what was Represented to me there—But <I> thought little of it then, tho
often of it since.—My mind being fully Settled & Determined; I prepared for my long
voyage. . . . [10]

Having taken farewell of my friends & Country (no Easie task) we went on
board at Learn[11] June: 10: 1734 and in yᵉ kind providence of God Landed all Safe at
new Castle on Delaware the 17th of August following being born in the old World and
landed in the new the very same Day of yᵉ year and hour of the Day which I then
observed.   in the Passage I was sore afflicted with Sea Sickness which brought me
very Low; but Recovered both health & strength before I Came aShore. I Escaped a
very Eminent[12] danger of being Lost in a Manner almost miraculous without any
mean<s> but yᵉ kind hand of providence   being accidently Cast over board in a
Dark & tempestuous night, <I> lay as on a bed of down on my back, on the Raging
Wave which tossed me back on yᵉ Ship's Side where I found holds & sprung aboard &
none aboard knew of it nor Did I Speak of <it> to any while at Sea.—this Evidence of
Divine Care I ought Ever to Remember with a Gratefull & thankfull heart to his
praise & Glory who made the proud wave a bed but not a Grave to Swallow me up
without Remedy

when I Came ashore I mett with an old acquaintence the Revᵈ Benjamin
Campbell then Minister of New-Castle[13]   he had been in the Country Some years,
and was very kind & friendly to me in Every Respect;   he was a very Judicious
Gentleman, Gave me a just account of the Country, and with Care advised me to Seek
aliving in a healthy place of the Country tho poor; gave me an account of the Ministry
and of men of parts among them which turn'd out Greatly to my advanta<ge>   he
was then Agueish,[14] & died about two Months after Greatly to my Grief

The Synod of Philadelphia Mett in September 1734[15] where I attended having
Several Letters of Recomme<n>dation from Ministers in Ireland to their
Correspondent ministers here and then had an opportunity to Deliver them   they

10. voige ms. Prayers of thanksgiving omitted.   11. Learn: Larne, Co. Antrim; spelling indicates Scots
pronunciation (rhymes with cairn).   12. Eminent: i.e., imminent.   13. Revᵈ Benjamin Campbell . . . of
New-Castle: born in Ireland, in 1729 Campbell emigrated to America, was received by the Presbytery of
Newcastle, and ordained sometime prior to September 1733; his death was reported to the Synod in September
1735.   14. Agueish: suffering from ague (a malarial fever).   15. The Synod of Philadelphia Mett in
September 1734 . . . : 33 Presbyterian clergy, about half of them Irish-born, attended the September 1734
meeting of the Philadelphia Synod; see n. 17.

were of service to me for the ministers used[16] me as well as a Stranger Could Expect, on that account—

It Gave me both Grief & Joy to see that Synod, Grief to See their Small Number & mean appearance, Joy to See their mutal Love & good order; & men of Solid Sense among them & Steady to ye Presbyterian Principles & against all innovations which began to appear at this Synod from an overture Read publickly by the Rev^d: Gilbert Tennent Concerning the Receiving of Candidates into the Ministry & Communicants to the Lords table & which he imbibed from one M^r. Freelinghouse a Low Dutch minister which Notions was then openly Rejected,[17] but afterwards prevail'd so far as to Divid the Synod & put ye Church of God here into ye utmost Confusion not yet rooted out tho Endeavoured

I now wanted a fixed Residence, finding it uneasy unprofitable & Expensive to wander about. But to find a place healthy where I Could gain my Bread and be under ye care of a minister able to help me was at that time very Difficult.—this I Endeavoured[18] to find at Several places and times for three months, but Still fail'd, which Greatly Distress'd my Mind as if God seem'd to frown upon me and bring me to Misery in a Strange Country among Strangers and vexed me with thoughts of Returning home, as if God had no Service for me here, but Such was the Love of God to me a poor Stranger that he would not Suffer me to Settle, but where I had all the things Desired to answer the Good End Ihad in view; I Saw here that a Steady Dependence on God far Exceeds humane Wisdom he at Last brought me to a healthy place, an home, a maintainance,[19] a faithfull & able friend a Sincere Christian ye Rev^d: John Thompson of Chesnut level[20] whose praise is Deservedly in ye Church, as being ye ins<t>rument in the hand of God of forming her into an organized Body here, & Defending her while he Lived

Now I began to foreget my Sorrow having my home with a poor but akind Stranger, and ye Sweet and improving Conversation of So Good & kind afriend here

---

16. used (spelling variants hereafter: **usd, us'd**): treated.   **17. an overture Read publickly by the Rev^d: Gilbert Tennent**: Craig refers to Gilbert Tennent's proposal (**overture**) or argument, before the 1734 Synod meeting, that the Westminster Confession of Faith required ministerial candidates to be examined not only in learning and doctrine but also for their "experimental knowledge of the salvation that they were to preach to others"—i.e., whether they had experienced personal conversions. However, the Synod passed only mild resolutions—urging greater care in examining candidates for the ministry and exhorting the clergy to greater diligence—instead of Tennent's overture (on Tennent, see chapter 47). **M^r. Freelinghouse**: Theodorus Jacobus Frelinghuysen (1691–ca.1748): a **Low Dutch** (i.e., from the Netherlands, as opposed to High Dutch "German") Reformed clergyman, skilled revivalist, and the first important preacher of the Great Awakening in the Middle Colonies; Frelinghuysen emigrated from Europe in 1720, responding to a call from the Dutch congregations of New Jersey's Raritan Valley; his emotional sermon style and his demand that both parishioners and clergy experience spiritual conversion were major influences on the evangelicalism of the Tennents and the other New Side Presbyterian clergy. **18. Endeavorured** ms.   **19. maintainance**: means of subsistence.   **20. Rev^d: John Thompson of Chesnut level**: see n. 8.

I Liv'd in Love & peace till ye year 1739 and then Remove<d> to augusta County in ye Colony of virginia

I taught School one year, and Read two years more Being Still affraid to Engage in So weighty awork & offices But being invited by ye Presbytery I entered on trials[21] & was Licenced by ye Presbytery of Donegal in Pensilvania in ye year 1737, but was still more affraid to undertake ye Charge of a Congregation tho Ihad Several Calls Given me, till I was Sent to a new Settlement in Virginia of our own Country people near 300 Miles Distant.   they were Encouraged to Settle there by ye honorable S^r: William Gooch then Governour of virginia a Good man & a father to the frontiers in the Colony who allow<ed> them the Benefit of the act of tolleration.[22]—No Presbyterians being Settled as an organized body in the Colony Since it was first Settled that I heard of.

from ye Dream I had before I left Ireland when I came to ye Settlement <I> knew it to be the plot in Christs vineyard where I was to Labour (I must Say I thought but Little of it[23] which perhaps was my Sin)   from them I had a Call & Durst Not Refuse it altho I well Saw that it wo[uld] Be attended with many & Great Difficulties; but Seing this So Clearly to be ye Call of providence and y^t I Should not Despise ye Day of Small things,[24] & that He could perfect His strength in my weakness, granting every necessary qualification gift and grace, for Carrying on his own work and Support ye agent Called by him to Do ye work, under Every Difficulty & Danger falling in the way while faith full   thus with aSteady Dependence on God for Light and Direction, aid and assistance, prudence & understanding I accepted their Call pass'd ordination trials & was ordain'd as their Pastor & was Received by their Commissioners in Dunegal the last of August 1740.[25] . . .

This is ye Last Scene of my Life to the End of my 60th year to which all ye preceding part was but as a preparative as to Labour, trials, temptations, Griefs, Dangers, Losses, Crosses &c

When I Came to the people of my Charge they Received me in the Most friendly manner, whose friendship (Except a very few) Continued Steady these thirty

---

21. trial: examination presented by presbyteries for licensing preachers and ordaining ministers; see **ordination trials** hereafter.   **22. S^r: William Gooch**: governor of Virginia (1727–1749); on Gooch and his role in settling the Scots-Irish in the Shenandoah Valley, see chapter 20; in response to the 1729 petition of Rev. James Anderson, Gooch guaranteed religious toleration to the Valley's Presbyterians.   **23. I thought but little of it**: "I was somewhat contemptuous of it (i.e., y^e **Settlement**)."   **24. Despise ye Day of Small things**: Zechariah 4:10: "For who hath despised the day of small things?" (King James Version); "A day for little things, no doubt, but who would dare despise it?" (Jerusalem Bible).   **25.** Robert Poag and Daniel Denniston headed the committee that invited Craig to minister at the Triple Forks of the Shenandoah. On 17 June 1740, Craig announced his acceptance of their call; on 3 Sept. 1740 he was formally ordained in Donegal Presbyterian Church, Lancaster Co., Pa., before moving to Augusta Co., Va. More of Craig's prayers and pious reflections are omitted from the text between this and the following paragraph.

years to our Mutual Comfort. In this I have been Most happy, but Destitute of all Conversation Direction or Advice of Fathers or Brethren for more than ten years being about 200 Miles from ye Nearest Presbyterian Minister   the place was a New Settlement, without place of worship, or any Church order; A wilderness in a proper Sense and a few Christians Settled in it, with Numbers of the Heathen[26] traveling among us, but Generally Civil tho Some people were Murdered by them about that time.   they March in Small Companies from twenty to fifty Sometimes more or Less.   they must be Supply'd at any house they Call at with victuals or they become their own Stuarts[27] & Cooks Spairing Nothing they Chuse to Eat or Drink[28] in the house and Carries with them bread and Meat as they please which was trouble Some times Expensive & Some times dangerous for they Go all Arm'd for war in their way.

A Company passing kill'd Some Cattle & horses,   Some neighbours Mett went & Enquired Why they Did So?   ye Indians Gave them No answer, but fir'd upon y^m[29]   the English[30] Returned ye fire made ye Indians give way;   in that Skirmish Eight men of ye English were kill'd & Severals wounded, & fifteen of ye Indians was kill'd, ye Rest fled.[31]   ye unExpected News Ran Swiftly thro ye Settlement which Greatly alarmed all the Inhabitants   Next Day a more dreadfull alarm Came of 500 Indians at ye Lower End of ye Settlement murdering all they Could find about ten miles off   the people gathered together & all y^t Could Carry arms went to meet them & happily found ye report false but ye Cries of women & Children Left without any Defence to Depend on was very Shocking to me   thes times was Distressing, as we were far from Zidon,[32] few of our Selves & fewer to Espouse our Cause heartily   For these Difficulties I was obliged to bear a part—

Another thing that gave me Great Concern, was how to Act So as to maintain Presbyterian order & Rules of Goverment in our Church, So as not to Give offence to ye Establish<ed> Church, and Goverment, with whom I had to Do, and in this Case, providence ordered Matters So that I obtain'd their approbation and Esteem   when

---

26. the Heathen: the Indians.   **27. Stuarts**: i.e., stewards.   **28. Dring** ms.   **29. y^m**: them.   **30. the English**: Craig's curious description here of his Scots-Irish Presbyterian compatriots as "English" (although described hereafter as members of his own ethnoreligious **Nation**) highlights the ambiguity of their eighteenth-century identity and perhaps can best be understood in Craig's specific context, i.e., of formal, bloody conflict between the Protestant "English" government's representatives on the American frontier and Catholic France's Indian allies. In seventeenth-century Ireland, Craig's usage of "English" to denominate *all* British settlers was common (although inaccurate), as "English" and "Irish" were the official political and cultural polarities of the colonial conflict between "civilized" settlers (invited to Ireland by what was prior to 1707 the English, not the British, government) and "barbarous" natives.   **31. in that Skirmish**: Craig refers to the skirmish between the Augusta Co. militia and the Iroquois, on 18 December 1742, in which Capt. John McDowell, brother of Mary Elizabeth Greenlee, was killed. At this time, the McDowells and Greenlees were members of Craig's congregation, probably at Tinkling Spring; see chapter 20.   **32. far from Zidon**: Judges 18:28 "And there was no deliverer, because it was far from Zidon" (King James Version).

we were Erected into a County & parish,[33] and had ministers[34] inducted, of which we had two they both in their turns wrote to me Making high Demands, I gave no Answer but Still observed our own Rules where there was No positive Law against them.—

Another Distressing affair to me being alone was the Division of our Church, having Seen yᵉ Conduct of ministers and People when I was in Pensyilvania, that Maintain'd these New Doctrines <I> Examined yᵉ Controversie, had free Conversation with both parties & apply'd to God for Light and Direction in yᵗ important Concern, which was Done with time & Deliberation, Not Instantly; I attain'd Clearness of Mind to join in yᵉ protest against these New and uncharitable opinions & yᵉ Ruin of Church Goverment[35]

This Gave offence to Some two or three families in my Congregation; who then Look'd upon me as an opposer of yᵉ work of God, as they Call'd it an Enemy to Religion &c. And apply'd with all keenness to their holy & Spiritual teachers,[36] to Come & preach & Convert the people of my Charge & free them from Sin & Satan and from me a Carnal wretch, upon whom they unhappily Depended for instruction to their Souls utter Destruction—they flying Speedily Came and thunder'd their New Gospel thro Every Corner of my Congregation & Some of them had yᵉ assurance to Come to my house & Demand a Dismission[37] for Some of my Subscribers who had invited them being tented[38] with these Notions formerly; but Providence So ordered that affair yᵗ they Gain'd None of my people more that I know of, my moral Character Stood Clear & Good Even among them but they freely Loaded me with these and yᵉ like[39]—poor, blind, Carnal, hypocritical Damn'd wretch—this Given to my face by Some of their Ministers and when I administered yᵉ Lords Supper to my people they mockingly Said to their Neighbours going to it, what are you Going to Craig's frolick?—I though't then that God had given me a Difficult plot to Labour in alone, among Strangers, not knowing how to trust any, in danger by the heathen, Reproached by Some of my own people & Nation,[40] our Religion from our own

---

33. when we were Erected into (i.e., formed into/established as) **a County & parish**: Augusta County was formally organized in 1745, but Presbyterians controlled the local Anglican vestries until 1769. **34. ministers**: i.e., of yᵉ **Establish<ed> Church** (of England). **35. protest**: Craig refers to the Old Side's "protestation," before the 1741 Philadelphia Synod, against the New Side revivalists for their denunciations of "unconverted" ministers and "invasions" of Old Side parishes. Signed by 12 ministers, nine of whom (including Craig) were born in Ulster, the protestation effectively expelled the New Side clergy from the Philadelphia Synod. In 1745 the New Side formed the rival New York Synod, but the two groups reunited in 1758. **36. their holy & Spiritual teachers**: Craig's sarcastic reference is probably to New Side ministers William Dean and Eliab Byram, itinerant preachers in Frederick and Augusta counties in the mid-1740s. More famous in Virginia were the revivals of Rev. Samuel Davies (1723–1761), but his ministry was confined to the area around Richmond, east of the Blue Ridge Mountains. **37. Dismission**: release (from the congregation). **38. tented**: i.e., tainted. **39. these and yᵉ like**: "the following epithets and others like them." **40. my own people & Nation**: my parishioners and compatriots (see n. 30).

Conduct our Enthusiastick & uncharitable Notions became the Jest of yᵉ wicked & profane, and had not God in his Great Goodness Directed Supported & Encouraged me I would fled[41] from yᵉ place as from an Enemy but I Ever Call'd upon him in trouble, & he Never fail'd to help

To Chuse a Session[42] to please yᵉ people & my Self and to unite their affections[43] when ordain'd Cost me much thought and Labour and God Granted that Blessing also which was the Strength & Stay of yᵉ Congregation.   it[44] was Large by Computation about thirty miles in Lenth & Near twenty in breath[45]   The people agreed to have two Meeting houses Expecting they would become two Congregations which is Now Come to pass (this prior to my Relation to them)[46]

That part Now Called Tinkling-Spring was most[47] in Number & Richer than the other and forward[48] & had yᵉ publick managment of yᵉ affairs of yᵉ whole Settlement, their Leaders proud Self interested Contentious & ungovernable all of them Closehanded about providing Necessary things for pious or Religious uses, and Could Not agree for Several Years upon yᵉ place or Manner where & how to build their meeting house, which Gave me very Great trouble to hold them together their Disputes Rose so high   Difference[49] happened between Coll John Lewis & Colˡ James Patton both Living in that Congregation which Continued while they Liv'd Which of them Should be highest in Commission & power which was hurtfull to yᵉ Settlement but Especially to me; they were Jealous of my interest[50] with the people to Such a Degree that I Could Neither Bring them to friendship with Each other Nor obtain both their friendshipes at once[51] Ever after;   they both had Good interest with yᵉ people of their own party; and one of them always by turns bitter Enemies to me which was very hurtfull both to my peace & Interests,   they by turns Narrowly watched Every Step of my Conduct—marred[52] my support to yᵉ utmost of their power— usd their interest with yᵉ people to Drive me from the place or Starve me out for want of Support, but to no purpose; for the people always intertain'd a Good opinion of me. My Character alway Stood Clear, tho they hurt my Estate[53] very much   this continued for 13 or 14 years till Colˡ Patton was murdered by the Indians,   at that time he was at peace with me   after his Death Colˡ Lewis was

---

41. I would fled: i.e., I would have fled. Craig also uses the standard English pattern; see **would I have prayed** and **I might have done** hereafter. The nonstandard pattern arises from the phonetic loss of the reduced form of **have** ("a" as in "I should a gone"); see chapter 1, n. 22.   **42. Session**: i.e., kirk-session: the lowest court in the Presbyterian church, composed of the minister and elders of the parish or congregation; Craig here refers to the election of such elders as would meet with his congregation's approval.   **43. to unite their affections**: to achieve a united disposition among them.   **44. it**: i.e., the (territorial) parish.   **45. breath**: i.e., breadth; see James McCullough's **with** "width" (chapter 21).   **46. this prior to my Relation to** ("connection with") **them**: i.e., the decision to build two meetinghouses occurred prior to Craig's ordination as minister.   **47. most**: greatest (in numbers of inhabitants).   **48. forward**: well advanced; (or) ardent, zealous.   **49. Difference**: disagreement, dispute, quarrel.   **50. interest**: personal influence.   **51. at once**: at one and the same time.   **52. marred**: damaged, impaired.   **53. Estate**: status, standing, dignity (OED, s.v., 3.a; archaic).

friendly to me till he Died   here God maintain'd my Cause & Supported me under base & Cruel usage but their wicked Devices Did not Die with them   my Estate Still Suffers by it and ye Congregation Continues a vacancy, the old Contentious Spirit Still Remaining amongst them[54]

To give one of many instances how basely I was us'd   Col^l. Patton, being a Magistrate, Sent[55] his precept[56] to the Common Constable on 100£ penalty to bring me immediately before his worship[57] designedly to fall out[58] on the Sabbath day   ye Constable as Soon as Divine Service was <over> Carried me off (I knowing No Cause or Reason for it) as the vilest Criminal   when I appear'd before him he asked me Some questions about a Runaway Servant and what he had Reported   I had Neither Seen ye man nor knew any thing of ye matter but his Design was to terrify & affront me, and provoke me[59] to Speak Something in passion where of he Might accuse me & drive me from my Charge and all this because I would Not become his Creature to Serve his interest

But a Just God, after he had born with him & prospered his Designs for a while Sent a Summons for him unexpectedly suddenly by merciless & Cruel officers, to answer more important questions & before a more awfull & Just Judge than he ask'd of me.

as to ye other part of the Congregation Now Called Augusta   the people Were fewer in Number & much Lower as to their worldly Circumstances; But a Good Natur'd prudent Governable people and Librally bestowed apart of what God gave them for Religious & pious uses, & Now Enjoy ye benefit in a Decent & becoming Manner, to their Great Satisfaction, Always unanimous among themselves Loving & kind to me these thirty years, with whom I Enjoy'd ye Greatest Satisfaction & Serve them with pleasure.   they Support me under the persecution (for it Deserves No better Name) of these ambitious men of the other part of the Congregation   I had no trouble with these about their Meetinghouse but to moderate & Direct them when Mett; they Readily fixed on the place, & Agreed on ye plan for building it and Contributed Cheerfully Mony & Labour to Accomplish the work; all in ye voluntary way, what Every man pleased

These hints will Serve to bring to Remembrance the whole Scenes of toil Labour & Suffering; and Satisfaction Comfort & pleasure Enjoy'd till the war brok out when Col^l. Washington was Defeated at Broad Meadows[60]

---

54. Craig resigned his charge at Tinkling Spring in autumn 1764; no regular pastor succeeded him until 1776.
55. **Send** ms., an earlier and now dialectal form of **sent**.   56. **precept**: a writ or warrant (issued by a court).
57. **his worship**: i.e., Patton.   58. **fall out**: take place, happen.   59. **provoke to me** ms.   60. **the war brok out when Col^l. Washington was Defeated at Broad Meadows**: Virginia militia colonel George Washington's surrender of Fort Necessity at Broad (or Great) Meadows, near the future site of Pittsburgh, on 3 April 1754, marked the beginning of what the colonists called the French and Indian War (1754–1763). To counter the French threat to the British colonial frontier, in 1755 London sent Gen. Edward Braddock and a small British army to Pennsylvania.

What made the times distressing and unhappy to all the frontiers, was the French and Indian war, which lay heavy on us, in which I suffered a part as well as others. When General Braddock was defeated and killed, our country was laid open to the enemy, our people were in dreadful confusion and discouraged to the highest degree.[61] Some of the richer sort that could take some money with them to live upon, were for flying to a safer place of the country. My advice was then called for, which I gave, opposing that scheme as a scandal to our nation, falling below our brave ancestors, making ourselves a reproach among Virginians, a dishonor to our friends at home, an evidence of cowardice, want of faith, and a noble Christian dependence on God, as able to save and deliver from the heathen; it would be a lasting blot to our posterity. . . . They required me to go before them in the work which I did cheerfully, though it cost me one-third of my estate. The people very readily followed, and my congregation in less than two months was well fortified.[62]

As to my private or Domestick State of Life, when fix'd in ye Congregation I found ye unseasonable[63] Calls, to visit the Sick, & baptize Sick Children and ye Like; prov'd trouble Some to ye place where I Lodg'd, and Not willing to trouble others I gave the More to my Self; which wearied me of that State of Life. I then purchased a plantation & began to improve upon it, and June 11: 1744 married a young Gentle woman of a Good family & character Born & brought up in ye Same Neighbourhood where I was born Daughter to M^r. George Russell by whom I had nine Children[64] Six Now alive and three Dead, & have been both happy in ye Relation hetherto, tho Not without our troubles trials and afflictions   our fortunes being Small we Endeavoured to increase it by our Labour Care and frugal Managment which we Cheerfully

61. **When General Braddock was defeated and killed . . . :** on 9 July 1755 Braddock's army, consisting of 1,400 regular British troops plus 450 colonials under Washington, was crushed by a force of nine hundred French and Indians at the Battle of the Wilderness, thus exposing the entire frontier to attack. Yet Virginia's backcountry suffered less than Pennsylvania's during the war, and the upper Shenandoah Valley, where Craig's congregations were situated, witnessed fewer Indian assaults than did the lower Valley.   62. The lines in this paragraph, from one of Craig's pages that has been lost since the mid–nineteenth century, were transcribed, regularized as to spelling, punctuation, etc., and in 1855 published by Rev. William Henry Foote in the second series of his *Sketches of Virginia, Historical and Biographical*. Although these lines were apparently located at the end of Craig's memoir, we have inserted them here for continuity with the surviving text. The paragraphing is ours, and the ellipses represent Foote's presumed omissions of material from the original manuscript. In his *Sketches* Foote also reproduced the memoir's now-missing first page, from which we have drawn for information on Craig's Irish origins, childhood, and early religious experiences.   63. **unseasonable:** untimely. 64. **nine Children:** the children of Craig and his wife, Isabella Helena Russell, were: Isabella Helena (b. and d. 1745); Mary (1746–1816), married Charles Baskin, buried at Tinkling Spring; John (b. and d. 1748); George (1749–1815), married Kitty Kennerly, inherited his father's farm, and was prominent in Staunton's Masonic lodge (est. 1786), but in 1805 he moved to Putnam Co., [West] Va.; an infant who died at birth (ca. 1751); Patience (1752–1822), wed William Hamilton, buried at Tinkling Spring; Joanna (ca. 1753–1835), married John Hamilton (brother of William), died in South Carolina; Analena (1754–?), wed Enos Atwater, buried at Tinkling Spring; and David (ca. 1754–ca. 1773).

Comply'd with as our Necessity Required: but God was pleased to try us with many Sharp and Sore afflictions heavy to be born in our persons family & Estate.

Having prepared a little house we Sett up housekeeping having Neither Servant Nor Slave to help us, only Employing hirelings[65] when we Could find them; the toil of Serving our Selves we Esteem'd No Burden.

The first Distressing Circumstance which happened to us was when My wife was Great with her first Child, Col[l]. Patton Sends y[e] Constable with a precept of an 100£ penalty to bring me before him   None of us knew for what I was to be Carri'd prisoner before him; My wife Never having Seen Ministers used in Such a Manner, Was very much terrify'd, fearing Some Dreadfull Evil She knew Not what, to befall me but Go I must & did (but She took uneasier[66] immediately)   he had Some trifling questions to ask me.   when I had Resolved them he Let me Go,   I had about 14 miles home & found my wife in a very Low Condition in which She Continued for five weeks with Some intervall till She was Delivered; During which time almost Every Night & Sometimes for y[e] Most part of the Night I had to Sit & hold her in My Arms, often not knowing Whether She was Living or Dead and none in the House but our Selves;   our Sufferings we Conceal'd as far as we possibly Could, least[67] we Should be made the Jest of Some that waited for our halting.   this was hard to bear, but God permitted Some thing harder to follow which Distressed me Even beyond Expression

While my wife was in Labour which was tedious and hard I being alone in alittle house, near where She was; Sometimes Reading, Sometimes Meditating, and offering up my Requests to heaven Suitable to my present Circumstances at that time: About Midnight I was Suddenly taken with a Stupid Dulness & pressure of Spirit So that I Could not Connect two Sentences, together, Nor So much as bid God bless me, and y[e] most bitter hatred arose in my mind against y[e] wife of my Bosom and object of my tenderest Love and the women all of them that was with her that I Could wish'd[68] house & all of them in it in one flame, but I knew not for what Reason or Cause, only my mind flam'd with Rage & bitter Revenge against them: In broken thoughts I Saw my Conduct was Wrong and fain would I have prayed to God to Deliver me from y[e] power of Satan but Could Not Express one Sensible Sentence.   the feurious agitation of mind So weakened & took away my Natural Strength y[t] I Could Scarce walk, tho I felt Neither bodily pain nor Sickness: when day appear'd I Resolv'd to Run away but knew Not where, Set out but was Not able to walk forty Rod[69] in an hour, but No words Can Convey Just Ideas of that Dreadfull horror anguish & agony I was In,   it Continued about Six hours, & went off as Suddenly as it Came, tho I was weak for Some time after: the Case[70] happened So that None knew of it but my Self

---

65. hirelings: paid help.   **66. took uneasier**: became more anxious.   **67. least**: lest; spelling indicates Scots pronunciation (rhymes with **east**).   **68. Could wish'd**; see n. 41.   **69. forty Rod**: 220 yards (1 rod = 5.5 yards).   **70. Case**: event, occurrence.

which I was well Satisfy'd with Ever after.—nor Did I Ever before or Since feal any thing Like it and I pray God may Never Suffer me to fall under Satan's Buffetings any More for it is merciless and Cruel Indeed.

Surely God permitt<ed> Satan to torment fill & inspire me with Evil thoughts & Designs to involve & Drive me into Some gross Sins & wick<ed>ness to Destroy me, Soul & Body   here God Let me See, I had No power to Resist him of my Self; but he Restrained him & kept me from the Evil I might have Done, & Desired to Do—I Should have thought Satan took a wrong time and found me at a very Different Exercise from his purpose,[71] yet at once Carries his Designs as far as permitted, and that without any External Cause or means, and in midst of Love & pity for a dutifull wife in pangs of Child Bearing and a keen Desire to See my first Born

Had Ever man a more Convincing proof of his own inability against So powerfull & Cruel an Enemy, and more Reason to Bless God who Lead Captivity Captive[72]   I was taken Carried off Shut up, but he opened the Strong prison Doors & Set me free again the world about me knowing nothing of it.   this happend May 29: 1745

another trial very Sharp in its Nature, but Not like the former,   My first born died October 4: 1745 being four months & Six days old which was a very Great Grief to us yᵉ parents being again Left alone.

In a few weeks after[73] providence permitted New trials to fall in our way of a Different kind from these mention'd   I had purchased a Stock of horses, breeding Mares, & Cows yᵉ Best I Could find in yᵉ Settlement upon which our Little mony was laid out for our us[e]   But in two or three weeks they all Died (I mean from the first yᵗ Died to[74] last was Dead)   I had Neither Child horse Nor Cow Left me;   Now, in Job<s> State Except his personal affliction I must travel a foot for No hor[se] of my property that Came on my plantation Liv'd a bove three or four Days,   I had Severals in the wood and brought them home as I had need when yᵉ Rest was dead But all of them Died   I Could Not Discover their Distemper tho I Search<ed> with all Diligence their Carcases,   Nor Did it Reach farther then my property   It was Court time; & we had many Strangers lodged with us taverans being few   their horse<s> went & fed with ours when Dying with the Disorder but theirs were all Safe & well: & after Some time when afriend Lent me an horse to Ride it was Safe and well and So[75] of all I had borrowed till Spring

but what Convinced me fully, My Brother[76] Liv'd with me on the place and our

---

71. took a wrong time and found me . . . : "chose the wrong moment and found me engaged differently from what his plan had anticipated." **72. God who Lead Captivity Captive:** Psalms 68:17–18: "the Lord is among them, as in Sinai, in the holy place. Thou hast ascended on high, thou hast led captivity captive" (King James Version). **73. after:** afterward. **74. to:** till. **75. So:** so it was, likewise. **76. My Brother:** According to J. L. Peyton's *History of Augusta Co., Va.* (1882), William Craig, "a relative of Rev. John Craig" and perhaps his brother, was one of the earliest settlers in Augusta Co. If William was indeed John Craig's older brother

Cattle pastur'd together a[ll] the Summer, and feed[77] together always Night & Day and Not one of his Die'd tho they Eat that very food that mine had Slobbered upon & Could Not eat when Dying; and they were all fat & Strong would Scarcely Eat fodder yᵉ food in yᵉ woods being then Good,   it was in yᵉ Month of December 1745

During that time my wife went & milk'd a fine young Cow that Gave a large quaintity of milk for Supper to our Selves & Some Strangers that was with us   we all Supp'd plentifully and by morning light She went out & found that Same Cow Dead Stife and Cold & this put us in Great fear Least yᵉ milk Should have affected us with yᵉ Same Disorder but None of us was yᵉ worse for it, only we feared of it   we feared that when the stock were destroyed we might Suffer in our persons Nothing Else being Left us; but our fears was mercifully Disappointed and our wordly loss gave us little trouble when we ourSelves were well.   But that winter was Spent by us Melancholy Enough

It was then Reported that yᵉ Cattle was kill'd by witch Craft, and indeed for Several Reasons that appeared to me in observing that Scene of affairs I Realy thought then & Now; that God had permitted Satan and his Emissaries to Destroy them to try my patience and Dependence on God: but I Conceal'd my opinion Carefully Guarding my whole Conduct to my power[78] So as Not to give offence to God or man; well knowing the Divel[79] had higher Designs than to kill Brutes.

Another Report was Raised that I used Charms and named Neighbours as the instruments of our loss   both these were Directly false; yet more Effectualy answered Satans Designs against me; as it open'd a door for Some of my Adversaries who watched my Steps to alienate yᵉ affection of my friends; who Speedily improved[80] yᵉ opportunity thinking they had now Gain'd their End Immediatly by their authority Call'ed and qualify'd wittnesses to prove these Charges against me Contrary to Justice or Equity as being both the accuser & Judge but Greatly to my advantage, as they Could find Nothing against me themselves being Judges which both Confused & disappointed them Greatly, hoping by that means they Could have Driven me away with Shame & Disgrace, which they Desired to Do.   But when my innocence appeared So Clearly the people wondered at my prudence & patience under So many Sharp trials & hard treatment.—

[Go]d Continued to Exercise me with trying Dispensations[81] in my family to teach me patience and Resignation to his will, but always mixed mercy & Goodness

---

and had proceeded him to Augusta Co., and perhaps also to America, this suggests secular motives for the latter's decisions to emigrate and/or to move to the Shenandoah Valley—motives that the pious Craig consciously omitted from his memoir.   **77. feed . . . Eat**: past tense forms. **Feed** has not undergone the vowel shortening seen in Standard English **fed**; **Eat** is pronounced [ett]. (Standard British and Southern Irish). **78. to my power**: "to the best of my ability."   **79. Divel**: general Hiberno-English pronunciation. **80. improved**: took advantage of (OED, s.v. improve, 2.c).   **81. Dispensation**: blessing or affliction dealt out to one.

with Chastisments   He took my first Child, & left ye Second with me; took ye third and left ye fourth with me; took ye fifth, and left ye Sixth with me: and gave me three More without any farther Breach to this Day.——Yet I found ye Lesson not Easy for Nature to Learn: Reason & Religion Could Silence Nature by arguments, But Corrupt Nature Could Yet Sourly whisper in my mind—all I have are his, he may take them all if he pleases—A thought too Sullen[82] to Evidence a free Resignation to ye will of God, which was Real Grief of heart to me, Especially as it might Justly provok even a merciful God to inflict Sharper Corrections to bend my Stuborn mind to obedience, which hitherto (I think) he has most mercifully averted, & Yet brought ye mind to Resignation & Contentment

As my family Encreas'ed So Did my Care & Expense to provi[de] for them food & Raiment & what Education I Could afford them as it was both Expensive & Difficult to be had in this Wilderness   ye people of my Congregations was all New Settlers, & Generally of Low Circumstances   their own Necessities Called for all their Labours,   they Could or did Do little for my Support Except a few, and Consequently fell Greatly in arear.   Yet to avoid the vile Reproach of Greed Commonly Cast on ye Clergy, & to prevent Reflections of Some who were No friends to my interest, & of the Established Church willing to find any thing to Cast in our teeth of this kind.—I Carefully observed Never to Demand Stipend, or for Marriage, or Supplying vacancies but when, and what they pleased to give, & received thankfully as if it had been a meer Bounty tho I kept a Just & Clear account of what I Received as all my people have freely acknowledg'ed   Yet one of my Congregations Refuse<d> to pay their Arear which they acknowledged to be sixty nine pounds   after I gave up my Charge of that Congregation Some years I modestly Desired them to pay ye Ballance Due   this Conduct obliged me & my family to be both industrious & frugal, and God So blessed our Endeavours. . . . [83]

Craig was not entirely truthful in his memoir, for he took at least one parishioner to court in an unsuccessful attempt to collect some arrears of his salary. Nor does the memoir describe his material "Endeavours" and acquisitions: for instance, his purchases and patents of at least one thousand acres of Valley land (650 of which his son, George, still held in 1780); or the hemp, livestock, and other goods that he raised on his farm for eastern markets; or his ownership of slaves, at least one of whom was freed by the Augusta County court in 1763, as having been "detain[ed] . . . contrary to law."[84]

Moreover, Craig's memoir only gives hints of his stubborn self-righteousness. According to tradition, Craig was so infuriated by his congregation's decision to locate his

---

82. Sullen: gloomy, dismal, melancholy.   **83.** This is the last surviving page (38) of Craig's original manuscript, which breaks off with the words "Endeavours, as we was."   **84.** Craig owned five slaves when he died in 1774. Quotation from L. Chalkey, *Chronicles of the Scotch-Irish Settlement in Virginia*, vol. 1, 103; see Sources, chapter 46.

first church at Tinkling Spring on Patton lands—instead of the place where he and his then-friend and patron, John Lewis, preferred—that he refused throughout his ministry to drink the waters from which the church derived its name. Likewise, his bitterness toward the New Side clergy never fully abated, and in poems he expressed his private scorn for those critics "who [although] inferior sit / Conceive themselves in conscience bound / To join and drag me to the ground."[85] Even after the split in the Church was formally healed in 1758, Craig resisted the reunited Synod's decision to remove the Valley's loyal Old Side congregations from the jurisdiction of Donegal Presbytery to that of Hanover Presbytery, in eastern Virginia, where the New Side clergy enjoyed a majority. Undoubtedly, the evangelicals' charismatic preaching (as well as their harsh personal attacks) had only increased Craig's feelings of insecurity. For in contrast to their extemporaneous and exuberant pulpit performances, his own sermons were "plain, unadorned, and strenuous": read from laboriously prepared texts and delivered in the old-fashioned, "exhaustive method"—during services that lasted from 10:00 A.M. to sunset, with only an hour's noon recess![86]

Nevertheless, John Craig was a dedicated pastor to his widely scattered parishioners. Neither financial nor moral scandals tarnished his reputation, as they did those of several Old Side clergymen in the Shenandoah Valley. In addition to his ministry at Tinkling Spring and Augusta, during his long career Craig not only conducted the first school in the Upper Valley but also established and periodically visited at least 13 other churches—one of them west of the Appalachians and several others as far south as North Carolina. Indeed, it was Craig's last great preaching tour through the backcountry, at age 60, that so impaired his health that he was inspired to write his memoir, in anticipation of impending death. Moreover, although officially "stern in his denunciation of sin,"[87] Craig personally was a kindly man, sensitive to personal slights but also to the suffering of others. According to local tradition, he refused his congregation's demand to try an old woman for witchcraft; neither did he believe in having women publicly whipped, nor that a man should spend a night in the stocks, for being absent from church, as the law required. On at least one occasion, he baptized and stood sponsor for an illegitimate child whose mother would not reveal the father's name. And, following his own parents' example, Craig adored and indulged his children: he drew loving pictures of them in his baptismal book and, during their five-mile Sunday walks between his farm and church, allowed them "to laugh and talk and sing and frolic along the way," despite censure from parishioners who regarded such conduct as Sabbath desecration.[88]

Finally, in the 1760s and early 1770s Craig, like most Presbyterian clergymen in the colonies, became in his old age an increasingly outspoken opponent of the Church of England, of British taxation, and of the threats they purportedly posed to "religious and

---

85. Cited in L. K. Craig, *Reverend John Craig . . .* , 30; see Sources, chapter 46.   **86.** H. McK. Wilson, *The Tinkling Spring . . .* , 99; see Sources, chapter 46.   **87.** H. McK. Wilson, *The Tinkling Spring . . .* , 97; see Sources, chapter 46.   **88.** L. K. Craig, *Reverend John Craig . . .* , 17; see Sources, chapter 46.

civil liberties." Thus, Craig supported the agitation that led to the American Revolution, although he did not live to witness the consequences, dying on 21 April 1774, aged 65, on his Augusta County farm. Twenty-four years later, the members of Augusta Stone Church erected a marble monument "to the memory of their late beloved pastor."[89] Perhaps reflecting his fatherly care as well as his religious devotion, seven generations later over 80 percent of Craig's descendants were still Presbyterians.

47 ✳

Rev. Samuel Blair, 1744

In the 1730s and 1740s the First Great Awakening in the Middle Colonies divided the Scots-Irish Presbyterian clergy into warring New Side and Old Side camps. The distinction between Ulster-born ministers who favored the revivals and those who opposed them was not strictly a generational one. Indeed, William Tennent, Sr. (1673–1746), the patriarch of the New Side and in 1726–1727 the founder of the famous "Log College" that trained many of the revivalists, was actually older than his principal clerical opponents. And his pupils—for example, his son Gilbert Tennent (1703–1764), Samuel Finley (1715–1766), and Charles Beatty (ca.1714–1772)—were roughly the same age as Old Side stalwarts Francis Alison (1705–1779) and John Craig (1709–1774).[1] The crucial difference lay not in date of birth but age at emigration. The Old Side clergy came to America in their early twenties, after completing much if not all of their education abroad. By contrast, the New Side ministers had emigrated in childhood or adolescence, and their formative experiences, including their training for the ministry, took place in the New World—particularly in districts where Scots-Irish Presbyterians comprised only one of several contending ethnic and religious groups.

In these respects, Samuel Blair was typical of the New Side revivalists. Born in Ulster[2] on 14 June 1712, Blair emigrated in early youth with his siblings and parents, probably landing at New Castle, Delaware. His family apparently settled on the tributaries of the Delaware River, between Brandywine and Red Clay creeks, in Pennsylvania's Chester County—an area the Scots-Irish had begun to settle in the late 1710s and early 1720s, in clusters interspersed with settlements of English and Irish Quakers and of German

89. Rev. W. H. Foote, *Sketches of Virginia . . .* , 33; see Sources, chapter 46.   **1.** On Craig and Alison, see chapters 46 and 55, respectively.   **2.** It is noteworthy that none of his contemporary or subsequent eulogists thought it important to mention Blair's precise birthplace in Ulster. Perhaps Blair himself thought the question insignificant, compared to the necessity of a spiritual "new birth" in America. However, the preponderance of Blair surnames in northwest Co. Antrim and northeast Co. Londonderry suggests that Samuel Blair's family probably lived in the Bann Valley between Lough Neagh and the river's mouth near Coleraine.

immigrants who professed a variety of faiths.[3] Like his future antagonist, John Craig, Blair enjoyed a childhood conversion and by all accounts was an exceptionally solemn and pious youth. In the early 1730s he studied for the ministry in William Tennent's Log College at Neshaminy in Bucks County, Pennsylvania. In late 1733, aged 21, Blair was licensed to preach by the Philadelphia Presbytery, and in 1734 he accepted the pastorate of two churches, Middletown and Shrewsbury, in what was then called East Jersey. Tall, "comely and well set, in aspect grave and venerable," Blair was well endowed by nature to preach "the terrors of the Lord" in sermons delivered, without notes, in a voice "clear and commanding." Although his efforts to spiritually revive the "very irreligious" members of his first congregations proved unavailing, in 1739–1740 he was called by and installed as minister of the Presbyterian church at Fagg's Manor, in Chester County's New Londonderry township.[4] It was here that Blair achieved his most spectacular successes as a revivalist. Within a year of his arrival, Blair also established his own academy—Fagg's Manor Classical School, modeled after the Log College—to train ministerial candidates for the New Side.

Even before his tenure at Fagg's Manor, Blair and his former schoolmates—especially the Tennent brothers[5]—had initiated the controversies that would split Presbyterianism in the colonies. In the early 1730s Gilbert Tennent, pastor at New Brunswick, East Jersey, had begun to preach a series of emotionally charged sermons, demanding that his parishioners experience conversion prior to their admission to the sacraments, and by the decade's end he and Blair had emerged as the most prominent leaders of a small but vociferous "revival party" in the Philadelphia Synod. In 1738 the Synod attempted to quarantine the New Side clergy in their own Presbytery of New Brunswick, but in late 1739 the arrival in the Middle Colonies of the famous Anglican revivalist George Whitefield (1715–1770) emboldened the evangelicals to launch a frontal attack, appealing for the laity's support against their clerical opponents. By 1741 the revivalists' inflammatory denunciations of Old Side clergymen as, in Blair's words, "dry, sapless, unconverted ministers,"[6] as well as their sometimes violent "intrusions" into Old Side parishes, precipitated their expulsion from the Synod and their formation of the schismatic Conjunct Presbyteries of New Brunswick and Londonderry. Three years later, to his friend and fellow evangelist, Rev. Thomas

---

3. A William Blair, perhaps Samuel's father, was an elder in the Brandywine (or Red Clay) Presbyterian church in 1729 and 1732. On Irish Quakers and others in Chester Co., see chapters 9, 30, and 61.   4. The New Londonderry settlement and Blair's church were located in the northwest corner of a seven-thousand-acre tract that William Penn had granted in 1682 to his daughter, Letitia, and named in honor of his wife's relative and another grantee, Sir John Fagg, of Sussex, England. Fagg's Manor (or New Londonderry) church was established in 1730 but had no regular pastor until Blair's arrival. By the late 1720s, Penn family agents reported that the Manor was "infested" with Scots-Irish squatters, among whom geographical mobility and turnover of lands were extensive. Such fluidity and uncertainty among the population may have provided an ideal setting for Blair's revivals. The quotations in this and the preceding sentence are from Webster, *Hist. Presby. Church*, 426, 429; see Sources, chapter 47.   5. Gilbert Tennent's younger brothers and fellow New Side ministers were: William, Jr. (1705–?); John (1707–1732); and Charles (1711–1771).   6. Webster, *Hist. Presby. Church*, 161; see Sources, chapter 47.

Prince of Boston,[7] Blair wrote for publication the following letter in which he described and defended the "remarkable" revival that had convulsed his own congregation in 1740.

> **Rev. Samuel Blair, Fagg's Manor, New Londonderry Township, Chester County, Pennsylvania, to Rev. Thomas Prince, Boston, Massachusetts, 6 August 1744**
>
> *Reverend* Sir,[8]
>
> I Do most gladly comply with your Desire in sending you some Account of the glorious Appearances of God in a Way of special Grace for us in this Congregation, and other Parts of this Country. . . . [9]
>
> That it may the more clearly appear that the Lord has indeed carried on a Work of true real Religion among us of late Years, I conceive it will be useful to give a brief general View of the State of Religion in these Parts before this remarkable Season.[10] I doubt not then, but there were still some sincerely religious People up and down;[11] and there were, I believe, a considerable Number in the several Congregations pretty exact, according to their Education, in the Observance of the external Forms of Religion, not only as to Attendance upon publick Ordinances[12] on the Sabbaths, but also, as <to> the Practice of Family Worship, and perhaps secret Prayer too; but, with these Things the most Part[13] seem'd to all Appearance to rest contented; and to satisfy their Consciences just with a dead Formality in Religion. If they perform'd these Duties pretty punctually in their Seasons,[14] and, as they thought with a good Meaning,[15] out of Conscience, and not just to obtain a Name[16] for Religion among Men, then they were ready to conclude that they were truly and sincerely religious. A very lamentable Ignorance of

7. Rev. Thomas Prince (1687–1758): born in Sandwich, Massachusetts, a scion of the earliest Puritan settlers; in 1709 Prince graduated from Harvard, and in 1718 he was inducted as cominister (with Rev. Samuel Sewall) of Boston's Old South Church; when Whitefield's preaching divided Boston's Congregational clergy, Prince became the evangelist's leading champion and published laudatory accounts of the revivals in *The Christian History* (1744–1745), a periodical edited by his son and namesake; Prince was exceptionally learned, owned one of New England's largest personal libraries, and wrote and published the first volumes of a projected, monumental history of Massachusetts Bay Colony.   **8.** As published in pamphlet form, Blair's letter was formally titled *A Short and Faithful Narrative of the late Remarkable Revival of Religion in the Congregation of New-Londonderry, and other Parts of Pennsylvania. As the same was sent in a Letter to the Rev. Mr. Prince of Boston. By Samuel Blair, Minister of the Gospel at New-Londonderry in Pennsylvania. Philadelphia. Printed and Sold by William Bradford at the Sign of the Bible in Second-street.* We have altered the eighteenth-century printer's "long s" into regular "s" in both the title and the following transcription of Blair's letter.   **9.** Additional introductory material omitted.   **10. in these Parts**: in this part of the country; **before this remarkable Season**: specifically, before the spring of 1740 when the revivals at Fagg's Manor commenced.   **11. up and down**: here and there (see the fuller variant hereafter: **up and down the Land**).   **12. publick Ordinances**: religious services, in particular the Lord's Supper (performed as ordained by the Church).   **13. the most Part**: the majority.
14. in their Seasons: at their appointed times.   **15. Meaning**: intention.   **16. Name**: reputation.

the main essentials of true practical Religion,[17] and the Doctrines nextly[18] relating thereunto very generally prevail'd. The Nature and Necessity of the *New-Birth*[19] was but little known or thought of, the Necessity of a Conviction of Sin[20] and Misery, by the Holy Spirits opening and applying the Law to the Conscience, in order to <achieve?> a saving Closure[21] with Christ was hardly known at all to the most. It was thought that if there was any need of a Heart-distressing Sight of the Souls Danger, and Fear of divine Wrath, it[22] was only needful for the grosser Sort of Sinners, and for any others to be deeply exercis'd this Way (as there might sometimes be some rare Instances observable) this was generally look'd upon to be a great Evil and Temptation that had befallen those Persons. The common Names for such Soul-Concern were, *Melancholy, Trouble of Mind, or Despair.*   These Terms were in common, so far as I have been acquainted, indifferently used as Synonimous; and *Trouble of Mind*, was look'd upon as a great Evil, which all Persons that made any sober Profession and Practice of Religion ought carefully to avoid. There was scarcely any Suspicion at all in general, of any Danger of depending upon Self-Righteousness, and not upon the Righteousness of Christ alone for Salvation: *Papists* and *Quakers* wou'd be readily acknowledged guilty of this Crime, but hardly any professed *Presbyterian.*   The Necessity of being first in Christ by a vital Union, and in a justified State[23] before our Religious Services can be well pleasing and acceptable to God, was very little understood or tho't of; but the common Notion seem'd to be, that if People were aiming to be in the Way of Duty[24] as well as they could, as they imagin'd, there was no Reason to be much afraid.

According to these Principles, and this Ignorance of some of the most Soul-concerning Truths of the Gospel, People were very generally thro' the Land careless at Heart, and stupidly indifferent about the great Concerns of Eternity. There was very little Appearance of any hearty Engagedness in Religion: And indeed the Wise, for the most Part, were in a great Degree asleep with the Foolish.[25] 'Twas sad to see with what a careless Behaviour the publick Ordinances were attended, and how People were given to unsuitable worldly Discourse on the Lord's Holy Day. In publick Companies,

17. **practical**: the system of religious belief as put into practice; active religious behavior, as opposed to passive religious knowledge. In succeeding passages Blair brings out the vital ("saving") difference between active and passive religion by the use of contrasting axes of vocabulary: **active** (practical religion, new birth, conviction of sin, practice, engagedness, renew, change, deeply exercised, righteousness of Christ, saving, awakening) versus **passive** (doctrine, profession, careless(ness), indifferent, secure, externals, dead formality, self-righteousness, dying, contented, unfruitful, unregenerate, asleep).   18. **nextly**: directly.   19. **the *New-Birth***: i.e., the conversion experience.   20. **Conviction of Sin**: acknowledgement of sin (following a rigorous examination of conscience).   21. **Closure**: union.   22. **Wrath. It** ms.   23. **justified State**: freedom from the penalty of sin, on the grounds of Christ's righteousness, by the infustion of grace (as received, according to the New Side clergy, through the conversion experience).   24. **to be in the Way of Duty**: "to be doing their duty/fulfilling their obligations."   25. **the Wise, for the most Part, were in a great Degree asleep with the Foolish**: an allusion to the parable of the wise and foolish virgins (Matthew 25:1–13).

especially at Weddings, a vain and frothy Lightness was apparent in the Deportment of many Professors;[26] and in some Places very extravagant Follies, as Horse Running, Fidling and Dancing, pretty much obtain'd on those Occasions.

Thus Religion lay as it were a dying,[27] and ready to expire its last Breath of Life in this Part of the visible Church: And it was in the Spring *Anno Domini* 1740, when the God of Salvation was pleased to visit us with the blessed Effusions of his Holy Spirit in an eminent Manner. The first very open and Publick Appearance of this gracious Visitation[28] in these Parts, was in the Congregation which God has committed to my Charge. The Congregation has not been erected[29] above Fourteen or Fifteen Years from this Time: The Place is a new Settlement, generally settled with People from Ireland. (as all our Congregations in *Pennsylvania*, except two or three, chiefly are made up of People from that Kingdom)   I am the first Minister they have ever had settled in the Place. Having been regularly[30] liberated from my former Charge in *East-Jersey,* above an hundred Miles North-Eastward from Hence (the Rev. Presbytery of *New-Brunswick* (of which I had the Comfort of being a Member) judging it to be my Duty, for sundry Reasons, to remove[31] from thence) at the earnest Invitation of the People here I came to them in the beginning of *November* 1739, accepted of[32] a Call from them that Winter, and was formally install'd and settled amongst them as their Minister in *April* following. There were some hopefully pious People here at my first coming, which was a great Encouragement and Comfort to me. I had some View and Sense of the deplorable Condition of the Land in general; and accordingly the Scope of my Preaching thro' that first Winter after I came here, was mainly calculated for Persons in a natural unregenerate Estate. I endeavour'd, as the Lord enabled me, to open up and prove from his Word, the Truths which I judged most necessary for such as were in that State to know and believe in order to their Conviction and Conversion. I endeavour'd to deal searchingly and solemnly with them; and thro' the continuing Blessing of God, I had knowledge of four or five brought under deep Convictions that Winter. In the beginning of *March* I took a Journey into *East-Jersey*, and was abroad[33] for two or three Sabbaths. A neighbouring Minister,[34] who seemed to be earnest for

---

26. Professors: (self-) declared Christians.   **27. lay . . . a dying**: an example of the older use of a previxed to a present participle when the latter complements a full verb; see Shakespeare, *Merchant of Venice*, 1.2.59: "he falls straight a cap'ring." Such examples are rarely attested in our texts, and it may be that here we have to do with an archaic stereotyped phrase. See chapter 36, n. 11.   **28. Visitations** ms.   **29. erected**: established, set up. **30. regularly**: i.e., not for any extraordinary reason (e.g. dishonorable behavior, doctrinal disputes, etc.). **31. remove**: move.   **32. accepted of**: took on the responsibilities of.   **33. abroad**: away from home.   **34. A neighbouring Minister**: almost certainly this was Rev. Alexander Craighead (or Creaghead), probably the son of Rev. Thomas Creaghead from Ulster and hence probably born in the colonies and educated by William Tennent, Sr.; in 1774 Craighead was licensed by Donegal Presbytery and called to Middle Octorara church, near Blair's congregation. A fervent revivalist and rigid Calvinist, Craighead was expelled by the Old Side from the Philadelphia Synod in 1741, but almost immediately he left the New Side presbytery because of its refusal to revive the seventeenth-century Scottish Solemn League and Covenant as a condition of communion and baptism. Afterward associated with the Reformed (or Covenanting) Presbyterians, he ministered to various

the Awakening and Conversion of secure[35] Sinners, and whom I had obtained to preach a Sabbath to my People in my Absence, preached to them, I think, on the first Sabbath after I left Home. His Subject was the dangerous and awful Case of such as continue unregenerate and unfruitful under the Means of Grace. The Text was *Luk. 13. 7. Then said he to the Dresser of his Vineyard, behold, these three Years I come seeking Fruit on this Fig Tree, and find none, cut it down, why cumbereth it the Ground?* Under that Sermon there was a visible Appearance of much Soul-Concern among the Hearers, so that some burst out with an audible Noise into bitter crying (a Thing not known in those Parts before.)   After I had come home there came a young Man to my House under deep trouble about the State of his Soul, whom I had look'd upon as a pretty light merry sort of a Youth: He told me that he was not any Thing[36] concerned about himself in the Time of hearing the above mentioned Sermon, nor afterwards, till the next Day that he went to his Labour, which was grubbing,[37] in order to clear some New-Ground; the first Grub he set was about a pretty large one with a high Top, and when he had cut the Roots, as it fell down those Words came instantly to his Remembrance, and as a Spear to his Heart, *cut it down   why cumbereth it the Ground?* So thought he, *may I be cut down by the Justice of God, for the Burning of Hell, unless I get into another State than I am now in.*   He thus came into very great and abiding Distress, which, to all Appearance has had a happy Issue: His Conversation[38] being to this Day as becomes the Gospel of Christ.

The News of this very publick Appearance of deep Soul-concern among my People met me an Hundred Miles from Home: I was very joyful to hear of it, in Hopes that God was about to carry on an extensive Work of converting Grace amongst them. And the first Sermon I preached after my Return to them, was from *Mat. 6. 33. Seek ye first the Kingdom of God, and his Righteousness.*   After opening up and explaining the Parts of the Text, when in the Improvement,[39] I came to press the Injunction in the Text upon the Unconverted and Ungodly, and offer'd this as one Reason among others, why they should now henceforth first of all *seek the Kingdom and Righteousness of God*, viz. That they had neglected too too long to do so already. This Consideration seem'd to come and cut like a Sword upon several in the Congregation, so that while I was speaking upon it they could no longer contain,[40] but burst out in the most bitter Mourning. I desir'd them, as much as possible, to restrain themselves from making a Noise that would hinder themselves or others from hearing what was

congregations in western Virginia and North Carolina, where he died in 1770.   **35. secure**: unanxious, untroubled.   **36. not any Thing**: in no way, not at all.   **37. grubbing**: clearing ground (usually of trees, by felling and rooting out); **grub . . . set**: "to set grub" is to mark a tree for grubbing (clearing).   **38. Conversation**: conduct, behavior.   **39. Improvement**: that portion of a sermon in which the minister explains how the **Text** is to be practically applied; here Blair refers to his explanation of the scriptural injunction "seek ye first the kingdom of God . . . "   **40. contain**: hold themselves in, restrain themselves.

spoken: And often afterwards I had Occasion to repeat the same Council. I still advised People to endeavour to moderate and bound their Passions, but not so as to resist or stifle their Convictions. The Number of the Awakened encreased very fast, frequently under Sermons there were some newly convicted, and brought into deep Distress of Soul about their perishing Estate. Our Sabbath Assemblies soon became vastly[41] large; many People from almost all Parts around inclining very much to come where there was such Appearance of the divine Power and Presence. I think there was scarcely a Sermon or Lecture preached here thro' that whole Summer, but there were manifest Evidences of Impressions[42] on the Hearers; and many Times the Impressions were very great and general: Several would be overcome and fainting; others deeply sobbing, hardly able to contain, others crying in a most dolorous Manner, many others more silently Weeping, and a solemn Concern appearing in the Countenance of many others. And sometimes the Soul Exercises[43] of some (tho' comparatively but very few) would so far affect their Bodies, as to Occasion some strange unusual Bodily Motions. I had Opportunities of speaking particularly with a great many of those who afforded such outward Tokens of inward Soul-Concern in the Time of publick Worship and hearing of the Word; indeed many came to me of themselves in their Distress for private Instruction and Council; and I found, so far as I can remember, that with by far the greater Part, their apparent Concern in Publick was not just a transient Qualm of Conscience, or meerly a floating Commotion of the Affections;[44] but a rational fix'd Conviction of their dangerous perishing Estate. They could generally offer as a convictive Evidence[45] of their being in an unconverted miserable Estate, that they were utter Strangers to those Dispositions, Exercises and Experiences of Soul in Religion, which they heard laid down from God's Word as the inseperable Characters of the truly regenerate People of God; even such as before had something of the Form of Religion; and I think the greater Number were of this Sort, and several had been pretty exact and punctual in the Performance of outward Duties. They saw that they had been contenting themselves with the Form, without the Life and Power of Godliness; and that they had been taking Peace to their Consciences from, and depending upon their own Righteousness, and not the Righteousness of JESUS CHRIST. In a Word, they saw that true practical Religion was quite another Thing than they had conceiv'd it to be, or had any true Experience of. There were likewise many up and down the Land brought under deep distressing Convictions that Summer, who had lived very loose Lives, regardless of the very Externals of Religion. In this Congregation I believe there were very few that were not stirred up to some solemn

---

41. **vastly:** a popular intensifier in the seventeenth and eighteenth centuries; close to American English "quite." 42. **there was scarcely a Sermon or Lecture preached here . . . but there were manifest Evidences of Impressions . . .** "there was scarcely a sermon or lecture preached here . . . in which there were not manifest evidences of impressions . . ." 43. **Soul Exercises:** spiritual exercises. 44. **a floating Commotion of the Affections:** "a passing agitation of the emotions." 45. **convictive Evidence:** evidence sufficient to prove.

Thoughtfulness and Concern more than usual about their Souls. The general Carriage[46] and Behaviour of People was soon very visibly alter'd. Those awakened were much given to reading in the Holy Scriptures and other good Books. Excellent Books that had lain by[47] much neglected, were then much perus'd, and lent from one to another; and it was a peculiar Satisfaction to People to find how exactly the Doctrines they heard daily preached, harmonize with the Doctrines maintain'd and taught by great and Godly Men in other Parts[48] and former Times. The Subjects of Discourse almost always when any of them were together, were the Matters of Religion and great Concerns of their Souls. All unsuitable, Worldly, vain Discourse on the Lord's Day seem'd to be laid aside among them. Indeed, for any Thing that appear'd,[49] there seem'd to be an almost universal Reformation in this Respect in our Publick Assemblies on the Lord's Day. There was an earnest Desire in People after Opportunities for publick Worship and hearing the Word. . . . [50]

Thus have I given a very brief Account of the State and Progress of Religion here, thro' that first Summer after the remarkable Revival of it among us. Towards the End of that Summer there seem'd to be a Stop put to the farther Progress of the Work, as to the Conviction and awakening of Sinners; and ever since there have been very few Instances of Persons convinced. It remains then, that I speak something of the abiding Effects and After-fruits of those Awakenings, and other Religious Exercises which People were under during the above mention'd Period. Such as were only under some slight Impressions and superficial Awakenings, seem in General to have lost them all again, without any abiding hopeful Alteration upon them: They seem to have fallen back again into their former Carelessness[51] and Stupidity: And some that were under pretty great Awakenings, and considerable deep Convictions of their miserable Estate, seem also to have got Peace again to their Consciences without getting it by a true Faith in the Lord Jesus, affording no satisfying Evidence of their being savingly renew'd: But, thro' the infinite rich Grace of God, (and blessed be his Glorious Name!) there is a considerable Number who afford all the Evidence that can reasonably be expected and requir'd for our Satisfaction in the Case of their having been the Subjects of a thorough saving[52] Change; except in some singular Instances of Behaviour (alas for

---

46. Carriage: demeanor or deportment, especially toward others.   **47. had lain by:** had been laid aside.
48. Parts: places.   **49. for any Thing that appear'd:** by all appearances.   **50.** Omitted: further accounts of Blair's preaching, alleging especially his careful, cautious examinations of his parishioners' spiritual condition and the revivals' beneficial and lasting behavioral consequences among his congregation. Blair admitted that there were some parishioners who merely "believed there was a good Work going on, that People were convinced, and brought into a converted State, and they desir'd to be converted too . . . and if they could come to weeping, or get their Passions so raised as to encline them to vent themselves by Cries," they deemed themselves saved by "an imaginary Conversion of their own making." Blair claimed, however, that he "endeavour'd to correct and guard against all such Mistakes so far as I discovered them in the Course of my Ministry."   **51. Carelessness:** lack of concern, untroubled attitude.   **52. savingly . . . saving:** leading to salvation.

them) which proceed from, and shew the sad Remains of Original Corruption even in the regenerate children of God while in this Imperfect State. Their Walk[53] is habitually Tender and Conscientious; their Carriage towards their Neighbour Just and Kind; and they appear to have an agreeable peculiar[54] Love one for another, and for all in whom appears the Image of God. Their Discourses of Religion, their Engagedness and Dispositions of Soul in the Practice of the immediate Duties and Ordinances of Religion, all appear quite otherwise than formerly. Indeed the Liveliness of their Affections in the Ways of Religion is much abated in General, and they are in some Measure humbly sensible of this and grieved for it, and are carefully endeavouring still to live unto God, much grieved with their Imperfections, and the Plagues they find in their own Hearts; and frequently they meet with some delightful Enlivenings of Soul, and particularly our sacramental Solemnities for communicating in the Lords Supper, have generally been very Blessed Seasons of enlivening and enlargement[55] to the People of God. There is a very evident and great Increase of Christian Knowledge with many of them. We enjoy in this Congregation the Happiness of a great Degree of Harmony and Concord: Scarcely any have appear'd to open Opposition and Bitterness against the Work of God among us, and else where up and down the Land, tho' there are pretty many such in several other Places thro' the Country. Some indeed in this Congregation, but very few, have separated from us, and join'd with the Ministers who have unhappily oppos'd this Blessed Work. . . . [56]

One of our Christian Friends, a Man about 50 Years of Age, was removed from us by Death in the Beginning of May last, of whom I can give some broken imperfect Account. . . . His Name was *Hanse Kirk Patrick,*   he was a Man of a pretty good Understanding, and had been, I believe a sober Professor for many Years, tho' he had not been very long in *America.* . . . [57] He dy'd of an Imposthume[58] and gradually wasted away for a long Time before his Death, and was for about two Months entirely

---

53. Walk: manner of behavior, conduct of life.   **54. peculiar**: particular, special.   **55. enlargement**: (in religious language) conscious "liberty," absence of constraint, as in prayer, etc. For a closely related meaning, see chapter 60, n. 19.   **56.** Omitted: Blair's account of the prolonged, agonizing conversion of a young, single woman in his congregation, assuring Prince that he had been "very careful to be exact in the Affair," especially in "my conversing with her" concerning her soul's "deep Distress." Significantly, Blair stressed that it was not only through his preaching but primarily through her "communion in the Lord's Supper"—the traditional focal point of Scots-Irish religiosity—that the woman at last achieved "clear Satisfaction and unspeakable Ravishment of her Soul."   **57.** Additional details of Kirkpatrick's conversion omitted. In view of the argument, made by several historians, that the individualistic implications of early religious revivalism proved most attractive among Americans engaged in entrepreneurial activities that often violated communal traditions, it is noteworthy that in March 1742 Thomas Dobbins accused Hanse Kirkpatrick, before the New Londonderry (Fagg's Manor) congregation, of "Breach of Bargain"—i.e., of selling his flaxseed to a "stranger" in order to take "advantage of the rising of the Market," instead of selling it to Dobbins, as he had promised, at a lower price. This incident is cited on p. 130 of P. Griffin, *The People with No Name: Ireland's Ulster Scots, America's Scots Irish, and the Creation of a British Atlantic World, 1689–1764* (Princeton, N.J., 2001), which otherwise appeared too recently for inclusion in our research.   **58. Imposthume**: i.e. **impostume** "swelling, cyst, abscess" (here probably a tumor or cancer).

confin'd to his Bed. He told me that for sometime before he was laid Bed-fast he had been full of very distressing Fears and Jealousies[59] about his Souls State, and was altogether unsatisfy'd about his Interest[60] in Christ; but that soon after he was confin'd to his Bed the Lord afforded him his comforting Presence, clear'd up his Interest, and remov'd his Fears. After this he continued still clear and peaceful in his Soul, and sweetly and wholly resign'd to the Lord's Will until Death. While he had strength to speak much, he was still free and forward to discourse of God and divine Things. One Time as two other of our Elders were with him he exhorted them to continue stedfast and faithful to God's Truths and Cause; for he said if he had a thousand Souls he could freely venture them all upon the Doctrines which had been taught them in this Congregation. One time when I took leave of him he burst out into Tears, saying, "I[61] had been the Messenger of the Lord of Hosts to him that the Lord had sent to call him out of the broad Way of Destruction." For some Days before his decease he cou'd speak very little, but to all Appearance with a great deal of serenity and sweetness of Soul he fell asleep in Jesus. . . . [62]

This blessed Shower of divine Influence spread very much thro' this Province that Summer, and was likewise considerable in some other Places bordering upon it. The Accounts of some Ministers being something[63] distinguish'd by their searching awakening Doctrine and solemn Pathetick[64] Manner of Address, and the News of the Effects of their Preaching upon their Hearers seem'd in some Measure to awaken People thro' the Country to consider their careless and formal Way of going on in Religion, and very much excited their Desires to hear those Ministers. There were several vacant Congregations without any settled Pastors, which earnestly beg'd for their[65] Visits, and several Ministers who did not appear heartily to put to their Shoulders[66] to help in carrying on the same Work, yet, then yielded to the pressing Importunities of their People in inviting these Brethren to preach in their Pulpits, so that they were very much call'd abroad[67] and employ'd in incessant Labours, and the Lord wrought with them mightily,   very great Assemblies would ordinarily meet to hear them upon any Day of the Week, and oftentimes a surprizing Power

---

59. **Jealousies**: apprehensions, anxieties.   60. **Interest**: right, title, claim (i.e., to salvation, through Christ's mercy).   61. **I**: i.e., Blair.   62. Omitted: Blair's account of two children, sisters aged nine and seven, who were "awakened by hearing the Word preached . . . in Sermons," who were thereby convinced of their "Sin against God" and that "they would surely go to Hell" unless they experienced conversion, and who eventually, through fervent prayer, were "fill'd with Sweetness and Delight." Afterward, "they seemed to be almost wholly taken up in Religion, that no Weather thro' the Extremity of Winter, would hinder them from going out daily to by-Places for secret Prayer, and if any thing came in the Way that they cou'd not get going out for Prayer at such times as they inclin'd and thought most proper, they wou'd weep and cry. Their Parents say they are very obedient Children, and strict observers of the Sabbath."   63. **something**: somewhat.
64. **Pathetick**: earnest, moving.   65. **their**: i.e., the (New Side) **Ministers'** (above).   66. **put to their Shoulders**: exert their shoulders, put their shoulders to work.   67. **call'd abroad**: summoned away from home.

accompanying their Preaching was visible among the Multitudes of their Hearers. It was a very comfortable[68] enlivening Time to God's People, and great Numbers of secure careless Professors, and many loose irreligious Persons thro' the Land were deeply convinced of their miserable perishing Estate, and there is abundant Reason to believe, and be satisfy'd that many of them were in the Issue,[69] savingly Converted to God. I my self have had Occasion to converse with a great Many up and down who have given a most agreeable Account of very precious and clear Experiences of the Grace of God, severals[70] even in *Baltimore*, a County in the Province of *Maryland*, who were brought up almost in a State of Heathenism, without almost any Knowledge of the true Doctrines of Christianity, afford very satisfying Evidence of being brought to a saving Acquaintance with God in Christ Jesus.

Thus Sir, I have endeavour'd to give a brief Account of the Revival of Religion among us in these Parts, in which I have endeavour'd all along to be conscientiously exact in relating Things according to the naked Truth, knowing that I must not speak wickedly even for God, nor talk deceitfully for HIM, and upon the whole I must say it is beyond all dispute with me, and I think it is beyond all reasonable Contradiction that God has carry'd on a great and glorious Work of his special Grace among us.

I am, Revd. Sir, your

very respectful Son

and Servant,

Samuel Blair.

In fact, Blair did not devulge to Rev. Thomas Prince all "the naked Truth" about the Fagg's Manor revival. For example, he had deigned to mention by name the notorious Rev. Alexander Craighead, the radical Covenanter whose sermons in early spring 1740 had first sparked the spiritual fires in Blair's congregation. He even omitted the fact that in the same year the controversial Anglican itinerant George Whitefield had twice preached at Fagg's Manor, before crowds of 12,000 screaming, weeping, and fainting enthusiasts.[71]

The primary reason for these and other omissions was that Blair's purpose in writing and publishing his letter, three years after the events he described had occurred, was not

---

68. comfortable: encouraging, comforting; see in the *Book of Common Prayer* the words said by the celebrant to the confessing congregants immediately following the absolution: "Hear what **comfortable** words our Savior Christ saith unto all those who truly turn to Him, 'Come unto me all ye that travail and are heavy laden, and I will refresh you.'"   **69. in the Issue**: in the end, as things turned out.   **70. severals**: several persons (Scots and American form, perhaps formed on **others**).   **71.** Of his first visit to Fagg's Manor, in May 1740, Whitefield wrote in his journal: "Look where I would, most were drowned in tears. The 'word was sharper than a two-edged sword.' Their bitter cries and tears were enough to pierce the hardest heart. . . . Some were struck as pale as death,—others lying on the ground,—others wringing their hands,—others sinking into the arms of their friends,—and most lifting up their eyes to heaven, and crying out to God for mercy. . . . They seemed like persons awakened by the last trump and coming out of their graves to judgment." Cited in Rev. W. B. Noble, *History of the Presbyterian Church of Fagg's Manor . . .* , 13; see Sources, chapter 47.

only to display God's "great and glorious Work" but also to lay the groundwork for a union between his yet-small, schismatic group of New Side clergy and the larger and more influential Presbytery of New York. The latter was composed primarily of New England–born and Yale–educated ministers who had long quarreled over doctrinal issues with the Ulster-born clergy who dominated the Old Side faction in the Synod of Philadelphia. It was mainly for that reason that the members of the New York Presbytery sympathized with Blair, Tennant, and the other New Side ministers whom the Old Side had expelled from the Philadelphia Synod in 1741. However, the staid New Englanders were distressed by reports of the revivals' boisterous and controversial features and thus they hesitated to embrace the New Side clergy.

It was to allay those apprehensions that in 1744 Blair penned a somewhat deceptive description of the Fagg's Manor revival.[72] In his letter to Prince, Blair tempered his formerly strident criticisms of his Old Side adversaries, yet above all he strove to refute their charges that the First Great Awakening threatened to destabilize the ordered hierarchies of colonial society. Thus, Blair minimized—and claimed he had tried to suppress—his parishioners' highly emotional and often bizarre physical responses to his preaching. Instead, he stressed the importance of Bible study and of traditional "sacramental Solemnities" in bringing people to "Christian Knowledge." Likewise, Blair emphasized the harmony between his sermons and "the Doctrines maintain'd and taught by great and Godly Men in . . . former Times," and, most important, he maintained that the revivals had produced lasting and beneficent spiritual and behavioral consequences. Most of his parishioners, Blair contended, had not merely experienced "a transient Qualm of Conscience" or "a floating Commotion of the Affections," as Old Side critics claimed. Rather, they had attained "a rational fix'd Conviction" of their sinfulness and dependence on "the Righteousness of JESUS CHRIST," which in turn had resulted in "an almost universal Reformation" among those who formerly "had lived very loose Lives."

Blair's reassurances—in conjunction with similar expressions by Gilbert Tennent and other New Side clergy—had their desired effect. In 1745 the New Englanders in the New York Presbytery deserted the Old Side's Philadelphia Synod and joined with the revivalists to form the New Side Synod of New York—and for the next 13 years, until the New and Old Side Presbyterians reunited, the former's congregations thrived and multiplied, while the Old Side clergy struggled in vain to maintain their numbers. Consequently, when the rival groups finally agreed to merge in 1758, their reunion in the Synod of New York and Philadelphia took place largely on the New Side's terms, and the new Synod fell firmly under New Side control. The remainder of Blair's short career was equally successful. He led the effort that culminated in 1746 with the establishment of the New Side's College of New Jersey (later Princeton University), and in his own academy at

---

72. In the same year, and for the same purpose, Blair also published a long and reassuringly learned and orthodox treatise on the Calvinist doctrine of predestination.

Fagg's Manor he trained several eminent Presbyterian ministers and laymen, including Rev. Samuel Davies (1723–1761), colonial Virginia's greatest Presbyterian revivalist and a future president of the College of New Jersey.[73] However, Blair's frequent one-hundred-mile journeys to attend the meetings of the College trustees, as well as his exhausting preaching tours in New England and the upper South, broke his fragile health. Thus, he supported but did not live to see the 1758 reunion between the New and Old Side clergy. Instead, he died at Fagg's Manor on 4 June 1751, aged only 39, leaving behind a wife and 10 children,[74] a younger brother—Rev. John Blair[75]—who succeeded him at Fagg's Manor, and a host of fervent admirers. Davies, Blair's former student, composed elegies in his honor, and Rev. Samuel Finley described him in his funeral sermon as "a public blessing to the Church, an honour to his people, an ornament to his profession, who 'magnified his office.' He spoke as he believed," Finley concluded; "he practised as he preached; he lived holy, and died joyfully."[76]

Decades after his death, Blair's elderly former parishioners remembered him with awe and reverence. However, Blair's and his New Side colleagues' triumph over their Old Side adversaries had several problematic legacies. In the long term, for example, the Presbyterian church could not withstand the logical consequences of fervent evangelicalism, and, ironically, in some respects Blair's and the other revivalists' oratorical successes east of the Appalachians proved more ephemeral than John Craig's steady, less spectacular efforts in the Shenandoah Valley. The New Side clergy's message—its popular, emotional style and its demand that individuals assume responsibility for their own conversions—implicitly contradicted traditional Presbyterian emphases on reason, education, and the necessity for a college-trained ministry, as well as the inexorable Calvinist logic of predestination. Thus, within a few decades after Blair's death, while western migration was depleting many New Side congregations, large numbers of New Side converts had begun to fall under the sway of Methodist, Baptist, and other ministers whose lack of education and unrestrained preaching style bore out the Old Side's direst fears.

73. Other Fagg's Manor alumni included: John Rodgers, moderator of the first General Assembly of the Presbyterian Church in America; John McMillan, pioneer minister and educator in western Pennsylvania; and David Ramsay, South Carolina's pioneer historian. On McMillan's pro-Federalist political activities, see chapters 62 and 67. 74. Blair's wife's name is unknown. Eight of their ten children survived to adulthood, and their only son, also Samuel (1741–1818), entered the ministry and, after Thomas Prince's death, served as copastor of Boston's Old South Church until ill health forced his early retirement to Germantown, Pa. In addition, four of Blair's daughters married Presbyterian clergymen, as did two of his sisters. 75. Rev. John Blair (1720–1771): born in Ulster; educated at William Tennent, Sr.'s Log College at Neshaminy, Pa., and licensed by the New Side after the 1741 schism. Considered his brother Samuel's equal as a theologian, but not as a preacher, between 1742 and 1748 John Blair served as pastor of several congregations in Cumberland Co., Pa.; in 1757 he succeeded his brother at New Londonderry, both as pastor and as head of Fagg's Manor academy; Blair played a major role in the Old Side/New Side negotiations that led to their reunion in 1758; in 1767–1769 he was professor of divinity and moral philosophy, and acting president, at the College of New Jersey, but he ended his career as a pastor at Wallkill, New York. 76. Cited in Sprague, *Annals Am. Pulpit*, vol. 3, 64–66; see Sources, chapter 47.

To be sure, in the late 1790s and early 1800s, Presbyterian clergymen—many of them trained by Blair and his successors—tried to export Calvinist revivalism across the Appalacians, thus initiating what would become known as the Second Great Awakening. They quickly discovered, however, that they could not control the religious enthusiams and innovations unleashed at Cane Ridge, Kentucky, and elsewhere in the West, and the primary results of their efforts were schisms and a further loss of parishioners to Methodist, Baptist, and other congregations.[77] Thus, whereas in 1776 the Presbyterians had ranked second among American denominations in numbers of churches, well ahead of the Methodists and Baptists, by 1850 they had fallen into third place behind both their evangelical rivals; and although the absolute number of Presbyterian congregations had risen, their proportion of the nation's churches had declined from 19 to less than 12 percent.

In addition, although some historians contend that the New Side's victory over the Old Side's alleged conservatism and élitism promoted democracy and egalitarianism in American society, generally, as well as in the Presbyterian church itself, the evidence is mixed at best. For instance, Old and New Side clergymen supported the American Revolution with equal enthusiasm, and it was the Old Side leader, Rev. Francis Alison, who played the most prominent role in the agitation that led to 1776.[78] In other respects, moreover, New Side ministers evinced little sympathy for democracy and equality in either church or politics. After 1758 the New Side majority exercised its sway over the Synod of New York and Philadelphia in ways that Alison and his Old Side colleagues decried as tyrannical and discriminatory. And in 1788, under the leadership of the Scottish-born Rev. John Witherspoon (1723–1794), president of the College of New Jersey from 1768, the New Side clergy reorganized their denomination as the Presbyterian Church in the United States, adopting an authoritarian "Scottish model" of ecclesiastical polity that was designed to marginalize if not root out the remaining Old Side ministers. Likewise, in the 1790s the great majority of Presbyterian clergymen, convinced that only their church stood between the new American republic and the forces of "anarchy" and "infidelity," defied the political sympathies of many if not most Scots-Irish Presbyterians by affiliating with the Federalist party and by condemning in turn the anti-Federalists, the French Revolution, the Whiskey Rebellion, and the Jeffersonian Republican party.[79]

Finally, New Side influences played a major role in reconfiguring the ethnic identities of Ulster-born Presbyterians and their descendants. On one hand, whereas the First and even the initial stage of the Second Great Awakening may have been grounded in traditional Scots-Irish religiosity, revivalism was inherently ecumenical, divorced from an imported Scots-Irish tribalism, and thus an avenue of assimilation to an "American" Protestantism that was panethnic as well as fluid across denominational boundaries. On the other

---

77. On Cane Ridge and similar western revivals, see chapter 14 and, especially, chapter 65.   78. On Alison, see chapter 55.   79. On the domestic political affiliations and radical Irish sympathies of many, perhaps most, Scots-Irish immigrants in late eighteenth- and early nineteenth-century America, see especially chapters 27, 38, 62, and 64, as well as appendix 3 (letters of Robert Crockett and David Robinson).

hand, however, Ulster-American Presbyterians' ethnic identity was not obliterated. Rather, it was transformed, and although the specific changes that occurred had deep historical roots, they also comported with the New Side clergy's sociocultural and political agendas.

For example, it was significant that, in his 1744 letter to Rev. Prince, Samuel Blair not only recounted his successes in inspiring personal conversions among his terrified parishioners but also linked his spiritual crusade to the suppression among them of transplanted rural Ulster customs, such as drinking, fiddling, dancing, and horse-racing on Sundays and at weddings and burials. Likewise, in the 1790s a typical New Side clergyman such as Rev. Elisha Macurdy, born in 1763 in Carlisle, Pennsylvania, and tutored by one of Blair's own students, strove to "civilize" as well as convert his Scots-Irish parishioners in the Ohio Presbytery—denouncing, for instance, their old custom of whiskey-drinking at funerals.

New Side ministers were also concerned about other "Irish" influences on their congregations. In 1773, for example, the New Side majority in the Synod of New York and Philadelphia made official what had long been their informal "non-importation" policy against Ulster-born and "foreign"-trained clergymen and licentiates who had not enjoyed conversion experiences, were "liberal" or Arminian on theological issues, and hence were potential recruits to Old Side ranks. Although this ban was inspired primarily by doctrinal differences, it also reflected ethnic jealousies and incipient nativism, and it served to reduce sharply the number of Irish-born Presbyterian clergymen in late eighteenth-century America, at a time when Scots-Irish immigration was peaking.[80] It represented as well the New Side ministers' growing antipathy to contemporary political developments in Ireland, as in 1798 the Presbyterian General Assembly in Philadelphia levied another formal "embargo" on all Irish émigré clergymen who had been associated with the United Irishmen. And in the same year of rebellion in Ireland, the Assembly, as well as many presbyteries and individual clergymen, redoubled their efforts to stamp out the "vice" and "immorality" they associated with Irish and French political radicalism.

Thus, the official unions of 1801–1808 between the American Presbyterian church and the Calvinist and (overwhelmingly Federalist) Congregational associations of New England—perhaps foreshadowed by the New Side's 1745 conjunction with the New York Presbytery—were politically as well as theologically and strategically logical. Outside New England, most of the new hybrid "Presbygationalists" eventually affiliated with Presbyte-

---

80. As a result, in the late eighteenth century immigrants whose churches had been suffused with liberal or New Light influences found Presbyterianism even in urban America strange and alienating. Thus, in 1789 Carlile Pollock, recently arrived in New York City, wrote to his uncle, Rev. William Campbell (1727–1805) of Armagh, one of Ulster's leading New Light clergy and a former moderator of the Ulster Synod: "you yourself wou'd not be a Presbiterian in this Country, such as they are here. I have attended their Church, but I have discontinued my attendance there, because they preach what I do not understand. They are of the Methodist class, and endeavour to bewilder the mind instead of enlightening it. . . . [F]ew of them are capable of distinguishing religion from ranting and declamation." Carlile Pollock, New York City, to Rev. William Campbell, Armagh, 23 June–29 July 1789; see Sources, chapter 47.

rian churches, thus augmenting the latter's numbers despite Methodist and Baptist competition. However, it may be that the New England Congregationalists' traditional contempt for the "Irish"—first revealed in the early 1700s in opposition to Ulster Protestant immigrants[81] but reinforced and politicized in the 1790s by Federalist hostility to all "wild Irish" Republicans—played at least a minor role in shaping their Presbyterian brethren's quest for a "Scotch-Irish" identity that would not only be "respectable" but also would enable them to claim that their ancestors, too—like the Pilgrims and Puritans—had been "founding fathers" of a "Protestant" American nation.[82]

48 ✳

Bernard M'Kenna, 1811

Irish immigrant schoolmasters, both Protestant and Catholic, were remarkably common in colonial America and in the early decades of the Republic—so much so they became prominent in frontier folklore, often as comic figures. Their training in Ireland, mode of emigration, and New World experiences varied widely. Some were excellent scholars,

---

81. On the New England Congregationalists' early antagonism to "Irish" immigrants (whether Anglicans, Presbyterians, or Catholics), see chapters 8, 17, 41, and 49. 82. Clearly, most Presbyterian clergymen in late eighteenth- and early nineteenth-century America were not involved in what historian Nathan Hatch has called "the democratization of American Christianity"—except perhaps as foils for the efforts of Methodist, Baptist, and other ministers whose doctrines, preaching and organizational styles, and political sympathies were more compatible with Jeffersonian Republicanism. Prominent among the latter, however, were several Irish-born or Irish-American clergymen. One was the Anglophobe James O'Kelly (1757–1826), who in the 1790s led the "republican Methodist" schism in the Upper South, declaring—in opposition to his English-born bishop's ecclesiastical authority—that he was "too sensible of the sweets of liberty, to be content any longer under British chains." ¶More important than O'Kelly were Thomas Campbell (1763–1854) and his son Alexander (1788–1866), Seceding Presbyterians who emigrated to the Ohio Valley from Richhill and Ahorey, Co. Armagh, in 1807 and 1809, respectively, and founded the American churches that were variously known as Christian, Churches of Christ, Disciples of Christ, or, popularly, as Campbellite. Seeking to unite all Protestants in Christian love, as a precursor to the Millennium, the Campbells rejected as divisive both evangelicalism and all "man-made" doctrines such as their own inherited Calvinism. Christians should return to the Bible alone, they preached, especially to the New Testament, to recreate the Christian communities of the first centuries after Christ's death. The Campbells were thus "primitivists" but not what were later called "fundamentalists"; rather, they rested their arguments on the Enlightenment belief that a "rational" reading of the Scriptures, understood in their historical contexts, would produce universal agreement on the essentials of Christian faith. In addition, they were not political conservatives, at least not initially; in 1829–1830 Alexander Campbell represented western Virginia at his state's constitutional convention, where he promoted Jacksonian political reforms and, equally in vain, argued for the abolition of slavery. Most religious historians have interpreted the Campbells' movement as quintessentially "American," but it is difficult to imagine that their goal of pan-Protestant unity (paralleling similar developments in early nineteenth-century Ireland itself)—as well as Alexander Campbell's Anglophilia and strident anti-Catholicism—were not at least partly a reaction to the interdenominational bloodshed that stained Co. Armagh's killing fields in the 1780s and 1790s.

trained (if Anglicans) at Trinity College, Dublin, or (if Presbyterians) in Irish dissenting academies and Scottish universities, or (if Catholics) in continental colleges and seminaries. Others were more haphazardly educated in Ireland's surreptitious "hedge schools," especially in the early eighteenth century when the Penal Laws barred both Catholics and Presbyterians from teaching school. Most probably emigrated as free men, searching for greater opportunities than Irish society could provide, but others came to America as indentured servants, redemptioners, and sometimes (if Catholics) even as transported felons. Indeed, colonial advertisements for runaway Irish servants often carried the description "pretends to be a schoolmaster."[1]

In America most Irish pedagogues were itinerants who labored in relative obscurity and poverty, teaching reading, writing, and simple mathematics to the children of back-country farmers, until they turned to more lucrative or secure occupations. Others, more learned or better connected, established successful and relatively permanent grammar schools or academies that catered to the offspring of the affluent and taught Latin and Greek, moral philosophy and theology, even fencing and dancing, as well as more mundane subjects such as "Bookkeeping, Geometry, Algebra, Conic Sections, Sir Isaac Newton's Laws of Motion, Trigonomety, Projection of the Sphere, Astronomy, Fortifications, Gunnery, Mensuration, Guaging, Surveying in theory, Dialing, Navigation, [and] Construction and the use of the Charts"—as Thomas Carroll advertised in 1766 of his school in New York City.[2] Many combined schoolteaching with other occupations, such as medicine, surveying, or the ministry. Their personal qualities were also extremely diverse: as in Ireland, the worst were brutal, "drunken, profane, [and] worthless,"[3] while the best inspired personal devotion and a love of learning among their grateful students. Yet all were important, in early America as in contemporary Ireland: they were usually the most literate—in Ireland often the *only* literate—members of their communities, besides the local ministers or priests, and hence served as crucial social, cultural, and political intermediaries between their countries' established or revolutionary élites and the "lower orders." Hence their position was pivotal and also at times highly controversial—especially, as in late eighteenth-century Ireland, when their influence or their often radical religious and political views competed with or contradicted those of the clergy.

Bernard M'Kenna was a Catholic schoolmaster on Long Island and in New York City during the late eighteenth and early nineteenth centuries. He was born in mid-Ulster about 1754, but his Irish abode cannot be located precisely. The M'Kennas were former Gaelic chieftains in the barony of Trough, in north County Monaghan, but Bernard M'Kenna's last residence before his flight to America in 1797 was the small linen-market

---

1. Cited in G. Koos, "Irish Immigrant Schoolmaster . . . "; see Sources, chapter 48. Also see chapter 32, on Francis Burdett Personel, a runaway servant who, merely because he was "well dressed, could write a passible hand, and understood some figures," could "set up for a Schoolmaster" in prerevolutionary Virginia.
2. Cited in M. O'Brien, "Irish Schoolmasters in the City of New York," 473–74; see Sources, chapter 48.
3. Cited in G. Koos, "Irish Immigrant Schoolmasters . . . "; see Sources, chapter 48.

town of Aughnacloy, in Carnteel parish and Dungannon barony, just on the County Tyrone side of the Monaghan border, while M'Kenna's brother James, who apparently accompanied him to the United States, had lived in Tyrone's Clonfeacle parish, immediately east of Carnteel.4 Thanks to the Plantation's effects, the middling ranks of Ulster's Catholic society were much smaller and poorer than in eastern and southern Ireland, and by the late 1700s most of the M'Kennas in southeast Tyrone and north Monaghan were petty farmers and cottage weavers. Clearly, however, Bernard M'Kenna's family had retained sufficient affluence to provide him with a good education, and his friendship and correspondence with Rev. Henry Conwell, vicar-general of Armagh archdiocese as well as parish priest of Dungannon town,5 also indicates his superior status.

From his letter it is equally clear that M'Kenna had emigrated under severe duress, almost certainly because of his involvement with the Catholic Defenders or the United Irishmen or both. Despite episcopal censure, in the turbulent 1790s many Catholic schoolmasters and even a few clergymen were engaged in plotting insurrection, and one of Ulster's most prominent rebels, Fr. James O'Coigley (b. 1761; executed 1798), was, like Conwell, a priest in the Armagh archdiocese. In 1797 M'Kenna was one of several thousand rebels, mostly Catholics and Presbyterians, who fled northern Ireland to escape the brutal disarming or "dragooning" of Ulster carried out by the British army, the Irish militia, and the Orangemen mobilized in the Protestant yeomanry corps. And M'Kenna may have had especially pressing motives for flight. On 17 May 1797 the government executed Owen and William M'Kenna, sons of a north Monaghan Catholic innkeeper of radical sympathies, on charges of subverting the loyalty of their fellow Monaghan militiamen. Bernard M'Kenna's hasty departure from Aughnacloy on 7 May, approximately the date of William and Owen's arrest and courtmartial, strongly suggests that the condemned men were his kinsmen and that he had good reason to fear the same punishment for similar activities. Thus, M'Kenna fled to Derry city and thence to America where, unfortunately, he would soon discover that sectarian bitterness prevailed even in what he called that "happy asylum for the banished children of oppression."

After disembarking at New Castle, Delaware, in mid-August 1797, Bernard M'Kenna parted from his brother and journeyed to New York City. Fourteen years after the Ameri-

---

4. For demographic data on Carnteel parish and Trough barony and their environs, see appendix 2.1c, on chapter 48. 5. Rev. Henry Conwell (ca. 1745–1842): born in Moneymore, Co. Derry, Conwell studied for the priesthood in Paris and in 1776 was ordained a priest in the Armagh archdiocese. Between ca. 1796 and 1820 Conwell served as archdiocesan vicar-general, but in 1819 Rome passed him over for the archbishopric of Armagh, offering instead his choice of the bishopric of Madras, India, or of Philadelphia. Unfortunately for Conwell, he chose the latter, and in 1820 he arrived in Philadelphia, where he was soon embroiled in the bitter public and legal controversies with Fr. William Hogan and the trustees of St. Mary's Church that resulted in the "Hogan schism" of the early 1820s. In 1826 the Vatican rejected Conwell's compromise with the trustees, in which he agreed to their demand for a veto over his appointment of pastors, and recalled him in disgrace to Rome. Conwell returned to Philadelphia without permission, was suspended from the administration of his diocese in favor of his coadjutor, Bishop Francis Kenrick, and spent his last years in secluded senility.

can Revolution, New York still barred Catholics from public office and would continue to do so until 1806. After a century of legal proscription, however, the state's Catholics now enjoyed religious freedom, and in 1785 several hundred of them established New York City's first Catholic church, St. Peter's, on the corner of Barclay and Church streets. From the beginning St. Peter's congregation was predominantly Irish, and although the church's trustees included laymen such as Dominick Lynch (1754–1825), a rich merchant who moved in the city's highest social circles, and future power brokers like William Mooney, the founder (in 1787) and the first Grand Sachem of the Tammany Society, most Irish parishioners were poor artisans, cartmen, and laborers whose families clustered in the emergent slums of the fifth, sixth, and seventh wards. Eventually, M'Kenna would join and strongly identify with Manhattan's Irish Catholic community. However, in the late 1790s yellow fever plagued American seaports; New York City's first Catholic school would not be established until 1801; and so, perhaps seeking a healthier environment as well as a teaching position, M'Kenna soon moved to Hempstead township, between Mosquito Cove and Oyster Bay, in what was then Queen's (now Nassau) County, on the north shore of Long Island.

M'Kenna must have cut a distinctive figure in the Queen's County countryside. His penchant for the big word (e.g. "I *conjectured* that I had *acquired* a cientific knowledge") and the verbose expression (e.g. "I should have been more *circumspect as to its better arrangement*") places him in the company of the philomaths, those favorite and respected characters of eighteenth- and early nineteenth-century Irish folklore. These were the "poor scholars," the "young priests," and, especially, the hedge schoolmasters who cultivated an ornate style of English speech and an orotund rhetoric—at bottom, a symbol of the Irish countryman's profound respect for education. For schoolmasters such as M'Kenna, the richness of language was paralleled by an abundance of knowledge in various "branches"—as, for example, in his own "arithmetical authors"—often pedantically displayed. Indeed, M'Kenna's speech and academic pretensions remind one of the fictional creations of his younger contemporary, William Carleton (1794–1869) of south Tyrone's Clogher Valley: of the schoolmaster Mat Kavanagh (based on the real-life Pat Frayne) in Carleton's short story "The Hedge School," who claimed a mastery of stereometry, Greek grammar, and Hebrew on the Masoretic text, in addition to less elevated subjects; and of the "young priest" Denis O'Shaughnessy, in "Denis O'Shaughnessy Going to Maynooth," with his baroque lexicon. Like Carleton's characters, M'Kenna shows a high-flown diction and a Latinate construction layered over a Gaelic linguistic substratum (successfully concealed in M'Kenna's case) and the dialect of the south Ulster countryside—the last shining through in M'Kenna's incongruous and almost stage-Irish "tagious" (for "tedious"). All this, filtered through a Tyrone accent, must have made M'Kenna's speech the object of bemused attention in America.

But in eastern Long Island bemusement and tolerance turned eventually to violent hostility. The region had been a nest of Toryism during the American Revolution and was a Federalist party stronghold in the 1790s. Its Quaker farmers and Dutch fishermen were proverbially insular and fiercely Protestant. In short, eastern Long Island was not a propitious place for an Irish Catholic schoolmaster with a radical past—as M'Kenna had learned to his cost by 1810 when, bereft of his American wife and exiled from his second home, he returned to New York City and, the following year, recounted his adventures since 1797 to his old friend in County Tyrone.

Bernard M'Kenna, New York City,
to Fr. Henry Conwell, Dungannon, County Tyrone, 15 September 1811

Ever dear and much respected friend,

After a long absence of fourteen years, I have had the great satisfaction of receiving a letter from you, and not I am sure, without much astonishment on my first perceiving your signature; which has excited various thoughts of the many sociable and jovial hours we have reciprocally spent together: and now had almost terminated in a total oblivion. But I hope my long silence, has not occasioned your being offended at me, or any suspicion that I have disregarded you.[6] If I was to offer at[7] a reason in excuse of it; it would be an invented one, for it has never been known to my self. But I was contented to know that my heart was always possessed of much affection towards you. I believe I may candidly say that there was no bounds to it. It has been observed to me by a certain person at the time of an indulgence[8] in Dungannon; that he perceived your regard for me was much declined,[9]   he said that he seen me salute[10] you and that you took but very little notice of it: the time I perfectly recollect; but however I intended to pass it unnoticed,[11] considering that you might have had a reason, wherefore I concluded that if you had a reason it must have been a very important one, knowing you to be a gentleman of too much good sense as to take notice of trifles. Now if there be any thing of this,[12] I sincerely request that you may communicate[13] it to me in your next, that I may have the satisfaction of knowing it. It never came within my recollection anything that I have said or done that would offend a single hair of your head: for as I have already observed to you, that I have born an unlimited affection for you. I could not forbear saying thus much to you on this head.[14]

Permit me here to trouble you with a sketch of some events which have occurred[15] to me since the time of my emigration from home. On the 7th of May

6. I have disregarded you: I have not thought of you, I have "forgotten" you.   7. to offer at: to attempt.
8. indulgence: probably the *occasion* of the proclamation of an indulgence (in Roman Catholicism a sacramental absolution resulting in the remission of part or all of the punishment due to sin).   9. was . . . declined: i.e., had . . . declined.   10. salute: greet.   11. intended to pass it unnoticed: "determined to let it pass unnoticed."   12. if there be any thing of this: "if there is anything consequential in this," "if this amounts to anything"; for the construction see the idiom what of it? "of what consequence is it?"
13. communicated ms.   14. head: subject, matter.   15. occurred: happened.

1797, I set out from Aughnacloy, and on the 8th, I sorrowfully took my leave of you, and on the evening of that day, I arrived at a small village within about three miles of Derry almost exhausted with fatigue of travelling and want of subsistance.[16] The yeoman made such a stir throug<h> the different villages, that I found it impracticable for me to make any delay without being detected: Therefore continuing my journey and was obliged to dispense[17] with one drink of milk and a small glass of spirits, except[18] water, which often proved very scant, and on my arrival in the village, had much difficulty in obtaining quarters, from the great commotion then of the times: and after regailing[19] myself that night, next morning set out for the city, and after my arrival, I agreed for a passage, and moved down to Movill,[20] where I impatiently lay,[21] untill the 7th day of June, when I took my departure for the United States of America, and after being some weeks out, we were boarded by a French Schooner after a two hours chace and several salutes from their guns, we were obliged to come to,[22] & after they had detained us for about the space of an hour, we were restored to liberty and on the 15th of August, we arrived at New-Castle,   here we landed on the blissful shore of America; a land of peace and plenty, and at this day may be called the Garden spot of the world; a happy asylum for the banished children of oppression. Now after spending a revery of some days[23] I concluded once more to revert[24] to the Delaware river for New-York where I arrived on the 12th of September; having spent a few days here, but not finding it suitable to my purpose, I crossed the East River for Long Island, and after a journey of thirtytwo miles; I met with some encouragement to teach a school in a very respectable neighbourhood, (it being now the 24th of September,) and soon got my self ingratiated into the good graces of the people. But soon after my commencement in the school, I found it highly requisit that I should improve my education, particularly in the following branches, (which I have been entirely dificient in,) Viz. English Grammar, Book-keeping, Geograph<y>, Navigation, with several arithmetical authors, (containing several abstruse problems,) which I have been unaquainted with,   Having then no other alternative than to have recourse to close[25] studies, and supplied my self with varieties of authors on the subject, for the better attainment of this arduous task: however I began my studies and gave myself up intirely to a recluse life appropriating every hour, (when absent from school,) to the business. In the summer season I frequently retired to the woods: here I spent time in solitude & in close retirement, as long as the temperance of the weather permitted; in the winter I shut myself up in the school house where I have spent whole nights: still continuing

---

16. subsistance: provender.   **17. dispense:** manage, make do.   **18. except:** apart from, in addition to. **19. regailing:** i.e., regaling "refreshing."   **20. Movill:** Moville town (Moville Lower parish, Inishowen East barony, Co. Donegal); although about 12 miles northwest of Derry city on the Inishowen penninsula, Moville was the passenger embarkation point for large transatlantic vessels leaving the port city.   **21. lay:** passed the time.   **22. come to:** come to a standstill (said of a ship).   **23. after spending a revery of some days:** "after spending some days enchanted" (i.e., with his new surroundings).   **24. revert:** return.   **25. close:** rigorous, concentrated; hereafter, describing retirement, "secluded."

myself[26] disengaged from every thing that I thought might retard my progress in the attainment of these desirable accomplishsments, for about the space of two years: by this time I conjectured that I had acquired a cientifick knowledge of thos<e> branches;[27] and now having received encouragement from a superior school, about the distance of fifteen miles from this, here I offered myself the first quarter as a probationar, but before the close of which, they built[28] an elegant School house for the purpose of establishing an acadamy.[29]   I advertised my self at the instance[30] of the superintendance,   the school began to get established and my pupils augmenting to the number of seventy, regularly taught under my direction. I taught here for three years at three hundred Dollars per year, and found in[31] everything but clothes, with every accomodation suitable to any gentleman, a horse, or horse an<d> chair,[32] anytime at my command.   I have been introduced by one of our neighbouring ladies to her sister, who was here upon a visit from New-York; and after several interviews, we seem<ed> to have a growing affection for each other, which moved my propensity[33] to a change of life, and after soliciting the consent of her brother, we got married by the Rev^d D^r OBryan;[34] subsequent to which and in private she made a recantation,[35] she formerly belong<ing> to the Quaker society,   her parents died when very young, and left her a handsome fortune independent;[36]   she was an amiable fine girl of most excellent accomplishments; and as to parentage she was of some of the first families on this Island.[37]   I shall now give you an account of some few occurances[38] in my

---

26. still continuing myself: always keeping myself.   **27. branch:** field (of study/knowledge).   **28. built** ms. **29. an acadamy:** perhaps the Oyster Bay Academy, founded in 1802 and one of a spate of academies established on Long Island in the two decades after the American Revolution; the Academy's first principal was a Baptist minister, Rev. Marmaduke Earl.   **30. instance:** solicitation, urging (i.e., of the school's **superintendance** [hereafter] = administration).   **31. found in:** furnished/provided with (i.e. as part of M'Kenna's salary).   **32. chair:** a light vehicle drawn by one horse, a chaise.   **33. moved my propensity:** "stirred my (already formed) inclination."   **34. Rev^d D^r OBryan:** Rev. William V. O'Brien (1740–1816): born in Ireland; educated at Bologna and Rome, where he entered the Dominican Order ca. 1761; O'Brien returned to Ireland in 1770 and pastored in and around Dublin until he emigrated to Philadelphia in 1786; in 1787–1807 he was pastor at St. Peter's Church in New York City, where his devotion to sick parishioners in the yellow fever epidemics of 1795, 1798, and 1805 won the respect of all New Yorkers; however, he quarreled with his assistant pastors, refusing even to speak to them, and eventually he was obliged to resign his pastorate in mysterious but "disagreeable circumstances" because of his "irregular conduct." Like other priests at St. Peter's, O'Brien occasionally visited the few Catholics on Long Island. Quotations from F. X. Curran, S.J., "The Jesuit Colony in New York . . . ," 97; see Sources, chapter 48.   **35. recantation:** a formal renunciation as erroneous of religious beliefs (in this instance, of the Society of Friends).   **36. independent:** (of a legacy/fortune) sufficient to make one financially independent.   **37.** M'Kenna's wife was almost certainly Phoebe Doty, whose family had attended the Quaker meeting at Jericho, in Hempstead township, since the late seventeenth century. Quaker records indicate she moved to New York City in 1791 and "married out" of the Society of Friends sometime before 2 May 1804. Isaac Doty (1764–1824), a kinsman and perhaps her brother or uncle, was a brewer in New York City's seventh ward and in 1814 was the only non-Irish executor of Bernard M'Kenna's will. Curiously, from the 1820s through at least the early 1840s Phoebe Doty's namesake and probable kinswoman was one of New York's most famous and financially successful prostitutes and brothel-keepers!   **38. occurances:** events.

marriage state. I had purchased a farm about two miles from my last residence,[39] upon which I built an elegant house, and after making some necessary arrangements on the place, I brought home my wife:[40]   here we spent some genial hours in the bonds of affection, and seemingly had gained the warm friendship of our neighbouring Quakers, who shewed upon all occasions a remarkable friendship and attachment to us, with frequent invitations to their meetings, which we always declined,   so we continued for near the space of five years, when my wife fell into a consumpson, which terminated her existence.[41] But now behold what succeeds, a scene of trouble most doleful.   sometime before her decease, she requested that I should send for the priest. I wrote for D[r] Byrn[42] to New York, about thirty miles from us, who immediately attended, and after discharging his duty, he told me he never visited so great a christian: her brother previous to this, had sent her a letter of admonition,[43]   the D[r] on seeing it wished very much that there should be an answer sent. However she answered the letter,[44] much to the astonishment of the D[r] who seen a copy of it afterwards,   But the quakers on hearing of the D[r] being come, several of them came seemingly much dismayed,   A few hours after the decease of my wife, I sat viewing her corpse absorbed in profound grief, thinking of what might be my future destiny;   my youngest child at this time was about fourteen months old, which I call Eleanor, and Mary Ann about three years old,   after spending some time deploring[45] my calamitous situation a blood vessel bursted, to the effusion of much blood.   I immediately communicated the matter to the company, and orderd a Doctor to be sent for, who attended me all night: next morning, Mary Ann on perceiving my alarming situation screamed out and seized hold of me in the bed,   I immediately ordered her to be taken away and sent to her aunts about a mile's distance—here I took my last farewell of her, (as I thought then,) it being the general opinion of many that I could not survive it,   at this time there were three Physicians attending me, who gave a more favourable opinion of my complaint. In about two days after the enterment of my wife, my servant girl left me,   my sister in law took away her daughter, who had been for some time wa<i>ting on[46] her aunt;   here all fled and forsook me;   the approach of night was a terror to me. But resigning myself with profound humility to the divine will of god, looking up to him for relief, whose goodness and mercies I have often

---

39. resident ms.   **40.** M'Kenna's farm was at Mosquito Cove, on the north shore of Queen's Co.; he still owned the property in 1814, when he described its location in his will.   **41.** According to M'Kenna's second letter to Fr. Conwell, dated 5 September 1812, his wife died on 10 February 1808.   **42. D[r] Byrn:** Fr. John Byrne, Irish-born assistant pastor at St. Peter's Church in 1804–1808; one of future saint Elizabeth Ann Seton's spiritual advisors and friends. Byrne fell into scandal with his fellow assistant pastor and drinking companion, Fr. Matthew O'Brien and was forced to resign (see n. 60). On Seton, see chapter 44.   **43. a letter of admonition:** i.e., a letter admonishing M'Kenna's wife for having called a priest to administer to her the Last Rites of the Catholic Church—or, more broadly, for her earlier but now-obvious conversion to Roman Catholicism.   **44. she answered the letter:** i.e., she had *already* answered the letter.   **45. deploring:** lamenting.   **46. wa<i>ting on** (of ms.): attending (specifically, a dying person).

experienced in the many vicissitudes of life;   after spending some time in meditating and reflecting with myself, the <h>our of sleep was nearly approaching, so I repaired with my children to bed. But having not long been in bed, when a little boy, (who hearing of my melancholy situation,) wanted to get in to keep me company, but not being able to give any assistance for his reception, he was obliged to come in through a window.   On the next day there came a woman to me, and offered her service for some time, untill I should be provided with a house keeper, to which I consented, and remained in this situation for some weeks,   She then went off, but had not been long gone, when I received a positive information[47] that she had taken away a great many articles with my wife's name on them;   her husband the night after her leaving me, made an attempt of robing me,   his plan I detected from finding the boults and latches so out of order as to prevent the doors from shuting close,   after securing the doors, the next night I wa<i>ted for his coming   accordingly[48] he attacked the house, but finding so unexpectedly his disappointment, he set up to the door outside a large stick[49] of a great weight, that on my opening thereof, it might have the good fortune of ending my existance, but through the providence of god, I have escaped this as well as many other dangers in life. Now as soon as I gained some strength I went to look after the Stolen things,   I got a constable and by virtue of[50] a search warrant, I entered the house and found said articles. I made them both prisoners, and made the husband discover[51] the whole plot,   he had killed my dog the night before lest he should make any alarm. I am strongly of an opinion that he had an intention to murder me had he got in,   never the less, I gave them their liberty.   As soon as I found my self in a tolorable state of health, I began my school as usual, and after teaching a few days, a party of Quakers came and turned me out of the school, and at the same time had a teacher along with them, to whome they gave posession,   my wife dying a catholick, here is Quaker revenge,   From these succeeding troubles[52] I found it impossible for me to live among such an uncultivated generation.[53] I rented out the Farm and came to New-York: the Catholick Free School at this time was vacant,[54] I was strongly advised by some, to give in[55] my proposal, altho several proposals were given in at this time; notwithstanding I gave in mine, and carried,[56] and after the

---

47. **a positive information**: an incontestable report.   48. **accordingly**: as expected.   49. **stick**: the word can designate a cut length of wood as massive as a tree trunk.   50. **by virtue of**: empowered by.   51. **discover**: divulge.   52. **From these succeeding troubles**: "Because of these successive troubles."   53. **uncultivated generation**: uncivilized class of persons.   54. **the Catholick Free School**: a charity school, established in 1801 for the children of St. Peter's poor parishioners. By 1805 the Catholic Free School was the largest denominational school in New York City, and in 1806, when the trustees successfully petitioned the New York state legislature for a share of the common school fund (est. in 1805), the school had about two hundred "scholars," all boys. In 1810 James Moffett, presumably M'Kenna's successor, was "Master of the Free School" with an annual salary of $400. Remarkably, the school remained in existence until 1935.   55. **give in**: submit.   56. **carried**: succeeded (i.e., in obtaining the teaching position).

BERNARD M'KENNA

expiration of one year, I resigned.   I found it too fatigueing on account of the great number of Scholars I had to teach. Shortly after my arrival in the city, I had received the news that there was a gentle man from New-York had taken possession of my Land, and claiming it as his, from an Indian deed, which he could produce: and further, he cut down the valuable fruit trees of every kind for fuel,   he continued in this manner for the space of a year. I watched my opportunity, and as soon as I found him in town, I put him under arrest for damages,   he gave 2000 Dollars security for his appearance in court,   on the first day of May last, I was obliged to take the disagreeable journey to the place for my rent,   I took a Constable of that neighbourhood along with me, but he refused to let us in,   he had his party insid<e> well fortified with unlawful weapons,   notwithstanding we entered the house, and carried off every single article, and left them in care with the constable, and in nine days after, he sold them at public vendue, and sent me the rent,   so after a tagious[57] suit, I obtained an order of Court, and a few days ago I sent the Sheriff to turn him out.   This person proves insolvent I am informed,   if so I must bear the cost.   Here I now remain enjoying my self in peace once more with my two little girls, (who is much admired by many,) and notwithstanding the many severe trials that I have experienced, the Lord has supported me and restored my health, and still have procured a handsome fortune for each of my children.

Now after closing my disastrous detail,[58] I shall proceed to give you a summary account of the ecclesiasticle order of our church, with the name of each ecclesiastick in succession from the year 1791 or there abouts, untill the present. Rev'd Father Whelen, Rev'd Father Newgent,*

––––––––––––––––––––

*who was anathematized by the Bishop for his acting inimical to the good government of the church. He commenced a revolution, and had seduced a party for the purpose of enabling him to carry his egragious views into effect: But his project being detected, he was tried by the laws of his country, and found guilty; and after subjecting himself to the penalties enflicted by the court, he took his flight to France.[59]

––––––––––––––––––––

Rev'd Father William OBryan, from Dublin, Rev'd Nicholas Burk, Rev'd Bartholomew McMaghen from Dublin, Rev'd Mathew OBryan from Cork, suspended, but I am informed that he is reinstated again, Rev'd Dr Kelly from Ireland, suspended and returned home, Rev'd Michael Hurley from Philadelphia, Rev'd Father Sepore from France   Rev'd Father Byrn from Dublin, dyed at Georgetown c<o>llege,   This puts an end to the Irish succession and for so far, has put an end to strife shame and

––––––––––––––––––––

57. tagious: i.e., tedious.   **58. detail:** account, narrative.   **59. *who was anathematized . . . to France:** this is M'Kenna's own footnote, separated by lines from the main text of his manuscript.

confusion,[60]   We have in the church now two most excellent divines, the Rev'd Anthony Kohlmann a German, Rev'd Mr Fanwick an American, both of which are subject to the order of the Jesuite<s>,[61]   Kohlman is Rector of the church,   each have 500 Dollars per year, paid quarterly, and live together in one house contiguous to the church,   the house they have rent free,   Our church was began in building

---

60. Over 40 priests are known to have ministered at St. Peter's between 1785 and 1815; of these, 16 were Irish, 14 French, 7 German, 3 American-born, and 2 Italian. **Rev'd Father Whelen**: Fr. Charles Whelan (1741–1806): Irish-born first pastor of St. Peter's in 1785–1786; a former chaplain in the French navy, his rough manners and poor preaching (he spoke better Irish and French than English) alienated the trustees, who forced him to resign in favor of Fr. Nugent. **Rev'd Father Newgent**: Fr. Andrew Nugent (1740–1795); born in Cork; officiated when St. Peter's was dedicated on 4 November 1786; his demands for a higher salary soon alienated many trustees, but his refusal to resign and his and his supporters' defiance of Bishop John Carroll ended in riot and legal action; in 1787 Nugent abandoned the struggle to retain St. Peter's and in 1790 he returned to France. **Rev'd Father William OBryan**: Fr. William V. O'Brien, successor to Fr. Andrew Nugent; see n. 34. **Rev'd Nicholas Burk**: Fr. Nicholas Burke (or Bourke, d. 1800): from the Irish Dominican convent in Lisbon; served as temporary rector of St. Peter's in 1792, when Fr. William O'Brien was fundraising in Cuba and Mexico. **Rev'd Bartholomew McMaghen**: probably Fr. Anthony McMahon; Irish-born Dominican; died in New York in 1800. **Rev'd Mathew OBryan**: Fr. Matthew O'Brien (1758–1815): born in Dublin, probably a relative of fellow Dominican Fr. William V. O'Brien (see n. 34), although their relationship at St. Peter's became hostile; emigrated 1795; pastor at Albany before his removal to New York City in 1799; assistant pastor at St. Peter's in 1799–1807; in 1805 he received into the church the Episcopalian convert Elizabeth Ann Seton (see chapter 44); although purportedly "a man of learning and eloquence" (Seton regarded O'Brien as her "kindest, most respectful confessor"), in 1807 he was forced to leave St. Peter's to avoid what Bishop Carroll called "the explosion of dreadful scandals" occasioned by his drunkenness; however, he was subsequently reinstated and served as pastor in Natchez, Philadelphia, and Baltimore, where he died. **Rev'd Dr Kelly**: perhaps Fr. Matthias Kelly, who arrived from Ireland in New York in 1806 but "proved neither hardworking nor abstemious"; or Fr. Patrick Kelly, who became "scandalous" and was eventually suspended for violently denouncing his personal foes from the pulpit. **Rev'd Michael Hurley**: Rev. Michael Hurley, O.S.A.; b. in Ireland ca. 1780; assistant pastor at St. Peter's from July 1805, when he befriended and provided spiritual counsel to Elizabeth Ann Seton; also sometime pastor of St. Augustine's church, Philadelphia, where he quarreled with Bishop Conwell. **Rev'd Father Sepore**: Fr. Louis Sibourd: born in France; a refugee from the French Revolution, in 1807 he succeeded Rev. William O'Brien as pastor of St. Peter's, but in 1808 was forced out by trustees who complained of his poor English; assigned to New Orleans in 1810. **Rev'd Father Byrn**: Fr. John Byrne (see n. 42). Quotations from M. J. Riordan, *Cathedral Records . . .* , 28; E. M. Kelly, ed., *Numerous Choirs: A Chronicle of Elizabeth Bayley Seton . . .* , vol. 1, 91; F. X. Curran, S.J., "The Jesuit Colony in New York . . . ," 52, 96; and A. M. Melville, *Louis William DuBourg . . .* , vol. 1, 462; see Sources, chapters 44 and 48.   **61. Rev'd Anthony Kohlmann**: Fr. Anthony Kohlmann, S.J. born in Alsace; educated at Fribourg; ordained in 1796 and joined the Fathers of the Sacred Heart; Kohlmann served as pastor, military chaplain, and seminary rector in Austria, Italy, Germany, the Netherlands, and (in 1798–1800) England, where he learned English; he joined the Jesuit Order after its restoration by Pius VIII and came to the United States in November 1806, at the invitation of the American Bishop John Carroll; Kohlmann first taught at Georgetown, Maryland, seminary, but in 1808 Carroll sent him to New York City, with the title of administrator and vicar-general. Because Luke Concanen, the first appointed bishop of New York, was stranded in Italy by the Napoleonic Wars and never reached his diocese, between 1808 and 1815 Kohlmann exercised a bishop's authority as well as the pastorate of St. Peter's; Kohlmann's stewardship revitalized Catholicism in the city, and in 1813 his refusal to testify in a court case established the sanctity of the confessional in American law; however, in 1815 he returned to Georgetown, and in 1828 he retired to Rome and joined the faculty of the newly reopened Jesuit seminary. ¶**Rev'd Mr Fanwick**: Fr. Benedict Joseph Fenwick (1782–1846): born into an

about the time of Father Whalen   it is incorporated,   it has gotten 158 Pews in it; the rent of those pews amounts to 1200 Dollars yearly out of which is paid all church expensis.[62]

There ar<e> nine Trustees elected every year, in whose power is vested the procuracy[63] to transact all the temporal business peculiar to the church. Every member of the congragation must pay some thing yearly, that he may be entitled to a vote. They have purchased a place out of town, on which they have built a College which cost 13000 Dollars, for the reception of scholars of every denomination, and have met with good encouragement. There are 50 scholars, and each one pays 200 Dollars per year for education and boarding,   the professors have no salary, as the<y> intend to belong to the ecclesiastical order themselves.[64] In the month of August last, they have made an other purchase about five miles out of town, which cost 8100 Dollars for the purpose of establishing a nunery: they are expecting nuns from Dublin.[65]

In the next place I shall proceed to give you a description of the order of the church. There are three masses selebrated on every day of the week—the Clergeyman walks into church dressed, from the vestry which is appendant to the church, with his hands joined and erect, proceded by four boys, (at the time of High Masses six,) dressed in white shirts with ther hands in like position.   On every festival and every first sunday of the month we have High Masses sung, with the greatest solemnity, and answered from the choire[66] on the gallery, with a most elated voice, in concert with the organs,

old Maryland Catholic family that had arrived with Leonard Calvert in 1634; educated at Georgetown and St. Mary's, Baltimore, seminaries. In 1806 Fenwick joined the Jesuits, and in 1808 he was ordained and accompanied Fr. Anthony Kohlmann to New York, where he served as assistant pastor of St. Peter's until 1817, when he returned to Georgetown; later Fenwick was vicar-general of Charleston, S.C. (1818–1822); president of Georgetown College (1822–1825); and bishop of Boston (1825–1846). **62.** In 1800 St. Peter's Church had a debt of $6,500, all but $2,000 of which was owed to the church's **trustees** (see hereafter), who had loaned money for the church's construction and furnishings. Since annual receipts, largely from pew rents, averaged only $1,500, while yearly expenses were about $1,400, the debt both limited parish activities and increased the trustees' power over the pastors. The lower annual receipts cited by M'Kenna in 1811 probably reflect the effects on the city's trade of the economic depression occasioned by the U.S. embargo acts of 1807–1810. **63. procuracy:** power, authority. **64.** In 1808 St. Peter's trustees, encouraged by Fr. Kohlmann, established a classical school, the New York Literary Institution, staffed by Jesuit priests and first located on Broadway. By early 1810, when it had 50 scholars, a new site was purchased far out in the country, between Fourth and Fifth avenues and Fiftieth and Fifty-first streets, opposite the botanic gardens. By 1813 the school had 74 students, all males, had acquired an excellent reputation, and was patronized by many of the city's wealthier Protestants as well as Catholics; however, in the summer of 1813, Fr. Grassi, superior of the Jesuit mission in America, ordered the faculty to return to Maryland and the Institution closed. **65.** In 1811 Fr. Kohlmann persuaded a group of Ursuline nuns, from Blackrock Convent, Cork, to come to New York City; in 1812 they established an academy and a charity school for girls, but both closed when the Sisters left the city in late 1814. **66. answered from the choire:** this passage refers to the fact that at High Mass the performance of the liturgy alternates between the celebrants (clergy) and the choir.

with incense and ten candles lit on the altar. Vespers[67] every sunday in the after noon is sung, attended with incense. At the time of procession, the Priests walk round the church with their Hymn Books, preceded by boys, one of which offers the incense moving in a retrograde order;[68] the Crucifix is carried round also, in an elevated position. Here follows the Fraternity[69] with their Hymn Books and a lit candle, the whole resounding with an united voice exhibiting a most festive appearance. Our altar is ornamented beyond my description, the Bishop's canopy on the one side and the pulpit on the other, with the picture of our Saviour on the cross above the alter, the picture of the Virgin Mary, and that of St Peter, on the one side and St. Joseph, and the Virgin Mary carrying the cross on the other with several other pictures. For every High Mass the priest gets from 15 Dol^{rs} to 20   for every mass for the dead he has one Dollar   for his attendance at funerals nine shillings, marriages and baptisms are optional. This is what is called his perquisites.

We are building a new church which is dedicated to St Patrick,   our present church is called St Peter's.   The foundation of our new church was laid 2 years ago last spring, and measures in its dimension on the foundation 120 feet by 80,   the work is going on but very slow.[70] Agreeable to your request I have made every necessary inquiry about the Rev'd Mr Fitzsimons, but cannot find any account of him. You are to forward your letter under this address. Rev'd Mr Fitzsimons Quebec care of the Catholick Bishop; or otherwise to the seminary in Montreal.   I have been also enquiring about D^r O Neil, but cannot find any intelligence about him either person or property. I have written to my brother, (who lives in Pennsylvania State,) about this business and have kept my letter open for a considerable time, for the reception of his intimation,[71] but have not received his answer: But had you confined me to narrower limits I could have with a greater degree of certainty found the property. In your next please to specify the name of the township and county that this property is situate in as the State alone is too great an extent for my enquiry: the information I suppose may be found in the demise,[72] through which, and my brother's exertion, I think I cannot fail

67. Vespers: the evening office, said or sung before supper; one of the daily round of canonical choir offices (matins, lauds, prime, terce, sext, none, vespers, and compline).   **68. the Priests walk round the church . . . moving in a retrograde order**: in processions the lay assistants and the lowest ranks of clergy are first in line.   **69. Fraternity**: a body or order of men organized for religious or devout purposes.   **70.** The cornerstone of "old" St. Patrick's cathedral, located "uptown" on the corner of Prince and Mott streets, was laid on 8 June 1809, but soaring construction costs were a terrible financial burden on the parish, especially because of the trade depression caused by the American embargo acts of 1807–1810 and then by the War of 1812; by the time it was dedicated on 6 November 1814, the cathedral had cost $90,000 and was still unfinished; and when Bishop John Connolly arrived in New York the following year, he inherited a $53,000 debt with 7 percent annual interest. Designed in neogothic style by Joseph Mangin, the cathedral was about 80 feet in height and reportedly had a "magnificent" interior—in marked contrast to St. Peter's plain brick church.   **71. intimation**: notification, but here used in the sense of "information."   **72. demise**: legal conveyance (i.e., will).

BERNARD M'KENNA

in finding the property, which no doubt will go the behoof[73] of the legatee.   Please to inform my brother's family (who formerly lived in Carrick Castle)[74] if you can that I have had a visit from him last October, the first sight I have seen of him since I took my leave of him in Wilmington[75] a few days after our arrival, but had several letters from him.   I understand by him that he has realized a pretty good fortune, but for whome I cannot tell. I have strictly reprimande<d> him for his long absence from his family, charging him with ingratitude which I have done frequently in my letters to him; he says he has sent to them, but did not say what, or how much. I should be very glad to know the certainty of this; he told me that he positively would send for them last spring,   my letters always found him at Westchester care of Charles M'Kenny Esq[r] Chester county State as above. He sometimes acts in the office of a constable which is looked upon here as a very respectable one, and often deputised by the Sherriff to act for him—cries all his vendues &[76]

Please to remember me to my sister, and to your brothers family whom I much esteem, to M[r] Small's family whose friendship I never shall forget. I wish to hear very much from Edward Conwell, William and Patt Small,   remember me to Arthur Devlin's family, the Erskins of Carnteel, James Curran and Thomas Hughes, &c. I have heard of the death of the unfortunate Judith, a considerable time ago, but I could never learn where or in what capacity or in what faith she died in. On my undertaking to answer your letter, it was my intention to take a transcript of it (when finished,) for the benefit of its correction,   otherwise I should have been more circumspect as to its better arrangement.   But finding my self much cramped for time, as well as my view in procuring the opportunity of sending with a vessel, which at this time was fitting out for her voyage to Ireland; has intirely frustrated my design; which I hope will plead an apology for its inaccuracy. I had often an ardent wish to know, if any change have taken place with you in the ministry, as by this time I am expecting that you are promoted to the emin<en>ce of a Bishop, a promotion I am sure would be very congratulatory[77] to me. I shall now take my leave of you; praying that you may long enjoy an uninterrupted state of good health, to preside with grace and ability over your flock, always displaying a christian pattern, which is my petition for you. After craving

---

73. go the behoof of: benefit (probably a reshaping of go *to* behoof of).   **74.** Carrick Castle: probably Carrycastle townland, in Clonfeacle parish, Middle Dungannon barony, Co. Tyrone; the townland's name in Irish is *Carraig an Chaisil;* M'Kenna's more accurate translation as **Carrick Castle** suggests he was bilingual, as were most mid-Ulster Catholics born in the mid- and late 1700s. In the 1820s a Patrick McKenna paid 2s. 3d. in tithes on four acres in Carrycastle.   **75. Wilmington**: in Delaware.   **76. vendues**: auction sales. As of 5 September 1812, when Bernard M'Kenna wrote his second letter to Fr. Conwell, M'Kenna's brother James still had not sent for his wife and children to join him in Pennsylvania; instead, he had resigned his post as Chester Co. subsheriff and joined the U.S. army on the western frontier in order, Bernard suspected, "to get clear of the family in case of their arrival."   **77. congratulatory**: welcome (i.e., worthy of M'Kenna's congratulations).

your blessing for myself and my children, I subscribe myself with the most profound veneration,

And fulness of esteem,

Your reverence's most dutiful

New-York   Humble and obliged servant.

   September 15th, 1811   Bernard M'Kenna

P.S. Direct your letter thus,

   Bernard M'Kenna   N.B. This \<is> my first letter to Ireland

   Teacher Bayard St. N\<o>. 70

        New-York

Relatively little is known about Bernard M'Kenna after his return to New York City. Directories recorded his address in 1810 at 16 Doyer, in 1811 at 70 Bayard, and in 1812–1814 at 48 Mott Street, where he and his young daughters shared a building with the families of two grocers, a cartman, and a sailor. Despite his resignation from the Catholic Free School, M'Kenna apparently continued his profession of schoolmaster, for all the directory entries list his occupation as "teacher." However, whether he taught in the short-lived Jesuit academy or in another Catholic charity school associated with the new St. Patrick's Cathedral (as his Mott Street address would suggest) or as a private instructor cannot be determined. Certainly the need for Catholic teachers was growing, as by 1815 the Catholic—and predominantly Irish Catholic—population of New York City had increased to about 15,000 out of approximately 100,000 inhabitants. And despite its overall poverty, already the city's Irish Catholic community was sufficiently stratified and pious to support Bernard Dornin's Catholic bookstore and publishing house (established in 1807—the first in the United States), which M'Kenna himself patronized. However, M'Kenna did not live long enough to witness the great influx of Irish immigrants that followed the War of 1812, as on 17 February 1814 he died of consumption, at 60 years of age, in New York City. M'Kenna's will, written two days before he died, instructed that his two daughters "should be instituted[78] and regularly brought up in the Roman Catholic Religion," and he bequeathed to them equal divisions of his Long Island farm, valued at $1,250, and seven shares in the Bristol Glass, Cotton, and Clay Company, plus furniture, silver, notes, and cash.

It would appear from these bequests that Bernard M'Kenna had found school-teaching more remunerative in America than in Ireland. Yet it is revealing that the Irish Catholic executors of M'Kenna's will were mere grocers, not prominent United Irish exiles such as the affluent physician William James Macneven.[79] This was an indication that M'Kenna, despite his superior education, had achieved membership only in the lower-

---

78. **instituted**: educated, instructed.   **79.** On Macneven, see chapter 66, n. 3.

middling ranks of New York City's Irish Catholic community. It also suggests that his social milieu and his identity in New York—in contrast to those of the Catholic former United Irishman John O'Raw in Charleston[80]—were shaped more by religious affinities than by former associations with a secular Irish rebellion.

Indeed, it is tempting to see M'Kenna as a transitional figure in Irish and Irish-American history—as representing a shift from the Enlightenment radicalism that affected many ambitious middle-rank Catholics in the late 1700s to the religious conservatism and ethnic insularity that characterized most members of the Irish and Irish-American Catholic bourgeoisie by the mid–nineteenth century. Even in the 1790s M'Kenna's political activities in Ulster may have been as much a reflection of his devotion to Catholicism, anger at the depredations of local Orangemen, and desire to recover lost family estates as a commitment to the United Irishmen's ecumenical republicanism. In this respect, it is intriguing that in 1807 M'Kenna was one of 318 subscribers to Bernard Dornin's American edition of the *General History of the Christian Church* (Dublin, 1790), by "Signor Pastorini," the pseudonym of Charles Walmesley, an English Catholic bishop, whose reading of the Apocalypse led him to predict that in about 1821 God would destroy Protestantism and all its adherents. Naturally, Walmesley's was not the millennial expectation that had inspired the leaders of the United Irishmen, but in the early 1800s "Pastorini's prophecies" raised Catholic peasants' anticipations and heightened Protestants' fears in an Ireland that was increasingly polarized and racked by sectarian and social violence.

To be sure, in 1811 M'Kenna's detailed description of New York Catholicism was probably not the product of spontaneous devotion but rather a response to Conwell's request for specific information about the state of the church in America.[81] Likewise, M'Kenna's position as a teacher in New York's Catholic schools, like Margaret Burke's in Baltimore a decade later,[82] undoubtedly obliged him to maintain both a pious reputation and his pastors' approval; by contrast, in Ireland Catholic schoolmasters were still largely independent of clerical authority and often flirted, as had M'Kenna, with radical politics that their priests and bishops condemned.[83] However, M'Kenna's first paragraphs suggest that his long estrangement from Conwell, probably occasioned by his political activities in Ulster, had caused him anxiety and grief. More important, his letter clearly shows that M'Kenna took great pride in his church and its progress in America—so

---

80. Of course, John O'Raw's Irish-American community in Charleston was much smaller than M'Kenna's in New York; in addition, the former was predominantly Protestant and included many of O'Raw's former neighbors and political associates, both Presbyterians and Catholics, from Co. Antrim; see chapter 13. **81.** It is likely that Conwell wrote M'Kenna in anticipation that he might be appointed bishop of New York after Rev. Luke Concanen, the first bishop and also Irish, had died in Naples in June 1810, before he could cross the Atlantic and assume his post; see n. 61. **82.** On Margaret Burke, see chapter 44. **83.** In the 1790s bishops in Ulster and elsewhere in Ireland threatened to excommunicate Catholics who joined the Defenders or the United Irishmen.

much so that, despite their Irish origins, he condemned the contentious priests who had sown so much "strife shame and confusion" among New York's Catholics, and he lauded the non-Irish clergymen Frs. Kohlmann and Fenwick who had restored order and discipline.

The conflicts to which M'Kenna referred were the first of a succession of "trusteeship crises" that scandalized the Catholic church in the United States during the late eighteenth and early nineteenth century. The poverty of early American Catholicism, coupled with Gallican traditions from the European church, encouraged heavy reliance on lay trustees to finance church-building, pay clerical salaries, and cover other expenses, just as the paucity of American-born priests required an equal reliance on clergymen, although often of dubious character, from Ireland, France, and elsewhere abroad. Elected by parishioners who could afford to pay pew rents, the trustees were almost invariably men of wealth. In theory, the trustees supervised their church's temporal affairs, while the priests concentrated on spiritual matters. In truth, factional competition and conflicts among trustees, priests, and bishops were endemic—over the appointment, salaries, and dismissal of clergy, for example, and the ownership of church property. Sometimes, as in early New York City, rival priests and their lay supporters literally battled for control of the pulpit. Often this strife had ethnic and political implications, as in the schism in John O'Raw's St. Mary's church in Charleston, and frequently it led to mob violence and to legal actions by trustees, rebellious clerics, and by bishops seeking to curb the trustees' powers.

In the late 1700s Irish-American trustees in cities such as New York and Philadelphia were often rich Federalists who regarded both their priests and the poorer parishioners as their social inferiors. By the early 1800s, when M'Kenna penned his account, this first generation of trustees had largely been superseded, sometimes in extremely contentious circumstances, by a new Irish-American urban élite whose members, although scarcely less affluent than their predecessors, were often former United Irishmen who in the United States affiliated with the Jeffersonian Republicans. Frequently they argued that they were defending a "democratic" mode of Catholic church governance that was more compatible with American republicanism than the hierarchical or ultramontaine system of clerical authority that Rome and their bishops sought to impose. However, the increasing numbers of poorer Irish Catholic immigrants, traditionally more deferential to the clergy than their American or European coreligionists,[84] resented the nouveau riche trustees' wealth and pretensions, and by the mid–nineteenth century the bishops—many of them Irish-born— had successfully mobilized their loyalties and prejudices to gain authority over priests and trustees alike.

84. E.g., see chapter 26.

Thus, it may indeed be significant that Bernard M'Kenna asked the city's humble Irish shopkeepers to execute his will and guard his daughters' faith. For it was the religious devotion and deference of Irish-Americans of that class, and lower, that in a few decades would enable bishops such as New York's John Hughes to discipline the clergy and suppress the trustees—and, ironically, in the process expunge from their church the radical republicanism that had once animated M'Kenna and the United Irishmen in mid-Ulster.[85]

85. On these themes, see also chapters 13, 26, and 63, as well as 44. Bishop John Joseph Hughes (1797–1864): born in M'Kenna's Co. Tyrone, Hughes emigrated to the United States in 1817 and was educated for the priesthood in Emmitsburg, Md. In early 1838 he was appointed coadjutor to the bishop of New York; in 1842 he became bishop and remained so until his death. Hughes staunchly defended his largely Irish flock against nativism, but one of his first actions as coadjutor was to suppress the wealthy Irish trustees of St. Patrick's cathedral, who were in rebellion against the French-born bishop John Dubois, partly on ethnic grounds. Although Anglophobic, Hughes was likewise indifferent or actively hostile to Irish and Irish-American nationalist movements (especially those led by radicals or Protestants), whose claims on immigrant loyalties competed, in his view, with those of the church. (On Hughes, also see chapter 44, n. 29.)

VII ✳
Irish Immigrants in Politics and War

49 ✳

Rev. James McGregor and John McMurphy, 1720–1730

Since the early eighteenth century, Ulster Presbyterians' motives for emigration and the definition and political implications of their ethnic identities in both Ireland and America have been sharply contested issues. Between 1650 and 1776 merely 10 percent of Ulster emigrants settled in New England, yet their leaders and descendants contributed disproportionately to these controversies. Of the early combatants, few were as important as Rev. James McGregor and his followers who in 1719 settled what became the township of Londonderry, New Hampshire.

James McGregor was born in 1677, a son of Colonel David McGregor, near Magilligan Point in the parish of Tamlaghtard in northwest County Londonderry. According to tradition, James received at least part of his education in Europe, but he graduated from the University of Glasgow and had returned to Ulster by 1701, when he was ordained as Presbyterian minister of Aghadowey parish, on the banks of the lower Bann River, in northeast County Derry.[1] Reportedly tall and of commanding appearance, in 1706 McGregor married Marion Cargill of Aghadowey, by whom he had 10 children.[2] Although in 1704 the Synod of Ulster had sharply admonished McGregor for intemperance, in 1710 the Synod commissioned him to preach in Ulster Irish (then virtually interchangeable with Scots Gaelic) to additional congregations in counties Derry, Antrim, and Tyrone.[3]

McGregor was still pastor of Aghadowey in 1717 when he and several other clergymen in the Bann Valley determined to transport themselves and their flocks to New England, as encouraged by Samuel Shute (1662–1742), then royal governor of Massachusetts. Thus, in early 1718, at the nearby seaport of Coleraine, McGregor delivered a farewell sermon, charging that he and his people were fleeing Ireland "to avoid oppression and cruel bondage, to shun persecution and designed ruin, to withdraw from the communion

---

1. For demographic data on Aghadowey parish and its environs, see appendix 2.1g, on chapter 49.
2. McGregor's wife was the daughter of Captain David Cargill of Aghadowey. James and Marion McGregor had 10 children, seven of whom were still living when their father died in 1729; McGregor's third son, David (ca. 1710–1777), married Mary Body and, like his father, was a Presbyterian minister in Londonderry, New Hampshire.   **3.** In 1710 the Synod reaffirmed its late seventeenth-century initiatives to convert Irish Catholics to Presbyterianism; the Synod reported that the Bible, the Westminster Confession, and the Catechisms had been published in translation, and it appointed McGregor and several other clergymen to preach in the Irish language. In 1720 Synod records claimed that 27 of its 130 ministers could preach in Ireland's native language, but the crusade soon faltered—partly because disputes over clerical subscription to the Westminster Confession consumed the Synod in the 1720s, partly because of the severe economic distress and high emigration that plagued Ulster in that decade.

of idolators and to have an opportunity of worshipping God according to the dictates of conscience and the rules of His inspired Word."[4]

McGregor's sermon set the tone for all subsequent popular, and some scholarly, interpretations of Ulster emigration as a communal exodus from "Egyptian bondage." However, Irish magistrates and Anglican clergymen dismissed Presbyterian claims of religious and political persecution as mere pretenses, arguing that their real reasons for emigration were economic. Certainly, economic concerns were crucial in stimulating this first great wave of Ulster emigration. In 1717–1720 crop failures sent provision prices soaring; smallpox and livestock diseases were epidemic; and rents increased sharply on the Clothworkers' and Mercers' estates, which included Aghadowey and adjacent parishes. These calamities afflicted Presbyterian tenants, cottage weavers, and clergymen alike, as by 1718 McGregor's own salary from his congregation was three years—over £80—in arrears.

Yet McGregor's and similar sermons were not entirely disingenuous. Not only was it customary for Ulster Presbyterians to interpret historical developments in eschatological terms, but in the early eighteenth century their longstanding conflicts with Irish Anglican officials and clergymen were particularly intense. In the 1690s the great Scottish migrations to Ulster had only heightened Irish Anglicans' traditional fears and prejudices, and by the early 1700s some contended that "the Scottish Ulster presbyterian[s]" were "a more knavish, wicked, thievish race than even the natural Irish of the other three provinces."[5] To be sure, by 1717–1718 the brief period of severe persecution during Queen's Anne's reign (1702–1714) had already ended, but Presbyterians remained bitterly aggrieved by the Irish results of a Glorious Revolution that had returned to power an Anglican establishment that questioned their loyalty to the crown, belittled their heroic sacrifices at the siege of Derry (1690), and in 1704 imposed a Sacramental Test Act that excluded Presbyterians and other dissenters from all civil and military offices, including membership of town corporations, grand juries, and the local magistracy. In addition, Presbyterians were harrassed by Church of Ireland ministers' demands for tithes and by their refusal to license non-Anglican schoolmasters or to recognize the validity of marriages performed by dissenting clergymen. Many affluent or ambitious Presbyterians converted to the established church to escape the Test Act's penalties, but emigration was another option for those suffering as well from economic distress. Thus, it was not illogical for McGregor to interpret his flock's departure in political terms, and his sermon was not only an act of self-exculpation but also a warning to Anglican officials in Dublin and London that northern Ireland might lose its Presbyterian garrison to emigration if Test Act was not repealed. In fact, the Act was suspended in 1719, a year after McGregor's company arrived at Boston, but Presbyterians remained subject to tithes and other disabilities.

McGregor may also have calculated his words to appeal to the sympathies of New England's Congregationalists—to their own memories of past persecutions at Anglican

---

4. Dickson, *Ulster Emigration*, p. 26. 5. Hayton, "Anglo-Irish Attitudes," 152; see Sources.

hands. If so, he must have been disappointed, for the approximately eight hundred to one thousand Ulster immigrants who landed at Boston in the summer of 1718 met a hostile reception from New Englanders who feared that ships from Ireland brought only famine, disease, paupers, and "papists." However, in late October McGregor successfully petitioned Governor Shute for a grant of land on the frontier of Maine, Massachusetts' northeastern province, and although McGregor himself first settled nearer Boston at Dracut, his brother-in-law, James McKeen,[6] and about three hundred of the immigrants went to Maine and spent the winter of 1718–1719 starving and shivering at Casco Bay. In the spring McKeen's family, with 16 to 19 others, abandoned Maine and sailed south to the Merrimack and up the river to Haverhill, Massachusetts, where they disembarked and traveled overland 20 miles northwest to an unsettled tract, called Nutfield for its abundance of chesnut, butternut, and walnut trees. On 12 April McGregor joined them, preached a memorable sermon describing their new home as "a great rock in a weary land" (Isaiah 32.2), and agreed to be pastor and effective leader of the first major and almost exclusively Ulster-Presbyterian settlement in the New World.

Unfortunately, however, Nutfield was in an area disputed by the governments of Massachusetts and New Hampshire, and although Shute was royal governor of both provinces, rival groups of proprietors and speculators, backed by their respective legislatures in Boston and Portsmouth, jealously contested ownership of the upper Merrimack Valley. Furthermore, both Shute and Massachusetts legislators were angry that the Ulstermen had left Casco Bay, and so in June 1719, when MacGregor and McKeen petitioned Boston for a land grant on the Merrimack, they were refused on the grounds that Nutfield was part of the territory belonging to Haverhill's proprietors. Consequently, in October the Nutfield settlers sent a similar petition to the General Court of New Hampshire. New Hampshire's lieutenant governor, John Wentworth (1672–1730), although Shute's nominal subordinate, was more sympathetic to the Nutfield colonists, perhaps because of his own family's Irish connections or because his son-in-law, Archibald Macpheadris (d. 1729), was both an Ulsterman and the richest merchant in Portsmouth, but more certainly because western settlements would increase New Hampshire's trade and population, create a barrier against Indian incursions, and, most important, strengthen his colony's claims to the upper Merrimack Valley.

In addition, while their petition to Portsmouth was pending Governor Shute's ultimate approval, McGregor and McKeen fortified their claim to Nutfield by purchasing from Colonel John Wheelright of Wells, Maine, the old deed to the area that Wheelright's grandfather had purportedly bought from the Indians in 1629. Despite this move, however,

---

6. James McKeen (1665–1756): of Ballymoney, Co. Antrim; according to family tradition, McKeen (like McGregor) took part in the siege of Derry; the reputed "patriarch" of the Londonderry, New Hampshire, settlement, McKeen served as moderator of its town meeting in 1719, 1729, and 1731 and its representative to the provincial legislature in 1727–1728.; his second wife was Annis Cargil (d. 1782), sister of Rev. McGregor's spouse.

during the winter of 1719–1720 the Nutfield settlers were harrassed, both legally and violently, by rival claimants from Haverhill and Boston, who alleged that the Ulstermen were not only illegal squatters but also "poor Irish," "not wholesome inhabitants," and, most damning of all, Roman Catholics. This was the context of the following "Humble Apology of the People of Nutfeild" that McGregor wrote and sent to Shute in late February 1720.

Petition 1.
Rev. James McGregor, Nutfield, New Hampshire,
to Governor Samuel Shute, Boston, Massachusetts, 27 February 1720

The Humble Apolegy of the People of Nutfeild to His Exelency Sam[ll] Shute Generall Govern[r]. and Commander in Cheife of his Majesties Provinces of the Massachusetts Bay and New Hampsh[r] in New England——[7]

May it Please Y[r] Exelency

The Subscribers having Seen a copy of Y[r] Exelencys Lett[r]. To Cap[t]: White & Cap[t]: Kembell, find themselves und[r]. a Nessessity of Vindicating themselves from the Charges given in against them; it being alowable by the Law of Nature & of Nations, to y[e] greatest Criminalls to Defend them selves when they Justly plead in their Own Vindication. We were Surprised to hear our Selves termed Irish People when we So frequently ventured our all for the Brittish Crown and Liberties against the Irish papists & gave all tests of our Loyalty w[ch] the Government of Ireland Required and are always ready to do the Same here w[n] demanded. Tho we Settled att Nutfeild yett we Used no Violence in the man[r]. of our Settlement, Seing no body in the Least offered to hinder us to Sett down in a desolate Wilderness; and we were So fare from hindering the English that Really had a mind to Plant[8] wth. us, that, many of them are now incorporated wth. us.   after our Settlement we found that two or three Different parties Claimed Nutfeild, by virtue of Indian deeds, and we were Given to understand, that it was Nessesary for us to hold the Soil by Some Right purchased from the Natives   accordingly we made applycation to the Hon[ble]. Co[ll]. Wheelwright of Wells, and Obtained his Indian right; w[ch] we have to Shew,[9] his Deed being of Ninety Years Standing, and Conveyed from the Cheife Sagamores[10] between the Rivers of Merimack and Piscattaqua, wth the Consent of the whole Tribe of the Indian Nation, and well Executed, is the most authentic we have Seen; and the Subscribers Could not in reason think that a deed w[ch] is not twenty years Old, of Land w[ch] is not Sufficiently butted and bounded,[11] from an Obscure Indian, Could Give any Right to Land w[ch]

---

7. Marginal notation in ms.: "A Copy of M[r]. M[c]gregor's lett[tr] to the Gov[r] [illegible] 1719."   8. **Plant**: settle, colonize (OED, s.v., 3.b; obsolete).   9. **wch we have to Shew**: "which we have available to place in evidence."   10. **Sagamores**: sachems, supreme chiefs.   11. **butted and bounded**: a legal cliché meaning "marked out."

had been Sold So many years before, by the Right owners. And the Subscribers hope they will be Excused, from Giving away So Good a Title, for Others that cannot pretend Rationally to be So well Supported; and wch they always refused to Warrantee and make Good, agst other Claimes. The Dutifull Applications wch we have made to both Courts, If we be inCorporated, in whatSoEver Province we fall[12] to be, will Witness for our respect to his Majesty's gov^{rmt}. If Affidavits have been Given agst one of our Number as useing Some threttning Expressions, we hope it will not be Imputed to the Community. If our accusers be permitted to Come up in troops, as they have done, and violently demolish'd one of our houses, and destroyed part of our hay, and threttned and Insulted us wth impunity, to the Great terror of our wives and Children, when we Suffered patiently, and then accuse us to our Rulers of violence, Injustice, fraud, force, insolence, Cruelty, dishonour of his Majesties Govern^t, & disturbance of his Majesties Subjects, injuries, and Offences to the English, and the like, when[13] we know our Selves to be Innocent, we think it hard measure; and must have Recourse to God, who forbideth to take up a bad report agst our Neighbour, and will, we hope, bring forth our Righteousness as the Light, and our Judgment as the Noon day. If we be Guilty of these disorders, we know we are Liable to a Legall Tryall and are not So weak as to Suppose our Selves to be out of the reach of Your Exelencys Government. The Subsscribers hope that If any other accusations come in agst them they will be allowed an Equall hearing before they be condemned; and as we Enjoy the liberty of the Gospell here, wch is So Great a mercy <we> Shall Improve it,[14] for Gods Glory; and as he has taught us be Dutifull to his Majesties Govern^t, Sett over us, and If possible live peaceably wth all men, Shall be Desierous of Peaceable Neighbours, that want to Settle wth us, and to help us to Subdue a part of this vast and uncultivated Wilderness; and we Shall not Cease[15] to pray for the Divine blessing on Y^r Exelency's person and Gov^t.

Done at Nutfield   Feb: 27: 1719/20 & Subscribed by——

James McGregore &c

McGregor's petition may have had its intended effect, for in April 1720 Governor Shute authorized Nutfield's inhabitants to choose their own officials. Moreover, in June 1722, at Wentworth's urging, the New Hampshire government gave the settlers full incorporation, with a grant of land 10 miles square, for a "town"[16] whose inhabitants, a

12. fall: happen, chance.   13. when: conjectural; ms. blurred.   14. Improve it: turn it to (spiritual) profit.   15. we Shall not Cease . . . : standard formula for closing a petition.   16. Eighteenth-century Londonderry was denominated a "town" according to New England usage but was never one in the usual sense of the word. Unlike the colonial capital, Portsmouth, Londonderry had no urban center and, although it contained storekeepers, millers, and other full- or part-time craftsmen, it was an overwhelmingly rural community dominated by farm families. Hence it was analogous to what elsewhere was usually called a township, e.g., Paxton or Donegal in Pennsylvania.

year later, officially renamed it Londonderry. Meanwhile, the settlement had grown rapidly—to 360 inhabitants by April 1721—as many of the 1718–1719 Ulster immigrants, who had initially settled elsewhere, plus newcomers directly from northern Ireland, converged on the upper Merrimack Valley, attracted by the free lands, Presbyterian worship, and refuge from Puritan prejudice that Nutfield-Londonderry offered. However, Londonderry's conflicts with Haverhill and Boston were just beginning, as the settlement now became the focal point of an intense political struggle between Massachusetts and New Hampshire for ownership of the region. The result was a boundary war, spearheaded by the proprietors of Haverhill, that assumed a variety of forms: endless petitions, arrests and trials for trespassing, seizures of property for nonpayment of taxes to Bay Colony authorities, destruction of crops and farm buildings, and physical assaults. On 5 March 1729, Rev. McGregor died in the midst of the strife, but in a town meeting held on 15 December 1729, Londonderry's inhabitants voted to send James McKeen, town moderator, and John McMurphy[17] to Portsmouth, to petition the New Hampshire government concerning "our Grivances with respect to Law Shuits that arises from our neighbouring town (viz) Heverhill." The following petition, probably written by McMurphy as town clerk, was in turn probably forwarded to London by Wentworth, as part of his own strategy to persuade the Crown to recognize his colony's title to the disputed area.

Petition 2.
John McMurphy, Town Clerk, and "the Rest of ye Proprietors of Londonderry," New Hampshire, to Lieutenant Governor John Wentworth, Portsmouth, New Hampshire, 17 March 1730

Honb^le S^r

You having been So kinde as to Prefere the Petition which Sund^ry the Inhabitants of this Town in behalf of the Rest Sent you in order to be Laid before His Majes^ty and Are Still so good as to offer us your Friendship and Assistance to help us out of the Difficulty we now are Under with respect to the Line between the Town of Haverhill & this Town of Londonderry—And that we make your Hon^r Sensable of the Hardships & Difficultys we have been in and Still Labour under we beg leave to make you this short Narrative

At our first Arrivall in New Engl^d altho we came in Severall Vessells & Landed in Various parte's of this Country yet as soon as we had surmounted the difficulties of Our passages which were many & great we Assembled ourselves & petitioned the Govr & Councill of New Hamp^r for a Tract of Land Lying to the North West of Haverhill which Town of Haverill is govern'd by the Massachusetts Governm^t and after

---

17. John McMurphy (ca. 1682–1753); Londonderry town clerk in 1721–1736 and member of the New Hampshire colonial legislature in 1732–1733 and 1746–1753.

the consideration of Gov[r] Shute then Gov[r] of Both New Hamp[r] and the Massachusetts he & the Councill there granted us a Township of Ten Miles Square at the afores[d] Place upon which we run out our Town Bounds & Laid out our first Divisions & with great Expense and Danger being in the Time of the Indian war   we cleared great parte of our s[d] first divition & had Enjoyed the Same for Seven years & Laid out all our substance by building & Improving thereon before Haverhill Town clamed the Same   Yet soit is[18] that the Inhabitants of s[d] Haverhill made great Inroads upon us & Dayly are carrying our people from their Houses & Labour, Cross[19] the river Marrimack to Courtes farr distant in that Gov[t] & Imprison Judge & Load them with Excessive Charges which besides the Loss of Improvement hath Cost many hundred Pounds, & are dayly perpetrating the Same things   We could bear the many scandalous & unjust reflections[20] which they cast upon us by saying we are romans & not good Subjects to his present Majesty being well assured your Hon[r] well knows to the Contrary haveing many of us Resolutely opposed both while in our own Country   Wittness the Trubles in Ireland at the Comeing in of King William of Blessed memory, our Present Minister & Severall of our People being at the Seige of Derry & had no small shear[21] in that Glorious Defence of Our religion & Country   now S[r] all that we ask y[r] Assistance in is that you would Use your Intrest[22] Some how or other to obtain Peace for us that once at Length[23] we may Enjoy the only thing we have Sought Since we came here which we Imagine can be don No Other way than by geting the Line Settled between the two Governm[ts] of the Massachusetts and New Hamp[r]

Dated at Londonderry March y[e] 17th 1729/30

James McKeen[24]	John Macmurphy Clerk
James Reid	John Barnat
David Morison	John Archbald
William Cochran	James Nesmith
James Leslie	John Gregg
Matthew Reed	James Moor
John Richay	Abraham Holms

In the name of the Rest of y[e] Proprietors of Londonderry

---

18. **Yet soit is**: "nonetheless it is a fact." 19. **Cross**: i.e., across. 20. **reflections**: imputations, reproofs. 21. **shear**: i.e., share. 22. **Intrest**: influence. 23. **at Length**: finally, at last. 24. On **James McKeen** and **John McMurphy**, see ns. 6 and 17. **James Reid** (or Reed; 1695–1755), one of the first settlers of Londonderry, N.H.; born in Scotland and reportedly a University of Edinburgh graduate; served as one of Londonderry's selectman in 1728–1732; probably a kinsman of **Matthew Reed**. **David Morison**: probably a son of John Morrison (ca. 1679–1776), an original Londonderry settler, who ca. 1759 moved to Peterborough, N.H., one of Londonderry's "colonies." **William Cochran**: an original settler; brother-in-law to James McKeen by the latter's first wife, Janet. **James Leslie**: probably James Lindsey, an original Londonderry, N.H., proprietor and a selectman in 1722 and 1728–1732. **John Richay** (Richey): also an original proprietor. **John Barnat** (Barnett): an original proprietor and a selectman in 1741–1743. **John Archbald** (Archibald): an original proprietor and

In 1740 London finally confirmed New Hampshire's ownership of the upper Merrimack Valley, separated its executive from that of Massachusetts, and appointed John Wentworth's son, Benning (1681–1770), as royal governor. Meanwhile, despite the troubles with Haverhill, Londonderry had flourished. By 1740 it was the second-largest settlement in the province, and by 1767 it had 2,389 inhabitants, and its overflowing population, augmented by modest but steady immigration from Ulster as well as by natural growth, had spawned a host of other communities in the Merrimack and Connecticut valleys. Although Londonderry's farms produced goods primarily for local exchange and consumption, as in Ulster its townspeople also developed a regionally unique and thriving industry in the household manufacture of linen yarn and cloth that were marketed throughout New England.

After the Revolution, new Ulster immigration to New Hampshire virtually ceased, and by the late 1700s superficial observers sometimes claimed, albeit wrongly, that save for unusual emphases on flax cultivation and linen production, there was little to distinguish the farmers of Londonderry and its satelite towns from northern New England's Congregationalists. However, in the early and mid-1800s the descendants of New Hampshire's Ulster Presbyterian settlers formally emerged as a distinct ethnic group, particularly in a series of centennial celebrations and authorized town histories whose orators and authors, usually clergymen, staked their ancestors' claims to "founding father" status. Most important, they argued vehemently that their forbears had not been "Irish"—although that had been the term most commonly applied to, and acknowledged by, Ulster Presbyterians in the late eighteenth century in America. Instead, their eulogists contended, the founders of Londonderry and other Ulster Presbyterian immigrants had been members of the "Scotch-Irish race," a group distinct in its Scottish origins and Protestant faith and, consequently, superior in its habits and morals to the "native Irish" Catholics against whom their ancestors had fought so valiantly in Ireland during the times of Cromwell and of William of Orange.

Since then, the controversy between the celebrants and the critics of what the latter sometimes called "the Scotch-Irish myth" has been unceasing and often acrimonious. Of importance here is the fact that "Scotch-Irish" spokesmen such as Rev. Edward L. Parker, the author of Londonderry's first town history, almost invariably buttressed their arguments by drawing on early statements such as those in the foregoing petitions, particularly on

a selectman in 1728–1733. **James Nesmith**; son-in-law of James McKeen, whom he accompanied from Ulster to New Hampshire in 1718; was Londonderry town moderator in 1730; one of his Irish-born sons, James, Jr. (1718–1815), fought at Bunker Hill in 1775. **John Gregg**: in 1718, aged about 16, he emigrated from Ulster with his Scottish-born father, Capt. James Gregg (b. 1690), another of James McKeen's brothers-in-law, who moderated the Londonderry town meeting in 1722, was a selectman in 1719–1722 and 1733–1734, and sat in the colonial legislature in 1736; John Gregg was also a selectman in 1734–1736, and he and his father were among Londonderry's wealthiest inhabitants. **James Moor**: an original Londonderry proprietor. **Abraham Holms** (Holmes; d. 1753): emigrated from Ulster in 1719 and soon after joined the Londonderry settlement where he became an elder in the Presbyterian church.

Rev. James McGregor's strenuous objection to the application of the label "Irish" to his people. Hence an analysis of the precise content and context of these petitions may be useful.

It is important to note that neither McGregor nor McMurphy identified their countrymen as "Scotch-Irish." Indeed, the petitioners essayed no positive ethnic identifications at all but focused on statements of what their people were *not*, thus illustrating a degree of uncertainty or fluidity in eighteenth-century ethnic identity that later generations, in an era of nationalist fervor, would find unacceptable. There were several specific reasons why McGregor, in his 1720 message to Boston, took pains to deny that his parishioners were "Irish." Of course, he desired to draw a sharp distinction between the Nutfield settlers and the native Irish, a few of whom had already come to New England as poor indentured servants and who were associated with a Catholicism that was abhorred ideologically and feared practically—especially in the danger it posed from French Quebec—throughout England's colonies. However, even McGregor's supporters in the New Hampshire government referred favorably to his flock as "a company of Irish at Nutfield," so it was already clear that disinterested or sympathetic observers would *not* confuse Irish Presbyterian and Catholic immigrants. Thus, there may have been additional reasons for McGregor's statements.

First was the fact that many, perhaps most, of McGregor's followers had migrated from Scotland to Ulster only during the reigns of James II (1685–1688) and William III (1688–1702), and in the Bann Valley "they had kept together in church relations, as well as in residence, more closely than most of the Scotch settlers"[25] in northern Ireland. Hence it would be natural if they had little identification with Ireland, even as a place, when they remigrated to New England scarcely 20 or 30 years later. In length of residence, then, the Nutfield colonists were certainly far less "Irish" than those Protestants whose ancestors had come to Ireland during the Ulster Plantation, the Cromwellian era, or even the reign of Charles II. Likewise, their identification with Ireland as homeland was far less secure than for the great majority of Ulster Presbyterians who would emigrate to America in the middle and later decades of the eighteenth century—three, four, or more generations after their ancestors had left Scotland.

Ironically, at least for the families that initially settled Nutfield, one of the truly "Irish" characteristics of their colony was its eventual name, Londonderry. Indeed, one wonders why, if the first settlers wished to clearly distinguish themselves as non-Irish, they did not name their community, say, "Argyle" or "Ayrshire," after their most common Scottish places of origin, or "Glasgow" in honor of Scottish Presbyterianism's ecclesiastical and educational center. Or why they did not name their settlement after one of the communities in the Bann Valley, whence most of them emigrated to the New World? The traditional explanation is that Nutfield's settlers naturally renamed their township to com-

25. Rev. A. L. Perry, *Scotch-Irish in New England* (Boston, 1891), 21.

memorate the walled Irish city in which so many of them had fought and suffered during the long, brutal siege of 1690. Allegedly, Rev. McGregor himself had fought on Derry's walls, although but a boy of 12 years old, and others supposedly had done so as well. To be sure, if all the Ulster immigrants who claimed they or their fathers held Derry for King William were credited, that city's walls would have needed to encompass a vast area. Yet there is no doubt that the siege of Derry had already assumed mythic proportions and become a symbol with which all Ulster Presbyterians wished to associate—perhaps especially in view of Irish Anglicans' denial of their prominence in the city's defense. However, given Londonderry's totemic significance, why did Nutfield's first colonists not rename their community at once, rather than four years after the initial settlement and a year after its incorporation?

There may have been some very pragmatic reasons for McGregor's and his people's choice of name and perhaps also for their precise timing. As McGregor probably—and Lieutenant Governor Wentworth certainly—were aware (and as Boston and London authorities were not), the Nutfield settlers' hold on their New Hampshire lands was extremely tenuous, not only because of Haverhill's competing claims but because the old 1629 Wheelright patent that McGregor's followers purchased in 1719, and that he defended in his 1720 petition, was a forgery, cleverly executed only a dozen or so years earlier by Portsmouth politicians. Hence, to reinforce their shaky title, Nutfield's leaders promulgated what became the traditional (albeit fallacious) explanation of their grant—namely, that it (or comparable lands elsewhere in America) had been a "free gift of King William," promised to the "faithful champions of his throne in the siege and defense of Londonderry."[26] Thus, the renaming of Nutfield not only symbolized its inhabitants' loyal Protestantism but also implied and justified an "ancient" title to their new possessions. The name "Londonderry" signified a northern fortress, not only against the Catholic French and their Indian allies above, but also against counterclaims from the men of Haverhill and Boston below, as even after its incorporation in 1722, the new community remained as besieged by "outsiders" as its settlers had formerly been threatened—first by rebellious Catholics and then by contemptuous Anglicans—in Ulster itself.

It may also be significant that, in his early petition from "Nutfield," Rev. McGregor did *not* specifically evoke the siege of Derry or "King William of Blessed memory." Not until after the township's rechristening, McGregor's death in 1629, and his replacement as Londonderry's parson by the 76-year-old Rev. Matthew Clarke (1659–1735),[27] a recent arrival whose scarred face clearly demonstrated *his* military service on Derry's walls, did those themes emerge and become prominent, as in John McMurphy's petition of 1730. Likewise, it may be illuminating that McMurphy did not repeat McGregor's denial that

---

26. Ibid., 23.   27. Rev. Matthew Clarke (1659–1735): Presbyterian minister of Boveedy, in Kilrea parish, Co. Derry, prior to his emigration in 1729; despite his advanced age, in January 1733 Clarke married Rev. James McGregor's widow.

the Nutfield-Londonderry settlers were "Irish." (Indeed, one wonders whether the date of McMurphy's petition, St. Patrick's Day, was merely an ironic coincidence.) Instead, he said only that they were not "romans," apparently assuming that the distinction between "Irish" Protestants and Catholics would be clearly understood. In his tactical shift, McMurphy may have presumed for his intended audience a greater sophistication than had McGregor, or the change may have reflected the sentiments of later settlers whose families had lived for generations in Ulster and who therefore regarded themselves as "Irish" at least in geographical origin.

Nevertheless, the religious distinction and political loyalism that McMurphy emphasized were crucial, and not only because of the virulent anti-Catholicism prevailing in the colonies but for another reason peculiar to Londonderry. During all the French and Indian wars that ravaged the northern frontiers from 1722 to 1760, Londonderry was never attacked, allegedly—as the townspeople believed—because McGregor and the Marquis de Vaudreuil, governor of Quebec in the 1720s, had been schoolmates and friends in the Netherlands and maintained a cordial correspondence in America, and so the marquis persuaded the Jesuits in Canada "to charge the Indians not to injure" McGregor's people, "as they were different from the English."[28] If true (and Vaudreuil's address was purportedly discovered in McGregor's papers after his death), this was a remarkable and fortuitous circumstance for Londonderry's inhabitants. However, it was also a coincidence that, if widely known outside the community, would have provoked intense suspicion and hostility at a time when Anglo-American colonists, and especially New England Congregationalists, regularly confused or conflated Protestant and Catholic immigrants from Ireland and often charged that "Irish papist" traders in the backcountry were inciting the Indians to war "in the French Interest."

Yet it is equally revealing that neither McGregor nor McMurphy described their people as "Scotch-Irish," for that term's origins and associations—both in the British Isles and in America—were highly problematic. From the late 1500s through at least the mid-1600s, apparently its most common British and Irish usage was pejorative, as both Irish Anglicans and Lowland Scots Presbyterians labeled as "Scotch-Irish" the Catholic, Gaelic-speaking McDonnells and other Highlanders who migrated back and forth between Argyll and the Western Isles and the coasts and glens of north Antrim, causing political and military problems for Protestant officials in Edinburgh and Dublin alike. By contrast, Scots Presbyterian settlers in Ireland were then and well into the early 1700s most commonly described as "Ulster-" or "northern Scots," as the "Scottish Interest" or "Nation" in Ireland, or occasionally as "British"—not in the later, inclusive sense, but to distinguish them from the "English."

To be sure, a few of the Ulster Presbyterian students at the universities of Glasgow and Edinburgh were officially registered, individually, as "Scottus Hibernicus," and some

28. Perry, *Scotch-Irish in New England*, 24.

scholars have argued that this was the origin of the modern term "Scotch-Irish" with its exclusively Protestant and positive connotations. In fact, however, Scottish university officials, faculty, and local magistrates almost invariably referred to such students as "Irish"—and often linked their "Irishness" to negative attributes (stupidity, drunkenness, insubordination) traditionally associated with their "papist" countrymen.[29] Moreover, by the mid-1700s Presbyterian spokesmen in Ulster itself were referring increasingly to their people as "Irish"—a development that reflected longer residence in Ireland, feelings of greater security from Catholic rebellion, and, as among Irish Anglicans, a growing "national" identification with the economic and political interests of "Ireland" versus "England."[30]

Spurring the latter development was the steady divergence between Scottish and Ulster-Presbyterian political conditions that had begun subsequent to the Glorious Revolution and widened after the Act of Union between England and Scotland. In Scotland after 1690 Presbyterianism was the legally established religion, and after the Union of 1707 the upper and middling ranks of Scottish Lowlands society rushed to seize the economic benefits of full membership in the Empire, strove to emulate the alleged superiority of English "civilization," and gloried in a new "North British" identity that obscured the realities of English contempt and their country's economic and political subordination to its larger, wealthier, and more powerful partner. By contrast, Ireland's Presbyterians bitterly resented their legally inferior status; ignored politically by their coreligionists in Scotland (and unable, for religious reasons, to sympathize with Catholic-Jacobite opponents to the new Scottish establishment), many became increasingly receptive to the rhetoric of Dublin's "patriot" politicians who promoted a vague but inclusively "Irish" or, at least, "Irish Protestant" nationalism that subsumed denominational differences and promised economic and political reforms. Consequently—and despite continuous traffic in trade, migrants, and university students between northern Ireland and Scotland—Ulster Presbyterians' political interests and identities were increasingly oriented to Ireland's capital city rather than to Glasgow, Edinburgh, or London. Thus, although in the eighteenth century Scottish and Ulster Presbyterians shared similar political *cultures*—based heavily, for example, on the works of the Ulster-born Francis Hutcheson, the "father of the Scottish Enlightenment"[31]—the very different contexts in which the political ideas of Scottish and Ulster Presbyterians operated determined equally different applications and conclusions.[32]

In America, during the eighteenth century Ulster Presbyterian identities appear to have developed along lines somewhat parallel to those in Ireland. From the early 1700s

---

29. Indeed, professor Thomas Reid, Scotland's famous "common sense" philosopher, scorned the Ulster Presbyterian students at his Glasgow University as "stupid Irish teagues!" I. McBride, "The School of Virtue: Francis Hutcheson, Irish Presbyterians and the Scottish Enlightenment," in Boyce et al., *Political Thought*, 89; see Sources.   **30.** On the development of "Irish" identification and nationalism among members of the Church of Ireland in the early eighteenth-century, see chapter 8.   **31.** See chapters 52 and 55.   **32.** All this began to change, of course, after 1800, when the Act of Union between Ireland and Great Britain dramatically reconfigured the political context.

Anglo-American colonists normally described all Ulster immigrants as "Irish"—as New Hampshire officials so labeled the Londonderry settlers. By contrast, the term "Scotch-Irish" was relatively rare and often had profoundly negative associations. Thus, in 1767 Rev. Charles Woodmason, an Anglican (and perhaps Irish-born) missionary described backcountry South Carolina's inhabitants as "a Sett of the most lowest vilest Crew breathing—Scotch-Irish Presbyterians from the North of Ireland," and during the Revolution the American general Charles Lee condemned the people of the Shenandoah Valley as "a Banditti of Scotch-Irish Servants or their immediate descendants."[33]

By contrast, to be "Irish" in a broad, ecumenical sense was meanwhile becoming useful, even fashionable, among wealthy or ambitious Ulster Presbyterians and other immigrants from Ireland. From at least the early mid-1700s, for example, many Ulster Presbyterian merchants and professionals in Boston, New York, Philadelphia, and other American seaports had joined with Anglican and even Catholic compatriots in celebrating St. Patrick's Day and in organizing specifically "Irish" (or "Hibernian") associations.[34] (Conversely, Scottish-born Presbyterians congregated separately in St. Andrew's societies.) Moreover, the American Revolution appears to have accelerated the tendencies of Ulster Presbyterian immigrants to embrace—and of Anglo-Americans to perceive—a generically inclusive "Irish" identity. Whether rebels or loyalists, both native and Irish Americans commonly viewed "Ireland's" proverbial discontent with English rule, now identified with the contemporary Protestant and genteelly led "Patriot" movement, as supportive of— even synonomous with—the American struggle for political freedom. Likewise, both associated (albeit not always accurately) the "Irish" in the United States with resistance to English rule, whereas by contrast Scottish immigrants were perceived generally (and more accurately) as loyal to the crown and, if merchants in America, as selfish and avaricious.[35] Thus, perhaps it was not surprising that, for several decades after the Revolution, the "Scotch-Irish" designation seems to have virtually disappeared from public print. Therefore, what *was* remarkable was that in the nineteenth century the term "Scotch-Irish" reappeared and soon became commonplace, and in the eyes of most Protestant native and Ulster-born Americans, it now enjoyed associations that were much more unambiguously favorable than in previous centuries.

For American scholars, "Scotch-Irish" *could* be a useful label, reflecting valid distinctions among immigrants (and their descendants) who were Ulster Presbyterians of Scottish ancestry, Irish Protestants of other faiths and origins, and finally, Irish Catholics of varying backgrounds. During the nineteenth century, however, in its popular usage the term soon broadened to embrace all Irish Protestant immigrants—as well as all Americans of Irish descent who, regardless of their ethnoreligious antecedents, were not Catholic at the mo-

---

33. Hooker, *Carolina Backcountry*, 14; Hart, *Valley of Va.*, 109; see Sources. **34.** See chapter 58. **35.** E.g., see chapter 58. But for examples of Irish Protestant Toryism during the American Revolution, see chapters 51, 53, and 60.

ment of its application. Among Irish-American Catholics, moreover, the "Scotch-Irish" label rapidly became a source of grievance and resentment. In large part this was because the term allegedly reemerged from obscurity shortly before and especially during the Great Irish Famine of 1845–1852, when middle-class Americans of Ulster Presbyterian birth or background—their Protestant consciousness already heightened by religious revivalism—rushed to distinguish themselves as "Scotch-Irish" Protestants and hence as different from and superior to the overwhelmingly Catholic, impoverished, and often Irish-speaking Famine refugees, whose ragged appearance and proverbially boisterous and drunken behavior scandalized genteel American Protestants. Certainly this explanation has merit, perhaps especially in New England, where from the 1820s increasing numbers of poor Irish Catholics had disembarked at Boston or migrated south through northern New England, sometimes through Londonderry itself, from their initial landing places at Quebec or in the Maritime Provinces.

However, the term "Scotch-Irish"—with its modern, positive connotations and its strident reassertion of the traditional dichotomy between Ulster Presbyterians and the now once-more exclusively Catholic "Irish"—began to take shape much earlier, in the 1790–1820 period, long before Irish Catholic immigrants or their churches had become numerous or significant factors in American life. Hence it is likely that the new "Scotch-Irish" ethnicity had other origins—that initially it was generated not by an external threat (real or perceived) from Irish Catholic immigation but rather by Ulster-American Presbyterian society's internal dynamics and by its relationship to native America's socioeconomic, cultural, and political hierarchies. Specifically, it is arguable that modernized "Scotch-Irishness" was in large part the product of an *intra*communal contest for political and cultural hegemony, led in New England (and elsewhere) by Ulster-America's politically conservative clergy and "respectable" laymen. Significantly, that contest in America mirrored a parallel struggle in contemporary Ulster between Presbyterians who embraced and those who rejected the ultrademocratic and ecumenical ideals of the United Irishmen.

After the American Revolution, during the so-called Federalist Period, genteel Ulster-Americans were often eager for acceptance and influence in an Anglo-American "society" that in New England was dominated by wealthy merchants and Congregational ministers who were leading members of the Federalist party. To achieve their goals, however, ambitious Ulster-Americans needed and desired to expunge from their own communities both the radical political tendencies and the "backward" sociocultural traits that offended native-American—especially Federalist—sensibilities *and* that were embarrassingly similar to those traditionally associated with the Catholic "Irish."[36] Not coincidentally, it was the Anglo-American Federalist pamphleteer, Congregational minister, and future Harvard president Jeremy Belknap (1744–1798) who—by discovering and publishing Rev. McGregor's old petition in his *History of New Hampshire* (1784–1792)—first pointed the

---

36. See chapters 47, 62, and 67 for parallel developments in western Pennsylvania.

region's conservative Ulster-stock Presbyterians toward a "Scotch-Irish" resolution of their political and cultural dilemmas. The message was clear: if the latter wished to avoid association with those whom Anglo-American Federalists stigmatized as "wild Irish" Republicans, it was desirable, indeed essential, that Ulster Presbyterian Federalists should follow McGregor's precedent and identify themselves and their people as the very antithesis of the proverbially barbaric, rebellious, and drunken "Irish," portraying them instead as conservative, law-abiding, and temperate "Scotch-Irish."

The problem, however, was that ordinary Ulster Presbyterians in New England often behaved in ways that were, at least in Congregationalists' eyes, suspiciously "Irish." From the start, Londonderry's first settlers were not only in danger of being confused with Irish "papists" in league with the French and Indians, but—like their countrymen on the Maine frontier[37]—they were embroiled with Massachusetts' officials and leading families in sometimes violent conflicts over land titles. To be sure, the American Revolution had forged a brief political alliance between New England's Scots-Irish farmers and its Congregational élites, but afterward that disintegrated rapidly. Thus, whereas the region's Presbyterian clergy joined Anglo-American Federalists in espousing law and order, deference and hierarchy, many of their parishioners were vociferous in demanding greater democracy and fairer taxes. In the winter of 1786–1787, for example, the inhabitants of Pelham and other Scots-Irish settlements in western Massachusetts openly sympathized with Daniel Shays' rebellion against the Boston government. In 1787–1788 most Ulster Presbyterian farmers in Londonderry and elsewhere in New England's backcountry opposed ratification of the U.S. Constitution. In 1794, the year of the Whiskey Rebellion in western Pennsylvania, many of them staged their own protests against Hamilton's excise. Afterward, most enlisted in the Republican party, and by 1798 the Irish-born Republican congressman from Vermont, Matthew Lyon, a former indentured servant turned radical journalist, epitomized everything New England Federalists feared and hated about Jefferson's "wild Irish" adherents.[38] Meanwhile, the old conflict between Maine's Scots-Irish farmers and Bay State officials and land companies continued to rage—escalating in the early 1800s into riots and murder. And finally, in the 1820s most of New England's Scots-Irish were still voting for Republican candidates—and then in the 1830s for Jacksonian Democrats.

New England's Presbyterian clergy and genteel laymen also had reason to be alarmed by the apparent cultural similarities between the local Scots-Irish and Irish Catholic peasants. For example, given their recent origins in Argyll and other parts of western Scotland

---

37. See chapter 17. 38. Matthew Lyon (1749–1822): born in Co. Wicklow, probably of Catholic ancestry, Lyon was elected from Vermont to the U.S. House of Representatives in 1796 and 1798; a violent partisan, in 1797 he outraged opponents by spitting in the face of Roger Griswold, a Connecticut Federalist, during a congressional debate; in 1798 a Federalist judge sentenced Lyon to a $1,000 fine and four months imprisonment for articles deemed defamatory of President John Adams under the newly passed Sedition Act; in 1801, after casting his electoral vote for Thomas Jefferson, Lyon moved to Kentucky and in 1803–1811 served as one of its Republican Congressmen.

where Scots Gaelic was still commonly spoken, as well as Rev. McGregor's former minis-tery to Ulster's Irish-speaking Presbyterians, it is likely that many of Londonderry's first settlers were so linguistically alien from New England's Congregationalists as to provoke their suspicion and contempt. Moreover, well into the late eighteenth century the immi-grants' offspring—as well as more recent arrivals—still spoke Ulster Scots (the language of commoners in the Scottish Lowlands and the Ulster Presbyterian countryside) or at least English in a "broad Scotch" accent that many Yankees found almost unintelligible. Perhaps equally important, even in the late 1700s the inhabitants of Londonderry and other Ulster settlements remained notorious among their Anglo-American neighbors for their alleged uncleanliness, their aversion to bathing bodies or clothes, their indifference to the rudest sanitary facilities, and their slovenly farmsteads and outbuildings. In addition, they had a notorious reputation as heavy drinkers—initially of potato-based Irish whiskey or *poitín*, later of New England rum—and their marriage ceremonies, wakes, and funerals were proverbially sodden, boisterous affairs that scandalized polite contemporaries. Finally, by virtue of Londonderry's 1722 charter its farmers enjoyed a uniquely "Irish" institution, a semi-annual fair that, like Catholic Ireland's Donnybrook, had by the mid-1700s become infamous for its "scenes of vice and folly." Indeed, even the fair's dates were suspiciously akin to those of two ancient and pagan Celtic festivals.

Perhaps it was little wonder, then, that McGregor and McMurphy had been so defensive—especially the former, given his own record of intemperance. Or that one hun-dred years later Rev. Edward L. Parker and other early "Scotch-Irish" eulogists blamed what they described as their people's political or cultural abberations—as their temporary and misguided deviations from Scots-Protestants' inherent virtues of order and sobri-ety—on their ancestors' brief, contaminating exposure to Ulster's Catholics. Inadvertently, however, their argument revealed that modern "Scotch-Irish" ethnicity was rooted ulti-mately in neither ancestral origin nor even religion, but instead was based on relatively novel "middle-class" behavioral standards. Thus, the law-abiding and genteel "Scotch-Irish" that Parker and his peers invented and celebrated were the products of neither seventeenth-century Scotland nor eighteenth-century Ulster; nor were they representative of the great majority of Ulster Presbyterian immigrants and their descendants in America during the eighteenth and early nineteenth centuries. Rather, their new image reflected the hegemonic imperatives of an emergent Ulster-American bourgeoisie whose goals and ascendancy remained woefully incomplete even in the early 1800s.

Not coincidentally, perhaps, the local clergy's first attempt to tame Londonderry's fairs occurred in 1798, the year of the Federalists' Alien and Sedition Acts in America as well as the United Irishmen's rebellion in east Ulster. However, not until 1839, in the midst of a regionwide temperance crusade, would they finally suppress what had long been an integral expression of their ancestors' traditional culture. Yet between those dates the poems of Robert Dinsmoor (1756–1836), grandson and great-grandson of two of London-derry's first settlers, from Ballywattick, County Antrim, heralded the changes that commercialization, evangelicalism, and the urge for gentility eventually wrought among New England's Ulster Presbyterians. The few scholars who have studied New Hampshire's self-styled "Rustic Bard" have portrayed him as an American analogue to the "Rhyming Weavers" of late eighteenth- and early nineteenth-century Ulster. But although both Dinsmoor and contemporary east Ulster poets such as James Orr of Ballycarry (1770–1816) wrote many of their poems in the language employed by Scotland's more famous bard, Robert Burns (1759–1796), otherwise they were strikingly different.

Like Burns, many and perhaps most of the Rhyming Weavers were liberal or even skeptical in religion, radical in politics, and defiant of genteel conventions. Because they wrote in the vernacular shared by the common people of Lowland Scotland and Presbyterian Ulster, some scholars in Northern Ireland have claimed them as cultural markers of a unique "Ulster Scots" ethnic and political identity—regionally distinct and definitively non-"Irish" and thus the equivalent of "Scotch-Irish" in America. In fact, however, many of the Rhyming Weavers' compositions evince a strong, clear sense of Irish nationalism, and indeed more than a few of these plebeian poets were involved with the United Irishmen and the 1798 Rebellion. By contrast, and despite his humble persona, Dinsmoor was an orthodox Calvinist and a fiercely conservative Federalist for whom the French Revolution and Jeffersonian Republicanism, as well as Roman Catholicism, literally represented the many faces of the antichrist. Perhaps most significant, in his poems, many of them published in New England newspapers, Dinsmoor linked American religious and political conservatism to both his Presbyterian heritage and his Scottish ancestry. "The highest pedigree I plead," he wrote, is a "Yankee born" of "true Scottish breed."[39]

Thus, McGregor's and McMurphy's search in the early eighteenth century for a definition—and for Anglo-American recognition—of their followers' non-"Irish" identity was realized in New England, a century later, in part through the poetry, hagiography, and sermons of Ulster-stock Presbyterians such as Robert Dinsmoor and Rev. Edward L. Parker. Indeed, so successful were the latter's efforts, and those of their counterparts in Pennsylvania and elsewhere, that soon their people's ambiguous origins and embarrassing "Irish" interlude were all but forgotten in the subsequent scramble for a purportedly timeless and respectable "Scotch-Irish" ancestry that eventually nearly all non-Catholic Americans of Irish descent would eagerly claim.

---

39. R. Dinsmoor, *Incidental Poems* . . . , 13; see Sources. Thus, Dinsmoor's compositions played in New England a role similar to the poems of his Federalist and self-styled "Scotch-Irish" contemporary, David Bruce, in western Pennsylvania; see chapter 67.

Dr. Charles Carroll, 1748

Despite their equally superior educations, it is difficult to envisage immigrants from Ireland more different in background and culture than Rev. James McGregor and Dr. Charles Carroll—the former of ordinary Scots-Presbyterian planter stock, the latter a descendant of Ireland's dispossessed Gaelic-Catholic gentry. No doubt Carroll would have agreed with McGregor's insistence that the settlers of Londonderry, New Hampshire, were not "Irish." Yet in some respects the question of nationality among Ireland's Catholics in the late seventeenth and early eighteenth centuries was nearly as ambiguous as it was for the island's English and Scottish settlers. Catholics of Gaelic origins, like the O'Carroll (Ó Cearbhaill) family, still resented those of Norman descent, whereas the latter, like the Blakes of Galway,[1] still took great pride in the alleged superiority of their "Old English" ancestry. To be sure, for their Catholicism both were condemned as "Irish" by Ireland's new Protestant conquerors; but during the seventeenth century religion alone had been insufficient to unite the two groups effectively, and their rebellions had not aimed to restore or create an independent Irish "nation" but rather to uphold the Stuart kings and thereby, they mistakenly believed, to protect or recover their estates and privileges.

Moreover, even the relationship between Catholicism and "Irish" nationality was then more problematic than it would later become, as beginning in the 1690s leading Irish Protestants proclaimed their own "Irish" patriotism. Finally, even Catholic converts to Protestantism were often driven to apostasy less by desires to embrace a new identity than by sheer necessity—by the urge to maintain or regain a status that was inseparable from inherited "Irish" notions of the place and power that their "ancient" families had long enjoyed. Despite conversion, many ex-Catholics remained loyal to their former coreligionists. Others turned against them, as did Dr. Charles Carroll, the subject of this chapter. Yet even the latter can be perceived not only as villains but as victims of a long, distorting process of conquest and colonization—the effects of which were psychological as well as military, economic, and cultural.

For centuries Dr. Charles Carroll's family was centered in mid-Leinster, in the adjacent baronies of Clonlisk and Ballybritt in what was shired in 1557 as the King's County (now Offaly). Clonlisk and Ballybritt formed the ancient heart of Ely O'Carroll, nearly four hundred thousand acres of Gaelic-held land wedged between the territories of two powerful Norman families, the FitzGeralds of Kildare to the north and east and the Butlers of Ormond to the south in Tipperary.[2] Throughout the Middle Ages the O'Carroll chiefs

---

1. See chapter 16. **2.** In the 1400s and 1500s Ely O'Carroll included not only Clonlisk and Ballybritt but also Eliograrty and Ikerrin baronies in north Co. Tipperary—in all, ca. 379,000 acres (103,000 in King's Co.). For demographic data on Clonlisk and Ballybritt baronies and their environs, see appendix 2.2c, on chapter 50.

had maintained their position by playing their enemies against each other—and against rival branches of their own clan. In the sixteenth century the O'Carrolls still pursued the same course: after Henry VIII crushed the Kildare Fitzgeralds in the 1530s, O'Carroll chieftains allied themselves with Ireland's new Protestant government, earning a knighthood in the process, to protect their lordship against both internal and external threats. However, the O'Carrolls declined to abandon Catholicism, and by the early 1600s their strategy had clearly failed. In 1600 the last O'Carroll to exercise authority under traditional Gaelic law was murdered; in 1605 Ely O'Carroll, already much reduced in size, was annexed to the King's County; and in 1619 the area's plantation by English Protestants began. Rebellion in 1641 only accelerated the O'Carrolls' downfall, as the Cromwellian conquest resulted in a total confiscation, which the Restoration of Charles II in 1660 failed to redress and which their equally futile rebellion of 1688–1691, in aid of the Catholic King James II, only reconfirmed. By the century's end, most of the descendants of Ely O'Carroll's Gaelic chiefs were struggling tenant farmers or Dublin artisans. The more enterprising, however, emigrated to Europe or America, some to reestablish on the banks of the Chesapeake the family fortunes that had been shattered in the Slieve Bloom mountains of the Irish midlands.

Dr. Charles Carroll (the "O" lost with the lordship) was born in 1691, probably in Clonlisk, a year after the decisive Jacobite defeat at the Boyne River. Carroll's genealogy cannot be traced precisely, but according to family tradition his father (also Charles) was the last baron of Ely O'Carroll and his mother, Clare, was a daughter of the O'Conor Don of County Roscommon. The O'Conor Don was a direct descendant of Gaelic Ireland's last high king, but he was also a pragmatist who, despite his Catholicism, had managed to retain a small portion of his ancestral property and thereby perhaps helped finance his grandson's medical education. The Penal Laws, passed by the Irish Parliament in Carroll's youth, forbade "papists" to purchase land or practice law, and although the practice of medicine was not explicitly proscribed, all the institutions that provided medical training and licensing (Irish and British universities, colleges of physicians, and guilds of barber-surgeons) were closed to Catholics. Thus, Carroll either attained his education on the continent (as did his brother John, at Lille in the 1720s), in defiance of the statutes that prohibited Catholic schooling abroad, or at home as an apprentice to one of the few Catholic physicians who, through conversion or concealment, survived the penal era.[3]

Around 1715, after qualifying as a surgeon, Charles Carroll, aged about 24, emigrated to Maryland. There he sought opportunities denied him at home—not only because of his religion but because Ireland's medical profession, like England's, was so rigidly stratified. Even had Carroll been Protestant, for example, his qualifications as a mere surgeon would have earned him in Ireland an income and status far below those of physicians, who

3. In 1718 Patrick Kelly and other former or clandestine Catholic physicians were instrumental in establishing Ireland's first hospital, Dublin's Charitable Infirmary.

confined their ministrations to society's upper ranks and disdained to work with their hands. By contrast, in the colonies—where very few physicians emigrated—trained practitioners of any kind were rare and, unlike Ireland and Britain, surgeons and even lowly apothecaries were popularly titled "doctors."

Yet for Dr. Charles Carroll, Maryland's greatest attraction was no doubt its reputation as a haven for persecuted Catholics. Such had been the intention of George Calvert (1580–1632), the first Lord Baltimore, when he established the proprietary colony in 1632. In fact, however, by 1710 only about a fifth of Maryland's 35,000 white inhabitants were Catholics (primarily of English origin). Moreover, in 1689 a local Protestant rebellion had overthrown the proprietary government, excluded Catholics from political office, and legally established the Church of England; for the next quarter-century Maryland was a royal colony. However, the Calverts still retained their lands and quitrents, and propertied Catholics still voted and comprised a disproportionate number of Maryland's wealthiest planters. And by 1715 the wealthiest of them all was Dr. Carroll's older kinsman from King's County, Charles Carroll "the Settler" (1660–1720).[4]

Fervently loyal to Catholicism, the Stuart kings, and the Calvert family, the elder Carroll had emigrated to Maryland in early 1688, with an appointment from the third Lord Baltimore[5] as the colony's attorney general. Unfortunately, he arrived just before the Glorious Revolution drove the Catholic James II from the throne, completed the Carroll family's ruin in Ireland, and, a year later, resulted in the overthrow of the Catholic-Calvert ascendancy in Maryland itself. With the advent of Protestant rule, the Settler lost his political positions; however, he retained lucrative offices in the Calverts' personal establishment and, despite his outspoken hostility to the new government, by the early 1700s he had become Maryland's largest land- and slave-owner. With nearly 68,000 acres, as well as a host of proprietary offices and revenues at his disposal, the Settler was well placed to advance Dr. Carroll and other immigrant kinsmen.[6] Moreover, the timing of Dr. Carroll's arrival seemed especially propitious, for by 1715 political developments in London had convinced Maryland Catholics that the Calverts would soon regain control of the colony and restore the Settler and his friends to the political power they had lost in 1689.

However, the Settler's expectations were cruelly dashed. In 1715 the British government indeed restored Maryland to the proprietary family, but only after Benedict Leonard Calvert, eldest son of the elderly third Lord Baltimore, had defied his father by renouncing Catholicism and converting to the Church of England. By the end of that year both he and his father had died, but Benedict's son Charles (1669–1751), now the fifth Lord, also changed religions and proved equally ruthless. Eager to prove his own loyal Protestantism,

---

4. The precise family relationship between Dr. Charles Carroll and Charles Carroll the Settler is uncertain.
5. Charles Calvert (1637–1715).   6. In the late 1600s and early 1700s, the Settler promoted immigration to Maryland by "some hundreds" of Irish Catholics, mostly indentured servants but others members of his and related families. However, his importations helped provoke Maryland's Assembly to pass laws designed to "prevent the growth of popery."

Charles Calvert ignored the Settler's three decades of fidelity and dismissed him from all his proprietary offices. Worse, in 1718 the young lord allowed Maryland's Assembly to pass new laws that stripped the colony's Catholics of the franchise and forbade them to practice law or worship in public.

Despite these calamities, Dr. Charles Carroll prospered in his new home. The old Settler's patronage, albeit now sharply reduced, still proved invaluable in securing affluent clients and business connections. Thus, in 1718 Dr. Carroll made his first acquisition of land, some 2,400 acres, in partnership with the Settler's youngest son, Daniel Carroll of Duddington (1707–1734). A few years later, Dr. Carroll married Dorothy Blake (1702–1734), thus forging alliances not only with his wife's affluent Catholic family but also with the Lloyds, her wealthy Protestant kinsmen. Indeed, Carroll's marriage allied him with some two dozen past, present, and future members of the Maryland Assembly, including Daniel Dulany (1685–1753), an Irish-born Protestant who, by the early 1730s, had become the wealthiest and most politically influential man in the province.

About the time of his marriage, Carroll largely discarded medicine and began a spectacular career as a tobacco planter, land speculator, merchant, ship-builder, and manufacturer. In 1731 he founded the fabulously profitable Baltimore Ironworks, in partnership with Dulany and the Settler's two sons, Daniel and Charles Carroll of Annapolis (1707–1782). Dr. Carroll's mercantile concerns were equally successful, as his ships traded tobacco, grain, lumber, sugar, and wine with England, the West Indies, the Iberian Penninsula, and the Wine Islands. By the late 1740s he owned plantations in Anne Arundel County totaling over 3,000 acres, in addition to speculations in at least 15,000 acres in Baltimore and other counties.

Carroll's abandonment of medicine was not unusual, for British-trained doctors often found American practice frustrating. Until the 1760s the colonies lacked professional medical societies, schools, and licensing laws, and so the few educated physicians and surgeons were vastly outnumbered by—and much less popular than—part-time practitioners and folk healers whose treatments were often gentler and more successful than the former's "scientific" methods of "bleeding, vomiting, blistering, [and] purging."[7] Very probably, Carroll quickly realized that he had exchanged a rigidly stratified social system, in which his profession had high status but few openings, for a more fluid society where opportunities for medical practice were so unlimited that professional prestige—and chances to attain wealth thereby—were virtually nonexistent.

In Maryland as in Ireland, however, medicine was a career that a Catholic could pursue legally and usually without inciting much religious prejudice. By contrast, Dr. Carroll's avid pursuit of wealth in lands and trade made him more visible and hence more

7. Popular manuals such as *Every Man His Own Doctor* (1734), by the Virginian John Tennent, and John Wesley's *Primitive Physic* (1747) urged medical self-reliance to readers who rightly suspected, as one physician admitted, that "Practice in our Colonies, is so perniciously bad, that . . . [f]requently there is *more Danger* from the Physician, than from the Distemper." Quotations in text and note from W. J. Bell, Jr., *The Colonial Physician* . . . , 8; see Sources.

vulnerable to Protestant resentment. Of course, even after 1718 Maryland's penal laws were less draconian than Ireland's. In Maryland "papists" could own and inherit land without restrictions, and a handful of affluent Catholic families dominated a colonial élite that, between 1720 and 1770, grew ever wealthier as Maryland's population rose from 62,000 to 220,000 and as the Chesapeake's annual tobacco exports soared from 40 million to 100 million pounds. But Maryland's population increase through immigration was accompanied by a further decline in its proportion of Catholics—to merely 10 percent by 1770. More critically, until the American Revolution Maryland Catholics remained legally and politically powerless and hence subject to legislative or judicial harrassment by jealous or unscrupulous Protestants. During periods of unusual tension, as during the 1745 Jacobite Rebellion in Britain or in the French and Indian War of 1754–1763, anti-Catholic animosity became so virulent that some wealthy Catholics, such as Charles Carroll of Annapolis, planned to remove their families to French Louisiana.[8]

Thus, Protestant prejudice imperiled all the Carrolls' efforts to rebuild in Maryland the family fortunes wrecked in Ireland by conquest and confiscations. Although once again holding great wealth, the Carrolls were politically impotent to protect it, and, although fiercely proud of their ancient lineage, they remained subject, as in Ireland, to the insults and depredations of Protestant "upstarts." Their American insecurity only exacerbated the anger they had transplanted from Ireland, since then compounded by feelings of betrayal over the Calverts' apostasy and shoddy treatment of the old Settler. Despite his own affluence, Dr. Charles Carroll fully shared the atavistic resentments that he and his kinsmen could safely disclose only in family correspondence. In 1748, over 30 years after his emigration to Maryland, Dr. Carroll penned a letter—to his second cousin in London[9]—that sharply revealed his continued bitterness over the political "Misfortunes" that had stripped his family of their ancient "Honours" and once-"ample Estates" in the Irish midlands.

**Dr. Charles Carroll, Annapolis, Maryland,
to Sir Daniel O'Carroll, London, 9 September 1748**

Annapolis in Maryland Sept[br] 9th 1748

S[r]

    This day I Rec[d] the favour of Y[rs] Dated London the first of May last and Embrace this first opportunity of acknowledgeing the same with an assureance of the

---

8. Maryland's Protestant assemblymen were especially prejudiced against *Irish* Catholics and frequently passed laws designed to curb their immigration. Animus was not confined to poor Irish Catholic servants and convicts: shortly before the Revolution, for example, Fr. George Hunter, a priest in Charles Co., warned a prospective Irish Catholic immigrant, whose name alone would not betray him, "against discovering [i.e. revealing] his Country" after arrival. J. B. Lee, *The Price of Nationhood . . .* , 21–22; see Sources. **9.** Sir Daniel O'Carroll: at the instance of the Duke of Ormond, in 1709 he was made a lieutenant colonel, in 1710 a colonel, of a British regiment; created a baronet by Queen Anne; also knight of the Order of Aragon in Spain; died in 1750 with the rank of lieutenant general of His Majesty's forces.

Pleasure I have in Hearing the Health of a Gentleman of My Name and so Nearly Related in famyly's tho by the Destiny and Revolution of Time and states separated from our Native soil where our Predecessors <from> time immemorial Inherited both ample Estates and Honours. Nothing More Contributes (next to Christian Patience) to alleviate My concerns for such Misfortunes, than the Consideration that the Macedonian and Roman Empires are no More, that the Grecian States with Many More within the Compass of Europe have been overturned. I therefore Comfort my self and Endeavour to get a Livelyhood in this wild Part of the Globe. I have not had the Pleasure of seeing either of Y^r Nephews or hearing of, or from them; and I can not say, but I am glad they have chose to fix at St Christophers[10] rather than here by Reason I think that or other west India Islands are the most Probable Places for Young Gentlemen to get into Business and make something of a fortune; I assure You if I were Young and had not the Charge[11] of a Famely and an Intrest,[12] wch I can not get Rid of I would not stay here. My Brother John[13] some Years ago had resolved to go to the West Indies, Spanish Islands, and Main;[14] and in his Passige with other Gentlemen from Barbados to Anteago[15] the Vessell and all were Lost. W^{hch} Leaves me the onely son of the Famely You Mention but by this I do not Expect to Inherit Clanlisk, Ballibrit, Leap, Castle Town, or any other Part, or a Foot in Ely O Carroll.[16] Transplantations sequestrations, acts of settlement, Explanations, Infamous Informations for Loyalty & other Evils forbid.[17] It will be a singular Pleasure to me at all times to hear from You and of Y^r Health and Happyness and that of all Y^r Famely to which I

---

10. St Christophers: commonly St. Kitt's; one of the British Leeward Islands.   11. Charge: responsibility.
12. Intrest: i.e. interest, "position, standing"; see Shakespeare, *Merchant of Venice*, 3.2.219: "my new int'rest here."   13. My Brother John: in 1726 Dr. Charles Carroll invited his younger brother, John, then a student at Lille, to join him in Maryland, which he did by 1729, but he shortly thereafter remigrated to the West Indies and perished en route.   14. Spanish . . . Main: the mainland of Spanish America (and, later, the sea adjacent to it); for main = mainland see John Donne's well-known words "no man is an Iland, intire of it selfe; every man is a peece of the Continent, a part of the maine" (*Devotions upon Emergent Occasions,* 17).
15. Anteago: Antigua, one of the British Leeward Islands.   16. Clanlisk (Clonlisk) and Ballybritt: adjacent baronies in southwest King's Co. and the heart of the Ely O'Carroll lands; also the names of two of the most important castles formerly held by the O'Carroll chiefs, the first of which is now in Kilcomin parish (Clonlisk barony), the latter in Aghacon parish (Ballybritt barony). Leap, Castle Town: two other O'Carroll castles, the former also in Aghacon parish, the latter near the town (and in the parish of) Kinnitty (Ballybritt barony).
17. Transplantations: Carroll probably refers to the "transplantation of Connacht," ordered by Cromwell's government in 1654, by which Catholic lands east of the Shannon were confiscated and their former owners removed to smaller properties in Connacht and Co. Clare. sequestrations: precise meaning unclear, but Carroll probably refers to land confiscations, generally. acts of settlement: in 1652 the English Parliament passed an Act of Settlement that provided for the confiscation of all lands held by Irish Catholic "rebels"; in 1660, after the Restoration, Parliament enacted another Act of Settlement that created a claims court to hear cases involving possible restoration of estates to "innocent papists." Explanations: in 1665 the English Parliament passed an Act of Explanation, directing Cromwellian landlords and soldiers in Ireland to yield one-third of their grants to their former owners; neither this law nor the 1660 Settlement Act satisfied Catholics, like the Carrolls, who never recovered estates forfeited in 1652. Informations for Loyalty: Carroll probably refers to the clauses in many Penal Laws, particularly that of 1704, rewarding informants who "discovered" Irish Catholics'

sincerely wish the same. Any Letters Directed for Me here and left under Cover for Mʳˢˢ John Philpot & Company Merchants in London at the Virginia & Maryland Coffee House near the Exchange[18] will come safe. If I hear anything of Yʳ nephews <I> shall not fail to acquaint You. I am with Great Esteem & Respect

> Sir
>
> Your affectionate Kinsman
>
> & Most Humble servant
>
> C Carroll

To The Honᵇˡᵉ Sir Daniel O'Carroll at Saint James's Coffee House[19] London

Charles Carroll's reflections in this letter were surely sincere: he could gain nothing by expressing them to a distant kinsman who had converted to Protestantism, become an officer in the British army, and been knighted by Queen Anne. It is all the more remarkable, then, that in 1738, seven years before he wrote to his cousin in London, Dr. Carroll himself had renounced Catholicism and joined the Church of England! There are many possible reasons for Carroll's conversion. Perhaps pragmatism, personal ambition, a desire to promote his children's future—and to protect them from inconvenience or proscription—had superceded religious devotion. In the early eighteenth century in Ireland, many members of the surviving Catholic élite made the same choice, albeit under much greater duress. Or perhaps Enlightenment ideas had led him to question Catholic doctines or to accept Protestant charges that "popery" was spiritually and politically despotic. In 1739, when Dr. Carroll transferred his protesting son from a Catholic school in Portugal to Eton College, England, he counseled him: "In point of Religion, be not too much attached to any [opinions] grown up with you," for "Bigotry and superstition in Religion is a grand Error," and the "Church of England as by Law Established is worthy of your consideration."[20]

In the last analysis, however, it is likely that Carroll's change of religion was motivated primarily, perhaps exclusively, by the fact that in Maryland, as in Ireland, Anglican-

---

violations of the laws prohibiting them from purchasing, renting, bequeathing, or inheriting land on equal terms with Protestants.   **18.** Patronized by merchants and ship captains, coffee houses were important dispatch and reception points for transatlantic correspondence in the eighteenth century in Britain and British America. In London the **Virginia & Maryland Coffee House**, on Threadneedle Street **near the** (Royal) **Exchange**, was a favored venue for merchants who traded with those colonies, especially in tobacco, and for expatriate or visiting planters; established at this location at least since 1728, the business was still operating in Freeman's (later, Newman's) Court, in London's Cornhill district until the mid–nineteenth century.   **19. Saint James's Coffee House**: perhaps the British capital's most famous eighteenth-century coffee house; established in 1705, near the palace of the same name, St. James's was a frequent resort for literary and political figures, including the Anglo-Irishmen Jonathan Swift and Richard Steele in the 1710s and 1720s and Oliver Goldsmith and Edmund Burke in the 1770s.   **20.** Dr. Charles Carroll, Annapolis, Md., to Charles Carroll, Jr., Lisbon, Portugal, 21 July 1739.

ism was "by Law Established" and thus guaranteed its members access to all the rights, honors, and privileges that Carroll no doubt felt that he, as a scion of Ireland's ancient nobility, truly deserved. Thus, by the perverted logic created by conquest and colonization, Carroll's rejection of Catholicism was deeply rooted in his inherited Irish pretensions and grievances as well as in a desire to transcend the limitations of that inheritance.[21] Indeed, Carroll's resentment for his lost ancestral estates may have promoted, rather than inhibited, his apostasy. After all, what had loyalty to the Stuarts and the Catholic Church brought the Carrolls except betrayal, defeat, and ruin? Even now in Ireland, Carroll must have known, leading Catholics' efforts to devise an oath that would enable them to pledge their loyalty to the Crown—a crucial first step toward gaining relief from the Penal Laws—were being thwarted, not by the British government but by the Vatican's refusal to abandon its alliance with the exiled Stuart Pretender.

Communion with the Church of England certainly proved "worthy" of Dr. Carroll's "consideration." It qualified him for the franchise and for public office, and in 1738— shortly after his conversion—he won election to the Maryland Assembly, in which he served for the rest of his life, first representing Annapolis and then Anne Arundel County. Reflecting perhaps his ancestors' drive for power, and perhaps their contempt for any authority but their own, Carroll was not content with merely a seat in the colonial legislature. Instead, he quickly became a primary leader or—as Maryland's governor declaimed— the "chief incendiary" of the popular "Country party" whose members assailed proprietary power and privileges.[22] Like his forefathers, Carroll was no democrat: the Country party represented the interests not of Maryland's small farmers and tenants but of those wealthy planters, merchants, and land speculators who were excluded from the governor's inner circle and who resisted paying proprietary fees and quitrents.[23]

Dr. Carroll's colleagues in the Assembly were, of course, all Protestants. Yet despite his apostasy, for a decade he remained intimate with his wealthy Catholic kinsmen and business associates. However, in 1750–1751 Carroll turned against his Catholic relatives and former coreligionists. Complaints by the Catholic Carrolls that he was cheating them in his management of the Baltimore Ironworks and, more damning, their charge that he had embezzled the late James Carroll's estate,[24] led the doctor to launch a vicious political offensive against the Catholic planter élite and the church to which he had formerly belonged. When Charles Carroll of Annapolis publicly exposed his cousin's chicanery, the doctor had him arrested for insulting a member of Maryland's Assembly. Then Dr. Carroll joined forces with an equally avaricious Protestant, Thomas Gantt of Prince George's

---

21. Note the similarities in motives and functions between Carroll's and the Presbyterian clergyman James MacSparran's rejections of their inherited faiths and conversions to the Church of Ireland; see chapter 8.
22. A. C. Land, *Colonial Maryland* . . . , 174; see Sources.   23. In 1733 the fifth Lord Baltimore had increased the quitrents in his colony by 250 percent, largely to maintain his extravagant lifestyle; his son, Frederick (1732–1771), the sixth and last proprietor, was even more dissolute.   24. James Carroll of Anne Arundel Co. (d. 1729) was a cousin of Charles Carroll of Annapolis.

County, who wanted to repossess estates that a Catholic ancestor had bequeathed to Maryland's Jesuits. Henceforth, the doctor and his allies enflamed Protestant fears of "popery," encited popular envy of Catholic wealth, and demanded that England's Penal Laws be fully enacted and enforced in Maryland, thus denying Catholics the right to own land in the colony.

For several years proprietary opposition blocked new anti-Catholic legislation.[25] However, Dr. Carroll's efforts were partly successful in 1756, during the anti-Catholic hysteria provoked by the French and Indian War, when the Assembly levied a double tax on Catholic-owned land to subsidize Maryland's defense. Carroll missed this small triumph, dying at age 64 in his Annapolis townhouse on 29 September 1755. During the 1750s alone he had patented over 28,000 acres in western Maryland, and at death he bequeathed to his children the unsold speculations, his plantations and slaves, and a personal fortune of at least £13,000.[26] Doubtless it is accurate to conclude that Dr. Carroll's implacable self-interest led him to reject a heritage of victimization and to enlist in the ranks of persecution. More than a few Catholic converts in Ireland itself, notably John FitzGibbon and Patrick Duigenon,[27] would follow the same path to political power. Carroll may also have been driven by the need to prove to suspicious Protestants the sincerity of his conversion. In addition, it may be that Carroll projected contempt for what he perceived as his family's mistaken and fatal loyalties—or even self-hatred stemming from the long-term psychological effects of colonization, or from shame for his own immediate betrayals—onto those who symbolized his former self and whose existence served as a standing reproach. Or perhaps Carroll was merely playing out in America the same intrafamilial conflicts whereby his ancestors had secured Ely O'Carroll by war, by assassination, and by enlisting whatever allies were available and necessary to crush rival kinsmen.

In any case, according to his obituary Dr. Charles Carroll died a "True Protestant": not for him the quixotic fealty that had ruined his family in Ireland and in 1715–1718 had broken the heart of his namesake and first patron, the old Settler. Ironically, Carroll remained more loyal to his abandoned profession than to his discarded faith, for he signed himself "Charles Carroll of the City of Anapolis Surgeon" to the end of his days. Yet perhaps even more ironic, in 1776 the son and heir whom he had dragged from Portugal, Charles Carroll "Barrister" (1723–1783), would rejoin his Catholic relations,[28] the Settler's descendants, to

---

25. Proprietor Charles Calvert's opposition to further Catholic proscription was not based on sympathy for his former coreligionists; instead it reflected his general resistance to the Country party's attempts to usurp proprietorial prerogatives.   **26.** Dr. Carroll's heirs were: Charles Carroll "Barrister" (1723–1783) and Mary Clare Carroll (b. 1727), wife of Nicholas Maccubbin (1709–1787); another son, John Henry (b. 1732) predeceased the doctor in 1754.   **27.** On John FitzGibbon, see chapter 35. Patrick Duigenan (1735–1816): judge, privy councillor, and member of the Irish (and, after 1800, the British) Parliament; the most virulently anti-Catholic politician in Dublin or London, despite (or because of?) his early education for the priesthood and later marriage to a devout Catholic.   **28.** Principal among them was Charles Carroll of Carrollton (1737–1832), son of Charles Carroll of Annapolis and the longest-lived signer of the Declaration of Independence.

declare Maryland's independence and to dismantle its penal laws, thus protecting their American estates against the government that had despoiled the O'Carrolls in Ireland.

51 ※

Silvester Ferrall, Charles Lewis Reily, Peter Warren Johnson, and George Croghan, 1745–1764

English colonization of Ireland, and the consequent links between the English and Irish governing and landlord classes, created opportunities for numerous Anglo-Irishmen in imperial administration and overseas patronage. Between 1745 and 1772, for example, lords Chesterfield, Dorset, Devonshire, Bedford, and Halifax served both as Irish lord lieutenants and as members of the British cabinet in London, where, as presidents of the Board of Trade or as secretaries of state for the colonies, they provided American "jobs" for their Irish allies, relations, and retainers. Likewise, the eighteenth century's most notorious "placemonger," the duke of Newcastle, secretary of state from 1724 to 1748, had Irish connections, and both he and Lord Hillsborough of County Down, president of the Board of Trade (1763–1766) and secretary of state for the colonies (1768–1772),[1] used (and abused) their power to foist on the American colonists a host of largely incompetent, avaricious, and occasionally—almost accidentally—highly competent Irish-born officials, who in turn appointed as subordinates their kinsmen, former neighbors, and even mere adventurers who presumed upon vague Irish associations.

Royal officials of Irish origin were common in the Southern colonies but particularly so in New York, where between 1683 and 1753 at least five royal governors were Irish landlords or had strong Irish alliances—the succession culminating disastrously with the autocratic, coarse, and venal William Cosby (1732–1736) and the well-meaning but ineffective and perhaps equally avaricious George Clinton (1743–1753). Moreover, during their administrations and until his death in 1760, the most powerful political figure in New York was James De Lancey (b. 1703), a brother-in-law of Admiral Sir Peter Warren (1703–1752), who had been born in County Meath and, thanks to his naval victories over the French at Louisbourg (1745) and Cape Finisterre (1747), was one of the wealthiest and most popular figures in Britain in the mid–eighteenth century. Warren's primary interests in New York were land and money: at his death he owned much of Manhattan Island plus at least 13,000 acres in the Mohawk Valley—the latter purchased in 1736, through De

---

1. Thomas Pelham-Holles (1693–1768), duke of Newcastle: secretary of state for the Southern Department of the Board of Trade (1724–1748); northern secretary (1748–1754); and first lord of the treasury (1754–1756); slow-witted but a master of patronage, bureaucratic minutiae, and electoral engineering. On the duke of Hillsborough, see n. 73.

Lancey's favor, for merely £110. It was the Newcastle-Cosby-De Lancey-Warren connection that launched in New York the spectacularly successful career of William Johnson, who in turn established perhaps the most remarkable Anglo-Irish patronage network in colonial America.

William Johnson was born about 1715 at Smithstown, in the parish of Killeen and the barony of Skreen, County Meath,[2] the eldest son of Christopher Johnson, who leased 199 acres from the Earl of Fingal, and of Anne Warren, sister of the future naval hero, Sir Peter, from nearby Warrenstown. The Warrens had come to Ireland with Strongbow in the late twelfth century, but Johnson's own ancestry is less certain; some evidence indicates Cromwellian origins, but Johnson's younger brother and offspring claimed descent from the royal Ulster house of O'Neill (with Mac Shane having been Anglicized to Johnson), and the fact that both the Johnson and Warren families were still Catholic in the early eighteenth century (Warren's father fought at the Boyne for James II) suggests that the O'Neill lineage may not be fanciful. However, Peter Warren was raised Protestant in England by a wealthy uncle and patron, and sometime before or shortly after his own emigration William Johnson also converted to the established church, perhaps at first for career motives but eventually becoming a sincere (although not bigoted) Anglican.

In late 1737 or early 1738, Johnson emigrated to New York, invited by his uncle, Peter Warren, to manage the Mohawk Valley property, which the latter had purchased two years earlier. Armed with a load of goods purchased by Warren, most of which proved unsuitable for frontier commerce, and accompanied by Warren's would-be tenants from Meath, Johnson settled on the south side of the Mohawk River, cleared the forests for farming, sold supplies to settlers and the military, and, most profitably, engaged in the fur trade. By background and training accustomed to straddle Irish and English, Catholic and Protestant societies, Johnson proved an ideal cultural intermediary between America's colonizing and native peoples, building a network of personal friendships and commercial and military alliances with the Six Nations of the Iroquois, particularly with the Mohawks, who dominated the other tribes in the northern colonies. By 1743 Johnson had left the Warren properties (much to his uncle's displeasure), moved to the north side of the river, and begun to amass what eventually became the largest personal estate in British America. There, in a fortified mansion named Mount Johnson, where he hosted sumptuous feasts for white and Indian guests alike, Johnson recreated on a crude but lavish scale the quasi-feudal lifestyle of an eighteenth-century Irish landlord (or even a preconquest Gaelic or Hiberno-Norman lord), surrounded by the camps of his Indian allies and by a host of Irish tenants, agents, and servants.

During his first decade in New York, however, Johnson rarely communicated with his family in County Meath. Perhaps he was alienated from his father, as some sources say, but Johnson was instinctively generous and hospitable, and it is more likely he was trying

2. For demographic data on Killeen parish and its environs, see appendix 2.2c, on chapter 51.

FIGURE 11
Portrait of Sir William Johnson (ca. 1715–1774), of the Mohawk Valley, New York, from an original painting ca. 1765 by Thomas McIlworth (1700–ca. 1800). Photograph (acc. no. 1896.2, neg. no. 6871) courtesy of the Collection of the New York Historical Society, New York City.

to avoid the supplications of impecunious relatives until his own fortunes were well established. Nevertheless, word of his growing prosperity and influence soon filtered back to Ireland, inspiring a small avalanche of requests for employment and assistance, such as the following plea by Silvester Ferrall, one of Johnson's many importunate in-laws.[3]

Letter 1.
Silvester Ferrall, Halifax, Nova Scotia, to "The Honble Willm Johnson Esqr. at Mount Johnson, at the Mohocks in the County of Albany," New York, 16 June 1745

      . . . I wrote you in my former letter posted[4] at Boston,[5] . . . that I had not gott into any employment by reason[6] of a New Governor been[7] expected here[8] . . . for this

3. The opening lines of this letter are too mutilated to permit even conjectural reconstruction of their meaning. The same is true of the concluding lines, save for the closing salutation and signature. **4. letter posted**: conjectural. **5. and likewise what [?] And** omitted between **Boston** and **that I. 6. employment by reason**: conjectural. **7. been**: i.e., being (phonetic spelling). **8. here**: conjectural; additional words lost in ms.

place, so that till he arives there is no likelyhood[9] of any buisness been Carry'd on in this place[10] . . . for as the present Governor is making arrangements for[11] his return to London everything in this place is at a stand,[12]   As for my part I have not ern'd one shilling[13] since I came to the Colloney, Yet I did everything in my[14] power to gett into some kind of buisness to[15] gett an honest and genteel livelyhood,   its true I have had[16] several promises, and Still have the Same from[17] Several of the gentlemen here, that as soon as some[18] of the Kings woorks begins to go forward,[19] that I should[20] be provided for,   that's fullfilling the old Proverb[21] Live horse and y^u. shall gett grass,[22] so that I Cant expect any relief till Such time as Coll: Hopson[23] . . . the New Governor Arives, and then but a Chance, for tis generally the Custom with New Governors to have many[24] followers,   You may belive that I am a good deal in debt for my dyet[25] and lodging Since I ariv'd here which is neer nine months, besides washing and other Expencess, so that if I be not reliv'd in a short time, I Shall be oblig'd to Sell my Cloaths and return to New: York,   I am inform'd by Several in this place that there is two Gentlemen of my Name that Lives at Monseratt,   they have great Plantations, and are vastly[26] rich and Keep a great Number of Negroes and has no Children,   they likewise inform me that they Came from Waterford in Irland,   they advise me to go to them, and that I need not fear been well provided for,   I have often herd my father Say that he had a brother and two Nephews that went from Irland when Young and that they were Setl'd in Some of the Island^s. there about so that its like[27] it may happen to be some of their Children,   If I had where with[28] to go there I dont doubt but it might turn to my advantage, but I shall wait y^r. advise what I shall do in this affair,   Mr Cartright Informs me that you have Setled y^r. affairs in New York to your Satisfaction, the which gave me pleasure. . . .

Y^r. Oblig'd, Sincere, well wish^r. and hu<m>ble Servt. to Command

Silv^r. Ferrall

According to John Johnson, William's brother in County Meath, Silvester Ferrall had "gone off from this Country to the prejudice of a great many with whom he has run greatly indebted, peticularly with our father who has suffered by him already above one

---

9. **arives there is no likelyhood**: conjectural.   10. **in this place**: conjectural; additional words lost in ms.
11. **arrangements for**: conjectural.   12. **place is at**: conjectural; **at a stand**: in suspended animation.
13. **shilling**: conjectural.   14. **in my**: conjectural.   15. **to**: conjectural.   16. **I have had**: conjectural.
17. **from**: conjectural.   18. **as some**: conjectural.   19. **go forward**: get under way.   20. **should**: conjectural.
21. **Proverb**: conjectural.   22. **Live horse . . .** : the proverb here is a translation of the Irish (**mair, a chapaill, agus iosfair féar** "live, horse, and you'll eat grass").   23. **Coll: Hopson**: Col. Peregrinus Thomas Hopson (d. 1759), governor of Nova Scotia (1747–1755), through the duke of Newcastle's patronage; his predecessor in the governorship was Sir Charles Knowles. One or more words illegible after **Hopson.   24. have many**: conjectural.   25. **dyet**: i.e., diet "board."   26. **vastly**: extremely, or often just "very"; **vastly** and **mighty** were favorite intensifiers in eighteenth-century English, the last surviving in colloquial American English to this day.   27. **like**: likely.   28. **where with**: i.e., wherewith "wherewithal, means."

hundred pounds. . . . [W]e would advise you," John warned, "to beware how you let him have the handling of your money."[29] Although susceptible to flattery, Johnson was a shrewd judge of character, and Ferrall's letter suggests that he had already visited the Mohawk Valley and that Johnson had sent him packing, perhaps with a letter of reference to military supply contractors in Halifax. Whether Ferrall eventually gained a "genteel livelyhood" through William Johnson's patronage is unknown, but it appears that British officials in Nova Scotia were equally eager to be rid of him, urging him to try "mending his tattered fortune"[30] among dubious kinsmen far away in the West Indies.

Johnson may have been more sympathetic to the following unusual letter from Charles Lewis Reily, whose implicit request for a position on Johnson's estate was penned in English, Irish, and, primarily, in a rather anglicized and unidiomatic form of Latin—the latter probably learned in one of north Leinster's famous hedge schools, taught by displaced Gaelic bards, and designed to impress Johnson, who also knew Latin, with Reily's claims to scholarship.

Letter 2.
Charles Lewis Reily, Goshen, New York, to William Johnson, "Mohawk Castle," Albany County, New York, 24 August 1749

Sir[31]

  I should be led to believe that men of learning interest you, on this account I Write in this manner, I was honored by your message sent to Charles Clinton

---

29. John Johnson, Dublin, to William Johnson, Mount Johnson, Albany Co., N.Y., 13 January 1749/50. This and other Johnson letters quoted hereafter are in the *Papers of Sir William Johnson;* see Sources. **30.** John Johnson, 13 January 1749/50. **31. Sir . . . :** Beginning here, approximately two-thirds of Reily's letter is written in Latin. Although editorial convention normally requires reproduction of the document text in the original language, with the English translation relegated to a footnote, for the reader's convenience we have instead inserted the translation in the body of the text; in the translation, however, we have reproduced the capitalization and punctuation of Reily's original Latin text, which follows: ¶Domine ¶Adducar ut credam te interesse doctos, hac causa hoc more Scribo, nuncio tuo misso Carolo Clinton Armigero decorabar, Responsoque, notum facio atque tibi affirmo ut gratia amicitiae egregiae subsistitur inter nostros Parentes, atque respectus teneo ulli ducenti originem a Patre tuo Domino Christophero Johnston habitante prope Dunshaghlin, ut magnopere gauderem si capax essem benefacere aut utilem esse tibi qua in re;——Interim Domine me dolet, ut, etsi, cupidus sim honorem familiaritatis tenendi tecum, tamen res nunc sic collocantur ut me non Sinunt uti ceremoniis assuetis bonorum morum Visendi sola gratia visitationis, Nihilominus maxime voluptati mihi Semper erit de valetudine tua audire, ob praedictas causas, quanto (ut Solitus es) Decori atque honori esse Patriae nostrae, & pro Viribus congratulor ¶Eruditio Juvenum nunc tempus consumit meum, Loco nonime Goshen, a quo licet mihi destituere termino Singulae quartae partis anni, adeo foederis articuli sunt, Octo Septimanae ab hoc tempore terminabunt postrema pacta hoc in loco, enim pactionem feci hiscum antequam ex te audivi Domino Clinton, aut ullo altero Sin aliter cum fama tua me meas venit ad aures, optato potireris visendo (His ita promissis) Si tibi conveniret, ut viserem te termino Septem aut octo Septimanarum, Significes Sententias mihi epistolis quam cite & convenienter ut poteris, & attendam tibi maxima cum Voluptate & alacritate; mittas Jussa mihi litteras dirigendo aut Domino Johanni Colden habitanti Albaniae aut Fratri Allexandri Colden Duci habitanti Newburgh hoc in ruri——uterlibet eorum industrie litteras tuas

Esquire,[32] and, in response, inform and assure you that the pleasure of a rare friendship exists between our Parents, and I have a regard for anyone who is descended from your Father Mister Christopher Johnston who lives near Dunshaghlin,[33] that I should greatly rejoice if I were capable of serving or being useful to you in any way;   Meanwhile Sir I regret that, though I crave the honor of familiar acquaintance with you, still circumstances are such that they do not permit me to follow the accustomed usage of good manners of coming to See you for the sole purpose of visiting,   Nevertheless it will always be especially pleasant to me to hear of your health, for the reasons mentioned, and how (as you are wont to do) you Adorn and honor our Country, and I congratulate you on your abilities

The Teaching of youth now consumes my time, at a Place named Goshen,[34] which I have the privilege of leaving at the end of a quarter; so the articles of agreement provide,   Eight Weeks from this time will end the contract in this place, for I made my agreement with these people before I heard from you, Mister Clinton or anyone else,   but If however since your fame has come to my ears, you would enjoy the desired visit (As it is promised) if it would suit you, that I should visit you at the end of Seven or eight Weeks, Signify your Wishes to me by letter as quickly as you

promovebunt; tanto quanto epistolas tuas acciperem citius gauderem, ex qua causa agam, eoque res Sic disponam ut Jussu adsim tibi illico, quousque maneo humilem Servum, aeque ac amantem compatriotam. . . . ¶P.S. Soror tua nupta fuit meo condiscipulo Gulielmo Fitzsymons filio Petri Fitzsymons Mercatoris Athboy, Frater meus erat pronubo Fratri tuo; Pater, Frater tuus atque Sorores valebant cum Vela Dedi Ventis, ¶Salus meo nomine detur Roberto Adams, Jacobo Rogers Petro Crotty & Erwin, omnibusque alteris hibernicis in illo loco. N.B. Pactionem alteram haud faciam, donec consilia tua meas pervenient ad aures, Efflagitoque, ut quam Cito poteris mihi nota Sint. Gratias Deo, Varias artes excolere possum tales aedificationes amnium generum Vehiculorum, et Lucro & Voluptati, ad hoc multa altera quibuscum Solitudine memet recreo; tunc deinde Siquando fatigatus essem, canendo variis musicis intrumentis, nunc tibiis Utricularibus nunc fistula germanica, tunc Sambuca, tum Cithara Minore aliis cum quo [words covered by seal?] recreativa mihi Sunt animum Remitto. **32. Charles Clinton Esquire**: Charles Clinton (1690–1773): a Presbyterian from Corbay, Co. Longford, Clinton emigrated with ca. four hundred of his neighbors and fellow dissenters in 1729, landing at Cape Cod after a horrific voyage in which 90 passengers, including two of his own children, died; settled at Little Britain in Ulster Co., N.Y., and engaged in farming, milling, surveying, and land speculation, attracting the favorable attention of Cadwallader Colden, the province's surveyor general, and of Colden's political ally, Governor George Clinton, probably a distant relative; served as justice of the peace, as lieutenant colonel of the New York militia during the French and Indian War, and in 1769–1773 as first judge of the Ulster Co. Court of Common Pleas. Clinton's son, George (1739–1812), was one of New York's most prominent revolutionary leaders, served six terms as state governor (1777–1795), and was twice elected U.S. vice president (in 1808 and 1812) under Jefferson and Madison; on George Clinton, also see chapter 66. **33. Dunshaghlin**: Dunshaughlin town (and parish), Ratoath barony, Co. Meath; the parish adjoins the Johnsons' Killeen parish on the southeast. **34. Goshen**: Goshen, Orange Co., N.Y.; first settled in 1712–1714, the town was the county seat from 1727; Charles Clinton (see n. 32) was one of the elders in the local Presbyterian church (est. 1721). In 1739 Goshen township (including the town itself) had 319 males above age 10. Before the Revolution, Goshen boasted a "select school of a classical character," where Reily may have taught and where, much later, Noah Webster was a "poor scholar."

conveniently can, & I shall attend you with the greatest Pleasure and promptness; send your commands to me addressing your letter either to Mister John Colden residing at Albany or his Brother Alexander Colden a leading Resident of Newburgh in this region[35]—either one of them will readily forward your letter; the sooner I receive your letter, the more delighted I should be, and on that ground I shall act, so disposing matters as to be with you at once on your direction, till that time I remain your humble Servant and affectionate compatriot

Charles Lewis Reily

Goshen in Orange County

August y^e. 24: 1749

P.S.[36]

Your sister was married to my school fellow William Fitzsymons son of Peter Fitzsymons a merchant at Athboy,[37] my Brother was best man to your brother, your Father, Brother and Sisters were well when I sailed.

Give my respects to Robert Adams, James Rogers Peter Crotty & Erwin, and all other irishmen in that place.[38] N.B. I shall not make a new agreement until your opinion reaches me, and I beg that it be made known to me as soon as may be. Thank God, I am able to practise various arts, such as the construction of all kinds of carriages, both for Gain and Pleasure; in addition to many other things with which I amuse myself in Solitude; then again if at any time fatigued, with playing various musical instruments, now the Bagpipes, now the german flute, then the Hautboy,[39] then the Violin—with other things when, as I engage in recreation, I relax my mind.[40]

P.S; I Shall greatly rejoice to be honour,d[41] by a letter from y^u, if y^u think convenient So to doe y^u may direct to me as affors,^{d} or to ye Care of the

---

35. John Colden . . . Alexander Colden: probably relatives of Cadwallader Colden (1688–1776), mentioned later in Reily's letter. An Anglican born in Scotland and educated at the University of Aberdeen, Cadwallader Colden emigrated in 1710 to Philadelphia, where he practiced medicine and trade, before moving in 1718 to New York, where he became surveyor general, a member of the Governor's Council (from 1721), and lieutenant governor of New York (from 1761) and served five terms as acting governor between 1760 and 1775. His estate, Coldingham, was in Orange Co., near the village of Newburgh. Like Johnson, Cadwallader Colden had unusual sympathy for the Iroquois and other Native Americans, as revealed in his *History of the Five Nations* (1727, 1747). **36. Goshen . . . P.S.**: in English. **37. Athboy**: a market town (and parish), Lune barony, Co. Meath. Reily's family history was accurate: one of William Johnson's sisters, Ellis, married William Fitzsimmons. **38. Robert Adams, James Rogers Peter Crotty & Erwin**: Robert Adams (or Adems), James Rogers (or Rodgers), and Joseph Irwin are mentioned in Johnson's *Papers* as his sometime employees or agents, and doubtless Peter Crotty was the same. In 1762 Rogers was a partner in upstate land speculation with the Ulster-born New York City merchant Waddell Cunningham, also one of Johnson's business associates (on Cunningham, see chapter 40). In his will (1774), Johnson refered to Adams, a former Dublin clerk and his lifelong bookkeeper, as "my faithful friend" and left him a small estate. **39. Hautboy**: oboe. **40. . . . mind**: the Latin portion of Reily's text ends here. **41. honour,d**: in the English portion of his letter, Reily employs commas instead of apostrophes in place of the missing letters in contractions: e.g. **affors,^{d}** and **couldn,t** hereafter.

Honourable Cadwallader Colden at Coldengham in ye Highlands or any other proper
way y^u. think,   the Sooner y^u acquaint me of y^r Desire the better for I couldn,t
understand y^r intentions by Mr Clinton or by James McCloghery,   If y^u think
Convenient when I goe up I,ll Carry Some tools with me to make y^u a Four wheeld
Chair or any Other pleasure carriage y^u. please; & Banaght Lath gu veke meh hu,[42]

    I Send this Letter to Captain Ross to forward to y^u,

Goshen August y^e. 24th: 1749

> I,ll also if y^u please bring with me
> all my musicall instruments
> Fiddle German flute Hautboy & Baggpipes

R eily's letter was a masterpiece of ingratiation, linking his prospects not only to Johnson's relatives at home but also to his political allies, Charles Clinton and especially
Cadwallader Colden, the chief adviser of the then-governor, George Clinton, who in
1746–1748 was using all his patronage powers to wage political warfare against the New
York Assembly and, with the help of Johnson and his Mohawk allies, a military campaign
against French Canada during King George's War (1744–1748). At Colden's urging, Johnson had been appointed New York's superintendent of Indian affairs and commander-in-
chief of the colony's militia, and in 1750 he became a member of the Governor's Council.
Reily clearly understood that Johnson's enhanced status might require his coach-building
skills, and that Johnson not only patronized schools on his estate but also entertained his
banqueting guests with Irish music—at various times employing a blind harpist from the
old country as well as several Irish fiddlers. Unfortunately, however, whether Reily entered
Johnson's employ is unknown: he does not appear in subsequent Johnson letters, unless he
was the "scoundrel" Luke Reily who betrayed Johnson's confidence and absconded to
Ireland in 1762.[43]

    After King George's War, Johnson retired from his official positions and concen-
trated on the fur trade. However, he reentered public life permanently and spectacularly
in the French and Indian War (1754–1763). In 1754 he attended the Albany Congress, and
in 1755 he was reinstated as New York's superintendent of Indian affairs and appointed
major general of colonial forces in the British campaign against the French stronghold of
Crown Point. On 8 September 1755 Johnson's colonial militia and Indian allies won a

42. Banaght Lath gu veke meh hu: i.e., *beannacht leat go bhfeicfe mé thu* "may a blessing go with you until I
see you [again]." Reily's phonetic spelling of Irish, based on English language orthography, shows the early
influence of English literacy on Ulster and north Leinster Irish-speakers. Phonetic spelling had been used since
the early eighteenth century, when it was introduced in a Protestant catchism intended for Rathlin Island, Co.
Antrim; Reily's usage suggests that in Ireland he may have taught in one of the "charter schools" established by
the Irish Parliament in 1733 to educate and convert Catholic children. However, most authorities argue that
native writers in Irish did not commonly employ phonetic spelling until the late eighteenth and early
nineteenth centuries, when it appeared in ballads and Catholic catechisms. **43.** Hugh Wallace, New York
City, to Sir William Johnson, Johnstown, Albany Co., N.Y., no date [early 1763].

great victory over the French at the Battle of Lake George; on 25 July 1759 his army captured Fort Niagara; and the following year he led New York's Indians in the British expedition that on 8 September forced the French to surrender Montreal. As a result of these triumphs, the British government made Johnson a baronet, granted him £5,000, and commissioned him "Sole Agent and Superintendent" of all the Indian tribes north of the Ohio River, with an annual salary of £600. It was now much easier for Johnson to comply with patronage requests from Irish relatives such as Peter Warren Johnson,[44] youngest brother of the new baronet, who in 1759 wrote the following letter on behalf of yet another member of their extensive family.

Letter 3.
Peter Warren Johnson, Dublin, to Sir William Johnson, Fort Johnson, Albany County, New York, 15 Oct 1759

Dublin   Oct[r]. 15th, 1759—

D[r]. Brother—

I wrote you two letters since I had any from you, but it gives me infinite pleasure to find by the publick papers that you are well after your great Success at Niagara   I pray Heaven to preserve you.

The Bearer M[r]. Michael Byrne is a Gent. in whose favour many have interested themselves that are & ought to be dear to us & who have Strongly Applyed to recommend him to your protection,   he formerly served in the Navy & was at the Bombardment of Pondichery,[45] upon the peace returned to Ireland and betook himself to Country Affairs[46] which he understands well but his Lease having expired without hopes of a renewal he Chuses to try the fortune of War in the Land Service,[47]   his Bro:[48] was Married to a near Relation of ours, and to whom I owe many Obligations a Gent. well worthy our esteem[49] a perticular friend and Acquaintance & so is the Young Gent. his Brother in whose favour I write,   his friends flatter themselves with the hopes of his prosperity from my recommendation as you may easily get him into some post or Commission by which he may get his bread and serve his Country which I

44. Johnson's youngest brother spent most of his early life in the British military, benefiting from the patronage of his uncle, Sir Peter Warren, and emphasizing that connection by styling himself "Warren Johnson." Naturally enough, on 4 August 1752, he wrote to William of the "Grief . . . unexpressible" which he and his family felt at Sir Peter's death, "for we have lost our all & all." (*Papers of Sir William Johnson*, vol. 1 (1921), 370–71.) In 1760–1761 Warren Johnson visited his brother in the Mohawk Valley, recorded his distaste for America in a journal that survives in the *Papers of Sir William Johnson*, and returned to Ireland where he died about 1790.   **45. Pondichery**: a major French port in southwestern India, captured by the British in the Seven Years' War.   **46. Country Affairs**: rural pursuits, farming.   **47. Land Service**: nonnaval service; in Warren's time this meant the army.   **48. his Bro**: probably John Byrne, who in 1763 sought letters of introduction from Warren to William Johnson; John Byrne's letters do not survive.   **49. worthy our esteem**: deserving, meriting our esteem (OED, s.v., 8.b).

earnestly recomend to your kind attention in the Warmest manner and shall take it as a perticular favour if you can serve him in any Shape.

in my last I Acquainted you of the Enquiery I made about Settlers at Rathkul[50] & was there myself   there are but few Families there inclinable[51] to go & those are of the German Extraction their Names Ebeny & Pemperton but upon so good a peace as we are likely to have am Certain of getting great Numbers,[52]

I am with Sincere good Wishes for your Health & prosperity My D[r]. Bro—

Y[rs]. most Affect[y]. and

faithfully—

Warren Johnson

O n this occasion, Sir William's patronage can be documented, for prior to his death in 1772 Byrne was one of Johnson's commissaries at Oswego, obtained warrants in partnership for about 30,000 acres in upstate New York, and despite the jibes in Johnson's correspondence—implying that Byrne was either homosexual or physically incapable of sexual intercourse—he married one of Sir William's daughters by his first Mohawk mistress and apparently fathered a son mentioned in Johnson's will.

In the decade after the Peace of Paris (1763), as Johnson's wealth and influence increased the numbers of Irish relations, tenants, and retainers in his employ and on his estate proliferated. Before his death at Crown Point, scapegrace brother-in-law Mathew Ferrall had been Johnson's commissary; and after the war nephew and son-in-law Guy Johnson became his secretary; nephew John Dease was his physician; Bryan Lefferty was family attorney; Thomas Flood (and, before him, his brother Patrick) was overseer; Patrick Daly was personal factotum; and so on, down to the Irish servants and dwarfs who served and entertained at the dinners in Johnson's new mansion, Johnson Hall. By the early 1760s Johnson's lands had become so populous that he constructed his own estate town, Johns-town, and in 1772 he persuaded New York's Assembly to make the town the seat of a new county, Tryon, over which he ruled as benevolent lord. Johnson was also grand master of New York's Masonic Order and a member of both the American Philosophical Society and the Society for the Propagation of the Gospel—the latter for his generous patronage to the Church of England and its missions to the Indians. Yet in 1773 he also defied New York's penal laws and protected the Irish-born Fr. Peter McKenna, who settled in Johnstown and held Catholic services for Johnson's Irish and Scots Highland tenants.

50. **Rathkul**: Rathcool townland (Ratoath parish and barony, Co. Meath); the site of a Palatine German settlement during the reign of Queen Anne.   51. **inclinable**: inclined, disposed (OED, s.v., 1.b; latest attestation 1826).   52. Warren Johnson was apparently successful in persuading Rathcool's inhabitants to emigrate, for in 1763 John Embury (**Ebeny**) and two dozen other Irish Palatine families petitioned for 25,000 acres in Albany Co., N.Y., and at least some settled on Sir William Johnson's lands.

Fort Johnson, Sir William Johnson's first mansion, erected in 1749, near Amsterdam, New York. Photograph of an "old French print" in Arthur Pound, *Johnson of the Mohawks: A Biography of Sir William Johnson* (New York, 1930).

Ultimately, however, as a royal official even Johnson's enormous influence derived from policies and patronage decisions conceived in the British capital. In early 1764, during the frontier crisis caused by Pontiac's Rebellion (1763–1764), Johnson authorized George Croghan—who was visiting London to secure compensation for his own losses in the Seven Years' War—to press his Indian policies and his land-grant claims on the British statesmen responsible for the North American colonies. Like Johnson, Croghan (ca. 1715–1782) was an Irish-born convert from Catholicism; after emigrating during the great Irish famine of 1741, he settled on the frontier, engaged in the fur trade, and by 1756, when Johnson appointed him Deputy Superintendent for Indian affairs, had gained great influence over the tribes in Pennsylvania and west of the Ohio. However, Johnson's friend was not an ideal emissary to London. As his monthly reports to Johnson demonstrate, Croghan was poorly educated,[53] far less urbane than his patron, and, despite his own reputation as a "vile rascal," appalled by both the venality of most of the English politicians he encountered and by their indifferent, ignorant, and even malevolent attitudes toward the American colonies. Although he found "Lord Hillsborrow . . . Much ples^d. when I tould him you

---

53. Croghan's origins are unknown, but his native Catholicism and his Ulster Scots speech, taken together with the geographic distribution of his surname (originally Crehan, sometimes anglicized to Creighton, sometimes confused with Cro(g)han), suggest that he came from the Laggan region of Co. Donegal or from the adjacent area of Co. Tyrone.

was . . . his Cuntryman,"[54] Croghan's long stay in London made him increasingly impatient and disdainful: "Nothing has been Don Respecting North aMerrica," he complained, as "the p[e]ople hear Spend thire Time in Nothing butt abuseing one aNother & Striveing who shall be in power with a view to Serve themselves & thire frends, and Neglect the publick. . . . I am Sick of London & wish To be back in aMerrica & Setle^d on a Litle farm where I May forgett the Mockery of pomp & Greatness."[55] Even two months later, he reported, "thire Lordshipes have Neaver Taken under thire Consideration Indian affairs. . . . [W]hen they May Sitt on Indian affairs is in My opinion very uncartian as y^e. Ministry and p[e]ople hear in power attend to Nothing Butt thire own privett Inrest. . . . [Y]^e. More I am Aquainted with those p[e]ople y^e. Less I find them Sinceer."[56] Not until early July could Croghan report, in the following letter, that the Grenville ministry had finally discussed and agreed to most of Johnson's recommendations.

Letter 4.

George Croghan, London, to Sir William Johnson, Johnson Hall, Johnstown, Albany County, New York, 12 July 1764

London July 12th. 1764

Hon^d. Sir

the Lords of Trade has had y^r. State of Indian affairs & that of M^r. Stewerts[57] under thire Consideration for Near Six weeks past and have form^d. a plan for y^e. futer Manidgement of y^r. Departments & the Indian Trade on which a Duty is to be Lay^d. of 5c ℔ which is to Defray the Expence of Indian affairs   you are to have three Deputys & M^r. Stewert two att 300 ℔ annum Each   you are to have an Interpreter & Smith att Each post of Trade & M^r. Stewart y^e. Same & there is to be a Commisery apointed att Each post to Inspect Trade   you are to have Seven thousand pounds ℔ annum alow^d. you for presents to y^e. Indians & other Expences   Mr Stewert five thousand   I Need Say No More on this Subject as you will Receive a Copey of the Plan from thire Lorshipes by this Packett——

thire Lordshipes Say that y^e. Commander in Cheefe will furnish you with what presents is Nesesary att present for y^e. Indians & hopes that y^e. Expedition under y^e. Command of Co^{ll}. Broadstreet[58] will putt an End to y^e. Indian Warr after which they

54. George Croghan, London, to Sir William Johnson, Johnstown, Albany Co., N.Y., 24 February 1764.
55. George Croghan, London, to Sir William Johnson, Johnstown, Abany Co., N.Y., 10 March 1764.
56. George Croghan, London, to Sir William Johnson, Johnstown, Albany Co., N.Y., 11 May 1764.
57. Mr Stewert: John Stuart (1718–1798): born in Scotland; emigrated in 1748 to South Carolina, where he engaged in the fur trade and gained influence with the Cherokees; appointed superintendent of the southern Indians, 1762. 58. Co^{ll}. Broadstreet: Col. John Bradstreet: his military expedition against Pontiac's Rebellion in the upper Ohio Valley, in summer and autumn of 1764, was a dismal failure.

hope the Duty on y^e. Indian Trade will be More then Sufisent to Defray y^e. Expence of your Department,   they Make very Light of y^e. Indian Warr. and give very Little attension to y^e. affairs of y^e. Colenys in Gineral,   M^r. Penn[59] has Don Every thing in his power to gett a Large present Sent you for y^e. Indians & has offerd to Joyn his preporsion in[60] itt butt None of the present Ministry wold agree to Give Six pence Towards that Service Except My Lord Halifax,[61] who is y^r. Sincear frend and aprove<s> all y^e. Meshers[62] you Recomm^d as to the Rest I Loock on what they Say as Meer froath & by Many questions w^h. they have putt to Me they Seem to be Jelous of y^r. being a popler[63] Man in Amerrica which they Seem to think att present Dangrouss,   In short they are Determined To Trust No power in y^e. hands of any person in Amerrica   they won't Suffer y^e. Commander in Cheefe for the futer to fill up any Commisions In aMerrica   the Cheefe Study[64] of the pople[65] in power hear att present is To Lay Heavy Taxes on the Colenys and tis Talkt of Laying an Internal Tax on them Next Cesion of parlament[66]——

the Lords of Trade has att Last Consented to Make a boundry between the Indians and us and has Made itt an Artickle of thire plan & Refer'd itt to your Honour to Setle[67] which was very hard to Gett them into[68] fer they wold have Chose to Lockt[69] on all the Indians Cuntry as Conquerd & Ceaded to us by the Last paice[70] on w^h. Account No Subject is to purchess any Land from the Indians as formerly the King only and when he purchess the Lands is to be Granted by the Lords of Trade & No More than twenty thousand acres to one person fer w^h. Grant there is to be paid hear a sume of Money besides ye Feess to y^e. Governer.

I Refer^d. a Memorial[71] to y^e. Lords of Trade for the Confirmation of y^e. Lands y^e. Six Nations gave Me formerly whch they Refused to Grant att which Time M^r.

---

59. M^r. Penn: Thomas Penn (1702–1775): proprietor of Pennsylvania and a warm admirer of Sir William Johnson; see chapter 53.   **60. Joyn . . . in**: contribute to.   **61. Lord Halifax**: George Montagu Dunk (1716–1771), second earl of Halifax: president, Board of Trade (1748–1761); Irish lord lieutenant (1761–1763); secretary of state (1765, 1771); during the mid-1700s the influence of his longtime mistress, Mary Anne Faulkner of Dublin, accounted for much Anglo-Irish patronage in the American colonies.   **62. Meshers**: i.e., measures.   **63. popler**: i.e., popular.   **64. Study**: effort, concern.   **65. pople**: i.e., people; the spelling represents a conscious attempt to relate the word to its Latin etymon **populus**.   **66. To Lay Heavy Taxes on the Colenys and . . . an Internal Tax**: as Croghan predicted, in 1765 Parliament imposed the notorious Stamp Act, which the colonists charged was an unconstitutional "internal tax."   **67. a boundry between the Indians and us . . .** : as per his instructions from London, on 5 November 1768, Johnson concluded the Treaty of Fort Stanwix, by which the Iroquois ceded to the crown most of western New York and Pennsylvania in return for what became a spurious guarantee that the government would prevent white settlements farther westward. **68. Gett them into**: "persuade them to do."   **69. to Lockt**: i.e., to a (i.e., to have) looked. An alternative explanation would see **Lockt** as containing the silent graphic t that in early Scots handwriting practice is very frequently added to final p, th, and ch/gh (e.g. **campt** "camp," **baitht** "both," **Edin burcht** "Edinburgh"); this archaic practice is attested as late as the middle of the nineteenth century in Ulster. See chapter 1, n. 22. **70. paice**: i.e., peace, elliptical for "peace treaty."   **71. Memorial**: memorandum.

Pownal[72] Menshon^d. y^r. honour haveing A Grant from y^e. Mohocks   thire Lordshipes Examined Me fer a Considerable Time how you obtaind itt & Wondred you had Nott Menshoned itt in your Leters to y^e. Board as they had Neaver herd of itt before   on which I tould them that I understood you had Wrote to M^r. Pownal to Lay itt before y^e. Board w^h. itt Seems he had Neaver Menshoned before and Lord Hillsborrough[73] was of opinion <it> was then two Late as they had Made a Rule of Granting Butt 20000. a<cres> to one Man and Seem^d. of opinion that No Indian Agent Should Make any Contracks with Indians fer Lands or be Concern^d. in Trade,   Sence that M^r. Pownall Desier^d. Me to aquaint you that he had nott been able to gett y^r. Grant Confirm^d. butt hoped he Shuld gett itt Don as Soon as a boundry was fixt with the Indians   Butt I Can ashure you that there is Litle Dependence to be putt in What he or his Brother Says   they are Greatt Indian Politicions & pretend to know as Much of Indian affairs as you Do and as there has been So Many Changes att y^e. Board Lately they are Imensly Ignerant and as Indiferent about itt as they are Nott Cartian[74] butt another Change will be this Next Cesion of parlament   I Came two Late to England to aply to the Last parlament for y^e. Losses Sustained Privous[75] to y^e. War   Seven hundred thousand p^d.[76] of y^e. Mony ariseing from y^e. Sales of y^e. Ships Taken from y^e. french on that Acount was apropriated before I Came   there is About £40000 Remaining which is y^e. only Chance I have of being Reimburst what I Lost and that must be by aplecation to parlem^t. w^h. M^r. Pen will undertake for Me as I Cant Stay My Self

tho Gineral Amhirst[77] has been Gineraly Condemd for his Conduct in Indian affairs his plan fer Chestiseing them is followed oweing I Blive to y^e. Litle attension paid by y^e. present Ministry to american affairs as they Study Nothing butt to keep them Selves in power[78]

I have Don Every thing in My power Respecting the Mohocks Complaints About y^e. Cayaderrussera patten<t> and that of y^e. Corperation of albany and thire

---

72. M^r. Pownal: John Pownall, Secretary of the Board of Trade in 1764; his more famous brother, Thomas (1722–1805), former governor of Massachusetts (1757–1760), was also a member of the Board. Despite Croghan's criticisms, with respect to North America the Pownalls were among the most knowledgeable and liberal-minded British statesmen.   **73. Lord Hillsborrough**: Wills Hill (1718–1793), second viscount (later earl of) Hillsborough, from 1789 the first marquis of Downshire; president, Board of Trade (1763–1766), and secretary of state for the colonies (1768–1772).   **74. Cartain**: i.e., certain; the spelling may represent a pronunciation **sartun**, although the usual Scots pronunciation is **saretun**.   **75. Privous**: i.e. previous; the form shows the frequent confusion in Ulster speech between the two forms of the suffix, -ous and -e/ious; cf. **serous** "serious," **courtously** "curteously," but **mischievious** "mischievous"; see chapter 67, n. 29. This kind of alternation probably explains James Wansbrough's form **peniall** "penal" (see chapter 1).   **76. p^d.**: i.e., pound(s).   **77. Gineral Amhirst**: General Jeffrey Amherst (1717–1797): commander of the British forces that captured Louisbourg, Cape Breton Island, on 26 July 1757; afterward commander-in-chief of all British forces in North America during the Seven Years' War, but criticized for his postwar policies, which alienated the Indians while weakening frontier defenses, thus provoking Pontiac's Rebellion (1763–1764).   **78. they Study Nothing butt to keep them Selves in power**: "they devote all their efforts to keeping themselves in power."

Lordshipes has att Last Agreed thet if y^e. asembly in New York will Nott Disanul[79] them patten<t>s by an act of asembly that they will have itt Don hear by an act of parlament

The Board of Trade was going to apoint the Comiserays to Inspect y^e. Indian Trade in y^r. Department hear Till I Lett Lord Hillsborrough know that those Comisereys Should be persons aquainted with y^e. Indians Customs and Maners & that I thought you Should have y^e. apointment of them as they were to act Imeidatly under y^r. Direction   To which he agreed and Said itt was proper you Should have y^e. apointment of y^r. own offisers in Such a Depertment Butt Said that in all other Depertments of his Majestys Service in Amerrica y^e. offisers Should be apointed hear by his Majestys Ministers which wold allways give them that Influence which they ought to have in this kingdom.

M^r. Penn Desiers Me to present his Complem^ts. to y^r. Honour & Says he will Write you by Me   Plese to Make Mine to M^r. John & Capt. Clause Capt. Johnson[80] & y^e. Ladys & blive Me with Greatt Sincerity y^r. Honours

Most obeident and

Humble Servant

Geo: Croghan

P.S.

M^r. Allan[81] before he Saild for Phill. Last Month Deliverd a State[82] of y^r. Services to M^r. Grinvill y^e. Lord high Tresuerer[83] Butt there had been Nothing Don in itt Nor Do I blive you will have any allowances Made you fer y^r. Extronerey Services Except you was to Come hear y^r. Self.   y^e. p<e>ople hear think you are Rich aNouffe and they heat[84] to hear of any amerrican being Either popler or welthey

E ventually, the Crown confirmed Johnson's grant from the Mohawks of one hundred thousand acres in upstate New York, but his plans for strict royal regulation of the

---

79. Disanul: nullify.   **80. M^r. John**: John Johnson (1742–1830), Sir William's eldest son and heir; commanded a loyalist regiment during the Revolution; afterward he settled in Canada, where he was superintendent-general of Indian affairs and colonel in the Canadian militia. **Capt. Clause**: Daniel Claus (1731–1787); born in Germany; husband of Sir William's eldest daughter, Ann (married in 1762), and his principal deputy among the New York Indians; removed to England after the Revolution. **Capt. Johnson**: Guy Johnson (ca. 1740–1788); born in Ireland; emigrated in 1756; Sir William's nephew and husband of his daughter, Mary, whom he wed in 1763; superintendent of Indian affairs after his father-in-law's death in 1774; during the Revolution Guy Johnson advocated a campaign of terror against the rebels, which backfired to the destruction of his and Sir William's estates; died an impoverished alcoholic in London. **81. M^r. Allan**: William Allen (1704–1795): of Ulster-born parents, one of Pennsylvania's wealthiest merchants and leader of that colony's so-called Presbyterian party, which was then in alliance with the Penn proprietorship; see chapter 53. **82. State**: account, detailed enumeration. **83. M^r. Grinvill y^e. Lord high Tresuerer**: George Grenville (1712–1770): chancellor of the exchequer and chief minister in 1764; advocate of stricter trade regulations and higher taxation for the American colonies. **84. heat**: i.e., hate.

Indian trade were only partly implemented. What eventually destroyed Johnson's unique, anachronistic world, however, was not the British ministers' personal jealousy but their new policies, which ended the long era of "salutary neglect" that had allowed the few competent royal officials, such as Johnson, to adjust London's edicts to colonial conditions. After 1763 ministerial arrogance and the higher taxes of which Croghan had warned polarized colonial politics and drove the Americans into rebellion.

Thus, Sir William Johnson's attempt to reestablish an Irish lordship in America ultimately failed, for his kinsmen—unlike those of Charles Carroll the Settler[85]—remained fatally loyal to Great Britain. Had Johnson lived to lead his white and Indian allies into battle for the Crown, the outcome of the Revolution might have been different, but he died on 11 July 1774, his liver rotted by decades of heavy drinking. Neither Sir William's son and heir, Sir John Johnson, nor his nephew, Guy Johnson, possessed his abilities, while Croghan, the only man with comparable influence among the Indians, sided with the Americans—his decision perhaps influenced by his negative experiences in London. After British general Burgoyne's defeat at Saratoga (17 October 1777), fratricidal strife ravaged the Mohawk Valley: an estimated two-thirds of its inhabitants were killed; the Johnson estate was devastated by war, then confiscated by the rebels; and most of Sir William's Irish and Iroquois relatives and friends fled to Canada.

52 ❋

Samuel Bryan, 1752

In 1752 Samuel Bryan of Dublin wrote to his son George in Philadelphia a letter that illustrates a common pattern in Irish emigration, particularly among families of middling or higher status: Irish parents' transmission of advice, as well as capital, to their offspring in America. More important, the elder Bryan's letter has unusual political and sociocultural significance—especially in light of George Bryan's exceptional, if ultimately tragic, career as one of Pennsylvania's most prominent Revolutionary leaders—for it demonstrates how the patterns and tensions of Irish political culture could also be transmitted, even in the most mundane guise, and adapted to the New World.

The eighteenth century was an especially didactic era: "courtesy books" enjoining polite conduct, manners, and civility, often composed as letters of fatherly advice to children, were immensely popular among the middle and upper ranks of British society. Samuel Bryan was typical of many affluent Irish fathers who sought to provide emigrant sons with parental guidance as well as the financial means and social connections requisite for success abroad. Of course, sheer distance between Irish and American societies, as well as

---

85. See chapter 50.

the latter's raw fluidity, inevitably attenuated parents' controls. However, their concern to maintain or improve family status in what was, after all, a transatlantic imperial, social, and cultural system—as well as the contemporary assumption that "enlightened" opinions and "proper" behavior were applicable everywhere—encouraged Irish parents to send lengthy epistles designed to reinforce in America the injunctions that, they hoped, their children had internalized prior to their departures.[1]

Samuel Bryan was a merchant, engaged in overseas trade, and a member of Dublin's Presbyterian community.[2] He and his wife, Sarah Dennis Bryan, were sufficiently wealthy to provide their eldest son George, born on 11 August 1731, with a superior education, probably in one of the capital's several Presbyterian academies. Most Presbyterians in Dublin traced their origins to late sixteenth- and seventeenth-century migrants from England (the Bryans' likely origin),[3] Scotland, and Ulster, although after 1685 they were joined by several thousand French Huguenot refugees. In the mid-1700s dissenters comprised less than one-fifth of Dublin's shrinking Protestant majority.[4] However, they were prominent in commerce, banking, and manufacturing, and the city's Presbyterians alone supported eight English, Ulster-Scottish, and French congregations.

Despite their affluence, as dissenters Presbyterians were excluded from the capital's social and political élite by the Anglican nobility, gentry, lawyers, and merchants who controlled both the Irish Parliament and the upper house, the Board of Aldermen, of the Dublin Corporation. In the late 1740s Presbyterians and other tradesmen mounted a political challenge to Dublin's oligarchy. Their spokesman was the nominal Anglican and "closet Presbyterian" Charles Lucas, a radical apothecary and journalist from County Clare.[5] In his newspapers, pamphlets, and speeches, Lucas condemned the city's "aristocrats" as corrupt and dissolute, touted the "middling sort's" humble "virtues" as superior to gentle

---

1. In a sense, these formal advice letters performed for literate emigrant families a ritualistic function, similar to the "American wakes" among pre- or recently literate Irish emigrants in the nineteenth century. In the latter, "proper" standards of behavior, especially family loyalty as expressed through monetary remittances from America, were enjoined through songs, proverbs, and other traditional, oral media.   2. In 1738 a "Samuel Bryan, cloth merchant," located at Old Bridge, Church Street, advertised his wares in Dublin's newspapers. 3. In 1677 Rev. Samuel Bryan, perhaps an ancestor of his 1751 namesake, was minister of Dublin's Presbyterian church on Cooke Street; he had been ejected from his former living of Aulseley, in Warwickshire, when the Stuart Restoration (1660) reestablished the Anglican church and purged it of dissenting clergy, several of whom migrated to Dublin.   4. In 1750 Protestants probably numbered about 50–60,000 of Dublin's approximately 100,000 inhabitants. For more demographic data on Dublin, see appendix 2.2b, on chapter 14. 5. Charles Lucas (1713–1771): born in Co. Clare to impecunious parents who moved to Dublin and apprenticed him to an apothecary; selected by the barber-surgeons' guild as member of Dublin's Common Council, 1741; in the *Censor* and other writings, Lucas championed the city's Protestant freemen and sharply criticized the oligarchical aldermen and the controlling "English interest" in the Irish government and the Church of Ireland; condemned by Parliament in 1749, Lucas fled to the continent where, in his 12-year exile, he studied medicine and earned an M.D. at Leyden in 1752; in 1761 Lucas returned to Ireland, and Dublin's freeholders elected him to the Irish Parliament, where he sat until his death; from 1763 Lucas published the *Freeman's Journal,* Ireland's leading "patriot" newspaper, in which he argued that British ministerial conspiracies threatened Protestant liberties in both Ireland and the American colonies.

birth or even great wealth as qualifications for public office, and, as one of Protestant Ireland's leading "patriots," condemned the Irish Parliament's legal subordination to London's authority.

However, Lucas's lowly origins and raucous political style made Dublin's Presbyterian merchants, bankers, and manufacturers uneasy; their instinctive preference was accommodation, not conflict. More commonly, therefore, they sought to join Dublin's aristocracy not only through material accumulation but also by emulating its culture of "polite manners." In this effort, they found models in the contemporary writings of the earl of Shaftesbury,[6] Addison and Steele,[7] and other Whig essayists who provided social guidance for Britain's nascent bourgeoisie. Borrowing heavily from John Locke's environmentalist or "sensationalist" psychology,[8] Shaftesbury and his followers shifted gentility's basis from its traditional, aristocratic criteria of land and pedigree to "expressive accomplishments"— such as civility, urbanity, and politeness—that could be attained by the "commercial classes" and even by those Shaftesbury called "the Poor Rivale Presbitereans," whom the Anglican élite generally disdained as "unpolite, unform'd, without Literature or Manners."[9] Shaftesbury thus moved the provenance of manners out of the royal court into the daily discourse of lowly-born but prosperous and ambitious citizens.

Shaftesbury and the authors of early eighteenth-century conduct books assumed that wealth, manners, and morals were, or should be, inextricable. Indeed, they usually argued that "virtue" alone constituted true nobility; it was not until 1774, when Lord Chesterfield's *Letters to His Son* was published,[10] that gentlemen's advice literature disconnected

6. Anthony Ashley Cooper (1671–1713), third earl of Shaftesbury: moral philosopher, sometime Whig statesman, and would-be political reformer; educated under John Locke's supervision; English M.P., 1695–1698, but due to ill health lived much of his later life in Holland and Naples, estranged both from Queen Anne's Tory government and from Whig opposition leaders; in 1711 he published *Characteristicks of Men, Manners, Opinions, and Times,* which included influential essays on virtue and sociability.   7. Joseph Addison (1672–1719) and Richard Steele (1672–1729): Whig politicians, dramatists, and essayists on society, manners, and politics—most famously in *The Tatler* (1709–1711) and *The Spectator* (1711–1712). Steele was born in Dublin, son of a wealthy attorney and former sheriff of Co. Tipperary, but was educated in England, where he met Addison and accompanied him to Oxford University. Both achieved political office and honors after the Hanoverian Succession (1714) ensured Whig ascendancy; in 1714–1715 Steele was knighted, elected a British M.P., and became manager of the Royal Theatre at Drury Lane. Addison's play *Cato* (1713) was an enormously popular exposition of classic republican principles.   8. John Locke (1632–1704), Whig statesman and philosopher; Locke expounded his theories of psychology in *An Essay Concerning Human Understanding* (1690) and *A Treatise on Education* (1693) but is perhaps most famous for his exposition of natural rights, contract theory of government, and the people's right of revolution against tyranny (thus justifying the Glorious Revolution) in his *Two Treatises of Government* (1690).   9. L. E. Klein, "Liberty, Manners, and Politeness . . . ," 588, 604; see Sources, chapter 52.   10. Philip Dormer Stanhope (1694–1773), fourth earl of Chesterfield: a Whig politician and statesman, Chesterfield sat in the House of Commons in 1715–1723 and in the Lords from 1726; George II appointed him privy councillor (1728), ambassador to the Hague (1728–1732), Irish viceroy (1745–1746), and secretary of state (1746–1748), but normally Chesterfield was in principled opposition to Robert Walpole's government; liberal and generous in public life (he was perhaps eighteenth-century Ireland's most sympathetic viceroy), Chesterfield outraged moralists by his succession of beautiful mistresses and by his worldly advice to his natural son, conveyed in letters written in 1737–1768 and published by his son's widow in 1774.

wealth and behavior from the constraints of morality. Nevertheless, Shaftesbury and his followers secularized and privatized the meaning of virtue. Thus, their teachings marked a fundamental revision of classic "republican," "commonwealth," or "country Whig" definitions of virtue, as expounded in England by James Harrington[11] and Lord Bolingbroke,[12] among others, and as adapted to Irish circumstances by Robert Viscount Molesworth[13] and later by Charles Lucas. Traditionally, "commonwealthmen" extolled rustic, "republican" (Spartan or early Roman) virtues—such as self-sufficiency, frugality, and a disinterested public spirit—which they attributed, almost exclusively, to an idealized, "independent" gentry. Conversely, they condemned self-interest, political "corruption" (their word for patronage), and urban luxury; they distrusted commerce and regarded bankers and speculators as "parasites."

Both the commonwealthmen and Shaftesbury's Whigs praised British "liberties" and opposed the concentration of political power, especially in the hands of the Stuart kings prior to the English Civil Wars of the 1640s and the Glorious Revolution of 1688. However, early eighteenth-century polemicists in the republican tradition were equally discomfited by Britain's new aristocracy of great wealth—by the "Robinocracy" that emerged under Robert Walpole and the Whig factions that governed Britain and controlled the Irish Parliament through patronage and rotton boroughs. Moreover, commonwealth ideals seemed antithetical to the main thrust of Shaftesbury's advice literature, attuned as it was to a society that was increasingly secular, urban, commercial, and individualistic. Shaftesbury's adherents tended to emphasize the performance of mere "social virtues"—as in the new coffee houses and drawing rooms that provided venues for congenial social climbing and stylized intercourse among otherwise competitive tradesmen.

---

11. James Harrington (1611–1677), radical political philosopher; Harrington supported the Parliamentary cause in the English Civil Wars (1642–1648) and championed the short-lived English Commonwealth (1649–1653) that preceded Oliver Cromwell's military government; Harrington described his ideal polity, an aristocratic republic, in *The Commonwealth of Oceana* (1656); imprisoned after the Restoration (1660) for his antimonarchical opinions, Harrington was eventually released but in broken health. **12.** Henry Saint-John (1678–1751), Viscount Bolingbroke: a leading Tory statesman under Queen Anne (1702–1714), Bolingbroke opposed the Hanoverian Succession (1714) and was involved in the Jacobite invasion of 1715; pardoned in 1723, Bolingbroke became a severe critic of Robert Walpole's Whig adminstration, especially of the "monied men," bankers and stockjobbers, who comprised Walpole's chief supporters; Bolingbroke coined the term "patriot" to describe the loose, oppositional alliance of Tories and discontented "country" or "real Whigs"; his book *The Idea of a Patriot King* (written in 1738, but not published until 1749) invoked the ideal of a harmonious, hierarchical society governed by a virtuous monarch. **13.** Robert Viscount Molesworth (1656–1712): born in Dublin and educated at Trinity College, Dublin, Molesworth supported the Glorious Revolution and in 1689–1690 and 1692–1694 served as William III's envoy to the Danish court, which he later criticized as tyrannical in *An Account of Denmark as it was in the Year 1692* (1694); returning to Ireland, Molesworth represented Dublin in the Irish Parliament (1695–1699) and was an Irish privy councillor from 1697; a friend of William Molyneux and Jonathan Swift, advocates of Irish legislative independence, Molesworth championed political, religious, and economic reform in political essays that were republished in 1775 as *The Principles of a Real Whig*.

SAMUEL BRYAN

Significantly, it was early eighteenth-century Presbyterian authors from Ulster and Scotland who played major roles in reconciling aristocratic, commonwealth notions of civic virtue with Shaftesbury's new emphases on bourgeois sociability and politeness, adding a democratic gloss to the old republican formula as well as stressing the public and religious dimensions of Shaftesbury's notions of civility. Perhaps most important were the teachings of Rev. Francis Hutcheson from County Down[14]—Molesworth's protegé and a teacher in one of Dublin's dissenting academies before assuming the Chair of Moral Philosophy at Glasgow University. Hutcheson contended that virtue's ultimate source was an innate, God-given, and universally shared "moral sense" that, in optimal circumstances, could overcome individual selfishness and inspire public benevolence as well as private morality. Ideally, he argued, society should be characterized by a roughly equal division of property, government should be both republican and broadly representative, education should be widespread, and religious establishments should be abolished; thus liberated from poverty, tyranny, ignorance, and superstition, the citizenry's moral sense would promote civic virtue and "general happiness."

Variously interpreted and elaborated, Hutcheson's ideas would inspire both the "moderate" literati of the eighteenth-century Scottish Enlightenment and the dissenter radicalism that flourished in America in 1776 and, less successfully, in east Ulster in the 1790s. In the 1740s, however, Dublin's wealthy Presbyterians remained torn, in their struggle for civil equality against the capital's Anglican élite, between public, political confrontation and individual, sociocultural adaptation. George Bryan's American career would epitomize the tensions between these conflicting strategies. Indeed, the failure of Lucas's political challenge to Dublin's aristocracy in 1749, when official repression forced him into exile, may have determined Samuel Bryan's decision to send George to America—as well as his parting admonition that polite manners and close attention to business were the only sure keys to self-advancement. Clearly, Samuel steered his son toward a career in transatlantic commerce, and in 1751 he arranged for George to become a business partner with James Wallace, an Irish-born merchant in Philadelphia, where one of George's maternal uncles also resided. Thus, in the spring or summer of 1752 George Bryan, aged 20, arrived in Philadelphia aboard one of his father's ships, the *Crawford*, and joined the new mercantile firm of Wallace & Bryan, located at the docks on the corner of Water and Market streets.[15]

Wallace & Bryan proved a highly profitable enterprise, trading in linens, flaxseed, servants, rum, wine, and other goods with the British Isles, Europe, and the West Indies. However, within a few months of George Bryan's arrival in Philadelphia, his father became alarmed, not only by the inadequacy of his son's first communications to Dublin but also by reports that young George had unwisely chosen "Low mean company" for his friends

---

14. Rev. Francis Hutcheson (1694–1746); professor of moral philosophy at the University of Glasgow (1730–1746); see chapter 55. 15. In its first advertisements, Wallace & Bryan offered for sale a cargo of less fortunate emigrants—indentured servants who had sailed in the *Crawford* with George Bryan.

FIGURE 13
Portrait of George Bryan
(1731–1791), painted by
Julius Augustus Beck
(1831–1918). Photograph
(acc. No. 1907.1) courtesy
of The Historical Society
of Pennsylvania (HSP),
Philadelphia.

and companions and with them had engaged in "Rustic" amusements. In retrospect, George Bryan's nocturnal activities appear harmless, but the contemporary conviction that environment—especially "good company"—was crucial in character formation, as well as for business and marriage prospects, no doubt inspired Samuel Bryan to fire off the following injunction to his disobedient son.

Samuel Bryan, Dublin, to George Bryan, Philadelphia, 23 September 1752

Dublin Septr 23^d 1752

Dear George

I received yours of 6 August last but so short a one does not please me. I am sure you knew of the Crawford's sailing some days before she came out, and you by that had no right to plead your being in a hurry, these are idle excuses & Letters writ in a hurry are never well done, I expected a list of occurrences since yours by the Jenny[16] & how the present Crops have proved both in Corn & flaxseed, very proper to

---

16. the Jenny: a 35-ton brigantine, owned by Wallace & Bryan and captained by Alexander Magee, also an Irish Presbyterian.

be taken notice of at the time of your writing——I am informed y^r. Evenings are taken up in boating on the River & down to M^r. Bleakly, this can in no way improve you as a man coming into Life. I recommended to you the best of company to keep, Men in Business, Men of Conversation[17] & good manners—that when I meet you again I may not meet with the Rustic or Tar,[18] but the genteel pretty agreeable fellow as well as the compleat sensible Merch^t, & this will never be the case if you proceed in your present Course, for you take the readiest method to lock yourself from what I have been recommending you to do. Mr Bleakly is an honest man but he is not a man of all men I should choose for my companion, he never saw anything in his young days that could polish his person & manners & I am afraid he has not improved either by going to Philadelphia. I gave you long letters before recommending your going into all companies where men of manners, Sense &^{c} were to be found, the Expence I valued not,[19] & those as good or better than yourself. Low mean company are a Scandal & a disgrace & nothing can so effectually lessen you in the opinion of Mankind——the amusements of Dancing, fencing, the use of the Small Sword taking a glass of wine or Punch with a few of Such <as> I am recommending at particular evenings, this w^d. after business is over be shewing yourself to Mankind to be known & regarded. Away with boating & Let me never hear more of such a thing unless on business or on a party of pleasure with good company.

Let not the carelessness of the world about you with respect to God & religion have any effect on you for if once you can lose sight of this you will be an easy prey to every vice which offers.[20] I conjure[21] <you> to take my advice and directions if you value & regard me as your tender affectionate father watchful of your happiness, willing & wishing you to be good & happy, could you but conceive my Joy in your attaining these happy ends you w^d. not stop in y^r pursuit 'till they were made y^r. own. I am doing everything in my power to advance you in the world and establish you as my son. Do not defeat it in any one Instance but resolve & I am sure you have resolution enough to surmount everything I can find fault with. For news little is going, nothing new in my family or among your friends who are well. Your uncles & Aunt & Cousins Jenny & Matty are all well & join in love to you. Your Mother joins me in hearty prayers to God for your health & prosperity here & your happiness to all Eternity. I am your tender, affectionate & watchful Father,

Saml Bryan

P.S. Do not omit to send your mother 2 or 3 kegs of cranberries & some pickles both peaches & cucumbers, as well as other pickles that are green & pretty. Send no more Sturgeon, it is very bad, what you sent already is so full of salt & Spice, that

---

17. Men of Conversation: "men who know how to conduct themselves in society." **18. Tar**: sailor. **19. the Expence I valued not**: "I did not reckon any expense too great." **20. offers**: presents itself. **21. conjure**: entreat.

it is not worth a penny   It is not saved in the Danzick way.[22] Send us some hickery sticks to make yards,[23] & if next Summer any Ship of yours or ours was coming here I wish you would send us one of y[r] best Pads,[24] one that is surefooted, goes well, fast & not rough & not old,   perhaps such may be picked up some time before that it might please for a thing of that kind could not be got to Satisfaction if bought when the Ship is going, but take<s> time & Opportunity,   we wrote about wax or Sperma cetti[25] candles,   the wetness of our season has spoiled all our bees, & wax next winter must be very dear so do not omit our order & let some candles be 2, 3, 4 or 5 to the pound some 6 & a few 8, but very few.

Inclosed is Your Uncle, I. Dennis's acc[t]. Curr[t].[26] for the balance of which press him immediately.

For nearly two decades, George Bryan followed his father's directions and amply fulfilled his expectations. After Wallace & Bryan wound up its affairs in 1755, Bryan embarked alone on an exceptionally successful career as an import-export and retail merchant, shipowner, army contractor, and land speculator. In 1757 he married Elizabeth Smith,[27] daughter of one of Philadelphia's prominent Presbyterian merchants, and by 1769 his property assessment in the city's Dock Ward was five times greater than that of Robert Morris, the future "financier of the Revolution." Bryan also assumed major public responsibilities. In 1758 Bryan, only 27 years old, was elected to the lay governing body of the First Presbyterian Church, and he soon became the leading spokesman for "the Presbyterian interest" in Philadelphia—"our own hero," in the words of one coreligionist[28]. Although he lacked formal training in law, in 1764 Bryan was appointed a judge of the orphan's court and court of common pleas. In the same year he was elected to represent the city in the Pennsylvania Assembly and, although defeated by Benjamin Franklin's "Quaker party" in the following election, in 1765 he joined John Dickinson as one of the colony's delegates to the Stamp Act Congress. In 1767–1770 Bryan played a leading role in the nonimportation agreement that Philadelphia's merchants signed to protest the Townshend Acts.[29]

However, in 1771 Bryan's fortunes collapsed, perhaps because of his strict fidelity to the trade embargo with Britain, and he declared bankruptcy and lost all his property. In

---

22. **saved in the Danzick way**: cured/preserved in the manner common in Danzig, a Hanseatic port city on the Baltic Sea. **23. yards**: rods, bars. **24. Pad**: an easy-paced horse. In his biography of Bryan, B. A. Konkle transcribes this as Cads. **25. Sperma cetti**: spermaceti: the waxy substance that separates from whale oil, especially that of the head cavity; used for making candles. **26. acc[t]. Curr[t]**: i.e. account current "a continuous account in which sums paid and received are entered in detail" (OED, s.v. account, 2.a).
27. Elizabeth Smith (1733–1799), daughter of Samuel Smith. George and Elizabeth Bryan's 10 children and their birthdates were: Sarah (1758), Samuel (1759), Arthur (1761), Francis (1764), Mary (1765), George (1767), Elizabeth (1769), William (1771), Thomas (1772), and Jonathan (1774). **28.** Foster, *Pursuit of Equal Liberty*, 35; see Sources. **29.** In 1768 Bryan was also elected a member of the American Philosophical Society. On George Bryan, Robert Morris, John Dickinson, and Pennsylvania politics in the 1760s and 1770s, generally, also see chapters 53, 55, 56, and 58.

addition, during the early 1770s three of his children died, and he exhibited first signs of the poor health that would plague the rest of his life. No longer a "compleat sensible Merch^t," Bryan was dependent on meagre salaries from public office for the remainder of his career.[30] Moreover, when he returned to political activity in the early days of the Revolution, it was as the champion of radical democracy and the political enemy of Robert Morris, John Dickinson, and other wealthy, former associates who were, at best, reluctant revolutionaries and who vehemently opposed the ultrademocratic Pennsylvania constitution of 1776. Under that constitution, Bryan was elected to the state's Supreme Executive Council (1776), as vice-president and then president of Pennsylvania (1777–1779), and as a representative to the state Assembly (1779) and to the septennial Council of Censors (1784). In 1780 he also became a judge of Pennsylvania's Supreme Court. Dedicated and energetic, Bryan successfully steered Pennsylvania through an "internal revolution" that was far more democratic than men such as Morris and Dickinson had desired, temporarily transforming the state into a kind of Spartan commonwealth. Between 1777 and 1779 Bryan's administration confiscated the Penn family's vast estates, imposed Test Acts (loyalty oaths) on Tories and pacifists, authorized price controls to curb inflation and speculation, radically reformed the College of Philadelphia, and shut down the city's theatres. Most significantly, perhaps, Bryan was primarily responsible for the 1780 law that abolished slavery in Pennsylvania—albeit more gradually than he would have preferred.

Inevitably, Philadelphia's conservative mercantile and financial élite despised him as an "archpartisan" and a "brawler." Bryan responded with equal contempt, always "identify[ing] himself with the *people*," as one critic complained, "in opposition to those who were termed the *well-born*."[31] Riches, Bryan declared, were merely the "inheritance of wise men and fools" and thus no prerequisite, as his opponents alleged, for political office; "wisdom and virtue alone," he argued, should distinguish those entrusted with governing

30. Ironically, in the end John Bleakly, the target of Samuel Bryan's contempt in his 1752 letter, far outstripped George in the race for riches. Bleakly (most commonly, Bleakley), an Ulster Presbyterian from rural Co. Armagh, may indeed have been unpolished in Ireland, as the urbane Samuel alleged. However, he was by no means a scoundrel or a failure in America, where he made a considerable fortune. In 1769 his property in Philadelphia was assessed at £402, the fifth-highest assessment in the city's North Ward, and in 1780 the same estate was valued at $36,000. Bleakly died sometime between 1769 and 1779. His son, John, Jr., inherited most of his father's fortune and was (along with the elderly George Bryan) an original member of Philadelphia's Hibernian Society (est. 1790) and from 1794 a member of the city's more exclusive Friendly Sons of St. Patrick. When John, Jr., died in 1802, he willed £2,000 in charity to poor widows and yellow fever victims. ¶Interestingly, among the elder John Bleakly's holdings was a section of Province or Fisher's Island, in the Schuylkill River, a frequent venue for the wealthy and politically influential members of the Fort St. David's and Schuylkill Fishing companies, two of Philadelphia's oldest and most exclusive clubs. (It is likely that Bleakly was the "John Blackney" listed in 1763 as a member of the Fort St. David's Company.) Thus, from a distance of three thousand miles, Samuel Bryan either had misjudged the context of George's boating excursions or, from the perspective of a more urbane and hierarchical society, had mistrusted the standards of a colonial élite in which a rustic like Bleakly could gain wealth and social acceptance. **31.** Foster, *Pursuit of Equal Liberty*, xiii–xiv; see Sources.

powers.[32] Unfortunately, Bryan's power base was confined largely to his fellow Calvinists among the Scots-Irish and German farmers in Pennsylvania's backcountry, and when the disfranchising Test Acts were repealed in the 1780s, his political enemies triumphed. Despite Bryan's efforts and anguished protests, Robert Morris's future Federalists first won control of the Pennsylvania Assembly, then secured the state's ratification of the federal Constitution (1787), and finally replaced the radical 1776 state constitution (1789–1790). Defeated, scorned, and impoverished, Bryan died in Philadelphia on 27 January 1791.[33]

Despite his financial and political failures, George Bryan did become "known" by all Pennsylvanians—highly "regarded" by many and hated by others. However, his career had diverged dramatically from that which his father had enjoined. While not neglecting "God & religion," Samuel Bryan had urged his son to perform "polite" accomplishments—"Dancing, fencing, the use of the Small Sword[,] taking a glass of wine or Punch"—to court the friendship and patronage of "men of manners." George did so successfully for two decades, although his political activities even prior to his 1771 bankruptcy suggest that commonwealth idealism, not genteel sociability, was his preferred métier. Significantly also, in the late 1760s Bryan worked closely with Francis Hutcheson's foremost disciple in America, Rev. Francis Alison from County Donegal, in opposition to the threatened establishment of Anglican bishops in the colonies.[34] Certainly after 1771 George Bryan's political trajectory remarkably paralleled that of Charles Lucas, the Dublin agitator of his impressionable youth. Like Lucas, Bryan became an apostate from the class that his father, and his own earlier ambitions, had urged him to join. And like the Irish "patriot," Bryan became, as one critic charged, "in the antipodes at all points, to whatever was English."[35]

George Bryan reportedly possessed a remarkable memory; had he not retained his father's letter to the end of his life, doubtless he would never have forgotten its contents.[36] Arguably, Bryan's political course may epitomize the eighteenth-century sociocultural "revolution against patriarchal authority" that, according to several scholars, was a crucial antecedent to the American Revolution. However, it is impossible to judge whether George Bryan viewed his father's advice as a flawed guide or a constant reproach. As both Bryans knew well, in the intensely, even viciously competitive real world of eighteenth-century trade and politics, wealth was the ultimate prerequisite to status. In Bryan's career after 1771, wealth was severed from his pretensions to public esteem, exposing him not only to the Philadelphia merchant élite's scorn of poverty but also to the religious and ethnic prejudices from which his former affluence had shielded him. Thus, his dramatic

---

32. Ibid., 83.   **33.** On Pennsylvania politics in the 1780s and 1790s, see chapters 58 and 62–63.   **34.** Rev. Francis Alison (1705–1779); see chapter 55.   **35.** Foster, *Pursuit of Equal Liberty*, xiv; see Sources.   **36.** In 1752 the will of a Samuel Bryan, merchant, was probated in Dublin. If this was George Bryan's father, then the 1751 letter was probably his *last* communication with George, which in turn would have greatly heightened its emotive power.

FIGURE 14
Portrait of William Findley
(1741–1821), of
Westmoreland County,
Pennsylvania, painted ca.
1805 by Rembrandt Peale
(1778–1860). Photograph
courtesy of the Independence
National Historical Park,
Philadelphia.

fall and subsequent quest to retain and justify status *without wealth* helped precipitate his transformation into an ardent champion of the common people's rights and "virtues."

To be sure, Bryan's vigorously democratic views were common among Irish Presbyterian emigrants, excluded as they had been from colonial aristocracies composed of wealthy Anglicans or, in Pennsylvania, Quakers. Like his radical Irish-born political associates, William Findley and John Smilie,[37] Bryan viewed the world in Manichean terms: as a struggle between freedom and tyranny, between Dissenters and Anglicans, and between the virtuous people and a selfish, dissolute aristocracy. However, Bryan's career differed significantly from those of Findley, Smilie, and other Scots-Irishmen who helped lead Pennsylvania's anti-Federalists and later its Democratic Republicans. They were men whom Samuel Bryan would have truly considered "Low mean company"—of humble, rural origins in Ulster and, prior to the Revolution, mere farmers or weavers in backcountry Pennsylvania, now prosperous and upwardly mobile but frustrated by the sociocultural barriers that Philadelphia's oligarchy strove to maintain. By contrast, George Bryan had

37. On John Smilie and/or William Findley, see chapters 12, 62, and 67.

endured the pain of social descent from the position to which men such as Findley aspired. Thus, it is arguable that Bryan's political career after 1771 represented either a belated rejection of his father's 1752 injunctions—of advice that had so signally failed him—or an effort to resolve the contradictions between those injunctions and his own traumatic bankruptcy. In either case, letters such as Samuel Bryan's suggest that even affluent, confident emigrants could not easily jetison the Old World's burdens and conflicts after they reached American shores.

53 ✳

Rev. Thomas Barton, 1758

Much of the life of Rev. Thomas Barton, an Ulster-born Anglican clergyman in Pennsylvania, was intentionally shrouded in ambiguity and misrepresentation. Nevertheless, Barton's career, like that of George Bryan,[1] bore several distinctively—albeit less salutary—"Irish" imprints. In 1758 Barton recorded in his journal a dramatic incident, the military execution of an Irish Catholic immigrant named John Doyle, that illustrated the sometimes tragic consequences of transplanted Irish prejudices and also illuminated the contradictions of Barton's own situation. Understood in its fullest contexts, Barton's account of Doyle's death suggests some remarkable parallels between the ethnoreligious conflicts that rent contemporary Pennsylvania and Ireland (especially Ulster) alike, as well as the conflicting roles that a minor member of the governing establishment was obliged to play in both colonial societies.

Born on the south Ulster frontier, surrounded by resentful Catholics whose lands his ancestors had expropriated, Barton spent most of his adult life in the Pennsylvania backcountry, ministering primarily to Ulster-born "planters" who faced savage attacks by the French (Catholic Ireland's perennial ally) and by the Delawares, Shawnees, and other tribes whose hunting-grounds had been seized by force and fraud. Like many Irish Anglicans of genteel origins, in times of peace Barton displayed a certain condescension for both Irish Catholics and Indians, hoping that in Ireland the former and in America the latter could be "civilized" and reconciled to English rule through education and proselytization. By contrast—and also reflecting traditional Anglo-Irish sentiments—Barton heartily disliked Protestant dissenters, including Quakers but particularly Scots-Irish Presbyterians. Like the Irish high churchmen Jonathan Swift and James MacSparran,[2] Barton scorned Presbyterians both as his social inferiors and for their allegedly "levelling," republican, and even regicidal principles. In America Barton especially despised New Side evangelicals for the disorderly "enthusiasm" of their revivals as well as for their crude and often violent prejudices against

---

1. See especially chapter 52.   2. See chapter 8.

FIGURE 15
Portrait of Rev. Thomas
Barton (1728/30–1780),
of Carlisle and Lancaster,
Pennsylvania, sketch from an
eighteenth-century portrait.
Photograph courtesy of
Walter Pencak, editor,
Pennsylvania History, and
Professor of History, Penn
State University, University
Park, Pennsylvania.

"papists" and Indians.[3] Yet in Pennsylvania as in Ireland, Barton's and his church's ultimate dependence on official patronage—as well as the demands for pan-Protestant solidarity when threatened by "native" uprisings—obliged Barton to swallow his contempt for the Scots-Irish and join them: first, by fostering the surge of anti-Catholic hysteria to which John Doyle fell victim; and second, a few years later, by excusing their massacres of Christianized Indians. In the short term, Barton was amply rewarded for betraying his sympathies. However, as his party's Scots-Irish allies became increasingly radical and moved toward the American Revolution, Barton—like most Angicans in late eighteenth-century Ireland itself—had no choice but to fulfill the logic of his background and status, collapsing in utter dependence on the Crown.

Thomas Barton was born in 1728 (or 1730—accounts vary), the son of William Barton III and Susan Bashford, in the overwhelmingly Catholic town and parish of Car-

3. On the New Side Presbyterians and the First Great Awakening, see chapters 46 and 47.

rickmacross (or Magheross), in the barony of Farney, County Monaghan.[4] The Bartons were originally Lancastershire gentry, but Thomas Barton's great-grandfather, William Barton I, was a merchant-tailor in London when, in 1656, he began to invest in south Ulster and north Leinster lands seized by the English in the Elizabethan period. Shortly after Cromwell's reconquest, William I's two sons, Thomas and William II (1640–1722, Rev. Thomas Barton's grandfather), settled permanently in south Ulster. William II was especially successful, acquiring ownership or long leases of large landholdings in Monaghan, Cavan, Tyrone, Louth, and Dublin. He also served several terms as a member of the Irish Parliament and as high sheriff of County Monaghan, while his nephew Richard Tenison was, successively, Church of Ireland bishop of Killala and Achonry, Clogher, and Meath.

However, in 1689 one of King James's armies sacked and burned Carrickmacross castle, William II's residence, and subsequently he moved to County Louth. Thus, if Thomas Barton was indeed born and raised in Carrickmacross castle, as family tradition asserts, he resided only in the gatehouse or in one of the turrets that had survived the Catholic attack. Ironically, the ruined castle symbolized Thomas's failure to inherit his grandfather's still-vast estates. Apparently, William II's son and Thomas's father, William Barton III (d. 1740s), was illegitimate, and William II willed all his lands to his only legitimate heir, a daughter whose marriage conveyed the Barton estates to the Tenison family. Consequently, instead of great wealth and high status, Thomas Barton inherited only genteel poverty, an obsessive fear of betrayal, and a desperate need to ingratiate himself with the rich and powerful in order to gain what he later called "a freedom from want—from low and abject dependence."[5] Given his circumstances, it was fortunate that Barton was both highly intelligent and able to attend Carrickmacross's celebrated "free school," taught in 1713–1745 by Rev. William Folds, a graduate of St. John's College, Cambridge. According to family tradition, Barton also studied at Trinity College, Dublin, and although poverty may have terminated his studies early—for Trinity has no record of his graduation—there is no doubt he had attained an exceptional education by about 1730–1731, when he emigrated to Philadelphia.

Soon after his arrival, Barton established a school at Norriton, about 20 miles outside Pennsylvania's capital, where he befriended and tutored the young David Rittenhouse (1732–1796), who later became eighteenth-century America's most celebrated astronomer and one of revolutionary Pennsylvania's most radical leaders. In late 1752 Barton returned to Philadelphia and became a tutor in the Academy (later, the College) of Philadelphia. There he gained the friendship and patronage of the school's future provost, Rev. William Smith (1727–1803)—a Scottish-born Anglican and a graduate of Aberdeen University, whose controversial career combined equal devotion to the Church of England, the Penn

4. For demographic data on Carrickmacross (or Magheross) parish and its environs, see appendix 2.1d, on chapter 53.   5. Rev. Thomas Barton, Lancaster, Pa., to the Society for the Propagation of the Gospel (S.P.G.), 16 November 1764 (in Perry, *Hist. Coll. Am. Colonial Church,* vol. 2; see Sources).

family's political interests, and his own ambitions for wealth and for appointment as the first American bishop. On 8 December 1753 Barton married Esther Rittenhouse (1731–1774), David's sister, and in summer 1754 he resigned his tutorship and embarked for England to seek ordination as an Anglican clergyman. Barton's decision may have been motivated by piety and ambition, and it may have been guided by Rev. Smith. However, his journey abroad may also have been flight from personal embarrassment—for his and Esther's first child was born only four months after their marriage, and Barton's entire career was marked by desires to flee the locales where he had suffered reverses or betrayed his principles.

Barton was ordained in England on 29 Jaunary 1755. Equally important and probably through Smith's recommendation, in London Barton met and befriended the able albeit avaricious Thomas Penn (1702–1775), son of Pennsylvania's founder and the chief proprietor of the province. It was through Penn's patronage that Barton became a missionary of the Society for the Propagation of the Gospel (S.P.G.), which ensured him a steady salary and a degree of independence from his future parishioners. However, his dependence on Penn ensured that, from 1755 until the American Revolution, Barton would be a loyal retainer of Pennsylvania's "Proprietary party." This loose political grouping, scarcely a "party" in any modern sense, was based on a pragmatic alliance between the colony's small Anglican minority, led by Smith and Rev. Richard Peters (1704–1776) of Philadelphia, head of the Governor's Council, and the much larger body of Scots-Irish Presbyterians. The latter in turn were led in Philadelphia by William Allen (1704–1795), a wealthy merchant and longtime provincial attorney general, and in the backcountry by Allen's lieutenants, such as the Fermanagh-born John Armstrong (1717–1795), a proprietary land agent, militia officer, and New Side elder in Carlisle.[6] Although normally hostile both in Ireland and the colonies, in Pennsylvania the Anglicans and Scots-Irish were united, albeit tenuously, by the lucrative land grants and official appointments with which Thomas Penn rewarded his adherents and by mutual antipathy to the "Quaker party" that controlled the colonial Assembly, denied western Pennsylvanians fair legislative representation, and

6. In 1759 Rev. William Smith estimated Pennsylvania's population as 250,000, of whom only 25,000 (10 percent) were Anglicans; 50,000 Quakers (20 percent); 55,000 Presbyterians (22 percent); and 95,000 (38 percent) German Lutherans, Calvinists, Mennonites, etc. Despite their demographic minority, the Quakers maintained control of Pennsylvania's Assembly throughout the colonial period, due to: (1) overrepresentation in the legislature of Bucks, Chester, and Philadelphia counties, where Quakers were heavily settled, and underrepresentation of the western counties (where the Scots-Irish predominated) and of Philadelphia city; (2) property qualifications, which excluded about half of adult males in rural areas and perhaps 90 percent of those in the capital city from voting; and (3) the longtime Quaker alliance with the Germans, particularly with the members of the pietistic sects. ¶In addition, although in 1761–1775 the Anglican church expanded dramatically in the colonies, especially in New England, there was little increase in Pennsylvania; in 1750 there were only 19 Anglican churches in Penn's colony, and in 1775 there were still only 23. Finally, even the province's Anglicans were not thoroughly united politically; in Philadelphia for example, the "Old Churchmen" in Rev. Richard Peters' Christ Church generally supported the Proprietors, but the "Liberal Churchmen" at St. Paul's followed their fellow (if nominal) Anglican Benjamin Franklin and usually adhered to the Quaker party.

challenged proprietary privileges.⁷ After his return to Pennsylvania, Barton corresponded regularly with Thomas Penn in London, sending reports on economic and political conditions in the backcountry as well as items of scientific curiosity. However, his primary duty was to defend Penn family interests by maintaining the volatile alliance between the Proprietary party's urban-Anglican leaders and the Scots-Irish frontiersmen. Barton's faithful compliance brought him material benefits but at the sacrifice of his integrity.

In April 1755 Barton returned to Pennsylvania and assumed the ministry of three Anglican churches, largely composed of Irish-born parishioners, at Huntingdon, York, and Carlisle, on the western side of the Susquehanna River and in what were then York and Cumberland counties. At first Barton enjoyed his pastorate on "the very Frontiers of the Messiah's Kingdom." His congregations were poor, his ministry was arduous (he regularly visited five additional churches), and the local Presbyterians were hostile to his efforts, but he found his parishioners to be "a worthy, well disposed and kind sort of people." Barton also found the Indians "willing to be instructed and . . . susceptible of good impressions"; recognizing they had been defrauded and debauched by unscrupulous agents and traders, he "entertained strong hopes" they could be Christianized and "civilized" by "Missionaries divested of sinister and selfish motives." Unfortunately, before Barton could begin "to do service among these tawny people," Braddock's defeat on 9 July 1755 unleashed horrific French and Indian attacks on Pennsylvania's western frontier. Within a few months and for three years thereafter, the backcountry suffered what Barton called "the sad effects of Popish Tyranny and Savage Cruelty!"⁸

Barton, like his Presbyterian peers, responded to the French and Indian War much as Protestant clergymen in Ireland typically reacted to Catholic rebellions. For instance, he obtained a militia captaincy from Pennsylvania's governor and organized his parishioners into armed companies to patrol the settlements; soon, he boasted, his "Churches [were] Churches militant indeed," and he had "the pleasure every Sunday (even at the worst of Times), to see my people crowding with their Muskets on their Shoulders; declaring that they will dye Protestants and Freemen sooner than live Idolaters and Slaves."⁹ Even more revealingly, he delivered a rousing sermon, "Unaminity and Public Spirit," which he plagiarized wholesale from a sermon first published in London, Dublin, and Belfast in 1745, during the anti-Catholic hysteria occasioned by the Young Pretender's invasion of Scotland. Barton's efforts not only helped rally the frontier's inhabitants but also greatly pleased Rev. William Smith and the Proprietary party's other leaders. Smith eulogized his friend as a "Watchm[a]n on the Walls of our HOLY ZION" and, not suspecting its dubious origin, rushed Barton's sermon into print, adding to it a long introduction that exonerated the

---

7. Another apparent link between Proprietary officials and agents was membership in Pennsylvania's Masonic Order, of which William Allen was grand master; it would not be surprising if Barton was a Mason, but we have discovered no clear evidence of his affiliation.   **8.** Thomas Barton, Huntingdon, Pa., to the S.P.G., London, 8 November 1756 (Perry, *Hist. Coll. Am. Colonial Church,* vol. 2; see Sources).   **9.** Rev. Thomas Barton, 8 November 1756.

proprietors and blamed the Quakers and the Assembly for the colony's inadequate defences against the minions of the papal antichrist. A few months later, Smith was mortified to discover he had published and endorsed a plagiarized work, but he suppressed the potential scandal: both Barton and his sermon had become too valuable to the proprietary cause to allow their public exposure. Indeed, as a partial reward for his services, in 1758 Smith and Richard Peters procured Barton's appointment as military chaplain to the Pennsylvania regiment that served in the British general John Forbes's expedition against Fort Duquesne, the French and Indian stronghold in western Pennsylvania.

However, Barton's sermon had several negative consequences. First, the Proprietary party's leaders' discovery and concealment of the sermon's true authorship placed Barton deeply in their debt, ensuring he would do their bidding on future occasions; in fact, they may have demanded that Barton accompany Forbes's army, to watch over proprietary interests. Second, the fame that Barton earned from the sermon apparently embittered several prominent Scots-Irishmen, especially John Armstrong, Barton's rival in Carlisle for proprietary favors and one of the three colonels of the Pennsylvania regiment that—alongside troops from the Southern colonies—accompanied Forbes on his march to Fort Duquesne. Indeed, Armstrong may have instigated the refusal by the regiment's overwhelmingly Scots-Irish soldiers to accept Barton's appointment as their official spiritual advisor.[10] As a result, Barton was obliged to serve only as a volunteer chaplain to the few Anglican soldiers in Forbes's command: "[M]uch pains hath been taken to prevent my going," Barton complained to Peters; "both the Church & I have been insulted. . . . Power in the hands of Bigots & Enthusiasts is a dangerous weapon."[11] The latter Barton learned only too well. For third and finally, Barton's sermon both justified and helped generate a wave of bigotry and persecution of Pennsylvania's tiny Irish and German Catholic minority.[12] Although Barton despised Presbyterian revivalists who preached "Cursed be he that keepeth back his Sword from Blood," his own pamphlet—not surprisingly, given its origins—was a rabid anti-"papist" diatribe, designed, as Smith wrote approvingly, to "inspire every bosom" with an ardent "zeal for our holy Protestant faith" and an equal abhorrence

10. In many companies from 50 percent to over 90 percent of the recruits were Irish-born; the great majority were Ulster Presbyterians, but there was a liberal sprinkling of native or "Catholic" Irish names—such as Doyle, Flannagan, O'Neale, etc. However, the recruitment of Roman Catholics, especially if they were Irish, was still discouraged or even forbidden in the colonies, as in Ireland itself. Although unofficial enlistment of Catholics in Ireland began in the 1750s, it did not become general and official until 1774; even then, the policy change did not reflect greater liberalism but rather the British military's desperate need for manpower. Hence it is likely that John Doyle's Scots-Irish officers would have regarded him with a suspicion or hostility that his desertion only confirmed.   11. Rev. Thomas Barton, Huntingdon, Pa., to Rev. Richard Peters, Philadelphia, 18 July 1758 (in Brown; also in *Pa. Arch.*, 1st ser., v. 3; see Sources).   12. In 1757, when frightened officials took a census of Pennsylvania's Catholics, they counted only 1,365 above age 12, of whom merely 416 were Irish and the rest Germans, scattered fairly evenly throughout the province. Nevertheless, the Protestant clergy thought the colony was "very much infested with Popery" and the government ordered the surveillance of Catholics by citizens responsible for their conduct.

of "popery" and its adherents. On 26 September 1758, Barton was obliged to face the awful consequences of the prejudice he had abetted.

On 7 July Barton left his home in York County, joined General Forbes's army at Carlisle, and began recording his military experiences in the journal excerpted here, a copy of which he later sent to Thomas Penn. Much of the journal is mundane, as Barton described western Pennsylvania's natural resources, with an eye to their future exploitation by the proprietors, and the agonizingly slow mobilization of the British and provincial forces at Raystown (later Bedford), where the soldiers were plagued by "Fluxes, Diarrhoas, Agues, Fevers, Small-Pox &C."[13] Problems of supplies and transport, plus Forbes's own illness, delayed the expedition, and although Barton enjoyed conversing with Colonel George Washington and other officers, given the paucity of Anglican soldiers there was little for him to do. Before September 19, when the excerpt here begins, Barton had merely preached nine sermons, baptized three children, drawn up one will, and buried one soldier.

Rev. Thomas Barton, Journal, Raystown Camp, Fort Bedford, Cumberland County, Pennsylvania, 19–26 September 1758

Tuesday September 19th. . . . A General Court Martial sat this Day to try a Number of Men for Desertion. . . . [14]

Sunday September 24th. . . . Receiv'd Orders from Major Halket[15] to attend John Hannah Soldier in the 1st Virginia Regt, Thomas Williams Soldier in the Maryland-Companies, Benjamin Murphy, & Salathiel Mixon of the N. Carolina Companies, & John Doyle of the Pennsylvania Regiment, who are all adjudg'd[16] to suffer Death by the general Court Martial, whereof Col. Mercer[17] was President, & ordered by the General to be shot at 7 O'Clock on Tuesday Morning next. . . . [18]

13. Rev. Thomas Barton, Journal, entry of 19 August 1758. 14. According to Gen. Forbes's orderly book, entries for 22–24 September, the court-martial met on 19 and again on 23 September. It tried 10 men, all but one for desertion: two were acquitted, including one of the alleged deserters; three of the guilty were sentenced to be whipped, five to be shot. W. A. Hunter, "Thomas Barton and the Forbes Expedition," 477, n. 195; see Sources. ¶Omitted before quotation: Arrival of the "melancholy News" of the failure of Major James Grant's advance expedition to Fort Duquesne, defeated by the French and Indians on 14 September, with heavy loses. ¶Omitted after quotation: entries of 20–23 September, describing arrivals at Raystown camp of additional supplies and troops, especially of a thousand Virginia militiamen commanded by Col. George Washington; successful results of an elk hunt; movement of troops and wagons to "Advanc'd Posts" toward Fort Duquesne. 15. Major Halket: Francis Halkett, captain (not major) of the 44th Royal Infantry Regiment and General Forbes's aide-de-camp. 16. adjudg'd: sentenced, condemned. 17. Col. Mercer: Col. Hugh Mercer (1725–1777), Scottish-born commander of the Third Pennsylvania Battalion, whose officers and men had rejected Barton's chaplaincy in favor of a Scots-Irish Presbyterian minister, Rev. Andrew Bay of Lower Marsh Creek, Pa., on 4 July 1758. 18. Omitted before quotation: Rev. Henry Monro, chaplain of the Highland Regiment, preached to the troops. Omitted after quotation: debate among Forbes's officers on the feasibility of building a military road for wagon traffic to Fort Duquesne.

Monday September 25th. At 6 O'Clock this Morning visited & pray'd with the Prisoners, who have not yet receiv'd their Sentence. . . . [19]

Receiv'd an Invitation from Major Halket Aid du Camp, to dine this Day with the General, who was very facetious[20] & in high Spirits at Table, tho' extremely weak & in a low State of Health:—He enquir'd much into the Moral State of the Army; declar'd he was concern'd at not being able to attend Divine Service; & that he was sorry I had so disagreeable an Office[21] upon my Hands at present, as that of attending Persons under Sentence of Death. . . . [22]

Visited the Prisoners in the Evening, who I found in Tears under terrible Apprehensions of approaching Death.— I pray'd with them; & examin'd into the State of their Souls, & their Preparations for Eternity;— but to my great Mortification[23] found very little Sense of Religion in any of them. Before I left them an Officer came in with the General's Pardon to John Hannah, Thomas Williams, Benjamin Murphy & Salathiel Mixon,—who seem'd more affected and more penitent at the Thoughts of Living than the Thoughts of dying; They were immediately discharg'd. . . . [24]

Tuesday September 26th. Very early this Morning visited & pray'd with John Doyle, who is to be shot to Death at 7 O'Clock A.M.—[25] He told me he was brought up a Papist; & as his Conscience never supply'd him with sufficient Reasons to renounce that Profession, he was resolv'd to dye one—yet as he made no Doubt but[26] the Prayers of good Men would avail much, he beg'd of me to stay with him the few Minutes he had to live, & attend him to the Place of Execution; to which I agreed.— In a little Time came in the Provost, & pin'd a Paper to his breast with these dreadful words— Viz—

"Camp at Rays Town September 26th 1758

"John Doyle, a Soldier in Captain Patterson's Company in the Pennsylvania Regt, is to be shot to Death for Desertion."——

I walk'd with him to the Place of Execution, surrounded by a strong Guard. He behav'd with uncommon Resolution;— exhorted his Brother-Soldiers to take Example

---

19. Omitted: arrival in camp of the wounded survivors of Major Grant's defeat on 14 September. **20. facetious:** amusing. **21. Office:** here and below "duty." **22.** Omitted: arrival from Philadelphia of news of British victories in Europe. **23. Mortification:** disappointment. **24.** Gen. Forbes's orderly book, entry of 25 September 1758: "John Hannah Soldier belonging to the 1st Virgn Regt Thomas Williams of the Maryland Compys Benjn Murphy & Salateel Mixon of the No Carolina Compys ordered by the Sentence of a Genl Court Martial to be shot tommorrow morning for desertion But their Officers from some favourable Circumstances and in hopes that the flagrant Example now before them of the Grossness of their Crimes in Cheating & Robing their King & Country will have a proper Influence upon their future Conduct, have Appeald to the Genl to pardon them; He therefore freely grants their request & orders them To Join their respective Corps to morrow after the Execution in hopes that it may have the desir'd Effect." (W. A. Hunter, "Thomas Barton and the Forbes Expedition," 481, n. 223; see Sources, chapter 53.) Omitted after quotation in text: problems of securing horses for the march to Fort Duquesne. **25. P.M.** ms. **26. made no Doubt but . . . :** was fully certain that . . .

by his Misfortunes;— To live sober Lives;— to beware of bad Company;— to shun pretended Friends, & loose wicked Companions, "who, says, he, will treat you with Civility & great Kindness over a Bottle; but will deceive & ruin you behind your Backs:"— But above all he charg'd them never to deser^t. When he saw the Six Men that were to shoot him, he enquir'd if they were good Marks-Men; and immediately strip'd off his Coat, open'd his Breast, kneel'd down, & said— "Come Fellow-Soldiers, advance near me,— do your Office well, point at my Heart,— for God's Sake do not miss me, & take Care not to disfigure me."— He would suffer no Handkerchief to be ty'd over his Face, but look'd at his Executioners to the last, who advanc'd so near him that the Muzzles of their Guns were within a Foot of his Body.— Upon a Signal from the Serjeant Major they fir'd, but shot so low that his Bowels fell out,— his Shirt & Breeches were all on Fire, & he tumbled upon his Side;— rais'd one Arm 2 or 3 Times, & soon expir'd. A shocking Spectakle to all around him; & a striking Example to his Fellow Soldiers—[27]

There are several suggestions that Barton was horrified by this incident—and perhaps not only by the harshness of military justice and by the apparently deliberate butchery of Doyle's executioners, but by the partiality of the predominantly Scots-Irish provincial officers who secured reprieves for the Protestant prisoners, leaving the only Irish Catholic among them to suffer the full penalty for desertion. One indication of Barton's response was the abrupt termination of his journal, although he accompanied Forbes's expedition all the way to its successful conclusion—the capture of Fort Duquesne on 25 November. Another sign of Barton's disapproval is the letter that his enemy, Col. Armstrong, wrote to the Proprietary party leader Richard Peters on October 3, only a few days after Doyle's execution, condemning Barton's character in apparent anticipation of the latter's own criticism of Armstrong's role in the affair. Finally, in the aftermath of his military experience Barton was desperate to leave Carlisle and his other Irish missions west of the Susquehanna, and in 1759 the S.P.G.—doubtless at Thomas Penn's urging—approved his transfer to the more prosperous congregation of St. James in Lancaster, a thriving market center of nearly six hundred houses, inhabited primarily by Germans, and the largest inland town in colonial America.

27. Gen. Forbes's orderly book, entry for 28 September 1758: "As the late example of Doyle who was shot to Death for Desertion by Sentence of a Genl Court Martial & the Clemency shown the others will it is hoped have a good effect upon the rest of the Army in preventing that Scandalous & infamous crime of Desertion by which they bring sure Ruin to themselves & shew their endeavours of betraying their Country to their enemies; the General therefore flatters himself that their will be no such thing for the Future & that though he is sensible that the Men have gone through a great deal of Fatigue during this Campaign, yet the remainder being so Short & the advance posts of the Army almost at ye Enemys Nose the Genl therefore with great confidence depends upon the Mens Alacrity & Steadiness in Carrying on the rest of the Service that we may shew our Enemys the danger of Rousing Britons fired & animated with Love of their King & Country."

At first, Barton enjoyed his new ministry, although he continually fretted that local dissenters, especially the New Side Presbyterians, were hostile and "likely to overrun us." He gained the respect of his parishioners, persuaded them to enlarge and improve the church, and joined with the town's other leading citizens to establish a fire company and a public library, stocking the latter with books and scientific equipment donated by Thomas Penn and his wife. With the French war drawing to a close, Barton was now again free to express his concern for Pennsylvania's Indians—"those poor Heathen who 'sit in darkness and the shadow of death.'"[28] Indeed, he hoped that his mission and his library might be the instruments that would lead them, "by the light of Knowledge, to lay aside their savage Nature, to become Members of Society; and even to serve the Public in some of its most honorable Offices."[29]

Yet once again Barton's paternalistic dreams were shattered by war and the demands of proprietary interests. In early May 1763 Pontiac's Rebellion convulsed the Pennsylvania backcountry: "our Country bleeds again under the Savage knife!" Barton reported, as thousands of Scots-Irish and other frontier families fled eastward from the "dreadful news of Murdering, Burning and Scalping."[30] In early August British troops crushed the Indians at Bushy Run, and by late November the crisis was over. However, on 14 and 27 December a band of Scots-Irish vigilantes, known as the Paxton Boys, sought easy revenge by massacring 20 Christianized Indians, mostly old men, women, and children, on their reservation at Conestoga Manor and in the Lancaster workhouse, where the survivors of the first attack had taken refuge. Then, in early February 1764, the Paxton Boys and several hundred supporters marched on Philadelphia, threatening to kill the remaining "friendly Indians" whom the Quakers were protecting.

There is little doubt that Barton was sincerely outraged, both by the murders of helpless natives and by the suspected complicity of John Armstrong and other local magistrates and proprietary agents. In his next communication to the S.P.G., Barton denounced the massacres as "inhuman" acts, praised his Anglican parishioners for their "obedience to civil authority," and condemned local Presbyterians for their involvement or acquiesence in the attacks.[31] However, the Proprietary party's leaders viewed the incident as but another opportunity for partisan warfare against the Pennsylvania Assembly and the Quaker party, especially since the latter, under Benjamin Franklin's leadership, publicly blamed Pontiac's Rebellion and the Paxton killings on Penn family misgovernment and Scots-Irish lawlessness, and, as the remedy for Pennsylvania's problems, petitioned the Crown to abolish the proprietorship and transform Pennsylvania into a royal colony. Consequently, Barton was again enlisted, by persuasion or coercion, in the Proprietary party cause. On 17

28. Rev. Thomas Barton, Lancaster, Pa., to the S.P.G., London, 6 December 1760 (in Perry, *Hist. Coll. Am. Colonial Church,* vol. 2; see Sources).   29. Rev. Thomas Barton, preface to the Catalogue of the Juliana Library Company of Lancaster, Pa. (in Landis, "The Juliana Library Company," see Sources).   30. Rev. Thomas Barton, Lancaster, Pa., to the S.P.G., London, 28 June 1763 (in Perry, *Hist. Coll. Am. Colonial Church,* vol. 2; see Sources).   31. Rev. Thomas Barton, 16 November 1764.

March 1764—"A Day dedicated to LIBERTY and ST. PATRICK"—he produced an anonymous pamphlet, *The Conduct of the Paxton Men, Impartially Represented*, that vilified the murdered Indians, blamed Pontiac's Rebellion on Quaker pacifism, and—in rhetoric strikingly similar to that employed by apologists for Ulster's Protestant paramilitary bands—justified the killings with "a series of biblical and Classical references designed to prove that a free people has the right to use force, even brutal and uncivilized force, in order to destroy traitors."[32]

Given his prejudices, it must have galled Barton to assume a Scots-Irish persona so effectively that one of his pamphlet's critics concluded that its author must be "a *Stark Naked Presbyterian*." Indeed, there is some evidence that Barton nearly suffered a nervous breakdown in the aftermath of yet another betrayal of his principles. In his reports to the S.P.G. Barton never admitted his authorship of *The Conduct of the Paxton Men*, and once again he became almost frantic to escape the scene of his duplicity. Although Barton had purchased a house and lot in Lancaster just a month before the massacres, he now begged the Society and his Proprietary friends to find him a ministry outside Pennsylvania altogether. However, Barton's self-interest and, perhaps, his Irish planter instincts soon overcame qualms of conscience. In late 1764 he urged that "the lands lately belonging to the Romish Clergy in Canada" should be confiscated, as in Ireland, to fund the Church of England's expansion and facilitate his proposed removal to Montreal.[33] More remarkably, Barton saw no contradiction between his derision of the former Paxton Boys, who, "under the ridiculous notion of a right by Conquest," had taken possession of the lands formerly held by the murdered Indians, and his own successful petition that Thomas Penn's agents should evict the squatters and convey to him lifetime possession of Conestoga Manor.[34] As in Ireland, it was the Protestant "rabble" who did the dirty work, but it was the Anglican gentry and clergy who reaped most of the spoils!

Ownership of the Conestoga farms, an increase in his S.P.G. salary, and a personal gift of £54 from Thomas Penn apparently reconciled Barton to life in Lancaster. By all accounts, he was a dedicated and effective pastor, active in church conferences, and zealous in combating the "cruel opposition" of Presbyterian "fanaticism" to the proposed appointment of an Anglican bishop in the colonies.[35] In unequal partnership with Sir William Johnson, the Anglo-Irish baron of the Mohawk Valley, Barton renewed his crusade for native missions and education, even boarding and tutoring Johnson's own half-Indian

---

32. Russell, "Thomas Barton," p. 327; see Sources. Barton's almost pornographic descriptions of Indian atrocities were also reminiscent of Protestant propaganda in the wake of the 1641 Rebellion in Ireland.
33. Rev. Thomas Barton, 16 November 1764. 34. Rev. Thomas Barton, Lancaster, Pa., to Edmund Physick, [Philadelphia?], 18 December 1770 (in *PMHB;* see Sources). Physick (1727–1804), a major figure in the Proprietary Party, was one of the Penn family's receivers-general of quitrents. Also see Barton to Sir William Johnson, May 1768 and 26 July 1770; and to Rev. Richard Peters, 24 August 1768 (in Brown and in *Sir William Johnson Papers*, v. 7; see Sources). 35. Rev. Thomas Barton, 16 November 1764; also see Barton to the S.P.G., 23 January 1766 and 15 November 1768 (in Perry, *Hist. Coll. Am. Colonial Church,* vol. 2; see Sources).

son.[36] Most of all, Barton indulged his scientific curiosity, aiding the experiments of his brother-in-law, David Rittenhouse, and accumulating large botanical and minerological collections. His own accomplishments, as well as Proprietary favor, won him election to the American Philosophical Society and honorary degrees from William Smith's College of Philadelphia and the Anglican-controlled King's College in New York.

However, yet another political storm ruined what might have been a peaceful twilight of Barton's career. In the late 1760s the controversy over a colonial bishop sundered the weak political bonds between Pennsylvania's Anglicans and what came to be known as the "Presbyterian party." In the early and mid-1770s most Anglicans, including virtually all the clergy, joined with the Quaker party, now led by Joseph Galloway (1731–1803), in defense of the Crown. By contrast, the Presbyterians—in Philadelphia led by Irish-born radicals such as George Bryan and Charles Thomson (1729–1824) and in the backcountry by men such as John Armstrong, Barton's old nemesis—thrust aside the aging loyalist William Allen and moved rapidly toward revolution and independence. Although Barton prayed for reconciliation and professed a benevolent neutrality, his sympathies (and perhaps his actions—the rebels accused him of complicity in Tory plots to seize Lancaster's arsenal) were clearly loyalist, as were those of virtually all S.P.G. missionaries. In the midst of the crisis Barton's wife Esther died, leaving him with eight children;[37] his own health began to fail, and now he and his Anglican friends became victims of the Scots-Irish mobs whose actions he had formerly justified. Yet despite public and legal pressure, Barton refused to omit prayers for the royal family from his services, and once the Revolution began, he was forced to shut the doors of St. James' church. When he also refused to take the loyalty oaths demanded by Pennsylvania's new government, he was at first confined to his rectory and finally given permission to sell his property and flee with his second wife (m. 1776) to

---

36. On Sir William Johnson, see chapter 51. Johnson and Thomas Penn were friends and political allies.

37. Thomas and Esther Barton's children were: William (1754–1817), a lawyer in Lancaster; Esther (b. 1756), who in 1774 married Paul Zanzinger, mayor of Lancaster after the Revolution; David Cradock (d. in infancy); Thomas, no data but spent his life in Lancaster; David (1768–1818), also of Lancaster; Mathias (1758–1798), a lawyer in Philadelphia and a member of the Pennsylvania legislature as well as an amateur naturalist and accomplished painter; Richard (1763–1821), who became a planter in Winchester, Va.; Benjamin (1766–1815), M.D. and from 1789 professor of natural history and botany (of medicine from 1813) at the University of Pennsylvania; member of the American Philosophical Society (1789) and president of the Philadelphia Medical Society (1808–1812); Susannah (d. in infancy); Juliana, in 1791 married a future attorney general and superior court justice of New Jersey. ¶Barton named at least three and perhaps five of his children for his proprietary patrons. However, Barton's offspring shared the radicalism of their maternal uncle David Rittenhouse (and perhaps of their mother as well), not their father's loyalism. Three sons, William, Mathias, and Richard, held political or military positions in Pennsylvania's revolutionary régime, and William was primarily responsible for designing the Great Seal of the new American republic. Barton's youngest son, Benjamin, inherited or rediscovered his father's ethnic identification as well as his scientific interests, joining Philadelphia's Hibernian Society at its inception in 1790.

the safety of British-controlled New York City.[38] There he died on 25 May 1780, just five days before the ship in which he had booked passage sailed for Ireland.

It would be tempting to conclude that at last Barton had found the courage to refuse to compromise his principles by bending to self-interest or political expediency—in effect, to display the fortitude he had admired in John Doyle. However, it may be more realistic to view Barton's loyalism as thoroughly consistent with his former behavior—as the last, logical stance of an Irish-born Anglican clergyman who knew, instinctively, that church and king were as inseparable and ultimately indispensable to the hegemony of his creed and class in America as they were in his native Monaghan.

54 ✳

Thomas Burke, ca. 1766–1767

After 1765 agitation and rebellion enormously expanded political opportunites for ambitious Irish immigrants who, unlike Rev. Thomas Barton, embraced the American Revolution. Among these perhaps no career was more meteoric than that of Thomas Burke. In 1760 Burke was merely 15 years old when he emigrated alone, friendless, and in disgrace, and in 1783 he was only 38 when he died in virtually identical circumstances. Yet between those years, Burke won honors as a self-taught physician, lawyer, and patriot poet; was a member of both the North Carolina legislature and the Continental Congress; helped draft both the 1776 North Carolina constitution and the Articles of Confederation; served as his state's wartime governor; and was the first to articulate the South's fateful doctrine of state sovereignty.

Throughout his career, Burke espoused the "classical" or "civic republican" ideals shared by eighteenth-century Anglo-Irish "patriots," British "country" or "real" Whigs, and many of the colonial politicians who, after 1765, opposed British taxation and eventually chose revolution and independence.[1] According to the republican creed, political history unveiled an eternal struggle in defense of liberty and virtue against government power and popular licentiousness. Those inextricable evils, rooted in man's susceptibility to corruption and lust for self-aggrandizement, required governments of checks and balances to guard against "tyranny" (whether by kings or by the "rabble"), and high property qualifications to ensure that voting and office-holding were largely if not entirely confined to the public-spirited members of an "independent" gentry. Based as it was on the assumption

---

38. In 1776 Barton married a widow with New York loyalist connections, Sarah De Normandie (1733–1826), née Baird; he sold his property to his son-in-law, Paul Zanzinger. **1.** On classical republicanism and radical whiggery, also see chapter 52.

that rational men could predict and control events and hence were directly responsible for the consequences of their actions, republicanism could easily foment suspicion and paranoia among its adherents. It also could encourage bitter strife and charges of hypocrisy, since every politician paraded his own patriotic virtue, assumed or charged that his opponents were motivated solely by selfish personal or factional interests, and ignored any contradictions between his own actions and professed ideals.

Strife and hypocrisy were especially characteristic of the Protestant gentry who controlled the Irish Parliament and of the plantation- and slave-owning oligarchy that dominated North Carolina's colonial assembly. The leaders of both groups adopted postures as selfless "patriots" and popular champions that often masked degrees of opportunism, avariciousness, and venality that were extraordinary even by eighteenth-century standards.[2] In fact, Burke appears to have been more idealistic and honest than the typical representatives of either political culture—the one that shaped him in Ireland and the one he served during the American Revolution. However, Burke's own character was a bundle of contradictions: high intelligence and intense ambition contrasted sharply with a profound sense of insecurity; extreme vanity was masked by a self-deprecatory pose that begged for reassurance; captivating charm alternated with irrascible, alienating behavior; a hunger for love, friendship, and popular approval mingled with intense suspicion, fear of betrayal, and contempt for the "monster multitude"; and an extreme sense of self-righteous honor blinded him to his own inconsistencies and provoked endless quarrels with political opponents. As a result, in Burke classical republicanism's benign and malign tendencies alike assumed obsessive, almost pathological proportions, as his political views and style were inseparable from a personality that had been warped by Irish experience.[3]

Born about 1745, the son of Ulick Burke of Tyaquin, County Galway,[4] and Janet Shaw of Galway city, Thomas Burke proudly traced his ancestry back to the Norman

---

2. In 1755, after his return to Ireland from a long sojourn abroad, the idealistic Lord Charlemont, future leader of the Volunteer movement, discovered that "the mask of patriotism is often assumed to disguise self-interest and ambition, and . . . the paths of violent opposition, are too frequently trod as the nearest and surest road to office and emolument. . . . [T]he pseudo-patriot resembles the Christian whose hopes are fixed upon an hereafter, and the death of patriotism is not unusually succeeded by a glorious resurrection into the paradise of court favor." Stewart, *Deeper Silence*, 33; see Sources.   **3.** It is arguable that civic republicanism, with its classical allusions, might be particularly appealing to Irish Catholic converts. Having embraced Protestantism for reasons largely or entirely instrumental, and lacking Anglicans' and especially Dissenters' traditional immersion in scriptural or millennial political imagery, they might find a pre-Christian and secular political discourse both appropriate and appealing in its ability to transcend Ireland's conflicting ethnoreligious legacies. Likewise, civic republicanism's pessimistic view of history would also speak to their particular situation; hence Dr. Charles Carroll's resigned reflection that "the Macedonian and Roman Empires are no More" (chapter 50). Thus, Burke's political style, as revealed in his epic poem on the Stamp Act, seems worlds removed from that of Irish bourgeois Dissenters such as George Bryan (chapter 52), Rev. Francis Alison (chapter 55), and James Caldwell (chapter 58), whose modes of expression reflect the more "modern" and "liberal" influences of John Locke, Francis Hutcheson, etc.   **4.** For demographic data on Tyaquin barony and its environs, see appendix 2.2c, on chapter 54.

adventurer Thomas de Burgh (d. 1205), who came to County Galway in the reign of Henry II. However, by the early eighteenth century Thomas Burke's "once affluent"[5] branch of the Tyaquin Burke family was much reduced by confiscations and penal laws.[6] Consequently, Thomas probably shared his friend and distant kinsman Ædanus Burke's contempt for the "scandalous partiality of the English,"[7] and it may be that, in the broadest sense, Catholic Ireland's bitter history shaped Thomas Burke's self-proclaimed passion for liberty and hatred of oppression. To be sure, Burke himself was not Catholic: apparently his father had conformed to the Church of Ireland,[8] thus enabling Thomas to attend Dublin's exclusively Protestant Trinity College, and later in the colonies Burke was an avowed deist. Yet intertwined with Burke's heritage of dispossession and apostasy were serious personal disabilities. A youthful case of smallpox had terribly scarred his face, leaving him blind in one eye and with a physical appearance that invited ridicule from political opponents. Perhaps equally important was his bitter estrangement from most of his Irish kinsmen. In his correspondence Burke scarcely ever mentioned his parents, and the dominant figure in his early life was a maternal uncle, Sir Fielding Ould (1710–1789), master of Dublin's Maternity Hospital and obstetrician to the Anglo-Irish élite. At first Ould had patronized the young Burke, perhaps subventing his Dublin education, but then, as a result of some quarrel or youthful misadventure, had abandoned him and precipitated his emigration.[9]

In later years, Burke would claim that "some Family misfortunes [had] reduced [him] to the alternative of domestick Indolent Dependence or an Enterprising Peregrination" and that he had "no reason to repent of" the latter choice.[10] In fact, however, the wounds of his uncle's "betrayal" scarred him far more deeply than the smallpox. He never forgot how he had been "persecuted with relentless rancour" by his relatives,[11] and in his letters to Ireland he made pitiable efforts to restore his reputation and impress his kinsmen with his American accomplishments. Indeed, in the colonies Burke "labored very hard to supply by Industry the Defects of Fortune" and, as he reported, soon succeeded in raising himself

5. Thomas Burke, Norfolk, Va., to John Bloomfield, nr. Birr, King's Co., 25 April 1772. **6.** In 1851 the Tyaquin estate still comprised nearly six thousand acres when financial circumstances obliged the Burkes to sell the property in the encumbered estates court; however, the estate had long since been alienated from Thomas Burke's branch of the family. **7.** On Ædanus Burke, see chapter 62. **8.** Between 1698 and 1709 several Ulick Burkes in Co. Galway, including (in 1704) one "gent[leman]" of Tyaquin, officially renounced Catholicism and conformed to the established church. **9.** Given his passionate avowals of devotion to "liberty," it is tempting to speculate that Burke's estrangement from his uncle and subsequent emigration may have been occasioned by the former's youthful involvement in Dublin's Anti-Union Riot of 3 December 1759, when Trinity College students joined poor Protestant weavers from the city's Liberties to protest a rumored plot to abolish the Irish Parliament. Certainly, Burke's participation would have horrified and embarrassed Ould, a pillar of the establishment, and would probably have resulted in Burke's expulsion from Trinity. Unfortunately, other than Burke's contemporary attendance at the College, no evidence survives to corroborate that suspicion. **10.** Thomas Burke, 25 April 1772. **11.** Thomas Burke, [Norfolk?], Va., to Sidney Shaw Jones, Dublin, ca. 1769; all subsequent quotations from Burke's correspondence are taken from this letter.

"from humble obscurity." However, despite his boasts—and his claim that in America "we have . . . every thing of Arcadia but its flocks and Fountains"—Burke regarded life in the colonies as "Exile," as "Banishment," as "a Sentence of Damnation," and his fondest hope was to achieve "a competent fortune" so he could return with honor to Ireland.

"[T]orn from all that [was] dear to him," Burke emigrated about 1760 to North America, "unknown to any Mortal in it and without any advantage of Circumstance." For reasons equally unknown, he settled initially in Northampton County, among the tobacco planters on Virginia's isolated Eastern Shore. His charm and intelligence must have secured him patronage and leisure sufficient to study medicine, for by 1763 he was practicing "Physic" and, "by Severe application and Methodical Study," had gained "a proficiency equall if not superior to most gentlemen in these climes." However, it was the Stamp Act crisis of 1765–1766 that first brought Burke public renown. In February 1766 Northampton's county court unilaterally declared the Stamp Act unconstitutional, and when word of the Act's repeal by Parliament reached the Eastern Shore in May, the local planters hosted a public celebration. Burke's poetic contribution to these festivities launched his political career. Doubtless, his personal experience of "oppression" had sharpened his antipathy to British policies. Likewise, Burke's sudden acclaim emboldened him to write the following letter, no doubt hoping that an inflated account of his American achievements would redeem his Irish reputation and win recognition from his hardhearted uncle.

**Thomas Burke, Northampton County, Virginia,
to Sir Fielding Ould, Dublin, ca. 1766–1767**

> Sir   You may please to recollect that one of the last times I had the pleasure
> of visiting you, you refused to see me   Since that day[12] I have held a long struggle
> between Indignation and Natural affection   The latter has at length prevailed and in
> Spite of every thing I must confess my Self full of Natures weak, Efeminate feelings: a
> Strong proof of it is my not being able to resist very Vehement Solicitations for the
> welfare of my relations in Ireland and Chiefly you next to my father and mother
> notwithstanding——I have wrote several letters, and repeatedly requested some acct of
> domestic concern but I suppose I have had the Misfortune to be thought a troublesome
> and Insignificant correspond^t best answered by Neglect. I cannot repine at this Fate
> when I consider it as common to all to whom Fortune has not been liberally Indulgent,
> but sure in my Example[13] there have been circumstances of a peculiarly Melancholy
> reflection, without a Crime nor prone to any Vice, one almost free even from the

---

12. pleasure of visiting you, you refused to see me   Since that day: conjectural; words omitted in ms., suggesting that this was a copy or initial draft of Burke's letter to Ould. **13. but sure in my Example**: "but certainly in my case." The use of **sure** as an asseverative particle has become characteristic of Hiberno-English, but it was once common in mainland English, as a perusal of seventeenth- and eighteenth-century correspondence shows.

Levity of Persons of <my> Age, abandoned, persecuted, denied even Justice, the common birth right of mankind——but I would not willingly trouble either your Imagination or my own with those excruciating Scenes which I hope are forgotten by all except one upon whom they have made so deep an Impression as my self and quem semper acerbatum——Semper honoratum Sic dii voluisti habebo[14]——My dear uncle after easing my Breast in this manner I will Venture to address you in the Manner Nature points out to me and first let me entreat you to forget the Boy of fifteen and consider much difference between him and the Man of twenty two——I cannot without reluctance unbosom my self to one whom I so much reverence and regard, and yet I know not to whom I should more properly do it   in Short Sir tho here placed in a Situation much fitter to provoke envy than Inspire Pitty having the first Men of a Country my Friends and Intimates and much more did not my Modesty prevent my Expression, I am far from being Happy,   I want the Bosom of my Friends and my Native Country   could I carry America to Ireland or bring Ireland hither I should be completely blest, but so tenderly am I attached to the one and So valuable and engaging are my connexions here that I should with much reluctance enjoy either at the Expence of the other   You will no doubt wonder what should procure me the Situation I have above hinted For I dare say you know me none of the most forward or Insinuating of Mankind——Indeed Sir I should wa<i>ve the Satisfying your Curiosity in this point were I not writing at the Distance of three thousand Miles and that gentleman on whom above all others I would wish to be informed of every thing concerning me,   another plea I will make in Excuse is that it must give you the pleasure alway attending Surprise and novelty for what can be more unexpected than my being at the head of the Literati of America Esteemed the Patern of Taste and Prince of Genius——I am sure the Surprise arising from the above relations[15] must require your taking Breath ere you can read the Manner of my coming by Such regard in points so unlikely   You must no doubt have heard of the American Stamp Act,   the unanimous opinion of America was that it was Illegal inexpedient and opressive   Such was mine,   as Such I confess I strenuously from my very Soul detested exposed and oposed it, for I am and ever shall be avowedly a passionate lover of liberty, and Hater of Tyranny,   the Essence of the former I take to be being govern'd by Laws made with constitutional consent of the community ultimately Judged by that community and enjo<y>ing and disposing of their Property only agreeable to Will, and the Latter is undeniably any thing Subversive of those Priviledges,   how far the Stamp Act was so sufficiently appears upon the very Face of it, and I shall say no more of it having introduced it only to let you know how I

---

14. **quem semper acerbatum——Semper honoratum Sic dii voluisti habebo**: "[The day has come] which I shall always hold in bitterness and honor (gods, you have wished this!)" (Vergil *Æneid* 5.50; Burke's Latin differs slightly from the standard texts and is incorrect; e.g., *voluisti* should be *voluistis*.)   15. **relation**: account, narrative, report.

became conspicuous.   then Sir I commenced Politician[16] and the Place where I reside having been most Strenuous and early in its Oppositions was also the first to celebrate its repeal with Singular Festivity   on this Occasion I wrote a prologue[17] which I shewd to one of my Intimates being notwithstanding fully determined to conceal the Author as much as might be and to give the Honor if any resulted from it to him whom I designd to Speak <of> it before the op<e>ning of the Entertainment,   but my hopes of remaining in obscurity were vain and in very few Hours it was not only in every Bodys Hands but even in every Mouth   every one of my acquaintance were no less surprised than I believe you will be upon this relation, and those who had the Influence of Friendship over me prevail'd upon me to give a very reluctant assent to its appearing in print   Indeed Sir I was not vain enough to think that any production of mine much less that of a Single Morning, which this was, could deserve Such regard and the Extravagant encomiums[18] given it by my Friends I ascribed rather to their affection than Judgement, but no sooner did it get abroad in print than universal Approbation reached from every Corner,   the author was look'd upon as a prodigy of Genius——but tis Time to leave a Subject which a man can not write even decently upon, and which I declare is far from being pleasing to me, nor Should I have gone thus far were not my Grand Maxim Magis Amicus Veritas.[19] I can with truth protest that I am not infected with the ridiculous Folly of Vanity,   I am displeased at being more conspicuous than is consistant with my Humble Fortune and Wishes,   the Esteem of my associates I had already acquired and the utmost of my Ambition always has been Secura Quies et nescia fallere Vita[20]——I make no doubt but your curiosity is much inflamed to See this Performance which produced such Miracles,   it is too long or I would gratify you [but] I will venture to give you a passage or two heartily wishing it may please you but entirely Indifferent whether it does the World or not   for being no Candidate for Fame it will be no disapointment to me not to acquire any   the Pasages I shall quote shall be a<s> short as [is] Possible   the Argument is an Exhortation to Festivity on so Joyous an Occation   mention is

16. commenced Politician: began to be a politician (OED, s.v. commence, 3.b; archaic).   **17. prologue**: prose or, usually, verse specially composed as an introduction, very commonly recited as the opening of an event or celebration.   **18. encomium**: expression (often florid) of high praise.   **19. Magis Amicus Veritas**: "a better friend is the truth"; a truncated, Latin version of a phrase in Aristotle's *Nicomachaean Ethics,* book 1, chapter 6: "for while both [Plato and the truth] are dear, piety requires us to honor truth above our friends." In the fifth century A.D., Aristotle's work was translated into Latin and subsequently anthologized; the phrase appears, for example, as a Latin quotation in *Don Quixote.* If Burke was familiar with the longer Latin passage, he may have understood it in either of two ways: (1) friendship is a dear thing, especially if the friend is very wise, like Socrates or Plato; yet one must tell the truth, even if it contradicts what the friend believes and even hurts him; (2) no matter how prestigious a friend (an authority) may be, the truth is superior.   **20. Secura Quies et nescia fallere Vita**: "carefree quiet and a life unmindful of disappointment"; (Vergil *Georgics* 2.467; Vergil's work (the title is from the Greek word for "tilling the soil" or "farmer") extols the beauties and joys of country life—a central theme of eighteenth-century classical republican thought—and hints at an antithesis: country life is simple and virtuous, urban life is complex and restless.

Made of several Material circumstances and M[r] Pitt[21] is introduced in the following Manner

> Triumph America thy patriot Voice
> has made the greatest of Mankind rejoice
> Immortal Pitt, ever glorious Name!
> Far, far unequalled in the rolls of Fame!
> What Breast? (for Virtue is by all approved
> And Freedom even by Asia's Slaves beloved)
> What Breast but glows with Gratitude to thee
> Boast of Mankind! great Prop of Liberty!

after this America is represented as pa<y>ing gratefull Homage to her guardian raised by his Hand and flourishing beneath his care, and even now recovering and smiling with fresh verdure under his Shade after which the Speaker burst into the following rapture

> Would 'twere in Pity to mankind decreed
> That Still a Pitt should to a Pit Succeed
> When proud Oppression would subvert the Laws
> That Still a Cambden[22] should defend the Cause
> Nor let's forget the gallant Barre's[23] Merrit
> His Tullys Periods and his Cato's Spirit
> His too an Honest independent Heart
> Where fear nor Fraud nor avarice have part

Sir Will[m] Meridith[24] is after wards respectfully Mentioned and the rapture is resumed

> Proceed great Names! your mighty Influence Join
> your country's arts and Pollicies refine
> Assist great Conway[25] and reform the State

---

21. **M[r] Pitt**: William Pitt, first Earl of Chatham (1708–1778); chief British minister (1756–1761, 1766–1768) and architect of British victory in the Seven Years' War; denounced the Stamp Act in Parliament (January–February 1766) and denied that body's right to tax the American colonies.   22. **Cambden**: Charles Pratt, earl of Camden (1714–1794); as chief justice of the Court of Common Pleas, in 1763 he ordered the release from prison of the radical Whig agitator John Wilkes (1727–1797), a hero in the American colonies, on the grounds that general warrants were unconstitutional.   23. **Barre**: Isaac Barré (1726–1802); born in Dublin; a graduate of Trinity College, Dublin (1745); colonel in the British army stationed in America during the Seven Years' War; British M.P. (1761–1790); a close political associate of William Pitt and a strenuous opponent of American taxation; Burke compares Barré's forceful orations against the Stamp Act to those of Cicero (**Tully**) and Cato, statesmen of the ancient Roman republic.   24. **Sir Willm Meridith**: Sir William Meredith (d. 1790), second baronet of Henbury, Cheshire; Whig M.P. (1754–1780) and an opponent of the Stamp Act. 25. **Conway**: Henry Seymour Conway (1721–1795); field marshal in the British army and British M.P. (1741–1784); in 1763–1764 Conway sided with Pitt and the Whigs in opposition to the government's arrest of

THOMAS BURKE

505

> Bid peacefull Commerce resume her Seat
> Bid British Navies whiten every Coast
> And British Freedom every Country boast

I shall Pass on now Sir to give you the address to the Ladies with which it[26] concludes

> and you, ye fair, on whom our Hopes depend
> Our future Fame and Empire <to> Extend
> Whose fruitfull Beds shall dauntless Myriads yield
> To fight for Freedom in some future Field
> Resign each Dear [. . .][27]
> Today let gladness beam in every Face
> Soften each smile and brighten every Grace
> While the glad roofs with lofty Notes resound
> With Grace Harmonious move the Mazy round[28]
> Make our Hearts feel the long forgotten Fire
> Wake into Flame each spark of soft desire
> Too long Indignant Tumults and alarms
> Have made us heedless of your lovely Charms
> But now beneath the downy wings of Peace
> With Freedom blest our care will be to please
> Each day the genial pleasure to improve
> and add new Sweetness to connubial love

I am Sensible nothing here will appear to you worthy of the regard I have mention<ed> But the Subject was Popular and it came from a plant the least promising of such fruit   true it was not my first Essay, for I have lisp'd in Numbers[29]   But I took all possible care to conceal my propensity having always dreaded the Idle Character of a Rhimer, but after this it were in vain to deny it and I have no hope of emerging from Ink befor my Emigration from America for tho by my knowledge of Short Hand I have been able to conceal every thing Heretofore yet I am not now able to resist the Importunity of my Friends for Such I will be bold to say I have——you are I suppose desirous of knowing what Studies chiefly engage me,   Moral and Natural Philosophy are my favorites but chiefly the Latter on acc^t of its utility in the Study and practice of Physic which I make entirely my Business   I proceed on the

---

the radical journalist John Wilkes, for which Conway was deprived temporarily of all civil and military offices; in February 1766 Conway moved Parliament's repeal of the Stamp Act. **26.** is ms. **27.** Remainder of line illegible. **28. let gladness . . . move the Mazy round:** "let gladness make its wandering journey." **29. I have lisp'd in Numbers:** "even in my earliest years I made verses"; **Numbers:** metrical units, lines; thus by synecdoche "verse, poetry."

certain Method of demonstration of Experiment, reject all Theory not reducible to proof,   I have endeavoured to acquire an accurate knowledge of The Animal Mechanism and econimy, the properties of aliments and Medicine<,> Medicinal Phenomena, History of diseases and Medicinal operations,   I am no Stranger to the Newtonian Principles and their application in Medicine   In a word Sir I am and Shall be indefatigable in observations and reading the best Authors I can procure, and am determined if I ever shall be happy Enough to See Europe again to endeavour for a degree in Some of the first Colleges,   while I am writing this I cannot help Lamenting that I cannot wth any certainty promise my Self an Answer which if I should be favor'd with I would wish to contain an account of every domestic occurrence of moment   it were endless to Mention every person by Name I should wish to be dear to, but a far more than ordinary regard is due for me to Mrs Kath: Ould and I hope I am incapable of Ingratitude   She cannot wish me more Affectionate to her than I am   I hope my Parents are well but I dread to mention them,   let me request you Sir to make Mention of me to Mr Shaw and his Lady and in a particular Manner to Miss Sidney[30]   That amiable young Lady has made herself doubly dear to me and I am certain she will be the last Person in Ireland or even the World whom I shall forget——if any of my Cozens remember me it must be your Son William   I wish him to be a good, Great, and Happy Man   I am at length constrain'd to take leave of you   Indeed tho my Life is a chearfull one, I have never Spent an Hour So agreeably Since my departure from Ireland as this wherein I have held conversation tho Imaginary with you,   I wish you long Life, Health and prosperity and hope you will never have reason to doubt or Indignate[31] my being your most dutifull and affectionate

Nephew and humblest
Tho Burke

Apparently, Ould never replied to his nephew, as a few years later Burke complained that he had "never yet received a Syllable of Answer" to any of his letters home. Indeed, not until the early 1770s, when Burke was firmly established in North Carolina, would other Irish kinsmen begin to communicate, begging for patronage and foisting his scapegrace brother, Redmond, upon him.[32] Meanwhile, Burke continued to build upon the modest fame earned in the Stamp Act controversy. About 1765 or 1766, realizing that medicine "was not a Field in which the most plentiful Harvest might be reaped," Burke "determined to Study Law which promised more profit and yet much less Anxiety."

---

30. **Miss Sidney**: Sidney Shaw, Burke's cousin; married David Jones in 1766.   31. **Indignate**: be indignant with someone for having done something unworthy.   32. In 1772 Redmond Burke emigrated to Boston, later joining his brother in North Carolina. In early 1773 he tried to seduce or rape Thomas Burke's wife, Polly, ironically while Thomas was visiting the colonial capital, Newbern, soliciting patronage for his brother from the royal governor. Expelled from Burke's household, Redmond migrated to South Carolina and, after the Revolution, turned up in London, petitioning the British government for compensation as a loyalist.

Amazingly, he claimed, after a few months of study he "was licenced by the Examiners upon the first Trial . . . with very great applause," and he was confident that "a few years will place me at the Head of my Profession." To further advance his prospects, in 1769 Burke moved across Chesapeake Bay to Norfolk, Virginia, a thriving port with about five thousand inhabitants, where he temporarily abandoned "patriotic" politics, alligned himself with the town's largely Scottish-born merchant élite, and on 28 March 1770 contracted what proved to be a very unhappy marriage with Mary "Polly" Freeman (b. ca. 1752–1755).[33]

By the early 1770s Burke had become a busy, prosperous lawyer, numbering among his friends and correspondents such luminaries of the Virginia bar as George Wythe and Thomas Jefferson. Although his earlier poems had eulogized American freedom and even denounced slavery as a "curse" and a "crime," in Norfolk Burke associated with future loyalists, fought a duel with the town's leading anti-British agitator, and purchased the first of the 15 slaves he owned at the time of his death. However, in 1771–1772 he decided to move to Hillsborough, the seat of Orange County, in the North Carolina backcountry. There were several reasons for Burke's migration: his later political poems had incurred ridicule from Norfolk's planter gentry; Orange County was much healthier than Norfolk's miasmic climate; and although Hillsborough contained only a few hundred inhabitants, the village was the primary trading and judicial center for an increasingly populous and commercialized region and hence offered "a fair field" for ambitious lawyers.

However, perhaps the most important factor in Burke's calculations was that in 1766–1771 Orange County had been the center of North Carolina's Regulator movement, an uprising of disgruntled backcountry farmers (many of them Scots-Irish) against the colony's eastern planters and their agents in the corrupt "courthouse rings" that operated out of western towns such as Hillsborough.[34] There is no evidence that Burke sympathized with the Regulators—quite the contrary—but ironically both their activities and their suppression provided him new career opportunities. In autumn 1770 rioting Regulators had driven away most members of Hillsborough's venal courthouse ring, thus vacating public offices that Burke could fill. Likewise, after Governor William Tryon's militia crushed the Regulators at the battle of Alamance (16 May 1771), thousands of farmers abandoned Orange County and fled west across the Appalachians, throwing on the market a vast amount of property that the land-hungry Burke could purchase cheaply.

Thus, in 1772 Burke purchased nearly six hundred acres of land outside Hillsborough, built a plantation that he named Tyaquin, and joined both the local élite and its allies among North Carolina's tidewater planters. In 1774–1776 those planters, perhaps motivated less by opposition to the Tea and Coercive acts than to the new royal governor's

---

33. Burke and his wife had only one child, Mary Williams Burke (b. ca. 1780), who died in Alabama, unmarried, after the Civil War. After Burke's death, his widow contracted an equally unhappy marriage to a Major Doherty.   34. On North Carolina's Regulators, also see chapter 57.

attempt to curtail their exploitation of backcountry farmers, led North Carolina into the American Revolution. In 1775–1776 Burke represented Orange County in the provincial congresses that dismantled royal authority and declared independence. In addition, he played a major role in drafting the 1776 state constitution that carefully preserved the dominance of the eastern planter oligarchy—and also barred non-Protestants from holding state office. In 1776–1781 Burke served as a member of the North Carolina Assembly and as a delegate to the Continental Congress, where his obsessive insistence on absolute state sovereignty shaped the Articles of Confederation and weakened Congress's ability to conduct the war. Indeed, by 1778 Burke's "obstinate Vanity," obstructionist tactics, and personal attacks on any delegates who tried to broaden the national government's authority had earned him Congress's formal censure for "disorderly and contemptuous conduct" and the detestation of most of its members.[35] Blinded by self-righteousness, Burke was incapable of acknowledging his own inconsistencies, as when he championed the interests of North Carolina's western land speculators or, after the British invaded the Carolinas in 1780, when he abandoned his commitment to state sovereignty and demanded that Congress assume virtually dictatorial powers to protect his state against British armies and loyalist militias.

Signaling their approval of his conduct, the planters who controlled the North Carolina Assembly not only sent Burke back to Congress but also, on 25 June 1781, elected him as chief executive of a state government that was near collapse, in a society that bordered on total anarchy. Burke performed energetically, but on 13 September he was captured by a loyalist band, turned over to the British army, and imprisoned near Charleston, South Carolina. After promising that he would not try to escape, Burke was paroled to James Island, but his fear of assassination by vengeful Tories overcame his sense of honor and on 16 January 1782 he broke his parole and absconded to North Carolina. He resumed his governorship but quickly discovered that no excuses or explanations could palliate his disgrace. Always poorly equipped to deal with failure or criticism, Burke reacted with the same anguish and bitterness that had marked his youthful emigration. He left office a broken, alienated man, convinced he had been betrayed by an ungrateful people, and died at his Tyaquin plantation, deserted by his wife and political associates, on 2 December 1783.

In many respects, Thomas Burke's Irish background and American career were very similar to those of Dr. Charles Carroll,[36] although posterity's and historians' evaluations of the two men have been very dissimilar. Both Burke and Carroll were of Catholic gentry origins and converts to the established church. Both sought to reestablish lost family fortunes in the New World, and each bore social and psychological scars that were at least partly attributable to Catholic Ireland's history of conquest and colonization. In America

---

35. J. N. Rakove, "Thomas Burke and the Problem of Sovereignty," 176; J. B. Sanders, "Thomas Burke in the Continental Congress," 32; see Sources. **36.** See chapter 50.

both men represented planter interests and each espoused classical republican or country Whig ideals—Carroll in his party's conflict with Maryland's proprietors, Burke in opposition to "British tyranny" and Congressional authority—that were sharpened by Irish circumstances and resentments. In America, however, the two men operated in very different political contexts. In early and midcentury Maryland, planter opposition to proprietary power was inextricably linked to the anti-Catholicism that Carroll eventually espoused. By the 1770s, in contrast, whereas anti-"popery" still played a major role in New Englanders' anti-British rhetoric, it had become a very minor theme in Southern planters' revolutionary discourse—although Burke's acquiescence, if not complicity, in North Carolina's exclusion of Catholics from political office suggests he may have shared Carroll's later opinions. For his time and place Carroll was as much a champion of "popular" interests as was Burke a quarter-century later, and neither was by any means a "democrat" in the Jeffersonian or Painite sense. Yet ironically, subsequent and more liberal generations would view them quite differently: Charles Carroll as an opportunistic if not unscrupulous bigot, Thomas Burke as an idealistic—albeit also fatally flawed—revolutionary hero.

55 ✳

Rev. Francis Alison, 1768

R ev. Thomas Barton's devotion to the Crown, although typical of S.P.G. missionaries in America, may have been intensified by his Ulster Anglican background.[1] By contrast, Rev. Francis Alison's Ulster Presbyterian heritage, as well as his exposure in Scotland to the teachings of Francis Hutcheson, no doubt heightened his sensitivity to what he and other Scots-Irish immigrants increasingly viewed, after 1763, as British threats to the political and religious liberties they enjoyed in the Middle Colonies. At least since the early eighteenth century, Ulster's Presbyterian clergy had characterized Scots-Irish migration to America as a flight from persecution, portraying their people as like the Israelites of the Old Testament, who had fled from Egyptian bondage to a "promised land." As Philadelphia's leading Presbyterian minister and educator, Francis Alison melded this tribal interpretation of Irish history with the perspectives of the Scottish Enlightenment and, perhaps more than any other public figure, helped prepare Pennsylvania's Scots-Irish for their prominent role in the American Revolution.

Alison was born in 1705 in the Foyle Valley of east County Donegal, in the religiously mixed parish of Leck[2] and the barony of Raphoe, the son of a Presbyterian weaver, Robert Alison (d. 1725), whose ancestors had migrated from Scotland to Ulster in the

---

1. On Barton, see chapter 53. 2. For demographic data on Leck parish and its environs, see appendix 2.1a, chapter 55.

early 1600s. Alison attended a charity school in Raphoe town and then, despite his parents' straitened circumstances, entered the University of Edinburgh. In January 1753 Alison received his M.A. degree from Edinburgh, and he and his disciples claimed that he also studied divinity at the University of Glasgow. In the early eighteenth century, both Edinburgh and Glasgow were centers of the "new learning" inspired by the empiricism of Newton and Locke, and although there is no record of Alison's attendance at Glasgow, it is virtually certain that he studied there with Francis Hutcheson (1694–1746), after 1730 professor of moral philosophy and, through his lectures and writings, the putative "father of the Scottish Enlightenment."

Hutcheson himself had been born near Saintfield, County Down, and educated at the University of Glasgow. In the 1720s Hutcheson was master of a dissenting academy in Dublin, where he mixed with Irish political and religious reformers such as Robert Viscount Molesworth and Rev. Thomas Drennan, whose son William would later help found the Society of the United Irishmen.[3] On his return to Glasgow, Hutcheson inspired his students with a modified and benevolent Calvinism. Hutcheson of course believed that human beings were inherently sinful and hence that their reason alone was an insufficient guide to God's will. However, he taught that men and women also possessed an innate "moral sense" that encouraged them to strive for virtue and—when informed by empirical knowledge of history and the natural world—made it possible for them to make benevolent as well as rational choices. Education, therefore, was essential—enabling enlightened citizens to pursue forms of personal happiness compatible with God's will and the public welfare alike and to construct social and political institutions that would promote progress, freedom, and charity. Furthermore, Hutcheson argued, since knowledge was expansive and beneficent, manmade religious and political dogmas and institutions that inhibited free inquiry and restricted social progress were anachronistic and unjust. Thus, citizens had the right—indeed, the duty—to oppose tyranny, whether in the forms of established churches, abusive governments, or oppressive social arrangements, such as African slavery. Indeed, in one fateful essay, clearly relevant to Ireland and America alike, Hutcheson contended that the inhabitants of a maturing colony had the right to "turn Independent."

Hutcheson's lectures and writings were seminal in the development of the Scottish Enlightenment, although the latter's exponents in Scotland, wedded as they were to an established church and to the benefits of the Act of Union of 1707, forswore the radical implications of much of Hutcheson's teachings. However, by the second quarter of the eighteenth century Hutcheson's brand of religious liberalism had permeated much of Ulster Presbyterianism, and his political ideas helped shape the Irish dissenter radicalism that flowered all too briefly at the century's end. Across the Atlantic, Hutcheson was probably the

---

3. Rev. Thomas Drennan (1696–1768): a graduate of the University of Glasgow and subsequently Presbyterian minister in Holywood, Co. Down, and in Belfast; most famously, the father of William Drennan (1754–1820), a physician, poet, and in 1791 (with Wolfe Tone and Thomas Russell) a founder of the Society of United Irishmen. On Molesworth, see chapter 52, n. 13.

FIGURE 16
Portrait of Rev. Francis
Alison (1705–1779) of New
London, Pennsylvania, and
Philadelphia. Photograph
courtesy of the Presbyterian
Historical Society,
Philadelphia.

most respected moral philosopher in the American colonies, and there Francis Alison was his foremost disciple and disseminator of his ideas.

In 1735 Alison emigrated to America, perhaps in part because, under Hutcheson's influence, he declined to subscribe to the Westminster Confession of Faith that Ulster's presbyteries often required of ministerial candidates. After landing at New Castle, Delaware, Alison first secured a temporary post as tutor in the Talbot County, Maryland, home of Samuel Dickinson, father of John Dickinson, the "Penman of the Revolution" and Alison's future ally and collaborator. He also enrolled as a probationer in the New Castle Presbytery, and in late 1735 and 1736 he supplied vacant pulpits at the Forks of the Brandywine. In 1737 Alison was ordained and installed as minister of the Presbyterian congregation of New London, in Chester County, Pennsylvania.[4] At New London he purchased a 50-acre glebe farm; persuaded his parishioners to build a larger church; and married Han-

---

4. New London's Presbyterian church had been established in 1728; Alison was its second settled pastor.

nah Armitage of New Castle, by whom he had six children.[5] Perhaps most important, upon discovering that "there was not a college, nor even a good grammar school" in all the Middle Colonies, in about 1740 Alison established at New London a classical academy which in 1743–1744 was expanded into a seminary to train ministerial candidates for the Old Side Presbyterians' Synod of Philadelphia.[6] Unfortunately, the Synod, its resources depleted by the 1741 schism, was unable to pay Alison's stipend with regularity. Eventually, the New London Academy was moved to Newark, Delaware, where it continued to prepare students for the Old Side ministry and, after the Revolution, evolved into the College—later the University—of Delaware. However, although Alison maintained close ties with his former institution, in 1752 financial exigencies prompted him to move to Philadelphia, where he took charge of the academy or Latin school that Benjamin Franklin had founded two years earlier. In 1755 the academy was reorganized and chartered as the interdenominational College of Philadelphia, headed by the Scottish-born Anglican, Rev. William Smith, as provost and by Alison as vice-provost and professor of moral philosophy. Alison held those positions, as well as the copastorship of Philadelphia's First Presbyterian church, until his death in 1779.

Like Alison, Smith—a graduate of the University of Aberdeen—was an exemplar of the Scottish Enlightenment and a sincere educational reformer, as well as an indefatigable fund-raiser for the College.[7] However, his penchant for political intrigue and frequent absences from Philadelphia obliged Alison to assume nearly all the teaching responsibilities. Despite his heavy Ulster accent, lack of social graces, chronic ill health, and a generally dour and irascible temperament, by all accounts Alison was a superb educator. Although not an original thinker, Alison was, as his admirers attested, "a living library" and perhaps "the greatest classical scholar" in the American colonies,[8] eventually receiving honorary degrees from Yale, Princeton, and Glasgow. At the College of Philadelphia he taught the classics, logic, geography, even the natural sciences, but his primary instruction was in moral philosophy, in which, like Hutcheson, he ranged from abstract deliberations on virtue and vice to concrete analyses of history, government, law, and economy. Although more orthodoxly Calvinist than his mentor, Alison also portrayed mankind as potentially

---

5. Hannah Armitage Alison (1715–ca.1805) was the daughter of James Armitage, who in 1702 had emigrated from Holmfirth, Yorkshire, and by 1738 was a justice of the peace in New Castle Co., Dela. Francis and Hannah Alison had six children, two of whom died in infancy; the others were: Francis, Jr. (1751–1813), a graduate of the College of Philadelphia, a surgeon in the American Revolution, and afterward a successful farmer in London Grove township, Chester Co.; Benjamin (1754–1781), also a College of Philadelphia graduate and a surgeon in the Revolution; Mary (1757–1827), who died in New London, unmarried; and Anna (b. ca. 1760), who in 1767 contracted an unhappy marriage to Alexander McCausland, who deserted her in South Carolina and died in the West Indies; ca. 1772 her father helped her settle in Northumberland Co., Pa., where she established a distillery and later married James P. Wilson.   6. Rev. Francis Alison, Philadelphia, to Rev. Ezra Stiles, Newport, R.I., 12 December 1767. On the Old Side–New Side schism in colonial Presbyterianism, see chapters 46–47.   7. On Rev. William Smith (1727–1803), also see chapter 53.   8. E. I. Nybakken, ed., "The Centinel" . . . , 20; see Sources.

rational and virtuous, with natural rights that were inalienable and defensible even to the point of revolution: "The end of all civil power is the public happiness," Alison taught, "& any power not conducive to this is unjust & the People who gave it may Justly abolish it."[9]

Although Alison hated public disputations, his strong convictions inevitably led him into religious and political controversies. During the Great Awakening, Alison "made a Stand against Enthusiasm & wild disorders y^t were like to destroy religion."[10] His belief that an educated clergy was vitally necessary to guide Pennsylvania's "vast multitude" of Scots-Irish immigrants—so "rude and unpolished in their tempers, disorderly in their Morals and unacquainted with the benevolent spirit of Christianity"—made him a natural leader of the Old Side Presbyterians.[11] However, from the moment of the 1741 schism, Alison strove for reconciliation. In 1758 he rejoiced when the Old and New Side clergy reunited, although subsequently the latter's persistent discrimination against Old Side and Irish-born ministers angered him and, in 1773, nearly provoked yet another division in colonial Presbyterianism. Yet in his last years Alison regarded as his single greatest accomplishment the creation of a life insurance program, based on Scottish models, that benefited New as well as Old Side clergymen.

Alison promoted harmony among warring Presbyterians for political as well as religious reasons. Prior to the 1760s Pennsylvania's Scots-Irish were largely apolitical, loosely attached to the Proprietary party and its predominantly Anglican leadership because the Quaker party refused to accord fair legislative representation to the western counties and to fund adequately the frontier's defense against the French and Indians. Despite these differences, Alison himself had remained friendly with Benjamin Franklin, the Quaker party's leader in the colonial Assembly, but in the early 1760s they became political adversaries as the relationship between the Scots-Irish and the Quakers worsened dramatically. In 1763–1764 Pontiac's Rebellion once again exposed western Pennsylvania's Scots-Irish to savage attacks, while the Paxton Boys' Christmas massacre of the Conestoga Indians and their February 1764 march on Philadelphia goaded the Quakers into a bitter pamphet war against the Presbyterians.[12] Alison was appalled by the apparently blatant hypocrisy of Franklin and his party: while denying funds for frontier defense, purportedly because of

---

9. Jasper Yeates, [Rev. Francis Alison's Lectures, at the College of Philadelphia, on] "Moral Philosophy in Three Books . . . Book 3: Of Oeconomics and Politics; Chapter 7: The Rights of the Supreme Power. . . . (1759)"; in the Rare Book Room, University of Pennsylvania Library, Philadelphia (courtesy of Professor Elizabeth I. Nybakken; see Sources). Yeates was one of Alison's students, as was Thomas Mifflin, whose notes on Alison's lectures are also preserved in his papers at the Library of Congress; on Mifflin, see n. 42.   10. Rev. Francis Alison, 12 December 1767.   11. [Rev. Francis Alison], "Memorial of the Rev. Mr. John Ewing and Hugh Williamson, M.D." (1773), a plea for financial assistance on behalf of New Ark Academy in Delaware, and carried to the British Isles by Ewing and Williamson on their unsuccessful fund-raising mission (sabotaged by Princeton's president, John Witherspoon, and other New Side clergy); the document is in the New Ark Academy Folder 359-A, Delaware Archives, Dover (courtesy of Prof. Elizabeth I. Nybakken; see Sources).   12. On the Paxton Boys affair and the subsequent pamphlet war, see chapter 53.

the Quakers' pacifistic principles, they displayed no scruples against arming themselves to repel the Paxton Boys, and then broke their promise to redress Scots-Irish grievances. However, Alison was even more alarmed when Franklin and his allies used the crisis as an excuse to petition the Crown for the abolition of proprietary rule and for Pennsylvania's transformation into a royal colony.

Although the Penns later rewarded Alison with a one-thousand-acre land grant, Alison was less concerned for the current proprietors than for William Penn's original Charter of Liberties (1701), which, by granting full civil and religious liberties to all settlers, had encouraged Scots-Irish Presbyterians to immigrate and in Pennsylvania had sheltered them from the official disabilities they had endured in their homeland. If Pennsylvania became a royal colony, there was no assurance the British government would honor Penn's guarantees; indeed, in Alison's view, after 1763 there was every indication it would not. By 1764 Parliament had already passed the Sugar Acts and the Quartering Act and had established special courts—without juries—to hear customs cases. Meanwhile, word of the impending Stamp Act had reached Philadelphia, and rumours abounded of government plans to revoke the charters of Connecticut and Rhode Island, to create an American peerage, and to restrict future colonial appointments—even professorships in American colleges—to members of the Anglican church. In this context, Alison believed that the Pennsylvania Assembly's petition for royal government was "madness,"[13] and in 1764 he played a leading role in mobilizing the Scots-Irish, who, combined with equally alarmed Germans and other voters, inflicted a stunning—if only temporary—defeat on Franklin's party in that year's election.

In the mid-1760s a "Presbyterian (or Scots-Irish) party" began to take shape in Pennsylvania politics, increasingly distinct from the old, loose proprietary coalition, and Alison was a major figure in its development. In the Stamp Act crisis of 1765, and later in response to the Townshend Acts of 1767, Alison led the Presbyterian clergy in opposition to the new British taxes; by contrast, most of the Proprietary party's Anglican leaders tried to discourage overt defiance. However, the crucial issue that galvanized the Presbyterian party into separate existence was the Anglican clergy's renewed effort to secure the appointment of Church of England bishops in the colonies. The question of an American episcopacy was not new, but, in the wake of the Stamp Act's repeal (1766), Anglican ministers in the Middle Colonies—led by Rev. Thomas Bradbury Chandler[14]—redoubled their pleas to London, arguing that the British government's "best Security in the Colonies does, and must always arise, from the Principles of Submission and Loyalty taught by the Church" of England, whose clergy "are constantly instilling these great Principles into the People."[15] Such statements only reinforced Alison's inherited fear that Anglican bishops, as in Ireland,

---

13. Rev. Francis Alison, Philadelphia, to Rev. Ezra Stiles, Newport, R.I., 15 April 1764.   14. Chandler (1726–1790), a convert from Presbyterianism, was a Church of England minister at Elizabeth, N.J.
15. Bridenbaugh, *Mitre & Sceptre*, 248; see Sources.

"were never friends to Liberty, but ever ready to flatter Princes, & to promote arbitrary Power." "[A]n Episcopate," Alison declared, "cannot be Established here, without an Act of Parlia[ment] & an Act of Parliam^t to Establish religion in ye Colonies, has ye same tendency with acts to destroy our assemblies, & to take away our Religious liberty, as ye oth[e]rs strip us of our property."[16]

To forestall what he now viewed as a concerted plot to suppress colonial rights, Alison took two complementary steps. In collaboration with John Dickinson and George Bryan,[17] Alison authored *The Centinel*, a series of 19 essays that appeared in the *Pennsylvania Journal* between 24 March and 28 July 1768. Exhaustively researched and, to his opponents, infuriatingly logical, Alison's essays systematically demonstrated that the history of established churches, whether Catholic or Protestant, "contains little else than the follies, absurdities, frauds, rapine, pride, domination, rage, & cruelty of spiritual tyrants."[18] Alison argued persuasively that, despite Rev. Chandler's contention that bishops in America would have strictly limited authority, in fact it would be impossible to prevent them from using the Common Law to demand tithes and in other ways grasp the authority they enjoyed in England and Ireland. After all, the infamous Stamp Act had proposed to tax documents pertaining to "ecclesiastical courts," although none yet existed in the colonies but surely would, Alison warned, if the bishops had their way.

Alison addressed his essays to all colonial dissenters, assuring Quakers and Germans (as well as liberal Anglicans) that in assailing the Church of England he and other Presbyterian ministers sought no spiritual or political ascendancy of their own, as their detractors warned, but only religious freedom for all and a strict separation of church and state. To illustrate his arguments, however, Alison drew heavily on his people's interpretation of the Presbyterian experience in northern Ireland: "Our Forefathers," he wrote, "harrassed by spiritual Courts and the Power of lordly Prelates . . . being likewise denied the Privilege of peaceably worshipping God in a Way the most agreeable to their Consciences, at last wearied out with Persecution, resolved to leave their Native Country, and seek Shelter in the Wilds of America. The Power of the Church of England by Law established, they

16. Rev. Francis Alison, Philadelphia, to Rev. Ezra Stiles, Newport, R.I., 7 May 1768.   17. John Dickinson (1732–1808): a nominal Anglican although born in Maryland of Quaker parentage, Dickinson resided primarily in Delaware; studied law in London, 1754–1756; was elected to the Delaware Assembly and chosen its speaker in 1760; he was elected to Pennsylvania's Assembly in 1762 but in 1764 broke with the Quaker party and opposed its petition for royal government. In 1765 Dickinson opposed the Stamp Act and attended the Stamp Act Congress; he wrote extensively in defense of colonial rights, most famously in his *Letters from A Pennsylvania Farmer* (1767), penned in opposition to the Townshend Acts; perhaps taking his cue from Alison or Bryan, in his *Farmer's Letters* Dickinson drew parallels between Britain's oppressions of Ireland and of the American colonies. Although a member of the First and Second Continental Congresses, Dickinson opposed American independence and retired to his farm in Dover; in 1779 he returned to politics as governor of both Delaware and Pennsylvania; in 1787 he was a member of the Constitutional Convention and wrote the "Fabius" essays in favor of ratification, but later he allied with Jefferson and the Democratic-Republicans in opposition to Federalist policies. On George Bryan, see especially chapter 52.   18. Rev. Francis Alison, *The Centinel*, no. 3 (7 April 1768).

imagined was confined to England"; until now "they had thought themselves secure from the oppressive Tyranny of any proud Ecclesiasticks."[19]

Alison's other strategy was to unite the Presbyterian clergy of the Middle Colonies with the Congregational ministers of New England in a formal, permanent, and fraternal union that would strengthen their opposition to the "Episcopal Plot." In this effort, his principal collaborator was Rev. Ezra Stiles (1727–1795), pastor of the Second Congregational church in Newport, Rhode Island, and future president of Yale College. In the following letter, Alison urged Stiles and his colleagues to action, and, recognizing the New Englanders' sense of relative security, drew again on Irish experience to drive home the dangers of an established church—in the process, revealing talents for biting satire and bitter sarcasm that he carefully suppressed in his *Centinel* essays.

Rev. Francis Alison, Philadelphia, to Rev. Ezra Stiles, Newport, Rhode Island, 29 March 1768

Philad[a] March y[e]: 29th 1768

To the Revr[d] D[r]. Ezra Stiles

Revr[d] & D[r] S[r]

I am not certain, but I think you ow<e> me a letter, but I complain that you Sent me no letter by Cap[t] Anthony tho you had Some months of which you might have Spared a few minutes for this purpose. I desire to know whether any thing is a doing[20] about D[r]: Chandlers Primitive Bishop in y[r]. Goverm[t], or whether y[r] Island is to be the place of his Residence.[21] If you admit him Cordially, he may posssibly be like foxes & Eagles, y[t] are Said to do most mischief at a distance; you may escape his oppression. The D[r]. puts on an air of modesty, but makes very high claims. they are y[e] church, y[e] american Church the Church of England in America & all others are but dissenters—none y[t] are dissenters from the national church have any right to any degree of Civil or military power—Their new Bishops are to protect & defend both the Clergy & the Laity; without Bishops he Says the church here y[t] is essentially y[e] same with y[e] Establishd Church in England, cannot long Subsist; & what Ruins y[e] one must in time destroy the other. Bishops he Says Should be granted,[22] if for no other Reason for y[e] sake of y[e] State; no other denomination of christians, but Episcopalians, can Support monarchy. That is y[e] old Cry, no king no bishop; & without[23] Bishops be

---

19. Rev. Francis Alison, *The Centinel*, no. 2 (31 March 1768). **20. a doing**: being done; see n. 37, and chapter 4, n. 45. **21.** Here and in the following sentences, Alison refers to—and quotes from—Rev. Thomas Bradbury Chandler's *Appeal to the Public in Behalf of the Church of England in America* (New York, 1767), which the convocation of colonial Anglican clergy published and sent to London in 1767. Although Chandler had tried to be moderate and reassuring, Alison—in both this letter (as he underlined) and in *The Centinel*—pounced on the former's unguarded expressions, arguing they revealed arrogant pretensions to ecclesiastical supremacy. **22. granted**: allowed, permitted. **23. without**: unless.

Speedily Sent to America, ye English Church, & State are in danger. Without a Bishop ye Negroes cannot be Converted, nor ye Indians Civilized. What wonders can be wrought by two or three men, at the most! What a Pity it is y^t ye men in powers, y^t ye Guardians of ye Nation, in the Parliament, would not hear their Complaints, & threatnings and cajolings, & Save ye Nation from Ruin by giving them Bishops without delay. But will it not be a hardship, that Bishops Should not have Courts for ye exercise of discipline; or that any but their Loyal followers, Should be alowed to fill any places of honor or profit in our Islands or Colonies? These things are Serious evils to us, who groand[24] under an Establishment, but are words of no force with you. A Sort of a Society in this city have determined to unmask him, & follow him thro all his doublings, & dark Shelters;[25] & we have publishd our first paper, Called the Centinel last Thursday in Bradfords Paper,[26] which will be continued. A paper called the american Whig is begun[27] after the Same manner in New York,[28] and we earnestly request you to Set Some paper on foot in like manner in y^r. free Goverm^t & excite the Sons of liberty in Connecticut, to do ye Same in New-haven. The attempt must be made to point out the Common Danger. Most nations in ye world have lost their liberty by not opposing the attempts of proud ambitious men in Season.[29] With as much propriety, may they Send Bishops into Scotland or Hanover, as to ye New England Colonies or to Maryland or Pensylvania. Ireland was long alowd greater Privileges than she enjoys there at Present   It was, if I remember right, in ye reign of queen Ann, that Presbyterians were disqualified by law to fill a better Post than that of a petty Constable,[30] and had these aspiring church men the power, they would think that they did God & ye State good Service to Serve[31] you all in the Same Manner. If ye King must nominate ye American Bishops, & if they are to be of Such Importance, why must they not be paid out of these new projected funds to pay Governors, &

---

24. groand: i.e., groaned "suffered"; Alison refers to the legal **Establishment** in his homeland of the Church of Ireland, which he and other Ulster Presbyterian immigrants (**us**) had experienced.   **25. doublings, & dark Shelters**: "twists and turns, and shadowy hiding places."   **26. Bradfords Paper**: the *Pennsylvania Journal*, long published by William Bradford, a leading Presbyterian in Philadelphia. Ironically, in 1756 it was Bradford who had threatened to reveal that Rev. Thomas Barton had plagiarized his sermon, "Unanimity and Public Spirit," but was dissuaded by Rev. William Smith, who was Barton's patron, Bradford's fellow associate in the Proprietary party, and Alison's colleague at the College of Philadelphia (see chapter 53).   **27. is begun**: has been started.   **28. the american Whig . . . in New York**: *The American Whig*: a series of essays opposing an American episcopacy; written primarily by William Livingston, New York lawyer and leader of that colony's nascent Presbyterian or Whig party; published in the *New York Gazette* in 1768.   **29. in Season**: at the opportune time.   **30. in ye reign of queen Ann . . . Presbyterians were disqualified by law . . .**: Alison's reference is to the Sacramental Test Act, passed by the Anglican-controlled Irish Parliament in 1704, which excluded Presbyterians and other Irish Dissenters from nearly all political offices, barred them from teaching school, and denied the validity of their marriages and funerals. Beginning in 1719, Parliament suspended many of the Act's clauses, but others remained in effect until the law's full repeal in 1784.   **31. Serve**: treat.

other officers of State,[32] & if we be taxd even to support them he tells us y^t he deserves not to be lookd on as a good subject that would think much to pay it; & will not ye same reasoning hold for a Support to ye missionaries?   thus ye Society[33] will be eased, & they will no longer be obliged to cut and Shufle, & make pretences to get money from the mother Countrey to Support ye Gospel, & they May greatly increase ye number of missionaries. Governor Dobbs,[34] a church biggot, has been unwearied in North Carolina, till he got a Law to oblige every County to maintain an orthodox minister, & as he Says, this goverm^t abounds with Sectaries of all denominations, especially the Anabaptists. They must all support the orthodox ministers of ye Episcopal persuasion, & he Say<s> in his letter to ye Society that by a Vestry law[35] of his procuring[36] every taxable[37] in that Goverm^t is obliged annually to pay ten Shillings to purchase Gleb<e>s, & to build gleb<e>-houses[38] &c; there is as he Says about 35 thousand taxables, which must Cost these poor people above 17-thousand pounds in that one article. See ye abstract of ye Societies proceedings for 1765 page 84. I earnestly entreat you to favor ye world with Such remarks on this attempt to bring us into bondage as you think Just, & let me know what is doing[39] in Boston or what they think will be ye Consequence of this appeal. We think in this place y^t it was a merciful providence, y^t directed him[40] to publish, & to give a timely alarm to see y^t our Liberties are in Danger. A letter by ye Post will be very acceptable to

Rev^d. S^r your Sincere friend & obedient humb^l Servt

Fra: Alison

Despite the New Englanders' temerity, Alison and Stiles were able to forge an ecumenical union of dissenting clergy. Between 1767 and 1775 their General Convention of Presbyterian and Congregational ministers met annually, eventually drawing mem-

---

32. . . . **to pay Governors, & other officers of State**: here Alison refers to the Townshend Acts of 1767, which provided that customs revenues collected from new taxes on imported goods would be used to pay the salaries of royal governors and other Crown officials, thus depriving the colonial assemblies of the "power of the purse"—i.e., the threat to deny legislative appropriations for official salaries—which the assemblies had employed to check royal authority in the colonies.   **33. ye missionaries** [of] . . . **ye Society**: the Anglican missionaries of the Society for the Propagation of the Gospel, whose colonial representatives, such as Rev. Thomas Barton, were conspicuously eager for an American episcopacy.   **34. Governor Dobbs**: Arthur Dobbs (1689–1765): born in Co. Antrim; royal governor of North Carolina (1754–1765); an earnest Anglican, Dobbs regarded his colony's "Sectaries" as "Evils" that "cannot be removed till there are proper Schools erected for the Education of Youth and qualifying them for holy Orders, and Bishops appointed in America to confer them." Despite Dissenters' opposition, in 1765 Dobbs persuaded the British government to approve legislation, passed by North Carolina's Assembly, that legally established the Church of England in that colony. Rhoden, *Revolutionary Anglicanism*, 31; see Sources.   **35. Vestry law**: law regulating parish affairs.   **36. of his procuring**: getting enacted.   **37. taxable**: taxable person.   **38. Gleb<e>s**: lands set aside for the use and income of the parish clergymen; **gleb<e> houses**: parsonages.   **39. doing**: being done.   **40. him**: i.e., Rev. Thomas Bradbury Chandler.

bers from as far away as the Carolinas, creating networks of correspondence and mutual concerns that proved invaluable as the conflict with Britain moved from rhetoric to rebellion.[41] To be sure, Alison did not welcome the ensuing crisis, for it disrupted his philanthropic endeavors, and Pennsylvania's revolutionary constitution of 1776, which created a unicameral legislature, violated his (and Francis Hutcheson's) belief in the virtues of a mixed or balanced government. Nevertheless, once the fighting began Alison supported the American cause wholeheartedly, but unfortunately he died in Philadelphia on 28 November 1779, before he could be sure of the Revolution's outcome.

Despite his misgivings, Alison's contribution to "the gathering storm" was enormous. Not only had he helped mobilize Pennsylvania's Scots-Irish as an independent political force but also, through his emphasis on freedom of conscience, he had laid the groundwork for an alliance between the Presbyterians and many of the colony's other dissenters. In the early 1770s that alliance evolved into a radical movement that overthrew both the proprietorship and the old Assembly, declared independence, and wrote the state constitution that brought the Scots-Irish and their allies to power. Inspired by his teachings, many of Alison's own former students, such as Charles Thomson, Thomas McKean, Thomas Mifflin, and George Read, led the agitation that maneuvered Pennsylvania and the neighboring colonies into the Revolution.[42]

---

41. Stiles not only cooperated with Alison in mobilizing New England's clergy against the "Episcopal Plot" but also sympathized with Alison's Old Side Presbyterians in their conflicts with the New Side–controlled Synod of New York and Philadelphia. Indeed, in 1773 Stiles urged Alison to break with the Synod and create a new, "distinct body"—"free from the alterations which arise from the ungenerous Aspersions of the English and the Scots"—to be led by the "Irish Brethren" in Philadelphia and based on the support of recent Ulster immigrants in the Middle and Southern colonies (Rev. Ezra Stiles, Newport, R.I., to Rev. Francis Alison, Philadelphia, 22 October 1773). Ironically, however, the association that the two men had cultivated between Presbyterian and Congregational clergymen had consequences that ran counter to Alison's religious goals, ethnic preferences, and, perhaps, his political sympathies. After the Revolution the close relationship that the New Siders developed with New England's Federalist clergy may only have reinforced the former's determination to "embargo" Irish-born ministers suspected of doctrinal liberalism and political radicalism. See chapters 47 and 49. **42.** Charles Thomson (1729–1824): born in Maghera, Co. Derry, Thomson emigrated as a 10-year-old orphan and was indentured for four years; however, he attended Alison's New London Academy and later tutored in the College of Philadelphia; like Alison, Thomson initially was an ally of Benjamin Franklin, but he broke with the latter's Quaker Party over the issues of frontier defense and royal government; in the early 1770s Thomson became a primary leader of the Philadelphia's Presbyterians and Sons of Liberty; at the height of his political career, between 1774 and 1789, he served as secretary of the Continental Congress; in retirement after 1789, he employed the Greek learned from Alison to author and publish (in 1808) a highly respected translation of the New Testament. ¶Thomas McKean (1734–1817): born of Ulster immigrant parents in Chester Co., Pa.; attended Alison's New London Academy; McKean practiced law and politics, becoming a member of the Delaware Assembly (1762–1776), a leading opponent of Stamp Act, and a member of the Continental Congress (1774–1783) and its president (1781); McKean signed the Declaration of Independence and played a major role in the machinations that pushed Pennyslvania into revolution; with George Read, McKean was the principal author of Delaware's state constitution; after his appointment as Pennsylvania's chief justice, McKean became more conservative, and in 1787 he supported Pennsylvania's ratification of the U.S. Constitution; however, in 1792 he broke with the Federalists over foreign policy issues and was elected Republican governor of Pennsylvania in 1799 and 1802; always a moderate, McKean's subsequent conflicts

More broadly, as John Adams later recalled, it was "the apprehension of Episcopacy [that] contributed . . . as much as any other cause, to arouse the attention . . . of the common people, and urge them to close thinking on the constitutional authority of Parliament over the colonies." Thanks largely to Alison, he wrote, "[t]he nature and extent of the authority of Parliament over the colonies was discussed everywhere, till it was discovered that [Parliament] had none at all."[43] Through his writings in the Anglican bishop controversy, Alison succeeded in melding Enlightenment theories of natural rights with the religious concerns and sensibilities that still gripped the great majority of his fellow colonists. In his work, the historical grievances and radical traditions of the Scots-Irish found fruition five thousand miles from their native Ulster.

56 ❈

John Morton, 1769

John Morton's life and letters illustrate the political vicissitudes of one of Philadelphia's Irish-born merchants, a member of the Society of Friends, during the Revolutionary era. Philadelphia's Irish merchant community was the largest and most affluent in

---

with Philadelphia's radical Republicans, led in part by Irish-American journalist William Duane, split the state party; but with Federalist and conservative Republican support, McKean was reelected governor in 1805. ¶Thomas Mifflin (1744–1800): born in Philadelphia of Quaker parents, Mifflin attended the College of Philadelphia; he became a wealthy merchant but died penniless because of his extravagance; an ardent Whig and member of the Pennsylvania Assembly (1772–1776), Mifflin broke with his fellow Quakers and was one of the youngest and most radical members of the Continental Congress; in 1775–1778 Mifflin served in the Continental Army as quartermaster general, but he resigned to intrigue with Horatio Gates against Washington's command; in 1787 a member of the U.S. Constitutional Convention, Mifflin opposed the 1776 Pennsylvania state constitution as too radical, and in 1789–1790 he chaired his state's second state constitutional convention; he was elected governor of Pennsylvania for three terms (1790–1799), first as a Federalist, later as a Jeffersonian. ¶George Read (1733–1798): born in Maryland of Irish Protestant parents, Read studied under Alison at New London; in 1753 he was admitted to Philadelphia's bar and in 1763 he secured an appointment as Delaware's attorney general; however, he resigned that post to protest the Stamp Act and was elected to the Delaware Assembly, serving from 1765 to 1776; a member of the First and Second Continental Congresses, Read signed the Declaration of Independence and, with McKean, coauthored Delaware's state constitution, under which he served as the state's vice-president (1776) and president (1777–1778); in 1787 he was a member of the U.S. Constitutional Convention and in 1788–1793 of the U.S. Senate. ¶In all, Alison taught, at New London or in Philadelphia, five future signers of the Declaration of Independence (McKean, Read, James Smith, Francis Hopkinson, and William Pacca), three members of the U.S. Constitutional Convention, 15 members and two chaplains of Congress, four generals in the Continental Army, over a dozen important officials in revolutionary Pennsylvania, Delaware, New Jersey, and the Carolinas, and the first president of the University of Pennsylvania (formerly Alison's College of Philadelphia). Only five of his former students are known to have been loyalists. **43.** E. I. Nybakken, ed., *"The Centinel"* . . . , [7]; see Sources.

America, numbering some 60 families at its height in the late 1760s. It was also a community that was sharply divided by religion and politics—but not according to Ireland's traditional divisions between Protestants and Catholics. Instead, political circumstances peculiar to colonial Pennsylvania separated Irish Quakers from the Irish-born members of all other denominations. Thus, Philadelphia's Irish Friends, like their coreligionists of British backgrounds, adhered to the Quaker party that controlled the colonial Assembly until 1776 and generally opposed the American Revolution. By contrast, the city's Irish Anglican, Presbyterian, and Catholic merchants supported the Penn family and the Proprietary party before the early or mid-1770s, when nearly all espoused or at least accepted American rebellion and independence. Likewise, prior to the Revolution affluent Irish Anglicans, Presbyterians, and Catholics interacted in the Friendly Sons of St. Patrick society, established in 1771, whereas few or no Irish Quakers joined that body until the 1780s and 1790s. To be sure, in 1765–1769 a common opposition to the Stamp and Townshend acts temporarily allied all of Philadelphia's Irish merchants, but in 1770 that unity crumbled, and by 1775–1776 virtually all the city's Irish (and other) Quakers were branded as loyalists and Tories. Not until the Revolution's end would common origins, shared economic interests, and conservative political instincts reunite most of Philadelphia's Irish merchants as Federalists in opposition to the agrarian democracy of backcountry Pennsylvania.

John Morton, born on 23 April 1739, and his older brother Samuel, born on 19 June 1730, were the sons of James and Sarah Morton[1] of Moyallon townland, a colony of Quakers established in 1685 in the parish of Tullylish and the barony of Lower Iveagh, on the County Down side of the River Bann.[2] The Morton family, perhaps originally from Aberdeen, Scotland, worshiped at the Friends' Meeting House at Grange Upper, in north County Armagh, with kinsmen such as John and Samuel's second cousin, Thomas Greer (1724–1803) of Bernagh, a prosperous merchant and linen manufacturer near the town of Dungannon in east County Tyrone. Greer would never leave Ulster, but he would become the Morton brothers' transatlantic business partner and correspondant after they emigrated to Philadelphia in 1748–1750 and entered the dry-goods trade.

The Mortons prospered overseas, both economically and socially, numbering among their friends some of Philadelphia's Quaker "grandees"—wealthy merchants, many of

---

1. James (b. 1701) and Sarah (née Whitsitt) Morton had at least four other children: Mary (1725–1814), who married William Greeves of Grange, Co. Tyrone; Susanna (b. 1728), who wed William Heazleton of Co. Tyrone and whose sons emigrated to Pittsburgh after the Revolution (see chapter 67); Ruth (b. 1734), who married James Nicholson; and Elizabeth (1744–1768), who in 1763 married Elias Dawson at Grange Meeting House and emigrated ca. 1765 to Philadelphia, where Elias was a merchant and died in 1805. 2. Moyallon townland, in Tullylish parish, comprised about four hundred acres. Many of Moyallon's first Quaker settlers appear to have immigrated from Scotland, particularly from Aberdeen, one of the few centers of Scottish Quakerism, in response to encouragement from Alexander Christy, a Scots Quaker who in 1685 purchased Moyallon and introduced linen manufacturing and bleaching to the area. In 1834 the townland's inhabitants were still "chiefly Quakers," and they had a meetinghouse large enough to accommodate about five hundred congregants. For demographic data on Tullylish parish and its environs, see appendix 2.1c, on chapter 56.

FIGURE 17
Portrait of John Morton
(1729–1838) of Philadelphia.
Photograph of an etching in
Lawrence Lewis, Jr., *A History
of the Bank of North America*
(Philadelphia, 1882).

whom also had Irish family or business connections—such as Henry Drinker, Abel James, Joshua Fisher, John Reynell, and the brothers Israel, James, and John Pemberton.[3] Eventually, the Mortons would own their own wharf on the Delaware River, a large counting-house in Water Street, and shares in at least two vessels. In 1769 their combined tax assessment was nearly £160, and, when he died in 1773, Samuel Morton was one of 84 Philadelphians, out of more than 30,000 inhabitants, who owned a carriage. As early as 1758 the Morton brothers were sufficiently affluent that Samuel could afford to marry,[4] turn the firm's daily operations over to John, and devote most of his time to the Quaker reform movement, led by James Pemberton, that sought to return Pennsylvania's Friends to the strict discipline of their ancestors.

3. Israel (1715–1779), James (1723–1809), and John Pemberton (1727–1795): wealthy Quaker merchants and philanthropists; leaders (especially James) of the pre-Revolutionary Quaker reform movement; their firm pacifism and their advocacy of friendly relations with Pennsylvania's Indians during the Seven Years' War and, later, of reconciliation with Britain antagonized the colony's Scots-Irish, who got revenge in 1777–1778 when the Pennsylvania government temporarily exiled all three brothers, with other leading Friends, to Winchester, Virginia.   4. On 7 September 1758, Samuel Morton married Phebe Lewis (1738–1812), daughter of Robert and Mary Lewis of Philadelphia, in the Friends' Meeting House on Arch Street. They had six children: Robert (1760–1786), who in 1784 married his step-sister, Hannah Pemberton, daughter of the Quaker leader James Pemberton; James (b. 1759); Sarah; Mary; Samuel, Jr. (b. 1766); and John (b. 1769).

In 1764 Samuel made an extended visit home to Ulster, where he arranged with Thomas Greer to trade American flaxseed for Irish linens. Fortunately, the crisis occasioned by the Stamp Act (1765) did not disrupt this profitable traffic. In November 1765 John and Samuel Morton and over four hundred other Philadelphia merchants protested the Act by signing a nonimportation agreement, but Irish goods sent directly to the colonies were exempt from the boycott. On this occasion, Quakers and other traders were virtually unanimous in opposition to British policy, but the next dispute with London would prove more divisive. In July 1767 word reached Philadelphia that Parliament had passed the Townshend Acts, imposing new taxes on imported British manufactured goods. Although Boston's merchants resolved in November 1767 to boycott British goods, at first Philadelphia's traders were averse to the economic losses that another nonimportation agreement might entail. Quaker merchants were especially opposed to any displays of disloyalty to the Crown, for their political leaders in the Assembly were meanwhile petitioning the British government to abolish the Penns' proprietorship and transform Pennsylvania into a royal colony. As a result, Philadelphia's first opposition to the Townshend Acts came from young Presbyterian and Anglican members of the Proprietary party, particularly from Charles Thomson, George Bryan, and John Dickinson, and between December 1767 and mid-February 1768 Dickinson's *Farmer's Letters* urged the city's merchants to action.[5]

Despite such pressures, Philadelphia's affluent traders continued to reject nonimportation, and the most conservative Quaker leaders feared that the agitation was merely a plot by Presbyterian radicals who "look[ed] upon this [crisis] as a favorable opportunity of establishing their Republican Principles."[6] However, while they feared disorder, most Quakers also opposed the Townshend Acts, and in November 1768 John and Samuel Morton, along with two hundred other traders, signed a letter addressed to London's merchants, requesting their aid in securing the Acts' repeal. This was their last attempt to resist the popular demand for nonimportation. Exasperated by Parliament's intransigence, on 6 February 1769 Philadelphia's merchants agreed to boycott all British goods after 10 March. Although Samuel Morton was on a religious visit to the Southern colonies, John Morton signed the Non-Importation Agreement in both their names. Like the 1765 boycott, that of 1769 allowed the importation of goods shipped directly from Ireland, but it obliged the Mortons to forfeit the benefits of the Linen Act of 1745, under which virtually all Irish linens shipped to North America were sent through England to collect a lucrative bounty on reexported cloth. Thus, in the following letters to Thomas Greer, one written just before and the other shortly after the boycott began, John Morton's apprehension of declining "Proffits" competed with his genuine opposition to Parliament's "Internal Taxation."

5. On Bryan and on Dickinson and Thomson, see chapters 52 and 55 (esp. n. 40), respectively. **6.** Thayer, *Pa. Politics*, 126; see Sources.

Letter 1.

John Morton, Philadelphia,

to Thomas Greer, Dungannon, County Tyrone, 22 February 1769

Philad[a] 2 Mon. 22 1769

D[r] Cousin

Our last was ⅌ Brig' Swallow via Cork to which we refer   this chiefly comes to inclose Willing & Morris's[7] & Bache & Cuthberts seconds of Exchange[8] for the Sums therein specified, the first of s[d]. Bills being sent by the Brig' above mentioned   we have not the least Apprehension of their meeting with Dishonor,[9] and if they should wou'd caution thee to take the necessary Steps in obtaining Protests,[10]   we have little material to say Only it's likely the Commerce carried on between Great Britain & her Colonies will be in a great Measure Stopped, if they dont repeal the late unconstitutional Revenue Acts which are very oppressive;   we have no other Means left in our Power in a Legal Manner to do ourselves Justice, but to omitt the taking off[11] their Manufactures,   we are resolved to be free from their Internal Taxation let the Event be what it may,   it's better to be Cloathed in a homely Garb & be free, than g<o>rgeously apparel'd & Submitt to Slavery, for what better than Slavery is it[12] if the Parliament of Great Britain can take away our Property without our Consent—So much for Politicks

I rece'd this Day a Letter from Brother Sam[l] who was in Charles Town, S. Carolina, the 4th Instant, accompanying my much esteemed Friend Rachael Willson from that[13] (North England)[14]   as I wrote thee before respecting his Journey <I>[15]

---

7. Willing & Morris: the merchant firm of Thomas Willing and Robert Morris was one of the most profitable partnerships in the late eighteenth century in Philadelphia. Willing and Morris were both Anglicans and leading, albeit young, members of the Proprietary party; reluctant revolutionaries at best (in 1776 Willing refused to vote for independence as one of Pennsylvania's delegates to the Second Continental Congress), they prospered during the war and in the 1780s through privateering, military contracting, commerce, banking, and speculation in lands and government securities, becoming leaders of the nascent Federalist party. On Willing and Morris, also see chapter 58.   **8. second of exchange**: the second in a series of bills of exchange. **9. Dishonor**: refusal to accept the bill of exchange.   **10. protest**: a formal declaration in writing that a bill of exchange has been presented and payment or acceptance refused (OED, s.v., 2).   **11. off**: i.e. of.   **12. what better than Slavery is it**: how is it any better than slavery. Ironically, "slavery" was commonly employed by American radicals, although many were themselves slaveowners, to describe the colonists' likely fate if their agitation failed. However, for Friends such as Morton the term had special (and less hypocritical) implications, because James Pemberton and other Quaker reformers were then in the midst of an ultimately successful effort to persuade the Society to denounce American slavery and to expel all Friends who refused to manumit their slaves.   **13. from that**: see chapter 11, n. 10.   **14. Rachael Wilson from . . . North England**: from Kendall, Westmorelandshire, Rachel Wilson (1715–1785) was a Quaker missionary whom Samuel Morton accompanied on her preaching tour of the Southern colonies between November 1768 and August 1769. The daughter of a tanner and the wife of Isaac Wilson (married 1740), a woolen manufacturer; according to evangelist George Whitefield, Rachel Wilson made a "fine figure and striking presence" and "was gifted with a clear, distinct voice and all the pathos of pure, unstudied eloquence." R. Larson, *Daughters of Light . . .* , 284, 318; see Sources.   **15. <I>**: an expected subject pronoun is often dropped in Ulster English in a noninitial clause, especially, as here, when it is identical with the subject pronoun of the preceding clause; see chapter 1, n. 110.

need not add, but that[16] he was well,   I dont expect to see him here before 5th Month next,   Wm. Johnson from your Parts was Setled in Charles Town & kept a School,   he died lately in that Place & was much lamented by his Acquaintance as an ingenious Man;   take a Paragraph from my Brother's Letter   "William Johnston is lately deceassed & left a Widow & five small Children,   she was bro'[17] to Bed two Days ago,   he is much lamented here being a general Loss to the Place on Acco' of the Youth he had under his Care,   he had a very large School & in a likely way to do well"—So it is, when we have strugled for a Series <of> Years with a fluctuating World & have some Reasons to hope for an Enjoyment of the Harvest of our Labour Iron Fisted Death comes as in a Moment & deprives us of all our Golden Dreames;   our Family is well   with Tender of dr Love to thee & all our Friends We remain

Thy affectionate Cousins
Saml & Jno Morton[18]

Letter 2.

John Morton, Philadelphia,
to Thomas Greer, Dungannon, County Tyrone, 4 April 1769

Philada 4 mo. 4 1769

Affectionate Cousin

Our last was (via Belfast) dated 2 mo 25 Inclosing Acco<unt> Sales of the last parcel of Linens we had from thee, since which have none of thy Favours;   we now inclose thee James Coopers Draft on John Strettle Mercht in London for £87 Stg Exchange at 60 ℗C in Curr<enc>y £139.4. which note accordingly——

The Merchants & Traders of this City have mutually covenanted & agreed with each other not to import any Goods from Great Britain untill the British parliament repeals some late Unconstitutional Revenue acts except such as were Shipp'd before the first of this Month; so that what Linens thou sends us, must come immediately from Ireland & by no Means go to England to recover the Bounty, except thou shou'd learn that the parliament had repeal'd the Act for laying a Duty on paper glass &c;   it's our Opinion they'll not be Suddenly repeal'd;   therefore wou'd submit to thy Judgment whether it wou'd be better to stop sending any more Linens for some Time, or send them immediately from Ireland, which wou'd deprive us of the Bounty, & consequently lessen our Proffits considerably;   what is become of the parcel of Linens thou wrote us was sent to L'pool long since,   its a Mistery to us what can detain them;   we are very hearty in the good Cause of Liberty & hope it will have the

---

16. <I> need not add, but that . . . : I need add only that . . .   **17.** bro': brought.   **18.** Saml & Jno Morton: Samuel Morton was still in the Southern colonies when John Morton wrote these letters, but he signed them in the name of the firm.

desired Effect of for ever deterring a corrupt Ministry from encroaching on the
Rights & Priviledges of a free people: our Family is well   with Love to all Friends
PS. Brother Saml is not returnd   We remain thy affectionate Cousins
but expect him in a Short Time   Saml & Jn°. Morton

Perhaps a combination of age (he was only 29 when he wrote these letters) and a transplanted resentment against British restrictions on Irish trade helps explain John Morton's youthful enthusiasm for "the good Cause of Liberty." A fortuitous combination of patriotism and profits may also have helped—for, thanks to the boycott, direct exports of Irish goods to America soared in 1769, and the Mortons were able to sell low-priced Irish linens at 150 percent—the more expensive cloths at 166 percent—above their invoice price, thus ensuring an ample income despite the loss of the reexport bounty. However, the Mortons' commitment to the Society of Friends and its wealthy, conservative leadership soon tempered their political convictions. In the late summer of 1769, Philadelphia's Monthly Meeting, led by James Pemberton, condemned Friends' involvement in nonimportation and urged Friends to withdraw. Also, on 2 November 1769 John Morton ensured his own élite status by marrying Esther Deshler (1740–1787), daughter of an affluent Quaker merchant who owned one of Philadelphia's finest mansions.[19] In May 1770, when word of the Townshend Acts' partial repeal reached Philadelphia, the wealthiest dry-goods merchants came out in opposition to continuing the boycott. Finally, on 20 September 1770, the city's most conservative tradesmen, led by Reynell, Fisher, Drinker, and other Quakers, met at Davenport's Tavern and voted to end nonimportation, despite the protests of Thomson, Bryan, Dickinson, and their allies. The result was a bitterly divided city: Philadelphia's merchant élite had split along political and religious lines; and the Quaker grandees would never again be able to lead or control protests against British policies. Henceforth, political power increasingly fell into the hands of Anglican and Presbyterian radicals.

The boycott's end also doomed the profitable relationship between the Mortons and Thomas Greer, for in 1771–1772 Irish linens (once again reexported through England) flooded the American market; the consequent low prices forced the Mortons to curtail orders and delay payments, much to Greer's displeasure, while overproduction in Ulster helped bring about severe depression in the Irish linen industry. On 16 February 1773, Samuel Morton died after a long illness (in 1775 his widow became James Pemberton's third wife), but John Morton's business continued to thrive, increasingly by shipping flour

---

19. Morton's father-in-law, David Deshler (d. 1792), was also a signatory to the 1765 and 1769 nonimportation agreements, and of the 1768 letter to London's merchants, but, like Morton, he apparently took no part in political activities thereafter. ¶John and Esther Morton had at least eight children: Robert; Sarah (married John Coats); Esther (wed D. B. Smith); Mary (b. 1771); James (b. and d. 1772); David (b. 1774); John, Jr. (1776–1812); and a second James (b. 1780). When John Morton, Jr., died, his personal property was inventoried at nearly $23,000.

to Europe and the West Indies. However, American protests against the Tea Act of 1773 began a chain of events that led to war, independence, and the persecution of Philadelphia's wealthy Quakers by the victorious radicals. In 1773–1774 John Morton's close friends, Abel James and Henry Drinker, became the targets of angry public meetings and mob violence for their attempts to import tea under the Act's provisions, and in summer 1774 the Philadelphia Friends' Meeting for Sufferings advised all Quakers to resign from the committees formed to protest the Coercive Acts. In November 1774, in a last attempt to control the agitation, John Morton and other affluent Friends ran for election to Philadelphia's first Committee of Observation, organized to implement the First Continental Congress's ban on trade with Britain; however, their "moderate" ticket was soundly defeated by the radical slate, dominated by Anglican and Presbyterian manufacturers and merchants of lesser wealth. In 1775 the city's Quaker Meeting denounced all "Insurrections, Conspiracies & illegal Assemblies" designed to destroy the "happy connection" between the colonies and the crown;[20] the Meeting also forbade Quakers to serve in the new militia or pay exemption fees, and it began to disown local Friends who persisted in revolutionary activities. By the summer of 1776, the Second Continental Congress had declared independence, an ultraradical government had forcibly replaced the old Pennsylvania Assembly, and Philadelphia's Quaker merchants were stigmatized as "notoriously disaffected" from the patriot cause.

It is uncertain whether John Morton should be classified as a "neutral" or a "loyalist" during the American Revolution. In 1777–1778, during the British occupation of Philadelphia, he consented to serve as a night watchman in Joseph Galloway's Tory administration, but the diary written by his nephew Robert (1760–1786) suggests that the Mortons soon became disillusioned by the British army's arrogance and wanton destruction. However, Pennsylvania's revolutionary government, led by George Bryan, made few or no distinctions: it persecuted all Quakers whose pacifistic principles forbade them to serve in the armed forces, hire substitutes, pay wartime taxes, sell supplies, handle Continental Currency, or take loyalty oaths. For his refusal to swear allegiance, John Morton was double-taxed in 1779 and, like other Quaker merchants during the Revolution, barred from engaging in trade. Others were treated more harshly: two Friends were hanged for aiding the British; and in 1777–1778 Morton's brother-in-law James Pemberton and his close friend Henry Drinker were among 20 Philadelphia Quakers exiled to western Virginia. It is uncertain whether Pennsylvania's government confiscated any of Morton's considerable estate,[21] but after the war he complained, in his last letter to Thomas Greer, that he had "Suffered very much in [his] Property."[22]

---

20. J. D. Marietta, *The Reformation of American Quakerism* . . . , 223; R. F. Oaks, "Philadelphians in Exile . . . ," 300; see Sources. 21. In the records of the Philadelphia Supply Tax of 1780, the patriot leaders Robert Morris and Isaac Cox are listed as paying taxes "for John Morton's estate." However, it is unclear whether this means that Morris and Cox had purchased Morton's confiscated property or that Morton had temporarily assigned his estate to Morris and Cox to avoid double-taxation. 22. John Morton, Philadelphia, to Thomas Greer, Dungannon, Co. Tyrone, 22 May 1783.

Despite his losses, John Morton's mercantile business, now in partnership with his nephew Robert, quickly recovered from the war, as transatlantic trade resumed in 1782–1783. Moreover, their mutual resentment of wartime inflation, paper money, price controls, and other radical policies reunited most of Philadelphia's Irish and other merchants—behind the leadership of Revolutionary financier Robert Morris—in a political alliance that, by 1790, would overthrow Pennsylvania's radical government and rewrite both the national and the state constitutions on conservative lines. In 1784 John and Robert Morton, along with other Quaker neutralists and loyalists, purchased shares in Morris's new Bank of North America (chartered in 1781), the financial engine of the nascent Federalist party. Morton's acceptance by the Bank's ruling clique—many of whom were former adherents of the old Proprietary party, members of the city's wartime political élite, and of Irish Anglican and Presbyterian background or birth—symbolized the triumph of shared socioeconomic interests over the religious and political divisions that the Revolution had exacerbated among the city's Irish merchants. Perhaps even more significant, in 1790 Morton became a founding—and virtually the only Quaker—member of the city's new Hibernian Society, whose first president, Pennsylvania's chief justice, Thomas McKean, of Ulster Presbyterian parentage, had sent Morton's Quaker friends into Virginia exile in 1777![23]

In 1792 John Morton was elected one of the Bank of North America's directors, as well as a member of the Philadelphia Common Council. He also became a director of the Hand-In-Hand Fire Insurance Company—another Federalist bastion that, prior to the Revolution, had had few Quaker members. By the late 1790s, if not before, Morton owned a carriage, and city directories listed him as a "gentleman" merchant (a "dealer in flour") in his residence at 116 Front Street. On 10 January 1809 he was unanimously elected president of the Bank of North America, succeeding the Irish-born Anglican John Nixon, another former patriot leader and member of the Proprietary party.[24] Morton served as Bank president until January 1822[25] and remained as a director until he died, aged 89, on 23 April 1828. A few days later, he was interred beside his wife in the Philadelphia Friends' burial ground.

By the time of his death, John Morton had already divided most of his estate among his children and grandchildren. Yet he still remained one of Philadelphia's wealthiest inhabitants, with personal property valued at nearly $25,000, including $15,000 in promissory

23. On McKean, see chapters 55 (esp. n. 42) and 63. In 1781–1785 John Morton was also a director of the Pennsylvania Hospital and in 1785–1828 a director of the Philadelphia Contributionship for the Insurance of Houses from Loss by Fire, the oldest fire insurance company in America. However, both the Hospital and the Contributionship were traditional Quaker institutions, and more revealing of Morton's postwar mobility across traditional tribal lines and into an interdenominational "Irish" milieu was his 1793 initiation into Philadelphia's Freemason's Lodge No. 2, which had a substantial Irish Presbyterian membership (including John Dunlap; see chapter 11) and close links with the Grand Lodge of Ireland. **24.** On John Nixon, see chapter 58. **25.** In view of the Quakers' testimony against war, it was ironic that during Morton's presidency the Bank of North America loaned the U.S. government ca. $650,000 to prosecute the War of 1812–1815.

notes and bonds, $1,400 in household furniture and books, almost $7,000 on deposit in the Bank of North America, $1,300 in stocks and shares, a gold watch worth $100, and $80 of "cash in house." Thus, unlike many of Philadelphia's revolutionary leaders, such as the impoverished George Bryan and the bankrupt Robert Morris, the suspected Tory John Morton survived the political crisis of 1775–1783, surmounted the economic upheavals of the postwar era, and fared quietly but spectacularly well.

57 ✳

John McDonnell, 1771

In retrospect the American Revolution may appear inevitable, but between 1770 and 1773 anti-British agitation abated as colonial élites resumed their traditional quest for power and patronage—in the process often engendering conflicts that divided Ulster Presbyterians and other Irish immigrants along regional and socioeconomic lines. North Carolina's Regulator movement of 1766–1771 epitomized—albeit in an extremely dramatic and unusually violent fashion—these "normal" political trends, as future rebels and Tories among the colony's tidewater planters and seaport merchants joined forces with royal governor William Tryon[1] to crush an agrarian uprising by backcountry farmers whose grievances were far more serious, and whose goals were much more democratic, than those that would animate North Carolina's Sons of Liberty in 1776.

Although Scots-Irish immigrants and migrants of Ulster ancestry from Pennsylvania, Maryland, and Virginia numbered heavily among the ranks of the Regulators, theirs was not an ethnic or a religious movement. Rather, in some respects, it resembled an intracommunal class war. Ever since the 1750s Ulster-born royal officials and land speculators, such as Governor Arthur Dobbs and Henry McCulloh,[2] had encouraged Ulster immigration and frontier settlement; however, they and their allies in the North Carolina Assembly had

---

1. William Tryon (1728–1788); royal governor of North Carolina, 1765–1771, and afterward the last royal governor of New York. Assailed by the tidewater planters during the Stamp Act crisis of 1765–1766, Tryon's strategy was to reconcile the provincial élite to royal authority by supporting the former in its exploitation of the backcountry and suppression of the Regulators. 2. Arthur Dobbs (1689–1765): born at Castle Dobbs, Co. Antrim; member of the Irish Parliament for Carrickfergus and surveyor-general of Ireland; in 1745 he and his partners acquired four hundred thousand acres in North Carolina, to which he encouraged Ulster emigration and settlement; royal governor of North Carolina in 1754–1765; also see chapter 55, n. 34. ¶Henry McCulloh: of Scottish ancestry and Ulster birth, from the 1720s McCulloh was an influential London merchant and power broker, deeply involved in colonial land speculation and politics; in 1737 the Privy Council granted McCulloh and his associates a patent of 1,200,000 acres in North Carolina, augmenting his earlier acquisitions. The unscrupulous behavior of McCulloh's land agents exasperated backcountry farmers, but both Dobbs and his successor as governor, William Tryon (n. 1), supported McCulloh interests.

also foisted on the newcomers a host of venal and avaricious county sheriffs, judges, clerks, and tax collectors. In addition, by the late 1760s the backcountry was afflicted by a swarm of lawyers and storekeepers who forged alliances with the corrupt "courthouse rings" in the county seats and enmeshed the farmers in webs of debt and litigation.[3] Many of these local "parasites" were Scots-Irish, and both they and their Anglican allies in the Assembly took care to cultivate the backcountry's Presbyterian clergy, who in turn supported North Carolina's rapacious oligarchy and, in 1766–1771, obligingly denounced the Regulators.

Although its author was a Quaker, the following letter by John McDonnell epitomizes the attitudes toward the Regulators of the Irish members—largely Anglicans and Presbyterians—of North Carolina's parvenu gentry. McDonnell was born on 3 April 1739, the son of Edward and Sarah (née Hobson) McDonnell, who leased at least 20 acres, from the earl of Manchester's estate, in Mullahead townland, Kilmore parish and Lower Orior barony, in north County Armagh.[4] The McDonnell surname normally connotes Highland Catholic origins, but by the late 1600s, at least, John McDonnell's ancestors were Scottish Quakers who, like John Morton's, probably migrated to Ulster from the 1680s through the early 1700s. The McDonnells and Mortons do not appear to have been closely related, and the former were associated primarily with the Quaker meeting at Ballyhagan, in Kilmore parish. However, some of the McDonnells' marriages and deaths were recorded in the Mortons' townland, Moyallon in west County Down, and John McDonnell's sole surviving letter was written to Thomas Greer, the wealthy linen merchant and bleacher at Dungannon, County Tyrone, who was also the Mortons' correspondent and business associate.[5]

According to Irish Quaker records, sometime prior to 1769 John McDonnell married Elizabeth Sinton,[6] also of Kilmore parish, and in that year he left his spouse in Mullahead and, like the Morton brothers before him, embarked for Philadelphia, hoping to make his fortune in transatlantic commerce. However, McDonnell may have found Philadelphia's dry-goods trade overly crowded and competitive. In any case, in 1770 or early 1771 he returned to Ulster and then sailed again, this time accompanied by his wife, "Betty," for Wilmington, North Carolina. Already in 1768 the Hinshaw brothers, McDonnell's and

---

3. See also chapter 54.   4. In 1788 Arthur McDonnell of Mullahead rented slightly more than 20 acres at a total rent of £20 5s., a very high valuation that suggests his involvement in linen bleaching, milling, or another lucrative branch of manufacturing; also in 1788 William McDonnell rented an additional 26 acres in Mullahead for £13 10s. In 1819 three local McDonnell families rented a total of nearly 60 acres at a cumulative annual rent of £108. For demographic data on Kilmore parish and its environs, see appendix 2.1c, on chapter 56.
5. See chapter 56.   6. Elizabeth Sinton McDonnell was born ca. 1747 and died in Cork city on 26 July 1831. She and John McDonnell had at least eight children, one of the first two of whom was probably the "fine thriveing Babey" mentioned in his 1771 letter from Wilmington: Elizabeth (d. near Cork, 1805); Sarah (disowned by the Cork meeting for marrying outside the Quaker faith); Margaret (b. 1779—in Cork, as were all of the following); Hannah (1780–1849; d. unmarried in Passage West, Co. Cork); Deborah (1782–1784); Ann (1785–1853; d. in Moyallon, Co. Down); John (1788–1791); and Rebecca (b. 1792; also disowned by Cork's Quakers, in 1811, for "marrying out").

Greer's kinsmen, had emigrated and settled in Orange County, North Carolina, but Mc-Donnell had no interest in emulating their modest success as backcountry farmers. As an ambitious merchant, McDonnell was attracted by North Carolina's expanding overseas trade in tobacco, timber, and naval stores. Wilmington, especially, was a good place to settle, despite its miasmic climate and high mortality rates. Although it only contained about 1,200 inhabitants, Wilmington was North Carolina's largest town and its only deep-water port, serving the wealthy planters and slaveowners who controlled New Hanover County and tapping the rich interior drained by the branches of the Cape Fear River. While in Philadelphia McDonnell may also have heard about native Wilmington traders' notoriously inefficient business practices, by comparison with which a Quaker merchant's proverbially steady and punctual habits might ensure his financial success.

Scanty evidence suggests that McDonnell easily assimilated to Wilmington's overseas merchant community, largely dominated by British and Irish traders. For example, despite his complaint that there were no Quaker meetings nearby (nearly all of North Carolina's 15,000 Friends lived in the backcountry), in 1771 he shared a pew in Wilmington's socially prestigious Anglican church, St. James; the same year he purchased a house lot fronting the river, and later he bought a one-hundred-acre property, Prospect Hall, on the town's outskirts. McDonnell's letter also indicates that he fully shared the conservative political attitudes of Wilmington's merchant élite, many of whom later became loyalists in the American Revolution. Thus, when writing to Greer, McDonnell studiously ignored the Regulators' genuine grievances: the western counties' gross underrepresentation in the North Carolina Assembly; the most corrupt and regressive tax system in all the colonies; the extortionate interest rates and fees charged by backcountry merchants, land speculators, and public officials; and the Assembly's draconian Riot Act of January 1771 which outlawed the Regulators and pushed them to the brink of civil war. Instead, McDonnell attributed frontier protests to a lack of "virtue . . . Religion [and] Morality," and, despite his Quaker pacifism, he obviously supported, if not relished, the government's bloody triumph at Alamance Creek on 16 May 1771.

John McDonnell, Wilmington, North Carolina, to Thomas Greer, Dungannon, County Tyrone, 2 June 1771

Wilmington   no Carolina   6 mo 2nd 1771

D^r friend

    I apprehend the news of a civil war been Comenced[7] in this province will make Some noise[8] at home, and as the Tragic Scene first apeared[9] in the neighbourhood of

---

7. **been Comenced**: i.e., being commenced "having commenced." **8. will make Some noise**: will be the subject of some comment and/or interest. **9. apeared**: reading conjectural; could also be read as **opened**.

Cane Creek[10] where a large boddy of friends are Setled with Satisfaction doth write thee[11] that they have behaved well in General and is Clear of Censure as far as I have Learned   yesterday I heard by our Express[12] to Governors Camp that the Troops was then within 3 miles of where the Hinshaws Lives   Either Jesse or william Sent their Respects to me and that they were all well[13]   the said Express brought us a Confirmation of the Battle Lately fought there and the advantj was on the Side of Goverment which I hope will be of Signal Service to this province,   ab^t 200 was killed in the Engagement and a Great many wounded[14]   most of the Chiefs amongst the Regulators are since fled and the Governors Letter Re^d yesterday Says upwards of 1400 has Since Come in and Surendered themself Took the oath of alegence and Got their pardon   one man Refused and they hung him up in Sight of the Rest   when the Express Came away the Troops was Destroying the houses and Plantaitions of such as was outlawed,[15]   their Cheief was one Husbands[16] who had his Education amongst

---

10. Cane Creek: in Orange Co., a tributary of the Yadkin River, where large numbers of Friends from the Middle Colonies, Britain, and Ireland had settled since midcentury, establishing Cane Creek Meeting before 1760.   **11. with Satisfaction doth write thee**: "I do with satisfaction write thee." The phrase illustrates the tendency, common in Ulster English, to drop a subject pronoun (in this case "I") in a noninitial clause of a sentence; when the pronoun is so dropped, the verb appears in the third person singular (here: **I do** becomes **doth**). See hereafter for further examples; also see chapter 1, n. 110.   **12. Express**: a specially dispatched messenger.   **13. the Hinshaws** (or Henshaws): Quaker relatives of the Greers and Mortons, from Clonfeacle parish, Co. Tyrone. Hinshaws had been emigrating from Grange Meeting since 1733, but the brothers **Jesse**, Absolam, and **William** Hinshaw migrated with their families to backcountry North Carolina in 1768. In a letter of 20 January 1769, William Henshaw reported to Thomas Greer that he had purchased 86 acres of "Deeded land with 12 acers Clear & midling houses for 25 pounds & now pays 3s & 4d yearly Rent," while Jesse had "Bought land not Deeded for 12 pounds," and Absolom was renting—in partnership with Moses Hammon—thirty acres for £2 per year. Greer Family Papers, D.1044/165, PRONI.   **14.** Historians estimate that Governor Tryon's miltia lost 9 killed and 61 wounded at Alamance, whereas between 17 and 20 Regulators were killed and over 100 wounded. Government forces numbered only about 1,186 militiamen against two thousand to three thousand Regulators, but the former were better organized and armed with cannon.   **15.** McDonnell's report of the hanging of one Regulator and the wholesale destruction of rebel property immediately after the battle is correct. In addition, on 19 June the government tried 14 Regulator prisoners under the Riot Act; 12 were found guilty and six hanged.   **16. Husbands**: Herman Husband (1724–1795); born in Cecil Co., Md.; christened an Anglican but joined the Quakers as a young man; migrated to North Carolina in the 1750s and settled near Hillsborough, Orange Co., where he became a fairly affluent planter and miller; in 1766 he organized his neighbors into the Sandy Creek Association, the first stage of the Regulator movement; elected by his supporters to the North Carolina Assembly in 1769–1770—but his expulsion and arrest for sedition in December 1770 helped trigger the violence that culminated at Alamance. Inspired by the millennialism of the First Great Awakening, Husband was more radical than most of his followers, especially in his opposition to slavery. Although disowned by Friends because of his political activities, Husband was true to the Quakers' pacifistic ideals; he championed the Regulators' refusal to pay taxes or recognize the province's corrupt courts, but he took no part in violence and tried to prevent the confrontation at Alamance. After the battle, Husband's property was confiscated, and he returned to Maryland; later he moved to western Pennsylvania, where in 1794 he was jailed for his part in the Whiskey Rebellion.

JOHN MCDONNELL

friends   by Character was a man of a Clear head but a Bad heart   he was Decried[17]
by friends Some years ago for his Captious Snarling amongst them,   all his faculties
was Employed to find faults without Endeavouring to mend them,   notwithstanding[18]
those men was on their march a few months ago to Take him out of newbern[19] Goal[20]
or Leve the Town in ashes which Efected his Liberty at that time, yet in the Very
Begining of the Battle he Deserted them and no Tidings is heard of him
Since   Severals[21] of the Regulators is gone in Sarch of him and Left Hostages in the
hands of Govert for their Return   providence Seemed to fav.[r] Goverment for
according to the Best acc.[ts] there was 2300 of them agst Less than 1000 and in an
Enemys Setlement and but 2 men was kill.[d] on the Governors Side and nine died since
of their wounds   they were Very Busie Raising Recruits here to Reinforce the
Governor but Since the Express arived they have Desisted and those that Lent money
for the purpose is to Recive it Back tomorrow an Indication that peace will Soon be
Established here again, I mean a Cesation from War as Real peace Can not be obtained
Where Vertue Ruleeth not, and neither Religion nor Morality is any way Esteemed by
9/10 of the People here,   as Soon as I Can Get my Debts Collected and Remited to
my Good friends at home doth Intend to move out of this province and in a few
weeks Intends[22] to set out for the northward to See Pensyl.[a] and Maryland in hopes
that I may find some place that will Suit for Trade and that I Can Live with more
Satisfaction and If not may probably Return home as Soon as I Can posably Get my
affairs Settled here   I dont Suppose that Trade has Gone against me since I Left home
only it was not in my Power to do any Business in Charles Town and the Quantity of
Linens that was Sent out was too much for this place so that it was Imposable I Could
Remit my friends in Due time which has Caused me Some unEasiness   howEver If
Some of my fr.[ds] here had not used me worse than I Expected Should[23] have owed But
Little at home now   Trade Rather Grows Better with me here, but as there is no
friends nor meeting near us I think its Dangerous to Tarry Longer than Necssity
Enforces   Sam.[l] Neile of Cork[24] was through this province Last winter but Ihad not
the Pleasure of Seeing him   I have Several times Contra[cd] with People to Get me
some Beetling Beams[25] which I intended for Tho[s] Christy and thee[26] but was always

---

17. Decried: publicly condemned (OED s.v. decry, 2).   **18. notwithstanding:** nevertheless.   **19. newbern:**
New Bern, North Carolina's provincial capital; the lavish expenditures of tax money on Governor Tryon's
"palace" at New Bern symbolized the abuses that the Regulators opposed.   **20. Goal:** gaol (jail).
21. Severals: when **several** means "several persons or things" it may in Ulster English have an overt plural
form **severals** (like Standard English others).   **22. doth Intend . . . and in a few weeks Intends:** "I do intend
. . . and in a few weeks intend" (see n. 11).   **23. Should:** "I should" (see n. 11).   **24. Sam.[l] Neile of Cork:**
Samuel Neale (b. 1729 in Dublin); after a reputedly dissolute youth, Neale experienced a spiritual reformation
and in 1753 became a Quaker minister and missionary, traveling frequently to America (as well as to Britain
and Europe) on religious journeys; his second wife, Sarah (married 1760), was the daughter of Joshua Beale of
Cork, a wealthy yarn merchant.   **25. Beetling Beams:** used in the finishing of linen cloth; usually made of
beech, but sycamore was rated second-best, and by 1771 supplies of good beechwood were running low.
26. thee: reading conjectural; could also be read **Sha** (i.e. **Sha<w>**).

Disapointed   the other day an aquaintance Sent me word he had provided Some
Sycamore ones of a Large Size and would Send them down as Soon as Posable but I
fear there will be no opper.^{ty} to Send them home sooner than Spring next   my
Brother w<u>m</u> wrote me to Take Care of the Effects that Billy Delap[27] Died Posessed of
but its out of my Power as he made a will and Chose an Executor[28] and Intirely out of
my way been at 100 miles Distance   I think the Best thing for Robt Delap would be
to Choose John Brownlow gaurdian who is on the Spot that he might Bring Robt
Rowan to an acc^t whats done[29] with the Effects,   we have Consolation as well as
Greevances here   Both Betty and me Enjoys much Better health in General nor[30]
when at home and has a fine thriveing Babey of apromising Sensibility to its
age   Betty Joins me with Dear and aff.^{te} Love to the<e> Wife and Children thy
Brother James[31] and family and Im thy welwishing friend &c

John McDonnell

Their hegemony assured by victory at Alamance, North Carolina's tidewater planters
would brook no interference from Josiah Martin, Tryon's successor as royal governor.[32] Indeed, it was their new governor's sympathy for backcountry grievances and his
promotion of judicial reforms, more than his autocratic temperament or their opposition
to the Tea Act, that propelled the province's Whig gentry into the American Revolution.
Ironically, in 1775 John McDonnell's devotion to authority made him a target of persecution by those whose interests he had supported against the Regulators. In January Wilmington's Committee of Safety, officered by New Hanover County's leading planters,
confiscated a shipload of McDonnell's imported goods, as violating the Continental Congress's strictures on British trade; and in March the Committee declared that McDonnell
and his friends were "unworthy of the rights of freemen & . . . Inimical to the Liberties of
their country" for their refusal to subscribe to the Continental Association.[33]

Apparently, these difficulties persuaded McDonnell and his wife to remove to
Charleston, South Carolina, but their stay there was temporary, as in 1777 they remigrated
to Ulster and, a year later, transplanted to the south of Ireland and settled in Cork city. It
is uncertain why John McDonnell moved to Cork. His 1771 reference to Samuel Neale,
Cork's famous Quaker missionary, suggests that John McDonnell already had contacts
there; and he may have accompanied an Edward McDonnell, perhaps his brother, who
left County Armagh for Cork at the same time. More broadly, Ireland's Friends were

---

27. Delap: Ulster pronunciation of the surname **Dunlap/Dunlop**.   **28. Executor . . . Distance . . . Choose**:
conjectural; words partly obscured by seal.   **29. whats done**: "what has been done."   **30. nor**: than.
31. Brother James: James Greer, brother of Thomas Greer, and one of the signators of the Lurgan (Co.
Armagh) monthly meeting's removal certificate, granted to John McDonnell on 30 July 1769, when the latter
first ventured to Philadelphia.   **32.** Josiah Martin (1729–1788); royal governor of North Carolina from August
1771 until his flight to the safety of a British warship in July 1775.   **33.** L. H. McEachern and I. M. Williams,
eds., *Wilmington-New Hanover Safety Committee Minutes . . .* , 21; see Sources.

highly mobile, with marriage and business alliances that traversed the entire island. In addition, with some 50,000 inhabitants (perhaps a fourth of them Protestants) Cork was Ireland's second largest seaport, and its Quaker community (numbering about four hundred to five hundred Friends) had flourished in manufacturing and in trade with North America (especially the West Indies), Britain, and Europe.[34] Finally, unlike Ulster, where the American Revolution depressed the linen trade, Cork's economy was booming in response to the British military's demand for salted beef, pork, and other provisions. In any case, although in 1783, at the Revolution's close, McDonnell made at least one more business trip to Philadelphia, he had decided to make Cork his permanent home, and on 31 March 1819 he died there, at his residence on Patrick Street, aged about 80 years. Likewise, McDonnell's widow and most of his children remained in the city, although the latter suffered from the steady shrinkage of Cork's Quaker population, as at least two of McDonnell's daughters died unmarried and two others were disowned for marrying outside the faith.

Nevertheless, McDonnell was probably wise to flee North Carolina at the onset of the Revolution. His Hinshaw kinsmen and North Carolina's other frontier Quakers were less fortunate, as the new state's revolutionary officials—already resentful at the Friends' opposition to slavery—interpreted their pacifism as treason and harassed them with quadruple taxes. As for North Carolina's former Regulators, most of those who had not fled west across the Appalachians after their defeat at Alamance strove during the war to preserve a precarious neutrality, singularly unimpressed by the democratic pretensions of their former persecutors.

58 ❋

James Caldwell, 1774

James Caldwell's correspondence of 1774 demonstrates the emergence among Ulster Presbyterians of an "Irish" identity, distinct from contemporary Scottish associations and linked to aspirations for political reform, on both sides of the Atlantic Ocean. More specifically, James Caldwell's own letter reflects the excitement and idealism of an ambitious, young Scots-Irish immigrant on the eve of the American Revolution, and his career in Philadelphia clarifies the economic, social, and political links that united the city's affluent Irish Presbyterian, Anglican, and Catholic merchants, across denominational lines, in the prewar Proprietary party and, later, as Whiggish revolutionaries, wartime patriots and profiteers, and postwar Federalists.

James Caldwell was born about 1745—probably in the town and parish of Bally-

---

34. For demographic data on Cork city and its environs, see appendix 2.2b, on chapter 57.

money, in the barony of Lower Dunluce, in north County Antrim—a younger son of Florence Ball (d. 1768), daughter of Ballymoney's Presbyterian minister, and John Caldwell (d. 1755), a prosperous linen bleacher, miller, and head tenant under the Earl of Antrim. Despite north Antrim's general prosperity, in the early eighteenth century emigration rates had been high, especially among the area's Protestant Dissenters: as early as 1718, James Caldwell's great-uncles had emigrated from Ballymoney to New Hampshire; and between 1734 and 1766 the number of Presbyterian households in the parish declined by 27 percent.[1] James Caldwell's older brother John (1742–1803)[2] inherited the family estate, and so in 1769, after his mother's death, James emigrated to Philadelphia. No doubt he took with him considerable amounts of capital, but, more important, he joined kinsmen who had been well established in Ulster-American trade and in Pennsylvania's capital for nearly two decades prior to his arrival.

For example, from the late 1740s one of James's elder kinsman, William Caldwell—from either the Ballymoney or the Strabane, County Tyrone, branches of the family—was a prosperous merchant in Londonderry town, a partner in the firm of Gregg, Vance & Caldwell; between 1748 and 1768 William Caldwell was coowner of at least 16 vessels that carried Irish linens, provisions, and emigrants to Philadelphia in return for flaxseed, flour, and wood products. Moreover, between 1749 and 1764 James's uncle, Andrew Caldwell, was master of at least three of William Caldwell's vessels, and by the late 1750s Andrew was permanently resident in Philadelphia as a shipping merchant. By 1767 Andrew Caldwell was sufficiently prosperous to purchase shares in William Caldwell's ships, and between that date and 1775 Andrew was either coowner or, increasingly, sole owner of at least 14 vessels, while he expanded his commercial ventures into smuggling, colonial land speculation, and the provision and wine trades with the West Indies and southern Europe. By 1769 Andrew Caldwell's Philadelphia property, including his counting-house at the Market Street wharf, was valued for taxes at nearly £97—in 1774 at over £104—and although he was not fabulously wealthy like the Quaker grandees,[3] he was clearly one of the more prosperous members of that rising group of relatively young Anglican and Presbyterian merchants who were affiliated with the Proprietary party and who, in the 1760s and early 1770s, aggressively challenged the Friends for economic and political dominance.

Andrew Caldwell's social and political network was led primarily by merchants of English birth or descent, such as Robert Morris and Thomas Willing.[4] However, it encom-

---

1. For demographic data on Ballymoney parish and its environs, see appendix 2.1g, on chapter 58. 2. For more information on John Caldwell (1742–1803), see chapter 68, in which this John Caldwell is titled "John Caldwell, Sr." to distinguish him from his son, "John Caldwell, Jr." (1769–1850), whose letter and life are the subject of chapter 68. 3. However, in 1769 Andrew Caldwell's taxable wealth did approximate that of Quaker merchants John and Samuel Morton, whose combined assessment that year was slightly less than £160. John Morton's rise to great wealth would begin with his marriage in late 1769; see chapter 56. 4. Robert Morris (1734–1806): born in Liverpool, Morris emigrated (with his father) about 1747; from the 1750s to 1793 he was the partner of Thomas Willing in Willing & Morris, one of Philadelphia's most prosperous merchant

passed many Irish traders such as Samuel Caldwell[5] and John Mitchell[6] (Andrew Caldwell's cousin and stepson, respectively),[7] James Mease (Samuel Caldwell's business partner) and his brother John Mease,[8] John Maxwell Nesbitt (partner in Conyngham & Nesbitt, Phila-

firms. Morris was prominent in opposition to the Stamp and Townshend acts, but as one of Pennsylvania's delegates to the Second Continental Congress, he did not vote for the Declaration of Independence on 1–4 July 1776. Morris was elected to Congress in 1777 and 1778. In February 1781 Congress chose him to be its superintendent of finance, in which post he served until November 1784. In December 1781 Morris organized the Bank of North America. In 1787 he was one of Pennsylvania's delegates to the Constitutional convention, and in 1788–1795 he was a U.S. senator. By 1790 Morris was immensely wealthy, but in the mid-1790s his speculations in western lands and Far Eastern trade failed, and he spent 1798–1802 in debtor's prison. Like his partner, Willing, Morris was an Episcopalian. ¶Thomas Willing (1731–1821): affluent lawyer, merchant, and banker; born and died in Philadelphia; the leading partner in Willing & Morris, shipping merchants. In 1767–1774 Willing was an associate justice of Pennsylvania's supreme court. He was a leader in opposition to the Stamp Act but became increasingly moderate thereafter. As one of Pennsylvania's delegates to the Second Continental Congress (1775–1776), Willing voted against the Declaration of Independence. Willing remained in Philadelphia during the British occupation (1777–1778)—and thereafter was tainted by suspicions of Toryism; however, in 1780 he subscribed £5,000 to supply the American army. In 1781–1792 he was the first president of the Bank of North America, and later he became first president of Hamilton's Bank of the United States (chartered by Congress in 1791).   **5.** Samuel Caldwell (ca. 1738–1798): probably born in Derry and emigrated about 1755 to Philadelphia, where he became a partner in the merchant firm of Mease & Caldwell and engaged heavily in colonial land speculation. Caldwell signed the nonimportation agreements of 1765 and 1769 and was secretary and treasurer of the Friendly Sons of St. Patrick in 1775–1792. He was on the losing "moderate" ticket in the August 1775 election for members of Philadelphia's Second Committee of Observation. An original member of the First City Troop of cavalry, Caldwell campaigned with Washington's army at Trenton and Princeton (December 1776–January 1777). During the Revolution Caldwell was active in persecuting Quakers, one of whom, Henry Drinker, called him "An unfeeling & inflexible man." (R. F. Oaks, "Philadelphians in Exile . . . , " 307; see Sources.) Associated with James Mease in supplying uniforms and other goods to the American forces, in spring 1780 Caldwell also subscribed £1,000 to the army. In 1781 an original investor in Morris's Bank of North America, in August 1787 Caldwell declared bankruptcy and retired from business; but in 1788 he was appointed one of Philadelphia's port wardens and in 1789 as clerk of the U.S. district court.   **6.** John Mitchell: born about 1730; a native of Ulster, perhaps a son of the wealthy Derry and Philadelphia merchant William Mitchell. Sometime in the 1750s John Mitchell emigrated to Philadelphia and entered the dry-goods trade in partnership with Randall Mitchell, his brother, and Thomas Barclay. Like Samuel Caldwell, John Mitchell signed the nonimportation agreements of 1765 and 1769. In 1773 he went bankrupt but was rescued by his creditors. In 1774 Mitchell was a member of Philadelphia's First Committee of Observation and of the First City Troop. During the Revolutionary War, Mitchell prospered as a wagon contractor for the American and French armies; he was also deputy quartermaster for Philadelphia, and he commanded several ships in Pennsylvania's navy. In 1780 a contemporary described him described as a "little fat, squat man, fifty years old, a great judge of horses." (Doerflinger, *Vigorous Spirit*, 144; see Sources.) In 1784 Mitchell went bankrupt again, but later he was appointed U.S. consul at Santiago de Cuba.   **7.** On 18 December 1768, Andrew Caldwell married Jane Mitchell, probably the widow of William Mitchell, who at midcentury was a prominent Ulster-born merchant in Philadelphia.   **8.** James Mease (ca. 1740–1785): born in Strabane, Co. Tyrone, in the 1750s Mease emigrated to join his uncle John (d. 1767), a wealthy Philadelphia merchant. He became a partner in the merchant firm of Mease & [Samuel] Caldwell. Mease signed the nonimportation agreements of 1765 and 1769 and was a member of the 1769–1770 enforcement committee. Later he was a member of Philadelphia's Committee of Correspondence (June 1774), the First City Troop (November 1774), the city's Committee of Safety (June 1775), and the Second Committee of Observation (Aug. 1775). In November 1774 Mease was appointed by Congress as paymaster and treasurer of the

delphia's most successful Irish firm) and his brother Alexander,[9] John Nixon,[10] Stephen Moylan,[11] and Thomas FitzSimons.[12] To be sure, these men differed in religion. The Caldwells and Meases were Presbyterians, and Andrew Caldwell was a member of Rev. Francis Alison's "Old Side" First Presbyterian church. By contrast, Nixon and probably Mitchell and the Nesbitts were Anglicans, while Moylan and FitzSimons were Catholics. However, they were united not only in competition with Philadelphia's Quaker oligarchy,

Continental Army, and in January 1777 Congress also named him the army's clothier-general. In 1780 he subscribed £5,000 to supply the American forces; after the war, Mease engaged in business until his death. ¶John Mease (ca. 1746–1826): brother of James Mease; born in Strabane and emigrated in 1754. John Mease also became a shipping merchant in Philadelphia; a member of the First City Troop (November 1774) and of the city's Committee of Safety (June 1775). During the Revolution, Mease served with the First City Troop in the New Jersey campaign (winter of 1776–1777); and in 1780 he subscribed £4,000 to help supply and pay the American army. From 1796 to 1825 he was admiralty surveyor of the port of Philadelphia. One of his sons, Dr. James Mease (1771–1846), became an eminent physician and scientist.   **9.** John Maxwell Nesbitt (1728–1802): born in Loughbrickland, Co. Down, in 1747 Nesbitt emigrated to Philadelphia, where he became clerk and in 1756 the partner of merchant Redmond Conyngham. Nesbitt signed the 1765 and 1769 nonimportation agreements and was also a member of the 1769–1770 enforcement committee. Like Samuel Caldwell, Nesbitt was on the losing, "moderate" ticket in the August 1775 election of the city's Second Committee of Observation. During the Revolution, Nesbitt served as paymaster of the Pennsylvania navy, as treasurer of the city's Committee of Safety, and as a member of the First City Troop in the New Jersey campaign (1777–1778). In 1780 he subscribed £5,000 to the American army for supplies. Between 1781 and 1792 he was director of Robert Morris's Bank of North America, and in 1792 he was the founder and first president of the Insurance Company of North America. Nesbitt served as president of the Friendly Sons of St. Patrick in 1773, and in 1790 he was one of Philadelphia's alderman. ¶Alexander Nesbitt (d. 1791): born in Loughbrickland, Co. Down, Alexander Nesbitt became a dry goods merchant in Philadelphia, a partner in the firm of Stewart & Nesbitt, and a member of the First City Troop; with Samuel Caldwell, in 1777 Nesbitt escorted Quaker exiles from Philadelphia to Winchester, Virginia (see chapter 56).   **10.** John Nixon (1733–1808): Nixon's grandparents emigrated from Wexford ca. 1700, and he was born into a Philadelphia merchant family. He signed the nonimportation agreements of 1765 and 1769. In 1774 Nixon was a member of Pennsylvania's first Committee of Correspondence, was in 1774–1775 a delegate to Pennsylvania's provincial conventions, and was a member of the Committee of Safety. During the Revolution he was lieutenant colonel of the third ("Silk Stocking") battalion of the Pennsylvania militia, in which he served in the Princeton campaign, at Valley Forge, etc. After the war Nixon was president of Robert Morris's Bank of North America from 1792 until 1808, when he was succeeded by John Morton (chapter 56); Nixon's son, Henry, married Morris's daughter and became fourth president of the Bank of North America when Morton retired.   **11.** Stephen Moylan (1734–1811): a merchant's son, Moylan was born in Cork, educated in Paris, and spent three years trading in Lisbon before 1768 when he emigrated to Philadelphia, where he became a successful merchant. In 1775 Moylan joined the U.S. army at the siege of Boston, and in 1776 he was appointed one of Washington's aides; in 1776–1777 he also served as quartermaster general of the Continental Army. He raised the first regiment of the Pennsylvania Cavalry and served at Valley Forge and later in the Southern campaigns, retiring with the rank of brigadier general. At the war's end Moylan resumed his mercantile career, and prior to his death was a U.S. loan commissioner. Stephen Moylan had three notable brothers: John—a merchant in Philadelphia and U.S. clothier-general during the Revolution; Jaspar—a prominent lawyer in Philadelphia; and Francis— Catholic bishop of Cork and an ardent supporter of the Crown and opponent of the United Irishmen in the 1790s and early 1800s.   **12.** Thomas FitzSimons (1741–1811): born in Ireland, FitzSimons emigrated as a youth to Philadelphia where he joined the merchant firm of George Meade & Company. After 1776 FitzSimons served on the Pennsylvania Council of Safety and the Navy Board; he also raised and commanded a militia company and in 1780 he subscribed £5,000 for military supplies. FitzSimons served several terms in the

and by their lucrative associations with the proprietary establishment, but also in a host of interdenominational ethnic and other social associations. These included the Hibernia Fire Company (est. 1751–1752), the Gloucester Fox Hunting Club, the Masonic Order (founded locally by Chief Justice William Allen, Philadelphia's wealthiest Ulster Presbyterian and a Proprietary party leader),[13] the Fort St. David's Fishing Company,[14] and the various "Irish clubs" that in early 1771 were formalized as the Friendly Sons of St. Patrick.[15] The Caldwells and their friends may also have been united by shared Irish resentments, as for a combination of transplanted and local reasons they all played significant roles in Philadelphia's protests against Britain's colonial policies. For example, in 1765 and in 1769 Andrew and Samuel Caldwell signed the nonimportation agreements in protest of the Stamp Act and the Townshend Acts, respectively, and in the latter year John Maxwell Nesbitt and James Mease were members, as was Robert Morris, of the committee elected to enforce the boycott.[16]

Arriving in Philadelphia in 1769, no doubt at the invitation of his uncle Andrew, James Caldwell was quickly integrated into this élite Irish network. He became his uncle's business partner and coowner in 1771–1773 of at least two of Andrew Caldwell's vessels and in 1769–1770 he helped orchestrate brutal mob violence, by sailors and dockworkers, against customs officials who tried to curtail the Caldwells' wine-smuggling activities. By the early 1770s James Caldwell had joined the Hibernia Fire Company and the Gloucester Fox Hunt, and eventually he became a member of the Friendly Sons of St. Patrick. Finally, on 21 September 1772, he married Sarah ("Sally") Mitchell, John Mitchell's sister and his uncle's stepdaughter.

Between 1769 and 1774, in letters now lost, James Caldwell sent stirring accounts of

Pennsylvania Assembly; in 1782–1783 he was a member of the Continental Congress, in 1787 a delegate to the U.S. Constitutional Convention, and in 1789–1795 a Federalist member of Congress. After the war FitzSimons was also president of the Philadelphia Chamber of Commerce, a director of John Maxwell Nesbitt's Insurance Company of North America, and a trustee of St. Mary's Catholic church (see chapter 63). Once wealthy, in 1805 FitzSimons went bankrupt through association with Robert Morris's failed speculations. **13.** On William Allen (1704–1795), also see chapter 53. **14.** In 1766–1768 the Fort St. David's Fishing Company's membership included the Irish merchants Andrew Caldwell, John Mease, George Meade, and Redmond Conyngham, as well as leaders of the anti–Quaker Party forces such as John Dickinson and the journalist William Bradford (1719–1791), the latter of Scots-Irish origins. In 1774 the Company's members, like those of the Friendly Sons of St. Patrick, joined the First City Troop of light-horse cavalry en masse. On the Fort St. David's and other élite fishing clubs, see chapter 52. **15.** Andrew and Samuel Caldwell were charter members of the Friendly Sons of St. Patrick, as were Moylan (its first president), Nesbitt, Mitchell, Nixon, Mease, Fitzsimons, and William Allen. Among the society's first honorary members were Robert Morris, John Dickinson, and Richard Penn of the Proprietary family, the selections clearly revealing the group's political affiliation. **16.** The names of the ships coowned by Andrew Caldwell and his relatives also reflect their political attitudes and affiliations, e.g., the *Liberty*, the *Independent Whig*, the *Pennsylvania Farmer*, and the *Richard Penn*. Likewise the classical names of many of their other ships (e.g., *Jupiter*, *Venus*, and *Minerva*) also suggest the Enlightenment's influence on their inherited Calvinism and hence their affiliation with the liberal Irish "New Light" and colonial "Old Side" Presbyterian churches.

American resistance to British authority back to Ballymoney, where his elder brother John rejoiced to learn of the "revival of that opposition to tyranny and [of] that attachment to the free and liberal principles of civil and religious liberty which animated our ancestors . . . who fled the land of their fathers and sought and found an asylum in the wilds of America."[17] However, as colonial protests against British policies became increasingly violent and as the role of Philadelphia's "mechanics" became more prominent, the Caldwells and their affluent allies hesitated at the brink of independence and bloodshed and, as a consequence, lost control of the resistance movement to Presbyterian and other radicals such as George Bryan and Thomas McKean.[18] Thus, whereas in November 1774 Andrew Caldwell helped organize Philadelphia's First City Troop of light-horse cavalry (whose affluent membership virtually duplicated that of the St. Patrick's society) and although in August 1775 he was elected a member of Philadelphia's Second Committee of Observation, to enforce Congress's ban on trade with Britain, in February 1776 neither he nor his friends (Morris, Mease, etc.) were selected as members of the Third Committee, whose radical leaders proceeded to dismantle Pennsylvania's proprietary establishment as well as the old Quaker-dominated Assembly and the authority of the British government.

James Caldwell's sole surviving letter to Ballymoney, written during the fervor occasioned by the Coercive Acts and by Congress's strong response, suggests that he shared his social group's Whiggish devotion to "rational liberty" and its ambivalence toward the prospect of war and independence, as he vacillated between enthusiasm for Patrick Henry's bellicose speeches and hope that the British government might yet regain the colonists' "affections and . . . friendships." More broadly, James Caldwell's analysis of Pennsylvania's political divisions deserves attention, as scholars continue to debate the role of ethnicity in shaping allegiances and attitudes toward the Revolution.

James Caldwell, Philadelphia,
to John Caldwell, Ballymoney, County Antrim, December 1774

My Dear Brother——   Philadelphia   December 1774——
Since my last I have received three letters from you & one from brother

---

17. John Caldwell, Ballymoney, Co. Antrim, to James Caldwell, Philadelphia, January 1774. At least by 1783–1784 John Caldwell was a captain in the Ballymoney unit of the Volunteers, formed in the late 1770s by Protestants in Belfast, Dublin, and throughout much of Ireland, ostensibly to protect Ireland from French invasion during the American Revolution but primarily to pressure the British Parliament to repeal legislation that restricted Irish trade and that codified the Irish Parliament's inferiority to Westminster. By 1782 the British government had acquiesced in those demands, and in 1783–1784 Caldwell's continued membership in the now-flagging Volunteer movement signified his and other Ulster Presbyterians' desires for yet more radical measures—e.g., for a democratic reform of Irish parliamentary representation and, increasingly, for the repeal of the remaining Penal Laws that circumscribed Catholic civil rights; thus, at a meeting in 1783–1784 Caldwell successfully insisted on the enrollment of Daniel Maxwell, a Catholic neighbor, in Ballymoney's Volunteer company.   18. On Bryan and McKean, see chapter 52 and chapter 55, n. 42.

Richard[19]—I have at length made up my mind to visit you the ensuing Spring, the last of our flaxseed ships has sailed & I shall have time to wind up my business, prepare my dear Sally to submit to my short absence and endeavour to reconcile myself to parting with her and my engageing little Kate[20]——Before I proceed further in this communication, I have to refer you to my various business Letters by the flaxseed ships—Unless I can accomplish my intended Spring visit, I foresee a state of things in the Political world that may prevent us meeting again for years and would to God your family, our brother Richard, Sisters, Uncles & Aunts would resolve to accompany me back again and enjoy the certain result of the glorious struggle which has already commenced——

Patrick Henry of Virginia,[21] one of our greatest Statesmen has already in Congress, expressed the determination of that leading Province which he represents—The Congress met in this City last month, when he asserted in his speech "That after all that has been said or done "We must fight" and I could mention a host of other great people, who think with him and will act with him—The minds of the People have been in a state of progressive improvement for years—It is now ten years (1764) since a M[r]. Otis,[22] a very eminent Lawyer of Boston published a tract entitled "The rights of British Colonies asserted" In which he assumes among other things as fundamental doctrine the following propositions "That the supreme and subordinate powers of legislation should be free and sacred in the hands where the community have once rightfully placed them" Again—"The supreme power cannot take from any man any part of his property without his consent in Person, or by his Representative" These points once conceded and established I fear not for the liberty and happiness of the

---

19. brother Richard: Richard Caldwell: in 1774 he was a partner in the Londonderry mercantile firm of Caldwell & Vance. According to some accounts, in 1776 he went to America with his brother James, after the latter's visit to Ulster, and settled in Baltimore. However, other and perhaps more reliable sources say that around 1776 Richard Caldwell and his family emigrated instead to Dominica, in the British West Indies, where he and his wife died about 1779; according to this account, Richard's orphaned children then returned to Co. Antrim but later remigrated to the United States with the family of their cousin, the United Irishman John Caldwell, when the latter was exiled after the 1798 Irish rebellion; see chapter 68. **20. Kate**: Catherine Caldwell (1774–1862), daughter of James and Sarah ("Sally") Caldwell; in 1795 she married Michael Keppele, mayor of Philadelphia in 1811. James and Sarah Caldwell later had three other children: Andrew (b. 1777); Elizabeth (1781–1858); and James, Jr. (1783–1857), born after his father's death. **21. Patrick Henry of Virginia** (1736–1799): orator and statesman; one of the strongest opponents of the Stamp Act and subsequent British measures. Henry's fiery orations in the Continental Congress swung the delegates against Joseph Galloway's reconciliation proposals and in favor of independence; in 1776–1779 and again in 1784–1786 Henry served as governor of Virginia; subsequently he opposed his state's ratification of the U.S. Constitution and was a leader in the demand for a Bill of Rights. **22. M[r]. Otis**: James Otis (1725–1783): Massachusetts lawyer; in 1765 Otis was the prime mover of, and a delegate to, the Stamp Act Congress; his famous pamphlet (cited inaccurately by Caldwell), *The Rights of the Colonies Vindicated* (1764), argued that in all questions relating to the expenditure of public money, the rights of a colonial legislature were as sacred as those of the House of Commons.

Country—I have frequently attended the debates in Congress & I am very much mistaken if the "tout ensemble"[23] of that Assembly does not far exceed and transcend your boasted Houses of Lords & Commons with all their decorations and gee gaws of Maces, gowns, big wigs and woolsacks[24]——

I have often write[25] to our Aunts and Sisters, but except by the flaxseed ships, the conveyance is so uncertain, that I fear my letters may not have reached them, as the Parental chastisement of the mother Country extends to the stoppage of letter intercourse between us, her almost[26] rebellious children, and such of our kindred, as may yet be nestling under the shadow of her wings,   but I shall hope that some worthy Clerk of the Post Office, in whose composition flows the milk of human kindness, may forward this epistle to relieve the anxiety of affectionate friends——

My little Catherine has just been innoculated for the small Pox,   the practice is becoming general in this city, notwithstanding the opposition of some bigoted Calvinists on the principles of Predestination which many of the prevailing sect of Quakers or as we call them here Friends, are said to adopt—These troubles and turmoils in our political relations must undoubtedly check for a time the trading prosperity of the Country; but it is yet in the power of the Parent State, to turn to its own advantage, that immense flow of wealth and property which must of course crown the efforts of increasing millions of yet Colonial subjects—this is the critical moment, the affections, and friendships of the Colonists can now be fixed or lost to Great Britain for ever—It is amusing to look at, and examine the principles by which the natives of the three Kingdoms who have emigrated here, seem to be actuated in political matters, now under discussion and altogether the leading topic——

The English are divided, some espousing our quarrel (as it is called) from real hatred to Tyranny, and others from attachment to the descendants of their Pilgrim relatives and Countrymen, and to the religion which they professed; but the greater part, at all hazard, determined to support the claims of the British Government be they right or wrong, to unconditional submission—The Scotch with very few exceptions are advocates for and friendly to those principles for which so many of them fought in 1715 & 1745[27] and of course opposed to the measures pursued by the Colonists; indeed

23. tout ensemble: general effect (French).   **24. woolsack:** the usual seat of the lord chancellor in the House of Lords, made of a large square bag of wool without back or arms and covered with cloth (OED, s.v., 1.b). **25. write:** i.e., wrote (rhymes with **bit**).   **26. almost:** obscured in ms., perhaps cancelled.   **27. 1715 & 1745:** the dates of the major Jacobite rebellions, in which many Scots, especially Catholic Highlanders, fought for the Stuart Pretender's claim to the British throne against the **house of Hanover**—i.e., against the Protestant or Hanoverian Succession, established by Parliament in 1715, after Queen Anne's death. Caldwell implies that past Scottish support for Stuart and High Tory principles (e.g., the divine right of kings) also predisposed their support for royal authority in the American colonies. His conflation of early eighteenth-century Scottish Jacobinism with the Scottish and Scots-immigrant toryism of the late 1700s was somewhat unfair but common among British and American reformers. The analogy held true for the Scots Highland immigrants in upstate

they seem anxious to wipe away the stigma & remembrance of their resistance and disafection to the house of Hanover, by the most unbounded loyalty to George the third & his measures, so true is it, that new converts are apt to become the most violent and jealous partizans; but among the Irish, nine tenths espouse the American Cause, and our Countrymen of the North add the sagacity and calmness of the calculating Scotch Lowlander, to the enthusiastic chivalry of the native of the Emerald Isle[28] in supporting the rights of the People, whilst our friend Charles Thompson from the County Derry records their resolutions and decrees as Secretary of Congress.[29] Among the worthies from our Country of our relatives are the Balls, the Caldwells, & the Hamiltons, and I understand of your wife's relations—The Agnews, the Ramseys, McCutcheons & the Kidds, all energetic & persevering, as is George Hughes the brother & Joseph Wilson the Cousin of Richards wife[30]—In fact the flame of Patriotic feeling is spreading far and wide & I doubt not its breaking forth in a radiance of glory,

New York and backcountry North Carolina, but the overwhelming majority of Scots who opposed the American Revolution, both at home and in the colonies, were Presbyterians who had no affection for the moribund Stuart cause. However, despite the prominence of James Wilson and of the president of Princeton College, John Witherspoon, both signers of the Declaration of Independence, Scottish immigrants (e.g., in the seaport St. Andrew's Societies) *were* disproportionately loyalists, and the writings of the radical British Whig, John Wilkes, had already predisposed the colonists to associate the Scots—especially Scottish politicians such as Henry Dundas, Lord Mansfield, and the earl of Bute—with the greatest corruption and the worst abuses of the British political system. In addition, many colonists, especially in the Chesapeake region, detested local Scottish tobacco merchants for their alleged clannishness, greed, and unprincipled business practices. Thus, whereas colonial revolutionaries rhetorically embraced the "Irish" as fellow "Americans" and "patriots," they denounced the Scots as "foreigners"—associations that in the nineteenth century most American Protestants would completely reverse. Also see chapter 49.   **28. the Emerald Isle**: i.e., Ireland; if John Caldwell, Jr.'s transcription of his uncle James's 1774 letter is accurate, the latter's usage of "Emerald Isle" antedates by some 15 years the supposed origination of the term by Belfast's Dr. William Drennan, a founder of the United Irishmen, in his poem "When Erin First Rose."   **29. Charles Thompson**: Charles Thomson (1729–1824); see chapter 55, n. 40.   **30.** Information about some of these families is elusive. The **Balls** of Ballymoney were James Caldwell's mother's family, but it is very questionable whether any of Caldwell's maternal kin in Philadelphia included the wealthy William Ball (1729–1810), a silver- and goldsmith whose property was valued for taxes in 1774 at £303, or Joseph Ball who in 1785 was a member of the Philadelphia Corporation. The name **Hamilton** was so common among both the Londonderry and Philadelphia merchant communities that it is impossible to trace possible Caldwell family relationships, although Caldwell's reference may be to kinsmen of a Dr. A. Hamilton of Ballymoney, who in 1795 was a founding member of that town's branch of the Society of United Irishmen. Likewise, the **Agnews, Ramseys**, and **McCutcheons** in Philadelphia cannot be identified, although the McCutcheons who in 1774–1776 still lived in Ballymoney supported the American cause. The **Kidd** (or Kydd) family of Philadelphia was prominent from at least the 1740s; in 1765 John and George Kidd, merchants, signed the nonimportation agreement; in 1774 John Kidd was elected to the Committee of Observation; and in 1781 he was an original subscriber (with Andrew and James Caldwell) to Robert Morris's Bank of North America. **George Hughes** was an officer in the U.S. navy during the Revolution, and in 1790 was one of Pennsylvania's Bankruptcy Commissioners; he died on 31 January 1799, and his burial in Andrew Caldwell's family vault, at Philadelphia's First Presbyterian church, was attended by members of Congress and of Pennsylvania's state legislature. **Joseph Wilson** in 1770–1773 was a coowner with Andrew Caldwell of three vessels engaged in trade between Philadelphia and Ulster; he died in 1779.

that will electrify and astonish the world, and crown our labours & exertions with lasting honor and happiness,   I have just got returns of the emigration from the <u>North</u> of Ireland in 1771 & 1772   it exceeds Seventeen thousand Souls & the influx for 1773 was twelve thousand[31]——

Rem^{br} me Affectionately to all friends—From   James Caldwell
                    Your aff^t brother

In 1775 James Caldwell made his promised visit to Ballymoney. By the time he returned, probably in the summer of 1776, war with Britain had begun, Congress had declared independence, and virtually all the members of the Friendly Sons of St. Patrick had enlisted in the patriot cause—despite their strong aversion to the ultrademocratic 1776 Pennsylvania state constitution. In December 1776–January 1777, during the American campaigns at Trenton and Princeton, James Caldwell served with "Gallantry" in the First City Troop; on 30 December he and five other volunteers (including Samuel Caldwell) captured 12 British soldiers. Andrew Caldwell also saw action: as commodore of Pennsylvania's navy, on 6 May 1776 he engaged in battle two British warships in the Delaware River. However, most of the Caldwells' wartime activities were more mundane—and more profitable. Through their close associations with Robert Morris, Congress's financial wizard, James and Andrew Caldwell built considerable fortunes—as did other Irish merchants, including Nixon, Nesbitt, Mease, Mitchell, and FitzSimons—through privateering, speculations in commodities and bonds, purchases of confiscated loyalist estates, and, most crucially, through contracts to sell foodstuffs, clothing, and military supplies to the American and Pennsylvania governments. Fortunately, the Caldwells and their friends were strategically situated to seize a wide array of economic opportunities: Andrew was a member of both the Pennsylvania Navy Board and the Council of Safety; John Mitchell, James's brother-in-law, was Philadelphia's deputy quartermaster; and Samuel Caldwell and his business partner, James Mease, shared the post of clothier-general and were responsible for supplying uniforms and other garments to the American forces. As a result of these connections, by the Revolution's end Andrew and James Caldwell's estates in Philadelphia were valued at more than £4,000.

To be sure, in the spring of 1780 James Caldwell subscribed £2,000 of his wartime profits to support the faltering war effort, but such generosity did not placate Philadelphia's radicals, who bitterly resented the power and profits that Morris and his "aristocratic"

---

31. Unfortunately, the returns to which Caldwell referred cannot now be located or identified, although apparently they included only immigrants whose vessels had sailed from Ulster ports and who debarked at Philadelphia, New Castle, and other points in the Delaware estuary. However, Caldwell's total figure of over 29,000 <u>North of Ireland</u> immigrants in 1771–1773 comports well with the estimates in R. J. Dickson's *Ulster Emigration to Colonial America, 1718–1785* (London, 1966) of 39,000–41,000 Ulster emigrants to *all* American destinations in 1770–1775.

friends were accumulating.[32] Moreover, in March 1779 James and Samuel Caldwell had joined James Mease, Nixon, and FitzSimons in founding Philadelphia's Republican Society, which, under Morris's leadership, agitated for the repeal of Pennsylvania's 1776 constitution and for the creation of a less democratic state government that would be more responsive to the city's mercantile interests. This inaugurated a decade of bitter political strife, as Morris's "Republicans" battled George Bryan's "Consitutionalists" over the meaning and future of Pennsylvania's Revolution. Already in 1779 James and Andrew Caldwell had incurred popular anger for their opposition to paper money and wartime price controls, and in 1780–1781 the state government charged their ally, the clothier-general James Mease, with corruption. Eventually, however, the conservatives were victorious, as the former leaders of the old Proprietary party joined hands with their prewar political foes, Pennsylvania's Quakers, to thwart the Scots-Irish radicals of the western counties. Morris's Bank of North America (chartered by Congress in 1781) subsidized the emergence of a new "Federalist" alignment that in 1787 secured Pennsylvania's ratification of the U.S. Constitution, in 1790 rewrote the state's constitution, and soon after evolved into the Federalist party. Again, the role of Philadelphia's Irish merchant élite was significant: James, Andrew, and Samuel Caldwell, along with Mitchell, James Mease, J. M. Nesbitt, Nixon, and FitzSimons, were original subscribers to Morris's Bank—and Andrew Caldwell was one of its first directors—while in 1787 FitzSimons signed the U.S. Constitution and crusaded for its ratification and, in 1789–1790, helped lead Pennsylvania's own constitutional counterrevolution.

Despite their political triumphs, however, many members of this group proved unable to consolidate their economic and political gains. On 6 September 1783 James Caldwell died, six days prior to the birth of his fourth child, and less than two years later James Mease followed him to the grave. Moreover, in 1784–1785 Philadelphia's merchant community reeled with the collapse of the postwar boom in dry-goods imports. John Mitchell, James Caldwell's brother-in-law, went bankrupt in 1785; so did Samuel Caldwell two years later; and before the century's end Thomas FitzSimons, John Maxwell Nesbitt, and even their great patron, Robert Morris, faced debtor's prison. Apparently, however, Andrew Caldwell not only survived the financial crisis of 1784–1785 but reaped another fortune in 1790–1791, when Congress redeemed in full the Continental securities in which he had speculated during the late 1780s. When he died in late 1793 or early 1794, Andrew Caldwell's Water Street property alone was valued at £12,000, and he bequeathed to his widow a £400 annuity and to his grand-children $17,500 in cash and in U.S. government bonds bearing 6 percent annual interest.

32. Indeed, Congress and the army used most of the funds donated in 1780 to purchase supplies from the Caldwells, Mease, Morris, and the other subscribers. Thus, the latters' generosity not only promoted the Revolution's success but also resulted in enhanced profits for the Caldwells and their fellow import merchants.

59 ✳

Matthew Patten, 1774–1776

Matthew Patten's rustic diary or "Day-Book" contrasts markedly in content and style with the urbane and self-conscious idealism that permeated merchant James Caldwell's 1774 letter, written in the political vortex of pre-Revolutionary Philadelphia.[1] For Patten portrays the crisis of 1774–1776 in his overwhelmingly rural and predominantly Scots-Irish community of Bedford, New Hampshire, where the Revolution's impact was refracted through intensely local concerns and controversies and where radical committee meetings and the news of battle mingled with the mundane continuities of family, farm, tavern, and Presbyterian meetinghouse.

Matthew Patten was born in Ulster, probably in the Foyle Valley, on 19 May 1719, the son of John Patten (1672–1746), who emigrated to Boston with his family in 1728. For 10 years the Pattens lived first in Chelmsford and then Dunstable, Massachusetts, but in September 1737 Samuel Patten (1713–ca.1792), Matthew's older brother, purchased a township right and a 50-acre lot in the new town of Souhegan East, New Hampshire, an offshoot of the Londonderry settlement, on the west bank of the Merrimack River and in what later became Hillsborough County.[2] In January 1738 Samuel bought a second township right and lot, which in April he sold to Matthew, and by spring both brothers had moved to Souhegan East and had begun clearing trees from their new farms. By 1749, when it was formally incorporated as Bedford, the settlement contained 56 families, nearly all of Ulster origin, and in 1775 the town had 485 white inhabitants, as well as 10 slaves.

Eventually, Matthew Patten and his brother each owned over 150 acres, which, in addition to their apparently superior educations and their status as original settlers and town proprietors, ensured their local importance. In addition, in 1750 Matthew married Elizabeth, daughter of John McMurphy (d. 1755), one of Londonderry's first settlers and, after Rev. James McGregor's death in 1729, its foremost political leader.[3] Thus, the first Bedford town meetings were held in Matthew Patten's barn; before the Revolution he held numerous town offices, including selectman and town clerk (1752–1772) and town treasurer (1757–1758); and in 1751 he was appointed justice of the peace, a post he held until his death in 1795. Brother Samuel was almost equally prominent.

---

1. See chapter 58.   2. Hillsborough Co. was established in 1769. On the origins and history of the Londonderry, N.H., settlement, see chapter 49.   3. On McMurphy, see chapter 49. Matthew and Elizabeth Patten had 11 children: Susanna (b. 1751), who married Thomas Taggart of Coleraine, a Scots-Irish settlement in western Massachusetts; John (1752–1776), see hereafter; Matthew (d. in infancy); James, who went to Ohio, fought under General Arthur St. Clair in the Indian wars, and was a prisoner of the Indians for four years; Elizabeth ("Betsy"), who wed Hugh Talford of Chester, N.H.; Robert, who married Jane Shirley of Goffstown, N.H.; David (1761–1836), a Bedford schoolmaster and surveyor who died unmarried; Mary ("Polly"), also died unmarried; Alexander, who married Lydia Atwood of Bedford; Jane and Sarah, both of whom died unmarried sometime after 1850.

Yet the Pattens were by no means affluent, especially compared with the members of Portsmouth's merchant oligarchy and its local representatives, such as "squires" Joshua Atherton and Benjamin Whiting—Anglicans who became loyalists in the Revolution. Although their acreages were slightly greater than average, and despite their occasional journeys to market in Portsmouth and Boston, the Pattens farmed primarily for subsistence, as did nearly all their Scots-Irish neighbors in the Upper Merrimack Valley, made almost all their own clothes and furniture, and subsisted largely on diets of barley broth and bread made of rye or Indian corn. As late as 1776 Matthew Patten's farm was taxed for merely two oxen, two cows, and a single horse. However, he was exceptionally versatile and supplemented the produce of his farm through fishing, fur-trapping, land speculation, and the local linen trade and by bartering his varied skills as surveyor, carpenter, auctioneer, and scribe in return for goods, labor, or, less frequently, paper money or even scarcer hard cash.

It was these economic transactions, plus daily records of farm work and descriptions of New Hampshire's severe winter weather, that comprised the overwhelming majority of the entries in Matthew Patten's diary, written between 1754 and 1788 in a tiny hand, sometimes four hundred words to a page, on pieces of paper measuring only six by three and a half inches and bound with linen thread. Indeed, it was not until the summer of 1774 that local responses to political developments in London, Boston, and Portsmouth began to appear in Patten's Day-Book. It may be, as historians of revolutionary New Hampshire have argued, that Patten and his neighbors shared—perhaps unconsciously prior

FIGURE 18
Matthew Patten's farmhouse (erected 1784) in Bedford, New Hampshire, in the early twentieth century. Photograph courtesy of the New Hampshire Historical Society, Concord.

to the crisis—a radical Whig or republican ideology that shaped their interpretations of the Coercive Acts (March–May 1774) and other British legislation. Perhaps also, as Presbyterians of Ulster birth or descent, the inhabitants of Bedford, Londonderry, and other Scots-Irish communities in the Merrimack Valley shared an inherited distrust of British authority and of the Anglican-dominated provincial government in Portsmouth. Likewise, given Ulster Presbyterians' traditional animus against "popery," their response to the Quebec Act of May 1774 may have been particularly negative, as was that of New Hampshire's revolutionary leader John Sullivan, whose parents were southern Irish-born converts to Protestantism. However, Patten's diary suggests that only slowly did such larger events and concerns impinge on his and his neighbors' intensely localistic world. Indeed, the only traces of political rhetoric or emotion that occur among the more than eight thousand entries in Patten's Day-Book were recorded when the Revolutionary War struck directly at the heart of his own family.

Certainly, as semisubsistence farmers in a virtually self-governing commonwealth, Patten and his neighbors would react adversely to British actions that threatened higher taxes or loss of political control, either of which might presage the imposition in America of the economic hardships and exclusive social and political systems from which they or their ancestors had escaped when they left Ireland. However, although New Hampshire's Scots-Irish appear to have been nearly unanimous in support of the Revolution, that conflict also exposed and exacerbated conflicts within their own communities, as earlier factional and familial strife now became politicized.[4] For Matthew Patten and his friends, the crisis of 1774–1776 provided opportunities not only to defy and supplant local magistrates of loyalist convictions but also to settle old scores with their own Presbyterian minister, John Houston (1723–1798). Born in Londonderry, New Hampshire, and educated at Princeton, in 1756 Houston was ordained as Bedford's clergyman, in a church that was built largely through the Patten brothers' efforts. However, relations between Houston and the Pattens quickly deteriorated, culminating by 1769–1770 in lawsuits and countersuits for slander. Matthew Patten's epithet for his adversary, "Priest Houston," suggests that in part their conflict was akin to those which in 1741–1758 rent the "Old Side" and "New Side" Presbyterians throughout the colonies, and the contents of Patten's library indicate that he was remarkably well-read in works of religious disputation, including those of revivalist Jonathan Edwards. If theological in origin, however, the controversy soon became bitterly personal, as Houston accused his foe of stirring "Strife & Debate Confusion and Evil Work," while Patten's wife charged that the minister was "fitter to stand in the pillory than in the pulpit." Bedford's clergyman may have been, as observers claimed, "stern & rigid," but Patten, too, was "Crabid as a Crab tree," and his role in the feud showed him to be petty, legalistic, mean, and vindictive.[5] The advent of the Revolution, when Hous-

4. On a larger and much more violent scale, this is apparently what happened among the backcountry Scots-Irish in revolutionary South Carolina; see chapter 60. 5. K. Scott, "John Houston, Tory Minister . . . ," 174, 180–81, 185, 195; see Sources.

ton made the politically fatal mistake of remaining loyal to King George, gave Patten the chance to drive him from the pulpit. However, Patten paid a high price for his opportunity, for whereas the Revolution made Bedford's social and political systems more open and fluid, it also exposed its sons to unprecedented dangers.[6]

Matthew Patten Day-Book, Bedford, New Hampshire, 14 July 1774–1 August 1776

<July> 14th <1774>   Was Generally[7] observed as a fast through this and the Bay province[8] att the desire of the Committees of correspondance[9]   altho M[r] Houston would not observe it in Bedford I and my famely keept[10] and I went to Meeting in Derryfield[11] and heard M[r] Strickland[12] preach from the 5th Verse of the 2[d] of Revelations[13]. . . .

<September> 19th   james Orr[14] mended my plow Shear that was broke in the wing[15]   he had a good deal of pains in the doing it   the charge unknown   and I went to a town meeting at Evening and the people intended to go to Amherst[16] tomorrow to Visit[17] M[r] Atherton[18] who[19] Insisted on my going with them and they

---

6. Most of Patton's daily entries and portions of entries that only concerned farmwork, economic transactions, and other mundane affairs have been omitted from this transcript; ellipses indicate where omissions occur. **7. Generally**: universally; see Shakespeare, *Henry VIII* 2.1.46: "This is noted, and **generally**; whoever the King favours, the Cardinal instantly will find employment."   **8. through this and the Bay province**: i.e., throughout New Hampshire and Massachusetts.   **9.** On 6 July 1774, radical members of the New Hampshire Assembly called for the towns to select delegates to the first New Hampshire Provincial Congress (which met at Exeter on 21 July) and recommended that their local **Committees of correspondence** observe 14 July as a day of fasting and prayer.   **10. keept**: miswritten for *kept it* or *keep it*.   **11. to meeting**: i.e. to church. **Derryfield**: a town in Hillsborough Co., adjacent to Bedford, across the Merrimack River; incorporated in 1766, Derryfield had 285 inhabitants in 1775; with the advent of its industrialization, in the early nineteenth century the town was renamed Manchester.   **12. M[r] Strickland**: John Strickland, Jr. (1741–1823), minister of Nottingham West Presbyterian church (Hudson and Derryfield, N.H.) in 1774–1782.   **13. 5th Verse of the 2[d] of Revelations**: "Remember therefore from whence thou art fallen, and repent, and do the first works; or else I will come unto thee quickly, and will remove thy candlestick out of his place, except thou repent"; **Revelations** is still a common mistake for the name of the final book of the New Testament, which is properly **Revelation** (of St. John).   **14. james Orr**: son or, more likely, grandson of John Orr (d. 1752), one of Bedford's earliest settlers; James Orr was crippled at the battle of Bennington (16 August 1777) but lived until 1823, when he died aged 75.   **15. plow Shear**: i.e., plowshare "the part of the plow that cuts the soil"; **wing**: the part of the plowshare that extends sideways and cuts the bottom of the furrow.   **16. Amherst**: the seat of Hillsborough Co.; incorporated in 1760, Amherst had 1,428 inhabitants in 1775.   **17. Visit** (and **Viset** hereafter): test; interrogate; also, deal with (sternly).   **18. M[r] Atherton**: Joshua Atherton (b. 1737), a prominent lawyer and loyalist in Amherst; in early September 1774, the First Continental Congress in Philadelphia adopted the Continental Association or boycott of British goods and urged each town to enforce it; it appears that Atherton was being persecuted for his criticism of the work of either the First Continental Congress, the first New Hampshire Provincial Congress that met at Exeter, or the New Hampshire Committee of Correspondence and its local branches. Unlike other loyalists, after the Revolution Atherton recovered his popular esteem; in 1788 he led the political forces opposed to New Hampshire's ratification of the U.S. Constitution and later became the state's attorney general; however, in the 1790s he became an ardent Federalist, lost popularity, and in 1798 resigned his office.   **19. who**: "and they" (i.e., the people); cf. Shakespeare, *Richard II*, 1.3.16-17: "my name is Thomas Mowbray, Duke of Norfolk, who [= and I] hither come engaged by my oath."

told me I must and Should go and that if I did not they would Viset me on which I said I would go

20th   james Orr and Shed[20] set the shoes on my horses fore feet and I went to Amherst and about 300 men assembled and chose a Commitie[21] who went to M[r] Atherton and he came to the people to the Court house and he Signed a Declaration and Read it to the people who accepted it   he Invited them to go to M[r] Hildreths[22] and Drink what they pleased   the people Dispersed about Midnight without Doing any Out Ragious act[23]   I stayd till morning. . . .

<February> 21st <1775>   Was a Meeting at Amherst of Amherst and Bedford <men> to chuse a Representative which I attended and Was chosen Moderator and We chose Paul Dudly Sergant[24] to Represent the two towns   he had 74 Votes and Col: Goffe[25] had 47 and I was chose one of the Commitee to prepare instruction for M[r] Sergant and I lodged at M[r] Hildreths. . . .

<April> 20th   I Rec[d] the Melancholy news in the morning that General Gages troops had fired on our Contrymen at Concord yesterday and had killed a large number of them[26]   our town was notified[27] last night   We Generaly met[28] at the meeting house about 9 of the Clock and the Number of twenty or more went Directly off from the meeting house to assist them. . . . And our john[29] came home

---

20. Shed: Nathan Shed, probably a laborer; in 1774 he was taxed 3s. 5d., but he did not appear in Bedford's 1776 tax list.   **21. a Commitie**: in late 1774 and early 1775, New Hampshire towns adopted the Continental Association (the boycott of British goods imposed by the First Continental Congress in September 1774) and appointed or elected local Committees of Safety and Inspection to enforce conformity.   **22. M[r] Hildreth** (Holdreth, etc.).: a tavern- and storekeeper in Amherst, New Hampshire.   **23. Out Ragious act**: offense (against the law).   **24. Paul Dudly Sergant**: Paul Dudley Sergeant (d. 1827) of Amherst; elected to represent Amherst and Bedford in the first, second, and third New Hampshire Provincial Congresses held at Exeter; this passage refers to his election to the second Congress that met on 25 January 1775 and assumed effective authority over the province.   **25. Col: Goffe**: Col. John Goffe (1701–1781); son of John Goffe, Esq. (d. 1748), one of Londonderry's and Bedford's first settlers. Probably the wealthiest farmer, mill-owner, and land speculator in Bedford, Col. Goffe was a militia officer in the French and Indian War, probate judge for Hillsborough Co. in 1771–1776, and a representative to the New Hampshire Assembly in 1762–1774. His son, Major John Goffe, fought in the American Revolution at Bunker Hill and elsewhere, as did several of Major Goffe's sons, two of whom died in the conflict.   **26. Concord**: the battles of Lexington and Concord, Mass., occurred on 19 April 1775, between American militiamen and British troops under the command of Gen. Thomas Gage, military governor of Massachusetts under the Coercive Acts. Immediately, hundreds of New Hampshire militiamen, who had been drilling for weeks in towns such as Bedford, marched south toward Boston. In 1850 Matthew Patten's elderly, unmarried daughters, Polly and Sarah, recalled the events of April 20–21: "[N]ever shall forget [how] Brother John came home that night, and we sat up all night, baking bread and making small clothes for brother John and John Dobbin, who went away early in the morning. The soldiers kept coming along, and we kept giving the bread and meat, and when night came, we had not a morsel left." Later, at the time of the Battle of Bunker Hill (17 June 1775), they reported, "we could hear the guns very distinctly" even in Bedford! *History of Bedford, New-Hampshire*, 489; see Sources.   **27. notified**: informed.   **28. Generaly met**: "met in a body."   **29. our john**: John Patten (1752–1776), Matthew Patten's oldest son and lieutenant of his militia company, which fought at Bunker Hill on 17 June 1775 and later in the Quebec campaign (see hereafter). Matthew Patten's sons Robert and James also served in the American forces, the former in New York, the latter in Rhode Island.

from being down to Pentuckett and intended to Sett off for our army to morrow morning and our Girls sit up all night bakeing bread and fitting things for[30] him and john Dobbin[31]

21st   our john and john Dobbin and my bro[r] Samu[ell] two oldest sons[32] sett off and joined Derryfield men and about Six from Goffestown[33] and two or three more from this town under the comand of Cap[t] john Moor[34] of Derryfield   they amounted to the N[o] of 45 in all   SunKook men and two or three others that joined them marched in about an hour after   they amounted[35] to 35   there was nine more went along after them belonging to Pennykook[36] or thereabouts and I went to M[c]Gregores[37] and I got a pound of Coffie on Credit

22[d]   I was wakoned in the morning by M[rs] Chandlers[38] comeing with a letters[39] from the Committee of the Provincial Congress for calling another congress of the Province[40] imeadeatly and I went with it as fast as could to john Bells[41] but he was gone to our army and both the others allso   and I went to Robert Alexanders[42] and got 4 bushell of Rie on credit and took it to Cap[t] Moors mill and got it groand[43] and I

30. **fitting things for**: outfitting (in this instance with small clothes "knee breeches"; see n. 26).   31. **john Dobbin**: Matthew Patten's hired man; as a private in the New Hampshire militia, Dobbin fought alongside John Patten at Bunker Hill and, in late 1775 and early 1776, in the campaigns in Quebec and upstate New York (see hereafter); in 1821 Dobbin died in Illinois.   32. **bro[r] Samu[ell] two oldest sons**: i.e., Matthew Patten's brother Samuel's two oldest sons: Samuel, Jr. (b. 1752) and John Patten (b. 1756).   33. **Goffestown**: Goffstown, Hillsborough Co., adjacent to Bedford; it was incorporated in 1748 and named after its principal proprietor, Col. John Goffe; in 1775 Goffstown had 831 inhabitants.   34. **Cap[t] john Moore**: a Bedford mill-owner; born in Ireland, Moore served in the French and Indian War and in 1761 and 1773 was moderator of Bedford's town meeting.   35. **amounted**: conjectural; ms. blurred.   36. **belonging to**: "coming from/being inhabitants of"; **Pennykook**: an old town and rural district, in Rockingham Co., out of which the town of Rumford, later named Concord, was incorporated in 1733; in 1775 Concord had 1,052 inhabitants. 37. **M[c]Gregores**: almost certainly a reference to a descendant of Rev. James McGregor of Londonderry (see chapter 49). At this time, Rev. David McGregor was Presbyterian clergyman of Londonderry's west parish; but the David McGregor referred to in Patten's diary appears to have been a tavern- or storekeeper near the Bedford–Londonderry ferry across the Merrimack River.   38. **M[rs] Chandlers**: probably the wife of Zachariah Chandler, Esq., taxed 8s. 9d. in the 1774 Bedford-Merrimack assessment.   39. **a letters**: perhaps represents a vacillation between **letter** in the ordinary sense and **letters** in the meaning of an official communication; see chapter 64, n. 9.   40. **calling another congress of the Province**: this was the call for delegates to the third New Hampshire Provincial Congress that met at Exeter in late April 1775.   41. **john Bell**: either John Bell, Jr., or John Bell III; John Bell, Sr. and Jr., were born in Ulster and settled in Bedford ca. 1736; John, Jr., was Bedford town clerk in 1773–1776; John III served in the New Hampshire militia at the battle of Bennington. 42. **Robert Alexander**: of Merrimack town; assessed 13s. 3d. in the 1774 Merrimack-Bedford tax list. 43. **groand**: i.e., ground (rhymes with **gown**); the unusual spelling employing **oa** to represent the sound heard in standard English **gown** or **round** is probably best explained as a miswriting in anticipation of the closely following **toal** (i.e. toll), perhaps favored by the fact that **toll** has alternating pronunciations rhyming with both **foal** and **towel**. The form **ground** is an importation from the standard language; the usual Scots form is **grun**, rhyming with **run**.

had the Toal[44] and I had ½ a bowle of Tody[45] at McGaws[46] for which I paid 4/ Lawful[47]

24th   my neck was so Stiff that I could not do anything with a cold I had got[48]

25th   I went and Notified on the River Road to meet[49] at the meeting house in the afternoon on our publick Distress and I went to Col: Goffes to ask his advice and met toward Evening and acted on what we thot necessary and my Brors jos:[50] helped me with their 3 pair of Oxen to cross plow[51]

26th   I went at the desire of the town to Col: Goffes and Merrils[52] and McGregores and Cautioned them to take Special care of Strangers and persons Suspected of being Torys crossing the River to Examin and Search if they judge it needful[53] and I got a pound of Coffe and nine flints from McGregore for which I paid him 11/8 Bay old tenor[54]

27th   **Was The Province Fast**[55] by the Governors Proclamation

28th   I began to Stock[56] Capt Blairs Gun and I went and got jamey Orr to forge me a Screw nail[57] for the breech[58] of the Gun and I fitted it and cut the Screws and he made me a burning iron all of my iron[59]. . . .

---

44. I had it the Toal ms. **Toal**: i.e., toll: a portion of the ground meal kept as payment by the miller. The meaning of **I had the Toal** is uncertain; perhaps "I was allowed to keep the toll" (i.e., "didn't have to pay it"), and it may be that Patten's exemption from paying the toll at Moore's mill (also see n. 94 below) was the result of a personal relationship with Moore or was a perquisite of the town offices that Patten held. **45. Tody**: i.e., toddy; any of a number of drinks made with rum or whiskey. **46. McGaws**: perhaps Jacob McGaw, Esq., of Merrimack, New Hampshire. **47. Lawful**: in 1750 the Massachusetts Assembly passed a law that provided for payments in specie only and fixed the value of the Spanish dollar, then in general use, at 4s. 6d. sterling and at 6s. **lawful** money, thus establishing what became known as the "New England currency." **48. my neck was so Stiff that I could not do anything with a cold I had got**: "my neck was so stiff with a cold I had gotten that . . . " **49. Notified . . . to meet**: called/announced a meeting. **50. my Brors jos**: i.e., my brother Samuel's (younger) son, Joseph Patten (b. 1758); see n. 32. **51. cross plow**: to plow across the old furrows. **52. Merrils**: probably Robert Merrill (or Morrial) of Bedford, whose land and livestock were valued at £50 in 1776; in 1779 Merrill served in the Continental Army. **53. to take Special care of Strangers . . . to Examin and Search . . .** : "to be particularly wary of strangers . . . , to examine and search them . . . "; **needful**: necessary. **54. Bay old tenor** (old Tenr or old tenor hereafter): depreciated Massachusetts Bay Colony paper currency; superceded in 1741–1742 by new paper currency ("new tenor"), but the latter also became so depreciated that by 1749, when the Massachusetts Assembly legalized payments only in specie or **lawful** money (see n. 47), both emissions of paper money had become known, collectively, as **old tenor**. **55. Was The Province Fast**: boldfaced in ms. **56. Stock**: to make a stock (the wooden support for the barrel of a gun); here (and hereafter) Patten details his repair of a muzzle-loaded musket, the normal ordnance employed in the Revolutionary War. **57. Screw nail**: a screw made to join separate parts of wood or metal. **58. breech**: the hindmost part of the bore of a gun. **59. burning iron**: branding iron; **all of my iron**: "using only my own iron."

MAY 1st   The boys planted potatoes and I worked at the Gun and William Barnet[60] gelded 3 lambs and a Boar for us and our john and john Dobbin came home

2d   Shed forged a Guard[61] and some Rods for pining on the Quils[62] and Stock on the Gun and I attended a Meeting of the town[63] on our affairs of the country and Capt Moor had a training[64] and our john and john Dobbin came home. . . .

From the 15th to the 20th Inclusive I fished at the falls[65]   I got 106 Ells[66] and how ma<n>y shad I cant Remember   on the 19th we finished planting corn   on the 16th we had a town meeting in Bedford at which we Voted to Shut the meeting house against Mr Houston and I was chosen to attend the county Congress next wednesday at Amherst.[67] . . .

29th   I went to Amherst and met the Rest of the Commitee[68] and we took the care of the Goal[69] and took from under his hand to Deliver it to us[70] the first Tuesday in July next and I came home at Break of day next morning   my Expences was 19/6 Bay old Tenr. . . .

<July> 3d   I hooped the pail I set up the first[71] and the afternoon I went with Samll Vose[72] my Brors[73] and Met john Bell at Adam Dickeys[74] And took his Wifes

60. William Barnet: a Bedford farmer, assessed for 9s. 4d. in 1774; Barnet died in service during the American Revolution.   **61. Guard**: trigger guard.   **62. Quils**: tubes containing combustable material. When the priming in the flash pan is sparked by the descending cock (activated by the trigger), the material in the quill tubes is ignited, conveying the combustion to the bore and exploding the powder behind the ball.   **63. a meeting of the town**: Patten was a member of Bedford's own Committee of Safety and Inspection, but this was probably a reference to an ordinary Bedford town meeting.   **64. a training**: i.e., a military training or drilling for the local militiamen.   **65. the falls**: Namoskeag (or Amoskeag) Falls on the Merrimack River. The inhabitants of Bedford and adjacent towns purchased shares in "companies," each comprising five or six men, that claimed fishing rights on specific sites at the Falls. Patten's seine was on the river's west bank, at the head of Smith's Falls. Salmon, shad, eels, alewives, etc. caught at the Falls were a major supplement to the local diet and often used as means of exchange in the region's semibarter economy.   **66. Ells**: i.e., eels.   **67. the county Congress next Wednesday at Amherst**: on 16 May 1775, Bedford chose Patten to attend the third Hillsborough Co. Congress, which announced as one of its purposes, "To go into some measure for the better security of the internal Polity of this County to prevent declining into a State of Nature." (R. F. Upton, *Revolutionary New Hampshire*, 37; see Sources.) The Congress's seizure of the county jail, referred to in Patten's next entry, symbolized its appropriation of the law-and-order functions of the former royal government. **68. the Commitee**: the Hillsborough Co. Committee of Safety and Inspection, the executive and enforcement arm of the Hillsborough Co. Congresses.   **69. Goal**: i.e., gaol "jail."   **70. took from under his hand to Deliver it to us**: "received his signed undertaking to deliver it to us."   **71. I hooped the pail I set up the first**: "I put hoops on the pail I had prepared July 1st."   **72. Samll Vose**: Samuel Vose or Voce, a Bedford mill-owner and militia lieutenant. Vose served as one of Bedford's selectman in 1768 and 1782, as town constable in 1769, and as moderator of the town meeting in 1777. On 16 January 1775, Bedford's town meeting elected Vose, Samuel Patten, and Daniel Moor to enforce the measures of the Continental Congress. In 1776 Vose was assessed £3 11s. 8d., one of the highest in Bedford. Vose's ancestors had emigrated from England in 1638.   **73. my Brors**: in light of the previous reference to Samuel Vose, Patten probably means here "my Brother's Samuel," i.e., his brother Samuel's eldest son and namesake; see n. 32.   **74. Adam Dickey**: a Bedford selectman in 1773 and 1775, and town constable in 1780.

Deposition and james Mathies and his son Roberts[75] of some Discourse M[r] Houston had to them Relating the cruel acts of Parliament. . . .

13th   I went to Amherst to judge Esq[r] Whiting[76] for his being a Tory and I took two Salmon with me that weighed 20 £[77]   I sold one to M[r] Holdreth and I gave him the other   I had 2/6 ℔ £ Bay old Ten[or]   my expences was 16/6 Bay old Tenor. . . .

17th   There was 4 <members> of Goffestown committee and 4 of Merrymac[78] and 2 from Derryfield met in Bedford by the desire of Bedford committee[79] to judge of M[r] Houstons being an Enemy to this country   They judged him Guilty and confined him to the county without leave[80] from the maj[r] part of one of the commitees of the towns who judged him   we broke up the next morning after day break. . . .

20th   Was the Continantal Fast and M[r] Cook[81] preached with us in Bedford   he preached with us last Sabath day which was the first preaching we have had since we shut the meeting house doors against M[r] Houston

NOVEMBER

1st   The boys digged about 17 bushel of poatoes being the last[82]   we have 170 bushell in all this year   we put them all in the Cellar and I spent the day framing a Complaint for the Selectmen to the Commitee of Safty for M[rs] Heppers casting her Daughter Hannahs child on the town and a Warrant to the Constable to Seize her goods to maintain the child and going with the constable and Selectmen to Seize the goods

<December> 5th   I went to Col: Moors mill and I took two bushell of Indian corn and a bushell and a half of Rie and got it Ground and the Commitee Recd The coppy of a letter from General Sullivan[83] to the Com[tee] of Safty for the Province for 19[84]

---

75. james Mathies and his son Roberts: James and Robert Matthews of Bedford; in 1774 the former's property was valued at £10 3s. 3d. Patton is collecting information from the Mathews family concerning Rev. Houston's pro-British **Discourse** "remarks" or "observations" (either in his sermons or in conversation).
76. Esq[r] **Whiting**: Benjamin Whiting of Hollis, former royal sheriff of Hillsborough Co. On 13 July 1775 the Hillsborough Committee of Safety convicted Whiting of loyalism, citing evidence he had called John Sullivan (**General Sullivan**; see hereafter) "a damn'd rebel, and deserves to be hanged." (R. F. Upton, *Revolutionary New Hampshire*, 121; see Sources.) Whiting fled New Hampshire to the British forces on Long Island, where in 1776 he became first lieutenant of a loyalist militia company organized by John Wentworth, New Hampshire's deposed royal governor.   77. £: Patten's shorthand often employs the symbol for British pound currency to denote "lb." or a pound's weight of measure.   78. **Merrymac** (below **Merrimac**): Merrimack, a town adjacent to Bedford in Hillsborough Co.; incorporated in 1746, Merrimack had 606 inhabitants in 1775.
79. **committee**: referring to the Committees of Safety and Inspection of Bedford and the other towns mentioned.   80. **without leave**: "unless he got permission"; i.e., Houston could not leave the county without securing permission to do so from one of the committees that had judged him guilty of treason.   81. **M[r] Cook**: perhaps Rev. Samuel Cooke (1709–1783).   82. **being the last**: "which were the last to be harvested."
83. **General Sullivan**: John Sullivan (1740–1795). About 1723 Sulivan's parents emigrated as redemptioners from counties Limerick and Cork to Maine, later moving to Somersworth, New Hampshire, where Sullivan

men to be Raised in the Province to fill the place of Conecticut men who were to be dismist the 6th Instant

6th   The town met at the Meeting House and there was 12 men Turned out and Enlisted   there was 7 Guns lacking[84] to Equip them and the Com[tee] is to procure them   my Bro[rs] Sam[ll][85] and I borrowed john McLaughlins[86] gun

7th   I spent the day in going to Lieut Moors[87] and other places to procure Guns for the men that goes out of this town but got none

8th   I went to McGaws to meet our men that listed[88] to go into the army   I got home the latter part of the night   My Expences was a pistereen[89] and I bo[t] an almanack for which I paid Six coppers[90]

9th   john set of<f> for the Army and Bob[91] went with him. . . .

<February> 5th <1776>   I went to Amherst and was Qualified[92] by M[r] Claget[93] and

was born. Sullivan may have hated England as a result of his native Irish background, but he was bitterly and outspokenly anti-Catholic. Sullivan studied law in Portsmouth, was a delegate to the First and Second Continental Congresses, and on 22 June 1775 was appointed brigadier general in overall charge of New Hampshire's armed forces. After the war, Sullivan was a member of the New Hampshire constitutional convention of 1782, governor of the state in 1786–1787 and 1789, and chairman of the state convention that ratified the U.S. Constitution in 1788. A military leader of questionable ability, Sullivan's mercurial temperament, oversensitivity, generosity, and political skills were often characterized or criticized by contemporaries as "typically Irish." Ironically, the harshest Congressional critic of Sullivan's military skills was the Irish-born Thomas Burke of North Carolina (on whom see chapter 54). **84. lacking:** needed. **85. my Bro[rs] Sam[ll]:** see n. 32. **86. john McLaughlin:** John McLaughlin, Jr.; born in Ireland in 1720 and emigrated with his parents to Bedford in 1735; served as Bedford's town clerk in 1750–1751 and as its treasurer in 1765. **87. Lieut Moors:** Lt. James Moor. **88. listed:** enlisted. **89. a pistereen:** a Spanish coin worth about one-fifth of a Spanish dollar; see n. 47. **90. Six coppers:** six copper pennies (6d.). **91. Bob:** Matthew Patten's younger son, Robert. Patten's reference is to his sons' joining the New Hampshire militia companies that were sent to reinforce the American army that had invaded Quebec in early September 1775, under the command of Gen. Richard Montgomery. After initial successes, capturing Montreal on 13 November, on 31 December the American forces failed in their assault on Quebec city, where Montgomery was killed. The Americans maintained a weak cordon around the city through the winter, but in April 1776 the army retreated to Chambly, where its commander and many soldiers died of smallpox, after which the remaining forces returned to Fort Ticonderoga on Lake Champlain. Montgomery, a scion of Ireland's Protestant aristocracy, had been born in 1738 at Swords, Co. Dublin, and was a distinguished British officer in the Seven Years' War, after which he settled in New York and married into the wealthy Livingston family. Nearly forgotten today, for many decades Montgomery's connections, character, and gallant death made him an American icon—in 1818 his remains were returned from Canada and reinterred in New York with great public ceremony—especially for Irish-American nationalists seeking to perpetuate the ecumenical patriotism of the United Irishmen and to link their own cause with the American Revolution; e.g., in the early and mid-1800s many Irish-American militia companies were named the Montgomery Guards. **92. Qualified:** given/bestowed with legal capacity. **93. M[r] Claget:** Wyseman Claggett, a lawyer from Litchfield, Hillsborough Co., who on 12 November 1776 was elected as Bedford's and Merrimack's representative to the New Hampshire General Assembly; Claggett also served as New Hampshire's attorney general during the Revolution.

Doct^r Nichols as judge of Probate and a justice and I lodged at Mr Heldreths and I took two bushel of corn and two of Rie to Col Moors mill and had it Ground and I had the Toal.[94] . . .

28th I went to Amherst to hold a Probate Court   we granted four administrations   the fees was 29/6   the Rigister gave me 10/6   I was chose to Represent Merrimac and Bedford in the General Court.[95] . . .

<March 9–23>   I sit in the General Court untill the adjournment which was the 23^d I Rec^d pay for 15 days attendance   my travil was 11/8   my wholl pay amounted to 5-1-8. . . .

<May> 16th I set out for Exeter[96] to attend as one of the Com^{tee} of Safty for the Colony and arived there that night

17th 18th 19th & 20th I attended at Exeter on the affairs[97] and set out for home the afternoon of the 20th and came to Chester[98] and lodged at Capt Underhills   I left a Gown and near 26 yards of Fustin[99] at Mr Barkers to Cloathiers to be dyed and dressed   My Expences was 13/4^1/$_5$ I bo^t 4/ worth of things viz 2 $\pounds$ of Tobacca a Rub ball for my breeches[100] and a Declaration for Independence[101]

21st I came home and went to[102] writing letters to Crown point[103] for on my journey down I got an account of my johns Death of the Small pox at Canada and when I came home my wife had got a letter from Bob which gave us a particular[104]

---

94. I had the Toal: see n. 44.   **95. the General Court**: on 28 December 1775, the fifth New Hampshire Provincial Congress at Exeter voted to resolve itself into a bicameral state legislature, or General Court, which in turn approved a state constitution by 5 January 1776. However, real authority remained in the New Hampshire Committee of Safety, many of whose members were also in the Council or upper house of the General Court. Patten was elected a member of the lower house or Assembly in 1776 and 1777 and was elected by the Assembly to the Council in 1778. In 1776 Patten was also a member of the New Hampshire Committee of Safety as well as those of Bedford and of Hillsborough County.   **96. Exeter**: a town in Rockingham Co., with a population of 1,741 in 1775. Exeter was New Hampshire's state capital during the Revolution.   **97. attended . . . on the affairs**: "was occupied with the business (of the New Hampshire Committee of Safety)."   **98. Chester**: a town in Rockingham Co., Chester in 1775 had a population of 1,599.   **99. Fustin**: i.e., fustian, a stout fabric woven of cotton and flax.   **100. a rub ball for my breeches**: a ball of some kind of material used to smooth the breech of a gun.   **101. a Declaration for Independence**: Richard Henry Lee did not propose his resolutions in favor of American independence to the Second Continental Congress at Philadelphia until 7 June 1776, so Patten's reference may be to Thomas Paine's *Common Sense*, first published in that city on 9 January 1776, although copies for sale did not reach New Hampshire until late spring. This supposition is reinforced by Patten's use, in his very next diary entry, of Paine's famous, derrogatory reference to King George III. However, Massachusetts's town meetings were debating independence, at the request of the lower house of its colonial assembly, from early May of 1776, and so it is equally likely that Patten was referring to a "declaration" or resolutions in favor of American independence passed in Haverhill or another nearby Massachusetts town.   **102. went to**: set to work.   **103. Crown point**: Crown Point, New York: a fortified U.S. army camp at the southern tip of Lake Champlain.   **104. particular**: detailed.

account   it informed us that he was sick of them[105] at Chambike and That they moved him to S[t] johns where they tarried but one night when They moved him to Isle of Noix[106] where he died on the 20th day of june   the Reason of Moveing him was the Retreat of the army which was very preceipatate and he must either be moved or be left behind   whether the moveing him hurt him he does not inform us but it seems probable to me that it did   He was shot through his left arm at Bunker hill fight and now was lead after suffering much fategue to the place where he now lyes in defending the just Rights of America to whose end[107] he came in The prime of life by means of that wicked Tyranical Brute (nea worse than Brute) of Great Britain   he was Twenty four years and 31 days old

22[d]   I writ at[108] letters to send to the army   in all I wrot four one <to> Col: Stark[109] one to Maj[or] Moor[110] one to Master Egan[111] and one to Bob. . . .

25th   I set out[112] to go to M[c]Gregores to meet the post[113] and Met M[c]Gregores boy comeing for me on the post horse and I gave the post four letters for the carriag of which I paid him 4/ and he Agreed to bring my johns things Except the Gun and accoutraments   toward his doing it I paid him 8/. . . .

August 1st   Col: Kelley[114] according to orders from the Com[tee] of Safty published INDEPENDENCE in Amherst   one of Amherst Companies under Cap[t] John Bradford and Lindborough[115] company under Cap[t] Clark attended under arms   The

---

105. he was sick of them: "he was sick with them (i.e., **the Small pox**)." The word **pox** was originally a plural (of **pock**; see for a similar usage **shingles**), but was later construed as a collective and then a singular; both usages (plural and collective/singular) coexisted for a time.   **106. Chambike . . . S[t] johns . . . Isle of Noix:** Chambly, St-Jean-sur-Richelieu, St-Paul-de-Île-aux-Noix: stages in the American army's retreat from Quebec city to Montreal and south via the Richelieu River to Lake Champlain in New York.   **107. to whose end:** to the accomplishment of which, for which purpose (refers to "defending the just rights").   **108. writ at:** worked at writing.   **109. Col: Stark:** John Stark (1728–1822): Stark's parents were Ulster emigrants who in 1720 settled as farmers at Londonderry, N.H. During the French and Indian War Stark served with distinction as an officer in Rogers' Rangers. During the Revolution, Stark was colonel of the New Hampshire militia at Bunker Hill, and in May 1776 he went to Canada and accompanied the American forces on their retreat south from Quebec; most famously, on 16 August 1777 Stark was the victorious American general at the battle of Bennington, Vt. At the war's end Stark retired with the rank of major-general. Other diary entries indicate that Patten and Stark were on intimate terms.   **110. Maj[or] Moor:** probably Major, later Col. Daniel Moor; born in 1730 in Londonderry, N.H., Daniel Moor was one of Bedford's selectman in 1776, when he commanded the ninth New Hampshire militia regiment in which Matthew Patten's son, John, was first lieutenant during the retreat from Quebec.   **111. Master Egan:** Luke Eagan, Bedford schoolmaster; born in Ireland and educated for the Catholic priesthood, Egan converted to Protestantism and emigrated to America; during the Revolution Egan served a short time in the American forces, but he drowned in the Merrimack River in 1776 or 1777.   **112. I went set out** ms.   **113. post:** mail.   **114. Col: Kelley:** Moses Kelley, a tavernkeeper in Goffstown; during the Revolution Kelly served as sheriff of Hillsborough Co. and as colonel of the ninth New Hampshire militia regiment; as sheriff he was notorious for his persecution of local loyalists.   **115. Lindborough:** Lyndeborough, Hillsborough Co.; incorporated in 1763, Lyndeborough had 713 inhabitants in 1775.

whole was conducted with decence and Decorum and the people departed in peace and good order   The prinsaple Gentlemen of the County attended But not any who have been suspected of being unfriendly to the Country attended   my Expences was 5/. . . .

For a brief moment in the mid-1770s, a wave of "history" as political upheaval had swept through Bedford, temporarily upsetting its people's mundane routine. When the waters of war receded, some of Matthew Patten's old neighbors had been washed away—leaving his family more prominent than before—yet new ones were swept in, as between 1775 and 1783 Bedford's population rose by over 50 percent to 762 inhabitants. In late 1778 Rev. Houston had acceded to communal pressure, had signed the oath of allegiance to New Hampshire's revolutionary government, and, despite Patten's protests, was allowed to live and farm the rest of his days in Bedford, although he never preached from the town's pulpit again. Eighty-two Bedford men had fought in the Revolution and twelve never returned: among the dead were William Barnett and John Patten, Scots-Irish; John Callahan and Valentine Sullivan, native Irish, whatever their religion; and Primas Chandler, Patten's neighbor's freed slave. With his eldest child already dead, Patten's diary evinced little interest in the war after 1778, when his last son to join the army, James, returned safely from the Rhode Island campaign. Patten declined further service in the state legislature and, judging from his Day-Book, the focus of his life once again narrowed to his flocks and fields, until finally he recorded that 10 July 1783 "was a day of Rejoicing in this town on acc^t of the peace." By this date, Patten was already 64 years old, but he lived on for another 22 years, until 27 August 1795, when he died sitting under a tree on his farm. To his widow and children he bequeathed nearly 60 years of accumulated Bedford property: land valued at $1,755; crops and livestock worth $281; household furniture, six silver spoons, kitchen utensils, and farm tools worth $145; clothes worth $15; and a small library of books on religion, law, and surveying valued at $13.30. Eventually, changes more sweeping than those of 1776 would obliterate Matthew Patten's hard-earned legacy, as the fields in which he labored and for which his son had died in Quebec now lie under the manicured greens of the local country club's golf course.

60 ✳

John Phillips, 1783

Although support for the American Revolution was nearly unanimous among the Scots-Irish farmers and frontiersmen of New Hampshire and Pennsylvania, many Ulster immigrants in the backcountries of New York and especially of the Carolinas and Georgia were ambivalent or opposed to the colonial rebellion. Most strove to remain neutral or shifted allegiance with the changing fortunes of war, whereas others, such as John Phillips, were adamantly loyal to the Crown, fought for the British, and suffered exile and the confiscation of their property.

John Phillips was born about 1730, probably in either Ahoghill or Kirkinriola parish, near the linen-market town of Ballymena, in west County Antrim.[1] Like nearly 80 percent of their neighbors, the Phillipses were Presbyterians. Perhaps impelled by the economic dislocations that inspired the Steelboys' uprising in 1770–1772,[2] or induced by the South Carolina government's offer of free land to frontier settlers, in late 1770 John Phillips emigrated via Charleston to the South Carolina backcountry, accompanied by his wife, Elizabeth (née Lurkan), their nine children, his brothers James and Robert, and his married sisters, Mary Dunsketh and Rachel Buchanan, and their families. In early 1771 Phillips took out a warrant for 450 acres on the springs of Little River, but he settled on another two-hundred-acre grant along Jackson's Creek, just north of the Broad River. Both holdings were located near the village of Winnsboro, in that part of Camden electoral district that later became Fairfield County. Phillips's siblings settled on adjacent or nearby farms, as did his Chesney and Miller kinsmen who came from Antrim in 1774–1775.

Within 10 years of his arrival in South Carolina, Phillips and his sons cleared and fenced 60 acres on Jackson's Creek. In addition, he still held his original grant of 450 acres on Little River, and he acquired 150 more acres on Rocky Creek from the estate of his deceased sister, Mary. With eight hundred acres in all, Phillips was a comfortable backcountry farmer, as well as a founding elder of the Lebanon Presbyterian church on Jackson's Creek. However, he was not an affluent indigo planter like Robert Witherspoon and the other Scots-Irish who had settled South Carolina's coastal plain 40 years earlier.[3] In his 1783 petition to the British government, Phillips claimed compensation for his crops of wheat, Indian corn, hemp, flax, and oats, as well as 19 horses, 38 cattle, 36 sheep, and 50 hogs. Although his wheat, hemp, and livestock were marketable in Charleston, Phillips owned no slaves, china, or silverware and had no more than £21 in cash when the rebels plundered his farm. And whereas he valued his lost furniture and farm tools at £80, he claimed no compensation for what must have been a large but cheaply constructed log house, similar to those of his poorer neighbors.

At the very beginning of the American Revolution, John Phillips declared his "Attachment to Great Britain" and refused a military commission from South Carolina's rebellious congress; in the summer of 1775, when the congress sent emissaries to enlist the backcountry in rebellion, Phillips persuaded nearly all the Jackson's Creek settlers (except

1. For demographic data on Kirkinriola and Aghohill parishes and their environs, see appendix 2.1f, on chapter 13. 2. On the Steelboys in east Ulster, see chapter 4. 3. On Witherspoon, see chapter 18.

his Buchanan kin) to remain loyal to the Crown. Eventually, Phillips became the commandant of Camden's loyalist militia, in which two of his sons and his brothers James and Robert were junior officers.

It is impossible to discern precisely why Phillips and other Scots-Irish in frontier South Carolina opposed American independence, while a majority joined or at least acquiesced in the rebellion. Certainly, the Scots-Irish Presbyterians in the Carolina and Georgia Piedmonts, generally, were more isolated from the agitation that preceded the Revolution than were their coreligionists in western Pennsylvania or in the Shenandoah Valley. They were also alienated from the largely Anglican coastal planters, slaveowners, and merchants who dominated the Carolina and Georgia legislatures and led their states into revolution. Backcountry South Carolinians, especially, had ample reasons to scorn the low-country élite's "Noise about Liberty" and "No Taxation without Representation." Although the Piedmont contained about three-fourths of the colony's white population, its inhabitants had only three seats in the colonial Assembly, and this and other injustices (for example, the legislature's refusal to locate courts and sheriffs in the western districts) had inspired the Regulation protests of 1767–1769. However, South Carolina's Regulators were much less radical and violent than those in neighboring North Carolina: the former's leaders were rising backcountry planters and slaveowners who wanted to replicate, not overthrow, coastal institutions and to emulate the low-country aristocracy.[4] Consequently, in 1775–1783 most of South Carolina's former Regulators supported the American Revolution. Moreover, Phillips did not settle in the Piedmont until after the Regulation was over.

Throughout America, however, there was a strong correlation between very recent immigration and loyalism, and Phillips and other nonslaveholding newcomers may have been estranged from both the lowland aristocracy and the backcountry's aspirant élite, many of whom were transplanted Virginians who, although often of Irish birth or ancestry, were "Americanized" by long residence in the colonies. In addition, very recent Ulster immigrants in South Carolina and Georgia had few quarrels with British officials. Instead, they had gained their lands through royal grants—rather than from proprietors (as in Pennsylvania) or from speculators (as in Virginia)—and may have chosen loyalty out of gratitude or fear of forfeiting title to their holdings. Other reasons for political loyalties were no doubt local, factional, and personal: the Carolina backcountry was a patchwork of relatively autonomous communities, each with its own social networks and "men of influence" whose idealism, ambitions, or prejudices drew neighbors and dependents to one side or the other. As for Phillips himself, some of Fairfield County's early chroniclers speculated

---

4. On North Carolina's Regulation movement of 1766–1771, see chapters 54 and 57.

that prior service in the British army or even past links to prominent figures in the Anglo-Irish governing classes may have ensured his fidelity to the Crown.[5]

Whatever the reasons for his loyalism, Phillips shared with other staunch Tories the shifting fortunes of war in revolutionary South Carolina: from suppression and persecution by the state's congress and its patriot militias in 1775–1778 to temporary triumph in 1778–1780, when British forces under Clinton and Cornwallis invaded the South, captured Savannah and Charleston, and crushed an American army at the battle of Camden (16 August 1780); and to ultimate disaster in 1780–1782, when Nathanael Greene's troops and the rebel militias defeated British and loyalist forces at King's Mountain (7 October 1780) and the Cowpens (17 January 1781), lured Cornwallis's main force north toward Virginia, and drove the remaining British regulars and over nine thousand loyalists out of the backcountry into Charleston and, by late 1782, into evacuation and exile overseas. John Phillips's written and oral testimony to the Loyalist Claims Commission in London provides a stark account of his own role in this "uncommonly Cruel" civil war, when rebel and Tory partisans "pursue[d] each other with the most relentless fury, killing each other whenever they" met,[6] and transforming the backcountry into a wasteland of burning farms and dead livestock.

John Phillips, Petition and Testimony
to the Loyalist Claims Commission, London, 6 May 1783[7]

The Memorial[8] of Col. John Phillips late of Camden District in the province of S° Carolina Sheweth

That at the Commencement of the Troubles in America your Memorialist[9] still retaining his unshaken Loyalty to his Majesty, endeavoured as much as possible to suppress the Rebellion *[although] in 1775 the Rebels offered him a Lieut. Col^s Comm^n.[10] if he wo^d join their party.*

In the Month of July 1775, the first Armed Association having been raised, a resolution was proposed to support the 13 States of America against Great Britain. All the Inhabitants of the parish wherein Claimant lived were gathered together in the meeting house and called upon to sign this Resolution when Claimant publickly opposed it and with such Success that nobody

---

5. According to one South Carolina tradition, for example, John Phillips had old associations "with the aristocracy of his native land"; specifically, "in the old country [he] had kept the race-horses of the father of Lord Cornwallis," the British general in command of the Southern campaign that ended in surrender at Yorktown, Va. (L. M. McMaster, "Ancestry of the Buchanan Family . . ."; F. Phillips, "Col. John Phillips of South Carolina . . . ," 73; see Sources); on Cornwallis, see n. 22.   6. R. M. Weir, "'The Violent Spirit': The Reestablishment of Order, and the Continuity of Leadership in Post-Revolutionary South Carolina," in Hoffman et al., *Uncivil War*, 77; R. Hoffman, "The 'Disaffected' in the Revolutionary South," 294; see Sources.   7. Due to their brevity and complementary nature, Phillips's written petition and the Loyalist Claims Commission's transcription of his oral testimony are here melded for continuity into a single, chronologically ordered text. Phrases in italics are from the oral testimony.   8. **Memorial:** memorandum.   9. **Memorialist:** writer of a memorial (memorandum).   10. **Lieut. Col^s Comm^n.:** lieutenant colonel's commission.

would sign it but two persons who had previously signed it. . . . [I]n consequence of this he became a marked Man. . . .

That on your Memorialist refusing to take up Arms in favor of the Rebel States he was enormously fined, as well for his two Sons as for himself, wch[11] greatly distressed your Memorialist and his Family——*He was first fined in Nov: 1775. It was an Arbitrary Fine. He had 2 Sons who were capable of doing duty in the Militia, and who refused likewise to join their Musters. All this time he rec<eiv>ed many Insults, but no personal Ill Treatment. . . .*

He cont[d12] *in this Situat*[n] *till 1778. In 1777, the beg<in>ing of the year Col. M*c*Laurin*[13] *sent in 2 Gentlemen from Saint Augustine. Col. M*c*Laurin was a Settler in Georgia who had taken an early & active part in favor of Britain. These Gentlemen were sent in to administer the Oaths of Allegiance to the King. Claimant took the Oath to the King and was impowered to administer it to all loyal Subjects, and to do everything in his power to support the King's Government with a promise that Troops should be sent to their Assistance. . . . [H]e administ*[d] *the Oath to four persons.*

In the begin[g] *of May 1778, the State Oath & the Oath of abjuration of Great Britain was tendered to him wch he positively refused to take as did both his Sons.* That on the imposition of the State Oath your Memor[ts14] two Sons with a number of Loyalists endeavoured to make their escape to Saint Augustine to join the British Army there but were taken on their retreat & made prisoners by y[e] Rebels who confined them in Irons in Orangeburge Goal in wch place one of your Memorialist's Sons, by the great Cruelty he rec<eiv>ed from the Rebels died, and the other after six Months Confinement was tried for his Life and released.

That on your Memorialist refusing to take the afo[d15] Oath he was made a prisoner & carried to the Rebel Army, then on their route against Saint Augustine, and so continued during a Campaign of Three Months and a March of about 800 Miles,[16] from thence he was conveyed to Camden Goal[17] where he lay confined for four Months, after wch he was tried for Sedition against the Rebel States and condemned to die, under wch Sentence he lay for 15 days *(The Gallows was erected before his Window)* when the British Army arrived in Georgia wch your Mem[t.18] imagines was the means of procuring his enlargement.[19] *[I]n consequence of the proclam*[n].

---

11. wch: which (abbreviation occurs frequently hereafter). **12. cont**[d]: continued. **13. Col. M**c**Laurin**: Evan Mclaurin, a loyal but hard-drinking Scottish-born trader, who had a store below the fork of the Broad and Saluda rivers; in August 1776 he escaped to British-held St. Augustine, was commissioned a major in the East Florida Rangers, and sent loyalist recruiters and raiding parties into the South Carolina and Georgia backcountries. **14. Memor**[ts]: memorialist's. **15. afo**[d]: aforesaid. **16. . . . a Campaign of Three Months . . .** : this was the American brigadier general Robert Howe's unsuccessful strike, in summer 1778, against the British base in East Florida. **17. Goal**: i.e., gaol "jail"; **he was conveyed to Camden Goal**: on 13 August 1778. **18. Mem**[t.]: memorialist; also abbreviated **Memorial**[t.] and as **Memor**[t] hereafter. **19. enlargement**: release from confinement; see Shakespeare, *Love's Labour's Lost*, 3.1.5: "take this key, give enlargement to the swain."

JOHN PHILLIPS

issued by Col. Campbell and Sir Peter Parker who had taken Savannah[20] wherein they promised Amnesty to all who had taken up Arms against the King, except such as had condemned loyal Subjects to death, 50 of the Rebels petitioned for Claimant's Life wch was granted. He then went home and remained quiet till after Charles Town was reduced.[21]

That after the reduction of Charles Town your Memorialist on receiv^g Orders embodied the Loyalists and joined the Royal Army at Camden then under Command of the Right Honble the Earl Cornwallis.[22]   *In April 1780 he rec<eiv>ed a Message from Sir Henry Clinton by Capt. Rewner. It was a gen^l. Instruct^n. to all loyal Subjects who had never taken an Oath to the Rebels to embody[23] themselves and seize upon all prisoners & amunition belong^g to the Rebels.*

That your Memorialist was appointed a Colonel of Militia and served under the command of L^d. Cornwallis during his Lords<hi>p's stay in Carolina. *He embodied at that time about 150[24] who chose him their Captain & as soon as Charles Town was taken marched out & seized upon and disarmed above 300 of the Rebels. He joined the British at Camden in June 1780 with about 50 Men who were all that were necessary to Guard the prisoners he brought in with him. When he completed his Reg^t.[25] it amounted to 5 or 600 Men. He was appointed Col of the Militia by Lord Cornwallis in June 1780. He cont^d from this time to serve with Lord Cornwallis till the time his Lords<hi>p marched into North Carolina. He never rec<eiv>ed pay till he joined Lord Rawdon[26] in Camden in Janry 1781 after L^d. Cornwallis's Departure, but rec<eiv>ed a complem^t.[27] from L^d. Cornwallis of 50 Gu<ine>as. From Janry 1781 he rec<eiv>ed 10/ a day till he left Charles Town on the Evacuation in 1782. He continued to serve under Lord Rawdon till the province was evacuated. When Lord Cornwallis marched away Claimant was left at Wynnsburgh[28] and sent 120 Waggon Loads of provision for the use of his Army wch they were in great want of. These were provisions belong^g to the Army. His Lordship was then at Rocky Creek.*

20. Col. Campbell and Sir Peter Parker who had taken Savannah: the brigadier general Sir Archibald Campbell (1739–1791) and the admiral Sir Peter Parker (1721–1811) commanded the British army and naval forces that captured Savannah on 29 December 1778.   **21. reduced**: captured; **Charles Town was reduced**: Sir Henry Clinton (1738–1795) and 14,000 British troops besieged Charleston from mid-February until 12 May 1780, when Gen. Benjamin Lincoln surrendered the city and three thousand American troops.   **22. Earl Cornwallis**: Charles Cornwallis (1754–1833), first marquis and second earl Cornwallis; after Clinton's return to New York on 5 June 1780, Cornwallis became commander of British forces in the southern colonies but surrendered at Yorktown, Va., on 19 Oct. 1781. After the Revolution Cornwallis served as governor-general of India (1786–1793) and lord lieutenant of Ireland (1798–1801) and enjoyed greater success in suppressing Indian and Irish rebellions.   **23. embody**: form into a military body.   **24. He embodied at that time about 150**: i.e., he had organized by that time about 150 militiamen.   **25. Reg^t.**: regiment.   **26. Lord Rawdon**: Francis Lord Rawdon (1754–1826), a member of the Anglo-Irish aristocracy; second earl of Moira and first marquis of Hastings; adjutant general during the British campaign in the southern colonies, Rawdon became commander-in-chief in South Carolina in January 1781, when Cornwallis led the bulk of his troops into North Carolina in pursuit of Greene's army; Rawdon left America for reasons of health in the summer of 1781. A member of both the Irish and the British House of Lords, in 1797 Rawdon denounced the "tyranny" of the Irish government, sympathized with the United Irishmen, and in 1799–1800 opposed the Act of Union.   **27. complem^t.**: i.e., compliment "gratuity."   **28. Wynnsburgh**: i.e., Winnsboro.

That shortly after the defeat of Col. Tarleton by the Rebel Genl. Morgan[29] your Memorialist was detached with a party of Militia by order of Lord Cornwallis to escort the British Officers who were wounded in that Action to Camden when on the 21st of January 1781 they were surrounded by a Party of Rebels four times their number and after a firing of 50 Minutes had sevl.[30] Men wounded & some killed, and your Memorialist was again made a prisoner together with his Son & remained so until Ld. Cornwallis got his Exchange. *They were carried into North Carolina and very inhumanely treated, being kept three days with no other provisions but water. He was exchanged in May 1781, and in August being sent for by Lord Rawdon to Charles Town, he left the Command of his Regimt. to his Son. . . .*

That after the departure of Ld. Cornwallis for Virginia your Memorialt. with his Regt. joined the Rt. Honble Lord Rawdon at Camden & marched with his Lords<hi>p to the relief of Ninety six,[31] continuing with him thro' all his fatiguing and difficult Marches, till Genl. Stuart[32] succeeded to the Command, at wch time yr. Memort. accompanied his Lords<hi>p to Charles Town,   the command of his own Regt. he left to his Son David Phillips until his return.

That your Memorialist's said Son being shortly after on a command was unfortunately taken prisoner and after being sometime confined was by the Rebels most inhumanely murdered

That soon after this Melancholy Event your Memorialist's Wife & eight Children were driven from their Habitation on Jacksons Creek in the sd. province to Charles Town in a distressed sitn.[33] & almost naked.[34]

That your Memorialist thro' his Attachment and Zeal for Great Britain, and by the part he took to suppress the Rebellion has lost all and every part of his property, as more fully appears by the annexed estimate & Vouchers.

Your Memt. therefore prays that his Case may be taken into your Con<siderati>on in order that yr. Memt. may be enabled under yr report to rec<eiv>e such Aid and relief as his Losses and Services may be found to deserve.

And your Memorialist as in duty bound shall ever pray

J. Phillips

---

29. the defeat of Col. Tarleton by the Rebel Genl. Morgan: on 17 January 1781, Brigadier General Daniel Morgan (1736–1802) defeated Major Banastre Tarleton's Irish Legion (a loyalist force raised in New York) at the battle of Cowpens, on the banks of the Broad River. "Bloody" Tarleton (1754–1833) was a dashing but brutal cavalry leader, hated for his massacre of surrendering American troops at the Waxhaws on 29 May 1780. **30. sevl.:** several.　**31. the relief of Ninety six:** the month-long defense of Ninety Six, the primary British base in the South Carolina backcountry, was the loyalists' most successful military engagement. In early June 1781 Lord Rawdon marched two hundred miles with a relief force of 1,700 men, including 84 loyalist militiamen from Camden District, under Phillips's command. Rawdon's men raised the seige but shortly afterward abandoned Ninety Six and escorted the area's loyalist refugees to Orangeburg and then to Charleston, leaving the backcountry in rebel hands.　**32. Genl. Stuart:** British General Alexander Stewart. **33. sitn.:** situation.　**34.** In 1781–1782 thousands of loyalists sought refuge in Charleston, and Phillips was appointed an "inspector" in charge of providing food, shelter, and medical care to the refugees from Camden District.

South Carolina's earliest historians were divided in their assessment of Colonel John Phillips's wartime conduct. At least one described him as the perpetrator of "many acts of cold blooded cruelty," and indeed in 1782 Phillips had justified the execution of a rebel leader as "a proper example, and Just reward for his treason and infidelity," lamenting that "the same mode of correcting rebels was so long deferred."[35] Surely Phillips had ample cause for vengeance, as his youngest brother, Robert, and two of his sons died at rebel hands, one of the latter butchered and beheaded while a helpless prisoner, while two more of his children perished of fever in the Charleston refugee camps. And whereas other commentators praised Phillips's "compassionate heart" and "kindness" to his rebel neighbors,[36] citing his alleged intercessions with Cornwallis on their behalf, such actions did not mollify the vindictive South Carolina legislature, which in 1782–1783 confiscated all his property and banished him from the state, under sentence of death should he return. Thus, Phillips had no choice but to abandon his adopted country, and in early December 1782 he and his wife and remaining children embarked from Charleston in a British troopship. In mid-April 1783 Phillips landed at Portsmouth, England, and proceeded to London to seek aid from the recently created Loyalist Claims Commission

From their refuges in Canada, the West Indies, and the British Isles, some 320 South Carolina loyalists (out of nearly three thousand total claimants) petitioned the Commission for £1,426,550 in compensation for lost real estate, slaves, and other property. A fourth of the South Carolina claimants were Irish-born, the highest proportion from any former colony. On average the petitioners received only 37 percent of the value of their losses. However, despite their aristocratic biases and Philips's "common" status, the Commissioners awarded him £850, over 45 percent of his £1,874 claim, thanks to strong support from Lord Cornwallis and other British officers who declared, "there cannot be a better Man in America than Colonel Phillips" or one whose family had "suffered more from their fidelity to their King and country."[37]

With his compensation, his officer's pension, and—according to reports circulated in South Carolina—a crown appointment secured through Cornwallis's influence, Phillips returned to his native County Antrim, lived to witness the United Irish Rebellion of 1798 (which his kinsman and fellow South Carolina loyalist exile, Alexander Chesney, helped suppress),[38] and died at his home in Ballyloughan, Ahoghill parish, on 2 December 1808, aged about 80 years. However, Phillips's unhappy experience did not discourage his relatives from emigrating to South Carolina. Indeed, at least one of his own sons returned

<hr />

35. L. M. McMaster, "Ancestry of the Buchanan Family . . . "; R. S. Lambert, *South Carolina Loyalists . . .*, 211; see Sources. 36. L. M. McMaster, "Ancestry of the Buchanan Family . . . "; see Sources. 37. H. E. Egerton, ed., *The Royal Commission on the Losses and Services of American Loyalists . . .*, 49; E. A. Jones, ed., "The Journal of Alexander Chesney . . . ," 62; see Sources. 38. Although logical, the Irish-born American exiles' active loyalism in Ireland itself during the 1790s has never been examined; our survey of the American loyalist claims and of historians' lists of Crown supporters and informers in 1798 Ulster has uncovered several identical names, in addition to that of Philips's young kinsman, Alexander Chesney.

there, and his brother James never left the state, petitioned successfully for both a pardon and the return of his property, reconciled with his rebel wife's family, and in 1819 was living happily in Fairfield County, "retired and independent" on a "large plantation," and on intimate terms with his former enemies.[39]

61 ❀

Job Johnson, 1784

Nearly half the Revolutionary War soldiers who fought in the Continental Army and state militia units raised in Pennsylvania were of Irish birth or descent, and in some companies (as of the seventh regiment) the proportion was as high as 75 percent. Most enlisted only for short terms, however. Job Johnson (or Johnston)[1] was one of a few Irish immigrants who served his adopted country throughout the conflict, surviving the New Jersey campaign, border warfare in western Pennsylvania and Ohio, and the climactic seige of Yorktown, Virginia—as well as numerous bouts of severe illness—to describe his military experiences in a letter to his brother in Ulster.

Job Johnson was born about 1745 and raised at Barley Hill, a small farm in Slaghty-bogy townland, in the parish of Maghera and the barony of Loughinsholin, in south County Londonderry. Economic motives, inextricably linked to south Derry's shifting religious balance, were no doubt paramount in Job Johnson's decision to emigrate. Johnsons (or Johnstons) had been present in south Derry at least since 1659, when Protestants already comprised between a fourth and a third of Maghera's inhabitants, and in the 1690s and early 1700s large numbers of migrants from Scotland sharply increased the area's Protestant population. Most of the region, however, was owned by the London Companies, and their high rents and oppressive leasing policies obliged most farmers to supplement their incomes through linen manufacturing. By a combination of famine in the early 1740s and heavy emigration thereafter, between 1740 and 1766 the number of Protestant households in Maghera declined by nearly 33 percent. By 1766 Protestants comprised less than 46 percent of the parish's population, and due to subsequent emigration by 1831 only a third of Maghera's inhabitants were Protestants, of whom nearly 78 percent were Presbyte-

---

39. John B. Phillips, Charleston, S.C., to his parents, Ballymena, Co. Antrim, 12 March 1819 (T.1449, PRONI). For ex–United Irishman John O'Raw's derrogatory remarks in 1809 about James Phillips in South Carolina, see chapter 13.   **1.** Job Johnson signed and addressed two of his three surviving letters, as well as his 1790 will, as "Johnson," and the family name in Maghera parish is so recorded in the Tithe Applotment Book (1828) and in Griffith's Valuation (1859). Consequently, we have followed that spelling, although Job Johnson signed himself "Johnston" in his 1784 letter, and although in the early 1830s the Ordnance Survey of Maghera parish spelled the family name as "Johnstone."

rians and other Dissenters.[2] Thus, Maghera's Protestant tenants needed to be very industrious to hold onto or increase the size of their farms, despite fluctuations in the linen industry and increasing Catholic competition for land and leases.

Job Johnson's family was both Presbyterian and exceptionally energetic. Indeed, during the late 1700s and early 1800s Job's brother, Robert, would purchase the leases of his emigrating neighbors, until by 1830 his widow possessed the largest farm (50 acres) and the only two-story, slate-roofed house in Slaghtybogy townland. Job Johnson shared his brother's industry and ambition but realized that, as a younger, noninheriting son, emigration was his own best option—especially as in his youth he had seen "Many Go to America worth nothing [and] some of them servants," who had returned "in two or three years worth more than they would have been by staying at home."[3] Consequently, in about 1765 Job Johnson and his brother William emigrated to Philadelphia or New Castle, and by late 1767 Job was teaching in "a very Large School" in Oxford township, in the southwestern corner of Chester County, Pennsylvania, while his brother "follow[ed] plantation business" nearby.[4]

In 1775 Job Johnson may have joined the Revolution because he was still single and still landless and because a military venture offered escape—and perhaps upward mobility—from the relatively poor wages of a country schoolmaster. For although Oxford township, with its predominantly Scots-Irish population, may have been socially congenial, most of the good soils had been settled before 1750, and during the late eighteenth century land values in Chester County increased enormously, farms became fewer and larger, and chances to acquire land through purchase or even tenancy grew scarce.[5] However, Job Johnson's prewar letters to Barley Hill reflected no discontent with his choice of settlement. Rather, he had eulogized Pennsylvania as "as Good a Country as any Man needs to Dwell in" and, like Robert Parke 40 years earlier,[6] had lavishly praised Chester County's prosperous farms and "Orchards laden with fruit to admiration." America "is Much better than I expected it to be in every way," Johnson wrote, "and I really likes it so well and it is so pleasant to me that it would be a good Estate in Ireland that would Make Me Stay there." In Chester County, he reported, the farmers "Make No other use of [oats] than to feed their horses," whereas in east Ulster oats were the primary staple of the farmers' diet. Indeed, Johnson declared he "never . . . had the Least Thought of returning home," save to visit his family one last time, for he knew no "one that has come here that Desires to

2. For demographic data on Maghera parish and its environs, see appendix 2.1b, chapter 61. **3.** Job Johnson, Oxford Township, Chester Co., Pa., to John, Robert, and James Johnson, Slaghtybogy, c/o James Barclay, Maghera, Co. Derry, 27 November 1767. **4.** Job Johnson, 27 November 1767. **5.** Oxford township was one of the earliest Scots-Irish settlements in Pennsylvania, with a Presbyterian church since 1725. Between 1759 and 1782 the average size of farms in Oxford township increased from 64–106 acres to 151–208 acres, while the value of land rose from £5.5–£6.2 per hundred acres to between £7 and £14 per *single* acre. Even in 1767 Johnson reported that "Land in this part is very high, selling Commonly at six and seven pounds per acre" (27 November 1767). **6.** On Parke, see chapter 9.

be in Ireland again . . . and would rather live in Slavery."[7] Thus, it is most likely that Johnson embraced the American Revolution to defend "this . . . Brave Country" from what he called "that Cursed . . . Stamp Act" and from other British policies that, in his view, threatened to reduce American society to an impoverished, rigidly stratified condition analogous to Ireland's and, in the process, circumscribe or destroy the remarkable opportunities that Pennsylvania seemingly offered to poor but ambitious Irish immigrants.[8]

Johnson's experiences in the Revolution, described here, did not dampen his patriotic enthusiasm for American "Independancy." However, his last surviving communication with his family in Ireland clearly indicates that he had undergone severe wartime hardships that only his Presbyterian piety, also evident in this letter, had enabled him to endure.

Job Johnson, Philadelphia, to Robert Johnson, Slaghtybogy, Maghera Parish, County Londonderry, 5 December 1784

Dear Brother——   Philadelphia   December 5th, 1784
          The pleasure I this morning feel of having through the Infinite and kind Redeemers goodness, a life like Mine prolonged Through a long and Severe War, the hardships I have been partaker of, But bless God who has at last given us the Victory, and established our Independancy. Oh happy peace, which enables me at this time through God, to take up My pen to enquire after your Wellfares, and to give you an Account of My own, and in the first place I Must tell you that a large Volume would not Contain what I would wish to writ on that Subject, Much less a letter,   Therefore let it but Suffice to give you to know, that your letters of 1775 being the last I received came to hand, and never After untill this day had I the happiness to answer them. The above year I enjoyed[9] a bad State of Health, and in the fall of that Said Year, being out in the Militia, as Quarter Master I took the Bloody Flux[10] at Perth Amboy State of New jersey, Which Continued with me for Seventeen Week, in Spite of Medicine and that was not wanting,[11] and at last ended in a

---

7. Job Johnson, 27 November 1767. 8. Job Johnson, 27 November 1767; and William and Job Johnson, Oxford Township, Chester Co., Pa., to John Johnston, Slaghtybogy, c/o James Barclay, Maghera, Co. Derry, 2 March 1766. In their 1766 letter the Johnsons lavishly praised American opportunities for Irish artisans. Thus, although the immigrant William Hay was still only an indentured servant, coming to Pennsylvania had been "the Best Step that He Could Take," because eventually "He May Come to [i.e., achieve] that which none of the Brethren Ever will come to by Staying at Home a Roasting of Potatoes." Likewise, if former neighbor George Given "Was Here He would make Well out at Making of Broomes [to] sweep Houses with, there Being a Great Call for Such Tradesmen [at] sixpence per Broom, so that If He is not Failed since we came away He Might Make Easily six of them Each Day Besides [having] Meat and Drink [such] as Slatabogie Never can Afford Him." 9. enjoy: see chapter 23, n. 37; also chapter 5, n. 16, and chapter 9, n. 12. 10. the Bloody Flux: severe dysentery. 11. and that was not wanting: "which was not spared."

Intirmiting fever, (or Ague) which Continued with Me Nine Months longer Being at this time got to Philadelphia, and <I> lay under the hands of two of the Ablest Phys<ic>ians here, was Several times given up for Death, But Yet through God was So far Recovered in Summer 1776 that I Could Ride alittle and did so and found Benefit thereby,   But Still a Complications of disorders attended Me, which I thought would Soon take Me out of this World of Troubles; Yet through Mercy he who Judges best for all Men alloted <me> To See a great deal more hardships, and thanks be to his Name who has brought Me through them all to this happy period,——For Shortly after I got So well, that I joined the Army again, Being Appointed by Congress, an Assistant Deputy Commissary General of Issues; for the Western department, of the State of Pennsilvania; in Which line of the Staff I bore that Commission for three Years & Six Month, being the Most of that time out against the Indians in the Western Army;[12]   This letter would not be able to Contain But a very small Description of that Savage people that we had to fight against, and their Cruelty to us when in their power,   the Battles <and> Skirmishes with them and the numbers slaine, with the hardshipp undergone by us While in their Country, I Must not fall on,[13] as it would swell My letter that I would writ Nothing else;   However, After being there three years, I was to My great joy, ordered to Philadelphia to Join the Army then going with his Excelency General Washington to besiege Lord Cornwallas, in little York State of Virginia. I left the Indian Country in August having Six hundred Miles to Philadelphia, and got there in time to join our Troops and the French then on their March to Williamsburgh,[14] being four hundred & Twenty Miles More, without having had one days rest Save two Nights at Billys[15] on my way whom I had Not Seen for the Above Times——We got to Wiliamsburg and began the Seige 28th of Sept <17>81 Which lasted untill the 19th of october, all which time, (to be Short on the Subject) was like Nothing but one Continued Clap of Thunder, between us & them; When at last they Surrendered;[16]   I will Say No More on the Subject of War, only that the preserver of all Men made me Fortunate enough to get through the whole without loss of Life, or

12. We have been unable to identify Job Johnson in published U.S. military records. However, it is probable that in western Pennsylvania and Ohio he served with or alongside the eighth Pennsylvania regiment, whose junior officers included Elizabeth Brownlee Guthrie's first and second husbands; on Guthrie, see chapter 22. **13. fall on**: get started on (OED, s.v. fall, 93.c; rare). **14. Williamsburgh**: Williamsburg, Virginia's colonial capital. **15. Billys**: conjectural, ms. blurred, but Job Johnson almost certainly is referring to his brother, William, who was last described as following "plantation business," in partnership with John Lewis, in Chester County's Haverford township (27 November 1767). In 1771 William Johnston held 80 acres, one horse, and one cow in Haverford, where John Lewis held 270 acres and John Lewis, Jr., another two hundred acres. **16.** The combined American and French seige of the British forces at Yorktown (**little York**), Va., began on 28 September 1781, as Job Johnson reported. On 17 October the British commander, Lord Cornwallis, opened negotiations for the surrender of his army; the articles of capitulation were signed the next day; and on 19 October the British army of nearly eight thousand men laid down their arms.

Members; Still though with an Ailing Constitution, for which I have the greater reason to bless God who Continued Me when Many Stout & Strong arround me fell——After Coming home from the hardships of the War There has Not been a year Since but what I have had aSevere Spell of either one disorder or another; the Flux once and Ague twice; and now Dear Brother, I am Just through providence got Just So far as to be able to Sit up to writ you this, for about four weeks ago No one that Saw me would have believed that ever I Should have wrot More in this world,   I was Bedfast for Seven weeks of a Nervous fever, and Indeed hardly can I now Sit to writ you; but anxious desire to let you hear from Me once More, and God only knows but it May please him to Make it the last.[17] I would have thought that you would have wrot Me before this but Not a line have I Received from one[18] in Ireland, only old Uncle John, and Brother Johnney; But I expect that you will. My Most kind Compliments to Sister Betty, and Children,   I would be glad to know what Children each of you has gotten, and their Names.——My Respects to all old Neighbours, Friends, and former Acquaintances; and let them all know I yet live, and would be glad to hear from them all. While I Remain Dear Brother with ardent good Wishes for your health and Prosperity, Together with that of your family.

> Your Most Affectionate brother,
> Job Johnston[19]

Unlike the Caldwells,[20] Job Johnson did not prosper after the Revolution, although his wartime services—and his sacrifice of what he had once called "that Precious Jewel Health"[21]—were infinitely greater than theirs. Apparently, Johnson purchased—or received as a bounty for his service—1,500 acres in Fayette County, Kentucky, but between 1784 and 1790 he remained in Philadelphia, once again teaching school, most likely because his health was too shattered to enable him to move westward. When he died in 1790, he directed that his Kentucky lands be sold to pay his debts and funeral charges.[22] To his "loving brother William," he willed his personal property, consisting of clothes, a silver watch, books, a pewter inkstand, and a tomahawk—the latter no doubt a souvenir of his western campaigns—all of which had a total value of merely £6 18s. 3d.

17. God only knows but it May please him to Make it the last: "God only knows whether/if it may please him . . . "   18. one: "anyone."   19. See n. 1.   20. See chapter 58.   21. William and Job Johnson, 2 March 1766.   22. Unfortunately, Johnson's Kentucky deeds were probably worthless, for Virginia's government had sold, warranted, or granted as soldiers' bounties far more Kentucky lands than actually existed; the resulting uncertainty of land titles ensured a bonanza for lawyers and speculators but became a nightmare for ordinary settlers, most of whom were obliged to become mere tenants or squatters. In 1784–1786 Job Johnson also had warranted or had surveyed a total of 770 acres in Westmoreland Co., in western Pennsylvania; apparently, he had disposed of these lands by 1790, however, as they were not mentioned in his will.

David Redick and Ædanus Burke, 1787–1788

In 1787–1788 American politicians of Irish birth or descent were unusually prominent—especially in Pennsylvania—in the anti-Federalist opposition to the federal Constitution. For example, the Ulster-born Presbyterian William Findley of Westmoreland County was the probable author of one major anti-Federalist tract, styling himself "An Officer of the Late Continental Army."[1] Likewise, George Bryan of Philadelphia, the elderly Dublin-born revolutionary, probably wrote the essays signed "An Old Whig," in collaboration with John Smilie, Findley's backcountry associate and also from east Ulster, and James Hutchinson, a physician at the now Presbyterian-controlled College of Philadelphia. Finally, George Bryan's son, Samuel (b. 1759), was the likely author of the eighteen *Centinel* essays that made perhaps the most influential and sophisticated of all the arguments against the Constitution.[2]

To be sure, it is debatable whether the writings of these and other Irish-Americans differed from those authored by anti-Federalists of non-Irish backgrounds. Like other anti-Federalists, Findley, Smilie, and the Bryans portrayed the contest over ratification as a struggle between "democracy" and "aristocracy." They favored state sovereignty, annual elections, and rotation in office. They distrusted the "British" system of "mixed" government—of checks and balances to curb the popular will—that American conservatives idealized. And they feared that concentrated federal power, especially to tax and maintain a standing army, would lead inevitably to corruption and tyranny. Our government, Findley wrote to a friend, must be one of "confidence . . . Supported by affection arising from an apprehension of mutual interest," not one based on power, "fear and apprehension."[3]

Such sentiments were common among many rising "new men," Irish and non-Irish alike, who feared that the Constitutional Convention was a conspiracy to reestablish the rule of America's prewar mercantile and landed oligarchies. Similarly, virtually all farmers,

---

1. In the Philadelphia *Independent Gazetteer*, 6 November 1787. William Findley (1741–1821): born in east Ulster of Scots Covenanter descent, in 1763 Findley emigrated to Pennsylvania and settled in Waynesboro, where he worked as a weaver and schoolmaster until the American Revolution, when he rose to prominence as a member of his county's committee of observation and as a captain in the Continental forces; in 1783 Findley moved across the mountains and settled in Unity Township, Westmoreland Co., whence he was elected in 1783 to Pennsylvania's Council of Censors and in 1785–1788 to the General Assembly. In 1787 Findley was a delegate to the convention that (over his opposition) ratified the U.S. Constitution, and in 1789–1790 he was a member of both the state's Supreme Executive Council and of the convention that wrote Pennsylvania's second constitution. Adapting to new realities, Findley served as a member of Congress in 1790–1797 and again in 1804–1817 and became a major figure in his state's Republican party.   2. On John Smilie and George Bryan, see chapters 12 and 52, respectively. George Bryan's son, Samuel, no doubt titled his *Centinel* essays in emulation of those his father in 1768 had coauthored (with Rev. Francis Alison and John Dickinson) in opposition to an Anglican espiscopacy in the American colonies; on Alison, see chapter 55. 3. William Findley, Philadelphia, to General William Irvine, Congress, New York City, 12 March 1788.

Irish and non-Irish, who inhabited frontier districts wanted state laws, providing cheap paper money and debtor relief, that the new Constitution would prohibit. Conversely, the Irish in the seaport towns and their immediate hinterlands (and in the Valley of Virginia, linked by waterways to eastern markets) generally favored ratification. Likewise, those Irish who during the Revolution achieved officer status in the Continental Army (as opposed to the state militias) and who later joined the Order of the Cincinnati were thoroughly assimilated into the new nation's cosmopolitan élite and so supported the Federalist cause; this was as true of western Irishmen such as General William Irvine,[4] recipient of the first letter printed hereafter, as of Philadelphia merchant-soldiers like James Caldwell.[5]

Nevertheless, there was to anti-Federalism an ethnoreligious dimension that, conflated with regional and social factors, located most Irish immigrants and their offspring among the most vociferous opponents of the Constitution. The tracts written by Findley, Smilie, and the Bryans, for example, were unusual in their radical egalitarianism and their acceptance of the new "liberal" notion that society—in America as in Ireland—was characterized by a plurality of competing interest groups. Among the great majority of rural Irish-Americans, moreover, the longstanding and continued political and social conflicts between backcountry farmers and eastern merchants and planters nurtured a sense of estrangement and reinforced a fear of tyranny that had been imbibed in Ireland and rooted alike in the dissenter radicalism of Ulster Presbyterians and in the civil alienation of the island's Catholics. Thus, frontier experience had confirmed imported traits and predispositions and made the Irish of inland New Hampshire, upstate New York, western Pennsylvania, and the Carolina backcountry unusually suspicious of political power, particularly when concentrated in remote metropolitan centers and among landed and commercial élites whose ethnic complexion and prejudices, and whose ideas of order, hierarchy, and deference, were strikingly similar to those held by the Anglo-Irish governing classes as well as by former British officials in the American colonies. Beset in the 1780s by a troubled economy and exploited by eastern-based speculators, land companies, and merchants, the frontier Irish could view their marginal, neocolonial status in postwar America as not dissimilar to what they or their ancestors had fled in Ireland and endured in the New World before the Revolution. Thus, the anti-Federalist literature produced by men such as Findley and the Bryans rang with "scriptual citations, and with words and phrases with a biblical and a

---

4. William Irvine (1741–1804): born near Enniskillen, Co. Fermanagh, Irvine was educated at Trinity College, Dublin, and served as a British navy surgeon during the Seven Years War; in 1764 he settled in Carlisle, Pa., where he practiced medicine. Irvine held various commands in the Continental Army during the Revolution; in 1779 he was appointed brigadier general and in 1781 was entrusted with the defense of the Pennsylvania frontier. After the war Irvine invested heavily in western lands, especially near Erie, Pa. A moderate Federalist, Irvine was a delegate to the Continental Congress in 1786–1788, to Pennsylvania's state constitutional convention of 1789–1790, and to Congress in 1793–1795; in 1794 he commanded the Pennsylvania troops that helped quell the Whiskey Rebellion. Irvine was one of the first members of Pennsylvania's chapter of the Order of the Cincinnati and its president at the time of his death. 5. On Caldwell, see chapter 58.

DAVID REDICK AND ÆDANUS BURKE

Nonconformist . . . flavor," reminiscent of the works of Rev. Francis Alison and of other Presbyterian critics of Anglican establishments in both Ireland and prewar America.[6]

Indeed, the Federalists themselves confirmed their opponents' ethnicity, especially in Pennsylvania, identifying them as "Irish" and disparaging them as "the sons of Paxton," as transplanted "*white* boys," and as "foreign renagadoes," unworthy of citizenship, "[w]ithout a foot of land, in our country, or property of any kind."[7] Such associations between ethnicity, social inferiority, disorder, and disloyalty were particularly offensive to Irish immigrants such as Findley and Smilie, former small farmers, schoolmasters, or weavers who had risen from poverty to wealth through a combination of Revolutionary activity and western migration. Now, they feared, the Anglo-American aristocracy they had challenged or, in Pennsylvania, even overthrown in 1776 was plotting a constitutional counterrevolution that would restore the old political, social, and ethnoreligious hierarchies.

The following letters, written in 1787 and in 1788 by immigrants David Redick of Pennsylvania and Ædanus Burke of South Carolina, respectively, illustrate backcountry Irish opposition to the new Constitution. Little is known of Redick's early life. A Presbyterian, apparently he emigrated from east County Down shortly before the American Revolution and first settled in Lancaster County, Pennsylvania. Redick was still landless in 1779, when he first appears in the new state's tax records, but at some point he married Ann Hoge,[8] whose father and uncles, also from Ulster, owned several thousand acres in south-

6. On Alison, see chapter 55. The quotation re "scriptual citations" is from Ireland, *Religion, Ethnicity, & Politics*, 119; see Sources, chapter 62.   7. Ireland, *Religion, Ethnicity, & Politics*, 121, 128, 130; see Sources, chapter 62. For the significance of the Federalists' reference to "the sons of Paxton," see chapter 53. The Federalists' analogy between the overwhelmingly Protestant Irish anti-Federalists and the Whiteboys is even more revealing, for the latter were members of the almost exclusively-*Catholic* secret societies, composed of small farmers and laborers, that employed intimidation and violence to oppose economic exploitation in Ireland's southern counties during the 1760s, 1770s, and 1780s. Although most of the Whiteboys' activities were restrained and reflected intracommunal conflicts (e.g., over access to land, the levels of farm wages and of subtenants' rents), in the 1780s the protests of the Rightboys (the Whiteboys under a new name) against tithes provoked leading members of Ireland's "Protestant Ascendancy" into a ferocious ideological (as well as military) response that proved a harbinger of the militant "Orange" conservatism that crushed Irish reformers and radicals in the 1790s. ¶Interestingly, anti-Federalists also countered with ethnic slurs. For example, one essayist labeled James Wilson (1742–1798), one of Pennsylvania's leading Federalists, "James de Caledonia," thus seeking to tar the Scottish-born Wilson with the Revolutionary-era prejudices against Scots as loyalists and reactionaries. However, the prominence of Scots such as Wilson and Princeton president John Witherspoon (1723–1794) in the Federalists' ranks, coupled with their association of anti-Federalism with "Irishness," may have begun in the 1780s a reversal of both Irish and Scottish connotations: a revival of the former's traditionally negative associations that culminated in the 1790s with Federalist diatribes against the "wild Irish" and a new association between "Scottishness" and positive attributes such as order, self-discipline, and industry.   8. Ann Redick (d. 1817) was the daughter of Jonathan Hoge and the niece of David Hoge, Esq., who employed Redick to lay out Washington town on his lands. Jonathan Hoge was a member of the Pennsylvania Assembly in 1776, 1778–1782, and 1788–1789 and a member of the state's Supreme Executive Counitl in 1778–1779. David and Ann Redick had at least eight children: Jonathan; David, Jr., an attorney who died in 1810; James; Sally, who married Thomas Swearingen; Nancy, who wed Dr. James Stevens; Peggy, who married [John?] Israel, probably a son of Israel Israel (see n. 32); and Eliza.

western Pennsylvania. In 1781, when Washington County was created, Redick surveyed that portion of the Hoge estate that became Washington town, the county seat, where he and his family settled.

Thereafter, Redick's rise to wealth and political prominence was rapid. During the next decade, he and his sons acquired title to at least one thousand acres in Washington County, as well as larger speculations elsewhere in western Pennsylvania and in the Ohio country. In 1782 Redick was admitted to the bar and soon became, along with Findley and Smilie, one of George Bryan's "Irish colonels," defending the democratic 1776 state constitution against conservative assaults. In 1786 Redick was elected to Pennsylvania's Supreme Executive Council, membership in which obliged residence in Philadelphia during the summer and autumn of 1787, when the Convention that wrote the new federal Constitution was at work. Writing in late August to William Irvine, then a congressman in New York City, Redick alternated between "verry Sanguine hopes" that the new framework of national government would be "wholsome," or at least "tollorably So," and apprehension that "artfull, plausable men of influence," who "may not be lovers of mankind," were calculating "to raise a few at the expence of the many" and "Strike at the liberties of the people."[9] Publication of the Constitution confirmed Redick's fears, and on 24 September, just a few days before the Pennsylvania legislature began debating the Federalists' call for a quick election of delegates to a state ratifying convention, Redick declared to Irvine his objections both to the document and to its most vocal supporters—the affluent Quakers and Anglicans who had opposed the backcountry Irish quest for political power both before and during the Revolution.

Letter 1.
David Redick, Philadelphia,
to Congressman William Irvine, New York City, 24 September 1787

Philadelphia   24th Sep^t 1787

Dr S$^{<r>}$

The new plan of goverment proposed by the convention has made a bustle in the city & its vicinity.   all people, almost, are for Swallowing it down at once with out examining its tendencies.——

I have thought it unsafe within the wind of huracane to utter a Syllable about it: but to you Sir I may venture to Say that in my oppinion the day on which we adopt the present proposed plan of goverment, from that moment we may Justly state the loss of american liberty,   perhaps my fears hath contributed principlly to this oppinion. I will change the moment that I See better. My dear Sir why is not the liberty of the press provided for? why will the Congress have power to alter the plan or mode of choosing

9. David Redick, Philadelphia, to William Irvine, New York City, 29 August 1787.

Representatives? why will they have power to lay direct Taxes? why will <they> have power to keep Standing Armies in time of peace? why will they have power to make laws in direct contradiction to the forms of goverment established in the Several States? why will they have power to collect by law ten Dollars for ever<y> German or Irishman which may come to Settle in America?[10] why is the Trial by Jury destroy^{d} in Civil causes before Congress? and above all I cannot imagine why the people in this city are So verry anxious to have it adopted instantly before it can be digested or deliberatly considered. If you were only here to See and hear those people, to observe the Means they are useing to effect this purpose, to hear the tories declare they will draw their Sword in its defence<,> to See the quaquers runing about Signing declarations and Petitions in favor of it before the<y> have time to examine it, to See gentlemen runing into the Country and neibouring towns haranguing the Rabble, I Say were you to See and hear these things as I do you would Say, with me that the verry Soul of confidince itself ought to change into distrust. If this goverment be a good one or even a tollarable one the Necessaties and the good Sense of America will lead us to adopt it.   if otherwise give us time and it will be Amended and then adopted; but I think the measures pursued here is a strong evidence that these people know it will not bear an examination and therefor wishes to adopt it first and consider it afterward. I hope Congress will be verry deliberate and digest it thoroughly before they Send it recommended to the States. I Sincerely hope that Such Gentlemen as were Members of Convention, and who have Seats in Congress, may not be considered as verry proper Judges of their own Works.——

I Pray a Spirit of Wisdem and a Spirit of integrety prevade Congress, more especially at this time,

I am D^{r} S^{r} your Most ob^{t} and verry humble

S^{t}

David Redick

Redick's suspicion that the Federalists wished Pennsylvania's voters "to adopt [the Constitution] first and consider it afterward" was well grounded. Employing intimidation and mob violence, as well as a large legislative majority, the proponents of ratification rammed through a bill that provided for a special election in early November, before the state's anti-Federalists could mobilize their forces. Consequently, the Federalists won two-thirds of the convention seats, and despite the anguished protests of Findley, Smilie, and the other anti-Federalist delegates—at least half of whom were of Irish birth or descent

10. Foreign-born Anti-Federalists, such as Redick, were perhaps especially disposed to interpret the Constitution's article 1, section 9—which declared vaguely (without using the word "slaves") that Congress could levy a tax, not exceeding $10 each, on imported Africans—as giving Congress the power to impose a prohibitive duty on indentured servants and other immigrants from Europe.

and primarily from the western counties—on 12 December Pennsylvania became the second state to ratify the Constitution.

Anti-Federalist opposition was much stronger in South Carolina. Indeed, most historians agree with Ædanus Burke's contention that at least 80 percent of the state's white inhabitants opposed the Constitution and that only the grossly unrepresentative nature of South Carolina's electoral system enabled a minority of Charleston merchants and low-country planters to impose ratification on an angry backcountry. Ædanus Burke was born in County Galway in 1743, into a once-affluent Catholic family whose estates had been confiscated after the battle of the Boyne. After attending the Jesuit college of St. Omer, France, in about 1766 Burke emigrated to Virginia, where he studied law with Thomas Burke[11] and with the Dublin-born John Mercer (1704–1768), one of that colony's most successful lawyers. In early 1770 Burke returned to Ireland, but in 1775 he remigrated, after a sojourn in the West Indies, to Charleston, South Carolina. At some point Burke made an expeditious conversion to the Anglican faith—as even after 1778, when South Carolina disestablished the Church of England, the state's constitution still barred non-Protestants from elective office. However, the ethnic taunts of Burke's political opponents, as well as his hatred of England, his prominence in Charleston's Hibernian Society, and his boast of descent from "the old Milesian race"—all marked him as distinctively Irish.[12]

Despite his recent arrival in South Carolina, as "a volunteer to fight for American liberty"[13] Burke enjoyed rapid upward mobility through his adherence to the radical, pro-independence faction of the state's lowcountry Whigs. After brief service as an officer in both the militia and the Continental Army, in 1778 Burke was appointed a judge of the Court of Common Pleas and General Sessions, and in 1779 he was elected to the first of several terms in the South Carolina General Assembly. Although Burke resided in Charleston and usually represented lowcountry parishes in the state legislature, his judicial circuit included much of the heavily Scots-Irish backcountry, particularly the district of Ninety Six. Burke's political beliefs were more reflective of eighteenth-century republicanism, with its emphasis on virtue and its anticommercial bias, than were those of Presbyterian anti-Federalists, such as Redick and Findley, in the Middle States.[14] Nevertheless, in many respects Burke was more representative of South Carolina's raw and largely Scots-Irish frontier than of the state's genteel, tidewater society. For example, Burke's "Irish rollicking character" and hard drinking, as well as his compassion and fairness on the bench, won respect and affection from backcountry farmers, while both his "Irish bulls"—his conversational "blunders, vulgarisms and Hibernianisms"—and his opposition to "aristocracy" only earned contempt from the state's planter élite.[15]

11. On Thomas Burke, see chapter 54. 12. J. C. Meleney, *The Public Life of Aedanus Burke . . .* , 18; see Sources. Charleston's Hibernian Society was founded in 1799, and Burke was one of its first presidents.
13. J. C. Meleney, *The Public Life of Aedanus Burke . . .* , 23–24; see Sources. 14. On republicanism (or civic humanism) in eighteenth-century Ireland and America, see chapters 52 and 54. 15. J. C. Meleney, *The Public Life of Aedanus Burke . . .* , 25–26, 33; see Sources.

FIGURE 19
Portrait of Ædanus Burke
(1743–1802), of Charleston,
South Carolina. Permission
to reproduce this photograph
courtesy of the Hibernian
Society of South Carolina,
Charleston.

In 1783 Burke gained national attention and signaled his deep suspicion of those who would become his Federalist opponents when he published a pamphlet that accused the recently formed Order of the Cincinnati of conspiring to overthrow the fragile new republic. Thus, although on 19 January 1788 Burke voted with a majority of South Carolina's legislators to authorize the election of delegates to a state ratifying convention, on 12 April he won a convention seat, from an upland district, as an avowed opponent of the federal Constitution. In mid-May, while the Charleston convention was in progress, John Lamb,[16] one of New York's leading anti-Federalists, sent letters to Burke and likeminded

16. John Lamb (1735–1800): born in New York City, Lamb was a manufacturer of mathematical instruments and a wine merchant who, during the Stamp Act crisis, emerged as a primary leader of the city's Sons of Liberty. Thereafter, Lamb was one of New York's most radical politicians. In 1783 Congress appointed him a brigadier general, and in 1784 the New York legislature named him customs collector for New York City. In 1787–1788 Lamb led the city's anti-Federalists and corresponded extensively with Patrick Henry, Richard

South Carolinians, proposing interstate cooperation against ratification. Unfortunately, Burke did not receive Lamb's letter until mid-June and, as he explained in the following reply, by that time the contest was over—thanks, Burke implied, to local British and ex-Tory influence and to the national machinations of George Washington and of the Order of the Cincinnati.

Letter 2.
Ædanus Burke, Charleston, South Carolina,
to John Lamb, New York City, 23 June 1788

Charleston 23[d] June 1788

Sir,

Your favour of the 19th of May I received the 18th of June inst.[17] That it came not to hand Sooner, I cannot account for; however, it came too late; for our Convention had acceded to the new Constitution on the 24th of May by a Majority of <149.> The minority consisting of 73.

It is now unnecessary perhaps to state to you the different causes, whereby the new Plan has been carried in South Carolina, notwithstanding $\frac{4}{5}$ of the people do, from their Souls detest it. I am convinced, from my Knowledge of the Country, that I am rather under, than over,[18] that proportion. In the first place, we in the Opposition, had not, previous to our Meeting, either wrote, or spoke, hardly a word against it, nor took any one step in the matter. We had no principle of concert or union, while its friends and abettors left no expedient untried to push it forward. All the rich, leading men, along the Seacoast, and rice settlements; with few exceptions, Lawyers, P<h>ysicians and Divines, the merchants, mechanicks, the Populace, and mob of Charleston. I think it worthy of Observation that not a Single instance in S[o]. Carolina of a Man formerly a Tory, or British adherent, who is not loud and zealous for the new Constitution. From the British Consul[19] (who is the most violent Man I know for it) down to the British Scavenger, all are boisterious to drive it down.[20] Add to this, the whole weight and influence of the Press was in that Scale. Not a printing press, in Carolina, out of the City. The printers are, in general, British journeymen, or poor Citizens who are afraid to offend the great men, or Merchants, who could work their

Henry Lee, and other leading opponents of ratification. Nevertheless, in 1789 President Washington appointed Lamb to the federal collectorship of New York port; but in 1797 a scandal forced his resignation and bankruptcy, and he died in poverty.   **17. June inst.:** this June.   **18. I am rather under, than over:** "I underestimate rather than overestimate."   **19. the British consul:** George Miller, stationed in Charleston as British consul for the Carolinas and Georgia, publicly urged ratification of the Constitution shortly before the South Carolina convention began its deliberations.   **20. boisterous to drive it down:** "noisy/violent in their efforts to force it on us."

DAVID REDICK AND ÆDANUS BURKE

ruin. Thus, with us, the press is in the hands of a junto, and the Printers, with most Servile insolence discouraged Opposition, and pushed forward publications in its favour; for no one wrote against it.

But the principle cause was holding the Convention in the City, where there are not fifty Inhabitants who are not friendly to it. The Merchants and leading Men kept open houses for the back and low country Members during the whole time the Convention sat. The sixth day after we sat, despatches arrived, bringing an account that Maryland had acceded to the Scheme.[21] This was a Severe blow to us; for next day, one of our best speakers in the Opposition, Doctor Fousseaux,[22] gave notice he would quit that ground, as Maryland had acceded to it. Upon which we were every day afterwards losing ground & numbers going over to the Enemy, on an idea that further Opposition was useless. But notwithstanding these Misfortunes, the few of us who spoke, General Sumpter,[23] Mr. John Bowman,[24] a gentleman of fortune and fine talents, of the low-country; myself and a few of the back country men, found it necessary, in supporting the Opposition, to exert the greater spirit and resolution, as our difficulties increased. Our Minority is a respectable one, and I can with great truth assure you, that it represents by far a greater number of Citizens than the Majority——The minority are chiefly from the back Country where the Strength and numbers of our republick lie——And although the Vote of the Convention has carried it, that has not changed the opinion of the great body of people respecting its evil tendency. In the interiour Country, all is disgust, sorrow, and vindictive reproaches against the System, and those who voted for it. It is true, the ratification of it was solemnized in our City, with splended procession and Shew. We hear from the back Country, however That in some places the people had a coffin painted black, which,

---

21. The South Carolina convention convened on 12 May; on 16 May the Charleston *City Gazette* reported that Maryland had ratified the Constitution on 28 April.   22. Doctor Fousseaux: Dr. Peter Fayssoux (1745–1795): born in Charleston of French Huguenot parentage, Fayssoux studied medicine at the University of Edinburgh and served in the American Revolution as senior physician to the American forces; an occasional member of the South Carolina legislature, in 1789 Fayssoux cofounded the Medical Society of South Carolina. 23. General Sumpter: Thomas Sumter (1734–1832): after serving in the French and Indian War, Sumter settled in the South Carolina backcountry, at Eutaw Springs, where he became a merchant and planter. During the Revolution Sumter was one of the most celebrated leaders of the patriot militias that fought the occupying British forces and their loyalist allies; after retiring with the rank of brigadier general, in 1781–1788 Sumter served in the South Carolina legislature, championing the backcountry's unsuccessful demand for paper money. Like that of his former comrade, Col. Thomas Taylor (see hereafter), Sumter's anti-Federalism in 1787–1788 stemmed largely from his wartime resentments against the superior airs assumed by Continental Army officers in South Carolina. After ratification, Sumter served in the U.S. Congress in 1789–1793 and (as a Republican) in 1797–1801, and in the U.S. Senate in 1801–1810.   24. John Bowman (ca. 1745–1807): born in Scotland and educated in law and medicine at Edinburgh and Paris, about 1766 Bowman emigrated to South Carolina where he married a sister of Thomas Lynch, Jr. (1749–1779), a signer of the Declaration of Independence, and became a wealthy rice planter at Peach Island on the Santee River.

borne in funeral procession, was solemnly buried, as an emblem of the dissolution and interment of public Liberty. You may rely upon it if a fair Opportunity offers itself to our back Country men they will join heart and hand to bring Ruin on the new Plan unless it be materially altered. They declare so publickly: They feel that they are the very men, who, as mere Militia, half-armed and half-clothed have fought and defeated the British regulars in sundry encounters————They think that after having disputed and gained the Laurel under the banners of Liberty, now, that they are likely to be robbed both of the honour and the fruits of it, by a Revolution purposely contrived for it. I know some able Men among us, or such as are thought so, affect to despise the general Opinion of the Multitude: For my own part I think that that Government rests on a very sandy foundation, the Subjects whereof are convinced that it is a bad one. Time alone will convince us.

This is the first time that I ever put pen to paper on the Subject, (to another) and it is not for want of inclinaton to do it. Nobody views this matter from the point of light and view in which I see it; or if any one did, he must be crazy, if he told his mind. The true, open, rising ground, no one has dared to take, or will dare to do it, 'till the business is all over. If you live two or three years, you will find the World will ascribe to the right Author,[25] this whole affair, and put the saddle on the right Horse, as we say. I find myself approaching too near to forbidden ground, and must desist. I am sorry it hath been my Lot not to be able to serve the Repub<lic> on the present Business. Virginia and New York adopting it (and of which I have no doubt) they will proceed to put it into Motion, and then you, and I, and all of us, will be obliged to take it, as we take our Wives, "for better, for worse". I have only one remark to make—Should any event turn up with you, that would require to be known to our republican Friends here, only make us acquainted with it. Should either Virginia or New York State reject it, the system will fall to pieces, tho other nine States may agree to it, and in such an Event, or in any other that may give us an occasion to serve the Repub<lic> your communication will be duly attended to by me. I forgot to mention, that Mr Lowndes,[26] would not serve in the Convention, declining to take his Seat; out

---

25. the right Author: i.e. George Washington, Burke's bête noire.   26. Mr Lowndes: Rawlins Lowndes (1721–1800): born in St. Kitts in the British West Indies, in 1730 Lowndes emigrated with his parents to South Carolina; although he was soon orphaned, a fortunate marriage brought him wealth, and in 1749 he won election to the General Assembly, of which he was speaker in 1763–1765 and 1772–1775. Albeit a strong opponent of British taxes and royal governors, Lowdes was a reluctant revolutionary and, although he served as his state's president in 1778–1779, he petitioned for reinstatement as a British subject during Cornwallis's occupation of Charleston. The Revolution brought Lowndes to the brink of financial and political ruin, but afterward he rebuilt his fortune and in 1787 won election to the South Carolina legislature. Lowndes's opposition to the Constitution was due primarily to his fear that the federal government would be controlled by anti-slavery Northerners. In 1789–1790 Lowndes ended his political career as mayor of Charleston.

of disgust to some leading men in the parish that Sent him, he abandoned a Cause, which, I believe, he thought a just one.

M^r. John Bowman is capable of serving any Cause he espouses. Col. Thomas Taylor of the Congarees[27]—Col Richard and Wade Hampton.[28]——These three are from the back Country; their gallantry in the War, their property, and Some talents, give them great influence in that part of the Country.

With great respect, I am Sir,

Your most obed^t humb^l Servt

Æ^s. Burke

With varying degrees of success and consistency, after 1787–1788 David Redick and Ædanus Burke continued their opposition to Federalist hegemony, and their subsequent careers overlapped and to a degree interacted with the more radical and more overtly ethnic Irish-American politics of the 1790s. As a "cautious democrat,"[29] Redick's later course was marked by inconsistency or ambivalence, perhaps reflecting his status in western Pennsylvania's infant aristocracy, many of whose members—especially in Washington town—were Federalists. Although he publicly urged acquiescence to the now-adopted Constitution, the Federalists accused him—along with Findley and Smilie—of instigating popular resistance to the new government. Certainly, Redick's initial opposition to ratification, as also to the Federalists' campaign for a new, less democratic state constitution, marked him for political punishment. Thus, although in October 1788 Redick served for a few weeks as Pennsylvania's vice-president, following the incumbent's early resignation, in November the Federalists denied him reelection. In 1790 Washington County's voters sent Redick to the state constitutional convention, but again Redick was in the minority, helpless to stem the Federalist tide. Redick never again held statewide office, but in 1791–1792 he was named prothonotary and clerk of the Washington County courts and later was appointed to survey and plat the lands adjacent to Pittsburgh.

27. **Col. Thomas Taylor** (1743–1833): born in Virginia, in 1754 Taylor migrated to backcountry South Carolina and settled in Camden District, at the future site of Columbia, on the Congeree River. Taylor served in South Carolina's first and second provincial congresses, as a militia colonel during the Revolution, and periodically thereafter as a state legislator. **28. Col. Richard . . . Hampton** (d. 1792): in 1774 Richard Hampton migrated with his kinfolk from Virginia to South Carolina, where he became a backcountry trader, eventually a wealthy planter; during the Revolution Hampton was colonel of the Orangeburgh District militia and afterward served in the upper house of the state legislature. His more famous and wealthier brother, **Wade Hampton** (1754–1835), served in 1782–1791 in the South Carolina legislature, where he championed increased political representation and economic development for the backcountry. Although he was an anti-Federalist delegate to his state's ratifying convention in 1788, Wade Hampton was elected to Congress in 1795 and 1803 and served as U.S. military commander in New Orleans in 1809–1811; he also took part in the disastrous American invasion of Canada in 1813. At his death, Hampton owned vast plantations and about one thousand slaves in South Carolina and Louisiana. **29.** R. Walters, Jr., "Spokesman of Frontier Democracy . . . ," 162; see Sources.

Along with Findley, Smilie, and the Swiss-born Albert Gallatin,[30] in the early 1790s Redick was an early leader of what became the Republican party in western Pennsylvania. Inspired by the French Revolution and calling themselves the "Friends of the Rights of Man," Redick and his associates organized and encouraged their region's opposition to Hamilton's economic policies, particularly to the 1791 excise on whiskey.[31] Likewise, Redick was a founding member of Washington town's Democratic-Republican Society—one of three in Washington County, all predominantly Irish.[32] In 1794, however, when popular animosity to the Whiskey Tax escalated into the Whiskey Rebellion, Redick quickly became "prominent in defense of law, order, and the constitution": he resigned his membership in the Democratic-Republican society, denounced the Whiskey rebels' "dreadful deeds," and joined William Findley in efforts to quell the agitation and so persuade President Washington that military intervention was unnecessary.[33] Chastened by the invasion of federal troops into western Pennsylvania and by renewed accusations that he had abetted "treason" and "anarchy," thereafter Redick drifted away from democratic politics and into increased land speculation, often in association with Scots-Irish Federalists such as William Irvine, his correspondent in 1787. Ironically, by 1796 Redick was embroiled with his tenants in bitter conflicts over rents, even threatening to use the state militia to evict them. Only after the 1800 election did Redick reemerge as an energetic Republican, and perhaps his youthful ardor for "the Rights of Man" had been rekindled not only by Jefferson's victory but also by the arrival in Washington town of Rev. Thomas Ledlie Birch, Redick's

30. Albert Gallatin (1761–1849): born in Geneva, Switzerland, Gallatin emigrated in 1780 and settled in the Pennsylvania backcountry, serving in 1790–1792 as a member of the state legislature and becoming a principal leader of western Pennsylvania's nascent Republican party. In 1793 Gallatin won election to the U.S. Senate, but its Federalist majority refused to seat him on the grounds that he had not been an American citizen for nine years. However, in 1795–1801 Gallatin served as a congressman and as Republican minority leader in the House and later became secretary of the treasury (1801–1814) under presidents Jefferson and Madison. **31.** Redick and some of his affluent friends may have had personal reasons for fomenting popular opposition to Hamilton's excise; for example, Redick's in-laws, the Hoges, were among the largest whiskey distillers in the region. **32.** The most radical and militant Democratic-Republican Society in western Pennsylvania, perhaps in the entire nation, was that of Mingo Creek, in Washington County. Formally named the Society of United Freeman, perhaps in emulation of the Society of United Irishmen in Ireland itself, the Mingo Creek society met in a Presbyterian meetinghouse, allegedly to plot the murder of excise collectors and rebellion against Federal authorities. ¶Redick was a member of the more moderate Democratic Society of Washington town; indeed, in 1795 he claimed that one of his purposes in founding the Society was "to prevent the people from undue influence at elections" (E. P. Link, *Democratic-Republican Societies . . .* , 202; see Sources). However, the vice-president of Redick's Society was David Bradford, who became a leader of the Whiskey Rebellion. William Hoge, Redick's brother-in-law, was treasurer; and Redick himself was a member of the corresponding committee. ¶Redick was also a leading member of Washington town's Masonic Lodge No. 54, the membership of which overlapped with that of the Democratic-Republican Society and also included kinsmen by marriage such as John Hoge and the son of Israel Israel (1745?–1822), Pennsylvania's grand master and a leader of Philadelphia's Republicans. **33.** B. Crumline, *History of Washington County*, 479; W. Miller, "The Democratic Societies and the Whiskey Insurrection," 344; see Sources.

fellow east Down Presbyterian and an exiled United Irishman.[34] Birch engaged the local Presbyterian clergy, virtually all arch-Federalists, in fierce battles for the region's political soul, although the church's future belonged to the conservative evangelicals.[35] On 28 September 1805, in the midst of the strife, David Redick died at his Washington County farm.

Ædanus Burke's political principles and record were more consistent than Redick's, perhaps because the former's reputation as an "unpredictable, hot-tempered, sometime rough Irishman" made him an isolated, idiosyncratic figure among South Carolina's haughty planters.[36] In autumn 1788 Burke won election from Beaufort and Orangeburgh districts to the new federal Congress, but he served only a single, frustrating term. Burke's failure to secure Constitutional amendments that would restore authority to the states, as well as his intense dislike for Hamilton and his financial policies, made the unreconciled anti-Federalist even more convinced that ratification of the Constitution had been the first "stage in the progess of a conspiracy" to destroy popular liberties.[37] After returning to South Carolina and resuming his judicial post, Burke further alienated the state's wealthy Federalists by supporting the French Revolution and embracing Edmund Genet, the inflammatory French ambassador to the United States. In 1794–1795 Burke strongly opposed Jay's Treaty and formed a political alliance with the Irish-born Pierce Butler, a wealthy lowcountry planter and former-Federalist-turned-Republican who, like Burke, believed that the Treaty was designed by scheming "Anglomen" who desired "returning under the British Yoke."[38] Burke survived the "dread and panic"[39] that the Federalists' Alien and Sedition Acts of 1798 inspired among Irish-born immigrants, and two years later he welcomed Jefferson's electoral victory. However, he died at his Charleston home on 30 March 1802. Never married, Burke left bequests to two Irish mistresses and one illegitimate son

34. Thomas Ledlie Birch (1754–1828): born in Gilford, Co. Down, and educated at the University of Glasgow, in 1776 Birch was ordained Presbyterian minister at Saintfield, Co. Down, where he was an enthusiastic supporter of the American Revolution and chaplain to the local Volunteer corps. Although theologically conservative, from the 1780s Birch advocated total Catholic emancipation and radical political reform; he became a member of Society of United Irishmen and participated in the 1798 Rebellion; exiled to Philadelphia in 1799, the following year Birch moved to Washington, Pa., where his political radicalism and contempt for New Side evangelicalism embroiled him in continual controversies with the Presbyterian clergy, especially with Rev. John McMillan (1752–1833), who in the 1790s had been western Pennsylvania's chief clerical antagonist to the Democratic-Republican societies, the Whiskey Rebellion, and the Republican party. On McMillan, also see chapter 67. **35.** On Presbyterianism in western Pennsylvania and elsewhere in the early 1800s, see chapters 47, 65, and 67. **36.** J. C. Meleney, *The Public Life of Aedanus Burke . . .* , 205; see Sources. **37.** Ibid., 177. **38.** Pierce Butler (1744–1822): an Anglican born in Co. Carlow, in 1771 Butler emigrated to South Carolina, where he was a state legislator in 1778–1782 and 1784–1789, and a fairly consistent champion of backcountry interests, although he resided in the coastal parish of Prince William. In 1787 Butler was a member of the U.S. Constitutional Convention and subsequently supported ratification, but later he became alienated from Hamilton's domestic and foreign policies and joined the Republican opposition. In 1789 and in 1792 Butler was elected to the U.S. Senate, but in 1796 he resigned to protest Federalist measures; he was reelected to the Senate in 1802 but resigned again in 1806. J. C. Meleney, *The Public Life of Aedanus Burke . . .* , 226, 232; see Sources. **39.** Ibid, 237.

and donated the rest of his property to aid poor Irish immigrants in South Carolina—a legacy that in 1818 became the trust of Charleston's Hibernian Society, dominated by former United Irishmen such as John O'Raw.[40]

63 ❋

Daniel McCurtin, 1798

The end of the American Revolution had unleashed a small flood of Irish emigration to the new United States. In 1783 at least five thousand Irishmen and -women left Ireland, in 1784 perhaps three or four times that number, and for the next three decades—until the Anglo-American war of 1812–1815 closed the sea lanes—annual departures averaged between three thousand and five thousand. Economically, the new immigrants generally prospered, usually as settlers on America's western frontiers but also in growing seaports such as Philadelphia, New York, and Baltimore. During the 1790s perhaps 27,000 Irish immigrants disembarked on the banks of the Delaware River, still their primary American destination, and approximately one-third of them remained in Philadelphia, helping to swell the city's population from 44,096 in 1790 to 61,559 in 1800. By the end of the eighteenth century, at least 12 percent of greater Philadelphia's inhabitants were Irish-born.

It is arguable that the Irish who emigrated after the Revolution—predominantly "comfortable farmers" and craftsmen, observers alleged, rather than indentured servants— were more affluent, skilled, and literate than their immediate predecessors of the early 1770s. It is also likely that they were more politically aware and sophisticated. Emigrants from Ulster and Leinster, whence came the great majority of the "new Irish," had experienced the nationalist fervor of the Patriot and Volunteer movements of 1778–1783, as well as the deep disillusionment that followed the Irish government's rejection in 1784 of both parliamentary reform and protective tariff legislation. In 1789 the example and ideals of the French Revolution rekindled agitation for political reform and, especially among Catholics, for repeal of the Penal Laws. From the late 1780s, large numbers of Catholics, particularly in mid-Ulster, were politicized through involvement in the Defender movement; and from its founding in 1791 perhaps as many as a half-million Protestants and Catholics— largely in the areas most prone to emigration—joined the Society of United Irishmen. Even prior to the 1798 Rebellion, government and loyalist repression forced many United Irishmen to flee to the United States, where the ecumenical spirit that characterized Irish republicanism was reinforced by Federalist hostility toward Irish Protestants and Catholics alike.

---

40. On O'Raw, see chapter 13.

For nearly a decade after 1783, Irish immigrants could anticipate a warm welcome in what many Irish newspapers touted as an American "asylum" where there was work, peace, religious freedom, and political liberty for all. In Dublin, Belfast, and Cork, radical Irish journalists such as Mathew Carey, Denis Driscol,[1] and John Daly Burk[2] wrote glowingly of "the land of liberty and brotherly love," of that "thrice happy America"[3] where eventually all three men would be exiled for their political activities at home. Likewise, during the 1780s Irish immigrants in their personal letters promised that newcomers would find the United States a congenial political clime as well as a "land of opportunity." "They are very fond of Irish Emigration here," assured one Ulsterman from Virginia in 1785; "it is Given as a Toast often at their Fairs," as the Americans "much applaud the Irish for their . . . Spirit of Independence."[4]

In reality, however, American politics in the eighteenth century's last decades were disappointing, sometimes bitterly disillusioning: both to the "old Irish" who had immigrated prior to 1776 and settled mainly in the backcountry and, especially, to the "new Irish" who disembarked in the late 1780s and the 1790s. In 1787–1788 most of the old

1. Denis Driscol (sometimes O'Driscol): born in 1762 into a Catholic family in Co. Cork, Driscol studied in Spain for the priesthood, but in 1789 he conformed to the Church of Ireland and became a curate in one of Cork city's Anglican churches and editor of the *Cork Gazette*. In 1791–1792 he lost his curacy, espoused the French Revolution, deism, and Irish nationalism and embarked on a career in radical journalism. One of the few United Irishmen who called for sweeping agrarian as well as political reforms, in 1794–1796 Driscol was imprisoned for seditious libel. On his release he played a major role in forging links between the United Irishmen and the Catholic peasants of Munster, but his precise role in the 1798 rising is unknown. In early 1799 he fled Dublin for New York, where he edited the *Temple of Reason*, Elihu Palmer's deist newspaper. Later Driscol migrated to Philadelphia, then to Baltimore, and finally to Augusta, Georgia, where from 1804 he published the *Augusta Chronicle*, a Republican newspaper. In America Driscol—like his friend John Daly Burk (see n. 2)—openly opposed slavery, although he muted his sentiments after moving to Georgia. **2.** John Daly Burk (1772–1808): the son of a Co. Cork schoolmaster, Burk was raised a member of the Church of Ireland and prepared for college by Rev. Paul Limerick of Cork city, the son or nephew of Rev. James MacSparran's correspondent in 1752 (see chapter 8). In 1792 Burk entered Trinity College, Dublin, where he joined the United Irishmen, wrote radical articles for the *Dublin Evening Post*, and tried to convert fellow students to deism. Expelled from Trinity in 1794, Burk spent the next two years organizing political clubs in working-class Dublin's radical underworld, devising the cellular structure later adopted by the United Irishmen as the basis of their military organization. In the spring of 1796, after several comrades had been arrested and executed, Burk fled to America, writing his first play, *Bunker-Hill; or The Death of General Warren,* on shipboard. Initially Burk settled in Boston, where his play was first performed, and published the *Polar Star,* the first daily newspaper in the United States. Burk's Republican and pro-French views were unwelcome in Federalist Boston, and in 1797 he moved to New York, where he edited another Republican party paper, the *Time Piece*, violently attacking the Adams administration until August 1798, when he was arrested for sedition. Bailed out by Aaron Burr, Burk fled to Amelia Co., Virginia, where he lived in hiding, writing a *History of the Late War in Ireland*, until after Jefferson's election. Although disappointed in his bid for a federal appointment in return for his sufferings in the Republican cause, Burk settled happily in Petersburg, Va., became a lawyer, married, and began to publish his monumental *History of Virginia* before he was killed in a duel with a Frenchman, whose nation he blamed for the failure of the 1798 Rebellion. **3.** *Volunteer's Journal* (Dublin), 10 November 1784; Durey, *Transatlantic Radicals*, 164–65; see Sources. **4.** John Joyce, Portobago Bay, Caroline Co., Va., to Rev. Robt. Dickson, Narrow Water, near Newry, Co. Down, 24 March 1785; see Sources, chapter 63.

frontier Irish in Pennsylvania, the Carolinas, even in New Hampshire, opposed the ratification of the federal Constitution, and in 1789–1790 those in Pennsylvania were doubly chagrined when the Federalists overthrew the state's first constitution. In addition, both old and new Irish generally despised the financial and foreign policies of the Washington administration: the Whiskey Tax of 1791, which burdened frontier farmers; the Land Act of 1796, which favored eastern (and usually Federalist) speculators over western settlers; and the Neutrality Proclamation of 1793 and, especially, Jay's Treaty of 1794, the latter of which, many Irish believed, effectively allied the American government with England against the French Revolution and against those in Ireland who sought French assistance to overthrow British rule.

In both seaport cities and western settlements, old and new Irish immigrants flocked into the new Democratic-Republican societies organized to oppose Federalist policies. In Philadelphia and New York City during the summer of 1793, pro-French mobs, largely composed of Irish-Americans, rioted against the Neutrality Proclamation, and in the following year Irish and other farmers on the frontiers of Pennsylvania, Maryland, Kentucky, and Ohio staged the abortive Whiskey Rebellion against Hamilton's hated excise. With Irish support, in late 1794 the nascent Republican party won key Congressional election victories in Philadelphia and New York City, and in 1795–1796 those cities' Irish-born politicians and emigré journalists played leading roles in the campaign to repudiate Jay's Treaty. But despite their efforts, Congress ratified and funded the Treaty, and in late 1796 the presidential election victory of John Adams unleashed a firestorm of Federalist nativism and persecution of Irish Republicans. Thus, in 1798, while United Irish rebels died by the thousands at home—struggling, as their exiled spokesmen claimed, for the principles of 1776—the Federalists in Congress passed the Alien and Sedition Acts to crush dissent and a new Naturalization Act that increased the residency requirement for citizenship and suffrage rights to 14 years: all three laws designed primarily to banish or exclude from politics the "hordes of wild Irishmen" who threatened Federalist hegemony.[5] Only in 1799–1800 did the tide begin to turn: first in Pennsylvania, where Thomas McKean,[6] a moderate Republican of Ulster parentage, won election as state governor; and nationally a year later when Thomas Jefferson was elected president with overwhelming Irish-American support.

The sense of betrayal shared by politicized Irish immigrants in the 1790s can be seen most clearly in the editorials and other publications by exiled journalists such as John Daly Burk, one of several Irish victims of the Federalists' Alien and Sedition laws, who recalled with bitter irony how in 1775 John Adams himself had drafted the Continental Congress's *Address . . . to the People of Ireland*, appealing for Irish support against the British government's "iniquitous schemes of extirpating liberty" in the colonies. Alas, Burk lamented,

---

5. E. C. Carter II, "A 'Wild Irishman' under Every Federalist's Bed . . . ," 334; see Sources.   6. On McKean, see chapter 55 n. 42.

the Irish emigrés' belief in "the supposed congeniality between their principles and those of the [United States] government" had been sadly mistaken.[7] Unfortunately, thanks to Irish government censorship of the mails in the 1790s, there is very little surviving transatlantic correspondence that reveals candidly the personal political sentiments of Irishmen and of Irish-Americans during the era of the French Revolution. In Ireland no doubt more than one correspondent felt obliged, as did Samuel Rogers of County Cavan in 1798, to write "GOD SAVE THE KING" across his letter, to ensure it reached its American destination.[8] Thus, among the few sources of privately expressed political opinions during this era are the letters of the Dublin-born exile and Philadelphia journalist Mathew Carey (1760–1839), whose messages to and from Ireland were often hand-carried across the ocean by friends and relations.[9]

In late 1784 Carey, the son of a wealthy Catholic baker, fled Irish government prosecution for the inflammatory editorials in his radical Dublin newspaper, the *Volunteer's Journal*. Settling in Philadelphia, in 1785 Carey commenced publishing the *Pennsylvania Evening Herald*; in 1787–1792 he would issue the *American Museum*, for a time the nation's most influential magazine. By the early nineteenth century Carey would be the leading publisher in the United States, nurturing his adopted country's historical myths and literary fashions through books such as Parson Weems's biographies of American heroes and James Fenimore Cooper's Leatherstocking novels. Well before his death in 1839, Carey would be honored by native American businessmen and politicians for his promotion of the Bank of the United States, high protective tariffs, and manufacturing.

In fact, from his very arrival in Philadelphia Carey had been an ardent American nationalist and proponent of economic development. In an age of Federalist paranoia, however, Carey's democratic ideals, Irish origins, and intense Anglophobia soon engendered harsh criticism, especially from pro-British journalists who charged: "As well might we attempt to tame the Hyena, as to Americanize an Irishman."[10] Thus, nativist reaction, as well as his own sympathies, encouraged Carey's emergence as ethnic leader of Philadelphia's new Irish immigrants. Indeed, Carey became a key link between the old Irish-American politics of the 1770s and 1780s and the new Irish-American radicalism of the 1790s. Although in 1787–1788 Carey supported ratification of the U.S. Constitution, he was close friends with many of Pennsylvania's leading Irish anti-Federalists, such as William Findley, Blair McClenachan, and the elderly George Bryan,[11] all of whom became charter

---

7. [Continental Congress], *An Address . . . to the People of Ireland* (Philadelphia, 1775), 10; Wilson, *United Irishmen*, 52–53; J. I. Shulim, "John Daly Burk . . . ," 35; see Sources, chapter 63.   **8.** Samuel Rogers, near Cootehill, Co. Cavan, to Jane Rogers, Washington, Ky., 24 July 1798; see Sources.   **9.** On Mathew Carey, see also chapters 14, 34–35, and 44.   **10.** Wilson, *United Irishmen*, 47; see Sources.   **11.** On Bryan and Findley, see chapters 52, 55, and 62 (esp. n. 1 on Findley). Blair McClenachan (d. 1812): a Presbyterian born in Co. Derry, McClenachan emigrated before the Revolution to Philadelphia, where he engaged in transatlantic trade, and during the war he became wealthy through military contracts, smuggling, and privateering. Despite his affluence and his business associations with Robert Morris, in the late 1770s and 1780s McClenachan supported George Bryan's Constitutionalists. In 1788 McClenachan was described as "the most violent anti-

members of the Hibernian Society for the Relief of Emigrants that Carey organized in Philadelphia in 1790. Although primarily a charitable organization, the Hibernian Society also served Carey's social and political goals: it mobilized the city's new Irish middle classes—the shopkeepers and manufacturers excluded from membership in the old, élite Friendly Sons of St. Patrick—and in the early and mid-1790s it led many of them into the Democratic-Republican societies and the agitation against Jay's Treaty. Later in the decade, at least a few Hibernian Society members, probably including Carey himself, also joined the American Society of United Irishmen, a shadowy support group for the revolutionaries in Dublin and Belfast.[12] Contemporary estimates of its size and influence varied widely, but in 1798 the Society and its purported threat to American institutions became the primary target of Federalist journalists and of official persecution.

At the beginning of the 1790s, however, Carey was still boundlessly optimistic about America's political future under its new Constitution and president, George Washington, whom Carey revered. Writing in 1791 to his friend, John Chambers, Dublin's wealthiest printer and a leading United Irishman,[13] Carey predicted that within three years the "happiness in this Country will be greater than any other Country under heaven."[14] "Remote from the Tyranny and ambition of Kings," he wrote, "we shall afford an example of the heights to which human felicity can be carried by good governments."[15] At first Chambers agreed, reporting that the American Constitution was "still more & more admired" in Ireland,[16] but by early March 1794, after Britain had declared war on the French Republic and begun a campaign of repression against Irish and British reformers, Chambers warned

federalist in America" and thereafter he became an equally vociferous Republican. At a public meeting in 1794, McClenachan, then president of the Democratic Society of Pennsylvania, symbolically linked the "old" and the "new" Irish politics when he embraced United Irish exile Archibald Hamilton Rowan and urged his largely Irish audience to "kick this damn [Jay's] treaty to hell," precipitating a major riot. In 1790–1795 McClenachan served in Pennsylvania's legislature, and in 1796 he won a seat in Congress, sweeping the Irish vote in the working-class Philadelphia suburbs of Southwark and the Northern Liberties. Wilson, *United Irishmen*, 41; see Sources.   **12.** According to Irish government informers, United Irish sympathizers in the United States smuggled gunpowder in flaxseed casks to Ulster and Dublin.   **13.** John Chambers (1754–1837): Chambers was a member of the Church of Ireland and the son of a Dublin wine merchant. After completing an apprenticeship, Chambers became Dublin's finest printer, with premises at 5 Abbey Street; from 1793 he was master of his guild, in 1789–1798 a member of Dublin's city council, and in 1797 a director of the Bank of Ireland. A founding member of the Society of United Irishmen in Dublin, Chambers was a member of its Leinster Directory when he was arrested in March 1798. Imprisoned in 1798–1802 at Ft. George, Scotland, with Thomas Addis Emmet, William James Macneven, and other United Irish leaders (see chapter 66), at his release he went to France and in 1805 remigrated to New York City, where he prospered on Wall Street as a printer and stationer. Active in New York Republican Party and Irish-American circles, in 1816 Chambers vainly petitioned Congress, on behalf of the New York Association for the Relief of Emigrant Irishmen, for a large land grant in Illinois to provide farms for poor Irish immigrants. In 1828–1833 Chambers was president of the city's Friendly Sons of St. Patrick. He married (1) in Ireland, Christian Mary FitzSimon, a Catholic, and (2) in America, Catherine Caldwell Parks, widowed sister of United Irishman John Caldwell (on whom see chapter 68).   **14.** Mathew Carey, Philadelphia, to John Chambers, Dublin, 9 September 1791.   **15.** Mathew Carey, Philadelphia, to John Chambers, Dublin, 12 September 1791.   **16.** John Chambers, Dublin, to Mathew Carey, Philadelphia, 12 April 1792.

that "the number [of Irishmen] is not Small who think they see a very Strong British Influence over your Federal Governm^t—God forbid!" he declared, for "If such were the fact, the world might then say, where will Liberty lay her head?"[17] Ever optimistic, for a time the Philadelphian resisted his old friend's logic, but by the summer of 1796 the Republicans' efforts to nullify Jay's Treaty had failed and Carey was beginning to despair. "On the score of Politics what shall I say to you?" Carey asked, for

> on which side soever I cast my eye the prospect appears sombre & distressing [and] it has become nothing more than problematical whether all the high bought[18] & delightful anticipations of happiness for this 'highly favoured land,' are not doomed to disappear like the Careless fabric of a vision, & leave not a wreck behind. . . . What will be the issue of these things, it is impossible to say. But this much is certain, that it is more than ever desirable to the friends of mankind that the French may finally triumph over their enemies. If they fail, it requires little penetration to see that our Republicanism will perish with them.[19]

By the end of 1796, Carey's outlook was even bleaker: "Our political horizon darkens," he wrote, fearing that the election of John Adams as president that year would surely "plunge us into . . . the worst of wars"—a "war with France . . . our only sister republic on earth."[20]

After this letter, there is a long break in the Carey-Chambers correspondence, as under the threat of the Alien and Sedition Acts Carey either ceased writing to Dublin or else destroyed both the messages he received from Irish radicals overseas and the copies of his replies that he normally transcribed in his letterbook.[21] However, one letter of anguished outrage does survive from the turbulent 1790s, written to Carey by Daniel McCurtin, an Irish schoolmaster on Maryland's Eastern Shore. McCurtin was born about 1745 in the village of Carrignavar, in the parish of Dunbolloge and the barony of Barrymore, in east County Cork, five miles from Cork city.[22] His Catholic parents were sufficiently affluent to afford him a classical education, perhaps in a continental seminary. McCurtin may have studied for the priesthood but, if so, he abandoned that calling, and the books he would later order from Carey's publishing house (the works of Voltaire, for example) suggest that he, like John Daly Burk and Denis Driscol, at some point became a deist as well as an enthusiastic admirer of the French Revolution.

In 1760 McCurtin's brother Thomas (d. 1793), who remained a devout Catholic, emigrated to America and settled in New Jersey, where he opened a school. The date of Daniel's departure from Ireland is unknown, but in June 1775 he was living at Hagerstown,

---

17. John Chambers, Dublin, to Mathew Carey, Philadelphia, 26 March 1794.   **18. bought**: conjectural.
19. Mathew Carey, Philadelphia, to John Chambers, Dublin, 7 June 1796.   **20.** Mathew Carey, Philadelphia, to John Chambers, Dublin, 11 December 1796.   **21.** Likewise, it may not be coincidental that the minutes of Carey's Hibernian Society for the 1790s were allegedly "lost or destroyed."   **22.** For demographic data on Dunbulloge parish and its environs, see appendix 2.2b, on chapter 63.

a largely German settlement in western Maryland's Frederick County, where he joined the Continental Army to fight what he called "the Butchers belonging to the Tyrant of Great Britain."²³ McCurtin's company of buckskin-clad riflemen marched north to take part in the siege of Boston—a bloody affair that he chronicled in a journal—and eventually he rose to the rank of quartermaster sergeant. At the end of the war McCurtin appeared briefly in Philadelphia, where his brother's family had resettled, but by 1785 he was in the village of Chestertown, in Kent County, Maryland, where he received an M.A. degree from Washington College, recently established by Rev. William Smith, the former provost of the College of Philadelphia.²⁴ McCurtin remained at Washington College for the next 20 years, from 1791 as a professor with an annual salary of £175; after 1802 he earned £200 per year as headmaster of the College's grammar school.²⁵ McCurtin was also an ardent Mason and, in 1793, secretary of the Chestertown chapter of Maryland's Society for Promoting the Abolition of Slavery.²⁶ Despite his radical views, McCurtin appears to have flourished in what was, in effect, an Episcopalian and a Federalist academy, patronized by the Eastern Shore's planter and slaveowning élite.²⁷

McCurtin began to correspond with Mathew Carey as early as 1787, at first merely to order books (for which he often had difficulty paying) and to make plaintive (and vain) requests that his self-proclaimed "elegant & sublime" poetical tributes to Masonry be published in Carey's *American Museum*. By 1796, however, Carey's involvement in the campaign against Jay's Treaty spurred McCurtin to write lengthier letters, inquiring as to the progress of those "generous, brave and enlightened [United] Irishmen, who had staked their all in the most glorious of all Causes—the vindication of the rights of their native land." "Would to Heavens!" McCurtin prayed, "that the Punishment of Sodom was in-

---

23. Daniel McCurtin, "Journal of the Times at the Siege of Boston" (August 1775–March 1776); see Sources. **24.** On Episcopalian minister William Smith, see chapters 53 and 55. **25.** By 1790–1796 McCurtin was married, but the names of his wife and children (if any) are unknown. The 1790 federal census recorded his household as including, besides himself, three white males of at least 18 years of age, four white males under 18 years, one white female, and two slaves. However, although McCurtin referred to his wife in one letter to Mathew Carey (12 April 1796), he never mentioned any children, and at least some of the "white males" listed in the 1790 census were probably Washington College students boarding at his residence. **26.** McCurtin's antislavery views were ideologically consistent but may also have been triggered by recent Maryland court cases in which slaves with Irish surnames—e.g., the Mahoney brothers and the descendants of "Irish Nell" Butler—had petitioned for freedom, successfully in the Butlers' case. The Butlers, Mahoneys, and many like them were the products of marriages or sexual liaisons between colonial Maryland's African slaves and Irish indentured servants. **27.** In 1790 Kent County had 12,836 inhabitants, 42 percent of whom were slaves. In 1795 Chestertown contained only seven hundred residents, and its population was virtually stagnant for the next three decades. ¶Any patronage links between Rev. William Smith and McCurtin can no longer be traced, but Smith himself was a leading Mason, the founder of Maryland's Grand Lodge. In addition, in 1785 Washington College granted an honorary degree to Maryland's John Carroll, the first Catholic bishop in the United States, suggesting that McCurtin's religious background would not be stigmatized by either College officials or a planter aristocracy that was partly Catholic. However, McCurtin's political opinions would have differed totally from Carroll's and from those of most Eastern Shore planters, Catholic and Protestant alike.

flicted on the British nation."[28] Carey's replies to such letters were usually circumspect, but McCurtin probably felt safe from Federalist reprisals in his "sequestered spot" on the Eastern Shore.[29] Certainly in the following letter, written in mid-1798, McCurtin threw caution to the wind, goaded as he was by the news of the Irish Rebellion and of Congress's imminent passage of the Naturalization and the Alien and Sedition acts.

Daniel McCurtin, Chestertown, Maryland, to Mathew Carey, Philadelphia, 13 June 1798

Chester Town, M^d,

My Dear Carey   13th June 1798

I have had it in Contemplation for some time past to become a Subscribor to "Carey's United States Recorder". [30] As I am unacquainted with the Editor's address You will be pleased to inform me of his terms, and Days of Publication. I wish to purchase "Volney's Syria"[31] & "Imison's School of arts".[32] I will thank you to inform me of their prices, which I will immediately remit to you.

Gracious God! what a horrid picture does our ill-fated country present to the friend^s of Man. 1641 vanishes before it.[33] I most sincerely pray and wish that the French may effect a landing in Ireland. If so! a long adieu to the infernal british despotism over that singularly unhappy Country. What think you of the Alien and Sedition bills? Such rapid strides towards Despotism are unexampled. Heavens! what a return to the generous efforts of the irish in favour of America both in Europe and in

---

28. Daniel McCurtin, Chestertown, Md., to Mathew Carey, Philadelphia, 29 April 1796. **29.** Daniel McCurtin, Chestertown, Md., to Mathew Carey, Philadelphia, 20 June 1792. **30.** "**Carey's United States Recorder**": from 1797 James Carey, probably with his brother Mathew's financial assistance, published in Philadelphia the *United States Recorder*, a violently pro-French, pro-Republican, and anti-Federalist newspaper. **31.** "**Volney's Syria**": Constantin-François Chasseboeuf, comte de Volney (1757–1820), French philosophe and deist. In 1798 an English translation of Volney's *Voyage en Syrie et en Egypte* (Paris, 1787) was published in New York. Volney inaugurated the chair of history at Paris's École Normal, and in his most important book, *Les Ruines, or, Meditation sur les Revolutions des Empires* (Paris, 1791), he argued that, despite cultural and racial differences, all men are brothers whose duty is to perfect the laws instilled in them by Nature. In the 1790s Volney was obliged to seek refuge from the French Revolution in the United States, but he returned to France in anticipation of the Alien Acts of 1798. **32.** "**Imison's School of arts**": John Imison (d. 1788), a clock- and watchmaker and printer in Manchester, England. Imison wrote and published several novels, but his most noted work was *School of Arts, or, An Introduction to Useful Knowledge* (1785), republished from 1794 through 1822 in an edition (revised by Thomas Webster) titled *Elements of Science and Art: Being a Familiar Introduction to Natural Philosophy and Chemistry, Together with their Application to a Variety of Elegant and Useful Arts*. **33.** 1641: McCurtin refers to the Catholic Irish rebellion of 1641, in which thousands of Ulster Protestants died. McCurtin was correct in predicting that rebel casualties in 1798 would be much higher than the numbers of Ulster Protestants killed in 1641. However, Tory propagandists would ignore the former and charge that the relatively small number of loyalists massacred in 1798 was analogous to the traditionally and grossly inflated number of Protestant casualties of 1641. See chapter 5, n. 24, and chapter 67, n. 39. In 1819 Mathew Carey wrote and published *Vindiciae Hibernicae: or, Ireland Vindicated*, to refute "the legendary tales of the pretended conspiracy and massacre of 1641."

this Country during the American war. Never had this Country more sincere friends. Ireland considered its emancipation inseperably connected with American Independence. This development of the American character must be singularly pleasing to the friends of tyranny all over the world. A Gov^t founded on the rights of man—A Representative republican Governm^t brands with every opprobrious term every nation attempting to imitate their example.

The naturalization law crowns the Climax. Were I near the press I should conceive myself bound to caution aliens against enlisting in the army or navy of the US. What! fight in defence of the rights of others, when absolutely deprived of them myself! I am d. . . . . d, if I would.

your Sincere friend

Daniel McCurtin

P.S. If you think any part of this scrawl worthy of publication, you may insert it in the "Aurora"[34] or "recorder", as an extract of a letter from C Town.

D M^c C—

After 1798 the letters that McCurtin and Carey exchanged once again became short and impersonal. Perhaps McCurtin was disappointed by his friend's reticence on political matters, but Carey had to operate in an urban environment where he was not only surrounded by suspicious native Protestants but also dependent financially on the patronage of affluent and politically conservative Irish-American Catholics such as Thomas FitzSimons, Philadelphia's Federalist congressman in 1789–1795, and James Gallagher, a wealthy merchant who backed Carey's loans from the Bank of Pennsylvania.[35] Like the bulk of the Irish Catholic clergy, both at home and in the United States, such men despised the French Revolution for its threats to order and religion, abhorred the prospect of rebellion in Ireland, regarded the United Irishmen as representatives of a Protestant-Jacobin plot, and viewed Jeffersonian Republicanism as the harbinger of anarchy and infidelity. As early as 1794 Gallagher had warned Carey that if Philadelphia's Democratic-Republicans ever gained power, "there would be as much Gu<i>llotining and as many innocent people suffer" as in France under Robespierre.[36]

Less than a year after McCurtin wrote his angry letter, an incident occurred in Philadelphia that dramatically illustrated the tensions between the religious and the secular,

34. the "Aurora": The Philadelphia *Aurora,* the leading Republican newspaper in the 1790s, first published by Benjamin Franklin Bache and, after his death in 1798 while imprisoned for seditious libel, by William Duane (1760–1835), perhaps the most radical of the Irish emigré journalists in Federalist America. On Duane, see chapter 38, n. 46. **35.** On Thomas FitzSimons, see chapter 58. Little is known about James Gallagher, beyond the data in the text of this chapter (and of chapter 44) and that he was a member of Carey's Hibernian Society. His son, Dr. James, Jr. (see below), was in 1790 a founding member of the Hibernian Society, one of its physicians, and in 1796 a member of its acting committee; he died in 1822. **36.** James Gallagher, Philadelphia, to Mathew Carey, Philadelphia, no date [1794?].

and the "American" and the "Irish," aspects of Irish-American Catholic identity. On a Sunday in mid-February 1799, a minor riot occurred when Dr. James Gallagher, Jr., the American-born son of Carey's wealthy patron, and several other trustees of St. Mary's Catholic church, violently expelled from the churchyard a handful of United Irish exiles who were soliciting signatures for their petition to Congress against the Alien Acts. At the subsequent trial, Dr. Gallagher declared that "no Jacobin petition had a right to a place on the walls" of his church and that he had felt himself "hurt by the injury and insult done to my religion"—most especially because there was not "a single Catholic" among the petitioners. Yet a defense witness, Thaddeus M'Carthy, only two years from Ireland, testified that the chief petitioner, Dr. James Reynolds,[37] was "a great Irish gentleman," and that "great numbers" of St. Mary's ordinary Irish congregants had been eager to sign. Even Gallagher admitted that, during the fracas, most of his fellow parishioners had given him "much abuse" for ejecting Reynolds and had threatened to punish Gallagher for "insulting their nation"—although, he added rather disingenuously, "they did not mention what nation."[38]

Clearly, there was a major ideological division, as well as a social gap, between St. Mary's affluent Federalist trustees and the artisans, carters, and laborers who composed the bulk of its congregation. The former regarded United Irish activities as an "insult" to Catholicism and a threat to their identity as citizens of a conservatively defined American "nation," whereas the latter viewed Gallagher's opposition to the United Irishmen as an "insult" to the Irish "nation" whence they had recently emigrated (or fled) and to Reynolds's and their own aspirations for its liberation from British rule. In the short run, Reynolds's Catholic sympathizers would win the battle for St. Mary's, as a year after the riot Gallagher, FitzSimons, and two other Federalist trustees lost their bids for reelection to four representatives of a rising group of Irish manufacturers and shopkeepers. However, these "new men" were in turn soon embroiled in ideological and financial controversies with their bishop and with priests who believed, with the Irish-born Fr. Patrick Kenny, that "all Irish Catholics taking shelter in the United States" should be "more faithful to

---

37. Dr. James Reynolds (d. 1808): a Protestant physician from Co. Tyrone and an early and leading member of the United Irishmen, Reynolds conspired with fellow deists John Daly Burk and Denis Driscol (see earlier) to radicalize and organize Dublin's working classes. Reynolds fled from Belfast to Philadelphia in May 1794, after the authorities learned of his complicity in plans for a French invasion of Ireland. In Philadelphia Reynolds practiced medicine and anti-Federalist journalism and was purportedly the chief organizer of the American Society of United Irishmen and hence a primary target of Federalist vitriol (including an alleged plot to assassinate him) and of government persecution under the Alien and Sedition Acts. After Jefferson's election in 1800, Reynolds joined William Duane's radical "Philadelphia" or "Old School faction" of Pennsylvania's divided Republican party (on which see chapters 38 and 64). In 1802 John Lithgow, a radical Scottish emigré, dedicated to Reynolds his *Equality: A Political Romance,* the first utopian socialist tract written and published in the United States. ¶The other petitioners at St. Mary's were: William Duane, editor of the Philadelphia *Aurora* (see earlier and chapter 38, n. 46); Robert Moore, a fugitive United Irishman from Co. Antrim; and Samuel Cuming, a young Irish printer, probably in Duane's employ. 38. W. Duane, *A Report of the Extraordinary Transactions . . . ,* 6–7, 16; see Sources.

their religious principles than enamour'd with the Political constitution" of the United States[39]—or with the United Irishmen's brand of secular and ecumenical nationalism.

From the early 1800s through the 1840s, these trusteeship controversies, both in Philadelphia and elsewhere in the United States, produced temporary schisms, occasional riots, and seemingly endless litigation, as upwardly mobile, pew-renting trustees tried to impose on the Church a "republican" model of ecclesiastical government, while clergymen such as Fr. Kenny denounced them as members of a "vile anti-catholick party" composed of "Free-masons [and] soi-disant Catholics" and supported by "olive-branch orange-men."[40] By midcentury, however, the Catholic bishops and those priests loyal to their authority had triumphed in these conflicts, largely by mobilizing the faith and prejudices of the poorest and most recent Irish immigrants—their religious devotion and traditional deference to the clergy, their socioeconomic grievances with the trustees, and their resentments against the Protestant bigotry that was increasingly evident and violent on both sides of the ocean.[41] New generations of middle-class Irish-American Catholics would conform to these strictures, and bourgeois Irish nationalism, as it developed in nineteenth-century America and Ireland alike, would become nearly inseparable from militant Catholicism and would reject, sanitize, or acknowledge only rhetorically the ideals and sacrifices of the United Irishmen—led and composed as they largely had been by "heretics" and "Jacobins."

Unfortunately, any comments McCurtin may have made on the St. Mary's church riot have not survived, and the brevity of his post-1798 letters to Carey may indicate that he was preoccupied with his own spiritual and economic struggles. From 1800 on, McCurtin's book orders—for example, of a copy of the Douai Bible, which Carey was the first to publish in the United States—suggest a return to the faith of his fathers, and in 1802 he remitted $30 to Irish relatives in care of Francis Moylan, the Catholic bishop of Cork, a sibling of Philadelphia's Federalist Moylan brothers, and a British loyalist who had threatened Munster's United Irishmen with excommunication. In addition, by the late 1790s McCurtin's Washington College was a financial and physical ruin, and in 1805, when the state legislature terminated its annual subvention, the College was forced to dismiss McCurtin and nearly all its other faculty. In 1808 he resurfaced briefly as principal of another

---

39. Rev. Patrick Kenny, Diary, 4 July 1817 (see Sources). Kenny (1763–1840) was born in Co. Dublin, was educated at the College of St. Sulpice in Paris, and immigrated to America in 1804. He resided on a farm outside Wilmington, Delaware, and, despite his chronically poor health, regularly ministered to at least five congregations in and between Wilmington and Philadelphia, including the DuPonts' colony of Irish workers at their gunpowder factory in northern Delaware.   **40.** Rev. Patrick Kenny, Diary, 9 April 1822. Kenny's references were to Philadelphia's famous "Hogan schism" of the 1820s, in which he was tangentially involved; Kenny also had severe difficulties with the "insolent" trustees of his Wilmington church. On the "trusteeship crises," also see chapters 13, 26, and 48.   **41.** This brief description of the trusteeship controversies is necessarily oversimplified. Much of the strife was interethnic—not confined solely to conflicts among Irish clergy, trustees, and parishioners. Often Irish or other parishioners resented French-born bishops and priests for ethnic and/or ideological reasons (e.g., see chapter 13), and German-American trustees and congregants frequently rebelled against increasing Irish dominance of the hierarchy and clergy. Nevertheless, it was an ostensibly panethnic but in fact "Irish-Catholic" version of Catholicism that ultimately gained hegemony.

academy in Maryland's Somerset County, but his tenure appears to have been short, perhaps because he was by then at least 60 or 65 years old. Thereafter Daniel McCurtin disappears from the historical record, except for a seemingly ironic but revealing postscript: the great-great-nephew of the former deist and revolutionary enthusiast was John Gilmary Shea (1824–1892), the pious, pioneer historian of American Catholicism, whose works interpreted the trusteeship and the ideological controversies that had riven the early nineteenth-century Church as simple conflicts between faith and infidelity.

64 ✳

Robert McArthur, 1802

On 1 May 1801 the United Irish exile John Daly Burk, lately a fugitive from both British laws and the Federalists' Alien and Sedition Acts, delivered an oration at Townes Tavern in Amelia County, Virginia, where since 1799 he had been hiding from the Adams administration. Finally free from persecution, he and other radical Irish emigrés could now savor "the sweetness and fragrance of Elysium," for the occasion of Burk's address was to celebrate Thomas Jefferson's election as president—to proclaim what Burk called "that wonderful revolution."[1]

Written over a year later, Robert McArthur's letter from backcountry Pennsylvania—like Samuel Brown's from Philadelphia in 1815[2]—demonstrates the satisfaction and vindication felt by most ordinary Irish immigrants when the Republican triumphs of 1799–1800 restored their sense of equal citizenship and opportunity in the "land of freedom." In addition, the history of the McArthur family illustrates how long residence in Ireland, the Irish reform movements of the 1770s, 1780s, and 1790s, and the political situation in America during the late eighteenth-century could converge to shape a broadly defined "Irish" identity among many Protestants both in Ireland and in the United States.

According to family tradition, the McArthurs came to Ulster in 1685 from Argyll in the Scottish Highlands. Thus, the McArthurs had migrated to northern Ireland at roughly the same time, from the same Scottish region, and for precisely the same reason—the Stuart kings' persecutions of Scots Presbyterians—as the followers of Rev. James McGregor, who in turn had remigrated to Boston in 1718–1720, settled in New Hampshire, and adamantly denied they were "Irish" in their petitions to colonial officials.[3] However, in 1685 the McArthurs had not gone from Argyll to east Ulster's Lower Bann Valley, where McGregor's people had settled. Instead, they had migrated to the west of the province, to County Donegal, where they settled on Lord Donegall's estate in Burt, the southernmost parish in the peninsula and barony of Inishowen, and farmed the hill overlooking Derry city, only

---

1. Durey, *Transatlantic Radicals*, 258; J. I. Shulim, "John Daly Burk . . . ," 36–37; see Sources, chapter 63.
2. On Brown, see chapter 38.   3. See chapter 49.

four miles away.[4] Robert McArthur was born in 1775, the second or third eldest of the five sons of John McArthur (1740–1820), who held at least 350 acres in the townlands of Carrowreagh, Bonemain, and Greenfort.

In most respects the family's situation in west Ulster was highly advantageous: the soils in the Foyle Valley were rich, two-thirds of Burt's inhabitants were Protestants (mostly Presbyterians), Lord Donegall's rents were unusually low, and the leases he granted tenants were long (John McArthur's were for 31 years). However, east Donegal's prosperous Protestant farmers—like the Crocketts a few miles south in Killea parish[5]—generally practiced impartible inheritance, and Lord Donegall's policy of charging new tenants exhorbitant entry fees made it difficult for noninheriting sons to acquire farms. As a result, many of the large farmers in Inishowen became middlemen, subletting much of their lands to undertenants (either Protestant noninheritors or ambitious Catholics) at rent levels two or three times higher than those that head tenants paid Lord Donegall. Perhaps it was to avoid such rack-rents that Robert MacArthur's elder brother William (ca. 1760–1822) emigrated to Philadelphia in 1783, followed by his younger siblings: first Andrew (1771–1851) about 1795, then Robert in 1797, and finally John, Jr. (1767–1843) in 1804.

The MacArthurs' emigration may have stemmed from political as well as economic motives. Inishowen's Presbyterians resented the Anglican monopoly of local offices, and farmers of all denominations resisted official efforts to suppress the illegal distillation of whiskey—a major regional industry in the late eighteenth century. Although east Donegal was never as politically active as Antrim or Down, from 1768 the area's Presbyterian voters sent "Patriot" candidates to the Irish Parliament; likewise, from 1778 they strongly supported local Volunteer companies (including one in Burt), several of which welcomed Catholic members. In 1793 the reform movement in east Donegal and Derry city faltered as middle-class Presbyterians became fearful of growing unrest among Catholic subtenants and laborers. By 1798 such concerns as well as official coercion had largely suppressed the local United Irishmen. Even after the Rebellion, however, liberal and even radical sympathies still prevailed among the McArthurs and many of their neighbors. For example, in 1800 John McArthur, Jr., then still in Donegal, declared to his brother Robert in Pennsylvania that "Experience has taught the reasoning part of Mankind The following simple truths—That in political institutions Nothing is stable that is not Just[,] that gross and increasing abuses lead necessarily[6] to Violence and revolution," whereas "Timely and effectual Reform" leads "to peace and security"; therefore, he argued, since "Violence . . . and revolution are but Desperate remedies for Desperate Evils . . . it is the extreme either of human folly or Depravity in Goverment to make Such remedies Seem generally Necessary." Such sentiments were now smothered in Ireland—"as politicks is a thing Not to be spoken of by any Irishman

---

4. For demographic data on Burt parish and its environs, see appendix 2.1a, on chapter 64.   5. On the Crocketts, see chapters 15 and 27.   6. **necessary** ms.

I lay aside that Subject," John McArthur had concluded[7]—but in the United States, especially after Jefferson's victory that same year, they could have full play.

By late 1797 when Robert McArthur disembarked at New Castle, Delaware, his brother William was well established at Meadville, a village of about four hundred souls that in 1800 would become the seat of Crawford County in far northwestern Pennsylvania. Since William's arrival in 1783, he had taught school in York County, Pennsylvania, studied surveying with Colonel Moses McClean, who in 1760–1763 had helped map the Mason-Dixon line, and married his mentor's daughter, Rebecca. Sometime in the early 1790s, William had migrated to northwest Pennsylvania, then densely forested and scarcely settled, and in 1795, at the behest of Meadville's founder, General David Mead, he resurveyed and remodeled the town, reproducing that familiar feature of urban Ulster, "the diamond," at the village's heart. For the rest of his life, William resided in Meadville, the region's unofficial political capital. An ardent Jeffersonian Republican, deeply suspicious of the slightest deviations from what he called "genuine Democratic principles,"[8] William held numerous county offices—treasurer in 1800–1802, surveyor in 1800–1806, prothonotary and clerk in 1809–1821, and recorder of deeds in 1812–1820. More important, in 1801 and again in 1805 the region's voters elected him to the state senate. In 1797 William purchased two hundred acres of land in Shenango township, in Crawford County's southwestern corner, and in a few years Shenango (later, South Shenango) held a substantial colony of Irish families from Burt parish. In 1798 the recently arrived Robert McArthur also purchased two hundred acres in Shenango, probably for $1.00 per acre, as did brother Andrew, who had preceded Robert to America. Soon afterward, a host of Scotts, Gambles, Cochrans, Works, Rankins, Latas, and other kinsmen and former neighbors from east Donegal also settled in the McArthurs' township. Thus, although Robert's 1802 letter admits his initial uncertainty whether to settle permanently in the United States, he was persuaded to remain by considerations of economic advantage, brother William's connections, and the confidence inspired by the victorious Republicans' repudiation of the Federalists' anti-Irish policies.

Robert McArthur, Shenango Township, Crawford County, Pennsylvania, to John McArthur, Carrowreagh, Burt Parish, County Donegal, 4 November 1802

Shenango   November the 4th 1802

Brother John

If these[9] Comes to your hand they will inform you that I am in good health at present and has enjoyed the same since the last time I wrote you   I have not Receiv'd

---

7. John McArthur, Greenfort, Burt Parish, Co. Donegal, to Robert McArthur, Shenango Township, Crawford Co., Pa., 27 May 1800. **8.** William McArthur, Meadville, Pa., to James Miller, Mercer Co., Pa., 15 June 1809; copy courtesy of R. D. Ilisevich, Crawford Co. Historical Society, Meadville, Pa. **9.** these: "this letter" (letter was formerly construed as plural—and still is in the case of official documents and in other stereotyped usages—because of its derivation from the Latin plural form *litterae* "letter," lit. "letters"). See also hereafter: **he will forward** *these* **letters**; and in the direction: *these* for **John McArthur**.

any letters from Ireland this year as yet which prevented me from writing to the last
moment   We Received the letters sent in the Care of James Gamble and James
Wark[10] which was the latest account we have had from Ireland   the linnen sent in
Care of James wark I understand is lost   he has not Come to this part of the Countrey
as yet   the last account I had of him he was in york County   the hats I belive is
save[11]   I do not know exactly how the linen was lost but report says it was when the
passengrs arrived in this Country   a number of them was sickly and was put into the
hospitall<,> their goods being put into a store<,> and some of them<,> getting well
before the rest<,> was able to make a start <and> took along with them the property
of others and by doing so, Compleatly broke the last great precept of the Morall Law,
which says you shall not Covet any thing that is thy Neighbours,   But as there[12] a
Class of mankind which stoops below the dignity of the human specious[13] in many
respects as well as Cov<e>tiousness we need not wonder at such things, but just
Conclude, that was the way <the> linnen went

Mr Gamble has been often telling me that he saw you diffrent times before he left that
Country, and that you Could[14] give him a very Good de<sc>ription of this part of the
Country, which[15] I was very Glad to Learn you was so well acquainted with the
history of this new Country   But as you mention that you have a desing[16] in Coming
to see this part of the world I think you will be able to give a more accurate account of
it to your friends when you return,   but Indeed Brother John, that is a Journey I
Could not advise you to undertake, as it would be attended with a Considerable
expence, the loss of time, and the danger of Crossing the seas, although if it was the
Case that you were to Come to this Country I should enjoy as much happiniss in the
visit as any person in the world, but I think if you Come to this Country you will not
return in haste or at any rate not so soon as you expect,   I know this was the Case
with respect to myself   when I Came to this Country I thought that Certainly I
would be in Ireland before this time (But I am here yet)   When a man settels in any
Country it is not easy for him to rise up and embark for another when he pleases
although he had a very Great mind to do it, and more so in this part of the world
where the people are partly purchasing their Estate by Actual Settlement   although
the price of lands were very low in the first settling of this Country again[17] the

---

10. **James Gamble and James Wark**: east Donegal emigrants to Crawford Co., Pa. In 1797 or 1798 John
Gamble purchased two hundred acres in Shenango township; shortly afterward his brothers, James and
Matthew, arrived and settled. The Wark [more commonly, Work] family had farmed land adjacent to the
McArthurs in Burt parish; in 1801 Joseph Work was a founding elder of Shenango's Presbyterian church, the
first of that denomination in Crawford Co.   **11. save**: safe (Scots form); see also hereafter: **he will forward
these letters . . . by a *save* hand**.   **12. there**: there is (Scots form); examples: **the'r** a big heidin in thà paiper
anent it "there's a big headline in the paper about it;" **the'r** nae hairm in buik-larnin "there's no harm in
education." Philip Robinson, *Ulster Scots* (Belfast, 1997), p. 186.   **13. specious**: i.e., species.   **14. Could**: here
factual rather than hypothetical: "were able to."   **15. which**: i.e., and; see chapter 3, n. 3.   **16. desing**: design
(Scots form).   **17. again**: by the time that.

ROBERT MCARTHUR

purchasor rec<k>ons all his Costs truble and expences it will stand[18] him something Considerable and as he was by his Bargain to settle on the land he Could not omit living in the Country and that five years,[19]   But the first settlers of this Country has no reason to regret their Coming to this parts, although many are the disconveniences incident to the settling of a new Countrey   as to my own part I entertain a very good oppinion of this part of the world and it appears the longer I live in it I like it the better   this may be from the Rappid progress it makes in improveing which surpasses my first expectations very much   there are severall natural advantages that the people of this part will enjoy, and receive Considerable benefits by and that of Navigation in particular   although this is an inland Country and a great distance from the sea yet every farmer Can have a watter Carrage[20] for every produce he has to dispose of very near him and a great many from their doors[21]   it would be too tedious for me at present to give you as de<s>criptive an account of this Countrey in General as I would wish to do   therefore I shall Content myself to[22] some other oppertunity   as with respect to politcks I have nothing paticular to Mention at present only that the Republicans seem to bear the sway[23] and Carry the elections by a great Majority both in this State and throughout the Union   our present Government dismantled and Repealed several laws that seemed a grievance to the people   the Sedition law Stamp act and excise law is entirely done away so the distiller Can work his Stills or let them stand idle as he pleases   so much for the distillers   and the Allien law Repealled in such amaner that a forienger who has been five years under the Jurisdiction of the United States and one of them years in the bounds of that State he now lives in by going forward to any Court of Record in the County he lives in and making the proofs requisite he shall be admited to take the oath of naturalization and have all the priviledges of a Citizen[24]   all this I have done   So much for the poor Irish, that was Alliens and that of the worst kind, as the firm Federals allowd[25] them to be

I have followed Distilling this two seasons past a<nd> Intends to be at it again in a short time   the Grain is not plenty[26] enough in this new Country To Carry on the

18. stand: cost.   19. and that five years: "and do that for five years."   20. watter Carrage: transportation by water.   21. In southern Crawford Co., where the McArthurs settled, the Venango, Allegheny, Shenango, and Beaver rivers and creeks flow south to the Ohio River.   22. to: until.   23. to bear the sway: be victorious. 24. According to the Naturalization Act of 1802, passed by the Republican-controlled Congress, free white males could apply for citizenship at any local court of record; they had to declare their intention at least three years prior to naturalization, and they had to be resident in the United States for five years and in the state where they applied for one year. In addition, they had to swear an oath to uphold the Constitution and renounce allegiance to any foreign sovereign. The 1802 Naturalization Act was far less restrictive than that of 1798 (see chapter 63) but less generous than that of 1790 (which had allowed naturalization after merely two years' residence in the United States) or even that of 1795. The latter act had merely required an alien to swear that he had been a United States resident for five years; by the Act of 1802 (as of 1798), he had to prove it with documentation.   25. allowd: declared.   26. plenty: plentiful.

Distilling all the year but I Can Get as much as I Can Still[27] in the winter season so I make allitle whiskey in the winter and farms alittle in the sumer and so makes out[28] to live as well as my Neighbours   you informed me you had not taken new leases which I think must be Good for you at present as I Understand Markets has taken a wonderfull turn[29] of late   it is perhaps a happy thing for <the> poor But how Can the farmer live that pays such a uncomon[30] rent for his land and taxes high in proportion to the Rents

My Father Mentioned to me that there was some of my honest old Neighbours speaking of me when the times was at the worst with them and that if I had been there I would be of use to them   but If I had some of them here I Could be of more use to them than ever I had it in my power to be there and willing I would be to serve them if it lay in my power but likely that is what will never be but still I am glad to think I still have the good wish of my old acquantances

Brother John I hope you will write every oppertunity as there is nothing more pleasing to me than hearing from you and the rest of my Relations and freinds in that part[31]   Joseph does not write as often I think as he might do and I wish you would tell him so   I would write oftener But my oppertunity of Conveyance is not so good as I wish

Brother W^m & An^d is both well   Moses Scoot[32] is well   the Rankins & W^m lata and family is well   in short all our Neighbours from your part of the Country is well   Brother W^m starts for the Sanate[33] in a few Days   he will forward these letters I expect by a save[34] hand and he will have an oppertunity of writing frequently which I have Charged him not to neglect   there is a Mr Willson a friend to the Rankins   perhaps he will be the Bearer of these letters

Brother John I must draw to a Conclusion but it is for want of time and more Blank paper   therefore I Beg to be excused for any Blunders or Bad writeing as there is not time to Coppy

---

27. **Still**: distill (Scots form).   28. **makes out**: manages.   29. **wonderfull turn**: remarkable/surprising change; McArthur refers here to a sharp decline in the market price for Irish grain, probably caused by a temporary cessation of the Napoleonic Wars.   30. **uncomon**: i.e., uncommon "extraordinary."   31. **in that part**: there. 32. **Moses Scoot**: Moses Scott, a McArthur kinsman. The Scotts and McArthurs were close neighbors in Burt parish. In December 1798 Moses Scott purchased two hundred acres in Shenango township; in 1809–1811 he was Crawford Co. treasurer. Scott died of tuberculosis on 6 May 1834 and was eulogized by the *Meadville Courier* (13 May 1834) as "one of the early settlers of this county, and . . . highly esteemed by all who knew him as an upright and honest man."   33. **Sanate**: i.e., the Pennsylvania state senate, which then met in Lancaster.   34. **save**: see n. 11.

ROBERT MCARTHUR

Be so good as to remember me To my Father and jean Joseph Rebeca & Moses Scoot[35] and Uncels & Aunts my Couzins in Burt and in short Give My best Respects to all my Frinds and Neighbours that wishes to inquire for me

So no more But Remains your

These for John McArthur   a[ffecti]onet Brother   Robert McArthur

For the rest of their lives, Robert, William, and Andrew McArthur, joined by brother John in 1804, remained in Crawford County and moderately prospered as its population grew from 2,346 in 1800 to nearly 9,400 in 1820 and to 31,724 by 1840—when only Andrew and John were still living. Robert, a farmer and distiller in South Shenango, married Mary Euphemia Linn, fathered eight children,[36] died in a sledding accident in late January 1836, and was memorialized by the *Meadville Courier* as "an upright and much esteemed citizen."[37] He and his brothers also had remained staunch Jeffersonians and eventually became equally ardent Jacksonians, voting Democratic long after most of the county's electorate had joined the Whig party. During the early nineteenth century, Crawford County was bitterly contested political ground, as a pragmatic alliance between Meadville's Federalist and "moderate" or "Quid" Republican merchants and speculators, who supported the claims of eastern land companies, was ranged against the radical-Republican "Friends of the People," including the McArthurs, who championed the interests of poor farmers who had squatted on company lands.[38] By the 1820s the companies had won court orders, evicted most of the "intruders," and forced those who remained to purchase their farms at company prices. However, although Crawford County's overt class conflicts ended when the ejected squatters migrated westward, the somewhat parallel ethnoreligious divisions—forged in the late 1790s—remained, as it appears that the townships that voted most consistently Jeffersonian-Republican and, later, Democratic were those that, like South

---

35. jean Joseph Rebeca & Moses Scoot: Jeanne and Rebecca were Robert McArthur's sisters, and Rebecca was the wife of Moses Scott, probably uncle of the Moses Scott who settled in Crawford Co. in the late 1790s (see n. 32). Joseph was Robert McArthur's brother; with his siblings' departures for America, Joseph inherited the family holdings in Burt; he was dead by 1832, when his son William (1806–1856) wrote his surviving uncles in Crawford Co., asking their advice concerning his own prospects in America. Neither William nor his widow, Jane, emigrated, but in the 1830s other, younger members of the McArthur family (e.g., George McArthur and Robert Scott) did so.   36. Mary Euphemia Linn (1783–1844) was the daughter of Joseph Linn. Robert McArthur's and her children were: Margaret (1806–1878); John (1808–1892), who from 1846 was a farmer in Winnegago Co., Illinois, and after 1870 in Story Co., Iowa; Euphemia (1810–1885), who married James Martin, a Crawford Co. farmer from Donegal; Rebecca (1812–1897); Robert, Jr. (1816–1846), who died of malaria; Hannah (1818–1856); Alexander (1819–1895); and William (1821–1888).   37. *Meadville Courier*, 2 February 1836; courtesy of C. W. P. MacArthur, Marble Hill, Dunfanaghy, Co. Donegal.   38. On the state level, the radical wing of Pennsylvania's Republican party was led in part by Irish Philadelphians William Duane (1760–1835) and, for a time, John Binns (1772–1860), both Protestants (although Duane was American-born of Irish Catholic parents) and former United Irishmen who had fled or been exiled to America; on Duane, see chapter 38. esp. n. 46, and chapter 63. Significantly, one of the radicals' goals was to restore many of the ultrademocratic provisions of George Bryan's 1776 Pennsylvania constitution.

Shenango, had been heavily settled by Ulster Presbyterian immigrants, whereas the Federalist, Whig, and—from 1856—Republican townships were dominated by Methodist and Baptist families from New York, New Jersey, and New England.[39]

65 ❈

John Nevin, 1804

The leaders of the United Irishmen—mostly Protestant merchants, manufacturers, and professionals—believed with Thomas Paine that the successful pursuit of "reason" would embolden Irishmen to break the shackles of aristocracy and to forswear the religious "passions" and prejudices that for centuries had so bitterly divided them. Yet it was the exiles' misfortune to land in America at the beginning of the greatest religious upheaval that the transatlantic world had ever witnessed, the Second Great Awakening, a series of emotional revivals that convulsed Protestant societies in the United States and Ireland alike and that, coupled with the rise in both countries of ultramontaine Catholicism, destroyed the milieu that had nourished the United Irish project of ecumenical radicalism. It was scarcely surprising, therefore, that when John Nevin, a rebel leader and a Presbyterian from north County Antrim, fled to the United States and settled on the waters of east Tennessee, his response to the first waves of frontier revivalism that he witnessed was one of horrified amazement and alarm.

John Nevin was the second son of James Nevin (d. 1796), one of three brothers who were prominent farmers and linen manufacturers in north Antrim. The Nevins' home farm was in Kilmoyle townland, in the parish of Ballyrashane and the barony of Lower Dunluce,[1] but in the late eighteenth and early nineteenth centuries they also leased the markets in nearby Coleraine, County Derry, and owned or rented over three hundred acres in several other north Antrim parishes. In 1797 a local magistrate described John Nevin as "one of the richest Countrymen in this Neighbourhood, and has several tenants under him."[2] Yet despite their affluence, the Nevins of Kilmoyle were at odds with the government from at least 1761, when they resisted paying tithes to the local Anglican clergy. The Nevins were members of a Seceding (Anti-Burgher) Presbyterian congregation in Ballywatt, a townland adjacent to Kilmoyle. Although traditionally alienated from the govern-

---

39. The dominance of Ulster Presbyterian immigrants in certain townships, such as Shenango, has been determined by the location and founding dates of their churches, which in turn match almost precisely the local prevalence of Jeffersonian-Republican and Democratic party voters from 1800 through the election of 1852 and, often, through that of 1860.   **1.** In 1832 the Nevins still held nearly 75 acres in Kilmoyle, valued at £62. For demographic data on Ballyrashane parish and its environs, see appendix 2.1g, on chapter 65.
2. Rev. T. H. Mullin, *Coleraine in Georgian Times*, 160; see Sources.

ments and established churches of both Ireland and Scotland, in general Seceding (or Associate) Presbyterian clergy and laymen were at best lukewarm to political reform; in
addition, as strict Calvinists they opposed the rational, tolerant "New Light" views that
prevailed among most of the Presbyterian ministers in east Ulster who joined or sympathized with the United Irishmen.[3] In north Antrim, however, the United Irishmen were
"mostly Roman Catholics or Seceders," according to one local informer.[4] In the late 1770s
and early 1780s, the Nevins' minister at Ballywatt, John Tennent, had been prominent
in the Volunteer movement; and although he later became more cautious, three of his
sons—merchants in Belfast—were among the first and most prominent United Irishmen
in that city.[5]

John Nevin apparently joined the United Irishmen in 1795, at a meeting in Ballymoney, County Antrim, when he was appointed captain of Ballyrashane parish, under the
immediate command of Richard Caldwell.[6] For the next several years, Nevin drilled his
men by moonlight in the nearby parish of Derrykeighan and labored to subvert the loyalty
of the militiamen stationed in Coleraine. When the rising in Ulster occurred, in early June
1798, Nevin marched his followers to Ballymena, County Antrim, which had been captured by the rebels. However, the revolt soon collapsed with the United Irishmen's defeat
at Antrim town, and Nevin became a fugitive, with a price on his head. After several
weeks in hiding, Nevin was smuggled through Coleraine in a barrel, made his way to
Magilligan, County Derry, and, disguised as a sailor, took ship for America.

According to family tradition, Nevin landed in Charleston, South Carolina, but soon
moved west to Knoxville, the frontier capital of the new state of Tennessee. Admitted to
the Union in 1796, by 1800 Tennessee had nearly 106,000 inhabitants, about a third of
Scots-Irish descent, concentrated primarily in the mountainous east, along the tributaries of
the Tennessee River. Knoxville's population was merely one thousand, but its merchants
conducted a lively trade in flour, cotton, and whiskey with New Orleans, via the Tennessee, Ohio, and Mississippi rivers, and sent huge droves of cattle and hogs to eastern seaports. Nevin became an Indian trader, licensed by the War Department to trade along the
Tennessee River with the Cherokees and Creeks, exchanging flour and what he called
"other articles" (probably—and illegally—including whiskey) for the cattle that he drove
down the French Broad River into North and South Carolina, probably encountering
James Patton's brother-in-law, Andrew Erwin of Asheville, en route.[7]

3. On Ulster's Seceding (Associate) Presbyterians, also see chapter 6, especially n. 7. **4.** Rev. T. H. Mullin,
Coleraine in Georgian Times, 159; see Sources. **5.** Rev. John Tennent (c. 1726–1808): educated at the
University of Glasgow; ordained in 1751 as minister of Ballywatt, Ballyrashane, and Roseyards churches;
considered emigration to America in 1751 and again in the early 1770s, when departures sharply reduced his
congregations, but instead remained and became a strong advocate of political reform as a spokesman for north
Antrim's Volunteers. (The relationship between heavy emigration by Ulster Presbyterians—e.g., in the early
1770s and again in the 1780s and early 1790s—and their clergy's support for Irish political and economic
reform seems obvious but remains unstudied.) On John Tennent's sons, see chapter 68, n. 39. **6.** On
Richard, brother of John Caldwell, see chapter 68. **7.** On Patton and Erwin, see chapter 43.

From Knoxville in 1804 John Nevin wrote to his siblings his only surviving letter from the New World. To his brother James in Kilmoyle, Nevin rejoiced that he now lived under "a Real Republickan Government and the Best in the Woreld," thanks to the election in 1800 of Thomas Jefferson, whose patronage to former United Irishmen probably aided Nevin to secure his trading license. However, although Nevin's letter suggests no estrangement from the Indians, he was clearly disturbed by the religious behavior of the local Scots-Irish and other settlers, as their frenzied revivals, sparked by the recent camp meetings at nearby Cane Ridge, Kentucky, deeply offended his faith in a "God of Order and not of Confusion."

John Nevin, Knoxville, Tennessee, to James Nevin, Kilmoyle, Ballyrashane Parish, County Antrim, 10 April 1804

Knoxville   Apr^l 10th 1804——Tennessee State

Dear Friends

     Happy in an oppertunity of writting I Now Embrace this[8]   your Last favours I Rec^d in Less then Ten Weeks from their Date   I have also seen a Mr Stewart from the Garden a few Days a Go on his way to Natchez which left Ireland in November Last and Informs me that Troublesume Times is not likely to be over yet.   O: that I Could but have you all in this Countery with the Value of your Property   here I Enjoy Equal Right and Priveledges of the Governor and I am an Equal Companion of our first Rank whilst you must Pour[9] out your Purse to Landlords and whiper ins[10] And your Hats in your hand at same Time   you have mentioned your desire to know my Business in the Ingin Nation and also in Charelston in South Carolina   I went Down the Tennessee river with a Boat Loaded with Flower and a Number of other articles   Sold that to the Ingins & Bought Steers off them And after stallfeeding the Oxen Drove them to Charelston— And I Just Now am waiting the Arrival of a Boat I have Bought to Go Down the river again And Expects to go in three Days from Now——No Dout you will think that a Dreadful Business to Tread[11] with the Ingins But you are Intirely Missinformed Respecting the Tread   you Expect that we that Go there must have Ingin wifes——True the white Men that Lives in the Nation has Mostely red women but that is their Pleasure[12]   I have my Licence from the Agent of War for one year and I Can Go and Come at my Pleasure During that Term without[13] Either woman or Man or what Company I See Cause to Take

---

8. **this**: i.e., this one.   9. **Pour**: conjectural; ms. torn.   10. **whiper ins**: i.e., whipper in (later: **whip**) is a parliamentary official whose function is to ensure that members of his party are present to vote on a given issue; here the term is used figuratively to designate a person (in Ireland, for example, an estate agent, or bailiff, sheriff, tithe proctor, etc.) who makes certain that subordinates obey the law and/or their socioeconomic superiors.   11. **Tread**: i.e., trade (reverse spelling).   12. **Pleasure**: desire, choice.   13. **without . . .** : Nevin appears to have left out some words here; the sense is: "without restriction of either woman or man or whatever company I see reason to take along."

along——I had intended being home Last Spring but it was Out of my Power but God willing I shall See you all this one Coming[14]——I am Sorry to Heir of So Many of my Countery men being Confined and Sume Executed But the Permissave will of God must be Done——you are Under the Rod of affliction in a high Degree and; o: that it may be Santifyed and Improven[15]   You Must Wait with Patience   your Deliverence (if not come before you receive this) is fast Hastening   you Complain of a Declintion[16] of Religion in me which I may with Shame Acknowledge in Part but Such Religion as we Now have here No Man hath Ever seen——I have Been yesterday at a Sacrement (an[17] Exercise as they Call it hath not been half so Bad as sume Other Meetings[18] I have Been at) But we have them here to Ly two or three Days as if Dead being struck Down at their Meetings And then to Break out into the Gratest Raptures of Prayer that the Minister is Sume times Oblyged to Quit Preaching to[19] they are Done Prayer[20]——and at their Meeting you Can See Sume Dancing Sume Running Sume Jumping Sume Jerking and twitching Like a Person in a Voilent Convulsive Fite[21]   Others Praying others Singing and others shouting Glory Glory as Loud as they Can Bawl And wringin and Clapping their hands And Such Other Conduct Sure[22] man Never Seen in Religious Worship and I wish it may be by the Direction of Heaven for it is fare[23] Beyond my Tongue or Pen to Describe——in my present atempt I am as far short of it as you may think I am beyond Anything you have Ever seen——and Althoug<h> it hath Alarmed me yet I Cannot Approve of it as God is a God of Order and Not of Confusion——We are Now in this Countery Under a Real Republickan Government and the Best in the World And has got into Possession of a New and Extensive Countery[24] which Ireland would not be a Garden to[25]——the river I go Down Goeth into it and perhaps I May Visit it Er I return   My Situation in Life[26] has Not Changed as yet and What is still worse No appearance of it   and for[27] my Health Thanks be to God alone, I never Knowen[28] (I may Say) what it is to be sick one Hour   if you Receive this in Time And it in your Powers Please send me on sume Linnen this season that it may be sume addition

---

14. this one Coming: "this coming spring."   **15. that it may be Santifyed and Improven**: that it may result in *spiritual* profit (**Santifyed**: earlier form of **sanctified**; **Improven**: Scots form of **improved**).   **16. Declintion**: i.e., declension "decay, falling off, decline."   **17. and** ms.   **18. Others Meeting** ms.   **19. to**: until.   **20. they are Done Prayer**: they have finished prayer/praying. The pattern **be done + X** "have finished X" is restricted to Scotland, Ireland, and the U.S. The element **X** can be represented by a verbal noun (e.g., praying) or its substitute (e.g., prayer, as here). Another pattern used is **be done + with + Object** (e.g. they are done with praying/prayer/us). Standard British English prefers **have** in all of these patterns. See chapter 13, n. 25; chapter 21, n. 44; and chapter 33, n. 22.   **21. Fite**: i.e., fit.   **22. Sure**: introductory, asseverative **sure** has become a hallmark of Irish, as opposed to English, colloquial speech, but in the seventeenth and eighteenth centuries it was very common in the latter.   **23. fare**: i.e., far.   **24. a New and Extensive Country**: i.e., the Louisiana Purchase territory, acquired from France in 1803.   **25. to**: in comparison to.   **26. Situation in Life**: i.e., marital status (Nevin died a bachelor).   **27. for**: as for (especially after **and** or **but**).   **28. Knowen**: knew.

to my Stock in going home[29]   Please Remember me to Brothers and Sisters Cousins and families, M[r] Step[h] Hunter, M[r] [. . .][30] family and Loughconaly People[31] and all friends[32] and Please make my appology for not writing as my Distance and few oppertunitys Puts out of my power to write to Every one———Whilst I Remain your Tender and Ever affectionate Brother till Death

John Nevin

Perhaps Nevin was fortunate that he traded primarily with the Indians in frontier Tennessee, for one consequence of the Second Great Awakening was a realignment of local economic relationships according to whether merchants and customers supported or opposed the revivals or according to their membership in one or another of the many competing denominations and sects that proliferated or expanded in the camp meetings' wake. However, as a republican (in both its Irish and American connotations) and as a traditional Calvinist, Nevin had even more profound reasons for concern. For in the late 1790s and early 1800s, many of the Presbyterian clergymen who initiated the Awakening in western Pennsylvania and Kentucky, albeit of Scots-Irish descent, were Federalists who viewed and promoted revivalism as an antidote to the French revolutionary radicalism that inspired the United Irishmen in Ulster and many of the Scots-Irish immigrants who became Jeffersonian Republicans in America.[33] Moreover, although those clergymen—like Nevin's Seceders in Ireland and in the United States—sought to combine orthodox Calvinism with the exigencies of evangelicalism, the latter's emphases on personal conversion and popular preaching challenged and quickly overwhelmed traditional beliefs in predestination and the necessity for a college-trained clergy. The result was repeated schisms within the main body of American Presbyterianism, and the churches that emerged and flourished after the revivals (the Cumberland Presbyterians, the Campbellites and Disciples of Christ, the Methodists, and most of the Baptists) embraced free-will theologies, often employed minimally trained or lay preachers, and generally eclipsed the Presbyterians in the South and West.[34]

---

29. that it may be sume addition . . . . : "that its sale may increase the profit I take with me when I return to Ireland."   **30.** Surname illegible.   **31.** Loughconaly People: i.e. John Nevin's kinsmen in Loughconnelly townland, in Skerry parish, north Co. Antrim; in 1862 the **Hunters** still held 235 acres in Loughconnelly.   **32.** friends: conjectural; ms. torn.   **33.** On the background and conservative political implications of the early phases of the Second Great Awakening, see especially chapters 47, 49, and 67.   **34.** Despite their own church's tradition of "lively preaching," the handful of Seceding Presbyterian clergy in the Ohio, Tennessee, and Cumberland valleys opposed the Second Great Awakening because of its theological deviations from strict Calvinism, the interdenominational and (as Nevin complained) the disorderly nature of many of its revivals, and their own adherence to a college-educated (and, if possible, Scottish-trained) ministry. Consequently, the revivals decimated the few Seceding congregations in Tennessee and Kentucky, but in any case, Nevin would have found Seceding Presbyterianism in the United States politically uncongenial, as its largely Scottish-born clergy regarded French and Irish revolutionary radicalism as "abhorrent." Although the various and relatively small American offshoots of the Seceding (and Covenanting) Presbyterian churches, unlike the main

Perhaps it was not surprising, therefore, that despite his enthusiasm for America's political institutions, John Nevin anticipated an early return to Ulster. However, the naval victory of the British admiral Horatio Nelson at Trafalgar, in October 1805, dashed Nevin's hope that the French would deliver Ireland from the "Rod of affliction," and he never went back to Kilmoyle, dying instead at Knoxville on 19 May 1806. In his will, Nevin bequeathed his "Estate in Ireland" and his American property to the siblings "who suffered persecution with me in Ireland for my political Opinions."[35] Back in Ballyrashane, someone wrote a popular ballad describing "Captain Nevin" as "a gallant hero," and his kinsmen commissioned the manufacture of a set of glazed earthenware jugs, inscribed "To the memory of John Nevin of Killmoyle, who was by the Foes of Reform Banish'd from his Native home . . . [and who] lived in the state of exile 7 years, 11 months, [and] 8 days."[36]

66 ❈

Thomas Addis Emmet, 1806–1807

As older Irish-American leaders, such as George Bryan and William Findley, either passed from the scene or adapted to the multiethnic exigencies of frontier politics, the "new Irish" immigrants of the late eighteenth and early nineteenth centuries, increasingly visible in the seaport cities, embraced the transplanted leadership of the exiled United Irishmen. Likewise, as Philadelphia's Irish leaders divided after 1800 along social, ideological, and factional lines, Irish-America's center of political gravity shifted to New York City—a trend made permanent after 1815 as the burgeoning Empire City, soon the gateway to the west via the Erie Canal, far outdistanced its urban rivals as the primary destination for the Irish immigrants who surged to the United States after the Napoleonic Wars. However, Irish-America's new leaders would not be radical journalists like John Daly Burk and the other polemicists who had borne the brunt of struggle against Federalist reaction in the 1790s but instead solid merchants and professionals who comprised, as one exile claimed, "the most respectable emigration which has taken place to your United States since the settlement of the New-England colonies."[1] Arriving for the most part after Jefferson's election victory, these men of "rank and property" found what one called a "happy country, where liberty is triumphant & cherished"[2]—and where Republican politicians,

---

Presbyterian denominations, remained distinctive and self-consciously Scots-Irish (and Scottish) ethnic enclaves in the nineteenth century in America, one of their most obviously "Irish" characteristics was an exceptionally pronounced anti-Catholicism, rather than the ecumenical liberalism or radicalism that had characterized much Presbyterianism in the late eighteenth century in Ulster. **35.** John Nevin's will, [signed] 16 May 1806; see Sources. **36.** A. McClelland, "A Link with the '98," 15; see Sources. **1.** [Rev. Thomas L. Birch], *A Letter from an Irish Emigrant to His Friend in the United States, Giving an Account of the Rise and Progress of the Commotions in Ireland* (Philadelphia, 1779). **2.** Thomas Addis Emmet, New York City, to Robert Simms, Belfast, 1 June 1805.

eager to enlist the exiles' aid in mobilizing the Irish vote, enabled the former United Irishmen to formalize claims to ethnic leadership through legal protection and party patronage. As a result, for the next several decades most of the new immigrants, Protestants and Catholics alike, assimilated as "Irish" into a party system that either validated (by the Republicans) or stigmatized (by the Federalists) the political principles and the bitter memories of British oppression that made them, albeit temporarily, "united" Irishmen in the New World.

In shaping this pattern of political adaptation, none was more significant than Thomas Addis Emmet who, along with his intimate friends and fellow New York exiles, William James Macneven[3] and William Sampson,[4] became the archetypal Irish leaders in the New World. Emmet was born in Cork city on 24 April 1764 and baptized in the legally established Church of Ireland. His ancestors had migrated from Lancashire and settled in County Tipperary during the mid-1600s; both his grandfather and his father, Robert (1729–1802), were physicians and modest landowners, and from his mother, Elizabeth Mason (d. 1803), Emmet would inherit several thousand acres in County Kerry. Shortly after their marriage in 1760, Emmet's parents moved to Dublin when a distant relation, then Irish lord lieutenant, secured his father the post of state physician. The second eldest of four surviving children (another 13 died in infancy), Emmet attended Trinity College, Dublin, and the University of Edinburgh, where he studied medicine. However, in 1788, after the death of his eldest brother, Emmet's father persuaded him to abandon medicine for a legal career. Accordingly, he studied law in London and in 1790 was admit-

---

3. William James Macneven (1763–1841): a Catholic whose ancestral holdings in Co. Galway were confiscated in the 1600s, Macneven was raised in Prague by his uncle, a baron and physician to the Austrian empress, and studied medicine there and in Vienna. With Emmet, Macneven was a member of the Leinster Directory of the United Irishmen and in 1798 was arrested and imprisoned in Ft. George, Scotland. Upon release, he sojourned in France and then joined Emmet in New York City, where he resumed his medical practice and also taught chemistry. Very prominent in founding and supporting Irish immigrant aid societies, in 1828 Macneven (with William Sampson) was a leader in organizing the Society for Civil and Religious Liberties and the Association of the Friends of Ireland in New-York, both of which supported Daniel O'Connell's campaign for Catholic emancipation in Ireland. However, in the early 1830s Macneven publicly criticized the Democrats for their attacks on the Second Bank of the United States, whereby he forfeited the loyalties of many of New York's middle- and working-class Irish, now allied with Tammany Hall and the Jacksonians. 4. William Sampson (1764–1837): born in Londonderry, the son of an Anglican clergyman, Sampson studied at Trinity College, Dublin, and law at Lincoln's Inn. It is uncertain whether Sampson actually joined the Society of United Irishmen, but he identified with their principles, methods, and goals, and became one of their most prominent legal advocates before the Irish bar. In 1798 he was arrested and imprisoned at Ft. George with Emmet and Macneven. On 4 July 1806 he disembarked at New York City, where he settled and resumed his legal practice. Several of Sampson's cases made legal history: e.g., in 1809, when he defended the city's cordwainers' union against conspiracy charges (with Emmet as opposing counsel for the prosecution); in 1813, when he argued successfully for the sanctity of the Catholic confessional against judicial inquiry; and in 1824 when, with Emmet, he defended the Irish Catholic weavers of Greenwich Village against riot charges that stemmed from their violent confrontation with local Orangemen on 12 July.

FIGURE 20
Portrait of Thomas Addis
Emmet (1764–1827) of New
York City, a mezzotint made
in Emmet's old age by John
Rubens Smith (1775–1849).
Photograph courtesy of the
National Portrait Gallery,
Smithsonian Institution,
Washington, D.C.

ted to the Irish bar. Two years later Emmet married Jane Patten (d. 1846), daughter of the
Presbyterian minister at Clonmel, County Tipperary.[5]

Albeit of slight stature, poor eyesight, and retiring personality, Emmet quickly won
fame as one of Ireland's most brilliant young barristers, earning over £1,000 per year, and
the government soon offered him official posts and honors to secure his loyalty. However,
during the late 1770s and 1780s Emmet's entire family had become radicalized, perhaps
through the influence of American relatives who returned to Ireland during the American
Revolution, and in the early 1790s Emmet became the chief legal advisor to the Dublin
Society of United Irishmen. In 1795–1796, after the Society was outlawed and became
overtly revolutionary, Emmet assumed increasing prominence among the United Irishmen
and helped solicit French military aid for an Irish rebellion. Always a sincere reformer but
a "reluctant revolutionary," Emmet's goal was an equality of rights, not of property; and

5. Emmet and his wife had 10 children, eight of whom reached adulthood: Robert, who became an eminent
lawyer and judge of the New York Superior Court; Thomas Addis, also a prominent New York lawyer, who
married Macneven's stepdaughter; John, trained by Macneven in medicine, who became professor of chemistry
at the University of Virginia and died in 1842; Temple, who died in the U.S. navy about 1822; Margaret, the
eldest daughter, who died unmarried; Elizabeth, who married a Mr. LeRoy and lived at Potsdam, New York;
Marianna, who wed a Mr. Graves; and Jane Erin, born during her parents' imprisonment at Ft. George,
Scotland, who married a Mr. McIver.

he believed that both élite leadership and the presence of a disciplined French army were essential to prevent insurrection from degenerating into "acts of outrage and cruelty" that "would give the nation lasting causes of grief and shame."[6] By mid-1797 Emmet was the leader of the United Irishmen in the south of Ireland, but on 12 March 1798 the government arrested him and nearly all the other members of the Leinster Directory.

After the Rebellion was crushed, Emmet, Macneven, and the other "state prisoners" bargained with Lord Cornwallis, the Irish lord lieutenant, agreeing to disclose the outlines of their conspiracy (without divulging names) in return for a cessation of executions and reprisals.[7] Implicit in the arrangement, or so Emmet and his comrades believed, was Cornwallis's pledge to permit their immediate emigration to Europe or the United States. However, the government reneged, in part, Emmet would later allege, because Rufas King, U.S. ambassador to Britain and an ardent New York Federalist,[8] refused to allow the United Irish leaders to seek refuge in America, where, he feared, they would range "themselves on the side of the [Republican] malcontents" and enlist "in mischievous combinations against our government."[9] Consequently, Emmet, Macneven, Sampson, and 17 other prisoners from Dublin and Belfast spent the next three years imprisoned at Fort George in Scotland. On his release in late June 1802, Emmet sojourned in Holland, then went to Paris with the expectation of joining a new French invasion of Ireland. However, Emmet's revived hopes for a successful Irish revolution were soon dashed. On 20 September 1803 his younger brother, Robert (b. 1778), was executed in Dublin for having led that summer's ill-fated rebellion, and by the autumn of 1804 Emmet had become disgusted by Napoleon's tyranny and deceitful conduct toward the Irish exiles. Thus, in October Emmet and his family embarked from Bordeaux for the United States, landing at New York on 17 November 1804.

Because of his abhorrence of slavery, Emmet rejected invitations to settle in the American South and for a time considered purchasing a farm in Ohio. However, the governor of New York, George Clinton,[10] and his nephew, De Witt Clinton,[11] the mayor

6. Durey, *Transatlantic Radicals*, 101; see Sources, chapter 66.   7. On Lord Cornwallis, see chapter 60, n. 22.
8. Rufas King (1755–1827): born in Maine, the son of a merchant, King graduated from Harvard in 1777 and served briefly as a militia officer in the Revolution before 1780, when he was admitted to the Massachusetts bar. In 1783–1785 King was a delegate to the Massachusetts General Assembly, in 1784–1786 to Congress, and in 1787 to the Constitutional Convention, where he may have inserted the clause prohibiting the states from impairing obligations of contracts. In 1786 he married into the Alsop family, wealthy New York City merchants and former Tories, and in 1788 he removed to New York. In 1789 the New York Assembly elected King to the U.S. Senate, where he strongly supported all the Federalists' domestic and foreign policies. In 1795 King was reelected to the Senate, and in 1796 he was appointed U.S. ambassador to Great Britain, where he served until 1803. King was the Federalist party's vice-presidential candidate in 1804 and in 1808, was elected again to the U.S. Senate in 1812, and was the Federalists' presidential candidate in 1816. Reelected once more to the Senate in 1820, King's opposition to the admission of Missouri to the Union as a slave state helped precipitate the nation's first major sectional crisis.   9. Twomey, *Jacobins & Jeffersonians*, 43; see Sources.
10. George Clinton (1739–1812); also see chapter 51, n. 32.   11. De Witt Clinton (1769–1828) was a leading New York state assemblyman and senator in 1797–1802 when, while serving on the state council of

of New York City, urged Emmet to remain in Manhattan and resume the practice of law. The elder Clinton, son of a Presbyterian immigrant from County Longford, was a sincere democrat and an admirer of the United Irishmen, but he also hoped to use Emmet's prestige to harness the Irish vote to the Clintonian faction of the state Republican party. Accordingly, when Emmet assented to Clinton's proposal, the governor persuaded the state supreme court justices to waive the usual residence requirements and admit Emmet to the New York bar, despite Federalist protests that he was a "fugitive Jacobin."[12] Emmet's first case, in defense of fugitive slaves, won widespread admiration and launched what became a spectacularly successful legal career. Within a few years he emerged as one of his adopted country's preeminent lawyers, with an annual income exceeding $10,000. It was not surprising, then, that merely two years after disembarking at New York, Emmet summarily rejected a suggestion from an old friend in Dublin, Peter Burrowes,[13] that he return to Ireland.

Letter 1.
Thomas Addis Emmet, New York City,
to Peter Burrowes, Dublin, 19 November 1806

New York   Novr. 19th
1806

My Dear Burrowes

I had the pleasure of receiving yours of July last in due time—& first as to the matter of business to which it alludes——I have inquired after Mr Fotterell's claim to property in Baltimore, and the result is pretty conclusively, that

appointment, he allegedly introduced the "spoils system" that signaly benefited Emmet and other Irish immigrants then and thereafter. Elected to the U.S. Senate in 1802, Clinton resigned to become mayor of New York City (then appointed by the state governor), in which post he served almost continuously from 1803 to 1815. As mayor and later as New York's governor (elected 1817, 1820, and 1825), Clinton was chiefly responsible for laying the foundations of New York's public school system and for the successful completion of the Erie Canal, both of which were especially beneficial to poor Irish immigrants in need of employment and free education.   12. R. R. Madden, *The Life and Times of Robert Emmet* . . . , 297; see Sources.   13. Peter Burrowes (1753–1841): born in Portarlington, Queen's Co., of a "respectable," Anglican family, Burrowes graduated with distinction from Trinity College, Dublin, and studied law at the Middle Temple, London. Although never a member of the United Irishmen, Burrowes strongly supported parliamentary reform and Catholic emancipation, was an intimate friend of Emmet and Wolfe Tone, and was defense counsel for several United Irish leaders, including Robert Emmet in 1803. An Irish M.P. for Enniscorthy, Co. Wexford, in 1799–1800, Burrowes strongly opposed the Act of Union, thereby earning the enmity of Tory politicians who refused to consider him for honors or promotions thereafter. Only in 1806–1807, when the Tories briefly fell from power and the Grenville ministry "of all the talents" was in office, did reformer Charles James Fox appoint Burrowes as first counsel to the Irish revenue commissioners, with fees alone averaging £14,000 per year. This was the appointment to which Emmet's letter refers. However, Burrowes lost the post in April 1807, when the Tories returned to office, and he refused on principle their offers of subsequent appointments. His only other official position was a judgeship of the insolvent debtors' court in Dublin.

nothing can now be done; & probably never could, even if the party entitled had come out here to urge his claim——Mr Puffer is at present in Baltimore, and I have furnished him with all the information I could get before his departure; & on his return shall put into his hands another letter I have since received——he therefore will I suppose write more particularly[14] than I have time to do. As to your late law arrangements I sincerely rejoice my good friend that promotion has fallen upon your head & those of some others where I think it will be bestowed——In the list of the promotions, however, there are Men of whom I never wish to think; because I cannot think of them without the strongest emotions of aversion & disgust—strong & warm as was my former friendship. In the conclusion of your letter, you ask a question, which, if I did not know the occasional absence of your thoughts, would have caused me much speculation——"Do you ever mean to visit us" says an influential officer of the Government of Ireland, to a proscribed exile, whose return would be death by law,[15] "or to send over any of your children." A man who was very anxious to return would catch at this offer; but that is not my case—I am settled here with the fairest prospects for my self & my Children,   my principles & my sufferings were my first passport & introduction here—& they procured me the effective friendship of the leading Characters of this State & in the Union at large——In proportion as I cherish those principles, I am respected, & every day's reflection & observation makes them dearer to me——Ought I to go, where they are treason—& sufficient ground for perpetual proscription? Besides my good friend, I am too proud, when vanquished to assist by my presence, in gracing the triumph of the Victor——And with what feelings should I tread on Irish ground?—as if I were walking over graves—& those the graves of my nearest Relatives & my dearest friends——No, I can never wish to be in Ireland, except in such a way, as none of my old friends connected with the Government, could wish to see me placed in——As to my Children—I hope they will learn here to love liberty too much, ever to fix a voluntary residence in an enslaved Country—— Nothing in their future prospects gives me more pain than the fear that my eldest boy will be obliged when he comes of age, to go to Ireland to dispose of some settled property; which, if I were worth a few thousand dollars more, I should wish rather in the hands of my greatest enemy than his——There is not now in Ireland an individual that bears the name of Emmet—I do not wish that there ever should, while it is connected with England—And yet it will perhaps be remembered in its history. With the very sincerest & warmest esteem—believe me

Ever Yours,

T: A: Emmet

---

14. **more particularly**: in greater detail.   15. **death by law**: in suggesting that Emmet revisit Ireland, Burrowes apparently had forgotten or ignored the terms of his friend's exile under the Banishment Act, which prescribed the death penalty for the return of unpardoned traitors; indeed, according to the Act, even Burrowes's correspondence with Emmet was a felony offense, punishable by transportation to the Australian penal colonies.

THOMAS ADDIS EMMET

In many respects, Emmet was supremely content in America; indeed, at times he could scarcely bear to "think of Ireland," so painful were his recollections. However, his private life revolved around Irish associations, as his family, the Macnevens, the Sampsons, and other exiles formed "a little Irish community" in New York City.[16] More important, much of Emmet's public life played upon the politics of ethnic memory and association. Emmet and his fellow exiles were prominent in the Hibernian Provident Society (est. 1802), the Shamrock Friendly Association (1816), and similar organizations designed to guide New York's new Irish immigrants and to protect and promote their interests. In part, Emmet's enormous prestige among his poorer countrymen stemmed from his own considerable abilities, his past sacrifices for Ireland, and his generous character. It also reflected the enormous popular respect for his martyred brother, Robert, whose memory was toasted at St. Patrick's Day observances more frequently than that of any other Irish hero. Ultimately, however, Emmet's influence was linked to the fortunes of the Clintonian wing of the state's Republican party, the source of the legal protection and patronage that succored and advanced Irish immigrants in a city whose economy was dynamic but perilous and whose laws and inhabitants' attitudes were often less than favorable to the newcomers. For example, it was only in 1802 that the city council outlawed the traditional "Paddy" effigies, whose flaunting by nativist mobs had frequently led to sectarian riots, and not until 1806 was the state's Test Act, which barred Catholics from public office, repealed—over Federalists' protests and largely through De Witt Clinton's efforts. Likewise, on Christmas Eve, 1806, major riots broke out when native Protestants disrupted services at St. Peter's Catholic church; again, only intercession by Clintonian politicians protected the Irish against legal reprisals.

Thus, to hold New York City's 10,000–15,000 Irish immigrants together, across denominational lines, in a political bloc that would command respect and rewards, it was essential that Emmet should both serve the Clintonian cause and emphasize the nonsectarian principles and common experiences of the United Irishmen. In spring 1807, during the election campaign for the New York state Assembly, Emmet seized the opportunity to achieve both goals, as well as gain a measure of revenge against Rufas King. When the Federalists tried to split the Irish vote by nominating Andrew Morris, an Irish-American Protestant, for an Assembly seat, Emmet's Hibernian Provident Society threatened to expel any member who voted for Morris. Then Emmet publicly attacked Rufas King, the city's leading Federalist and his party's gubernatorial candidate, for having prevented the Irish state prisoners from emigrating to the United States in 1799. Alleging that King was "unfit to be trusted . . . with any kind of delegated power," Emmet charged that his enemy's "unwarrantable and unfeeling interference . . . [had] degraded the dignity and independence of the country you represented," for "you abandoned the principles of its govern-

16. R. R. Madden, *The United Irishmen . . .*, vol. 4, 190; see Sources.

ment and . . . became the tool" of British tyranny.[17] The Federalists responded with fury, made the New York Irish their primary campaign issue, and called on the voters to reject "being led and governed by the outcasts of Europe," by "foreign vagrants" and "imported incendiaries." The Clintonians countered by identifying the Irish struggle against England with the American Revolution: "No man can be an enemy to the Irish," they argued, "who is not sold to England."[18]

In the short run, at least, Emmet's strategy was successful: the Clintonians won a large majority of Assembly seats; King himself was denied election, as was Morris; and the Republicans had embraced a central tenet of United Irish doctrine—the affinity between 1776 and 1798. However, the strategy also threatened "discord and hatred" between native and naturalized citizens, as the Federalists (rather hypocritically) charged, and for the Federalists and their political successors the Irish came to symbolize corruption, vulgarity, and violence. In the aftermath of the 1807 election, however, Emmet was confident, as he revealed in the following letter to Robert Simms of Belfast, once a fellow prisoner at Fort George.[19] Indeed, given the recent disgrace of the Clintonians' chief rival, Aaron Burr[20]

---

17. Thomas Addis Emmet, New York City, to Rufas King, New York City, 9 April 1807; in R. R. Madden, *The Life and Times of Robert Emmet . . .* , 308, 310–11; see Sources, chapter 66. Emmet's accusations against King were disingenuous in several respects. First, it is by no means clear that Emmet intended emigrating to the United States in 1799; indeed, because of the yellow fever epidemic then raging in American seaports, as well as the anticipated hardship of the voyage upon his children, Emmet had expressed a preference for exile in Germany. Second, King had not acted alone: his attitude toward the United Irishmen clearly reflected the spirit, if not the express wishes, of the Adams administration. Finally, it does not appear that King intrigued with the Irish and British governments to deny the state prisoners access to the United States; rather, King's opposition to their exile caused Lord Cornwallis's administration considerable consternation. However, Emmet was not privy to the latter circumstances, and his contempt for King, his party, and his principles was entirely sincere. **18.** H. Strum, "Federalist Hibernophobes in New York . . . ," 9–11; see Sources. **19.** Robert Simms: with his brother and business partner, William (also mentioned in Emmet's letter), Simms was an affluent merchant, tanner, and paper manufacturer in Belfast and a founder of that city's United Irishmen (1791) and of their newspaper, the *Northern Star*. In November 1797 Robert Simms was elected the United Irishmen's military commander in Co. Antrim. However, he accepted the post reluctantly, citing his lack of military experience, and in June 1798 he resigned his command, amid charges of cowardice or treachery, refusing to lead a rebellion in the absence of French military assistance. Imprisoned with Emmet, Macneven, and others at Ft. George, Simms was released in 1802, returned to Belfast, and resumed his mercantile career, declining Emmet's encouragement to emigrate to America. Although apparently uninvolved in Robert Emmet's 1803 conspiracy, Simms and his brother never disavowed their radical principles and remained subject to government surveillance. **20.** Aaron Burr (1756–1836): in 1772 a graduate of the College of New Jersey, Burr served on Washington's staff during the Revolution. One of the chief organizers of the Republican party in New York City, Burr served as state attorney general (1789–1791), as U.S. senator (1791–1797), and several terms in the state assembly before his controversial election in 1800–1801 as Jefferson's vice president. After killing Alexander Hamilton in a duel (11 July 1804), Burr fled New York, and in 1806 he became involved in a conspiracy the precise nature of which—whether to conquer Mexico or to persuade the western states and territories to secede from the Union (as Emmet apparently believed)—has never been clarified. Tried for treason and high misdemeanors at the U.S. circuit court in Richmond, Virginia, Burr was acquitted, primarily (or so Emmet and other Republicans believed) because of the Federalist partiality of the presiding judge, John Marshall, chief justice of the U.S. Supreme Court.

and, more important, the British attack in June 1807 on the U.S. warship *Chesapeake*[21]—an incident that united Irish immigrants with most Americans in a frenzy of hatred for England—it seemed that Emmet had every reason to be sanguine about his people's future in their adopted country.[22]

Letter 2.
Thomas Addis Emmet, New York City,
to Robert Simms, Belfast, 2 November 1807

New York   Nov[r] 2nd 1807—

Dear Simms

I was extremely gratified by the receipt of yours of the 22nd of August last, & particularly so by finding that you approved of the steps I was induced to take here in politics. I have been compelled by a sense of duty, & the foolish scurrility of the federalists to make myself very prominent by my controversy with Rufas King. Their malignity (if they had succeeded) would have pursued me with as much fury &

---

21. On 22 June 1807, off the Virginia coast, the British commander of H.M.S. *Leopard* demanded that the U.S. frigate *Chesapeake* surrender four of its sailors, claiming they were deserters from the British navy. When the *Chesapeake*'s captain refused, the *Leopard* opened fire—killing three and wounding 18—and seized the alleged deserters. In response, on 2 July President Jefferson ordered all British vessels to leave U.S. territorial waters, but on 17 October the British government ordered an even more vigorous prosecution of its policy of impressing British subjects from neutral vessels. On 22 December the Republican-controlled Congress passed, at Jefferson's behest, an Embargo Act that interdicted virtually all American commerce with Britain and other foreign countries. On 18 June 1812, the issues of British impressment of U.S. citizens and of freedom of the seas for American commerce, as well as American ambitions to conquer Canada and Florida, led to a U.S. declaration of war against Britain.   **22.** An 1807 letter from William Sampson, a 1798 exile and one of Emmet's closest friends, described New Yorkers' initial reaction to the *Leopold*'s attack on the *Chesapeake,* as well as the array and political complexion of the city's Irish-American societies. After witnessing the local Fourth of July celebration, Sampson wrote: "All the militia and Volunteer troops were paraded at 6 Oclock on a beautiful spot called the battery, and there reviewed by their General. They then about 9 or ten marched through the principal Streets in the Town and made a very good figure. Then came the Civil associations such as the Tammany society so called from an Indian Saint or Patron [and t]he Hibernian provident Society, instituted by Irish Emigrants for purposes of Charity, and chiefly to provide for Such poor Countrymen as arrive from their native country, and <u>provide</u> them occupation there fore called <u>provident</u>. . . . Emmet & M[c]Nevin are of it. It was charged by the Federal or English party with having turned the [1807] election in favor of the Republicans and was of course much abused by the opposition. There are many Belfast men in it old acquaintances & some old clients of mine. It had a complete political triumph. . . . But what animated this days ceremonies was the resentment felt and universally expressed against the attack of the English Ship Leopold upon the american Ship Chesapeake   in this resentment all parties joined and the most hostile united to express by unanimous resolutions their determined resentment and indignation and to pledge themselves to . . . make every sacrifice to preserve their national honor and independance. War is generally expected in consequence. . . . This day I was entertained by an Irish corps of volunteers called the Republican greens. We had a band of volunteer music which made dinner pass agreeably." William Sampson, New York City, to Grace Sampson, [Belfast?], 4 July 1807; see Sources, chapter 66.

effect as that of the Orangemen in Ireland—but thank God they are powerless. Even beaten as they are, they combined to do me every professional injury in their power—but finding the combination of no avail, a sense of individual interest forces them to abandon it. Rufas King is placed in public opinion just where he ought to be; & unless the federalists possess the power of reviving the dead, I hope & believe will never again do much mischief—but that they can do a great deal too much is manifest from the issue of Burr's trial. That man, whom they hated while he appeared to be a Republican, whom they never tolerated till he became a Renegado, & never openly upheld until he attempted to sever the Union & establish a monarchy within the territory of the United States—that man is acquitted by their intrigues & interference—by their partiality & exertions, tho' his guilt is fully developed,[23] & no man affects to doubt it. It is very possible however that his acquittal will do good—it will cause a revisal of some defective parts of our criminal law, & perhaps an investigation of the conduct & opinions of some of our judges, who stand at the head of the federalists, & continued in office notwithstanding the overthrow of their Party. Jefferson's administration is I think entitled to all your praise—& as he will not serve again, I think his probable successor (the present vice President)[24] will equally claim your approbation for his uprightness, &, what in these times is very necessary, for his decision & firmness. On the subject of war, most people judge here differently from what I apprehend you do in Europe. We expect it. The calamities it will produce are known to every body—universally spoken off & admitted—the ruin of our commerce & of every occupation connected with it is held up in the strongest point of view by the English agents & factors—& underrated by no one—but nevertheless (except the English agents & factors) almost every one is ready & willing to bear his share of those inconveniences & calamities. With the English agents & factors must be counted the leading Mercantile federalists in the commercial cities—if in truth they are not the same thing with different names—but the other federalists in the Country parts[25] partake very much of the general Spirit. The claims of Great Britain to the right of search & impressment might have remained undecided upon, but for the affair of the Chesapeak & the report of the West India Committee[26] which insists upon the necessity of destroying almost all neutral commerce with belligerents—these have now brought into discussion the whole of her pretensions & awakened the remembrance of

---

23. developed: exposed, revealed.   **24.** Jefferson's . . . probable successor (the present vice President): i.e. George Clinton of New York. Emmet miscalculated, as James Madison of Virginia, not Clinton, was the Republican party's victorious presidential candidate in 1808; however, Emmet's patron was reelected as vice president in Madison's first administration.   **25.** the Country parts: i.e., the rural areas (of the United States). **26.** the West India Committee: the British parliamentary committee partly responsible for the policies that in 1805–1806 authorized a sharp increase in British seizures of American vessels trading with the French West Indies.

all her conduct towards America since 1793.[27] The result is that the most moderate feel the necessity of repressing those pretensions & resenting that conduct at some period; & the most reflecting imagine that no period can promise better than the present. The first consequences of the war are admitted & calculated upon—but the ultimate effects of it on the colonial system manufactures & commerce of England, & even upon her naval strength if she should fail in the Baltic, & be unable to supply herself with Naval stores from thence, are anticipated as fully equivalent to the misfortunes of its commencement. French politics have nothing to say to these sentiments—tho' undoubtedly in the event of a rupture, America would endeavour to turn to the best advantage the alliance with france—& in the West India seas the two powers united, & the ports of each opened to the cruisers & ships of the other would embarrass England much beyond what she has ever experienced in that quarter. Adieu my good friend. M[rs] E & my three eldest unite in the most affectionate remembrance with yours

very sincerely

T. A. Emmet

I request you will remember me most kindly to your brother & such of my old friends as still feel an interest for me

On the surface, the remainder of Emmet's life in America was marked by repeated triumphs. He practiced before the U.S. Supreme Court (for example, in the famous *Gibbons v. Ogden* case of 1824), as well as before the New York bar, and his fame and wealth continued to increase. In 1812 the Clintonians secured his appointment as state attorney general, and during the Anglo-American war of 1812–1815 he commanded an Irish militia regiment assigned to defend Manhattan against British attack. And when Emmet died in court on 15 November 1827, his funeral was the largest public spectacle ever seen in New York City: the city council adjourned in his honor and attended en bloc; all business was suspended throughout the city, and the flag of every vessel in the harbor remained at half-mast during the ceremony; and De Witt Clinton, Martin Van Buren, and other dignitaries served as pall-bearers. No wonder that his old comrade, Macneven, eulogized Emmet for "the beneficial influence he has shed upon the Irish character in the United States," dispelling nativist prejudices through "the bright example of [his] great personal worth."[28]

Even before Emmet's death, however, cracks had appeared in the façades of Irish-native American and of Irish-American unity. In 1808 the United Irish exiles divided acrimoniously between the rival candidacies of the elderly George Clinton, Emmet's patron, and of James Madison for the Republican party's presidential nomination; by 1816

---

27. since 1793: i.e., since the outbreak of war between Britain and the French Republic, when London inaugurated its policy of forbidding neutral counties to trade with France or with French allies and colonies, resulting in the British navy's seizure and condemnation of American merchant ships so engaged.   **28.** Potter, *Golden Door*, 214–16; see Sources.

Emmet, Macneven, and other Irish Clintonians had been ousted from the Hibernian Provident Society, joining in response a newer organization, the Shamrock Friendly Association. In addition to factional strife, class tensions also began to rend the New York Irish community. As early as 1809 Emmet's prosecution of the city's cordwainers' union—ironically, on conspiracy charges under English Common Law—had exposed potential conflicts between middle- and working-class immigrants; and after the War of 1812 the Shamrock Friendly Association—as well as Emmet's own advice letters in Irish newspapers—warned poor Irishmen away from New York City and urged them to migrate westward and shun whiskey, in part so they would not provoke nativist scorn and embarrass Irish-America's urban bourgeoisie. In 1817–1818 Emmet's and his friends' unsuccessful effort to persuade Congress to grant the Irish large tracts of land in Illinois, where they could settle as yeomen farmers, followed the same logic. Most ominous, on 12 July 1824 the Orange-Green riots in Greenwich Village, which pitted recently arrived Irish Protestants against Irish Catholic weavers, signaled both the transplantation to America of the vicious sectarianism that had become common in Ireland since the Act of Union and the beginning of the disintegration of the United Irishmen's ecumenical ideals in the United States. Finally, in 1817 Tammany Hall's refusal to nominate Emmet for the state Assembly revealed the depth of nativism current even among many Republicans, while Tammany's later, cynical courtship and manipulation of the working-class Irish vote helped destroy what remained of the United Irishmen's claims to ethnic leadership. Thus, by 1832 when the New York Irish gathered at St. Peter's Episcopal cemetery, where Emmet was buried, to unveil a 30-foot-tall white marble obelisk in his honor, the occasion also symbolized the entombment of Emmet's dream of Irish and Irish-American amity.

67 ✳

William Heazelton, Jr., 1814

Many of the reasons for the ultimate demise of Emmet's dream can be traced in the letters of William Heazelton. To be sure, Heazelton's own career merely exemplifies several mundane patterns of eighteenth- and early nineteenth-century Irish emigration: movement abroad by members of middle-rank and often downwardly mobile Irish Protestant families and the transfer of Irish capital—in the forms of rents and inheritances—to more lucrative fields of investment. More important, however, William Heazelton's letters illustrate the transplantation and overseas nurture of an Irish Protestant political conservatism that would doom the United Irishmen's ecumenical project as completely in the New World as in the Old.

In Ireland during the late eighteenth and early nineteenth centuries, politically conservative Protestants were distinguished by their loyalism and, from the mid-1790s, usually by membership in the Orange Order and often by the evanglicalism of the so-called New Reformation—a series of Protestant revivals and missionary efforts, funded by pious Britons and Irish landlords, that flourished first among Heazelton's Methodists but soon engaged many Anglicans and doctrinally and politically conservative Presbyterians. In contemporary America, conservative Irish Protestant immigrants usually adhered to the Federalist and, later, to the Whig and Republican parties. In addition, and despite their own foreign birth, immigrants such as Heazelton were frequently associated with American nativist movements that targeted Irish Catholic newcomers and their church, as well as Irish-born radicals of all denominations.

From the 1780s William Heazelton's home in mid-Ulster's "linen triangle" was the epicenter of fierce conflicts between roughly equal numbers of Catholics and Protestants— the latter finely balanced between Anglicans and dissenters and between those sympathetic and those opposed to political reforms. In the 1790s the French Revolution and the agitation of the United Irishmen sharply divided the region's Presbyterians, but local Anglicans, Quakers, and Methodists tended to be staunchly loyal, the latter especially so. In the early and mid–eighteenth century, the Heazeltons had been Quakers. William the emigrant was a son of William Heazelton and Susanna Morton (b. 1728), sister of John and Samuel Morton, who had emigrated to Philadelphia in 1764,[1] and of Mary Morton (1725–1814) who married William Greeves (1719–1766). The latter's son, John Greeves of Bernagh (1761–1843), was William Heazelton the emigrant's cousin and the recipient of his letters from America.

Both the Greeves and the Heazelton families worshiped at the Friends' meetinghouse at Grange Upper, in north County Armagh, but their homes were a few miles away in east County Tyrone, between Moy and Dungannon—primarily in the parishes of Killyman and Clonfeacle, where they held lands under the earls of Ranfurly.[2] In the late 1700s Ulster Quakerism was waning as the wealthiest and most ambitious Friends joined the Church of Ireland while many of their poorer coreligionists embraced Wesleyan Methodism. The family of John Greeves of Bernagh retained affluence as linen drapers, tanners, and large farmers and remained loyal to their ancestors' Quaker faith. However, their relatively poor relation, William Heazelton, apparently inherited only about 30 acres in Culnagrew townland, in Killyman parish, and sometime in the late 1700s he joined the Methodists.

William Heazelton's letters and other family correspondence suggest that it was his Irish debts—as well as a failed marriage—that obliged his emigration at a fairly advanced age. Heazelton probably disembarked at Philadelphia, but he quickly migrated to Pittsburgh, either accompanying relations or joining them there sometime prior to October 1810, when he wrote his first surviving letter to his cousin in Bernagh. As early as 1807–

---

1. On the Mortons, see chapter 56. 2. For demographic data on Killyman parish and its environs, see appendix 2.1c, on chapter 67.

1808 Pittsburgh's newspaper had recorded the presence of several "Hazletons," and in the former year Edward Heazelton, apparently William's brother, was a founding member of the city's first Methodist church (actually built in 1810), as was his brother-in-law and business partner, Nathaniel Holmes. In 1813 the first Pittsburgh directory listed both William and Edward Heazelton as merchants—the former on Market Street, between Diamond and Fifth streets, and the latter (with Holmes) at the corner of Market and Fifth.

Early nineteenth-century Pittsburgh, "gateway to the west" via the Ohio River, was an ideal setting for William Heazelton's efforts to recoup his fortune. Between 1800 and 1820 the city's population rose from 1,565 to 7,248, and its business community flourished: trading with Philadelphia and downriver as far as New Orleans; supplying migrants to the Ohio country; and, especially during the War of 1812, manufacturing commodities such as iron, glass, and textiles. However, William Heazleton apparently enjoyed only a modest and precarious success in his new home. "I am Now begining the World in the new and as Usual <am> hard put to it," he wrote in 1810, while begging his cousin to remit him the rents of Culnagrew. "[Y]ou know my Capital here was Small and house Rents very Dear," he complained, for "I pay 190 Dolars p^r yeare for a Store and 2 Rooms and on so Small a Sum as I had I Cannot Lay in goods Sufficient to make the Rent. . . . [Y]ou have heard many acct^s of this Country," he continued, "and I now for my part think that if the people would be as Indoustrous at home the<y> might Doe as Well" in Ulster as in America; "for them that has not money heare the<y> must Work harder than I ever Saw them doe in Ireland."[3] Although by 1814 Heazelton was doing "a great Dale" of trade in dry goods, his letter that year, printed hereafter, indicates his continued reliance on infusions of Irish capital.

Heazelton's Pittsburgh was also a mecca for Irish immigrants, especially for Presbyterians (and some Catholics) from Ulster. Thus, in 1810 he exclaimed that "the 9/10 of the people of pittsburg is Irish and the<y> are flocking here Every day." Yet Heazelton clearly was alienated from many of his transplanted fellow countrymen, primarily but not exclusively from "the Lower order of the Irish," who were, he alleged, the city's "Least Respected" inhabitants. Heazelton's condemnation of the latter's propensity for "hot Liqures<,> which is the Ruin of many of the Irish here,"[4] was routine among ambitious Irishmen of all faiths and political persuasions.[5] However, Heazelton's 1814 letter suggests that in Ireland he had joined "the orang<e> men," and certainly he expressed opinions that, at this early date, were still quite uncommon among Ulster immigrants: contempt for those he called "the Blagaird Runaway united Irish men" and opposition to the Jeffersonian Republican Party and to the War of 1812, both of which most Irish-Americans supported wholeheartedly.

3. William Heazelton, Pittsburgh, to John Greeves, Bernagh, Co. Tyrone, 22 October 1810.   4. William Heazelton, 22 October 1810.   5. E.g., see chapter 26.

William Heazelton, Pittsburgh, Pennsylvania,
to John Greeves, Bernagh, Killyman Parish, County Tyrone, 29 May 1814

Pittsburgh   29 May 1814

Dr John

I have wroate often to you but have not Recd an answer   I onst[6] more wright
to you   perhaps Some of them you may Receive   I Sopose you think that we are all
Killd in this Contry but some of us is still alive and well   as to my part I am well and
has my Health as well as Ever I had in my life and hopes that you and your good
family Injoys health and hapiness in the like manner   Dr John I think Long[7] to heare
from you and my Friends and how the<y> are Doeing,   I am Still keeping a Store
and has but one Clark and my Self which does my buisiness[8] and I doe asure you I doe
a great Dale[9] in drie goods and Groseries and also Defrent[10] articles of the projuse of
this Contry   we must have our hand in many things to meake[11] a living here as house
Rents is high and Vituling Remarkble dear   the Rates[12] at present is   my house
Rent is 300 Dollars pr year   flower 6 Dollars pr hundred[13]   butter 37½ Cents by the
pound   beef 10.c   beacon 20c   potatoes 1 Dollar pr Bushell and Every thing Else in
proportion as the Crops mist in this Country Laste year and produse buying up[14] for
the army   this warr is not a popular warr here   Some for it and some against it but I
think it would be Better for this Country the<y> had never begun it and how it will
End god only Knowes   as for my part I wish it was over and the Seaes Clear   I
would Soon be home with you if provedance would permit me   Jo Will Left me last
June and took a trip to new orleanes Where he got in to Imployment with a gentle
man whome was a kind of Comasary to the people here Call<ed> patriotts and have
hard[15] that he was killed the 24 July Last in an ingagement with the Spaniards near new
mexicoe[16]   Jo Got to be a very fine boy but he though<t> to meake his fortune at

---

6. onst: i.e., once; the final t is excresent, as in whilst. Excresent t is frequently heard after n, s, and f in Ulster
speech; as in sartint "certain" (see Alient hereafter) twicet "twice," clift "cliff."   7. think Long: be anxious.
8. does my buisness: is enough for me (Gaelicism: déanfaidh sé sin mo ghnó "that'll do my business,"
"that'll be enough").   9. Dale: i.e., deal; I doe a great Dale in drie goods "I do a great deal of business in
drygoods." Dale is a phonetic spelling, showing the preservation of Middle English long open e in Hiberno-
English generally.   10. Defrent: spelling shows Ulster pronunciation.   11. meake: i.e., make. The text of
Heazelton's letter abounds in such spellings: weare "were" [wayr], ingeaged "engaged" (see ingagement
above), teaking "taken," tread "trade," Streangers "strangers," Every pleace "everyplace," nopleace
"noplace," Weating "waiting," teade "take."   12. Rates: prices, cost.   13. hungred ms.   14. produse
buying up: produce being bought up; see chapter 4, n. 45.   15. hard: Scots and general Ulster for heard.
16. Apparently, Jo Will was killed while engaged in a privately organized military expedition in aid of the
Mexican Revolution (1810–1821) against Spanish rule. The specific reference may be to Guitiérrez de Lara's
abortive invasion of Texas (then a province of Spanish Mexico), with the connivance of U.S. authorities, in
1812–1813; in the spring of 1813 de Lara's army, partly composed of American mercenaries, captured San
Antonio but was soon defeated by royalist forces led by José Joaquin Arredondo, who subsequently executed
over three hundred invaders and rebels.

onst but his Expectations and [. . .] weare Disapointed   it was not with my Concent he went to the Southard[17] or ingeaged in any party afaires[18] in this Country   for my part I Keep as Quiet as I Can here tho not in Sulted buy any Respectable people but am teaking[19] by the hand   the better Sort of people heare treates me as well as my heart Could wish and my Creddit is as good as I could Ever Expect   I doe asure you I have not been Idle   I met with Some Losses in tread which you Can hardly avoid in this Country   the Lower order of the Irish is the worst and Least Respected but where the<y> are a Clever honest man the<y> farr Exceed any other Streangers[20] that Comes here   the Blagaird[21] Runaway united Irish men makes a Great fuss here but Getting out of Creddit Rapaidly   they are the onely people that I dislike for their bad Conduct and lying Stories that the<y> propagate a gainst Ireland but the<y> are Coming fast down[22] as the Real americans dont Like them on any acc[t]   what I mean by Real[23] Americans is the better Sort of people Call<ed> Federlists   but there is good and bad of all Kinds Every pleace   D[r] John Let me Know how you Get my Rents paid   I hope you meake them pay up as I know it is all one thank[24] and Iam in Need of money as Soon as it Can be Sent Safely to me   if the warr was over and my affairs Setled I would Go home and Live the Remainder of my days Quietly——— your Nephew John G. Greeves is well   he Lives in new Orleanes and has a good Sallery for being a Clark to a Merchant there   I heard from him a few days agoe   he had to Leave orlanes on acc[t] of the Alient act[25] and Live in the Country which Cost him Some Money   he wroght to me he would be heare in the fall as Every Alient Must be 40 miles from the Sea Which has drove a Great Deal of People to this Westring[26] Country   there is nopleace in the union Improving So fast as pittsburgh

---

17. the Southard: the part of the country lying to the south (OED, s.v., B); here, the Spanish southwest.
18. party afaires: i.e., partisan politics; the expedition in which **Jo Will** lost his life was undoubtedly organized by Republicans who sympathized with the Mexican Revolution and/or hoped to annex Spanish territory to the United States.   **19. teaking**: i.e., taken (reverse spelling).   **20. Streangers**: foreigners.   **21. Blagaird**: blackguard; spelling reflects Scots and Ulster Scots pronunciation [**blugaird**] (stress on second syllable).
22. Coming fast down: quickly losing respect.   **23. Leal** ms. In contemporary Scots, **leal** was a somewhat archaic adjective meaning "true" or "good" (SND). Thus, although it is clear that Heazelton's intention was to expand here on the definition of what he had called, in his preceding sentence, **Real americans**, he may have been thinking simultaneously of the virtues of whose whom he regarded as **leal**; i.e., "leal Americans" = "real" or "true Americans" (both were common self-appellations among American Protestant nativists in the early and mid-1800s).   **24. one thanks** ms.; **it is all one's thank**, normally "it is all the gratitude one can expect," spoken of a perfunctory return of thanks, which disappoints the recipient (SND, s.v. thank); in the present context Heazelton's meaning is obscure, but he may perhaps be saying that his relationship with his tenants is purely a hardheaded matter of business in which rent is agreed to and paid and no finer feelings are involved.
25. the Alient act: In February 1813 the U.S. State Department ordered all "alien enemies" (including unnaturalized Irish as well as British immigrants) who lived within 40 miles of the seacoast and were engaged in commerce to move inland; those so situated but not employed in commerce had to apply for permission to remain. Ironically in view of Heazelton's strictures against the United Irish exiles, theirs were the loudest protests against these restrictions, as impugning recent Irish immigrants' loyalty to their adopted country.
26. Westring: i.e., westren (i.e., western); transposed spelling (-eur for –ure).

Since the Warr Comenced   Building and Manufecturies[27] are Gowing on[28] Wrapedly
as the people are flocking from all the Seacosts here——

D[r] John let me know how Sam[l] Douglass and famely are Doing and all the Rest of my
Relations which is two Numerious[29] to mention   Let John Kerr Know that all his
Children are well heare and Give my love to all my friends that Deserves it   let me
know how the Verners and the Louds are and how the orang\<e> men is
Doeing   Give my best Respects to your good family Cosen peggy all the
Children   Remember me to your Mother and your Brother Wiliam   Jo Williams
&c and Excuse my Wrighting as the gentleman is Weating to teake this Letter to New
york   no more at present but your affectionat

W[m] Heazelton

William Heazelton died in 1815, only a year after he wrote this letter. He left behind an estate worth \$4,106.50—including \$3,548 in goods sold at auction and uncollected debts of \$215, which his sister and her husband in Pittsburgh refused to pay. However, Heazelton's own debts amounted to \$2,149, and, after his American kin had cannibalized the estate, there was nothing left to fulfill his legacies to poor Irish relations, such as his brother-in-law and sister, Samuel and Susy Douglass, who had guaranteed William's old Irish debts and lost Culnagrew in consequence. No wonder that John Greeves of Bernagh eventually concluded that the American Heazeltons "are a people that I w[d] wish not to have anything further to do with."[30]

Politically as well as socially, William Heazelton appears at first glance to have been a lonely and somewhat anomalous figure, for in the early nineteenth century most Ulster Protestant immigrants, especially on the western frontier, still urged relatives to join them overseas with economic and political arguments that signified their rejection of Ireland's "despotic tyrant[s]" and their embrace of America's "sweets of liberty."[31] To be sure, Heazelton's antipathy to Jeffersonian Republicanism may have been characteristic of western Pennsylvania's relatively few Irish Methodist immigrants, for those in remote Crawford County also voted Federalist during this era, in contrast to the county's Ulster Presbyterian settlers.[32] In general, however, the Ohio Valley's Methodists—most of them migrants from Maryland and Virginia—appear to have been strong Jeffersonians; in Ohio itself, for example, Methodists controlled the Republican party in alliance with that state's Scots-Irish inhabitants. Moreover, by the 1810s the Republicans also dominated western Pennsylvania politics and their party attracted most members of Pittsburgh's rising and heavily Ulster-

---

27. Manufecturies: i.e., manufactories "factories, workshops" (OED, s.v. manufactory, 3).   **28. Gowing on**: in progress, proceeding (OED, s.v. go, 86.e).   **29. Numerious**: see chapter 51, n. 75.   **30.** John and Jane Greeves, Armagh, Co. Armagh, to William and Anne O'Brien, [Smithsville, N.Y.?], 7 February 1826.   **31.** For example, see David Robinson's and Robert Crockett's letters in appendix 3.   **32.** On Ulster Presbyterian settlers in Crawford Co., Pa., see chapter 64.

American business, manufacturing, and professional classes. Among the latter, a large majority worshiped in the city's First Presbyterian church, not with socially inferior Methodists like Heazelton, who still clung for patronage to the old-élite and largely Anglican leaders of the moribund Federalist party.[33]

Yet western Pennsylvania had already witnessed the beginnings of an Irish-American Protestant political conservatism as well as the genesis of a reactionary reformulation of Irish ethnic identities. In 1794, for example, Rev. John McMillan of Washington County and other local Presbyterian clergymen, of Ulster parentage and Federalist party affiliation, had denounced the Whiskey Rebellion from their pulpits and even withheld the sacraments from unrepentent rebels. Afterward McMillan was virtually a Federalist party election agent, and during the early stages of the Second Great Awakening, he and many of his fellow ministers continued to rail against the French Revolution, Jeffersonian Republicanism, and any United Irish exiles, such as the radical Presbyterian divine Thomas Ledlie Birch, who settled in the area.[34]

Perhaps more portentiously—and although in 1814 William Heazelton had still described *all* his transplanted countrymen as "Irish"—it was southwestern Pennsylvania's David Bruce, an immigrant from Ulster (or Scotland—accounts differ) and a Federalist propagandist and Ulster-Scots dialect poet, who in the mid-1790s was one of the first American public figures to employ the term "Scotch-Irish" in positive and recognizably modern ways.[35] Bruce's poetry, published in Pittsburgh's newspapers, emphasized Ulster Presbyterian immigrants' Scottish ancestry and Protestant faith and, most important, linked that heritage specifically to social respectability and political conservatism. Thus, Bruce's idealized "Scotch-Irish" contrasted sharply with the intemperate and disputatious "Irish" adherents of local Republican radicals such as the Ulster-born Presbyterians William Findley, John Smilie, and David Redick.[36] Almost simultaneously, it was western Pennsylvania's Hugh Henry Brackenridge (1748–1816), a Scottish immigrant and a conservative Republican judge, who in his serialized novel *Modern Chivalry* (1792–1815) satirized his socially inferior Irish Protestant political rivals—first the Presbyterian weaver-turned-legislator Findley, later the Anglican radical journalist William Duane[37]—as the fictional "Teague O'Regan," whose name and characteristics—his blundering ignorance, his erratic, drunken, and violent behavior, and his absurdly anarchic political opinions—were stereotypically "native" and Catholic "Irish."

McMillan's, Bruce's, and Brackenridge's messages were as clear as those of their conservative contemporaries in New England.[38] If Irish Protestant immigrants, especially

---

33. From the mid-1790s, Pittsburgh's Scots-Irish Presbyterians had opposed the local growth of Methodism—perhaps on ethnopolitical as well as social and religious grounds, since as late as 1807 a visiting Methodist preacher reported that the members of the city's fledgling congregation were still "principally English." In 1812 Pittsburgh's Methodists numbered merely 147 whites and 20 "colored" members; and by 1817 total membership had risen merely to 280.   **34.** On Birch, see chapter 62, esp. n. 34.   **35.** Unusually, Bruce actually wrote the term as "Scots-Irish."   **36.** On Smilie and on Redick and Findley, see chapters 12 and 62 (esp. n. 1), respectively.   **37.** On Duane, see chapters 38 (esp. n. 46) and 63.   **38.** See chapter 49.

Ulster Presbyterians, and their descendants sought social ascent and acceptance by those whom Heazelton called "the better Sort" of "Real Americans," they had to disprove Federalist and conservative Republican accusations that they were "wild Irish": a term laden with historic connotations of *native* Irish barbarism, treachery, and violence— especially the violence associated with Irish Catholics' 1641 rising against the Ulster Plantation.[39] Of course, American conservatives knew well that the overwhelming majority of those they stigmatized as "wild Irish democrats" were not Catholics but Ulster Presbyterians. In effect, however, they were accusing the latter of forfeiting, even of betraying, their ancestral claims to ethnic and religious superiority by behaving politically and socially in ways that were traditionally associated with despised "papists" alone. Logically, the only recourses for Ulster Americans who shrank from such imputations were to disavow both the ecumenical Irish nationalism of the United Irishmen and the ultrarepublicanism of radical Jeffersonians such as Findley and Duane and to disassociate themselves as well from Irish-American Catholics, generally, by emphasizing, exaggerating, and if necessary even fabricating the ethnoreligious, cultural, and behavioral traits that purportedly and eternally distinguished all the "Scotch-Irish," regardless of social status, from all Irish Catholics.

Thus, poor William Heazelton had died too soon, for although in the 1810s his political tendencies were still unusual among Ulster American Protestants, in succeeding decades they would become commonplace and, by the century's end, almost universal. After 1815 the arrival from Ireland of larger numbers of Protestant and Catholic immigrants, many of them poor and militantly sectarian, both exacerbated the strains of American urbanization and early industrialization and helped promote new waves of Protestant evanglicalism and, in response to the growth of Irish-American Catholicism, increasingly frequent outbreaks of nativist violence. In addition, as some Ulster-American Presbyterians grew more wealthy and influential, positive definitions of "Scotch-Irish" identity became more formal, elaborate, and pervasive—assuming the same hegemonic functions in their communities as did the exclusive identification of "Irish" with devout Catholicism among the new immigrants of that faith.

39. English and Scottish Protestant propagandists, eager to blame the 1641 massacres on King Charles I and his putative alliance with Irish "papists" against "Protestant liberties," variously claimed that between 50,000 and a half-million British settlers in Ulster had been killed in the 1641 Rising. By contrast, modern scholars estimate that between 4,000 and 10,000 died, and the rebellion's leaders had ordered that Ulster's *Scottish* settlers should be spared and protected, as many were. Neither of those facts suited the political needs and religious prejudices of Scotland's and England's Protestant politicians, themselves allied in rebellion against Charles I. However, the main point here is that, given the known patterns of Scots migrations to northern Ireland (much heavier after 1650, and especially after 1690, than before), it is highly probable that the ancestors of the great majority of the later Scots-Irish emigrants to America in the eighteenth and nineteenth centuries were living in Scotland, not in Ulster, when the 1641 massacre occurred. (Likewise, many of their forebears were not yet in northern Ireland by 1689, when the equally famous Siege of Derry took place.) Nevertheless, both in 1641 and subsequently, political imperatives and religious mythologies converged to ensure that communal "memories" of 1641's atrocities (as of Derry's valiant defense) became and remained central motifs in most Ulster Protestants' sense of history and identity.

Perhaps it was no wonder, then, that as early as 1812 the elderly William Findley—formerly the scourge of economic élites and chartered financial monopolies but soon to be a supporter of (and stockholder in) the Second Bank of the United States—would, in his memoir, designate his ancestry as "Scotch-Irish," although in the late 1700s he had been an "Irish" politician to friend and foe alike. Thus, the broader connotations of "Irish" identity, ironically first developed by Anglican "patriots" in the early 1700s, soon disappeared, as did the old negative connotations of "Scotch-Irish" and, more broadly, the confusing but creative possibilities of eighteenth-century Irish-American ethnicity. Thus, bereft of an alternative and "respectable" ethnic appellation, the relatively few Irish Protestant immigrants to America in the nineteenth century who were Anglicans, Methodists, or members of other denominations—along with many Irish Catholic converts to Protestantism—increasingly joined those who were truly of Ulster Presbyterian origins to proclaim and celebrate their allegedly "Scotch-Irish" heritage.

WILLIAM HEAZELTON, JR.

✳

Epilogue

68 ✳

John Caldwell, Jr., 1802

John Caldwell's life and his 1802 letter from New York City provide in several ways an appropriate conclusion to this book. For instance, Caldwell's letter offers a catalog of United Irish exiles, mostly minor figures and Protestants such as Caldwell himself, who in the early 1800s comprised much of the economic and political leadership of Manhattan's Irish-American society. In addition, John Caldwell's is one of the earliest and most detailed "advice letters" that describe the opportunities and perils of American life for the "new Irish" immigrants who flocked to the United States after 1798 and, especially, after 1815. Generally optimistic, sometimes even eulogistic, Caldwell's injunctions reflect his urban-commercial milieu and hence nicely complement the rural focus of other advice letters, earlier and contemporary, such as those by Robert Parke and Edward Toner.[1]

Most important, John Caldwell's family saga is a virtual analogue of early modern Irish history and emigration. In Ireland itself, the family's experiences and memories stretched from King James I's Plantation of the early 1600s (when the Caldwells left Scottish Ayrshire and Renfrewshire and settled in Ulster), to the siege of Derry in 1689 (in which John Caldwell's great-great-uncles, William Caldwell[2] and Thomas Ball allegedly participated), to the liberal reforms of the 1770s and 1780s inspired by the American Revolution (for which John Caldwell's father and uncle shared such enthusiam), and finally in the 1790s to the revolutionary radicalism of the United Irishmen, whose failure precipitated John Caldwell's forced migration at the century's end. Likewise, the family's history exemplifies early Irish migration to North America, dominated as it was by Ulster Presbyterians from 1718, when William Caldwell and Thomas Ball emigrated from the Bann Valley to New England, to 1769 when uncle James Caldwell debarked in Philadelphia, down to—and for several decades after—John Caldwell's own exile to New York in 1799.[3] The Caldwells' story also illustrates changes in the patterns of Ulster migration and settlement. For although the great majority of Ulster immigrants in the eighteenth century became farmers in rural America—as did John Caldwell's great-great-uncles in Londonderry and then Bedford, New Hampshire—his uncle James's settlement in Philadelphia and his own migration to New York City presaged the Irish-American urbanization, spearheaded by the more skilled and affluent, that despite Caldwell's own misgivings became increasingly prevalent among poor Irish immigrants during the early and mid-1800s. In addition, John Caldwell's choice of New York City, like Thomas Addis Emmet's, symbolized the early

---

1. On Parke and Toner, see chapters 9 and 26, respectively.   **2.** William Caldwell was born about 1670.
3. On early Ulster emigration to Boston and elsewhere in New England, see chapters 17 and 49; on James Caldwell, see chapter 58.

nineteenth-century shift from Philadelphia to the Empire City as Irish-America's unofficial political capital.[4]

Perhaps equally illuminating, succeeding generations of Caldwell emigrants illustrated the changes that took place during the 1700s in the religious and political culture of much of Ulster Presbyterianism: from the traditional Calvinism of John Caldwell's great-great-uncles, for example, to the liberalizing impacts of the Scottish Enlightenment and New Light rationalism on the religious beliefs of his father and uncle, and to the even more radical influences of the French Revolution and of Thomas Paine's writings on John Caldwell himself. Even more dramatically, John Caldwell's family demonstrates the remarkable transformations in national identities and political allegiances among large numbers of Ulster Presbyterian emigrants. From the ethnoreligious tribalism and British loyalism of his New Hampshire ancestors in the 1720s; to the élitist but interdenominational Whiggery of uncle James Caldwell and the other members of Philadelphia's St. Patrick's society during the 1770s; to the ecumenical radicalism of John Caldwell and his exiled United Irish brethren in the 1790s and early 1800s: members of the Caldwell family moved from an exclusive religious identity, grounded in Presbyterian struggles against Scottish and Irish "papists" and expressed in loyalty to the Crown and the Protestant Succession, to an inclusive sense of "Irishness" that transcended religious and, to a degree, even social differences and was based on democratic ideals and a shared antipathy to British monarchy, Irish aristocracy, and American Federalists.

John Caldwell was born on 3 May 1769, the eldest son of Elizabeth Calderwood (d. 1796) and John Caldwell, Sr. (1742–1803), a prosperous farmer, miller, and linen manufacturer whose estate, Harmony Hill, held under a small head rent from Lord Antrim, was situated near the linen-market town of Ballymoney in north County Antrim.[5] From an early age, Caldwell later remembered, he felt shame for the "wrongs" his ancestors had inflicted on Ulster's natives,[6] and from one of his father's Catholic servants or undertenants Caldwell learned enough Irish so that, decades later in America, he could still compose odes and toasts in that language. Caldwell's parents first sent him to school in Derry city, where he devoured letters from his kinsmen in Philadelphia. Then he went to Bromley, in Middlesex, where he contrasted what he perceived as his English schoolmates' vulgarity with their pretensions to membership in "a superior race of beings." Meanwhile, the American Revolution made young Caldwell an early convert to the "ideas of liberty" that

---

4. On Emmet, see chapter 66. **5.** In addition to John, Jr., the Caldwells of Harmony Hill had eight other children who survived infancy and went into American exile: Flora (1768–1814), who by 1791 had married John Parks of Ballymoney; Mary (d. 1822); Catherine (1775–1856), who married (1) her sister Flora's brother-in-law, James Parks, in 1805 and (2) the Dublin United Irish exile, John Chambers, in 1837; Richard (1780–1812); Andrew James (1782–1862); Margaret (1785–1805); William Alexander (1787–1846); and Elizabeth (1789–1862). For demographic data on Ballymoney parish and its environs, see appendix 2.1g, on chapter 58. **6.** Unless otherwise noted, all quotations from John Caldwell's writings are taken from his memoir, "Particulars of History of a North County Irish Family"; see Sources.

FIGURE 21
Portrait of John Caldwell, Jr.,
of New York City and
Salisbury Mills, Orange
County, New York.
Photograph courtesy of Mrs.
Polly Midgely, Briarcliff,
New York.

also enthused his parents and many other north Antrim Presbyterians. During the early 1780s his father led a company of Volunteers who espoused Catholic emancipation and, at his insistence, admitted Catholic members. And in American exile Caldwell would charge that, although his father never joined the United Irishmen, his liberality "became the object of malignant hatred to the aristocracy and petty squireality of the land," who marked his family for future "persecution and destruction."

In February 1784 Caldwell went to Belfast and was apprenticed to Samuel Brown, whose mercantile firm traded with Baltimore and other American ports.[7] Despite his youth, he rapidly became prominent among Belfast's wealthy Presbyterian merchants and professionals. In 1787–1788 Caldwell became Brown's business partner, as well as clerk in the Northern Bank that the latter helped establish, and in 1793 went into the shipping business on his own, establishing the trading contacts with New York that would later prove his lifelines to America. Although he continued to attend Presbyterian worship, Caldwell was soon "persuaded" that most religious dogma was "merely the offspring of

---

7. On the Browns of Belfast and, later, Baltimore, see chapter 45.

JOHN CALDWELL, JR.

priestcraft, Kingcraft, and moneycraft."[8] Accordingly, he became an enthusiastic Mason; in 1792 he joined the city's radical reformers in petitioning for parliamentary reform and for total repeal of the Penal Laws; and he was an early member of the first branch of the Society of United Irishmen, established in Belfast in 1791.

Despite his intimacy with Wolfe Tone,[9] the United Irishmen's primary emissary to the French Republic, Caldwell would later deny that he had desired or helped invite a French invasion of Ireland, and he resigned his military commission in the United Irishmen before the 1798 Rebelion commenced. However, there is no doubt he was deeply involved in the inner workings of the Society's Ulster Directory. Moreover, in 1795 Caldwell's kinsmen by marriage, John and James Parks, had founded the Ballymoney branch of the United Irishmen; and when the rising took place, his younger brother, Richard, commanded the rebel forces from north Antrim. Thus, loyalists regarded Caldwell's entire "family and connections" as "notoriously disaffected,"[10] and in early June 1798, shortly after the fighting began, vengeful loyalists burned the Caldwells' house and mills at Harmony Hill.

On 19 May 1798 John Caldwell himself was arrested and charged with high treason. After interrogation, he was incarcerated for eight weeks at Dublin Castle and then transferred to prison in Belfast, where he learned for the first time that his father's property had been destroyed and that his brother Richard had been tried and condemned to death. John Caldwell expected the same fate, but fortunately his family still had powerful friends, and through their intercession and the leniency of Lord Lieutenant Cornwallis, Richard Caldwell's death sentence was commuted in return for his father's agreement that the entire clan would go into American exile. Richard sailed immediately on 1 September 1798, followed by John and five of his siblings in early May 1799, by their father (after selling his remaining Irish property) in July 1799, and finally by brother Andrew, sister Flora and her husband John Parks, and an elderly aunt in the spring of 1800.

Aged 30, John Caldwell disembarked at New York on 12 June 1799, and although the other ships carrying his kinsmen landed at different ports, the family soon reunited in Manhattan and on the farm that his father rented on Long Island. By October 1802, when

---

8. Caldwell's usage of "priestcraft" should not be interpreted as evidence of anti-Catholic prejudice. To be sure, Irish Protestant liberals and radicals disliked what they regarded as the authoritarian and obscurantist character of the Catholic Church, but they denounced the same tendencies in all religions and clergymen, especially in the legally established Church of Ireland, but also in Presbyterian synods and divines who preached submission to religious or political dogmas and officials. **9.** Theobald Wolfe Tone (1763–1798): born in Dublin, the son of an Anglican coach-maker, and educated at Trinity College, Tone was primarily responsible for forging the alliance between east Ulster Presbyterians and radical Catholics that eventuated in the Society of the United Irishmen; he was also one of the first United Irishmen to move from reformism to republicanism and the necessity for revolution, and he played the major role in persuading the French government to provide military support to an Irish rebellion. In November 1798, after he was captured while accompanying an abortive French expedition to Ireland, Tone allegedly committed suicide in prison to escape execution for treason. **10.** Rev. T. H. Mullin, *Coleraine in Georgian Times*, 161, see Sources.

John wrote the following letter to his old friend in Belfast, fellow United Irishman and former cellmate Robert Simms,[11] the Caldwells appeared supremely well adjusted to life in the United States, surrounded by friends and fellow exiles, and well on the road to prosperity. John had already joined one of New York City's Masonic lodges (patronized by the state's grand master, the mayor of New York City, De Witt Clinton)[12] as well as the Friendly Sons of St. Patrick, and he and brother Richard had established on Water Street a promising trading partnership that soon included their brother-in-law, John Parks. And as John Caldwell predicted in his letter to Simms, one month later his father purchased Salisbury Mills, an estate in Blooming Grove township, near Newburgh in Orange County, where the family might replicate the independence and enterprise they had formerly enjoyed at Harmony Hill.

John Caldwell, New York City, to Robert Simms, Belfast, 18 October 1802

Newyork   18th October 1802

My Dear Friend

I only received your Letter dated in December a few days since[13] by Docter Cumming,[14] who seems to be a deserving worthy Man,   I trust he will do well here,   an eminent surgical character[15] strongly recommended & with good Certificates from Edinburgh or elsewhere of his Professional abilities could not fail of succeeding,   a Man may its true be a Man of Merit without all these appendages, but then he has to struggle with perhaps the prejudices of strangers & if he is lucky he will overcome them——Doctor Johnston[16] formerly of Downpatrick was an eminent Practitioner,   he was much encouraged to make this the place of his settlement, but previous to his coming here, he had made an engagement with Mr Richard formerly of

---

11. On Robert Simms, see chapter 66, n. 19. Before Simms was incarcerated with Emmet, Macneven, and others, at Ft. George, Scotland, he and Caldwell had been berthmates in the stifling hold of a prison ship in Belfast Lough. **12.** On De Witt Clinton, also see chapter 66, n. 11. **13.** since: ago. **14. Docter Cumming**: George Cumming (or Cuming), Presbyterian, apothecary and physician; born about 1768 in Newry, Co. Down, Cumming removed to Co. Kildare, where he joined the Leinster Directory of the United Irishmen. Cumming was arrested in Dublin on 12 March 1798 with Emmet, Macneven, Henry Jackson, etc., and imprisoned for three years in Ft. George, Scotland. On his release, in the autumn of 1802 he emigrated to New York City, where he became a leading local Republican politician and office-holder. Generally, Cumming was a member of the Republican party's Clintonian faction, although he supported James Madison over De Witt Clinton in the 1812 presidential election because he could not stomach the latter's Federalist supporters; in 1816 he was appointed city inspector at a salary of $1,250. Cumming was an officer in John Caldwell's Erin Masonic Lodge and also a member of the Friendly Sons of St. Patrick in New York. In 1827 he chaired the Irish meeting at Tammany Hall that resolved to erect the marble monument in memory of Thomas Addis Emmet; at $200 his was the largest individual subscription (see chapter 66). **15. character**: reputation. **16. Docter Johnston**: Perhaps the "Johnston" whose house near Bangor was burned by British soldiers in 1798, in retaliation for his role in the rebellion. In 1792 a Hugh Johnson was one of the Presbyterian signatories to the Belfast radical reformers' declaration in favor of Catholic emancipation; other cosigners included John Caldwell, Samuel Neilson, William Tennent, and Robert Simms.

the Antrim Militia to visit & make a trial of the Genesee Country——they there settled in the most beautiful spot you can imagine Bailey Town, on the West Bank of Lake Seneca, between that Lake and Lake Cayuga, 360 Miles from this place, but notwithstanding the Doctors being a firm Man & of strong mind, he had not within himself sufficient resources against crisis & being deprived of Society, the pursuit of his Distilling business & other avocations of his Industry could not make up for the void he felt in his breast & he litterally became a victim to despair & died a Martyr to his own obstinacy in refusing the advise of his friends in a settlement in this place   I am the more particular in this narrative, as you seem to wish me to enter intimately into the every thing that might be supposed to operate on, to influence, or to affect an Emigrant coming to this Country——the United States do undoubtedly promise much to Emigrants of every description—provided they are Industrious & well conducted, but no Country under Heaven throws more obstacles in the way of an Idle & dissolute Man procuring a livlyhood——We are too apt when we approach these shores & hail this Land of Liberty & Peace to be too sanguine in our expectations, & as Docter Franklin[17] Jocosely observed to expect the Dollars on the Sea shore the Apple Pyes hopping down the Chimnie & the little birds Perching on your Shoulders crying "come who'll eat me"   but in general, every Stranger coming here, is inclined to encrease his wealth by some means or other,   the misfortune is that many of us mistake the way——the Scotch farmer or Labourer on his arrival in a transatlantic Town, calls on his Country men, advises with them,[18] goes back to the Country & becomes a farmer & of course a respectable member of Society——the Dutch & Germans frequently with two & three Hundred Pounds Sterling of property, will bind themselves to the Pensylvania Farmer & while the Husband attends his employer through his avocations,[19] the wife will be learning the more domestick business of the farm, as suited to her sex——when the engagement of the People expire—they again emigrate to an uncleared Piece of Land & sett an example of Industry by blessing the Country with the fruits of their Labour   I wish I could say so much for our Country men——the Labourer, the farmer, the weaver, on coming here, all incline to live in large Towns,   this may arise from the known character of the Irish——we are to use a trite saying, so warm hearted, we wish to live together & to be in the way[20] of hearing often from our friends, but this disposition is often attended with ruin to Individuals and dishonour to our National character——I have often seen the Man, who with his family might have made a figure a 100 Miles from Town & there been respectable as a Citizen & a man—lose[21] his little property in the dram shop he kept—lose his time by attending to Political controversy & matters that as an Alien did not concern him or at all events which his interference could not better, & lose the

---

17. Docter Franklin: i.e., Benjamin Franklin (1706–1790).   **18. calls on . . . advises with them**: visits . . . gets advice from them.   **19. through his avocations**: as he (= the employer) goes about his various occupations.   **20. be in the way**: have the opportunity.   **21. lose**: waste.

respectability of himself & his family by the consequences which must generally arise from such a line of conduct——The general establishment of Banks, the easy means for People of good character 'tho of small Capital, to acquire accommodation of Money,[22] gives the Industrious & careful Trader considerable advantage——Its true Imprudent & speculative Men, have been ruined by availing themselves improperly of the credit offer'd them, but such People are closely watched & if your Neighbours can hear of your doing any business out of your line, your credit is at an end——thus a Hardware Merch^t is hard looked at[23] if he is known to speculate in Pot Ashes & we have withdrawn credit from Houses in our line, whom we discovered to be dabbling in Shipping business——In fact there is no Country w<h>ere a prudent Alien who has been brought up to Mercantile life, can make a better livlyhood, particularly by avoiding all foreign or shipping Speculation——The Importing Merchant offers his Cargo for Sale—ten or twelve of us will call on him, purchase it & sell it out to the Count<r>y or the retail Grocer——Our worthy, dear, & respected friend Joseph Stevenson[24] sailed a few days ago—we most severely feel & sincerely lament being deprived of his Society—you will be much gratified by an hour or twos conversation with him on the variety of subjects which will occur to you respecting this Country— this Ne plus Ultra[25] for a great part of the Emigrants both Vagabonds, Rebels, traitors & Gentlemen, from our native land—for when a fellow turns out badly at home, the family consult & according to their different grades in Society—they determine if he is stupid—or good natur'd, to educate him for the Church, if he is a devil for the Army, if he is a spend thrift to Sea with him, but if he is a nar do well[26] send him to America 'tho of all places in the world, it is where he is most unlikely to succeed——the Tavern at the falls of Niagara is now kept by a "Gentleman" whom I have seen make a conspicuous figure in the side boxes of Crow Street & Belfast Theatre[27]   but here every business, every calling is honorable that is honest, every pursuit respectable that is respectable,   here indeed People are subject to the like Passions, as elsewhere——We see too often Malice, Hatred & Revenge prevail & we can only place it to the account of poor human nature, whom we blame so often, & so often unjustly   discontent, with certainly as happy a form of government & with laws administered at least as wisely, as elsewhere on the globe—prevails but you will not find discontent among the farmers who certainly compose that body properly

---

22. to acquire accommodation of Money: to be accommodated/furnished with money (i.e., **credit** hereafter). **23. hard looked at**: closely scrutinized.   **24. Joseph Stevenson**: perhaps a relative of James Stephenson, who signed the 1792 Belfast Presbyterian declaration in favor of Catholic emancipation, with John Caldwell, Robert Simms, etc. Apparently, Joseph Stevenson returned to Ireland permanently, as Caldwell was addressing letters to him there in 1806.   **25. Ne plus Ultra**: Latin "no further," a point beyond which one cannot go, the acme, the culmination.   **26. nar do well**: i.e., ne'er-do-well.   **27. Crow Street**: Crow Street in Dublin, running north from Dame Street, was the location of the Crow Street Theatre, which lasted in business from 1758 until 1820, rivaling the city's more famous Smock Alley Theatre (1662–1815). The **Belfast Theatre** was established by 1768 at the Millgate.

JOHN CALDWELL, JR.

denominated the People———but no more on this subject!!!!   My father since he came here has rented a farm at Flushing Bayside in the County of Queens Long Island—the situation is truly beautiful, but the land in general poor as you may suppose for the Rent of 200 Dollars ℔ annum within 17 Miles of N. York, but the house is good,   they have plenty of fuell[28] for the Cutting & a sufficient q[ty][29] of Land under Grass & tillage for the purpose of raising necessaries for the family, Cattle &c &c,   but notwithstanding all this, My father intends removing up the North River,[30] so soon as he can get a place to purchase to his liking———Our family is Large & every one of them inclined to Industry———a place just now offers[31]—it contains about 150 Acres of tollerable Land, with a Merchant Mill & a Country Mill,[32] a good comfortable dwelling House, a large Store for the reception of Wheat, Bark &c & for the vending of Merchant goods or rather for their barter—a Bark Mill & a snug neat Tan Yard—all within 60 Miles of this Town eight Miles off the North River—4 from West point & 8 from Newburgh—4 Miles from General Clintons[33] in a full settled Country—on an excellent Road & a plentyfull supply of Water———15,000 Dollars is asked for this place, but how much will be taken[34] is another point———It comes up so every way to[35] such a place as would have suited you had you come here, that I dwell on it perhaps too long———If my father gets it, our great end will be accomplished Viz[t][36] to find full scope for the Industry of two branches of the family, without risking much Capital, & without grating[37] our feelings by parting or seperating our family, at least to any distance, as between this Town & Newburgh, there is daily communication,   that little rising Town alone, employs 16 Sloops of from 60 & 90 Tons between this place & that———every bit of Leather tanned at the farm I mention is vended[38] on the spot to the Country People & Newburgh Traders & if your Capital is stinted you may either take in the Rough hides & tan them for payment, or purchase them & pay in dressed Leather———thus you see business can be carried on to good acc[t] in a variety of methods, but still provided, Speculation, is kept in the back ground———I had planned in my own mind just such a settlement as this for you & for our friend Tennent[39] a bustling life of Town trade,   In such a situation as I have described our friend

---

28. fuell: firewood.   **29. q[ty]:** quantity.   **30. the North River:** the Hudson River.   **31. offers:** has come up (i.e., for sale).   **32. Merchant Mill:** a mill engaged in the grinding of grain for the purpose of trade (OED, s.v.). **Country Mill:** by contrast, presumably a mill where grain is ground for the local farmers, i.e. not prepared for trade.   **33. General Clinton:** George Clinton, then governor of New York and patron of Thomas Addis Emmet and other United Irish exiles in the state; also see chapters 51 and 66.   **34. taken:** accepted; "but how much [less than the asking price] will be accepted [by the owner] is a different question." **35. comes up . . . to:** reaches the standard of; "Thus in every respect it meets the standard of the sort of place that would have suited you."   **36. Viz[t]:** abbr. of Latin *videlicet* "namely."   **37. grating:** wearing on. **38. vended:** traded.   **39. Tennent:** probably William Tennent (1759–1832): born near Dervock, Co. Antrim, the eldest son of an Associate (Seceding) Presbyterian minister (see chapter 65). Tennent was a wealthy merchant and banker in Belfast when in 1791 he was a founding member of the city's Society of the United

Henry Jackson[40] might have been happy, but in his present place of abode he has to combat the prepossession of his family in favor of their native Country & to lead a life of inactivity, in as much as farming, cannot be so congenial to his long settled habits & ways of thinking, as the more active pursuits of Mechanical profession or calling——— there is no Man of your acquaintance become a more enthusiastick American than Docter White,[41]   he has adopted their ways & manners & admits he never felt real comfort & happiness to the degree he now enjoys—in the Land he left——— He is held in high estimation & what is extraordinary, by the very violent Political People of both parties———Cranston[42] & Alexander[43] are worthy respectable young Men & among our most intimate connections—as is Wm Bailey[44]———we have too among the circle of

Irishmen and of its newspaper, the *Northern Star*. However, in 1798 he was a reluctant revolutionary and protested his innocence when arrested and confined in Ft. George, Scotland, with Emmet, Cuming, etc. Tennent returned to Belfast on his release and died there, apparently without ever visiting America. Brothers George and John Tennent (1772–1813) were also prominent United Irishmen; John spent 1797–1798 in France, lobbying for a French invasion of Ireland; after the 1798 rising failed, he joined Napoleon's Irish Legion, became a lieutenant colonel, and was killed at the battle of Lowenberg. In 1784 another brother, Robert (1765–1837), emigrated to the West Indies and in 1793–1799 was a surgeon in the British navy; returning to Belfast, his exertions helped win brother William's release from Ft. George.   **40. Henry Jackson**: from Co. Monaghan, Jackson was a Presbyterian who moved to Dublin, where he became a wealthy iron-founder and one of the United Irishmen's most radical leaders. Jackson was related by marriage to William Tennent (n. 39) and the father-in-law of the Dubliner Oliver Bond, also a Presbyterian and a leading United Irishman, who died in Kilmainham Prison in 1798 (see chapter 5, n. 8). Although a member of Dublin's city council, Jackson was in charge of weapons manufacture and procurement for the United Irishmen; he also was instrumental in radicalizing the city's working classes, and in 1797–1798 he urged immediate revolution without waiting for French aid. Arrested with Emmet, Bond, Cumming, etc., in March 1798, Jackson was imprisoned in Ft. George until 1802, when he emigrated to America, taking with him considerable capital. Initially he settled on a farm in Pennsylvania, but he found life there too rustic. In about 1807 Jackson returned to Europe but subsequently remigrated to the United States; with his widowed daughter, Mrs. Bond, he settled in Baltimore, where he died in the early 1840s.   **41. Docter White**: John Campbell White, a Belfast apothecary and Presbyterian and an original member of the Belfast Society of United Irishmen and a member of its Ulster Directory. After the 1798 rebellion, White settled in Baltimore, where he prospered under the patronage of the city's Presbyterian merchant élite. A staunch Jeffersonian Republican, in 1803 White founded Baltimore's Hibernian Benevolent Society.   **42. Cranston**: probably Alexander Cranston, of Alex. Cranston & Co., New York merchants, and a member of the city's Friendly Sons of St. Patrick as early as 1805; probably the same as—or a kinsman of—the Alexander Cranston who in 1794 helped found Belfast's Linen Hall Library; its first librarian was Thomas Russell, a leading United Irishman and Wolfe Tone's closest friend, who in 1803 was executed for his part in Robert Emmet's rising of that year.   **43. Alexander**: perhaps John Alexander who, like Richard Caldwell, was a United Irish commander in Ulster in 1798, although merely in his twenties, and who was permitted to transport himself to America after the rebellion; or Joseph Alexander, secretary of New York City's Friendly Sons of St. Patrick in 1827–1828; or Rev. Thomas Alexander of Cairncastle, imprisoned in 1798 and exiled to America; or John Alexander (1748–1832), whose inn at Peter's Hill in Belfast was one of the United Irishmen's chief meeting places.   **44. Wm Bailey**: from Co. Down; a captain in the British East India Company before returning from the Indies to England, where he was a member of the radical London Corresponding Society and the United Britons. In January 1798 Bailey returned to Ireland, with United Irishmen Benjamin Binns and Fr. James Coigley of Armagh (executed 1798), to pledge English radicals' support for an Irish rising. After the rebellion Bailey fled to France and then to New York City, where in 1805–1806 he was practicing law.

our visiting & friendly acquaintances a great many others, so many that it is almost invidious to particularize a few——in short—from what I know of you & your willingness even to make the best of a bad situation, you would have been agreeably disapointed,[45] nay, you would have been highly delighted with the State of things in general here——As to Religion I must own[46]—tho' the People are strictly moral, yet I cannot discover much fervency of Devotion——We too often see either the most violent Enthusiasm,[47] or a total Apathy in these matters——there are a few but a very few who profess Deism——there are I believe 30 Churches & upwards in this Town—most of them crowded twice every Sunday, & yet ask a simple question to these seeming godly People on the subjects of what they heard & they will profess their ignorance or want of Memory——We have a seat in the Wall Street Meeting House[48] & for ought I know one of the Seats, occupied by the Dragoon Horses of his Imperial Britannick Majesty during the War, for they converted this Meeting House into a Stable—for which we pay nine Pounds or twenty three & one half Dollars ℔ Annum——I own I do not implicitly believe every thing the Parson says—'tho they are Men whose words or Oaths would be taken in any Court of Justice or even with you, but I think it necessary to join my Household or family at least once a week in publick offering of prayer & praise——the number of Lawyers here exceeds belief & but few among them of bright or transcendant abilities,   among these however in this place is Hamilton[49] & even he I have hopes of seeing exceeded by Emmett, if he makes this his place of residence——It is said the Period of Naturalization will yet be short<e>ned, perhaps to three years,[50] which will be a material point[51] to Men of Professional pursuits——In the case of a Purchase of Lands made by my father, John Parks[52] was obliged to put the Lawyers right in three or four very Capital[53] instances & they were obliged to admit their being wrong——the little enquiry made[54] by Purchasers, becomes a source of endless litigation & many, many, a Lawsuit is

45. you would have been agreeably disapointed: i.e. (given your equable and charitable temperament, and since American conditions are not in fact bad) you would probably have been "happily disappointed" to be left without cause for not having to make the best of a bad thing (or "agreeably frustrated" at not having to tolerate something that is indeed much better than tolerable).   **46. own**: admit.   **47. Enthusiasm**: religious emotionalism (e.g., as characteristic of the revivals of the contemporary Second Great Awakening).   **48. the Wall Street Meeting House**: the First Presbyterian church, established in 1716 by Rev. Francis Makemie's followers and located on the north side of Wall Street, near Nassau St.; during the American Revolution, the British army used the church as a barracks and then a stable.   **49. Hamilton**: Alexander Hamilton (1755–1804), Washington's secretary of the treasury and architect of Federalist financial and foreign policies; his fatal duel with Aaron Burr on 12 July 1804 helped pave the way for Thomas Addis Emmet's ascendancy among New York's barristers (see chapter 66).   **50.** Caldwell refers to the Naturalization Act of 1802, then under Congressional debate (see chapter 64).   **51. a material point**: a very consequential matter.   **52. John Parks**: married by 1791 to John Caldwell's sister Flora. An attorney in Ballymoney, Parks was a founding member of the United Irishmen in north Co. Antrim; he went into exile with the Caldwells and died about 1814 at Salisbury Mills, New York. His brother, James Parks, was also a Ballymoney lawyer, the Antrim County coroner, and a United Irishman; after confinement in Carrickfergus jail, in 1802 he emigrated and joined the Caldwells in New York, where in 1805 he married John Caldwell's sister, Catherine, but died shortly afterward.
53. Capital: important, significant.   **54. little enquiry made**: failure to ask sufficient/adequate questions.

bought with a farm & the curse of it entailed as well as the Acres on Posterity——
Joseph Cuthbert[55] is here,   I have little doubt of his doing well,   he is industrious,
attends to his business, & does not interfere with Politicks,   he has got already a good
trade & I hope will be able to keep it——We have besides of Belfast People here
Thomas Storry[56]—the Quinns[57] & Brysons of Newtonards,[58] Nixon the apothecary[59]
(gone to Savannah) Tho⁵ Kean,[60] Robᵗ Wilson,[61] & a variety of others—— Tom

55. Joseph Cuthbert: born in Belfast about 1762; a Presbyterian master-tailor of some means, Cuthbert was one of the most radical and bellicose United Irish leaders in Ulster. Although arrested (and released) as early as 1793, in 1795–1797 Cuthbert played a major role in forging the alliance between the United Irishmen and the Catholic Defenders, in subverting the loyalties of Irish militiamen, and, allegedly, in assassinating informers. Imprisoned in Ft. George, Scotland, until 1802, Cuthbert emigrated to New York, resumed his tailoring trade, and apparently prospered.   **56. Thomas Storry**: Thomas Storey (d. 1827), a Belfast printer in partnership with his brother, John; both United Irishmen, they published rebel songs that allegedly subverted the loyalties of the government's militiamen. During the 1798 rising, John Storey was a commanding officer at the battle of Antrim, after which he was captured, tried, and executed; his severed head was displayed on a pike at Belfast's market house. Thomas Storey was also apprehended and taken to Belfast, but he escaped from prison before his trial and fled to America, where he lived about 16 years before he returned to Ireland, secured a pardon, and spent the rest of his life in business in Belfast and Antrim.   **57. the Quinns**: John Quinn; sentenced to 14 years' transportation to New South Wales, Quinn was at length permitted to exile himself and his family to America; perhaps related to Arthur Quin, in 1794 a founding member of Belfast's Linen Hall Library.
58. Brysons of Newtonards: Andrew Bryson, Sr., a Presbyterian and prominent United Irishman, of Newtownards, Co. Down, accompanied John Caldwell into exile in 1799. His son, Andrew, Jr., was also a United Irishman and took part in the rebel attack on Newtownards. Andrew, Jr., was arrested and convicted, but his death sentence was commuted to 20 years' service in the "condemned regiments" of the British army in the West Indies. His brother, David, also a United Irishman, escaped arrest, fled to the United States, and then went to Antigua, where he rescued his brother and brought him to New York City. In New York the family prospered in the grocery trade, but Andrew may have returned to Newtownards with his brother-in-law, James McKittrick, also an exiled rebel. In New York David Bryson was intimate friends with Emmet and Macneven. He became a prominent local politician and a city alderman and between 1802 and 1816 he was many times an officer of the Hibernian Provident Society, affiliated with the Clintonian faction of the New York Republicans. A kinsman, William Bryson of Belfast, signed the Presbyterian radicals' petition for Catholic emancipation in January 1792 and was the father-in-law of Samuel Neilson, editor and publisher of the *Northern Star*, who also fled to America, where he died in 1803.   **59. Nixon the apothecary**: probably Jacob Nixon of Belfast, arrested by the government in April 1796.   **60. Tho⁵ Kean**: Thomas Kane of Belfast; a Presbyterian, Kane was the clerk of Samuel Neilson, editor of the *Northern Star*, and a prominent United Irishman in his own right. Aide-de-camp to the rebel general Henry Monro during the rising in Co. Down, Kane escaped to America after the battle of Ballynahinch and settled in New York. His brother William, also a United Irish commander, was captured but escaped from his Belfast prison and also fled to the United States; in 1803 he was living in Philadelphia.   **61. Robᵗ Wilson**: perhaps Dr. Wilson of Cullybackey, Co. Antrim, a moderate United Irishman; or perhaps a relative of Dr. Thomas Wilson of Magherafelt, Co. Derry, a United Irishman who spent a brief exile in America before returning to Ireland; or possibly a kinsman of another Dr. Thomas Wilson (d. 1817) of Newtownards, Co. Down, who spent a few years in American exile before returning to Ulster. Finally, Robert Wilson may have been a relative of the more prominent Hugh Wilson (1772–1829): born in Belfast, Wilson moved to Dublin, where he became a clerk in the Bank of Ireland and close friends with Oliver Bond, Emmet, and other United Irishmen; arrested and imprisoned at Ft. George, Wilson was released in 1802 and spent the rest of his life prosperously as a merchant in Charleston, South Carolina, the West Indies, New York, New Orleans, again in New York, and in Copenhagen, where he married a Danish heiress, settling afterward at St. Croix, in the Virgin Islands; he died at New Haven, Connecticut, during one of his frequent visits to New York.

JOHN CALDWELL, JR.

Bashford[62] went to St Jago de Cuba & is expected soon back again———Robt M:Hinch is making Money & adding Respect to our National character,　he is worthy of honorable mention———

31st October　I have been so much & so variously engaged since I began this Letter, that you will find it I fear unconnected & I shall not recorrect it—so you must take it as it is for better for worse———the News of the conflagration at Liverpool has spread much consternation here, as it is not doubted but that there has been much American Property destroyed,[63]　that & other accounts have caused a spurt in the Cotton Market, which is now 19^cts & scarce for Upland[64]———I have said nothing yet of the domestick habits & amusements of the People of this Town———the old settlers principally the descendants of Dutch, are extremely cautious & jealous of Strangers, but if your character bears scrutiny, after a pretty severe ordeal, they become friendly & Neighbourly———the European settlers live in a degree of style & Splendor that would astonish you & the very poorest Man, if industrious can live as comfortable & as well as the Mayor of the Town———there are 900 Carmen[65] here under licence———We employ one who keeps two horses & we have actually paid for Cartages of goods in & out of our Store from 1200 to $1500 ℔ Annum———there is a very elegant Theatre & a tolerable sett of Performers, but I have been very seldom one of the Audience———they have a Musseum—Circusses—& here as with you—repeated exhibitions of Mammoth Ox's—Monsters with two heads, five feet—extraordinary tails, &c &c &c　The Publick walks of the Park & the Battery, but particularly the latter must I think be[66] the finest in the world———there is elegant gravel walks, wood & water & the top of the Battery has been by the present Mayor[67] decorated with Pallisadoes[68] & Seats all round for the accommodation of the Citizens, to whom the property belongs———Last Summer presented so Novel a scene at this spot, that the account of fairy Land or the Arabian Nights Entertainments came alone up to it[69]———An Assemblage of at least 5000 well dressed People of both sexes would meet & walk about from eight till

62. Tom Bashford: Thomas Gunning Bashford, Jr.: a Belfast shopkeeper and member of the Ulster Directory of the United Irishmen, in May 1798 Bashford denounced Robert Simms and other cautious United Irish leaders and urged an immediate rising in the north of Ireland. Although proclaimed in the Fugitive Act of 1798, Bashford escaped to the United States where he became a merchant, trading with Santiago (St Jago hereafter), Cuba, and elsewhere in the West Indies. **63. conflagration at Liverpool:** on 15 September 1802 fire destroyed Liverpool's extensive Goree warehouses and their contents; total estimated damage was £323,000, including American cotton valued at £30,000; the fire was so intense that the ruins continued to burn for three months. **64. Upland:** i.e., upland cotton, a short staple variety grown on high ground; "19 cents for upland cotton, which is moreover scarce." **65. Carmen:** carters. **66. by ms. 67. the present Mayor:** De Witt Clinton, nephew of Governor George Clinton (see earlier and chapter 66). Fenced, planted, and landscaped in 1785–1791, the Battery and the Park at the tip of Manhattan Island were a popular promenade in the 1790s, but by 1807 they had "become too common," according to one visitor, and the city's "fashionable" people crowded Broadway instead. Bushman, *Refinement*, 165; see Sources. **68. Pallisadoes:** palisades, here "rows of trees and/or bushes." **69. the account of . . . came alone up to it:** "only the account of . . . came up to it" (see n. 35).

ten OClock, during which they were entertained by the Mayors orders with a Band of Musick on shore, while a select party of Amateurs[70] in highly decorated boats, followed by a train of boats all superbly illuminated, entertained themselves & the Company on the battery by very exquisite performances——the brightness of the clear & unclouded hemisphere—the view of the most beautiful Harbour in the world, the prospect of the opposite Banks of the Hudson & the Shores of Long Island, the <u>happy look</u> of the Multitude & the Personal independence of every Individual, made the scene most truly enchanting——this entertainment continued some weeks, but the Nights becoming moist, occasioned frequent colds & the good Citizens were obliged to recreate themselves otherwise——Our House has written your R & WS[71] to their Letter I refer you for Mercantile news——Mean while I remain with best wishes for your success in your renovated firm & with Aff[t] respects to M[rs] Simms & family My Dear Sir Your Obliged & Aff[t72] friend

John Caldwell

Initially, John Caldwell and his family flourished in what his father called "the free and blissful regions of the United States of America,"[73] and in the spring of 1803 his mercantile future appeared sufficiently promising to enable him to wed Ann Higenbotham, daughter of a clergyman from County Waterford.[74] Likewise, at first the family estate at Salisbury Mills prospered, as newly constructed turnpikes channeled the produce of upstate New York through Orange County for processing and transshipment down the Hudson to Manhattan. After his father's death in late 1803, Caldwell's brother Richard left New York City and assumed management of the family estate; in 1806 John Caldwell boasted that Richard would soon have "the most handsome farm in the County," surrounded by industrious tenants engaged in "shop-keeping, farming, currying, shoe-making, weaving, spinning, smith's work, coopering, [and] milling of every description."[75]

Unfortunately, however, the damp autumnal weather that Caldwell described in 1802, as scattering the festive crowds on New York's Battery, served as an apt metaphor for his family's fortunes in America. Caldwell's partner in the Water Street firm, brother-in-law John Parks, turned out to be incompetent, and brother Richard's mismanagement of the Salisbury estate drained both their father's fortune and his own firm of capital. James Parks, Caldwell's other brother-in-law, took over at Salisbury Mills, but he also laid out too much money on "great improvements"—"the rock on which we all split," Caldwell later and ruefully recalled. In 1808 John Caldwell's mercantile concern suspended payment.

---

70. Amateurs: nonprofessional performers.　71. R & WS: Robert & William Simms, the Belfast merchant firm of Caldwell's correspondent.　72. Aff[t]: affectionate.　73. John Caldwell, Sr., Account of his exile, 1799 (1 April 1803), in New York Genealogical and Biographical Society, New York City.　74. John and Ann Caldwell had two children: Margaret Elizabeth (1804–1836), who married Thomas M. Shapter; and Elizabeth Ann (1805–1867), who wed her brother-in-law, James S. Shapter.　75. John Caldwell, Jr., New York City, to Robert Simms, Belfast, 15 May 1806 (D. 1759/3B/6, PRONI).

Through a voyage as supercargo on a merchant vessel, he managed to satisfy his creditors; then he moved to Orange County in an effort to save the family estate from bankruptcy. But in 1812 his brother Richard embarked on a quixotic quest for revenge against the British government, enlisting as captain in a New York militia regiment; within six months of the war's commencement, Richard was dead of exposure at Lake Champlain, leaving a widow and two young children in John's care. Eventually, Richard's son would salvage and farm two hundred acres of Salisbury Mills, but, despite all John Caldwell's efforts, the rest of the estate was lost through foreclosure or at auction sale to satisfy the enormous debts his kinsmen had incurred.

After his wife died in 1818, Caldwell moved back to Manhattan and recommenced trade, this time in partnership with another brother who resided in Charleston, South Carolina. Again, however, the results were disappointing, and in 1827 Caldwell could muster merely a $12 contribution toward the cost of the monument that the city's Irish commissioned in Emmet's memory. By 1834 Caldwell was "entirely out of business," but his political friends secured him an appointment as collector of arrear taxes for New York City and County; by good management, he made the post sufficiently lucrative so that, when he retired in 1839, he could spend his old age at Salisbury Mills, in a rented house on the verge of his nephew's farm. When John Caldwell died on 17 May 1850, shortly after his eighty-second birthday, his total assets were valued at $8,337, but most of it consisted of mortgaged Manhattan property, bank stock, and unrecoverable debts owed by impecunious relatives; his household goods—which included no china or silverware— were valued at merely $376.

Finally, the imagery of Caldwell's 1802 letter can also serve as a metaphor of general disenchantment, as the cold winds of change dispelled the United Irishmen's dream that their exiled Protestant and Catholic countrymen would be united, by common principles and fraternal affection, with each other and with like-minded American republicans. To be sure, Caldwell himself, despite his financial embarrassments, remained active in New York's Irish-American society, serving in 1805–1808 as treasurer and in 1828 as vice-president of the city's Friendly Sons of St. Patrick, as well as master of the Erin Masonic Lodge. And in 1843, when the American Repeal Association, dedicated to the abolition of the Act of Union between Ireland and Britain, held its second national convention in Manhattan, the Irish-American repealers, overwhelmingly Catholic, honored the elderly Presbyterian as one of the last surviving United Irish exiles. Indeed, one could argue that, in his longevity and his presence at the Repeal meeting, John Caldwell provided a living as well as a symbolic link between the Irish revolutionaries of 1798 and those convention delegates who would later support the Young Ireland revolt of 1848 and the Fenian rebellion of 1867 against the "British tyranny" that Caldwell never ceased to condemn.

However, the disjunctions between the late eighteenth and the mid–nineteenth centuries were more striking than the apparent continuities. From the 1820s on, New York City—and the rest of urban-industrializing America—was riven with overlapping class, ethnoreligious, and political conflicts that divided Irish immigrants along social and denominational lines. Indeed, only one year after New York's Repealers honored the legacy of 1798, Irish Protestants and Catholics engaged in bloody religious warfare in the streets of Philadelphia.[76] To be sure, pockets of Irish Protestant radicalism survived to the American Civil War—perhaps primarily in rural settlements, such as Robert McArthur's Crawford County, Pennsylvania.[77] In general, however, the United Irishmen's ecumenical ideals and shared antipathies to England flourished only briefly in a Jeffersonian and Jacksonian America where, from the 1820s onward, economic growth was increasingly dependent on British markets and capital investments [78]—and where upper- and middle-class status were increasingly measured by élite or bourgeois British standards of taste and civility.

During John Caldwell's long life, stretching into the Great Irish Famine and its mass migrations of 1845–1855, the United Irishmen's ideals were at length overwhelmed and submerged by new waves of Protestant and Catholic immigrants who espoused the religious tribalism and confessional politics that produced such bitter strife on both sides of the ocean. The rise of the Orange Order, the escalating fervor of Protestant evangelicalism—linked in Ireland to British loyalism; in America to the Federalist, later to the Whig and Republican parties, and on both shores to a strident anti-Catholicism—and bitter competition for Irish farms and American jobs: all drove Irish immigrants apart socially and politically, both before and after their migrations. So did also the growing assertiveness of the Irish and Irish-American Catholic clergy and the political crusades of Daniel O'Connell, Catholic champion of early nineteenth-century Ireland, neither of which included any tolerance for the United Irishmen's political goals and methods. Indeed, the sad reality was that John Caldwell was merely a token figure at the 1843 Repeal convention, dominated as it was by an aggressively Catholic, Irish-American bourgeoisie, most of whose members took their political cues from O'Connell or their clergy, not from Wolfe Tone, and whose sense of ethnic identity linked "faith and fatherland" in ways that, inadvertently if not intentionally, marginalized or ignored Ireland's Protestants and the "men of '98."

76. On the Philadelphia riots of May 1844, see chapter 25, n. 121. 77. On McArthur and the Ulster Presbyterians of Crawford Co., Pa., see chapter 64. 78. The U.S. Coinage Act was especially noteworthy in this regard; by adopting the gold standard, the law aligned the U.S. and British currencies, which in turn encouraged a flood of British investments in the American economy, especially in internal improvements and urban infrastructure. As the historian Gary Lawson Browne puts it, through the Coinage Act American domestic economies were "thus drawn into closer dependency upon Great Britain's through finance at the same time that the American national market economy was brought"—through Liverpool—"into greater alignment with that of the British." (G. L. Browne, *Baltimore in the Nation. . .* , 127; see Sources.) Perhaps unsurprisingly, it was usually the state governments, which guaranteed the bonds sold to build internal improvements, that exercised primary responsibility for employing legal and military force to suppress strikes and riots by Irish workers on the canals and railroads financed in large part by British capitalists—thus reproducing in America the British state's relationship with Irish landlords and peasants in Ireland itself.

Thus, it was not the seeds of liberty's tree that Emmet had hoped to plant but instead the noxious weeds of prejudice sown by immigrants such as William Heazelton[79]—himself on the cutting edge of the new, symbiotic Irish relationship among evangelicalism, social conservatism, and political loyalism—that found the most fertile ground in mid-nineteenth-century America. By 1850, when John Caldwell died, Irish identities both at home and in the United States had come full circle: as mutually antagonistic now as they had been over 130 years earlier when, in Londonderry, New Hampshire, John Caldwell's ancestors had signed the petitions[80] that provided their eulogists with "historical evidence" for an exclusive and purportedly eternal "Scotch-Irish" identity that denied both the real ambiguities and the fleeting unities of early Irish emigration—as well as what some have lamented as the "lost opportunities" of Irish and Irish-American history.

79. On Heazelton, see chapter 67.   **80.** See chapter 49.

�

Appendices

APPENDIX 1 ❋ Text and Language

BRUCE D. BOLING

The centerpiece of each chapter of this volume is a document, or series of documents—typically personal letters—chosen to illustrate a particular aspect of Irish immigration to North America from the late 1600s to the end of the Napoleonic wars. In addition to serving as auxiliaries to the writing of history, these documents are in themselves cultural artifacts of the highest interest as products of a given time, place, and mentality. These considerations have determined our decision to present the documents as their writers left them, altering them as little as the requirements of clarity allow. We realize that this way of proceeding places unusual demands on the modern reader, who is accustomed to standardized spelling, grammar, and punctuation. We have therefore compromised absolute strictness of transcription with judicious emendation of the texts, alerting the reader whenever the original has been altered. Changes that do not affect the *meaning* of the text are, however, not noted; such are the silent omission of repetitions and cancellations and the relocation of matter written above or below the line to its logical place in the sentence. In addition, serious obstacles to understanding posed by dialect forms, idiomatic expressions, exotic spellings, changes over time in the meaning of words and phrases, and the like are discussed in the footnotes. The consequence of our care to reproduce the original appearance of the documents is a certain amount of editorial clutter, but we hope that the balance struck between emendations and notes has reduced this to a tolerable level.

EDITORIAL CONVENTIONS (TEXT)

The following will illustrate the types of emendations we have used.

- When emendations are simple and straightforward we have inserted square or angled brackets as in the examples below.
- Square brackets enclose matter originally present in the text which is now either gone altogether (because, for example, there is a tear or hole in the paper) or obscured (because, for example, it lies on a fold). Examples: **She and Georg Preste Came in here together [. . .]** (hole in the ms.; chapter 28). More often than not it is possible to restore part or all of the missing matter on the basis of context or likelihood: **I am Dear Br[other] yours till Death** (chapter 4, letter no. 1); **the Creator of us [. . . an]d give my love and servis to my Cossens in generall** (several words illegible; chapter 1, letter no. 2).
- Angled brackets indicate that a letter, word, or phrase is missing in the original. Example: **we have given them < . . . >** (sentence incomplete; chapter 30). It is frequently possible to supply the absent element: **Bis<h>ops** (chapter 2); **un<con>cidret** "inconsiderate" (chapter 2); **Whilst <living>** (letter-writing formula; chapter 24). In some instances an incomplete written form is not a mistake or oversight but represents a conventional spelling or a phonetic rendering, which may be confusing or distracting to the modern reader. These stumbling blocks can often be removed by using brackets. A good example is furnished by the phonetic spelling **the** for **they**: in northern Hiberno-English the definite article **the** and the

pronoun **they** fall together in favor of **the** (see W. McMordie's strictures on this nonstandard pronunciation in his *Our Ulster Accent and Ulster Provincialisms* [Belfast, 1897], p. 13). Whenever the spelling **the** represents **they** we emend to **the<y>**. **They** is also frequently written **thy**; when this is the case, we emend the form to **th<e>y**. To give a slightly more complicated example, the manuscript spelling **to** may represent either a phonetic or an incomplete spelling and, depending on meaning, may remain **to** ("to") or be emended to **to<o>** or **t<w>o** when phonetic or to **to<w>** ("kind of flax"; rhymes with **cow**) when incomplete.

- Cancellations made by the writer (e.g., erasures, cross-outs) are usually not specially noticed unless they contain matter that is particularly interesting in shedding additional light on the contents of the document.

- Frequently the desired emendation is beyond the scope of the simple device of bracketing; in these cases we have provided an explanatory note. Such notes are mostly self-explanatory, and a few examples will be enough to illustrate the various types.

  1. **six or seven**: conjectural, written above cancelled **five**.
  2. **Bein being** ms. [the manuscript spells the word **Bein**, then corrects it to **being**; editors give only **being** in their transcription].
  3. Ms. torn (six to eight words missing).
  4. **held** ms. [the manuscript has **held**, which the editors have corrected to **help** in their transcript].

EDITORIAL CONVENTIONS (CONTENT)

By far the greatest number of notes are devoted to illuminating the historical background and to explaining linguistic matters. The former need no illustration. The latter are specifically concerned with spelling, grammar (phonology, morphology, syntax), meaning (definitions, paraphrases), and dialect. A few examples follow.

  1. **ithath**: i.e., it hath.
  2. **asa[f]e**: i.e., a safe.
  3. **Burdings**: i.e., burdens (reverse spelling).
  4. **hith**: i.e., height; see n. 4.
  5. **carty fie**: i.e., certify "inform officially."
  6. **direction**: address.
  7. **Sence . . . deed**: "since I cannot, [you are to] take . . . "
  8. **Within Compass**: without exaggeration.
  9. **Would Ahad me to Agon**: A represents the phonetic reduction of **have** to **[u]**: "would have had me to have gone (i.e., would have had me go)." When functioning as the complement of a verb in the past tense, the present infinitive can be replaced by its past counterpart (as here: **go** is replaced by **to have gone**); such usage is particularly popular in the written language of the Early Modern period but is later abandoned.
  10. **least**: i.e., lest (spelling indicates Scots pronunciation).

In providing notes on the linguistic aspect of the texts it has sometimes been necessary to discuss sound. This has been done in two ways. If we wish merely to indicate how a form is pronounced, we have recourse to rhyme (e.g., **Learn** "Larne," rhymes with cairn); if the matter is more complicated, we use an adaptation of the system devised by Sir James Wilson, which uses symbols from the ordinary alphabet. The consonants have their usual English value, except [kh], which represents the sound in lo<u>ch</u> [lokh], and [ng], which is always the sound in si<u>ng</u>er [singur], never that in fi<u>ng</u>er [finggur]. The vowels are: [aa] as in <u>a</u>re, [ay] as in s<u>ay</u>, [e] as in b<u>e</u>t, [ee] as in f<u>ee</u>d, [ey] as in s<u>i</u>de, [aw] as in <u>aw</u>e, [o] as in l<u>o</u>t, [oa] as in c<u>o</u>urt, [oo] as in b<u>oo</u>t, [ow] as in <u>ow</u>l, [u] as in b<u>u</u>t and also as the sound in s<u>e</u>rious, when in an unstressed syllable.

All questions of the meaning of English words and phrases can be assumed to have been referred as a matter of course to the *Oxford English Dictionary*. Only when the definition provided there differs in any significant way from the common acceptation is a specific citation made (e.g., OED, s.v., 3). Definitions of Scots words and phrases can likewise be assumed to have been checked against the *Scottish National Dictionary* and the *Concise Ulster Dictionary*. Definitions taken from more specialized dictionaries are always accompanied by a citation.

LANGUAGE

The documents in our compilation are not uniform in language. Among their authors there are the usual class and educational differences, but more fundamentally there are differences of dialect. When we speak of dialect we do not have in mind some lower order of human speech brimming with misused pronouns and barbarous participles or an isolated rural patois with its Elizabethan syntax perfectly preserved. We rather refer to the fact that language varies through space and over time. London English, for example, is notably different from that spoken in New York. As for temporal change, the language of the pre-Conquest epic *Beowulf* is incomprehensible to the ordinary English speaker of the twentieth century, and letters written at the beginning of the Modern English period (ca. 1450–1500) are distinctly exotic. The spatial varieties of a given language are called dialects. It often happens for various complicated reasons that one dialect out of the many gains prestige and rises to the status of a standard. If the spatial extent of a language is large enough, several *regional* standards may emerge; so we have, for example, Standard British English, Standard American English, Standard Australian English, and so on. Those dialects that do not achieve the rank of standard are designated by linguists as "nonstandard," meaning that they are different from, but not inferior to, the standard language, as far as their status as a language is concerned and whatever their social standing may be.

Ireland has two major dialect areas, Southern Hiberno-English and Northern Hiberno-English. Southern Hiberno-English is *roughly* the speech of what is today the Irish Republic minus the three counties of Cavan, Donegal, and Monaghan, and came to Ireland with settlers from the southwest and the West Country of England. Northern Hiberno-English is *roughly* the speech of the province of Ulster—that is, of what is today Northern Ireland, plus counties Cavan, Donegal, and Monaghan. (County Louth also, although not part of historical Ulster, belongs to the northern dialect region.) Moreover, within Ireland's northern region there are two quite distinct dialect areas: Ulster Scots (in counties Antrim, Derry, north Down, and east Donegal) and Mid-Ulster (elsewhere). Ulster Scots (also called Ullans) has developed from the variety of Lowland Scots brought by settlers from the west and southwest of Scotland, whereas Mid-Ulster has its origins in the north and north midlands of England.

When referring to matters of dialect in the notes we will use the following conventions:

Hiberno-English	throughout Ireland
Southern	confined to the southern region
Ulster	Ulster Scots + Mid-Ulster
Ulster Scots	confined to the Ulster Scots region
Mid-Ulster	confined to the Mid-Ulster region
Scots	Scots + Ulster Scots

In annotating linguistic phenomena it is not our purpose to furnish a systematic dialect grammar of Hiberno-English but merely to provide help in understanding unfamiliar forms and constructions and incidentally to suggest that Irish dialects of English are to be taken seriously. It was tempting to go further into linguistic detail than we did, but two factors tempered our enthusiasm: one, this is a work of social history, not dialectology; and two, the resulting book would have been too expensive for the market. However, one of the authors, Bruce Boling, has compiled and analyzed all the dialect data in the documents and hopes to publish this very valuable material separately in due course.

In line with our desire to assist our readers, we have not stinted in the matter of notes; we have also not hesitated on occasion to duplicate notes from one chapter to another, to serve those who pick and choose the chapters they wish to read or to assist those through-readers whose memory of a note they saw ten chapters earlier is faulty. We also add here some remarks about certain fundamental aspects of Hiberno-English dialect spelling and syntax that may render the texts less exotic and formidable.

SPELLING

Reverse Spellings

When a sound change takes place, the spelling that represented the original sound may persist as the spelling of the new sound. This allows the conservative spelling to be extended beyond its original reach.

A good example of this phenomenon can be seen in the "reverse" spelling of the word **burden**. Early on in the history of Modern English the sound [ng] (as in si<u>ng</u>) following an unstressed vowel at the end of a word (as in si<u>ng</u>ing) became [n] (as in sin). If *singing* persisted as a way of spelling the new sound (which ought properly to be **singin**), then **ng** could be used to represent final [n], whatever its origin. This is what happens in the spelling **burding** for **burden**; the latter word of course never in its history ended in the sound [ng].

Another clear example is furnished by the spelling **roiet** for **riot**. A number of very common Scots words have a root vowel [ey] (as in [meyn] "mine") corresponding to Standard English root vowel [oy] (as in [koyn] "coin"); e.g., Scots **bile**, **jine** = English **boil**, **join**. The presence of these corresponding pairs allows the *spelling* **oi** to be used to represent the *sound* [ey], yielding such spellings as **goile** for Scots **jile** "gaol/jail" and **roiet** for Scots (and English) **riot**.

Spellings with <u>ea</u>

The graph **ea** represents the reflex in Modern English of the Middle English long open [e], approximately [ay] as in [mayd] "made." This [ay]-reflex later fell together with [ee] (as in <u>feed</u>) in Standard English, but remained in the various dialects spoken in Ireland, so that, for example, Hiberno-English has [draym] "dream" corresponding to Standard English [dreem]. The persistence of the original reflex in Ireland allows **ea** to become one of the means available to spell the sound [ay] whatever its origin. Thus, for example, **made [mayd]** can be spelled **made, maid, med, mad,** as well as **mead**. The use of **ea** in this way can give rise to serious confusion, since the result is sometimes in appearance an entirely different word, as in the case of the form **mead**, just exampled above: the modern reader is likely at first glance to interpret the word as "alcoholic drink made from honey" rather than the past tense of **make**. The same can be said of the form **tread** "trade," which occurs several times in this compilation. To obviate such confusion the editors have annotated spellings where **ea** is not historically justified.

Analytic and Synthetic Spellings

Analytic spelling refers to the practice of breaking written words into constituent parts (usually two). Synthetic spelling refers to the opposite process, which combines independent words into a single form. These two processes are as old as the restoration of English to official status in the fourteenth century, and they are abundantly attested in the texts presented in this compilation. Except in the most obvious cases the editors have annotated such spellings.

Below are a few examples from the texts.

Analytic spellings

carty fie	"certify"	(chapter 1, James Wansbrough)
Im Presion	"impression"	(chapter 2, Alexander Crawford)
A Merica	"America"	(chapter 24, John and Jane Chambers)
a piel	"appeal"	(chapter 29, JohnKennedy)
Out Ragious	"outrageous"	(chapter 59, Matthew Patten)

Synthetic spellings

Ronoute	"run out"	(chapter 1, James Wansbrough)
Amatick	"a mattock"	(chapter 21, James McCullough)
Iwas	"I was"	(chapter 23, Daniel Kent)
InProportion	"in proportion"	(ibid.)
withus	"with us"	(ibid.)

Examples from Henry Ellis, ed., *Original Letters Illustrative of English History*, 2nd ser., vol. 1 (London, 1827): **un to** your heigh astate (letter no. 1); our liege **lord es** comaundment (ibid.) (see **thomas es** "Thomas's," in our chapter 1); **with owten** doute (letter no. 2); **bemy** trowthe "by my troth" (letter no. 6).

It is clear in all of these examples that the location of the split in analytic forms is not arbitrary but corresponds to the boundary between what are perceived to be meaningful grammatical or lexical elements. Synthetic spellings in turn reflect the fact that in speech certain words are closely bound syntactically, typically with loss of stress on one of the constituents, and form a kind of compound word.

SYNTAX

Northern Concord Rule

A prominent grammatical feature of the letters in this compilation is the Northern Concord Rule, the operation of which may mislead readers into assuming that Irish immigrant writers were "semi-literate."

The Northern Concord Rule governs the formal relationship between the subject and the verb and is valid for the northern regions of English speech (northern England, Scotland, and the north of Ireland). The operation of the rule gives a very distinct character to northern English and is accountable for more examples of dialect usage in our collection than any other aspect of dialect grammar.

According to the Northern Concord Rule, the verb stands in the third-person singular unless closely preceded or followed by a *simple* subject personal pronoun (i.e., I, you, he, she, it, we, or they); e.g., **they SOW** their crops, but **the farmers SOWS** their crops.

In the present tense the rule applies to all verbs except the modal auxiliaries (**can, may, shall, and will**); e.g., **they CAN** sow their crops; **the farmers CAN** sow their crops.

In the past tense only the verb "to be" is affected by the rule, since it is the only verb to distinguish singular and plural in that tense: was vs. were). (In some usages was and were are distinguished in the past tense only in the third person: he was vs. they were, but I/we was; e.g., **he was** sowing his crops; **they were** sowing their crops; but **we was** sowing our crops, instead of the expected **we were** sowing. . . .)

Below are examples, taken from the texts of the letters, of the patterns produced by the operation of the Northern Concord Rule.

With plural subject noun:
> Very Few **Men was** able to buy A Brown Webb (chapter 4, Henry Johnston)
> Our public **prints has** given us several accounts (chapter 15, George Crockett).

In both these examples the verb is closely preceded by a plural subject noun (not a simple personal subject pronoun, in which case the second example would regularly be: **they have** given us several accounts).

With coordinate noun (noun + noun, noun + pronoun):
> send me word how **my Cousin John tate and all his Brothers is** (chapter 24, John and Jane
>   Chambers)
> **he and his family is** well (ibid.)

With plural demonstrative pronoun ("these, those"):
> **them is** found by the owner of the Building (chapter 38, Samuel Brown) "those are provided
>   by the owner of the building"

With Plural Indefinite Pronoun ("some"):

> **they Plow** an Acre, nay **Some Plows** 2 Acres a Day (note the difference in treatment between the simple personal pronoun ("they") and the non-personal, indefinite pronoun ("some"); (chapter 9, Robert Parke)

With relative pronoun ("who, which, that"):

> my un[con]cidret Lines **which** Justly **merits** Rebuk (chapter 2, Alexander Crawford)
> all **that was** taken for the Roiet (chapter 4, Henry Johnston) "all who were arrested for rioting"

With zero:

> We plow & likewise **Sows** our wheat with 2 horses (= we plow & likewise **[we]** sow (chapter 9, Robert Parke)
> I live hapy and well and **Expects** so[on] to By A place of My Own (chapter 26, Edward and Mary Toner)

It should be understood that the Northern Concord Rule is not perfectly observed in the letters. All writers from the northern region would have been able to speak the standard language in varying degrees of competence and would have been consciously or unconsciously influenced by it. Those who had any schooling would have been warned against such uncouth usage in their early years and would doubtless have remembered the sanctions.

Syntax, James Wansbrough, and the Quakers

To close this appendix we present a short commentary on a section of James Wansbrough's first letter (chapter 1), which we think illustrates how a coalition of linguistic and socio-cultural analysis might work to illuminate important aspects of Irish social history.

In James Wansbrough's letter of May 4, 1700, the form **nevies** "nephew's"—along with the forms **hith** "height," **wher** "whether," and perhaps **this** "these"—together with the preservation of Middle English long open [e] (usually written **ea** in Modern English), point to the Dorset-Somerset-Wiltshire area as the locus of origin of Wansbrough's speech. This is consistent with the fact that the surnames of the Wansbrough family and their To(w)ler/Toller cousins are derived from habitation names in Wiltshire and Dorset respectively. Since the Cromwellian settlement of the south of Ireland drew heavily from the population of England's West Country, Wansbrough's letters give us perhaps the largest corpus so far available of the founding stage of Southern Hiberno-English.

A jarring note in Wansbrough's southwest English speech is sounded by the strong presence in it of the Northern Concord Rule (see above), which is otherwise a hallmark of the northern dialects (north of England, Scotland, and northern Ireland). However, a scrutiny of the letters in this collection sharing the anomaly with the Wansbrough letters reveals that they share another feature that is sociological: whether from north or south, they are all written by Quakers or by those living in close familial contact with Quakers. This coincidence suggests that this deeply conservative religious community, which originated in the north of England, preserved—perhaps as a badge of identity and as a living sign of their uniqueness—a reminder of their origin to be passed down the generations. A very suggestive example of this coupling of religion and language is furnished by the letters of Daniel Kent. Kent had left his native Limerick a Methodist, but soon after his arrival in America he converted to Quakerism, and over the subsequent course of his life as an American Quaker his letters show a steady increase in the use of the Northern Concord Rule. Conversely, the letters of Kent's father, who remained a Methodist in Limerick, show not a trace of the Northern Concord Rule. A less striking, but equally interesting, example is found in the letters of Joseph and Hannah Wright of Dublin and County Wexford (chapter 25), in which an educated veneer employing the Southern Concord Rule of the standard language frequently peels back to reveal a perfect use of the nonstandard Northern Concord Rule. A third example of northern usage in southern territory is seen in the letter of Robert Parke (chapter 9), where the initial use of standard syntax gives way, as the letter progresses, to the northern, as if the standard usage is too artificial to maintain. Toward the end of the letter the use of standard syntax is resumed.

Sources

William Grant, ed., *Scottish National Dictionary* (Edinburgh, 1940–1976); C. I. Macafee, ed., *A Concise Ulster Dictionary* (Oxford, 1996); W. McMordie, *Our Ulster Accent and Ulster Provincialisms* (Belfast, 1897); *Oxford English Dictionary*, 2nd ed. (Oxford, 1989); Philip Robinson *Ulster Scots* (Belfast, 1997); and the following books by James Wilson, *Lowland Scotch as Spoken in the Lower Strathearn District of Perthshire* (London, 1915), *The Dialect of Robert Burns, as Spoken in Central Ayrshire* (London, 1923), and *The Dialects of Central Scotland* (London, 1926).

APPENDIX 2 ※ Irish Migration and Demography, 1659–1831

KERBY MILLER AND LÍAM KENNEDY[1]

In the eighteenth century, Irish magistrates and others often commented with alarm on the "great numbers" of people—particularly Ulster Presbyterians—leaving Ireland for America. Since then, scholars on both sides of the Atlantic have attempted to quantify early Irish emigration. For example, in his classic study *Ulster Emigration to Colonial America, 1718–1785* (London, 1966), R. J. Dickson estimated that prior to 1776 perhaps 120,000 emigrants left Ulster for North America. Other estimates include those in: B. Bailyn, *Voyagers to the West: A Passage in the Peopling of America on the Eve of the Revolution* (New York, 1986); Bríc, "Ireland, Irishmen"; Cullen, "Irish Diaspora," in Canny,

---

1. In 1985–1986 Kerby Miller and Líam Kennedy of the Queen's University of Belfast, assisted by Keith Brown and Mark Graham, began a study of Irish religious demography, 1659–1926, some of the initial results of which are published here for the first time. Two works that proved invaluable in tracing parishes—despite their frequent name and boundary changes—from the late 1600s to the early 1800s, and in amalgamating the 1831 diocesan- and parish-based data into their respective counties, are: S. Lewis, *A Topographical Dictionary of Ireland,* vols. 1–2 (London, 1837; repr. Baltimore, 1984); and B. Mitchell, *A New Genealogical Atlas of Ireland* (Baltimore, 1988). Also of enormous value were: W. J. Smyth, "Society and Settlement in Seventeenth-Century Ireland: The Evidence of the '1659 Census,'" in Smyth and K. Whelan, eds., *Common Ground: Essays on the Historical Geography of Ireland* (Cork, 1988), 55–83; and especially the seminal article by Dickson, Ó Gráda, and Daultrey, cited in the text.

Europeans; Doyle, *Ireland, Irishmen*, whence (p. 85) the 1790 estimates of Irish-Americans in the introduction; A. S. Fogelman, "From Slaves, Convicts, and Servants to Free Passengers: The Transformation of Immigration in the Era of the American Revolution," *JAH*, 85, no. 1 (June 1998), 43–76; H.-J. Grabbe, "European Immigration to the United States in the Early National Period, 1783–1820," *Proc. Am. Phil. Soc.*, 133 (June 1989), 190–214; M. A. Jones, "Ulster Emigration"; G. Kirkham, "Ulster Emigration to North America, 1680–1720," in Blethen & Wood, *Ulster & No. America*, 76–117; Lockhart, *Some Aspects;* Truxes, *Irish-Am. Trade;* and Wokeck, *Trade in Strangers.* (For full citations, see list of abbreviations in Sources.)

The estimates in these and other works often vary enormously. Indeed, very recently some historians have radically minimized the numbers of Irish—particularly of Ulster—emigrants to America in 1700–1776: to as low as 60,000 from all Ireland and as few as 35,000 from Ulster. Minimalist estimates are based heavily on North American (especially Philadelphia) port records, and their authors have discounted earlier and much higher totals, as set forth by Dickson and by Audrey Lockhart, for example, as little more than erroneous extrapolations of passenger numbers from fallacious ship tonnage figures advertised in eighteenth-century Irish newspapers.

We disagree with the minimalist trend and continue to rely on Dickson's older research. Contrary to his critics, Dickson did not base his estimates solely on tonnage figures as reported only in Ulster shipping advertisements. Rather, he found considerable data on tonnage *and* passengers, for the *same* ships and voyages, in Ulster *and* in American newspapers, and it was from these varied sources that he devised a tonnage–passenger ratio that he could apply to the bulk of less well-documented voyages. However, Dickson's critics also contend that Irish shippers invariably exaggerated their vessels' tonnages when advertising for passengers in Irish newspapers, in order to lure passengers with false claims as to their vessels' size and accommodations; consequently, Dickson's reliance on inflated tonnage figures inadvertently inflated his estimates of passenger numbers. Yet Dickson's critics have overlooked several issues. First, to avoid colonial port taxes, merchants had equal if not more reasons to *under*estimate their ships' tonnage when they arrived in American seaports. Therefore, the low tonnage figures reported in America (on which Dickson's critics have largely relied for their own low estimates of immigrant arrivals) are hypothetically even *less* accurate than those printed in Irish newspapers. Second, J. J. McCusker's authoritative article, "The Tonnage of Ships Engaged in British Colonial Trade during the Eighteenth Century," in his *Essays in the Economic History of the Atlantic World* (London, 1997), pp. 43–75, identifies reasons for variations in eighteenth-century ships' recorded tonnages that are much subtler but far more significant than those postulated by Dickson's critics. Most important, McCusker's conclusions as to the relationships between tonnage and passenger numbers largely corroborate Dickson's research.

More broadly, a wide array of scholars, exploring migration among a number of different countries, have discovered that—even in the more statistically minded and bureaucratic nineteenth century—official port and passenger records commonly undercounted emigration/immigration totals by as much as one-third or more. Moreover, when historians look closely at the evidence (as did Graeme Kirkham at Ulster emigration in 1680–1720 and Maurice Bríc at all Irish migration in 1783–1815), almost invariably they discover more voyages, departures, and arrivals than previously known. Indeed, given the paucity of surviving eighteenth-century newspapers from Londonderry, west Ulster's primary embarkation point during most of the 1700s, as well as from minor ports serving northern emigrants, it is very likely that Dickson's high-end figures are far too low and that Ulster emigration before 1776 may have ranged up to 250,000 or more.

Finally, we posit that the demographic data presented hereafter suggest levels of early migration from Ulster—particularly by Presbyterians—and from southern Ireland by Protestants, generally, that far exceed minimalist estimates.

From 1659 to 1831 Ireland's population was counted in several religious "censuses," sometimes undertaken as part of tax assessment and collection processes, sometimes—as in 1740 and in 1766—because the Irish Parliament wished to compare Protestant numbers with "the progress of popery," and lastly—in 1831 (and 1834)—to measure the educational needs of Ireland's religious communities. These enumerations were of widely varying reliability and were based on criteria that changed over time. For example, the "census" data (actually, the poll-tax returns) of 1659 were enumerated by counties, baronies, parishes, and townlands, but subsequent name and boundary changes, as parishes were subdivided or amalgamated, make it difficult to correlate 1659 parish data with those of 1766 and later. Likewise, the 1731–1733 "censuses" (hearthmoney returns) were counted only by county and barony (and several baronies are missing), whereas the actual censuses of 1766 and of 1831 were based on civil (or Church of Ireland) parishes.

Likewise, the enumeration of 1659 included only adults, that of 1740 only Protestant households, and that of 1766 usually only Protestant and Catholic households or families. In 1766, however, persons (as well as households) were occasionally enumerated, and in a few parishes Protestants (persons or households/families) were distinguished as Anglicans or Dissenters (sometimes even as Anglicans, Presbyterians, or Quakers) and counted separately. Finally, the 1831 census enumerated individual Catholics, Anglicans, Presbyterians, and members of other Protestant denominations.

Consequently, a major problem has been to apply to the 1740 and 1766 data a household-to-persons multiplier that would make possible a comparison between parish populations in 1740 or 1766 and in 1831. Unless otherwise indicated hereafter, we have used the generic multipliers of 4.99 persons per Ulster household and 5.15 persons per Leinster household, as devised by D. Dickson, C. Ó Gráda, and S. Daultrey, "Hearth Tax, Household Size, and Irish Population Change, 1672–1821," *Proceedings of the Royal Irish Academy*, 82C, no. 6 (1982), 125–50.

Nevertheless, the annual growth rates computed hereafter, primarily for 1766–1831, appear misleadingly precise; furthermore, a simple comparison of Catholic and Protestant annual growth rates does not *necessarily* indicate differences in levels of out-migration among members of the various communities. As some 1766 data reveal, Catholic households were usually larger than Protestant ones; in addition, it is likely that in 1766 (as in the earlier "censuses") Catholic households in at least some parishes were undercounted. To a degree, these factors qualify the pattern that the data suggest in much of Ulster and in southern Ireland, that is, of significantly higher Catholic than Protestant annual growth rates in 1766–1831. However, they do not affect findings of *generally low* yearly increases among Protestants in 1766–1831, and these can be compared with the estimated provincial growth rates calculated for 1753–1831 by Dickson, Ó Gráda, and Daultrey: namely, between 1.512 and 1.709 for Ulster, and between 1.104 and 1.277 for Leinster. Nor does Catholic undercounting in 1766 undermine our findings in those Ulster parishes where Protestant annual growth rates in 1766–1831 *exceeded* those of Catholics—quite the reverse—or where growth rates among Dissenters and Anglicans can be isolated and compared.

Despite the difficulties involved, therefore, the 1659–1831 data—if employed carefully and evaluated tentatively—can illuminate broad regional patterns of absolute or relative demographic change among the members of Ireland's religious denominations. In turn, these patterns do not only suggest the overall volume of early Irish emigration. In addition, they reveal the regional and denominational variations in emigration—or at least of out-migration. Finally, they shed light on what appear to be the highly regionalized and denomination-specific demographic consequences of the Irish political and sectarian conflicts of the late eighteenth and early nineteenth centuries, particularly in the area known as mid-Ulster.

The sources most commonly employed in this research (and referred to by number in the essays hereafter) are as follows:

1. S. Pender, *A Census of Ireland, circa 1659* (Dublin, 1939).
2. An Abstract of the Number of Protestant and Popish Families as Returned to the Hearth Money Office in 1731 (MIC 310/1, Public Record Office of Northern Ireland, Belfast).
3. *Abstract of the Number of Protestant and Popish Families in the Several Counties and Provinces of Ireland, Taken from the Returns made by the Hearthmoney Collectors . . . in the Years 1731 and 1733* (Dublin, 1736; copy in the Linen Hall Library, Belfast).
4. 1734 Religious Census of Cary, Dunluce, and Kilconway baronies, County Antrim (Séamus Ó Casaide Papers, Ms. 5456, National Library of Ireland, Dublin).
5. 1740 Census of Protestant Householders (T.808/15,208, PRONI).
6. 1766 Religious Census (T.808/15,264, PRONI).
7. 1766 Religious Census (T.808/15,266, PRONI).
8. 1766 Religious Census of County Antrim (T.808/14,900, PRONI).
9. 1766 Religious Census of County Armagh (Rev. T. Groves Papers, Ms. 2677, NLI).
10. 1766 Religious Census (Rev. T. Groves Mss., Representative Church Body Library [hereafter RCBL], Dublin).
11. 1766 Religious Census, Some Surviving Parliamentary Returns (Ms. 1A.46.49, Irish National Archives, Dublin).
12. 1766 Religious Census, Cork and Ross Dioceses (Dr. B. O'Keefe Papers, M.4921 [1C.29.64], INA).
13. 1766 Religious Census, in Rev. M. Comerford, *Collections Relating to the Dioceses of Kildare and Leighlin* (Dublin, 1883).
14. Rev. Terence O'Donnell, "Parliamentary Returns for the Diocese of Raphoe, 1766," *Donegal Annual,* 3, no. 1 (1954/55), 74–77.
15. 1831–1834 Religious Censuses, in First Report of the Commission of Public Instruction, Ireland, *British Parliamentary Papers,* H.C. 1835, xxxiii.
16. J. B. Leslie, *Armagh Clergy and Parishes* (Dundalk, 1911).
17. J. B. Leslie, *Clogher Clergy and Parishes* (Enniskillen, 1929).
18. J. B. Leslie, *Derry Clergy and Parishes* (Enniskillen, 1937).
19. J. B. Leslie, *Raphoe Clergy and Parishes* (Enniskillen, 1940).
20. W. E. Vaughn and A. J. Fitzpatrick, eds., *Irish Historical Statistics: Population 1821–1971* (Dublin, 1978).

1. ULSTER

1a. West Ulster and the Foyle Valley

This region already had a sizeable Protestant population in 1659, but between that year and 1731–1733 more British in-migration increased the relative size of the Protestant population—to majority status in the areas of richest soils. Between the early 1730s and 1766 the pattern is mixed: in some parishes the relative size of the Protestant population increased, but in others the reverse occurred. However, between 1766 and 1831 population growth was low overall and the Protestant proportion of the region's population shrank considerably. Where measurable, in 1766–1831 Presbyterian annual growth rates were invariably lower than those of Anglicans as well as of Catholics, but Anglican growth rates were usually also lower than Catholic growth rates.

Chapter 2. Alexander Crawford, 1736

Killymard parish, Banagh barony, County Donegal. Between 1732–1733 and 1831 the Protestant proportion of County Donegal's entire population declined from 57 to 30 percent, and the annual growth rate among the county's Protestants was less than 1.11, compared with over 2.29 for Catholics. Between 1766 and 1831 the Protestant and Catholic growth rates in 26 Donegal parishes were 0.70 and 1.86, respectively. In Crawford's Killymard parish between 1766 and 1831 the growth rate among Protestants was at most 1.50 per annum (and perhaps as low as 0.84), whereas the Catholic growth rate was 2.69 (probably due to in-migration as well as natural increase). *References:* 1, 3, 7, 15, 19, and W. McAfee, "The Demographic History of Ulster, 1750–1841," in Blethen & Wood, *Ulster & No. America,* 41–60.

Chapter 11. James Orr, 1811

Camus-Morne (or Strabane) parish, Strabane Lower barony, County Tyrone. Between 1732 and 1766, the Protestant proportion of Strabane barony's population rose from 49 to 57 percent, but by 1831 it had declined to 51 percent. In Camus-Morne parish, between 1765–1766 and 1831 the Protestant share of the population declined steeply, from 70 to 52 percent. In the same period the Presbyterian proportion of the parish's inhabitants fell from 40 to 29 percent, while the Anglican share declined only from 30 to 23 percent. Annual growth rates in 1765–1831 were 0.37 among Presbyterians, 0.46 for Anglicans, and 1.60 among Catholics. Comparable changes indicating disproportionately heavy Presbyterian emigration occurred in adjacent Ardstraw parish, where in 1765–1831 the Presbyterian share of the population fell from 53 to 41 percent, while that of Anglicans rose from 11 to 16 percent and of Catholics from 35 to 43 percent. *References:* 2, 3, 7, 15, 20, and Religious [Hearthmoney] Return of Strabane District . . . 1765 (T.808/15,261, PRONI).

Chapter 15. George Crockett, Jr., 1797–1807

Killea parish, Raphoe barony, County Donegal. Between 1659 and 1732–1733, the Protestant share of County Donegal's inhabitants increased from 28 to 57 percent, although in Raphoe barony it was stable at ca. 58–61 percent. In the mid- to late 1700s and early 1800s, however, east Donegal's population experienced very little growth, especially among Protestants, probably due to migration overseas. Thus, between 1740 and 1766 the Protestant population of the Donegal portions of Templemore parish (later the parishes of Muff and Burt) had an annual growth rate of merely 1.00. More broadly, between 1766 and 1831 the Protestant share of the populations of seven east Donegal parishes (Leck, Killea, Raphoe, Raymoghy, Stranolar, and Taughboyne) declined from 63 percent to less than 54 percent, while their absolute numbers rose from ca. 14,100 to merely 15,700. By 1831 County Donegal's entire population was only 30.1 percent Protestant.

In the Crocketts' Killea parish, between 1766 and 1831 the Protestant population increased by only 10 percent, and its share of the parish's inhabitants declined from nearly 90 percent to

73 percent. Killea Protestants' annual growth rate in 1766–1831 was merely 0.14, whereas among Catholics, whose numbers rose 243 percent, it was 1.89. Similar patterns prevailed in adjacent east Donegal parishes such as Donaghmore and Taughboyne (including All Saints); and in Raymoghy, where in 1766 Presbyterians and Anglicans were enumerated separately, their annual growth rates in 1766–1831 were 0.44 and 1.07, respectively, with 1.13 among Catholics. *References:* 1, 2, 3, 5, 7, 15, and 19.

Chapter 22. Elizabeth Guthrie Brownlee Guthrie, 1755–1829

Londonderry city (Templemore parish, part), County Londonderry. According to the local Anglican dean's census, in 1771 Londonderry city had 8,700 inhabitants, of whom only 21 percent were Catholics; of the city's Protestant majority, 57 percent belonged to the Church of Ireland, and 43 percent were Presbyterians. Sixty years later, the city's religious composition had changed radically. In 1831 the population of that part of Templemore parish that included Derry city and its suburbs had risen to 18,972, of whom 52 percent were Catholics and 48 percent were Protestants, and of the latter only 35 percent were Anglicans, the rest Presbyterians and other Dissenters. *References:* 15 and Census of Derry, 1771 (T.808/15,259, PRONI); and C. Thomas, "The City of Londonderry: Demographic Trends and Socio-Economic Characteristics, 1650–1900," in O'Brien, *Derry & Londonderry.*

Chapter 33. James Patton (1), 1783–1789

Tamlaght Finlagan parish, Keenaght barony, County Londonderry. Between 1659 and 1766 the Protestant proportion of the population of Keenaght barony (including a portion of Banagher parish in Tirkeeran barony) rose from 45 to 63 percent but subsequently declined to less than 57 percent by 1831. However, there were major differences within the barony: in the northeastern parishes with the richest soils, Protestant annual growth rates in 1766–1831 were dramatically lower than those among Catholics (e.g., 0.50 vs. 1.46 in Aghanloo), but in the southern and mountainy parishes of Banagher and Dungiven, the pattern was strikingly different (see sec. 1.b, on chapter 8).

In 1659 the population of Patton's Tamlaght Finlagan parish was already 64 percent Protestant. Between 1740 and 1766 the number of Protestant households rose from 388 to 721 (an annual growth rate of 2.41), and in the latter year Protestants comprised 85 percent of the parish's inhabitants (based on household-to-person multipliers [4.551 for Protestants, 4.747 for Catholics] derived from contiguous Balteagh parish). However, between 1766 and 1831 the Protestant annual growth rate was merely 0.82 (compared with 1.76 among Catholics), and the Protestant share of Tamlaght Finlagan's inhabitants declined to less than 72 percent, suggesting heavy Protestant out-migration, probably coupled with considerable Catholic in-migration from County Donegal (as reported in adjacent Tamlaghtard or Magilligan parish). In 1831 Presbyterians accounted for 87 percent of the parish's Protestants.

The 1766 data for Tamlaght Finlagan does not distinguish Anglicans and Presbyterians, but they do in three of Keenaght barony's parishes: Aghanloo, Bovevagh, and Drumachose. Presbyterians predominated among Protestants in all three parishes, but in Bovevagh and Drumachose there were striking differences in 1766–1831 between Anglican and Presbyterian annual growth rates: 2.71 vs. 1.34 in the former, 1.34 vs. 0.94 in the latter. *References:* 1, 5, 7, 15, and S. Butler, Statistical Account of Tamlaghtard Parish, 1824 (T.3239/1, PRONI).

Chapter 55. Rev. Francis Alison, 1768

Leck parish, Raphoe barony, County Donegal. Between 1659 and 1732 the Protestant share of the inhabitants of Raphoe barony remained stable at about 60 percent, and between 1659 and 1766 the Protestant share of the households in Alison's Leck parish rose from 45 to 55 percent—although in 1766 the numbers of Leck's *inhabitants* (based on multipliers derived from adjacent Lettermackaward) were more evenly balanced between Protestants and Catholics. However, estimated annual growth rates in 1766–1831 were 1.05 among Protestants and 1.51 among Catholics, and by 1831 only 42.5 percent of Leck's inhabitants were Protestants, of whom nearly four-fifths were Presbyterians, the rest Anglicans. In the Deanery of Raphoe (which included Raphoe parish), Protestant and Catholic growth rates in 1766–1831 were 0.49 and 0.74, respectively, and the Protestant share of the deanery's population fell from ca. 45 to 39 percent. Again, the data suggests very heavy out-migration, particularly among Protestants. *References:* 1, 2, 7, and 15.

Chapter 64. Robert McArthur, 1802

Burt parish, Inishowen West barony, County Donegal. Between 1659 and 1732–1733 the Protestant proportion of Innishowen barony's inhabitants increased from 15 to about 60–65 percent. In 1659 Burt parish was already about one-third Protestant, but no parish data for the 1700s can be located. However, in the contiguous parish of Muff, between 1766 and 1831 the Protestant share of the population fell from 62.5 to 57 percent, while the Presbyterian proportion of the parish's Protestants declined from 70 to 66 percent. All annual growth rates 1766–1831 in Muff were very low—Presbyterians 0.36; Anglicans 0.69; and Catholics 0.63—indicating high rates of out-migration, generally, but especially among Dissenters. *References:* 1, 2, 3, 7, 15, and 19.

1b. South and Mid-Derry

With the exception of the mountainous parish of Dungiven (and adjacent Banagher) in mid–County Derry, the parishes in this region exhibit demographic patterns similar to those in west Ulster. Limited evidence suggests a stable or slightly declining Protestant presence in south Derry in 1740–1766, followed by significant proportional declines among Protestants (vs. Catholics) and among Presbyterians (vs. Anglicans) in 1766–1831. These patterns contrast sharply with those in the adjacent mid-Ulster or "Linen Triangle" region just to the southeast in east Tyrone, Armagh, and west Down.

Chapter 3. David Lindsey, 1758

Desertmartin parish, Loughinsholin barony, County Londonderry. Between 1766 and 1831 the Protestant share of Desertmartin's population remained fairly stable at 40–45 percent, but the proportion of Presbyterians and other Dissenters (mostly Quakers) declined from 35 to 26 percent, while the Anglican share rose from 11 to 17 percent. Annual growth rates in 1766–1831 were 1.57 for Desertmartin's Catholics, 1.41 among all Protestants, but only 1.05 among Presbyterians and other Dissenters. Although the 1766 household figures were obviously "rounded," the data indicate significant Protestant emigration, especially among Dissenters, in the late 1700s and early 1800s. *References:* 5, 7, 15, and 18.

Chapter 8. Rev. James MacSparran, 1752

Dungiven parish, Kennaght barony, County Londonderry. Between 1740 and 1766 the number of Protestant households in mid-Derry's mountainous Dungiven parish rose by more than 60 percent, and in the latter year 55 percent of the parish's households were Protestant. However, between 1766 and 1813–1814 Protestant growth slowed to less than 48 percent, whereas Catholic numbers rose by over 70 percent. Finally, between 1813–1814 and 1831 both Protestants and Catholics experienced heavy out-migration, as their respective populations declined nearly 10 percent and over 35 percent. Indeed, in the early 1800s Catholic out-migration was so extensive that between 1766 and 1831 the Protestant share of Dungiven's population actually increased from less than 45 to nearly 50 percent, in marked contrast to the general south Derry experience. (A proportional increase of Protestants also occurred in the adjacent and equally rugged Banagher parish.) Also anomalous is that between 1813–1814 and 1831 the Presbyterian proportion of Dungiven's inhabitants rose from 29 to nearly 38 percent, while the Anglican share remained stable at 12 percent; in the same period the absolute number of Presbyterians fell merely 2 percent but that of Anglicans declined by a fourth. Thus, it may be that mid-Derry's mountains and bogs represented a "last stage" of the Ulster Plantation, begun in the early 1600s, and that some noninheriting Protestant (especially Presbyterian) farmers' sons and laborers from the Foyle Valley or from County Derry's richer parishes chose internal colonization on one of Ulster's "last frontiers" rather than overseas emigration. *References:* 1, 7, and 15; 1740 Census of Protestant Householders (T.808/14,905, PRONI) and W. S. Mason, *Statistical Account, or Parochial Survey of Ireland,* vol. 1 (Dublin, 1814), whence we derived the household-to-persons multiplier employed here.

Chapter 61. Job Johnson, 1784

Maghera parish, Loughinsholin barony, County Londonderry. In 1659 the parishes of Maghera, Killelagh, Termoneeny, and Ballyscullion contained 205 Protestant families, 37 percent of the total, and by 1740 these had increased to 633 and by 1766 to 726, when they comprised about 53 percent of all families. However, between 1766 and 1831 the annual growth rate among Maghera's and Killelagh's Protestants was only 1.53, compared with 2.32 among local Catholics, and by 1831 the Protestant proportion of the two parishes' inhabitants was only 33 percent. (Anglicans and Dissenters were not differentiated until 1831, when Presbyterians comprised 22.5 percent of all Protestants in Maghera and Killelagh.) Protestant decline began even earlier in Termoneey and Ballyscullion: between 1740 and 1766 their number of Protestant households fell 7 percent, and between the latter year and 1831 the Protestant share of the population declined from ca. two-thirds to 53 percent. *References:* 1, 5, and 15.

1c. Mid-Ulster and the "Linen Triangle"

Demographic patterns in this region—roughly bounded by Lisburn to the east, Newry to the south, and Dungannon to the west—were dramatically different, at least in 1766–1831, from all other Ulster regions. Apparently because of a combination of economic and political factors, explored hereafter, except on the region's fringes, Protestant annual growth rates were often dramatically higher than among Catholics. Perhaps even more remarkable is that, where measurable, Anglican growth rates were much higher than for Presbyterians (as well as for Catholics), far exceeding the "normal" Anglican–Presbyterian discrepancies found in west Ulster and south Derry. To be sure, in 1766 much of this region's Protestant population was already predominantly Anglican, but in 1766–1831 members of the Church of Ireland either substantially increased their majorities (or minorities) or established new ones at the Catholics' and Presbyterians' expense. Indeed, it may be said that in this era—spanning the birth of the heavily Anglican Orange Order and the vicious sectarian and political conflicts of the 1780s and 1790s—the loyal adherents of the Church of Ireland "conquered" mid-Ulster in their own, their landlords', and the Crown's interests.

Chapter 4. Henry Johnston, 1773–1800

Aghaderg parish, Iveagh Upper barony, County Down. Situated in west Down, on the eastern fringe of the Linen Triangle, Aghaderg's demographic patterns are not quite as startling as those in north and mid-Armagh or in east Tyrone but are nonetheless different from those in west Ulster and south Derry. Between 1766 and 1831 the Protestant share of Aghaderg's inhabitants declined from 70 to 57.5 percent, but the proportion of Dissenters (nearly all Presbyterians) fell even more steeply, from nearly 60 to less than 43 percent; by contrast, the Anglican share of Aghaderg's population rose from 10 to nearly 15 percent. Boundary uncertainties make it difficult to determine Aghaderg's annual growth rates in 1766–1831; our best guess is 0.29 for Presbyterians and other Dissenters, 1.37 for Anglicans, and 1.23 for Catholics. In adjacent Seapatrick parish, the rates were 1.38 for all Protestants and 2.48 among Catholics.

More dramatic are the data for nearby Moira parish, in northwest County Down. In 1766 Moira's population was 34 percent Anglican, 34 percent Presbyterian, and 32 percent Catholic. However, by 1831 the Anglican share of Moira's inhabitants had increased to 53.5 percent, while the proportion of Catholics had declined to 27.5 percent and that of Presbyterians to merely 19 percent. These radical alterations may reflect not only the common disparities, as in west Ulster, between Ulster Presbyterian and Anglican emigration, but also the effects of official and unofficial repression in a parish whose Presbyterian inhabitants were notoriously rebellious in 1798. Barring wholesale conversions to the established church, surely only drastic pressures, such as post-Rebellion changes in local landlords' leasing policies—discrimination against "disloyal" Dissenters (and Catholics, to a lesser degree) and favoritism to "loyal" Anglican migrants from other parishes—can account for such dramatic revisions of Moira's ethnoreligious composition. *References:* 3, 6, 8, and 15; fragments of the 1766 Religious Census in T.808/15,255 (PRONI).

Chapter 6. Margaret Wright, 1808

Donaghmore parish, Dungannon Middle barony, County Tyrone. On the western fringe of the Linen Triangle and generally characterized by poor, mountainous soils, Donaghmore's demographic patterns were more "normal" than in most of mid-Ulster, although the unusual stability of the Catholics' share of the local population suggests that their out-migration was greater than in most parishes outside mid-Ulster. Between 1764–1766 and 1831 the Protestant share of the population in Donaghmore parish (including adjacent Pomeroy) remained very stable at between 35 and 37 percent. In the latter year Anglicans accounted for 17 percent of the inhabitants, Presbyterians and other Dissenters nearly 18.5 percent. The consistency of their shares of Donaghmore's and Pomeroy's population suggests that Protestants and Catholics emigrated in roughly equal proportions, and the magnitude of the total outflow is indicated by the parishes' low annual growth rate (1.15) and relatively low population increase in 1764–1831: 117.5 percent, compared with 168 percent in 1766–1831 for David Lindsey's Desertmartin parish in south County Derry and 172 percent for Seapatrick parish in Henry Johnston's west County Down. *References:* 2, 7, 15, and 16.

Chapter 24. John and Jane Chambers, 1796

Ballymore parish, Orior Lower barony, County Armagh. In 1766 Ballymore parish, in east Armagh bordering County Down, contained 901 households; in 1831, it had 12,161 inhabitants; and between the two dates the Protestant proportion of Ballymore's inhabitants remained stable at about two-thirds. In 1831, 46 percent of the parish's Protestants were Anglicans, with 54 percent Presbyterians plus a handful of Quakers and Methodists.

However, Ballymore's similar Protestant and Catholic growth rates in 1766–1831 contrast markedly with those in north and mid-Armagh, which in turn may reflect the drastic effects of the anti-Catholic pogroms launched by the Peep 'o Day Boys in the mid-1780s and by the Orangemen and the Protestant Yeomanry in the mid- to late 1790s. For example, in the parishes of Mullaghbrack and Kilcluny, the annual Protestant growth rate in 1766–1831 was 2.62, whereas that of local Catholics was merely 0.81, causing the Catholic proportion of the population to fall from 59 to 31 percent. Likewise, in Kilmore parish the Catholic share of the population declined from one-third to one-fourth.

Moreover, the Presbyterian share of north and mid-Armagh's inhabitants also fell sharply in this period. For instance, in Loughgilly, Killevy, and Forkhill parishes, the 1766–1831 annual growth rate among Presbyterians was merely 1.17, compared with 4.03 among Anglicans (and 1.91 for Catholics), and the Presbyterian proportion of the parishes' population declined from 34 to 23 percent. Comparably startling discrepancies between high Anglican and low Presbyterian (and low Catholic) annual growth rates, 1766–1831, also occurred in the parishes of Derrynoose (e.g. 1.56 vs. 0.30), Loughgall, and Seagoe. To be sure, in 1766 the Protestant populations of Loughgall and Seagoe were already heavily Anglican (79 and 77 percent, respectively), and of course by 1831 had become more so (81 and 88 percent). However, in Armagh parishes where Presbyterians predominated among local Protestants, the Anglican shares of the Protestant populations also sharply increased at the Presbyterians' expense: from 5 percent to 26 percent in Loughgilly-Killevy-Forkhill and from 15.5 percent to 29 percent in Derrynoose.

Thus, as in nearby Moira (see earlier), it appears that the "normal" disparities between Ulster Anglican and Presbyterian annual growth and emigration rates were greatly exacerbated in County Armagh during the 1780s, 1790s, and perhaps long thereafter by discriminatory leasing policies, as well as overt repression, that targeted politically disaffected Presbyterians (as well as Catholics) and that favored (and were orchestrated by) Anglican landlords, magistrates, and paramilitary bands. (A possible alternative explanation to massive Presbyterian out-migration is widespread Presbyterian conversions to the Church of Ireland, perhaps not unlikely in the circumstances during and after the late 1790s.) *References: 6 and 15.*

Chapter 26. Edward and Mary Toner, 1818

Desertcreat parish, Dungannon Upper barony, County Tyrone. Between 1766 and 1831 the Catholic proportion of Desertcreat's population remained stable at about 52–54 percent; in the latter year Presbyterians comprised over 60 percent of the parish's large Protestant minority. As expected, in 1766–1831 Catholic and Protestant annual growth rates were similar: 1.58 and 1.48, respectively. These patterns are comparable to those in Margaret Wright's Donaghmore (and Pomeroy) parish, although the latter had larger Catholic majorities in both 1766 and 1831.

However, Desertcreat was not far from the western border of County Armagh, where loyalist pressures apparently decimated many Catholic and Presbyterian communities. For instance, in Clonfeacle, which straddles the Tyrone-Armagh border, the annual growth rate among the parish's predominantly Anglican Protestants was 1.43 versus merely 0.93 among local Catholics. In addition, in 1766–1831 several east Tyrone parishes witnessed sharp differences between Anglican and Presbyterian growth rates. In Artrea and in Donaghenry, for instance, Anglican growth rates were 1.88 and 2.48, respectively, while among local Presbyterians they were only 1.28 and 1.18; as a result, the Anglican shares of the Protestant populations rose from 41.5 to 51 percent in Artrea and from 25 to 44 percent in Donaghenry. *References: 6, 7, and 15.*

Chapter 45. Mary Cumming, 1814–1815

Blaris parish, Massereene Upper barony, County Antrim, and Iveagh Lower barony, County Down. Lisburn town is located on the County Antrim side of the parish of Blaris (or Lisburn), which is divided by the Lagan River between County Antrim's Upper Massereene barony and the baronies of Lower Iveagh (Upper Half) and Upper Castlereagh in County Down. In 1831 Blaris parish contained 13,240 inhabitants, nearly half of whom were members of the Church of Ireland and a third of whom were Presbyterians and other Dissenters; merely 17.7 percent of Blaris's inhabitants were Catholics.

Although no eighteenth-century data survive for Blaris, some does for four adjacent Lagan Valley parishes: Derryaghy, Lambeg, Magheragall, and Magheramesk. In 1766 each of their populations was heavily Protestant, and by 1831 the Protestant proportions of their respective inhabitants had increased: in Derryaghy from 69 to 80 percent; in Lambeg from 82 to 88 percent; in Magheragall from 87 to 90 percent; and in Magheramesk from 75 to 84 percent. In all four parishes, 1766–1831 annual growth rates among Protestants were unusually low, ranging from 0.36 in Derryaghy to 1.02 in Magheramesk. However, Catholic annual growth rates were even lower (0.19 and 0.15 in Magheragall and in Magheramesk, respectively, and Derryaghy and Lambeg experienced negative Catholic growth rates of –0.56 and –0.37, respectively.

Such low or negative growth rates must reflect heavy out-migration, either overseas or to the nearby industrial city of Belfast. Presumably, economic factors were the primary determinants, but religious and political factors also may have been involved. Although the 1766 data does not distinguish between Anglicans and Presbyterians, it may be significant that in 1831 Anglicans constituted the great majority of these parishes' inhabitants—from 64 percent in Lambeg to 86 percent in Magheramesk. Viewed in light of other mid-Ulster data, we posit that these figures suggest a positive (perhaps even a causal) relationship between high Anglican proportions of local populations and unusually low growth (and high out-migration) rates among Catholics and Presbyterians. *References: 8, and 15; 1766 Religious Census data in T.808/15,255 (PRONI).*

Chapter 48. Bernard M'Kenna, 1811

Carnteel parish, Dungannon Lower barony, County Tyrone (and Donagh and Errigal Trough parishes, Trough barony, County Monaghan). Between 1659 and 1732 the Catholic proportion of the inhabitants of County Monaghan's Trough barony fell from 88 to 69 percent, thanks to heavy in-migration by Anglicans (esp. in Errigal Trough parish) and by Presbyterians (esp. in Donagh parish). Thereafter, the Catholic share remained fairly steady—at 70 percent in 1766 and 72 percent in 1831.

Catholics were only a minority, however, in Bernard M'Kenna's Carnteel (and Aghaloo) parish, in County Tyrone, comprising only about a third of the inhabitants both in 1766 and in 1831—when Presbyterians and Quakers constituted 59 percent of the Protestants. Yet many of the adjacent parishes had fairly consistent Catholic majorities in 1766–1831, declining from 61 to 53.5

percent in Clonfeacle (County Tyrone) but remaining stable or slightly increasing in Killeshill (Tyrone: 61.5 to 59 percent), Errigal Keeroge (Tyrone: 63 to 66 percent), Donagh (Monaghan: 56 to 60.5 percent), and Errigal Trough (Monaghan: 85 to 86 percent).

In general, Catholic annual growth rates in 1766–1831 are lower than those among Protestants in the parishes that are closest to Dungannon and to the border between Tyrone and north and mid-Armagh, the epicenter of sectarian violence in the 1780s and 1790s. Thus, in Clonfeacle, a border parish where M'Kenna's brother lived prior to his emigration, the Catholic growth rate was only 0.93, versus 1.43 among local Protestants. By contrast, to the south and southwest, in Carnteel and Aghaloo, Catholic and Protestant growth rates were 1.61 and 1.41, respectively, and even further south in north Monaghan's Trough barony, Catholic and Protestant rates were 1.48 and 1.18 in Donagh parish and 1.29 and 1.18 in Errigal Trough. The 1766 census enumerated Anglicans and Presbyterians separately only in Killeshill and Donagh parishes. In both parishes Anglican growth rates in 1766–1831 exceeded those for Presbyterians (and for Catholics)—only slightly in Killeshill but substantially so in Donagh (1.56 vs. 0.94). *References:* 1, 2, 7, 15, and 16.

Chapter 56. John Morton, 1769

Tullylish parish, Iveagh Lower barony, County Down. Between 1659 and 1732–1733 the Protestant proportion of Iveagh barony's population rose from about one-third to one-half, while that of County Down as a whole increased from ca. 43 percent to ca. 72 percent. Subsequent baronial data is unavailable, but in 1831 65.2 percent of County Down's inhabitants were Protestants, and of the latter 26.7 percent were Anglicans, 71.4 percent Presbyterians, and 1.8 percent Quakers and other Protestants. In Morton's Tullylish parish, between 1766 and 1831 the Protestant proportion of the local population increased from ca. 57 to 70 percent, and in the latter year 51 percent of the parish's Protestants were Anglicans, 47 percent Presbyterians, and 1.4 percent (106 people) were Quakers. As in many parishes to the west, in strife-ridden County Armagh, in 1766–1831 the annual growth rate among Tullylish's Protestants (3.39) markedly exceeded that among local Catholics (1.01). The same pattern prevailed in the nearby parishes of Magheralin (1.74 vs. 0.94) and Drumcree (1.90 vs. 0.99), but in parishes that lay east of the Bann (e.g. in Magherally, Donaghmore, and Shankill) Catholics' annual growth rates exceeded those for Protestants (1.64 vs. 1.13 in Magherally).

The 1766 data for Tullylish and nearby parishes do not distinguish Anglicans and Dissenters, but we suspect there is a correlation between high Anglican proportions of local populations and low Catholic (and Presbyterian) growth rates in 1766–1831. E.g., in 1831 Anglicans comprised 69 and 88.5 percent of the inhabitants of Magheralin and Drumcree, respectively, but only 17 percent of those in Magherally. An examination of estate and parish records would be necessary to determine whether the large relative increase in Tullylish's Protestant population, between 1766 and 1831, reflected a sharp rise in the numbers of Anglican inhabitants, at the expense of local Presbyterians (and Catholics), as was the case in many parishes in the Linen Triangle. *References:* 1, 2, 3, 7, and 15.

Chapter 57. John McDonnell, 1771

Kilmore parish, Orior Lower barony, County Armagh. In 1766 Kilmore parish's 1,192 households were approximately two-thirds Protestant, one-third Catholic. As in other heavily Anglican north and mid–County Armagh parishes, however, between 1766 and 1831 the Protestant proportion of Kilmore's population markedly increased while annual Protestant and Catholic growth rates were 1.60 and 1.01, respectively. By 1831 nearly three-fourths of Kilmore's 14,940 inhabitants were Protestants, of whom 73 percent were members of the Church of Ireland, nearly 8 percent Quakers and Methodists, and the remainder Presbyterians. *References:* 7, 15, and 16.

Chapter 67. William Heazelton, Jr., 1814

Killyman and Clonfeacle parishes, Dungannon Middle barony, County Tyrone. Between 1766 and 1831 the Protestant share of Killyman's inhabitants rose from less than 39 percent to 50 percent, conforming to the common pattern in the border parishes between north Armagh and east Tyrone. In 1766–1831 the annual growth rate among Killyman's Protestants was 2.05 and among Catholics 1.19. In 1831 members of the Church of Ireland comprised almost 92 percent of Killyman's Protestants and nearly 61 percent of those in Clonfeacle, and both parishes contained relatively large numbers of Quakers and Methodists (123 in Killyman, 192 in Clonfeacle). *References:* 7 and 15.

1d. South Ulster

In this heavily Catholic region, comprising counties Cavan, Fermanagh, and Monaghan, heavy Protestant settlement in 1659–1730s was offset by Protestant proportional (and often absolute) declines from the 1740s. For example, in 1766–1831 the annual growth rate among County Cavan's Protestants was only 1.71, quite respectable when compared with Protestant rates of increase in, say, the Foyle Valley but considerably less than the 2.03 growth rate among Cavan's Catholics. (In 1766–1831 County Cavan's total population increased by over 250 percent, with an overall annual growth rate of nearly 2.00.) At least from 1766, moreover, it appears that south Ulster's Anglicans were less susceptible than the region's Presbyterians to the lures or pressures conducive to out-migration.

Chapter 7. Anonymous Poet, Mid- to Late 1700s

Derryvullan parish, Tirkennedy barony, County Fermanagh. Between 1744 and 1776–1777 the number of Catholic families in Derryvullan increased both absolutely (from 171 to 225) and proportionately (from less than 34 to more than 41 percent of the total), and by 1831 the Catholic share of Derryvullan's inhabitants had risen to 46 percent. Of the Protestant families enumerated in 1777, a significant number may have been Presbyterians, as the hearthmoney returns listed only 150 "communicants" of the Church of Ireland out of 318 Protestant families. In 1831, however, less than 2 percent of the parish's Protestants were counted as Presbyterians, the remainder as Anglicans. In 1744–1831 Derryvullan's Catholic and Protestant populations rose by 474 and 243 percent, respectively, and their annual growth rates were 2.01 and 1.41. *References:* 7, 15, and 17.

Chapter 19. James Magraw, 1733

Aghalurcher parish, Magherastephana barony, County Fermanagh. Between 1659 and 1732 heavy English (and some Scottish) immigration had increased the Protestant shares of the populations of Magherastephana barony and County Fermanagh from 22 to nearly 60 percent and from 25 to 58 percent, respectively. Between 1732 and 1766, however, the Protestant shares of their inhabitants had fallen—to 57 percent in Magherastephana and to 45 percent in County Fermanagh. In 1766 Protestants comprised 54 percent of the population of Aghalurcher parish (up from only 26 percent in 1659), but by 1831 the Protestant share of Aghalurcher's inhabitants had declined to 49 percent, while those of Magherastephana and of County Fermanagh had further declined to 46 and 43.5

percent, respectively. In 1831 Anglicans constituted 84 percent of Aghalurcher's Protestants, 41 percent of the parish's total population. *References:* 1, 2, 7, 15, and 17.

Chapter 48. Bernard M'Kenna, 1811.

Trough barony, County Monaghan. For data on north Monaghan, see sec. 1.c, on chapter 48.

Chapter 53. Rev. Thomas Barton, 1758

Carrickmacross (or Magheross) parish, Farney barony, County Monaghan. One source alleges that County Monaghan's English plantation never recovered from the Jacobite Wars of 1688–1691, but between 1659 and 1732–1733 the Protestant share of the population rose from 11 to 36 percent, while that of Farney barony, in south County Monaghan, increased from 7 to nearly 29 percent. However, steep declines occurred thereafter: by 1766 Protestants comprised only 10 percent of Farney's population, by 1831 merely 4.4 percent. In the latter year only 27.4 percent of County Monaghan's inhabitants were Protestants, of whom 53 percent were Anglicans, the rest Presbyterians. A similar decline occurred in Barton's Magheross parish (as it was called in the 1700s): in 1766 the parish's 114 Protestant households comprised 16 percent of the total, but in 1766–1831 the Protestant annual growth rate was only 0.62 (vs. 2.15 among Catholics), and by the latter year Magheross's 848 Protestant inhabitants (65 percent of whom were Anglicans) made up only 7 percent of the population.

As elsewhere in south and west Ulster in 1766–1831, Presbyterian attrition appears to have been the primary reason for Protestant decline in south Monaghan. In the parishes of Donaghmore and Magheracloone, for example, Presbyterians experienced negative growth rates, while their Anglican populations grew by yearly averages of 1.18 and 2.57. As a result, between 1766 and 1831 the Presbyterian shares of Donaghmore's and Magheracloone Protestant populations fell from 49 to 25 percent and from 58 to 14 percent, respectively. *References:* 1, 2, 3, 7, and 15; 1785 Census of Protestant Males in Clogher Diocese (T.808/15,262, PRONI).

1e. Northeast Down and Belfast

This region was heavily Protestant at least from 1659 and apparently became more so through the mid–eighteenth century. However, between 1766 and 1831 the Protestant proportion of the area's inhabitants declined slightly, and low Protestant growth rates indicate heavy out-migration, both overseas and to industrializing Belfast. Some data suggest that Anglicans were less prone than Presbyterians to out-migration, whereas Catholics may have been more likely than Protestants to migrate to Belfast.

Chapter 10. John Rea, 1765

Magheradrool parish, Kinelarty barony, and Drumbo parish, Castlereigh Upper barony, County Down. Between 1659 and 1732 the Protestant share of Castlereagh barony's population rose from 59 to 95 percent; later baronial data is unrecoverable, but between 1732–1733 and 1831 Protestant numbers in all of County Down declined slightly from ca. 71–73 percent to 67.5 percent. Unfortunately, eighteenth-century census data for Magheradrool and Drumbo parishes do not survive. In 1831, 19.5 percent of Magheradrool's inhabitants were Anglicans, 52 percent Presbyterians, and 28.5 percent Catholics; in Drumbo the figures were 17 percent Anglicans, 80 percent Presbyterians, and 3 percent Catholics.

We suspect that in this part of Down, as in much of mid- and west Ulster, Presbyterian attrition was primarily responsible for whatever relative declines occurred in Protestant populations; however, Presbyterian losses were often counterbalanced by (if not directly related to) much higher growth rates among Anglicans (and, to a lesser degree, among Catholics). Data for 1766–1831 in seven parishes adjacent to Drumbo and Magheradrool indicate positive relationships between large Anglican majorities and substantial increases in Protestant proportions of local populations. Thus, in 1766–1831 the proportion of Derryaghy's inhabitants who were Protestants (of whom 72 percent were Anglicans in 1831) increased from 69 to 80 percent and in Magheramesk (where Anglicans comprised 86 percent of Protestants in 1831) from 75 to 84 percent. By contrast, in heavily Presbyterian Annahilt, Moira, and Saintfield parishes, the Protestant proportions remained stable or declined slightly. *References:* 1, 2, 3, 8, and 15; fragments of the 1766 Religious Census in T.808/15,255 (PRONI).

Chapter 12. John Smilie, 1762

Greyabbey parish, Ards Lower barony, County Down. In 1659 Protestants already comprised ca. 60 percent of the inhabitants in Greyabbey parish, and between that year and 1732 the Protestant shares of the populations of County Down and Ards barony rose from 43 and 60 percent, respectively, to about 71 and 76 percent. By 1766 over 98 percent of Greyabbey's inhabitants were Protestants, declining only slightly to 95.3 percent by 1831. In the latter year, Presbyterians comprised 86 percent of Greyabbey's inhabitants and 97 percent of those in adjacent Bangor parish. However, the annual growth rate in 1766–1831 among Greyabbey's Protestants (essentially, that is, among its Presbyterians) was a low 1.06, reflecting the effects of heavy out-migration. *References:* 7, 10, and 15.

Chapter 38. Samuel Brown, 1793–1815

Shankill parish (Belfast), Belfast Upper barony, County Antrim. In 1766 Protestants headed 89.5 of the 2,433 households (ca. 12,140 inhabitants) in Shankill parish, which included Belfast and its immediate hinterland. By 1831 Shankill had 60,388 (Belfast 53,287) inhabitants, of whom Protestants comprised 67.2 percent—with Presbyterians 39 percent and Anglicans 27 percent. Thnaks to their disproportionately heavy in-migration from the Ulster countryside, Catholics now constituted nearly a third of Shankill/Belfast's population. *References:* 8, 15, and 20.

1f. Mid- and West Antrim

In 1659 a large percentage of this area's population was already Protestant, and by the 1730s Protestants (overwhelmingly Presbyterians) were a large majority of the inhabitants. Between 1766 and 1831 the *overall* balance in the region between Protestants and Catholics (and between Presbyterians and Anglicans) appears to have remained relatively stable, but there were significant variations within the area. In about half the parishes surveyed, annual growth rates for Protestants (i.e. Presbyterians) exceeded those for Catholics, but the heavily commercialized and industrializing areas around Ballymena and Antrim towns were major exceptions. In general, it appears that, unlike their brethren in mid-Ulster, the Presbyterians in mid- and west Antrim were so dominant (demographically and socially) that they were no more susceptible to pressures for out-migration than were local Anglicans and Catholics.

Chapter 13. John O'Raw, 1811

Kirkinriola (or Ballymena) parish, Toome Lower barony, County Antrim. Early data for Toome barony do not exist, but between 1659 and the early 1730s the Protestant shares of the populations in the adjacent baronies of Antrim and Kilconway rose from 42 to 95 percent and from 28 to 64 percent, respectively; in 1734 over 80 percent of Kilconway's Protestants were Presbyterians. As for O'Raw's Kirkinriola parish (which included Ballymena town), the Protestant proportion of its inhabitants declined, from ca. 96 percent to between 83 and 75 percent, between 1766 and 1831, when over 80 percent of Kirkinriola's Protestants were Presbyterians. Similar relative declines among Protestants also occurred in several neighboring parishes (Dunaghy–Newtown Crommlin and Ahoghill-Craigs-Portglenone), where (as in Kirkinriola) Catholic annual growth rates were significantly higher than among Protestants and, when measurable, Anglicans' growth rates slightly exceeded those among Dissenters. However, in other adjacent parishes (e.g. Skerry-Racavan) the Protestant/Catholic shares of the populations remained virtually identical in 1766–1831, and Protestant annual growth rates slightly exceeded those among Catholics—although both were so low as to indicate very heavy out-migration. In general, the data for this part of west Antrim suggests greater emigration among Protestants (especially Presbyterians) than among Catholics, with the latter preferring intraregional, rural-to-urban migration (i.e. to Ballymena). *References:* 1, 2, 4, 5, 7, 8, 9, 15, and 20.

Chapter 46. Rev. John Craig, 1734–1769/70

Donegore parish, Antrim Upper barony, County Antrim. Between 1659 and 1732, the Protestant proportion of Antrim barony's inhabitants soared from 42 to 95 percent, although by 1831 it had fallen to ca. 84 percent. In Craig's Donegore and its affiliated parishes, between 1766 (employing household-to-persons multipliers derived from nearby Connor parish) and 1831 the proportions of Protestants and Presbyterians remained virtually identical at 95–96 percent and 95–93 percent, respectively, of the total population. Likewise, the Protestant shares of the populations in most mid-Antrim parishes adjacent to Donegore remained both stable and very high (e.g., 98–97 percent in Ballynure, 91–88 percent in Connor). However, Protestant growth rates 1766–1831 were usually below or at the low end of those calculated by Dickson, Ó Gráda, and Daultrey for all of Ulster's inhabitants, indicating that local Protestant (i.e., Presbyterian) out-migration was generally high. *References:* 1, 2, 7, 8, and 15; and S. T. Carleton, ed., *Heads and Hearths: The Hearth Money Rolls and Poll Tax Returns for Co. Antrim 1660–69* (Belfast, 1991).

1g. The Lower Bann Valley: Northeast Derry and North Antrim

As in mid- and south Antrim, between 1659 and the 1730s the population became more heavily, in some areas overwhelmingly, Protestant (and usually Presbyterian). However, between the latter date and 1766 Protestant communities experienced only very slight growth or even absolute declines, presumably the effects of very heavy emigration. And between 1766 and 1831 the region's demographic trends exhibit as much internal variation as in mid- and west Antrim. Thus, in 8 of the 18 parishes surveyed, Protestant annual growth rates in 1766–1831 actually exceeded those for Catholics, and, where measurable, annual growth rates among Presbyterians challenged the provincial trend and exceeded those among Anglicans.

Chapter 42. Thomas Shipboy, Jr., 1774

Coleraine town and parish, and Agherton (or Ballyraghan) parish, Liberties of Coleraine, County Londonderry. Between 1659 and 1766, heavy British immigration (especially in the 1690s) increased the Protestant proportion of Coleraine parish's population from ca. 75 to nearly 95 percent and in the adjacent parish of Agherton (or Ballyaghran) from ca. 33 to 97 percent. By 1831 almost 86 percent of Coleraine parish's inhabitants remained Protestants—almost 70 percent of them Presbyterians; in Agherton the comparable figures were 92 and nearly 78 percent.

Between 1740 and 1766, however, Protestant growth in the area had been quite low, perhaps reflecting the famine of 1740–1741 as well as heavy out-migration—especially after 1718, when leases expired and rents escalated on the Clothworkers' estates. Likewise, between 1766 and 1831 Protestant annual growth rates lagged behind those of Catholics, again probably due to Protestant emigration, stimulated in part by another wholesale reletting of the Clothworkers' estates in the late 1760s and early 1770s. Thus, in 1766–1831 (employing a 1766 household-to-persons multiplier derived from nearby Macosquin) Coleraine parish's Protestant population increased merely 0.82 per year, compared with a Catholic annual rise of 2.29. In rural Agherton, the Protestant growth rate was substantially higher, 1.45, but still less than half the 3.02 Catholic increase. *References: 1, 4, 5, 8, and 15;* fragments of the 1766 Religious Census in T.808/15,255 (PRONI) and in the Rev. T. Groves Mss., vol. 6231, in the Manuscript Library of Trinity College, Dublin.

Chapter 49. Rev. James McGregor and John McMurphy, 1720–1730

Aghadowey parish, Coleraine barony, County Londonderry. Thanks to heavy British immigration, between 1659 and 1732–1733 the Protestant share of County Londonderry's population increased from ca. 30 percent to perhaps 76 percent; by 1831, due to Protestant emigration, that figure had fallen to 56 percent. However, in 1659 already half of the inhabitants in McGregor's Aghadowey parish were Protestants, and their share had risen to nearly 82 percent by 1831, when Presbyterians comprised almost 78 percent of the parish's total population and 95 percent of its Protestants.

Unfortunately, for Aghadowey no eighteenth-century data survive that can be compared with the 1831 figures. However, a 1740 census of household heads as well as 1766 religious census data exist for three adjacent parishes—Errigal, Kilrea, and Macosquin—and these indicate that between 1740 and 1766 famine and heavy emigration produced absolute declines in the numbers of Protestant households in Kilrea and Macosquin, with only a slight increase in those for Errigal. By contrast, between 1766 and 1831 Protestants in the same parishes enjoyed annual growth rates that were higher than the provincial average and higher than those for local Catholics, causing relative increases in the Protestant shares of their populations. Likewise, in contiguous Desertoghill parish, the Presbyterian annual growth rate in 1766–1831 was much higher than among Anglicans (or Catholics), causing the Presbyterian share of the parish's population to rise from 47 to 63 percent. *References: 1, 3, 5, 7, and 15.*

Chapter 58. James Caldwell, 1774

Ballymoney parish, Dunluce Lower barony, County Antrim. Thanks to famine (1740–1741) and heavy emigration, between 1734 and 1766 the number of Protestant households in Ballymoney parish fell by about one-fifth—from 743 to 585—with the greatest decline (to 582) occurring between 1734 and 1740; moreover, between 1734 and 1766 Presbyterian households declined numerically by over one-fourth (692 to 502) and proportionately from 93 to 86 percent of the parish's Protestant households and from 90 to 80 percent of all households. However, the relative sizes of Ballymoney's Protestant and Presbyterian populations stabilized between 1766 and 1831; in the latter year Protestants and Presbyterians comprised nearly 88 and 79 percent, respectively, of Ballymoney's inhabitants, while Presbyterians made up nine-tenths of the parish's Protestants. In 1766–1831 annual growth rates among local Presbyterians was 1.73 (vs. 1.03 for Anglicans and 2.12 among Catholics). *References: 4, 5, 8, and 15; fragments of the 1766 Religious Census in the Rev. T. Groves Mss., vol. 6231, Manuscript Library, TCD.*

Chapter 65. John Nevin, 1804

Ballyrashane parish, Dunluce Lower barony, County Antrim. In 1659 Nevin's Ballyrashane's population was already about 76 percent Protestant, but the parishes to the east and south of Coleraine (e.g. Derrykeighan and Dunluce) remained predominately Catholic. Due to more British immigration, however, between 1659 and 1734 the Protestant share of the inhabitants of north Antrim's Cary, Dunluce, and Kilconway baronies rose from ca. 28 to 74 percent (in 1734 ca. three-fourths of their Protestants were Presbyterians), and by the latter year Derrykeighan and Dunluce were 85–88 percent Protestant. Unfortunately, no eighteenth-century demographic data survive for Ballyrashane parish (most of which was in County Derry, in the Liberties of Coleraine); in 1831 nearly 95 percent of Ballyrashane's inhabitants were Protestants, of whom 96 percent were Presbyterians. In general, however, between 1734 and 1766 the Protestant percentages of the populations of north Antrim parishes remained high and steady, although low annual growth rates (e.g., 0.54 among Dunluce's Protestants) reflect either high famine mortality in 1740–1741 or heavy emigration or both. Between 1766 and 1831 demographic patterns are more varied: in some parishes, Protestant annual growth rates were both relatively high (e.g., 1.65 in Dunluce, 2.09 in Armoy) and exceeded those among Catholics, but in other parishes (e.g., −0.16 in Culfeightrin, 1.09 in Ballintoy) the opposite was the case. Overall, however, in 1766–1831 the Protestant proportion of the area's inhabitants remained high and stable, and the Presbyterian share of the three baronies' Protestant inhabitants actually increased to 82 percent.

Very broadly, we suggest that perhaps some parts of north Antrim (like Dungiven parish in mid-Derry) remained quasi-frontier zones of Protestant (especially Presbyterian) settlement into the late 1700s; that in 1766–1831 the region's Presbyterians were too dominant to be susceptible to the kinds of pressures that apparently induced heavy emigration among Dissenters in mid- and south Ulster; and that the area might even have afforded a refuge for Presbyterians from other parts of the province. *References: 1, 4, 5, 7, 8, and 15; fragments of the 1734 and 1740 Religious Censuses of County Antrim in T.808/14,905 and T.808/15,263 (both PRONI), and Rev. J. Dubordieu, Statistical Survey of the County of Antrim (Dublin, 1812).*

2. SOUTHERN IRELAND

Demographic trends in southern Ireland can be summarized fairly easily. Between 1659 and the 1730s English immigration and settlement usually increased the absolute and relative sizes of local Protestant (overwhelmingly Anglican) minorities. However, Protestant populations generally declined thereafter, often most dramatically in urbanized areas—that is, in cities and in parishes where in 1831 at least 20 percent of their inhabitants lived in towns. In Leinster, for example, in 29 rural parishes in counties Carlow, Kildare, King's, and Queen's, between 1766 and 1831 the Protestant share of their total populations fell from 19 to 12 percent, and in nine urbanized parishes the decline was from 23 to 14 percent; Protestant growth rates in both sets of parishes were 0.58. Likewise, between 1731 and 1800 the number of Protestant families in rural County Kilkenny fell by 14 percent and in Kilkenny city by 38 percent. Similar Protestant declines took place in Munster and in east Connacht. For instance, in 1766–1831 County Waterford's Protestant populations declined absolutely, as well as proportionately, and between 1749 and 1831 the Protestant share of the population in the Anglican diocese of Elphin (including most of counties Roscommon and east Sligo) fell from 10 to 5 percent, with an annual growth rate of merely 0.97 (vs. 1.54 among Catholics).

Within these time frames, we cannot determine the precise timing of southern Protestant decline, nor can we determine the relative effects of conversion to Catholicism vs. out-migration. However, we suggest that the Protestant attrition that occurred in County Longford in 1732–1766 and in County Kilkenny in 1731–1800 indicates that causal factors *other* than sectarian and political pressures (as in the 1790s–1820s), or even simple economic competition from Catholics, should be considered as primary explanations for southern Protestant decline. More important, we posit, were the local and regional influences of market forces (e.g., in promoting or discouraging tillage, grazing, and urban or industrial development), of landlords' leasing and eviction policies, and of the social structures of local Protestant communities—the status and permanence of Protestant middlemen and "yeomen" families, for instance. We suggest also that southern Irish Dissenters (minorities within the overall Protestant minority but, unlike Anglicans, without favorable connections to landlords and public officials) were more prone to emigration than members of the legally established Church of Ireland.

References: Rev. M. Comerford, *Collections Relating to the Dioceses of Kildare and Leighlin* (Dublin, 1883); Rev. T. P. Cunningham, "The 1766 Religious Census, Kilmore and Ardagh," *Briefne,* 1 (1961), 352–62; Elphin Diocesan Census, 1749 (Irish National Archives, Dublin); Kennedy & Miller, "Long Retreat"; K. A. Miller, "The Lost World of Andrew Johnston," in J. S. Donnelly, Jr., and Miller, eds., *Irish Popular Culture, 1650–1850* (Dublin, 1998), 222–41; Rev. W. H. Rennison, *Succession List of the Bishops, Cathedral, and Parochial Clergy of the Dioceses of Waterford and Lismore* (n.p., 1920); and W. Tighe, *Statistical Observations on Co. Kilkenny* (Dublin, 1802).

2a. Southeast Leinster

Chapter 5. Walter Corish Devereux, 1798

Rosdroit parish, Bantry barony, County Wexford. In 1831 nearly 93 percent of the 1,976 inhabitants of Devereux's Rossdroit parish were Catholics. Unfortunately, no eighteenth-century census data survive for Rossdroit or almost any other Wexford parishes. However, between 1659 and 1732 the Catholic shares of Bantry barony's and County Wexford's populations may have declined slightly from 96 and 88 percent, respectively, to 91 and 83 percent, rising again by 1831 to 92 and 88 percent. Probable undercounting of Catholics in 1659 and/or 1732 makes it likely that the overall Catholic–Protestant ratio remained even more stable than these figures suggest. Yet in any case, the data do not indicate a dramatic Protestant exodus resulting from the 1798 Rebellion in Wexford; indeed, given the likelihood that birthrates and family size were higher among Catholics than Protestants, it is probable that one result of the Rebellion and subsequent repression was a higher rate of Catholic than of Protestant out-migration. *References:* 1, 2, and 15.

Chapter 9. Robert Parke, 1725

Fennagh parish, Idrone East barony, County Carlow. Between 1659 and 1732 the proportion of "English" Protestants in County Carlow was stable at 14 to 15 percent, but—thanks in part to heavy Anglican and Quaker emigration—by 1831 it had declined to less than 11 percent. The fragmentary and confusing condition of County Carlow's 1766 census returns makes it impossible to determine precisely the Protestant populations of Fennagh or the adjacent parishes in which the Parkes held land: our best estimates range from 16 to 26 percent in 1766, falling to 4 percent or 13 percent by 1831. More reliably, between 1766 and 1831 the Protestant share of the populations in nearby Carlow and Killeshin parishes declined from 27 to 12 percent. *References:* 1, 2, 3, and 15; Rev. M. Comerford, *Collections Relating to the Dioceses of Kildare and Leighlin* (Dublin, 1883).

Chapter 25. Joseph and Hannah Wright, 1801–1817

Liskinfere parish, Gorey barony, County Wexford. In 1831 Liskinfere (or Clough) parish contained 517 Anglicans and 24 Quakers, in addition to 672 Catholics, who comprised 55 percent of the parish's 1,213 inhabitants. No pre-1831 census data survive to reveal if Liskinfere's religious demography underwent significant change in the late 1700s or early 1800s, as a result, for instance, of the turmoil associated with the 1798 Rebellion. Between 1659 and 1732 the Protestant share of Gorey barony's population rose from ca. 13.5 to 25 percent, and our best estimate is that in 1831 Protestants still comprised about a fifth of Gorey's inhabitants. *References:* 1, 2, 3, and 15.

2b. Urban Areas

Chapter 14. Thomas Hinds, 1795

Dublin city, County Dublin. In the eighteenth century the population of Dublin roughly tripled, from around 60,000 in 1700 to about 180,000 in 1800, when Ireland's capital was perhaps the sixth largest city in western Europe. Urban infant mortality rates were so high, however, that the city's remarkable growth in the late 1600s and early 1700s was primarily due to Protestant immigration from England, and in the mid-1700s and thereafter to Catholic migration from rural Leinster. The latter inflow was so large that, coupled with emigration by Protestant artisans and laborers, it reduced the Protestant (predominantly Anglican) share of Dublin's inhabitants from over two-thirds in 1732 to about a third in 1800 and a fourth by 1831. *References:* L. M. Cullen, "The Growth of Dublin, 1600–1900," in F. H. A. Aalen and K. Whelan, eds., *Dublin City and County* (Dublin, 1992), 252–77; and Hill, *Patriots to Unionists.*

Chapter 23. Daniel Kent, 1786–1794

Limerick city, County Limerick. According to the 1659 poll-tax returns, Protestants then headed nearly 53 percent of Limerick city's 1,367 families. By 1732 the hearthmoney returns indicated that 3,339 families inhabited the city but that the Protestant proportion had fallen to less than 42 percent. In 1810 the local Anglican bishop reported that less than a tenth of Limerick's people were Protestants, and the 1831 religious census enumerated only 3,599 (7.6 percent) of the city's 47,334 inhabitants as Protestants, merely 206 of whom (including 144 Methodists) were not members of the Church of Ireland. *References:* 1, 2, and 15; E. Wakefield, *An Account of Ireland, Statistical and Political,* vol. 2 (London, 1812).

Chapter 40. Robert Pillson, 1764

Drogheda, County Louth. In 1766 about a fifth of Drogheda's 975 households were headed by Protestants—mostly Anglicans, as were the Brabazons; the Presbyterian presence, although dating from the 1690s, was small. By 1831 the Protestant share of the town's population had declined by half. *References:* 7 and 15; M. Corcoran, "Drogheda Census List of 1798," *County Lough Arch. & Hist. J.,* 17, no. 2 (1970), 91–96.

Chapter 57. John McDonnell, 1771

Cork city, County Cork. According to the 1659 poll-tax returns and the 1732 hearthmoney lists, between those dates the Protestant share of Cork city's population rose from 19 to 32 percent. The 1766 Cork census is incomplete, but by 1831 the Protestant proportion of Cork city's 80,882 inhabitants had declined to less than one-fifth; in 1831 (as earlier) the overwhelming majority of the city's Protestants were members of the Church of Ireland, as Quakers and other Dissenters totaled only 835 persons. *References:* 7, 12, and 15.

Chapter 63. Daniel McCurtin, 1798

Dunbolloge parish, Barrymore barony, County Cork. On the outskirts of Cork city, Dunbolloge was one of the five united parishes of St. Peter's, part of which lay inside the city's boundary. In 1766 only 20 of Dunbolloge's inhabitants were Protestants (vs. 1,162 Catholics), but the population of the entire St. Peter's union was nearly 39 percent Protestant. By 1831 Dunbolloge had only 31 Protestant inhabitants (vs. 4,603 Catholics), and the Protestant share in St. Peter's union had fallen to 20 percent. Virtually all the local Protestants (over 96 percent) were Anglicans. *References:* 7 and 15.

2c. The Midlands and Meath

Chapter 1. James Wansbrough, 1700–1728

Killoscully parish, Owney and Arra barony, County Tipperary (North Riding). Between 1659 and 1732 the Protestant share of the North Riding's population rose from ca. 9 to 11 percent; however, the increase occurred within the Ormond baronies (11–15 percent Protestant by 1732), and in Owney and Arra barony the Protestant proportion of the population may have declined from 19 to 7 percent. Moreover, between 1766 and 1831 the Protestant share of the inhabitants of Kilnerath union (including Wansbrough's Killoscully parish) fell from 12 percent (574 persons) to less than 5 percent (537). In 1831 all the Protestants in Kilnerath were Anglicans, except for only six "other Protestants" (presumably Baptists). Equally drastic relative declines in 1766–1831 occurred in four other north Tipperary parishes; absolute declines took place in two of them; and by 1831 less than 6 percent of the entire North Riding's inhabitants were Protestants—merely 103 of whom (out of 10,150) were not members of the Church of Ireland. *References:* 1, 2, 7, and 15; fragments of the 1766 Religious Census in Ms. 8487 and Ms. 8908 (NLI), and in Rev. St. John D. Seymour, *The Succession of Parochial Clergy in the United Dioceses of Cashel and Emly* (Dublin, 1908).

    Rathconrath parish, Rathconrath barony, County Westmeath. Between 1659 and 1732–1733 the Protestant proportions of the populations of Rathconrath barony and of County Westmeath rose from ca. 4 and 6 percent, respectively, to 7.5 and 14 percent. Subsequent baronial data is unrecoverable, but by 1831 Protestants comprised less than 8 percent of the county's inhabitants. As for Wansbrough's second home parish of Rathconrath, in 1733 it contained 46 Protestants, rising to 106 in

1802–1803, but falling to 89 by 1831, when they comprised 3.1 percent of the parish's population. However, Protestant minorities in 1831 were larger in some adjacent parishes: e.g., nearly 10 percent in Leney union and almost 8 percent in urbanized Mullingar. *References:* 1, 2, 3, and 15; Bishop O'Beirne's Meath Diocesan Censuses, 1802–1803 and 1818 (including fragments of the 1733 Hearthmoney Returns and the 1766 Religious Census), in the Bishop O'Beirne Mss. in the RCBL and in the Meath Diocesan Archives, Trim, County Meath.

Chapter 28. Benjamin Chandlee, 1705

Carbury parish, Carbury barony, County Kildare. Protestant settlement in County Kildare's Carbury barony appears to have been heaviest between 1659 and 1732, when the Protestant share of its inhabitants rose from 3 to 11 percent. In 1766 Protestants comprised 9 percent of the population of the united parishes of Carbury, which covered virtually all of the barony. Surprisingly, by 1831 the Protestant share of Carbury union's inhabitants had increased slightly to 11 percent—although only 19 Protestants were Quakers, the overwhelming majority Anglicans.

If reliable, these figures suggest that in Carbury between 1659 and 1732 heavy Protestant inmigration outpaced emigration, followed in 1732–1766 by a period of Protestant stagnation or decline caused by distress and emigration and, more tentatively, between 1766 and 1831 by a consolidation of small farms into large holdings for grazing, which benefited the wealthy Protestant farmers who remained at the expense of Catholic smallholders and laborers who migrated elsewhere. (In addition, the possibility of selective leasing policies favoring Protestants cannot be discounted, especially in the aftermath of the 1798 Rebellion.) Carbury's patterns are thus rather unique in midLeinster, where in general the absolute and relative size of Protestant communities declined sharply after 1766, due to high out-migration among noninheriting farmers' sons and from the middling, artisanal, and lower ranks of Protestant society. For instance, between 1766 and 1831 the Protestant share of the inhabitants of Monasteroris parish (adjacent to Carbury and containing the Quaker center at Edenderry town) fell from 29 to less than 18 percent, and by 1831 the parish held only 67 Quakers (less than 9 percent of its Protestants). *References:* 1, 2, 3, 7, and 15; Rev. M. Comerford, *Collections Relating to the Dioceses of Kildare and Leighlin* (Dublin, 1903).

Chapter 50. Dr. Charles Carroll, 1748.

Clonlisk and Ballybritt baronies, King's County (now County Offaly). Between 1659 and 1732–1733 the Catholic proportion of the population in Clonlisk and Ballybritt baronies declined from about 87 to 77 percent, while the Protestant share of King's County's entire population remained stable at around 15–16 percent. Later baronial data does not exist, but by 1831 Catholics comprised nearly 90 percent of King's County's inhabitants. *References:* 1, 2, 3, and 15.

Chapter 51. Silvester Farrell et al., 1745–1764

Killeen parish, Skreen barony, County Meath. In 1659 the population of Taragh (or Tara) parochial union, which included Killeen parish, was nearly 94 percent Catholic, as was the population of Skreen barony in that year and in 1732–1733. In 1766 Taragh union's Protestants numbered only 20 "souls," but they had increased to 58 by 1802–1803 and to 125 by 1831, when they comprised 8 percent of the inhabitants. Given the overall decline in the relative size of County Meath's Protestant population (from ca. 10 percent in 1732–1733 to less than 6 percent in 1831), the increase in Taragh union appears anomalous. As in Chandlee's Carbury barony in County Kildare, however, the data for Taragh suggests that midlands parishes—often subject to wholesale evictions and consolidation of farms for grazing cattle—could witness heavy out-migration by Catholic smallholders and laborers, resulting in proportional increases among favored Protestant populations. *References:* 1, 2, 3, and 15; Bishop O'Beirne's Meath Diocesan Censuses, 1802–1803 and 1818 (including fragments of the 1733 Hearthmoney Returns and the 1766 Religious Census), in the Bishop O'Beirne Mss., Library of the Representative Church Body, Dublin, and in the Meath Diocesan Archives, Trim, County Meath.

Chapter 54. Thomas Burke, ca. 1766–1767

Tyaquin barony, County Galway. Early demographic information on County Galway is scanty. According to the 1732–1733 hearthmoney returns, 97 percent of Tyaquin barony's inhabitants (and 95 percent of County Galway's) were Catholics. In 1831 Catholics comprised 97 to 100 percent of the population of every parish in Tyaquin and 98 percent in the entire county. *References:* 2, 3, and 15.

APPENDIX 3 ✳ Additional Documents

Robert Crockett, Gallatin, Tennessee,
to George Crockett, Sr., Drumnashear, County Donegal, 23 December 1825

. . . you appear to be on the alarm about the Roman Catholicks of your Country   I Should not wonder if they did not try to have their rights guaranteed to them as they have been deprived of <them> So long   there must be Something Rotton in the State of affairs in that goverment that would oppress one party and favour another but the real fact is all parties is oppress[d],   when you are Compelled to pay twenty pounds in Tithes and Taxes for one year when the Sallary of the Royal family alone amounts to Some Millions of Money it is not Surprising that your Taxes would amount to twenty pounds   I think Such an extravagant family Could be Very well dispenced with and even the Roman Catholicks that has to pay a full proportion of all goverment expences and yet not allowed the Same privileges of other Citizens it appears Cruel in the extreme,   when all Men are of right equal or at least ought to be So for what reason would you deprive them of their rights<?>   was it because their property was Confiscated in times of Old that you are affraid they would try to get back their Just dues—they are entitled to them and let them have them and there is no doubt in my mind but that class of People would make as loyal Subjects as any other, but then your Lords would <be> strip[d] of all they now possess and if their titles is not good and Just let them loose them for every person is entitled to their Just rights under every goverment whatever and why not in England that goverment that boasts so much of their liberty—They carried on a twenty years war against France to Suppress liberty and Established the Holy Alliance in full power in Europe,   that Same Holy Alliance will ere long bind England in fetters if the United States do not lend them their aid,   they had no more right to enter into that war with France than the Emperor of China has to wage war with the Creek Indians—you gained nothing by it and has increased your national debt beyond all possibility of ever being able to pay the Interest   our Neighbours in South America has Established their independence and a Republican form of

Goverment but they have an established Church which will terminate I am afraid in complete anarchy, for there is nothing so dangerous in a Government as an established Church our Goverment has given full proof on that Score we have no Established churches nor Popes nor Bishops nor Fryers nor even Rectors to pay Tythes for and yet there is more true Religion in this country than any other whatever. . . .

Peter O'Connor Petitions, 1797–1798

Petition 1.
Peter O'Connor, Philadelphia Almshouse,
to Mathew Carey, Philadelphia, 4 November 1797

Nov.ᵣ 4.ᵗʰ 1797——

Sir——

Please Excuse the liberty I have taken in addressing you, to the following purport, but having been Encouraged by Some of (I presume) your well wishers and the Church to which I Belong, to lay my Case Before you in hopes (agreeable to the good Character you Bear) that you would Endeavour to make afamily happy by Geting me in Some way of Employment at my Business (Bookbinding) I have Tryed most, or all I Know of the Bookbinders in this City for work, but they Either are Slack in work — have hands Enough or Many App<r>entices and no Room — in Short Sir they all have Some obstacle or other, particularly the Great Scarcity of Money, to purchace Materials or pay any Wages —— Therefore Sir, most probably through your Interest, the Gentlemen Booksellers of my Nation Could furnish me with tools Enough to Make aBeginning — as Doubtless they Could with work Enough my terms Shall be such as you may Reasonably please to Establish your Self, as I only Aspire to Make a living Barely for my family and Self I Require no Settlement before it may Suit my Employers, Except Sufficient for food fuel and Rent, in the Cource of one year — also if it might Suit — in a Short time I Could pay for the tools I am a Native of, and Served my Apprenticeship in the City of Dublin, and have Been in the United States about Eight years. I have work,ᵈ in Several parts of the Union Since, with Credit and flatter Myself that I Could Please any Reasonable Person, Either with my Behaviour or performance in point of Business. my wife is an Excellent folder and sewer which would Contribute to Dispatch. I am acquainted with Making all Manner <of> Pocket Books, Etwee Cases,[1] Traveling and Surgical Instrument Cases, Slate paper or any thing in that way, as good as any Imported, Specimens of which may be Seen at Mᵣ. Thoˢ Allens NYork as I made Several Dozens for him —— with Regard to my honesty, the Gentlemen for whom I have work,ᵈ: I doubt not will Give me that Character in this City (Viz, Mᵣ. Rob,ᵗ Aitkin, Mᵣ. Wᵐ Woodhouse and Mᵣ. Condy and you may not Doubt my Sobriety as I Drink no manner of Strong Liquors but have Some time Agoe Been Guilty of it at times, to my loss Only. Afew Days before this late Sickness I got a

---

1. Etwee (étui) **Case**: an ornamental case for one or more articles in daily use, e.g., toiletries, glasses, scissors, needles.

Small wound on my ankle, and being unable Either to work if I Could have got it, or Employ a Surgeon I was Oblidged to go into the Alms House and soon after got well — where I Since Remained on Account of the Bad times. I would not Object to labouring work, but Since I was Sick at Bush hill I have had a Debility in my left leg, which Occasions alameness — but hinders me not the least from my Own Business —— if you^l. please Sir to let the Bearer Thos. Wilkinson Know if I may wait on you Some Saturday —— if such a Circumstance would be worth your notice Between this and Spring I hope you^l. have no Reason to Repent Encouraging your Most Obed^t Servant Humbly Subscribed ——————————

Peter O Connor

NB — if it wont Suit you yet Sir to trouble your Self about the Above My Wife would be glad to Accept of aplace of Service for the present   She Can produce Excellent Recommendations from divers persons of Respectability   She has lastly Nursed Twins for M^r. W^m. Patten Printer whose wife Died in Childbed

Petition 2.
Peter O'Connor, Philadelphia Almshouse,
to Mathew Carey, Philadelphia, 17 February 1798

Worthy Sir —   alms House   Feby 17th 1798 ——
I Humbly Intreat you to Notice the following Lines, as my hopes are Entirely Centered in your Goodness to Comply with my Request — tho as yet I have Merited nothing of you — I would be far from Making Such an application as This — if my limbs would permit me to attend Journeywork at Binding — for if I am not Befriended by Such a Character as you I may Still Languish here from My Family, and in the Flower of my Days But to the Reverse may through you Become aUcefull Member to Society and Happy in Myself, and fall in to Some way to Recover the Natural Strength[2] of my Knees Being Very healthy Otherways. Doctors here are No more than Matter of Form —— I Being Concious that my Intentions are Honest an<d> Honourable in Repaying any Small Sum that might be lent me through you, from those Gentlemen of the Hibernian Society who wish to Encourage Industry Virtue and Change wrechedness of Family into Happiness I am perswaded that in a Short time, you will Pronounce me a Deserving Object of your Notice   God will Undoubtedly Reward Such aWork ——

I would Intimate that I Request no more than the Loan of 20 Dollars or less (Please Sir Excuse my Mentioning any Sum) to be paid at a Certain Time in Cash, or in pocket Books to you: to purchase Leather paper, and Some few Tools to Begin,   you Shall have the preferance of the first Choice of Every thing I make viz. pocket Book<s> of all Descriptions, Ladys Etwee Cases, Genuine Slate paper port Folios, Surgical Instrument and

---

2. Strenght ms.

Traveling Cases &ᶜ and my pay in the Goods of your Store —— if the Money is Granted for Charity, I will prove my Self Deserving the Same by the United Industry of my wife and me. I am perswaded that you are pestered with applications of this Kind by Individuals, who Never Intend Doing Credit to your Bounty —— for which Reason, Permit me Mᵣ Carey to Solicit your Serious Concideration on the Matter, for your Complyance being the Result — will Bind me in Duty, to Ever Esteem you My Benefactor, to Dayly Offer up My prayers for your Prosperity in this Life and Felicity in the Next, and my Infants Shall Lisp the Name of Carey in their Prayers. I Call God to witness the purity of my Views in only Aspiring to Get an Honest living out of this Asylum for the Miserable and Wicked —— and have an Opportunity to Attend my Church Regular and lead a pious Life in future   My Wife Has as Much Furniture as may answer a Small Room which we will Take on the 1st of March Before which time I will wait on you for your Reply   perhaps Sir, your Shewing what I have made Bold to Write you — to Some of the Humane Gentlemen might prove Favorable — I beg pardon for Declaring myself so much at large, Beging that youˡ. Concider My Cace,   may God Strenghten you in Doing Good

most Humbly
Subscribed   Peter Connor

NB if I Should have a Good Call for My Business with God Help I may be Enabled to purchace Some Binders Tools next Fall, and Some Musical Instruments to Teach Music in the Winter Evenings — as I am Capable ——

David Robinson, Lexington, Kentucky,
to Mary Robinson, Londonderry city, 4 May 1817

Lexington May 4ᵗʰ 1817

Dear Mother

I sit down to inform you of my health and happiness both of which I am so confident you will be glad to hear of—I have never enjoyed better health than I had last winter—I am now more hearty and weighs more than perhaps you have ever seen me—I am fatter than I ever recollect of except at the time I arrived in America—then I weighed 150ˡᵇˢ a few pounds more than I weigh at present—but as [. . .] probable I shall soon become lean as I generally fall off very much in warm weather—Therefore possessing health, having plenty to eat drink and to ware of the best and enjoying at present the Company of good sociable and religious friends—besides I live with my old friend Mr Campbell a man who has at all times been very indulgent to me—you will be apt to conclude if that I am unhappy it must proceed from some bad quality in myself—I received in good order the Shirts, which you were so kind as to send me, for which I return you my sincere thanks—them with what I had will probably last me untill I pay a visit to Ireland, the time I have not yet determined.

I am sorry to hear of the distressing accounts with which every newspaper is filled of the deplorable State of Ireland—I hope it is not as bad as represented   it appears that you are in a state of Starvation,   I wish all the inhabitants of Ireland were in the back woods of America, where they could obtain a sufficiency of every thing their heart could wish,   the millions of uncultivated acres would give employment to all them who wished it, and those who would be above working would soon become poor indeed except they would make their bread by some other usefull employment—this is a bad place for idlers—We are all free here, and all possesses a spirit of independence—the man who earns his bread by the swet of his brow, speaks his sentiments with as much boldness and freedom as the legislator who represents him in Congress—that would be the principal objection with me from ever living in Ireland—a man who has once enjoyed the sweets of liberty could never brook the idea of cringing to a despotic tyrant—

I wrote some time ago, giving it as my oppinion that my Brother Richard had better come to this country after Business would get better, I still give it as my oppinion that he had better come—what can he promise himself in Ireland—nothing but indigence and poverty all his life—here there is a good prospect, if not making a fortune at least of making a comfortable living—there is millions of acres of vacant land now to be sold by the United States Government, up the Missoura there is to be sold some of as fine land as in the world—it generally sells from 2 to 3 dollars ℔ acre and after that is paid, there is no renewing of lease, nor paying of rents—nothing to pay but a small tax to defray the expences of government and that does not amount to the one tenth of the taxes they have to pay in Ireland, also, there is a large track of land, adjoining the State of Georgia, which General Jackson gained from the Creek Indians to be sold in a short time, to which there is a vast emigration this spring the emigration to the Missoura Country last fall in the space of three Months was computed at seven thousand souls—If Richard comes I think he had better leave his family at home for some time untill he would provide a place of residence for them—there is but few people who are reconciled to a strange country at first—it takes some time before the manners and customs becomes familiar and unto that takes place they are generally discontented—therefore I would advice any man who has a family, if he can any way make it convenient to leave them behind untill he could first get a knowledge of the country—

I was sorry to hear of the distresses of my countrymen last year at New York—which was occasioned by such a vast number emigrating to the same place and their ignorance of the country—had they on their arrival pushed back into the country they would have all found employment in large towns on the Seabord is now I believe nearly as bad for the poor emigrant as where he left

I intend going to Philadelphia in the course of the Summer, I think in June I have been keeping Store in this State now better than six years I have got tired, I wish to try some other ways of living, I wish to get in to some better way of making money—however, when I arrive at Philadelphia, I will write you what I intend to do—I wrote you some time ago of the death of your Aunt, also of the expected death of William Hopkins, he died in January last laving a son and three daughters to lament their loss—their Mother being dead some time before

In consequence of the great demand for breadstuffs in Europe marketing of that kind is much higher, here, than formerly Wheat now sells for one dollar ℔ Bushel double its usual price Indian corn meal half a doller ℔ Bushel and all other grains in proportion—

Tobacco is but slow sale this year at four dollars ℔ 100 pound   last year it sold rapidly at ten dollars—

Give my love to my Grandmother to all my uncles & aunts   give my best respects to my Brothers & sisters—I hope long ere this Sister Sarah has recovered to her fomer State of health   Remember me to all my cousins friends and acquaintances   Tell James Cochran I have for a long time, been expecting a letter from him   I wrote him a long letter giving him a description of my travil through the State of Tennessee and the Mississipy Territory—which I have never heard of

I remain Dear Mother
your obt Son
David Robinson

Direct your letters as usual—all that is necessary is this—David Robinson
Lexington   Kentucky— The two last letters I received had been opened   the directions being so awquardly <written> excited the curiosity of some unprincipled fellow—have the directions in a better hand than usual

✳
Sources

ABBREVIATIONS IN SOURCES ✳

Archives and Libraries

Bur. Arch. & Hist., PHMC	Bureau of Archives and History, in PHMC
HSP	Historical Society of Pennsylvania, Philadelphia
HSWP	Historical Society of Western Pennsylvania, Pittsburgh
INA	Irish National Archives, Dublin
NLI	National Library of Ireland, Dublin
NYGBS	New York Genealogical and Biographical Society
NYPL	New York Public Library
PHMC	Pennsylvania Historical and Museum Commission, Harrisburg
PRONI	Public Record Office of Northern Ireland, Belfast
TCD	Trinity College, Dublin

Primary Sources

Census of Ireland 1821: Occupations	Abstract of the Answers and Returns made pursuant to an Act of the United Parliament, passed in the 55th Year of the Reign of His Late Majesty George the Third, Intituated, "An Act to provide for taking an Account of the Population of Ireland. . . . " *British Parliamentary Papers,* 1824, xxii.
Evans' Early Am. Imprints	*Evans' Early American Imprints: 1639–1800,* C. K. Shipton, ed. (Worcester, Mass., 1967–74).
Griffith's *Valuation*	Sir Richard Griffith, *Primary Valuation of Ireland, 1848–64.* (Bound copies for Ulster in PRONI; bound or microfilm copies for Leinster, Munster, and Connacht in NLI; Mss. Library, TCD; and INA.)
TAB	Tithe Applotment Book(s). (TABs for Ulster are located in PRONI, for the rest of Ireland in NLI.)
White, *Geneal. Abstracts*	V. D. White, comp., *Genealogical Abstracts of Revolutionary War Pension Files,* 2 vols. (Waynesboro, Tenn., 1993).

Dictionaries and Encyclopedias

ACAB	*Appleton's Cyclopedia of American Biography*
ANB	*American National Biography*
DAB	*Dictionary of American Biography*
DCB	*Dictionary of Canadian Biography*
DNB	*Dictionary of National Biography*

Hinshaw, *Encycl. Am. Quaker Geneal.*	W. W. Hinshaw, *Encyclopedia of American Quaker Genealogy* (places and dates vary)
NCE	*New Catholic Encyclopedia*

Journals, Serials, and Newspapers

AHR	*American Historical Review*
Am. J. Sociology	*American Journal of Sociology*
Am. J. Legal Hist.	*American Journal of Legal History*
Am. Q.	*American Quarterly*
Bul. NYPL	*Bulletin of the New York Public Library*
Bul. Presby. Hist. Soc. of Ire.	*Bulletin of the Presbyterian Historical Society of Ireland*
Cath. Educ. Rev.	*Catholic Educational Review*
Cath. Hist. Rev.	*Catholic Historical Review*
Coll. Dutchess Co. Hist. Soc.	*Collections of the Dutchess County [N.Y.] Historical Society*
Co. Lough Arch. & Hist. J.	*Co. Lough Archaeological and Historical Journal*
Ga. Hist. Q.	*Georgia Historical Quarterly*
Hist. Educ. Q.	*History of Education Quarterly*
Hist. J.	*Historical Journal*
Hist. Mag. Prot. Episc. Ch.	*Historical Magazine of the Protestant Episcopal Church*
Hist. N.H.	*Historical New Hampshire*
Hist. Pub. Soc. Col. Wars Pa.	*Historical Publications of the Society of Colonial Wars in the Commonwealth of Pennsylvania*
IESH	*Irish Economic and Social History*
IHS	*Irish Historical Studies*
JAH	*Journal of American History*
JAIHS	*Journal of the American Irish Historical Society*
J. Am. Ethnic Hist.	*Journal of American Ethnic History*
JAS	*Journal of American Studies*
J. Brit. Studies	*Journal of British Studies*
J. Econ. Hist.	*Journal of Economic History*
J. Fam. Hist.	*Journal of Family History*
J. Interdis. Hist.	*Journal of Interdisciplinary History*
J. Lanc. Co. Hist. Soc.	*Journal of the Lancaster County Historical Society*
J. Presby. Hist.	*Journal of Presbyterian History*
J. Presby. Hist. Soc.	*Journal of the Presbyterian Historical Society*
J. So. Hist.	*Journal of Southern History*
Md. Hist. Mag.	*Maryland Historical Magazine*
NCHR	*North Carolina Historical Review*
N.J. Arch.	*New Jersey Archives*
N.J. Geneal. Mag.	*New Jersey Genealogical Magazine*
N.Y. Hist.	*New York History*
O'Callaghan, *Doc. Hist. N.Y.*	E. O'Callaghan, *Documentary History of the State of New York* (Albany, 1849–1851).

Ohio Arch. & Hist. Q.	Ohio Archaeological and Historical Quarterly
P & P	Past and Present
Pa. Arch.	Pennsylvania Archives (Harrisburg, Pa.)
Pa. Gazette	Pennsylvania Gazette
Pa. Hist.	Pennsylvania History
Pa. J.	Pennsylvania Journal
Papers Lanc. Co. Hist. Soc.	Papers of the Lancaster County [Pa.] Historical Society
Parl. Hist.	Parliamentary History
Perry, Hist. Coll. Am. Colonial Church	W. S. Perry, ed., Historical Collections Relating to the American Colonial Church (1870–1878; repr. New York, 1969)
Perspectives Am. Hist.	Perspectives in American History
PMHB	Pennsylvania Magazine of History and Biography
PRIA	Proceedings of the Royal Irish Academy
Proc. Am. Ethnol. Soc.	Proceedings of the American Ethnological Society
Proc. Am. Phil. Soc.	Proceedings of the American Philosophical Society
Proc. Mass. Hist. Soc.	Proceedings of the Massachusetts Historical Society
Proc. So. Car. Hist. Soc.	Proceedings of the South Carolina Historical Society
QH	Quaker History
Rec. Am. Cath. Hist. Soc. Phila.	Records of the American Catholic Historical Society of Philadelphia
Rhode Is. Geneal. Reg.	Rhode Island Genealogical Register
So. Car. Hist. Mag.	South Carolina Historical Magazine
Sprague, Annals Am. Pulpit	Rev. W. B. Sprague, Annals of the American Pulpit; or Commemorative Notices of Distinguished American Clergymen of Various Denominations, 9 vols. (New York, 1857–69).
Tenn. Hist. Q.	Tennessee Historical Quarterly
Trans. Am. Phil. Soc.	Transactions of the American Philosophical Society
Trans. R.H.S.	Transactions of the Royal Historical Society
U.S. Cath. Hist.	U.S. Catholic Historian
U.S. Cath. Hist. Soc., Hist. Rec. & Studies	United States Catholic Historical Society, Historical Records and Studies
U.S. Gazette	United States Gazette (Philadelphia)
VMHB	Virginia Magazine of History and Biography
WMQ	William and Mary Quarterly
WPHM	Western Pennsylvania Historical Magazine

Books

Adams, Printed Word	J. R. R. Adams, The Printed Word and the Common Man: Popular Culture in Ulster, 1700–1900 (Belfast, 1987).
Ahlstrom, Religious History	S. E. Ahlstrom, A Religious History of the American People (New Haven, 1989).

Albert, *Westmoreland Co.*   G. D. Albert, *History of the County of Westmoreland, Pennsylvania* (Philadelphia, 1882).

Bailyn & Morgan, *Strangers*   B. Bailyn and P. D. Morgan, eds., *Strangers within the Realm: Cultural Margins of the First British Empire* (Chapel Hill, N.C., 1991).

Barnard, *Cromwellian Ireland*   T. C. Barnard, *Cromwellian Ireland: English Government and Reform in Ireland, 1649–1660* (London, 1975).

Barratt & Sachse, *Freemasonry in Pa.*   N. S. Barratt and J. F. Sachse, *Freemasonry in Pennsylvania, 1727–1907: As Shown by the Records of Lodge No. 2, F. and A.M. of Philadelphia* (Philadelphia, 1908), vols. 1–2.

Bartlett, *Fall and Rise*   T. Bartlett, *The Fall and Rise of the Irish Nation: The Catholic Question, 1690–1830* (Dublin, 1992)

Bartlett & Hayton, *Penal Era*   T. Bartlett and D. W. Hayton, eds., *Penal Era and Golden Age: Essays in Irish History, 1690–1800* (Belfast, 1979).

Bartlett & Jeffery, *Military History*   T. Bartlett and K. Jeffery, eds., *A Military History of Ireland* (Cambridge, England, 1996).

Baseler, *"Asylum for Mankind"*   M. C. Baseler, *"Asylum for Mankind": America, 1607–1800* (Ithaca, N.Y., 1998).

Bayor & Meagher, *N.Y. Irish*   R. H. Bayor and T. J. Meagher, eds., *The New York Irish* (Baltimore, 1996).

Beckett, *Protestant Dissent*   J. C. Beckett, *Protestant Dissent in Ireland, 1687–1780* (London, 1948).

Beeman et al., *Beyond Confederation*   R. Beeman, S. Botein, and E. C. Carter II, eds., *Beyond Confederation: Origins of the Constitution and American National Identity* (Chapel Hill, N.C., 1987).

Bell, *Patriot-Improvers*   W. J. Bell, Jr., *Patriot-Improvers: Members of the American Philosophical Society*, vol. 1, *1743–1768* (Philadelphia, 1998).

Bishop, *Hist. Am. Manuf.*   J. L. Bishop, *A History of American Manufactures from 1608 to 1860* (Philadelphia, 1868).

Blethen & Wood, *Ulster & No. America*   H. T. Blethen and C. W. Wood, Jr., eds., *Ulster and North Ameria: Transatlantic Perspectives on the Scotch-Irish* (Tuscaloosa, Ala., 1997).

Blumin, *Emergence Middle Class*   S. M. Blumin, *The Emergence of the Middle Class: Social Experience in the American City, 1760–1900* (Cambridge, England, 1989).

Bolton, *Scotch-Irish Pioneers*   C. K. Bolton, *Scotch-Irish Pioneers in Ulster and America* (Boston, 1910).

Bonomi, *Cope of Heaven*   P. U. Bonomi, *Under the Cope of Heaven: Religion, Society, and Politics in Colonial America* (New York, 1986).

Bonomi, *Factious People*   P. U. Bonomi, *A Factious People: Politics and Society in Colonial New York* (New York, 1971).

Bowen, *Protestant Crusade*   D. Bowen, *The Protestant Crusade in Ireland, 1800–70* (Dublin, 1978).

Boydston, *Home & Work*   J. Boydston, *Home and Work: Housework, Wages, and the Ideology of Labor in the Early Republic* (New York, 1990).

Boyce et al., *Political Thought*   D. G. Boyce, R. Eccleshall, and V. Geoghegan, eds., *Political Thought in Ireland since the Seventeenth Century* (London, 1993)

Bridenbaugh, *Cities in Revolt*   C. Bridenbaugh, *Cities in Revolt: Urban Life in America, 1743–1776* (New York, 1968).

Bridenbaugh, *Cities in the Wilderness*   C. Bridenbaugh, *Cities in the Wilderness: Urban Life in America, 1625–1742* (New York, 1938).

Bridenbaugh, *Mitre & Sceptre*   C. Bridenbaugh, *Mitre and Sceptre: Transatlantic Faiths, Ideas, Personalities, and Politics, 1689–1775* (New York, 1962).

Bridenbaugh, *Rebels & Gentlemen*   C. and J. Bridenbaugh, *Rebels and Gentlemen: Philadelphia in the Age of Franklin* (New York, 1942).

Brock, *Scotus Americanus*   W. R. Brock, *Scotus Americanus: A Survey of the Sources for Links between Scotland and America in the Eighteenth Century* (Edinburgh, 1982).

Brooke, *Ulster Presbyterianism*   P. Brooke, *Ulster Presbyterianism: The Historical Perspective, 1610–1970* (Dublin, 1987).

Brunhouse, *Counter-Rev. in Pa.*   R. L. Brunhouse, *The Counter-Revolution in Pennsylvania, 1776–1790* (Harrisburg, 1971).

Burtchaell & Sadlier, *Alumni Dublinenses*   G. D. Burtchaell and T. Ulick Sadlier, eds., *Alumni Dublineses: A Register of the Students, Graduates, Professors and Provosts of Trinity College in the University of Dublin, 1593–1860*, 2nd ed. (Dublin, 1936).

Bushman, *Refinement*   R. L. Bushman, *The Refinement of America: Persons, Houses, Cities* (New York, 1962).

Butler, *Sea of Faith*   J. Butler, *Awash in a Sea of Faith : Christianizing the American People* (Cambridge, Mass., 1990).

Campbell, *Friendly Sons of St. Patrick*   J. H. Campbell, *History of the Friendly Sons of St. Patrick and the Hibernian Society of Philadelphia* (Philadelphia, 1892).

Campbell & Skinner, *Scot. Enlight.*   R. H. Campbell and A. S. Skinner, eds., *The Origins and Nature of the Scottish Enlightenment* (Edinburgh, 1982).

Canny, *Europeans*   N. Canny, ed., *Europeans on the Move: Studies on European Migration, 1500–1800* (Oxford, 1994).

Carey, *People, Priests, & Prelates*   P. Carey, *People, Priests, and Prelates: Ecclesiastical Democracy and the Tensions of Trusteeism* (Notre Dame, Ind., 1987).

Carwardine, *Transatlantic Revivalism*   R. Carwardine, *Transatlantic Revivalism: Popular Evangeli-*

	calism in Britain and America, *1790–1865* (Westport, Conn., 1978).
Casey & Rowan, *No. Leinster*	C. Casey and A. Rowan, *North Leinster: The Counties of Longford, Louth, Meath and Westmeath* (London, 1993).
Chesnutt & Wilson, *Meaning So. Car. Hist.*	D. R. Chesnutt and C. N. Wilson, eds., *The Meaning of South Carolina History: Essays in Honor of George C. Rogers, Jr.* (Columbia, S.C., 1991).
Clark, *Eastern Frontier*	C. E. Clark, *The Eastern Frontier: The Settlement of Northern New England, 1610–1763* (New York, 1970).
Clark, *Hist. Manuf. U.S.*	V. S. Clark, *History of Manufactures in the United States, 1607–1860* (Washington, D.C., 1916).
Clark, *Irish in Philadelphia*	D. Clark, *The Irish in Philadelphia* (Philadelphia, 1973).
Clark et al., *Maine in Early Republic*	C. E. Clark, J. E. Leamon, and K. Bowden, eds., *Maine in the Early Republic: From Revolution to Statehood* (Hanover, N.H., 1988).
Claydon & MacBride, *Protestantism*	T. Claydon and I. MacBride, eds., *Protestantism and National Identity: Britain and Ireland, c. 1650–c. 1850* (Cambridge, England, 1998)
Cohen, *Linen, Family & Community*	M. Cohen, *Linen, Family and Community in Tullylish, County Down, 1690–1914* (Dublin, 1997).
Connolly, *Religion, Law & Power*	S. J. Connolly, *Religion, Law and Power: The Making of Protestant Ireland, 1660–1760* (Oxford, 1992).
Countryman, *People in Revolution*	E. Countryman, *A People in Revolution: The American Revolution and Political Society in New York, 1760–1790* (Baltimore, 1981).
Cremin, *Am. Educ. Col. Exper.*	L. A. Cremin: *American Education: The Colonial Experience, 1607–1783* (New York, 1970).
Crimmins, *St. Patrick's Day*	J. D. Crimmins, *St. Patrick's Day: Its Celebration in New York and Other American Places, 1737–1845* (New York, 1902).
Crow & Tise, *So. Exper. Am. Rev.*	J. J. Crow and L. E. Tise, eds., *The Southern Experience in the American Revolution* (Chapel Hill, N.C., 1978).
Cullen & Smout, *Comparative Aspects*	L. M. Cullen and T. C. Smout, eds., *Comparative Aspects of Scottish and Irish Economic and Social History, 1600–1900* (Edinburgh, 1977).
Curtin, *United Irishmen*	N. J. Curtin, *The United Irishmen: Popular Politics in Ulster and Dublin, 1791–1798* (Oxford, 1994).
Daiches, *Scottish Culture*	D. Daiches, *The Paradox of Scottish Culture: The Eighteenth-Century Experience* (London, 1964).
Daly & Dickson, *Origins Pop. Literacy*	M. Daly and D. Dickson, eds., *The Origins of Popular Literacy in Ireland: Language Change and Educational Development, 1700–1920* (Dublin, 1990).

Daniell, *Col. N.H.*   J. R. Daniell, *Colonial New Hampshire: A History* (Mill-wood, N.J., 1981).

Daniell, *Experiment*   J. R. Daniell, *Experiment in Republicanism: New Hampshire Politics and the American Revolution, 1741–1794* (Cambridge, Mass., 1970).

Day & McWilliams, *OSM*   A. Day and P. McWilliams, eds., *Ordnance Survey Memoirs of Ireland* (Belfast); later vols. also coedited by N. Dobson.

Devlin & Fanning, *Religion & Rebellion*   J. Devlin and R. Fanning, eds., *Religion and Rebellion: Historical Studies 20* (Dublin, 1997).

Dickson, *New Foundations*   D. Dickson, *New Foundations: Ireland 1660–1800* (Dublin, 1987).

Dickson, *Ulster Emigration*   R. J. Dickson, *Ulster Emigration to Colonial America, 1718–1785* (London, 1966).

Dickson et al., *United Irishmen*   D. Dickson, D. Keogh, and K. Whelan, eds., *The United Irishmen: Republicanism, Radicalism and Rebellion* (Dublin, 1993).

Doerflinger, *Vigorous Spirit*   T. M. Doerflinger, *A Vigorous Spirit of Enterprise: Merchants and Economic Development in Revolutionary Philadelphia* (Chapel Hill, N.C., 1986).

Dolan, *Am. Catholic Experience*   J. P. Dolan, *The American Catholic Experience: A History from Colonial Times to the Present* (Garden City, N.Y., 1985).

Donovan, *No Popery in Scotland*   R. K. Donovan, *No Popery and Radicalism: Opposition to Roman Catholic Relief in Scotland, 1778–1782* (New York, 1987).

Doyle, *Ireland, Irishmen*   D. N. Doyle, *Ireland, Irishmen and Revolutionary America, 1760–1820* (Dublin, 1981).

Dunaway, *Scotch-Irish of Col. Pa.*   W. F. Dunaway, *The Scotch-Irish of Colonial Pennsylvania* (Chapel Hill, N.C., 1944).

Durey, *Transatlantic Radicals*   M. Durey, *Transatlantic Radicals and the Early American Republic* (Lawrence, Ks., 1997).

Egnal, *New World Economies*   M. Egnal, *New World Economies: The Growth of the Thirteen Colonies and Early Canada* (New York, 1998).

Ekirch, *"Poor Carolina"*   A. R. Ekirch, *"Poor Carolina": Politics and Society in Colonial North Carolina, 1729–1776* (Chapel Hill, N.C., 1981).

Elliott, *Partners in Revolution*   M. Elliott, *Partners in Revolution: The United Irishmen and France* (New Haven, 1982).

Ellis, *Catholics in Col. Am.*   J. T. Ellis, *Catholics in Colonial America* (Baltimore, 1965).

Ferguson, *Early W. Pa. Politics*   R. J. Ferguson, *Early Western Pennsylvania Politics* (Pittsburgh, 1938).

Finke & Stark, *Churching of America*   R. Finke and R. Stark, *The Churching of America, 1776–*

	1990: Winners and Losers in Our Religious Economy (New Brunswick, N.J., 1992).
Fisk, *Scottish High Church Tradition*	W. L. Fisk, *The Scottish High Church Tradition in America: An Essay in Scotch-Irish Ethno-Religious History* (Lanham, Md., 1995).
Foner, *Tom Paine*	E. Foner, *Tom Paine and Revolutionary America* (New York, 1976).
Ford et al., *As By Law Established*	A. Ford, J. McGuire, and K. Milne, eds., *As By Law Established: The Church of Ireland since the Reformation* (Dublin, 1987).
Foster, *Pursuit of Equal Liberty*	J. S. Foster, *In Pursuit of Equal Liberty: George Bryan and the Revolution in Pennsylvania* (University Park, Pa., 1994).
Frantz & Pencak, *Beyond Philadelphia*	J. B. Frantz and W. Pencak, eds., *Beyond Philadelphia: The American Revolution in the Pennsylvania Hinterland* (University Park, Pa., 1998).
Futhey & Cope, *History of Chester Co.*	J. Futhey and G. Cope, *History of Chester County, Pennsylvania* (Philadelphia, 1881).
Galenson, *White Servitude*	D. Galenson, *White Servitude in Colonial America* (Cambridge, England, 1981).
Gillespie, *Devoted People*	R. Gillespie, *Devoted People: Relief and Religion in Early Modern Ireland* (Manchester, England, 1997).
Greaves, *God's Other Children*	R. L. Greaves, *God's Other Children: Protestant Nonconformists and the Emergence of Denominational Churches in Ireland, 1660–1700* (Stanford, Cal., 1997).
Green, *Lagan Valley*	E. R. R. Green, *The Lagan Valley, 1800–1850: A Local History of the Industrial Revolution* (London, 1949).
Greenberg, *Crime & Law*	D. Greenberg, *Crime and Law Enforcement in the Colony of New York, 1691–1776* (Ithaca, N.Y., 1976).
Grubb, *Quakers*	I. Grubb, *The Quakers in Ireland, 1654–1900* (London, 1927).
Guthrie, *John McMillan*	D. R. Guthrie, *John McMillan: The Apostle of Presbyterianism in the West, 1752–1833* (Pittsburgh, 1952).
Haire, *Challenge & Conflict*	Rev. J. L. M. Haire, ed., *Challenge and Conflict: Essays in Irish Presbyterian History and Doctrine* (Antrim, 1981).
Harper, *Western Pa.*	R. E. Harper, *The Transformation of Western Pennsylvania, 1770–1800* (Pittsburgh, 1991).
Hart, *Valley of Va.*	F. H. Hart, *The Valley of Virginia in the American Revolution, 1763–1789* (Chapel Hill, N.C., 1942).
Hatch, *Democ. Am. Christ.*	N. O. Hatch, *The Democratization of American Christianity* (New Haven, 1989).
Hennesey, *Am. Catholics*	J. Hennessey, *American Catholics: A History of the Roman Catholic Community in the United States* (New York, 1981).

Herlihy, *Irish Dissenting Tradition* K. Herlihy, ed., *The Irish Dissenting Tradition, 1650–1750* (Blackrock, County Dublin, 1995).

Herlihy, *Politics of Irish Dissent* K. Herlihy, ed., *The Politics of Irish Dissent, 1650–1800* (Dublin, 1997).

Herlihy, *Religion of Irish Dissent* K. Herlihy, ed., *The Religion of Irish Dissent, 1650–1800* (Dublin, 1996).

Higgins, *Rev. War in South* W. R. Higgins, ed., *The Revolutionary War in the South: Power, Conflict, and Leadership* (Durham, N.C., 1979).

Hill, *Patriots to Unionists* J. Hill, *From Patriots to Unionists: Dublin Civic Politics and Irish Protestant Patriotism, 1660–1840* (Oxford, 1997).

Hoffman & Albert, *Religion in Rev. Age* R. Hoffman and P. J. Albert, eds., *Religion in a Revolutionary Age* (Charlottesville, Va., 1994).

Hoffman & Albert, *Sov. States* R. Hoffman and P. J. Albert, eds., *Sovereign States in an Age of Uncertainty* (Charlottesville, Va., 1981).

Hoffman et al., *Through a Glass Darkly* R. Hoffman, M. Sobel, and F. J. Teute, eds., *Through a Glass Darkly: Reflections on Personal Identity in Early America* (Chapel Hill, N.C., 1997).

Hoffman et al., *Uncivil War* R. Hoffman, T. W. Tate, and P. J. Albert, eds., *An Uncivil War: The Southern Backcountry during the American Revolution* (Charlottesville, Va., 1985).

Hooker, *Carolina Backcountry* R. J. Hooker, ed., *The Carolina Backcountry on the Eve of the Revolution: The Journal and Other Writings of Charles Woodmason, Anglican Itinerant* (Chapel Hill, N.C., 1953).

Hutson, *Pa. Politics* J. H. Hutson, *Pennsylvania Politics, 1746–1770: The Movement for Royal Government and Its Consequences* (Princeton, 1972).

Ireland, *Religion, Ethnicity, & Politics* O. S. Ireland, *Religion, Ethnicity, and Politics: Ratifying the Constitution in Pennsylvania* (University Park, Pa., 1995).

Jensen, *Mar. Commerce* A. L. Jensen, *The Maritime Commerce of Colonial Philadelphia* (Madison, Wis., 1963).

Kilroy, *Protestant Dissent* P. Kilroy, *Protestant Dissent and Controversy, 1660–1714* (Cork, 1994).

Klein, *Unification of Slave State* R. Klein, *Unification of a Slave State: The Rise of the Planter Class in the South Carolina Backcountry, 1760–1808* (Chapel Hill, N.C., 1990).

Klett, *Presby. in Col. Pa.* G. S. Klett, *Presbyterians in Colonial Pennsylvania* (Philadelphia, 1937).

Land Owners in Ireland, 1876 *Land Owners in Ireland. Return of Owners of Land of One Acre and Upwards in the Several Counties . . . in Ireland* (1876; repr. Baltimore, 1988).

Laurie, *Working People of Phila.* B. Laurie, *Working People of Philadelphia, 1800–1850* (Philadelphia, 1980).

Lebsock, *Free Women of Petersburg*   S. Lebsock, *The Free Women of Petersburg: Status and Culture in a Southern Town, 1784–1860* (New York, 1984).

Leerssen, *Mere Irish*   J. Leerssen, *Mere Irish and Fíor Ghael: Studies in the Idea of Irish Nationality, Its Development and Literary Expression prior to the Nineteenth Century* (Notre Dame, Ind., 1997)

Lemon, *Best Poor Man's Country*   J. T. Lemon, *The Best Poor Man's Country: A Geographical Study of Early Southeastern Pennsylvania* (New York, 1972).

Levy, *Quakers & Am. Family*   B. Levy, *Quakers and the American Family: British Settlement in the Delaware Valley* (New York, 1988).

Lewis, *TDI*   S. Lewis, *A Topographical Dictionary of Ireland . . . with Historical and Statistical Descriptions* (1837; repr. Baltimore, 1984).

Leyburn, *Scotch-Irish*   J. G. Leyburn, *The Scotch-Irish: A Social History* (Chapel Hill, N.C., 1962).

Light, *Rome & New Republic*   D. B. Light, *Rome and the New Republic: Conflict and Community in Philadelphia Catholicism between the Revolution and the Civil War* (Notre Dame, Ind., 1996).

Lockhart, *Some Aspects*   A. Lockhart, *Some Aspects of Emigration from Ireland to the North American Colonies between 1660 and 1775* (New York, 1976).

McAvoy, *Cath. Church in U.S.*   T. T. McAvoy, C.S.C., *A History of the Catholic Church in the United States* (Notre Dame, Ind., 1969).

McBride, *Scripture Politics*   I. R. McBride, *Scripture Politics: Ulster Presbyterians and Irish Radicalism in the Late Eighteenth Century* (Oxford, 1998).

McBride, *Siege of Derry*   I. McBride, *The Siege of Derry in Ulster Protestant Mythology* (Dublin, 1997).

McCormick, *New Jersey*   R. P. McCormick, *New Jersey from Colony to State, 1609–1789* (Princeton, 1964).

McCusker & Menard, *Econ. Brit. Am.*   J. J. McCusker and R. R. Menard, *The Economy of British America, 1607–1789* (Chapel Hill, N.C., 1991 ed.).

Miller, *Emigrants & Exiles*   K. A. Miller, *Emigrants and Exiles: Ireland and the Irish Exodus to North America* (New York, 1985).

Miller, *Phila.—Federalist City*   R. G. Miller, *Philadelphia—The Federalist City: A Study of Urban Politics, 1789–1801* (Port Washington, N.Y., 1976).

Mitchell, *Appalachian Frontiers*   R. D. Mitchell, ed., *Appalachian Frontiers: Settlement, Society, and Development in the Preindustrial Era* (Lexington, Ky., 1991).

Moffat, *Pop. Hist. of E. U.S. Cities*   R. Moffat, comp., *Population History of Eastern U.S. Cities and Towns, 1790–1870* (Metuchen, N.J., 1992).

Moody & Vaughn, *NHI 4*   T. W. Moody and W. E. Vaughn, eds., *A New History of Ireland*, vol. 4, *Eighteenth-Century Ireland, 1691–1800* (Oxford, 1986).

Murphy, *Derry, Donegal*   D. Murphy, *Derry, Donegal and Modern Ulster, 1790–1921* (Londonderry, 1981).

Myers, *Irish Quakers into Pa.*   A. C. Myers, *The Immigration of Irish Quakers into Pennsylvania, 1682–1750* (Swarthmore, Pa., 1902).

Nash, *Urban Crucible*   G. B. Nash, *The Urban Crucible: Social Change, Political Consciousness, and the Origins of the American Revolution* (Cambridge, Mass., 1979).

Nolan & O'Neill, *Offaly*   W. Nolan and T. P. O'Neill, eds., *Offaly: History and Society. Interdisciplinary Essays on the History of an Irish County* (Dublin, 1998).

Nolan et al., *Donegal*   W. Nolan, L. Ronayne, and M. Dunlevy, eds., *Donegal: History and Society. Interdisciplinary Essays on the History of an Irish County* (Dublin, 1995).

O'Brien, *Derry & Londonderry*   G. O'Brien, ed., *Derry and Londonderry: History and Society. Interdisciplinary Essays on the History of an Irish County* (Derry, 1999).

O'Brien, *Parl., Politics, & People*   G. O'Brien, ed., *Parliament, Politics, and People: Essays in Eighteenth-Century Irish History* (Blackrock, County Dublin, 1989).

Ó Ciosáin, *Print & Pop. Culture*   N. Ó Ciosáin, *Print and Popular Culture in Ireland, 1750–1850* (London, 1997).

O'Flanagan & Buttimer, *Cork*   P. O'Flanagan and C. G. Buttimer, eds., *Cork: History and Society. Interdisciplinary Essays on the History of an Irish County* (Dublin, 1993).

Potter, *Golden Door*   G. Potter, *To the Golden Door: The Story of the Irish in Ireland and America* (Boston, 1960).

Power & Whelan, *Endurance*   T. P. Power and K. Whelan, eds., *Endurance and Emergence: Catholics in Ireland in the Eighteenth Century* (Dublin, 1990).

Prendergast, *Cromwellian Settlement*   J. P. Prendergast, *The Cromwellian Settlement of Ireland* (Dublin, 1922).

Proudfoot, *Down*   L. Proudfoot, ed., *Down: History and Society. Interdisciplinary Essays on the History of an Irish County* (Dublin, 1997).

Ramsay, *Carolina Cradle*   R. W. Ramsay, *Carolina Cradle: Settlement of the Northwest Carolina Frontier, 1747–1762* (Chapel Hill, N.C., 1964).

Rhoden, *Rev. Anglicanism*   N. L. Rhoden, *Revolutionary Anglicanism: The Colonial Church of England Clergy during the American Revolution* (New York, 1999).

Robbins, *Commonwealthman* C. Robbins, *The Eighteenth-Century Commonwealthman: Studies in the Transmission, Development and Circumstance of English Liberal Thought from the Restoration of Charles II until the War with the Thirteen Colonies* (Cambridge, Mass., 1959).

Robinson, *Plantation of Ulster* P. Robinson, *The Plantation of Ulster: British Settlement in an Irish Landscape, 1600–1670* (Dublin, 1984).

Roebuck, *Plantation to Partition* P. Roebuck, ed., *Plantation to Partition: Essays in Ulster History in Honour of J. L. McCracken* (Belfast, 1981).

Rosen, *Courts & Commerce* D. A. Rosen, *Courts and Commerce: Gender, Law, and the Market Economy in Colonial New York* (Columbus, Ohio, 1997).

Rowe, *Mathew Carey* K. W. Rowe, *Mathew Carey: A Study in Economic Development* (Baltimore, 1933).

Royster, *Rev. People at War* C. Royster, *A Revolutionary People at War: The Continental Army and American Character, 1775–1783* (Chapel Hill, N.C., 1979).

Ryerson, *Rev. Now Begun* R. A. Ryerson, *The Revolution Is Now Begun: The Radical Committees of Philadelphia, 1765–1776* (Philadelphia, 1978).

Sachse, *Old Masonic Lodges* J. F. Sachse, *Old Masonic Lodges of Pennsylvania: "Moderns" and "Ancients," 1730–1800* (Philadelphia, 1912), vol. 1.

Salinger, *"To Serve Well & Faithfully"* S. V. Salinger, *"To Serve Well and Faithfully": Labor and Indentured Servants in Pennsylvania, 1682–1800* (Cambridge, England, 1987).

Scharf & Westcott, *Hist. of Phila.* J. T. Scharf and T. Westcott, *History of Philadelphia, 1609–1884*, 3 vols. (Philadelphia, 1894).

Schmidt, *Holy Fairs* L. E. Schmidt, *Holy Fairs: Scottish Communions and American Revivals in the Early Modern Period* (Princeton, 1989).

Schultz, *Republic of Labor* R. Schultz, *The Republic of Labor: Philadelphia's Artisans and the Politics of Class, 1720–1830* (New York, 1993).

Schwartz, *"Mixed Multitude"* S. Schwartz, *"A Mixed Multitude": The Struggle for Toleration in Colonial Pennsylvania* (New York, 1987).

Sheils & Wood, *Churches* W. J. Sheils and D. Wood, eds., *The Churches, Ireland and the Irish* (Oxford, 1989).

Shields, *Civil Tongues* D. S. Shields, *Civil Tongues and Polite Letters in British America* (Chapel Hill, N.C., 1997).

Shy, *People Numerous* J. Shy, *A People Numerous and Armed: Reflections on the Military Struggle for American Independence*, rev. ed. (Ann Arbor, Mich., 1990).

Slaughter, *Whiskey Rebellion* T. P. Slaughter, *The Whiskey Rebellion: Frontier Epilogue to the American Revolution* (New York, 1986).

Sloan, *Am. College Ideal*   D. Sloan, *The Scottish Enlightenment and the American College Ideal* (New York, 1971).

Stevenson, *Scottish Covenanters*   D. Stevenson, *Scottish Covenanters and Irish Confederates: Scottish-Irish Relations in the Mid–Seventeenth Century* (Dublin, 1981).

Stewart, *Deeper Silence*   A. T. Q. Stewart, *A Deeper Silence: The Hidden Origins of the United Irish Movement* (London, 1993).

Stewart, *Summer Soldiers*   A. T. Q. Stewart, *The Summer Soldiers: The 1798 Rebellion in Antrim and Down* (Belfast, 1995).

Taylor, *Liberty Men*   A. Taylor, *Liberty Men and Great Proprietors: The Revolutionary Settlement on the Maine Frontier, 1760–1820* (Chapel Hill, N.C., 1990).

Thayer, *Pa. Politics*   T. Thayer, *Pennsylvania Politics and the Growth of Democracy, 1740–1776* (Harrisburg, Pa., 1953).

Tillson, *Gentry & Common Folk*   A. H. Tillson, Jr., *Gentry and Common Folk: Political Culture on a Virginia Frontier, 1740–1789* (Lexington, Ky., 1991).

Trinterud, *Forming Am. Tradition*   L. J. Trinterud, *The Forming of an American Tradition: A Re-examination of Colonial Presbyterianism* (Philadelphia, 1949).

Truxes, *Irish-Am. Trade*   T. M. Truxes, *Irish-American Trade, 1660–1783* (Cambridge, England, 1988).

Tryon, *Household Manuf.*   R. M. Tryon, *Household Manufactures in the United States, 1640–1860* (Chicago, 1917).

Twomey, *Jacobins & Jeffersonians*   R. J. Twomey, *Jacobins and Jeffersonians: Anglo-American Radicalism in the United States, 1790–1820* (New York, 1989).

Tully, *Forming Am. Politics*   A. Tully, *Forming American Politics: Ideals, Interests, and Institutions in Colonial New York and Pennsylvania* (Baltimore, 1994).

Vann & Eversley, *Friends in Life*   T. Vann and D. Eversley, *Friends in Life and Death: The British and Irish Quakers in the Demographic Transition, 1650–1900* (Cambridge, England, 1992).

Wacker, *Land & People*   P. O. Wacker, *Land and People: A Cultural Geography of Preindustrial New Jersey* (New Brunswick, N.J., 1975).

Wacker & Clemens, *Land Use in N.J.*   P. O. Wacker and P. G. E. Clemens, *Land Use in Early New Jersey: A Historical Geography* (Newark, N.J., 1995).

Walker, *Intimate Strangers*   G. Walker, *Intimate Strangers: Political and Cultural Interaction between Scotland and Ulster in Modern Times* (Edinburgh, 1995).

Webster, *Hist. Presby. Church*   Rev. R. Webster, *A History of the Presbyterian Church in America . . . with Biographical Sketches of Its Early Ministers* (Philadelphia, 1858).

Weir, *Col. So. Car.*   R. M. Weir, *Colonial South Carolina: A History* (Mill-
                                          wood, N.Y., 1983).

Weis, *Col. Clergy New England*   F. L. Weis, *The Colonial Clergy and the Colonial Churches
                                          of New England* (Lancaster, Mass., 1936).

Westerkamp, *Triumph of Laity*   M. J. Westerkamp, *Triumph of the Laity: Scots-Irish Piety
                                          and the Great Awakening, 1625–1760* (New York,
                                          1988).

Whelan, *Wexford*   K. Whelan, ed., *Wexford: History and Society. Interdisci-
                                          plinary Essays on the History of an Irish County* (Dub-
                                          lin, 1987).

Wighan, *Irish Quakers*   M. J. Wighan, *The Irish Quakers: A Short History of the
                                          Religious Society of Friends in Ireland* (Dublin, 1992).

Wiley, *Chester Co.*   S. T. Wiley, *Biographical and Portrait Cyclopedia of Chester
                                          Co., Pa.*, ed. and rev. by W. S. Garner (Richmond,
                                          Ind., 1893).

Wilson, *United Irishmen*   D. A. Wilson, *United Irishmen, United States: Immigrant
                                          Radicals in the Early Republic* (Ithaca, N.Y., 1998).

Wokeck, *Trade in Strangers*   M. S. Wokeck, *Trade in Strangers: The Beginnings of
                                          Mass Migration to North America* (University Park, Pa.,
                                          1999).

Wood, *Creation of Am. Rep.*   G. S. Wood, *The Creation of the American Republic,
                                          1776–1787* (Chapel Hill, N.C., 1969).

Wood, *Radicalism of Am. Rev.*   G. S. Wood, *The Radicalism of the American Revolution*
                                          (New York, 1993).

Woolverton, *Colonial Anglicanism*   J. F. Woolverton, *Colonial Anglicanism in North America*
                                          (Detroit, 1984).

York, *Neither Kingdom*   N. L. York, *Neither Kingdom nor Nation: The Irish Quest
                                          for Constitutional Rights, 1698–1800* (Washington,
                                          D.C., 1994).

Young, *Am. Rev. Radicalism*   A. F. Young, ed., *The American Revolution: Explorations
                                          in the History of American Radicalism* (DeKalb, Ill.,
                                          1976).

Articles, Book Chapters, and Dissertations

Bartlett, "Protestant Nationalism"   T. Bartlett, "Protestant Nationalism in Eighteenth-Cen-
                                          tury Ireland," in M. O'Dea and K. Whelan, eds., *Na-
                                          tions and Nationalisms: France, Britain, Ireland and the
                                          Eighteenth-Century Context* (Oxford, 1995), 79–88.

Bríc, "Ireland, Irishmen"   M. J. Bríc, "Ireland, Irishmen, and the Broadening of
                                          the Late Eighteenth-Century Philadelphia Polity"
                                          (Ph.D. diss., Johns Hopkins University, 1991).

Calhoon, "Aedanus & Thos. Burke"   R. M. Calhoon, "Aedanus Burke and Thomas Burke:

	Revolutionary Conservatism in the Carolinas," in Chesnutt & Wilson, *Meaning So. Car. Hist.*
Carter, "Mathew Carey"	E. C. Carter II, "The Political Activities of Mathew Carey, Nationalist, 1760–1814" (Ph.D. diss., Bryn Mawr College, 1962).
Chinnici, "American Catholics"	J. P. Chinnici, "American Catholics and Religious Pluralism, 1775–1820," *J. of Ecumenical Studies,* 16 (fall 1977).
Crawford, "Economy & Society"	W. H. Crawford, "Economy and Society in South Ulster in the Eighteenth Century," *Clogher Record,* 7 (1975), 241–58.
Cullen, "Irish Diaspora"	L. M. Cullen, "The Irish Diaspora of the Seventeenth and Eighteenth Centuries," in Canny, *Europeans,* 112–49.
FitzGerald, "Irish-Speaking"	G. FitzGerald, "Estimates for Baronies of Minimal Level of Irish-Speaking amongst Successive Decennial Cohorts: 1771–1781 to 1861–1871," *PRIA,* 84C, no. 3 (1984), 117–55.
Hayton, "Anglo-Irish Attitudes"	D. Hayton, "Anglo-Irish Attitudes: Changing Perceptions of National Identity among the Protestant Ascendancy in Ireland, ca. 1690–1750," in J. Yulton and L. E. Brown, eds., *Studies in Eighteenth-Century Culture,* 17 (1987), 145–58.
Hollingsworth, "Irish Quakers"	G. Hollingsworth, "Irish Quakers in Colonial Pennsylvania: A Forgotten Segment of Society," *J. Lanc. Co. Hist. Soc.,* 79 (1975), 150–62.
Hood, "Presbyterianism"	F. J. Hood, "Presbyterianism and the New American Nation, 1783–1826: A Case Study of Religion and National Life" (Ph.D. diss., Princeton University, 1968).
Jones, "Ulster Emigration"	M. A. Jones, "Ulster Emigration, 1783–1815," in E. R. R. Green, ed., *Essays in Scotch-Irish History* (New York, 1969).
Kelly, "Resumption of Emigration"	J. Kelly, "The Resumption of Emigration from Ireland after the American War of Independence, 1783–1787," *Studia Hibernica,* 24 (1984–88), 61–88.
Kennedy & Miller, "Long Retreat"	L. Kennedy and K. A. Miller, "The Long Retreat: Protestants, Economy and Society, 1660–1926," in R. Gillespie and G. Moran, eds., *Longford: Essays in County History* (Dublin, 1991), 31–62.
Lockhart, "Quakers & Emigration"	A. Lockhart, "The Quakers and Emigration from Ireland to the North American Colonies," *QH,* 77 (fall 1988), 67–92.

Mac Suibhne, "Up Not Out" B. Mac Suibhne, "Up Not Out: Why Did Northwest Ulster Not Rise in 1798?" in C. Póirtéir, ed., *The Great Irish Rebellion of 1798* (Cork, 1798).

McAleer, "'Civil Strangers'" Margaret H. McAleer, "'Civil Strangers': Philadelphia's Irish in the Early National Period" (Ph.D. diss., Georgetown University, 1997).

McBride, "School of Virtue" I. McBride, "The School of Virtue: Francis Hutcheson, Irish Presbyterians, and the Scottish Enlightenment," in Boyce et al., *Political Thought,* 73–99.

Middleton, "Interments" Rev. T. C. Middleton, "Interments in St. Mary's Burying Ground, Philadelphia, from 1788 to 1800," *Rec. Am. Cath. Hist. Soc. Phila.,* 5 (1894), 19–87.

O'Hare, "Quakerism" M. P. O'Hare, "Quakerism in the Carlow and Kildare Area, 1650–1850," *J. of the County Kildare Archaeological Society,* 17 (1991), 106–17.

Shankman, "Democracy in Pa." A. Shankman, "Democracy in Pennsylvania: Political, Social, and Economic Arguments in the Jeffersonian Party, 1790–1820" (Ph.D. diss., Princeton University, 1997).

Wangler, "Religious Exercises" T. E. Wangler, "Daly Religious Exercises of the American Catholic Laity in the Late Eighteenth Century," *Rec. Am. Cath. Hist. Soc. Phila.,* 108, nos. 3–4 (fall–winter 1997–98), 1–23.

Weis, "Col. Clergy Middle Colonies" F. L. Weis, "The Colonial Clergy of the Middle Colonies: New York, New Jersey, and Pennsylvania, 1628–1776," *American Antiquarian Society, Proceedings,* 66, part 2 (1957).

Wells, "Famine of 1799–1801" R. Wells, "The Irish Famine of 1799–1801: Market Culture, Moral Economies and Social Protest," in A. Randall and A. Charlesworth, eds., *Markets, Market Culture and Popular Protest in Eighteenth-Century Britain and Ireland* (Liverpool, 1996), 163–93.

Wingo, "Politics, Society, & Religion" B. C. G. Wingo, "Politics, Society, and Religion: The Presbyterian Clergy of Pennsylvania, New Jersey, and New York, and the Formation of the Nation, 1775–1808" (Ph.D. diss., Tulane Univerity, 1976).

SOURCES ✳

Irish demographic sources, both published and unpublished, are listed separately in appendix 2.

1. James Wansbrough, 1700–1728
Because of the conversion of several descendants to the Society of Friends, the Sheppard-Wansbrough letters are located in the Quaker Collection in the Haverford College Library, Haverford,

Pennsylvania, and catalogued as Ms. 858. We wish to thank the Haverford College Library for permission to publish, and Eva W. Myer of the Quaker Collection, Carl L. West, librarian at the Cumberland County Historical Society, Greenwich, New Jersey, and especially Dr. Kevin Herlihy of St. Joseph's University, Philadelphia, for research assistance.

On late seventeenth-century emigration from southern Ireland, generally, see: Cullen, "Irish Diaspora"; and Lockhart, *Some Aspects*. Published works on the Baptists in Ireland include: H. D. Gribbon, "Irish Baptists in the Nineteenth Century: Economic and Social Background," *Irish Baptist Historical Society J.*, 16 (1983–84), 4–18, and "Prominent Irish Baptists of the Eighteenth Century," *Irish Baptist Historical Society Journal,* 4, no. 8 (1996–97), 25–44; J. Thompson, "The Irish Baptist Association in the Eighteenth Century," *Irish Baptist Historical Society Journal,* 17 (1984–85), 18–29; and especially the following essays by K. Herlihy: "'A Gay and Flattering World': Irish Baptist Piety and Perspective, 1650–1780," in Herlihy, *Religion of Irish Dissent,* 48–67; "The Early Eighteenth Century Irish Baptists: Two Letters," *IESH,* 19 (1992), 71–76; and "'The Faithful Remnant': Irish Baptists, 1650–1750," in Herlihy, *Irish Dissenting Tradition,* 65–80, as well as the accompanying essays by R. Gillespie and T. C. Barnard. On Irish Baptists and other Cromwellian settlers in their social, religious, and political contexts, also see: Barnard, *Cromwellian Ireland*; N. Canny, "English Migration into and across the Atlantic during the Seventeenth and Eighteenth Centuries," in Canny, *Europeans,* 39–75; Connolly, *Religion, Law & Power,* and "The Defence of Protestant Ireland, 1660–1760," in Bartlett & Jeffery, *Military History,* 231–46; and especially Greaves, *God's Other Children*; Kilroy, *Protestant Dissent*; and Prendergast, *Cromwellian Settlement*. On Baptist–Quaker relationships, see the aforementioned works by Barnard (*Cromwellian Ireland*), Greaves, Herlihy, and Kilroy, as well as T. L. Underwood, *Primitivism, Radicalism, and the Lamb's War: The Baptist–Quaker Conflict in Seventeenth-Century England* (New York, 1997).

On Baptists and other New English in County Tipperary, see: I. Murphy, *The Diocese of Killaloe in the Eighteenth Century* (Dublin, 1991); T. P. Power, *Land, Politics, and Society in Eighteenth-Century Tipperary* (Oxford, 1993); W. Nolan and T. G. McGrath, eds., *Tipperary: History and Society* (Templeogue, County Dublin, 1985); and on their early nineteenth-century emigration, B. S. Elliott, *Irish Migrants in the Canadas: A New Approach* (Montreal, 1988). Modern scholarship on County Westmeath is much sparser, but see: Casey & Rowan, *No. Leinster*; and (for Rathconrath barony) Kennedy & Miller, "Long Retreat."

On the Irish Quaker origins of the proprietors and promoters of West Jersey colonies, see: Grubb, *Quakers;* and W. Stockdale, *The Great Cry of Oppression* (Dublin, 1683). References to the Shepherds/Sheppards or their colony on the Cohansey River are in: T. Cushing and C. E. Sheppard, *History of the Counties of Gloucester, Salem, and Cumberland* (Philadelphia, 1883); McCormick, *New Jersey*; J. E. Pomfret, *The Province of West New Jersey, 1609–1702* (Princeton, 1956); W. L. Sheppard, "Some Early Immigrants from Ireland to New Jersey," *American Genealogist,* 50 (1974), 153–55; T. Shourds, *History and Genealogy of Fenwick's Colony* (1876; repr. Baltimore, 1976); G. Thomas, *Historical Description of the Province and Country of West-New-Jersey in America* (London, 1698); Wacker, *Land and People;* Wacker & Clemens, *Land Use in N.J.;* and W. A. Whitehead et al., *N. J. Arch.,* 1st ser., vols. 2 (1881); 4 (1882); 5 (1882); 23 (1901); 30 (1918); and 32 (1924).

2. Alexander Crawford, 1736

Crawford's letter of 21 July 1736 is located in the National Archives of Scotland, Edinburgh, catalogued as doc. 10/1421/12/489 in the Broughton and Cally Muniments Mss. (G.D. 10), which also contain other letters, petitions, etc., relevant to Alexander Murray's Irish estates. We are grateful to Dr. Graeme Kirkham of Eynsham, Oxford, for bringing Crawford's letter to our attention, the National Archives of Scotland and the Murray Usher Foundation, Cally Estate Office, Gatehouse of Fleet, Scotland, for permission to publish, and David J. Brown of the Scottish Record Office and especially Ann Barry of Edinburgh for research assistance.

On the Ulster Plantation and eighteenth-century Ulster society and emigration, generally, we have drawn on numerous studies for this and the following chapters, including: J. Bardon, *A History of Ulster* (Belfast, 1992); Blethen & Wood, *Ulster & No. America,* especially G. Kirkham, "Ulster Emigration to North America, 1680–1720," 76–117; Canny, *Europeans,* especially the essays on English and Scottish migration to Ireland by Canny and by T. C. Smout et al., respectively; Crawford, "Economy and Society"; W. H. Crawford, *Domestic Industry in Ireland: The Experience of the Linen Industry* (Dublin, 1972); Dickson, *Ulster Emigration;* M. W. Dowling, *Tenant Right and Agrarian Society in Ulster, 1600–1870* (Dublin, 1999); R. Gillespie, *Colonial Ulster: The Settlement of East Ulster, 1600–1641* (Cork, 1985); W. A. Macafee, "The Movement of British Settlers into Ulster during the Seventeenth Century," *Familia,* 2, no. 8 (1992), 94–111; M. Perceval-Maxwell, *The Scottish Migration to Ulster in the Reign of James I* (London, 1973); Robinson, *Plantation of Ulster;* Roebuck, *Plantation to Partition,* especially the essays by Macafee and Morgan, Kirkham, and Roebuck; Stevenson, *Scottish Covenanters;* and A. T. Q. Stewart, *The Narrow Ground: Aspects of Ulster, 1609–1969* (London, 1977).

Specifically on County Donegal, Killymard parish, and the Murray estates, see: W. H. Crawford, ed., "The Murray of Broughton Estate, 1730: 'The Several Answers and Remarks made by Thomas Addi of Donnaghadee . . . ,'" *Donegal Annual,* 12 (1977), 22–39, quotations in text from p. 37; Day & McWilliams, *OSM,* vol. 39, *Parishes of County Donegal II* (1997); Lewis, *TDI,* vol. 2; Nolan et al., *Donegal,* chapters 10–13; and especially the following essays by G. Kirkham: "Economic Diversification in a Marginal Economy: A Case Study," in Roebuck, *Plantation to Partition;* "'No More to Be Got off the Cat but the Skin': Management, Landholding and Economic Change on the Murry of Broughton Estate, 1670–1755," in Nolan et al., *Donegal,* 357–380, quotations in text from pp. 364, 371; and "'To Pay the Rent and Lay Up Riches': Economic Opportunity in Eighteenth-Century Northwest Ulster," in R. Mitchison and P. Roebuck, eds., *Economy and Society in Scotland and Ireland, 1500–1939* (Edinburgh, 1988).

3. David Lindsey, 1758

A copy of David Lindsey's 1758 letter is located in T. 2439 (formerly in T.2269), in PRONI, with additional family materials in D.1660. We are grateful to the Ulster Historical Foundation, Belfast, and to the Deputy Keeper of Records, PRONI, for permission to publish, and to Dr. Ann McVeigh of PRONI, Helen M. Wilson of the Historical Society of Western Pennsylvania, Pittsburgh, and John C. Shelly of the Bureau of Archives and History, Pennsylvania Historical and Museum Commission, Harrisburg, for research assistance.

On eighteenth-century Ulster society and emigration, see Dickson, *Ulster Emigration,* and the other works cited for chapter 2. On County Derry and Desertmartin parish, 1740–1830s, see: Day & McWilliams, *OSM,* vol. 31, *Parishes of Co. Londonderry XI, 1821, 1833, 1836–7* (1995); Lewis, *TDI,* vol. 1; and O'Brien, *Derry and Londonderry,* especially the essays by McCourt, Currie, and Bell. On the immigrant Lindseys and their offspring, see M. I. Lindsay, *The Lindsays of America: A Genealogical Narrative* (Albany, N.Y., 1889); and the eighteenth-century Pennsylvania tax and land records, published by county in *Pa. Arch.,* 3rd ser., vols. 11–26 (Harrisburg, Pa., 1897).

4. Henry Johnston, 1773–1800

The Henry Johnston letters are catalogued as T.3578 in PRONI; for permission to publish, we are grateful to Mrs. Henrietta Gerwitz of West Valley, New York, and to the Deputy Keeper of Records, PRONI; thanks also to John C. Shelly of the Bur. Arch. & Hist., PHMC, for data on Moses Johnston's military service in the American Revolution, and to Professor Emeritus A. T. Q. Stewart of Queen's University, Belfast, for research assistance.

On late eighteenth-century County Down, see: W. H. Crawford, "Change in Ulster in the Late Eighteenth Century," in Bartlett and Hayton, *Penal Era*, 186–203; Cohen, *Linen, Family & Community*; W. A. Maguire, *The Downshire Estates in Ireland, 1801–1845* (Oxford, 1972); and Proudfoot, *Down*. Other sources include: Lewis, *TDI*, vol. 1; and Day & McWilliams, *OSM*, vol. 12, *Parishes of County Down III, 1833–8* (1992); and Census of Ireland 1821: Occupations (Ulster), 319.

On sectarian and political developments in east Ulster, see: N. Curtin, *United Irishmen*, and "Rebels and Radicals: The United Irishmen in County Down," in Proudfoot, *Down*, 267–96; J. S. Donnelly, Jr., "Hearts of Oak, Hearts of Steel," *Studia Hibernica*, 21 (1981), 7–73; Elliott, *Partners in Revolution*; M. Hill, B. Turner, and K. Dawson, eds., *1798 Rebellion in County Down* (Newtownards, County Down, 1998); W. A. Maguire, "Lord Donegall and the Hearts of Steel," *IHS*, 21, no. 84 (September 1979), 351–76; D. W. Miller, "The Armagh Troubles, 1784–95," in S. Clark and J. S. Donnelly, Jr., eds., *Irish Peasants: Violence and Political Unrest, 1780–1914* (Madison, Wis., 1983), 155–91, and *Peep O' Day Boys and Defenders: Selected Documents on the County Armagh Disturbances, 1784–96* (Belfast, 1990); and Stewart, *Summer Soldiers*.

On Lancaster County, Pennsylvania, see: A. Harris, *A Biographical History of Lancaster County* (Lancaster, 1872); F. Ellis and S. Evans, *History of Lancaster County* (Philadelphia, 1883); and Lemon, *Best Poor Man's Country*. On the Genesee country, New York, see: F. W. Beers, ed., *Gazeteer and Biographical Record of Genesee County, N.Y.* (Syracuse, N.Y., 1890); and L. R. Doty, ed., *History of the Genessee Country*, vol. 1 (Chicago, 1925). For specific references to Moses Johnston, see: *Pa. Arch.*, 3rd ser., vol. 17 (1897), p. 286 (1782 Pa. Supply Tax list); *History of Monroe County, New York* (Philadelphia, 1877), p. 20 (1800 New York tax records); the 1790 U.S. Census Mss. (Leacock Township, Lancaster County, Pa.), p. 136; and the 1810 U.S. Census Mss. (Riga, Genessee County, N.Y.), p. 143.

5. Walter Corish Devereux, 1798

Walter and Catherine Devereux's letters are among the Devereux Papers in the Friedsam Library Archive at St. Bonaventure University, St. Bonaventure, New York. The authors wish to thank the St. Bonaventure University Archive for permission to publish; Lorraine Welsh, assistant archivist, for her assistance; and, especially, John Devereux Kernan of Hamden, Connecticut, for his advice in preparing this essay. Thanks also to Mr. Kernan and to Matthew Garrett for permission to publish the portrait of John C. Devereux of Utica.

On early Catholic and southern Irish emigration to North America, generally, see: Bríc, "Ireland, Irishmen"; Cullen, "Irish Diaspora"; Doyle, *Ireland, Irishmen*; Kelly, "Resumption of Emigration"; and Lockhart, *Some Aspects*.

On County Wexford and the United Irish Rebellion, see: Elliott, *Partners in Revolution*; D. Gahan, *The People's Rising: Wexford, 1798* (Dublin, 1995); D. Keogh and N. Furlong, eds., *The Mighty Wave: The 1798 Rebellion in Wexford* (Blackrock, County Dublin, 1996); T. Packenham, *The Year of Liberty* (London, 1969); and the following studies by Kevin Whelan: "The Catholic Community in Eighteenth-Century Wexford," in Power & Whelan, *Endurance*, 129–70; "The Religious Factor in the 1798 Rebellion in County Wexford," in P. O'Flanagan, P. Ferguson, and Whelan, eds., *Rural Ireland: Modernisation and Change, 1600–1900* (Cork, 1987), 62–85; and Whelan, *Wexford*, especially chapters 8–11.

On Walter C. Devereux's family in Wexford and America, see: C. Lewis III and J. D. Kernan, *Devereux of the Leap: Nicholas Devereux, 1791–1855* (St. Bonaventure, N.Y., 1974). On the Devereux brothers' careers in Utica, see: M. M. Bagg, ed., *Memorial History of Utica* (Syracuse, N.Y., 1892); P. Jones, *Annals and Recollections of Oneida County* (Rome, N.Y., 1851); A. G. Noble, *An Ethnic Geography of Early Utica, New York* (Lewiston, N.Y., 1999); H. G. Spafford, *A Gazetteer of the State of New York* (Albany, 1813); and D. E. Wager, ed., *Our County and Its People: A Descriptive Work on Oneida County* (Boston, 1896). References to the Devereuxs' assistance to later Irish immigrants are in P. Bates, *Donabate and Portrane—A History* (Cork, 1988), for which reference we thank Prof. Kevin Kenny of Boston College.

6. Margaret Wright, 1808

The McNish Family Papers (including the Wright, Kerr, and Beatty letters, as well as McNish property tax assessments, etc.) are catalogued as Ms. 754 in the Division of Rare and Manuscript Collections, Cornell University Library, Ithaca, New York. We are grateful to the Cornell University Library for permission to publish Margaret Wright's 1808 letter and to its archivists, Kathleen Jacklin and Elaine Engst, to Dr. Peter Robinson of the Ulster Folk and Transport Museum, Cultra, Holywood, County Down, and to Dr. Brian Trainor, former director of the Ulster Historical Foundation, Belfast, for research assistance.

On early nineteenth-century Ulster emigration, see: Doyle, *Ireland, Irishmen;* Miller, *Emigrants & Exiles,* chapter 5; and Jones, "Ulster Emigration." For Irish local and regional background, see especially: W. H. Crawford, "Change in Ulster in the Late Eighteenth Century," in Bartlett and Hayton, *Penal Era and Golden Age,* 186–203; Crawford, "Economy and Society"; and B. McEvoy, "The United Irishmen in County Tyrone," parts 1–2, *Seanchas Ardmhacha,* 3, no. 2 (1959), 283–314, and 4, no. 1 (1960–61), 1–32. On Associate (Seceding) Presbyterians in Ulster and America, see: Fisk, *Scottish High Church Tradition;* Rev. R. Lathan, *History of the Associate Reformed Synod of the South* (Harrisburg, Pa., 1882); Rev. D. Stewart, *The Seceders in Ireland, with Annals of Their Congregations* (Belfast, 1950); and Rev. J. B. Woodburn, *The Ulster Scot: His History and Religion* (London, 1914); and on Irish Seceders' political conservatism, see: McBride, *Scripture Politics.* On the occupational structure of Donaghmore parish, see: Census of Ireland 1821: Occupations (Ulster), 319; and Lewis, *TDI,* vol. 1. On the size, rent, and value of John Kerr's and Charles Beatty's farms, see: Rent Rolls on Lord Ranfurly's Estate, ca. 1771 (D.235/56, PRONI); List of Lessees and Tenants on Lord Ranfurly's Estate, 1771 (D.235/158, I.239, PRONI); and TAB: Donaghmore Parish (1826) in PRONI.

Information on the New Perth/Salem settlement and the McNish family is in: *History and Biography of Washington County* (Richmond, Ind., 1894); M. S. and E. F. Jackson, comps., *Death Notices from Washington County, New York, Newspapers 1799–1880* and *Marriage Notices from Washington County, New York, Newspapers, 1799–1880* (both Bowie, Md., 1995); C. Johnson, *History of Washington Co.* (Philadelphia, 1878); Moffat, *Pop. Hist. of E. U.S. Cities;* H. G. Spafford, *A Gazetteer of the State of New York* (Albany, N.Y., 1813); W. L. Stone, ed., *Washington County, New York: Its History to the Close of the Nineteenth Century* (New York, 1901); and H. Williams et al., *The Salem Book: Records of the Past and Glimpses of the Present* (Salem, N.Y., 1896). On McNish's war service and marriage, see: Revolutionary War Bounty Applications, U.S. National Archives, microfilm 804, reel 1699 (Sarah McNish, 1837/8). McNish's family is listed in the U.S. Census Mss., New York, Washington County, Salem, 1790–1840 (microfilm).

7. Anonymous Poet, Mid- to Late 1700s

The poem was collected in the field and published in E. Ó Muirgheasa, comp., *Céad de Cheoltaibh Uladh* (Dublin, 1915), 139–40; trans. by B. D. Boling. For data on Derryvullan parish and County Fermanagh, see: J. Crawford, comp., *Lisbellaw and Surrounding District: A Gazetteer* (Enniskillen, 1992); Day & McWilliams, *OSM*, vol. 14, *Parishes of Co. Fermanagh II, 1834–5* (1992); Lewis, *TDI*, vol. 1; FitzGerald, "Irish-Speaking"; and Robinson, *Plantation of Ulster*. On Irish Catholic traditional culture, literature, and early emigration, generally, see: N. Canny, "The Formation of the Irish Mind: Religion, Politics and Gaelic Irish Literature, 1680–1812," *P & P*, 95 (1982), 91–116; D. Corkery, *The Hidden Ireland: A Study of Gaelic Munster in the Eighteenth Century* (Dublin, 1924); Doyle, *Ireland, Irishmen;* Miller, *Emigrants & Exiles,* chapters 3–4; J. Wooding, ed., *The Otherworld Voyage in Irish Literature and History* (Dublin, 1999). We thank Brian McGinn of Alexandria, Virginia, for bringing the 1490s English references to the "New Isle" to our attention.

8. Rev. James MacSparran, 1752

Only three copies of *America Dissected* are known to exist, one of them in the John Carter Brown Library of Brown University, Providence, Rhode Island, and reproduced on microcard in *Evans' Early Am. Imprints*. Our text is an edited replica of the original published in Wilkins Updike, *A History of the Episcopal Church in Narragansett, Rhode Island* (1847), second enlarged ed. by Rev. D. Goodwin (Boston, 1907). Unpublished correspondence by and about MacSparran, 1715–24, is in the Society for the Propagation of the Gospel (S.P.G.) Letterbooks, series A, vols. 10–18 (on microfilm). For research assistance, we are grateful to Prof. Patricia U. Bonomi of New York University and Raymond Refaussé, librarian and archivist at the Representative Church Body Library, Dublin.

General works on religion and the Anglican church in colonial America include: Bonomi, *Cope of Heaven;* Bridenbaugh, *Mitre & Sceptre;* Butler, *Sea of Faith;* F. V. Mills, Sr., "Anglican Expansion in Colonial America," *Hist. Mag. Prot. Episc. Ch.,* 39 (1970), 315–24; B. E. Steiner, "New England Anglicanism: A Genteel Faith," *WMQ,* 3rd ser., 27 (1970), 122–35; Rev. H. P. Thompson, *Into All Lands: The History of the Society for the Propagation of the Gospel in Foreign Parts, 1701–1950* (London, 1951); and Woolverton, *Colonial Anglicanism.*

In addition to Updike, *History*, and Bridenbaugh, *Mitre & Sceptre*, published information on MacSparran, his church, and neighbors in Rhode Island can be found in: S. G. Arnold, *History of the State of Rhode Island and Providence Plantations,* vol. 2 (New York, 1860); T. W. Bicknell, *History of the State of Rhode Island and Providence Plantations,* vol. 2 (New York, 1920); J. Clement, comp., "Anglican Clergymen Licensed to the American Colonies, 1710–1744, with Biographical Sketches," *Hist. Mag. Prot. Episc. Ch.,* 27, no. 3 (September 1948), 207–50; Rev. D. Goodwin, ed., *A Letter Book and Abstract of Out Services Written during the Years 1743–1751 by the Rev. James MacSparran* (Boston, 1899), quotations in text from pp. xv–xvi, xli, and xliii; S. V. James, *Colonial Rhode Island: A History* (New York, 1975); W. G. McLoughlin, *Rhode Island: A Bicentennial History* (New York, 1978); W. W. Manross, comp., *The Fulham Papers in the Lambeth Palace Library: American Colonial Section,*

Calendar and Indexes (Oxford, 1965), for correspondence by and about MacSparran, 1719–1754; Sprague, *Annals Am. Pulpit*, 5 (1861); Weis, *Col. Clergy New England*; and entries for MacSparran in *DAB* and *DNB*.

On MacSparran's Scottish background, see: R. Blaney, *Presbyterians and the Irish Language* (Belfast, 1996); J. H. Ohlmeyer, *Civil War and Restoration in the Three Stuart Kingdoms: The Career of Randal MacDonnell, Marquis of Antrim, 1609–1683* (Cambridge, England, 1993); Stevenson, *Scottish Covenanters*; D. S. Thomson, *The Companion to Gaelic Scotland* (Oxford, 1983). Recent historical literature relevant to the issue of seventeenth- and eighteenth-century Irish "national" identities is voluminous, but see especially: Bartlett, *Fall and Rise;* Bartlett, "Protestant Nationalism"; Claydon & MacBride, *Protestantism;* Connolly, *Religion, Law & Power;* R. Eccleshall, "Anglican Political Thought in the Century after the Revolution of 1688," in Boyce et al., *Political Thought*, 36–72; Hayton, "Anglo-Irish Attitudes"; Hill, *Patriots to Unionists;* Leerssen, *Mere Irish;* J. G. Simms, *Colonial Nationalism, 1698–1776: Molyneux's "The Case of Ireland . . . Stated"* (Cork, 1976); and York, *Neither Kingdom*.

On the Church of Ireland, see: T. C. Barnard, "The Government and Irish Dissent," in Herlihy, *Politics of Irish Dissent*, 9–27; D. Bowen, *History and the Shaping of Irish Protestantism* (New York, 1995); and the essays by T. Barnard, S. J. Connolly, and D. Hayton in Ford et al., *As By Law Established*. On the Money Bill dispute, see: Dickson, *New Foundations;* J. L. McCracken, "The Rise of Colonial Nationalism, 1714–1760," in Moody & Vaughn, *NHI 4*, 105–22; and D. O'Donovan, "The Money Bill Dispute of 1753," in Bartlett & Hayton, *Penal Era*. For data on Dungiven parish see: W. S. Mason, *Statistical Account, or Parochial Survey of Ireland*, vol. 1 (Dublin, 1814); and Lewis, *TDI*.

Biographical data in the footnotes are from: Burtchaell and Sadlier, *Alumni Dublinenses*, on Rev. Paul Limrick and the Carys; W. Maziere Brady, *Clerical and Parochial Records of Cork, Cloyne, and Ross*, vol. 1 (Dublin, 1863), on Rev. Limrick; Webster, *Hist. Presby. Church,* on Rev. Hugh Conn; *Land Owners in Ireland, 1876*, on the Hamiltons of Ballyfatten, County Tyrone; and *Burke's Peerage* (1967 ed.), on Lady Cork. For the Mather family's Irish associations, see: Brock, *Scotus Americanus;* Greaves, *God's Other Children;* R. Middlekauff, *The Mathers: Three Generations of Puritan Intellectuals, 1596–1728* (New York, 1971); and S. ffeary-Smyrl, "'Theatres of Worship': Dissenting Meeting Houses in Dublin, 1650–1750," in Herlihy, *Irish Dissenting Tradition*, 49–64.

9. Robert Parke, 1725

Robert Parke's 1725 letter is located in the Chester County Miscellaneous Papers, 1684–1847, vol. 1, pp. 87–92, in the Historical Society of Pennsylvania, Philadelphia; it appears to be a first draft, hence the blank spaces for data to be filled in later. We are grateful to Jeffrey Webb of the University of Chicago for alerting us to the location of this document; to Linda Stanley, manuscripts and archives curator, HSP, for research assistance; and to the HSP for permission to publish. There are also at least two early published variants of Parke's letter in: C. A. Hanna, *The Scotch-Irish* (1902; repr. Baltimore, 1998), vol. 2, 64–67; and in Myers, *Irish Quakers into Pa.*, 69–79, which also provides extensive information on the Parke family. Vital data on the Parkes and Valentines in Ireland are in the Carlow Monthly Meeting's Marriage, Birth, and Death Registers, now deposited in the Historical Library of the Religious Society of Friends in Ireland, in Dublin, whose curator, Mrs. Mary Shackleton, we thank for her research assistance. The Parke family in Chester County is also mentioned in the diary of Ketchtichia Sudbury, a Carlow Quaker missionary to America, 1725–1727 (microfilm p.1560, NLI); we thank Dr. Kevin Herlihy of Villanova University for a typescript of this manuscript.

On early southern Irish emigration, generally, see: Doyle, *Ireland, Irishmen;* and Lockhart, *Some Aspects;* and on its causes in the 1720s, J. Kelly, "Harvests and Hardship: Famine and Scarcity in Ireland in the Late 1720s," *Studia Hibernica,* 26 (1991–92), 65–106. On the Quakers in Ireland, see: T. C. Barnard, "Identities, Ethnicity and Tradition among Irish Dissenters, c. 1650–1750," 29–48, and R. S. Harrison, "'As a Garden Enclosed': The Emergence of Irish Quakers, 1650–1750," 81–95, both in Herlihy, *Irish Dissenting Tradition;* Beckett, *Protestant Dissent;* Greaves, *God's Other Children;* Grubb, *Quakers;* Kilroy, *Protestant Dissent;* O'Hare, "Quakerism"; Vann & Eversley, *Friends in Life;* and Wighan, *Irish Quakers.*

On Irish Quaker emigration and settlement in Pennsylvania, see: Hollingsworth, "Irish Quakers"; Lockhart, "Quakers & Emigration"; and especially Myers, *Irish Quakers into Pa.* On eighteenth-century Chester County, generally, see: Futhey & Cope, *History of Chester Co.;* C. W. Heathcote, *A History of Chester County* (Harrisburg, 1932); Lemon, *Best Poor Man's Country;* R. S. Warden, "Chester County," in Frantz & Pencak, *Beyond Philadelphia,* 1–22; and Wiley, *Chester Co.,* which contains specific data on the Parke and Valentine families. On the Parke, Thornton, Coates, and other holdings in late eighteenth-century Chester County, see the tax lists in: *Pa. Arch.,* 3rd ser., vols. 11–12 (1897).

10. John Rea, 1765

John Rea's letter was published in the 3 September 1765 issue of the *Belfast News-Letter,* copies of which are available in the Ulster Linen Hall Library, Belfast. In addition, transcripts of Rea's letter are located in D.3561 and MIC 19/Reel 14 in PRONI. Rea's letter and other items pertinent to the Queensborough project are reprinted in "The Irish Settlements in Colonial Georgia: Extracts from the *Belfast News-Letter,* 1763–76," a typescript in the Georgia Historical Society, Savannah. We thank Jan Flores, archivist at the Georgia Historical Society, Mark Graham of Belfast, and especially Prof. Michael Montgomery, University of South Carolina, for research assistance.

On County Down, generally, see: Proudfoot, *Down.* On Magheradrool, Drumbo and adjacent parishes, see: Day & McWilliams, *OSM,* vol. 7, *Parishes of County Down II, 1832–4, 1837,* and vol. 17, *Parishes of County Down IV, 1833–7* (1991 and 1992); Lewis, *TDI;* and Griffith's *Valuation:* Drumbo (1863), in PRONI.

On colonial Georgia, see: E. J. Cashin, ed., *Colonial Augusta: "Key of the Indian Countrey"* (Macon, Ga., 1986); K. Coleman, *Colonial Georgia: A History* (N.Y., 1976); H. E. Davis, *The Fledgling Province: Social and Cultural Life in Colonial Georgia, 1733–1776* (Chapel Hill, N.C., 1976); H. H. Jackson and P. Spalding, eds., *Forty Years of Diversity: Essays on Colonial Georgia* (Athens, Ga., 1984); and T. R. Reese, *Colonial Georgia: A Study in British Imperial Policy in the Eighteenth Century* (Athens, Ga., 1963). For estimates of Georgia's Irish-stock population in 1790, see Doyle, *Ireland, Irishmen,* 75–76.

On John Rea, George Galphin, and the Queensborough settlement, see: Dickson, *Ulster Emigration,* 164–73; J. E. Doan, "How the Irish and Scots Became Indians: Colonial Traders and Agents and the Southeastern Tribes," *New Hibernia Review,* 3, no. 3 (autumn 1999), 9–19; G. F. Fenwick, "Portrait of an Irish Entrepreneur in Colonial Augusta: John Rae, 1708–1772," *Ga. Hist. Q.,* 83, no. 3 (fall 1999), 427–47; F. P. Hamer, "Indian Traders, Land and Power—Comparative Study of George Galphin on the Southern Frontier and Three Northern Traders" (M.A. thesis, University of South Carolina, 1982); D. K. MacDowell, "George Galphin: Nabob of the Backwoods," *South Carolina History Illustrated,* 1, no. 1 (February 1970), 51–56; M. Montgomery, "A Tale of Two

Georges: The Language of Irish Indian Traders in Colonial America," in J. Kallen, ed., *Focus on Ireland* (Amsterdam, 1996); Savannah Unit, Georgia Writers' Project, "Rae's Hall Plantation," *Ga. Hist. Q.*, 26 (1942), 236–41; and especially E. R. R. Green, "Queensborough Township: Scotch-Irish Emigration and the Expansion of Georgia," *WMQ*, 3rd ser., 17 (1960), 183–99. Other references to John Rea and Queensborough are in: K. Coleman and M. Ready, eds., *Colonial Records of the State of Georgia*, vols. 27–28 (Athens, Ga., 1976), vols. 27–28; E. Merton and A. B. Saye, eds., *A List of the Early Settlers of Georgia*, 2nd ed. (Athens, Ga., 1967).

11. James Orr, 1811

John Dunlap's correspondence, including James Orr's 1 June 1811 letter, is catalogued as T.1336/1 in PRONI; we thank Canon W. A. Delap and the Deputy Keeper of Records, PRONI, for permission to publish Orr's letter. William and Ann Stewart's 1762 passport and Robert McNaire's 1762 transfer certificate are catalogued as T.2439/2 and T.1315, respectively, also in PRONI.

On the Strabane region, see: J. Bradley et al., *The Fair River Valley: Strabane through the Ages* (Belfast, 2000); J. Dooher, "Strabane and the North West in the Decade of Rebellion," *Ulster Local Studies*, 19, no. 1 (1997), 7–31; Lewis, *TDI*; Mac Suibhne, "Up Not Out"; and Murphy, *Derry, Donegal*. On Strabane in the American Revolution, see: S. Conway, *The British Isles and the War of American Independence* (Oxford, 2000), ch. 8. On the Orr and Rutherford families in Strabane, see: W. Crawford, *A History of Ireland, from the Earliest Period to the Present Time* (Strabane, 1783), vol. 1, list of subscribers; D. S. Schlegel, comp., *Irish Genealogical Abstracts from the "Londonderry Journal," 1772–1784* (Baltimore, 1990); and *Pigot's Irish Directories* (Dublin, 1820, 1824).

On the Rutherfords' 1811 voyage to America, see: M. Tepper, ed., *New World Emigrants: A Consolidation of Ship Passenger Lists*, vol. 2 (Baltimore, 1988). In Philadelphia, for Alexander Rutherford, tanner, see F. White, *The Philadelphia Directory* (1785), and Barratt & Sachse, *Freemasonry in Pa.*; Thomas Orr, merchant, can be found in various Philadelphia directories from 1793 through 1811. On John Dunlap, see *DAB*, vol. 3; Campbell, *Friendly Sons of St. Patrick*; Barratt & Sachse, *Freemasonry in Pennsylvania*; and Scharf & Westcott, *Hist. of Philadelphia*. On Irish immigrants in early Philadelphia, generally, see: Bríc, "Ireland, Irishmen"; Clark, *Irish in Philadelphia*; and McAleer, "'Civil Strangers.'" On the Irish in Philadelphia politics during the Revolutionary and Federalist periods, see chapters 52, 56, 58, and 63.

12. John Smilie, 1762

John and Robert Smilie's letters are in the 13 May 1763 issue of the *Belfast News-Letter*, original and microfilm copies of which are in the Linen Hall Library in Belfast; the letters are also printed in Dickson, *Ulster Emigration*, 288–90. Information on Smilie families in north County Down are available in the TABs and in Griffith's *Valuation*, both in PRONI, for the parishes of Bangor, Greyabbey, Magheradrool, and Newtownards.

On eighteenth-century voyage conditions, see Dickson, *Ulster Emigration*, and Wokeck, *Trade in Strangers*. For data on the *Sally* and Captain James Taylor, see Dickson, *Ulster Emigration*, 288–90, as well as "Ship Registers for the Port of Philadelphia, 1726–1775," *PMHB*, 27 (1903), 346–70. On John Smilie's American career, see: E. Everett, "John Smilie, Forgotten Champion of Early Western Pennsylvania," *WPHM*, 33 (September–December, 1950), 77–89; R. C. Henderson, "John Smilie, Antifederalism, and the 'Dissent of the Minority,' 1787–1788," *WPHM*, 77 (1988), 235–61; and Wood, *Creation of Am. Republic*. Smilie's economic progress can be traced in the 1771–85 Pennsylvania tax lists and land warrants, in *Pa. Arch.*, 3rd ser., vols. 20 and 22–26, whence the term "Over the Mountains" describing tax-payers in western Pennsylvania (e.g. in 1782).

13. John O'Raw, 1809

John O'Raw's 1 April 1809 letter is catalogued as D.3613/1/2 in PRONI, along with biographical data supplied in 1963 by Dr. Michael Tierney, then president of University College, Dublin, to Prof. E. R. R. Green of the Queen's University, Belfast. We thank Mrs. Eibhlin Tierney and the Deputy Keeper of Records, PRONI, for permission to publish O'Raw's letter; Brian Moore O'Hara of Ballylesson, County Antrim, for Irish background information; and Patricia G. Bennett of the Charleston Library Society; Oliver B. Smalls, archivist at the College of Charleston; Kathleen Howard at the South Carolina Historical Society, Charleston; and Rev. Paul K. Thomas, archivist of the Archdiocese of Baltimore, for research on O'Raw's American career.

On Ballymena, Ballyclug, and the O'Raws there, see *Pigot's Irish Directories* (Dublin, 1820–24); Day & McWilliams, *OSM,* vol. 23, *Parishes of County Antrim VIII, 1831–5, 1837–8* (1993); Lewis, *TDI,* vol. 1; Griffith's *Valuation:* Ballymena (1863) in PRONI; and Ballymena Observer, *Old Ballymena* (Ballymena, 1938).

Sources of data on O'Raw and his relations in South Carolina include: J. W. Hagy, ed., *People and Professions of Charleston, 1782–1802* (Baltimore, 1992); B. H. Halcomb, comp., *South Carolina Naturalizations, 1783–1850* (Baltimore, 1985); K. Scott, comp., *British Aliens in the United States during the War of 1812* (Baltimore, 1979); A. H. Mitchell, *The History of the Hibernian Society of Charleston, S.C., 1799–1981* (Barnwell, S.C., 1981); *Charleston Directory and Stranger's Guide* (titles vary slightly), 1816–25; and the manuscript schedules for the 1820 U.S. Census, South Carolina, p. 36-A (on microfilm).

On the commerce in goods and emigrants between Ireland and Charleston before the Revolution, see: Truxes, *Irish-Am. Trade.* On emigrant voyages in the 1783–1814 period, see: Dickson, *Ulster Emigration,* 201–20; Miller, *Emigrants & Exiles,* 154–55 and 169–70; and D. A. Dunleavy, "Irish Emigration to the United States in the Early National Period, 1783–1830" (M.A. thesis, University College, Dublin, 1987). For background information on early nineteenth-century Charleston and South Carolina, see: W. J. Fraser, Jr., *Charleston! Charleston! The History of a Southern City* (Columbia, S.C., 1989); Klein, *Unification of Slave State;* and D. D. Wallace, *South Carolina: A Short History, 1520–1848* (Columbia, S.C., 1961); with population data from Moffat, *Pop. Hist. of E. U.S. Cities.* On Catholicism in South Carolina during the early 1800s, see: Dolan, *Am. Catholic Experience,* chap. 4; R. M. Miller and J. K. Wakelyn, eds., *Catholics in the Old South* (Macon, Ga., 1983); and P. Carey, *An Immigrant Bishop: John England's Adaptation of Irish Catholicism to American Republicanism* (Yonkers, N.Y., 1982). For opposing views of the "Charleston schism," see: Carey, *People, Priests, & Prelates;* and P. Guilday, *The Life and Times of John England, First Bishop of Charleston, 1786–1840,* two vols. (New York, 1927).

On Daniel O'Connell's crusade for Catholic emancipation and its repercussions among Irish Protestants, see: Bowen, *Protestant Crusade;* Brooke, *Ulster Presbyterianism;* F. O'Ferrall, *Catholic Emancipation: Daniel O'Connell and the Birth of Irish Democracy* (Dublin, 1985); and J. A. Reynolds, *The Catholic Emancipation Crisis in Ireland, 1823–1829* (New Haven, 1954). On competing "Irish" and "Scotch-Irish" identities in the American South, see: K. A. Miller, "'Scotch-Irish,' 'Black Irish,' and 'Real Irish': Emigrants and Identities in the Old South," in A. Bielenberg, ed., *The Irish Diaspora* (Harlow, England, 2000), 139–57.

14. Thomas Hinds, 1795

Thomas Hinds's petition is located in the Edward Carey Gardiner Collection, Historical Society of Pennsylvania, Philadelphia. We thank the Historical Society for permission to publish Hinds's petition, and Dr. Maurice Bríc of University College, Dublin, and Prof. Elizabeth A. Perkins of Centre College, Danville, Kentucky, for research assistance.

On late eighteenth-century Dublin, see: F. H. A. Aalen and K. Whelan, eds., *Dublin City and County: From Prehistory to Present* (Dublin, 1992), especially chapter 9 by L. M. Cullen; M. Craig, *Dublin, 1660–1860: A Social and Architectural History* (Dublin, 1969); Hill, *Patriots to Unionists;* and C. Maxwell, *Dublin under the Georges, 1714–1830* (London, 1936). On Rev. Henry Dabzac of Rathmines, see: Burtchaell & Sadleir, *Alumni Dublinenses.*

On Mathew Carey and the Hibernian Society, see especially: M. Carey, *Autobiography* (Brooklyn, 1942); Carter, "Mathew Carey"; J. N. Green, *Mathew Carey, Publisher and Patriot* (Philadelphia, 1985); Rowe, *Mathew Carey;* and Campbell, *Friendly Sons of St. Patrick.* On brassworkers and other artisans in mid- and late eighteenth-century Philadelphia, see: C. Bridenbaugh, *The Colonial Craftsman* (Chicago, 1964); C. S. Olton, *Artisans for Independence* (Syracuse, N.Y., 1975); and "Order of Procession . . . 4 July 1788," broadside reproduced in R. F. Weigley, ed., *Philadelphia* (New York, 1982), 165.

On the Kentucky background, see: H. E. Everman, *History of Bourbon County, 1785–1865* (Baltimore, 1977); W. H. Perrin, *History of Bourbon, Scott, Hamson, and Nicholas Counties* (Chicago, 1882); and, more generally, S. Aron, *How the West Was Lost: The Transformation of Kentucky from Daniel Boone to Henry Clay* (Baltimore, 1996); T. F. Craig, ed., *The Buzzel about Kentuck: Settling the Promised Land* (Lexington, Ky., 1999); and E. A. Perkins, *Border Life: Experience and Memory in the Revolutionary Ohio Valley* (Chapel Hill, N.C., 1998).

The 1800–1810 Kentucky censuses, land, tax, marriage, and other records were searched without conclusive results. However, see the 1794 Kentucky militia enlistment records for William Hinds, in M. J. Clark, *American Militia in the Frontier Wars, 1790–1796* (Baltimore, 1990). Also see Mrs. Hinds's brief memoir, provided in 1844 to Rev. John D. Shane, in the Draper Mss., Kentucky Papers, vol. 11 CC, p. 5 (microfilm, Western Historical Manuscripts Collection, University of Missouri, Columbia).

15. George Crockett, Jr., 1797–1807

We thank the late Mrs. Elizabeth Reeve of Orient Point, New South Wales, and her brother, James Crockett of Heversham, Cumbria, England, for permission to publish some of the 38 Crockett letters, 1796–1851, in the latter's possession, although copies are deposited in the Cumbria Record Office, Kendal. We are also grateful to Walter T. Durham of the Sumner County Historical Society, Gallatin, Tennessee, for research assistance. An earlier version of this chapter is: D. N. Doyle and K. A. Miller, "Ulster Migrants in an Age of Rebellion: The Crocketts of Raphoe," *IESH,* 22 (1995), 77–87; we thank Dr. Mary Daly of University College, Dublin, then editor of *IESH,* for permission to republish. James Steele's letter of 19 April 1796 is in the Ephraim Steele Papers (acc. 3876), Southern Historical Collection, University of North Carolina, Chapel Hill.

On County Donegal in the 1790s, see: Murphy, *Derry, Donegal;* and Nolan et al., *Donegal,* especially chapter 14 by D. Dickson. On the United Irishmen in east Donegal, see: Mac Suibhne, "Up Not Out." Other data are derived from: Lewis, *TDI,* vol. 1; and Day & McWilliams, *OSM,* vol. 39, *Parishes of County Donegal II, 1835–6* (1997). On the Crocketts' Irish holdings, see: TAB: Killea Parish, 1830 (PRONI); and Griffith's *Valuation:* Drumnashear (1858), in PRONI. On Rev.

Francis Makemie of Ramelton, County Donegal, see: Rev. J. M. Barkley, *Francis Makemie of Ramelton: Father of American Presbyterianism* (Belfast, 1981); and B. S. Schlenther, ed., *The Life and Writings of Francis Makemie* (Philadelphia, 1971).

On Scots-Irish families in Ulster and America, see: H. Donnan and G. McFarlane, "'You Get on Better with Your Own': Social Continuity and Change in Rural Northern Ireland," in P. Clancy et al., eds., *Ireland: A Sociological Profile* (Dublin, 1986), 380–99; G. K. Neville, "Kinfolks and the Covenant: Ethnic Community among the Southern Presbyterians," in J. Bennett, ed., *Proc. Am. Ethnol. Soc.* (1973), 258–74; and R. Reid, "Church Membership, Consanguineous Marriage, and Migration in a Scotch-Irish Frontier Population," *J. Fam. Hist.*, 13, no. 4 (1988), 397–414.

The Crocketts and their relations in the United States were traced in the U.S. Census, *Heads of Families . . . 1790: Tennessee* (Washington, D.C., 1908), and *North Carolina* (Baltimore, 1973); W. H. Dumont, *Tax Lists, Westmoreland County, Pennsylvania, 1786–1810* (Washington, D.C., 1968); *The New Baltimore Directory and American Register for 1800 and 1801* (Baltimore, 1800); *The Shamrock or Hibernian Chronicle* (New York, 14 September 1811), reprinted in "Some Irish Arrivals in New York and Other Ports," *JAIHS*, 3, no. 7 (1926), 24; B. Sistler, *1830 Census: Middle Tennessee* (Evanston, Ill., 1971); S. E. Lucas, Jr., *Marriages from Early Tennessee Newspapers, 1794–1851* (Eastley, S.C., 1978); and *Pa. Arch.*, 3rd ser., vols. 23–24 (1897).

The Crocketts' socioeconomic, religious, and political contexts and associates in Tennessee are described in: B. M. Barrus, M. L. Baughn, and T. H. Campbell, *A People Called Cumberland Presbyterians* (Memphis, 1972); C. A. Campbell, *The Development of Banking in Tennessee* (Nashville, 1932); T. H. Campbell, *Good News on the Frontier: A History of the Cumberland Presbyterian Church* (Memphis, 1965); W. T. Durham, *James Winchester, Tennessee Pioneer* (Gallatin, Tenn., 1979), and "Wynnewood" and "Mexican War Letters to Wynnewood," *Tenn. Hist. Q.*, 33 (1974), 149 and 389–409; S. J. Folmsbee, R. E. Corlew, and E. L. Mitchell, *Tennessee: A Short History* (Knoxville, Tenn., 1969); A. S. Goodstein, *Nashville, 1780–1860: From Frontier to City* (Gainesville, Fla., 1989); *Goodspeed's History of Tennessee, from the Earliest Time to the Present* (Chicago, 1887); F. M. Jones, *Middlemen in the Domestic Trade of the United States, 1800–1860* (Urbana, Ill., 1971); B. W. McDonnold, *History of the Cumberland Presbyterian Church* (Nashville, 1899 ed.); P. C. Welsh, *Tanning in the United States to 1850* (Washington, D.C., 1964); and [J. Woolridge et al.], *History of Nashville, Tennessee* (Nashville, 1890).

On the Sumner County background, the Fultons, Hugh Rogan, and early Gallatin, see: J. G. Cisco, *Historic Sumner County* (Nashville, 1909); W. T. Durham, *The Great Leap Forward: A History of Sumner County, Tennessee* (Gallatin, Tenn., 1969), and *Old Sumner: A History of Sumner County* (Gallatin, Tenn., 1972); C. S. Hankins, "Hugh Rogan of Counties Donegal and Sumner: Irish Acculturation in Frontier Tennessee," *Tenn. Hist. Q.*, 54 (winter 1995), 306–23; D. T. Herndon, *Centennial History of Arkansas* (Chicago, 1922), vol. 1; and L. J. White, *Politics on the Southwestern Frontier: Arkansas Territory, 1819–1836* (Memphis, 1964). For U.S. population data, see R. M. McBride and O. Meridith, eds., *Eastin Morris' Tennessee Gazeteer, 1834* (Nashville, 1971); Moffat, *Pop. Hist. of E. U.S. Cities;* and J. C. Smith, *Harper's Statistical Gazeteer* (New York, 1855). On Felix Grundy and Gen. James Winchester, see their entries in *DAB*.

16. John Blake, 1675–1676

John and Henry Blake's letters should be deposited in Mss. 10,789–90, NLI, but cannot be located. We have reproduced the least modernized transcriptions available, published in V. L. Langford, ed.,

Caribbeana, vol. 1, pt. 2 (London: April 1909), 51–57; but also see the transcripts in M. J. Blake, *Blake Family Records, 1600 to 1700* (London, 1905), which also contains genealogical data and other documents. Additional West Indian Blake correspondence, 1730s, is in M.6936/1, in the Irish National Archives, Dublin. For research assistance, we thank Prof. Marion Casey of New York University; Robert St-Cyr of New York City; Prof. Riva Berleant-Schiller of the University of Connecticut, Torrington; and especially Brian McGinn of Alexandria, Virginia.

On the Blakes and other Galway Tribes in Ireland and in West Indian and European trade, see: D. Ó Cearbhaill, ed., *Galway: Town and Gown, 1484–1984* (Dublin, 1984), esp. the essays by G. Mac Niocaill, N. Canny, and L. M. Cullen; L. M. Cullen, "Merchant Communities, the Navigation Acts, and Irish and Scottish Responses," in Cullen & Smout, *Comparative Aspects*; P. Melvin, "The Composition of the Galway Gentry," *Irish Genealogist*, 7 (1986), 81–96; G. Moran and R. Gillespie, eds., *Galway: History and Society* (Dublin, 1996), especially the chapters by B. Cunningham, S. Mulloy, and P. Melvin; M. D. O'Sullivan, *Old Galway: The History of a Norman Colony in Ireland* (Galway, 1983 ed.), quotation in text from p. 452; and Truxes, *Irish-Am. Trade*.

On seventeenth-century Irish migration, transportation, and settlement in the West Indies, see: H. McD. Beckles, "A 'Riotous and Unruly Lot': Irish Indentured Servants and Freemen in the English West Indies, 1644–1713," *WMQ*, 47 (1990), 503–22; J. W. Blake, "Transportation from Ireland to America, 1653–60," *IHS*, 3, no. 2 (March 1943), 267–281; H. A. Fergus, "Montserrat 'Colony of Ireland': The Myth and the Reality," *Studies*, 70 (winter 1981), 325–40; A. Gwynn, "Documents Relating to the Irish in the West Indies," *Analecta Hibernica*, 4 (October 1932), 139–286, and three articles by the same author in *Studies*, "Early Irish Emigration to the West Indies (1612–1643)," 18 (1929), 377–93 and 648–63, "Indentured Servants and Negro Slaves in Barbados (1642–1650)," 279–294; and "Cromwell's Policy of Transportation," 19 (1930), 607–23; B. McGinn, "How Irish Is Montserrat?" *Irish Roots*, 1, 2, and 4 (Cork: 1994); J. C. Messenger, "The 'Black Irish' of Montserrat," *Éire-Ireland*, 2, no. 1 (spring 1967), 27–40, and "Montserrat: The Most Distinctively Irish Settlement in the New World," *Ethnicity*, 2 (1975), 281–303; Prendergast, *Cromwellian Settlement*; and D. B. Quinn, *Ireland and America: Their Early Associations, 1500–1640* (Liverpool, 1991).

On Barbados and the Leeward Islands (including Montserrat), generally, see: H. McD. Beckles, *A History of Barbados: From Amerindian Settlement to Nation-State* (New York, 1990); R. Berleant-Schiller, "Free Labor and the Economy in Seventeenth-Century Monsterrat," *WMQ*, 46, no. 3 (July 1989), 539–64; C. and R. Bridenbaugh, *No Peace beyond the Line: The English in the Caribbean, 1624–1690* (New York, 1972); M. Craton, "Reluctant Creoles: The Planters' World in the British West Indies," in Bailyn & Morgan, *Strangers*; R. S. Dunn, *Sugar and Slaves: The Rise of the Planter Class in the English West Indies, 1624–1713* (Chapel Hill, N.C., 1972), quotations in text from p. 27, and "The English Sugar Islands and the Founding of South Carolina," in T. H. Breen, ed., *Shaping Southern Society: The Colonial Experience* (New York, 1976); V. T. Harlow, *A History of Barbados, 1625–85* (Oxford, 1926); C. S. S. Higham, *The Development of the Leeward Islands under the Restoration, 1660–1688* (Cambridge, England 1921); G. A. Puckrein, *Little England: Plantation Society and Anglo-Barbadian Politics, 1627–1700* (New York, 1984); L. M. Pulsipher, "The Cultural Landscape of Montserrat, West Indies, in the Seventeenth Century" (Ph.D. diss., Southern Illinois University, 1977); J. McR. Sanders, *Barbados Records: Wills and Administrations*, vol. 2, 1681–1700 (Houston, 1980), on William Carpenter; J. Sheppard, *The "Redlegs" of Barbados: Their Origins and History* (Millwood, N.Y., 1977); and R. B. Sheridan, *Sugar and Slavery: An Economic History of the British West Indies, 1623–1775* (Baltimore, 1974).

SOURCES

17. Samuel McCobb, 1729–1772

Samuel McCobb's deposition of 23 October 1772 is located in the Lincoln County Registry of Deeds, Lincoln County Courthouse, in Wiscasset, Maine, and we thank Jane S. Tucker, volunteer archivist at the Lincoln County Historical Association, Wiscasset, for locating this document, and William Blodgett, Chairman, Lincoln County Commissioners, for permission to publish. McCobb's deposition is also published, with shorter depositions by John Beath, William Fullerton, and William Moore, in F. B. Greene, *History of Boothbay, Southport and Boothbay Harbor, Maine, 1623–1905* (Portland, Maine, 1906), 116–22. A petition from Boothbay's inhabitants to the Massachusetts royal governor, dated 1774 and perhaps written by McCobb, is published in J. P. Baxter, ed., *Collections of the Maine Historical Society: Documentary History*, 2nd ser., vol. 14 (1910), 166–71. For research assistance, we are especially grateful to Barbara Rumsey of the Boothbay Region Historical Society, Boothbay Harbor, for sharing with us both her own research on Boothbay's early settlers and also the genealogical research of Allan McCobb of Enid, Oklahoma.

On early Ulster emigration to and settlement in Maine and New England, generally, see: Bolton, *Scotch-Irish Pioneers;* Clark, *Eastern Frontier;* Dickson, *Ulster Emigration;* C. B. Fobes, "Path of the Settlement and Distribution of Population in Maine," *Economic Geography*, 20 (1944), 66–67; F. B. Greene, *History of Boothbay*, which contains detailed information about the McCobb family and other Ulster settlers; J. Johnston, *A History of the Towns of Bristol and Bremen* (Albany, N.Y., 1873); Leyburn, *Scotch-Irish;* D. McCourt, "County Derry and New England: The Scotch-Irish Migration of 1718," in O'Brien, *Derry & Londonderry*, 303–20; L. K. Mathews, *The Expansion of New England* (Boston, 1909); B. Rumsey, "The Long House," *Boothbay Register* (11 April 1991) and "William McCobb, Blacksmith," *Boothbay Register* (15 December 1994); R. S. Wallace, "The Scotch-Irish of Provincial New Hampshire" (Ph.D. diss., University of New Hampshire, 1984), quotations in text from pp. 63, 83, 107, and 111; and W. D. Williamson, *History of the State of Maine* (Hallowell, Maine, 1832).

On the conflicts between settlers and proprietary companies in post-Revolution Maine, see: Clark et al., *Maine in Early Republic;* and Taylor, *Liberty Men;* on Irish Catholic settlers in Lincoln Co., see: E. T. McCarron, "The World of Kavanagh and Cottril: A Portrait of Irish Emigration, Entrepreneurship, and Ethnic Diversity in Mid-Maine, 1760–1820" (Ph.D. diss., University of New Hampshire, 1992); and on Anglo-Irish middlemen in the Pemaquid region, see: E. T. McCarron, "In Pursuit of the 'Maine' Chance: The North Family of Offaly and New England, 1700–1776," in Nolan & O'Neill, *Offaly*, 339–70.

18. Robert Witherspoon, 1734–1780

Our transcript of Robert Witherspoon's memoir derives largely from Mary Stevens Witherspoon's "Genealogy of the Witherspoon Family" (1894), a photocopied manuscript in the South Caroliniana Library, University of South Carolina, Columbia, supplemented by the published version in the *History of Williamsburg* (Columbia, S.C., 1923) by W. W. Boddie, who purportedly made a "true copy" of the original manuscript, then in the possession of "the descendants of the late Dr. J. R. Witherspoon, of Alabama." Another somewhat conflicting transcript of Robert Witherspoon's memoir is in J. B. Witherspoon, *History and Genealogy of the Witherspoon Family (1400–1972)* (Fort Worth, Tex., 1979). Boddie's and Witherspoon's books also contain data on the family and their settlement, as does D. Ramsay, *The History of South Carolina from 1670*, vol. 1 (Charleston, 1809), and G. Howe, *History of the Presbyterian Church in South Carolina*, vol. 1 (Columbia, S.C., 1870). We thank the South Caroliniana Library for permission to publish and Herbert J. Hartsook, curator of manuscripts at the South Caroliniana Library, for research assistance.

On County Down, see: Proudfoot, *Down*. For historical background on the Williamsburg settlement, see: Klein, *Unification of Slave State;* C. F. Kovacik and J. J. Winberry, *South Carolina: A Geography* (Boulder, Colo., 1987); G. L. Johnson, Jr., *The Frontier in the Colonial South: South Carolina Backcountry, 1736–1800* (Westport, Conn., 1997); E. McCrady, *South Carolina under Royal Government* (New York, 1899); R. L. Meriwether, *The Expansion of South Carolina, 1729–1765* (Kingsport, Tenn., 1940); W. S. Robinson, *The Southern Colonial Frontier, 1607–1763* (Albuquerque, N.M., 1979); M. E. Sirmans, *Colonial South Carolina* (Chapel Hill, N.C., 1966); D. D. Wallace, *South Carolina: A Short History* (Columbia, S.C., 1961); and Weir, *Col. So. Car.* On John Barnwell, see *DAB*.

19. James Magraw, 1733

According to W. H. Burkhart, *The Shippensburg Story, 1730–1970* (Shippensburg, Pa., 1970), James Magraw's letter was "found among the archives and colonial records at Harrisburg," Pennsylvania's state capital, and first published, about 1866, in the *Shippensburg News*. In 1881 W. H. Egle, one of Dauphin County's earliest historians, saw the original letter and vouched for its authenticity. Since then, the manuscript has disappeared, and our rendering of the letter is a composite of four slightly different versions published in Burkhart; [J. F. Richard], *History of Franklin County, Pennsylvania* (Chicago, 1887); Egle, *Notes and Queries: Historical and Genealogical*, Ser. 1, part 4 (Harrisburg, 1881); and C. P. Wing, *History of Cumberland County, Pennsylvania* (Philadelphia, 1879). For research assistance, we thank Myrtle Yohe of the Shippensburg Historical Society, Michelle Hornung of the Cumberland County Historical Society in Carlisle, Pennsylvania, and the staff of the Bureau of Archives and History at the Pennsylvania Historical and Museum Commission in Harrisburg.

On settlement, society, and emigration in eighteenth-century County Fermanagh, see: Crawford, "Economy and Society"; Dickson, *Ulster Emigration;* FitzGerald, "Irish-Speaking"; and Robinson, *Plantation of Ulster.*

For background information on the Scots-Irish in Shippensburg, the Cumberland Valley, and Pennsylvania, generally, see also: S. P. Bates, *History of Cumberland and Adams Counties* (Chicago, 1886); W. H. Burkhart, *Cumberland Valley Chronicles* (Shippensburg, Pa., 1976); H. M. Cummings, *Scots Breed and Susquehanna* (Pittsburgh, 1964); G. P. Donehoo, ed., *History of the Cumberland Valley in Pennsylvania* (Harrisburg, 1930); Dunaway, *Scotch-Irish of Col. Pa.;* W. H. Egle, *History of the Counties of Dauphin and Lebanon* (Philadelphia, 1883); S. W. Fletcher, *Pennsylvania Agriculture and Country Life, 1640–1840* (Harrisburg, 1950); G. W. Frantz, *Paxton: A Study of Community Structure and Mobility in the Colonial Pennsylvania Backcountry* (New York, 1989); Klett, *Presby. in Col. Pa.;* Leyburn, *Scotch-Irish;* I. H. M'Cauley, *Biographical Annals of Franklin County* (Chicago, 1905), and *Historical Sketch of Franklin County* (Chambersburg, Pa., 1878); A. Nevin, *Men of Mark of Cumberland Valley, Pa., 1776–1876* (Philadelphia, 1876); and I. D. Rupp, *History and Topography of Dauphin, Cumberland, Franklin, Bedford, Adams, and Perry Counties* (Lancaster, Pa., 1846). On farming methods and implements in colonial America, see: P. D. McClelland, *Sowing Modernity: America's First Agricultural Revolution* (Ithaca, N.Y., 1997). For references to the Steens, Rippeys, and others mentioned in Magraw's letter, see: Rupp, *History and Topography*; and *Pa. Arch.*, 3rd ser., vol. 20 for Cumberland County tax lists, 1778, and vol. 24 for Pennsylvania land warrants (Harrisburg, 1897–98).

20. Mary Elizabeth McDowell Greenlee, 1737–1754

Mary Elizabeth McDowell Greenlee's 1806 deposition in the Peck-Borden Chancery Suit is filed in the District Court Record Book (September 1789-April 1793), in the Augusta County Clerk's Office, Staunton, Virginia. For copies of this and other court records, including the 1763 appraisal of

James Greenlee's estate, we thank the late Mrs. Katherine G. Bushman of the Augusta County Historical Society, Staunton. For research assistance, we are equally grateful to the late Prof. David Wakefield of the University of Missouri, Columbia; to Dr. Katharine L. Brown, former director of research, Frontier Culture Museum of Virginia, Staunton; to Alice Williams, curator of the Rockbridge Historical Society, Lexington, Virginia; and especially to Lisa McCown, special collections archivist at the Leyburn Library, Washington and Lee University, also in Lexington.

For information on the Greenlee, McDowell, and Lewis families, see especially: L. Chalkey, *Chronicles of the Scotch-Irish Settlement in Virginia*, 3 vols. (Rosslyn, Va., 1912); W. Couper, *History of the Shenandoah Valley*, vol. 1 (New York, 1952); W. H. Foote, *Sketches of Virginia, Historical and Biographical*, 2nd ser. (Philadelphia, 1855); R. S. Greenlee and R. L. Greenlee, *Genealogy of the Greenlee Families* (Chicago, 1908); I. Frazier, "John Lewis—Founder and Patriarch," *Augusta Historical Bulletin*, 3, no. 2 (fall 1967), 5–12; I. Frazier, M. W. Cowell, Jr., and L. F. Fisher, *The Family of John Lewis, Pioneer* (San Marino, Calif., 1985); J. L. M. Kinkead, *Our Kentucky Pioneer Ancestry: A History of the Kinkead and McDowell Families of Kentucky* (Baltimore, 1992); O. F. Morton, *History of Rockbridge County, Virginia* (1920; repr. Baltimore, 1980); J. L. Peyton, *History of Augusta County, Virginia* (1882; repr. Bridgewater, Va., 1953); and the old McDowell family histories and memoirs in the Davidson Papers, Ms. 113, folders 11–14, in the Leyburn Library, Washington and Lee University.

On Scots-Irish and others settlers in the Shenandoah Valley and western Virginia, generally, see: T. P. Abernathy, *Three Virginia Frontiers* (University, La., 1940); R. R. Beeman, *The Evolution of the Southern Backcountry: A Case Study of Lunenburg County, Virginia, 1746–1832* (Philadelphia, 1984); Blethen & Wood, *Ulster & No. America*, especially the essay by W. R. Hofstra, "Land, Ethnicity, and Community at the Opequon Settlement, Virginia, 1730–1800," 167–88; Dunaway, *Scotch-Irish of Col. Pa.*; Hart, *Valley of Va.*; W. R. Hofstra, "Land Policy and Settlement in the Northern Shenandoah Valley," in Mitchell, *Appalachian Frontiers*; W. R. Hofstra, "'The Extension of His Majesties Dominions': The Virginia Backcountry and the Reconfiguration of Imperial Frontiers," *JAH*, 84, no. 4 (March 1998), 1281–1312, and "The Virginia Backcountry in the Eighteenth Century," *VMHB*, 101, no. 4 (October 1993), 485–508; W. R. Hofstra and R. D. Mitchell, "Town and Country in Backcountry Virginia: Winchester and the Shenandoah Valley, 1730–1800," *J. So. Hist.*, 59, no. 4 (November 1993), 619–646; P. G. Johnson, *James Patton and the Appalachian Colonists* (Verona, Va., 1973); F. B. Kegley, *Kegley's Virginia Frontier* (Roanoke, Va., 1938); Leyburn, *Scotch-Irish*; T. McCleskey, "Rich Land, Poor Prospects: Real Estate and the Formation of a Social Elite in Augusta County, Virginia, 1738–1770," *VMHB*, 98, no. 3 (July 1990), 449–486; R. D. Mitchell, *Commercialism and Frontier: Perspectives on the Early Shenandoah Valley* (Charlottesville, Va., 1977); M. J. Puglesi, ed., *Diversity and Accommodation: Essays on the Cultural Composition of the Virginia Frontier* (Knoxville, Tenn., 1997), especially the essays by W. R. Hofstra, "Ethnicity and Community Formation on the Shenandoah Valley Frontier, 1730–1800," 59–81, and R. K. MacMaster, "Religion, Migration, and Pluralism: A Shenandoah Valley Community, 1740–1790," 82–98; Tillson, *Gentry & Common Folk*; and J. A. Waddell, *Annals of Augusta County, Virginia, from 1726 to 1871* (1888; Staunton, 1902 ed.). On the Valley after 1800, see the essays in K. E. Koons and W. R. Hofstra, eds., *After the Backcountry: Rural Life in the Great Valley of Virginia, 1800–1900* (Knoxville, Tenn., 2000).

Rev. Ezekiel Stewart's 25 March 1729 comment on Ulsterwomen's promotion of emigration is in D.2092/1/3/141 (PRONI); on gender in early Virginia, see K. M. Brown, *Good Wives, Nasty Wenches, and Anxious Patriarchs: Gender, Race, and Power in Colonial Virginia* (Chapel Hill, N.C., 1996); and on gentility in colonial America, see Bushman, *Refinement*.

21. James McCullough, 1748–1758

James McCullough's journal is in the possession of Charles J. Stoner of Mercersburg, Pennsylvania, whose own ancestor is mentioned in one of McCullough's entries. We thank Mr. and Mrs. Stoner for their generosity in allowing the journal's publication and for their aid in its transcription and in background research. Thanks also for research assistance to Lillian Colletta of the Kittochtinny Historical Society, Chambersburg, Pennsylvania; Charles H. Glatfelter of the Adams County Historical Society, Gettysburg, Pennsylvania; the staff of the Coyle Free Library in Chambersburg; and Dr. Vivienne Pollock, history curator of the Ulster Museum, Belfast.

For information specific to the McCullough family, see W. H. Egle, "Warrantees of Land in . . . Pennsylvania, 1730–1898, v. 3," in *Pa. Arch.*, 3rd ser., vol. 26 (1897), 721–25; J. L. Finafrock, *Traditions and Records of a Pioneer Family* (Chambersburg, Pa., n.d. [1921?]); C. J. Stoner, "The Journal of James McCullough," *Kittochtinny Historical Society Papers*, vol. 19 (1989), 257–66; and J. McCullough III, *Genealogy of the McCullough Family* (Harrisburg, Pa., 1912), which contains the memoir of John McCullough, the redeemed captive, also published in J. Pritts, comp., *Mirror of Olden Time Border Life*, 2nd ed. (Abingdon, Va., 1849).

On the Conococheague settlement and Franklin County, see: D. G. Beer, *Atlas of Franklin County* (Philadelphia, 1868); [G. Norcross, et al.], *Centennial Memoir of the Presbytery of Carlisle*, 2 vols. (Harrisburg, 1889); C. H. Sipe, *The Indian Wars of Pennsylvania* (1929; repr. New York, 1971); and, The Woman's Club of Mercersburg, Pa., *Old Mercersburg* (New York, 1912); in addition to the works by Burkhart, Cummings, Dunaway, Fletcher, Klett, M'Cauley, Nevin, Richard, Rupp, and Wing listed in the Sources for chapter 19. On the socioeconomic characteristics of Scots-Irish farming communities in colonial Pennsylvania, generally, see: Lemon, *Best Poor Man's Country;* V. Pollock, "The Household Economy in Early Rural America and Ulster: The Question of Self-Sufficiency," in Blethen & Wood, *Ulster & No. America,* 61–75; and D. Snydacker, "Kinship and Community in Rural Pensylvania, 1749–1820," *J. Interdis. Hist.,* 13, no. 1 (1982), 41–61. On use of the Bible in eighteenth-century Ulster, see: Gillespie, *Devoted People.*

22. Elizabeth Guthrie Brownlee Guthrie, 1755–1829

The original manuscript of Elizabeth Guthrie's 1829 petition no longer exists, but a purportedly verbatim transcript was published in the 24 May 1899 issue of the *Westmoreland Democrat* (Greensburg) and was reprinted in Anna L. Warren, *A Captive's Tale: The Story of Elizabeth Brownlee Guthrie* (Greensburg, 1977). William Guthrie's 1818 and Joseph Brownlee Guthrie's 1847 federal pension applications are catalogued in file 804–383 in the Revolutionary War Pension Records in the National Archives, Washington, D.C.; the latter is also summarized as entry W3245 in White, *Geneal. Abstracts.* We thank Ms. Warren, archaeological supervisor at the Westmoreland County Historical Society, Greensburg, for her generosity in allowing us to use the results of her own research on the Guthries; and we also are grateful to Mrs. Dolores T. Yeaney of Summerville, Pennsylvania; Bessie Wenner, assistant librarian at the Clarion County Historical Society, Clarion, Pennsylvania; Bruce Norman of Washington, D.C.; and Prof. Michael Montgomery of the University of South Carolina for research assistance.

On Londonderry city, see: B. Lacy, *Siege City: The Story of Derry and Londonderry* (Belfast, 1990); and C. Thomas, "The City of Londonderry: Demographic Trends and Socio-Economic Characteristics, 1650–1900," in O'Brien, *Derry & Londonderry,* 359–77.

Information on the Guthries, Brownlees, and/or the Hannastown raid can be found in: Albert,

Westmoreland Co.; A. J. Davis, *History of Clarion County* (1887; repr. Rimersburg, Pa., 1968); W. H. Egle, "Warrantees of Land in . . . Pennsylvania, 1730–1898, v. 3," *Pa. Arch.*, 3rd ser., vol. 26 (1897); L. R. Guthrie, comp., *American Guthrie and Allied Families* (Chambersburg, Pa., 1933); E. W. Hassler, *Old Westmoreland: A History of Western Pennsylvania during the Revolution* (Pittsburgh, 1900); C. H. Sipe, *The Indian Wars of Pennsylvania* (1929; repr. New York, 1971); and H. A. Thomas, "A Lonely Historic Grave," *WPHM*, 48, no. 2 (April 1965), 175–83. For general background, also see: V. K. Bartlett, *Keeping House: Women's Lives in Western Pennsylvania, 1790–1850* (Pittsburgh, 1998); S. J. and E. H. Buck, *The Planting of Civilization in Western Pennsylvania* (Pitsburgh, 1939); Dunaway, *Scotch-Irish of Col. Pa.;* Harper, *Western Pa.;* and G. T. Knouff, "Soldiers and Violence on the Pennsylvania Frontier," in Frantz & Pencak, *Beyond Philadelphia*, 171–93.

23. Daniel Kent, 1786–1784

Daniel Kent's and his parents' letters, as well as Kent's indenture and other family mss., are located in the Friends Historical Library of Swarthmore College, Swarthmore, Pennsylvania, and we are grateful to the Library and to its successive curators, Mary Ellen Chijioke and Christopher Densmore, for permission to publish, and to its archivists, Susanna Morikawa and Pat O'Donnell, and to Dr. Robert Doan, then a graduate student at Temple University, Philadelphia, Dr. Liam Kennedy of Queen's University, Belfast, and Prof. John Wigger of the University of Missouri, Columbia, for research assistance.

    Transcripts of the Kent letters, plus biographical and genealogical data, are published in: D. Kent, *Letters and Other Papers of Daniel Kent, Emigrant* (Baltimore, 1904). Other sources of information about the Kents, Hawleys, etc., include: Futhey & Cope, *History of Chester Co.;* and *Pa. Arch.*, 3rd ser., esp. vols. 11–12 (Pennsylvania taxpayers' lists, 1765–85). For general background on late eighteenth-century Chester County, see: Lemon, *Best Poor Man's Country,* and three articles by L. Simler: "Tenancy in Colonial Pennsylvania: The Case of Chester County," *WMQ*, 43 (1986), 542–69; "The Landless Worker: An Index of Economic and Social Change in Chester County, Pennsylvania, 1750–1820," *PMHB*, 114 (1990), 163–99; and (with P. G. E. Clemons), "The 'Best Poor Man's Country' in 1783: The Population Structure of Rural Society in Late-Eighteenth-Century Southeastern Pennsylvania," *Proc. Am. Phil. Soc.*, 133 (1989), 234–61; plus R. S. Warden, "Chester County," in Frantz & Pencak, *Beyond Philadelphia*, 1–22. On the Methodists in Philadelphia, see: D. E. Andrews, *The Methodists and Revolutionary America, 1760–1800: The Shaping of an Evangelical Culture* (Princeton, 2000); and R. Schultz, "God and Workingmen: Popular Religion and the Formation of Philadelphia's Working Class, 1790–1830," in Hoffman & Albert, *Religion in Rev. Age*, 124–55. On the re-creation of personal identities in early America, see: Hoffman et al., *Through a Glass Darkly,* especially M. Sobel, "The Revolution in Selves: Black and White Inner Aliens," 163–205.

    On Limerick city, see: R. A. Butlin, ed., *The Development of the Irish Town* (London, 1977); and P. J. O'Connor, *Exploring Limerick's Past: An Historical Geography of Urban Development in County and City* (Newcastle West, County Limerick, 1987); and E. Wakefield, *An Account of Ireland, Statistical and Political,* vol. 2 (London, 1812). On Irish Methodism (and its American connections) in the eighteenth century, see: Carwardine, *Transatlantic Revivalism;* Rev. W. Crook, *Ireland and the Centenary of American Methodism* (Belfast, 1866); C. H. Crookshank, *History of Methodism in Ireland* (London, 1885); D. N. Hempton, "Methodism in Irish Society, 1770–1830," *Trans. R.H.S.*, 5th ser., vol. 36 (1986), 117–42; and the journals and other writings of John Wesley (1703–91), especially in vols. 9 and 18–23 of R. E. Davies, ed., *The Works of John Wesley* (Nashville, 1989–93; vols. 18–23 ed. by

E. R. Ware). On the socioeconomic distress described in William Kent's last letters, see, Wells, "Famine of 1799–1801."

24. John and Jane Chambers, 1796

John and Jane Chambers' letter is in the New-York Historical Society, New York City (and a copy is catalogued as T.2299 in PRONI). We thank the New-York Historical Society for permission to publish this document (catalogued as Misc. MSS Chambers), and for research assistance we are grateful to: Bette Barker, archivist at the New Jersey State Archives in Trenton; Fred W. Oser of the Monmouth County Library in Manalapan, New Jersey; and Jane Reynolds-Peck of the Monmouth County Historical Society Association in Freehold, New Jersey

For background information on the Tanderagee district of County Armagh, see the published works on mid-Ulster and County Down listed for chapter 4. Rent rolls for the Duke of Manchester's Ballymore and Kernan estates, 1790–92, are catalogued as D.1248/R99 and /R100 in PRONI.

Scattered references to Chambers families in Freehold township and elsewhere in Monmouth County can be found in the *N.J. Geneal. Mag.*, vols. 43, 45, and 49; and also in Freehold's "List of ratables, Taken in the Month of July 1785 . . . [by] John Campbell, assessor," among the Monmouth County tax lists, 1773–1822, in the New Jersey State Archives, Trenton. Published sources include: F. Ellis, *History of Monmouth County, New Jersey* (Philadelphia, 1885); *History of Monmouth County, New Jersey* (New York, 1922); W. S. Horner, *This Old Monmouth of Ours* (Freehold, N.J., 1932); McCormick, *New Jersey*; E. A. Salter, *History of Monmouth and Ocean Counties* (Bayonne, N.J., 1890); Wacker, *Land and People;* and Wacker & Clemons, *Land Use in N.J.* On Scottish (and Scots-Irish) settlement in central New Jersey, see: N. C. Landsman, *Scotland and its First American Colony, 1683–1765* (Princeton, 1985).

25. Joseph and Hannah Wright, 1801–1817

The Wright family letters and relevant Quaker records are located in the Historical Library of the Religious Society of Friends in Ireland, in Dublin, whose curator, Mrs. Mary Shackleton, we thank for permission to publish and for research assistance. For the latter we also acknowledge the invaluable aid of Mildred E. Wilkins, Barnesville, Ohio, and Richard Thompson, Belmont, of the Belmont County Chapter of the Ohio Genealogical Society (OGS hereafter), Huton Memorial Library, Barnesville; of Jeff Thomas, reference archivist at the Ohio Historical Society, Columbus; and Kevin King, assistant archivist at the Ohio University Library in Athens.

On County Wexford and on Irish Quakers, generally, see: Grubb, *Quakers;* Whelan, *Wexford;* and Wigham, *Irish Quakers.* On the Wright family holding in Ballinclay, County Wexford, see the TAB: Liskinfere (1831), and Griffith's *Valuation:* Liskinfere (1853), both in the NLI.

On the Wrights in Ohio, the Belmont County Chapter of the OGS has local census, deed, marriage, and probate records, and the Ohio Historical Society holds pertinent Belmont County tax records. The 1820 Belmont town census schedule is reprinted in the OGS, Belmont County Chapter *Newsletter,* 10, no. 3 (winter 1987), 15. Published works that mention Wright family members or their Ohio settlement include: *Belmont County, Ohio, Atlas* (n.p., 1888); J. A. Caldwell, *History of Belmont and Jefferson Counties* (Wheeling, W. Va., 1880); Hinshaw, *Encycl. of Am. Quaker Geneal.,* vol. 4, *Ohio* (Ann Arbor, Mich., 1946); H. L. Ingle, *Quakers in Conflict: The Hicksite Reformation* (Knoxville, Tenn., 1986); and A. T. McKelvey, ed., *Centennial History of Belmont County* (Chicago, 1903). On Joseph Wright's sons, Benjamin and Smithson, and their descendants, see *The Past and*

Present of Rock Island County [Illinois] (Chicago, 1877), and A. E. Lee, *History of the City of Columbus, Ohio*, vol. 2 (Columbus, 1892), respectively. For the Baltimore-Ohio Quaker connections, see A. J. Wright, "Joel Wright, City Planner," *Ohio Arch. & Hist. Q.*, 56 (1947), 287–94.

On settlement, land purchase, society, and politics in frontier Ohio, generally, see: J. P. Brown and A. R. L. Cayton, eds., *Pursuits of Public Power: Political Culture in Ohio, 1787–1861* (Kent, Ohio, 1994); A. R. L. Cayton, *The Frontier Republic: Ideology and Politics in the Ohio Country, 1780–1825* (Kent, Ohio, 1986); B. H. Hibbard, *A History of the Public Land Policies* (New York, 1939); R. D. Hurt, *The Ohio Frontier: Crucible of the Old Northwest, 1720–1830* (Bloomington, Ind., 1996); D. J. Ratcliffe, *Party Spirit in a Frontier Republic: Democratic Politics in Ohio, 1793–1821* (Columbus, Ohio, 1998); M. J. Rohrbough, *The Land Office Business: The Settlement and Administration of American Public Lands* (New York, 1968), and *The Trans-Appalachian Frontier: People, Societies, and Institutions* (New York, 1978); W. T. Utter, *The Frontier State, 1803–1825* (Columbus, Ohio, 1942); and H. G. H. Wilhelm and A. G. Noble, "Ohio's Settlement Landscape," in L. Peacefull, ed., *A Geography of Ohio* (Kent, Ohio, 1996), 80–109. On Abraham Shackleton, Hannah Barnard, and Elias Hicks, see the relevant entries in *DNB, ANB*, and *DAB*, respectively.

26. Edward and Mary Toner, 1818–1819

Edward Toner's letters are catalogued as Ms. 2300 in the National Library of Ireland, Dublin. The Toner letters are the property of the Council of Trustees of the National Library of Ireland and have been reproduced in this book by the Council's permission. We thank Agnes Tomichek of the Westmoreland County Historical Society, Greensburg, Pennsylvania, and Mrs. Helen Wilson of the Western Pennsylvania Historical Society, Pittsburgh, for research assistance concerning the Toners' naturalization, baptism, marriage, probate, and other records located in their archives. We are grateful as well to Elizabeth Pollard Grayson of the University of Texas, Austin, for references to published sources on Rev. Charles B. Maguire.

On Desertcreat and adjacent parishes, see: TAB: Desertcreat (1825), in PRONI; Day & McWilliams, *OSM*, vol. 20, *Parishes of County Tyrone II, 1825, 1833–5, 1840: Mid and East Tyrone* (1993); Lewis, *TDI;* Griffith's *Valuation:* Knockavaddy (1859), in PRONI; and *Land Owners in Ireland, 1876*. On the Defenders and United Irishmen in late eighteenth-century Tyrone, see: B. McEvoy, "The United Irishmen in Co. Tyrone," *Seanchas Ardmhacha*, 3, no. 2 (1959), 283–314, and 4, no. 1 (1960–61), 1–32. And on the religious background, see: S. J. Connolly, "Catholicism in Ulster, 1800–50," in Roebuck, *Plantation to Partition*, 157–71, and *Priests and People in Pre-Famine Ireland* (Dublin, 1982); Gillespie, *Devoted People;* and O. P. Rafferty, *Catholicism in Ulster, 1603–1983* (Columbia, S.C., 1994). For an intimate perspective on Catholics in pre-Famine County Tyrone, see William Carleton's *Life . . .*, ed. by D. J. O'Donoghue (London, 1896), and *Tales and Stories of the Irish Peasantry* (New York, 1864).

On the Toners in western Pennsylvania, their environment, and its early Catholicism, see: Albert, *Westmoreland Co.;* S.N. and D. G. Beers, *Atlas of Westmoreland County* (Philadelphia, 1867); J. Boucher, *History of Westmoreland County*, vol. 1 (New York, 1906); *Catholic Baptisms in Western Pennsylvania, 1799–1828: Father Peter Helbron's Greensburg Register* (Baltimore, 1985); J. Connolly, ed., *History of the Archdiocese of Philadelphia* (Philadelphia, 1976); Harper, *Western Pa.;* S. Jones, *Pittsburgh in the Year 1826* (Pittsburgh, 1826); Rev. A. A. Lambing, *History of the Catholic Church in the Dioceses of Pittsburg and Allegheny* (New York, 1880); M. E. Maloney, *Fág An Bealach: The Irish Contribution to . . . Western Pennsylvania* (Pittsburgh, 1977); M. Szarnicki, *Michael O'Connor: First Catholic Bishop of Pittsburgh, 1843–60* (Pittsburgh, 1975); and S. T. Wiley, *Biographical and Historical Cyclopedia of Westmoreland County* (Philadelphia, 1890).

On Rev. Charles Bonaventure Maguire, see: Fr. A. Faulkner, "Letters of Charles Bonaventure Maguire, O.F.M. (1768–1833)," *Clogher Record,* 9 (1981), 284–303, and "Charles Bonaventure Maguire, O.F.M. (1768–1833)," *Clogher Record,* 10 (1982), 77–101, and 11 (1983), 187–213; as well as Charles F. E. Tourscher, trans., *Diary and Visitation Record of the Rt. Rev. Francis Patrick Kenrick* (Lancaster, Pa., 1916). On early American Catholicism, generally, see: Chinnici, "American Catholics"; Dolan, *Am. Catholic Experience,* esp. chapter 4; Ellis, *Catholics in Col. Am.;* Carey, *People, Priests, and Prelates;* Light, *Rome & New Republic;* and Wangler, "Religious Exercises."

27. James and Hannah Crockett, 1822

On the provenance of the Crockett family's letters and on their Irish background, see Sources for chapter 15. In addition to the gratitude we there expressed to the donor and others, we wish to thank the staff of the Luzerne County Recorder's office, in Wilkes-Barre, Pennsylvania, for research assistance.

Unfortunately, nearly all Luzerne County records pertinent to James Crockett have been lost or destroyed. However, see the 1850 U.S. Census schedule: Ross Township, Luzerne County, p. 101 (microfilm). Published primary sources include: Anon., *History of Luzerne, Lackawanna and Wyoming Counties* (New York, 1880), and S. Pearce, *Annals of Luzerne County* (Philadelphia, 1866).

For more general background information on conditions in Crockett's central Pennsylvania society in transition, see: D. Ball and G. Walton, "Agricultural Productivity Change in Eighteenth-Century Pennsylvania," *J. Interdis. Hist.,* 13 (1982), 45–59; R. Berthoff, "The Social Order of the Anthracite Region, 1825–1902," *PMHB,* 89 (1965), 261–91; S. W. Fletcher, *Pennsylvania Agriculture and Country Life,* vol. 1, *1640–1840* (Harrisburg, 1950) and vol. 2, *1840–1940* (Harrisburg, 1955); W. A. Gudelunas and W. G. Shade, *Before the Molly Maguires: The Emergence of the Ethno-Religious Factor in the Politics of the Lower Anthracite Region, 1844–1872* (New York, 1976); M. R. Haines, "Fertility, Marriage and Occupation in the Pennsylvania Anthracite Region, 1850–1880," *J. Fam. Hist.,* 2 (1976), 30–51; K. Kenny, *Making Sense of the Molly Maguires* (New York, 1998); G. L. Laidig et al., "Agricultural Variation and Human Fertility in Antebellum Pennsylvania," *J. Fam. Hist.,* 6 (1981), 201–23; K. Martis, *Historical Atlas of Political Parties in the U. S. Congress* (New York, 1989); G. Palladino, *Another Civil War: Labor, Capital, and the State in the Anthracite Regions of Pennsylvania, 1840–68* (Urbana, Ill., 1990); and N. B. Wilkinson, "Land Policy and Speculation in Pennsylvania, 1779–1800" (Ph.D. diss., University of Pennsylvania, 1958).

28. Benjamin Chandlee, 1705

A contemporary copy of Benjamin Chandlee's letter is in the Quaker Records (portfolio 4), at the Historical Library of the Religious Society of Friends in Ireland, in Dublin, and was published (with a second Chandlee letter dated 1707) in O. Goodbody, ed., "Two Letters of Benjamin Chandlee," *QH,* 64, no. 2 (autumn 1975), 110–15 (the Goodbody transcription has slight errors). We thank the Friends' Historical Library and its curator, Mrs. Mary Shackleton, for permission to publish and for providing Chandlee genealogical data.

On the Cotteys and Chandlees, also see: E. E. Chandlee, *Six Quaker Clockmakers* (Philadelphia, 1943); and Hinshaw, *Encycl. Am. Quaker Geneal.,* vol. 2 *(Pennsylvania)* (Baltimore, 1938). For published sources on the Quakers in Ireland and colonial Pennsylvania, see those listed in the Sources to chapter 9 in addition to R. L. Greaves, *Dublin's Merchant-Quaker: Anthony Sharp and the Community of Friends, 1643–1707* (Stanford, Calif., 1998). On the spread of potatoes in the Irish diet, with reference to Chandlee's letter, see: L. M. Cullen, *The Emergence of Modern Ireland, 1600–1900* (London, 1981).

On the colonial American economy and urban society, generally, see: Blumin, *Emergence Middle Class;* Egnal, *New World Economies;* McCusker & Menard, *Econ. Brit. Am.;* Nash, *Urban Crucible;* and E. J. Perkins, *The Economy of Colonial America* (New York, 1980). On craftsmen, clock-making, and other industries in early Pennsylvania, see: Bishop, *Hist. Am. Manuf.;* Bridenbaugh, *Cities in the Wilderness:*; C. Bridenbaugh, *The Colonial Craftsman* (New York, 1950); and H. Terry, *American Clock Making: Its Early History* (Waterbury, Conn., 1870).

29. John Kennedy, 1753

John Kennedy's petition is in box 7 of the NYC Misc. Mss., 1753, at the New-York Historical Society, New York City. We thank the Society for permission to publish; its library director, Margaret Heilbrun, for research assistance; and Dr. Thomas M. Truxes of Hartford, Connecticut, for bringing this document to our attention. For research aid we are also grateful to: Ray Jorgenson of the Fishkill Historical Society and the Van Wyck Homestead Museum, Fishkill, New York; R. W. Link of the Dutchess County Genealogical Society in Poughkeepsie, New York; and, especially, Mrs. Mary Lou Davison, genealogical researcher at the Dutchess County Historical Society, in Poughkeepsie.

Published data on Kennedy can be found in: F. Hasbrouck, ed., *History of Dutchess County* (Poughkeepsie, 1909); New-York Historical Society, *Collections for the Year 1891* (New York, 1982); and W. W. Reese and H. W. Reynolds, *Eighteenth Century Records of the Portion of Dutchess County, New York, That Was Included in Rombout Precinct and the Original Town of Fishkill (Coll. Dutchess Co. Hist. Soc.,* vol. 6 [1938]). Also on Dutchess County, see: [no author], *Historical and Genealogical Record [of] Dutchess and Putnam Counties* (Poughkeepsie, 1912); J. H. Smith, *History of Duchess County, New York* (Syracuse, N.Y., 1882); and P. H. Smith, *General History of Duchess County* (Pawling, N.Y., 1877).

On colonial New York's economy, society, and the background to the anti-Rent War, see: Bonomi, *Factious People;* Countryman, *People in Revolution;* Sung Bok Kim, *Landlord and Tenant in Colonial New York* (Chapel Hill, N.C., 1978); and Rosen, *Courts and Commerce.* On the Irish in colonial New York, see: Doyle, *Ireland, Irishmen;* J. D. Goodfriend, *Before the Melting Pot : Society and Culture in Colonial New York City, 1664–1730* (Princeton, N.J., 1992); R. J. Purcell, "Irish Contribution to Colonial New York," *Studies,* 29 (1940), 591–604, and 30 (1941), 107–20, and "Irish Cultural Contribution in Early New York," *Cath. Educ. Rev.,* 35 (October 1937), 449–60, and 36 (January 1938), 28–42.

On cooperage and the flaxseed trade, see: Bishop, *Hist. Am. Manuf.;* C. Bridenbaugh, *The Colonial Craftsman* (New York, 1950); Clark, *Hist. Manuf. U.S.;* F. E. Coyne, *The Development of the Cooperage Industry in the United States, 1620–1940* (Chicago, 1940); P. Linebaugh, *The London Hanged: Crime and Civil Society in the Eighteenth Century* (Cambridge, England, 1992); McCusker & Menard, *Econ. Brit. Am.;* Truxes, *Irish-Am. Trade;* and Tryon, *Household Manuf.*

30. Philip McRory, Ruth McGee, Edward Curry, Rosanna Stewart,
Patrick M'Cullen, Ann Dougherty, Thomas Ralph, and Michael Wade, 1735–1774

The Philip McRory, Ruth McGee, Edward Curry, Rosanna Stewart, Patrick M'Cullen, Ann Dougherty, and Thomas Ralph petitions and Michael Wade's testimony are located in the Court of Quarter Sessions, Servant and Apprentice Papers, at the Chester County Archives, West Chester,

Pennsylvania. For research assistance, we are especially grateful to Laurie Rofini, Chester County archivist, and Kathleen Ryan of the University of Pennsylvania, Philadelphia.

Background data on a few of the petitioners (M'Cullen and Ralph) and on nearly all of the masters and magistrates can be located in one or more of the following sources: the unpublished Chester County Tax and Court Records, in the Chester County Archives; Futhey & Cope, *History of Chester Co.*; the 1831–34 Irish Religious Censuses (for Ralph's Comber, County Down); Lockhart, *Some Aspects;* Myers, *Irish Quakers into Pa.; Pa. Arch.*, 3rd ser., vols. 11–12 (tax lists) and 22 (Ralph), and 5th ser., vol. 3 (M'Cullen); the *Pa. Gazette*, 14 June 1739 (Curry); and *PMHB*, vols. 3, 5, and 73 (Whitesides), 30 (Howell), 31 (Powell), 32 (Benson, Rea), 34 (Rea), 37–38 and 52 (Lightfoot), and 58 (Dougherty); and Wiley, *Chester Co.*

On Irish and other indentured servants, see: Doyle, *Ireland, Irishmen;* A. S. Fogelman, "From Slaves, Convicts, and Servants to Free Passengers: The Transformation of Immigration in the Era of the American Revolution," *JAH,* 85, no. 1 (June 1998), 43–76; Galenson, *White Servitude;* F. K. Geiser, *Redemptioners and Indentured Servants in the Colony and Commonwealth of Pennsylvania* (New Haven, 1901); F. Grubb, *Runaway Servants, Convicts, and Apprentices Advertised in the "Pennsylvania Gazette," 1728–1796* (Baltimore, 1992), and "Servant Auction Records and Immigration into the Delaware Valley, 1745–1831: The Proportion of Females among Immigrant Servants," *Proc. Am. Phil. Soc.,* 133 (June 1989), 160–67; C. A. Herrick, *White Servitude in Pennsylvania: Indentured and Redemption Labor in Colony and Commonwealth* (Philadelphia, 1926); Salinger, *"To Serve Well & Faithfully";* A. E. Smith, *Colonists in Bondage: White Servitude and Convict Labor in America, 1607–1776* (Chapel Hill, N.C., 1947); and Wokeck, *Trade in Strangers.*

For recent studies of society in eighteenth-century Chester County, see: D. E. Ball, "The Dynamics of Population and Wealth in Eighteenth-Century Chester County, Pennsylvania," *J. Interdis. Hist.,* 6, no. 4 (1976), 621–44; Lemon, *Best Poor Man's Country;* L. Simler, "The Township: The Community of the Rural Pennsylvanian," *PMHB,* 106, no. 1 (January 1982), 41–68; Simler's articles listed in the Sources for chapter 23; and R. W. Warden, "Chester County," in Frantz & Pencak, *Beyond Philadelphia,* 1–22. On rents in mid-eighteenth-century New York City, see: E. Blackmar, *Manhattan for Rent, 1785–1850* (Ithaca, N.Y., 1989).

31. John Grimes, John Fagan, and John Johnston, 1765

The only known copy of John Grimes's, John Fagan's and John Johnson's *Last Speech* (Burlington, N.J., 1765) is located in the Library Company of Philadelphia, but it was republished in slightly modernized form in F. Shelley, ed., "The Departing Confessions of Three Rogues," *Md. Hist. Mag.,* 52 (1957), 343–46. We thank both Mary Anne Hines, chief of reference at the Library Company of Philadelphia, and Robert J. Brugger of Baltimore, editor of the Maryland Historical Society's *Magazine,* for permission to publish; Norman V. Blantz, Ph.D., of the Burlington County Historical Society, Burlington, N.J., for research assistance; and Prof. Michael Montgomery, University of South Carolina, for bringing this document to our notice.

The fate of Grimes, Fagan, and Johnson can be followed in the *Pa. Gazette,* issues of 25 July, 1 and 22 August, and 5 September, 1765, sometimes reprinted in W. Nelson, ed., *N.J. Arch.,* 29 (Patterson, N.J., 1902), 577–86. Rev. Campbell's death was recorded in the *Pa. J.,* 14 August 1766. A possible runaway advertisement for John Grimes is listed in F. Grubb, *Runaway Servants, Convicts, and Apprentices Advertised in the "Pennsylvania Gazette," 1728–1796* (Baltimore, 1992), 68, but the actual notice could not be located in the issue (14 February 1763) where it purportedly appeared.

On Burlington County, New Jersey, see: J. E. Pomfret, *Colonial New Jersey: A History* (New York, 1973); Wacker and Clemens, *Land Use in N.J.;* and E. M. Woodward and J. F. Hageman, *History of Burlington and Mercer Counties, New Jersey* (Philadelphia, 1883).

In addition to Grubb's *Runaway Servants,* historical studies of Irish (and other) convicts in eighteenth-century America include: Doyle, *Ireland, Irishmen;* A. R. Ekirch, *Bound for America: The Transportation of British Convicts to the Colonies, 1718–1775* (Oxford, 1987); K. Morgan, "Convict Runaways in Maryland, 1745–1775," *JAS,* 23, no. 2 (August 1989), 253–68; and A. E. Smith, *Colonists in Bondage* (Chapel Hill, N.C., 1947). See also the works on indentured servants cited in the Sources for chapter 30.

On crime, law enforcement, and punishment in early America, especially in New Jersey and New York, see: Bridenbaugh, *Cities in Revolt;* G. W. Edwards, *New York as an Eighteenth Century Municipality, 1731–1776* (New York, 1917); Greenberg, *Crime & Law;* D. Greenberg, "Crime, Law Enforcement, and Social Control in Colonial America," *Am. J. Legal Hist.,* 26 (October 1982), 304–25; L. P. Masur, *Rites of Execution: Capital Punishment and the Transformation of American Culture, 1766–1865* (New York, 1989); K. Preyer, "Penal Measures in the American Colonies: An Overview," *Am. J. Legal Hist.,* 26 (October 1982), 326–53; A. Taylor, "'The Unhappy Stephen Arnold': An Episode of Murder and Penitence in the Early Republic," in Hoffman et al., *Through a Glass Darkly,* 96–121; and H. B. Weiss and G. M. Weiss, *An Introduction to Crime and Punishment in Colonial New Jersey* (Trenton, N.J., 1960).

On crime and punishment in eighteenth-century Dublin and London, see: B. Henry, *Dublin Hanged: Crime, Law Enforcement, and Punishment in Dublin, 1780–1795* (Dublin, 1993); P. Linebaugh, *The London Hanged* (New York, 1992); C. Maxwell, *Dublin under the Georges, 1714–1830* (London, 1936). On the popularity of criminal biographies in eighteenth-century Ireland, see: Ó Ciosáin, *Print and Pop. Culture;* and D. Ó hOgáin, "Folklore and Literature: 1700–1850," in Daly & Dickson, *Origins Pop. Literacy,* 1–13.

On Rev. Colin Campbell, see: Weis, "Col. Clergy Middle Colonies"; and on his ethnoreligious background, see: R. Blaney, *Presbyterians and the Irish Language* (Belfast, 1996); Brock, *Scotus Americanus;* Daiches, *Scottish Culture;* D. Dobson, *Scottish Emigration to Colonial America, 1607–1785* (Athens, Ga., 1994); and Donovan, *No Popery in Scotland.*

32. Francis Burdett Personel, 1773

Francis Burdett Personel's *Authentic and Particular Account* is item no. 12,936 in *Evans' Early Am. Imprints.* It is reprinted in full and edited, along with contemporary newspaper and other accounts, in D. E. Williams, *Pillars of Salt: An Anthology of Early American Criminal Narratives* (Madison, Wis., 1993), and summarized in Greenberg, *Crime & Law.* In addition to the newspaper accounts of Personel's execution cited by Williams, see also *Rivington's New-York Gazette* of 16 September 1773. On Irish indentured servants, crime, and punishment in early America, see the works cited in the Sources for chapter 31, especially those by Doyle, Greenburg, Lockhart, Morgan, and Taylor. On the spectacular growth of prerevolutionary Virginia's Baptist congregations, one of which Personel tried to join, see: R. Isaac, *The Transformation of Virginia, 1740–1790* (Chapel Hill, N.C., 1982).

33. James Patton (1), 1783–1789

Written in March 1839, in Asheville, North Carolina, the *Letter of James Patton, One of the First Residents of Asheville, North Carolina, to his Children,* was first published, privately, by William Patton, one of James's sons, in Racine, Wisconsin, in 1845, and republished verbatim in 1890, in 1930, and again in 1970 by Helen Patton of Racine and George Patton of Philadelphia. We wish to thank Helen Patton of Franklin, North Carolina, for permission to publish excerpts from the *Letter of James Patton*, and Rory Fitzpatrick, with Ulster Television in Belfast in 1985, for first bringing this document to our attention.

For background information on James Patton, see H. Tyler Blethen and Curtis W. Wood, "A Trader on the Western Carolina Frontier," in Mitchell, *Appalachian Frontiers, 150–65*. Blethen's and Wood's thorough research has obviated our usual need to consult primary sources for biographical and contextual data. However, on County Londonderry see: O'Brien, *Derry & Londonderry,* especially the chapter by E. A. Currie. On Tamlaght Finlagan and adjacent parishes, see: Day and McWilliams, *OSM*, vol. 25, *Parishes of Co. Londonderry VII, 1834–5: North-West Londonderry* (1994); and Lewis, *TDI*. On the Ogilby estates, see *Land Owners in Ireland, 1876.*

On late eighteenth-century society in the Pennsylvania regions where Patton labored in 1783–89, see the relevant works in the Sources for chapter 21. For data on Pennsylvanians mentioned in Patton's memoir, see also J. Gibson, ed., *History of York County, Pennsylvania* (Chicago, 1886), and *Pa. Arch.*, 3rd ser., vols. 14–16 (1897). For Irish workers on America's earliest canals, see R. Shaw, *Canals for a New Nation, 1790–1860* (Lexington, Ky., 1990); and P. Way, *Common Labour: Workers and the Digging of North American Canals, 1780–1860* (Cambridge, England, 1993).

34. Thomas McMahon, William Sotherin, and John Justice, 1789–1793

The McMahon, Sotherin, and Justice petitions are located in the Lea and Febriger Papers, Mathew Carey Incoming Correspondence, 1785–1796, in the Historical Society of Pennsylvania, Philadelphia, as are the petitions by Patrick Morgan (17 December 1796) and Peter O'Connor (1797–1798, in appendix 3). We thank Dr. Maurice Bríc of University College, Dublin, and Prof. Michael Montgomery of the University of South Carolina for bringing these documents to our attention; and the Historical Society of Pennsylvania for permission to publish. On John Justice, see: *McPherson's Directory for the City and Suburbs of Philadelphia* (1785); James Hardie, *The Philadelphia Directory and Register* (1794); *The Philadelphia Directory* (1798); and C. W. Stafford, *The Philadelphia Directory* (1800), all published in Philadelphia. On Thomas McMahon and on William Sotherin's creditors and references, see all the Philadelphia city directories from 1785 through 1808, as well as Governor Mifflin's and Bishop White's entries in *DAB*, and Nixon's and Fuller's biographies in Campbell, *Friendly Sons of St. Patrick.* The burial records of William Southern's children are in: Middleton, "Interments."

On Mathew Carey, see: M. Carey, *Autobiography* (Brooklyn, 1942); Campbell, *Friendly Sons of St. Patrick;* E. C. Carter, "Mathew Carey in Ireland, 1760–84," *Cath. Hist. Rev.*, 51 (1966), 503–27; Carter, "Mathew Carey"; J. N. Green, *Mathew Carey, Publisher and Patriot* (Philadelphia, 1985); McAleer, "'Civil Strangers'"; and Rowe, *Mathew Carey.*

On the working classes, poverty, and poor relief in late eighteenth- and early nineteenth-century Philadelphia, see: D. R. Adams, "Wage Rates in the Early National Period: Philadelphia, 1785–1830," *J. Econ. Hist.* (September 1968); J. K. Alexander, *Render Them Submissive: Responses to Poverty in Philadelphia, 1760–1800* (Amherst, Mass., 1980); P. F. Clement, *Welfare and the Poor in the Nineteenth-Century City: Philadelphia, 1800–1854* (Rutherford, N.J., 1985); Foner, *Tom Paine;* Laurie, *Working People of Phila.;* G. B. Nash, "Poverty and Poor Relief in Pre-Revolutionary Philadelphia," *WMQ*, 3rd ser., 33 (1976), 3–28, and "Up from the Bottom in Franklin's Philadelphia," *P & P*, no. 77 (1977), 57–83; Schultz, *Republic of Labor;* C. Shelton, *The Mills of Manayunk: Industrialization and*

Social Conflict in the Philadelphia Region, 1787–1837 (Baltimore, 1986); and B. G. Smith, "Struggles of the Independent Poor: The Living Standards of Philadelphia's 'Lower Sort,'" *WMQ*, 3rd ser., 38 (1981), 163–202, and *The "Lower Sort": Philadelphia's Laboring People, 1750–1800* (Ithaca, N.Y., 1990). On the Irish in Philadelphia, generally, see: Bríc, "Ireland, Irishmen"; Clark, *Irish in Philadelphia;* Doyle, *Ireland, Irishmen;* and McAleer, "'Civil Strangers'"; and on the city's Irish poor and their relationships with local African Americans, see: N. Ignatiev, *How the Irish Became White* (New York, 1995), and G. B. Nash, *Forging Freedom: The Formation of Philadelphia's Black Community, 1720–1840* (Cambridge, Mass., 1988).

35. James Doyle, 1789

Doyle's letter of 17 October 1789 is in the Lea and Febriger Papers, Mathew Carey Incoming Correspondence, 1785–96, in the Historical Society of Pennsylvania, to which we are grateful for permission to publish. Thanks also to Dr. Maurice Bríc of University College, Dublin, for alerting us to this document; and to Prof. Jeff Pasley of the University of Missouri, Columbia, and, especially, to Miss M. Lamoureux of the American Antiquarian Society, Worcester, Massachusetts, for research assistance.

On Irish printing, see: Adams, *Printed Word;* R. L. Munter, *The History of the Irish Newspaper, 1685–1760* (Cambridge, England, 1967); J. W. Phillips, *Printing and Bookselling in Dublin, 1670–1800: A Bibliographical Inquiry* (Dublin, 1998); T. Wall, *The Sign of Dr. Hay's Head* (Dublin, 1958); and R. E. Ward, *The Prince of Dublin Printers: The Letters of George Faulkner* (Lexington, Ky., 1972). On John FitzGibbon, Mathew Carey's political nemesis—as of Dublin's other liberal and radical printers—see: A. C. Kavanaugh, *John FitzGibbon, Earl of Clare* (Dublin, 1997).

On Mathew Carey, see especially the works by Bríc and Carter cited in the Sources for chapter 34, as well as Durey, *Transatlantic Radicals,* and Wilson, *United Irishmen.* On other Irish immigrant printers, see: P. L. Ford, ed., *The Journals of Hugh Gaine, Printer* (New York, 1902); A. L. Lorenz, *Hugh Gaine: A Colonial Printer's Odyssey to Loyalism* (Carbondale, Ill., 1972); and D. Kaser, *Joseph Charless: Printer in the Western Country* (Philadelphia, 1963), on the County Westmeath–born first printer and newspaper publisher west of the Mississippi.

On early American printing and political journalism, generally, see: J. Axelrod, *Philip Freneau* (Austin, Tex., 1967); C. Brigham, *History and Bibliography of American Newspapers*, 2 vols. (Worcester, Mass., 1947); M. A. Lause, *Some Degree of Power: From Hired Hand to Union Craftsman in the Preindustrial Printing Trades, 1778–1815* (Fayetteville, Ark., 1991); D. C. McMurtrie, *History of Printing in the United States*, vol. 2 (New York, 1969 ed.); R. Remer, *Printers and Men of Capital: Philadelphia Book Publishers in the New Republic* (Philadelphia, 1996); R. G. Silver, *The American Printer, 1787–1825* (Charlottesville, Va., 1967); and I. Thomas, *History of Printing in America* [1810], ed. by M. McCorison (New York, 1970). References to James Doyle's religious publications in Georgetown, Maryland, can be found in Wangler, "Religious Exercises." Biographical data on William Dunlap, Francis Childs, and other printers mentioned in Doyle's letter were discovered in the Printers Authority File at the American Antiquarian Society, Worcester, Massachusetts.

36. Stephen Fotterall, 1791

Stephen Fotterall's 15 June 1791 petition is in the Lea and Febriger Papers, Mathew Carey Incoming Correspondence, Historical Society of Pennsylvania. Again we thank the HSP for permission to publish this document and Dr. Maurice Bríc for bringing it to our attention. On the Fotterall family in Ireland, see: H. Fanning, ed., *The Fottrell Papers, 1721–39* (Belfast, 1980); and Sir. A. Vickars, *Index to the Prerogative Wills of Ireland* (Dublin, 1897), 179. On Stephen Fotterall's career in the United States, see: Campbell, *Friendly Sons of St. Patrick;* W. A. N. Dorland, "The Second Troop, Philadelphia City Cavalry," *PMHB*, 53 (1929), esp. 380–81; *Pa. Arch.*, 6th ser., vols. 4 and 9; P. W. Philby, *Philadelphia Naturalization Records, 1789–1880* (Detroit, 1982); *Stephens's Philadelphia Directory* (Philadelphia, 1796); and Stephen Fotterall's Will 1839/197, in the Registry of Wills, Philadelphia City Hall. On the Hubly family, see *PMHB*, 10 (1886), 414–15; 33 (1909), 129–30; and 43 (1919), 30–42. On indentured servants in Philadelphia, generally, see: Doyle, *Ireland, Irishmen*, 96–106; Galenson, *White Servitude;* F. Grubb, "Servant Auction Records and Immigration into the Delaware Valley, 1745–1831: The Proportion of Females among Immigrant Servants," *Proc. Am. Phil. Soc.*, 133, no. 2 (June 1989), 154–69; and Salinger, *"To Serve Well & Faithfully."*

37. Charles O'Hagan and Mary Dunn, 1796

O'Hagan's petition is in the Lea and Febriger Papers, Mathew Carey Incoming Correspondence, 1785–96, in the Historical Society of Pennsylvania; thanks again to the HSP and to Dr. Maurice Bríc. On O'Hagan and Dunn, see: C. Biddle, *The Philadelphia Directory for 1791* (Philadelphia, 1791); *Stephens's Philadelphia Directory for 1796* (Philadelphia, 1796); C. W. Stafford, *Philadelphia Directory for 1799* (Philadelphia, 1799), and *Philadelphia Directory for 1800* (Philadelphia, 1800); and P. W. Filby, *Philadelphia Naturalization Records, 1789–1880* (Detroit, 1982). Mary Dunn's and Sarah O'Hagan's burial records can be found in Middleton, "Interments." On Irish female poverty in late eighteenth- and early nineteenth-century Philadelphia, see the works by Alexander, Clement, McAleer, Salinger, and Smith in the Sources for chapter 34. Also relevant is K. Wulf, *Not All Wives: Women of Colonial Philadelphia* (Ithaca, N.Y., 2000).

38. Samuel Brown, 1793–1815

The Brown family papers are catalogued as D.3688/F/1–14 and T.3525 in PRONI. We thank the Deputy Keeper of Records, Public Record Office of Northern Ireland, and C. MacLaughlin, Esq., for permission to publish Samuel Brown's letters, and we also thank Mrs. Neddy Seagraves, director of the Genealogical Society of Pennsylvania, and Louise T. Jones and Joel T. Loeb of the Historical Society of Pennsylvania, both in Philadelphia, for research assistance.

On the Brown family business in Belfast, see J. Pigot's *Commercial Directory of Ireland* (Dublin, 1820) and *City of Dublin and Hibernian Provincial Directory* (Dublin, 1824), and the *Belfast Directory, 1831–32*. On Belfast, generally, see: J. C. Beckett and R. E. Glasscock, eds., *Belfast: Origin and Growth of an Industrial City* (London, 1967); Green, *Lagan Valley;* and W. A. Maguire, *Belfast* (Keele, 1993).

The Browns were traced in numerous Philadelphia city and trade directories, from E. Hogan's *Prospect of Philadelphia* (Philadelphia, 1795) to Robert Desilver's *Philadelphia Directory and Stranger's Guide* (Philadelphia, 1833). Thomas and Samuel Brown's wills are catalogued as 1836/200 and 1851/336, respectively, in the Registry of Wills, Philadelphia City Hall. Their nephew James Brown *may* be the individual listed in K. Scott, comp., *British Aliens in the United States during the War of 1812* (Baltimore, 1979), 263. For demographic data on urban and suburban Philadelphia, see: Moffat, *Pop. Hist. of E. U.S. Cities.*

On late eighteenth- and early nineteenth-century Philadelphia, generally, and on the impacts of industrialization and of Republican party factionalism on its Irish and other inhabitants, see: S. W. Higginbotham, *The Keystone in the Democratic Arch: Pennsylvania Politics, 1800–1816* (Harrisburg

1952); Miller, *Phila.—Federalist City;* J. H. Powell, *Bring Out Your Dead: The Great Plague of Yellow Fever in Philadelphia in 1793* (Philadelphia, 1949); Scharf & Westcott, *Hist. of Phila.*, vol. 1 (Philadelphia, 1884); R. Schultz, "God and Workingmen: Popular Religion and the Formation of Philadelphia's Working Class, 1790–1830," in Hoffman & Albert, *Religion in Rev. Age*, 125–55; Shankman, "Democracy in Pa."; T. W. Smith, "The Dawn of the Urban-Industrial Age: The Social Structure of Philadelphia, 1790–1830" (Ph.D. diss., University of Chicago, 1980); R. F. Weigley, ed., *Philadelphia: A Three-Hundred-Year History* (New York, 1982); and also the works by Adams, Clark, Foner, Laurie, McAleer, Schultz, and Shelton, listed in the Sources for chapter 34.

On Jeffersonian liberalism and its contradictions, see: J. Appleby, *Capitalism and a New Social Order: The Republican Vision of the 1790s* (New York, 1984). On the Philadelphia journeymen cordwainers' strike and trial of 1805–1806, also see: T. Lloyd, *The Trial of the Boot & Shoemakers of Philadelphia, on an Indictment for a Combination and Conspiracy to Raise their Wages* (Philadelphia, 1806), reprinted (with accounts of similar trials) in J. R. Commons, et al., eds., *A Documentary History of American Industrial Society*, vol. 3, *Labor Conspiracy Cases* (Cleveland, 1910), 59–248; and C. L. Tomlins, *Law, Labor, and Ideology in the Early American Republic* (New York, 1993). On William Duane and Michael Leib, also see their entries in *ANB*, and on the former: Campbell, *Friendly Sons of St. Patrick;* and K. T. Phillips, "William Duane, Philadelphia's Democratic Republicans, and the Origins of Modern Politics," *PMHB*, 101 (1977), 365–87.

39. Francis Campble, 1737–1742

Campble's journal, formally titled his "Thoughts, Transactions and Incidents," no longer survives, but the introductory segments were published, with modernized spelling and punctuation (as printed herein), in the 3 April 1880 issue of the *Shippensburg News* and republished in W. H. Burkhart, *Cumberland Valley Chronicles: A Bicentennial History* (Shippensburg, Pa., 1976), which also contains biographical information. We are grateful to the Shippensburg Historical Society, Shippensburg, Pennsylvania, for permission to publish the excerpts from Campble's journal that appeared in the late W. H. Burkhart's *Cumberland Valley Chronicles*. For research assistance, especially into Campble's tax and probate records, we thank Christa L. Bassett, librarian, and Joby Maclay of the Cumberland County Historical Society in Carlisle, Pennsylvania, and Myrtle Yohe and Beverly Rensch of the Shippensburg Historical Society.

For additional data on Campble and Shippensburg, see: S. P. Bates, *History of Cumberland and Adams Counties, Pennsylvania* (Chicago, 1886); C. H. Browning, "Francis Campbell," *PMHB*, 28 (1904), 62–70; W. H. Burkhart, *The Shippensburg Story, 1730–1970* (Shippensburg, Pa., 1970); I. H. M'Cauley, *Historical Sketch of Franklin County* (Chambersburg, Pa., 1878); B. M. H. Swope, *History of the Middle Spring Presbyterian Church* (Newville, Pa., 1900); and C. P. Wing, *History of Cumberland County* (Philadelphia, 1879). In addition, see the Sources for chapter 19, esp. the works by Cummings, Dunaway, Klett, and Leyburn.

On early American economic growth; its social consequences, and implications for the Irish immigrant merchants, shopkeepers, etc., described in this and the other chapters in this part, see: Blumin, *Emergence Middle Class;* T. H. Breen, "An Empire of Goods: The Anglicization of Colonial America," *J. Brit. Studies*, 25 (October 1986), 467–99, and "'Baubles of Britain': The American and Consumer Revolutions of the Eighteenth Century," *P & P*, 119 (May 1988), 73–104; Bushman, *Refinement;* Doyle, *Ireland, Irishmen;* Egnal, *New World Economies;* S. L. Engerman and R. E. Gallman, eds., *The Cambridge Economic History of the United States.* vol. 1, *The Colonial Era* (Cambridge, England,

1996); Lockhart, *Some Aspects;* McCusker & Menard, *Econ. Brit. Am.;* E. J. Perkins, *The Economy of Colonial America* (New York, 1980); Truxes, *Irish-Am. Trade;* G. M. Walton and J. F. Shepherd, *The Economic Rise of Early America* (Cambridge, England, 1979); and Wood, *Radicalism of Am. Rev.* For overviews of the eighteenth-century Irish economy, see: L. M. Cullen's chapters in Moody & Vaughn, *NHI 4;* and Dickson, *New Foundations.*

40. Robert Pillson, 1764

Robert Pillson's letters (Ms. 10,360) are the property of the Council of Trustees of the National Library of Ireland, Dublin, and are reproduced with its permission. Thanks also to Dr. Thomas M. Truxes of Westbrook, Connecticut, and Prof. Jim Smyth of the University of Notre Dame for research assistance. Pillson's emigration and application for the Lake George land grant are cited in H. L. Porter III, *Destiny of the Scotch-Irish: An Account of a Migration from Ballybay, Ireland, to Washington County, New York* (Winterhaven, Fla., 1985); and the sale of his New York property in M. J. O'Brien, "Irish Property Owners and Business Men of New York City in the Seventeenth and Eighteenth Centuries," in O'Brien, *Irish Settlers in America,* vol. 1 (Baltimore, 1979).

On Newry and on Pillson landowners in nineteenth-century County Down, respectively, see: T. Canavan, *Frontier Town: An Illustrated History of Newry* (Belfast, 1989); and *Land Owners in Ireland, 1876.* On the Corrys of Newry, see Isaac Corry's entry in *DNB.* On Drogheda and the Brabazons, see, in *Co. Lough Arch. & Hist. J.,* M. Corcoran, "A Drogheda Census List of 1798," 17, no. 2 (1970), 91–96; J. Fitzgerald, "The Drogheda Textile Industry, 1780–1820," 20, no. 2 (1981), 36–48; D Mac Iomhair, "Clergy and Churchwardens of Termonfeckin Parish (1724–1799)," 17, no. 2 (1970), 84–88; and P. Ó Snodaigh, "Notes on the Volunteers, Militia, Yeomanry, and Orangemen of Co. Louth," 18, no. 4 (1976), 279–93.

On the economy and merchants of colonial New York City, generally, see: V. D. Harrington, *The New York Merchant on the Eve of the Revolution* (New York, 1935); and C. Matson, *Merchants and Empire: Trading in Colonial New York* (Baltimore, 1998). On Irish-American trade and New York's Irish merchant community, see: R. C. Murphy and L. J. Mannion, *History of the Society of the Friendly Sons of Saint Patrick in the City of New York, 1784 to 1955* (New York, 1962); R. C. Nash, "Irish Atlantic Trade in the Seventeenth and Eighteenth Centuries," *WMQ,* 42 (1985), 329–356; T. M. Truxes, ed., *Letterbook of Greg & Cunningham, 1756–57: Merchants of New York and Belfast* (Oxford, 2000); and especially Truxes, *Irish-Am. Trade.*

41. John O'Kelly, 1773

O'Kelly's letter is in the George Peabody Wetmore Papers at the Massachusetts Historical Society, Boston, and was published (in slightly modernized form and as by John O. Kelly) in that Society's *Collections,* vol. 9, *Commerce of Rhode Island, 1726–1800* (Boston, 1914), pp. 456–57, which also contains Asa Champlin's 17 September 1773 letter to his brother Christopher. O'Kelly's letters to Aaron Lopez, dated 4 May and 6 July 1772, are in the Aaron Lopez Collection (MSS 541), Rhode Island Historical Society, Providence. O'Kelly's Revolutionary War pension file is W13579, on film at the National Archives in Washington; for an abstract of his will, see L. B. Beaman, "Abstracts of Warren Wills," *Rhode Is. Geneal. Reg.,* 4, no. 3 (January 1982), 265; for the inventory of his estate and related papers, see the Warren Town Council records, in the Warren Town Clerk's Office; and for tax and military service records, see the Warren Town Records, 1738–1878 (microfilm), and the Rhode Island Military Papers (MSS 673), in the Rhode Island Historical Society.

We thank the Massachusetts Historical Society's director, Louis L. Tucker, for permission to publish O'Kelly's letter to Champlin, and its reference librarian, Jennifer Tolpa, for research assistance. For research aid we are also grateful to Bertram Lippincott III and Ronald M. Potvin of the Newport Historical Society; to Richard Stattler and Meredity Sorozan of the Library of the Rhode Island Historical Society, Providence; to Elizabeth A. Johnson of the Town Clerk's Office, Warren, R.I.; and to Bruce Norman of Washington, D.C. Special thanks are due to Dr. Thomas M. Truxes of Westbrook, Connecticut, for bringing the O'Kelly letter to our attention.

On the O'Kellys in County Galway, see: M. Patrick, "The Composition of the Galway Gentry," *Irish Genealogist*, 7 (1986), 82–96; and in Jamaica, T. Burnard, "European Migration to Jamaica, 1655–1780," *WMQ*, 53 (October 1996), 769–96. On Irish emigration from Newfoundland and Galway, see: Lockhart, *Some Aspects;* and Cullen, "Irish Diaspora." On the flaxseed trade, see: Truxes, *Irish-Am. Trade*; and "Connecticut in the Irish-American Flaxseed Trade, 1750–1775," *Éire-Ireland*, 19, no. 2 (summer 1977), 34–62. On the Irish in early Rhode Island, see: T. H. Murray, *Irish Rhode Islanders in the American Revolution* (Providence, 1903); R. J. Purcell, "Irish Builders of Colonial Rhode Island," *Studies* (June 1935), 289–300, and "Rhode Island's Early Schools and Irish Teachers," *Cath. Educ. Rev.*, 32 (1934), 402–15; and the following articles in the *JAIHS:* J. J. Cosgrove, "The Irish in Rhode Island," 9 (1910), 365–68; and T. M. Hamilton, "Commerce between Ireland and Rhode Island," 6 (1906), 31–36, and "The Irish Vanguard of Rhode Island," 4 (1904), 109–33.

For background data on Warren, Newport, and colonial Rhode Island, generally, see: V. Baker, *History of Warren, Rhode Island, in the War of the Revolution, 1776–1783* (Warren, R.I., 1901); T. W. Bicknell, *History of the State of Rhode Island and Providence Plantations*, vol. 2 (New York, 1920); E. F. Crane, *A Dependent People: Newport, Rhode Island, in the Revolutionary Era* (New York, 1985); G. M. Fessenden, *The History of Warren, R.I.* (Providence, 1845); E. Field, ed., *State of Rhode Island and Providence Plantations at the End of the Century: A History* (Boston, 1902); S. V. James, *Colonial Rhode Island* (New York, 1975); W. G. McLoughlin, *Rhode Island* (New York, 1978); and R. H. Rudolph, "Eighteenth-Century Newport and Its Merchants," *Newport History*, 51, no. 170 (spring 1978), 21–38, and no. 171 (summer 1978), 45–60.

Biographical data on Christopher Champlin are based on his obituary in the Newport *Mercury* (4 May 1805), the Champlin Genealogy in the Newport Historical Society, and the Guide to the Champlin Papers (1992) at the Rhode Island Historical Society; J. Hugo Tatsch, *Freemasonry in the Thirteen Colonies* (New York, 1933); and (for the MacSparran connection) W. Updike, *A History of the Episcopal Church in Narragansett, Rhode Island* (1847), 2nd ed. by Rev. D. Goodwin (Boston, 1907). On Aaron Lopez, see his entry in *ANB* and S. F. Chyet, *Lopez of Newport* (Detroit, 1970).

42. Thomas Shipboy, Jr., 1774

Shipboy family correspondence is catalogued as D.530/22 in the Public Record Office of Northern Ireland, Belfast. We thank the Deputy Keeper of Records, PRONI, and A. Deane, Esq., for permission to publish Thomas Shipboy, Jr.'s only surviving letter. Most of the biographical data on the Albany Shipboys was located in primary sources by Dr. Stefan Bielinski of the Colonial Albany Social History Project and by Coreen P. Hallenbeck, also of Albany, and we are very grateful for their assistance.

Information on the Albany Shipboys can also be found in J. Munsell, *Collections on the History of Albany*, vols. 1, 3, and 4 (Albany, 1865–71); and in K. Scott, *Rivington's New York Newspaper: Excerpts from a Loyalist Press, 1773–83* (New York, 1973). On the Shipboys of Coleraine, see Rev.

T. H. Mullin, *Coleraine in Georgian Times* (Belfast, 1977); and Truxes, *Irish-Am. Trade*. On Coleraine, Agherton (or Ballyaghran), and adjacent parishes, see Lewis, *TDI*.

On eighteenth-century Albany and its merchants, see: D. A. Armour, *The Merchants of Albany, New York, 1686–1760* (New York, 1986); S. Bielinski, "How a City Worked: Occupations in Colonial Albany," in N. A. McC. Zeller, ed., *A Beautiful and Fruitful Place: Selected Rensselaerswijck Seminar Papers* (New York, 1991), and "The People of Colonial Albany, 1650–1800: The Profile of a Community," in W. Pencak and C. E. Wright, eds., *Authority and Resistance in Early New York* (New York, 1988); Bonomi, *Factious People;* Countryman, *People in Revolution;* D. G. Hackett, *The Rude Hand of Innovation: Religion and Social Order in Albany, New York, 1652–1836* (New York, 1991); G. R. Howell et al., *History of the County of Albany* (New York, 1886); and Rosen, *Courts & Commerce,* esp. p. 28 (Peter Kalm).

On the Irish in early Albany, see: F. M. Danaher, *Early Irish in Old Albany, N.Y.* (Boston, 1903); and W. E. Rowley, "The Irish Aristocracy of Albany, 1788–1878," *N.Y. Hist.*, 52 (1971), 275–304. On Sir William Johnson, see the Sources for chapter 51 and Greenberg, *Crime & Law.*

43. James Patton (2), 1789–1839

Again, we thank Helen Patton of Franklin, North Carolina, for permission to publish. Perhaps our greatest debt is to professors H. Tyler Blethen and Curtis W. Wood, of Western Carolina University, in Cullowhee, North Carolina, whose essay, "A Trader on the Western Carolina Frontier" (see Sources for chapter 33 for full citation), provides ample background data on Patton and his locale, drawing on sources such as probate records and F. A. Sondley, *History of Buncombe County*, 2 vols. (Asheville, N.C., 1930). On Scots-Irish migration and entrepreneurial patterns, see: Doyle, *Ireland, Irishmen;* and Dunaway, *Scotch-Irish of Col. Pa.* Census figures for 1790 are derived from *A Century of Population Growth: From the First Census of the United States to the Twelfth, 1790–1900* (Baltimore, 1989); and for Asheville in 1800 and 1850 from Moffat, *Pop. Hist. of E. U.S. Cities.*

44. Margaret Carey Murphy Burke, 1798

Margaret Carey Murphy Burke's correspondence with her brother, 1792–1815, is located in the Mathew Carey Incoming Correspondence and Letterbooks, in the Lea and Febriger Collection at the Historical Society of Pennsylvania, Philadelphia, which we thank for permission to publish Margaret Carey Murphy's 1798 letter. Mathew Carey's own *Autobiographical Sketches* (New York, 1970 repr.) and *Autobiography* (Brooklyn, 1942 repr.) unfortunately contain no mention of his sister. However, primary data on Margaret Carey, her husbands, and their children can be found among the Philadelphia city directories in 1794–1807; in the baptismal register of Old St. Joseph's Catholic church, in the Philadelphia Archdiocsan Archives; the Philadelphia Register of Wills; and especially in the archives of Mount St. Mary's College and Seminary, and of the Daughters of Charity, St. Joseph's Provincial House, both in Emmitsburg, Maryland. The archives of the Daughters of Charity also contain copies of Margaret Burke's letters to Cecelia O'Conway [Sr. Marie de l'Incarnation], 1825–1841 (the originals of which are located in the archives of the Ursuline Convent in Montreal), as well as Mother Seton's correspondence. Equally valuable were the Baltimore city directories of 1816–1851; the U.S. Census manuscripts for Baltimore, 1810–1850; the Baltimore Cathedral cemetery records; and the Baltimore City Register of Wills and Estate Inventories, at the Maryland State Archives, Baltimore. Burial records for Margaret Carey Murphy's first husband and children are in Middleton, "Interments." On the Murphys' tavern, see B. and M. Boggs, "Inns and Taverns of

Philadelphia," ms. (no. Am.3032) in the Historical Society of Pennsylvania, Philadelphia, for research in which we thank Laura E. Beardsley, HSP research services coordinator.

For research assistance, we are particularly grateful to: Victoria Pitt Allan, reference archivist at the Maryland State Archives; Sr. Rebecca Fitzgerald, C.A., archivist and director of special collections, Mount St. Mary's College and Seminary; Christine Friend and Steve Paolino of the Philadelphia Archdiocesan Archives; Dr. Margaret McAleer of the Library of Congress, who located and copied the Carey correspondence at the HSP; Sr. Betty Ann McNeil, D.C., archivist at St. Joseph's Provincial House, Emmitsburg; Fr. Paul K. Thomas, archivist of the Baltimore Archdiocese; and Dr. Peter Thompson of St. Cross College, Oxford, for sharing his knowledge of late eighteenth-century Philadelphia taverns. In addition, we wish to thank Dr. David Barnwell of ITE/The Linguistics Institute of Ireland, in Dublin, for sharing the results of his research on Matthias O'Conway, particularly with respect to the latter's political convictions.

For advice on Catholic female education and women religious in late eighteenth-century Ireland, we thank: Professor Nancy Curtin of Fordam University, Yonkers, N.Y.; Sr. Maire Kealy, O.P., of Dublin; Dr. Maria Luddy of the University of Warwick, England; Dr. Mary O'Dowd of Queen's University, Belfast; Dr. Margaret Ó hOgartaigh and Dr. Carla King of St. Patrick's College, Drumcondra, Dublin; and Dr. Rosemary Raughter of University College, Dublin. Finally, we are grateful to Prof. Linda Reeder and Prof. LeeAnn Whites, of the University of Missouri, for their insightful comments on Margaret Carey's correspondence.

On women, women's education, and women religious in Ireland during the late 1700s and early 1800s, see: C. Clear, *Nuns in Nineteenth-Century Ireland* (Dublin, 1987); Sr. Mary Genevieve, P.O., "Mrs. Bellew's Family in Channel Row," *Dublin Historical Record,* 22 (1968), 230–41; J. Kingston, "The Carmelite Nuns in Dublin, 1644–1829," *Reportorium Novum: Dublin Diocesan Historical Record,* 3, no. 2 (1964), 331–60; M. Luddy, *Women and Philanthropy in Nineteenth-Century Ireland* (Cambridge, England, 1995), and *Women in Ireland, 1800–1918: A Documentary History* (Cork, 1995); M. MacCurtain and M. O'Dowd, eds., *Women in Early Modern Ireland* (Edinburgh, 1991); M. P. Magray, *The Transforming Power of the Nuns: Women, Religion, and Cultural Change in Ireland, 1750–1900* (New York, 1998); G. O'Flynn, "Some Aspects of the Education of Irish Women through the Years," *Capuchin Annual* (Dublin, 1977), 164–79; J. Prunty, *Dublin Slums, 1800–1925: A Study in Urban Geography* (Dublin, 1998), and *Margaret Aylward, 1810–1889* (Dublin, 1999); Rev. M. V. Ronan, "Catholic Schools of Old Dublin," *Dublin Historical Record,* 12, no. 3 (August 1951), 65–81; and more broadly, P. J. Corish's *The Catholic Community in the Seventeenth and Eighteenth Centuries* (Dublin, 1981), and *The Irish Catholic Experience* (Dublin, 1985).

On American women in the late eighteenth and early nineteenth centuries, see: Boydston, *Home & Work;* Bridenbaugh, *Cities in Revolt;* P. Cleary, "'She Will Be in the Shop': Women's Sphere of Trade in Eighteenth-Century Philadelphia and New York," *PMHB,* 119 (July 1995), 181–202; N. F. Cott, *The Bonds of Womanhood: "Woman's Sphere" in New England, 1780–1835* (New Haven, 1977); E. F. Crane, "Dependence in the Era of Independence: The Role of Women in a Republican Society," in J. P. Greene, ed., *The American Revolution: Its Character and Limits* (New York, 1987), 253–75; J. R. Gundersen, *To Be Useful to the World: Women in Revolutionary America, 1740–1890* (New York, 1996); R. Hoffman and P. J. Albert, eds., *Women in the Age of the American Revolution* (Charlottesville, Va., 1989), esp. the essays by Kerber, Norton, Salmon, Shammas, and Smith; A. Jacob, "The Woman's Lot in Baltimore Town: 1729–97," *Md. Hist Mag.,* 73, no. 3 (fall 1976), 283–95; J. J. Kenneally, *The History of American Catholic Women* (New York, 1990); L. K. Kerber,

Women of the Republic: Intellect and Ideology in Revolutionary America (Chapel Hill, 1980); Lebsock, *Free Women of Petersburg*; M. B. Norton, *Liberty's Daughters: The Revolutionary Experience of American Women, 1750–1800* (Boston, 1980); M. P. Ryan, *Womanhood in America: From Colonial Times to the Present*, 3rd ed. (New York, 1983); C. Shammas, "The Female Social Structure of Philadelphia in 1775," *PMHB*, 107 (1983), 69–83; B. Welter, "The Cult of True Womanhood, 1820–1860," *Am. Q.*, 18, no. 2 (pt. 1) (summer 1966), 151–74; J. Hoff Wilson, "The Illusion of Change: Women and the American Revolution," in Young, *Am. Rev. Radicalism*, 383–445; L. Wilson, *Life after Death: Widows in Pennsylvania, 1750–1850* (Philadelphia, 1992); N. Woloch, *Women and the American Experience*, 2nd ed. (New York, 1994); and K. Wulf, *Not All Wives: Women of Colonial Philadelphia* (Ithaca, N.Y., 2000). Also relevant is: C. Shammas, M. Salmon, and M. Dahlin, *Inheritance in America: From Colonial Times to the Present* (New Brunswick, New Jersey, 1987).

On the Irish in late eighteenth-century Philadelphia, see: Bríc, "Ireland, Irishmen"; McAleer, "'Civil Strangers'"; and Miller, *Phila.—Federalist City*. On Mathew Carey, see: Carter, "Mathew Carey"; Rowe, *Mathew Carey*; and Wilson, *United Irishmen*, in addition to Carey's autobiographical writings (cited earlier).

On taverns and gambling in the late eighteenth and early nineteenth century in Philadelphia and urban America, generally, see: Bridenbaugh, *Cities in Revolt*; H. Asbury, *Sucker's Progress: An Informal History of Gambling in America* (New York, 1938); H. Chafetz, *Play the Devil: A History of Gambling in the United States* (New York, 1960); A. Fabian, *Card Sharps, Dream Books, and Bucket Shops: Gambling in Nineteenth-Century America* (Ithaca, N.Y., 1990); J. M. Findlay, *People of Chance: Gambling in American Society from Jamestown to Las Vegas* (New York, 1986); W. J. Rorabaugh, *The Alcoholic Republic: An American Tradition* (New York, 1979); and especially P. Thompson, *Rum Punch and Revolution: Taverngoing and Public Life in Eighteenth-Century Philadelphia* (Philadelphia, 1999).

On Baltimore in the early 1800s, see: G. L. Browne, *Baltimore in the Nation, 1789–1861* (Chapel Hill, N.C., 1980); S. H. Olson, *Baltimore: The Building of an American City* (Baltimore, 1980); J. T. Scharf, *History of Baltimore City and County* (1881; repr. Baltimore, 1971); and C. G. Steffan, *The Mechanics of Baltimore: Workers and Politics in the Age of Revolution, 1763–1812* (Urbana, Ill., 1984). For population data, see: Moffat, *Pop. Hist. of E. U.S. Cities*.

On the Catholic church in the United States, generally, during the early 1800s, see: Dolan, *Am. Catholic Experience;* and Hennesey, *Am. Catholics*. Published works on early women religious and their communities in the United States include: M. Ewans, *The Role of the Nun in Nineteenth-Century America* (New York, 1978); J. J. Kenneally, *The History of American Catholic Women* (New York, 1990); K. Kennelly, C.S.J., ed., *American Catholic Women: A Historical Exploration* (New York, 1989), esp. the essay by Ewans; J. G. Mannard, "Maternity . . . of the Spirit: Nuns and Domesticity in Antebellum America," *U.S. Cath. Hist.*, 5, nos. 3–4 (summer/fall 1986), 305–24; B. Misner, "Highly Respectable and Accomplished Ladies: Early American Women Religious, 1790–1850," *Working Papers Series, Center for the Study of American Catholicism, University of Notre Dame*, ser. 8, no. 1 (fall 1980); M. S. Thompson, "Discovering Foremothers: Sisters, Society, and the American Catholic Experience," *U.S. Cath. Hist.*, 5, nos. 3–4 (summer/fall 1986), 273–90, and "Women and American Catholicism, 1789–1989," in S. J. Vicchio and V. Geiger, eds., *Perspectives on the American Catholic Church, 1789–1989* (Westminster, Md., 1989), 122–44; and J. M. White, ed., *The American Catholic Religious Life* (New York, 1988).

General works on the Catholic Church and Catholic schools in the early nineteenth century in Maryland include: Rt. Rev. O. B. Corrigan, *The Catholic Schools of the Archdiocese of Baltimore*

(Baltimore, 1924); M. J. Riordan, *Cathedral Records, from the Beginning of Catholicity in Baltimore* (Baltimore, 1906); J. G. Shea, *Life and Times of the Most Rev. John Carroll, Bishop and First Archbishop of Baltimore* (New York, 1888); and T. W. Spalding, *The Premier See: A History of the Archdiocese of Baltimore, 1789–1989* (Baltimore, 1988). On the Sulpician priests in Maryland and elsewhere, see: C. J. Kauffman, *Tradition and Transformation in Catholic Culture: The Priests of Saint Sulpice in the United States* (New York, 1988); and J. W. Ruane, *The Beginnings of the Society of St. Sulpice in the United States* (Washington, D.C., 1935). Biographical studies of Mother Seton and her spiritual directors and acolytes, many of which briefly mention Margaret Carey Murphy Burke or, more commonly, her daughter, Sr. Maria Murphy, include: J. I. Dirvin, C.M., *Mrs. Seton: Foundress of the American Sisters of Charity* (New York, 1962); E. M. Kelly, ed., *Numerous Choirs: A Chronicle of Elizabeth Bayley Seton and Her Spiritual Daughters* (Evansville, Ind., 1981); E. Kelly and A. Melville, eds., *Elizabeth Seton: Selected Writings* (New York, 1987); A. M. Melville, *Elizabeth Bayley Seton* (New York, 1951), and *Louis William DuBourg: Bishop of Louisiana and the Floridas* (Chicago, 1986), vol. 1; Rt. Rev. R. Seton, *Memoir, Letters and Journal of Elizabeth Seton* (New York, 1869), vol. 1; R. Shaw, *John Dubois: Founding Father* (Yonkers, N.Y., 1983); S. T. Smith, "Philadelphia's First Nun [Cecilia O'Conway]," *Rec. Am. Cath. Hist. Soc. Phila.*, 5 (1894), 417–522.

See also: M. M. Meline, *The Story of the Mountain: Mount St. Mary's College and Seminary* (Emmitsburg, Md., 1911), vol. 1; and the relevant entries in M. Glazier and T. J. Shelley, eds., *The Encyclopedia of American Catholic History* (Collegeville, Minn., 1997). On Matthias O'Conway, see his correspondence in Ms. 21,533, National Library of Ireland, Dublin; and L. F. Flick, "Matthias O'Conway, Philologist, Lexicographer and Interpreter of Language, 1766–1842," *Rec. Am. Cath. Hist. Soc. Phila.*, 10 (1892), 257–99, 385–422, and 11 (1893), 156–77.

45. Mary Cumming, 1814–1815

We could not locate the original ms. copies of Mary Cumming's letters. However, handwritten and typescript copies are catalogued as T.1475 and T.2757 in PRONI, and similarly modernized renditions (as reprinted in this chapter) were published in J. Irvine, ed., *Mary Cumming's Letters Home to Lisburn from America, 1811–1815* (Coleraine, 1982), which also contains biographical and other information on the Cumming and Craig families in Ireland and America. For permission to publish, we wish to thank Miss A. McKisack; the Deputy Keeper of Records, PRONI; and Tom McDonald of Impact Printing, of Coleraine, County Derry, who also graciously permitted our reproduction of Mary Cumming's portrait. For research assistance and advice, we are grateful to Dr. Brian Trainor, former director of the Ulster Historical Foundation, Belfast; Minor Weisiger, archivist, Virginia State Library, Richmond; Suzanne Savery, curator of the Petersburg Museum; and Prof. Linda Reeder and Prof. LeeAnn Whites of the University of Missouri.

On Lisburn and vicinity, see: Day & McWilliams, *OSM*, vol. 8, *Parishes of Co. Antrim II, 1832–8; Lisburn and South Antrim* (1991); and Green, *Lagan Valley*.

On William Cumming in Petersburg, see R. V. Jackson, et al., eds., *Virginia 1810 Census* (Bountiful, Utah, 1976); and his will and estate inventory in the Petersburg City Hustings Court Will Book 2, 1806–1827 (reel 18, pp. 214a, 220–221a), at the Virginia State Library. On early Petersburg, see: E. S. Gregory, *A Sketch of the History of Petersburg* (Richmond, 1877); Lebsock, *Free Women of Petersburg*; J. G. Scott and E. A. Wyatt IV, *Petersburg's Story: A History* (Petersburg, Va., 1960); and E. A. Wyatt IV, *Along Petersburg Streets: Historic Sites and Buildings of Petersburg, Virginia* (Richmond, 1943). On Baltimore and its Irish merchants and Presbyterian clergy, see: T. D. Bilhartz,

Urban Religion and the Second Great Awakening: Church and Society in Early National Baltimore (Rutherford, N.J., 1986); D. T. Gilchrist, *The Growth of the Seaport Cities, 1790–1825* (Charlottesville, Va., 1967); J. C. Brown, *A Hundred Years of Merchant Banking: A History of Brown Brothers and Company* (New York, 1909); S. W. Bruchey, *Robert Oliver, Merchant of Baltimore, 1783–1819* (Baltimore, 1956); A. Ellis, *Heir of Adventure: The Story of Brown, Shipley & Co.* (London, n.d.); and F. R. Kent, *The Story of Alex. Brown & Sons* (Baltimore, 1950); in addition to brief references to United Irish exiles Brown, Dickey, and Sinclair in Durey, *Transatlantic Radicals,* and in Wilson, *United Irishmen.*

In addition to Lebsock, *Free Women,* on women and gender in the early nineteenth-century South, see: C. A. Kierner, *Beyond the Household: Women's Place in the Early South, 1700–1830* (Ithaca, N.Y., 1998); and J. Sidbury, *Ploughshares into Swords: Race, Rebellion, and Identity in Gabriel's Virginia, 1783–1810* (New York, 1997); and, more broadly, Boydston, *Home & Work*; and L. Davidoff and C. Hall, *Family Fortunes: Men and Women of the English Middle Class, 1780–1850* (Chicago, 1987). On the U.S. government's regulations of aliens during the War of 1812, see: Baseler, *"Asylum for Mankind,"* and Wilson, *United Irishmen.*

46. Rev. John Craig, 1734–1769/70

Rev. John Craig's memoir is located in the John Craig Papers, in the archives of the Presbyterian Church (U.S.A.), Presbyterian Historical Society, Montreat, North Carolina. We thank William B. Bynam, acting deputy director at Montreat, for permission to publish and for providing a photocopy of the original ms. For research assistance, we are also grateful to the staff of the Presbyterian Historical Society, Philadelphia, and to Prof. Elizabeth I. Nybakken, formerly of Mississippi State University.

On the Craigs in Donegore and adjacent parishes, see: S. T. Carleton, ed., *Heads and Hearths: The Hearth Money Rolls and Poll Tax Returns for Co. Antrim 1660–69* (Belfast, 1991). On Irish and Scottish influences on Presbyterianism in eighteenth-century America, see: Brooke, *Ulster Presbyterianism;* E. J. Cowan, "Prophecy and Prophylaxis: A Paradigm for the Scotch-Irish," in Blethen & Wood, *Ulster & No. America,* 15–23; Rev. J. G. Craighead, *Scotch and Irish Seeds in American Soil . . .* (Philadelphia, 1878); R. F. G. Holmes, *Our Irish Presbyterian Heritage* (Belfast, 1985); E. I. Nybakken, "New Light on the Old Side: Irish Influences on Colonial Presbyterianism," *JAH,* 68, no. 4 (March 1982), 813–32; S. O'Brien, "A Transatlantic Community of Saints: The Great Awakening and the First Evangelical Network," *AHR,* 91, no. 4 (October 1986), 811–32; and Westerkamp, *Triumph of Laity.*

On religion, the Great Awakening, and Presbyterianism in colonial America, generally, see: Ahlstrom, *Religious History;* R. Balmer and J. R. Fitzmier, *The Presbyterians* (Westport, Conn., 1993); Bonomi, *Cope of Heaven;* Butler, *Sea of Faith;* W. B. Bynum, "'The Genuine Presbyterian Whine': Presbyterian Worship in the Eighteenth Century," *American Presbyterians,* 74 (fall 1996), 157–70; Cremin, *Am. Educ. Col. Exper.;* Finke & Stark, *Churching of America;* W. M. Gewehr, *The Great Awakening in Virginia, 1740–1790* (Durham, N.C., 1930); P. N. Mulder, "Choosing God's People: Religious Identity in the Era of Awakenings" (Ph.D. diss., University of North Carolina, Chapel Hill, 1995); *Records of the Presbyterian Church in the United States of America* (Philadelphia, 1841); Webster, *Hist. Presby. Church;* E. T. Thompson, *Presbyterians in the South,* vol. 1 (Richmond, Va., 1963); and Trinterud, *Forming Am. Tradition.*

On the early Shenandoah Valley and for biographical data on Craig and his contemporaries, see: W. Couper, *History of the Shenandoah Valley,* vol. 1 (New York, 1952); L. K. Craig, *Reverend John Craig, 1709–1774* (New Orleans, 1963); L. Chalkey, *Chronicles of the Scotch-Irish Settlement in*

Virginia, vol. 1 (Rosslyn, Va., 1912); Rev. W. H. Foote, *Sketches of Virginia, Historical and Biographical*, 2nd ser. (Philadelphia, 1855); Hart, *Valley of Virginia;* P. G. Johnson, *James Patton and the Appalachian Colonists* (Verona, Va., 1973); J. L. Peyton, *History of Augusta County* (1882; repr. Bridgewater, Va., 1953); R. F. Scott, "Colonial Presbyterianism in Virginia, 1727–1775," *J. Presby. Hist.*, 35, nos. 2–3 (1957), 71–92 and 171–92; Tillson, *Gentry and Common Folk;* J. A. Waddell, *Annals of Augusta County* (1888; Staunton, Va., 1902 ed.); Webster, *Hist. Presby. Church;* and H. McK. Wilson, *The Tinkling Spring: Headwater of Freedom* (Fisherville, Va., 1954). Also see the Sources for chapter 20.

47. Rev. Samuel Blair, 1744

The published pamphlet containing Rev. Samuel Blair's 1744 letter to Rev. Thomas Prince is item 5342 in *Evans' Early Am. Imprints.* On Blair and his Fagg's Manor church and academy, see: Rev. A. Alexander, *Biographical Sketches of the Founder and Principal Alumni of the Log College* (Philadelphia, 1851); Dunaway, *Scotch-Irish of Col. Pa.;* Futhey & Cope, *History of Chester Co.;* Klett, *Presby. in Col. Pa.;* Rev. W. B. Noble, *History of the Presbyterian Church of Fagg's Manor . . .* (Parkesburg, Pa., 1876); Sprague, *Annals Am. Pulpit,* vol. 3 (New York, 1868); J. B. Turner, "Records of Old Londonderry Congregation, Now Faggs Manor, Chester Co., Pa.," *J. Presby. Hist. Soc.,* 8 (1916), 343–79; J. D. E. Turner, "Rev. Samuel Blair, 1712–1751," *J. Presby. Hist. Soc.,* 29 (1951), 227–36; W. W. Thomson, *Chester County and Its People* (Chicago, 1898); and Webster, *Hist. Presby. Church.* Also see the *DAB* and the *ACAB* entries for Samuel Blair, his brother John, and Rev. Thomas Prince—also described in Weis, *Col. Clergy New England.*

On Presbyterians and the First Great Awakening, especially in Pennsylvania, see the works by Ahlstrom, Balmer and Fitzmier, Bonomi, Butler, Bynum, Nybakken, Trinterud, Webster, and Westerkamp cited in the Sources for chapter 46. In addition, see: T. H. Cornman, "Securing a Faithful Ministry: Struggles of Ethnicity and Religious Epistemology in Colonial American Presbyterianism" (Ph.D. diss., University of Illinois, Chicago, 1998); T. D. Hall, *Contested Boundaries: Itinerancy and the Reshaping of the Colonial American Religious World* (Durham, N.C., 1994); N. Landsman, "Presbyterians, Evangelicals, and the Educational Culture of the Middle Colonies," *Pa. Hist.,* 64, supp. issue (summer 1997), 168–82, and "Revivalism and Nativism in the Middle Colonies: The Great Awakening and the Scots Community in East New Jersey," *Am. Q.,* 34 (1982), 149–64; M. Lodge, "The Crisis of the Churches in the Middle Colonies, 1720–1750," *PMHB,* 95 (1971), 195–220; G. W. Pilcher, *Samuel Davies: Apostle of Dissent in Colonial Virginia* (Knoxville, Tenn., 1971); and Sloan, *Am. College Ideal.*

For American Presbyterianism and religion, generally, in the late 1700s and early 1800s, also see: Carwardine, *Transatlantic Revivalism;* P. K. Conkin, *Cane Ridge: America's Pentecost* (Madison, Wis., 1990); T. H. Cornman, "Securing a Faithful Ministry: Struggles of Ethnicity and Religious Epistemology in Colonial American Presbyterianism" (Ph.D. diss., University of Illinois, Chicago, 1998); Rev. D. Elliott, *The Life of the Rev. Elisha Macurdy* (Allegheny, Pa., 1848); Finke & Stark, *Churching of America;* K. L. Griffin, *Revolution and Religion: American Revolutionary War and the Reformed Clergy* (New York, 1994); Guthrie, *John McMillan;* Hatch, *Democratization;* A. Heimert, *Religion and the American Mind* (Cambridge, Mass., 1966); Hoffman & Albert, *Religion in Rev. Age;* Hood, "Presbyterianism"; B. R. Lacy, Jr., *Revivals in the Midst of the Years* (Richmond, Va., 1943); R. W. Long, "The Presbyterians and the Whiskey Rebellion," *J. Presby. Hist.,* 43 (March 1965), 28–36; Wingo, "Politics, Society, and Religion"; and Wood, *Radicalism of Am. Rev.*

Carlile Pollock's 1789 letter to his uncle, Rev. William Campbell of Armagh, is in file 49 of the T. F. G. Patterson Ms. Collection in the Armagh County Library in Armagh town and is reprinted in: Rev. W. D. Patton, "'My Dear Uncle': A Letter from New York, 1789," *Bul. Presby. Hist. Soc. of Ire.*, 23 (1994), 20–24. We are grateful to: Prof. Michael Montgomery of the University of South Carolina for bringing this document to our attention; Rev. W. Donald Patton of Belfast for his generosity in sharing with us his research on Rev. Campbell; and Catherine McCullough, curator of the Armagh County Museum, for granting us permission to publish Pollock's letter.

For interpretations of James O'Kelly and the Campbells, see: P. K. Conkin, *American Originals: Homemade Varieties of Christianity* (Chapel Hill, N.C., 1997), as well as Hatch, *Democ. Am. Christ.* (although the Campbells are misidentified as "Scottish"). On O'Kelly, also see: C. F. Kilgore, *The James O'Kelly Schism in the Methodist Episcopal Church* (Mexico City, 1963); and W. E. MacClenny, *The Life of Rev. James O'Kelly* (Raleigh, N.C., 1910); and on the Campbells and their churches: A. Campbell, *Memoirs of Elder Thomas Campbell* (Cincinnati, 1861); D. E. Harrell, Jr., *Quest for a Christian America: The Disciples of Christ and American Society to 1866* (Nashville, 1966); H. L. Lunger, *The Political Ethics of Alexander Campbell* (St. Louis, Mo., 1954); L. G. McAllister, *Thomas Campbell: Man of the Book* (St. Louis, Mo., 1954); R. Richardson, *Memoirs of Alexander Campbell* (Philadelphia, 1868); and R. F. West, *Alexander Campbell and Natural Religion* (New Haven, 1948).

48. Bernard M'Kenna, 1811

Bernard M'Kenna's three letters, 1811–1812, comprise part of Ms. 2300, which is the property of the Council of Trustees of the National Library of Ireland, Dublin, which we thank for permission to publish. For research assistance, we are grateful to: Prof. Diana Ahmad of the U. of Missouri-Rolla; William Asadorian, archivist, Queen's Borough Public Library, Jamaica, New York; Prof. Marion R. Casey of New York University; James Driscoll, director of research, Queen's Historical Society, Flushing, New York; Anne Hartfield of San Marino, California; Dr. Greg Koos, executive director, McLean County Historical Society, Bloomington, Illinois; Christine McCullough, assistant archivist, Archdiocese of Philadelphia Archives, Overbrook, Pennsylvania (where Bishop Conwell's papers are located); John O'Connor of New York City, who found M'Kenna's record in that city's Death Registers; Robert P. Rushmore, secretary, Nassau County Historical Society, Garden City, New York; Joseph M. Silinonte of Brooklyn, New York; and the staff of the New York Genealogical and Biographical Society, New York City.

M'Kenna's will is in the New York County Wills, vol. 51, p. 365 (on film at the NYGBS) and in R. C. Sawyer and G. A. Barber, *Abstracts of New York County Wills, 1801–1856* (typescript at Brooklyn Historical Society), vol. 3, p. 5; and for references to M'Kenna's wife and her kin, see: E. A. Doty, *The Doty-Dotten Family in America* (Brooklyn, 1897); Hinshaw, *Encycl. Am. Quaker Geneal.*, vol. 3 (Ann Arbor, Mich., 1940); and T. J. Gilfoyle, *City of Eros: New York City, Prostitution, and the Commercialization of Sex, 1790–1920* (New York, 1992).

Patrick McKenna's holding in Carrycastle is valued in TAB: Clonfeacle Parish (n. d. [1824–38]) in PRONI. On the M'Kennas of north County Monaghan, see: E. Eugene Swezey III, *The MacKennas of Truagh* (Bowie, Md., 1993). The executions of the M'Kenna brothers and two other Monaghan militiamen were commemorated by William Sampson's revolutionary song "Death before Dishonor; or the Four Irish Soldiers"; see M. H. Thuente, *The Harp Re-strung : The United Irishmen and the Rise of Irish Literary Nationalism* (Syracuse, N.Y., 1994).

On schoolmasters, Catholics, and political conflict in late eighteenth-century Ulster, generally, see: Adams, *Printed Word;* S. J. Connolly, "Catholicism in Ulster, 1800–50," in Roebuck, *Plantation to Partition*, 157–71; Daly & Dickson, *Origins Pop. Literacy*, especially the essays by L. M. Cullen and N. Ó Cíosáin; P. J. Dowling, *The Hedge Schools of Ireland* (Dublin, 1935); M. Elliott, "The Defenders in Ulster," in Dickson et al., *United Irishmen*, 222–33; Fitzgerald, "Irish-Speaking"; B. McEvoy, "The United Irishmen in Co. Tyrone," *Seanchas Ardmhacha*, 3, no. 2 (1959), 283–314, and 4, no. 1 (1960–61), 1–32; R. R. Madden, *The United Irishmen, Their Lives and Times*, vol. 4 (London, 1842–45); O. P. Rafferty, *Catholicism in Ulster, 1603–1983* (Columbia, S.C., 1994); and A. T. Q. Stewart, *Summer Soldiers*.

On education and Irish schoolmasters in early America, see: Cremin, *Am. Educ. Col. Exper.*; G. Koos, "Irish Immigrant Schoolmasters in Early American Education" (unpub. essay, 1995); E. Nybakken, "In the Irish Tradition: Pre-Revolutionary Academies in America," *Hist. Educ. Q.*, 37, no. 2 (summer 1997), 163–84; M. O'Brien, "Irish Schoolmasters in the American Colonies" and "Irish Schoolmasters in the City of New York," in O'Brien, *Irish Settlers in America*, vol. 2 (Baltimore, 1979); R. J. Purcell, "Irish Cultural Contributions in Early New York," *Cath. Educ. Rev.*, 35 (October 1937), 28–42; and Sloan, *Am. College Ideal*.

For background information on Queen's County, New York, see: [Anon.], *History of Queen's County* (New York, 1882); J. H. French, *Gazetteer of the State of New York* (Syracuse, N.Y., 1860); H. G. Spafford, *Gazetteer of the State of New-York* (Albany, N.Y., 1813); and H. Onderdonk, Jr., *The Annals of Hempstead, 1643 to 1832* . . . (Hempstead, N.Y., 1878).

On the early Catholic church and clergy in New York City, see: J. R. Bayley, *A Brief Sketch of the Early History of the Catholic Church on the Island of New York* (New York, 1870); W. H. Bennett, *Catholic Footsteps in Old New York* (New York, 1909); M. L. Booth, *History of the City of New York* (New York, 1880); Carey, *People, Priests, & Prelates;* Sr. M. P. Carthy, O.S.U., *Old St. Patrick's: New York's First Cathedral* (New York, 1947); Rev. Msgr. F. D. Cohalan, *A Popular History of the Archdiocese of New York* (Yonkers, N.Y., 1983); F. X. Curran, S.J., "The Jesuit Colony in New York, 1808–1817," U.S. Cath. Hist. Soc., *Hist. Rec. & Studies*, 42 (1954), 51–97; J. P. Dolan, *The Immigrant Church: New York's Irish and German Catholics, 1815–1865* (Baltimore, 1975); A. Hartfield, "Profile of a Pluralistic Parish: Saint Peter's Roman Catholic Church, New York City, 1785–1815," *J. Am. Ethnic Hist.*, 12, no. 3 (spring 1993), 30–59; Hennesey, *Am. Catholics;* J. M. O'Toole, "From Advent to Easter: Catholic Preaching in New York City, 1808–1809," *Church History*, 63, no. 3 (September 1994), 365–77; Rev. L. R. Ryan, *Old St. Peter's: The Mother Church of Catholic New York* (New York, 1935); J. K. Sharp, *History of the Diocese of Brooklyn*, vol. 1 (New York, 1954); and L. J. Walsh, "Life among the Early Irish Immigrants," *Catholic World*, 154 (March 1942), 716–21.

On trusteeism, generally, see: Carey, *Priests, People, & Prelates;* Chinnici, "American Catholics"; Light, *Rome & New Republic;* and the relevant chapters of Dolan, *Am. Catholic Experience*, and McAvoy, *Catholic Church in U.S.* On bishops Conwell and Fenwick, see the entries in *DAB* and *NCE*. Additional information on the priests mentioned in M'Kenna's letter can be found in the works on Mother Seton and Baltimore Catholicism by Dirvin, Kelly, Melville, Riordan, Shaw, and Shea listed in the Sources for chapter 44.

49. Rev. James McGregor and John McMurphy, 1720–1730

Rev. James McGregor's letter to Samuel Shute of 27 February 1720 is located in the Jeremy Belknap Papers, volume 61.A.81, in the Massachusetts Historical Society, Boston, whose governing body we thank for permission to publish. Modernized texts of MacGregor's petition are published in: J. Belknap, *The History of New-Hampshire* (Dover, New Hampshire, 1812), vol. 2, pp. 260–63; and in

N. Bouton, ed., *Documents and Records Relating to the Province of New Hampshire*, vol. 3 (Manchester, N.H., 1869), pp. 770–71. The 17 March 1730 petition by John McMurphy et al. is catalogued as CO5/871 ff.186–87 in the New England correspondence of the Papers of the Board of Trade and Secretaries of State (America and West Indies) in the British Public Record Office in Kew, England, and a nearly accurate transcript was published in J. P. Baxter, ed., *Collections of the Maine Historical Society: Documentary History*, 2nd series, vol. 11 (1908), 18–19. For research assistance we are grateful to: Sharon Carson of Londonderry, New Hampshire; Prof. James E. Doan of Nova Southeastern University; Nicholas Graham, reference librarian at the Massachusetts Historical Society; Dr. Ann McVeigh at PRONI; Prof. Michael Montgomery of the University of South Carolina; Prof. James P. Myers of Gettysburg College; and Robert W. O'Hara of Kew, England.

On Presbyterian grievances and Anglican hostility in early eighteenth-century Ireland, see: J. M. Barkley, "The Presbyterian Minister in Eighteenth-Century Ireland," in Haire, *Challenge and Conflict*, 46–71; Beckett, *Protestant Dissent;* Hayton, "Anglo-Irish Attitudes"; Herlihy, *Irish Dissenting Tradition,* especially the essays by T. C. Barnard and R. Gillespie; Herlihy, *Politics of Irish Dissent,* particularly the chapters by T. C. Barnard and D. W. Hayton; Kilroy, *Protestant Dissent*; and McBride, *Siege of Derry*. On Scots-Gaelic and Irish-speaking Presbyterians in the 1600s and 1700s in Ulster, see: R. Blaney, *Presbyterians and the Irish Language* (Belfast, 1996). On Protestant political identities in eighteenth-century Ireland, see: Connolly, *Religion, Law & Power;* Hayton, "Anglo-Irish Attitudes"; McBride, *Scripture Politics;* and additional relevant works in the Sources for chapter 8.

On Rev. James McGregor, the Londonderry settlers, and early Ulster migration to New England, generally, see: Bolton, *Scotch-Irish Pioneers;* G. W. Browne, ed., *Early Records of Londonderry, Windham, and Derry, New Hampshire, 1719–1762,* 2 vols. (Manchester, N.H., 1908 and 1911); Clark, *Eastern Frontier;* Daniell, *Col. N.H.;* Dickson, *Ulster Emigration;* J. E. Doan, "The 'Eagle Wing' and Presbyterian Memoirs" (unpublished conference presentation, 1999); D. McCourt, "County Derry and New England: The Scotch-Irish Migration of 1718," in O'Brien, *Derry & Londonderry,* 303–20; Rev. E. L. Parker, *The History of Londonderry* (Boston, 1851); Rev. A. L. Perry, *Scotch-Irish in New England* (Boston, 1891), which contains a detailed and (especially considering its initial delivery to a Scotch-Irish Congress) remarkably candid account of eighteenth-century Londonderry; J. Smith, "The Massachusetts and New Hampshire Boundary Controversy, 1683–1740," *Proc. Mass. Hist. Soc.,* 43 (1909–10), 77–88; R. S. Wallace, "The Scotch-Irish of Provincial New Hampshire" (Ph.D. diss., University of New Hampshire, 1984); and D. J. Watters, "Fencing ye Tables: Scotch-Irish Ethnicity and the Gravestones of John Wight," *Hist. N.H.,* 52 (spring/summer 1997), 2–18. In his research for *Fighters of Derry: Their Deeds and Descendants* (London, 1932), W. R. Young could not find Rev. James McGregor's name listed "by any seige authority" among Derry city's 1690 defenders. On New England royal governors Shute and Wentworth, see their entries in the *DAB*.

On Scots-Irish political activities in the late eighteenth and early nineteenth centuries in New England, see: Clark et al., *Maine in Early Republic;* D. B. Cole, *Jacksonian Democracy in New Hampshire, 1800–1851* (Cambridge, Mass., 1970); Daniell, *Experiment;* R. P. Formisano, *The Transformation of Political Culture: Massachusetts Parties, 1790s-1840s* (New York, 1983); and Taylor, *Liberty Men.* On Matthew Lyon of Vermont, see: A. Austin, *Matthew Lyon: "New Man" of the Democratic Revolution, 1749–1822* (University Park, Pa., 1981). For Jeremy Belknap, see his entries in *DAB* and *DNB*.

Discussion of the so-called Scotch-Irish myth is often fraught with controversy and acrimony. However, for critical analyses of ethnic nomenclature and identity, see (in addition to Wallace, "The

Scotch-Irish of Provincial New Hampshire"): M. A. Jones, "The Scotch-Irish in British America," in Bailyn & Morgan, *Strangers;* and the appendix to Leyburn, *Scotch-Irish,* the text of which also contains a brief history of Ulster Presbyterian settlement in New England. For derogatory references to the "Scotch-Irish" in eighteenth-century America, see also: Hart, *Valley of Virginia;* and Hooker, *Carolina Backcountry.* On the images of Scotland and Scottish immigrants in revolutionary America, see: Brock, *Scotus Americanus;* and A. Hook, *Scotland and America: A Study of Cultural Relations, 1750–1835* (Glasgow, 1975), both of which contradict P. Ross's hagiographical history *The Scots in America* (New York, 1896).

On Scotland in the 1700s, see: A. C. Chitnis, *The Scottish Enlightenment: A Social History* (London, 1976); Daiches, *Scottish Culture;* Donovan, *No Popery in Scotland;* C. Harvie, "Scott and the Image of Scotland," in R. Samuel, ed., *Patriotism: The Making and Unmaking of British National Identity* (London, 1989), 173–92; B. Lenman, *Integration, Enlightenment, and Industrialization: Scotland, 1746–1832* (Toronto, 1981); McBride, "School of Virtue"; N. Phillipson, "The Scottish Enlightenment," in R. Porter and M. Teich, eds., *The Enlightenment in National Context* (Cambridge, England, 1981), 19–40; N. T. Phillipson and R. Mitchison, eds., *Scotland in the Age of Improvement* (Edinburgh, 1970); R. B. Sher, *Church and University in the Scottish Enlightenment* (Edinburgh, 1985); and R. Sher and A. Murdoch, "Patronage and Party in the Church of Scotland, 1750–1800," in N. MacDougall, ed., *Church, Politics and Society: Scotland, 1408–1929* (Edinburgh, 1983), 197–220.

On socioeconomic, political, and cultural relationships between Ireland/Ulster and Scotland in the 1700s, see: L. M. Cullen, "Scotland and Ireland, 1600–1800: Their Role in the Evolution of British Society," in R. A. Houston and I. D. Whyte, eds., *Scottish Society, 1500–1800* (Cambridge, England, 1989), 226–44; J. Erskine and G. Lucy, eds., *Cultural Traditions in Northern Ireland. Varieties of Scottishness* (Belfast, 1997); E. W. McFarland, *Ireland and Scotland in the Age of Revolution* (Edinburgh, 1994); I. S. Wood, ed., *Scotland and Ulster* (Edinburgh, 1994); and Walker, *Intimate Strangers.*

On the Ulster Scots language and the Rhyming Weavers, see: G. B. Adams, *The English Dialects of Ulster,* ed. by M. Barry and P. Tilling (Holywood, Co. Down, 1986); J. Erskine and G. Lucy, eds., *Cultural Traditions,* especially the essays by Herbison, Kay, and Lunney; J. Hewitt, *Rhyming Weavers and Other Country Poets of Antrim and Down* (Belfast, 1974); L. McIlvanney, "Robert Burns and the Ulster-Scots Literary Revival of the 1790s," *Bullán: An Irish Studies Journal,* 4, no. 2 (winter 1999/spring 2000), 125–44; M. B. Montgomery and R. J. Gregg, "The Scots Language in Ulster," in C. Jones, ed., *The Edinburgh History of Scots* (Edinburgh, 1997). On specific Ulster poets, see: J. R. R. Adams, "A Rural Bard, His Printers and His Public: Robert Huddleston of Moneyrea," *Linen Hall Review,* 9, nos. 3/4 (Belfast: winter 1992), 9–11; D. H. Akenson and W. H. Crawford, *James Orr: Bard of Ballycarry* (Belfast, 1977); J. Campbell, *The Poems & Songs of James Campbell of Ballynure* (Ballyclare, Co. Antrim, 1870); I. Herbison, *Webs of Fancy: Poems of David Herbison, the Bard of Dunclug* (Oxford, 1980); J. Orr, *Poems on Various Subjects . . .* (Belfast, 1936 ed.); P. Robinson, ed., *The Country Rhymes of James Orr, the Bard of Ballycarry, 1770–1816* (Bangor, Co. Down, 1992); and E. McA. Scott and P. Robinson, eds., *The Country Rhymes of Samuel Thomson, the Bard of Carngranny, 1766–1816* (Bangor, Co. Down, 1992).

On Robert Dinsmoor ("The 'Rustic Bard'"), see his *Incidental Poems . . . and Sketch of the Author's Life* (Haverhill, Mass., 1828); and M. Montgomery, "The Problem of Persistence: Ulster-American Missing Links," *J. of Scotch-Irish Studies,* 1 (2000), 105–19. On the Presbyterian clergy's crusade to suppress traditional religious customs in the United States as in Scotland and Ulster during the late 1700s and early 1800s, see: Schmidt, *Holy Fairs*. On the Celtic feasts of Bealtaine and Samhain, the dates of which (8 May and 1 November, respectively) closely coincide with those of Londonderry's fairs, see: A. and B. Rees, *Celtic Heritage* (London, 1961).

50. Dr. Charles Carroll, 1748

Dr. Charles Carroll's 1748 letter to his London cousin is in the Dr. Charles Carroll of Annapolis Letterbooks, MS. 208.1, pp. 198–99, in the Manuscripts Division of the Maryland Historical Society Library (MHSL), Baltimore; the Letterbook also contains Carroll's 1739 letter to his son in Lisbon. We thank the MHSL and its curator of manuscripts, Jennifer A. Bryan, for permission to publish. The 1748 letter is also published, in slightly modernized form, in the *Md. Hist. Mag.*, 22, no. 4 (December 1927), 376–77, along with other Dr. Charles Carroll correspondence. For research assistance, we are grateful to Dr. Jacqueline Hill of the National University of Ireland at Maynooth; to Dr. J. B. L. Lyons and Dr. James McGuire of University College, Dublin; to Prof. Ronald Hoffman, director of the Institute of Early American History and Culture, Williamsburg, Virginia; and especially to Prof. Beatriz B. Hardy of Coastal Carolina University, Conway, South Carolina, who most generously brought this letter to our attention, allowed us to read her unpublished doctoral dissertation, and provided both an accurate transcription of Dr. Carroll's letter and invaluable information about him.

For the fullest account of the O'Carroll family of King's County (Offaly), see: R. Hoffman with S. D. Mason, *Princes of Ireland, Planters of Maryland: A Carroll Saga, 1500–1782* (Chapel Hill, N.C., 2000); I. Murphy, *The Diocese of Killaloe in the Eighteenth Century* (Blackrock, Co. Dublin, 1991); and the chapters in Nolan & O'Neill, *Offaly*, by T. Venning, R. Loeber, and H. Murtagh.

On the Catholic community and its dispossessed gentry in the late seventeenth and early eighteenth centuries in Ireland, generally, see especially: Bartlett, *Fall and Rise*; P. J. Corish, *The Catholic Community in the Seventeenth and Eighteenth Centuries* (Dublin, 1981), and *The Irish Catholic Experience: A Historical Survey* (Dublin, 1985); P. Fagan, *Divided Loyalties: The Question of an Oath for Irish Catholics in the Eighteenth Century* (Dublin, 1997); Leerssen, *Mere Irish*; C. D. A. Leighton, *Catholicism in a Protestant Kingdom* (Dublin, 1994); Power & Whelan, *Endurance*, especially Power's "Converts," 101–27; and M. Wall, *Catholic Ireland in the Eighteenth Century*, ed. by G. O'Brien (Dublin, 1989).

On Dr. Carroll and his Maryland context, see: L. G. Carr, P. D. Morgan, and J. B. Russo, eds., *Colonial Chesapeake Society* (Chapel Hill, N.C., 1988); F. Emory, *Queen Anne's County, Maryland* (Baltimore, 1950); G. A. Hanson, *Old Kent: The Eastern Shore of Maryland* (Baltimore, 1876); R. B. Harley, "Dr. Charles Carroll—Land Speculator," *Md. Hist. Mag.*, 46 (1951), 93–107; R. Hoffman, "'Marylando-Hibernus': Charles Carroll the Settler, 1660–1720," *WMQ*, 45, no. 2 (April 1988), 207–36; R. Hoffman with S. D. Mason, *Princes of Ireland*; A. C. Land, *Colonial Maryland: A History* (Millwood, N.Y., 1981); J. B. Lee, *The Price of Nationhood: The American Revolution in Charles County* (New York, 1994); Lockhart, *Some Aspects*; "'News' from the 'Maryland Gazette,'" *Md. Hist. Mag.*, 23, no. 1 (March 1923), 30 (Carroll's 1755 obituary); E. C. Papenfuse et al., eds., *A Biographical Dictionary of the Maryland Legislature, 1635–1789*, vol. 1 (Baltimore, 1977); R. J. Purcell, "Irish Colonists in Colonial Maryland," *Studies*, 23 (June 1934), 279–294; H. D. Richardson, *Side-Lights on Maryland History*, 2 vols. (Baltimore, 1913); J. D. Warfield, *The Founders of Anne Arundel and Howard Counties* (Baltimore, 1905); and especially, B. B. Hardy, "Papists in a Protestant Age: The Catholic Gentry and Community in Colonial Maryland, 1689–1776" (Ph.D. diss., University of Maryland, College Park, 1993).

On the medical profession in early eighteenth-century Ireland and Britain, see: C. S. Cameron, *History of the Royal College of Surgeons in Ireland* (Dublin, 1913); W. Doolin, *Dublin's Surgeon-Anatomists*, ed. by J. B. L. Lyons (Dublin, 1987); M. D. R. Leys, *Catholics in England, 1554–1829: A Social History* (London, 1961); J. B. L. Lyons, "Aspects of Medicine in Hibernia Magna," *Irish Medical J.*, 80 (August 1987), 235–39; E. MacLysaght, *Irish Life in the Seventeenth Century* (Cork, 1939); E. O'Brien, *The Charitable Infirmary, Jervis Street, 1718–1987* (Dublin, 1987); and D. Riesman, "The Dublin Medical School and Its Influence upon Medicine in America," *Annals of Medical History*, 4 (1922), 86–96. On medicine in colonial America, see: W. J. Bell, Jr., *The Colonial Physician and Other Essays* (New York, 1975); J. H. Cassedy, *Medicine in America: A Short History* (Baltimore, 1991); R. H. Shryock, *Medicine and Society in America, 1660–1860* (New York, 1960); and P. Starr, *The Social Transformation of American Medicine* (New York, 1982). On eighteenth-century coffee houses, see: B. Lillywhite, *London Coffee Houses: A Reference Book* (London, 1963); and Shields, *Civil Tongues.*

51. Silvester Ferrall, Charles Lewis Reily, Peter Warren Johnson, and George Croghan, 1745–1764

The original manuscripts of the Silvester Ferrall, Charles Lewis Reily, and Peter Warren Johnson letters are in the Sir William Johnson Papers at the New York State Library, Albany; the George Croghan letter of 12 July 1764 no longer exists in manuscript, and we have republished the copy printed in the *Papers of Sir William Johnson*, vol. 4 (Albany, 1925), 462–66. For permission to publish, we are grateful to the New York State Library; and for research aid, we thank: James Corsaro and Billie Aul, Manuscripts and Special Collections, at the New York State Library; Jeffrey W. Hall of the Goshen, New York, Public Library and Historical Society; and, for assistance with Reily's Latin, Prof. Charles Nauert and Prof. Mark Smith of the University of Missouri, Columbia.

On Sir William Johnson's family and environment in Ireland, see: Casey & Rowan, *No. Leinster*; and F. B. Recum, *The Families of Warren and Johnson of Warrenstown, County Meath* (New York, 1950), in addition to the early chapters in the Johnson biographies listed in the following paragraph. For information on early eighteenth-century Irish schoolmasters and the use of phonetic Gaelic (in Charles Lewis Reily's letter), see: D. Hayton, "Did Protestantism Fail in Early Eighteenth-Century Ireland? Charity Schools and the Enterprise of Religious and Social Reformation, ca. 1690–1730," in Ford et al., *As By Law Established*; Ó Ciosáin, *Print & Pop. Culture*; and the chapters by Ó Ciosáin and L. M. Cullen in Daly & Dickson, *Origins Pop. Literacy.*

For background information on Sir William Johnson and his colonial American milieu, see: Bonomi, *Factious People*; Doyle, *Ireland, Irishmen*; Countryman, *People in Revolution*; J. T. Flexner, *Lord of the Mohawks: A Biography of Sir William Johnson* (Boston, 1979); M. W. Hamilton, *Sir William Johnson, Colonial American* (New York, 1976); S. N. Katz, *Newcastle's New York: Anglo-American Politics, 1732–1753* (Cambridge, Mass., 1968); *Papers of Sir William Johnson*, 14 vols., various eds. (Albany, N.Y., 1921–62); A. Pound, *Johnson of the Mohawks: A Biography of Sir William Johnson* (New York, 1930); R. J. Purcell, "Irish Contribution to Colonial New York," *Studies*, 29 (1940), 591–604, and 30 (1941), 107–20, and "Irish Cultural Contribution in Early New York," *Cath. Educ. Rev.*, 35 (October 1937), 449–60, and 36 (January 1938), 28–42; W. L. Stone, *The Life and Times of Sir William Johnson, Bart.*, 2 vols. (Albany, N.Y., 1865); and the entries on Sir William and Guy Johnson in

DAB, DNB, and *DCB.* Biographical data about some of Johnson's Irish tenants and dependents (e.g., Fr. Peter McKenna) can be found in the American Loyalists' petitions, especially vols. 17–24 (see the Sources for chapter 60 for full citation).

For American data pertinent to Charles Lewis Reily, see: S. W. Eager, *An Outline History of Orange County* (Newburgh, N.Y., 1847); R. Headley, ed., *The History of Orange County* (Middletown, N.Y., 1908); and E. M. Ruttenber and L. H. Clark, *History of Orange County* (Philadelphia, 1881); O'Reilly's letter is also published in V. F. O'Reilly, "An Irish Schoolmaster's Letter," *JAIHS,* 23 (1924), 190–92. On Charles Clinton, see the early chapters of his son's biographies: J. P. Kaminski, *George Clinton: Yeoman Politician of the New Republic* (Madison, Wis., 1993); and E. W. Spaulding, *His Excellency George Clinton* (New York, 1938). On Cadwallader Colden, see: A. M. Keys, *Cadwallader Colden* (New York, 1906); and *DAB.* On George Croghan, see: A. T. Vowiler, "George Croghan and the Westward Movement, 1741–1782," *PMHB,* 46 (1922), 273–311; N. B. Wainright, *George Croghan, Wilderness Diplomat* (Chapel Hill, N.C., 1959); and *DAB.* On Sir Peter Warren and the other British statesmen and colonial officials mentioned in the letters, see their entries in the *DNB, DAB,* or *DCB.*

52. Samuel Bryan, 1752

A copy of Samuel Bryan's letter of 23 September 1752, typed in the early twentieth century, is in the George Bryan Papers at the Historical Society of Pennsylvania, Philadelphia The location of the original manuscript is unknown; according to the historian Burton A. Konkle, in 1922 it was in the possession of William F. Bryan, Peoria, Illinois. We wish to thank the Historical Society of Pennsylvania for permission to publish Samuel Bryan's letter; and for bibliographical and research assistance we appreciate the aid of Prof. Ted Koditschek of the University of Missouri, Columbia, and Kathleen Ryan and John Smolenski at the University of Pennsylvania.

Biographies of George Bryan are: Foster, *Pursuit of Equal Liberty;* and B. A. Konkle, *George Bryan and the Constitution of Pennsylvania, 1731–1791* (Philadelphia, 1922). Also see Bell, *Patriot-Improvers.* Unfortunately, these works contain scant information on Samuel Bryan of Dublin, but he is listed in the following primary sources: *A Directory of Dublin for the Year 1738* (Dublin, 2000); "An Alphabetical List of the Freemen and Freeholders of the City of Dublin, who Polled at the Election for Members of Parliament . . . 1749 (Dublin, 1750; copy in Haliday Pamphlets (HP), vol. 214, Royal Irish Academy, Dublin); G. Thrift, comp., Roll of Freemen, City of Dublin, 1575–1774 (Mss. 76–79, NLI); and Sir A. Vicars, comp., *Index to the Prerogative Wills of Ireland* (Dublin, 1897).

On eighteenth-century Dublin dissenters and politics, and on the career of Charles Lucas, see: Rev. J. Armstrong, *History of the Presbyterian Churches in the City of Dublin* (Dublin, 1829); Dickson, *New Foundations;* Haire, *Challenge & Conflict;* Herlihy, *Irish Dissenting Tradition,* especially the essays by T. C. Barnard and S. ffeary-Smyrl; Herlihy, *Politics of Irish Dissent,* particularly the chapters by T. C. Barnard and D. W. Hayton; Kilroy, *Protestant Dissent;* McBride, "School of Virtue"; S. Murphy, "Charles Lucas and the Dublin Election of 1748–49," *Parl. Hist.,* 2 (1983), 93–111; York, *Neither Kingdom;* and especially the following works by Jacqueline Hill: "Biblical Language and Providential Destiny in Mid-Eighteenth-Century Irish Protestant Patriotism," in Devlin & Fanning, *Religion & Rebellion,* 71–83; "Dublin Corporation, Protestant Dissent, and Politics, 1660–1800," in Herlihy, *Politics of Irish Dissent,* 28–39; and *Patriots to Unionists.*

The classic works on the "republican" and "commonwealth" traditions in British and American political thought include: B. Bailyn, *The Ideological Origins of the American Revolution* (Cambridge,

Mass., 1967); J. G. A. Pocock, *Virtue, Commerce, and History: Essays on Political Thought and History* (Cambridge, England, 1985); Robbins, *Commonwealthman;* and Wood, *Creation of Am. Rep.* For a critical view, see: I. Kramnick, *Republicanism and Bourgeois Radicalism: Political Ideology in Late Eighteenth-Century England and America* (Ithaca, N.Y., 1990), which argues for the primacy of Lockean liberalism on Britain's and America's emergent bourgeoisie. On Shaftesbury, Addison, Steele, Locke, Chesterfield, Harrington, Bollingbroke, and Molesworth, see also their entries in *DNB.*

On the contexts of George Bryan's mercantile and political careers in Philadelphia, see especially: Doerflinger, *Vigorous Spirit;* and Ireland, *Religion, Ethnicity, & Politics;* plus the many works on Pennsylvania politics in the 1760s to 1790s, cited in the Sources for chapters 53, 55, 56, 58, and 62.

On the social order, gentility, manners, and courtesy and parental advice books in eighteenth-century Britain and colonial America, see: Blumin, *Emergence Middle Class;* Bushman, *Refinement;* J. Fliegelman, *Prodigals and Pilgrims: The American Revolution against Patriarchal Authority, 1750–1800* (Cambridge, England, 1982); Hoffman et al., *Through a Glass Darkly,* especially the essays by K. A. Lockridge and P. Greven; L. E. Klein, "Liberty, Manners, and Politeness in Eighteenth-Century England," *Hist. J.,* 32, no. 3 (September, 1989), 583–606, and *Shaftesbury and the Culture of Politeness* (Cambridge, England, 1994); P. Langford, *A Polite and Commercial People: England, 1727–1783* (Oxford, 1989); J. E. Mason, *Gentlefolk in the Making: Studies in the History of English Courtesy Literature* (Philadelphia, 1935); M. Morgan, *Manners, Morals, and Class in England, 1774–1858* (New York, 1994); Shields, *Civil Tongues;* Wood, *Radicalism of Am. Rev.;* and L. B. Wright, ed., *Advice to a Son: Precepts of Lord Burghley, Sir Walter Raleigh, and Francis Osborne* (Ithaca, N.Y., 1962).

For fragmentary data on John Bleakly (Bleakley), see: Campbell, *Friendly Sons of St. Patrick;* Scharf & Westcott, *Hist. of Phila.;* and *Pa. Arch.,* 3rd ser., vols. 20 and 22–26. On eighteenth-century Philadelphia's fishing clubs, see: [Anon.], *A History of the Schuylkill Fishing Company . . .* (Philadelphia, 1889); [William Milnor], *An Authentic Historical Memoir of the Schuylkill Fishing Company . . .* (Philadelphia, 1830); J. P. Simms, "The Fishing Company of Fort St. Davids," *Hist. Pub. Soc. Col. Wars Pa.,* 7, no. 4 (1951), 3–30; and N. B. Wainwright, *The Schuylkill Fishing Company* (Philadelphia, 1982).

53. Rev. Thomas Barton, 1758

Thomas Barton's "Journal of an Expedition to Ohio . . . 1758" (Am. 8153) is located in the Library of the Historical Society of Pennsylvania, which we thank for permission to publish this extract. For research assistance we are particularly grateful to Prof. James P. Myers, Jr., of Gettysburg College, Gettysburg, Pennsylvania, whose published essays represent by far the most insightful and scholarly treatments of Barton's career. Much of Barton's correspondence has been published, especially in Perry, *Hist. Coll. Am. Colonial Church,* vols. 2 and 5 (1871; repr. New York, 1969). Additional letters by, to, and about Barton (including those quoted in this chapter) can be found in S. E. Brown, Jr., ed., *Rev. Thomas Barton (1728–1780) and Some of His Descendants* (Berryville, Va., 1988); the *Sir William Johnson Papers,* vols. 5, 7, and 11 (Albany, N.Y., 1927–53); O'Callaghan, *Doc. Hist. N.Y.,* vol. 4 (Albany, N.Y., 1851); *Pa. Arch.,* 1st ser., vols. 3, 5, and 7 (Harrisburg, 1853); *PMHB,* 4 (1880), 119; and H. W. Smith, *Life and Correspondence of the Rev. William Smith, D.D.,* vol. 1 (Philadelphia, 1879).

On Barton's Irish background, see: Prendergast, *Cromwellian Settlement;* D. M. Schlegel, "The Barton Estate and Lough Bawn in County Monaghan," *Clogher Record,* 15 (1995), 104–21; and E. P. Shirley, Esq., *History of the County of Monaghan* (London, 1879). On Protestant settlement and society in County Monaghan, see: Crawford, "Economy and Society"; W. A. Macafee, "The Movement of British Settlers into Ulster during the Seventeenth Century," *Familia,* 2, no. 8 (1992),

94–111; and P. Roebuck, "The Economic Situation and Functions of Substantial Landowners, 1600–1815," in R. Mitchison and P. Roebuck, eds., *Economy and Society in Scotland and Ireland, 1500–1939* (Edinburgh, 1988), 81–92. On Irish Anglicans, generally, see: R. Eccleshall, "Anglican Political Thought in the Century after the Revolution of 1688," in Boyce et al., *Political Thought,* 36–72; and Ford et al., *As By Law Established.*

On Barton's American career and locales, see: W. Barton, *Memoirs of the Life of David Rittenhouse* (Philadelphia, 1813); Bell, *Patriot-Improvers,* although Barton is omitted; S. E. Brown, Jr., *Rev. Thomas Barton;* Butler, *Sea of Faith;* F. Ellis and S. Evans, *History of Lancaster County* (Philadelphia, 1883); M. E. Flower, *John Armstrong: First Citizen of Carlisle* (Carlisle, Pa., 1971); J. Gibson, ed., *History of York County* (Chicago, 1886); A. Harris, *A Biographical History of Lancaster County* (Lancaster, Pa., 1872); W. A. Hunter, "Thomas Barton and the Forbes Expedition," *PMHB,* 95, no. 4 (October 1971), 431–83; T. W. Jeffries, "Thomas Barton (1730–1780): Victim of the Revolution," *J. Lanc. Co. Hist. Soc.,* 81 (1977), 39–64; H. M. J. Klein, ed., *Lancaster County, a History,* 4 vols. (New York, 1924); H. M. J. Klein and W. F. Diller, *The History of St. James' Church (Protestant Episcopal), 1744–1944* (Lancaster, Pa., 1944); C. I. Landis, "The Juliana Library Company in Lancaster," *PMHB,* 43 (1919), 24–52, 163–81, 228–50; J. P. Myers, Jr., "Preparations for the Forbes Expedition, 1758, in Adams County, with Particular Focus on the Reverend Thomas Barton," *Adams County History,* 1 (1995), 4–26, "The Rev. Thomas Barton's Authorship of *The Conduct of the Paxton Men, Impartially Represented* (1764)," *Pa. Hist.,* 61 (1994), 155–84, "The Rev. Thomas Barton's Conflict with Colonel John Armstrong, ca. 1758," *Cumberland County History,* 10 (1993), 3–14, and "Thomas Barton's *Unanimity and Public Spirit (1755):* Controversy and Plagiarism on the Pennsylvania Frontier," *PMHB,* 119, no. 3 (July 1995), 225–48; J. L. Mombert, *An Authentic History of Lancaster County* (Lancaster, Pa., 1869); I. D. Rupp, *History of Lancaster County* (1844; repr. Spartanburg, S.C., 1984); M. F. Russell, "Thomas Barton and Pennsylvania's Colonial Frontier," *Pa. Hist.,* 46 (1979), 313–34; C. W. Rutschky, Jr., "Thomas Barton's Collection of Minerals," *Pa. Hist.,* 8 (1941), 148–50; Sprague, *Annals Am. Pulpit,* vol. 5 (New York, 1861); J. H. Wood, Jr., *Conestoga Crossroads: Lancaster, Pennsylvania, 1730–1790* (Harrisburg, 1979); W. F. Worner, "The Church of England in Lancaster County," *Papers Lanc. Co. Hist. Soc.,* 41 (1937), 41–91; and A. H. Young, "Thomas Barton: A Pennsylvania Loyalist," *Ontario Historical Society,* 30 (1934), 33–42.

For general background information on mid-eighteenth-century politics and religion in Pennsylvania, see: Bonomi, *Cope of Heaven;* T. M. Brown, "The Image of the Beast: Anti-Papal Rhetoric in Colonial America," in R. O. Curry and T. M. Brown, eds., *Conspiracy: The Fear of Subversion in American History* (New York, 1972); M. H. Buxbaum, *Benjamin Franklin and the Zealous Presbyterians* (University Park, Pa., 1975); Hutson, *Pa. Politics;* J. E. Illick, *Colonial Pennsylvania* (New York, 1976); R. L. Ketcham, "Conscience, War, and Politics in Pennsylvania, 1755–1757," *WMQ,* 3rd ser., 20 (1963), 416–39; B. Newcombe, *Political Partisanship in the American Middle Colonies, 1700–1776* (Baton Rouge, La., 1995); D. Rothermund, *The Layman's Progress: Religious and Political Experience in Colonial Pennsylvania, 1740–1770* (Philadelphia, 1961); Schwartz, *"Mixed Multitude";* Thayer, *Pa. Politics;* L. Treese, *The Storm Gathering: The Penn Family and the American Revolution* (University Park, Pa., 1992); Tully, *Forming Am. Politics;* and G. B. Warden, "The Proprietary Group in Pennsylvania, 1754–1764," *WMQ,* 3rd ser., 21 (1964), 367–89. For additional works of relevance, see the Sources for chapters 55, 56, and 58.

On Irish-born soldiers in the Seven Years' or French and Indian War, see: Bartlett, *Fall and Rise;* Lockhart, *Some Aspects;* and M. C. Ward, "An Army of Servants: The Pennsylvania Regiment during the Seven Years' War," *PMHB,* 119 (January/April 1995), 75–94. On the Paxton Boys specifically, see: P. A. Butzin, "Politics, Presbyterians and the Paxton Riots," *J. Presby. Hist.,* 51 (1973), 70–84; J. E. Crowley, "The Paxton Disturbance and Ideas of Order in Pennsylvania Politics," *Pa. Hist.,* 37 (1970), 317–39; H. M. Cummings, "The Paxton Killings," *J. Presby. Hist.,* 44, no. 4 (December 1966), 219–43; J. R. Dunbar, ed., *The Paxton Papers* (The Hague, 1957); B. Hindle, "The March of the Paxton Boys," *WMQ,* 3rd ser., 3, no. 4 (October 1946), 461–86; J. M. Kirby, "The Return of the Paxton Boys and the Historical State of the Pennsylvania Frontier, 1764–1774," *Pa. Hist.,* 38 (1971), 117–33); A. Olson, "The Pamphlet War over the Paxton Boys," *PMHB,* 123 (January/April 1999), 31–55; and A. T. Vaughan, "Frontier Banditti and the Indians: The Paxton Boys' Legacy, 1763–1775," *Pa. Hist.,* 51 (1984), 1–29.

On Pennsylvania's Anglican clergy and their loyalism during the Revolution, see: F. V. Mills, "Anglican Expansion in Colonial America, 1761–1775," *Hist. Mag. Prot. Episc. Ch.,* 39 (September 1970), 315–24; E. L. Pennington, "The Anglican Clergy of Pennsylvania and the American Revolution," *PMHB,* 63 (1939), 401–31; Rhoden, *Rev. Anglicism;* and Woolverton, *Colonial Anglicanism,* in addition to the works on loyalism by Brown, Calhoon, Nelson, and Norton listed in the Sources for chapter 60.

54. Dr. Thomas Burke, ca. 1766–1767

Thomas Burke's letters are catalogued as Acc. 104, Folder 18A, and as Microfilm no. 1-653 in the Library of the University of North Carolina, Chapel Hill, whose permission to publish Burke's letter to Sir Fielding Ould we gratefully acknowledge. For additional research assistance, we thank Brooks M. Barnes, librarian, Eastern Shore Public Library, Accomac, Virginia, who located records of Burke's activities in the Northampton County Minute Book, vol. 25 (1754–61). Our gratitude is due also to Prof. Larry Okamura of the University of Missouri, Columbia, for aiding us with the translations and literary origins of Burke's Latin quotations; and to Dr. Patrick Melvin of the Oireachtas Library, Leinster House, Dublin, for sharing his research on the Tyaquin Burkes.

Burke has been the subject of several studies, most of which have judged his political opinions as more "democratic" than we do. See: Calhoon, "Aedanus & Thomas Burke"; E. P. Douglass, "Thomas Burke, Disillusioned Democrat," *NCHR,* 26 (1949), 150–86; J. N. Rakove, "Thomas Burke and the Problem of Sovereignty," in *The Beginnings of National Politics* (New York, 1976); J. B. Sanders, "Thomas Burke in the Continental Congress," *NCHR,* 9 (1932), 22–37; R. Walser, ed., *The Poems of Governor Thomas Burke of North Carolina* (Raleigh, N.C., 1961); R. M. Weir, "Rebelliousness: Personality Development and the American Revolution in the Southern Colonies," in Crow & Tise, *So. Exper. Am. Rev.;* and especially the following works by J. S. Watterson III: "Poetic Justice; or, an Ill-Fated Epic by Thomas Burke," *NCHR,* 55, no. 3 (July 1973), 339–46; "The Ordeal of Governor Burke," *NCHR,* 48 (1971), 95–117; and *Thomas Burke: Restless Revolutionary* (Washington, D.C., 1980). On Ædanus Burke, see: J. C. Meleney, *The Public Life of Aedanus Burke* (Columbia, S.C., 1989); *State Records of North Carolina,* 15 (Goldsboro, N.C., 1898), 676–80; and the Sources for chapter 62.

Little is known of Burke's precise Irish origins, but for general background, see: P. Melvin, "The Composition of the Galway Gentry," *Irish Genealogist,* 7 (1986), 81–96; G. Moran and R. Gillespie, eds., *Galway: History and Society* (Dublin, 1996), especially the chapters by S. Mulloy, J. Kelly, T. C. Barnard, K. Harvey, and P. Melvin; and E. O'Byrne, ed., *The Convert Rolls* (Dublin, 1981). On Sir Fielding Ould, see his entry in *DNB.* On eighteenth-century Irish and British political thought, see the Sources (Bailyn, Pocock, etc.) for chapter 52, as well as T. J. Leersen, "Anglo-Irish Patriotism and Its European Context: Notes Towards a Reassessment," *Eighteenth-Century Ireland,* 3 (1988), 7–24. On the devious opportunism of eighteenth-century Irish politicians, including many onetime "patriots," see Dickson, *New Foundations* and Stewart, *Deeper Silence*. On the 1759 incident that may have precipitated Burke's estrangement from his uncle and subsequent emigration, see: S. Murphy, "The Dublin Anti-Union Riot of 3 December 1759," in O'Brien, *Parl., Politics, & People,* 49–68.

For general information on the history and society of Burke's various American locales, see: W. M. Billings, J. E. Selby, and T. W. Tate, *Colonial Virginia: A History* (White Plains, N.Y., 1986); L. S. Butler and A. D. Watson, eds., *The North Carolina Experience* (Chapel Hill, N.C., 1984); Ekirch, *"Poor Carolina"*; P. Guilday, *The Life and Times of John England, First Bishop of Charleston (1786–1842)* (N.Y., 1927), vol. 1, in which Guilday argues for Burke's Catholicism; R. D. Higginbotham, "James Iredell and the Revolutionary Politics of North Carolina," in Higgins, *Rev. War in South*; H. T. Lefler and A. R. Newsome, *North Carolina: History of a Southern State,* 3rd ed. (Chapel Hill, N.C., 1973); H. T. Lefler and W. S. Powell, *Colonial North Carolina: A History* (New York, 1973); H. R. Merrens, *Colonial North Carolina in the Eighteenth Century* (Chapel Hill, N.C., 1964); T. C. Parramore, *Norfolk: The First Four Centuries* (Charlottesville, Va., 1994); and R. T. Whitelaw, *Virginia's Eastern Shore: A History of Northampton and Accomack Counties* (Richmond, Va., 1951). For additional works on colonial North Carolina and especially on its Regulator movement, see Sources, chapter 57. The best study of the controversy that launched Burke's political career remains E. S. and H. M. Morgan's *The Stamp Act Crisis,* rev. ed. (New York, 1962).

55. Rev. Francis Alison, 1768

Rev. Francis Alison's 29 March 1768 letter, with other Alison-Stiles correspondence quoted in this chapter, is located in the Rev. Ezra Stiles Papers, in the Beinecke Rare Book and Manuscript Library, Yale University, New Haven, Connecticut. For research assistance, we thank Vincent Giroud, curator, and Paul C. Allen, assistant curator, of the Beinecke Library. For research aid, we are especially grateful to the foremost Alison scholar, Prof. Elizabeth A. Ingersoll Nybakken, formerly of Mississippi State University.

On County Donegal in the early 1700s, see: Nolan et al., *Donegal,* especially chapters 9–15. On Francis Hutcheson and Irish dissenter radicalism, see: T. D. Campbell, "Francis Hutcheson: 'Father' of the Scottish Enlightenment," in Campbell & Skinner, *Scot. Enlight.*; M. Elliott, *Watchmen in Sion: The Protestant Idea of Liberty* (Derry, 1985); McBride, *Scripture Politics*; McBride, "School of Virtue," and "William Drennan and the Dissenting Tradition," and P. Tesch, "Presbyterian Radicalism," in Dickson et al., *United Irishmen,* 49–61; Robbins, *Commonwealthman*; C. Robbins, "'When It Is That Colonies May Turn Independent': An Analysis of the Environment and Politics of Francis Hutcheson, 1694–1746," *WMQ,* 11 (April 1954), 214–51; D. Smyth, ed., "Francis Hutcheson," a supplement to *Fortnight #308* (Belfast, 1990); Stewart, *Deeper Silence*; and Walker, *Intimate Strangers.* On the Scottish Enlightenment, generally, see also the works cited in the Sources for chapter 49.

On Rev. Francis Alison and his American influence and milieu, see: Bell, *Patriot-Improvers* (from 1744 Alison was a corresponding member of the American Philosophical Society); D. Berman, "Irish Philosophy and the American Enlightenment during the Eighteenth Century," *Éire-Ireland,* 24 (spring 1989), 28–39; Bridenbaugh, *Mitre & Sceptre*; Cremin, *Am. Educ. Col. Exper.*; Doyle, *Ireland, Irishmen*; Futhey & Cope, *History of Chester Co.*; K. L. Griffin, *Revolution and Religion: American*

Revolutionary War and the Reformed Clergy (New York, 1994); E. A. Ingersoll [Nybakken], "Francis Alison: American *Philosophe, 1705–1779*" (Ph.D. diss., University of Delaware, 1974); "Letter of Rev. Francis Alison, 1776," *PMHB*, 28 (1904), 379; J. L. McAllister, Jr., "Francis Alison and John Witherspoon: Political Philosophers and Revolutionaries," *J. Presby. Hist.*, 54 (1976), 33–60; D. F. Norton, "Francis Hutcheson in America," *Studies in Voltaire and the Eighteenth Century*, 114 (1976), 1553–65; E. I. Nybakken, "In the Irish Tradition: Pre-Revolutionary Academies in America," *Hist. Educ. Q.*, 37, no. 2 (summer 1997), 163–84; E. I. Nybakken, ed., *"The Centinel": Warnings of a Revolution* (Newark, Del., 1980); T. C. Pears, "Francis Alison," *J. Presby. Hist.*, 30 (1952), 213–25; Sloan, *Am. College Ideal;* Sprague, *Annals Am. Pulpit*, vol. 3 (New York, 1861); and Webster, *Hist. Presby. Church.*

On Presbyterianism in mid- and late eighteenth-century Pennsylvania, see the Sources for chapter 46 and, especially, chapter 47. On political and ethnoreligious conflicts in Pennsylvania from the 1750s through the beginning of the American Revolution, see the relevant publications listed in the Sources for chapters 53, 56, and 58. On John Dickinson, George Bryan, Ezra Stiles, Thomas Bradbury Chandler, Charles Thomson, etc., also see their entries in *DAB* and *DNB*. On Arthur Dobbs, see: D. Clarke, *Arthur Dobbs, Esquire, 1689–1765* (Chapel Hill, N.C., 1957); and Rhoden, *Revolutionary Anglicanism.*

56. John Morton, 1769

John and Samuel Morton's correspondence is located in the Greer Family Papers, D.1044/176 and 179 (also in MIC. 531/1) in the Public Record Office of Northern Ireland, Belfast; we are grateful to the Deputy Keeper of Records, PRONI, and to J. A. Greeves of Belfast for permission to publish John Morton's letters. For research assistance, we thank: Mary Ellen Chijioke, curator, Friends' Historical Library, Swarthmore College, Swarthmore, Pennsylvania; Bill Crawford, Ph.D., of Belfast; Prof. Donald Disbrow of Ypsilanti, Michigan; Dr. Thomas M. Doerflinger of Summit, New Jersey; J. A. Gamble of Belfast; Prof. Kevin Herlihy of St. Joseph's University, Philadelphia; Nellie Jester of Westfield, New Jersey; Joy H. Jones of Colorado Springs, Colorado; John W. McConaghy, Ph.D., of Bangor, County Down; Kathleen Ryan of the University of Pennsylvania; Neddy Seagraves, director, Genealogical Society of Pennsylvania, Philadelphia; Mrs. Mary Shakleton, curator of the Library of the Society of Friends, Dublin; and the staffs of the HSP and the Philadelphia City Archives.

For information on the Mortons, Greers, and other Quakers in eighteenth-century Ulster (and Scotland), see: M. Bell, "Notes on the Quakers of Mid-Ulster," *Ulster Local Studies*, 16, no. 1 (summer 1994), 63–78; *Burke's Irish Family Records* (London, 1976); Cohen, *Linen, Family & Community;* D. Dobson, *Scottish Emigration to Colonial America, 1607–1785* (Athens, Ga., 1994); Lockhart, "Quakers & Emigration"; J. W. McConaghy, "Thomas Greer of Dungannon, 1724–1803, Quaker Linen Merchant" (Ph.D. diss., Queen's University of Belfast, 1979); Myers, *Irish Quakers into Pa.;* Vann & Eversley, *Friends in Life;* and Wighan, *Irish Quakers.* On Tullylish parish see: Day & McWilliams, *OSM: Parishes of County Down III, 1833–8;* vol. 12, *Mid-Down* (1992); and Lewis, *TDI.*

Published and unpublished primary source data on the Mortons can be found in: *ACAB* (Robert Morton); Barratt & Sachse, *Freemasonry in Pa.;* "Births, Burials, and Marriages, 1772–1870. Southern District Monthly Meeting, Philadelphia" (Philadelphia, 1924; in the library of the Genealogical Society of Pennsylvania [hereafter GSP], Philadelphia); Campbell, *Friendly Sons of St. Patrick;* G. Cope, "Abstract of the Minutes and Records of New Garden Mo[nth]ly Meeting, Chester Co., Pa., 1718–1768" (1884; in GSP); E. F. Crane, ed., *The Diary of Elizabeth Drinker* (Boston, 1991);

"Diary of Robert Morton, Kept in Philadelphia While That City Was Occupied by the British Army in 1777," *PMHB*, 1, no. 1 (1887), 1–39; Hinshaw, *Encycl. Am. Quaker Geneal.*, vol. 2 (Baltimore, 1994 ed.); "List of Original Certificates of Removal, in possession of Arch Street Meeting, Phila., 1758–1772" (in GSP); J. Mease, *The Picture of Philadelphia* (Philadelphia, 1811); J. Morton, Jr., Will and Estate Inventory (1812/94, Philadelphia City Archives); "Names of Persons Who Took the Oath of Allegiance to the State of Pennsylvania, 1776–94," *Pa. Arch.*, 2nd ser., vol. 3; "Permits for Interment in Friends' Burial Ground, Philadelphia" (in HSP); Philadelphia city directories (1785, 1791, 1793, etc.); "Philadelphia Monthly Meeting (Arch St.) Marriages, 1672–1871" (Philadelphia, 1915; in HSP); "Philadelphia Monthly Meeting Records: Abstracts of Minutes, Vol. 3 (1730–1785)" (in GSP); Phebe Morton, "Memoir of Samuel Morton," in the Friends' Historical Library, Swarthmore College; A. Ritter, *Philadelphia and Her Merchants, as Constituted Fifty and Seventy Years Ago* (Philadelphia, 1860); Scharf & Westcott, *Hist. of Phila.*; "Ship Registers for the Port of Philadelphia, 1726–1775," *PMHB*, 27 (1903) and 28 (1904); and *U.S. Gazette* (Philadelphia), 29 April 1828 (John Morton's death notice). Also see the published Philadelphia tax lists in *Pa. Arch.*, 3rd ser., vols. 14 (for 1769 and 1779), 15 (1780–81), and 16 (1782); and John Morton's will and estate inventory (24 September 1845) in W55–1828 in the Registry of Wills, Registrar's Office, Philadelphia City Hall.

On Philadelphia's Quakers before and during the American Revolution, see: H. Barbour and J. W. Frost, *The Quakers* (Westport, Conn., 1988); R. Bauman, *For the Reputation of Truth: Politics, Religion, and Conflict among the Pennsylvania Quakers, 1750–1800* (Baltimore, 1971); K. L. Carroll, "Irish and British Quakers and Their American Relief Funds, 1778–1797," *PMHB*, 102, no. 4 (October 1978), 437–56; J. W. Frost, *The Quaker Family in Colonial America* (New York, 1973); Hollingsworth, "Irish Quakers"; S. V. James, *A People among Peoples: Quaker Benevolence in Eighteenth-Century America* (Cambridge, Mass., 1963); W. C. Kashatus III, *Conflict of Convictions: A Reappraisal of Quaker Involvement in the American Revolution* (Lanham, Md., 1990); R. L. Ketcham, "Conscience, War, and Politics in Pennsylvania, 1775–1777," *WMQ*, 3rd ser., 20 (1963), 416–39; Levy, *Quakers & Am. Family*; J. D. Marietta, *The Reformation of American Quakerism, 1748–1783* (Philadelphia, 1984); A. J. Mekeel, *The Relation of the Quakers to the American Revolution* (Washington, D.C., 1979); R. F. Oaks, "Philadelphians in Exile: The Problem of Loyalty during the American Revolution," *PMHB*, 96 (July 1972), 298–325; I. Sharpless, *A Quaker Experiment in Government* (Philadelphia, 1902); T. G. Thayer, *Israel Pemberton: King of the Quakers* (Philadelphia, 1943); and F. B. Tolles, *Meeting House and Counting House: The Quaker Merchants of Colonial Philadelphia, 1682–1763* (Chapel Hill, N.C., 1948). On English Quaker missionary Rachel Wilson, see: R. Larson, *Daughters of Light: Quaker Women Preaching and Prophesying in the Colonies and Abroad, 1700–1775* (New York, 1999).

Published works on business, society, and politics in late eighteenth-century Philadelphia (some of which mention the Mortons) include: Bridenbaugh, *Rebels & Gentlemen*; S. Brobeck, "Changes in the Composition and Structure of Philadelphia Elite Groups, 1756–1790" (Ph.D. diss., University of Pennsylvania, 1973); Brunhouse, *Counter-Rev. in Pa.*; Doerflinger, *Vigorous Spirit*; R. A. East, *Business Enterprise in the American Revolutionary Era* (New York, 1938); R. M. Gough, "A Theory of Class and Social Conflict: A Social History of Wealthy Philadelphians, 1775 and 1800" (Ph.D. diss., University of Pennyslvania, 1977), and "Can a Rich Man Favor Revolution? The Case of Philadelphia in 1776," *Pa. Hist.*, 48, no. 3 (July 1981), 237–45; D. Hawke, *In the Midst of a Revolution* (Philadelphia, 1961); C. E. Hutchins, ed., *Shaping a National Culture: The Philadelphia Experience, 1750–1800* (Winterthur, Del., 1994), especially the essays by Gough, Rosswurm, and Soderlund; Hutson, *Pa. Politics;* Ireland, *Religion, Ethnicity, & Politics;* Jensen, *Mar. Commerce;* S. E. Lucas,

Portents of Rebellion: Rhetoric and Revolution in Philadelphia, 1765–76 (Philadelphia, 1976); McCusker & Menard, *Econ. Brit. Am;* B. Newcombe, *Political Partisanship in the American Middle Colonies, 1700–1776* (Baton Rouge, La., 1995); R. F. Oaks, "Philadelphia Merchants and the American Revolution, 1765–1776" (Ph.D. diss., University of Southern California, 1970), and "Big Wheels in Philadelphia: Du Simitière's List of Carriage Owners," *PMHB*, 115, no. 2 (July 1971), 351–62; A. M. Ousterhout, *A State Divided: Opposition in Pennsylvania to the American Revolution* (Westport, Conn., 1987); G. D. Rappaport, *Stability and Change in Revolutionary Pennsylvania: Banking, Politics, and Social Structure* (University Park, Pa., 1997); E. E. Rasmusson, "Capital on the Delaware: The Philadelphia Upper Class in Transition, 1789–1801" (Ph.D. diss., Brown University, 1962); S. Rosswurm, *Arms, Country, and Class: The Philadelphia Militia and "Lower Sort" during the American Revolution, 1775–1783* (New Brunswick, N.J., 1987); Ryerson, *Rev. Now Begun;* A. M. Schlesinger, *The Colonial Merchants and the American Revolution* (New York, 1924); Schwartz, *"Mixed Multitude";* Thayer, *Pa. Politics;* and Truxes, *Irish-Am. Trade.*

On the Bank of North America, also see: M. L. Bradbury, "Legal Privilege and the Bank of North America," *PMHB*, 96, no. 2 (April 1972), 139–66; E. J. Ferguson, *The Power of the Purse: A History of American Public Finance, 1776–1790* (Chapel Hill, N.C., 1961); B. Hammond, *Banks and Politics in America from the Revolution to the Civil War* (Princeton, 1957); F. C. James, "The Bank of North America and the Financial History of Philadelphia," *PMHB*, 64, no. 1 (January 1940), 56–96; L. Lewis, Jr., *A History of the Bank of North America* (Philadelphia, 1882); R. Redlich, *The Molding of American Banking: Men and Ideas,* part 1, *1781–1840* (New York, 1947); and J. Wilson, "The Bank of North America in Pennsylvania Politics, 1781–1787," *PMHB*, 66, no. 1 (January 1942), 3–28.

57. John McDonnell, 1771

McDonnell's letter (and the Hinshaw correspondence) is in the Greer Family Papers, D.1044/294 (and MIC.531/2) in PRONI; once again, we thank the Deputy Keeper of Records, PRONI, and J. A. Greeves of Belfast for permission to publish. For research assistance, we are also grateful to John W. McConaghy, Ph.D., of Bangor, County Down; Mrs. Mary Shakleton of the Library of the Society of Friends, Dublin; Neddy Seagraves of the Genealogical Society of Pennsylvania, Philadelphia; and, especially, Diane Cashman of the Lower Cape Fear Historical Society Archives, Wilmington, North Carolina; and Carole Treadway, Librarian, Friends Historical Collection, Guilford College, Greensboro, North Carolina.

Biographical information on John McDonnell and his kin can be found in: the Lurgan Monthly Meeting Marriage Certificates, the Cork Meeting Removal Certificates, and the Cork Family and Burial Records, all in the Historical Library of the Religious Society of Friends in Ireland, in Dublin, and also in the abstracts of the Philadelphia Friends' Monthly Meeting Records, which are located in both the Genealogical Society of Pennsylvania and the Friends Historical Collection at Guilford College. On McDonnell's Irish background, see: R. S. Harrison, *Cork City Quakers, 1655–1939: A Brief History* (Cork, 1991); in addition to the published works on Ulster Quakers (including Thomas Greer) cited in the Sources for chapter 56. On the McDonnells of Mullahead, see: Manchester Estate Leases (D.1248/L, PRONI); TAB: Kilmore Parish (1833) in PRONI; and *Griffith's Valuation:* Kilmore (1864), also in PRONI. On late eighteenth- and early nineteenth-century Cork city, see: I. d'Alton, *Protestant Society and Politics in Cork, 1812–1844* (Cork, 1980); and O'Flanagan & Buttimer, *Cork,* especially chapters 13 and 16, by O'Flanagan and W. J. Smyth, respectively.

For mention of John McDonnell in North Carolina, see: L. H. McEachern and I. M. Williams, eds., *Wilmington-New Hanover Safety Committee Minutes, 1774–1776* (Wilmington, N.C., 1974); E. F. McCoy, *Early New Hanover County Records* (Wilmington, N.C., 1973), and *Early Wilmington Block by Block from 1733 On* (Wilmington, N.C., 1967); *St. James Church Historical Records, 1737–1852* (Wilmington, N.C., 1965; typescript in Lower Cape Fear Historical Society Archives); and W. L. Saunders, ed., *Colonial Records of North Carolina*, vol. 9, *1771 to 1775* (Raleigh, N.C., 1890).

On the Lower Cape Fear region, Wilmington, and its merchants and planters, see: E. W. Andrews, ed., *Journal of a Lady of Quality, being the Narrative of a Journey from Scotland to the West Indies, North Carolina, and Portugal, in the Years 1774 to 1776* (New Haven, 1923); D. C. Cashman, *Cape Fear Adventure: An Illustrated History of Wilmington* (Woodland Hills, Cal., 1982); Jensen, *Mar. Commerce*; L. Lee, *New Hanover County: A Brief History*, rev. ed. (Raleigh, N.C., 1977), and *The Lower Cape Fear in Colonial Days* (Chapel Hill, N.C., 1965); Truxes, *Irish-Am. Trade;* and A. M. Waddell, *A History of New Hanover County and the Lower Cape Fear Region, 1723–1800* (Wilmington, N.C., 1909). On the North Carolina Quakers, see: S. B. Hinshaw, *The Carolina Quaker Experience* (Davidson, N.C., 1984); Lockhart, "Quakers & Emigration"; Ramsay, *Carolina Cradle;* and on the Hinshaws, Myers, *Irish Quakers into Pa.*

On North Carolina politics, generally, and the Regulator movement, see: D. Clarke, *Arthur Dobbs, Esquire, 1689–1765* (Chapel Hill, N.C., 1957); R. DeMond, *The Loyalists in North Carolina during the Revolution* (Durham, N.C., 1940); Ekirch, *"Poor Carolina";* A. R. Ekirch, "The North Carolina Regulators on Liberty and Corruption, 1766–1771," *Perspectives Am. Hist.,* 11 (1977–78), 199–256, and "Whig Authority and Public Order in Backcountry North Carolina, 1776–1783," in Hoffman et al., *Uncivil War;* M. L. M. Kay, "The North Carolina Regulation, 1766–1776: A Class Conflict," in Young, *Am. Rev. Radicalism;* M. L. M. Kay and L. L. Cary, "Class, Mobility, and Conflict in North Carolina on the Eve of the Revolution," in Crow & Tise, *So. Exper. Am. Rev.;* W. S. Powell, J. K. Huhta, and T. J. Farnham, eds., *The Regulators in North Carolina: A Documentary History* (Raleigh, N.C., 1971); C. G. Sellers, "Making a Revolution: The North Carolina Whigs, 1765–1775," in J. C. Sitterson, ed., *Studies in Southern History* (Chapel Hill, N.C., 1957), and "Private Profits and British Colonial Policy: The Speculations of Henry McCulloh," *WMQ,* 8 (October 1951), 535–51; A. D. Watson, "The Committees of Safety and the Coming of the American Revolution in North Carolina, 1774–1776," *NCHR,* 73 (April 1996), 131–55; and J. P. Whittenburg, "Planters, Merchants, and Lawyers: Social Change and the Origins of the North Carolina Regulation," *WMQ,* 34 (1977), 215–38; in addition to the works by Butler and Watson, Lefler and Newsome, and Lefler and Powell cited in the Sources for chapter 54.

58. James Caldwell, 1774

The whereabouts of James Caldwell's original December 1774 letter is unknown. In 1849 it was transcribed by his nephew, John Caldwell, Jr., in the latter's memoir, entitled "Particular of History of a North County Irish Family" (1849). A typescript of this memoir is catalogued as T.3541/5/3 in PRONI, and the original manuscript is in the New York Genealogical and Biographical Society, New York City. We wish to thank Mrs. R. V. T. Edie and the Deputy Keeper of Records, PRONI, for permission to publish the typed text of the Caldwell letter, which we have restored according to the 1849 transcription in the NYGBS. For research assistance, we thank: Paul Burns of PRONI; Thomas Doerflinger, Ph.D., of Summit, New Jersey; Prof. James P. Myers of Gettysburg College,

Gettysburg, Pennsylvania; and especially Alice Naughton of New York City and Polly Midgley of Briarcliff, New York.

On Ballymoney parish and the Caldwells, see: Antrim Estate Leases, 1783–89 (D.2977/3B/4, PRONI); Ballymoney Museum and Heritage Centre, *Ballymoney and the Rebellion [of] 1798* (Ballymoney, 1998); Rev. T. H. Mullin, *Coleraine in Georgian Times* (Belfast, 1977); Stewart, *Summer Soldiers;* and Truxes, *Irish-Am. Trade.*

Primary sources of data on the Caldwells in Philadelphia include: Andrew Caldwell Shipping Records, 1757–64, and John Caldwell Family Papers, 1798–1800 (NYGBS); Andrew Caldwell, Will and Probate Records (1794/36, Registry of Wills, Philadelphia City Archives); Caldwell Family Papers (D.1518, PRONI); Campbell, *Friendly Sons of St. Patrick;* E. T. Langford, "Five Generations of Caldwells of Ballymoney, Co. Antrim, Ireland, and Salisbury Mills, Orange Co., New York" (typescript in NYPL); Philadelphia City Directories, 1785–1793; "Names of Persons Who Took the Oath of Allegiance to the State of Pennsylvania, 1776–94," *Pa. Arch.*, 2nd ser., vol. 3, pp. 3–99; A. Ritter, *Philadelphia and Her Merchants* (Philadelphia, 1860); Scharf & Westcott, *Hist. of Phila.;* "Ship Registers for the Port of Philadelphia, 1726–1775," *PMHB*, vols. 23–27 (1899–1907); and Philadelphia tax lists, 1769–83 (titles vary), in *Pa. Arch.*, 3rd ser., vols. 14–16. Also see scattered references to Caldwells in *PMHB*, vols. 3, 8, 15, 19, 30, and 48; and in *Pa. Arch.*, 2nd ser., vol. 2, and 6th ser., vols. 1 and 13. For biographical data on FitzSimons, Nesbitt, etc. see their entries in *ACAB, ANB,* and *DAB,* as well as in Campbell, *Friendly Sons of St. Patrick.*

For studies of business, society, and politics in late eighteenth-century Philadelphia (some of which mention the Caldwells), and on the Bank of North America, see the Sources for chapter 56, especially the works by: Brunhouse, Doerflinger, East, Ireland, Jensen, Oaks ("Philadelphia Merchants"), Ryerson, and Truxes. Also see: J. P. Simms, "The Fishing Company of Fort St. David's," *Hist. Pub. Soc. Col. Wars Pa.,* 7, no. 4 (1951), 3–30. On the images of Scotland and of Scottish immigrants in revolutionary America, see: Brock, *Scotus Americanus;* A. Hook, *Scotland and America* (Glasgow, 1975); and N. C. Landsman, "The Provinces and the Empire: Scotland, the American Colonies, and the Development of British Provincial Identity," in L. Stone, ed., *An Imperial State at War: Britain from 1689 to 1815* (London, 1994), 258–87.

59. Matthew Patten, 1774–1776

The Matthew Patten Diary, 1754–99, is in the manuscripts collections of the New Hampshire Historical Society, Concord, New Hampshire, and we thank the Society's manuscripts curator, Elizabeth Hamlin-Morin, for permission to publish these excerpts. For research aid, we are grateful to: Prof. Charles E. Clark of the University of New Hampshire, Durham; Prof. Patricia Kelleher of Kutztown State University, Kutztown, Pennsylvania; and especially to Sharon M. Carson of Londonderry, New Hampshire.

A full and virtually accurate transcript of Patten's Day-Book was published as *The Diary of Matthew Patten of Bedford, N.H.* (Concord, N.H., 1903); nonetheless, in this chapter we have relied on the original manuscript. Additional primary sources include: the Patten-Tolford Papers and eighteenth-century land and tax records in the New Hampshire State Archives, Concord; Patten wills and estate inventories in the Probate Records Office of the Hillsborough County District Court in Nashua; and the collections of the New Hampshire and the Bedford historical societies. We thank the relevant officials for allowing Sharon M. Carson to do research in these institutions on our behalf. On the value and interpretation of diaries or journals such as Matthew Patten's, see: Bushman, *Refinement;* and V. Pollock, "The Household Economy in Early Rural America and Ulster: The Question of Self-Sufficiency," in Blethen & Wood, *Ulster & No. America,* 61–75.

Published works on Matthew Patten and his community include: Bedford Historical Society, *History of Bedford, N.H., 1737–1971* (Bedford, N.H., 1972); Clark, *Eastern Frontier;* J. Farmer, *Historical Sketch of Amherst* (1837; repr. Somersworth, N.H., 1972); *History of Bedford, New-Hampshire* (Boston, 1851); D. H. Hurd, *History of Hillsborough County* (Philadelphia, 1885); T. Savage, *A Historical Sketch of Bedford, N.H.* (Manchester, N.H., 1841); K. Scott, "Bedford's Meeting House," *J. Presby. Hist. Soc.,* 24, no. 4 (December 1946), 236–40, and "John Houston, Tory Minister of Bedford," *J. Presby. Hist. Soc.,* 22, no. 4 (December 1944), 172–97, and "Matthew Patten of Bedford, New Hampshire," *J. Presby. Hist. Soc.,* 28, no. 3 (September 1950), 129–45; R. S. Wallace, "The Scotch-Irish of Provincial New Hampshire" (Ph.D. diss., University of New Hampshire, 1984); and G. Woodbury, *John Goffe's Legacy* (New York, 1955). On Londonderry, N.H., also see the Sources for chapter 49, especially those by Leyburn, Parker, and Perry.

On late eighteenth-century New Hampshire, generally, see: Daniell, *Col. N. H.,* and Daniell, *Experiment;* E. M. Hunt, *New Hampshire Town Names and Whence They Came* (Peterborough, N.H., 1970); C. E. Potter, *The Military History of the State of New-Hampshire* (1866–68; repr. Baltimore, 1972); and especially R. F. Upton, *Revolutionary New Hampshire* (Hanover, N.H., 1936).

On New Hampshire's Scots-Irish soldiers in the Revolution, see also: Shy, *People Numerous,* chapter 7; and on General Richard Montgomery, see: Royster, *Rev. People at War;* and H. T. Shelton, *General Richard Montgomery and the American Revolution* (New York, 1994). For an explanation of eighteenth-century New England currency, see: J. Johnston, *A History of the Towns of Bristol and Bremen* (Albany, N.Y., 1873); and on preliminary "declarations of independence" in New England, see: P. Maier, *American Scripture: Making the Declaration of Independence* (New York, 1997). On John Stark and John Sullivan, see their entries in *ANB* and *DAB;* also see O. G. Hammond, ed., *Letters and Papers of Major General John Sullivan* (Concord, N.H., 1930), vol. 3, for Sullivan's Irish correspondence.

60. John Phillips, 1783

For research assistance, we are indebted to Ruth M. Stevenson of the Fairfield County Museum in Winnsboro, South Carolina, and Prof. Emeritus Robert S. Lambert of Clemson University, Clemson, South Carolina. The original transcripts of John Phillips's petition, oral testimony, and corroboratory references are in the Audit Office Series (AO) 12/13, in the British Public Record Office, Kew, London. We have relied on the verbatim Bancroft Transcripts of the Audit Office 12/13 series, in the New York Public Library and available on microfilm from Marquette University in Milwaukee. The Phillips materials republished here are in vol. 52 (reel 17), pp. 267–89, of the Bancroft Transcripts, but also see vol. 4 (reel 1), 476–77; vol. 7 (reel 2), 553; and vol. 11 (reel 3), list of claims and awards; and H. E. Egerton, ed., *The Royal Commission on the Losses and Services of American Loyalists, 1783 to 1785* (Oxford, 1915).

For abstracts and transcripts of original documents by and about James Phillips, see: A. S. Edwards, ed., *State Records of South Carolina: Journals of the Privy Council, 1783–1789* (Columbia, S.C., 1971); F. Phillips, "Col. John Phillips of South Carolina: His Claim for Losses in the War of Independence," *Familia,* 2, no. 5 (1989), 73–80; John B. Phillips, letter of 12 March 1819 (T.1449, PRONI); and T. J. Thompson, ed., *State Records of South Carolina: Journals of the House of Representatives, 1783–84* (Columbia, S.C., 1977). Also on Phillips's loyalist kinsmen, see: E. A. Jones, ed., "The

Journal of Alexander Chesney," *Ohio State University Studies*, 7 (1921), 1–166; Chesney's journal is also in PRONI as D.2260 and T.1095).

On Kirkinriola and Ahoghill parishes and Ballymena town, see: Day & McWilliams [and Dobson], *OSM: Parishes of County Antrim VIII, 1831–5, 1837–8*; vol. 23 (1993); and Lewis, *TDI*. On Phillips and Fairfield County, South Carolina, see: Anon., *Fairfield's Heritage* (Winnsboro, S.C., n.d.); F. H. McMaster, *History of Fairfield County* (Spartanburg, S.C., 1980 ed.); L. M. McMaster, "Ancestry of the Buchanan Family of Fairfield County" (1945), typescript in the Fairfield County Museum; and Mrs. B. H. Rosson, Jr., comp., *Ederington's History of Fairfield County* (Tuscaloosa, Ala., n.d.).

Studies of South Carolina before and during the Revolution include: R. M. Brown, *The South Carolina Regulators* (Cambridge, Mass., 1963); Crow & Tise, *So. Exper. Am. Rev.*; Higgins, *Rev. War in So.*; R. Hoffman, "The 'Disaffected' in the Revolutionary South," in Young, *Am. Rev. Radicalism*; Hoffman et al., *Uncivil War*; G. Howe, *History of the Presbyterian Church in South Carolina* (Columbia, S.C., 1870); L. P. Jones, *The South Carolina Civil War of 1775* (Lexington, S.C., 1975); Klein, *Unification of Slave State*; E. McCrady, *The History of South Carolina in the Revolution, 1780–83* (New York, 1902); R. L. Meriwether, *The Expansion of South Carolina, 1729–1765* (Kingsport, Tenn., 1940); J. J. Nadelhaft, *The Disorders of War: The Revolution in South Carolina* (Orono, Maine, 1981); J. S. Pancake, *This Destructive War: The British Campaign in the Carolinas, 1780–1782* (University, Ala., 1985); D. Ramsay, *The History of South Carolina*, 2 vols. (Charleston, 1809); D. D. Wallace, *South Carolina: A Short History, 1520–1948* (Columbia, S.C., 1961); and Weir, *Col. So. Car.*

On American loyalists, generally, see: W. Brown, *The Good Americans: The Loyalists in the American Revolution* (New York, 1969), and *The King's Friends: The Composition and Motives of the American Loyalist Claims* (Providence, 1965); R. McC. Calhoon, *The Loyalists in Revolutionary America, 1760–1781* (New York, 1973); R. McC. Calhoon, T. M. Barnes, and G. A. Rawlyk, eds., *Loyalists and Community in North America* (Westport, Conn., 1994); W. H. Nelson, *The American Tory* (Oxford, 1961); and M. B. Norton, *The British-Americans: The Loyalist Exiles in England, 1774–1789* (Boston, 1972). On toryism in South Carolina, see: R. W. Barnwell, Jr., "Migration of Loyalists from South Carolina" and "Reports on Loyalist Exiles from South Carolina, 1783," in *Proc. So. Car. Hist. Soc.* (1937), 34–46; M. J. Clark, *Loyalists in the Southern Campaign of the Revolutionary War*, 3 vols. (Baltimore, 1981); and especially R. S. Lambert, *South Carolina Loyalists in the American Revolution* (Columbia, S.C., 1987). On Irish-born American loyalists, see: Doyle, *Ireland, Irishmen*.

61. Job Johnson, 1784

A few years ago, the Job Johnson letters were in the possession of the late Dr. Charlotte C. Arnold of Belfast, but transcriptions exist in T.3700 (PRONI) and in A. C. Davies, "'As Good a Country as Any Man Needs to Dwell In': Letters from a Scotch-Irish Immigrant in Pennsylvania, 1766, 1767, and 1784," *Pa. Hist.*, 50, no. 4 (October 1983), 313–22. We thank the Deputy Keeper of Records, PRONI, for permission to publish, yet our transcription of Johnson's 1784 letter is based on photocopies of the original manuscript supplied by Dr. Alun C. Davies of Queen's University, Belfast, for whose assistance and generosity we are very grateful.

On Maghera and adjacent parishes, see: W. Macafee, "The Colonization of the Maghera Region of South Derry during the Seventeenth and Eighteenth Centuries," *Ulster Folklife*, 23 (1977), 70–91; W. S. Mason, *A Statistical Account, or Parochial Survey of Ireland*, vol. 1 (Dublin, 1814); and O'Brien, *Derry & Londonderry*. For details of the Johnson's holdings in Maghera, see: TAB: Maghera Parish (1828), in PRONI; Day & McWilliams, *OSM*, vol. 18, *Parishes of Co. Londonderry V, 1830*,

1833, 1836–7: Maghera and Tamlaght O'Crilly (1993); and *Griffith's Valuation:* Maghera Parish (1859) in PRONI.

Job Johnson died too young to appear in the American Revolutionary pension records, and we were unable to locate him or identify precisely his military units in published lists of Revolutionary officers or in histories of the western, Yorktown, and other campaigns. However, Johnson's will is catalogued as 1790/207 in the Registry of Wills in Philadelphia City Hall; and references to him and his brother, William, can be found in *Pa. Arch.,* 3rd ser., vols. 11–12 and 25–26. For general background information, see: C. P. Neimeyer, *America Goes to War: A Social History of the Continental Army* (New York, 1996); and on the Scots-Irish in Chester County, see: Dunaway, *Scotch-Irish of Col. Pa.;* Futhey & Cope, *History of Chester Co.;* C. W. Heathcote, *A History of Chester County* (Harrisburg, 1932); Klett, *Presby. in Co. Pa.;* W. W. Thomson, ed., *A History of Chester County* (Chicago, 1898); Wiley, *Chester Co.;* and especially, Lemon, *Best Poor Man's Country.*

62. David Redick and Ædanus Burke, 1787–1788

David Redick's letters (and several by William Findley) are in the General William Irvine Papers at the Historical Society of Pennsylvania, Philadelphia, and Ædanus Burke's letter is in the John Lamb Papers, Box 5, at the New-York Historical Society, New York City. We thank each institution for permission to publish. A slightly modernized version of Burke's letter is in: J. P. Kaminski and G. J. Saladino, eds., *The Documentary History of the Ratification of the Constitution,* vol. 18, *Commentaries on the Constitution, Public and Private,* vol. 6 (Madison, Wis., 1995), 55–57. For research asssistance we are grateful to the staff of the Washington County Historical Society, Washington, Pennsylvania; to Emilie S. Staisley of the Historical Society of Western Pennsylvania, Pittsburgh; and to Dr. Ann McVeigh of the Public Record Office of Northern Ireland, Belfast.

Primary data on David Redick, e.g., abstracts of his will, deeds, and marriage record, are located in the Washington County Historical Society; also see the Pennsylvania tax records and deed warrants in *Pa. Arch.,* 3rd ser., vols. 20, 22, and 26. On Redick's local context, see: Albert, *Westmoreland Co.;* A. Creigh, *History of Washington County . . .* (Harrisburg, Pa., 1871); R. G. Crist, "Cumberland County," in Frantz & Pencak, *Beyond Philadelphia,* 107–32; B. Crumrine, *History of Washington County* (Philadelphia, 1882), and *The Courts of Justice, Bench, and Bar of Washington County* (Washington, Pa., 1902); Harper, *Western Pa.;* W. A. Huss, *The Master Builders: A History of the Grand Lodge of Free and Accepted Masons of Pensylvania,* vol. 3 (Philadelphia, 1986); J. F. McFarland, *20th Century History of the City of Washington and Washington County* (Chicago, 1910); and Sachse, *Old Masonic Lodges.*

On Redick's political milieu and associates (William Findley, John Smilie, etc.) and adversaries, see: M. Allen, "The Federalists and the West, 1783–1803," *WPHM,* 61 (1978), 315–32; Brunhouse, *Counter-Rev. in Pa.;* S. Cornell, *The Other Founders: Anti-Federalism and the Dissenting Tradition in America, 1788–1828* (Chapel Hill, N.C., 1999); J. A. Davis, "The Democratic-Republican Societies of Pennsylvania, 1793–1796" (Ph.D. diss., Washington State University, 1996); Doyle, *Ireland, Irishmen;* E. G. Everett, "Some Aspects of Pro-French Sentiment in Pennsylvania, 1790–1800," *WPHM,* 43 (1960), 23–41; Ferguson, *Early W. Pa. Politics;* Foster, *Pursuit of Equal Liberty;* Ireland, *Religion, Ethnicity, & Politics;* E. P. Link, *Democratic-Republican Societies, 1790–1800* (New York, 1942); J. T. Main, *The Anti-Federalists* (Chapel Hill, N.C., 1961); R. A. Ryerson, "Republican Theory and Partisan Reality in Revolutionary Pennsylvania: Toward a New View of the Constitutionalist Party," in Hoffman & Albert, *Sov. States,* 95–133; C. Schramm, "William Findley in Pennsylvania Politics," *WPHM,* 20 (1937), 31–40; M. Sioli, "The Democratic Republican Societies at the End of the

Eighteenth Century: The Western Pennsylvania Experience," *Pa. Hist.*, 60 (July 1993), 288–304; H. M. Tincom, *The Republicans and Federalists in Pennsylvania, 1790–1801* (Harrisburg, 1950); R. Walters, Jr., "The Origins of the Jeffersonian Party in Pennsylvania," *PMHB*, 66, no. 4 (October 1942), 440–58, and "Spokesman of Frontier Democracy: Albert Gallatin in the Pennsylvania Assembly," *Pa. Hist.*, 13, no. 3 (July 1946), 161–84; "William Findley of Westmoreland, Pa.," *PMHB*, 5, no. 4 (1881), 440–50; G. S. Wood, "Interests and Disinterestedness in the Making of the Constitution," in Beeman et al., *Beyond Confederation*, 69–109, and Wood, *Creation of Am. Rep.* and *Radicalism of Am. Rev.*

On the Whiskey Rebellion, specifically, see: L. D. Baldwin, *Whiskey Rebels: The Story of a Frontier Uprising* (Pittsburgh, 1939); S. R. Boyd, ed., *The Whiskey Rebellion: Past and Present Perspectives* (Westport, Conn., 1985); R. V. Gould, "Patron-Client Ties, State Centralization, and the Whiskey Rebellion," *Am. J. Sociology*, 102 (September 1996), 400–429; R. W. Long, "The Presbyterians and the Whiskey Rebellion," *J. Presby. Hist.*, 43 (March 1965), 28–36; W. Miller, "The Democratic Societies and the Whiskey Insurrection," *PMHB*, 62, no. 3 (July 1938), 324–49; and Slaughter, *Whiskey Rebellion*.

On Ædanus Burke and his political context, see: Ædanus Burke letter to Thomas Burke, 2 December 1739, in W. Clark, ed., *The State Records of North Carolina* (Winston, Goldsboro, and Raleigh, N.C., 1895–1914), vol. 15, pp. 676–80; Calhoon, "Aedanus & Thomas Burke"; S. Cornell, "Reflections on 'The Late Remarkable Revolution in Government': Aedanus Burke and Samuel Bryan's Unpublished History of the Ratification of the Federal Constitution," *PMHB*, 112 (January 1988), 103–30; S. Cornell, *The Other Founders*; Crimmins, *St. Patrick's Day*; Klein, *Unification of Slave State*; J. C. Meleney, *The Public Life of Aedanus Burke: Revolutionary Republican in Post-Revolutionary South Carolina* (Columbia, S.C., 1989); J. J. Nadelhaft, "'The Snarls of Invidious Animals': The Democratization of Revolutionary South Carolina," in Hoffman & Albert, *Sov. States*, 62–94; and D. D. Wallace, *South Carolina: A Short History, 1520–1848* (Columbia, S.C., 1961).

On anti-Federalist fears that the Constitution gave Congress the power to tax and thereby prevent European immigration to the United States, see: Baseler, *"Asylum for Mankind."* On Pierce Butler, Dr. Peter Fayssoux, Wade Hampton, William Irvine, John Lamb, Rawlins Lowndes, and Thomas Sumter, as well as William Findley, see their respective entries in the *ANB* and *DAB*; data on the other South Carolinians cited in footnotes were located in the *So. Car. Hist. Mag.* Also on Findley and Irvine, see: Campbell, *Friendly Sons of St. Patrick*; and H. Simpson, *The Lives of Eminent Philadelphians, Now Deceased* (Philadelphia, 1859). On Rev. Thomas Ledlie Birch, see: Durey, *Transatlantic Radicals*; and especially the informative (albeit rather disparaging) treatment in Wilson, *United Irishmen*.

63. Daniel McCurtin, 1798

The letters of Daniel McCurtin, John Chambers, James Gallagher, and Mathew Carey are located in the Lea and Febriger Collection and the Edward Carey Gardiner Collection at the Historical Society of Pennsylvania, Philadelphia. We thank the HSP for permission to publish McCurtin's letter, and for research assistance we are grateful to: Dr. Maurice Bríc of University College, Dublin; Dr. Edward C. Carter II, librarian at the American Philosophical Society, Philadelphia; Lynn Conway, special collections librarian, Georgetown University, Washington, D.C.; Donn Devine, archivist, Wilmington Archdiocesan Archives, Wilmington, Delaware; Prof. Jay P. Dolan of Notre Dame University; Prof. Lynn Dumenil of Occidental College, Los Angeles; Prof. Beatriz B. Hardy of

Coastal Carolina University, Conway, South Carolina; Dr. Timothy Meagher at the Catholic University of America, Washington, D.C.; Kathleen Ryan and John Smolenski of the University of Pennsylvania, Philadelphia; the staff of the Kent County Public Library, Chestertown, Maryland; Rev. Paul K. Thomas, archivist, Baltimore Archdiocesan Archives, Baltimore; Dr. Kevin Whelan of Notre Dame University; Dr. C. J. Woods of the Royal Irish Academy, Dublin; and most especially to Patricia Joan O. Horsey and Prof. Emeritus Robert Janson-La Palme of Chestertown, Maryland, to Dr. Margaret H. McAleer of the Library of Congress, and to Dr. David Wilson of the University of Toronto.

On McCurtin's Dunbolloge parish and St. Peter's union, see: Lewis, *TDI.* On the image of America in late eighteenth-century Ireland, see: M. R. O'Connell, *Irish Politics and Social Conflict in the Age of the American Revolution* (Philadelphia, 1965). John Joyce's 1785 letter from Virginia is reprinted in "Virginia in 1785," *VMHB*, 23 (1915), 407–14, with a notation that the original document is in the Virginia Historical Society at Richmond. Samuel Rogers's 1798 letter from County Cavan is located in the Kemper Family Papers (Ms. qK32s, no. 56) at the Cincinnati Historical Society.

On Philadelphia in the 1790s, generally, see especially: Miller, *Phila.—Federalist City.* On the effects of the 1798 Naturalization and Alien and Sedition Acts, see: Baseler, *"Asylum for Mankind";* J. C. Miller, *Crisis in Freedom: The Alien and Sedition Acts* (Boston, 1951); J. M. Smith, *Freedom's Fetters: The Alien and Sedition Laws and American Civil Liberties* (Ithaca, N.Y., 1956); and L. E. Tise, *The American Counterrevolution: A Retreat from Liberty, 1783–1800* (Mechanicsburg, Pa., 1998).

On the "new Irish" immigrants in Philadelphia and the radical Irish emigrés' political careers in America, see: Bríc, "Ireland, Irishmen"; Carter, "Mathew Carey"; E. C. Carter II, "A 'Wild Irishman' under Every Federalist's Bed: Naturalization in Philadelphia, 1789–1806," *PMHB*, 94 (July 1970), 331–46; Durey, *Transatlantic Radicals;* Kelly, "Resumption of Emigration"; McAleer, "'Civil Strangers'"; J. I. Shulim, "John Daly Burk: Irish Revolutionist and American Patriot," *Trans. Am. Phil. Soc.*, 54, pt. 6 (October 1964), 1–60; Twomey, *Jacobins & Jeffersonians;* and Wilson, *United Irishmen.* On John Chambers specifically, see: M. Pollard, *Dublin's Trade in Books, 1500–1800* (Oxford, 1989), and "John Chambers, Printer and United Irishman," *Irish Book*, 3 (1964), 1–22. On Dr. James Gallagher, see Campbell, *Friendly Sons of St. Patrick.*

On Daniel McCurtin and his various locales and associations, see: "A Muster Roll of Capt. Thomas Price's Company of Rifle-Men in the Service of the United Colonies," *Md. Hist. Mag.*, 22 (1927), 275–83; T. Balch, ed., *Papers Relating Chiefly to the Maryland Line during the Revolution* (Philadelphia, 1857), which includes McCurtin's "Journal of the Times at the Siege of Boston"; W. Barroll, "Washington College, 1783," *Md. Hist. Mag.*, 6 (1911), 164–79; C. B. Clark, ed., *The Eastern Shore of Maryland and Virginia*, 3 vols. (New York, 1950); R. B. Clark, "Washington Academy, Somerset Co., Md.," *Md. Hist. Mag.*, 44 (1949), 200–209; F. W. Dumschott, *Washington College* (Chestertown, Md., 1980); P. Guilday, "John Gilmary Shea," U.S. Cath. Hist. Soc., *Hist. Rec. & Studies*, 17 (July 1926), 9–171; *Index to Revolutionary War Service Records*, vol. 3 (Waynesboro, Tenn., 1995); *Maryland Eastern Shore Newspaper Abstracts*, vol. 1 (1790–1805); *Pa. Arch.*, 3rd ser., vol. 15; J. T. Scharf, *History of Maryland . . .* , 3 vols. (1879; repr. Hatboro, Pa., 1967), and *History of Western Maryland*, 2 vols. (Philadelphia, 1882); *1790 U.S. Census, Heads of Families: Maryland* (Washington, D.C., 1907), 81; F. G. Usilton, *"City on the Chester": History of Chestertown . . .* (Chestertown, Md., 1899); T. S. Whitman, *The Price of Freedom: Slavery and Manumission in Baltimore and Early National Maryland* (Lexington, Ky., 1997); and T. J. C. Williams, *A History of Washington County, Maryland* (Hagerstown,

Md., 1906). References to McCurtin's Masonic lodge in Chesterton can be found in: Sachse, *Old Masonic Lodges,* vol. 1; and E. T. Schultz, *History of Freemasonry in Maryland* (Baltimore, 1884).

On Catholicism in late eighteenth- and early nineteenth-century Philadelphia and elsewhere in the United States, see: Carey, *People, Priests, & Prelates;* Chinnici, "American Catholics"; Dolan, *American Catholic Experience;* Hennesey, *Am. Catholics;* J. L. J. Kirlin, *Catholicity in Philadelphia, From the Earliest Missionaries Down to the Present Time* (Philadelphia, 1909); Light, *Rome & New Republic;* McAleer, "'Civil Strangers'"; and McAvoy, *Cath. Church in U. S.*

The best account of Dr. James Reynolds's American career is in Twomey's *Jacobins and Jeffersonians.* On the 1799 St. Mary's church riot, Wilson's account in *United Irishmen* should be supplemented by the trial testimony in W. Duane, *A Report of the Extraordinary Transactions which Took Place at Philadelphia in February 1799* (Philadelphia, 1799), in *Evans' Early Am. Imprints,* 1st ser., no. 35424. On Fr. Patrick Kenny, see: J. Wilcox, "Biography of Rev. Patrick Kenny, A.D. 1763–1840," *Rec. Am. Cath. Hist. Soc. Phila.,* 7 (1896), 27–79. Kenny's original diary is in the American Catholic Historical Society of Philadelphia, at St. Charles Borromeo Seminary, Overbrook, Pennsylvania; we have relied on the published entries in: [J. Wilcox], "Diary of Rev. Patrick Kenny," *Rec. Am. Cath. Hist. Soc. Phila.,* vols. 7–10 (1896–1899); some installments are titled "Extracts from the Diary of Rev. Patrick Kenny" and are ed. by M. I. J. Griffin.

64. Robert McArthur, 1802

Robert McArthur's 1802 letter, plus five other letters sent from Ireland to Crawford County in 1798–1832, are in the possession of Col. Francis M. McMunigle, U.S.A.F. retired, of Tucson, Arizona. Two additional McArthur letters, dated 1847 and 1858, are held by C. W. P. MacArthur of Marble Hill, Dunfanaghy, County Donegal. We are very grateful to Col. McMunigle for allowing publication of Robert McArthur's letter; to Martha Western of Denver, Colorado, for sharing her research in the Crawford County deed books; and Dr. Robert D. Ilisevich of the Crawford County Historical Society, Meadville, Pennsylvania, for research assistance. We are especially thankful to Mr. C. W. P. MacArthur of Marble Hill for bringing these documents to our attention, for his generous responses to our research inquiries, and for sharing his knowledge of the McArthur family history—including data he gleaned from Commander J. P. B. Ellison, Royal Navy, retired; Marie Penar of Grove City, Pennsylvania; and Clifton King of Colo, Iowa.

On the MacArthur family's Irish background and late eighteenth-century emigration, see: D. Dickson, "Derry's Backyard: The Barony of Inishowen, 1650–1800," in Nolan et al., *Donegal,* 405–46; Kelly, "Resumption of Emigration"; Jones, "Ulster Emigration"; Miller, *Emigrants & Exiles,* chap. 5; Mac Suibhne, "Up Not Out"; and Murphy, *Derry, Donegal.* On Burt parish, see: Lewis, *TDI,* vol. 1; and Day & McWilliams, *OSM,* vol. 39, *Parishes of County Donegal II, 1835–6* (1997).

On the McArthurs and their neighbors in Crawford County, see: S. D. Bates, *Our County and Its People: A Historical and Memorial Record of Crawford County* (Boston, 1899); [R. C. Brown], *History of Crawford County* (Chicago, 1885); R. D. Ilisevich, "Class Structure and Politics in Crawford County, 1800–1840," *WPHM,* 63, no. 2 (April 1980), 95–119, and *David Mead: Pennsylvania's Last Frontiersman* (Meadville, Pa., 1988); J. S. Hanson and T. L. Yoset, "Holland Land Company Sales in the Meadville District," *Crawford County Genealogy,* 18, no. 1 (February 1995), 53–58; E. W. MacArthur, comp., *The MacArthur Family Genealogy* (Meadville, Pa., 1921); and J. E. Reynolds, *In French Creek Valley* (Meadville, Pa., 1938).

For broader political context, see: M. Allen, "The Federalists and the West, 1783–1803,"

WPHM, 61 (1978), 315–32; S. J. Buck and E. H. Buck, *The Planting of Civilization in Western Pennsylvania* (Pittsburgh, 1939); Ferguson, *Early W. Pa. Politics;* and Shankman, "Democracy in Pa." On the naturalization laws of 1790–1802, see: Baseler, *"Asylum for Mankind."* On John Daly Burk, see the works by Durey, Shulim, and Wilson cited in the Sources for chapter 63.

65. John Nevin, 1804

A photocopy and typescript of John Nevin's letter are catalogued as T.3721/1 in PRONI, but the original manuscript is apparently in the Archives of the Religious Society of Friends, Ulster Quarterly Meeting, in Lisburn, County Antrim. We thank George L. Stephenson of Lisburn and the Deputy Keeper of Records, PRONI, for permission to publish, and we are also grateful to Professor Ruth-Ann M. Harris of Boston College; Dr. Líam Kennedy of Queen's University, Belfast; and Steve Cotham, head, McClung Historical Collection, Knox County Public Library, Knoxville, Tennessee, for research assistance.

On the Nevins of Ballyrashane, see: Ballywatt Presbyterian Church Records (MIC IP/379, PRONI); TAB: Ballyrashane (1832) in PRONI; Griffith's *Valuation:* Ballyrashane (1861) in PRONI; A. McClelland, "A Link with the '98," *Ulster Folk Museum Yearbook* (1966–67), 14–15; Rev. T. H. Mullin, *Coleraine in Georgian Times* (Belfast, 1977) and *Families of Ballyrashane* ([Belfast], 1969). On the Associate (Seceding) Presbyterians in Ulster, see: Brooke, *Ulster Presbyterianism;* McBride, *Scripture Politics;* D. Miller, "Presbyterianism and 'Modernization' in Ulster," *P & P*, 80 (August 1978), 66–90; and Rev. D. Stewart, *The Seceders in Ireland, with Annals of their Congregations* (Belfast, 1950).

On the United Irish Rebellion in north County Antrim and John Nevin's role, see: Stewart, *Summer Soldiers;* and on John Nevin and other United Irish exiles in America, see: Durey, *Transatlantic Radicals;* and Wilson, *United Irishmen.* Nevin's will is in the Knox County Estate Book 1, p. 216, in the McClung Historical Collection, Knox County Public Library. On the Seceding Presbyterians in America, see: Fisk, *Scottish High Church Tradition;* Rev. R. Lathan, *History of the Associate Reformed Synod of the South* . . . (Harrisburg, Pa., 1882); and J. P. Miller, *Biographical Sketches and Sermons of Some of the First Ministers of the Associate Church in America* . . . (Albany, 1839).

On the early history of east Tennessee and Knoxville, see: T. D. Clark and J. D. W. Guice, *Frontiers in Conflict: The Old Southwest, 1795–1830* (Albuquerque, N.M., 1989); R. E. Corlew, *Tennessee: A Short History,* 2nd ed. (Knoxville, Tenn., 1981); *Goodspeed's History of Tennessee* (1887; repr. Nashville, 1972); R. Horsman, *The Frontier in the Formative Years, 1783–1815* (N.Y., 1970); and M. U. Rothrock, ed., *The French Broad-Holston Country: A History of Knox County, Tennessee* (Knoxville, Tenn., 1946). On frontier revivalism in early nineteenth-century Tennessee and Kentucky, see: J. B. Boles, *The Great Revival, 1787–1805* (Lexington, Ky., 1972); P. K. Conkin, *Cane Ridge: America's Pentecost* (Madison, Wis., 1990); B. R. Lacy, Jr., *Revivals in the Midst of the Years* (Richmond, Va., 1943); and Schmidt, *Holy Fairs.* And for the broader religious context, see: Ahlstrom, *Religious History;* Hatch, *Democ. Am. Christ.;* Hood, "Presbyterianism"; and Wingo, "Politics, Society, & Religion."

66. Thomas Addis Emmet, 1806–1807

Thomas Addis Emmet's letter of 19 November 1806 is in the Peter Burrowes Papers (23.K.53/5.1) at the Royal Irish Academy, Dublin. His 2 November 1807 letter, with other correspondence from United Irish exiles in America to Robert Simms in Belfast, is in the Presbyterian Historical Society of Ireland, Belfast; in addition, typescripts of all the Simms letters are catalogued as D.1759/3B/6 in PRONI. For permission to publish and for research assistance, we thank Ms. Íde Ní Thuama of the Royal Irish Academy, and Rev. Dr. W. D. Baile, chairman, Rev. Dr. Joseph Thompson, and

R. H. Bonar of the Presbyterian Historical Society of Ireland. Additional primary sources include the R. R. Madden Papers at Trinity College, Dublin, and the William Sampson Papers (including his 1807 letter), in microfilm #13,611 at the Library of Congress, Washington, D.C. In addition, one of Emmet's advice-to-immigrants letters appears in the 17 September 1818 issue of the *Dublin Evening Post*, available in the National Library of Ireland, Dublin.

On Emmet, his comrades, and his milieux in Ireland, France, and the United States, see: R. G. Albion, *The Rise of New York Port* (New York, 1939); Curtin, *United Irishmen;* Dickson et al., *United Irishmen,* especially M. Burke, "Piecing Together a Shattered Past: The Historical Writings of the United Irish Exiles in America," 297–306; Doyle, *Ireland, Irishmen;* Durey, *Transatlantic Radicals;* Elliott, *Partners in Revolution;* T. A. Emmet, *Memoir of Thomas Addis and Robert Emmet,* 2 vols. (New York, 1915); P. A. Gilje, "The Development of an Irish American Community in New York City before the Great Migration," in Bayor & Meagher, *N. Y. Irish,* 70–83; R. R. Madden, *The Life and Times of Robert Emmet; also a Memoir of Thomas Addis Emmet* (N.Y., 1886), and *The United Irishmen, Their Lives and Times,* 8 vols. (London, 1847); Miller, *Emigrants & Exiles;* J. Mushkat, *Tammany: The Evolution of a Political Machine, 1789–1865* (Syracuse, N.Y., 1971); S. I. Pomerantz, *New York: An American City, 1783–1803* (New York, 1938); Potter, *Golden Door;* H. Strum, "Federalist Hiberno-phobes in New York, 1807," *Éire-Ireland,* 16 (winter 1981), 7–13; Twomey, *Jacobins & Jeffersonians;* W. J. Walsh, "Religion, Ethnicity, and History: Clues to the Cultural Construction of Law," in Bayor & Meagher, *N.Y. Irish,* 48–69. On Peter Burrowes, see: W. Burrowes, *Select Speeches of the Late Peter Burrowes, Esq., K.C., . . . with a Memoir* (Dublin, 1850), which contains a modernized text of Emmet's letter (as does Emmet, *Memoir*). Some biographical data on Robert Simms can be found in Stewart, *Summer Soldiers,* in addition to the works by Curtin, Dickson et al., Elliott, and Madden, already cited. On Rufas King, see his entries in *ANB* and *DNB*.

67. William Heazelton, Jr., 1810

William Heazelton's letters are catalogued in PRONI as D.592/10 and /13; the collection also includes (as /16) a letter from Pittsburgh by Nathaniel Holmes, dated 21 November 1815, which provides data on the deceased Heazelton's assets and debts. We thank the Deputy Keeper of Records, PRONI, the late Col. J. R. H. Greeves of Crawfordsburn, County Down, and J. A. (Tony) Greeves of Belfast for permission to publish Heazelton's 1814 letter. For research assistance, we are grateful to Prof. Michael Montgomery of the University of South Carolina; Mrs. Mary Shackleton, curator, Friends' Historical Society Library, Dublin; Helen Wilson, librarian, Western Pennsylvania Historical Society, Pittsburgh; Prof. John Wigger of the University of Missouri, Columbia; and to Greeves descendants J. A. Gamble and Tony Greeves of Belfast; Nellie Jester of Westfield, New Jersey; Prof. Donald Disbrow of Ypsilanti, Michigan; and, especially, Joy H. Jones of Colorado Springs, Colorado, who kindly loaned copies of transcriptions, made by the late Col. Greeves, of additional Greeves/O'Brien letters, including that of John and Jane Greeves, dated 7 February 1826, quoted in this chapter. For the reference to Guitiérrez de Lara's 1812–13 invasion of Spanish Mexico, we are grateful to Dr. Graham Davis of Bath Spa University, Bath, England.

Irish background information on the Greeves/Heazeltons and their locales is in: *Burke's Irish Family Records* (London, 1976); TAB: Killyman (1836) in PRONI; Griffith's *Valuation:* Killyman (1860) in PRONI; and A. C. Myers, *Irish Quakers into Pa.*

On Irish Methodism in eighteenth- and early nineteenth-century Ireland, see: Bowen, *Protestant Crusade;* Rev. W. Crook, *Ireland and the Centenary of American Methodism* (Belfast, 1866); C. H. Crookshank, *History of Methodism in Ireland* (London, 1885); D. N. Hempton, "Methodism in Irish

Society, 1770–1830," *Trans. R.H.S.,* 5th ser., vol. 36 (1986), 117–42; D. N. Hempton and M. Hill, *Evangelical Protestantism in Ulster Society, 1740–1890* (London, 1992); and M. Hill, "Popular Protestant-ism in Ulster in the Post-Rebellion Period," in Sheils & Wood, *Churches,* 191–202. On early Meth-odism's U.S.-British-Irish connections, see: Carwardine, *Transatlantic Revivalism;* and on Methodism in early nineteenth-century America, especially in western Pennsylvania and Ohio, see: E. S. Bucke, gen. ed., *The History of American Methodism,* vol. 1 (New York, 1964); D. J. Ratcliffe, *Party Spirit in a Frontier Republic: Democratic Politics in Ohio, 1793–1821* (Columbus, Ohio, 1998); and W. G. Smeltzer, *Methodism on the Headwaters of the Ohio* (Nashville, 1951).

William and Edward Heazelton appear in Pittsburgh's first directory, *The Honest Man's Extra Almanac* (Pittsburgh, 1813). On early nineteenth-century Pittsburgh, see: L. D. Baldwin, *Pittsburgh: The Story of a City* (Pittsburgh, 1937); J. N. Boucher, ed., *A Century and a Half of Pittsburgh and Her People* (Chicago, 1908); C. W. Dahlinger, *Pittsburgh: A Sketch of Its Early Social Life* (New York, 1916); L. C. Frey, *The Land in the Fork: Pittsburgh, 1753–1914* (Philadelphia, 1955); *History of Allegheny Co., Pennsylvania* (Philadelphia, 1878); S. Lorant, ed., *Pittsburgh: The Story of an American City* (Garden City, N.Y., 1964); *The People & Times of Western Pennsylvania: Pittsburgh Gazette Abstracts, 1806–1811,* vol. 3 (Pittsburgh, n.d.); J. F. Rishel, *Founding Families of Pittsburgh: The Evolution of a Regional Elite* (Pittsburgh, 1990); and E. Wilson, ed., *Standard History of Pittsburgh* (Chicago, 1898). On the U.S. government's regulations of Irish and other aliens during the War of 1812, see: Baseler, *"Asylum for Mankind,"* and Wilson, *United Irishmen.*

On Republican and Federalist politics in late eighteenth- and early nineteenth-century west-ern Pennsylvania, see the Sources for chapter 62, especially those by Brunhouse, Ferguson, Slaughter, and Tincom, in addition to Guthrie, *John McMillan.* William Findley's 1812 autobiographical letter is reprinted in full in "William Findley of Westmoreland, Pa.," *PMHB,* 5, no. 4 (1881), 440–50. On David Bruce, see his *Poems Chiefly in the Scottish Dialect, Originally Written under the Signature of the Scots-Irishman, . . . By A Native of Scotland* (Washington, Pa., 1801); in addition to M. Montgomery, "The Problem of Persistence: Ulster-American Missing Links," *J. of Scotch-Irish Studies,* 1 (2000), 105–19; and H. R. Warfel, "David Bruce, Federalist Poet of Western Pennsylvania," *WPHM,* 8 (1925), 175–234. On Hugh Henry Brackenridge, see: Ferguson, *Early W. Pa. Politics;* Slaughter, *Whiskey Rebellion;* and S. A. Watts, *The Republic Reborn: War and the Making of Liberal America, 1790–1820* (Baltimore, 1987). On Ulster Protestant historical realities vs. mythologies, see: McBride, *Siege of Derry;* and J. H. Ohlmeyer, "The Wars of Religion, 1603–1660," in Bartlett & Jeffrey, *Military History,* 160–87. On the Ulster-Scots language poets of late eighteenth-century east Ulster and New England, see the Sources for chapter 49.

68. John Caldwell, Jr., 1802

John Caldwell's letter of 18 October 1802, plus another to Robert Simms dated 1806, is located in the Presbyterian Historical Society of Ireland, Belfast; for permission to publish, we are grateful to the Society, chairman Rev. Dr. W. D. Bailie, R. H. Bonar, Society librarian, and Rev. Joseph Thompson of Belfast. Transcripts of the following Caldwell manuscripts are available in the Public Record Office of Northern Ireland (PRONI), Belfast: John Caldwell, "Particulars of History of a North County Irish Family" (1849), in T.3541/5/3; the Caldwell-Simms letters of 1802–1806, in D.1759/3B/6; Caldwell family leases, 1783–1789, in D.2977/3B/4; and additional papers in D.1518. In addition, the New York Genealogical and Biographical Society, in New York City, has an origi-nal copy of Caldwell's 1849 memoir, John Caldwell, Sr.'s account of his family's exile, two family histories by Harriet B. Caldwell and E. T. Langford, and additional family and business papers. Also, the R. R. Madden Papers (Ms. 873) in Trinity College, Dublin, include an 1842 letter from Caldwell (item 436). Other primary sources include: Caldwell's will and estate inventory, 1850, in the Orange County Surrogate's Court, Goshen, New York; the various New York City directories, 1800–1836; and lists of New York's Masonic lodges and their officers, in the New-York Historical Society.

In addition to the PRONI staff, for invaluable research assistance we thank: Prof. Marion Casey of New York University; Janet Dempsey, town historian of Cornwall, New York; Nancy Husor of the Orange County Surrogate's Court in Goshen; Helen Ver Nooy Gearn, city historian of Newburgh, New York; and especially Dr. A. T. Q. Stewart, retired, of Queen's University, Belfast; and Caldwell descendants Polly Midgley of Briarcliff, New York; Mrs. Midgley's late mother, Mrs. R. V. T. Edie, who deposited the Caldwell mss. in the NYGBS; and Alice Naughton of New York City. Finally, we are grateful to Margaret Evans, assistant curator of the Maritime Archives and Library, Liverpool, for information on that city's great fire of 1802, mentioned in Caldwell's letter.

Information on the lives in Ireland and America of John Caldwell and other 1798 exiles mentioned in his 1802 letter can be traced in the following published sources: W. Barrett, pseud. [J. A. Scoville], *The Old Merchants of New York City* (New York, 1885 ed.); Crimmins, *St. Patrick's Day;* Curtin, *United Irishmen;* C. Dickson, *Revolt in the North: Antrim and Down in 1798* (Dublin, 1960); Dickson et al., *United Irishmen;* M. Durey, ed., *Andrew Bryson's Ordeal: An Epilogue to the 1798 Rebellion* (Cork, 1998); Durey, *Transatlantic Radicals;* Elliott, *Partners in Revolution;* M. Elliott, *Wolfe Tone: Prophet of Irish Independence* (New Haven, 1989); T. A. Emmet, *Memoir of Thomas Addis and Robert Emmet,* vol. 1 (New York, 1915); R. R. Madden, *Antrim and Down in '98* (Glasgow, n.d.), and *The United Irishmen: Their Lives and Times,* 7 vols. (Dublin, 1846); Rev. T. H. Mullin, *Coleraine in Georgian Times* (Belfast, 1977); the various *New York City Directories,* 1800–1836; Potter, *Golden Door;* J. Savage, *'98 and '48: The Modern Revolutionary History and Literature of Ireland* (New York, 1856); J. Smyth, *The Men of No Property: Irish Radicals and Popular Politics in the Late Eighteenth Century* (Dublin, 1992); Stewart, *Summer Soldiers;* Wilson, *United Irishmen;* R. J. Wolfe, "Early New York Naturalization Records in the Emmet Collection; with a List of Aliens Naturalized in New York, 1801–1814," *Bul. NYPL,* 67 (April 1963), 211–17; and R. M. Young, *Ulster in '98: Episodes and Anecdotes* (Belfast, n.d.). On the United Irishmen, generally, also see: K. Whelan, *The Tree of Liberty: Radicalism, Catholicism and the Construction of Irish Identity, 1760–1830* (Cork, 1996).

Works describing early nineteenth-century Orange County, New York, the first of which mentions the Caldwells of Salisbury Mills, include: E. M. Ruttenber and L. H. Clark, comps., *History of Orange County* (Philadelphia, 1881); and H. G. Spafford, *A Gazetteer of the State of New-York* (Albany, 1813). Works on—or relevant to—the history of the Irish in early to mid-nineteenth-century New York City include: Bayor & Meagher, *N.Y. Irish,* especially chapters 2 and 3; R. Ernst, *Immigrant Life in New York City, 1825–1863* (New York, 1949); P. A. Gilje, *The Road to Mobocracy: Popular Disorder in New York City, 1783–1834* (Chapel Hill, N.C., 1987); H. P. Rock, *Artisans of the New Republic: Tradesmen of New York City in the Age of Jefferson* (New York, 1979); C. Stansell, *City of Women: Sex and Class in New York, 1789–1860* (New York, 1982); R. B. Stott, *Workers in the Metropolis: Class, Ethnicity, and Youth in Antebellum New York City* (Ithaca, N.Y., 1990); and S. Wilentz, *Chants Democratic: New York City and the Rise of the American Working Class, 1788–1850* (New York, 1984). On the effects of the U.S. Coinage Act of 1834, see G. L. Browne, *Baltimore in the Nation, 1789–1861* (Chapel Hill, N.C., 1980).

Appendix 3. Additional Documents

Robert Crockett, 1825

Thanks again to the late Mrs. Elizabeth Reeve of Orient Point, New South Wales, and her brother, James Crockett of Heversham, Cumbria, England, for permission to publish this and the other Crockett letters (see the Sources for chapters 15 and 27).

Peter O'Connor Petitions, 1797–1798

O'Connor's petitions are in the Lea and Febriger Papers, Mathew Carey Incoming Correspondence, 1785–1796, in the Historical Society of Pennsylvania, Philadelphia. We thank the HSP for permission to publish and Meg McAleer for bringing them to our attention.

David Robinson, 1817

We thank the Deputy Keeper of the Public Record Office of Northern Ireland, in Belfast, for permission to publish Robinson's letter, catalogued as D.2013/1.

INDEX ❋

Note: Alternate spellings of names are in parentheses

College of Philadelphia, 484, 489, 513
colonial nationalism, 7–8, 71–72
Comber town and parish, Co.
    Down, 264
Commander, Samuel, 138
commerce. *See* foreign trade;
    merchants and traders
Committees of Correspondence
    (N.H.), 550
Committees of Correspondence and
    Safety (Maine), 134
Common Sense (Paine), 557n.101
commonwealthmen, 479
companionate marriage, 368
Concanen, Luke, 425–26n.61,
    430n.81
Concord, battle of (1775), 551
conduct books, 478–80
*Conduct of the Paxton Men, Impartially
    Represented, The* (pamphlet), 497
Conestoga Indians, 514
confessions, criminal, 268–74, 275,
    276–79
Congregationalists, 133–34, 197,
    383n.5
    American Presbyterian church
        and, 414–15, 517–20
    anti-Catholicism and, 445, 449
    in Boston, 402n.7
    MacSparran (James) and, 56–57,
        58–59
    Ulster immigrants and, 436–37,
        448–50
Conjunct Presbyteries of New
    Brunswick and Londonderry,
    401
Conn, Hugh, 63
Connacht, Ireland, 4, 457–58n.17
Connecticut, 249, 328, 515
    Congregationalism and, 57,
        383n.5
    MacSparran's (James) description
        of, 65–66
Connemara, Co. Galway, 127
Connolly, John, 427n.70
Conococheague settlement (Pa.),
    157, 158, 178, 285–86
Constitution, U.S., 8, 94, 449, 485,
    546
    anti-Federalist opposition to,
        572–82, 587
Constitutional Convention, U.S.,
    520–21n.42, 572–73, 575,
    576–77
Continental Army, 3, 178, 180, 253,
    262, 567, 573
Continental Association, 334n.13,
    550n.18, 551n.21
Continental Congress, 520–21n.42
    British trade restrictions and, 335,
        528, 535
    Burke (Thomas) as delegate to,
        499, 509
    First, 334n.13, 335, 528

Henry (Patrick) and, 542
Irish support for, 587–88
printer to, 87, 292
convent schools, 350–51
conversions
    to Anglicanism, 3, 70, 452, 454,
        458–60
    of Catholics, 3, 452, 454, 458–60,
        500n.3, 627
    to Church of Ireland, 620
    to Methodism, 412, 413
    to Presbyterianism, 23, 223
    to Quaker belief, 188–89, 192–93
    revivalism and, 227, 412, 413
convicts, Irish, 38n.46, 122, 270
Conway, Henry Seymour, 505
Conwell, Henry, 224, 228n.14, 417,
    419, 430
Conyngham, Redmond, 540n.14
Conynghan & Nesbitt, 538–39
Cookstown, Co. Tyrone, 28
Cooper, Anthony Ashley, earl of
    Shaftesbury, 478–80
Cooper, James Fenimore, 588
Cooper family, 133n.24
coopers, 250, 251
Cork, city and county, Munster, 4,
    13, 39, 73, 535–36, 586
Cork, Lady, 64
Cornwallis, Charles, 562, 564, 565,
    566, 570, 611, 634
Corry, Edward, 324, 325
Corry, Isaac, 324, 325
Corry, Isaac (Edward's son), 325n.6
Cosby, William, 461, 462
Cosgrave, James, 269n.3
Cottey, Abel, 245, 249
Cottey, Sarah, 249
cottier-weavers, 31
cotton gin, 95
cotton industry, 95
Country Party, 459
courtesy books, 476, 478–79
courthouse rings, in North Carolina,
    508, 531
Coutance, Catherine, 299
Covenanting (or Reformed)
    Presbyterians, 135–36n.1, 148,
        385, 404–5n.34
Cowman, Jeremiah, 76, 79
Cox, Isaac, 528n.21
craftsmen, 185, 104
    American demand for, 243, 250
    British emigration restrictions and,
        86
    Brown, Samuel, 4, 302n.13,
        303–13, 596
    Chandlee, Benjamin, Sr., 243–49,
        255
    Doyle, James, 292–96
    emigration to West Indies, 121,
        122
    Kennedy, John, 250–53
    labor unions and, 312

McMahon, Thomas, 4, 289, 291
    post–Revolutionary War immi-
        gration of, 288, 291, 303, 585
    status in America, 303
    women as, 357
    See also specific trades and crafts
Craig, Agnes Park, 381
Craig, Andrew, 364, 377
Craig, David, 381
Craig, George, 398
Craig, Isabella Helena Russell,
    394n.64
Craig, James (Mary Cumming's
    brother), 364, 377
Craig, John, 3, 4, 381–400, 401, 412
    memoir of, 386–98
Craig, Margaret, 363, 364, 369, 376
Craig, Mary McCully, 364
Craig, Rachel, 364, 376
Craig, William, 396–97n.76
Craighead, Alexander, 404–5n.34,
    410
Crane, Stephen, 253n.26
Cranston, Alexander, 639
Crawford, Alexander, 24–27
    letter from, 25–27
Crawford, Hugh, 25
Crawford County, Pa., 598, 602–3,
    624, 645
Creek Indians, 82, 604
criminals, 416
    confessions of, 268–74, 275,
        276–79 as immigrants, 243
    Irish convict transports, 38n.46,
        122, 270
    Philadelphia convictions of, 288
Crockett, Ann, 239–40
Crockett, Catherine, 118
Crockett, David (frontiersman),
    109n.6
Crockett, David (George, Jr.'s
    brother), 108, 114, 115, 118,
    235–36
Crockett, Eliza, 108, 118
Crockett, George (cousin), 110, 114,
    116–17
Crockett, George, Jr., 4, 107–18,
    235, 236
    letters from, 111–14, 115–16
Crockett, George, Sr., 107–8, 111,
    115, 236–37, 238
Crockett, George Alexander (James's
    son), 238, 239–40
Crockett, Hannah, 237
    letter from, 237–38
Crockett, James, 108–9, 110, 118,
    235–40
    letters from, 236, 237–38
Crockett, Robert, 108, 111, 114,
    116–17, 118, 235, 236, 238,
    239–40, 678–79
Crockett, William, 108, 114, 115,
    118
Crockett family, 233, 311, 312, 597

convent schools, 350–51
hedge schools, 416, 465
Hutcheson's (Francis) view of, 511
schoolmasters, 227, 228n.14,
    415–32, 436, 568, 571, 590,
    591, 595–96
schoolmistresses, 357, 360, 361
See also specific institutions
Edwards, Jonathan, 549
Eighth Pennsylvania Regiment, 180,
    181n.5
Ely O'Carroll (Ireland), 452, 453, 460
Emancipation Act of 1829 (Ireland),
    102n.56
Embargo Acts of 1807–10 (U.S.), 45,
    96n.13, 426n.62, 616n.21
Embury, Philip, 186n.8
emigration, Irish
    advice letters and, 75, 631
    business ventures and, 82
    causes of, 4–9, 13–50, 197,
        292–93, 317–18
    charitable organizations and, 103,
        288–92
    in early nineteenth century, 4, 13,
        608–9, 611–18, 626
    economic factors and, 5–8, 20, 25,
        27, 35, 89, 436, 567
    guidebooks and, 55, 59, 75
    patronage and, 461–76
    of political exiles, 4, 586, 594n.37,
        596, 608, 609, 613n.15, 614,
        618–19, 631, 632, 634–35, 644
    political factors and, 4–8, 15,
        20–21, 34–35, 46, 292–93, 417,
        430, 435–36
    post–American Revolution,
        585–89, 594–95, 608
    processes of, 53–118
    religious issues and, 5–6, 14, 15
    transatlantic correspondence and,
        9, 72–73
    transatlantic passages and, 90–93,
        94, 96–98
emigration agents, shippers' use of,
    28
Emmet, Robert (Thomas's brother),
    202n.8, 611, 614, 639n.42
Emmet, Robert (Thomas's father),
    609
Emmet, Thomas Addis, 42n.7,
    608–19, 610, 631, 635n.14, 640,
    641n.58, 644, 646
    letters from, 612–13, 616–18
Emmitsburg, Md., 359
England. See Great Britain
England, John, 95, 102
English Civil Wars (1642–48), 479
Enlightenment, 227, 385, 430, 458,
    480, 510, 511, 521, 632
epidemics, yellow fever, 292, 296,
    304, 305, 352
Episcopalians. See Anglicans; Scottish
    Episcopalians

Erie Canal, 39, 44, 608, 611–12n.11
Erin Masonic Lodge (N.Y.C.), 644
Erwin, Andrew, 346, 347, 348, 604
Essay Concerning Human Under-
    standing, An (Locke), 478n.8
ethnic identity
    commerce and ethnoreligious
        linkages, 318
    early nineteenth-century
        immigrants and, 609, 614,
        626–27
    "Irish," 8–10, 70, 71–72, 447, 536,
        543–44n.27, 574, 626–27, 632
    Irish Catholics and, 8, 102–3, 452,
        593–95, 626
    Irish Protestants and, 8, 71–72,
        442–51, 596
    post–Revolutionary War issues of,
        593–95
    "Scotch-Irish," ix, 8, 70, 72n.76,
        103, 442–51, 625–27, 646
    Ulster Presbyterians and, 103, 413–
        14, 435, 442–51, 536, 626, 632
    working-class issues of, 312–13
evangelicalism, 227, 234, 308, 626,
    645
    camp meeting revivals and, 607
    New Reformation revivals and,
        620
    Presbyterians and, 102, 103,
        384–85, 399, 401, 412, 607
    Protestant conservatives and, 620
    working classes and, 312, 313
    See also Great Awakening
Evans, Eleanor, 219
Ewing, John, 514n.11
Exeter, N.H., 557
exports, 317, 324

factory system, 303
Fagan, John, 268–71, 274
    confession of, 272–73
Fagg, John, 401n.4
Fagg's Manor (New Londonderry,
    Pa.), 401, 410, 411
    Classical School, 401, 411–12
Fairfax, Lord, 147
famines, Irish, 20, 25, 567
    Great Famine (1845–52), 103, 239,
        263, 448, 645
farmers and planters, 121–240
    American Revolution and, 508–9
    anti-Catholicism and, 510
    Blake, John, 121–28
    Burke, Thomas, 508–10
    Carroll, Charles (doctor), 455–56
    Chambers, John and Jane,
        196–200
    Crockett, James and Hannah,
        108–9, 110, 118, 235–40
    exports by, 317
    Greenlee, Mary, 3, 4, 147–56,
        179, 226
    Guthrie, Elizabeth, 3, 179–84

indentured labor and, 253,
    254–55, 258–59
Kent, Daniel, 4, 184–96, 200, 255,
    297
land companies and, 602
Magraw, James, 143–46, 226
McCobb, Samuel, 128–35
McCullough, James, 156–79
Patten, Matthew, 547–59
post–Revolutionary War
    immigration and, 585
Regulator movement and, 508,
    530–36, 561
Toner, Edward and Mary, 4,
    224–34, 235, 631
U.S. Constitution ratification
    debate and, 572–73
Witherspoon, Robert, 3, 4,
    135–43, 560
Wright, Joseph and Hannah, 4,
    200–224, 236, 249n.68, 362
See also tenant farmers
Farmer's Letters (Dickinson), 524
Faulkner, Mary Anne, 473n.61
Fayssoux (Fousseaux), Peter, 580
Federalist Party, 8, 94, 609
    anti-Irish legislation and, 587, 614
    Bank of North America and, 529
    as Catholic trustees, 431
    Irish immigrant supporters of, 111,
        573, 620, 625, 626
    in New York, 611, 612, 614–17
    in Pennsylvania, 135n.31, 287,
        308, 309, 312, 485, 520–21n.42,
        522, 525n.7, 536, 546, 574, 576,
        587, 594–95, 602–3, 624
    Philadelphia class alignment and,
        308, 309
    Presbyterian clergy support of,
        135n.31, 413, 520n.41, 584
    Quakers as, 222, 308
    revivalism and, 607
    Scots-Irish Presbyterians and, 415,
        448–49
    U.S. Constitution ratification and,
        574, 576, 582, 587
    See also anti-Federalists
Female Orphan Asylum (Petersburg,
    Va.), 364, 369
Fenian rebellion of 1867, 644
Fennagh parish, Co. Carlow, 73
Fenwick, Benedict Joseph,
    425–26n.61, 431
Fenwick, John, 14
Ferguson, Robert, 108
Fermanagh County, Ireland, 55
Ferrall, Mathew, 470
Ferrall, Silvester, 463–65
    letter from, 463–64
financiers, 317
Finch, William, 253n.26
Findley, William, 226n.7, 486, 486,
    487, 572–77, 582, 583, 588–89,
    608, 625, 626, 627

Presbyterians (*continued*)
  Scottish Episcopalian repression
      by, 269n.2
  Seceding Presbyterians, 45–46,
      46–47n.7, 324, 328n.30, 385,
      603–4, 607
  in South Carolina, 24, 101, 103,
      135–43, 447, 559–61
  in Ulster, 3, 4, 5, 24–25, 27, 28,
      31, 35n.33, 36–37, 45, 70, 89,
      135–36, 381, 384–85, 435–36,
      443, 445–46, 510, 511, 596–97,
      620
  in Virginia, 383–400
  Westminster Confession of Faith
      and, 36n.43, 46–47n.7, 388n.17,
      435n.3, 512
Presbytery of Donegal (America),
    383, 389, 399
Presbytery of Hanover, 399
Presbytery of New Brunswick, 401
Presbytery of New York, 411, 414
Presbytery of Philadelphia, 401
priests, Roman Catholic, 357–59,
    426n.64, 445, 460
primitivists, 415n.82
Prince, Thomas, 401–2, 410
Princeton University (formerly
    College of New Jersey), 411,
    412, 513
printing industry, 292–96
prisoners. *See* convicts
Pritchard, William, 294, 295
property qualifications, for suffrage,
    499
proprietary companies, 129
Proprietary Party (Pa.), 490–92,
    496–97, 514, 515, 522, 524,
    529, 536, 537, 546
proselytization
  Anglican, 57
  New Reformation and, 620
  Presbyterian, 70
  See also evangelicalism
Protestants
  American radicalism and, 645
  Catholic converts to, 3, 452,
      458–60, 500n.3, 627
  Catholic strife with, 5, 8, 10, 35,
      36n.35, 37, 40–41, 44, 226–27,
      239, 240, 430, 452, 620
  colonial nationalism and, 7–8,
      71–72
  emigration by, 3–8, 13, 53, 55, 89,
      624
  evangelicalism by, 102, 103, 227,
      234, 308, 312, 313, 384–85,
      399, 401, 412, 645
  indentured servitude and, 253,
      261, 275
  in Ireland, 5, 6, 7–8, 13–15, 20,
      24, 28, 34–35, 70–71, 73–74,
      185–86, 452–53, 567–68,
      619–20

Irish gentry and, 500
New Reformation and, 620
political conservatism (late
    eighteenth and early nineteenth
    century) and, 619–21, 624–26
revivalism by. *See* evangelicalism
schoolmasters and, 415–16
Scots-Irish. *See* Scots-Irish
women's perspective, 350
See also specific denominations
Providence, R.I., 329
publishing industry, 292–96, 429,
    588
Puritans, 402n.7, 415
  hostility toward Catholics by, 328,
      330
  Ulster Presbyterian immigrants
      and, 128, 129, 328, 440
putting-out system, 31, 303

Quakers, 385
  American Revolution and, 528,
      529, 536, 538n.5
  Barton's (Thomas) disdain for, 487
  converts to Church of Ireland
      from, 620
  emigration to North America by,
      3, 4, 24, 200, 201, 243–45
  Hicksite schism, 222, 223
  as indentured servant masters,
      255–57, 258–59, 261
  in Ireland, 13–14, 73, 74,
      200–202, 244, 522, 531,
      535–36, 620
  as "Irish New Lights," 201
  Kent's (Daniel) conversion to
      188–89, 192–93
  "marrying out" by, 74, 202, 222
  in New Jersey, 14, 23, 73, 268
  in New York, 418–19
  in North Carolina, 73, 532–34,
      536
  in Ohio, 214, 218–19, 222–23,
      249n.68
  in Pennsylvania, 14, 63–64, 73–75,
      81, 87, 188, 244–45, 249, 308,
      400, 490–92, 496–98, 514–16,
      521–24, 527–29, 537, 538n.5,
      546
  in Rhode Island, 58, 328
  in Scotland, 522n.2, 531
  as slavery opponents, 525n.12, 536
  in South Carolina, 73
  transatlantic correspondence and,
      72–73
  transfer certificates and, 86
  U.S. Constitution ratification and,
      575
Quartering Act of 1764 (Britain), 515
Quebec, Canada, 443
Quebec Act of 1774 (Britain), 549
Queen Anne's War, 129
Queensborough, Ga., 85–86
Quid Republicans, 312, 602

Quin, Thomas, 193
Quinn, John, 641
quit rents, 63n.40, 83n.7, 152, 153
  in Maryland, 454, 459

railroads, 117
Ralph, Thomas, 255, 264–65
  petition by, 264–65
Ramsay, David, 142, 412n.73
Ranfurly, earls of, 46, 620
rapparees, 269
Rathconrath parish, Co. Westmeath,
    14
Rathcool townland (Rathkul),
    Rathoath parish and barony,
    Co. Meath, 470
rationalism, 385, 511, 603, 632
Rawdon, Francis Lord, 564, 565
Rea, Catherine, 82
Rea, David, 82
Rea, James (indentured servant
    "soul-driver"), 259n.19, 260
Rea, James (John Rea's half-
    brother), 85
Rea, John (father), 82–86, 147
  letter from, 83–84
Rea, John (son), 85
Rea, Matthew, 82, 83, 84, 85
Rea, Robert, 82, 85
Read, George, 520
redemptioners, 75, 187n.20, 243, 416
Redick, David, 574–76, 577, 582–
    84, 625
  letter from, 575–76
Reed, Matthew, 441–42n.24
Reed family, 133, 134
references, personal, 86
Reformation, 121
Reformed Presbyterians. *See*
    Covenanting (or Reformed)
    Presbyterians
regium donum, 383
Regulator movement, 508, 530–36,
    561
Reid, James, 441–42n.24
Reid, Thomas, 446n.29
Reily, Charles Lewis, 465–68
  letter from, 465–68
Reily, Luke, 468
religion
  church-state separation and, 516–17
  as emigration factor, 5–6, 14, 15,
      436
  tolerance in America, 6, 14, 58
  See also clergymen; Roman
      Catholics; Protestants; *specific
      denominations and sects*
republicanism, 478n.7, 479, 499–500,
    577
Republican party (founded 1854), 313
Republican party (Jeffersonian), 8
  Catholic trustees and, 431
  conservative Protestant opposition
      to, 620, 621, 624, 626

early election victories of, 587
former United Irishmen and, 431,
    585, 587, 588–91, 593–96, 607,
    608–9, 612, 614–19
Irish Catholic clergy opponents
    to, 593
Irish immigrants and, 135n.31,
    299, 308–9, 312, 431, 449, 596,
    598, 608–9, 612, 614–15,
    618–19
Jay's Treaty and, 590
Jefferson's election as president
    and, 596, 598
Methodists as, 624
in New York, 587, 612, 614, 615,
    618–19
Ohio Valley Methodists and, 624,
    625
in Pennsylvania, 308–9, 312, 313,
    449, 486, 583, 587, 593, 602–3,
    624
Philadelphia class alignment and,
    308, 309, 312, 313
Presbyterian clergy's opposition
    to, 413, 625
Scots-Irish and, 486, 607
See also Anti-Federalists; Federalist
    party
Republican Society (Philadelphia),
    546
revivalism. See evangelicalism; Great
    Awakening
Revolutionary War. See American
    Revolution
Revolution of 1782 (Ireland), 34–35
Reynell, John, 523, 527
Reynolds, James, 594
Reynolds, John, 319–20
Rhode Island, 57–58, 515
    American Revolution and, 331
    Anglicans and, 3, 57, 58
    Baptists and, 58, 328
    Catholics and, 58, 329–31
    MacSparran (James) and, 57, 58,
        66–67, 69, 329n.2
    merchants and traders, 328–29
    O'Kelly (John) and, 328–31
    Quakers and, 58, 328
Rhyming Weavers, 451
Ribbon Lodges, 224, 226, 233n.77
Rice, John, 295
Rice, Thomas, 131
rice plantations, 253
Richay (Richey), John, 441–42n.24
Rightboys, 574n.7
Riot Act of 1771 (N.C.), 532,
    533n.15
riots
    New York City, 614, 619
    Philadelphia, 222–23n.121, 312,
        645
Rippey, Hugh, 144, 146
Rippey, Samuel, 320
Rippey family, 146, 318

Rittenhouse, David, 489, 498
Rittenhouse, Esther, 490, 498
Roberts, John (Baltimore merchant),
    214
Roberts, John (Pa. state senator),
    93n.13
"Robinocracy," 479
Robinson (David), 681–83
Rockbridge County, Va., 147, 148,
    154–55, 156
Rodgers, John, 412n.73
Rogan, Hugh, 114
Rogers, George, 86n.1
Rogers, James, 467
Rogers, Samuel, 588
Roman Catholics, 3, 5–6, 268
    in Antrim County (Ireland), 94–95
    Barton's (Thomas) disdain for, 487
    British reconquest of Ireland
        (1649–50) and, 13
    British repression of, 5, 102,
        457–58n.17, 492n.10
    Charleston (S.C.) schism, 102,
        103, 431
    converts to Protestantism, 3, 452,
        454, 458–60, 500n.3, 627
    in Donegal County (Ireland), 110
    ethnic identity and, 8, 102–3, 452,
        593–95, 626
    female domestic servants, 300
    female religious orders, 350, 351,
        358–61, 426n.65
    Hogan schism, 417n.5
    immigration by, 4, 5, 8, 24,
        39–40, 44, 53, 121, 224–28,
        229n.26, 243
    indentured servitude and, 3, 39,
        121, 122, 253, 255, 261–63, 443
    Irish land confiscations from, 13,
        14, 16n.14, 40, 121–22, 501
    Irish nationality and, 452
    Irish outlaws, 269n.3
    Irish Penal Laws and, 16n.13, 71,
        102n.56, 351, 352, 416, 453,
        457–58n.17, 459, 460, 501, 585,
        634
    Irish poverty and, 7, 317
    Irish Rebellion of 1641 and, 5,
        121, 453, 592n.33, 626
    Irish resurgence of 1690s and, 14
    Kilkenny Confederation, 121
    in Maine, 134n.27
    male religious orders, 357–59,
        426n.64, 445, 460
    in Maryland, 7, 128, 202, 453–61
    nativist movements against. See
        nativism
    in New England, 329–30, 443
    in Pennsylvania, 6, 224–26, 234,
        287, 300–303, 312, 487,
        491–92, 522, 536, 539
    Protestant strife with, 5, 8, 10, 35,
        36n.35, 37, 40–41, 44, 226–27,
        239, 240, 430, 452, 620

Puritan hostility toward, 328, 330
religious publications of, 296
reluctance to emigrate by, 53–55
in Rhode Island, 58, 329–31
Ribbon Lodges, 224, 226, 233n.77
as schoolmasters, 227, 228n.14,
    415–32
as schoolmistresses, 357, 360, 361
"Scotch-Irish" term and, 447–48
secret societies, 574n.7
in South Carolina, 95, 102, 103
trusteeship crises in America and,
    431–32, 594–95, 596
in Ulster, 5, 24, 31, 35n.33, 37,
    39, 89, 94–95, 110, 224, 226–27
ultramontanism and, 603
in West Indies, 39, 121, 122–28
women's perspective, 349–50,
    357–62
See also anti-Catholicism
Rossdroit parish, Co. Wexford, 40
Rowan, Archibald Hamilton,
    588–89n.11
Russell, Thomas, 511n.3, 639n.42
Rutherford, Alexander, 89n.15
Rutherford, John, 86, 87, 88–89
Rutherford, Mary, 89
Rutherford, Robert, 87
Rutherford, Sarah, 89
Rutherford, William, 87, 89
Rye House Plot of 1683 (Ireland),
    15

Sacramental Test Act of 1704
    (Ireland), 436, 518n.30
St. Andrew's societies, 447
St. Bonaventure College (N.Y.), 44
St. Christopher (island), 122, 127
St. James's Church (Lancaster, Pa.),
    495–96, 498
Saint James's Coffee House
    (London), 458n.19
Saint-John, Henry (Lord
    Bolingbroke), 479
St. Joseph's House (Md.), 359, 360
St. Mary's Catholic Church
    (Philadelphia), 417n.5, 594, 595
St. Mary's Catholic Church
    (Charleston, S.C.), 95, 102, 431
St. Mary's Free School for Girls
    (Baltimore), 361
St. Patrick's Cathedral (N.Y.C.),
    427, 429, 432n.85
St. Patrick's Day, 447
St. Patrick's Society (Philadelphia),
    522, 632
St. Paul's Church (Narragansett,
    R.I.), 57, 58, 69
St. Peter's Catholic Church
    (N.Y.C.), 418, 421n.34,
    424–27, 614
Salem, Mass., 156n.51
Salem, N.Y. See New Perth, N.Y.
Salem County, Pa, 14, 23

Talbot, Jeremiah, 262
Talbot, Richard, 16n.12
Tamlaght Finlagan parish, Co.
Londonderry, 280
Tammany Hall (N.Y.C.), 609n.3,
619
tanning industry, 114
Tarleton, Banastre, 565
tavernkeepers, 351
Burke, Margaret Carey Murphy,
4, 351–56
Campble, Francis, 322–23
Greenlee, Mary Elizabeth
McDowell, 155
women as, 350, 353
Taylor, George (Declaration of
Independence signer), 255n.3
Taylor, George Keith (Va. state
legislator), 370
Taylor, James, 91, 93
Taylor, Thomas, 580n.23, 582
Tea Acts of 1773 (Britain), 508, 528,
535
Teague, meaning of term, 58n.6
temperance crusades, 450
Temple-Bar (London), 271
tenant farmers
Anti-Rent War (1766; N.Y.), 253
impartible inheritance and, 107, 597
in Ireland, 20, 25, 27, 28, 31, 35,
196–97, 280, 567–68, 596–97
Irish emigrants as, 4, 193, 196,
197, 200, 224
tenant-right, 108
Tenison, Richard, 489
Tennent, Charles, 401n.5
Tennent, George, 638–39n.39
Tennent, Gilbert, 385, 388, 400,
401, 411
Tennent, John (Antrim County
minister), 604
Tennent, John (Gilbert's brother),
401n.5, 455n.7
Tennent, John (minister John's son),
638–39n.39
Tennent, Robert, 638–39n.39
Tennent, William (Belfast reformer),
635n.16, 638
Tennent, William, Jr., 401n.5
Tennent, William, Sr., 400, 401, 411
Tennessee, 4, 109–10, 114, 116–18,
604–5, 607
Terbush, Isaac, 253
Terry, Eli, 249
Test Act (1704; Ireland), 418n.30,
436
Test Act (1806; N.Y.), 614
Test Acts (1777–79; Pa.), 484, 485
testimonials, 86, 189
Texas, 622n.16
Third Philadelphia Regiment, 299
Thomas, George, 322
Thomson, Charles, 255n.3, 498, 520,
524, 527, 544

Thomson (Thompson), John, 385,
386, 388
Thornton, Matthew, 255n.3
Thornton, Samuel, 75, 79
Tinkling Spring Church (Va.), 383,
392, 399
Tipperary County, Munster, 14
Tirkennedy barony, Co. Fermanagh,
55
tithes, 6, 14, 15, 25, 74, 436, 516
tobacco farming
indentured labor and, 253
in Maryland, 128, 455, 456
in Virginia, 364, 367
in West Indies, 122, 123
tolerance, religious, 6, 14, 58
Toler family, 14, 20–21n.94
Tone, Wolfe, 511n.3, 612n.13, 634,
639n.42, 645
Toner, Edward, 4, 224–34, 235, 631
letter from, 228–33
Toner, Joseph M., 234
Toner, Mary, 224–34
letter from, 228–33
Toner, Meredith, 234
Toner, Nancy, 233
Toner, Peter, 233
Tories. See American Revolution;
Great Britain; loyalists
Townsend (Maine settlement), 129,
130
Townshend Acts of 1767 (Britain),
483, 515, 519n.32, 522, 524,
527, 540
trade. See foreign trade; merchants
and traders
trade unions. See labor unions
transatlantic correspondence, 9,
72–73, 121, 243, 458n.18
transatlantic passages, 90–93, 94,
96–98
transfer certificates, 86
transport, commercial, 317
Treatise on Education, A (Locke),
478n.8
Treaty of. See key word, e.g.,
Utrecht, Treaty of
Trinity Church (Newport, R.I.), 58
Trinity College (Dublin), 416, 501
Trumbull family, 39
trustees, Roman Catholic, 431–32,
594–95, 596
Tryon, William, 508, 530, 534n.19
Tryon County, N.Y., 470
"Tuckahoes," 106
Tullylish parish, Co. Down, 522
Tyaquin barony, Co. Galway, 500
typhus, 90
tyranny
anti-Federalists' fear of, 572, 573
Hutcheson's (Francis) view of, 511
in republican theory, 499
Tyrone County, Ireland, 45, 224,
226

Ulster
American Revolution and, 536
Anglicans and, 24, 31, 620
contemporary problems, 10
cotton industry, 95
emigrant reasons for leaving, 5,
27, 35
emigrants from, 3–6, 8, 24, 28, 30,
34, 45, 114, 128–30, 133,
135–37, 143–44, 146, 147, 156,
179, 224, 280, 287, 303,
311–13, 317, 318, 324, 328,
332, 336, 337, 381, 386, 400,
435–51, 510, 530–31, 536, 547,
549, 561, 585, 603, 624–27,
631–32
emigration's impact on, 5, 89
folksong tradition, 53
indentured servants from, 254, 255
linen industry, 7, 25, 27, 28, 31,
46, 328, 536
political upheaval in, 36–37, 417,
430
Rhyming Weavers and, 451
Roman Catholics and, 5, 24, 31,
35n.33, 37, 39, 89, 224, 226–27
Steelboys protest, 31, 33n.27,
324n.3, 560
See also specific place names
Ulster Plantation, 24, 381, 384, 417,
443, 453, 626, 631
Ulster Presbyterians, 3, 4, 5, 24–25,
27, 28, 31, 35n.33, 36–37, 45,
46–47n.7, 70, 89, 135–36, 381,
384–85, 435–36, 443, 445–46,
510, 511, 596–97, 620. See also
Scots-Irish
Ulster Scots (language), 450
ultramontaine Catholicism, 603
Union, Pa., 238–39
unions. See labor unions
United Irishmen. See Society of
United Irishmen
United Irishmen's Rebellion of
1798, 7, 39, 40–41, 42n.7,
43–44n.24, 45, 95, 195, 227,
309, 368–69n.28, 450, 451, 587,
597, 604, 611, 634
United Kingdom. See Great Britain
United States
Alien and Sedition Acts (1798),
299, 302, 450, 584, 587, 590,
592, 596
Articles of Confederation, 499,
509
Catholic repression in, 6, 10, 58,
454–61, 510
Civil War, 645
Coinage Act, 645n.78
Constitution, 8, 94, 449, 485, 546,
572–76, 587
Constitutional Convention,
520–21n.42, 572–73, 575,
576–77